DATE DUE

PRINTED IN U.S.A.

CLASSICAL
AND MEDIEVAL
LITERATURE
CRITICISM

Guide to Gale Literary Criticism Series

For criticism on	Consult these Gale series
Authors now living or who died after December 31, 1999	*CONTEMPORARY LITERARY CRITICISM (CLC)*
Authors who died between 1900 and 1999	*TWENTIETH-CENTURY LITERARY CRITICISM (TCLC)*
Authors who died between 1800 and 1899	*NINETEENTH-CENTURY LITERATURE CRITICISM (NCLC)*
Authors who died between 1400 and 1799	*LITERATURE CRITICISM FROM 1400 TO 1800 (LC)* *SHAKESPEAREAN CRITICISM (SC)*
Authors who died before 1400	*CLASSICAL AND MEDIEVAL LITERATURE CRITICISM (CMLC)*
Authors of books for children and young adults	*CHILDREN'S LITERATURE REVIEW (CLR)*
Dramatists	*DRAMA CRITICISM (DC)*
Poets	*POETRY CRITICISM (PC)*
Short story writers	*SHORT STORY CRITICISM (SSC)*
Black writers of the past two hundred years	*BLACK LITERATURE CRITICISM (BLC)* *BLACK LITERATURE CRITICISM SUPPLEMENT (BLCS)*
Hispanic writers of the late nineteenth and twentieth centuries	*HISPANIC LITERATURE CRITICISM (HLC)* *HISPANIC LITERATURE CRITICISM SUPPLEMENT (HLCS)*
Native North American writers and orators of the eighteenth, nineteenth, and twentieth centuries	*NATIVE NORTH AMERICAN LITERATURE (NNAL)*
Major authors from the Renaissance to the present	*WORLD LITERATURE CRITICISM, 1500 TO THE PRESENT (WLC)* *WORLD LITERATURE CRITICISM SUPPLEMENT (WLCS)*

ISSN 0896-0011

Volume 37

CLASSICAL AND MEDIEVAL LITERATURE CRITICISM

Excerpts from Criticism of the Works of World
Authors from Classical Antiquity through the
Fouteenth Century, from the First Appraisals
to Current Evaluations

Jelena O. Krstović
Editor

Detroit
New York
San Francisco
London
Boston
Woodbridge, CT

STAFF

net Witalec, *Managing Editor, Literature Product*
Jelena Krstović *Editor*
Mark W. Scott, *Publisher, Literature Product*

Elisabeth Gellert, *Associate Editor*
Tom Schoenberg, *Assistant Editor*
Patti A. Tippett, Timothy J. White, *Technical Training Specialists*
Kathleen Lopez Nolan, Lynn M. Spampinato, *Managing Editors*
Susan M. Trosky, *Content Director*

Maria L. Franklin, *Permissions Manager*
Edna Hedblad, Kimberly F. Smilay, *Permissions Specialists*
Erin Bealmear, Sandy Gore, Keryl Stanley, *Permissions Assistants*

Victoria B. Cariappa, *Research Manager*
Andrew Guy Malonis, Barbara McNeil, Gary J. Oudersluys, Maureen Richards, Cheryl L. Warnock, *Research Specialists*
Tamara C. Nott, Tracie A. Richardson, *Research Associates*
Scott Floyd, Timothy Lehnerer, Ron Morelli, *Research Assistants*

Dorothy Maki, *Manufacturing Manager*
Stacy Melson, *Buyer*

Mary Beth Trimper, *Composition Manager*
Evi Seoud, *Assistant Production Manager*
Carolyn Fischer, Gary Leach, *Composition Specialists*

Mike Logusz, *Graphic Artist*
Randy Bassett, *Image Database Supervisor*
Robert Duncan, *Imaging Specialist*
Pamela A. Reed, *Imaging Coordinator*
Kelly A. Quin, *Image Editor*

Library of Congress Catalog Card Number 88-658021
ISBN 0-7876-4379-3
ISSN 0896-0011
Printed in the United States of America

10 9 8 7 6 5 4 3 2 1

Contents

Preface vii

Acknowledgments xi

Preface

Since its inception in 1988, *Classical and Medieval Literature Criticism* (*CMLC*) has been a valuable resource for students and librarians seeking critical commentary on the works and authors of antiquity through the fourteenth century. The great poets, prose writers, dramatists, and philosophers of this period form the basis of most humanities curricula, so that virtually every student will encounter many of these works during the course of a high school and college education. Reviewers have found *CMLC* "useful" and "extremely convenient," noting that it "adds to our understanding of the rich legacy left by the ancient period and the Middle Ages," and praising its "general excellence in the presentation of an inherently interesting subject." No other single reference source has surveyed the critical reaction to classical and medieval literature as thoroughly as *CMLC*.

Scope of the Series

CMLC provides an introduction to classical and medieval authors, works, and topics that represent a variety of genres, time periods, and nationalities. By organizing and reprinting an enormous amount of critical commentary written on authors and works of this period in world history, *CMLC* helps students develop valuable insight into literary history, promotes a better understanding of the texts, and sparks ideas for papers and assignments.

Each entry in *CMLC* presents a comprehensive survey of an author's career, an individual work of literature, or a literary topic, and provides the user with a multiplicity of interpretations and assessments. Such variety allows students to pursue their own interests; furthermore, it fosters an awareness that literature is dynamic and responsive to many different opinions. Early commentary is offered to indicate initial responses, later selections document changes in literary reputations, and retrospective analyses provide the reader with modern views. The size of each author entry is a relative reflection of the scope of the criticism available in English.

An author may appear more than once in the series if his or her writings have been the subject of a substantial amount of criticism; in these instances, specific works or groups of works by the author will be covered in separate entries. For example, Homer will be represented by three entries, one devoted to the *Iliad*, one to the *Odyssey*, and one to the Homeric Hymns.

CMLC continues the survey of criticism of world literature begun by Gale's *Contemporary Literary Criticism* (*CLC*), *Twentieth-Century Literary Criticism* (*TCLC*), *Nineteenth-Century Literature Criticism* (*NCLC*), *Literature Criticism from 1400 to 1800* (*LC*), and *Shakespearean Criticism* (*SC*).

Organization of the Book

A *CMLC* entry consists of the following elements:

- The **Author Heading** cites the name under which the author most commonly wrote, followed by birth and death dates. Also located here are any name variations under which an author wrote, including transliterated forms for authors whose native languages use nonroman alphabets. If the author wrote consistently under a pseudonym, the pseudonym will be listed in the author heading and the author's actual name given in parenthesis on the first line of the biographical and critical information. Uncertain birth or death dates are indicated by question marks. Single-work entries are preceded by a heading that consists of the most common form of the title in English translation (if applicable) and the original date of composition.

- The **Introduction** contains background information that introduces the reader to the author, work, or topic that is the subject of the entry.

- A **Portrait of the Author** is included when available.

- The list of **Principal Works** is ordered chronologically by date of first publication and lists the most important works by the author. The genre and publication date of each work is given. In the case of foreign authors whose works have been translated into English, the list will focus primarily on twentieth-century translations, selecting those works most commonly considered the best by critics. Unless otherwise indicated, dramas are dated by first performance, not first publication. Lists of **Representative Works** by different authors appear with topic entries.

- Reprinted **Criticism** is arranged chronologically in each entry to provide a useful perspective on changes in critical evaluation over time. The critic's name and the date of composition or publication of the critical work are given at the beginning of each piece of criticism. Unsigned criticism is preceded by the title of the source in which it appeared. All titles by the author featured in the text are printed in boldface type. Footnotes are reprinted at the end of each essay or excerpt. In the case of excerpted criticism, only those footnotes that pertain to the excerpted texts are included. Criticism in topic entries is arranged chronologically under a variety of subheadings to facilitate the study of different aspects of the topic.

- A complete **Bibliographical Citation** of the original essay or book precedes each piece of criticism.

- Critical essays are prefaced by brief **Annotations** explicating each piece.

- An annotated bibliography of **Further Reading** appears at the end of each entry and suggests resources for additional study. In some cases, significant essays for which the editors could not obtain reprint rights are included here. Boxed material following the further reading list provides references to other biographical and critical sources on the author in series published by Gale.

Cumulative Indexes

A **Cumulative Author Index** lists all of the authors that appear in a wide variety of reference sources published by the Gale Group, including *CMLC*. A complete list of these sources is found facing the first page of the Author Index. The index also includes birth and death dates and cross references between pseudonyms and actual names.

Beginning with the second volume, a **Cumulative Nationality Index** lists all authors featured in *CMLC* by nationality, followed by the number of the *CMLC* volume in which their entry appears.

Beginning with the tenth volume, a **Cumulative Topic Index** lists the literary themes and topics treated in the series as well as in *Nineteenth-Century Literature Criticism, Twentieth-Century Literary Criticism,* and the *Contemporary Literary Criticism* Yearbook, which was discontinued in 1998.

A **Cumulative Title Index** lists in alphabetical order all of the works discussed in the series. Each title listing includes the corresponding volume and page numbers where criticism may be located. Foreign-language titles that have been translated into English are followed by the titles of the translation—for example, *Slovo o polku Igorove* (*The Song of Igor's Campaign*). Page numbers following these translated titles refer to all pages on which any form of the titles, either foreign-language or translated, appear. Titles of novels, dramas, nonfiction books, and poetry, short story, or essay collections are printed in italics, while individual poems, short stories, and essays are printed in roman type within quotation marks.

Citing *Classical and Medieval Literature Criticism*

When writing papers, students who quote directly from any volume in the Literary Criticism Series may use the following general format to footnote reprinted criticism. The first example pertains to material drawn from periodicals, the second to material reprinted from books.

T. P. Malnati, "Juvenal and Martial on Social Mobility," *The Classical Journal* 83, no. 2 (December-January 1988): 134-41; reprinted in *Classical and Medieval Literature Criticism,* vol. 35, ed. Jelena Krstović (Farmington Hills, Mich.: The Gale Group, 2000), 366-71.

J. P. Sullivan, "Humanity and Humour; Imagery and Wit," in *Martial: An Unexpected Classic* (Cambridge University Press, 1991), 211-51; excerpted and reprinted in *Classical and Medieval Literature Criticism,* vol. 35, ed. Jelena Krstović (Farmington Hills, Mich.: The Gale Group, 2000), 371-95.

Suggestions are Welcome

Readers who wish to suggest new features, topics, or authors to appear in future volumes, or who have other suggestions or comments are cordially invited to call, write, or fax the Managing Editor:

Managing Editor, Literary Criticism Series
The Gale Group
27500 Drake Road
Farmington Hills, MI 48331-3535
1-800-347-4253 (GALE)
Fax: 248-699-8054

Acknowledgments

The editors wish to thank the copyright holders of the excerpted criticism included in this volume and the permissions managers of many book and magazine publishing companies for assisting us in securing reproduction rights. We are also grateful to the staffs of the Detroit Public Library, the Library of Congress, the University of Detroit Mercy Library, Wayne State University Purdy/Kresge Library Complex, and the University of Michigan Libraries for making their resources available to us. Following is a list of the copyright holders who have granted us permission to reproduce material in this volume of *CMLC*. Every effort has been made to trace copyright, but if omissions have been made, please let us know.

COPYRIGHTED EXCERPTS IN *CMLC*, VOLUME 37, WERE REPRODUCED FROM THE FOLLOWING PERIODICALS:

American Journal of Archeology, v. 67, July, 1963. Reproduced by permission.—*Romance Notes*, v. XIV, Autumn, 1972. Reproduced by permission.

COPYRIGHTED EXCERPTS IN *CMLC*, VOLUME 37, WERE REPRODUCED FROM THE FOLLOWING BOOKS:

Barron, W. R. J. From *English Medieval Romance*. Longman Group UK Ltd., 1987. © Longman Group UK Limited, 1987. All rights reserved. Reproduced by permission of Pearson Education Limited.—Boussard, Jacques. From *The Civilization of Charlemagne*. Translated by Frances Partridge. McGraw-Hill Book Company, 1968. © Jacques Boussard. Reprinted by permission of Frances Partridge.—Bullough, Donald. From *The Age of Charlemagne*. Elek Books Limited, 1965. © Paul Elek Productions Limited, 1965. Reproduced by permission of the author.—Caulkins, Janet H. From "Narrative Interventions: The Key to the Jest of the Pelerinage de Charlemagne," in *Etudes de Philologie Romane et d'Histoire Litteraire*. Edited by Jean Marie D'Heur and Nicoletta Cherubibi. Liege, 1980. Reproduced by permission of the author.—Clark, James M. From *The Great German Mystics: Eckhart, Tauler and Suso*. Basil Blackwell, 1949. Ganshof, F. L. From *The Carolingian and the Frankish Monarchy: Studies on Carolingian History*. Translated by Janet Sondheimer. Cornell University Press, 1971. © 1971 by Longman Group Limited. Used by permission of the publisher, Cornell University Press. Reproduced in United Kingdom by permission of Pearson Education Limited.—Garrison, Mary. From "The Emergence of Carolingian Latin Literature and the Court of Charlemagne" (780-814), in *Carolingian Culture: Emulation and Innovation*. Edited by Rosamond McKitterick. Cambridge University Press, 1994. © Cambridge University Press 1994. Reproduced by permission.—Glover, T. R. From "Strabo: The Greek in the World of Caesar," in *Greek Byways*. The Macmillan Company, 1932. Copyright 1932 by The Macmillan Company.—Kay, Sarah. From "The Character of Character in The Chansons de Geste" in *The Craft of Fiction: Essays in Medieval Poetics*. Edited by Leigh Arrathoon. © by Solaris Press, Rochester, Michigan 48063. All rights reserved. Reproduced by permission.—Kelley, C. F. From the introduction to *The Book of the Poor in Spirit*. Longmans and Green & Co., 1954. Reproduced by permission of Pearson Education Limited.—Lamb, Harold. From *Charlemagne: The Legend and the Man*. Doubleday & Company, Inc. Copyright 1954, Harold Lamb. Renewed 1982 by Ruth Barbour Lamb. Used by permission of Doubleday, a division of Random House, Inc. In the United Kingdom by permission of the author and Curtis Brown, Ltd.—Schmidt, Josef. From the introduction to *Johannes Tauler: Sermons*. Paulist Press, 1985. Copyright © 1985 by Maria Shrady. Reproduced by permission.—Scholz, Bernhard Walter. From the introduction to *Carolingian Chronicles: Royal Frankish Annals and Nithard's Histories*. University of Michigan Press, 1970. Copyright © by The University of Michigan 1970. All rights reserved. Reproduced by permission.—Winston, Richard. From *Charlemagne: From the Hammer to the Cross*. The Bobbs Merrill Company, Inc, 1954. Copyright 1954, by Richard Winston. Renewed 1982 by Clara Winston.

Charlemagne
742-814

(Also known as Charles the Great, Charles I, Karl der Grosse, and Carolus Magnus.) King of the Franks (768-814) and Emperor of the Western World (800-14).

INTRODUCTION

Beloved ruler of western Europe, Charlemagne brought forth a rebirth in learning at a time when few of his subjects could even write their own names. A patron of literature and the arts and the founder of many schools, Charlemagne through his leadership encouraged and inspired others to read, write, and learn, bringing forth what has been called the Carolingian Renaissance. Charlemagne, already a legend in his own time, became a prominent character in the body of literature known as the Carolingian cycle or the Matter of France, and through these *chansons de geste*, he continued to influence millions of people in numerous countries for centuries.

BIOGRAPHICAL INFORMATION

Charlemagne was born to Pepin the Short and Bertrade in northern Europe; his exact birthplace is unknown. He inherited half the kingdom of the Franks upon the death of his father in 768. Three years later, upon the death of his brother Carloman II, who had shared the Frankish empire, he became King of all the Franks. Skilled in strategy and tactics (his work on these subjects was later to be studied by Napoleon Bonaparte), Charlemagne set forth to Christianize the land. He battled the pagan Saxons for more than three decades, finally conquering them in 804. In 773-74 he conquered Lombardy, restoring the land to the Pope. He waged dozens of campaigns, including expeditions against the Saracens in northeastern Spain in 778. It was in a surprise attack against Charlemagne's rear forces that the Basques killed one of his nobles, Roland—the hero of the *Chanson de Roland*. By the end of the century Charlemagne ruled most of western Europe, uniting much of the land once under the Roman empire. Pope Leo III crowned him Emperor of the Western World in 800. Charlemagne improved conditions for the common people to an extent never before accomplished through reforms in government, the military, commerce, farming, and education. The latter was available for peasants as well as nobles; he went so far as to consider universal free schooling. Charlemagne died in 814, leaving his only surviving son, Louis, as ruler. Louis lacked the command or organizational skills of his father and the empire was quickly invaded.

MAJOR WORKS

Charlemagne himself did not write any literary works; indeed he could not write at all until his old age, and then only barely. He could, however, read Latin and some Greek. Thus, it is not as author but as a character that Charlemagne is known in literature. Of mythical, legendary proportions, he is featured in a great body of work which includes the epic *Chanson de Roland*. For centuries after Charlemagne's death, many common folk refused to believe that he was dead, even envisioning him as leading the Crusades. Others believed him always ready to protect the land, resting in a cave until such a time as he was needed. By the middle of the century of his death, this devotion was expressed through making him the subject of many songs and tales, the practice continuing through the next two centuries. The *Chanson de Roland* was written by an anonymous French poet (some believe him to have been the Norman poet Turold) sometime between the Norman Conquest and the first Crusade in 1096. The epic of four thousand lines is an embellished conflation of many lesser tales about Charlemagne. Fighting for the King (considered French by the poet), Roland is vanquished by overwhelming numbers but does not lose his honor. Charlemagne finds the slain Roland, prays over his body, and the newly-inspired French chase the Saracens into a river where they drown. For more than five centuries, until the Renaissance, the *Chanson de Roland* remained popular and is still France's most famous poem. In *Le Pèlerinage de Charlemagne,* another classic poem of nearly 900 lines, Charlemagne seeks out Hugo the Strong of Constantinople. In Jerusalem, on their way, Charlemagne and his fellow travelers are given relics. When they eventually meet up with Hugo they make extravagant claims which Hugo calls on them to perform. Charlemagne and his men accomplish their tasks with the help of God. In what is assumed to be a joke at the end of the poem, the assertion is made that Charlemagne is a greater man than Hugo because Charlemagne is the taller of the two. No doubt the popularity of works which feature Charlemagne can be credited in no little part to the public's adoration of the King, who was adopted as one of their own by France, Germany, Scandinavia, Poland, and Spain.

REPRESENTATIVE WORKS

Poetry of the Carolingian Renaissance (poetry) (edited by Peter Goodman) 1985

The Pilgrimage of Charlemagne (poetry) (translated by Glyn S. Burgess) 1988

The Song of Roland (epic) (translated by D. D. R. Owen) 1990

CRITICISM

Edward L. Cutts (essay date 1882)

SOURCE: "The Revival of Learning" and "The Ecclesiastical Work of Charles" in *Charlemagne,* E. & J. B. Young and Co., 1882, pp. 306-36.

[*In the following excerpt, Cutts explores Charlemagne's encouragement of learning and examines his religious policy, edicts, and controversial theological decisions.*]

THE REVIVAL OF LEARNING

The feature of Charles's character and work to which the historian naturally turns with the greatest sympathy is his love of learning and the wise and strenuous encouragement of it from which dates the revival of letters in Europe.

The elegant culture of which the letters of Sidonius have given us so charming a glimpse, had long since died out of the countries between the Alps and the English Chan-

nel. The Imperial schools, which we have seen still existed in the towns of Gaul in the time of the grandsons of Clovis, had fallen into neglect and decay. If the Frank conquerors had gradually progressed from their original barbarism, the civilization of the conquered race had gradually deteriorated in the midst of perpetual war, until at last, about the time of Charles Martel, the whole people had reached the lowest point of civilization to which Gaul had sunk since it learnt the language and the manners of Rome.

Letters had taken refuge in the monasteries; but the monastic schools did not fulfil the place of the old Imperial schools. Pagan literature was very naturally disliked and discouraged by the Church, and the schools of the monasteries took a narrower range.

The advantages of learning were indeed recognized by the Frank princes from the first, and Clovis, and his sons and grandsons, encouraged some of their young nobility to qualify themselves for high places in the State and in the Church. No doubt Pepin and Carloman, with the assistance of Boniface, in regulating and reforming the Frankish Church, did something to encourage learning. Pepin, we have seen, had the Italian scholar, Peter of Pisa, at his court as tutor to the young princes and the young nobles of the court. But the adoption of general measures to revive learning throughout the kingdom was the work of Charlemagne, and is one of his best claims to the gratitude of posterity.

It was about the year 780 that he induced an eminent Lombard scholar, Paul the Deacon, to take up his residence at his court, and to undertake the instruction of all who chose to attend his lectures. In the following year he met with the scholar whose name is more especially associated with that of Charles in the revival of learning.

It was at Parma, during Charles's expedition to Italy, that a group of Anglo-Saxon ecclesiastics were introduced to him, who had been to Rome to fetch the pallium for Eanbold, the newly elected Archbishop of York. Chief of them was Alcuin, who held the honourable office of master of the schools of York, in which he had succeeded the new archbishop.

The schools of Britain and Ireland had at this time a considerable reputation. The school of York was one of the most famous of them. Theodore of Tarsus, Archbishop of Canterbury, and the Abbot Adrian, the companion of his labours, were both men of considerable learning, and they had taken pains to establish schools in England. Bede (673-735) had gained for himself and for the Northumbrian schools a European reputation; Egbert, his scholar and friend, had maintained the high character for learning of the school of York; Egbert had been the master of Elbert, and Eanbold the new archbishop, and Alcuin, had been school-fellows under Elbert. When Elbert succeeded Egbert as archbishop, Eanbold succeeded Elbert in the schools; when Eanbold was in turn raised to the see, Alcuin succeeded him as *scholasticus;* so that Alcuin was a scholar of great reputation, and in a position in which he might naturally expect to succeed in his turn to the see of York. The school of York had maintained the Roman traditions derived from its founders; it taught the theology of Augustine and of Gregory the Great, and it regarded Rome as the mother of Western Christendom.

In the scholasticus of York, King Charles recognized the kind of man he needed to take the lead in that revival of learning on which he was intent. Alcuin listened to his proposals, and agreed to accept his offers, provided that when he reached England, in discharging his embassy, the archbishop and the Northumbrian king should give their consent; and in 782 Alcuin took up his residence at the court of the King of the Franks, as master of the Palatine school. The king gave him two abbeys to afford him an income—one near Troyes, and another, Ferrieres, in the diocese of Sens—and no doubt he cared for the well-being of the houses from which he derived his emoluments; but his duties were the teaching of the Palatine school, and the promotion of education throughout the Frank dominions. The king at this time was forty years of age, the scholar was forty-seven.

It was a strangely wandering life which was led by the court of the great Charles. Wherever the military or political affairs of his wide dominions made it necessary for him to fix his residence for a few months, thither his wife and children, his counsellors and secretaries, in short, his whole court, accompanied him,—now in Saxony, now in Aquitaine, now in Lombardy, now on the banks of the Rhine.

The duties of the master of the Palatine school were very much the same as those of the master of any of the great schools of the period. He was a professor, who delivered public lectures. But seeing he was here the sole professor, he had to lecture on all subjects which he desired that his pupils should learn.

Charles himself had a great thirst for knowledge, and a great desire to encourage learning. He frequently set the example of attending the master's lectures, and such an example was sure to be followed by all who desired to stand well with the king. Still more frequently in conversation he availed himself of the great scholar's supposed capability of solving all questions on all subjects. We take leave to quote a few paragraphs, which place the scene vividly before us:[1]—

> We find Charles and his courtiers plying the *Vates* from across the Channel with innumerable questions, often blundering strangely and misapprehending wildly, but forming a circle which even at this lapse of time it is impossible to contemplate without interest. The monarch himself, in the ardour of a long unsatisfied curiosity, propounding queries on all imaginable topics; suggesting, distinguishing, objecting, disputing;—a colossal figure, gazing fixedly with bright blue eyes on his admired guest, and altogether a presence that might

well have disconcerted a less assured intellect. Alcuin, however, holding fast by his Boethius, Cassiodorus, and Isidorus, is calm and self-possessed; feeling assured that so long as he only teaches what 'Gregorius summus' and 'Bæda venerabilis' believed and taught, he cannot go very far wrong. Around him, as the years went by, he saw successively appear the three royal sons, born in rightful wedlock: Charles, the future ruler of Neustria and Austrasia; Pepin, the acknowledged lord of Italy; and Lewis, who almost from his cradle had worn the crown of Aquitaine,—the graceful young athlete and mighty hunter, his mind already opening to that love of learning which, through all the good and evil of his chequered life, he cherished so fondly in his later years. There, again, was Charles's much-loved sister Gisela, Abbess of Chelles, who from her girlhood had renounced the world, but whom the fame of the great teacher drew from her conventual retirement. Thither also came the last and best-loved of Charles's wives, Liutgarda, of the proud Alemannic race, hereafter to prove among the firmest of Alcuin's friends; and the royal daughter, Gisela, whose parental affection held her too dear for the proudest alliance. There, too, was Charles's son-in-law, Angilbert, chiefly distinguished as yet for his fondness for the histrionic art, but afterwards the saintly Abbot of St. Riquier. There, too, were the royal cousins, the half-brothers Adelhard and Wala, whose after action shook the whole fabric of the Carolingian Empire. There, too, was Riculfus, destined ere long to fill the chair of St. Boniface and rule the great see of Mayence; Eginhard, the royal biographer, the classic of the ninth century; and Fredegis, Alcuin's youthful countryman, poet, and philosopher, not always faithful to his master's teaching.

> It appears to have been a frequent affectation in mediæval times for distinguished men to assume a literary or historic *alias;* and to this custom we must attribute the fact that Alcuin usually in his correspondence addresses the members of this circle under another name. Charles's second name would seem to have really been David, and this fact may account for the assumption of scriptural names by some of his courtiers. Pepin was Julius; Gisela (the sister), Lucia; Gisela (the daughter), Delia; Queen Liutgarda was Ava; Adelhard was Antony; Wala, Arsenius; Eginhard, with reference perhaps to his destined state avocation, was Besaleel; Riculfus, Flavius Damoetus; Rigbod, Machairas; Angilbert, Homer; Fredigis, Nathanael.

There appears, however, little to support the popular idea of a regular Athenæum, or academy of adult members of Charles's court.

For the first five years after Alcuin's arrival (782-787) the mind of the king was occupied with the wars in which he was incessantly engaged; but when, in 785, Witikind laid down his arms and embraced Christianity, Charles had more leisure to turn to the designs of peace. During his residence at Rome, in the winter of 786-7, Charles had secured in the capital of Western learning several teachers of repute, whom, on his return, he distributed among the principal Frank monasteries to aid in the work of educational revival. Shortly after he issued the famous capitulary of A.D. 787. The copy which has been preserved is that addressed to the Abbot of Fulda:—

Charles, by the grace of God King of the Franks and of the Lombards, and Patrician of the Romans, to Bangulfus Abbot, and to his whole congregation, and to the faithful committed to his charge:

Be it known to your Devotion, pleasing to God, that in conjunction with our faithful we have judged it to be of utility that in the bishoprics and monasteries committed by Christ's favour to our charge, care should be taken that there shall be not only a regular manner of life and one conformable to holy religion, but also the study of letters, each to teach and learn them according to his ability and the Divine assistance. For even as due observance of the rule of the house tends to good morals, so zeal on the part of the teacher and the taught imparts order and grace to sentences; and those who seek to please God by living aright, should also not neglect to please Him by right speaking. It is written, 'By thine own words shalt thou be justified or condemned;' and although right doing may be preferable to right speaking, yet must the knowledge of what is right precede right action. Every one, therefore, should strive to understand what it is that he would fain accomplish; and this right understanding will be the sooner gained, according as the utterances of the tongue are free from error. And if false speaking is to be shunned by all men, especially should it be shunned by those who have elected to be the servants of the truth. During past years we have often received letters from different monasteries, informing us that at their sacred services the brethren offered up prayers on our behalf; and we have observed that the thoughts contained in these letters, though in themselves most just, were expressed in uncouth language, and while pious devotion dictated the sentiments, the unlettered tongue was unable to express them aright! Hence there has arisen in our minds the fear lest, if the skill to write rightly were thus lacking, so too would the power of rightly comprehending the Holy Scriptures be far less than was fitting; and we all know that though verbal errors be dangerous, errors of the understanding are yet more so. We exhort you, therefore, not only not to neglect the study of letters, but to apply yourselves thereto with perseverance, and with that humility which is well pleasing to God, so that you may be able to penetrate with greater ease and certainty the mysteries of the Holy Scriptures. For as these contain images, tropes, and similar figures, it is impossible to doubt that the reader will arrive far more readily at the spiritual sense according as he is the better instructed in learning. Let there, therefore, be chosen for this work men who are both able and willing to learn, and also desirous of instructing others; and let them apply themselves to the work with a zeal equalling the earnestness with which we recommend it to them.

It is our wish that you may be what it behoves the soldiers of the Church to be,—religious in heart, learned in discourse, pure in act, eloquent in speech; so that all who approach your house in order to invoke the Divine Master, or to behold the excellence of the religious life, may be edified in beholding you, and instructed in hearing you discourse or chant, and may return home rendering thanks to God most High.

Fail not, as thou regardest our favour, to send a copy of this letter to all thy suffragans, and to all the monaster-

ies; and let no monk go beyond his monastery to administer justice, or to enter the assemblies and the voting-places. Adieu.

This capitulary appears to have been issued from Augsburg, where he had just received the submission of the rebellious Tassilo.

It was probably some time after this that Charles sent round to the Churches a homilary or collection of sermons, corrected by the hand of Paulus Diaconus (at that time probably engaged in teaching at Metz), accompanied by the following instructions:—

Desirous as we are of improving the condition of the Churches, we impose upon ourselves the task of reviving with the utmost zeal the study of letters, well-nigh extinguished through the neglect of our ancestors. We charge all our subjects, as far as they may be able, to cultivate the liberal arts, and we set them the example. We have already, God helping, carefully corrected the books of the Old and New Testaments, corrupted through the ignorance of transcribers. And inasmuch as the collection of homilies for the service at Nocturns was full of errors . . . we have w illed that these same should be revised and corrected by Paul the Deacon, our well-beloved client; and he has presented us with readings adapted to every feast-day, carefully purged from error, and sufficing for a whole year.

Two years after the appearance of the famous capitulary of 787, Theodulphus, Bishop of Orleans, one of the Missi Dominici, and who appears to have succeeded Alcuin, on his retirement to Tours, as a kind of "minister of education," addressed a document to the clergy of his diocese, which appears to have been widely adopted in other dioceses, in which he describes study as "a means whereby the life of the righteous is ennobled, and the man himself fortified against temptation." In this, he requires his clergy to open schools in every town and village of his diocese, and to receive "the children of the faithful" for instruction, demanding in return no payment, though permitted to accept a gift spontaneously offered. Theodulphus himself was one of the cluster of learned men about the Frankish court. The library of his cathedral was famous for the number and beauty of the manuscripts he had gathered together. He has left us one monument at least which has in our days, in a translation, obtained a new popularity— the hymn "Gloria Laus et Tibi Honor"—

"All glory, laud, and honour
To Thee, Redeemer, King," etc.

In the year 795, the abbacy of Tours became vacant. It was, perhaps, the wealthiest of all the preferments in the wide dominions of Charles. The Archbishop of Toledo, in a controversy with Alcuin, made it a subject of reproach, that as Abbot of Tours he was the master of 20,000 slaves—the serfs upon his wide domains.

Here Alcuin continued his labours as teacher. He sent some of his monks to England to bring back books for the abbey library. Scholars flocked to him from all parts of the Frankish dominions, and many from his native England. He continued to correspond with the king,[2] and continued to exercise a great influence on the literary progress of the kingdom.

He was immediately succeeded in the mastership of the Palatine school by Witzo, who had accompanied him from York; and he, after a short time by Fredegis, another scholar of York. But within about two years there arrived from Ireland two men, in secular learning and in the Sacred Scriptures incomparably learned,[3] named Clement and Albinus, and they seem to have eclipsed Alcuin and his disciples in the regard of Charles.

The scholars of the Celtic school seem indeed to have had some advantages over the scholars of the school of York. We have seen that Alcuin and his school walked along the narrow path of Augustinian theology and Roman tradition. The Celtic scholars were familiar with the Greek Fathers. Manuscripts of Origen and other Greek authors, written in the beautiful character distinctive of the Celtic school of caligraphy, long remained at Luxeuil, St. Gall, and Bobbio, the great foundations of Columbanus, which long maintained their Celtic traditions. They were, by temperament as well as by training, more speculative than the steady Saxons. Clement appears, also, to have had a greater acquaintance with natural science than Alcuin. In one of Charles's letters to Alcuin, we find that Clement had given some different explanation of astronomical phenomena from those which Alcuin had previously given. Charles expresses the hope that he will not be too proud to admit that he was wrong if he sees reason to think so. It is interesting to find Alcuin quoting, with reference to Clement, Virgil's story of Dares and Entellus, which Jerome had quoted when Augustine opened a controversy with him.[4] We find the influence of these new Celtic teachers opposed also by Theodulphus, Bishop of Orleans, and Benedict of Aniane, whose character and abilities gave great weight to his opinions on all theological questions. On the other hand, Clement and his companions, if viewed with suspicion at Tours, and in the cell by the Anianus, and at Orleans, would find sympathy and support in the great monastery of Luxeuil and in its daughter-house of St. Gall, which were among the most famous of the religious communities of the time. It is from the monk of St. Gall that we have several stories about Clement, one of which is worth transcribing, as an illustration of Charles's encouragement of learning among the young men of his court.

On his return from Italy (probably the expedition of A.D. 786-7), Charles called before him the youths who had been under Clement's instructions, and found those of the middle and lower class more advanced than those of the noble class. Charles, with gracious looks and kind words, encouraged the former to persevere in their studies, promising them noble sees and abbeys as their reward. Then he turned to the others, and thundering at them rather than speaking to them, he reproached them with trusting to their noble birth and riches and good looks, and neglecting his orders and their own glorification, postponing their studies to luxury and play, idleness and useless exercises. Lifting his august head and unconquered right hand to heaven, he swore, with his accustomed oath, by the King of Heaven, "I do not care much for your nobility and your good looks, though others admire you; be sure of this, that unless you speedily repair your former negligence by diligent study, you shall never get any good from Charles."[5]

We return, for a moment, to our countryman Alcuin. The king invited him to accompany him in the journey to Rome, in which he received the Imperial crown and title, but ill health prevented the Abbot of Tours from being present with his master on that memorable occasion. The last two years of his life, his growing infirmities led him to devolve much of the business of his great and laborious position upon others, while he continued his devotions and his studies, and awaited his end. He had been accustomed to express a wish that he might depart this life on the festival of Pentecost; and so it came to pass. He died on the day of Pentecost, in the year A.D. 804.

The sense of the signal service rendered by Alcuin to his age must not lead us to exaggerate his merits or powers. He was a scholar, one of the foremost scholars of his age; and, through the wise and powerful patronage of Charles, he was instrumental in doing much for the revival of learning on the continent of Europe, when it had fallen to its lowest point of neglect. He was a vigorous upholder of the faith, and he exhibited the example of a pure and blameless life in the midst of a rude and licentious court. But, as a scholar, he had nothing of genius; he was merely the painstaking teacher of the traditions of his school. The plans for the extension of learning, of which he was a chief agent, were those of Charles. He left no work of genius, like Eginhard's Life, or Theodulphus's Hymn. There was no heroic spirit of self-devotion, like that of Columbanus or Boniface. He was in his place as master of the school of York; he might, like his predecessors in that office, have risen to be Archbishop of York; he accepted Charles's invitation to be master of his Palatine school, and he was recompensed with the abbacy of Tours.

Of Charles's own literary attainments it is difficult to speak. On one hand we are told that he spoke Latin fluently and forcibly, that he understood Greek, that he had an insatiable thirst for knowledge, and was industrious in its acquisition. The authorship of the hymn "Veni Creator Spiritus" is attributed to him. He ordered a collection to be made of the Teutonic ballads which had come down from old times. He was correcting the Latin version of the New Testament by reference to the Greek at the time of his death. Yet we are told that, not having learned the art of writing in youth, he in vain tried to acquire it in manhood, though he took persevering pains to do so. It is probably an error on our part to overlook the many evidences with which history supplies us, that a good memory and a strong understanding will enable a man to acquire an amount of knowledge and an intellectual training which we think unattainable by a man who does not possess our keys to learning—the arts of reading and writing.

. . . . .

The Ecclesiastical Work of Charles.

The religious side of Charles's character is of the greatest interest in the study of his remarkable character as a whole, and his religious policy led to the most important and durable results of his reign.

He inherited an ecclesiastical policy from his father; the policy of regulating and strengthening the influence of the Church in his dominions as the chief agent of civilization, and a great means of binding the various elements of the empire into one; the policy of accepting the Bishop of Rome as the head of Western Christianity, with patriarchal authority over all its Churches.

We have seen that he required the bishops and abbots to maintain the sacred buildings in their guardianship in good repair. The Domkirche at Aix is the principal ecclesiastical building which he himself erected. We have seen that he diligently attended the services of the Church, took great interest in the details of the service, and interfered personally in their conduct.

He seems to have taken completely into his own hands the nomination to all the bishoprics and abbeys, and, having a sincere desire for the efficiency of the Church, his appointments were usually good. We have no charges that he received presents from candidates for his patronage. Still, he allowed those about him to solicit patronage for their friends and dependents; and he sometimes selected his nominees in a way which savours of caprice. We will only relate one of the anecdotes of the monk of St. Gall in illustration of the subject.

On one occasion, when it was announced to him that one of the bishops had died, Charles asked whether, out of his good or labours, he had sent anything before him ("utrum de rebus vel laboribus suis ante se præmitteret aliquam"). The messenger, apparently misunderstanding the question, and thinking the king asked how much the bishop had left behind him, answered, "Not more than two pounds of silver." A young clerk of the king's chapel, who happened to be standing by, muttered in a low tone to himself, "A small viaticum for so long a journey." Charles overheard, and said to him, "Do you think, if you received the see, you would take care to make better provision for that long journey?" The clerk, swallowing the words like premature grapes falling into a gaping mouth, fell at his feet and said, "My lord, that depends on the will of God and your power." The king bade him stand behind the curtain which was behind his chair, and he would hear how many suitors he had for that honour. The news of the vacancy had become known in the palace, and there came a number of the courtiers begging for it for one man and for another. The Queen Hildegardis first sent a message, and then came herself, to beg for the vacant see for her own clerk; and

the monk laughingly records the honeyed phrases with which the beautiful queen asked her boon of her mighty spouse: "Sweetest lord, my king, my glory and my refuge" ("Domine dulcissime, mi rex, gloria mea et refugium meum"). The clerk felt that his grapes were very likely to be intercepted before they could fall into his mouth, and said from behind the curtain, "Lord king, hold fast your courage, and let not any one wrest from your hands the power which God has entrusted to them" ("Domine rex, tene fortitudinem tuam, ne potestatem a Deo tibi collatam de manibus tuis quisquam extorqueat"). Then the most strong lover of truth (so he calls Charles) called the clerk out from behind the curtain before all, and said to him, "Take that see, and provide diligently that you send greater expenditure and a viaticum for the long and irrevocable journey before thyself and before me."[6]

Charles's assumption of the patronage of the sees and abbeys of his dominions was indefensible in theory, submitted to because it could not be resisted, and made tolerable by appointments which were for the most part good. That it was considered an irregularity and a grievance, is shown by the fact that when Louis the Pious succeeded to the throne and published edicts for the better regulation of the discipline of the Church, he restored the right of canonical election.

The policy of Charles towards the see of Rome was a continuation of that already inaugurated by his father. He maintained the Bishop of Rome in the possession of the territories which Pepin had added to the endowments of the see, and even made some considerable additions to them from time to time. The Bishop of Rome held these possessions of his see on the same conditions as all the rest—the same conditions on which the bishops of Gaul held the landed endowments of their sees. He exercised a virtual lordship over them, subject to the sovereign authority. The authority of the bishop over the possessions of his see, is to be distinguished from the authority which he possessed as the most wealthy and powerful man in Rome, who had thereby attained to the political leadership of the *Respublica Romana*. Ultimately they became confounded. But when the Bishop of Rome accepted from Pepin the exarchate of Ravenna and the Pentapolis as endowments of his see, the Roman Republic still continued to acknowledge the Eastern emperor as its sovereign. It was not until Leo placed the crown on the head of Charles, at the Christmas festival of 800, that the Roman Republic formally withdrew its allegiance from the Eastern emperor; and by the same act it acknowledged a similar sovereignty in the newly elected emperor of the West, and the pope and the magnates of Rome did homage to Charles as their political lord. It was when, under the successors of Charles, his empire fell in pieces, and each great division asserted its independence, that the bishops of Rome, like the rest, were able to assert a practical independence—still, however, subject in theory to Imperial rights, which a strong emperor, in some special conjuncture, from time to time found himself able to enforce.

From the edict of Leo the Isaurian (A.D. 724), the prohibition of images in the Eastern Church had been maintained by successive emperors, till the Council of Nicæa, 786, when the use and adoration of pictures (not statues) was restored, and the long schism which had existed on this subject between the East and West was terminated.

The Pope Adrian, on receiving the acts of the Nicene Council, communicated a copy to the Frankish Church, clearly anticipating that the decision of a so-called general council would be accepted by the Franks. But the Churches north of the Alps appear never to have fallen into the abuse of images, which had grown up in the Churches of the East and of Italy. And the customs and convictions of these Churches made them unwilling to accept the decisions arrived at in the synod of Nicæa. Charles sent the decisions of the synod to Alcuin, who was then on a visit to England, and it is said that the English bishops joined in desiring their illustrious countryman to write against the council. Alcuin wrote some remarks, in the form of a letter to Charlemagne; others of the Frankish divines are said to have also written on the subject. Out of these writings grew a treatise in four books, known as the Caroline Books, because the king took a kind of editorial part in the compilation, and finally put the book forth in his own name. The tone of the book is firm and dignified. Great deference for the Apostolic See is professed, but the views of the Frankish Church are resolutely maintained,—that the use of images for the ornamentation of churches, and as historical memorials, is allowable and laudable, but that adoration of them is superstitious and to be forbidden. The views, both of the worshippers of images and of the breakers of images, are unsparingly criticized. Adrian sent a long reply to the king's book, but his arguments are feeble; his tone seems to show both a sense of the weakness of his cause and a fear of offending the king.

The general tendency of the theology of the age was to follow with implicit trust the system of doctrine which the genius of Augustine had recommended to Latin Christendom. Gregory the Great is the chief link of transition between the period of the Fathers and the mediæval period, and he chiefly follows Augustine. Isidore of Seville (595-636), a large and intelligent contributor to the literature of Spain, in his theological writings transcribes Augustine and Gregory. Bede (672-735) has no theological originality; he follows the Fathers, and especially Augustine; Egbert of York, and Alcuin follow, without any originality of thought, the teaching of their school.

The great controversy, which disturbed the theological serenity of the age of Charles, sprang up in Spain, whose Church, though not oppressed by the dominant race, yet lay under such disadvantages that we should hardly have expected to find in it any exceptional originality of thought. Felix, Bishop of Urzel, a town on the south side of the Pyrenees, in the country subject to the Frank monarchy, was the most able teacher of the new opinions; Elipandus, Archbishop of Toledo, the first see of the Spanish Church, was their most prominent and ardent partisan. The system

of doctrine which Felix of Urzel taught seems to have had many points of likeness to that of the Antiochean school of the fifth century, which was condemned in the third general council at Ephesus. It may have been derived from a study of the Syrian writers of that time, such as Theodore of Mopsuestia; or Felix may have come to something of the same conclusions from approaching the subject of the divinity of Christ from the same side and in the same spirit—the spirit of rational inquiry, giving prominence to that which in the Person of Christ answers to the analogy of human nature. The general result was a sort of revived Nestorianism—a lowering down of the doctrine of Christ's divinity.[7] As in the Nestorian controversy the word *Theotokos* had been forced into undue importance, and taken as the keyword of the controversy, so now the phrases *"adopted son"* and *"adoption"* gave a title to the whole type of doctrine, and the controversy is known as the Adoptionist controversy.

The controversy was conducted with great acrimony in Spain, each side denouncing the other as unworthy of the name of Christian. From Spain it spread into the Frank Empire, disturbing the minds and unsettling the faith of many. Charles caused the question to be considered by an assembly convened at Regensburg, in the year A.D. 792. Felix of Urzel, his see being under the metropolitan jurisdiction of Narbonne, was cited to appear before the council. His doctrine was condemned, and he consented to a recantation. The king thereupon sent him to Rome, where his explanation was not considered satisfactory, and he consented to a further recantation. But on his return home he betook himself to the adjoining part of Spain, which was under the Moorish dominion, where he could express his real opinions without fear of persecution, and withdrew his recantations. Upon this Elipand and other Spanish bishops wrote two letters, one to Charles and another to the Frankish bishops, defending. Adoptionism; and they proposed a re-examination of the question, with a view to the reinstatement of Felix in his see. These letters the king sent to Pope Adrian for his information; but without waiting for any expression of opinion from him, he brought the matter before a council at Frankfort-on-the-Main, in August 15th, 794.

It was an assembly not unworthy to be compared with the earlier councils of the Western Church. Three hundred bishops were assembled, from Gaul, Germany, Lombardy, with some representatives of the English Church, and two legates from the Bishop of Rome. Alcuin was also admitted to a place, at the king's suggestion, on account of the service which his learning might be able to render. The meetings were held in the great hall of the palace. Charles, like Constantine at Nicæa, assisted at the council, and opened the proceedings with an address. Paulinus of Aquilæa, who was himself present, tells us "the venerable prince rose from his throne, and from the elevation of the dais he pronounced a long address upon the interests of religion which were in question. He concluded thus: 'It is for you to pronounce. Since the time, already far past, when the plague arose, its violence has not ceased to increase, and the contagion of the error has spread to the frontiers of my kingdom. It is necessary, then, to take steps to suppress it, by a precise definition of the faith.'" Then some days were given to the assembled Fathers in which to give in their opinions in writing; and not one defender of Adoptionism was found among them.

The question of the worship of images was also laid before the assembly for its decision, and was dealt with in a way which showed that the council was no more disposed to be bound by the decisions of Rome than of Constantinople; for it endorsed, by a formal conciliar act, the views which Charles and the Frankish theologians had already set forth in the Caroline Books.

The decisions of the council were notified by Charles, or at least in his name, to the bishops of his own dominions, and to the Spanish bishops and others beyond his own kingdom.

The decision of the Council of Frankfort by no means at once restored peace to the Church. Other lesser councils repeated the condemnation of the Fathers of Frankfort; one at Friuli (796), and one at Rome (799). The controversy continued between Felix and Alcuin, and between Elipand and Alcuin. Leidrad, Archbishop of Lyons, Nefred, Bishop of Narbonne, and Benedict, Abbot of Aniane, were sent into the district which had been infected by the Adoptionist teaching, to preach and argue, and reclaim those who had been perverted; and it is said by Alcuin that, in the course of two such missionary journeys, they made twenty thousand converts—bishops, clergy, and laity. Felix was induced to appear again before a council held at Aix, where Alcuin met him in a discussion which lasted six days, and Felix at last professed himself convinced by his adversary's arguments. But his former vacillations told against him now. He was not permitted to return to his diocese, but was committed to the care of the Archbishop of Lyons; and ultimately died in this kind of exile, leaving behind him papers which showed that it had not been an unnecessary precaution.

Another very important theological controversy of the reign of Charles is that on the question of the procession of the Holy Ghost.

The Council of Toledo, held under King Reccared, A.D. 589, at which the Visigothic Church of Spain formally abjured Arianism and adopted the orthodox faith, put forth a version of the great creed of Nicæa, in which they had interpolated an additional clause, which stated that the Holy Ghost proceeded from the Father "and from the Son" (*Filioque*). Under what influence the council took upon itself to make an addition to the creed of the universal Church is unknown. It is probable that the motive of the addition was to make a stronger protest against the Arian denial of the co-equal Godhead of the Son. The Spanish Church naturally took a special interest in the addition it had made to the symbol of Nicæa, and sustained it in subsequent councils. It became of special importance in the Adoptionist controversy, when it afforded a weapon drawn out of their own armoury against the Spanish heresy. The Frankish Church seems to have early adopted it from their Spanish neighbours, since at the Council of Gentilly (A.D. 767), under Pepin, when ambassadors from the Greek Emperor Constantine Copronymus were present, both the question of images and this question of the *filioque* were discussed, as points of difference between the two Churches; but the details of the proceedings of that council have not come down to us.

The question was brought before a council held at Aix in A.D. 809, in the form of a complaint that some Frank pilgrims to the Holy Land, visiting the famous monastery of St. Saba, near Jerusalem, had been accused of being heretics on the ground of this interpolation in the Catholic Creed, and an attempt had been made to drive them away from the monastery. The council formally approved of the addition to the creed, and Charles sent two bishops and the Abbot of Corbie to Rome, to request the pope's concurrence in the decision. Leo, at a conference with the envoys, expressed his agreement with the doctrine, but strongly opposed its insertion into the creed. And it is said that he caused copies of the creed in its genuine form, in Greek and Latin, to be engraved on two silver shields, and set up in the basilica of St. Peter as a protest against any alteration. Notwithstanding the pope's protest, the addition was adopted throughout the Frankish Empire. When the Emperor Henry V. was crowned at Rome, A.D. 1014, he induced Pope Benedict VIII. to allow the creed with the *filioque* to be chanted after the Gospel at High Mass; so it came to be generally used in Rome; and at length Pope Nicholas I. (858-867) insisted on its adoption throughout the West. At a later period the controversy was revived, and it became the ostensible ground of the final breach (A.D. 1054) between the Churches of the West and those of the East.[8] The growing opinion of the English Church of the present day probably is that Pope Leo III. was in the right; that though the doctrine is true, it was undesirable to insert it in the creed of the universal Church on any authority less than that of a general council.

Two curious features of the proceedings at Frankfort ought not to be omitted. Peter, Bishop of Verdun, who had been accused of participation in the conspiracy of Prince Pepin, was arraigned before the council. There was not sufficient proof to convict him, and he was allowed to prove his innocence if he could, after the Teutonic custom, by the oaths of conjuratos—the oaths of two or three of his brother bishops, or of his metropolitan alone, that they believed him to be innocent. But they all declined to give this testimony. Then he offered to clear himself by another Teutonic custom, the appeal to "the judgment of God" by proxy. We are not told what the nature of the ordeal was, but his "man" came safely through it, and the bishop was acquitted.

The Duke of Bavaria, dispossessed and sent to Jumièges six years before, was also brought before the council, and made to confess his treason, and to recognize the justice of his sentence, to surrender for himself and his family all his hereditary rights, and to commend his children to the mercy of the king. We can hardly doubt that this painful scene was submitted to by the unhappy duke under the coercion of threats and promises, and that its object was to extinguish in Bavaria the last hopes of a recovery of its autonomy. He was sent back to his cell, and this is the last time he or any of his dynasty, the oldest in Germany, appear on the stage of history.

Notes

1. "The Schools of Charles the Great," by J. B. Mullinger. London, 1877.

2. Among his scholars of this period were Raban Maur, Haymo, and other eminent men of the next generation.

3. The Monk of St. Gall, i. 1.

4. "The Fathers for English Readers," S.P.C.K.: Jerome, p. 216; Augustine, p. 130.

5. Monk of St. Gall, i. 3.

6. Lib. i. c. 4.

7. Neander, "Church History," vol. v. p. 215, etc. Bohn's ed.

8. Mr. Ffoulkes, "The Church's Creed and the Crown's Creed."

J. I. Mombert (essay date 1888)

SOURCE: "Famous Men.—Literature.—Libraries.—Architecture.—Public Works" in *A History of Charles the Great (Charlemagne),* D. Appleton & Co, 1888, pp. 253-79.

[*In the following excerpt, Mombert profiles noteworthy men in Charlemagne's circle and discusses Charlemagne's interest in astronomy and architecture, particularly the Rhine bridge at Mayence.*]

Besides Alcuin other men of note, already mentioned by name, stood in near personal relations to Charles.

Perhaps the oldest and most intimate of his friends was Adalhard, a son of count Bernhard, a grandson of Charles Martel, and cousin-german of Charles. Early in life he chose the monastic calling, and was abbot of Corbie, and founder of the abbey of Corvey in the Saxon country, where he died in 826. He wrote several works, but the most celebrated of them, his "Treatise of the Order and State of the Palace throughout the Frankish Realm," exists only in the reproduction of Hincmar, archbishop of Rheims. Charles consulted him on important matters and employed him in positions of the highest trust, such as imperial *missus,* administrator and *baiulus* of Bernhard, King of Italy, etc. He was a man of singular purity and strength, and one of the brightest ornaments of this reign.

Angilbert had been brought up with Charles and was essentially a man of the Court. His taste and habits were scholarly; much reading and culture, the gift of poetry, quick observation, and conversational power, made him a delightful companion. The king made him his *auriculus,* or privy councillor, and often singled him out as his representative on occasions requiring tact, good judgment, and statesmanship. The story of his love affair with the princess Bertha has been told. His cordial relations to Charles remained undisturbed to the last, and, by a singular coincidence, the abbot of St. Riquier died in his monastery about the time when Charles breathed his last at Aix-la-Chapelle.

Next to Alcuin, Einhard is believed, by some, to have been the most learned, and a very influential man at Court. A native of the Maingau, he was sent to school at Fulda; his bright ability attracted attention and led to his introduction, by the abbot, to Charles. He took an interest in him and placed him, as the companion of his own children, in the Palace School.

He rose rapidly, and successively filled the positions of superintendent of public works, councillor, and notary, or private secretary to Charles. He enjoyed to a remarkable degree the confidence of his sovereign, and to his influence is ascribed the designation of Louis, King of Aquitaine, as the associate of Charles in the imperial throne.

His biography is a masterpiece, constructed upon the model of the Life of Augustus by Suetonius. His portraiture is valuable both for what it states and suppresses; it was written in the next reign, and the fact that Louis was even more bountiful to him than his father, appears to be the true explanation of his vexatious silence and occasional perversions.

He is generally credited with the authorship of the Annals, which are among the most valuable authorities for this portion of history and generally cited by his name; but a collection of "Epistles" as well as the "History of the Translation of the Relics of St. Marcellinus and St. Peter Martyr" are unquestionably products of his pen.[1]

He was abnormally small in stature, and all the contemporary writers at the Court allude to him, but in a pleasant spirit, as a "manikin." Theodulf, Alcuin, and Walafrid Strabo jest about it, rehearse his praise, and express surprise that so much power, wisdom, and excellence should be housed in so very small a dwelling.

He was married to a certain Emma, or Imma, who is described in one of several worthless epitaphs at Seligenstadt, as the *legitimate* daughter of the great emperor Charles.[2]

The well-known legend of Einhard and Imma rests upon the unsupported authority of the chronicle of the monastery of Lauresheim, an establishment endowed by Einhard. Had the writer been a contemporary, or possessed accurate information, his statements might be entitled to respect. But he wrote more than three centuries after the death of Einhard, introduced the name of Imma as that daughter of Charles who at one time was affianced to the emperor Constantine, and applied to her the part performed by the sister of Emperor Henry III., as told by William of Malmesbury in the Chronicle written about forty years before his own. This stamps the legend as purely fictitious; its mythical character is further apparent from the language in which Einhard refers to the daughters of Charles, which he would hardly have used if one of their number had been his wife,[3] and from the total silence of the lists as to the existence of a royal daughter who bore the name of Imma.[4]

It is impossible to determine if Imma was related to Charles or how, but there is no uncertainty whatsoever as to the affection in which the king held Einhard, or the intimacy of their relations.

This is stated best in his own words.

> "To these reasons," he writes in the Prologue to his Life of Charles, "comes yet another, which in my opinion outweights the rest, and of itself not only justifies, but necessarily compels me to write. I mean, the tender care bestowed upon me since my childhood, as well as the constant friendship with which both King Charles and his sons have favored me ever since I began to live at the Court.

> "I feel bound to him by so many tokens of kindness, that I must needs cherish for him, now that he is dead, the same gratitude which I bore to him when he was alive. Indeed I should be an ingrate if, forgetful of the benefits he ever lavished upon me, I could suffer his memory to pass away without narrating the most glorious and illustrious achievements of the man to whom I owe everything, and suffer his life to remain as if he had never lived, without the memorial and tribute of praise to which his shining merit entitles him."[5]

Einhard and Imma had an only son, called Vussinus, who seems to have chosen the monastic profession, and after a preliminary education at Seligenstadt, was sent to the great monastery at Fulda and placed under the celebrated Rhabanus Maurus, its abbot from 822 to 847.

A letter of Einhard addressed to that son at the time of his departure for Fulda, opens an insight into his heart, and proclaims the man. No true parent will read it without profit or emotion.

> "To my most dearly beloved son Vussinus, greeting in the Lord.

> "I greatly fear that, when you have left the sheep-fold [his home at Seligenstadt], you may be alike forgetful of yourself and me, for inexperienced youth, unless held in by the bridle of discipline, is apt to forsake the ways of righteousness.

> "Strive, therefore, dear child, to follow good example, and in no way give umbrage to the excellent man whom I have set before you as your model; as much as you

are able, and your master may direct, remember your calling, and apply yourself to study.

> "If you follow in practice his instructions, you will not fall short in vital knowledge. As I have advised you by word of mouth, so I now urge you to persevere in study that you become skilled in all the sciences which the brilliant genius of the eminent orator, your master, may unfold to you.

> "But, above all things, endeavor to imitate his great virtues, for grammar, rhetoric, and the rest of the liberal arts, are vain things and hurtful to the servants of God, unless grace divine convince us to subordinate them to good morals, for 'knowledge puffeth up, but love edifieth.'

> "I would rather know that you were dead, than that you are stained with vice and pride, for the Saviour enjoins us to learn and copy His gentleness and humanity, but He nowhere bids us imitate His miracles.

> "What more shall I say? These and similar counsels you have often heard from my lips. God grant that by His grace you may sincerely love whatever promotes purity in heart, and purity in body. . . . "[6]

Among the personal friends of Charles and the royal family, Theodulf, bishop of Orleans, held a distinguished, honored, and prominent position. He was the recognized poet of the Court, and in the Palace School bore the pseudonym of *Pindar*. His merits were considerable, and quite a number of his poems have been preserved. Some of his graphic descriptions are already familiar to the reader, as lively delineations of persons and incidents. This makes them peculiarly interesting and instructive. His perceptions were accurate, his vocabulary large, his culture considerable, his expression fluent and telling.

One of his poems describes a royal dinner, and the episcopal bard narrates a curious episode or incident when, after the courses of eatables had been despatched, he rose for the purpose of reading one of his compositions. They might be pleasant enough to the king, the royal family and members of the Palace School, but not over interesting to the bibulous sons of Mars present, one of whom, sarcastically introduced as "Wibodus the hero," appears to have been an absent-minded hearer; he struck his thick head three or four times, and fiercely glared at the poet. The king watched him closely and either frowned or expressed his disapprobation. The broad-shouldered and huge-limbed warrior thereupon set in motion the vast machinery of his frame, whose middle portion by reason of its hilly character was ever in the van, and with shaking knees pursued an oblique line of retreat, to the intense mirth of the spectators, who needs thought of Vulcan when they beheld his feet, and of the thunders of Jove when they heard his voice.[7]

In spite of his high culture and sacred vocation, he occasionally dipped his pen in vitriol, and threw off unepiscopal adjectives and epithets in great profusion. Thus he lashed most unmercifully, in a carmen addressed to Angilbert (who by the by was also a graceful poet and would relish the thrust), an unfortunate Irish schoolmaster, who somehow had disobliged him and obtained his reward; he calls him *Scottus, sottus, cottus,* dubs him "a thing," dire, atrocious, savage, vile, infamous, pestiferous, and worse. His crime seems to have been the unpardonable one of contradicting the bishop in argument, and, the savage assault implies as much, worse than all, defeating him.[8] Some think that the castigation was intended for the Irish Clement, of whom the ever-communicative monk of St. Gall draws, however, a very different picture.

> "It so happened," he says, "that one day there arrived in Gaul two Scotchmen from Ireland,[9] fine scholars, well versed in letters sacred and profane. They had no merchandise to sell, but day after day cried in the market-place: 'Whoso desireth knowledge may have it of us, for we sell it.' This was only a figurative way of theirs, for they perceived that even then people were wont to value what they received, not according to its intrinsic worth, but according to what they paid for it.
>
> The matter being reported to Charles, he sent for the merchants of knowledge, and asked them if it was true that they carried knowledge about with them, as he had been told.
>
> 'Yes,' said the men, 'we have it and are willing to part with it to such as sincerely seek it, for the glory of God.'
>
> Their answer pleased the king, and he committed to the care of one of them a number of children, belonging to the nobility, the middle and the lower classes, to teach them. This was Clement.
>
> After a long absence the most victorious Charles returned into Gaul, and caused the children, whom he had left with Clement as his pupils, to be brought before him. He required them to be examined, and was amazed at the commendable progress of the poorer class of children, whose written productions were most creditable to them. On the other hand, those of illustrious parentage showed very poor specimens of their skill.
>
> He then set the good scholars on his right, and the poor on his left, saying: 'I praise you much, dear children, for your excellent efforts, and desire you to continue so that you may attain unto perfection; then I intend to give you rich bishoprics, or splendid abbeys, and shall ever regard you as persons of merit.'
>
> Then he turned in anger to those on his left, who trembled at his frowns and the sound of his voice, which resembled the roll of thunder, as he cried out to them: 'Look here, ye scions of our best nobility, ye pampered ones who, trusting to your birth or fortune, have disobeyed me, and instead of studying, as you were bound, and I expected you to do, have wasted your time in idleness, on play, luxury, or unprofitable occupation.'
>
> He then took his accustomed oath, and with uplifted head and arm, said in a voice of thunder: 'By the king of heaven, let others admire you as much as they please; as for me, I set little store by your birth or beauty; understand ye and remember it well, that unless you give heed speedily to amend your past

negligence by diligent study, you will never obtain anything from Charles."[10]

Peter of Pisa, a fine grammarian, taught grammar at the Court. Charles found him at Pavia, and claimed him as part of the spoil when he took that city. He was much beloved by Charles, Alcuin, and Angilbert. Alcuin heard him in his youthful days in a public disputation with Lullus, at Pavia, and sundry tributes to his memory have been preserved. He was advanced in years and died before 799; a grammar of his is still extant.[11]

Speaking of grammar, the name of Smaragdus, who taught it with great success at St. Mihiel on the Meuse, occurs, of whom it is known that he wrote a commentary on Donatus in which he selected his examples, not from the classics, but from the Bible and the Fathers. This he did in order to silence the objections of ultra-orthodox Christians and lazy scribes, who were wont to denounce grammar as a heathenish study.[12]

Among the men of note whom Charles drew to his court, Paulus Diaconus, the son of Warnefrid, deserves to be specially mentioned. He was a native of Friuli, born about 720-725, of noble parentage, and received his education at the court of Rachis in Pavia; he was also warmly attached to Desiderius, and much beloved by him. His daughter Adelperga, the wife of Arigiso, duke of Benevento, was his pupil, and at the time of the fall of the Lombards he found an asylum at the Beneventan Court.

Arigiso was a man of intellectual tastes, and his Lombard wife fully sympathized with him. She was highly educated and an enthusiastic student. Her tenacious memory stood her in good stead, and she was wont to grace her conversation with apt citations from the classical poets and the ancient philosophers. Paulus Diaconus placed in her hands the historical compend of Eutropius, but his gifted and diligent pupil deemed it unsatisfactory both on account of its great brevity and total silence concerning sacred history.

She induced him to enlarge the history and supplement the necessary references to sacred subjects. Paulus performed the work but not independently, for his additions are taken mostly from Orosius, Jerome, Jordanis, and others, and not very skilfully welded together. He extended the narrative of Eutropius from the reign of Valens to Justinian, but never carried out a projected continuation to his own time.[13] It so happened that his brother Arigiso, or Arichis, who was implicated in the Friulian revolt, had been taken prisoner and carried into Francia. Six years after that event, Paul, convinced of the clemency of Charles, addressed, and presented in person, an elegy to him, in which he made intercession for that brother.

Charles accorded to him a friendly reception, and induced him to spend several years in Germany. Paulus bore the reputation of being a very learned man, and men fabled of his proficiency in Greek and Hebrew. It was reported that he taught Greek to the Metz clergy, and Peter of Pisa, on the strength of that report which had reached the king's ears, by his command and in his name, indited a poetic epistle to Paulus, desiring him to instruct the companions of Princess Rothrud, then still affianced to the Emperor Constantine, in Greek. The deacon declined the offer, and his reply shows that his own estimate of himself was much more modest, for he wrote that if the Metz clergy spoke only the Greek they had learned of him, they would, like dumb statues, be the laughing stock of all who heard them.[14]

During his stay in Germany, Paul, who was a fair historian, and wrote poetry, composed a history of the bishops of Metz, and took pains, it is thought, to dwell at great length on the family and ancestry of Charles, with the evident design of representing the Carlovingian usurpation as justifiable, and the whole race entitled to the throne by virtue of its saints.[15] But this is hardly a fair statement of the case, and a gratuitous reflection on his character as a historian.[16]

While there is no reason to doubt his ultimate loyalty and sincere attachment to Charles, it is nevertheless certain that both were less profound than his strong feelings for the Lombard family. It is said that he never would suffer a word injurious to the memory and character of his former master, the King of the Lombards. The Franks reported the matter to Charles, and in the excess of their loyalty recommended the savage remedy of cutting off his hands, and putting out his eyes.

But Charles would have none of their counsel, and stopped the matter saying: "God forbid that I should thus treat so excellent a poet and a historian." Whatever may be the worth of the anecdote, it certainly is alike creditable to the king and the deacon.

Paulus was not a first-class historian. His best work, the *History of the Lombards,* unfortunately closes with the death of Liutprand (744); had he lived to continue it through his own time, his excellent information and unquestioned veracity would have made it a most valuable contribution to the history of that important and interesting period.[17]

At any rate he returned to Italy, and we know that he composed epitaphs for Queen Hildegard and other members of the Frankish family, as well as for Arigiso, duke of Benevento.

A list of his works is given below.[18] One of them, more especially connected with the history of Charles, is the collection of homilies which he prepared at the king's express request.

As his father, King Pepin, had directed his efforts towards the introduction of the Gregorian chant into the churches of Francia, so it was his desire to supply the want of a good collection of homilies. Those in use were utterly inadequate, and Charles denounced their intolerable and offensive solecisms. He accordingly requested Paulus to supply the deficiency. Paulus, who was then at Monte Casino, associating with himself his monastic father and friend, the abbot Benedict, selected the best homilies he could find among the tracts and sermons of the Fathers, in sufficient number to cover the entire circle of the church year, edited them in two volumes, and presented them to Charles. The king having read and approved them, set them forth, accompanied by a remarkable circular letter in which he commended them to the "readers." This Book of Homilies, known as the *Homiliarium,* has often been printed between 1482 and 1569, and translated into German and Spanish.[19]

Among those, who, like Einhard, were indebted to Charles and the Palace School for their education, may be named Angilbert; Adalhard and Wala, the king's cousins; Tatto, afterwards master of the monastery school at Reichenau; Walafrid Strabo, his pupil; Grimald,[20] subsequently abbot of St. Gall; Bernald, a Saxon, who became bishop of Strasburg, and others.[21]

Other schools in different parts of his empire enjoyed the munificent patronage of Charles. The school at Tours, under the direction of Alcuin, was one of the most celebrated; it sent forth a large number of distinguished men, and almost every man of parts of the next age was a pupil of Alcuin; Wizo, Fridugisus, Adalbert, Rhabanus Maurus, Hatto, Haimonus, and many more are said to have been his disciples.

The Missionary School of Utrecht, which flourished in the time of Gregory, bore an enviable reputation, and was much frequented.

The celebrated Rhabanus (Hrabanus)[22] Maurus taught at Fulda; Smaragdus at St. Mihiel on the Meuse; the schools at Würzburg, Reichenau,[23] Hirschau, St. Aniane in Aquitaine,[24] St. Wandrille, St. Germain d'Auxerre did noble work. Laidradus, archbishop of Lyons, had excellent "singing schools," and "reading schools;" of the former he wrote to the emperor, that such was the proficiency of the pupils that they had not only mastered the art of chanting the service, and conducted it after the pattern of the imperial chapel at Aix-la-Chapelle, but instructed others; concerning the "reading schools" he reported that the pupils not only read well, and gave evidence of their understanding what they read, but studied the Scriptures and were competent to explain the spiritual sense of the New Testament. This was truly remarkable.

The impetus to education, moreover, was general throughout the Frankish empire. In the diocese of Orleans, Theodulf charged the parochial clergy to found village schools, and provide for the gratuitous instruction of youth, reminding them that "teachers should shine as the brightness of the firmament, and they that turn many to righteousness as the stars forever and ever."[25]

In a cell or hermitage near St. Wandrille sat the presbyter Harduin, and taught a large number of pupils the arts of writing and arithmetic. He bore a good reputation for morals and learning, and allied to the contemplative habits of the hermit the more practical avocations of a teacher. The history of the cell, consecrated to a famous martyr, and built by the illustrious founder of the neighboring monastery, might stimulate profitable meditation, for St. Vandrille or Wandregesilus, was a remarkable man in his day and generation; he was a near relative of Pepin of Landen, and consequently connected with the ancestry of Charles; an energetic and zealous worker, who in spite of his austerities attained the rare old age of ninety-six. Harduin not only mused upon the virtues of the martyr and the saint, but spent much of his time in useful employment, and like St. Vandrille reached an exceptionally old age; he died, 811, in the abbacy of Trasarus.[26]

At St. Denis, and later at Pavia, Dungal, the Scot, taught astronomy and other branches; in fine, every monastery and cathedral became a centre of intellectual activity, and the enlightened views of Charles are abundantly set forth in circular letters and capitularies still extant.[27]

Without going into greater detail it may suffice to say that the intellectual life of the Frankish empire, its culture and influence for ages to come, are due to the intelligence, liberality, patronage, zeal, and enthusiasm of Charles. It is impossible to resist this conclusion, attested by Alcuin, Einhard, Angilbert, Theodulf, Rhabanus Maurus, Hincmar, Nithard, Otfried, and many other illustrious men.

Indeed we ought to say more on this head, at least, in one or two additional observations. As every school, and every church, stood in need of books, their supply gave an impetus to the art of writing and the production of libraries.

Thus the aged Harduin not only taught youth the art of writing in the cell of St. Saturnine, but copied quite a number of books, among them a book of the Gospels in uncial letters, which he bequeathed to the abbey of St. Wandrille.[28] Willehad, afterwards bishop of Bremen, engaged in the same occupation during his residence at Echternach; Laidradus, archbishop of Lyons, caused many volumes to be copied by monks and others; Angilbert collected at St. Riquier a library of two hundred volumes; Benedict of Aniane displayed a similar activity in the collection of books; and there is no doubt that Charles himself formed a most valuable library, some speak of several libraries, at Aix-la-Chapelle. It would lead too far to mention by name the magnificent specimens of the calligraphy of the Caroline age extant, but they are a feast to the eyes of all lovers of the beautiful, and standing monuments to the intelligence of Charles.[29]

Before passing on to other topics, the interest he took in astronomical subjects may detain us a little longer. He spent much time in the study, and corresponded on it with Alcuin;[30] he acquired the art of the computation of Easter,[31] and there is evidence that astronomy was much cultivated at the Court.

Two solar eclipses, one on the 5th of July, and the other on November 30th, 810, occasioned direct inquiries made of Dungal, then at St. Denis.[32] The nature of the observations, and the manner of their record, indicating the state of astronomical science, will appear from the following notice for one year beginning September 1st, 806:

> On the 4th nones of September occurred an eclipse of the moon; the sun stood in the sixteenth degree of the sign of Virgo, the moon in the sixteenth degree of Pisces.
>
> This year on the day before the kalends of February, the moon being seventeen days old, the planet Jupiter seemed to make the transit of the moon.
>
> On the 3d ides of February, about noon, an eclipse of the sun took place; the two stars stood in the twenty-fifth degree of Aquarius.
>
> Again, on the 4th kalends of March there was an eclipse of the moon, and that same night many meteors of astounding magnitude were seen; the sun standing at the time in the eleventh degree of Pisces, the moon in the eleventh degree of Virgo.
>
> On the 16th kalends of April, the planet Mercury appeared on the sun like a small black spot, and it was observed for the space of eight days slightly above the centre of that star; but clouds prevented our noting the exact time both of its entrance of the sun's disc and of its exit.
>
> In the month of August also, on the 11th kalends of September, occurred an eclipse of the moon in the third hour of the night, the sun standing in the fifth degree of Virgo, the moon in the fifth degree of Pisces.
>
> Thus from the month of September of the last year to the month of September of the present year, the moon was obscured three times, and the sun once.[33]

In a former paragraph the breadth, and vast range of the king's interest in every conceivable variety of subjects were mentioned; in this we may furnish some illustrations.

He noticed the inconvenience arising from the deficient method then in vogue of designating the quarters of the heavens by the four cardinal points only, and forthwith applied himself to the device of a scheme for defining the regions with greater accuracy, and upon its completion, gave the names and the bearings he had gained to the winds.[34]

His partiality for German, his mother-tongue, was remarkable; it grieved him to think that the vast capabilities of that noble language should lie fallow or droop into decay. With that feeling, Charles encouraged its study, recommended its use in preaching and reading, in the collection of songs, poems, and laws, and with a view to freeing it from foreign and barbarous admixtures, and elevating it to the rank of the dead languages, especially Latin, began to compose a German grammar. For throughout his reign Latin reigned supreme in the realm of letters; everything was written in Latin: the Scriptures, laws, epistles, poems, and even history; for instance, all the authorities of contemporary origin pertaining to his reign are *written* in Latin, although Latin had long ceased to be spoken.

He also invented a set of German names of the months instead of the Latin and barbarous designations in use.

The Latin names, however, could not be displaced, and his list, though ingenious, and in some of the names poetical, was never adopted. It possesses, nevertheless, a philological interest as showing what passed for good German in his day.[35]

The medical profession also was represented at the court of Charles, but its representatives appear to have been sadly deficient in knowledge. As a class they were known as the "Sect of Hippocrates," and even the inventive genius of Alcuin could say nothing better of them than that they bled their patients, compounded mixtures of herbs, and boiled poultices.

It seems that they practised medicine in connection with other avocations; perhaps they were monks or clerics otherwise provided for in the matter of support, or he would not have recommended the gratuitous dispensation of their art in order that the blessing of Christ might rest upon the labor of their hands.[36]

One of these physicians, the king's physician in ordinary, was a friend of Alcuin's; his name was Winthari. The aged and infirm Sturmi, abbot of Fulda, being about to travel from the Eresburg to his monastery, was placed by royal command in charge of the said Winthari, in the expectation that the arrangement would minister to his comfort and possibly lead to his recovery. The nature of his ailing is not known, but Eigil, the biographer of Sturmi, narrates as follows: "On a certain day the doctor made him take I know not what potion of his art, thinking it would lessen the pain, and improve the condition of the patient. But it had the opposite effect; he grew worse and worse, and the most alarming symptoms of the disease appeared in the most aggravated form. The poor abbot said full of anxiety, that the physician, who ought to have lessened the malady, had inflicted a worse evil."[37] Sturmi protested, but in vain, his case was beyond the skill of the royal physician in ordinary, for he soon died.

Charles had a very indifferent opinion of the medical profession and made light of their advice. Being generally in robust health himself, and watching their experience in the case of others, he conceived the notion that he could prescribe for himself far better than they were able. He was in the habit of confiding in the healing power of nature, and considered plentiful physical exercise, together with temperance and an occasional fast, the medicine best suited to his constitution. Sometimes he consulted the medical poem of Serenus Sammonicus and followed his advice.[38]

But as a rule he preferred his own inclinations to medical directions, and in the last years of his life, almost hated

physicians, "because they wanted him to give up roasts, to which he was accustomed, and eat boiled meat instead."[39]

The king encouraged to an uncommon degree the introduction and development of art, especially in connection with architecture. Palaces on a grand and imperial scale rose at Nimeguen,[40] Ingelheim, and Aix-la-Chapelle, but the grandest of his architectural undertakings were churches, not palaces.

The most beautiful of these was the basilica at Aix-la-Chapelle, erected in honor of the Virgin Mary, built throughout in the most massive style, of cut stone and exquisite symmetry, and, in the opinion of competent critics equal, if not superior, to the best and most ancient specimens then extant.

He summoned the most skilful workmen from every part of Europe, and imported the choicest columns, marbles, and mosaics from Rome and Ravenna.[41] The mosaics were used in the ornamentation of the walls and pavements. This splendid cathedral, adorned with gold and silver, superb candelabra, railings and doors of solid brass, and admired as a masterpiece of the age, is said, but on doubtful authority, to have been consecrated by Leo III.

Master Odo of Metz was the architect of this celebrated cathedral; the roof was covered with tiles of lead, and ornamented with a golden apple on the dome.

Two entertaining, but unsubstantiated, anecdotes relate to this period. Charles, says the Monk of St. Gall, set the most skilful of all his architects over the workmen employed in the building of the cathedral. He was an abbot, but that did not prevent his being a sharper. "The moment the emperor left home, the overseer undertook upon his own authority to discharge a number of the mechanics for the sole purpose of extorting from them bribes for their reappointment. As for those who were unable to pay the bribe, or for whom their masters refused to pay, they were in sore plight, for the abbot, after the example of the Egyptian overseers, laid grievous burdens upon them, and never gave them a moment's rest.

> By such nefarious means he accumulated a large fortune in silver and gold, and silk garments. He showed only the least valuable of his treasures openly in his room, but carefully concealed the most precious of them in chests and closets. One day he heard that his house was on fire; he ran home and rushing through the flames made his way to the room in which his gold lay secreted; eager to save as much as possible, he was not content with removing one chest at a time, but placed several boxes on his shoulders, and was on the point of leaving the burning chamber, when suddenly a huge beam, undermined by the flames, gave way, and falling on him, delivered his body to the tongue of terrestrial fire, but his soul to the unquenchable flames of hell. Thus did divine justice protect the cause and interest of Charles, when by reason of other and more important matters of his empire, he could not be present in person.

Such is the pious reflection of the chatty monk, who continues that "on these selfsame works was employed a singularly expert artificer in metal and glass. Tanchon, a monk of St. Gall, having cast a very fine bell of sweet tone, which greatly delighted the emperor's ear, the aforesaid skilful artificer said to him: 'May it please Your Majesty to command copper in large quantities to be delivered to me, and in order to make it absolutely pure in the casting, to direct that in place of tin, as is usual, the necessary weight of silver be placed at my disposal, not less than a hundred weight; let this be done, and I will make you a bell within the hearing whereof that of Tanchon shall seem dumb!'"

The speech pleased the emperor, who, "though immensely rich," did not set his heart on his riches, and commanded that the man should have all the precious metal and the copper he had asked for. The wretch, however, immediately after receiving it, went his way rejoicing, and purified the copper as well as he knew how to do it, not with silver but with tin thoroughly refined; nevertheless even of this debased metal he contrived to produce a bell which was in all respects superior to the first; it was tested, and in due course presented to the emperor. He much admired the elegance of its shape, ordered the clapper to be attached, and the bell to be raised to the belfry.

"And so it was done forthwith, even as he commanded." The bell, it seems, though hoisted to its proper place, and made fast by proper rule, was unmanageable. The guardian of the church, the chaplains of the imperial establishment, the most able and skilful mechanics, in turn tried to ring the bell, but tried in vain. "At last, the maker, even the same who had cast it, and been guilty of such unparalleled knavery, grasped the rope, and pulled the bell; suddenly the iron cross-piece to which it was fastened gave way and fell upon his head already weighted with so much iniquity; it went clean through his body and killed him outright. It was an appalling spectacle;" it was the judgment of heaven; "all the silver was found, which the most just Charles distributed among the poorest of the palace servants."[42]

Of the alleged prodigies connected with this church we shall speak on a subsequent page, but note here the partial denudation of the roof in an earthquake which shook Aix-la-Chapelle in the year 829.

A portion of it remaining in the present cathedral is improperly called "the nave." It is an "octagon in the style of S. Vitale at Ravenna, fifty feet in diameter, surrounded by a sixteen-sided gallery, and terminates in a cupola [which in the words of the Saxon poet 'climbs to the stars']. It is one of the most remarkable monuments of early Christian architecture, but unfortunately marred by modern disfigurements." The marble and granite columns, and the gates of the archways of the upper gallery date from the time of Charles.

> As long as his health allowed he was a daily worshipper at this church, going morning and evening, even after nightfall, besides attending mass; and he took care that all the services there conducted should be administered with the utmost propriety, very often warning the sextons not to let any improper or unclean thing be brought into the building, or remain in it. He provided it with numerous sacred vessels of gold and silver, and ecclesiastical vestments in great abundance, so that not even the door-keepers, who fill the humblest office in the church, were obliged to wear their ordinary clothes when in the exercise of their duties. He was at great pains to improve the church reading and psalmody, for he was well skilled in both, although he neither read in public nor sang, except in a low voice, and with others.[43]

The basilica was connected by a porticus with the royal palace, which among other peculiarities riveted attention by a bronze eagle with outspread wings which crowned the pinnacle, and the magnificent equestrian statue of Theoderic, which also came from Ravenna. It impressed Charles more than any other similar work of art he had ever seen. It was of colossal dimensions, and represented a snorting charger, the nostrils distended, and the opened mouth showing a terrible set of teeth. The spirited figure of the rider displayed a shield protecting the left shoulder, and holding a lance in the act of hurling in the uplifted right hand. The birds of the air chose the body of the horse for their nests, and flew in and out by the nostrils and the mouth.

The statue, it is said, was in the first instance set up in honor of the Emperor Zeno, and Theoderic only placed his name on it.[44]

The Rhine-bridge at Mayence was one of the most remarkable public works erected by Charles. Though only a wooden structure, it was of prodigious strength throughout its entire length of five hundred paces, and seemed as if it must last forever. This fine bridge, which associated his name with Cæsar's, had been ten years building, and constructed with admirable skill, was so completely destroyed by fire in the space of three hours that not a splinter of it was left except what was under water.[45] It must have been a marvel for strength; the Saxon poet states at the close of the ninth century that the piers of stone and earth remained visible as monumental ruins of its former splendor; nine hundred years later the submerged portions of the wooden buttresses had not yet disappeared (in 1881); but stranger still, this is contradicted, the intimation being, that the ancient oaken buttresses are not remnants of the bridge of Charles which was burned in 813, but of the Roman bridge built probably before the Christian era![46]

The accidental character of the fire, however, has been disputed; but the explanations offered instead are far from convincing. One says, that it was either the work of robbers who came at night in quest of discharged merchandise lying on the bridge, or of incendiaries desirous of building up a profitable ferry business. Others pretend that Richulf, archbishop of Mayence, ordered the bridge to be set on fire as the best method of stopping the highway robberies enacted on the bridge, and often attended by the murder of luckless passengers and their disappearance in the river. This is incredible, for such an act on the part of the archbishop would necessarily imply the express approbation of his imperial master; the loss of the bridge, moreover, was regarded as a national disaster of ominous significance, and it is known that Charles entertained the idea of replacing it by one in stone.[47]

His death prevented the execution of his purpose, and the Saxon poet describing the ruins, about the close of the century, breaks forth in lamentation, and predicts with gloomy forebodings that the work would never be performed.[48]

This prophecy proved true for nearly a millennium, for the first stone bridge over the Rhine at Mayence was not erected until 1862.

In the same connection deserves to be mentioned the grandiose scheme of a system of canalization designed primarily to establish a water-way from the Rhine to the Danube, and ultimately, from the North Sea to the Euxine.

It came up during the war with the Avars, as a feasible plan for the transportation of armies by water from and to the seat of war. The military advisers of Charles represented that troops, material of war, and especially pontoonbridges, which until then had to be carried in sections overland, might, by means of a short canal connecting two given points, be conveyed from the heart of Francia, and at a vast saving in time and expenditure, to any locality in the enemy's country suitable for military operations.[49]

The projected canal contemplated the connection of the Altmühl and the Rednitz, or more accurately, of the Suabian Rezat, a tributary of the latter. The scheme pleased Charles, and he commanded the work to be undertaken at once. A large force of men was detailed for its execution, and such was his interst that he proceeded in person, accompanied by the entire court, to the designated spot. The royal party sailed up the Danube and the Altmühl and disembarked at Sualafeld,[50] one of the termini. There was no lack of energy in the prosecution of the work, and the personal presence of Charles animated and encouraged all engaged in it. It was vigorously pushed forward throughout the autumn, and the workmen began to make the necessary excavations for the distance of two thousand steps at the width of three hundred feet; the data of the depth are not known.

But in spite of the most unremitting zeal and perseverance, the enterprise made no headway, and the bright prophecy of its easy and speedy accomplishment was falsified by the event. It was a grand and total failure.

Canal-building was one of the things which neither Charles nor his engineers understood. It is doubtful if the survey rested on accurate data touching the water-level of the respective rivers, and if the objective points were practicable; at any rate the skill of the engineers was not equal to the local difficulties of the line they selected. It ran through a low and swampy region, and the naturally soft character of the soil was aggravated by continuous rain.

The greatest obstacle they encountered was found in a section called the "Ried,"[51] where a quicksand baffled their efforts. The shifting andslippery nature of the spot forbade all progress; the superstitious workmen said that the devil was in it; that the place was bewitched and under the spell of fiends more potent than the labor of thousands of Christian hands; it had an invisible, unfathomable, omnivorous maw which devoured during the night the multitudinous loads of mud which the workmen dug out during the day.[52]

It was an unholy and evil enterprise, thought or muttered the monks; nor stopped at the thought and the speech, but set it down in writing, for we read in the Annals, drawn up in the neighboring archiepiscopal establishment at Salzburg, that "it was an idle work. But prudence and counsel cannot prevail against the Lord." This was evident by the result, for "afterwards might be heard every night the hurlyburly din of hideous noises, roaring defiance, and exulting in the laughter of derision."[53]

The record does not say if the nocturnal din and the ominous voices troubled Charles; but he ordered the work to be stopped.

Archæologists indicate Bubenheim on the Altmühl as the initial point of the "ditch," a place called "Graben" (*i. e.,* ditch), as a station, and "Weissenburg" on the Rezat, as its extreme terminus. Traces of the "Karlsgraben" (*i. e.,* the ditch of Charles) remain there to this day.[54]

By a strange coincidence this undertaking, like that of the permanent bridge at Mayence, remained unexecuted until the present century. The scheme, which so greatly interested Charles, was taken up more than a thousand years later by Louis I., King of Bavaria, and pushed to a successful termination. The canal, called after him the "König Ludwig Kanal," connects the river systems of the Danube and the Rhine by a different and much longer line. Its length of twenty-three German miles, however, bears no proportion to its width and depth, which are unfortunately inadequate to the requirements of a remunerative navigation, and a successful competition with the railroads.

In these respects it is an absolute failure.[55]

Notes

1. Wattenbach, *l. c.* I., 186 sqq.

2. They are published in Weinken, *Eginhartus Illustratus,* pp. 16, 21.

3. Vita Caroli, c. 19.

4. See the passage relating to the legend in Bouquet, V., 383. It is rejected by Bouquet, Guizot, Teulet, and the best writers generally.

5. Vita, Prologus.

6. "Ad Vussinum filium suum," in Einh. Epist. ed. Teulet, II., 45 sq.

7. Theod. Carm. *Ad Carolum Regem.*

8. Idem, *Ad Angilbert.*—Migne, cv., 322.

> Haec ita dum fiunt, dum carmina nostra leguntur
> Stet Scotellus ibi, res sine lege furens,
> Res dira, hostis atrox, hebeo horror, pestis acerba,
> Litigiosa lues, res fera, grande nefas.
> Res fera, res turpis, res segnis, resque nefanda,
> Res infesta piis, res inimica bonis.
> Et manibus curvis, paulum cervice reflexa,
> Non recta ad stolidum brachia pectus eant.
> Anceps, attonitus, tremulus, furibundus, anhelus,
> Stet levis aure, manu, lumine, mente, pede,
> Et celeri motu nunc hos nunc comprimat illos,
> Nunc gemitus tantum, nunc fera verba sonet. . . .
> Plurima qui didicit, nil fixum, nil quoque certum,
> Quae tamen ignorat, omnia nosce putat.
> Non ideo didicit, sapiens ut possit haberi,
> Sed contendendi ut promptus ad arma foret.

9. Dungal, mentioned in a later paragraph, Clement, a certain Joseph (on terms of friendship with Alcuin and Liudger), and perhaps Dicuil, were Scotchmen from Ireland.

Joseph versified and addressed several metrical pieces, remarkable for artificial acrostics, to Charles.—Hagen, *Carmina Medii Aevi,* p. 116, sqq.; Poet. Latin. aevi Carolin., I., 149 sqq.

Dicuil wrote a work, *De mensura orbis terrae;* verses on grammar, and a metrical manual of astronomy in four books, remaining in manuscript.—Dümmler, *N.A.,* IV., 256, and Poet. Latin. aevi Carolin., I., 666.

10. Monach. Sangall. I., 3, Bouquet, V., 107. On Clement, see Simson, *Jahrb. Ludw. d. Frommen,* II., 256 sqq.

11. Alcuini ep. 112 (Jaffé); Einh. Vita Caroli, c. 25; Alc. Carm. IV., 42 sqq., Angilb. Carm. II., 19 sqq. al. in Poet Latin. Carolin., I.

12. Mabillon, Vet. Analect. nov. ed. p. 358; Wattenbach, *Schriftwesen im Mittelalter,* 2 ed. p. 37.

13. MG. Auct. antiquiss. II., 4 sq.; Simson, *l. c.* I., 365.

Paulus seems to have continued at the court of Arigiso a number of years, probably until 781, when circumstances introduced a change.

14. Bouquet, V., 849; Poet. Lat. I., 48 (Dümmler). Some think that the lines of Peter, written as stated, in the name of Charles, establish the fact that he did instruct the Frankish ecclesiastics designated to accompany the princess to Constantinople. They read as follows:

> Haud te latet, quod iubente
> Michaele comitante,
> ad tenenda sceptra regni
> Christo nostro filia,
> sollers maris spatia
> transitura properat.
> Hac pro causa Graecam doces
> nostros, ut in eius pergant
> et Graiorum videantur
> Clericos grammaticam
> manentes obsequio
> eruditi regulis.

15. Bethmann, in Archiv., X., 303.

16. Bonnell, *Anfänge,* p. 45.

17. For an estimate of Paulus as a historian, see Wattenbach, *l. c.* I., 160 sqq.

18. The works of Paulus Diaconus, now extant, embrace the following: 1. "Eutropius historiographus, et post eum Paulus Diaconus de historiis Italicae provinc. ac Romanor."; 2. "De gestis Langobardorum libri sex."; 3. "Gesta episcoporum Mettensium."; 4. "Homiliarium." Of his poetry, besides the verses printed by Waitz in Monum. Germ. Hist. Langob. Saec. VI.-IX., p. 12 sq., the hymn for the feast of St. John, "Ut queant laxis," etc., is of special interest in the history of music; see "Guido d'Arezzo" in the cyclopedias.

19. Caroli epistola generalis, 786-800? apud Boretius, *Capitul.* p. 80. Compare the Dedication of Paulus in "Poet. Lat. aev. Carol." I., 68, No. 34. An entry in Bernold. Chron. 781. apud MG. SS. V., 418, states that the two volumes were completed in A.D. 808.

The Dedication referred to runs thus:

> En iutus patris Benedicti mira patrantis
> Auxilio meritisque piis vestrique fidelis
> Abbatis dominique mei, etsi iussa nequivi
> Explere ut dignum est, tamen, o pietatis amator,
> Excipe gratanter, decus et mirabile mundi,
> Qualemcumque tui famuli, rex magne, laborem;
> Quodque sacro nuper mandasti famine condi, etc.

For notice of a collection of homilies in two volumes by Alcuin see V. alch. 12 (Jaffé VI); Pertz, *Archiv.* IX., 469; Werner, *Alcuin,* p. 38.

20. Ne vero oblivisci vel neglegere videar de Albino, hoc vere de industria vel meritis eius agnovi, quod de discipulis eius nullus remansit, qui non abba sanctissimus vel antistes extiterit clarissimus. Apud quem et domnus meus Grimaldus primo in Gallia, post vero in Italia liberalibus est disciplinis imbutus.—Monach. Sangall. I., 9 (Jaffé).

21. Concerning Bernald, Ermoldus Nigellus (Eleg. I., 147 sqq. MG. SS. II., 519) writes:

> Quem Carolus, sapiens quondam regnator in orbe,
> Doctrine studiis imbuit atque fide,
> Saxona hic equidem veniens de gente sagaci.
> Sensu atque ingenio nunc bene doctus homo, etc.

Simson *l. c.* II., 572 n. 5 adds the following references: Mommsen's Fragment of his epitaph

(*Rhein. Museum für Philologie N. F.,* IX., 1854, p. 309); Erchenbald, Vers. de episc. Argentin. Boehmer Fontt., III., 2.

22. The successors of Sturmi as abbots of Fulda were: Baugulf (780-803); Ratgar (803-817); Eigil (817-822); Rhabanus (822-842). Of these Rhabanus is the most celebrated. He was a pupil of Alcuin, who called him Maurus after the favorite pupil of St. Benedict. About 804, the year of Alcuin's death, Rhabanus presided already over the school at Fulda, which enjoyed the patronage of the best society throughout the Frankish Empire. The students at Fulda might according to their intended vocation pursue an ecclesiastical or a secular course of studies. Many of course entered the Church, but quite a number followed the secular discipline. Rhabanus was an advanced thinker, and held that the study of the Classics was indispensable to the right understanding of the Scriptures.—Schneider, *Fulda,* p. 4 sqq.; Wattenbach, *l. c.* I., 221; Kunstman, *Hrabanus Magnentius Maurus,* Mainz, 1841.

23. Heito, afterwards bishop of Basel, was at the head of the monastery school of Reichenau. Among his pupils was a noble youth, called Erlebald, who ultimately became his successor. Heito, it seems, only taught him the Scriptures, and he acquired the seven liberal arts under the direction of a learned Scot, not improbably Clement.

See a collection of references in Simson, *Jahrb. Ludwigs des Frommen,* II., 256 sqq. (concerning Clement) and Abel-Simson, *l. c.* II., 575 (concerning Erlebald). The following passage is interesting:

> Post septem denosque petit venerabilis annos
> Insulanense solum: sociatu fratribus illis
> Atque magisterio Hettonis contraditur almi.
> Quo monstrante, sacris non parva ex parte libellis
> Imbuitur, variaeque vetant ne traderet artes
> Septenas curae, antiqui quas auribus indunt
> Nobilium; namque illa refert scriptura Joannis
> Ante retroque animalia sancta oculata fuisse.
> Sensusadest: sic doctus homo ex ratione biformi
> Ante superna videt, retro terrena cavetque
> Hac ex parte foret ne clauso lumine caecus.
> —Visio Wetini metr. 3. Mabillon A. S. o. s. Ben. IV., 1, p. 260.

24. On St. Aniane, and its founder, see Chapter IX., and Index.

25. Dan. XII., 3.

26. See note 2, page 267.

27. Epistola generalis, 780-800; "De litteris colendis," Capp. reg. Franc. I., 1, p. 79; see also Boretius, *l. c.* p. 78.—See on the most important schools of the period, Monnier, *Alcuin et Charlemagne,* p. 79; Werner, *Alcuin.* p. 37.

28. Gesta abb. Fontanell., c. 16, MG. SS., II., 202.

29. See on this subject: Wattenbach,*Das Schriftwesen im Mittelalter,*2 ed., p. 111; and Mabillon, A. S., s. B.

ed. Ven. IV., 1, p. 110, on the Evangeliarium with letters of gold, illuminations in silver, and precious stones.

30. See Appendix D.

31. Vita Alch., 6, Jaffé, VI., 17.

32. Epist. Carol., 30, Jaffé, IV., 396 sqq.

33. Annal. Einh, a. 807.

34. See Appendix, E.

35. See Appendix, F.

> Accurrunt medici mox, Hippocratica secta:
> Hic venas fundit, herbas hic miscet in olla,
> Ille coquit pultes, alter sed pocula praefert.
> Et tamen, o medici, cunctis impendite gratis,
> Ut manibus vestris adsit benedictio Christi.

36. Alc. Carm. 26. vv. 12-16.

37. Vita Sturmii, MG. SS. II., 377. Alcuin called him simply "Winter" (Uinter); he mentions his name in connection with a promised present of choice wine.—Alc. ep. 16 (Jaffé, VI., 171).

38. Teuffel, *Gesch. der römischen Literatur,* ed.4, p. 877 sqq. Compare on the medical profession in the next reign, Simson,*Jahrb. unter Ludw. d. Frommen,*II., 255, No. 4.

39. Vita Caroli, c. 22.

40. Vita Caroli, c. 17: Erm. Nigell. III., 583 sqq.; IV., 179 sqq.; Poeta Saxo, V., 429 sq. The last named author says of Ingelheim:

> Ingylemhem dictus locus est, ubi condidit aulam,
> Aetas cui vidit nostra parem minime.
> Quorum multiplicem si quis describere laudem
> Curabit, longum texet opus nimium.

The best and fullest description of this palace, and the church at Ingelheim, is that of Ermold. Nigell. *l. c.*

41. The use, for the purpose named, of those at Ravenna, was granted by Hadrian, as appears from his epistle to Charles:

Praefulgidos atque nectareos regalis potentiae vestrae per Aruinum ducem suscepimus apices. In quibus referebatur, quod palatii Ravennate civitatis mosivo atque marmores ceterisque exemplis tam in strato quamque in parietibus sitis vobis tribuissemus. Nos quippe libenti animo et puro corde cum nimio amore vestre excellentiae tribuimus effectum et tam marmores quamque mosivo ceterisque exemplis de eodem palatio vobis concedimus abstollendum.—Cod. Carol. 89 (Jaffé, IV., 268). The alleged use of marbles and mosaics from Trèves (Gesta Trever. 25, MG. SS. VIII., 163) and Verdun (MG. SS. VIII., 352) is legendary.

42. Monach. Sangall. I., 30, 31; Bouquet, V., 118 sq.

43. Vita Caroli, cc. 26, 27; Franc. Petrarcha, I., ep. 3; Petrus à Beek, *Aquisgrano,*c. IV., Cod. Carol. ep. 77

(Jaffé); Bädeker, *Northern Germany,* p. 5.—Also, Vita Caroli., c. 32; Annal. Einh., a. 829.—Vita Hlud. 43

44. Agnelli, *Lib. pontif. Raven.,* c. 94; cf. Vita Caroli, c. 26; and Cod. Carolin., 89 (Jaffé).

45. Vita Caroli, c. 32.

46. Dümmler, *Allg. D Biogr.,*XV., 147; Simson, *l. c.,* II., 512.

47. Monach. Sangall., I., 30, Marian. Scot. Chron. a. 835; Annal. Wirz., a. 813; Disibodenberg, a. 813.

48. Poeta Saxo, V., 601 sq.

49. Annal. Lauresh., Guelf., Einh. *al.*

50. Annal. Guelf. The locality does not agree with the names given by later writers.

51. Eckhart, Franc. Orient., II., 750; he gives a diagram.

52. Annal. Einh. a. 793; Mosell. 792; Lauresh.

53. Annal. Salisb., MG. SS. XIII., 23.

54. Auctarium Ekkehardi Altahense, 792, MG. SS. XVII., 362. Riezler, *l. c.* I., 181, no. 1.

55. Daniels, *l. c.* I., 233; Heigel, *Ludwig I., König von Bayern,* p. 170 sq.—Riezler, *l. c.* I., 181.

Thomas Hodgkin (essay date 1897)

SOURCE: "Results" in *Charles the Great*, Macmillan and Co., Limited, 1914, pp. 232-51.

[*In the following excerpt, originally published in 1897, Hodgkin summarizes Charlemagne's accomplishments in the fields of the Church, literature, science, law, and the state-system of Europe.*]

No ruler for many centuries so powerfully impressed the imagination of western Europe as the first Frankish Emperor of Rome. The vast cycle of romantic epic poetry which gathered round the name of Charlemagne, the stories of his wars with the Infidels, his expeditions to Constantinople and Jerusalem, his Twelve Peers of France, the friendship of Roland and Oliver and the treachery of Ganelon—all this is of matchless interest in the history of the development of mediæval literature, but of course adds nothing to our knowledge of the real Charles of history, since these romances were confessedly the work of wandering minstrels and took no definite shape till at least three centuries after the death of Charlemagne.

In this concluding chapter I propose very briefly to enumerate some of the chief traces of the great emperor's forming hand on the western church, on Literature, on Laws, and on the State-system of Europe.

I.

Theologically, Charles's chief performances were the condemnation of the Adoptianist heresy of Felix of Urgel

by the Council of Frankfort (794): the condemnation of the adoration of images by the same Council; and the addition to the Nicene Creed of the celebrated words "Filioque," which asserted that the Holy Spirit "proceedeth from the Father *and the Son.*" In these two last performances Charles acted more or less in opposition to the advice and judgment of the pope, and the addition to the Creed was one of the causes which led to the schism between the eastern and western churches, and which have hitherto frustrated all schemes for their reunion.

In the government of the church Charles all through his reign took the keenest interest, and a large—as most modern readers would think a disproportionate—part of his Capitularies is dedicated to this subject. Speaking generally, it may be said that he strove, as his father before him had striven, to subdue the anarchy that had disgraced the churches of Gaul under the Merovingian kings. He insisted on the monks and the canonical priests living according to the rules which they professed: he discouraged the manufacture of new saints, the erection of new oratories, the worship of new archangels other than the well-known three, Gabriel, Michael, and Raphael. He earnestly exhorted the bishops to work in harmony with the counts for the maintenance of the public peace. While not slow to condemn the faults of the episcopacy he supported their authority against mutinous priests: and preeminently, by the example which he set to Gaul in the powerful and well-compacted hierarchy which he established in Germany, he strengthened the aristocratic constitution of the church under the rule of its bishops. At the same time there can be no doubt that by his close relations with the Roman Pontiff and by the temporal sovereignty which he bestowed upon him, he contributed, consciously or unconsciously, to the ultimate transformation of the western church into an absolute monarchy under the headship of the pope. That Charles, with all his zeal for the welfare of the church, was not blind to the faults of the churchmen of his day is shown by the remarkable series of questions—possibly drawn up from his dictation by Einhard—which are contained in a Capitulary of 811 written three years before his death:

> We wish to ask the ecclesiastics themselves, and those who have not only to learn but to teach out of the Holy Scriptures, who are they to whom the Apostle says, 'Be ye imitators of me': or who that is about whom the same Apostle says, 'No man that warreth entangleth himself with the business of this world': in other words, how the Apostle is to be imitated, or how he (the ecclesiastic) wars for God?
>
> Further, we must beg of them that they will truly show us what is this 'renouncing of the world' which is spoken of by them: or how we can distinguish those who renounce the world from those who still follow it, whether it consists in anything more than this, that they do not bear arms and are not publicly married?
>
> We must also enquire if that man has relinquished the world who is daily labouring to increase his possessions in every manner and by every artifice, by sweet persuasions about the blessedness of heaven and by ter-

rible threats about the punishments of hell; who uses the name of God or of some saint to despoil simpler and less learned folk, whether rich or poor, of their property, to deprive the lawful heirs of their inheritance and thus to drive many through sheer destitution to a life of robbery and crime which they would otherwise never have embraced?

Several more questions of an equally searching character are contained in this remarkable Capitulary.

II.

If doubts may arise in some minds how far Charles's ecclesiastical policy was of permanent benefit to the human race, no such doubts can be felt as to his patronage of literature and science. Herein he takes a foremost place among the benefactors of humanity, as a man who, himself imperfectly educated, knew how to value education in others; as one who, amid the manifold harassing cares of government and of war, could find leisure for that friendly intercourse with learned men which far more than his generous material gifts cheered them on in their arduous and difficult work; and as the ruler to whom more perhaps than to any other single individual we owe the fact that the precious literary inheritance of Greece and Rome has not been altogether lost to the human race. Every student of the history of the texts of the classical authors knows how many of our best MSS. date from the ninth century, the result unquestionably of the impulse given by Charles and his learned courtiers to classical studies. It is noticeable also that this reign constitutes an important era in paleography, the clear and beautiful "minuscule" of the Irish scribes being generally substituted for the sprawling and uncouth characters which had gone by the name of Langobardic. In one of his Capitularies Charles calls the attention of his clergy to the necessity for careful editing of the Prayer-books; otherwise those who desire to pray rightly will pray amiss. He enjoins them not to suffer boys to corrupt the sacred text either in writing or reading. If they require a new gospel, missal, or psalter, let it be copied with the utmost care by men of full age. In another Capitulary, he expresses his displeasure that some priests, who were poor when they were ordained, have grown rich out of the church's treasures, acquiring for themselves lands and slaves, but not purchasing books or sacred vessels for the church's use.

Something has already been said as to the Academy in Charles's palace, which was apparently founded on the basis of a court-school established in his father's lifetime, but became a much more important institution in his own. Probably it was then transformed from a school for children into an Academy for learned men, in the sense in which the word has been used at Athens, Florence, and Paris. Alcuin, after his departure from court, founded a school at Tours, which acquired great fame; and we hear of schools also at Utrecht, Fulda, Würzburg, and elsewhere. Doubtless, most of these schools were primarily theological seminaries, but, as we have seen in the case of Alcuin, a good deal of classical literature and mathematical science was, at any rate in some schools, taught alongside of the correct rendering of the church service.

The Monk of St. Gall (who wrote, as we have seen, two generations after Charlemagne, and whose stories we therefore accept with some reserve) gives us an interesting and amusing picture of one of the schools under Charles's patronage. After giving a legendary and inaccurate account of the arrival of two Irish scholars in Gaul, named Alcuin and Clement, he goes on to say that Charles persuaded Clement to settle in Gaul, and sent him a number of boys, sons of nobles, of middle-class men and of peasants, to be taught by him, while they were lodged and boarded at the king's charges. After a long time he returned to Gaul, and ordered these lads to be brought into his presence, and to bring before him letters and poems of their own composition. The boys sprung from the middle and lower classes offered compositions which were "beyond all expectation sweetened with the seasoning of wisdom," but the productions of the young nobility were "tepid, and absolutely idiotic." Hereupon the king, as it were, anticipating the Last Judgment, set the industrious lads on his right hand and the idlers on his left. He addressed the former with words of encouragement, "I thank you, my sons, for the zeal with which you have attended to my commands. Only go on as you have begun, and I will give you splendid bishoprics and abbacies, and you shall be ever honourable in my eyes." But to those on his left hand he turned with angry eyes and frowning brow, and addressed them in a voice of thunder, "You young nobles, you dainty and beautiful youths, who have presumed upon your birth and your possessions to despise mine orders, and have taken no care for my renown; you have neglected the study of literature, while you have given yourselves over to luxury and idleness, or to games and foolish athletics." Then, raising his august head and unconquered right hand towards heaven, he swore a solemn oath, "By the King of Heaven, I care nothing for your noble birth and your handsome faces, let others prize them as they may. Know this for certain, that unless ye give earnest heed to your studies, and recover the ground lost by your negligence, ye shall never receive any favour at the hand of King Charles."

There was one branch of learning in which Charles was evidently not enough helped by his friends of the classical revival, and in which one cannot help wishing that his judgment had prevailed over theirs. Einhard tells us that he reduced to writing and committed to memory "those most ancient songs of the barbarians in which the actions of the kings of old and their wars were chanted." Would that these precious relics of the dim Teutonic fore-world had been thought worthy of preservation by Alcuin and his disciples!

He also began to compose a grammar of his native speech; he gave names to the winds blowing from twelve different quarters, whereas previously men had named but four; and he gave Teutonic instead of Latin names to the twelve months of the year. They were—for January, *Wintarman-*

oth; February, *Hornung;* March, *Lentzinmanoth;* April, *Ostarmanoth;* May, *Winnemanoth;* June, *Brachmanoth;* July, *Hewimanoth;* August, *Aranmanoth;* September, *Witumanoth;* October, *Windumemanoth;* November, *Herbistmanoth;* December, *Heilagmanoth.*

III.

It is of course impossible to deal with more than one or two of the most important products of Charles's legislative and administrative activity.

1. In the first place, we have to remark that Charles was not in any sense like Justinian or Napoleon, a codifier of laws. On the contrary, the title chosen by him after his capture of Pavia, "Rex Langobardorum," indicates the general character of his policy, which was to leave the Lombards under Lombard law, the Romans under Roman law; even the Saxons, if they would only accept Christianity, to some extent under Saxon institutions. To turn all the various nationalities over which he ruled into Ripuarian Franks was by no means the object of the conqueror; on the contrary, so long as they loyally obeyed the great central government they might keep their own laws, customs, and language unaltered. As this principle applied not only to tribes and races of men, but also to individuals, we find ourselves in presence of that most peculiar phenomenon of the early Middle Ages which is known as the system of "personal law." In our modern society, if the citizen of one country goes to reside in the territory of another civilised and well-ordered country, he is bound to conform to the laws of that country. Where this rule does not prevail (as in the case of the rights secured by the "capitulations" to Europeans dwelling in Turkey or Morocco) it is a distinct sign that we are in the presence of a barbarous law to which the more civilised nations will not submit. But quite different from this was the conception of law in the ninth century under Charles the Great and his successors. Then, every man, according to his nationality, or even his profession,—according as he was Frank or Lombard, Alaman or Bavarian, Goth or Roman, layman or ecclesiastic,—carried, so to speak, his own legal atmosphere about with him, and might always claim to be judged *secundum legem patriae suae.* Thus, according to an often-quoted passage, "so great was the diversity of laws that you would often meet with it, not only in countries or cities, but even in single houses. For it would often happen that five men would be sitting or walking together, not one of whom would have the same law with any other."

But though Charles made no attempt, and apparently had no desire, to reduce all the laws of his subjects to one common denominator, he had schemes for improving, and even to some extent harmonising, the several national codes which he found in existence. But these schemes were only imperfectly realised. As Einhard says, "After his assumption of the imperial title, as he perceived that many things were lacking in the laws of his people (for the Franks have two systems of law, in many places very

diverse from one another), he thought to add those things which were wanting, to reconcile discrepancies, and to correct what was bad and ill expressed. But of all this naught was accomplished by him, save that he added a few chapters, and those imperfect ones, to the laws [of the Salians, Ripuarians, and Bavarians]. All the legal customs, however, that were not already written, of the various nations under his dominion, he caused to be taken down and committed to writing."

While Charles's new legislation was in general of an enlightened and civilised character, a modern reader is surprised and pained by the prominence which he gives, or allows, to those barbarous and superstitious modes of determining doubtful causes—wager of battle, ordeal by the cross, and ordeal by the hot ploughshares. As to the first of these especially, the language of the Capitularies seems to show a retrogression from the wise distrust of that manner of arriving at truth expressed half a century earlier by the Lombard king, Liutprand.

2. A question which we cannot help asking, though it hardly admits of an answer, is, "What was Charles's relation to that feudal system which, so soon after his death, prevailed throughout his empire, and which so quickly destroyed its unity?" The growth of that system was so gradual, and it was due to such various causes, that no one man can be regarded as its author, hardly even to any great extent as its modifier. It was not known to early Merovingian times; its origin appears to be nearly contemporaneous with that of the power of the Arnulfing mayors of the palace; it must certainly have been spreading more widely and striking deeper roots all through the reign of Charlemagne, and yet we can hardly attribute either to him or to his ancestors any distinct share in its establishment. It was, so to speak, "in the air," even as democracy, trades' unions, socialism, and similar ideas are in the air of the nineteenth century. Feudalism apparently had to be, and it "sprang and grew up, one knoweth not how."

One of the clearest allusions to the growing feudalism of society is contained in a Capitulary of Charles issued the year before his death, in which it is ordained that no man shall be allowed to renounce his dependence on a feudal superior after he has received any benefit from him, except in one of four cases—if the lord have sought to slay his vassal, or have struck him with a stick, or have endeavoured to dishonour his wife or daughter, or to take away his inheritance. In an expanded version of the same decree a fifth cause of renunciation is admitted—if the lord have failed to give to the vassal that protection which he promised when the vassal put his hands in the lord's, and "commended" himself to his guardianship. Other allusions to the same system are to be found in the numerous Capitularies in which Charles urges the repeated complaint that the vassals of the Crown are either endeavouring to turn their *beneficia* into *allodia,* or, if possessing property of both kinds,—a *beneficium* under the Crown and an *allodium* by purchase or inheritance from their fathers,—are starving and despoiling the royal *beneficium* for the benefit of their own *allodium.*

3. An institution which was intended to check these and similar irregularities, and generally to uphold the imperial authority and the rights of the humbler classes against the encroachments of the territorial aristocracy, was the peculiarly Carolingian institution of *missi dominici,* or (as we may translate the words) "imperial commissioners." These men may be likened to the emperor's staff-officers, bearing his orders to distant regions, and everywhere, as his representatives, carrying on his ceaseless campaign against oppression and anarchy. The pivot of provincial government was still, as it had been in Merovingian times, the Frankish *comes* or count, who had his headquarters generally in one of the old Roman cities, and governed from thence a district which was of varying extent, but which may be fairly taken as equivalent to an English county. Under him were the *centenarii,* who, originally rulers of that little tract of country known as the Hundred, now had a somewhat wider scope, and acted probably as *vicarii* or representatives of the count throughout the district subject to his jurisdiction. These governors, especially the count, were doubtless generally men of wealth and great local influence. They had not yet succeeded in making their offices hereditary and transmitting the countship, as a title of nobility is now transmitted, from father to son. The strong hand of the central government prevented this change from taking place in Charles's day, but it, too, like so much else that had a feudal tendency, was "in the air"; and it may have been partly in order to guard against this tendency and to keep his counts merely life-governors that Charles devised his institution of *missi.*

But a nobler and more beneficial object aimed at was to ensure that justice should be "truly and indifferently administered" to both rich and poor, to the strong and to the defenceless. It is interesting in this connection to observe what was the so-called "eight-fold ban" proclaimed by the Frankish legislator. Any one who (1) dishonoured Holy Church; (2) or acted unjustly against widows; (3) or against orphans; (4) or against poor men who were unable to defend themselves; (5) or carried off a free-born woman against the will of her parents; (6) or set on fire another man's house or stable; (7) or who committed *harizhut*—that is to say, who broke open by violence another man's house, door, or enclosure; (8) or who when summoned did not go forth against the enemy, came under the king's *ban,* and was liable to pay for each offence sixty solidi (£36). Here we see that three of the specified offences were precisely those which a powerful local count or *centenarius* would be tempted to commit against the humbler suitors in his court, and which it would be the business of a *missus dominicus* to discover and report to his lord.

The *missi* had, however, a wide range of duties beyond the mere control and correction of unjust judges. It was theirs to enforce the rights of the royal treasury, to administer the oath of allegiance to the inhabitants of a district, to enquire into any cases of wrongful appropriation of church property, to hunt down robbers, to report upon the morals of bishops, to see that monks lived according to the rule of their order. Sometimes they had to command armies (the brave Gerold of Bavaria was such a *missus*) and to hold *placita* in the name of the king. Of course the choice of a person to act as *missus* would largely depend on the nature of the duties that he had to perform: a soldier for the command of armies or an ecclesiastic for the inspection of monasteries. As Charles, in his embassies to foreign courts, was fond of combining the two vocations, and sending a stout layman and a subtle ecclesiastic together to represent him at Cordova or Constantinople, so he may often have duplicated these internal embassies, these roving commissions, to enquire into the abuses of authority in his own dominions.

We have, in one of Charles's later Capitularies, an admirable exhortation which, though put forth in the name of the *missi,* surely came from the emperor's own robust intellect:—"Take care," the *missi* say to the count whose district they are about to visit, "that neither you nor any of your officers are so evil disposed as to say 'Hush! hush! say nothing about that matter till those *missi* have passed by, and afterwards we will settle it quietly among ourselves.' Do not so deny or even postpone the administration of justice; but rather give diligence that justice may be done in the case before we arrive."

The institution of *missi dominici* served its purpose for a time, but proved to be only a temporary expedient. There was an increasing difficulty in finding suitable men for this delicate charge, which required in those who had to execute it both strength and sympathy, an independent position, and willingness to listen to the cry of the humble. Even already in the lifetime of Charles there was a visible danger that the *missus* might become another oppressor as burdensome to the common people as any of the counts whom he was appointed to superintend. And after all, the *missus* could only transmit to the distant regions of the empire as much power as he received from its centre. Under the feeble Louis the Pious, his wrangling sons and his inept grandsons, the institution grew ever weaker and weaker. Admirable instructions for the guidance of the *missi* were drawn up at headquarters, but there was no power to enforce them. With the collapse of the Carolingian dynasty towards the close of the ninth century the *missi dominici* disappear from view.

4. Another institution was perhaps due to Charles's own personal initiative; at any rate it was introduced at the outset of his reign, and soon spread widely through his dominions. It was that of the *scabini,* whose functions recall to us sometimes those of our justices of the peace, sometimes those of our grand-jurors, and sometimes those of our ordinary jurors. Chosen for life, out of the free, but not probably out of the powerful classes, men of respectable character and unstained by crime, they had, besides other functions, pre-eminently that of acting as assessors to the *comes* or to the *centenarius* in his court of justice.

Seven was the regular number that should be present at a trial, though sometimes fewer were allowed to decide. As in all the earlier stages of the development of the jury system, they were at least as much witnesses as judges—their own knowledge or common report forming the chief ground of their decision. It is not clear whether their verdict was necessarily unanimous, but it seems certain that the decision was considered to be theirs, and not that of the presiding functionary, whether *comes, vicarius,* or *centenarius.* It was, moreover, final; for, as one of the Capitularies distinctly says, "After the *scabini* have condemned a man as a robber, it is not lawful for either the *comes* or the *vicarius* to grant him life."

The *scabini* were expected to be present at the meetings of the county—probably also, to some extent, at those of the nation, and they joined in the assent which was there given to any new Capitularies that were promulgated by the emperor. It is easy to see how, both in their judicial and in their legislative capacity, the *scabini* may have acted as a useful check on the lawless encroachments of the counts. There was probably in this institution a germ which, had the emperors remained mighty, would have limited the power of the aristocracy, and have formed in time a democratic basis upon which a strong and stable monarchy might have been erected.

IV.

Lastly, a few words must be said as to the permanent results of Charles's life and work on the state-system of Europe. In endeavouring to appraise them let us keep our minds open to the consideration not only of that which actually was, but also of that which might have been, had the descendants of Charles been as able men as himself and his progenitors.

The three great political events of Charles's reign were his conquest of Italy, his consolidation of the Frankish kingdom, and his assumption of the imperial title.

1. His conduct towards the vanquished Lombards was, on the whole, generous and statesmanlike. By assuming the title of King of the Lombards he showed that it was not his object to destroy the nationality of the countrymen of Alboin, nor to fuse them into one people with the Franks. Had his son Pippin lived and transmitted his sceptre to his descendants, there might possibly have been founded a kingdom of Italy, strong, patriotic, and enduring. In that event some of the glorious fruits of art and literature which were ripened in the independent Italian republics of the Middle Ages might never have been brought forth, but the Italians, though a less artistic people, would have been spared much bloodshed and many despairs.

But we can only say that this was a possible contingency. By the policy (inherited from his father) which he pursued towards the papal see, Charles called into existence a power which would probably always have been fatal to the unity and freedom of Italy. That wedge of Church-

Dominions thrust in between the north and south would always tend to keep Lombardy and Tuscany apart from Spoleto and Benevento; and the endless wrangle between Pope and King would perhaps have been renewed even as in the days of the Lombards. The descendants of the pacific and God-crowned king would then have become the "unutterable" and the "not-to-be-mentioned" Franks, and peace and unity would have been as far from the fated land as they have been in very deed for a thousand years.

2. Charles's greatest work, as has been once or twice hinted in the course of the preceding narrative, was his extension and consolidation of the Frankish kingdom. One cannot see that he did much for what we now call France, but his work east of the Rhine was splendidly successful. Converting the Saxons,—a triumph of civilisation, however barbarous were the methods employed,—subduing the rebellious Bavarians, keeping the Danes and the Slavonic tribes on his eastern border in check, and utterly crushing the Avars, he gave the Teutonic race that position of supremacy in Central Europe which, whatever may have been the ebb and flow of Teutonism in later centuries, it has never been forced to surrender, and which, with all its faults, has been a blessing to Europe.

3. As to the assumption of the imperial title, it is much more difficult to speak with confidence. We have seen reason to think that Charles himself was only half persuaded of its expediency. It was a noble idea, this revival of the old world-wide empire and its conversion into a *Civitas Dei,* the realised dream of St. Augustine. But none knew better than the monarch himself how far his empire came short of these grand prophetic visions; and profounder scholars than Alcuin could have told him how little it had really in common with the state which was ruled by Augustus or by Trajan. That empire had sprung out of a democratic republic, and retained for centuries something of that resistless energy which the consciousness of self-government gives to a brave and patient people. Charles's empire was cradled, not in the city but in the forest; its essential principle was the loyalty of henchmen to their chief; it was already permeated by the spirit of feudalism, and between feudalism and any true reproduction of the *Imperium Romanum* there could be no abiding union.

I need not here allude to the divergence in language, customs, and modes of thought between the various nationalities which composed the emperor's dominions. The mutual antagonism of nations and languages was not so strong in the Middle Ages as it has been in our own day, and possibly a succession of able rulers might have kept the two peoples, who in their utterly different languages swore in 842 the great oath of Strasburg, still one. But the spirit of feudalism was more fatal to the unity of the empire than these differences of race and language. The mediæval emperor was perpetually finding himself overtopped by one or other of his nominal vassals, and history has few more pitiable spectacles than some that were presented by the rulers of the Holy Roman Empire—

men bearing the great names of Cæsar and Augustus—tossed helplessly to and fro on the waves of European politics, the laughing-stock of their own barons and marquises, and often unable to provide for the ordinary expenses of their households.

But all this belongs to the story of the Middle Ages, not to the life of the founder of the empire. It would be absurd to say that he could have foreseen all the weak points of the great, and on the whole beneficent, institution which he bestowed on Western Europe. And whatever estimate we may form of the good or the evil which resulted from the great event of the eight hundredth Christmas day, none will deny that the whole history of Europe for at least seven hundred years was profoundly modified by the life and mighty deeds of Charles the Great. . . .

Henry W. C. Davis (essay date 1899)

SOURCE: "Legislation—Religious Policy—The Renaissance; 774-800 A.D." and "Fate of the Franks—The Legend of Charlemagne" in *Charlemagne (Charles the Great): The Hero of Two Nations*, 1899, pp. 155-86; 312-31.

[*In the following excerpt, Davis describes the* missi, *Charlemagne's agents in many matters of law; Alcuin and his Palatine school; and Charlemagne's own scholarly interests and achievements. He also explains the demise of the Frankish empire and the development of the Charlemagne legends and song cycle.*]

LEGISLATION—RELIGIOUS POLICY—THE
RENAISSANCE 774-800 A.D.

The influence of the Church moulded the career of Charles as a conqueror; the same influence is equally conspicuous when we turn to his legislation. We have seen that his first capitulary was ecclesiastical in matter; when, after ten years, he again takes up the pen, the constitution and discipline of the Frankish Church are still his usual themes. More secretly and indirectly the Church affected his secular legislation; very many of his injunctions to the laity bear reference to offences against morality and the canons; others dealing with commerce, education, the administration of justice seem to be inspired by contact with Rome. Each visit to Italy was followed by important reforms in Church or State. Sometimes the King returns with artists, teachers, theologians in his train; more often we discern that the general sense of responsibility as the custodian of a great Christian society is quickened in him by the lofty ideas which Hadrian, greater in his words than in his acts, communicated to the Patrician of the Holy See.

The enactments of this period are not particularly copious. Two relate to Saxony, eight to Italy, five to the whole body of the realm, while several instructions addressed to the *missi* illustrate the detail of administration. Neither are they systematic. The important measures lie buried in lists of canons literally copied from ancient councils, among

exhortations to keep the Lord's Day, to attend mass, to love justice, and to believe in the one true God.

One constitutional change can be discerned, namely, the more systematic employment of royal *missi*. This office was not unknown in Merovingian times; any commissioner despatched from the royal palace with a special purpose bore the name of *missus*. But from the year 789, when the conquest of Bavaria seemed to have completed the process of expansion, the *missi* become the recognised agents through whom Charles the Great transmits his laws and edicts to the provinces, or gathers information, or investigates and redresses the abuses of local administration. To all appearance, the *missi* of this kingly period (768-800) went their rounds at irregular intervals in any part of the realm to which the attention of their master was particularly called. Thus, in 790, on discovering that through the neglect of Lewis the Pious, the finances of the Aquitanian crown had fallen into an embarrassed state, Charles sent a pair of *missi* to effect the needful economies and reforms. Once or twice commissioners went on circuit through the whole kingdom. In 789 and 792 they were charged to exact the oath of fealty from all men: "Thus I promise to my lord, Charles, and to his sons, that I am their faithful man and will be all the days of my life." On the latter occasion they also enquired in every province whether the counts judged all men by their own national law, as the King's will was. The first duty of the *missi* was to hear complaints against a count and, if necessary, to compel him to do justice. In cases of contumacy they paid a visit to the count's official residence and resided there as his proper charges until he bought them off by doing whatever they required in the interests of the injured suitor. Next they were expected to assist the count if any great vassal of the King obstructed the path of justice. Thirdly, they joined the bishop in periodical visitations, and punished laxities of discipline among the clergy, both secular and regular. Fourthly, they inspected the beneficial estates which the King had granted from the crown-lands of the province, reported any cases of improper use or waste, and exacted the usual dues and services. Fifthly, they enquired how the obligation of military service was discharged; and whether the count enforced it as he should.

As yet the office was in its infancy. We hear of no fixed circuits at this time, nor have the *missi* any law-court distinct from that of the count; when they make an appearance they supersede him for the time being, or sit on the bench beside him to see that he judges without fear or favour. Many functions hereafter to be conferred upon them are not mentioned in these early laws. The men employed were of no considerable station, but usually chosen from among the poorer vassals of the Crown.

Next in interest come the measures which deal with commerce and public order. For the first time in the history of the Frankish kingdom a uniform system of weights and measures was introduced.[1] Similarly the coinage was reformed within a few years after the Lombard conquest. Before 774 there were no less than sixty-seven local mints;

of these the greater number were now suppressed. The standard, too, was changed; henceforth twenty shillings went to the pound of silver, and twelve pennies to the shilling. To refuse coins of full weight and bearing the royal monogram became a serious offence against the King's peace. Coins not satisfying these conditions might be refused with impunity. In Italy the use of the old Lombard coinage was prohibited from August 1, 781. The new currency compares favorably with the old in purity, in weight, and in artistic workmanship. Unfortunately for us, it never before the year 800 bears the portrait of the King, although from time to time we find his emblem—a temple or the gate of a city—stamped upon one side.

Ordinances forbidding usury and fixing the price of corn prove that Charles borrowed his ideas of economics from the teaching of the Church. No canonist could blame severe measures against those who attacked travellers upon the highway or levied illegal tolls; and to this extent the interests of merchants were protected. The repeated denunciations of gilds are due in part to the semi-pagan cults which some had fostered, in part to the conspiracies of the Thuringians and Pepin the Hunchback; later capitularies show that mercantile associations for mutual insurance were not regarded as contrary to law.

The King defends his ecclesiastical laws from the charge of presumption, by a reference to those of King Josiah— "not that I profess myself his equal in holiness, but because we are enjoined to follow in all things the examples of the saints." The apology is not superfluous. Sometimes in a mixed assembly of laymen and religious persons, less often in a purely ecclesiastical synod, he regulated the constitution, the discipline, and the doctrine of the national church. The constitution—for following in the footsteps of St. Boniface he restored the authority of the metropolitans and defined their provinces, confirmed the jurisdiction of abbots over their monks, of bishops over their clergy; made the payment of tithe a legal duty incumbent on all laymen, and the sentence of excommunication enforceable at law; regulated the privileges of "immunities," ordered suits between clerks and other persons to be heard by the count and bishop jointly. The discipline—for he forbade the clergy to marry or keep concubines, to enter taverns, to carry arms, to hunt or hawk, to meddle in worldly business. He lectured the bishops on the nature of their duties. He informed the laity of three cases in which they might lawfully work upon the Sabbath, viz.: to bring up the baggage of the army, to transport food, to bury the dead. He altered the liturgy and church music; he introduced a new book of homilies; he ordered special fasts and services whenever he thought proper. In all these measures the opinion of the Pope is seldom asked. On one occasion Hadrian is allowed to delimit the provinces of Aix, Embrun and Tarentaise; on another to sanction the continued residence at court of Archbishop Angilramn. At times the Pope suggests a reform; command them he cannot, even in the Lombard kingdom.

In matters of doctrine the Pope's intervention would have seemed only natural. Then, as now, he was the recognised oracle of the faith. A book composed under the eye of the King himself, asserts that only those books are canonical and only those doctrines orthodox upon which the chief of all the Apostolic Sees has set the seal of its approval. In dealing with the Adoptianist heresy Charles was careful to put his theory into practice. The belief that Christ was a human being, adopted by, and therefore inferior to, the Father, was an old and popular tenet among the Spanish Christians. Some however impugned it; and Elipand, the Archbishop of Toledo, commissioned Bishop Felix of Urgel to confute them. The see of Felix, as belonging to the province of Narbonne, was subject to the Frankish church. Charles resolved to correct the bishop's errors. He submitted them to the Pope,[2] and on obtaining from him a formal expression of disapproval proceeded to confute and crush the heresy in a series of councils, at Regensburg (792), Frankfort (794), and Aachen (799). On the first occasion Felix, having recanted, was sent to Rome, where he repeated his statement before Hadrian. In 799 Leo held a synod at Rome simultaneously with that of Aachen, and reached the same conclusions. At Frankfort, two envoys from the Pope were present.

In the last named synod, however, Charles gave a remarkable proof of his independence even in doctrinal questions. Seven years previously the Empress Irene and her creature Tarasius, whom, from a well-grounded belief in his servility, she had preferred while yet a layman to the Patriarchate, convened the second Council of Nicæa and restored the worship of images with a difference; assigning to them adoration, not in the absolute sense, but such as becomes the symbol and dwelling-place of the divine.[3] The legates of Pope Hadrian were present at the council and he cordially approved of its decrees. The Latin Church had consistently maintained the use of images as aids to devotion and as a means of instructing the unlettered in the history of the church. Hadrian agreed that proper respect should be paid to them, and accepted the fine-spun distinction which the Greeks had drawn between worship and reverence. To Charles and his mentor Alcuin this distinction was incomprehensible. They drew up and sent to the Pope the famous *Libri Carolini* in which they proved, by the authority of the Scriptures and the Latin fathers, that the worship of images or pictures is mere idolatry. The conclusion is just, but beside the mark. Its exponents too were hampered by the necessity of admitting that the soundest authorities tolerated and that they themselves practised the worship of relics and of the true cross. This fact alone must prevent us from hailing them as the precursors of those Protestants who cited the *Libri Carolini* in the sixteenth and seventeenth centuries. Hadrian returned an elaborate reply, which failed to produce conviction. The synod of Frankfort condemned the decrees of Nicæa, and apparently a schism was only prevented by the submission of Hadrian. Döllinger supposes a political motive for this departure from the principle of obedience to the Holy See. Already, he thinks, Charles had resolved to assume the Imperial title. His object at Frankfort was not so much to repudiate what he believed to be a heresy, as to discredit Constantine and Irene in the eyes of Christendom. Some facts may be alleged in support of this hypothesis. Hadrian evidently suspected an ulterior motive. In his reply to the *Libri Carolini,* he says that, although he cannot brand the Emperor and his mother as heretics on account of decrees so undoubtedly orthodox, he is willing to attack them on another ground, because they are in unlawful possession of estates belonging to St. Peter. In the *Libri Carolini* themselves—which were circulated at least among the clergy of the Frankish kingdom—Irene and Constantine are personally criticised. The style of their documents, it is said, would make them the equal of God and His Apostles. The veneration paid to them and to their portraits is idolatrous. They call their own parents and predecessors heretics. In that case it is clear that they were educated by heretics and their faith comes from a tainted fount. And who ever heard before of a woman sitting and speaking in a council of the Church?

But these are arguments of a kind familiar to controversialists; and no special motive is needed to explain their introduction. Hadrian was engaged at the time in squabbles with Charles respecting the estates and jurisdictions of the Papacy, and was hardly in a position to know the true intentions of the King. The general tone of the *Libri Carolini* is that of men who are honestly engaged in the defence of the Catholic tradition, and really unable to understand the hair-splittings of their opponents. Moreover the authority of Gregory the Great was clearly on their side. To Charles and even to Alcuin it was incredible that there could be any legitimate excuse for the logical development of dogma. If a distinction was new they held that it could not possibly be true. Many passages in the correspondence of the latter prove his nervous fear lest the slightest appearance of innovation should produce a deadly schism. To Felix of Urgel he writes: "The end of the world is at hand. The love of many waxes cold. What should we weak mortals do but hold fast by the doctrine of apostles and evangelists." "The seamless robe of Christ" is a metaphor which he employs with great effect.

Thus Alcuin, nurtured in the tradition of Theodore and Gregory the Great, proved himself more Roman than the Romans. Of Irish Platonism and Arabian rationalism he was entirely innocent. In his conflict with the Pope he relied upon the authority of previous Popes. Never was the influence of Rome more powerful in Francia than at the period when he was the final authority of Charles in matters ecclesiastical. The temporary estrangements between his master and Hadrian were ripples on the surface; they did not affect the broad stream of Frankish policy.

Had Alcuin been a mere theologian this fact would interest us little. He was also a teacher and an organiser of education. He initiated an intellectual movement, and inspired the legislation by which it was fostered. Here also he was dominated by Roman ideas, which in his Northumbrian home had preserved more of their original vitality than in the soil from which they sprang.

Although the conquest of the Lombards brought to the notice of Charles Paul the Deacon, Peter of Pisa, and Pauli-

nus, afterwards patriarch of Aquileia; although the last named certainly and the others probably became, within a few years, honoured teachers at the Frankish Court, still the Carolingian Renaissance of learning hardly dates its commencement from their spasmodic and uncoördinated essays in education. Before any notable awakening of intellectual curiosity could be effected there must arise a brighter star of scholarship than any of these excellent grammarians. Their special knowledge was, for those times, very considerable, their industry unwearied. Paulinus had judgment, Peter a sense of scholarship, and Paul a sprightly intellect. But all three were men of the cloister, absorbed in barren trivialities or in the pursuit of learning for its own sake. The preceptor of the Frankish King and his nobles should be a man of the world, versed in affairs and with a wide range of sympathies; he must conquer their respect by proving his superiority in their own fields of thought and action. He must have the insight to see the dumb perplexities of the untutored mind, the art to enlighten without arrogance, the tact to avoid those subjects for which his pupils were unfitted, and the eloquence to impress them with the charms of those towards which they showed the slightest inclination. Method would be needed, but the method must be the opposite of pedantic. Each pupil would have to be attacked on a different side; the matter and manner of the lesson must be varied in each individual case. Above all, the teacher would require to be furnished with a ready answer for the question, To what end? He must show the applications of his lessons to the conduct of life and the government of the State. Such teachers are never common, but Charles was fortunate enough to find one possessing all these requisites, and to find him just when the times were ripe for his influence.

Alcuin was the scion of a noble Northumbrian house which had already rendered good service to Francia in producing St. Willibrod, the apostle to the Frisians. The future schoolmaster of the Empire cherished the memory of his illustrious kinsman, and was at the pains to write his biography in Latin verse. He himself became known to the Frankish Court in early life. A man of wealth who had embraced the clerical profession chiefly to avoid the entanglements and distractions of Northumbrian politics, he had travelled more than once through Gaul and Lombardy in quest of books and teachers. On one of these occasions he appeared at the court of Charles. The date must have been somewhere between 767 and 780. He was charged with a message from the King or the Primate of Northumbria, and thus came in contact with the ruler of the Franks. The scholar and the conqueror parted with feelings of mutual esteem, but probably with no idea of the close connexion in which they were afterwards to live. In 781 they met again at Parma, and this time the King extorted a promise that Alcuin would obtain the permission of his superiors for a protracted visit to the Court of Aachen. We are left to infer that Alcuin's fame for learning was already established. This may well have been the case. He had received his education in the famous School of York from teachers who had sat at the feet of the Venerable Bede, and he had assimilated all the learning, patristic, classical, scientific, which, from Canterbury, Rome, and Iona, had found its way to that greatest of English seminaries. He fulfilled his promise in 782, and, except for a few visits in the years 786-793, never revisited his native land. Northumbria had fallen on evil days. Civil wars, the Danish invasions, and the decline of the School of York—all these were pressing reasons why a peaceful scholar should cast about to find a new field for his energies. And in Mercia or Wessex, Alcuin would have been less at home than he was among the Franks.

He was forty-seven years of age when he came to Charles. Though loaded with rich benefices by his friend and master, he neither desired nor accepted an official position, and remained a simple deacon until his death. Strife and hurry were to him, he said, as smoke to sore eyes. His energies were unobtrusively bestowed upon the labours of writing, legislating, and teaching. In 796 he retired from court to the abbey of St. Martin at Tours, the most important of those which Charles had given him; and no solicitations could tempt him back. Shortly after the imperial coronation he asked and obtained leave to abandon all his preferments; and from that time till 804, when he was carried off by a paralytic stroke, he lived a life of rigid asceticism and meditation. In his epitaph he describes himself with characteristic modesty as merely one who was "a wanderer on the face of the earth" and "always a lover of wisdom." Yet to the last no personal influence was more widely felt in Francia and in Europe than that of the secluded English scholar.[4]

In the first period of his career (782-790) he organised the School of the Palace and others of a similar kind; in the second he fought and vanquished the Adoptianist and Iconodulic heresies; in the third he founded at Tours a monastic school which became the parent of many more and fixed the type of such institutions for centuries to come. In all three periods he stands forth as the general adviser of his patron, as the centre of a literary circle, as the great authority to whom scholars, theologians, and practical statesmen resort for the solution of their difficulties.

The School of the Palace may have enjoyed an amorphous existence from the earliest times. Ambitious youths of good families resorted to the courts of the Merovingians and their mayors in the expectation of learning whatever a ruler ought to know. It would be to the interest of their patrons to provide such instruction. The royal chaplains and secretaries were possibly ordered to teach the aspirants in their intervals of leisure. But until Alcuin's day the school had neither organisation nor a curriculum which deserved the name, and the general body of the Frankish aristocracy remained innocent of the slightest trace of culture. Under Alcuin the school became an important factor in national life; it developed into a well-defined and highly favoured institution. Any magnate might send his sons, nor were humble antecedents allowed to exclude a boy of talent. Plebeian or patrician, it mattered nothing to Charles; he singled out the most proficient with rare impartiality and promoted them to vacant offices or preferments. Alcuin taught in person and enlisted all the other literati in the service. The King set the fashion of taking lessons, and all his family were put to school. Being a Court affair, the school accompanied the royal household in its wanderings. It was not hampered by elaborate paraphernalia. Alcuin sent envoys far and wide to purchase books for his pupils, but the library which he gathered must have been both small and portable. The primers of the elementary subjects—orthography, grammar, rhetoric, and dialectic—were written by himself. They are extant and printed in his works.

The knowledge imparted in the school was rudimentary. Alcuin himself knew no more of the liberal arts than could be gathered from the meagre compilations of Cassiodorus and Martianus Capella, from the encyclopædia of Isidore of Seville, from imperfect translations of the *De Interpretatione* and the Categories of Aristotle. Of astronomy he knew virtually nothing, of arithmetic and geometry very little. Though Boethius had rendered into Latin the standard works of Nicomachus, Euclid, and Ptolemy on these subjects, we are forced to conclude that Alcuin had never seen or never mastered these authors. His logic is confused, his rhetoric a glossary of technical terms. Of Greek and Hebrew he knew only so much as could be gathered from the quotations in St. Jerome. He was familiar with Virgil and the minor tracts of Cicero; but, in later life at least, discouraged on principle the study of pagan authors. Others, however, were less narrow in their preferences. Eginhard shows a considerable acquaintance with Suetonius and Livy; Theodulf of Orleans defends the classics, on the ground that they present profound moral truths in the form of allegory. Both these men were pupils of Alcuin. Paul the Deacon and Peter of Pisa contributed to the general stock a finer scholarship than his, and some knowledge of Greek, of history, and of classical antiquities.

Theology formed the chief occupation of the advanced students. Charles in the famous encyclical of 789 defends all other studies on the ground that they minister to this. "Since in the holy pages there are tropes, figures of speech, and the like, there is no doubt that a man grasps their meaning in proportion as he is trained in letters." The pupils made great progress in the study thus commended to them as the final cause of all their labours. Gisla, the sister, and Rotrude, the daughter of the King, write urgently to Alcuin in his retirement at Tours for explanations of doubtful passages in the Fourth Gospel. They tell him that since receiving his lessons they have the keenest desire to be more deeply instructed. He sends them in return two bulky volumes of exegesis, and finds it necessary to excuse himself for not sending more. Lewis the Pious was already, before his father's death, despised by the Frankish warriors as one whose training had made him a monk at heart. The King, also, became a proficient in the science, though it must be owned that in his case the effect was the reverse of softening. It was his favourite recreation to bombard the Pope and Alcuin and any bishop whose opinion he valued, or whose flagging interest he wished to stimulate, with such questions as these: "What is meant by the ritual in the baptismal service? and what is the sevenfold grace of the Holy Ghost?" We do not know how Leo acquitted himself on these occasions. But one of the bishops, whom we suspect to have been a mighty hunter, solved his perplexities by persuading the good-hearted Theodulf of Orleans to write him a set of answers. Alcuin praises his master on the ground that he sets himself "to sharpen the wits of young men and to remove the rust of slothfulness" by these impromptu examinations. We gather from the case we have cited that the wits were sharpened, but hardly according to the royal intentions. At all events, the King set a good example to men of greater leisure than himself. A day or two before his death he was engaged in correcting the text of the Vulgate, with the help of Greek and Syrian scholars who translated their own versions to him. Nor was this a new departure. He had always been ready to defend the faith with the pen when his sword was unemployed. The general opinion is that he took some considerable part in drawing up the *Libri Carolini*. In his correspondence with Alcuin he is ready to suggest and criticise. In the confutation of the Adoptianist heresy he took the keenest interest. He even wrote with his own hand, for the benefit of the Spanish bishops, a statement of the true doctrine touching the Incarnation and the dual nature of our Lord. The beginning is not unimpressive: "This is the Catholic faith; since Catholic, therefore ours; we hope that it is yours also: That there is one faith and one baptism and one Lord Jesus Christ, very God and very Man, two natures in one person, the Mediator between God and men." But argument and open-minded discussion are not his forte. He passes rapidly from exposition to warning and expostulation. "Correct yourselves and hasten with a pure faith to join the unity of the Holy Church of God. Whence do you imagine—you who are so few—that you have discovered something more true than that which is held by the Universal Church in all the world?" Torquemada himself could not have expressed more forcibly the Church's abhorrence of the human reason. In controversy as in war Charles was always "the terrible King."

His attainments other than theological were, for the time, considerable. He knew enough Greek to understand the speeches of the Byzantine envoys. He learned his Latin grammar with Peter of Pisa, the other liberal arts with Alcuin. In the latter's dialogue on Rhetoric he appears as an interlocutor. Eginhard says that he began to learn writing, and kept the materials always under his pillow, but made little progress. This may mean that finer kind of writing used in making copies of books; yet it is far from incredible that even in his correspondence the King was dependent on a secretary. He was fascinated by the study of astronomy, although he had not even the Ptolemaic system for a guide. Among his treasures we are told of a planisphere made of precious metals, carved with the signs of the zodiac and the courses of the planets. Eager for knowledge of every kind, he turned his attention to several branches of science which lay outside the ordinary curriculum. By enquiries from foreigners and travellers he gained some knowledge of distant lands; histories, too, he loved and would have them read to him at meals. He caused the Frankish sagas to be collected, and began a grammar of his native tongue. He impressed upon his officials the necessity of studying law, and made medicine a compulsory subject in his schools. But he showed his usual prudence in refusing to let the Galens of the time prescribe for his ailments. We have a story relating to the Court physician which says little for his skill. His name was Wintar. Wintar was sent to attend upon old Abbot Sturm in his last illness, and gave him a mysterious potion. From that hour the Abbot grew worse instead of better. At length he cried with a lamentable voice, "The leech has undone me," and shortly afterwards breathed his last. In fact, the Palatine school and its kindred institutions retained, in spite of the King's attempt to make them the training-ground of practical men, a strongly theological bias and bred in their alumni a morbid suspicion of all other learning.

The special enactments by which Charles attempted to promote the revival of learning are not without their interest, and may conveniently be noticed in this place. In 786 he brought back from Italy Roman singers to improve the services of his church. He established them at Metz and Soissons, and sent them the precentors of many churches to be instructed. This reform, projected but never carried out by Pepin the Short, was in itself of no great importance, but it illustrates the essentially Roman character of the Carolingian Renaissance. We are told that at Rome Charles heard the choristers of his chapel disputing with Italians as to the merits of their respective styles. He said to the former, "Tell me, now: Which is the better, the living fountain or the streams which flow from it?" They answered with one voice, "The fountain." He retorted, "Return, then, to the fountain of St. Gregory, for you have plainly corrupted the music of the Church." In the same spirit he reformed the Frankish liturgy, expelling the interpolations of local usage, revised the ritual on the Roman model, forbade the unauthorised introduction of new cults, and employed Paul the Deacon to compile from the works of the most revered Latin fathers a Homiliarium which supplanted the ill-chosen selections previously in use in Northern Europe, and afterwards became the basis of that now authorised by the Roman Church. It was the ignorance of the clergy which necessitated such reforms, and he set himself to remove this fundamental evil. About the year 787 he addressed to the bishops and abbots a circular letter on the subject of education. The study of letters, he says, is an essential part of the religious life. Good works are better than knowledge, but without knowledge good works are impossible. He has noticed with pain, in the letters addressed to him by the religious, that laudable sentiments are too often obscured by uncouth language. He, therefore, bids those in authority to find schoolmasters and see that all beneath their care are duly instructed. In the preface to the Homiliarium he deplores the decay of letters which the neglect of his ancestors had permitted, remarks on the corrupt state of the sacred texts, and invites his subjects to coöperate with him in removing their blemishes. In 789 he orders that in every diocese be established schools where boys may learn the Psalms, musical notation, chanting, arithmetic, and grammar. They are to be supplied with well-corrected copies of the Catholic books.

At a later period he commanded that every clerk should learn, among other things, reading and writing, the creeds, the Lord's Prayer, the book of the Sacraments and the book of Offices, the Penitential, the *Liber Pastoralis* of St. Gregory, and the pastoral letter of Pope Gelasius. Every layman should at least be instructed by his priest in the Apostles' Creed, the Lord's Prayer, and the doctrine of the Trinity.

These efforts were not thrown away. Leidrade of Lyons reports in 813-814 that he has schools of singers, some of whom are qualified to teach others, and of readers who have learned to expound the Scriptures, as well as to avoid solecisms in pronunciation. Theodulf of Orleans established throughout his diocese parochial schools in which the clergy taught all children whose parents cared to send them, taking no reward except in the form of spontaneous offerings.

It will be observed that this system of education was entirely theological. Even arithmetic was introduced principally to enable pupils to calculate the dates of festivals. Those who could never hope to rule in Church or State had no occasion for the wider course of studies followed at the Palace. Alcuin's school at Tours is the type of the provincial academies. When he founded it his contempt for secular learning had risen almost to the point of fanaticism. Virgil and other profane texts were rigidly excluded. The school contained two grades or classes. In the first, beyond which laymen rarely passed, instruction was confined to the subjects prescribed in the Capitulary of 789; in the second, monks and other persons destined for the Church studied the Scriptures, the fathers, the canons, and so much of the seven liberal arts as might assist them in exegesis. The men who issued from this course usually became the abbots of German or Frankish monasteries. Raban Maur is the most distinguished of them; his chief title to fame is that he originated the school of Fulda. The other schools founded on the model of Tours (for example, Corbie, St. Wandrille, St. Gall) were almost without exception monastic and intended for the education of churchmen. Within this narrow field their beneficial effect was considerable. But the general level of culture among the laity was not raised. Very few even learned to read or sign their names.

To posterity these schools rendered a double service. They restored Latin to the position of a literary language, resisting on the one hand the invasion of German words, on the other the Gallo-Roman corruptions of inflections and of syntax. A correct orthography was reintroduced and a style formed which, if it owed more to St. Augustine than to Cicero, was none the less an adequate medium for the expression of current ideas. In the second place, the pupils became editors and copyists of such authors as had survived the wreck of ancient learning. The Vulgate, the Latin fathers, liturgical books, the works of Cassiodorus, Boethius, Bede, and those classical texts which contained nothing to shock the susceptibilities of the orthodox were carefully amended; and the chances of total loss were diminished by the multiplication of manuscripts. Alcuin laid down the first principles by which such labours must be guided; he also gave a splendid example of their application in his recension of the Vulgate. By collating a number of copies and by utilising the quotations to be found in Augustine and Jerome, he expelled many errors of long standing and gave to the Western Church a text of the Scriptures far superior to those possessed by the Greeks.[5] The work was presented to Charles at Rome on Christmas Day, 800. Under the influence of Alcuin the scriptoria of Tours, Fulda, and the other leading monasteries were peopled with skilful penmen. The manuscripts of this period are second to none in accuracy and artistic finish. Often written in gold upon a purple parchment, and adorned with exquisite initial letters and illuminations, they are still more to be admired for the regular and legible alphabet, modelled upon the ancient uncial, which they brought into fashion. Slight as this merely mechanical reform may appear, it had the important results of making books more accessible and of diminishing the chances of error in future copies.

From the schools we pass on to the men who made them and were made by them. The pupils and assistants of Alcuin are in general more attractive as human beings than as authors. Their books are as barren as their lives are rich in interest. Devoting themselves, like their master, to minute theological researches, they produced a number of long and tiresome treatises in which the results of wide reading and painful lucubrations are brought to bear upon such problems as the inner meaning of baptism, the mode of the Incarnation, the grace imparted by the Spirit. In vain we turn them over and over to find any passage which displays in a marked degree the merits of ordered exposition, closely woven logic, or perspicuous language. The lighter effusions of the school are scarcely more interesting. Master and pupils alike are prolific of banal epigrams and turgid compliments, of trifling riddles and insipid allegories. Were these written in a vernacular tongue they might at least have pleased by their ingenuous puerility. But they are in Latin verse of a peculiarly lame and formal kind. The prosody of Alcuin would at times disgrace a fifth-form schoolboy. Sometimes an unexpected touch of nature, a passing flash of satire, or an accidental piece of self-revelation lends interest to the shorter pieces; otherwise their value is merely historical. Of all the Court poets, Theodulf is the most readable. A native either of Spain or Italy, he is led by his warm southern nature sometimes to good-natured badinage of his equals, sometimes to fierce denunciation of the evils which ate like a canker-worm at the heart of the Frankish State. In his *Advice to Judges* he describes, with fiery contempt, the drunken count, the suitors coming with their bribes, the heartburnings and intrigues of the provincial law-court.

We owe to him a sketch of the Palace circle, which shows quite another Alcuin than the grave figure of the *Acta Sanctorum*—a burly convivial figure, eating and drinking largely, and between the courses laying down the law on all things human and divine. Of Alcuin's own poetry, the following dialogue between Spring and Winter is perhaps the most favourable specimen:

> *Ver.*—I am fain for the cuckoo's coming, the bird that I love the best;
> And there's not a roof where the cuckoo deigns to pause in his flight and rest
> And pipe glad songs from his ruddy beak, but will call him a welcome guest.
> *Hiems.*—Delay me the coming of cuckoo! The father of toils is he;
> And battles he brings, and all men in the world, however weary they be,
> Must rouse them from rest at his trumpet to brave land-farings and perils at sea.
> *Ver.*—The note of the cuckoo brings flowers and gladdens with honey the bee.
> Sends the landsman to build up his homestead, the ship to the unruffled sea,
> And the nestlings are hatched by his music, and the meadow glows green and the tree.

Beyond question, the greatest literary monument of the age is the biography which Eginhard wrote of his patron. Educated with the royal children, and afterwards employed at Court as director of public works, the future historian of the age had unrivalled opportunities for acquiring his material at first hand; from a careful study of classical historians he derived not merely a severe and weighty style, but also a true conception of artistic form. Both in manner and matter he is the best historian of the early Middle Ages. He is not absolutely impartial; he ascribes to his hero an antique gravity which hardly agrees with the impressions to be derived from other sources: the ostentation, the love of adventure, the often naïve ambition by which the true Charles was characterised pass unnoticed in the pages of Eginhard. Of doubtful transactions he professes a prudent ignorance or supplies an ingenious defence; in some few cases he appears consciously or unconsciously to distort the facts. In reading him we must always remember the personal equation. Eginhard shared to the full the foibles and the prejudices of his time. The true man stands confessed in his tract, *The Translation of SS. Marcellinus and Petrus.* He tells us with the utmost simplicity how he sent to Rome to buy relics for his monastery. The supply was running short and the Pope had forbidden further exportations. But, with the help of a roguish cicerone, the historian's agent plundered a crypt and returned rejoicing. And Eginhard, secure in his remoteness from Rome, calmly records the pious theft to vindicate before posterity the genuineness of his treasures.

A tale of the twelfth century assigns Eginhard as a lover to a certain Princess Emma, whom it calls the daughter of Charlemagne. It is true that the wife of Eginhard was named Emma, but there is no evidence to connect her with the royal family; and the severity with which her husband adverts upon the amours of the princesses precludes the idea that she was one of the culprits. Concerning Anghilbert, the fellow-scholar of Eginhard, more authentic scandals are related. Anghilbert became private secretary to the King and used his opportunities to form a liaison with the Princess Bertha. They had already two children when Charles, to stop the mouth of slander, allowed their marriage; and since Anghilbert was already in orders, the marriage was even more reprehensible than the intrigue by which it had been preceded. Four years later they took monastic vows together and entered the same religious house—yet another infraction of church discipline. Finally they quarrelled and separated; Bertha returned to the Court, where she was not long in finding other lovers; Anghilbert became arch-chaplain and one of the two chief ecclesiastical ministers of the King. The story illustrates at once the laxity of Court morals and the high standing which literary attainments conferred in this reign. Anghilbert owed his position chiefly to the scholarship which won for him the surname of Homer. He is not the only instance in point. The King encouraged all learned men to converse with him on a footing of equality. A society resembling the Italian academies of the eighteenth century formed itself under his patronage. In his intercourse with the initiated he took the name of David; Alcuin was Flaccus; Eginhard, Bezaleel; the ladies of the Court were admitted, also under classical names. The members exchanged verses and compliments; from time to time they banqueted at Court, criticised each other's works, and debated on topics of general interest. Meanwhile the wine cup circulated freely. Charles himself was temperate; the same could not be said of all his companions. Theodulf describes how faithful vassals, privileged to attend these feasts of reason, grew hot and argumentative with their potations or fell asleep while Alcuin held discourse.

In this patronage of literature we may discern something of vanity. The Austrasian chief aspires to be Augustus and Mæcenas in one; he must have his Virgil and Horace to sing the praises of his kingdom. It pleased him, also, to have men at hand who could answer the questions which occurred to his insatiable curiosity. Yet beneath these trivial motives there lay a settled policy, namely, that of utilising in his government all the available supply of intellect. The questions of Charles were not invariably frivolous; as head of the Church, he asked for clear ideas on the subjects of theological controversy; as head of the State, for assistance in forming a conception of his duties. And no scholar entered his service without finding himself, sooner or later, enjoined to undertake some work of public utility. To such men, as to the rude warriors whom he led into battle, he imparted some of his own fiery enthusiasm for the regeneration of society. If they had not genius, they were at least compelled to be industrious. "Work! for the night cometh," is the precept of Alcuin to his royal pupils; and Alcuin himself attests how literally Charles fulfilled this ideal, and lets us learn that he, for one, wore himself out in the service of this exacting master. Nor did the King confine his exhortations to the teachers. A variety of anecdotes bear witness to the minuteness with which he tested the working of his educational laws. At one time we find him coming to the Palatine school and questioning the boys; he puts the idle on one side and delivers a severe lecture to them, saying that industry, not noble birth, is the passport to his favour. At another he enters a cathedral, sees children brought to the font, and interrupts the service to catechise both them and their sponsors; they prove to be ignorant of the rudiments of the faith; he sends them home to get better instruction from their parish priests. Nowhere in the kingdom, says the Monk of St. Gall, were clerks better trained than in the royal chapel; the fear of their master was upon them. They never knew beforehand which of them would be called upon to read the lessons; at the proper moment in the service Charles would point with his staff to someone; he must begin at once and read on until the King, by clearing his throat, gave the signal to stop; and woe to the reader who mispronounced or could not find his place.

We must not exaggerate the importance of this Renaissance, or the abilities of the men by whom it was initiated. The scholars of the fifteenth and sixteenth centuries drew upon the purest sources, ascended through their classical studies to the first principles of literary art and philosophic thought, and were original even in their plagiarisms. In the eighth century the intellectual horizon was bounded by the Latin fathers and the tradition of the Church—to interpret and to codify the established theology was the highest ambition of the student. Any approach to rationalism, any independent exercise of the intellect, was the signal for a storm of contumely and persecution. We have seen the fate of Bishop Felix, whose error was at worst a venial one, touching only the highest metaphysics of the faith. But for royal protection his fate would have been shared by Dungal, a brilliant Irish scholar who came to Court after the retirement of Alcuin. The mysticism which Dungal inherited from the teachers of his own country, his dialectical powers, his unusual erudition, were traits which at once excited the hostility of his more sober predecessors. "A wild man of the woods, a plaguey litigious fellow, who thinks he knows everything, and especially the things of which he knows nothing." Such is the verdict of Theodulf. Alcuin accuses Dungal not obscurely of Alexandrian gnosticism and is lavish in warnings to all and sundry of his pupils. By such attacks the influence of the Irishman was neutralised, and the results, such as they were, of Celtic thought snatched from the Frankish Church.

These are the defects of the Carolingian intellectual movement. Its merits can only be appreciated when we compare the meagre chronicle of Frédégaire with the annals of Lauresheim and the writings of Eginhard, or the Latin of Marculf with that of Alcuin and of Hincmar; when we turn from the copious treatises and disputations of the ninth-century theologians to mark the blank silence and stagnation of the preceding epoch; or when we run over the list of monasteries planted by the authors of the movement in Saxony and Western Germany—veritable dykes to stem the tide of paganism and ignorance which otherwise must infallibly have swept back upon the newly conquered lands

in the chaos of the following century. For all these results the great King must take the principal credit. It was he who collected the teachers and set them to work, who furnished them with resources, who pointed out to them the direction in which their efforts would be most profitably expended.

. . . . .

FATE OF THE FRANKS—THE LEGEND OF CHARLEMAGNE

To all intents and purposes the Frankish Empire was buried in the grave of Charles at Aachen. Five of his descendants wore the imperial title: Lewis the Pious (840), Lothaire (855), Lewis II. (875), Charles the Bald (877), Charles the Fat (888). Theoretically the Empire only came to an end when the German nobles deposed Charles the Fat and chose Arnulf of Carinthia to be their king. In reality the last seventy years of its history had been one long death-agony; its fall was welcomed with delight by the nations which had belonged to it; only at the Papal Court and among some families claiming descent from the first Emperor was there any affection for the old idea of European unity.

As we have seen above, the causes of decay are principally to be found in the internal organisation of the Empire. Charles the Great ruled by the help of the Church and of a rude feudalism. Presuming on his control of the hierarchy, trusting to his personal influence with the Holy See and with national synods, he allowed the wealth and power of the clergy to increase without limit; conscious that all the nobles were his vassals, and over-confident that their special oath of fealty would keep them loyal to his successors, he watched with indifference, or at least neglected to check, the process by which all freeholders were forced to group themselves round the banner of count or bishop. It was the duke and the count, the abbot and the bishop, who sapped the vigour of the Carolingian Empire.

But special and accidental causes accelerated the downfall. The Frankish nation, which for so many generations had imposed its yoke upon Teuton and Latin alike; which had furnished Charles with warriors, administrators, ecclesiastic; which more than any other race had assimilated the Imperial idea—this nation came to a sudden and a violent end through the weakness of Lewis the Pious and the savage ambitions of his family. Bewildered by the arguments with which they were plied by the several factions of the royal house, loving the Empire, but uncertain in which line the Empire should rightfully descend, the flower of the race were drawn some to this camp and some to that; Franks fought against Franks for the possession of the Empire, and knew not that the prize for which they fought was crumbling away to nothingness. These fatal feuds began in the year 817 when Lewis the Pious first broached the calamitous project of admitting his children into partnership; like Lear, he put off his clothes before he went to bed, and the fate of Lear was his reward. The Franks, among whom he had thrown the apple of discord, survived him but a few years. Their power as a nation was broken on the field of Fontanet (841). At Fontanet the sons of Lewis fought for supremacy; it was the bloodiest battle remembered in the annals of the Franks; forty thousand of their best and bravest were left upon the field. Regino of Prum remarks that from that day they who had been the conquerors of the world could barely muster men enough to guard their own frontiers.[6] The result is seen in the treaty of Verdun (843). It recognises three kingdoms. The greater part of Gaul, the greater part of Germany, have broken away from the Frankish supremacy; though ruled by princes of the Carolingian stem, they owe no obedience to the Emperor Lothaire. He and his Franks were left to content themselves with a straggling Middle Kingdom. This kingdom was indeed of no inconsiderable extent. It reached from the Rhine to the borders of the Papal States; it included the Lombard Plain and the valley of the Rhone, Alsace and Lorraine, the country between the Rhine and Meuse, also, westward of that river, the province known as Old Francia, from which Clovis had started on his career of conquest. But for the nation of Charles and the heir of his title the treaty of Verdun was a cruel humiliation.

There was, however, worse to come. The Franks were paralysed by the weight of two hostile nations on their frontiers. They could not hold even the Middle Kingdom. On the death of Lothaire in 855 it was divided between his three sons. Italy became a separate state; the Rhone valley followed suit.[7] Only Lotharingia remained to the men of Aachen and Tournay. They had ceased to be the masters of the other nations; next they ceased to be masters of themselves. On the death of their king, Lothaire II., in 869, his uncles, Lewis the German and Charles the Bald, made haste to divide the prey. They were the sovereigns of Germany and Gaul respectively—or, to use the deceptive terminology of that age, of the East Franks and the West Franks. By the treaty of Mersen in 870 they completed the partition of Lotharingia. The boundary as then defined ran from Herstal on the Meuse to Metz upon the Rhine. The Franks living west of that line were incorporated with France; those to the east with Germany. Henceforth the struggle for the Empire was to be waged, not between the Austrasian and his subjects, but between the kings of the various national states which had taken shape within the husk of the Empire. The Imperial pretensions of Lewis II. (855-875) were based upon the kingdom of Italy, those of his successor, Charles the Bald (875-877), upon the kingdom of the West Franks. Charles the Fat enjoyed his brief supremacy (882-887) only because the three kingdoms, France, Germany, and Italy, one after another, chose him for their sovereign and lord. The Empire had come to be the merest gewgaw, an empty title of honour, conferring on the holder no accession of power, entailing no new responsibilities.

As for the Franks, the Northmen completed what fraternal strife had begun. About the year 880 the long ships came to Frisia. The invaders found the land defenceless. They pitched their camp at Maestricht and sallied unhindered up the Meuse and up the Rhine where their fancy led them.

All the great cities and strongholds of the Franks—Tongres, Liège, Julich, Köln, Trier, Nimeguen—fell before them. The flames consumed what the spoilers could not carry away. As a crowning outrage, the vikings plundered Aachen and stabled their horses in the dome which Charles had built.[8] In time they departed; in time church and town arose from their ashes. But it was no longer as the capital of the Franks, no longer as the seat of Empire that Aachen was to figure in the history of Europe. The hand of the Danes fell heavily enough upon the rest of Northern Europe. Already they had swept the northern frontier of Germany, burning Hamburg and chasing away its bishop, in the time of Lewis the Pious. The valour of Lewis III. could only purchase a temporary respite for France; and a few years later they wrested the duchy of Normandy from his successor to be a lasting trophy of their successes. France and Germany were humbled. But the ancient homeland of Charles the Great was laid completely waste. So far as buildings and landmarks were concerned, the country might almost never have been inhabited since the withdrawal of the Romans. The very name of the Franks was no longer to be found in the lands between the Meuse and Rhine. Franconia on the east, the Isle of France on the west, still serve to remind us of the vanished nation. But the intervening tract of country ceases to be known as Frankland. Lotharingia is the only designation which it bears henceforth.

The Franks, however, left behind them memorials of another kind than words and masonry. Through devious paths we can for generations to come trace their influence upon history. Until the year 911 Germany was ruled by a dynasty of the right Frankish blood. The Saxon dukes who took up the sceptre when it fell from the hands of Conrad the Franconian, claimed relationship on the female side with the line of Charles the Great. At Laon until 987 there ruled another Carolingian family speaking the Frankish tongue and cherishing the tradition of the Frankish monarchy divinely ordained and sacrosanct. The House of Capet, which succeeded them, was still at pains to maintain the connexion with the past. The Empire which had flourished so gloriously for a short fifteen years was not forgotten. It lent to the two greatest mediæval European states the support of a romantic idealism, the sanction of a cloudy but imposing political theory. Charlemagne is the chosen saint of rulers so dissimilar as Barbarossa and Louis XI.

The practical statesmanship of the first Frankish Emperor had a surprisingly slight influence upon his successors. His Capitularies and his commissions produced the merest ripples on the surface of the deep waters of customary law. Even in the ninth century the institution of the *missi* was flung aside as useless; it is by other means that Henry the Fowler and Louis le Gros will curb the centrifugal tendencies of feudalism. His frontier policy is also reversed. France retires from the Ebro; Germany advances far beyond the Elbe. In some few cases his example has a definite effect. Lewis the German takes in succession for his counsellors Otgar and Raban Maur, pupils both of

Alcuin's schools, the most Frankísh of ecclesiastics, the most Carolingian of statesmen. In the next century Otto the Great will be guided by his brother Bruno, in whom the ideals of Otgar and Raban Maur are still a living force, and from Bruno will learn the arcanum of the Carolingian Empire—the maxim that the road to universal sovereignty runs through Rome. Later still, in the astute and complaisant Gerbert we can hardly fail to trace the thoughts of Hincmar, his predecessor in the See of Rheims; the grandiose dreams of Otto III. are fed by distorted recollections of Charles and Alcuin. Even in details there are now and then some imitations. Stray Capitularies are revived by the Saxon emperors. The coinage, the weights and measures, the trade regulations of medieval Germany, bear witness to the influence of Charles upon certain aspects of her social life. But for all this the more ambitious measures and expedients of Charles lay forgotten, as though they had never been. New nationalities required a new form of government. It is neither surprising nor inappropriate that Charles, the administrator, should be best remembered in after centuries for his ecclesiastical innovations, for the interpolation of the Nicene, and the vulgarisation of the Athanasian Creed; for his vigorous, though illogical and incomplete, protest against the more degrading superstitions of Eastern Christianity. He was not a Frenchman; he was not a German. If his training drew him to the Latins, his origin bound him to the Teutons. His aspirations may, perhaps, be termed Latin; the traditions of social and political life, to which he rendered an unwavering homage, are most certainly Teutonic. Both strains met and mingled in his many-sided nature. He belonged, in fact, to no nation of modern growth, but to the only nation which, in his day, deserved the name, to that nation in which local and racial differences were suppressed or transcended,—to the nation of the Catholic Church. As the servant of the Church he humbled the Saxon, treated with the Dane, and cowed the Slav; as the servant of the Church he led his armies first across the Alps and then across the Pyrenees. The civilisation which he fostered was catholic, like his religion, and the patrimony of Christendom at large.

"At the prayer of Monseigneur St. Jacques our Lord gave this boon to Charlemagne, that men should speak of him so long as the world endureth." The words are those of a Frenchman. The prophecy found its accomplishment in the lays of French minstrels. The very name by which he is best known in history is the product of French invention. To his contemporaries the Emperor was Karolus or Karl. To us he will always be Charlemagne. The word is a hybrid compound of a Latin with a Teutonic stem; also it may be reprobated for the "suggestio falsi" which it carries. Still it has earned the right to exist, and the French nation may legitimately boast that Charles is theirs by adoption. He owes much to them, and they to him. On the one hand, they invested him with a cycle of romance; on the other, they borrowed from him the more imaginative ideas of his policy—the reverence for the Holy See, the interest in the eastern outposts of Christendom, the crusading zeal, of which we have seen no obscure traces in his career.[9]

Germany, too, possessed certain legends of Charles; but those of them that entered into popular mythology were sparse and bare. He became a pale copy of the gods of Valhalla, he appropriated the mount of Odin[10]; the belated traveller heard him riding through the thunder-storm or along the Milky Way in the chariot of Thor. To learn the histories of Roland and of Turpin, of Ganelon and Marsila of the voyage to Jerusalem, of the twelve peers, of the wars with the Saracen in every land of Europe, we must repair to French poetry. The fact may [seem] strange to those who reflect that Germany did and France did not owe national existence to Charles. It is not so strange when we remember that Charles first appeared before the Germans in the light of a ruthless conqueror, and the destroyer of the individualism which they held so dear. Bavarian and Saxon, Thuringian and Saxon, quickly forgot the peace which he had given them in his declining years. They chiefly remembered the period in which he had swept to and fro like a whirlwind through their borders, crushing rebellion and dragging their youth away to fight in distant wars. To Gaul, on the other hand, he had been at all times a deliverer and defender. He had warded off an old enemy in the person of the Saracen, a new one in the person of the Dane. In spite of his ceaseless wars, the country had enjoyed comparative security; and those wars, costly as they were, had been waged in the interests of Gaul, and of ideas with which she was never slow to sympathise.

The origins of the Charlemagne cycle are wrapped in obscurity. We can say with certainty only this much: that the foundations of it were laid in the ninth century and the early part of the tenth. Numberless stories concerning the House of Arnulf were current among the inhabitants of Gaul. Minstrels seized upon striking episodes, such as the siege of Pavia or the rout at Roncesvalles, and composed short, stirring lays which took for granted in the auditors a knowledge of the outlines of events. Cycles of ballads clustered round the names of great warriors—of Eric of Friuli, of Gerold of Bavaria, of Eggihard the seneschal, of Duke William of Toulouse.[11] And, far from being content with the bare facts, the authors added episodes from their own fancy, or from stories relating to earlier heroes. The exploits of Dagobert and of Charles Martel were confused with those of more modern conquerors. Old tales were frequently passed off under new names. Thus the popular tradition developed almost independently of literary authorities. The earlier *Chansons de gestes* reveal some acquaintance with the Court annals, with the biography of Charles by Eginhard, with that of Lewis the Pious by the Limousin Astronomer. But the information which they draw from these sources is of the vaguest and most general kind; it is freely altered to suit poetic requirements. The teaching of patriotic churchmen such as Hincmar and Notker had a more powerful effect upon the cycle at its commencement; for these writers moralised upon the character of Charles and made him a type of the perfect warrior and statesman.

During the ninth century there is a certain continuity of the literary tradition respecting Charles. Notker himself, whose book is a mirror of the tales which passed from mouth to mouth among the lower strata of society, nevertheless observes a certain caution. He himself had seen the Emperor; he had also talked much with men who had served in the Emperor's wars. However uncritical he may be, he has had means of information too full and good to admit of his straying very far from the path of history. But after him there comes a break. The literary world loses touch with the Carolingian period. It has lost sight of all landmarks, and readily lends itself to the task of expanding mere myths and legends. Thus Benedict of Soracte falsifies the narrative of Eginhard to prove that the Emperor in person visited Jerusalem. When this is done by a comparatively learned and sober chronicle, we may imagine what liberties were taken with the elastic framework of oral legends.

Of deliberate and sustained romance we have early examples, both in Latin and French. To the former class belong the first five chapters of the so-called "Chronicle of Turpin." These chapters, written before 1100, form a story, short but complete, of the Emperor's Spanish conquests. The author is interested in the shrine of St. James at Compostella, with which it is his object to connect Charles. Such a story can only be the work of a clerk attached to the shrine or of a zealous pilgrim. We have seen above how he brings the Emperor into Spain through the intervention of St. James. Having led him thither, he is not much concerned with any part of his feats except the visit to Compostella. He tells of the taking of Pampeluna, and how the walls fell down of themselves before the Franks. He also informs us that Charles remained three years in Spain and utterly destroyed all the idols except those in Andalusia. Archbishop Turpin makes his appearance in the story, but merely as a missionary who accompanies the Emperor and baptises all those of the Saracens who submit. Obstinate unbelievers are, of course, either put to death or enslaved. Finally Charlemagne returns across the Pyrenees without any reverses. Apparently the author does not know or does not care to tell of Roncesvalles.

A greater success was achieved by the unknown author who, after the Conquest of England but before the First Crusade, composed the *Song of Roland*. Apparently a Norman minstrel who had lived in England he wrote for recitation to a popular audience. Still he is a great literary artist, and his poem has, in addition to its other excellencies, a fine dramatic unity. It is not to be confounded with the ballad which Taillefer sang as he led the Norman charge at Hastings, and which must have been in essentials like the Frankish sagas, written, that is to say, in abrupt strophes with lines of no great length. The *Song of Roland* contains about four thousand lines and is in a style more adapted to recitation than song. The author had at his command a number of well known lays to which he occasionally refers in passing. His poem is evidently intended to fill a place in a long cycle. The Emperor has already been seven years in Spain before the tale begins. With the exception of Marsila's strong-hold of Saragossa, he has conquered Spain from sea to sea. The auditor is presumed to be familiar

with the sieges of Noble, Pine, Tudela, Seville, and Cordova; with the circumstances under which two Frankish envoys Basan and Basile, had been treacherously murdered by the infidel; with the personalities of the Emperor, of Roland and Oliver, of Geoffrey of Anjou, of Garin of Lorraine, and of many others. Also the poet reminds us that many famous feats of arms have already been performed by the Paladins in other lands. The past of the snow-haired Emperor contains whole epics of conquest. Says Roland to his sword Durendal:

> By thee did I win him Anjou and Bretagne, and Poitou and Maine.
> Won Normandy land of the free, Provence did I win, Aquitaine;
> Lombardy, all the Romagna, Bavaria, Flanders I won;
> Bulgaria, Poland, and homage hath Constantinople done;
> Saxony doeth his pleasure, and Scotland for him did I gain,
> Welshland and Ireland and England he made of his royal domain.
> 12

Early as this poem is, it diverges very widely from the tone and spirit of the ninth century. New threads of interest are imported into the time-worn story; the leading ideas are of a kind appropriate to the age when the crusading spirit was beginning to stir the hearts of men. The treachery of Ganelon, the love of Roland for the damsel Alde, the glorification of a feudal nobility, which includes in its ranks the progenitors of the great French families, the romantic enthusiasm of the exiled army for "la dulce France"—all these are striking innovations. In the hands of the later poets there is an ever-increasing tendency to develop these subsidiary motives at the expense of the central figure. The Emperor becomes a peg on which to hang stories of a modern kind.

Hence in the period of the great crusades the epic legend enters upon a new phase of development. It was widely believed that Charlemagne had risen from the dead to lead the first crusade. The minstrels seized upon the hint; they produced a new biography of the first Western Emperor in which he was depicted as the pattern crusader, and his life as one long war against the infidel. They elaborated the fiction of a voyage to Jerusalem and a subsequent visit to Constantinople. They corrupted the old ballads which told of national struggles against the Frank in Aquitaine, in Brittany, in Saxony, and Lombardy. Everywhere they brought in the Saracen. Witikind himself becomes a Saracen in the *Chanson des Saisnes* of Jean Bodel. Didier undergoes a similar transformation in the *Chevalerie Ogier*, and in *Aspremont*. We find a Saracen Emperor domiciled in Brittany. Naturally Spain was not forgotten. The pseudo-Turpin took up the Compostellan legend and added to it, besides the tale of Roncevaux, that of a great war between Charlemagne and Argolander, King of the Africans; the romance thus fabricated was published in the shape of an epistle from Turpin of Rheims to an archdeacon of his acquaintance. The pacific Archbishop Tilpin, of whom we find occasional mention in Carolingian documents, would have been not a little astounded at the marvels to which he was made to lend the sanction of his name. But Frederic Barbarossa adduced the Chronicle to justify an anti-pope in canonising Charles; it became famous and, except the *Song of Roland,* no other work had a greater effect upon the development of the cycle.

In the thirteenth century another element in the old stories was brought into prominence. After the crusades were over the attention of Europe was concentrated on the well-nigh universal struggle between feudalism and royalty. The historic Charlemagne had his vassals and found them disobedient enough. The *Chansons de geste* (drawing, perhaps, upon the experience of his unhappy descendants at Laon) credited him with many others of whom history bears no record. The sympathy of the minstrels is on the side of the rebels. Accordingly, the character of the Emperor is degraded in order to throw the virtues of his nobles into relief. He becomes a sovereign of the Merovingian type, a sovereign like Charles the Simple. Gerard of Roussillon, Raoul of Cambrai, Guillaume of Montreuil, Renaud of Montauban, and their compeers are the true heroes of the cycle in this its third stage. To enumerate the poems relating to them would be tedious and unprofitable; for the vigour of the minstrels wanes as they wander from the original outlines of their theme, and the great ideas which animated the older epics vanish away with the triumph of individualism. The prologue to the *Chanson des Saisnes* of Jean Bodel affords a favourable specimen of the new manner. It opens with an attack by Witikind upon Cologne. He has heard of the death of the twelve peers in Roncevaux; he has gathered the Saracens together that he may chase Charlemagne of Aix away from France. At Cologne he slays Duke Milo, and the beautiful Helissant is carried away to prison in Saxony. Then the scene shifts to Laon, where Charlemagne is keeping the feast of Pentecost. Fourteen kings sat down at table with the Emperor. Bishops and abbots without number were there. Pope Milo himself sang mass before the Court. The festival is disturbed by the news of Witikind's inroad. Charlemagne declares for war. But his barons protest; they have fought too much already. Let him tax the Hérupois for the war. He has favoured this people too much already; it is time that they bore a share of the burden. The Hérupois are the men of Normandy, Maine, and Brittany. They are indignant at the breach of their privileges. They threaten to gather their hosts together and to make war upon the Emperor. A hundred thousand of them will ride forth to burn his towns, his castles, and his boroughs. But later on they resolve to adopt a more moderate course. They march towards Laon in battle array with their tribute on the points of their lances. When the Emperor heard this he was sitting in his marble palace. The Pope was reading to him the life of St. Martin and explaining the Latin as he read. The Emperor rose and rode out to meet the rebellious barons. He was ashamed and repentant when he saw them. He declared that he had repented of his unjust design. He would only ask them for their personal service against the heathen. This request is cheerfully granted; and King and barons ride off to the Saxon war together.

It will be observed that the first part of this animated story is based upon good historical tradition. The *Chanson des gestes* continually tantalise us in this manner. The authors of the longer poems worked into their fabric all the old material which fell in their way and seemed suitable. In works of so late a date as the *Chevalerie Ogier* and the *Gestes de Charlemagne devant Carcassonne et Narbonne,*[13] we find at intervals a touch of detail which appears to come direct from the ninth century. Sometimes we recognise an extent authority,—Eginhard, or the Limousin astronomer, or the *Acta Sanctorum*—often we are left to vain conjectures. Highly ingenious attempts have been made to separate the different strata of legend in particular groups of the cycle; especially in those dealing with the wars of Narbonne, and with the birth of Charlemagne. But our store of historical facts can hardly be said to have been augmented by these researches. Local feeling, the desire to compliment great families, the thirst for novelties, the utter disinclination to discriminate between true and false—all these influences have tended to confusion. And the confusion increases as the poems become more pretentious and more systematic. Raimbert of Paris, Adenès, Gerard of Amiens, Jean Bodel, and their anonymous compeers could lend interest to their already well-worn themes only by the lavish use of embroidery.

As the Charlemagne cycle reaches its completion in France it begins to find imitators in other lands. About the year 1150 Germany gives birth to the *Ruotlands Liet,* a free version of our *Chanson de Roland;* in the same century a metrical history of Charlemagne, containing an independent version of the war in Spain, is woven into the fabric of the *Kaisercronik.* In the fourteenth century a German poet paraphrases the tale of Charles Mainet. King Hakon, the destroyer of Norwegian heathenism, introduces the *Chansons des gestes* as a civilising influence among his countrymen. From Norway, Scandinavian translations find their way to Iceland and give birth to the Karlamagnus Saga. Spanish chroniclers, resenting the arrogance of their French neighbours, take up the tale of Roncevaux and the wars of Spain in order to prove that the Emperor is over-rated. He was, they tell us, no deliverer, but a bandit. He attacked Alphonso the Chaste from ambition and was gloriously repulsed by Bernard de Carpio.[14] The Italians in a less serious spirit cast ridicule upon the chief events and personages of the cycle. In their hands Charlemagne becomes a dotard, Orlando a bombastic knight-errant. The nature of their treatment of the subject may be seen in the *Morgante Maggiore* of Luigi Pulci and the *Orlando Furioso* of Ariosto. In short, the legendary Charlemagne was a native of France; transported into other lands, he became a pale abstraction or a caricature.

Notes

1. His system of weights, known in medieval Germany as "Karl's weight," survives in the English Troy weight.

2. Mansi, *Concilia* xiii., 759. Letter of the Pope to the bishops of Spain and Gaul.

3. For the whole of this incident v. Hefele *Councils* (English translation vol. vii.) and the *Libri Carolini*, which are printed in Migne's *Patrologia* among the *Opera Karoli Magni*.

4. To avoid a multiplicity of references, I may mention at once the chief authorities consulted for the following sketch of the Carolingian Renaissance: 1. The Capitularies, which I quote by their dates as given in the edition of Boretius (*M. H. G.*). 2. The letters of Alcuin as edited by Jaffé, and his other works in Migne's edition. 3. The poems of Alcuin, Theodulf, Paul the Deacon, and Peter of Pisa (in the edition of Dümmler). 4. Eginhard's biography and the Monk of St. Gall. 5. The letters, etc., of Charles in Jaffé's edition. 6. Eginhard's tract on *The Translation of SS. Marcellinus and Petrus* (ed. Teulet). I must also express my obligations to the monographs of Mr. Bass Mullinger and M. Hauréau; to the Bishop of Oxford, as an authority for the facts of Alcuin's life (article *Alcuin*, in *Dictionary of Christian Biography*); to Mignet, *Études Historiques* (pp. 144-157); to Mühlbacher's chapter in his *Geschichte unter den Karolingern;* and to the *Histoire Littéraire de la France.*

5. Errors of the Eastern versions are quoted and reprobated in the *Libri Carolini*.

6. *M. H. G. Scriptores,* i., 568.

7. The sons of Lothaire I. were: Ludwig II., who obtained Italy with the title of Emperor, Lothaire, from whom the kingdom of Lotharingia took its name, and Charles. The latter took the kingdom of Provence, comprising Provence proper, the Duchy of Lyons, and Upper Burgundy. In 856 Upper Burgundy was wrested from him by his brothers; in 888 by the great treaty of partition it became an independent kingdom.

8. Regino in *M. H. G. Scriptores,* i., 592, s. a. 781. So the *Annals of Fulda:* "In capella regis equis suis stabulum fecerunt." The relics were saved by being taken to Stablo; possibly some of the articles still shown at Aachen, as having been the property of Charlemagne, were among these relics.

9. In entering upon the poetic history of Charlemagne I must express my obligations to the valuable works of MM. Gaston Paris and Léon Gautier.

10. Gudensberg in Hesse. It was said that Charles lay there waiting for the time of his second appearance. The same legend was afterwards annexed to the name of Frederic Barbarossa.

11. Of the stories respecting Gerold we have a trace in the vision of the monk Wettin (Bouquet, v., 399). Wettin saw him in Paradise among the martyrs. Eric of Friuli is the subject of a Latin poem attributed to Paulinus of Aquileia. The exploits of Duke William find their way, in a confused form, into the Provençal cycle. We learn from the Astronomer (*M. H. G. Scriptores,* ii., 608) that even in the ninth century many stories were current about Roncesvalles.

12. I have ventured to use the spirited translation of Messrs. Spencer & Way (Nutt, 1895).

13. This is a poem of the thirteenth century. It professes to be from the hand of Philomena, the secretary of Charlemagne.

14. The *Cronica general d'España* compiled by, or at least under the direction of, Alphonso X. of Castile.

Jessie L. Weston (essay date 1905)

SOURCE: "The Charlemagne Romances" in *The Romance Cycle of Charlemagne and His Peers*, David Nutt, 1905, pp. 5-45.

[*In the following essay Weston describes how the Arthur and Charlemagne cycles differ in their characteristics and asserts that the Charlemagne stories, while superior in content, are stylistically inferior to those about Arthur.*]

> *"Ne sont que trois matières à nul home entendant*
> *De France, de Bretagne, et de Rome le grant."*

The Middle Ages were, as we know, the ages of Romance; Romance embodied in Prose—pseudo-historic chronicles, pseudo-biographical accounts of noted heroes; in Poetry—short *lais,* longer poems (metrical romances as we call them), some independent, the greater number falling into groups round some one central figure, and in their entirety forming what we call cycles of Romance. To the mind of a writer of the twelfth century, whose words are quoted above (Jean Bodel, author of *La Chanson des Saisnes*), there were three of such cycles, and to them alone might the attention of a poet of that day be worthily directed; and of these cycles the respective centres were Charlemagne, Arthur, and Alexander.

Today this seems a somewhat inadequate method of classification, ignoring as it does the great mass of Northern tradition (Siegfried is surely a hero worthy of attention), yet it provides those who pursue the study of mediæval literature with a useful formula of designation for the two great bodies of French romance, the cycles of Charlemagne and of Arthur; the *Matières* of France and of Britain.

In the introductory number of these studies the Charlemagne romances have been alluded to, and incidentally discussed, but the subject matter of the study, *The Influence of Celtic upon Mediæval Romance,* was naturally far more closely connected with the second branch of Romantic literature, the Arthurian cycle; with Charlemagne Celtic legend has but little to do. In its later stages, when the *Matière de France* came into contact with the Arthurian story, the very soul of which is Celtic, it borrowed certain features from the *Matière de Bretagne,* but even then the fairy element, inseparable from the latter, presents itself partially, at least, under a Teutonic form. It was the *Matière de Bretagne* rather than that of France which was discussed in the opening study of this series. In the fourth number the various romances constituting the Arthurian cycle were described and classified, and in the fourteenth the Grail romances, forming a distinct section of that cycle with which their connection is late and artificial, was similarly treated; but so far the Charlemagne cycle has not received the notice which its importance demands.

It is natural that alike to English writers and English readers the cycle which Jean Bodel reckoned second in value should stand first in charm and attraction; indeed, it may be doubted whether those for whom he wrote did not judge even as we do; in purely *literary* value the Arthurian cycle is probably superior to that of Charlemagne; the latter can count on its roll no such names as those of Chrétien de Troyes, Hartmann von Aue, or Wolfram von Eschenbach.[1]

So far as the French literary presentment is concerned, the Charlemagne cycle is the elder, and the poems composing it, though the versions that have descended to us are not the earliest versions of the tales they tell, are as a rule cast in a form more primitive than that adopted by the writers of the Arthurian cycle. The prevailing form of the French Arthurian romance, one not found before the twelfth century, is a poem of eight syllabic lines, each pair rhyming; whereas in the Charlemagne *Chansons de Geste* we find *laisses* or *tirades* of varying length distinguished by a mono-rhyme, with, in the earliest copies, a vowel assonance prevailing throughout the *laisse.* This metrical form may be compared with the alliterative verse which in the Germanic languages was replaced by various forms of the rhyming couplet or stanza. Yet, in so far as the subject matter is concerned, dealing as it does largely with mythic and pre-historic elements, the Arthurian cycle may be deemed the older.

Before entering into a detailed discussion of the romances dealing with the *Matière de France,* it will, I think, be not unprofitable to make clear to our own minds the distinctive characteristics of these two great bodies of romance; both of them of extreme importance in the history of literature, yet differing so widely the one from the other that even where they have come into contact the influence resultant has been of the slightest and most superficial character. In general terms we may express this difference by saying that the groundwork of the Arthurian cycle is mainly mythical, that of the Charlemagne cycle mainly historical. This does not imply that there are no historical elements in the former cycle, and no mythical in the latter, or that, as contrasted with the great Emperor of the Franks, Arthur is a mere creation of the imagination. On the contrary, in all probability the leading lines of the Arthurlegend proper, the King's fights with the Saxons, his betrayal by wife and nephew, and death in battle have a foundation in fact, while the Charlemagne of legend is in many respects a wide departure from the Charlemagne of

history. But the real charm and abiding fascination of the Arthurian story lies in the realm of fancy and not of fact— *realms,* perhaps we should rather say, for the student of Arthurian romance is free of more than one kingdom: the land of faëry whose horizon is lost in the mists of Celtic heathendom, and the brighter, but no less elusive, land where ideal chivalry has sworn a close alliance with Christian mysticism.

It is true that not all chronicled in the Charlemagne romances has its parallel in historic reality; myth has certainly played a part in the stories of the hero's birth and early trials, but in its main lines the character of these romances is determined by historic facts. Such heroes as Huon de Bordeaux and Girard de Viane may be creatures of imagination, but the struggles of the feudal nobles against their over-lord are facts of stern reality; Vivien may never have lived, and rashly vowed, and shed his blood heroically at the gates of Arles, but at least the varying fortunes of the contests between Christian and Saracen for the fertile lands of Southern France are as historical as the fights of our ancestors with Saxon and Dane; and if Ganelon never betrayed his king and country, yet Roland died at Roncevaux.

Again, the Charlemagne story has its supernatural element, but it is not that of wizardry and faëry as in the Arthurian story; there is no shape-shifting Merlin, no treacherous Morgain, or beneficent Lady of the Lake. Nor is it laden with wondrous hints and revelations of divine doctrines and mysteries as in the Grail romances. The supernatural machinery is celestial and strictly simple; a guardian angel watches by the emperor's pillow, and shields him from his foes; in answer to his prayer a hart shows his army the ford across the swollen stream; at his death St. James of Compostella is beheld in a vision casting into a balance, wherein the devil weighs the emperor's good and evil deeds, the churches and shrines Charlemagne has erected in his honour.

When, in the last stage of its development, the fairy element enters the Charlemagne cycle it is manifestly due to the influence of Arthurian romance; thus Huon of Bordeaux is aided by Oberon, the fairy king (who is, indeed, rather a Teutonic elf (*albe*) than a Celtic fairy), but Oberon is the son of Morgain, and the rightful heir to his kingdom, with whom Huon must come to terms, is Arthur. Ogier and Renouart alike live on in fairyland (though each is supposed to have ended his days as a monk!), but that fairyland is Avalon. The supernatural element proper to the legend is presented under the simplest and most obvious form, that of direct Divine protection.

That the characterisation of the Charlemagne cycle should be more forcible than that of the Arthurian is only what we should expect; the authors of the *Chansons* were dealing with real men and women, like to, if not of, themselves. Charlemagne plays a far more important *rôle* than does Arthur. The British king is, after all, little more than a picturesque centre for a series of adventures in which he himself takes no part. He certainly leads his hosts to battle, but it must be admitted that the wars of the Arthurian story are its least interesting and most wearisome portion; otherwise, Arthur presides in a dignified manner at feasts, and invites adventures, which his knights achieve; as a personality he is not convincing.

And of his knights Gawain, with all his grace and courtesy, has about him that note of elusiveness that makes one realise that his proper destination is, like Arthur, the land of faëry. Lancelot is but a stage lover; Galahad a painted-window saint. Perceval and Tristan, as we meet them first, are indeed human, very creatures of flesh and blood, but the Arthurian story is not content to leave them so, the former it turns into a being scarcely less shadowy than Galahad, the latter into a lover as conventional as Lancelot.

But in the Charlemagne romances it is otherwise. The old Emperor, with his long white beard, is a majestic figure, which even the hint of years impossibly prolonged cannot rob of its reality. His intense family affections, his uncontrolled temper, violent fits of rage, savage revenge and unreasoning tyranny are all real. We feel the relationship between him and Roland to be no mere literary convention. The younger man, with his fierce temper, indomitable pride, and reckless courage, is exactly what we should expect Charlemagne's next of kin to be. Oliver, equally brave but less hot-headed, ready to temper his valour with discretion, is quite as real as his friend. Very real, too, that doughty champion of the church militant, Archbishop Turpin; and Ganelon, whose treason is in truth the attempt of a cowardly man to revenge himself upon one who has thrust him against his will into a post of danger.

> "Rollanz m'fors-fist en or et en aveir,
> Pur que jo quis sa mort e sun destreit;
> Mais traïsun nule n'en i otrei."

Convincing, too, is William of Orange; now battling valiantly against the overpowering force of his Saracen foes; now melting into tenderness over his dying nephew; and again wrathfully demanding aid from his pious and peace-loving brother-in-law, King Louis—who wishes himself otherwhere. The impression left upon us is that if these heroes did not really live, they might well have done so. We are not surprised that in his journey through the other world Dante beheld a goodly group of souls of the Charlemagne heroes, while of the Arthurian he saw none, save Tristan. Apart from their literary interest, the Charlemagne cycle appeals rather to the student of History, the Arthurian cycle to the student of Folk-lore.

The literary development of the two cycles not only sets the above-noted differences in a vivid light, but illustrates their true nature, and enables us to realise the history reflected in the Charlemagne cycle. The great Emperor died in 814, and with him died, as we can see, the conception of a France forming an integral portion of a vast Germano-Roman Empire. The warriors who followed Clovis and Dagobert, the companions of Charles the Hammer and of Pepin the Little, had in the course of centuries been putting off their Germanhood, been differentiating themselves from their kinsmen across the Rhine. The popular songs commemorating the mighty feats of Merwing and Karling kings, songs of which monkish chroniclers have preserved us a few scraps in their barbarous verse, or of which they have partially rendered the substance in their dreary prose—these songs, originally German, gradually passed into *Roman,* the language of the conquered race, as the Germanic element weakened. After Charlemagne's death his empire broke up, the *Roman* portion was cut definitely loose from the German-speaking world, and in less than a century the last traces of German speech vanished. The descendants of Frankish and Burgundian conquerors became French, and every fragment of German hero-song either put on a *Roman* dress or else died out. Small wonder if in the process the historic basis was shifted, if the deeds of earlier chiefs and warriors got transferred to the great Emperor. The fame and achievements of the latter would indeed have sufficed to inspire popular minstrels; but he also inherited the renown of many predecessors, and thus the earliest singers of his glory found themselves from the outset in possession of no inconsiderable stock of poetic material. The songs accumulated during the ninth century, and the decadence of the later Carolingians, threw into stronger relief the prowess and fame of Charlemagne.

As early, perhaps, as the first third of the tenth century, certainly by the middle of the century, *Chansons de Geste,* as distinguished from the popular songs on which they were based, had begun to appear, professing to narrate events of Charlemagne's lifetime. Throughout the tenth, eleventh, and early twelfth centuries these *Chansons* were being enlarged, worked over, adapted to cyclic requirements. These two hundred years were fertile in strong characters, in fierce passions, in events and movements which transformed the old Franko-Roman Empire into modern France. The Carolingian polity decayed and passed away; the Capets, embodying the aspirations and ideals of a new nationality, rose to power, and founded a monarchy destined to last for eight hundred years, and to incarnate, far more than was the case in England, the national genius. The pangs and throes which accompanied the birth of modern France were fierce and prolonged; Norman and Saracen assailed from without; king and feudatory grappled in deadly struggle within. All this we find mirrored in the *Chanson de Geste.* Itself the record of a nation's formation, it exercised, we cannot doubt, a formative influence, the force of which it were hard to overestimate. Germanic in its pristine essence as it was, Germanic as it remained in many of its animating ideas, it is in its highest moments a magnificent record of French patriotic feeling, an ardent fosterer of devotion to the fair land apostrophised by Roland—

> "Tere de France, mult estes dulz païs!"

From this, the creative period of the French epic, we possess comparatively little in an authentic and ungarbled form. Chief of what has come down to us is the earliest version of the *Chanson de Roland,* and even this, there can be little doubt, represents a fairly advanced stage of development. The great bulk of Charlemagne romances belong to a period reaching from the early twelfth into the fourteenth century. The main outlines of the *Chanson de Geste* had been determined, its leading types of character and incident had been settled, it had acquired a prodigious stock of conventions, it still in a large measure reflected the religious and social ideas of the time; thus it could not escape the hands of the adapter, the rearranger, the hack writer who thought more of dressing up time-honoured stories according to the literary fashion of the moment than of preserving their original spirit and form. From the middle of the twelfth century it was exposed to the competition of the Arthurian stories—a competition against which, as we have seen, it largely defended itself by adopting the tone and style and temper of its rival.

How different was the fate of the Arthurian romance on French soil! It came into French hands with a stock of incidents and characters, above all with an æsthetic, and what, in default of a better term, must be styled an ethical character of its own, which persist despite the modifications imposed by the alien French genius. Its period of evolution is comparatively short; in from fifty to one hundred years it runs its full course; its development is not determined by nor does it mirror the political situation or the political changes of the period. Vast and far-reaching social changes it does indeed herald and record, but indirectly and symbolically, not, as is the case with the *Chanson de Geste,* directly and realistically. The one body of literature is a monument of French intellect and French artistry exercising themselves upon an alien and imperfectly comprehended subject matter; the other is the nation typified, recording as it does its fierce birth-pangs, its wild and dour *enfances,* the exultant spirit of its early manhood.

It would be difficult to exaggerate the popularity, in mediæval times, of the Charlemagne cycle, or its importance as a factor in the history of European literature. In Italy it was the parent of a literature scarcely less extensive than that from which it sprang; indeed, the evolution was more complete. Italy yields pseudo-historical chronicles and metrical romances representing the legend at every stage: from that of historic reality, as typified by the rough-hewn figures of Roland and Oliver at the portal of Verona Cathedral, to that of pure fantasy, as in the *Orlando Amoroso* and *Orlando Furioso.* In Spain the Charlemagne story, as related in the *Chronica* of Alfonso X., gave impetus to the formation of a national cycle, the heroes of which— Bernardo del Carpio, the children of Lara, and the Cid— should rival in popularity the heroes of the earlier *gestes.* In Scandinavia and in Germany the romances found translators and imitators, while in England we fail to realise that our *Sir Bevis of Hampton* is but an imitation of a French poem, and is reckoned by scholars as an offshoot of the cycle; while a nobleman and statesman like Lord

Berners thought the translation of the tale of *Huon of Bordeaux* a task not unworthy of his time and labour. And have not we here in England the honour of possessing, in the MS. of the Bodleian Library, the oldest known copy of the most famous song of the cycle, the *Chanson de Roland?*

To undertake to give, in the small compass of one of these studies, an adequate account of so large and important a body of literature (M. Leon Gautier, in his *Épopées Françaises,* reckons *eighty* chansons as belonging to what he terms "la geste du roi" alone, without considering the subordinate cycle of the Narbonnais) would of course be impossible; the utmost that can be done is to describe the general character of the cycle, the lines into which it falls, and note the romances which will best repay the attention of the ordinary student of literature. Those who desire a more detailed account will do well to consult M. Leon Gautier's monumental work, *Les Épopées Françaises,* or the shorter but no less scientific, and, it may be, better arranged *Histoire Poétique de Charlemagne,* by M. Gaston Paris.

The dividing line of the Charlemagne romances is less individual than in the case of the Arthurian cycle; there, it is comparatively easy to classify the romances according to the knight who is hero of the tale. The leading heroes of the Round Table form so many centres round which the romances respectively group themselves, and the collective mass of these smaller groups or subsidiary cycles make up the great Arthurian legend. But with Charlemagne and his peers this guiding principle will no longer serve us. There are certainly many romances borrowing their title from the hero of the adventures they relate, but none of Charlemagne's warriors save William of Orange, the Marquis *au court nez,* have anything like such a body of romance connected with them as have Gawain, Perceval, or Lancelot, or can fairly be described as hero of a "cycle." The Charlemagne romances deal rather with families than with individuals; they are *Chansons de Geste,*[2] lays dealing with the feats of a race rather than of a person. The tendency is to look upon qualities, not as the individual characteristics of *one* member of a family, but as the natural and inevitable inheritance of all. Valour and loyalty, cowardice and treachery, alike pass from father to son. Thus one group of poems deals with the heroic virtues of the descendants of Garin de Montglane, another with the treacherous race of Doon de Mayence.

But the more convenient method of classification, that followed by M. Gaston Paris, is to group the romances according to their subject matter as relating to the Emperor, for Charlemagne, as we have noted above, plays a far more important part in his cycle than does Arthur. Following these lines, we shall find one group of poems dealing with the personal history of the monarch, his birth, his youthful adventures, his domestic trials, his fabled journey to the East, and final coronation of his son as his successor. A second and more important group deals with his various wars, principally those with the Saxons and the

Saracens,[3] and is connected with the subsidiary but highly interesting cycle of the Narbonnais, the heroic family of Aimeri de Narbonne, whose son, William of Orange, is the champion of Christianity against the Moslem invaders of the South of France. The third sub-division includes the romances which relate the internecine struggles of the great vassals with their over-lord, and counts among its number some of the most popular legends of the whole cycle.

While thus practically following historical lines, the compilers of the chansons have, however, by no means limited themselves to events occurring during the reign of the great Emperor, but freely transfer incidents from one period to another at their pleasure, ascribing to Charlemagne's reign what really happened under his predecessor, Charles Martel, or his successor, Charles le Chauve, and presenting the heroes of the *gestes* as living now under Charlemagne, now under his son Louis, thus involving the attainment of a truly patriarchal age. According to the author of the *Chanson de Roland,* Charlemagne was over two hundred years old at the date of Roncevaux, and, to rightly understand the historical background of the cycle, we must bear in mind that the conditions, social and political, there represented actually obtained for some three hundred years or so, and were by no means limited to the period covered by the reign of the son of Pepin. The anachronism exists, but it is not of such a nature as to destroy the value of the poetical representation.

In the romances dealing with the youth of Charlemagne[4] we are on mythical rather than on historical ground. The story of his mother, *Berte aux grans piés,* is the familiar and oft-told tale of "The False Bride," the waiting-maid substituted for her mistress, and as such belongs to the domain of Folk-lore. Equally the tale of his youthful adventures, when he flies from the death by poison prepared for him by the sons of the false maid, and under the name of *Mainet* takes refuge with the King of Spain, frees him from his enemies, and marries his daughter, is a creation of fiction, and has no historical basis. The chronicle of Eginhard distinctly states that nothing definite concerning Charlemagne's youth was known, and the author therefore judged it inadvisable to write of it. But it seems doubtful whether the name by which the great Emperor is known did not take its rise in this popular fiction, and Charlemagne be not derived from *Charles Mainet,* the two names being often coupled together, rather than from *Carolus Magnus.* In any case it is to be regretted that so many English writers of the present day substitute the common-place translation Charles the Great, for the time-honoured and far more impressive Charlemagne.

These tales, and other scattered legends relating to the personality of the great Emperor, are to be found in the vast compilation of the Venice Library, consisting of a number of the *Chansons* collected together under the name of *Charlemagne;* also in the Icelandic *Karlomagnus Saga,* which latter, however, begins the record of his adventures at a rather later date. A German poem, *Karl Meinet,* has preserved the account of his residence in Spain.

Purely fabulous, too, are the accounts of Charlemagne's journey to Jerusalem, accompanied by his twelve peers, and the extravagant feats they perform in fulfilment of their *gabs* or boasts; and of the false accusation of his Queen Blanchefleur, by the traitor Macaire—a version of which, under the title of *La reine Sibille,* enjoyed a widespread popularity.

The real interest of the legend lies not in Charlemagne's domestic life, but in his public actions; the energy with which he defended Christianity, and consolidated the Empire. This is, as we have said above, the historical element of the legend which, reflected in the romances, constitutes the distinctive feature and real importance of the cycle. The Emperor's object was obtained only at the cost of wars, foreign and domestic, and with such struggles the majority of the romances are concerned.

For poetical purposes the foes of the Emperor beyond his border were the Saxons and the Saracens; both were alike enemies of God and of Holy Church, but the poems dealing with the latter are not only more numerous, but strike a stronger and a truer note. This may, of course, be largely owing to the fact that much of the struggle was fought out on the soil of France, and the reality of the contest was thus more forcibly brought home to the imagination of the writers. The gulf of nationality, too, was wider; there was less difference between the barbarous Saxon and semi-civilised Frank, both white races, than between the latter and the dusky hordes that swarmed from Africa through Spain into Southern France, even though these latter might be representatives of a civilisation older than that of the West. Wotan and Thor, barbarous as were their rites, never seem to have raised half as much horror and antagonism in the minds of mediæval Christians as did the fabulous gods of the Saracens, Mahmoud, Termagant, and Apollo! In mediæval romance the iconoclastic followers of Islam are represented as idolaters of a monstrous type, a quintessence of all the evils of paganism and heathenism, and they are provided with a motley pantheon borrowed from classic tradition, supplemented by the fertile imagination of romancers. Over and over again these heathen hordes are represented as besieging Rome, sometimes as having gained possession of the Imperial city, and holding in their power the most precious relics of Christendom. More than once Charlemagne marches to the relief of *l'Apôtre*—as the Pope is generally termed in French romance—which relief is as a rule effected by a single combat between one of the Christian Paladins, and a giant more or less malicious, more or less willing to be converted, representing the Saracen host. It is the "motif" of David and Goliath repeated *ad nauseam.*

For such romances as *Aspremont, Les Enfances Ogier,* and *Fierabras,* there is no real foundation in history. The most that can be said is that they represent a distorted reminiscence of the siege of Rome by the Lombards.

But when we come to the group of poems dealing with Charlemagne's expedition to Spain, and culminating in the

Chanson de Roland, we are on surer ground; history has indeed been modified under the influence of the Saracen nightmare, but we are dealing with modification, not with invention. Briefly related, the facts as chronicled by Eginhard and others are these:—In 778 two Moorish emirs from Spain presented themselves before the Emperor and declared their desire to become his vassals. Encouraged by this, Charlemagne marched with a large army into Spain, besieged and took Pampeluna, and laid siege in vain to Saragossa. (This part of the expedition is found, much embellished, in the following romances: *L'Entrée en Espagne, La Prise de Pampelune,* and *Gui de Bourgogne.*) On the return of the army to France, the rear guard was surprised by the Gascons in the defile of Roncevaux, in the Pyrenees, and practically exterminated, Roland, prefect of the marches of Brittany, being among the slain. M. Leon Gautier remarks that this defeat must have been of far more importance than the chroniclers care to admit. Certain it is, that they pass over in but few words an event which has left an indelible impression on the popular mind, and the echoes of which can be caught at every subsequent period of French history. It is probable, too, that the Saracens lent a helping hand to the Gascon ambuscade. It is certain that tradition has forgotten the real authors of this shattering blow to the Emperor's prestige, and attributes it to the hereditary foe of Christianity, the Moslem.

But whatever be the true history of Roncevaux, the legend is the culminating point of the Charlemagne tradition. French scholars have vied with each other in praise of the *Chanson de Roland,* its dignity, its simplicity, and the lofty tone of courage, devotion, and patriotism which inspires it, and any unprejudiced critic must largely agree with them. It is not the work of a finished poet like Chrétien de Troyes, it has not the easy literary grace which marks the *lais* of Marie de France, but the force and directness of its language, and the universality of the feelings to which it makes appeal, can never fail to awake a response. We sympathise alike with Roland in his desire to fight unaided the unequal combat; with Oliver in his calmer appreciation of the overwhelming odds against them, and his vain attempts to induce his headstrong friend to realise the truth; with Archbishop Turpin as he solemnly absolves the doomed army, and, having thus performed his duty as a Christian and cleric, gives valiant account of himself as man and warrior. All alike are inspired by one spirit, by the desire that none shall hereafter sing *male cançun* regarding their end.

Perhaps the most impressive and affecting part of the poem is the lament of Charlemagne over the dead body of his heroic nephew, when in pathetic words he paints the picture of his return to France, how he shall sit throned in the hall of Laon, and the representatives of the races subdued by Roland's aid shall come before him and ask tidings of the valiant captain of his host, and he must needs answer, "In Spain he lieth dead!" Then they, taking courage at the tidings, shall rebel against him, and who shall put them down? The poem might well have ended here, as indeed, in the earlier versions, it doubtless did.

The defeat of the Saracen army, and the punishment meted out to Ganelon and his race, come somewhat as an anticlimax.

It may be worth while to ask here, what is the historic foundation for the heroic character of Roland? The chronicle of Eginhard, relating the catastrophe of Roncevaux, simply says: "Anselmus comes palatini, *et Hruodlandus Britannici limitis præfectus,* cum aliis compluribus interficiuntur."[5] Thus, here, Roland is simply prefect of the marches of Brittany, and no word is said of his relationship to the Emperor. It may seriously be doubted whether such a relationship did, in fact, exist. History records that Charlemagne had but one sister, who early became a nun, and thus could not possibly have been the mother of Roland. The relationship of uncle and nephew, as subsisting between the royal centre of an epic cycle and the hero of that cycle, is so general (*e.g.* the instances of Conchobar and Cuchulinn, Finn and Diarmid, Mark and Tristan, Arthur and Gawain), that it does not seem improbable that the Charlemagne legend may have been affected by the prevailing tradition. This supposition is strengthened by the fact that certain twelfth century texts represent Roland as not merely the *nephew,* but also the *son* of the Emperor, a feature manifestly borrowed from tradition, and highly primitive in character. Such is the relation between Sigmund and Sinfiotli in the Volsungasaga, Arthur and Mordred (in the first instance it was probably Gawain), and, in some versions of the story, between Conchobar and Cuchulinn. Thus, while we may take it as settled that history determined the character and fate of Roland, it yet seems probable that his relationship to Charlemagne was due to the influence of mythic tradition.

The twelve peers, Roland's companions, who, according to the poem, shared his fate at Roncevaux, owed their origin, M. Gautier considers, to Germanic custom. Among primitive German tribes it was the rule for certain warriors to associate themselves closely with the chief of the clan, to share with him his dangers and his spoil. They were his *pairs.* Hence, M. Gautier[6] thinks the *douze pairs,* their number being an imitation of that of the Apostles. M. Gaston Paris is, however, inclined to consider the institution of later date. The names of the peers vary in different poems, and two of the most famous of Charlemagne's warriors—Naimes de Baviere and Turpin—do not appear to have belonged to this body. According to *Girard de Viane,* it was Naimes who persuaded the Emperor to institute the order, as a kind of superior tribunal of judgment (cf. *supra*). The extreme popularity of the peers is shown by the introduction of their title into English mediæval romance, where we often find the word "*dosypere*" as equivalent for a valiant knight.

Compared with the *Chanson de Roland,* the poems dealing with the Saxon wars, *Guiteclin* and *La Chanson des Saisnes,* are far inferior in interest, marked by inordinate length and wearisome repetition of incident.

The third group of romances, those which relate the story of the Emperor's struggle with his rebellious vassals, is, taken as a whole, the most interesting of the three. Two among the number, *Renaud de Montauban (les quatre fils Aymon)* and *Huon de Bordeaux,* were in all probability the most popular and widely known of the Charlemagne romances, and have more or less retained that popularity to our own time.

Good mediæval translations of both are published by the Early English Text Society. The former gives a very fine picture of the relations between a vassal and his feudal lord, and the manner in which, among the nobler natures of the time, the obligations imposed by feudal service were realised and fulfilled. Charlemagne is entirely in the wrong in his treatment of the four brothers, but the old knight, Aymon, feels himself compelled by his oath of fealty to extend no aid or countenance of any kind to his sons. When in dire need they throw themselves upon the protection of their mother, who receives them with open arms, Aymon leaves the castle at their disposal and goes forth; he will not break his vow by aiding them, nor will he forbid his wife to follow the instincts of natural affection. Renaud, the principal hero of the tale, has as keen a sense of honour as his father; when his clever and resourceful cousin Maugis, whose wiles have been the salvation of the brothers, casts the Emperor into a magic slumber, and thus conveys him into the castle he has been besieging, Renaud refuses to profit by what he deems a disloyal action, and sends Charlemagne again to his host in safety: a forbearance which, it must be owned, the Emperor's conduct does not justify! The four sons of Aymon and their gallant steed, Bayard, were deservedly popular; indeed, in folk tradition Bayard still roams the forests of Ardennes.

Here we may point out the gradual declension which the character of the Emperor, as represented in the romances, undergoes. In the *Chanson de Roland* he is a venerable but an imposing and dignified figure; in *Renaud de Montauban* and *Huon de Bordeaux* he is capricious, tyrannical, given to fits of senile rage, cruel and unjust in the highest degree; his barons openly flout him, and the authors do not hesitate to stigmatise him as *un vieil radoté.* How are we to account for so fundamental a change of conception? It seems clear that it was due to historic causes, and was the outcome of a radical change in the relations between sovereign and subject. Under the feebler rule of the great Emperor's successors the power of the feudatory barons became increased to an alarming extent. The later romances, faithfully reproducing the characteristics of their age, have shifted the point of interest from the feeble and vacillating monarch to the rebellious but powerful vassal.

If the authors had maintained throughout the identity of the king during whose reign the romance was compiled, or remodelled, the picture would have been complete; but the position of Charlemagne as centre of the *Matière de France* was so firmly grounded, that they continued to retain him as representative of a system entirely alien to his methods. The relations between William of Orange and King Louis,

in *Aliscans,* are quite possible, and a legitimate and artistic presentment of the situation as conceived under the reign of that king; postulated of Charlemagne they are incorrect and misleading. The character of the Emperor has really suffered from the continued popularity of his cycle, and the need of adjusting the romances to contemporary social conditions.

The romance of *Ogier le Danois,* consisting of no fewer than twelve branches, belongs, in so far as the older portion is concerned, to the earlier and better period of the Charlemagne cycle, but it is somewhat marred by the barbarous fierceness and savagery of the hero.

Nevertheless, certain portions of the story have an epic force and vigour which raise them to the first rank of romantic legend. Such is the account of the prolonged siege of Chastelfort by the Emperor, a siege lasting for over seven years, during the progress of which all Ogier's men are slain; but the undaunted hero makes figures of wood, and clothing them in the armour of the dead knights, succeeds in deluding his foes into the belief that the castle is fully garrisoned. Also the charming story of the recognition of Ogier, after many years' imprisonment, by his faithful steed, *Broiefort,* which has been made the draught-horse of the neighbouring monastery, but retains sufficient spirit to carry its aged master to victory once more.

This story of a hero and his faithful steed was extremely popular in mediæval times, and we find it ascribed to Walter of Aquitaine (Waltharius) in the *Chronica Novalense,* an interesting monkish compilation of romantic legend; to Heimi, in the *Thidrek Saga;* and to William of Orange, in the *Moniage Guillaume;* in the two first cases the hero being a monk, and in the third a hermit—not a prisoner, as Ogier. The monastic version M. Gaston Paris holds to be the earliest form of the story, of which the *Chronica* probably gives the oldest extant version, the *Thidrek Saga* being probably borrowed from a Lombard chronicle.

In the older parts of the Ogier romance we have an account of Charlemagne's war with the King of the Lombards, at whose court the hero seeks shelter. This is an historic feature, and of the more value in that, as we have noted above, the tendency of the later romances is to ignore the wars with the Lombards, and in the traditions relative to the siege of Rome to replace them by the Saracens.

The character of the hero appears to be more or less founded on fact; there was certainly at Charlemagne's court a valiant soldier of the name of *Oggerius,* or Otkar, but his nationality is doubtful. Certain chronicles speak of him as of the family of Pepin, in which case he would, of course, be a kinsman of the Emperor. The title *Danois* is by some modern scholars held to be a misreading of the original *Ardennois,* and Ogier is thought to have been of the Ardennes rather than of Denmark. In its final stages the tale shows distinct traces of Celtic influence; and this modern scholars have strongly felt. Mr. Nutt, in the study already referred to, remarks that Huon and Ogier are "Arthurian heroes who have strayed by accident to the court of Charlemagne;" and the late William Morris, in that fascinating collection of legendary tales, *The Earthly Paradise,* gives the story of *Ogier the Dane* to a Breton sailor. Nevertheless, in its essential spirit the tale appears to be Germanic rather than Celtic.

According to the testimony of the chroniclers, Ogier was one of the most popular of mediæval heroes, but the numerous romances connected with his name have not retained their popularity as have *Renaud de Montauban* and *Huon de Bordeaux.* To-day most of us probably only know him through the medium of Hans Andersen's tales, though but few realise that the slumbering Danish hero Olge Danske is identical with the paladin of Charlemagne.

Both the romance of *Ogier le Danois* and that of *Renaud de Montauban,* if classified according to the family method suggested by M. Gautier, would belong to the *Geste* of *Doon de Mayence;* but the fact that that scholar himself was obliged also to include them in the *Geste du roi* seems an argument for the simpler method adopted by M. Gaston Paris, and followed in these pages.[7]

The tale of *Huon de Bordeaux* is less characteristic of any special age. The interest lies rather in the marvellous adventures of the hero, and the aid and protection extended to him by the fairy king Oberon. It is a tale of faëry not only in the loose but in the strict sense of the word, Huon's adventures reproducing closely those of the hero upon whom a task is laid which he can only accomplish by supernatural aid familiar to us in so many fairy tales, and as such it is one for all time. From it Shakespeare borrowed his fairy king, and Weber the libretto of his opera.

Among the romances of this class *Girard de Viane,* one of the oldest, is interesting as giving the account of the first meeting between Roland and Oliver; they fight themselves into friendship beneath the walls of Viane.

In most of these tales Charlemagne is represented as in extreme old age, in fact, as we have shown above, an unreasoning dotard, *un vieil radoté!* We therefore feel that the situation depicted in the *Couronnement Looys* is natural and inevitable; it may be considered as practically closing the cycle of Charlemagne and opening that of William of Orange, though there are, of course, poems dealing with the earlier history of that hero.

In the *Couronnement* we find the aged Emperor laying aside his crown in favour of his young son Louis, who, gentle and timid in disposition, shrinks from the responsibilities awaiting him. A certain Hernaud, of the traitorous race of Ganelon, comes forward with an offer to rule the kingdom till Louis feels himself prepared to take up the reins of government, but *William Fierabras,* detecting the traitorous purpose concealed beneath the offer, fells the traitor to the ground, and announces that he will be the protector and champion of the young king, a task he loyally performs.

The historic personality underlying the epic figure of this William, the hero of the important cycle of the *Narbonnais,* is not clear. Investigation discloses even more forcibly than elsewhere in the cycle of how composite a texture it really is, and how it welds together in one picture, periods separated by the stretch of centuries, regions separated by the width of France. Monsieur Gaston Paris considers that the legendary hero represents a reminiscence of the feats of at least four historical Williams, *i.e.* William *Fierabras,* William *au court nez,* William of Toulouse, and William of Orange. Of these William *Fierabras* (who may, but this is doubtful, have borne the appellation *au court nez*) and William of Aquitaine, later of Orange, were contemporaries of the great Emperor, but the one belonged to northern, the other to southern France. William of Toulouse, undoubtedly an historical character, and one of whom we possess a fair amount of authentic record, belonged to the tenth century. His was a striking personality, and he seems to have attracted stories belonging to the earlier William of Orange. Moreover, in the epic, William, when old, turns monk, and here would seem to have borrowed traits from two southern French saints, S. William *du Désert* and S. William *le Pieux.* Certain it is that the titles *Fierabras, au court nez,* and *d'Orange,* are all applied to one hero. But in those days *William* was the most common of Christian names. In a certain assemblage of nobles out of five hundred present three hundred and eighty were William; a fact which goes far to explain any confusion of identity which may have crept into the legend.

According to the romances, however, the parentage and personality of this William, though his surnames may vary, are distinct enough. He is the son of Aimeri de Narbonne, a descendant of that Garin de Montglane who, as we mentioned at the outset of our study, represents the heroic family or *geste* of the cycle. An extensive Italian compilation of the fourteenth century, under the title of *Storie Nerbonese,* recounts all the doings of the valiant family of Narbonne.

M. Gautier reckons twenty-four *chansons* composing this cycle, but here we need only enumerate those directly connected with the life and deeds of the hero, *Les Enfances Guillaume,*[8] *Siège de Narbonne, Le Charroi de Nîmes, La prise d'Orange.* These trace the history of William from his earliest years to his establishing himself as lord of Orange, from which city he has driven out the Saracens, and married the wife of their king. The loves of William and Orable, who in the later poems is known by her baptismal name, Guibourc, occupy a great portion of the story.

At this point another hero appears upon the scene, Vivien, the nephew of William, whose valiant deeds and untimely death appear to have been intended as a parallel to Roland in the earlier story. The poems directly connected with this young hero are *Les Enfances Vivien, Le Covenant Vivien,* and the famous *Aliscans;* this last being the crown and centre of the "William" cycle, even as the *Chanson de Roland* is of that of Charlemagne. Both poems relate the defeat of the Christians by the Saracens, and in both the catastrophe is due to the rashness of the youthful hero.

In the *Covenant Vivien* we learn how the youth, on receiving knighthood, makes a solemn vow never to retreat before the Saracens, a vow which even his uncle William, no model of prudence, condemns as unduly rash. A large Saracen fleet appears on the river beyond the plains of Aliscans (Aliscans-Aliscamps = Elysian Fields, and is the name of the famous cemetery beyond the walls of Arles). Vivien urges on his young comrades to attack them, which the lads do with an wholly inadequate force, and are put to the worse. Under pressure Vivien allows one of his cousins to ride to his uncle William and demand aid, and the poem of *Aliscans* opens at the conclusion of the fatal struggle. William has seen all his men slain, his young nephews, his brother's sons, taken captive, and is compelled to fly from the field. But first he must know the fate of Vivien; he seeks him at imminent risk to himself, and at last finds the lad mortally wounded, and at the point of death, beside a spring. The scene that follows is exceptionally fine; the count at first yields to a natural out-burst of grief at the death of one so young and valiant, but suddenly he recalls himself to a sense of his duty. No priest is at hand; Vivien is dying fast; it devolves upon William as nearest of kin to render the consolations of religion. The warrior becomes a priest; taking the dying boy in his arms he rests his head against his breast and bids him confess his sins. Vivien can think of nothing save that he has broken his vow, and retreated before the enemy. William pronounces absolution; for the first time gives him *le pain béni,* and commends his soul to God.

> "Dex reçoif s'arme par ton digne commant
> Qu en ton sierviche est mors en Aliscans!"

This scene of the first communion and death of Vivien has been held by critics equal, if not superior, to that of the death of Roland.

The author of *Aliscans* is not a literary artist, he repeats himself, indulges in lengthy description, but the subject-matter with which he is dealing in the first half of the poem is exceptionally good, and he rises to the occasion. Very fine is the description of the arrival of William, a fugitive, and alone, disguised in the armour of a dead Saracen, at the gates of his own city of Orange. His wife does not know him in such guise; William would never have returned without the lads he went to succour; and not till the pursuers are close on his heels does Guibourc recognise and admit her husband. Then she shows herself the stronger of the two; it is she who comforts the Count, broken down by the disaster which has overtaken his house, and bids him hasten at once to demand succour from King Louis; she and her maidens dressed in armour, will delude the Saracens into the belief that Orange is fully garrisoned, and keep them at bay. William goes to the court of the king whom he has protected and aided, and who has wedded his sister, only to be treated with scorn and contempt. This is one of the finest parts of the

romance. Eventually Louis yields, in sheer terror of his truculent brother-in-law, and William is provided with a new army—and the poem with a new hero in the person of Renouart, the gigantic brother of William's wife, Guibourc, who, stolen from his people in early youth, is acting the part of scullion in Louis' kitchen.

The latter part of the poem is taken up with the recital of the valiant deeds of Renouart in the second battle of Aliscans, which results in a crushing defeat of the Saracens. Finally Renouart marries Aaliz, the king's daughter, and in the *Bataille de Loquifer* (a poem probably by the author of *Aliscans,* but much inferior to that work) is carried off to Avalon, where he combats the monster Chapalu in the presence of Arthur, King of Avalon.

The poem of *Aliscans* undoubtedly rests upon historical tradition; in the opinion of M. Leon Gautier, it represents the welding together of two widely separated events—the defeat of William of Aquitaine by the Saracens at Villedaigne in 793, and the defeat of the Saracens by William I., of Provence, in 976. The leading "motif" of the *geste* of the Narbonnais, the long-continued struggle between Christian and Moslem for the South of France, is genuinely historical.

The end of William's career is related in two romances, both bearing the same name, *Le Moniage Guillaume,* and generally referred to by scholars as *Moniage I.* and *Moniage II.,* in which we read how the hero eventually quitted the world and retired to the hermitage, where (after again issuing forth to combat the enemies of his country) he died in the odour of sanctity. A similar romance bears the name of Renouart, and relates how that hero also became a monk; but it is impossible to take any real interest in a figure so completely the creation of imagination. Renouart is never more than a serio-comic character, and distinctly out of place beside so strenuous a hero as William; nevertheless he appealed to the fancy of the Middle Ages, and was certainly a more living and persistent element in folk-tradition than the far more sympathetic Vivien.[9]

With the battle of Aliscans it seems fitting that we should close this brief sketch of the great French cycle. That the Charlemagne romances will ever offer to English students so tempting a field of inquiry as that of the Arthurian legend is doubtful. The subject-matter of this latter, consisting as it does largely of the mythical elements which lie at the root of all history and all belief, must always make an appeal to a wider circle than that represented by professed students of history or literature. We have adopted Arthur as a national hero, and as such take a pride in his name and fame, but the interest of the Arthurian story lies deeper than our interest in Arthur the King, and the ideas he symbolises are not those which inspire the *Matière de France.* The Charlemagne legend, on the other hand, is of direct national interest; it appeals above all to the children and lovers of *La douce France.* Nor from a literary point of view is it of equal value. Probably the four best romances, in the opinion of literary scholars, would be reckoned to be the *Chanson de Roland, Renaud de Montauban, Huon de Bordeaux,* and *Aliscans;* but not one of these could bear comparison, as a piece of literature, with any one of the masterpieces of Arthurian romance. I have suggested above that it may be owing, in a great measure, to this deficiency in literary form, and consequent failure to satisfy the more exacting literary taste of the twelfth century, that the Charlemagne cycle was superseded so completely in popular favour by the Arthurian romances. If, however, we distinguish content from manner, the *Matière de France,* as an epic cycle, ranks above the Arthurian, which is not strictly epic; regarded in this light, the *Chanson de Roland* has few rivals. And were it only as a picture of the impression produced by a great man upon the minds and imaginations of the people of his day, an unrivalled collection of documents showing how fancy deals with facts, and history becomes folk-tale, the *Matière de France* would be well worth our study; our fathers found pleasure in these old stories, and we shall not do ill if we follow their example.

Notes

1. In saying this I do not ignore the high epic value of the *Chanson de Roland,* I rather refer to a conscious effort after perfection of literary form.

2. The translation of the word *Geste* is somewhat difficult; the meaning appears to have been originally chronicles = feats, then the feats or actions of a particular family = family or race. In this sense M. Gautier employs it, but I incline to think that the earlier meaning is the more correct; the concluding words of the *Chanson de Roland,* "Ci falt la Geste que Turoldus declinet," cannot possibly have the signification of *race* or *family.*

3. For romantic purposes the wars with the Lombards practically do not count, as the authors of the romances have largely confounded them with the Saracens. We shall refer to this again in connection with *Ogier le Danois.*

4. I only refer in the text to the more important members of each subdivision; they will be found fully enumerated in the bibliographical appendix.

5. Eginhard, *Vita Caroli IX.,* quoted by M. Gautier, *Épopées Françaises,* ii. p. 363.

6. *Épopées Françaises,* vol. ii. p. 173.

7. The romances belonging to the *Doon* family are found in a collected form in a MS. of the Montpellier Library. They are the following:—*Doon de Mayence, Gaufrey, Les Enfances Ogier, La Chevalerie Ogier, Aye de Avignon, Gui de Nanteuil, Parise la Duchesse, Maugis d'Aigremont, Vivien l'amachour de Monbranc, Renaud de Montauban.* Of these only the two mentioned above are of the first rank. *Parise la Duchesse* is a variant of the *Berte* and *Macaire* stories.

8. Perhaps it may be well to explain that *Enfances* is a technical term applied to the account of the deeds of a hero before he receives knighthood. The tendency of later research is to prove that the "William" cycle was of greater importance than generally supposed.

9. The story of scullion turned hero seems to have been popular in mediæval times. There is a version of it in the Low German Thidrek Saga.

K. G. T. Webster (essay date 1906)

SOURCE: "Arthur and Charlemagne," *Englische Studien,* No. 36, 1906, pp. 337-69.

[*In the following essay Webster compares and contrasts certain aspects of the ballad of King Arthur and King Cornwall with the* Pilgrimage of Charlemagne.]

In the following sketch[1], after a few suggestions toward the reconstruction of the fascinating and puzzling ballad of *King Arthur and King Cornwall,* I shall attempt to explain the relation of Queen Guinevere, not only to King Cornwall, but also to several other still more important personages. These are certain of those remarkable characters in Old French and Middle High German romance who dispute Arthur's right to his queen. The claimant, as a rule, makes the apparently preposterous statement that he is an accepted suitor, or even the rightful husband of Guinevere, and finally he carries her off. This person's claims, I hope to show, are much better founded than they appear to be. Then, inevitably led from the *Arthur and Cornwall* to the *Pilgrimage of Charlemagne,* I shall venture to propose what I believe to be a new explanation for that entertaining poem, namely, that it is at bottom an other-world visit, of a kind not so very unlike that in the English ballad-romance of the *Turk and Gawain.* This tentative article I shall consider to have accomplished its object if it serves to call the attention of more competent scholars to the problems here discussed.

I. Certain points in the reconstruction of the ballad.

At the gap before stanza 21 of the fragmentary *Arthur and Cornwall* it would be natural from the words "Our Lady was borne", with which the narrative begins again, to infer that the palmers had told of a visit to Jerusalem or to Nazareth, reputed birth-places of the Virgin[2]. This supposition would be supported by the circumstance that the little book which they had found by the side of the sea was written by our Lord's own hand[3]: such a book they would be more likely to discover on a strand of Palestine than elsewhere. In the third place Palestine is the spot palmers would most naturally seek. The objection to this view of the conversation in the missing portion of the poem is that the information there conveyed is of such a kind as to make Cornwall think that the palmers had been in Britain, i. e., Little Britain. Professor Child, therefore, who considered that a pilgrimage formed no part of Arthur's programme, supposed that some shrine of our Lady in

Little Britain had been mentioned[4]; and Mr. W. D. Briggs does not cite this passage in support of his contrary belief that a pilgrimage to Jerusalem is an essential feature of the ballad[5]. However, it is difficult to imagine how the words of our text could well apply to any shrine in either Britain, and it seems not quite so difficult to imagine that the wide travels related by the palmers might have made Cornwall suppose that they had visited Little Britain as well as remoter places.

In the gap after stanza 28 Professor Child[6] and Mr. Briggs[7] agree that a sword was one of the possessions Cornwall exhibited. Yet it should be noticed that as the golden yard and the powder are only appliances secured by Bredbeddle to enable Marramiles and Tristrem to fulfill their boasts, and had doubtless not been mentioned before, so the sword is but another tool procured to help Arthur carry out his boast and should likewise not have been mentioned. Similarly Hugo's sword with which Charlemagne was to perform in the *Pilgrimage* is not noticed beforehand.[8]

The gap at stanza 38 Professor Child[9] fills by supposing that Tristrem here bragged he would *carry off* Cornwall's horn, Marramiles his steed and Bredbeddle his sword. Mr. Briggs[10] merely observes, "Marramiles and Tristrem make boasts regarding the sword and horn". It seems, perhaps, best to consider that the gabs of the two first knights were simply to *blow* the horn and to ride the horse. That is all we can be sure is done, and that required magic. As the horn was rent up to the midst by Tristrem's effort, it may well be doubted if it at any rate was carried off; and Roland's parallel boast in the *Pilgrimage of Charlemagne* was only that he would blow a peculiarly effective blast[11]. The horse is like Chaucer's horse of brass; the feat is to make this kind of steed budge and to manage him. As to Bredbeddle, it is not quite certain whether he makes a vow or not: there is no evidence to show that he vowed to carry off the sword. Mr. Briggs calls his offer to fight Burlow Beanie his vow[12], which it may very well be; but it is not formally termed a vow, as are Arthur's and Gawain's, the only two preserved. Bredbeddle's position is peculiar in that he resembles a "helpful companion" rather than an ordinary member of Arthur's Round Table[13].

II. The relation between Guinevere and King Cornwall.

In stanza 24 Cornwall declares:

> . . . seven yeere I was clad and fed,
> In Little Britain in a bower;
> I had a daughter by *King* Arthur's wife,
> *That* now is called my flower;
> For *King* Arthur, that kindly cockward,
> Hath none such in his bower.
> 25 'For I durst sweare, and save my othe,
> *That* same lady soe bright,
> That a man *that* were laid on his death bed
> Wold open his eyes on her to have sight'.
> 'Now by my faith', says noble *King* Arthur
> 'And that's a full faire wight'!

To this Professor Child[14] compares the passage ll. 3313-4888 in Heinrich von dem Türlin's *Crône*[15], of which passage he gives a synopsis in ten lines. As the *Crône* is a peculiar, valuable and neglected compilation I shall at the risk of being tedious give a somewhat detailed account of the whole episode therein (ll. 3356-5370, 10113-12588).

One cold day after a hunt, as King Arthur sat warming himself by the fire, the queen began to poke fun at him. "You are not so hot", she said, "as a knight I know: he rides all night, summer and winter, in nothing but a white shirt, and sings love-songs all the while. His horse is ermine white, his shield white, his banner white on his red lance; and he haunts the ford before Noirespine". Then she was sorry she had spoken "wider ir selbes êre" (l. 3433). The king in great indignation went to consult the only three knights left with him, Kei, Gales Lischas and Aumagwin. In accordance with Aumagwin's advice they went that very night to the ford; and took up their stations each in a different place (l. 3626) so that the strange knight could in no way escape them. It was extremely cold. Kei fell asleep upon his shield in a ditch, and there the knight they were seeking found and waked him (l. 3694). This knight's equipment was strange and rich. He refused to tell the reviling Kei his name, easily dismounted him and led away his horse (4000). The same fortune happened to the courteous Gales; and to the Red Aumagwin, who was stationed at the ford (4243). When Artus saw the victor come leading the three horses, he taunted him with having stolen them; after more conversation, in which the king vainly tried to find out the stranger's name, it came to fighting. Artus had the advantage. He then renewed his demand that the other tell his name (4684); whereto the stranger replied that he would tell it to nobody but King Artus. He would not, however, believe that his opponent was Artus till the king made him put his finger into the well-known scar on his head (4765). The stranger then disclosed himself as Gasozein de Dragoz; and having obtained permission to speak further, with a promise of just treatment for any claim he might make (l. 4789), he proceeded: "You have had in your house more than seven years my captive, taken by you against my will" (4804-4812). Artus disclaimed all knowledge of any such captive. "Daz ist Gînôver diu Künigin, Der reht âmîs ich immer bin, Diu mir wart bescheiden von den nahtweiden Dô sie êrste wart geborn (4837-4841). That I am not exaggerating this girdle will prove. Gawein won it for her and she gave it to me. It has such virtue that it makes the wearer invincible and universally beloved. A rich fairy, Giranphiel, and her sister made it for Finbeus of Karlin (4885)".

Gasozein continued: "I am her real husband and you are wrongly with her. She loved me in the first hour that she began to speak, and I possessed her from the cradle up. She would rather be a year with me than a day with you (4968). Nevertheless I am willing if you will bring her hither to-day, to stake her on a single combat in order to end this miserable strife (5001). Then even if I win her I will not touch her for a year; but waiving my right, fight for her again at the end of that time against any of your knights (5027). Artus proposed instead one final combat at Karidol in six weeks; to which his opponent agreed. Then Gasozein gave Artus the captured horses and departed (5081). The four rode back to Tintaguel (5370).

At l. 10 113 we find that Artus called a council on the day before that set for the combat, to consider the matter. When he related it to them, they declared that the affair must come off as arranged. The queen, who had sent a maid to bring her the news, when she heard this, said — "Christ protect my wifely honour" (10 394). Gasozein rode into the lists in unimagined splendour, clad in the arms furnished him by his sister Galamide the rich fairy (10 500). His coat of arms was a gold lion rampant on an azure field; and his horse was "harmblanc".

Artus first warned his men that none of them should in any event come between him and Gasozein (10 575); and then welcomed the challenger (10 618). At the first swift course Gasozein evaded his opponent's blow and let the king drive by; wherefore, on returning into the ring Artus taunted him (10 687) sharply. Gasozein replied courteously that they might both incur disgrace abroad if the reason for their fighting became known (10 745); moreover two such princes need not wage a judicial combat like ordinary persons. Artus did not quite see how they could do otherwise, for he did not believe there was any truth in Gasozein's claim. Then the latter proposed that they should let Ginover choose between them (10 860). Artus being very willing to decide the matter thus, they rode back to Karidol. Arrived there, they went from the gate to the court hand in hand, and there before the great company the king declared the cause of the strife and bade Ginover choose which of the two she would have for husband (10 964)[16]. Then the queen stood long in anguish; she did not know what to do or whom to choose (10 980). The eager Gasozein reproached the king with attempting to force her choice by the presence of the crowd; whereat Artus quieted his knights and bade the queen choose freely (11 002). She then declared she knew nothing of Gasozein and begged the king not to send her away. Gasozein was deeply wounded at this, and immediately departed without leavetaking. But Artus politely kept him company (11 036).

Ginover's trials were not yet over. The good knight, Graf Gotegrin, son of good King Garlin of Galore, and brother of Ginover by father and mother (11 093), had come with 40 men and lay near Karidol. From his mountain hiding place he sent a spy to see what should happen. The spy beheld everything and reported to Gotegrin that if it had not been for fear and shame, Ginover would have gone over to Gasozein (11 088). Enraged at this news Gotegrin raced to the palace, 'where he found the queen standing on a stone awaiting Artus' return from accompanying Gasozein. He seized her by the hair, swung her on to his horse and hurried a mile into the wood before any pursuer could saddle his steed (11 122). All the entreaties of the victim herself, and of Gotegrin's band, for her life were of no

avail. Ginover cried aloud—"Help God! I perish for nothing but a jesting word against the king" (11 206). Gotegrin rode with her deeper into the wood, and twisting one hand in her hair, was brandishing his sword with the other, when lo—Gasozein appeared and hurled him from his horse so that his arm and "halsbein" broke (11 282). Gasozein took the fainting queen in his arms, and tying Gotegrin's horse to his own, spurred on into the wood (11 313). When his burden came to herself he begged her to reward him by riding to his kingdom. She entreated him to have done with such talk and to lead her back to Karidol (11 379). This Gasozein would by no means do; and the queen thought it better to ride on with him than to risk his forcing her there in the wood far from all help (11 461).

Meanwhile Gotegrin's men had discovered their master wounded on the grass and had borne him to Karidol, where Artus, likewise returned, now learned the dreadful news (11 518). No mourning ever described was so great as that which afflicted the court (11 607). But Gasozein, who had taken many a kiss on the way, was now arrived at a natural bower, where his lustful passion caused him to dismount and toy with the queen under a linden tree (11 634). Fear made her grant him every familiarity but the last; and as he strove by force to win that, Gawein appeared, riding home to Karidol from one of his adventures (11 748). The queen would gladly have concealed her shame, but it was impossible. Gawein asked her if the knight had her there of her own free will, and she told him the whole escapade. Then Gawein would lead her home; to which Gasozein objected. Thereupon began a tremendous and ridiculous battle (11 854-12 256)[17], in which neither hero could overcome the other. At length they agreed to postpone the final struggle till each was recovered, and now to go to Karidol (12 345). As there was only a single horse, Gasozein, the weaker, was set on his back; and the queen and the wounded Gawein took turns leading the horse and sitting behind the wounded Gasozein. It was daylight when they came to Karidol. Then all three got on the horse's back to enter the city. A little maid brought the news to Artus (12 437); and Kei, greeting the queen, declared that she ought to be made a knight of the Round Table for capturing such prizes[18]

After a year's care Gasozein had recovered quite, Gawein almost (12 538). His wounds festered and did not close: he had exerted himself more than Gasozein, because he let the latter ride. Gasozein then went before Artus and declared his queen innocent, admitting that his pretensions had been mere lies. He was willing to suffer punishment, but was forgiven by all and remained at court (12 588).

On this passage Professor Child makes the following comment: "Very possibly to be found in some French predecessor[19], which recalls the relations of Cornwall King and Guinevere. The queen's demeanor may be an imitation of Charlemagne's (Arthur's) wife's bluntness, but the *liaison* of which Cornwall boasts appears to be vouched for by no other tradition, and must be regarded as the invention of the author of the ballad"[20]. This view of the relations of

Guinevere and Gasozein hardly agrees with the evidence in the abstract of the *Crône* just given. Gasozein there declares that Guinevere was promised to him at her birth by the witches[21], that Cupid conspired with them; he is her right *ami,* her proper husband, Arthur not; she loved him from the first hour, and he possessed her from her cradle until Arthur deprived him of her seven years ago. This is more than a *liaison.* In fact the position of the two lovers is reversed. In the *Crône* Gasozein is (or claims to be) the rightful husband, but the queen had been seven years with Arthur; in the ballad Arthur is the proper husband, and it is Cornwall (Gasozein) who has lived seven years with the queen. This indicates plainly what I take to be, relatively speaking, the original form of the story: Guinevere was the wife of another before Arthur won her, and the first husband still pressed his claims upon her after her second union. Such a conception could not exist in fashionable romance as Arthur grew in popularity; it is an archaism even in the thirteenth century *Crône.* Arthur could certainly come to be looked upon as the rightful and only husband, while the other, his previous claims forgotten, would be considered merely a lover of the queen, good or bad, favoured or not, as the case might be. In a ballad it would not be surprising if the older unpolished tradition lived on, with such results as we see in *Arthur and Cornwall;* but on the other hand it would also not be surprising if popular rhymsters reduced a romance in which hints of the old state of things remained to what we find in our ballad. It is the old question of survival or reversion, oral or written sources. With the direct source of the ballad, however, we are not much concerned at present: it is rather the relations of Guinevere and Cornwall, of Guinevere and her fairy husband—or of Arthur and his fairy wife. This matter, which I have considered, not fully but at length, in another place[22], I shall here merely outline.

An older and more orderly account of the queen's rape is found in Ulrich von Zatzikhaven's *Lanzelet*[23]. This German poem of about 1194 is a translation, probably an accurate one, of a French biographical romance of Lancelot which must have been written before Chrétien's *Charrette,* that is before 1170. Paris dates it at 1160[24]. Here we find a splendid prince, lord of a strange castle, who comes to Arthur's court and declares that Guinevere belongs by right to him, because she was promised to him *before she was of marriageable age.* Arthur will not give her up, and the stranger loses the duel on which they agree to stake her (cf. the Gasozein-Gawain duel). But a year later he captures her in a wood and carries her to his castle. Arthur tries in vain to get her back with his army. Finally he procures the aid of a magician, who studies his black books and puts the inhabitants of the castle to sleep, so that it is easily stormed and Guinevere recovered. This wonderful stranger, here called Valerin, is of course the same person as Gasozein and makes the same claim of a previous right to the queen.

If we go back further yet in pursuit of our story we come to the Latin version in the *Vita Gildae*[25], ascribed to Caradoc of Llancarvan, and dated with considerable uncertainty

at c. 1145. Here we are told that Melwas, ruler of Aestiva Regio or Somerset, violently captured Guinevere and took her to Glastonbury, a place strong on account of the surrounding marshes. Arthur, after searching a year, brought the armies of Cornwall and Devon thither to rescue her; but the Abbot of Glastonbury and St. Gildas reconciled the two monarchs, persuading Melwas to give back the queen peaceably. Both Melwas and Arthur, in a proper spirit of gratitude, presented lands to the abbey. This is still plainly our story in spite of the alterations of the pious narrator. The events have been localized by him at Glastonbury, the site of the great and scheming abbey, instead of in a vague strange land[26]; the splendid ravisher is spoken of depreciatingly as *iniquus;* the queen is restored to Arthur not by the aid of a damnable wizard, but by the good abbot and St. Gildas. If any proof of the story was demanded could not the broad lands still be pointed at, which the appreciative monarchs had bestowed on the abbey?

So far our search has not made the relations of Guinevere and Arthur's rival much clearer than the extract from the *Crône* did; but if we proceed still westward and backward, to Ireland, and consider the ancient tale of the *Wooing of Etain*[27], I believe that a fairly complete illumination will take place. Etain was the favorite wife of the fairy king Mider. An envious rival transformed her into a fly and blew her over Ireland till she fell into the cup of a certain mortal queen. In due time she was born as the daughter of this queen; and by and by Eochaid Airem, supreme king of Ireland, married her. Her old husband Mider came a-wooing her and tempting her with songs and claims of previous rights to return to his kingdom; but she would not—not without her husband's consent. So Mider appeared one day to King Airem and proposed a game of chess for any stakes the victor chose. He let Airem win and had to perform a prodigious task. Then Mider proposed a second game with the same stakes. This time Mider won and demanded the queen. "Come again in a month", said Airem. Mider did, appearing suddenly in the midst of the warriors set to guard the queen. He spirited her away from them to his fairy mound of Bri Leith. Airem with his army could not recover her. He told his druid to get her back. A year the druid sought, and at last by his ogams and yew-twigs he discovered that she was in the mound. They destroyed the mound and regained the queen.

Here at length, I believe, is the explanation of the relation of Guinevere and her various lovers and abductors, of which illustrious line King Cornwall is the last and a not unworthy scion: the same story was told of Arthur in Britain as of Airem in Ireland[28]: Guinevere was at one time a fairy, and Cornwall her other-world husband[29]. Now it becomes apparent why the abductor (in spite of his reprehensible conduct) is generally represented as an unusually splendid and formidable prince; why his land is so peculiar and so rich; why Guinevere is not blameworthy in spite of these escapades, and Arthur no cuckold—till late ballad times at least; why Guinevere is never maltreated in any of her "captivities", and why she is in no hurry when "rescued" to return to her legal spouse, or even finds difficulty in deciding between Arthur and Gasozein,—and numerous other details which need not be considered here. It may be well to observe, however, that the previous marriage has developed in quite a natural way. It became in the *Lanzelet,* as we have seen, an early promise to marry; in the *Crône* the original state of affairs is emphatically expressed by the old husband, but he afterwards admits that his pretensions are all false, which is a feeble and exasperating device of the poet's to get out of this difficult situation. In the more polite romances of the *Charrette* and *Durmart,* which also treat of the rape of Guinevere; in the prose versions which depend upon the former of these poems; and in the moral life of Gildas, which was only meant to tell so much of the story as would connect Arthur and Melwas with Glastonbury Abbey—in these, the awkward circumstance of Guinevere's first marriage is not mentioned. In our ballad it is plainly represented by Cornwall's *liaison*[30]

III. THE PILGRIMAGE OF CHARLEMAGNE.

Any consideration of the ballad of *King Arthur and King Cornwall* inevitably leads one to the famous old *geste* of the *Pilgrimage of Charlemagne* or the *Journey of Charlemagne to Jerusalem and Constantinople*[31]. To get at the kernel of this tale, our intention in the present chapter, we may immediately abandon the pilgrimage portion proper, with its visit to Jerusalem and its incongruous relics[32]. The persons and places then remaining we cannot suppose to be more than local habitations and names[33]. With the personality of Charlemagne and his peers gone, the number of gabs is left uncertain. The fact that only three are performed, renders it probable that the original gabs, feats or tests—whatever they might have been—were fewer than those in the present *Pilgrimage*[34]. Lastly it must be observed that the reproving wife episode is by no means such an essential part of the *Pilgrimage of Charlemagne* as it is of *Arthur and Cornwall.* Arthur's wife was known to be a lady of spirit, with a wonderful other-world lover whom it was quite natural that she should throw at Arthur's head; and of this relation Cornwall himself boasts to his unhappy guest in no delicate fashion. In the *Pilgrimage of Charlemagne,* however, not the least reason is given why Charles's wife should prefer Hugo to him; Hugo appears to know nothing of her. Moreover, the poet's treatment of the queen, after the opening scene, is not entirely satisfactory. In the first fifty-seven lines she comes into the action energetically enough, furnishing Charles with a sufficient motive for his journey; but thereafter she is only mentioned with great brevity, and sometimes quite awkwardly, five times in the 800 lines. At line 92, she is left weeping (one line): at ll. 234–235 Charles on leaving Jerusalem recollects his wife and her words (2 lines); at l. 365 Charles after viewing Hugo's palace recollects his wife whom he had threatened (one line); at ll. 813–815 (the crown-wearing) the French say that the queen had spoken folly, for Charles is superior to Hugo (3 lines); and in the last three lines of the poem we are told that on Charles's arrival the queen throws herself at his feet and he forgives her fault for love of the Holy Sepulchre, which he had adored; though as a matter of fact nothing has been said

about his adoring the Holy Sepulchre[35]. Then again the emphasis laid on the crown wearing is strange. Charles says to the queen at the beginning, "Wife, did you ever see any king under Heaven, whom his sword and his crown on his head became so well? I shall yet conquer cities with my sword". She who was not wise responded foolishly, "Emperor, you esteem yourself too highly. I know one who looks better when he wears his crown among his knights; on whose head it is more becoming". Then at the end of the story the two kings wear their crowns together, and Hugo wore his not quite so lofty (810) and was one foot three inches shorter than Charles. This appears sophisticated and unconvincing. The three considerations just mentioned, though perhaps only the first is of great weight, are sufficient to make one wonder if the reproving wife episode is an integral portion of the story, if it has not been prefixed to the Constantinople visit simply to get the hero started[36]

At this point it may be well to consider how our story has hitherto been classified. All[37] commentators, so far as I know, have followed Paris in not separating the reproving wife episode from the happenings in Constantinople. In the words of Prof. Child[38] the story is "one of a cycle of tales of which the frame-work is this: that a king who regards himself as the richest or most magnificent in the world is told that there is somebody who outstrips him, and undertakes a visit to his rival to determine which surpasses the other, threatening death to the person who has disturbed his self-complacency, in case the rival should turn out to be his inferior". Concerning this classification, I should like to remark in the first place that the analogies cited by Paris and Prof. Child in this connection are by no means close. Thus in the moral tale of Haroun Alraschid, the king, when he is reproved by his vizier, threatens the vizier with death if his words shall not prove true, and starting off, finds a more generous man. How very unlike Charlemagne's exciting experience. In the *Gylfaginning* and the *Vafdrudnismal* the heroes start of their own accord, the contest is one of wisdom only and Gylfi's life is not at stake, if Odin's is. Why Thor visits Geirrödr we are not told, only that Loki promised that giant he would persuade Thor to come unarmed; and therefore, although the resemblance in detail noted by Paris and by Child is significant, this story as it stands does not belong in the cycle described[39]. *Biterolf and Dietlieb* has only this similarity, that Biterolf, started by a palmer, seeks the superior court of Attila; and the tale of Jatmundr (Hlödver) in the *Magus Saga Jarls,* cited in Child's note, relates only that the boasting king on being told by a minister that he needs a wife to complete his glory, goes to Constantinople (Miklagard), and by asking obtains the Emperor Hugo's daughter as his wife. Finally, Professor Child himself points out the insufficiency as analogues of the large class of eastern tales which he mentions in the introduction to the *Elfin Knight*[40]: here the demand is made not in person but through an ambassador; the king who happens to be the hero is delivered by the sagacity of his minister or the minister's daughter; and "the tasks are always such as require ingenuity of one kind or another, whether in devising practical expedients, in contriving subterfuges, in solving riddles or even in constructing compliments". It is therefore unnecessary to examine these narratives. The second observation I have to make on Paris's classification of the *Pilgrimage* is, that when the hero's wife is the person who abases his pride by telling him of a superior, we may reasonably expect a special variation of the type, a variation in which a love affair between the wife and the personage mentioned plays an important part. This is so in the *Crône, Rigomer*[41] and *Arthur and Cornwall*[42]. Thus our examination of the parallels offered by Paris and Child discloses nothing at variance with the conclusions reached in the last paragraph: not one of these parallels contains the reproving wife, and in only one, the visit of Thor to Geirrödr, is there anything that resembles at all closely the happenings at Constantinople. Therefore, we may disregard the old classification of our story, and still consider that the reproving wife episode is no essential part of the *Pilgrimage of Charlemagne,* that the actual kernel of the tale is the happenings at Constantinople. To this most interesting portion we will now turn our attention.

Cornwall, I have tried to show, is an other-world monarch; and the question very naturally arises, is not Hugo one also? I believe we shall find not a few good reasons besides his likeness to Cornwall for considering him such. One of the most striking of these is the nature of Hugo's land. Charles found in a blooming garden (l. 262) near the shining, towered city 20,000 well-clad knights playing chess and tables and carrying falcons; he beheld likewise 3000 beautiful damsels with an equal number of cavaliers. Hugo (l. 283) was ploughing with a gold plough, himself seated in a rich litter drawn by mules[43]. There were no thieves in this land (l. 324). The most gorgeous palace, which was painted within and without with figures of all beasts, serpents, creatures and birds[44], revolved rapidly when a wind came from the sea[45]. Whoever heard the statuettes about making music thought he was in Paradise (l. 376). A tempest of wind, snow and hail quickly came and quickly went[46]. Charles' bedroom was lighted by a single carbuncle; and the coverlets of his bed had been made and presented to Hugo by a friendly fairy Maseüz (430). It is but reasonable, I think, to suppose that the poet is here describing a sort of fairyland. This view is not invalidated, but rather strengthened, by the fact that the scene is localized at Constantinople, the city of Hugo, emperor of Greece and of Constantinople; for in mediæval Irish stories the other world is regularly placed in Greece[47]; and in the 12th century French romance of *Parthonopeus de Blois* the undisguised fairy heroine lives in Besance[48]

This view of Hugo's land provides an explanation of the confused geography of the poem, which so exercises commentators[49]. To Jerusalem the journey is explicit and mostly comprehensible (100–108); from there to Constantinople (261–262) it is brief and perplexing. But if we have here to do, not with the actual city on the Golden Horn at all, but with what may be loosely termed the other world, we should not expect geographical preciseness.

Again, if Hugo is an other-world monarch, then we can understand the self-denial of Charles when Hugo offers him departing all his treasures, and Charles refuses, saying that the French have already as much as they can carry (839–844). It is true that the poet makes Hugo become Charles' vassal (l. 787 f.), but the episode is by no means convincingly told; and we feel throughout that Hugo is a richer and more powerful king than Charles. The story teller succeeds in making his hero more than a match for the emperor of Constantinople at the feats and the crown-wearing, but he cannot quite bring himself to exhibit a fairy king as a genuine vassal of France, or Charles as bearing home other-world treasures[50]. Such deference for other-world monarchs even when faded and almost indistinguishable, is common, and surprises us until we recognize the illustrious being: thus apologies are made for the killing of Valerin, and neither Arthur nor Gawain is allowed to overcome Gasozein.

An other-world monarch often imposes upon his guests prodigious tests. These are generally such as cannot be performed by a mortal without supernatural aid. It may not be unreasonable to propose that the gabs in their wild extravagance represent tests of this kind, where the relics and the angel take the place of some magic helper, just as in the *Vita Gildae* St. Gildas and the abbot replace the older wizard or druid. An interesting example of a genuine other-world visit, and a closer parallel to the happenings at Constantinople than any yet adduced, is the rude and mutilated romance of *The Turk and Gawain*[51]. Here a Turk (i. e. dwarf) comes to Arthur's court and takes a buffet from Gawain. To receive his buffet back Gawain agrees to follow the Turk at all hazards. So for several days they journey northward together until they come to a hill, which opens for them and closes again. Within they pass through storm and dark. At a gap in the poem the Turk appears to warn Gawain against eating, drinking and talking in this land. They arrive at a deserted castle where viands are laid out; but his guide forbids Gawain to touch them, and brings him safe food. Gawain demands his buffet, but the Turk (at a gap) apparently refuses to give it. After this they sail over the sea in a boat to the fair castle of the heathen King of Man, who possesses a retinue of hideous giants. Here the Turk tells Gawain that he shall see strange things, such as a huge tennis ball, and be well assayed; but that he need have no fear, because the Turk will preserve him. When the king invites Gawain to sit at the board, he refuses, demanding first the adventures. At the king's command his 17 giants bring out the ball of brass such as no man in England could carry: they thought to play with Sir Gawain and strike out his brain. At a gap here Gawain's "boy", the Turk[52], appears to overcome the giants at the tennis play, and moreover at casting the axletree—as the poem begins again he has just stuck a giant with the axletree. At this the king remarks that the third and last adventure will be more trying for the boy. Then a giant bids Gawain lift an enormous "chimney", or grate laden with coal and wood[53]. Gawain tells the giant to begin and he or "boy" will answer him. The giant lifts the chimney with his hand, whereat Gawain is aghast; but the boy picks it up and flings it about his head. The tests proper appear to end here; but after a gap the king, who declares he has already killed "the flower" (of Arthur's knights?) and will let nobody who belongs to King Arthur escape, is overheard by the Turk, here clad in invisible weeds[54], plotting to kill Gawain. Gawain is led "into steddie" (l. 238) where is "a boyling leade", and before it a giant with an iron fork. The king says to the giant "Here is none but wee tow let see how best may bee" (ll. 248–249). But when the giant catches sight of Gawain's boy he writhes in dread[55]; and no wonder, for the boy picks him up, throws him into the lead and holds him down with the fork until he is dead[56]. The king spits on Gawain, whereat the Turk flings him into the fire. After this Gawain cuts off the Turk's head with a sword, and the misshapen dwarf becomes a stalwart knight. The two release many captives, ladies and men. They eat, restore the ladies to their husbands and return to Arthur's court. Sir Gromer, the former dwarf, becomes king of Man.

In this primitive story we have a situation, the similarity of which to Charlemagne's predicament at Constantinople cannot be overlooked. Gawain in the mysterious Isle of Man must perform the same sort of feats as Charles and his peers in Constantinople; he like the Frenchmen will lose his life if unsuccessful; and like them he succeeds by supernatural aid. The most striking similarity is in the nature of the feats; there is the same imaginative and grimly humorous exaggeration of physical strength in both cases. Even certain details correspond: William of Orange performs with a huge *pelote,* the Turk with a great brass tennis ball[57]: Ernalz will sit in molten lead, the Turk holds the giant down in the same; Aimer has a *tarnkappe,* and the Turk an equally virtuous garment of 'invissible gray'.

In yet another other-world visit, though here the original state of things is very much disordered by attempts at rationalizing and christianization, can be found important resemblances to Charlemagne's adventure at Constantinople. This is Wolfdietrich's sojourn with King Belian in the *Great Wolfdietrich*[58]. The same episode in a considerably different form occurs in Ulrich von Zatzikhoven's *Lanzelet*[59]; but it will suffice for the present to give only the version bearing the greatest resemblance to the *Pilgrimage of Charlemagne.*

(*Great Wolfdietrich* § 1060.) Wolf came to a fine castle, on every pinnacle of which but one stuck a head. King Belian received him hospitably, but told him that every guest there had to sleep with his beautiful daughter Marpali; and if he did not succeed in making her his wife that night, then his head came off and went on a pinnacle. Every guest so far—some 500 of them—had lost his head. Aghast at the prospect Wolf rode out again, but was stopped by a lake at the door, that Marpali had conjured up. So he had to return and take his chances (l. 1097). Then Marpali was brought in attended by sixty maids, whom she outshone like a rose among other flowers. They had a feast that evening, at which the porter, who liked Wolf, signed to him to touch nothing. This repast was under a great cast-

metal linden tree full of jewelled birds[60] to which silver tubes went up from bellows below; so that when the bellows were blown the birds all sang. At night (1136) Wolf went to the bedroom with Marpali, to whom her father whispered—"You know how to entertain him". But Marpali had fallen in love with Wolf, and she threw away the sleeping draught (drugged wine) brought to them in their room, which had rendered all the previous guests incapable of touching her (1143). Then she wooed Wolf frantically but vainly, for the Virgin helped him to remain cold to one who would not be baptized. Now Belian was accustomed to come to his daughter's room in the morning and capture the knights in bed; and he came to the door this morning (1169) saying: "Tell me, daughter, has the guest loved you? did not my clear wine protect?" "No," she replied, "Avenge me. I threw out the wine." "You will have to fight me now or lose your head," said Belian to Wolf. "Very well," answered Wolf, "I never refuse an even fight." First Belian showed him Death, one of his idols. Wolf smashed it and laughed—"Ha, ha. I have broken your death, now you must live forever;" but Belian was vexed (1175). Then Belian jumped a moat nine klafters wide by putting a shield under his armpit. But Wolf in the same way jumped farther yet[61]. Next came the knife play, which the author relates at length with great gusto. This peculiar kind of combat seems to have reached a high stage of development; it reminds one of the various "arts" and showy performances with weapons, of which the Irish stories make so much. Its technique appears to have consisted of three parts: the *schirmen,* or defense with a span-wide shield; the *sprunc,* or dodge and jump; and the *wurf,* or throw. The contestants, at least in *Wolfdietrich,* stand on peculiar stools[62]

> Wir müsen in zwen hemden uf zwen stülen stan,
> die sind durchgossen mit blie uf dri stecken smal,
> daz uns die füsze beide gend übereinander hin zu tal.

1184

In *Wolfdietrich* to touch the foot to the ground was death. Each combatant has a little shield and three knives[63]. The great master of this art was Berchtung of Meran, Wolf's mentor. He had learned it from King Anzius of Constantinople; and taught it again to Belian and to Wolf. He concealed one dodge and one throw from Belian, but showed Wolf all. It had been foretold to Belian that Wolf should slay him (12, 334–345). Accuracy of throwing is of course the most desirable accomplishment of a knife player; each contestant names his shot before taking it. After a most entertaining contest (1184-1235) Wolf split his opponent's heart so exactly in two that there was not a hair's difference between the halves. A fight now ensued with Belian's followers, who were overcome and baptized in a miraculous font. Marpali would not be baptized. Her Wolf carried off with him; but after she had bedevilled him in most embarrasing ways, she turned into a crow amid an infernal stench, and flew to a tree (1277).

In this extraordinary narrative the parallels which concern us are these: the hero, arrived at the strange castle which corresponds in beauty and terror to Hugo's city[64], has to perform certain feats to escape with his life. These feats are to sleep with the daughter and make her his wife, which may be compared to Oliver's adventure with Hugo's daughter; to leap the moat by the device of putting a shield under the arm, which is nothing less than flying with shields as Bertram in the *Pilgrimage* bragged he would do[65]; and finally to excel the host at knife throwing, which strongly reminds one of Gerin's gab that he will throw a heavy sword at two pennies placed on top of a tower half a league away: the top penny he would knock off without jarring the other, and he will run fast enough to catch the sword before it reaches the earth[66]. A minor incident in both poems is that the father in the morning comes to the daughter's door to find how she has fared.

It is from such other-world visits as these two stories, *The Turk and Gawain* and the visit of Wolfdieterich to King Belian, that I conceive Charlemagne's experiences at Constantinople to have evolved. Thor's visit to Geirrödr the giant, already cited by Paris and Child[67], is the same sort of tale; which is one reason why Thor's performances on this, as on other of his visits to the giants, fundamentally resemble those of Charlemagne's followers: they are grotesque feats of strength, which, successfully done in the presence of an actually superior power, enable the visitor to escape with his life; indeed sometimes to slay his formidable host. To be a little more definite, I think that the germ of this part of the *Pilgrimage* may have been an ancient version of the King Belian episode, for this offers the daughter, who is, in a way, the central figure of the whole affair[68]. What might almost be called an intermediate stage of the tale, that is, one based on the old material yet influenced by the new, is found in the *Libro del Danese* described by Rajna in *Romania* IV 402-417. Here Orlando, Rinaldo and Ulivieri spend the night at the court of the heathen king, Carcasso (Gargagi). In their bedroom is this inscription, "Whoever sleeps here must make a gab before he goes to bed". So Orlando declares that with his lance he will pierce King Carcasso clad in whatever armour he pleases to wear. Ulivieri boasts that he will stay three days with the king's daughter Gismonda without ever eating or drinking. Rinaldo says that alone he will take the field against any and all heathen. Carcasso demands the fulfillment of the gabs under penalty of death, calling Ulivieri's first. By miraculous help Ulivieri accomplishes his boast, and moreover resists the frantic wooing of the daughter. The other gabs are also fulfilled and thus Carcasso loses his life. It seems reasonable to consider this somewhat unsatisfactory narrative a decayed version of the King Belian episode under the influence of the *Pilgrimage of Charlemagne,* rather than simply a weakened imitation of the Pilgrimage[69]

I wish to meet one objection that may be offered to the view of Charlemagne's visit to Constantinople just proposed. The accepted explanation of the poet's description of Constantinople is that he is following travellers' accounts of the actual place. Paris says of the fantastic picture of Hugo's city and palace, that it was "bien ainsi que l'imagination des occidentaux, excitée par les récits des pèlerins qui avaient traversé Constantinople en allant en Terre-Sainte, se représentait la ville des merveilles"[70]. We must therefore look at the resemblances cited by Paris between the actual Constantinople as depicted by these travellers, and the Constantinople of our poem, premising, however, that even if Paris' view be judged correct, the possibility that in the poem we still have to do with a localization of the other world, would not be excluded.

Beyond a general magnificence, the noteworthy parallels which Paris gives are these: "Qu'on se rappelle les descriptions laissées par les historiens du *chrysotriclinium:* 'C'était une grande salle octogone a huit absides, où l'or ruisselait de toutes partes . . . Dans le fond s'élevait une grande croix ornée de pierreries, et toutà l'entour des arbres d'or, sous le feuillage desquels abritait une foule d'oiseaux émaillés et décorés de pierres fines, qui par un ingénieux mécanisme, voltigeaient de branche en branche et *chantaient au naturel . . .* En même temps se faisaient entendre les orgues placées à l'autre extrémité de la salle'. Je ne parle pas des fameux lions d'or qui se dressaient sur les pattes en rugissant; mais ces oiseaux qui chantent sur des arbres d'or, cet orgue où le vent des soufflets fait passer de suaves melodies, n'ont-ils pas visiblement servi de typeà la description de notre poeme? Ces merveilles furent exécutées au IXe siècle; Liudprand, qui les vit au Xe, nous dit que les arbres d'or etaient simplement en bois doré; mais cela ne changeait rien à l'aspect, qui dut rester pareil jusqu'à la prise de Constantinople par les Francs. La salle où sont dressés les treize lits des Français semble aussi devoir quelque chose au souvenir du *Triclinium au onze lits,* dans le même palais, où des colonnes d'argent supportaient au-dessus du lit réservé a l'empereur les plus riches draperies".

I do not think that upon examination any of these details will be found of very great significance. It is surely not allowable to compare the enamelled birds that hopped and sang on the golden trees of the supposedly real palace with the flying birds, which, together with all other creatures, were painted on Hugo's palace. The singing of these birds and the music which the wind made on the aeolian harp or organ bears some resemblance to the performance of the two hundred[71] cherubs of Hugo's hall, who blew their horns when the palace turned in the wind; but this by itself counts for little. As to the bedrooms, certainly nothing should be made of what similarity they possess, because we may be sure that in whatever palace Charles and his peers spent a night we should be quite likely to find a room with thirteen beds. A much closer parallel, in fact a striking one, for Charles' bedroom can be observed in the ancient Irish story of the *Wooing of Emer* in the *Leber na h'Uidre*[72]. So it seems to me that it still remains to be proved that our Constantinople owes anything, even its situation, to the real Constantinople. Indeed it might not be altogether folly to consider whether some of the wonders which early travellers and historians declared to exist in Constantinople were not mere other-world features transferred to the place where the other world was localized,—for instance these very trees of singing birds.[73]

IV.

If the inferences of the previous sections are sound, their bearing on the ballad of *King Arthur and King Cornwall* is important. This piece, apparently so like the *Pilgrimage of Charlemagne,* we should now have to consider as different fundamentally. In the ballad the reproving wife episode and the other-world visit are inseparably connected. This latter portion may be greatly influenced by other tales, such as the *Pilgrimage of Charlemagne,* or the horse, horn and sword story that Professor Child suggests[74]; but it is nevertheless at bottom the kind of adventure we should expect from the introduction. In the *geste* this is not the case. Moreover, we have observed attached to Arthur another combination of pilgrimage to Jerusalem and visit to a great king—that is the romance of *Golagros and Gawain*—which is probably independent of the *Pilgrimage of Charlemagne.* Any argument that derives the ballad from the *geste* on account of similarity of plot must take these two circumstances into consideration. Another difficulty in the way of such a theory is the genuine romantic archaism of the ballad in the many details wherein it differs from the *geste*[75]. This state of things points rather to a common origin in part[76] for the two poems, with direct influence later of the Pilgrimage upon the ballad[77]

The opposite view to that just mentioned, namely that the *Pilgrimage of Charlemagne* is an imitation or a variation of the original *Arthur and Cornwall,* with the intrigue omitted, might seem too preposterous to mention. Yet there is perhaps still too much uncertainty about the relations of the Arthurian and the Carlovingian cycle to permit us to pass over such a notion without remark. Arthur is an older hero than Charlemagne, although he did not so soon attain a European popularity. Brittany, a home of Arthurian romance, played no small part in the development of the Carlovingian cycle, for the Roland was composed in the French portion of Brittany, and not long before the *Pilgrimage*[78]. A third explanation of the poem may be preferred by some. They may assume that much the same story was once told of Charlemagne in France that was told of Airem in Ireland and of Arthur in Britain; that Hugo, accordingly, corresponds to the otherworld lover of the queen, but that the writer of the *Pilgrimage* is either ignorant of this earlier feature of the tale, or purposely alters it[79]. The objection to this hypothesis is that no trace of such a story is found. It is true that Charles' wife, Sebille, is according to a popular and wide spread tale the daughter of the King of Constantinople[80]; but in the versions that have come down to us there is no hint that her father is supernatural. Both of these hypotheses retain the reproving wife as an essential part of the tale. However in the light of what has been said above on this point, it seems better to abide by the view there expressed, that the reproving wife and the visit at Constantinople are unrelated episodes combined by the narrator of the *Pilgrimage of Charlemagne.*

The origins suggested in these pages, if they should prove at all correct, would tend to strengthen the growing belief that mediæval romance owes a great deal more to sources commonly called Celtic than scholars formerly supposed. Professor Thurneysen[81] in 1884 remarked out that the closest resemblances to the gabs of Charlemagne's peers were to be found in the "cless, die Bravourstücke" of the old-Irish warriors, and suggested that in the *Pilgrimage of Charlemagne* we might have, as it were, "an afterglow of old Celtic story-telling preserved among the folk". The juggling and leaping[82] feat of Archbishop Turpin was pointed out by Thurneysen as characteristically Irish. To half a dozen more of the gabs and to the general situation at Constantinople we have noticed instructive illustrations or fairly close parallels in the *Turk and Gawain* and *Wolfdietrich;* the former of which, with its other world in the Isle of Man, has a decidedly Celtic tinge, and the latter at least nothing out of harmony with Celtic conceptions. The striking resemblances between Charlemagne's bedroom and that of Conchobar described in the *Wooing of Emer* has been indicated, likewise briefly the likeness of Hugo's realm to the Celtic other world. Many more of such similarities would probably occur to any Celticist who should make a careful examination of the poem.

Notes

1. This paper, in a considerably different form, was read at a ballad course at Harvard College in the spring of 1902.

2. Cf. Mandeville's *Travels,* cap. XIII, for Nazareth, and the Seigneur d'Anglure's *Saint Voyage de Jherusalem,* § 62, for Jerusalem.

3. Stanzas 46 and 47.

4. *The English and Scottish Popular Ballads,* Vol. I, p. 279. Prof. Child appends the following note:—"Arthur is said to have 'socht to the ciete of Criste' in 'Golagros and Gawane', Madden's 'Syr Gawayne', p. 143, v. 302. The author probably followed the so called Nennius c. 63." Certain further resemblances of the confused romance of *Golagros and Gawane* to the *Pilgrimage of Charlemagne* should be noticed. There we find Arthur and a small troop going toward Tuskane, "hym to seek ouer the sey that sacklese wes sald" (l. 3). They get lost, but are entertained royally and set right by the lord of a fair city. Continuing their journey they reach another beautiful city begirt with 30 towers, situated on a rich river. Golagros, the master of this place, which is impregnable, holds of nobody but God. Arthur, on hearing this, resolves to make him his man when he returns from his pilgrimage. So he goes on and seeks the city of Christ over the salt flood; and having made his offering, returns. He comes to Rome (which appears to be identified with the beautiful city that had excited his cupidity) and undertakes a siege of the place. Single combats occur. Golagros wins Gawain through Gawain's generosity. Arthur and his men sup with Golagros, who, to their surprise, submits to Arthur; but Arthur refuses to receive his homage and leaves him "Fre as I the first fand With outen

distance". In this poem, then, we have Arthur going on a pilgrimage to Jerusalem (the city of Christ), and stopping on his return at an extraordinary city in order to make its remarkable king who had no superior but God, acknowledge Arthur's superiority. The king finally submits, as Hugo does, but yet Arthur declines to receive his oath and leaves him free, just as we feel that Hugo is left in spite of the fact that the French poet makes him become Charles's man. If *Golagros and Gawane* can thus be brought into the set of poems under discussion and contains a pilgrimage of Arthur to Jerusalem, then the probability that *Arthur and Cornwall* also contained such a pilgrimage is somewhat increased. Here also we have a third combination of pilgrimage and visit, which slightly weakens the force of Mr. Briggs's argument in vol. III of the *Journal of Germanic Philology* p. 347, that the ballad of *King Arthur and King Cornwall* and the *Pilgrimage of Charlemagne* could hardly be independent of each other, since they make the same combination of pilgrimage and visit. To Arthur's pilgrimage should be compared the various more sober early accounts of Charlemagne's journey to Jerusalem or to Constantinople to procure relics: cf. *Die Legende Karl's des Grossen,* Gerhard Rauschen, p. 141; *Histoire Poétique de Charlemagne,* G. Paris, bk. I, cap. III; *Les Épopées Françaises,* T. Gautier, 2nd ed., III 282 f.; G. Paris in *Romania* IX 16.

5. *Jour. of Germ. Phil.* III 342, *King Arthur and King Cornwall.*

6. *Ballads* I 279.

7. *Op. Cit.* 344.

8. G. Paris, *Romania* IX 17 remarks that Charlemagne and his peers borrowed arms, offensive and defensive, because they brought none of their own. Arthur's party should have no arms; nevertheless Bredbeddle seems to possess enough of good ordinary weapons in st. 42. There may be magic virtue in the weapons of the strange king.—That the horn and the Burlow Beanie were exhibited, as Prof. Child and Mr. Briggs agree, there appears no reason to doubt. The fragment of stanza 29 which closes this gap " . . . Nobody say . . . But one *that's* learned to speake", may allude to a charm necessary to quell the Burlow Beanie, which Bredbeddle fortunately found in the "little book".

9. p. 280.

10. p. 344.

11. Line 470.

12. p. 344.

13. If Bredbeddle represents a supernatural helper like the Turk in the *Turk and Gawain* (*Bishop Percy's Folio MS.,* ed. Hales and Furnivall, vol. II), he should make no boast; but if he is considered merely one of Arthur's knights, he should boast like the others. It preserves the symmetry of the poem to have him boast.

14. *Ballads* I 279.

15. *Diu Crône,* ed. G. H. F. Scholl, Stuttgart 1852, vol. XXVII of the Bibliothek des litterarischen Vereins in Stuttgart. . . .

16. Dr. E. C. Armstrong in his dissertation, *Le Chevalier à L'Epée,* Baltimore 1900, p. 65, is probably incorrect in saying that this situation seems to have been suggested to Heinrich von dem Türlin by the French "Maiden and Dog" story. It is rather an unavoidable dilemma of Guinevere's.

17. The prolixity and vulgarity of the *Crône* are strikingly exemplified in the last thousand lines. No combat more senselessly amplified, no meeting of lovers more voluptuous can be found in the Arthurian romances.

18. Kei mentions four prizes Guinevere had captured "sît gestern": Gotegrin, Gawein, Gasozein, and Auguintester (12 490).

19. The assumption of a French source for most of the *Crône* is, I believe, general: see Scholl's introduction, p. XI; O. Warnatsch, *Der mantel,* p. 120 (*Germanistische abhandlungen* II). For thinking that this particular portion is so I can give a specific reason. In the *Prose Lancelot* is a passage wherein mention is made of Gawain's severe wound which Gasoain gave him at the time when Gawain accused Gasoain of *desleiauté* and fought with him before the king (Jonckbloet, *Roman van Lancelot,* II, p. XX). This must refer to the prodigious combat described in the *Crône,* and must be supposed taken from the French source of the *Crône;* for it is highly improbable that the French compiler of the *Prose Lancelot* would have gone to the German *Crône,* Indeed he could not have, because he represents Gawain and Gasoain as having fought before the king, a thing which the *Crône* only hints at after describing an encounter in the woods; but which there is reason for believing actually occurred in a very old French version (non-extant) of the rape of Guinevere. This point I have discussed at length in a paper which I hope to publish shortly.

20. *Ballads* I 279 n. Cf. Madden's note, *Syr Gawayne* p. 357: This intrigue "is nowhere, as far as I recollect, hinted at in the romances of the Round Table".

21. "Von den nahtweiden", 4840.

22. In a dissertation entitled *Lancelot and Guinevere, a Study in the Origins of Arthurian Romance,* presented to the Harvard Faculty of Arts and Sciences for the degree of Ph. D. in 1902.

23. Ed. K. A. Hahn, Frankfurt 1845; ll. 4972—5360, 6710—7423.

24. *La Littérature Française au Moyen Age,* 2nd ed., p. 247.

25. *Monumenta Germaniae* XIII 109. For the date v. Sir F. H. Hardy, *Descriptive Catalogue etc.* I 151 f.; Stevenson's *Gildas,* Introd.; E. A. Freeman in

Macmillan's Magazine XLII 463; la Borderie, *Etudes Historiques Bretonnes* I 356; Paris, *Rom.* X 490 f.; Rhys, *Arthurian Legend* p. 52; T. Wright, *Biographia Britannia Literaria* I 119, 120; F. Lot, *Rom.* XXVII 566.

26. It is possible that before the *Vita Gildae* was written popular tradition had localized the realm of the mysterious Melwas at Glastonbury Tor; that this hill was considered by the Britains a fairy mound: v. Rhys, *Arthurian Legend,* p. 31; Nutt, *Studies in the Legend of the Holy Grail,* p. 223; Freeman, *Macmillan's Magazine,* XLII 468; Paris, *Rom.,* X 491; E. Brugger, *Zeitschr. für frz. spr.,* XX 99; Zarncke, *Paul and Braune's Beiträge* III 325; F. Lot, *Rom.,* XXIV 329 and XXVII 567; Zimmer, *Zeitschr. für frz. spr.,* XII 245.

27. This brief outline I make from Zimmer's full account of the tale in the *Zeitschrift für Vergleichende Sprachforschung (Kuhn's Zeitschrift)* XXVIII, pp. 585–594, with some help from O'Curry's *Manners and Customs of the Ancient Irish,* II 192 f., and Nettlau in *Revue Celtique* XII 229–241. For further references to the *Tochmarc Etain* and for the nature of the story, v. Kittredge in *Harvard Studies and Notes in Philology and Literature* VIII 192, 196 and notes.

28. For other supposed correspondences between Arthur and Airem v. Rhys, *Arthurian Legend,* cap. II.

29. Prof. Kittredge has already brought Guinevere into the large class of fairy wives, *fées* won by a mortal husband from an immortal, who return to their former husband only to be won back again by the mortal; and he has pointed out that the fée's "return to fairie with her immortal partner is not regarded as an offence, and she is not liable to punishment for unfaithfulness". *Harvard Studies and Notes* VIII 261, cf. 190, 195.

30. In that this *liaison* takes place after Arthur's marriage to Guinevere, it corresponds in position to Mider's wooing. The original wooing seems to have left traces in the *Crône,* where Guinevere tells how Gasozein haunts the neighborhood singing love songs.

31. *Karl's des Grossen Reise nach Jerusalem und Constantinopel,* ed. Koschwitz, 4th ed., Leipzig 1900.

32. So Paris, *Rom.,* IX 8; Child, *Ballads,* I 282; Koschwitz XXVI, XXX, XXXV.

33. "Originairement étranger à Charlemagne aussi bien qu'à Constantinople", Paris.

34. Yet the possibility that the number twelve was a primitive feature, must be admitted; for a hero with a band of twelve is not uncommon in ancient French and German romances. V. Rajna, *Le Origini dell' Epopea Francese,* pp. 393, 415 f. Conchobar in the *Wooing of Emer* has twelve principal chariot chiefs, whose twelve beds are about his as those of the peers about Charlemagne's, cf. below.

35. Of course, too much should not be inferred from this feeble ending. The poet was in a bit of a dilemma. He knew that Hugo was superior to Charles and that therefore the queen was exonerated; but he was obliged to represent Hugo as inferior, thereby putting the queen under sentence of death. So he was compelled to make Charles forgive her and to slur over the incident. Guinevere, who in the *Crône* is still more injudicious in that she publicly hesitates whether to go with the lover or the husband, gets no word of blame from Arthur, although she is punished by her brother. Cf. above.

36. Prof. Kittredge by another method of reasoning has already arrived at the same conclusion: "We are not to suppose", he says, that the feature in question first came into existence when the *Pèlerinage* was composed. It is rather an incident which the author of the poem knew independently of the story of the *Pèlerinage* and which he utilized (with superb effect) to motivate Charlemagne's journey". *Harvard Studies and Notes* VIII 213.

37. Excepting Prof. Kittredge, as noted above.

38. Child, *Ballads,* I 282, is following freely Paris (*Rom.* IX 8), who says: "Réduit a ses éléments les plus simples, il peut s'analyser ainsi: un roi, qui se croit le plus noble et le plus magnifique du monde, entend dire qu'un autre le surpasse; il se rend a sa cour pour s'en assurer, promettant, si ce n'est pas exact, de punir ceux qui se seront joués de lui; arrivé là, et bien que reelment ébloui par la magnificence dont il est témoin, il se livre à des vanteries imprudentes, dont son hôte exige l'exécution, et qu'il parvient, à la grande terreur de celui-ci, à executer grâce à la protection divine; il résulte d'ailleurs de la comparaison finale que le roi étranger ne l'emportait pas sur lui comme on l'avait prétendu".—The category of Paris is thus a little narrower than that of Prof. Child, and therefore suits worse the illustrations offered.

39. v. below.

40. *Ballads* I 283 and 11.

41. Cited by Paris, *Histoire Littéraire de la France,* XXX 110; synopsis do. 92.

42. In the ballad of *Young Waters* (Child II 343) we may possibly have a very late version of the reproving wife *motif,* where any improper relation between the queen and Young Waters—if it ever existed—has been lost sight of. Mr. W. W. Confort in a paper read at a meeting of the Modern Language Association of America in Providence, Dec. 1904, emphasized the similarity between the opening of *Young Waters* and that of *Arthur and Cornwall.* [The paper has in the meantime been printed in Mod. Lang. Notes 20, 115.]

43. Paris, *Histoire Poétique de Charlemagne,* p. 343 n., and Briggs, *Four. Germ. Phil.* III 351, cite historical illustrations to Hugo's ploughing; the former the

annual furrow of the Chinese emperor, the latter the field work of the first Ottoman emperor, Othman. But it is in mythology, rather, that we should seek an explanation. Cf. Rhys' *Arthurian Romance,* cap. II, where an interesting attempt is made to prove Airem and Arthur ploughers and culture gods.

44. Such figures often characterize fairy belongings, e. g., the magic tent that was an *irdisch paradîs* in the *Lanzelet,* 4735 f.; and the celebrated mantel in the same poem, 5812 f.

45. On revolving castles as a feature of the Celtic other world v. A. C. L. Brown's *Iwain,* pp. 76 and note, 79, 80 n., in *Harvard Studies and Notes in Philology and Literature* VIII.

46. Such storms may have formed, like revolving entrances, one of the barriers of the other world. Cf. *The Turk and Gawain* l. 69. Is this the meaning of the artificially raised storm in Chrétien's *Iwain,* l. 438 etc.? Dr. Brown in the articles already mentioned has shown sufficient reason for believing *Iwain* to be an other-world adventure. Cf. Miss Lucy Allen Paton's *Studies in the Fairy Mythology of Arthurian Romance* (Radcliffe College Monographs No. 13) p. 169.

47. Brown, *Iwain* 97; Kittredge, *Arthur and Gorlagon,* in the same volume of *Harvard Studies and Notes* (VIII), p. 176 n.

48. A reference for which I am indebted to Dr. Schofield.

49. v. Paris, *Rom.* IX, 26-28; Koschwitz' ed., note to ll. 100 and 260.

50. Morf (*Rom.* XIII 209) explains this thus: The French writer wished to represent Charles as the conqueror of Constantinople; but as he knew well enough that Constantinople never belonged to France, he made Charles decline to become its master. It should be noted, however, that an explanation different from both of these offered can be found in the pseudo-historical *Descriptio* etc., an eleventh century relation of how Charles sought precious relics at Constantinople for the church at Aix-la-Chapelle. The emperor there offered Charles great gifts, but he refused them and begged for a few relics only. Cf. Gautier, *Les Epopées Françaises* III 285 f.; Rauschen, *Die legende Karl's des grossen* pp. 97 f., 141 f., text p. 110 f.; Morf (as above) p. 231.

51. In Madden's *Syr Gawayne* p. 243, *Bishop Percy's Folio MS.* ed. Hales and Furnivall I 88. On the archaic nature of the central episode in *The Turk and Gawain* v. Kittredge, *Journal of American Folk Lore* XVIII, p. 1 f.

52. Perhaps we should suppose that Gawain, by the Turk's direction, laughed at the notion that such feats were difficult, and said "I don't care to waste my strength on trifles; my boy will do these small tricks". The situation in *King Estmere,* Child II 49,

is similar: King Estmere disguised as a harper, with his brother Adler Yonge as "boy soe faine of fighte" to help him, goes to win the daughter of King Adland. When he arrives at King Adland's court, he finds Bremor of Spain there on the same errand. After King Estmere has stabled his steed so audaciously at the hall-board, he speaks to the angry king of Spain:—

51   'My ladde he is so lither', he said,
      'He will do naught that's meete;
      And is there any man in this hall
      Were able him to beate?'
52   'Thou speakst proud words' says the King
of Spaine:
      'Thou harper, here to mee:
      There is a man within this halle,
      Will beate thy ladd and thee.'
53   'O let that man come downe', he said,
      A sight of him wold I see;
      And when he hath beaten well my ladd,
      Then he shall beate of mee.'

Compare especially this stanza 53, with lines 204 f. of *The Turk,* cf. below. *King Estmere* and the related *King Adler* (Hales and Furnivall II 296) may be other-world adventures; v. Kittredge, *Harvard Studies and Notes* VIII 194 n.

53. There appears to be mispunctuation at lines 204-205 of the Percy MS. as printed by Hales & Furnivall and by Madden. Instead of "A giant bad gawaine assay, and said, 'Gawain begin the play!'", we should read "A giant bad gawaine assay; and said Gawain, 'Begin the play!'"

54. "The turke was clad inuissible gay", MS. l. 232; "clad in invissible gray", Child amends. Probably the Turk puts on for the occasion a magic garment like Aimer's *tarnkappe* in the *Pilgrimage.*

55. Cf. the kemperye man of the heathen King of Spain in *King Estmere.* After looking King Estmere's "ladd" in the ear, this champion shrank back:

55   And howe now, Kempe, said the kyng of
Spaine,
      And how, what aileth thee?
      He Saies It is writt in his forhead,
      All and in gramarye,
      That for all the gold that is under heaven,
      I dare not neigh him nye.

In st. 41 it tells that what the two brothers have written in their foreheads is, "That we towe are the boldest men that are in Christentye".

56. In Ellis's account of *Sir Ferumbras* we hear how Duke Naymes, incensed because the Saracen Lukafere had burnt his beard at an odd game, beat out Lukafere's eyes with a brand, and throwing him into the fire held him there with the fire-fork till he was burned to death. *Specimens of Early English Metrical Romances* p. 395 (ed. Halliwell, London 1848).

57. Paris (*Rom.* IX 5) calls the ball stone; Prof. Child (*Ballads* I 277), metal. Metal better suits the

description "Entre or fin et argent guardez com bien i at!" (*Pilgrimage* 509). The ball is of iron in the Welsh version, of gold in the Norse (*Sechs Bearbeitungen etc.*, ed. Koschwitz, Heilbronn 1876, p. 30; *Karlamagnus Saga ok Kappa Hans*, Unger, Christiania 1860, p. 474). Hugo's *pelote,* the ball for the *jeu de paume,* is probably exactly the same as the King of Man's tennis ball.

58. *Der grosse Wolf-Dieterich,* ed. A. Holzmann, Heidelberg 1865. The episode is not notably different in the other versions of *Wolfdietrich* given in Amelung and Jänicke's *Ortnit und die Wolfdietriche,* Berlin 1871-73. Prof. Kittredge first called my attention to this valuable reference.

59. In the *Lanzelet,* l. 705 f., the hero and two companions arrive at the castle of the terrible Galagandreiz, who is reputed to slay his daughter's lovers. At night the fair daughter tries to become the bedfellow of first one and then the other of Lancelot's friends: but they are too much afraid of the father to have ado with her. The reckless, young Lancelot, however, welcomes her. The grim father comes in the morning and compels him to play the knife game, at which Lancelot kills him by running in and stabbing him.

60. Golden tree and birds in *Wolfdietrich* B, §§ 555-556.

61. This leaping is not in *Wolfdietrich* B.

62. There are no stools in the *Lanzelet:* the contestants stand against a wall:

63. *Lanzelet,* one knife.

64. The adventure of Belian's castle is clearly a rationalized fairy mistress or lustful demon story of the well known giant and daughter type.

65. Bertram will fly much further, and cry fearfully meanwhile. *Pilgrimage* 591 f. Cf. Koschwitz' note to l. 593.

66. *Pilgrimage* 602 f.

67. v. above.

68. As a mere exercise of fancy I will indicate what might conceivably have been the development of the story. The emperor's daughter, like Marpali, Galazandreiz' daughter and Carcasso's daughter, was originally the wooer, and a fée. Her lovers had to undergo hard tests. The successful hero probably slew Hugo, as the father is slain in the versions just mentioned, and as Arthur slew Cornwall. A certain refinement, with ignorance of the older story, caused the monarch to be spared, and the gab which meant his death to be directed against one of his followers. The action was limited to one night, not two. By the change of the feats or tests to gabs, and by the addition of the spy, the events were made to occupy two nights and the climax was thereby heightened.

69. The latter is the view of Paris, found in *Rom.* IX 10: "On pourrait croire retrouver là une forme plus

ancienne du conte des *gabs;* mais il est beaucoup plus probable que c'est simplement un arrangement rationaliste (et, pourvoir le *gab* d'Oliver, tout à fait édifiant) de notre conte; les Italiens l'ont connu par *Galien.*"

70. *Rom.* IX II. Stengel, *Litteraturblatt für germ. und rom. Philologie* 1881, p. 287, and Koschwitz p. XXVIII admit the possibility of "saga material" also.

71. Cf. Koschwitz l. 352 note.

72. "The bed of Conchobor was in the front of the house, with boards of silver, with pillars of bronze, with the glitter of gold on their headpieces and carbuncles in them, so that day and night were equally light in it, with its silver board above the king to the highest part of the royal house. Whenever Conchobor struck the board with a royal rod, all the men of Ulster were silent thereat. The twelve beds of the twelve chariot-chiefs were round about that bed." Translation of Kuno Meyer, *Archeological Review* I 69.

73. We saw this tree of automatic birds at Belian's castle in *Wolfdietrich*. Remarkable trees of singing birds are a prominent feature of the Celtic other-world landscape; v. Brown's *Iwain* p. 82 f.

74. *Ballads* I 282 n.

75. Beside the *liaison* of Cornwall and Guinevere, such are: making wealth rather than looks the subject of contention (but cf. Child I 282 n.), the fewer followers, the fine porter, the one night's stay, the exhibiting of treasures, the manner in which the feats are performed with Bredbeddle as helpful companion, and the killing of Cornwall.

76. "In part", because the two other-world visits may very well have been distinct types.

77. Cf. the incident in the *Libro del Danese* discussed above, p. 37.

78. *Rom.* IX 43, *La Littérature Française au Moyen Age,* pp. 43, 61.

79. One passage reminds us of the seven years Cornwall had spent with the queen, and the seven years Gasozein had missed her; namely where Hugo at line 310 tells Charles that he first heard of him seven years ago.

80. For Sebille (or Blanchefleur) v. Paris, *Histoire Poetique de Charlemagne,* p. 389 f.; Rajna, *Le Origine dell'Epopea Francese,* cap. VIII; Gautier, *Les Épopées Françaises,* cap. XXVII. It is tempting to speculate as to the manner in which Charles in lost romances may have got possession of Sebille.

81. *Keltoromanisches* (Halle), pp. 18-21, a welcome reference given me by my friend Dr. A. C. L. Brown after the practical completion of this paper.

82. The gab of Naimes in the Norse and Welsh versions includes even greater leaping. Berengier's gab, to

leap from a tower upon sword points, reminds one of the spear feat mentioned several times in the *Wooing of Emer,* which was twisting around the points of spears, and jumping and performing on their points.

F. L. Ganshof (essay date 1951)

SOURCE: "The Use of the Written Word in Charlemagne's Administration" in *The Carolingians and the Frankish Monarchy: Studies in Carolingian History,* translated by Janet Sondheimer, Cornell University Press, 1971, pp. 125-42.

[*In the following essay, first published in French in 1951, Ganshof describes some of the types of written documents that Charlemagne caused to be used—including agendas, minutes, instructions, authorizations, circulars, mobilization orders, reports, and descriptions—in order to foster clarity and efficiency in his realm.*]

It is known that the use of the written word for administrative purposes survived, in at least some parts of the territory ruled by the Frankish monarch, as a debased legacy from the Later Empire. In the formulary of Marculf, which was compiled in the Paris region during the first half of the seventh century, documents used in administrative practice are given some prominence.[1] If we turn to the *Lex Ribuaria,* we find that it contains provisions which mention a *cancellarius,* who seems to have been a scribe attached to the county court and qualified to draw up charters. Some of these provisions may belong to the oldest part of the text, in which case they date from the second quarter of the seventh century; they show traces of borrowings from the Burgundian law, and through this intermediary from Roman institutions.[2] It is by no means established, however, that the 'chancellor' of the *Lex Ribuaria* was called on to write documents which formed part of an administrative routine. After the middle of the seventh century there is nothing further, or at all events nothing of which we can be certain.[3] From that time onward, the only use for written records seems to have been to furnish proof of individual rights, or to assist in such proof.

So far as we can judge from the sources, the use of the written word for administrative purposes started to revive under Pippin III, though only to a very modest extent. His rare capitularies deal chiefly with church affairs, and administrative documents do not enter the picture. With one exception. In 768, when Pippin sent his commissioners into a subdued Aquitaine, he armed them with a memorandum of their basic instructions, as elaborated during an assembly; this was a summary of the measures they were expected to implement, some being of permanent application, others no doubt related to issues of current importance. In almost every case, the purpose of the measures was to make authoritative intervention in support

of religion, the royal power and the rights of communities and subjects.[4] A new form of administrative document had made its appearance, the document shortly to be known as a *capitulare missorum.*

When we come to the reign of Charlemagne we find a change in the situation. The number of sources to enlighten us about administrative records becomes more plentiful; and although more numerous for the period after the imperial coronation, they are spread over the entire reign. This abundance of documentation is novel and revealing.

Whatever the field, Charlemagne attached great importance to setting things down in writing. We find an increase in the documents designed to furnish or facilitate proof of individual rights. Existing legal provisions regarding both Church[5] and state were grouped together and published, and new ones promulgated; in the period immediately following the imperial coronation there was even an attempt, admittedly abortive, to commit to writing all the national laws currently in force within the realm and to make judges adhere to the written text of the laws.[6] In judicial matters we find an unmistakeable preference for written evidence.[7] The same preoccupation shows itself in procedure: a new rule, first laid down by a capitulary of 794 and repeated in several subsequent capitularies, prescribed that parties or witnesses directed by civil or ecclesiastical authorities to appear before the royal court at the Palace should go armed with a document prepared for the occasion.[8]

The foregoing facts have been mentioned as a necessary introduction to the business of this present article, which is to examine the use of the written word for administrative purposes. They are important as an aid to placing the measures taken by Charlemagne in this field within their general context.

We should start by examining the documents which originated in the Palace. They fall into several groups, the first consisting of documents drawn up for the use of the monarch. We know that two acts of great political importance were recorded in writing. One was Tassilo III's solemn and final renunciation of all his rights over Bavaria, made at Frankfurt in 794 and recorded in a document made in as many as three copies.[9] The other was Charlemagne's disposition of the succession, effected at Thionville in 806 and recorded in a solemn *instrumentum* drafted with particular care, a copy of which was even sent to Rome to receive the pope's subscription.[10] This *Divisio Regnorum* may have been the first Carolingian arrangement for the succession ever recorded in writing.

Another type of document prepared for the use of the monarch was the written agenda listing questions for deliberation with the lay and ecclesiastical magnates at the general assembly. Whether such documents were regularly produced is not known; the examples we have relate to the assemblies of 808 and 811.[11] There may have been occasions when one or two important people were given copies of the agenda in advance of the meeting.[12]

Sometimes the points discussed at the assembly and the decisions taken were recorded afterwards in a minute. A few such minutes have survived, all dating from the period after Charlemagne became emperor; they were apparently used as the basis for drafting instructions to *missi,* or for framing capitularies more general in scope.[13]

In a second group we can place documents sent out from the Palace, first and foremost those connected with the activities of the *missi dominici.* What these 'itinerant commissioners' frequently received was a *memorandum* containing instructions to themselves and a note of the communications they were to make to the agents of power and inhabitants in the localities, communications concerned in some cases with permanent orders of general application and in others with matters of immediate interest; action on the orders they brought with them was usually left to the *missi* to initiate.[14] We have here the development of a document first met with under Pippin III, the *capitulare missorum.* Three such survive from the period before the imperial coronation, and perhaps seventeen from the period after it.[15] Some of these *capitularia missorum* were drawn up for the use of *missi ad hoc,* for example the *missi* sent on a special mission to Aquitaine in 789 and the *missi* made responsible in 807 and 808 for mobilising the army in a particular region;[16] others were prepared for *missi* on regular tours of inspection, who when appropriate received a copy which included articles relating specifically to a particular group of counties they were visiting.[17] With the exception of the great *capitulare missorum* of 802, which embodies a religious and political programme promulgated after Charlemagne had assumed the imperial title,[18] these texts show a great economy in drafting, some of the articles even taking the form of headings or allusions.[19]

Another administrative document carried by *missi* was the *tractoria,* an authorisation to requisition transport, lodgings and provisions.[20]

Along with the *capitularia missorum* we should notice the analogous document sometimes issued to bishops, abbots and counts—by no means all of whom acted as *missi dominici*—on their departure for home at the conclusion of a general assembly: it listed the measures, chiefly administrative, to be notified to local populations and implemented. This written memorandum was clearly a reinforcement to instructions given orally. We have the text of one of these documents, dating probably from 808.[21]

Written instructions might also be issued to ambassadors sent on embassies abroad. Two sets have survived, both relating to missions to the pope; one of them specifies the exact words the ambassadors were to use, the other takes the form of a letter addressed to the ambassador, who was a very distinguished person, namely Angilbert.[22]

We have been concerned so far with administrative documents issued by the Palace and handed directly to agents of the royal authority. But there were also those the Palace despatched to various parts of the country, some of which were what we would describe as circulars. The earliest surviving circular, sent out between 779 and 781, was addressed to the secular agents of royal authority in Italy, to remind them of certain general principles of government and to order the enforcement in Italy of regulations laid down in the capitulary of Herstal.[23] Another circular, issued between 25 December 792 and 7 April 793 and sent probably to all bishops, abbots and counts, instructs the clergy, counts, and royal vassals in the pious exercises and almsgiving appropriate to times of famine or political crisis. Circulars with a similar theme were also sent out in 807—we have the copy addressed to bishop Gerbald of Liège—and perhaps again in 810.[24] Also to be classed as circulars are the celebrated *Epistola de litteris colendis,* issued between 789 and 800 to bishops and abbots enlisting them in a campaign for education—we have the copy addressed to Abbot Baugulf of Fulda—and the *Epistola generalis* of 786-801, ordering the clergy to use the homiliary composed by Paul the Deacon.[25] Finally, there is the *Capitulare de villis,* issued between 770 and 800 to administrators of *fisci,* in an attempt to 'bring a modicum of order into the by now defective management' of the royal domains.[26]

Another type of document sent out directly from the Palace was the written mobilisation order, when it was not transmitted through the intermediary of a *missus.*[27] This order, addressed in any case to counts and to bishops and abbots whose churches enjoyed immunity, would specify the place and time for the army to assemble and might also include details about the type of fighting men, equipment and war material required. We know of one such mobilisation order, dated 806 and addressed to Abbot Fulrad of St Quentin.[28]

The Palace also despatched administrative documents direct to individuals. Comparable with our modern despatches, they dealt with some particular affair or class of affairs,[29] usually issuing some directive; they are often called by the traditional name, *indiculum.*

We hear of two further types of administrative document sent directly from the Palace. There is the type which can broadly be described as written directives issued by Charlemagne to his sons who ruled autonomous kingdoms. Instructions of this kind must have been drawn up for Louis when he was king of Aquitaine, though no trace of them has survived. But we have a capitulary promulgated by Pippin as king of Italy which was based on written instructions (*sceda*) from his father, and also a letter from Charlemagne to his son in which he refers, *inter alia,* to the fact that the capitulary of 803 is an obligatory addition to all the national laws.[30] The other type is exemplified by the set of instructions (*ammonitio*) handed down by the emperor to the Fathers of the five reforming councils which met in 813, listing the chief matters requiring discussion.[31]

The various administrative documents so far discussed have one thing in common: they all issued from the Palace. The documents we now turn to were issued either by the 'itinerant commissioners' sent out by the king (or emperor), or by agents of royal (or imperial) authority in the localities.

On occasion the *missi* seem to have used the written word in their dealings with the inhabitants of their *missaticum,* or with the royal agents it was their duty to inspect. The documents of this nature which have survived all date from the imperial period. One of them, comprising thirteen articles, contains directives which the emperor ordered the *missi* sent out in the spring of 802 to communicate to the people; it may well be that this is the Latin summary form of their *adnuntiatio,* the announcement the *missi* were required to make to the free men attending their *placitum.*[32] We also have examples of written instructions sent or handed to counts by *missi*—all well-known personages—on ordinary tours of inspection, as a guide to the performance of their duties. In one of them it is stressed that the written directive is merely a summary, complementing their oral instructions; counts in doubt over its meaning should seek enlightenment from the *missi* by sending them a deputy capable of understanding their explanation.[33] We also have the text of a speech in the exhortatory vein composed by a *missus,* doubtless an ecclesiastic and probably an Italian, for the edification of the clergy, royal agents and inhabitants of his *missaticum.*[34]

It could happen that *missi* were doubtful over the meaning of instructions they had received from the Palace, or about the measures they should take, and we know that some sought to resolve their difficulty by writing to the Palace for further instructions. To one such request a *missus* received a somewhat impatient response (still extant), displaying a very clear disposition to leave him to shoulder his own responsibilities.[35]

We are much less well informed about the use made by counts of the written word in the administration of their counties; it can only have been on a very restricted scale. We have a formula for an *indiculum de comite ad vicarium,*[36] but it is hard to believe counts often made use of it to remind subordinates of basic rules for the exercise of their office. We know that during the imperial period a count might be called on to supply a written report to the *missi* on some specific matter, for example acts of rebellion.[37] And that is all. Certain texts suggest, however, that in Italy the counts made a more extensive and systematic use of written documents,[38] which should not surprise us.

A group of administrative documents comprising reports and returns addressed to the king or emperor merits particular attention. The work of compiling them often fell to the *missi,* and we hear of them performing this task from quite early in the reign. One such report still extant was drawn up in 780 by Vernarius, one of the *missi* appointed *ad hoc* to investigate alleged encroachments on properties belonging to the church of Marseilles: it is a lengthy and muddled document, showing no sign that it was compiled to any standard pattern.[39]

Particularly important are the reports the king commanded from every part of the Frankish and Lombard kingdoms on the administration of the oath of fidelity he imposed on all his subjects in 793. The basic document, as we learn from the capitulary promulgated on the occasion, was a list drawn up by the count, *centena* by *centena,* giving the names of all who had taken the oath and distinguishing natives of the *pagus* from those who had come as vassals from elsewhere; defaulters had to be listed under a separate heading. Having compiled their list, the counts were to hand it over to the *missi* who would deliver it to the Palace, but not before they had added their own return, giving the names of all persons from whom they themselves had taken the oath, hands between hands, and a numerical statement, based on the count's lists, of the total number of oath-takers in their *missaticum.*[40] It will be appreciated that the actual execution of such an order may well have fallen far short of what was intended.

After Charlemagne's accession to the empire we hear of more and more details to be reported by *missi* at the end of their tours, although we cannot always be sure whether the headings are for a general report[41] or for one of more limited scope. In any case, the *missi* were required to report in writing to the emperor all public pronouncements they made in the course of their tours (*breves de adnuntiatione*), and they were reminded of their duty to inform him of their interventions and decisions (*de opere*).[42] They had to report serious professional misdemeanours by counts,[43] they had to submit lists of important personages, lay or clerical, who absented themselves from the *placita missorum,*[44] they had to send in the names of any *scabini, advocati* or 'notaries' they themselves had appointed.[45] They are told to report, county by county, on the upkeep of benefices held from the king or from other lords within their *missaticum,* and at a later date to submit a full list of all such benefices with a *descriptio* of each, detailing the state of upkeep, encroachments on the king's rights, and the numbers of vassals living *casati* on lands which formed part of the benefice.[46] On yet another occasion they are asked for a full list of nonautochthonous elements in the population.[47] Lastly, when a capitulary was promulgated as an addition to one or all the national laws, the *missi* had to supervise the subscription of a copy by the counts, subordinate officials and *scabini,* and presumably convey the copy back to the Palace.[48]

The Palace also received reports and returns relating to the administration of the royal domains. In 787 we find Charlemagne demanding descriptions—we can, I think, call them polyptychs—of all the Italian domains he had assigned to Hildegarde, his deceased queen. This is a text which applies to lands in the Italian peninsula, but there is nothing specifically Italian in the preoccupation which inspired it.[49] In any case, we also have the *Capitulare de villis,* which is quite general in its application[50] and demands from the *iudices,* or chief administrators of the *fisci,* a multiplicity of reports and returns. The annual returns to be compiled and sent to the Palace were as follows: a statement of the product derived from cultivation (*laboratio*), submitted before the money raised from it (*argentum de nostro laboratu*) was paid in on the day appointed, which was Palm Sunday; a statement of the commodities available for consumption during Lent, after the court's allocation had been subtracted; three separate returns of the total production of the *fiscus,* the first showing everything allocated to the king's service or the army, or still in hand for some special purpose, the second showing what had been distributed to *prebendarii,* set aside for sowing and so forth, the third accounting for all the rest, for example everything sold; and a general survey, to be submitted each Christmas, showing production, revenues of various kinds, and the resources of the *fiscus* in human and material equipment and reserves, all set out under the appropriate headings.[51] It is well to bear in mind that we are dealing here with instructions; how far they were carried out may have been another matter.

Further orders on estate management were issued after Charlemagne's accession to the empire. Between 802 and 813 he demanded returns, to be sent to the Palace, of the wool and flax issued to women who worked in the *gynaecaea* on the royal domains, and a statement of the number of garments woven.[52] In 811 he wanted *descriptiones* not only of benefices held from the Crown but also of all royal domains not granted out in benefice: and to give him a clearer picture of the imperial properties, the descriptions had to be made by *missatica.*[53] The descriptions of the fiscs of Annappes, Cysoing, Somain (France, Nord), Vitry (Pas-de-Calais) and Triel (Seine-et-Oise), known to us from the *Brevium exempla,* were possibly made in response to this command.[54]

To the reports and returns dealing with the administration of the royal domains we must add those demanded in respect of the landed properties of great ecclesiastical establishments. We know that in 787 Charlemagne ordered two *missi*—Abbot Landri of Jumièges and count Richard—to compile an inventory of the possessions of St Wandrille. This is unlikely to have been an isolated case. Furthermore, the *Brevium exempla,* which were intended as models for *descriptiones* of domains, contain not only *brevia* for *fisci* but also some fragmentary descriptions—of a different type—of church properties (belonging to the bishopric of Augsburg and the abbey of Weissenburg); these descriptions obviously owed their existence to the intervention of *missi.* When we think of the use the Carolingians made of church property, the interest of such documentation becomes apparent.[55]

All the administrative documents so far discussed can be attributed to the activity of the Palace, *missi,* local officials, or administrators of domains. But we also hear of written records we are unable to connect with the activity of any known institution or agent. Who, for example, drew up the list of Saxon hostages and their custodians, the gist of which has come down to us? Was it compiled in the Palace, or by some commander in the field? We do not know. What we do know is that the *commendaticiae,* the letters of recommendation which a priest who had served one *Eigenkirche* had to present to his new master before being accepted to serve another, were issued not by a

representative of public authority but by the lord of the *Eigenkirche* the priest was leaving: even so, we are still dealing with a document which Charlemagne's legislation made obligatory.[56]

Just how administrative documents were produced is difficult to establish. As regards the documents which issued from the Palace (*capitularia missorum,* circulars, despatches, instructions of various kinds), we are completely in the dark: there is nothing to indicate whether or not they were produced by what is conventionally known as the chancery.[57] In all probability they were written, on orders from the monarch or one of his advisers, either by a cleric serving in the Palace or by some young man preparing himself for public or ecclesiastical office, one of the *pueri palatini.*[58] There seems to have been no regular writing office with the capacity to produce copies of the same document in reasonable quantity. In 808, when Charlemagne issued a capitulary concerning mobilisation in a particular region, he ordered it to be made in four copies: one for the *missi* conveying the capitulary, one for the count involved, one for the *missi* who would command the army once it had mobilised, and one for the chancellor. Since the capitulary must have affected several counts, we can only suppose that each was expected to take note of its contents, if necessary making a copy, before passing it on; providing a copy for all the counts affected was apparently beyond the resources of the Palace. Still in the later part of the reign, we hear that a document whose content was to be notified to local officials and populations through the *missi* could not be supplied to each group of commissioners: those who had a copy were expected to pass the information on to the rest.[59] With such methods of transmission there was obviously plenty of scope for error. Presumably, the 'notary' who in all probability accompanied the *missi* to attend to their written business in many cases made copies or notes of documents for them, which could partly account for the great divergencies in the manuscript tradition of certain capitularies.

Documents purporting to be written by *missi* or counts must in practice have been the work of a notary when they had one, or of some cleric pressed into service for the occasion. Some places had a *cancellarius* or *notarius* appointed for the county and charged with the drawing up of deeds: where this was so, we can assume he would normally have attended to the count's written business.[60] In the period after his accession to the empire, Charlemagne gave orders that bishops and abbots, as well as counts, should each have a notary;[61] if a count had failed to appoint one, the *missi* had the emperor's instructions to appoint one themselves.[62] It is questionable whether this order was everywhere obeyed.[63]

The use of the written word for administrative purposes supposes the existence of archives, since without them records cannot play their proper role. That archives of a kind existed at the Palace is not in doubt. We know that two copies of Tassilo's solemn renunciation of 794 were destined for preservation at the Palace. The same is true of one of the copies of the mobilisation capitulary of 808, and of one text of the canons issued by each of the five reforming councils of 813.[64] It was presumably in the Palace archives that Einhard, private secretary to Louis the Pious,[65] found the letters Charlemagne received from the king of Galicia and Asturias, and from the Irish kings.[66] This was the *archivum palatii;*[67] it seems to have been placed under the authority of the chancellor, though whether the deposit was a dependency of the 'chapel' is impossible to say.[68] We know nothing of the way it was organised, nor even whether the Dogvulfus *scriniarius,* to whom Alcuin addressed a letter, was attached to the deposit.[69] It is known that along with documents received the archive also housed drafts of documents sent out, as was certainly the case with some of the capitularies.[70] But we cannot tell if this was a general rule, and if so, how far it was observed.

Documents concerning the royal domains and their administration, when they were kept, may have formed a separate deposit. A reference in a capitulary from the imperial period suggests that they went to the *camera* or chamberlain's office;[71] when a general superintendent of the domains was appointed, he may perhaps have taken charge of them.[72]

As for the counts, we know that in the imperial period, at least, they were requested to make a collection of the capitularies and other instructions addressed or communicated to them, which according to exhortations they received from their *missi* they were to read and re-read.[73] It is doubtful whether the counts' collections can ever have been very complete.

We must now consider what conclusions are to be drawn from the foregoing exposition.

The fuller use of the written word to administer the Frankish realm under Charlemagne stands in contrast with the modest role it played under Pippin III and its insignificance in the preceding reigns. Unmistakeable signs of this fuller use appear as early as the 780s and 790s: it reflects aspirations towards a clearer view of things and a concern for order, stability and system in state and society, goals characteristic of Charlemagne, which the written word could help to promote. In the years following the imperial coronation we find still greater emphasis on written records, as is consistent with what we know of the emperor's efforts, admittedly somewhat fruitless, to make his government more efficient, and thus better equipped to combat a growing number of abuses. These developments in the use of written records during the latter part of the reign are no doubt also partly accounted for by the emperor's decreasing mobility. However that may be, there seems to me no doubt that the use of the written word for administrative purposes was an act of policy.[74]

It was a policy which continued to be applied, and with greater emphasis, under Louis the Pious; in *Francia Occidentalis* it even continued under Charles the Bald. But

thereafter, from the end of the ninth and in the succeeding centuries, the use of the written word to administer the states produced by the dissolution of the Carolingian empire progressively diminished, until it almost reached vanishing point. This is a fact so well known that it hardly needs to be recalled.

It must also be said that even under Charlemagne the written word was not fully exploited. It is highly characteristic, for example, that no trace has survived of any diploma of appointment to important offices, for example that of count,[75] although we know that such a diploma existed in the sixth and early seventh centuries. Furthermore, it seems certain that many of the records ordered to be made were never in fact compiled, or if they were, only in unsatisfactory fashion. One reason, of course, was the deficiency of personnel, both in quality and quantity. This can be illustrated by considering two particular cases. I have already described the returns demanded in connection with the oath-taking of 793: would every county have had a scribe capable of compiling them, by *centena* or *vicaria,* with the necessary clarity and precision? That *some* returns were compiled is not in doubt; we can be equally certain that others were never produced, or if produced, that they left something to be desired.[76] Again, what of the many returns demanded from the *iudices* who managed the *fisci?*[77] To compile them, these officials would have needed assistance not only from scribes but also from expert accountants. Where were such men to be found? As in the first instance, we need not doubt that *some* returns were made; but few can have met the requirements laid down, and many probably never saw the light of day.

When these documents—reports, lists, returns and so on—arrived at the Palace, were they all used, or indeed useable? The answer is undoubtedly that they were not. We find no trace at the Palace of the departments needed to sort, study and classify documents of this kind. *Some* of them were used, just a few were referred to more than once—very important texts preserved with especial care, or others whose survival was due to chance—but the bulk must have piled up in a confused heap, or vanished completely. We have to set this mass of documents arriving at the Palace beside the mass of business which had to be transacted there, but could not be dealt with, or was handled inefficiently.[78] Admittedly, these remarks apply only to the Frankish or imperial *Palatium;* in the departments and archives of the *Palatium* of Italy better order may well have prevailed.

Effective use of written documents demands a minimum of intellectual training. At the period under discussion this was a very weak point, particularly among the laity. We have only to look at the questions counts asked of the Palace, and the replies which came back, to realise that the mental capacity of both sides was strictly limited. When a *missus* invited a count to send a subordinate to receive instructions, he had to stress it should be someone capable of understanding them.[79] Even the scribes—and they were clerics—were not clear in their work. The report submitted by the *missus* Vernarius in 780 would be incomprehensible if we did not also have the report of a *placitum* to enlighten us.[80] We have only to look at a few capitularies—*capitularia missorum* in particular—to realise just how faulty and obscure they are in composition, even at the end of the reign. Documents of this kind must have produced some dire confusions.

But when all is said, the fuller use made by Charlemagne—and Louis the Pious—of the written word in the administration of their realm is a fact of great historical importance. For despite all the imperfections and failings, it gave a powerful stimulus to the formation and development of social and political cadres which have left a profound and distinctive mark on countries once part of the Carolingian empire.[81]

Notes

1. MGH *Formulae, Form. Marculfi,* i, nos 5, 6, 8, 11, 19, 23, 26-9, 37; on the date and origins of the formulary I share the views of L. Levillain, 'Le formulaire de Marculf et la critique moderne', *Bibliothèque de l'Ecole des Chartes* (1923). See also F. Lot, *L'impôt foncier et la capitation personnelle sous le Bas-Empire et à l'époque franque* (Paris, 1928), 83 ff.

2. *Lex Ribuaria,* lix and lxxxviii, ed. R. Sohm, MGH *Leges,* v, pp. 247-50, 267. As regards this text, I accept the views of F. Beyerle, 'Volksrechtliche Studien. I. *Die Lex Ribuaria.* III. Das Gesetzbuch Ribuariens', *Zeitschrift der Savigny-Stiftung für Rechtsgeschichte. Germanistische Abteilung* (1928 and 1935).

3. Formula no. 6 (which is a charter from the king designating someone bishop of a *civitas*) of the *suppl. Marculfi*—a collection dating apparently from the mid-eighth century—is still thoroughly Merovingian (MGH *Formulae,* p. 109); formula no. 33 (ibid., p. 155: royal command to a count to take action against a *pagensis* who has failed to appear before the king's court) of the Tours collection—generally considered to date from about the middle of the eighth century—is largely a reproduction of Marculf i, 37, but has been given an *intitulatio* which conforms to that of Pippin III: it would be rash to assert that this formula reproduces a document which actually existed.

4. MGH *Cap.,* I, no. 18: the only articles dealing with judicial activities are c. ix and x.

5. For a typical passage see the introductory section to the *Admonitio generalis* of 789 (MGH *Cap.,* I, no. 22): in order to make whatever reforms are necessary in the life and organisation of the Church, Charlemagne is sending *missi* on a visitation of bishoprics and abbeys; furthermore, *sed et aliqua capitula ex canonicis institutionibus, quae magis nobis necessaria videbantur subiunximus.*

6. I have in mind manifestations of law-making such as the publication and revision of the national laws, the promulgation of general regulations, intended to be permanent, in capitularies of various types, and the promulgation, starting in 803, of *capitularia legibus addenda.* On attempts to commit law (with revisions) to writing see *Annales Laureshamenses,* 802 (MGH *SS,* I); Einhard, *VK,* xxix. For the judges' obligation to observe the written law, see *Ann. Lauresh.,* loc. cit., and *Capitulare missorum generale,* 802, xxvi (MGH *Cap.,* I, no. 33). In Italy, not surprisingly, the superiority of written over customary law is asserted as early as 787 (MGH *Cap.,* I, no. 95, x); for the date see C. de Clercq, *La législation religieuse ·franque de Clovis à Charlemagne,* (Louvain, 1936), 165-7.

7. See for example the *Capitulare legibus additum* (803), c. vii (MGH *Cap.,* I, no. 39) and the reply to questions put by a *missus,* (802-14), ibid., no. 58, c. vii. On the implications of the attempt to institute a 'chancellor' or 'notary' for each county, which at latest dates from 803, see A. de Boüard, *Manuel de diplomatique française et pontificale,* II. *L'acte privé* (Paris, 1948), 129-30.

8. Synod of Frankfurt, 794, c. vi (MGH *Cap.,* I, no. 28): if, in a dispute lying within his competence, a bishop is unable to secure the appearance or submission of the defendant either before himself or before the metropolitan, *tunc tandem veniant accusatores cum accusatu cum litteris metropolitano, ut sciamus veritatem rei. Capitulare missorum generale* issued at Thionville, 805, c. viii (ibid., no. 44): if one of the parties to a suit is unwilling either to acquiesce in the judgment or to make a charge of false judgment and wants to apply to the Palace, then that party must produce the request and . . . *cum custodia et cum ipsis litteris . . . ad palatium nostrum remittantur.* Capitulary issued at Aachen, 809, c. xiv (ibid., no. 61): oath-helpers are ordered . . . *cum indiculo aut sigillo ad palatium venire.* Bavarian synod held in 799 or 800 at Freising and presided over by Arn, archbishop of Salzburg, c. xxvi (ibid., no. 24): same rule as in the Frankfurt capitulary, . . . *cum litteris commendatitiis dirigere eum studeat ad regem.* A capitulary issued by Pippin III (751-55) provides for similar cases (MGH *Cap.,* I, no. 13, c. vii: on the date see De Clercq, op. cit., pp. 131-2), but makes no mention of written documents.

9. Synod of Frankfurt, c. iii (MGH *Cap.,* I, no. 28). See below, n. 64.

10. *ARF,* 806: *De hac partitione et testamentum factum et iureiurando ab optimatibus Francorum confirmatum et constitutiones pacis conservandae causa factae, atque haec omnia litteris mandata sunt et Leoni papae ut his sua manu subscriberet per Einhardum missa.* The text is printed MGH *Cap.,* 1, no. 45.

11. 808, MGH *Cap.,* 1, no. 51: *In anno octavo. Capitula cum primis conferendis.* Thirteen articles follow, in

the form of short headings (1, *De latronibus et furibus*. 2. *De falsis testibus* etc.). 811, ibid., 1, nos 71, 72, 73: in two manuscripts no. 71 is headed *De interrogatione domni imperatoris de anno undecimo* and c. i runs as follows: *In primis separate volumus episcopos, abbates et comites nostros et singulariter illos alloqui.* The three capitularies are of the same character; the first is mixed, the second ecclesiastical and the third secular. On the whole topic see De Clercq, op. cit., 210-11, 213-15.

12. MGH *Cap.*, 1, no. 71, xiii: *Ista conservetis sicut vobis decet; et in vobis confido, piissimi pontifices, et in quantum investigare possum vobis mittere seu scribere non dubito.*

13. G. Seeliger is probably right when he says (*Die Kapitularien der Karolinger,* Munich, 1893, 71) that MGH *Cap.*, 1, no. 63 minutes decisions taken during an assembly held at Aachen in 809; no. 61 could be a *capitulare per se scribendum* promulgated at the conclusion of that assembly, and no. 62 a memorandum for the *missi* who were charged, amongst other things, to see that the measures decided on were executed. For the assembly of 810, no. 65 would play the same role as no. 63 for that of 809 and no. 64 the same role as no. 62. Seeliger (op. cit., 82) thinks we should regard both nos. 65 and 64 as minutes of the assembly's decisions, but his view is difficult to reconcile with c. ii, viii and xii of no. 64, which certainly look like instructions to *missi.*

14. Articles which make this last duty plain are to be found in a number of capitularies: the *capitulare missorum* of 803 (MGH *Cap.*, no. 40), c. iii, v, xvii, xix; the *capitulare missorum generale* issued at Thionville, 805 (ibid., no. 44), xiii, xix; the *memoratorium de exercitu preparando* of 807 (ibid., no. 48), c. iii; the *capitula a missis cognita facienda* of 803-813 (ibid., no. 67), c. iv; the Bavarian *capitulare missorum* of 802-813 (ibid., no. 69; cf. De Clercq, op. cit., 221). Seeliger argues (op. cit., 69-71) that several of these texts should not be classed as *capitularia missorum,* but the passages just cited are already enough to weaken his case.

15. The documents I accept as *capitularia missorum* are as follows, all printed MGH *Cap.*, 1: nos 23, 24, 25; 33, 34, 40, 43, 44, 46, 48, 49 (in part), 50, 53, 60, 62, 64, 66, 67, 69, 83.

16. ibid., nos 24, 48, 50.

17. The list of instructions issued to the *missi* who were despatched throughout the empire in the spring of 802 has survived in copies made for the *missatica* of Paris, Le Mans, and Orleans (MGH *Cap.*, 1, no. 34). Certain articles (xiiia, xiiib, xviiia), notably those which apply to coastal regions, figure only in the copies intended for the Paris and Le Mans *missatica.*

18. MGH *Cap.*, 1, no. 33. cf. F. L. Ganshof, 'La fin du règne de Charlemagne. Une décomposition',

Zeitschrift für Schweizerische Geschichte, XXVIII (1948), 440-2, translated below, Ch. XII.

19. For example: *cap. miss.,* 802 (see above n. 17), c. vii. *De periuria.* c. viii. *De homicidia.* c. x. *De illis hominibus qui nostra beneficia habent distructa et alodes eorum restauratas. Similiter et de rebus ecclesiarum.*

20. Known to us from *Formulae Imperiales* no. 7 (MGH *Formulae,* p. 292); this collection dates from the reign of Louis the Pious, in whose chancery it was compiled. Despite this late date, the formula agrees so well with information to be gleaned from some of Charlemagne's capitularies (no. 32, xxvii; no. 40, v and xvii and no. 57 ii), that I feel justified in using it here. cf. F. L. Ganshof, 'La Tractoria', *Revue d'histoire du droit,* VIII (1927), 88-90. The *intitulatio* of *Formulae Marculfinae aevi carolini* no. 20 (MGH *Formulae,* pp. 121-2) has a Carolingian look to it, but for our present purpose is of no interest, since it is an almost word for word copy of *Form. Marculfi,* 1, xi.

21. MGH *Cap.*, 1, no. 54: *Capitula quae volumus ut episcopi, abbates et comites qui modo ad casam redeunt per singula loca eorum nota faciant et observare studeant, tam infra eorum parochias et missaticos seu ministeria eorum convicinantium qui in exercitu simul cum equivoco nostro perrexerunt.* There follow six articles dealing with aid to the needy, mobilisation, brigandage and the monastic life.

22. MGH *Cap.*, I, no. III (ambassadors sent with gifts for Pope Hadrian I, presumably 785); MGH *Epist.*, IV, pp. 135-6 (mission to Pope Leo III, 796).

23. MGH *Cap.*, I, no. 97; on the date see De Clercq, op. cit., 161-2.

24. MGH *Cap.*, I, no. 21; on the date see F. L. Ganshof, "Note sur deux capitulaires non datés de Charlemagne", *Miscellanea L. van der Essen,* I (Brussels), 123-8; Merkel's formula no. 63 (MGH *Formulae,* p. 262) presumably represents written instructions given by a *missus* to a bishop. MGH *Cap.*, I, no. 124 and note the allusion in no. 127.

25. MGH *Cap.*, I, no. 29, later in date than *Admonitio generalis* lxxii (789: ibid., no. 22), but prior to Charlemagne's assumption of the imperial title, ibid., I, no. 30; on the date see F. L. Ganshof, 'La révision de la Bible par Alcuin', *Bibliothèque d'Humanisme et Renaissance,* IX (1947), 12. (p. 31 above).

26. MGH *Cap.*, I, no. 32; on the date see M. Bloch, 'L'origine et la date du *Capitulare de Villis'*, *Revue Historique,* CXLIII (1923), from which the passage in inverted commas is taken, and F. L. Ganshof, 'Observations sur la localisation du *Capitulare de Villis'*, *Le Moyen Age* (1949), 203-4.

27. MGH *Cap.*, I, no. 54 (805-8), iii, instructions in case of mobilisation: *Ut omnes praeparati sint ad*

Dei servitium et ad nostram utilitatem, quandoquidem missus aut epistola nostra venerit, ut statim nobiscum venire faciatis.

28. MGH *Cap.*, I, no. 75, which Boretius dates 804-811; my reasons for assigning it a more precise date will be justified elsewhere.

29. MGH *Cap.*, I, no. 122 (to Bishop Gerbald of Liège; De Clercq, rightly in my opinion, dates it 801-810, op. cit., 222-3). *Cartae Senonicae* no. 26 and *Formulae Marculfinae aevi carolini* no. 18 (MGH *Formulae*, pp. 196, 121) are also relevant even though they may be adaptations of earlier texts (i.e. *Form. Marculfi* i nos. 37 and 29, ibid., pp. 67, 60-1). *Cartae Senonicae* no. 18 (ibid., p. 193) is definitely not taken from a document issued by the palace.

30. MGH *Cap.*, I, no. 94 (Pavia, 787-8; De Clercq, op. cit., 165-7): *Incipit capitula de diversas iustitias secundum sceda domni Caroli, genitoris nostri*, ibid. no. 103 (806-810; the capitulary to which he alludes is that of 803, ibid., no. 39).

31. Council of Mainz, c. iv and vi, MGH *Concilia* II, no. 36; Council of Tours, c. li, ibid., no. 38.

32. MGH *Cap.*, I, no. 59; two articles (ii and xi) are still in the second person.

33. MGH *Cap.*, I, no. 85 (802-813; cf. De Clercq, op. cit., 226), c. iv: *. . . si aliquid de omni illo mandato . . . quod vobis domni nostri aut scribendo aut dicendo commendatum est, dubitetis ut celeriter missum vestrum bene intelligentem ad nostra mittatis, qualiter omnia et bene intelligatis et adiuvante Domino bene perficiatis.*

34. MGH *Cap.*, I, no. 121 (800-813).

35. ibid., I, no. 58 (802-813; cf. De Clercq, op. cit., 222).

36. *Formulae Salicae Merkelianae*, no. 51 (MGH *Formulae*, p. 259; its date must be 790-800).

37. MGH *Cap.*, I, no. 85, iii: *Deinde ut quicumque vobis rebelles aut inobedientes fuerint . . . inbreviate illos quanticumque fuerint et aut antea, si necesse fuerit, remandate aut nobis ipsis cum insimul fuerimus dicite. . . .*

38. See, for example, Pippin of Italy's capitulary of 782-7 (MGH *Cap.*, I, no. 91) c. vi, and another promulgated by the same ruler at an assembly held in Mantua between 802 and 810 (ibid., no. 80; on the date see De Clercq, op. cit., 218-19), c. ii and iii.

39. J. H. Albanès and U. Chevalier, *Gallia Christiana Novissima* II (Marseilles-Valence, 1899), no. 41. On this text see F. L. Ganshof, 'Les avatars d'un domaine de l'église de Marseille à la fin du VIIe et au VIIIe siècle', *Studi in onore di Gino Luzatto*, I (Milan, 1950), 55-6.

40. MGH *Cap.*, I, no. 25, i, ii, iii, iv (25 Dec. 792-7 Apr. 793): on the date see Ganshof, 'Note sur deux capitularies', 128-32.

41. That the *missi* of spring 802 submitted a general written report seems certain: MGH *Cap.*, I, no. 33, xl.

42. MGH *Cap.*, I, no. 40 (803), xxv.

43. MGH *Cap.*, I, no. 85 (802-813), vi: *sciatis certissime quod grandem exinde contra vos rationem habebimus* (the *missi*, addressing themselves to the counts of their area).

44. MGH *Cap.*, I, no. 58 (imperial period), c. v: *et qui tunc venire contempserint, eorum nomina annotata ad placitum nostrum generale nobis repraesentes* (the emperor addressing the *missi*).

45. MGH *Cap.*, I, no. 40 (803), iii: *et eorum nomina, quando reversi fuerint, secum scripta deferant.*

46. MGH *Cap.*, I, no. 49, iv (which in my view has no connection with the preceding articles; it must in any case be later than the great *capitulare missorum* of spring 802, ibid., no. 33). The article sets out the various headings which should figure in the report. Ibid., I, no. 80, (811), c. v: *ut missi nostri diligenter inquirant et describere faciant unusquisque in suo missatico, quid unusquisque de beneficio habeat vel quot homines casatos in ipso beneficio.* c. vi: *Quomodo eadem beneficia condricta sunt, aut quis de beneficio suo alodem comparavit vel struxit.* These two articles form a group with the succeeding article, c. vii, which applies *expressis verbis* only to benefices held of the king (see below, n. 53).

47. MGH *Cap.*, I, no. 67 (803-813), iv: *De adventiciis ut, cum missi nostri ad placitum nostrum venerint, habeant descriptum quanti adventicii sunt in eorum missatico et de quo pago sunt eorum seniores.*

48. MGH *Cap.*, I, no. 40 (803), xix (orders) and the note preserved in Paris, lat. 4995, f° 19 v° (their execution), documents connected with the *capitulare legibus additum* of 803 (MGH *Cap.*, I, no. 39).

49. MGH *Cap.*, I, no. 95 (787: cf. De Clercq, op. cit., 165), c. xiv: *De rebus quae Hildegardae reginae traditae fuerunt, volumus ut fiant descriptae per breves et ipsae breves ad nos fiant adductae.*

50. MGH *Cap.*, I, no. 32: cf. the articles by M. Bloch and F. L. Ganshof cited n. 26, above.

51. c. xxviii. c. xliv: *et quod reliquum fuerit nobis per brevem . . . innotescant.* c. lv: *Volumus ut quicquid ad nostrum opus iudices dederint vel servierint aut sequestraverint, in uno breve conscribi faciant, et quicquid dispensaverint, in alio; et quod reliquum fuerit, nobis per brevem innotescant.* c. lxii: *. . . omnia seposita, distincta et ordinata ad Nativitatem Domini nobis notum faciant, ut scire valeamus quid vel quantum de singulis rebus habeamus.* My interpretation of these texts agrees with that of M. Bloch, 'La organización de los dominios reales carolingios y las teorias de Dopsch', *Anuario de historia del derecho español* (1926).

52. MGH *Cap.*, I, no. 77 (802-813), xix: *. . . et perveniant ad cameram nostram per rationem.*

53. MGH *Cap.,* I, no. 80 (811), vii: *Ut non solum beneficia episcoporum, abbatum abbatissarum atque comitum sive vassallorum nostrorum sed etiam nostri fisci describantur, ut scire possimus quantum etiam de nostro in uniusquisque legatione habeamus.* E. Lesne, *Histoire de la propriété ecclésiastique en France,* II, 2 (Lille, 1926), 73 ff. and III (1936), 3, thinks that the benefices of the bishops, abbots and abbesses in question are their *episcopatus* or *abbatia.*

54. MGH *Cap.,* I, no. 128, xxv ff. These texts date from the reign of Charlemagne or Louis the Pious (probably at latest before 836-7); cf. Ganshof, 'Observations sur deux capitulaires', 204, n. 8. See P. Grierson, 'The identity of the unnamed fiscs in the *Brevium exempla ad describendas res ecclesiasticas et fiscales' Revue Belge de Philologie et d'Histoire,* XVIII (1939), and J. Vannérus, 'Une énigme toponymique: *Treola', Bulletin de la Commission royale de Toponymie et de Dialectologie,* XXII (1948).

55. *Gesta Sanctorum Patrum Fontanellensis Coenobii,* xi, 3 (ed. F. Lohier and J. Laporte, Rouen and Paris, 1936, p. 82). *Brevium exempla* c. i ff. and c. x ff. cf. E. Lesne, op cit. II, I (Lille, 1922), 64 ff. and III (1936), 1-4.

56. List of hostages: MGH *Cap.,* I, no. 115; *commendatitiae:* when Charlemagne found himself obliged to regularise the status of the *Eigenkirche* he applied to it an ancient rule of canon law which forbade the acceptance of a cleric from one diocese by another without *commendatitiae* (see, e.g. *Admonitio generalis* of 789, MGH *Cap.,* I, no. 22, c. iii). The texts which concern us here are canon xxvii of the Synod of Frankfurt (ibid., no. 28) and for Italy c. viii of Pippin's capitulary of 802-810 (ibid., no. 102; cf. de Clercq, op. cit., 218).

57. H. Bresslau, *Handbuch der Urkundenlehre für Deutschland und Italien,* I, (2nd edn, Leipzig, 1912), 381.

58. See the letter from Alcuin, MGH *Epistolae,* IV, p. 282 (no. 171); cf. E. Lesne, op. cit., V, 'Les Ecoles de la fin du VIIIe siècle à la fin du XIIe', (Lille, 1940), 39.

59. MGH *Cap.,* I, no. 50, c. viii: *Istius capitularii exemplaria quatuor volumus ut scribantur: et unum habeant missi nostri, alterum comes in cuius ministeriis haec facienda sunt, ut aliter non faciant neque missus noster neque comes nisi sicut a nobis capitulis ordinatum est, tertium habeant missi nostri qui super exercitum nostrum constituendi sunt, quartum habeat cancellarius noster;* cf. Seeliger, op. cit., pp. 22-3. MGH *Cap.,* I, no. 67, c. vi: *Quicumque ista capitula habet, ad alios missos ea transmittat qui non habent, ut nulla excusatio de ignorantia fiat;* cf. Seeliger, op. cit., 23.

60. In Carolingian texts, where the existence of a person drafting deeds for a county is mentioned, as in texts where there is mention of a person employed to do the count's writing for him, I think *cancellarius* and *notarius* are synonymous. In favour of this view are Bresslau, op. cit., I, 2nd edn, 592-3 and H. Brunner and C. von Schwerin, *Deutsche Rechtsgeschichte,* II (2nd edn, Munich and Leipzig, 1928), 249; against, O. Redlich, *Die Privaturkunden des Mittelalters* (Munich and Berlin, 1911), 65, and A. de Boüard, op. cit., II, 130-1.

61. Ecclesiastical capitulary issued at Thionville in 805, MGH *Cap.,* I, no. 43: Wolfenbüttel (*fonds* Blankenburg) ms. 130.52 adds to the heading *De notariis* at c. iv *ut unusquisque episcopus aut abbas vel comes suum notarium habeat;* the lessons to be learned from this manuscript strike me as deserving serious consideration.

62. *Capitulare missorum* of 803 (MGH *Cap.,* I, no. 40, c. iii: *Ut missi nostri scabinios, advocatos, notarios per singula loca elegant et eorum nomina, quando reversi fuerint, secum scripta deferant.* The power of appointment here vested in the *missus* looks to me like a reserve power. That the count himself normally appointed his 'notary' or 'chancellor' seems implied by a passage c. ii of the *Vita S. Eparchii,* composed at the beginning of the ninth century (MGH *SS rer. Merov.,* III, p. 553), which is noted by Bresslau, op. cit., I, 2nd edn, 592 n. 2. The county *cancellarius* is also mentioned in the reply to questions put by a *missus,* printed MGH *Cap.,* I, no. 58, c. ii, and in a fragment of a lost capitulary preserved Ansegisus, iii, 43 (ibid., I, p. 430), but these passages do not touch on his administrative role.

63. The county 'chancellor' or 'notary' lingered on in the Burgundian regions and nearby southern Swabia much longer than elsewhere, perhaps an indication—though this is sheer hypothesis—that Charlemagne's plans met with greater success in those parts.

64. Synod of Frankfurt, MGH *Cap.,* I, no. 28, c. iii: *Unde tres breves ex hoc capitulo uno tenore conscriptos fieri praecepit: unum in palatio retinendum, alium praefato Tassiloni . . . dandum tertium vero in sacri palacii capella recondendum fieri iussit.* MGH *Cap.,* I, no. 50, c. viii: see above, n. 59. *ARF,* 813: *. . . quamquam et in archivo palatii exemplaria illarum habeantur.*

65. MGH *Epistolae,* v, pp. 111 and 115 (Einhard's letters, nos 4 and 12).

66. Einhard, *VK,* xvi.

67. See above, n. 64.

68. See above, n. 59. Bresslau, op. cit., I, 2nd edn, p. 163, basing himself on texts which relate to the early part of Louis the Pious's reign, disputes the connection between the *archivum* and the chapel postulated by T.(von) Sickel, *Acta regum et imperatorum Karolinorum,* I (Vienna, 1867), 9. But

Bresslau's argument assumes the existence of a chancery as an institution quite distinct from the chapel, an assumption which seems undermined by the more recent work of H. W. Klewitz, 'Cancellaria', *Deutsches Archiv für Geschichte des Mittelalters,* I (1937) and G. Tessier, 'Originaux et pseudo-originaux du chartrier de Saint-Denis', *Bibliothèque de l'Ecole des Chartes,* CVI (1945-6).

69. MGH *Epistolae*, IV, p. 115 (Alcuin's letters, no. 73, *c.* 789-796).

70. e.g. the copy of which there is direct mention in the capitulary of 808; see above, n. 59. The text of the Herstal capitulary (MGH *Cap.*, I, no. 20 (779)) must have been preserved in the Palace archives: how otherwise can we account for the detailed references to its provisions in later capitularies? There is record of draft copies (but not of *the* draft copies) in the reign of Louis the Pious (Bresslau, op. cit., I, 2nd edn. 163).

71. See above, n. 52.

72. For example the count Richard, *villarum suarum provisorem,* mentioned by the Astronomer, *Vita Hludowici,* vi (MGH *SS,* II, 610), who held office in the reign of Charlemagne (794). This must surely be the count Richard who in 787 was ordered with the abbot of Jumièges, to make a 'description' of the landed possessions of St Wandrille (see above, n. 55).

73. MGH *Cap.*, I, no. 85: introduction, *Nunc autem admonemus vos ut capitularia vestra relegatis et quaeque vobis per verba commendata sunt recolatis . . . c. vii: Deinde ut istam epistolam et saepius legatis et bene salvam faciatis, ut ipsa inter nos et vos in testimonium sit, utrum sic factum habeatis sicut ibi scriptum est aut non habeatis . . .*

74. A conclusion parallel to the one reached by Redlich, op. cit., 65, and A. de Boüard, II, 130, in the matter of Charlemagne's preference for written documents as instruments of proof.

75. There is no specimen diploma of appointment to a countship among the *Formulae Imperiales* (see above, n. 20). Numbers 13, 14, and 15 of the *Formulae Marculfinae aevi carolini* (MGH *Formulae,* 119-20), although relating to the consecration of a bishop or the appointment of a count, merely reproduce Merovingian formulae, with slight modifications, and do not come into the picture.

76. For the lists required at the oath-taking see above, p. 130. A list of 180 persons who took the oath of fidelity in an Italian county has come down to us (MGH *Cap.*, I, no. 181); if this list dates from the reign of Charlemagne, which is not certain, the directions given in the *capitulare missorum* of 792-3 have not been followed.

77. See above, p. 131.

78. See e.g., MGH *Cap.*, I, no. 64, c. i; ibid., c. xiii and no. 74, c. iv; no. 80, c. ii.

79. Ibid., nos. 85, c. iv and 58. cf. above, p. 129.

80. See above, n. 39.

81. The basic ideas developed in this article formed the subject of a paper read to the Legal History Section of the Ninth International Congress of the Historical Sciences held at Paris in 1950. In the discussion which followed helpful remarks, for which I am most grateful, were made by Professors C. G. Mor, of the University of Modena, G. Tessier, of the Ecole des Chartes, and F. Vercauteren, of the University of Liège, who was in the chair.

Abbreviations

I. *Sources*

ARF = *Annales Regni Francorum,* ed. F. Kurze, Hanover, 1895.

VK = Einhard, *Vita Karoli Magni,* ed. O. Holder-Egger, Hanover, 1911.

MGH = Monumenta Germaniae Historica.

MGH *Cap.* = MGH *Capitularia Regum Francorum:* vol. I, ed. A. Boretius, 1883; Vol. II, ed. A. Boretius and V. Krause, 1897.

MGH *Concilia* = MGH *Concilia:* vol. I, ed. F. Maassen, 1893; vol II, ed. A. Werminghoff, 1904-8, Supplement to vol. II, *Libri Carolini,* ed. H. Bastgen, 1924.

MGH *Diplomata Karol.* = MGH *Diplomata Karolinorum,* ed. E. Mühlbacher, 1906.

MGH *Epist.* = MGH *Epistolae* in quarto. Vol. III contains *inter alia* the *Codex Carolinus* ed. W. Gundlach, vol. IV contains *inter alia* the correspondence of Alcuin, ed. E. Dümmler, 1895.

MGH *Formulae* = MGH *Formulae Merowingici et Karolini aevi,* ed. K. Zeumer, 1886.

MGH *Poetae* = MGH *Poetae Latini aevi Carolini,* Vols. I and II, ed. E. Dümmler, 1880-81, 1884.

MGH *SS* = MGH *Scriptores* in folio.

MGH *SS rer. Merov.* = MGH *Scriptores rerum Merovingicarum,* in quarto. Vol. I, 2nd edition contains the historical work of Gregory of Tours, ed. B. Krusch and W. Levison, 1951; the hagiographical works are to be consulted in vol. I, 1st edition by W. Arndt and B. Krusch, 1884; vol. II contains the chronicle of Fredegar and its continuations, ed. B. Krusch, 1888.

W-H = *The Fourth Book of the Chronicle of Fredegar with its continuations,* ed. with English translation by J. M. Wallace-Hadrill, London, 1960.

2. *Periodicals*

HZ = *Historische Zeitschrift.*

Meded. d. Kon. Vla. Acad. v. Wet., Kl. Lett. = *Mededelingen van de Koninklijke Vlaamse Academie voor*

Wetenschappen, Letteren en Schone Kunsten van België, Klasse der Letteren.

MIÖG = Mitteilungen des Öesterreichischen Instituts für Geschichtsforschung.

SSCI = Settimane di Studio del Centro Italiano di Studi sull' alto medioevo.

ZKG = Zeitschrift für Kirchengeschichte.

Richard Winston (essay date 1954)

SOURCE: "The World of Culture" in *Charlemagne: From the Hammer to the Cross,* The Bobbs-Merrill Company, Inc., 1954, pp. 138-55.

[*In the following excerpt, Winston examines the accomplishments of two of Charlemagne's greatest scholars: Alcuin, who was charged with improving literacy and who initiated a teacher-training program, and Paul, a natural scientist and historian who wrote the* History of the Lombards.]

A recent French historian has disdainfully dismissed the Carolingian revival of learning in a few words: "What possible point can there be in trying to rehabilitate this gloomy age, to glorify this abortive renaissance? Neither Charlemagne nor his companions were responsible for its failure. They were too close to their barbaric past, and were not ripe for civilization."[1]

Monsieur Sedillot has fallen into the trap that awaits historical tourists who pay only the briefest of visits to a past civilization and then flit on to the next point of interest. Like the American in Europe who sees only the inadequacy of local plumbing, he has judged and found wanting a culture that does not meet the standards of urban industrialism. Is it not obvious that our contemporary concern with schools of existentialism, say, or with the distinctions among capitalism, communism and socialism, will seem a thousand years hence as incomprehensible to historians of his temper as the eighth century's concern with adoptianism, iconoclasm or the *filioque* controversy? The human mind has always worked with the materials it had at hand. It is risky to judge and condemn the intellectual achievements of one age by the standards of another. Aristotle was not a fool because he thought the universe consisted of fifty-five concentric hollow spheres—any more than Niels Bohr was a fool when he framed his "solar system" model of the atom. Both men were working with the information available to them, and both men were adding to man's understanding of the universe. Physical science has moved so rapidly in modern times that Bohr's brilliant theory had to be abandoned within ten years after it was conceived (and Bohr himself was foremost in abandoning it), whereas a variant of Aristotle's conception continued to be accepted for well over a millennium and a half. The slower pace of scientific development in the past does not mean that every thinker from Ar-istotle to Copernicus was an intellectual dwarf. The modern schoolboy is not greater than Euclid because he knows far more about mathematics.

Charles, King of the Franks and Lombards, was the Alexander rather than the Aristotle of his time. Yet his mind, which had hitherto expressed itself principally in political action, in conquest and consolidation, was now beginning to range wide in less practical realms. He had begun studying grammar with the aging Peter of Pisa, and grammar included "literature," the examination and interpretation of literary and above all scriptural texts. He was seeking someone to teach him astronomy, to give him lessons in music and versification, to help him with Biblical and patristic criticism, to answer his questions about the origins of things, to discuss ethical and theological problems with him. He was a great talker, so much so that the members of his court thought him a bit loquacious. Now he wanted people around him with spry and subtle minds who could hold up their end of a conversation on subjects other than hawking and hunting—although he, in common with all noble Franks of his day, dearly loved to speak of his falcons and hounds, his successes or failures on the great hunts which all his life were to take up much of his leisure time.

To satisfy his longing for intellectual stimulus he began gathering around himself both reputable scholars and bright young men. The Monk of St. Gall, who as always embroiders the facts of Charles's life with charming fantasies and yet so often hits on essential traits of Charles's character, has constructed a fine legend out of this activity. The Monk writes:

> Now it happened, when Charles had begun to reign alone in the western parts of the world, and the pursuit of learning had been almost forgotten throughout all his realm . . . that two Scots came from Ireland[2] to the coast of Gaul along with certain traders of Britain. These Scots were unrivaled for their skill in sacred and secular learning; and day by day, when the crowd gathered around them for business, they exhibited no wares for sale, but cried out, 'Ho, everyone that desires wisdom, let him draw near and take it at our hands; for it is wisdom we have for sale.' Now they declared that they had wisdom for sale because they said that people cared not for what was freely given, but only for what was sold. . . . For so long did they make their proclamation that in the end . . . the matter was brought to the ears of King Charles, who always loved and sought after wisdom. Wherefore he ordered them to come with all speed into his presence and asked them whether it were true that they had brought wisdom with them. They answered, 'We both possess and are ready to give it, in the name of God, to those who seek it worthily.' Again he asked them what price they required for it, and they answered: 'We seek no price, O king. We ask only a fit place for teaching and quick minds to teach, and besides these food and clothing. . . . '

This answer filled the king with great joy, and first he kept both of them with him for a short time. But soon, when he had to go to war, he made one of them named Clement reside in Gaul, and to him he sent many boys both of noble, middle and humble birth, and he ordered as much food to be given them as they required, and he set aside for them buildings suitable for study.

Although the two "Scots" probably never attempted to cry wisdom in the market place, the Monk conveys a true picture of Charles's pleasure in finding men of learning, of his zeal in setting up schools for boys of all classes and of his generosity toward good teachers. His own thirst for learning made him value education highly. Moreover, he recognized that only by raising educational standards could he recruit the corps of administrators he needed for his rapidly expanding kingdom. Under the Merovingian kings of Frankland enough of the Roman schools had survived to supply educated laymen for the offices of government. But that system had broken down during the disorders of civil wars and Saracen invasions in the early part of the eighth century, and even the ecclesiastical schools were in a bad way.

The most important secular school in the Frankish realm was, of course, the Palace School, in which Charles's own boys and the sons of his chief nobles were being or were to be educated. For this school Charles wanted to find the best available teacher.

The Monk goes on to tell us: "When Albinus [Alcuin], an Englishman, heard that the most religious Emperor[3] Charles gladly entertained wise men, he entered into a ship and came to him. Now Albinus was skilled in all learning beyond all others of our times, for he was the disciple of that most learned priest Bede, who next to Saint Gregory was the most skillful interpreter of the Scriptures."

The association had not begun in quite this fashion. It was due partly to a lucky accident. On his recent visit to Italy Charles had stopped for a short time at the city of Parma. There, by good fortune, he had met the famous Anglo-Saxon scholar who was returning from a mission to Rome.

Alcuin was about ten years older than Charles himself. Born around the time that the Venerable Bede died at Jarrow, he had been raised in the Cathedral School at York in the tradition of Archbishop Egbert, one of Bede's disciples. It was a great tradition, for in the early part of the eighth century, while on the Continent Boniface was bemoaning the ignorance and license he found even among the clergy, England was a center of learning.

The emphasis in the studies at the Cathedral School was on the history and doctrines of the Church, of course; but the "seven liberal arts"—grammar, rhetoric, dialectic, arithmetic, music, geometry and astronomy—were not neglected. In the library at York, of which Alcuin soon became the head as he became also director of the Cathedral School, the ardent young disciple of Egbert was able to study the works of Pliny, Cicero, Vergil, Ovid and possibly also Horace and Terence. Most of the Roman classics, however, were known to him only at second hand, through the sixth-century writings of Boethius and Cassiodorus, or through the encyclopedic compilations of the seventh-century Spanish bishop Isidore. But the greatest influence on Alcuin would naturally be the Venerable Bede, whose simple, clear and classical Latin style Alcuin imitated to advantage.

Latin required intensive study in England, for in the Anglo-Saxon kingdoms there was no tradition of Latin speech as there was on the Continent in Spain, Gaul and Italy. Precisely because the classical language was unaffected by a related "vulgar" tongue, a "purer" Latinity flourished among the English scholars than was to be found anywhere on the Continent. Bede's great gifts as a stylist enabled him to make the best possible use of this classical tradition in his *Ecclesiastical History,* which is not only the best and almost the only source on the early history of England, but which is a book that still makes lively reading. It might well have served Alcuin's contemporaries as a model of intelligence and coherence.

Yet it was to Bede's theological books, with their emphasis on allegorical interpretation of the Scriptures, that Alcuin's bright but essentially conventional and highly orthodox mind was most attracted. He was excited by these lessons which, as he wrote, "opened out the mysteries of Holy Scripture and gave us to look into the abyss of law ancient and unfulfilled."[4] Through Alcuin's popularization of Bede's method, allegorical exegesis (a method whose roots go back to Origen and Augustine) became the characteristic medieval approach to the Scriptures. The historical significance of the Bible was almost entirely neglected.

Essentially Alcuin was a schoolmaster, content to cull from the writings of the past and put together textbooks whose contents were adapted to the needs of students. That he was one of the great teachers of the age is evident from the devotion of his many talented pupils, to whom he gave such thorough preparation that they fitted easily into high ecclesiastical posts all over Europe. Nor did he lose touch with his pupils once they had gone out into the world of the Church. With all of them he kept up a warm correspondence in which a somewhat pedantic didacticism is always mingled with his genuine friendliness. Sometimes his letters were in verse, most of it mediocre.

In the year that Charles embarked on his disastrous Spanish expedition (778) Alcuin was given complete charge of the school and library of the York Cathedral, which he had unofficially headed for some time. Here, with his placid and retiring temperament, he might have remained, quietly teaching for the rest of his life. But a new archbishop, Eanbald, was installed at York in 780 and, following the custom, sent to Rome for his pallium—that woolen band ornamented with crosses which was originally conferred by the pope as a sign of favor but which by the late eighth century had become a necessary symbol of the archbishop's authority and of his submission to the pope as head of the Church. The honor of fetching the pallium from Rome went to Alcuin.

The journey was one Alcuin undertook with pleasure, not only because he was eager to visit Rome and speak with the pope but because it gave him the opportunity to visit many friends and former pupils on the way. Travel was not too difficult; there was constant intercourse by sea between Frisia and England, and many Frisian traders were settled in the Anglo-Saxon kingdoms. The Frisians—the ancestors of the Dutch—were already noted for trade and their thriving dairies; we find Alcuin in a poem greeting Bishop Alberic of Utrecht as "lord of many cows." From Utrecht Alcuin apparently made his way down the Rhine and the Moselle to what is now Southern France, and thence into Italy.

In the course of his return trip from Rome, bearing the pallium for his archbishop, Alcuin and Charles met at Parma. The delight Charles took in this cultivated Englishman can be surmised from the warm friendship that so rapidly developed between them. Charles promptly invited Alcuin to come to his court and be director of the Palace School. He indicated that Alcuin would be also in general charge of educational affairs in the Frankish kingdom. There was much work to be done in Frankland, he urged. He often received letters from monasteries stating that the brethren were offering pious prayers on his behalf, but most of these letters were characterized by "correct thoughts and uncouth expressions." As he himself wrote, "What pious devotion dictated faithfully to the mind, the tongue, unskilled for want of study, was not able to express in the letter without error." He needed an inspiring teacher whose authority in the field of knowledge was unchallenged. To such a teacher he would give all the support needed to carry out an ambitious program. Would Alcuin consent to "sow the seeds of learning in Frankland" as he had already done in his native England?

The worldly rewards that Charles offered were tempting, even though Alcuin had inherited wealth of his own back home. But more appealing than these to a man of Alcuin's caliber was the opportunity for a wider sphere of activity than he could ever find as head of a school in the small kingdom of Northumbria, which in recent years had been racked by political disturbances. A lover of stability and legitimacy, Alcuin was deeply troubled by the bloody uprisings which had driven two kings into exile within six years. In Northumbria no one was free from fear; the earth, as he was to write later, "was stained with the blood of rulers and kings." Charles, on the other hand, was the secure ruler of a great and growing state which stood in the closest relations with Alcuin's beloved Church.

Alcuin was also favorably impressed by this candid and outspoken giant of a man, with his rather large nose and high-pitched voice, who showed a schoolboy's eagerness to learn. For the great king plied Alcuin with respectful questions on the Scriptures and the stars, humbly addressed him as "Father"—though he was a mere deacon—and assured him that if he accepted and came to Frankland he would find a king and all his courtiers among his pupils. Alcuin knew how rare it was to find love of learning

combined with political power. Then too the king's ability to understand and speak Greek was a formidable accomplishment to Alcuin, and a further recommendation. For Alcuin himself had no facility or easy familiarity with Greek; the tags of Greek in his writings are borrowed from his predecessors. The prospect of being at a court where he could learn as well as teach was a further enticement; for, the king informed him, there would be a Greek teacher at court. In the arrangements for the betrothal of Rotrud to young Constantine it had been agreed that a Byzantine official named Elissaeus would reside at Charles's court (or, rather, travel about with it) in order to instruct the princess in the Greek language and in the customs of the Empire of the Romans.

Alcuin agreed to the king's proposal, provided that Archbishop Eanbald and his own king gave their consent. Then he returned to England with the pallium for Eanbald.

Alcuin and Eanbald had long been engaged in directing the rebuilding of York Cathedral, which had burned down in Alcuin's boyhood, the year before Charles was born. But the work was now done, and the archbishop had no reason to hold Alcuin back from a greater destiny than he could offer him. King Elfwald of Northumbria also was not averse to having one of his subjects at the court of Charles. Good relations with the King of the Franks might provide him with sufficient prestige to maintain his shaky position, in spite of his turbulent nobles and the claims of his great neighbor, King Offa of Mercia, who styled himself king of all the English.

The way, then, was clear, and Alcuin, with many a backward glance at York (he wrote at this time a versified history of the city), crossed to the Continent and made his way to the royal vill at Quierzy, near Paris, where King Charles was spending the winter.

With Alcuin's arrival at Charles's court there began that many-sided intellectual activity which was to be the ornament of Charles's reign and to influence significantly the next thousand years. Alcuin had come primarily as a schoolmaster, and it is as teacher and minister of education that his activities were most important in the earlier years. His active role in doctrinal controversies belongs to the latter part of his life and of Charles's reign; his function as Charles's friend, riddle maker, question answerer and general mentor was incidental to his main work. Because he did that work so well, Charles would have kept him at his post even if there had not existed between the two men such strong mutual respect and affection.

The foremost task Alcuin faced was the improvement of literacy, which was at a woefully low level even in the monasteries. There were not enough schools, and the textbooks used were faulty. These faulty texts were further corrupted because they were copied by half-literate boys. Attempts were made to remedy this situation in a number of decrees issued by Charles but no doubt written by Alcuin. Every abbey was required to have a school where boys[5] might learn reading, the Psalms, musical notation, singing, arithmetic and grammar. If copies of the Gospel, Psalter or Missal were needed, these were to be made by mature men.

Alcuin and Charles insisted also on the instruction of upper-class children—which may seem strange until we recall that the Frankish nobles were primarily fighters, not scholars. One of the stories of the Monk of St. Gall tells how Charles, visiting a school, found the work of the lower-class children immensely superior to that of the young scions of the nobility:

> Then the most wise Charles, imitating the judgment of the eternal Judge, gathered together those who had done well upon his right hand and addressed them in these words: 'My children, you have found much favor with me because you have tried with all your might to carry out my orders. . . . Now study to attain perfection and I will give you bishoprics and splendid monasteries and will always honor you.' Then he turned severely to those who were gathered on his left . . . and flung at them in scorn these terrible words, which seemed thunder rather than human speech: 'You nobles, you sons of my chiefs, you superfine dandies, you have trusted to your wealth and have set at naught my orders which were for your own good; you have neglected learning and gone in for luxury and sport, idleness and profitless pastimes. . . . By the King of Heaven, I take no account of your noble birth and your fine looks, though others may admire you for them. Know this for certain, that unless you make up for your laziness by vigorous study, you will never get any favors from Charles.'

The point was, of course, that Charles needed educated young noblemen for administrators in his expanding realm. But it is unfair to put too utilitarian an interpretation on his policy. We must recognize that he believed in widespread education for its own sake.

At the beginning of Alcuin's activity the prime necessity was to teach teachers and to halt that progressive corruption of texts which, in an age when all books had to be reproduced by hand, resulted from the ignorance of copyists. So successful was Alcuin in his teacher-training program that after fifteen years, when he retired to the Monastery of Tours and his work was taken over by Bishop Theodulf of Orléans, it was possible to propose *universal free education.* "The priests are to have schools in the towns and villages," Theodulf ordered, "and if any of the faithful wish to recommend their children for the learning of letters, the priests must receive and teach these children. . . . And they are to charge no fee for their teaching and to receive nothing except what the parents may offer of their own free will and out of affection." The tremendous importance of this step can scarcely be exaggerated. Although the Carolingian school system suffered severely in the disorders that followed the reign of Charles, the aim and the ideal had been set for all time.

In addition to organizing education and overseeing the two monasteries of which Charles had promptly appointed him abbot, Alcuin obtained from England books which were not available in Frankland and began building up a library for Charles. Since elementary text books were sadly wanting, he also wrote a number of his own. These are cast in dialogue form, which Alcuin judged best suited for beginners and which also expressed the direct and personal relationship he liked to establish with his pupils. These textbooks were scarcely specimens of brilliant organization or logical treatment. Alcuin, for example, divides grammar into twenty-six "varieties": words, letters, syllables, clauses, dictions, speeches, definitions, feet, accents, punctuations, diacritical marks, spellings, analogies, etymologies, glosses, differences, barbarisms, solecisms, faults, metaplasms, schemata, tropes, prose, meters, fables and histories. Classification was certainly not Alcuin's strong point. But his writings on grammar, rhetoric, orthography and arithmetic were highly esteemed in their day—and long afterward—and they served their purpose. In Alcuin's schools the teachers were superior to their textbooks.

One of Alcuin's texts—the *Disputation between the Royal and Most Noble Youth Pepin with Albinus the Schoolmaster*—affords a remarkable insight into the medieval mind, with its obliqueness, fancifulness and love of epigrammatic formulations. Some of the questions are simple; some are the basic human questions with which philosophers and scientists have wrestled throughout the ages. But what strikes us about all the answers that Alcuin gives is the indirectness, the total absence of the natural-scientific point of view. Everything is reduced to a symbol. Egon Friedell[6] has remarked, in a striking exaggeration, that the medieval mind was really interested in only two things: God and the soul. Certainly Friedell has gone too far, but the dialogue between Pepin and Alcuin suggests how much truth there is in his statement. For example:

PEPIN	ALBINUS
What is writing?	The guardian of history.
What is speech?	The revealer of the soul.
What produces speech?	The tongue.
What is the tongue?	The lash of the air.
What is air?	The guardian of life.
What is life?	The joy of the good, the sorrow of the wicked, the waiting for death.
What is man?	The bondsman of death, a passing way-farer, a guest upon earth.
What is man like?	An apple [a play on words: *homo, pomo*].
What is sleep?	The image of death.
What is faith?	Certain belief in an unknown and wondrous thing.

Questions on the parts of the body also lend themselves to succinct replies that to the modern mind are hardly informative, to the medieval mind were satisfactory and above all stimulating. For instance:

What is the beard?	The distinguisher of sex, the honor of age.
What are the lips?	The doors of the mouth.
What is the mouth?	The nourisher of the body.
What is the stomach?	The cook of food.
What are the feet?	A movable foundation.

More revealing still of the radical difference between the medieval and the modern approach are the answers to questions on natural science:

What is the sun?	The splendor of the universe, the beauty of the sky, the glory of the day, the divider of the hours.
What is the moon?	The eye of night, the giver of dew, the foreteller of storms.
What are the stars?	Pictures on the roof of the heavens, guides of sailors, the ornament of night.
What is winter?	The exile of summer.
What is spring?	The painter of the earth.
What is summer?	The reclother of the earth, the ripener of fruits.
What is autumn?	The barn of the year.

Evidently Alcuin and his contemporaries preferred to define things in terms of their effects; the modern mind makes an effort to include causes in a definition. There is no reason for us to smile at these answers as childish. Even had Alcuin known that the moon was a planetary body about one fourth the diameter of the earth, revolving around the earth at a mean distance of 240,000 miles, he would not have been interested. What mattered about the moon or any other heavenly body was their effect on human beings, their value as symbols of the divine order and their usefulness for calculating the date of Easter. Ptolemy and Aristotle, with their comprehensive and mathematically logical, if erroneous, astronomical systems, were forgotten in the time of Alcuin and Charles—forgotten because no one really wanted that kind of knowledge.

It must be remembered also that these texts of Alcuin's served to teach a foreign language to the German-speaking Frankish boys. As language lessons they were certainly superior to the "I-see-the-book-of-my-father-on-the-table-of-my-uncle" sort of thing which until quite recently represented the highest achievement of Western civilization in the art of language teaching. Even the Romance-speaking peoples of Frankland had to apply themselves to the study of Latin. They had to learn the complex case forms which the vulgar tongue had dropped, and the classic and late classic Latin vocabularies, in order to understand the Fathers of the Church. A good part of the woeful "decay of learning" over which Alcuin and his

contemporaries lamented was a decline in the knowledge of Latin—the inevitable result of the widening gap between the common speech and the written language.

Alcuin was too much the professor even to consider the common languages, whether German or the *lingua romana rustica,* suitable subjects for study. Although a well-established tradition of vernacular literature already existed in England, Alcuin had no use for such studies. Writing to the Bishop of Lindisfarne, he warned against songs from *Beowulf:* "Let the words of God be read at table in your refectory. The reader should be heard there, not the flute player. What has Ingeld to do with Christ?"

In this respect his master Charles showed a more liberal and scientific bent. Charles took lessons in Latin grammar from Alcuin, and applied them by beginning to write a grammar of German. He also gave German names to the months and to the winds and, as we have mentioned, became the first German folklorist by making a collection of the traditional German lays. Though his successors did not think these works worth preserving, something of Charles's enlightened attitude toward his native speech lived on in his grandson, the talented historian Nithard, who wrote down the texts of the Strassburg oaths in their original languages.[7]

Around the Palace School as an institution in which the young people of the court were educated there grew up a kind of higher academy composed of the faculty proper of the school, the king and those among the officials of the court who had intellectual interests. This academy had no definite meeting place, no fixed composition, none of the appurtenances of the modern university. Much of the intercourse among the members was carried on by letter. Its sessions might be held after dinner, during or after a hunt, even—in later years—in the baths at Aachen. Informality was the rule.

Membership in the academy widened greatly in the later years of Charles's reign. But at the time Alcuin first arrived the chief intellectuals at the court were Peter of Pisa, who was considered strictly a grammarian; Paulinus, who became Alcuin's special friend and whom Charles later appointed Patriarch of Aquileia; and Paul Warnefried, who was called Paul the Deacon. Paul was by far the most interesting and talented of these older men.

A Lombard by birth, Paul had come to the court of Charles on a mission of mercy. Paul's brother had taken part in the ill-fated uprising of Hrodgaud of Friuli and had been brought to Frankland by Charles and cast into prison along with a number of other rebellious Lombards. There he remained for six years, until Paul wrote to Charles pleading for his brother's release. His petition was in the form of an elegy which Paul either delivered in person or followed up by a visit to the king's court. The poem spoke of "my brother, a captive going on seven years now, naked, in need and heartsore, while in her homeland his wife begs for food with trembling lips." By this ignoble trade, Paul goes on to say, she can barely keep her four children in rags.

Paul had evidently heard that well-turned verses were the surest way to move Charles. When he appeared at the court, around the same time that Alcuin arrived there, Charles received him amicably and respectfully but firmly refused to release Paul's brother or the other Lombard prisoners until he had extracted from Paul a reluctant promise to stay at the court as a teacher. Thus he exchanged one captive of the Warnefried family for another. Paul's captivity, however, was of the most pleasant and luxurious sort. He was offered land and money and was flattered by the king and his companions. Charles had Peter of Pisa write a poem to Paul praising him as the most learned of men, a Homer in Greek, a Vergil in Latin, a Philo in Hebrew, a Horace in verse, and so on, and urging him to put aside his homesickness and strike roots in Frankland.

Homesickness was not the only reason for Paul's reluctance to stay with Charles. He was deeply attached to the family of the deposed Lombard king, Desiderius, and in particular to that king's daughter, Adalperga. In the "good old days" of Lombardy's independence Paul had been Adalperga's mentor. Because that highly intelligent lady found fault with the commonly used history of Rome by the fourth-century writer Eutropius, Paul undertook to write a "Roman History" for her which would be more comprehensive than that of Eutropius and would include Christian history as well.

Paul's loyalty to the old Lombard dynasty continued strong after Charles's conquest of Lombardy, and his national pride stood in the way of his serving Charles wholeheartedly. He had become a monk in middle life, probably after the collapse of the Lombard kingdom, and throughout his stay in Frankland he chafed to return to his beloved Monte Cassino. In one of his letters to his abbot at the famous monastery he wrote:

> I live among good Christians here, am well received by all . . . but compared to your cloister this court seems to me a prison; compared to the peace a mong you, life here is a tempest. Only my poor weak body clings to this country; with my whole soul, which is the only sound part of me, I am with you and imagine myself listening to the sweetness of your songs, or in the refectory with you refreshing myself more from the reading than the food, or watching each of your various occupations, seeing how the old and the sick are faring, or crossing the holy threshold which is as dear to me as paradise. Believe me, my master and father and all you devout flock, only the emotion of pity, only the commandment of love, only the demands of the soul are keeping me here for a while. These, and what is more than all of these, the silent might of our lord king.

When, after a few years, Paul was at last allowed to leave the Frankish court he returned to Monte Cassino and there spent the remaining years of his life writing his *History of the Lombards,* which has remained the best and virtually the only source for the history of that people whose independence Charles had destroyed. Unfortunately for historians, Paul did not bring the history down to his own day, either because he died before he could complete it or, more likely, because he was unwilling to recount the downfall of the dynasty with which he was linked by lasting ties of affection.

In spite of his loyalty to the family of Desiderius, however, and in spite of his grievance against a king who had kept his brother imprisoned for so many years, Paul formed equally strong ties of affection with Charles, who reciprocated his feeling. There was a fundamental similarity in the minds of the two men. Both had a wider range of emotion and a deeper interest in the real world than, say, those of which Alcuin was capable. Where Alcuin was a grammarian and teacher, Paul was a historian and—in the limited sense that it was possible for a medieval man to be—a natural scientist. His history of the Lombards opens with the curious speculation that northern climates are more healthful than southern climates and more favorable for the propagation of mankind, and on this ground he accounts for the numerous population of Germany. He comments on the greater length of the days in the northern summers. While staying with Charles at the royal villa of Thionville one Christmas he compares the declination of the sun with that of Italy in the same season by actually measuring his own shadow—an incredibly original act of experimentation for a man of his time.

It was in this practical, skeptical, essentially "modern" turn of mind that Paul resembled Charles. Where Alcuin turned automatically for information to a scriptural or patristic text, both Charles and Paul were inclined—again it must be stressed: within the limitations of the age—to look to the natural world for answers. Charles, indeed, sometimes embarrassed Alcuin with his persistent questioning and his fundamentally common-sense approach. He was capable of asking Alcuin wherein lay the essential difference between Christians and the pagan philosophers who also believed in dignity, nobility, virtue and pure morals. Alcuin lamely replied that the difference was "faith and baptism," which certainly did not satisfy the king. Or Charles wondered why the hymn which Jesus and his disciples must have sung before the Last Supper had not been recorded in any of the Gospels—a question which sounds like that of a schoolboy trying to trap the master. Charles also tried to extend the study of astronomy beyond its conventional function, which at that time was the calculation of the dates for Easter. He instituted a program of careful observation and recording of astronomical matters. In this he received the assistance of Irish scholars like Dungal of St. Denis or the Clement previously mentioned who afterward took over the Palace School when Alcuin retired. Charles was, in fact, passionately interested in astronomy and sought a deeper knowledge of it than any of his contemporaries were capable of giving him.

These practical studies, in which Paul and Charles shared a common interest, Alcuin could never fully understand. Alcuin was always content to study what had already been done, to compile from the writings of the Church Fathers, rather than to make any original contributions of his own. "What better purpose shall we ordinary men be able to devise," he once wrote, "in these loveless days of the world's last age, than that we should follow . . . the doctrine of the apostles, not inventing new terms, no t bringing forth anything unfamiliar."

For all the respect in which Alcuin was held, he must sometimes have found it hard to keep up with some of the younger, quicker and perhaps more cynical minds in the court circle. The composition of this circle changed, of course, with the passage of time, as new persons moved into and out of official positions, were rewarded for their services by being appointed abbots of monasteries (like Chancellor Itherius, who became Abbot of Tours around 775 and remained in charge of that huge and wealthy monastery until his death, whereupon Charles gave it to Alcuin), or were sent on missions by the king. But the circle itself remained, loosely organized as a kind of informal academy whose members met at intervals to listen to lectures, read poems to one another, discuss questions of theology or astronomy and, in lighter moments, to exchange riddles. Alcuin brought with him from England the Anglo-Saxon fondness for riddles and found it matched by the Germanic traditions of his hosts.

Alcuin, too, introduced among the members of the court circle the use of nicknames by which they addressed one another. In the intimate circle Charles was addressed as King David, Alcuin himself as Flaccus, Charles's sister Gisla as Lucia, Charles's daughter Rotrud as Columba. Theodulf of Orléans was known for his poetic gifts as Pindar. Another poet of distinction, Charles's chaplain and intimate adviser Angilbert, was called Homer. And the future biographer of Charles, Einhard, was dubbed Bezaleel after the architect of the tabernacle (Exodus, 31). Alcuin himself justified this nicknaming in a letter to Charles's cousin Gundrada, the sister of Adalhard and Wala. "Intimate friendship often calls for a change of name. Thus the Lord himself changed Simon to Peter and called the sons of Zebedee the 'sons of Thunder.'" This whimsy became a Carolingian custom that lasted well into the next two generations.

Among all the brilliant men around him Charles easily stood out as the leading spirit, if not always the best informed. He was humble, and freely acknowledged his indebtedness to Alcuin, Paul or Peter. But he was not easily fooled or put off and was quite capable of criticizing his teachers and companions. "You say it is not worth while repeating what is already known," Alcuin once wrote plaintively to Charles. "Well, then, I don't know what the countryman Flaccus can say to the wise David that he won't know."

Like the medieval man he was, Charles pondered the mysteries of the Trinity and subtle metaphysical questions; like Socrates he examined the nature of justice and the distinctions between justice and law; and like the universal men of the Renaissance he interested himself in architecture, canal building, music, liturgy, languages, textual criticism of the Bible, poetry, sculpture and a host of other matters. Since he was also a man of action, an administrator, general and diplomat as well as hunter, swimmer and fighter, the portrait of a man seven hundred years in advance of his times is complete. No man of comparable many-sidedness can be found in the Middle Ages, and it is no wonder that his contemporaries—even those famous wits, poets and scholars of the court and Palace Academy who saw him every day at close quarters—should have stood in awe of him. It is the more remarkable that they also loved him fervently. "I loved so much in you," Alcuin wrote, "what I saw you were seeking in me." The warmth of his personality, his generosity, his hospitality (Einhard remarks that he was so fond of foreigners and entertained them in such numbers that they were a burden on both palace and kingdom), his loyalty to his friends and readiness to reward them, his kindliness and his affection for his wives, concubines and children—all these traits enabled him to live among people rather than above them, and saved him from that painful isolation which is the ordinary lot of great rulers.

It is important for us to bear this in mind, for Charles was now entering on a dark period of his life when the acids of political action were beginning to corrode his genial liberality and leave permanent scars on his personality. Just after the arrival of Alcuin, when the gay and earnest sports of the mind were giving Charles the greatest pleasure and when the whole culture of the Roman world was being thrown open to him, he was forced to turn his attention once more to the grim struggle with barbarians. He marched to the contest resentful of the interruption to his studies but with a clearer consciousness of which side he was on, of what principle he represented. During the next few decisive years he was more Roman than the Romans, and he fought his German cousins with the fury of a convert to a higher and more glorious cause.

Notes

1. René Sedillot, *An Outline of French History,* New York, Alfred A. Knopf, 1953.

2. The Irish were universally called Scots at this time.

3. A characteristic slip on the part of the Monk. Charles was at this time only king.

4. Cited by Eleanor Duckett, *Alcuin, Friend of Charlemagne,* New York, The Macmillan Company, 1951. In the discussion of Alcuin I have leaned heavily on Miss Duckett's excellent biography, and used some of her translations. She is, however, in no way responsible for my conclusions.

5. No provision was made officially for the education of women. Nevertheless, women obtained education somehow, for there were a good many highly cultivated ladies at the time—in particular Charles's own daughters and sister, and the wives of his rivals, Tassilo and Arichis.

6. In *Kulturgeschichte der Neuzeit.*

7. In the spring of 842 two of the warring sons of Louis the Pious, Charles and Louis, formed an alliance against their brother Lothar. They took solemn oaths to observe this alliance faithfully; if they failed to do so, each of their subjects might consider himself released from his personal oath of allegiance to his king. Louis' men spoke German, Charles's men the *lingua romana*. In order for the oaths to be understood by the men of the other army, Louis swore in the Roman tongue and Charles in the *lingua teudisca* (*teudisca—teutsch, deutsch*). Nithard, who wrote the history of these troubled times at the request of his cousin Charles, was a product of Alcuin's schools and demonstrated the excellence of his early training by producing a thoroughly original work of history.

Harold Lamb (essay date 1954)

SOURCE: "Growth of a Legend" in *Charlemagne: The Legend and the Man*, Doubleday & Company, Inc., 1954, pp. 282-311.

[*In the following excerpt, Lamb narrates the final months of the aged and ailing Charlemagne through his death and its aftermath, and explains how and why his legend grew even while his kingdom was being invaded.*]

It came first in quiet voices from the land. A boy picked herbs for medicine in a garden close. Bending low, he drew in the fragrance of hyssop and thyme, and he thought how when he carried the herb basket to the door where the old Benedictine waited, he would add his words, although he could not make much of a poem as yet. "Such a little gift, my father, for so great a scholar—if you were sitting here in this green darkened garden, all your boys of the school would be playing here under the apple growth. All your laughing boys of the happy school. Will you, my father, who can make a book out of thoughts, prune and shape these my words so they can be a poem?"

This boy grew up to attend the school, and he did make a poem which he called *About Gardening* and explained that it was a very poor gift from Walafrid Strabo to the venerable abbot of St. Gall.

Then, walking by the sandy bank of the Loire, Fredugis, who had taken Alcuin's place, tried to bring back the thoughts of his master, of "the field flowers yielding herbs that heal, where the birds sing together their matins, praising God who made them. Where the fragrance of apple orchards creeps into the cloisters. Like the memory of your voice, echoing within the walls."

These small voices in strained cadence bespoke, however, a new hope and peace of mind. The boys thronging into the growing School of Tours, the books flowing from the writing chamber in the fine clear script, going on to Reims and Reichenau, where the monks painted in more lifelike saintly figures, out to the fields of Brittany and the heights of the Asturias, where artisans worked with forge and pliers to shape new lamps like the Moors of Córdoba—this quiet in labor, this articulation of joy, came out of the peace of those few brief years.

In his chamber at Orléans where a map of the world had been painted, the busy Theodulf remembered Rothaid, who had brought apples to her father, and who now "shone in royal splendor of precious metal and jewels." At St. Denis upon the highway to the obscure, overgrown island of Paris, the former Lombard, Fardulf, announced that the hostel palace he had built in gratitude awaited the arrival of Charlemagne. A sleeping chamber, kept in order for him with damask on the couch, overlooked the distant Seine. It awaited him—would he not visit it again in the Hay Month?

A stranger riding to Aix beheld these river lands and spoke of them as "Flowering Francia." They reminded him of the Florentian city in Italy.

There is no mistaking the meaning of the voices. The land was at peace. In the mind of the stripling Walafrid, and the wayfarer alike, the aspect of this land had been brought about by Charlemagne. Who else? What province or diocese of Christendom did not obey him?

"Since the beginning of the world," the Irish Dungal asked, "when has there been a king in the lands now ruled by the Franks so wise and strong as he?"

These speakers express an awareness of something taking place around them. However moved by their hopes, they sense an ending of barbarism, while a great Christian community extends as far as the outposts of the Church. Inwardly it gains understanding of itself, and it goes on its way with no other aid than religion.

In spite of Einhard's fondness for calling it a revival of Rome, few others behold in it anything to do with the empire of Rome. One or two speak vaguely of the golden time of Romulus, at the founding of the other empire. And of course, the word *Imperator* stands on the coins of new weight and fineness—like the new measures and weights for scales. Most of them, beholding the paintings covering the walls of Reims and Ingelheim, as well as the pages of the fresh Bibles, think of the domain of King David, or of Moses, leading his people away from the peril of the Red Sea crossing.

Oddly enough, there was a meeting of minds between the monks who never left their cloisters and the veterans of the wars. The old soldiers remembered how after Irminsul was overthrown the thirst of the drouth-stricken army was quenched by a miraculous torrent of rain. On the walls of Fritzlar—did not two unknown warriors in shining white appear to aid the Christian swordsmen? These twain the monks identified as Sts. Martin and Denis. To cap that, the soldiers chanted the refrain of Sigiburg—how in the shield ring of the Christians appeared two shields flaming as with living fire, frightening the pagans to their doom.

Such were the *cantilènes* that the grandsons of Kerold heard in the camps. The cause of such celestial intervention, in the minds of the old soldiers, could only have been Charlemagne. That time he fell from his horse and his spear flew twenty feet from his hand marked the almost miraculous death of his enemy, Godfried the Dane king. The spear flying away from his hand gave a sign that he would not need it. And certainly the time of the double eclipse in the sky, of the sun and moon, had been that of the deaths of his two sons, Charles and Pepin.

Thus while Charlemagne lived the semblance of the second Charlemagne, the king of legend, was forming around him. And the massive Arnulfing took pains to encourage the legend. It helped to control troops led into an Avarland, or to quiet villagers frantic with fear of the plague. Tall and impressively round in body, he rode at the head of gleaming dukes, lords, and bishops, with the standard of Jerusalem going before and a remarkable elephant following after. He sang with the chanters at the altars and the drinkers in the taverns. This combination of most potential monarch and artful comedian always pleased the crowds.

Yet he could not have anticipated the consequences of his acting an emperor in this fashion.

Being confined now to the palace at Aix, Charlemagne no longer heard the songs of the camps or the miracle tales of the monastic refectories. Because he limped heavily he wore a long mantle edged with ermine. The apple-wood stick had been discarded for a long staff of carved ivory head, the gift of Frisian seal hunters.

At his dawn rising, he allowed himself to be shaved, and even waited for the barber to brush his gray mustache out on both sides. Now that his hair had turned white as old Sturm's, he let it grow down below his ears, so that it resembled a gleaming helmet, bound by the thin gold of the diadem.

The morning that he heard about the fire, he managed to step through the chamber curtains with an even stride, bracing himself against the pain that shot through his joints.

He greeted Burchard, and Einhard the fosterling, hearing from them that Arno had sent Croat Christians to take oath to him, and that the count waited with the case of the Saxon family.

The lawmen made much of this suit of the slain Westfalian grandsire. In Witukind's day, this Saxon grandsire had been baptized. Although a Christian and a sword-bearing noble, he had been slain by mishap when Charles the king's son had ravaged the Westfalian *pagus.* Then the Saxon's son had renounced claim to a death amend by

swearing loyalty to Charles. So far, it was well enough. Yet in the disorder of the last campaigns in Saxonland, this father, a free man and vassal of Charles, had been carried off into exile with his family by the dragnet that swept so many into new homes in Frankland. Now the three sons, tall youths bearing weapons, brought suit to recover their ancestral lands in Westfalia, since they were the heirs of the dead grandsire who had possessed the lands.

Being Saxons, these three appealed to Saxon law. But were they exiles or free men? In the archives at Aix they were written down as exiles. Saxon law laid down that "Only by the king's will may an exiled noble be granted possession of his property again."

The lawmen had argued the case with determination, without finding an answer. Reluctantly the Count of the Palace had granted their appeal to the lord king.

Charlemagne looked toward the three young Saxons. Straight they stood, flushed with excitement, their blue eyes reflecting awe and expectancy. At their age, they knew him only as the great king who had driven the raiding Northmen from Westfalia. They would make the best soldiers—

"I grant it," he announced. "As loyal servants, they shall inherit the property."

Burchard, making a note on his tablet, muttered something like, "And how many other thousand Saxons!"

As he passed the kneeling boys, Charlemagne could not resist glancing at their exultant faces. He looked at the Croats, dark men with white felt cloaks and silver armlets. They had brought him a rude silver processional cross, and he was glad that Burchard had selected more valuable gold arm bands as Charlemagne's gifts to them.

He progressed through the throng as far as the stairhead and was listening for the chime of the metal clock that would sound the past-noon hour when he could lead the way to the dining hall, and after staying his hunger could take off his shoes, mantle, and girdle to sleep for two hours or even three.

Then the messenger from the Rhine courier boat came through to report the fire that destroyed the great bridge at Mainz. It had been built with massive strength, to stand forever above the flood waters. Drunken roisterers had dropped their torches into the wooden beams, instead of the river, and in three hours the charred bridge fell into the water.

"We will build it again of stone," he said curtly. But when he dozed that afternoon he could not rest in sleep for wondering how masonry could be arched between stone piers, and how any piers could be raised in midstream. The force of the river was too great.

The force of a spring storm toppled over the covered colonnade that sheltered him on the way to his church. His masons could not bind stones together like the Romans, who had raised the aqueducts. . . . How long had it taken them to build their monumental Rome? Four centuries, Einhard said. That was nonsense that Alcuin could have banished with a jest. These younglings, raised in his palace, told him the *words* of books, not the meanings. Even if those words were clearly inscribed in the new small letters, they could accomplish no more than tiny sticks laid for a fire. The mind itself had to seize on the words and kindle with understanding, as if flame had caught in the sticks.

Yet if understanding came, and the mind strove with clear purpose to achieve something, how could that something be achieved unless by the will of God, the Almighty Father?

No lawmen could answer that question. They looked to him. Burchard waited for his word to plant the new seed grain from Africa; Arno sent the Croats to him. The broken colonnade, the fallen bridge, the graves of the plague-slain and the beseeching of their thousands of sons all waited to be preserved by him. . . .

When he stirred up from his nap, the pages of the sleeping chamber found him limping in his blue mantle toward the stair that led to the church. They called Rothaid from the gossiping ladies, to tell him this was the hour when he must take his throne seat to hear the fiscal reports of the Thuringian bishops, and the codification of his judgments in law matters.

At this time in the afternoon the body fire that the physicians called fever wearied him, and confused his thoughts. Often he looked at the faces ranged around him, to remember what he must do next. Burchard urged him to send for his surviving son, by Hildegard. But Louis was on the Spanish March with the host of Aquitaine; the boy had his duties there. Charlemagne put Burchard off, and did not send for Louis.

There in the south the sea border was aflame. The Saracen fleets did not hold back for the truce signed at Córdoba. The Moors of Spain joined with their brethren from Africa; they swept over Corsica again, and Sardinia, landing on the mainland at Nicaea (Nice) and at Narbona, and the Tuscan coast. Leo's forts could not move to meet the incoming ships. One hope Charlemagne held to. A Byzantine fleet had been sighted off Sicily.

If the arm of the other emperor reached out from Constantinople to aid him, in this fashion, the two of them might keep the coasts safe, even if the isles were lost.

Charlemagne nursed that hope. He had failed to launch strong fleets; his clumsy craft of green wood had been scattered and driven as if by blasting winds. When he sat down at the silver table he studied the plan of Constantine's great city. Surely it had mighty harbors and an arsenal, with the buildings called University where—his envoys said—the Greeks made an unquenchable flame named Sea Fire, because it burned on the water. This Greek flame could destroy enemy vessels.

Who was his envoy at Constantinople? Hugo, the young count of Tours, and Amalhar the bishop. Hugo reported faithfully that the peace treaty could not be signed because the weak Michael had been exiled by a stronger soldier called the Armenian. No one could be certain of this Armenian's policy, except that he did not favor images. . . . Strange it was that Irene, a scheming woman, had been devoted to the holy images. . . . Charlemagne waited for Amalhar to return with the peace treaty sign ed.

Anxiety weighed on him since the loss of Charles and Pepin. Both his hands had rested on those two strong sons. Now he labored alone, using his ivory staff as if it were a new kind of scepter, walking slowly bareheaded through the broken corridor, waiting for tidings that would ease his despair.

He counted the weeks until he could put aside his staff, and robes, to mount for the hunting. When he could take the road to the Ardennes with his huntsmen, the devil of fever would leave him, and he could sleep until sunrise showed the tree branches in shadow shapes upon the tent over his head.

Before then would come the assembly of the seigneurs, and the plans for the next year. This year the assembly must be at Aix.

When he told Burchard that, the Constable nodded, in silence.

"Bernard must make the journey from Pavia to be at the gathering. Adalhard can wait at Rome."

His officer assented and said gravely that the Count of the Breton March could not leave his post, because of restlessness among the Breton folk. And the lords of the Basque mountains with the Gascons could be counted out; they had deserted the armed host of Aquitaine.

The words stirred memories in the aged king. Thirty and five years before, Roland had been the Warden of the Breton March, and the armed host had fallen before the Basques at Roncesvalles—the place no one mentioned now.

"You say the Basques have deserted?" he asked.

His sharp tone alerted his commander of the armed forces. "The report is, Lord King, they have left the standard of Louis the king, and disappeared into their mountains."

"Where—does Louis bear his standard?"

"Toward Huesca, by the Ebro."

Charlemagne had known that. He only wanted the officer to confirm it. Huesca had revolted from his rule; it lay near to Saragossa.

In memory he beheld the red heights of Spain, against the thin blue of the sky. He felt the heat of the sun striking through him at dawn. A land of treachery and hidden danger. In his mind he weighed the heedlessness of Louis, the boy's blind trust in the protection of the Lord. The Basques had vanished into their mountains. Again he searched his memory, listening to the warning of the warrior, William of Toulouse. Above the road the empty hills were a sign of danger, because the shepherds had driven off their flocks. The memories brought deep foreboding.

One son he had left to him. What his labor had created depended now on the survival of Louis, the heir. The flames of torches tossed away had destroyed his Rhine bridge, massive and enduring. How much more fragile was the rule of a dozen peoples!

"Lord Constable," he said, formally, "send at once to Louis, my son, my wish and command that he return at speed from the Ebro March. With his standard and the armed levies."

His memory quested along the valley of the Ebro, climbing to the two passes, one perilous and one safe. Burchard, surprised and attentive, waited for him to finish speaking.

"I wish the route of his return to be by Urgel, the town, and the pass of the Perch, to his city of Toulouse, then hither in his own good time."

"By Urgel and the pass of the—Perch," murmured Burchard, who had a way of repeating orders. Curiously he stared up at the old man, who seemed to be lost in brooding. Had he anything more to add?

Twisting the signet ring on his thick finger, Charlemagne roused from brooding. The summer's assembly would be festive, he said slowly, and the lay and ecclesiastical lords would come not for a campaign but to render fealty to Louis, his son, as emperor. It was time that his son received the crown. (He said nothing of summoning Leo, the Pope, to bestow it.) Let the lord Seneschal prepare to entertain mighty people in all their numbers.

"For joyous tidings have come to us by land and by sea," Charlemagne informed his paladins. "Never have our land and our folk been more blessed by the mercies of the Lord God. It is fitting that in peace and glory, the Lord aiding, my son shall take the title of emperor, together with me, to be emperor alone at my death."

So great appeared his anticipation that his paladins felt relief and joy in their turn. Einhard told the physicians and they were glad that the sick man had at last called his strong son to his side.

Alone in his sleeping chamber that night, Charlemagne counted over the weeks to come, and decided that Louis would begin his journey by early Hay Month, and the coronation would he held at Second Cropping. Then, by the moon of the Vintage Month he could summon his huntsmen and take the road to the Ardennes.

The legend grew that summer. Where the lords' cavalcades filled the highroads, they held festival. Where the monastic trains of hooded folk wound down from the hills, they chanted prayers for the emperors twain. From Orléans, where Theodulf joined him, to Theodo's Villa the folk made holyday when Louis passed with the array of his kingdom. Yet when the throngs cried acclaim they shouted also for the mighty Charlemagne in his city of glory.

It was a fortunate journey, said the seigneurs of Provence, for they had come unharmed through the Pyrenees, despite the trap laid for them by the treacherous Basques, "as they are wont to do."

Although short in stature as his grandsire, Louis made a brave appearance, broad in shoulders and erect, zealous in praying at the shrines. Gentle they called him, handsome and pious.

The throngs filled the valley of the Würm, and pavilions rose on the far hills. For Charlemagne had summoned in all bishops and abbots; for weeks he held them in council "to decide among themselves all matters for the good of the empire." On the reading stand before Hildebald—who had come from the Colony to be archchaplain of Aix—lay the great Bible of Alcuin's making.

Long did these lords of the churches debate the new laws, the tithes, and benefices, while Charlemagne waited with his staff, on his field stool by the Mary Church. They went out to him with their opinions and his high voice exhorted them to greater things. "You have numbered the vices of these, my people; now list what good works you have done . . . there is no dignity save in merit of works . . . you say there is peace and accord; show me the compacts of peace you have made with my counts who accuse you of quarreling . . . for after the emperor, the duty of governing the people of God lies between you and those counts!"

Not speedily did these lords of minsters and monasteries reach agreements that pleased their emperor. The rumor of their debates passed out to the farmers and the pilgrims at evensong.

Some of the visitors noticed how beggars showed their sores at the portals of the palace; vagabonds skulked by walls to slit purses. Prostitutes rode in with the merchants' carts from Pavia and Passau. In ribbons and pheasant plumes they walked the courtyards with eyes for ermine cloaks passing and the flash of jeweled hands. For a silver solidus or whispered promise of a lusty half hour the doorkeepers let in the women. Servitors in the corridors took more money from them and snickered, whispering that the birds of finest feather nested upstairs in the royal chambers, and charged a higher price.

Bernard the young king came in from Italy with his four half-grown sisters and knew not where to quarter them because the women's chambers babbled and reeked like a brothel. Charlemagne quartered the young girls, his grandchildren, among the girls of his concubines. Sometimes he could not remember the names of the younglings. With the elfin Rothaid, Adelinda the Saxon beauty reigned in this roost, because she was mother of Thierry, the seven-year boy, last to be born to him.

To Bernard the old emperor babbled how his enthroned son and grandson must nourish and minister to this tender brood of children.

When Louis the Pious came in, he eyed with disdain the bedizened women, thinking of the good Hildegard, his mother. He took up his residence with Hildebald, and his father allowed it.

Charlemagne greeted his son with tears of joy, for now in his weakness he wept and laughed easily. Anxiously his glance swept the faces behind Louis, recognizing with relief Bera the Visigoth. But Sancho the Wolf, hero of the Basques, was not in the king's following; Rostaing of the Gironne, who had carried the standard, had not come.

So the disloyal had deserted his son. Louis, joyful at beholding the gold dome of the Chapel, recked little of it. Yet loyalty was the first link in the chain that bound together the Christian people. Without loyalty there could be neither good will nor honesty. How many links were needed to make strong the chain? Nourishment from the harvests joined to trustworthy money, they stretched all the way to the anchor link of armed force, by sea and land. That last link he had never been able to forge. He had tempered it in the blood of his champions, of Roland and Eric, Gerold and Audulf.

Now, enthroned before the western windows, he greeted his liegemen assembled in the great hall. When he heard murmurings of evil tidings from the Campanian coast, he told his liegemen of final peace, by Adalhard's making, with the last of the Lombards, the Beneventans. The peril of the Saracen fleets had allied together Greeks, Lombards, and Franks, to resist them. When the Count of the East reported the pressure of Slavs, he retorted that Hohbuki had been won back. If Huesca had been lost, the watch castles of the Pyrenees stood safe, owing to the merit of Louis the king, and the providence of the Lord God.

Every day he searched the faces before him for that of Amalhar the bishop, who was on the road from Constantinople. If Amalhar could arrive, to set between his hands the signed peace of the other emperor—then the coronation of Louis would be fortunate in omen.

By the dawn of the coronation day, Amalhar had not arrived. Charlemagne limped from his curtain and eased his weight down on the bench, with a grateful sigh, to be shaved and combed.

The sky over the hills seemed to be clear. Pointing at it, he said, "A good sign. Are not the storms of strife and famine ending? Never has a day come with so much of peace and charity awaiting us."

Then, feeling the iron knife edge caressing his jaw and the ivory comb stroking his head, he slumbered. The illness had taken from him the small store of strength remaining at his age of seventy-one. He had become a mask, a moving image of majesty. One step following the other, he drew himself through the ritual of ruling, sustained by a reflex of his will. He could no longer separate in his mind his brood of grandchildren, the younglings of his family, from the empire he had made. The need of the gangling bastard Thierry joined with the necessity of Amalhar's coming. . . .

In the full morning of that eleventh of September, 813, he entered the nave of his church, while they sang, "The Cross of the faithful. . . . " One step after the other, he passed between the dark columns toward the myriad lights of the altar. Leaning on the strong shoulder of his son, he did not need his staff. His head bore the imperial crown, on his chest a heavy chain of gold bore the regal insignia. As nearly as Charlemagne could tell, he wore the robes of the ancient emperors.

Beheld in this manner by the priesthood at either side and by the nobility in the gallery, Charlemagne towered among them in majesty. Kneeling in prayer, rising to turn at the altar, where rested the other crown, he seemed to them to be vital with hope and power. When he spoke of Louis as a true son and true servant of the Lord, they shed tears of rejoicing. When he asked if they were agreed that he should grant the crown of the empire to this son, the king of Aquitaine, they responded with one voice that it should be done, "by the will of God and the interest of the empire."

Only when Charlemagne faced his son and questioned him as to his will to carry out the duties of ruler did his voice ramble unexpectedly. After demanding of him the protection of all churches, the charity toward all in misery, Charlemagne went on, "And to be at all times merciful to your sisters, to your nephews and nieces, as well as all others of your blood."

Again he asked his son to swear to do so, and Louis gave his oath. Then Charlemagne placed the crown upon the head of his son, and prayed: "Blessed is the Lord God who gave my eyes to behold this day a son of mine upon my throne."

The throng shouted, "Long life to Louis, emperor and Augustus!"

Hildebald advanced to the altar to celebrate the Mass, and the song began, "Come Holy Spirit . . . "

To the watchers at that moment, Charlemagne was clothed in more than majesty. He stood by the altar, summoning them forward like an apostle of the old, miraculous age. The boy, Bernard, came forward for consecration as king of the Lombards.

They held festival that afternoon with high heart. For days the lords of the realm swore fealty to Louis, their co-emperor, and Charlemagne heaped upon his son the richest gifts. No one except Burchard, and Charlemagne himself, remembered that Amalhar had not returned from Constantinople.

Yet they were surprised when Charlemagne bade his son journey back to Aquitaine, where his duties awaited him. "So that," a chronicler explained, "the Lord Emperor might retain his title with accustomed honor."

The physicians and Einhard were deeply disturbed, because the ailing father had need of the son's strength. Moreover the place of an emperor of the realm was not far off, in Aquitaine. But there seemed to be no realization in Charlemagne that another could share his rule at Aix. Obediently Louis departed, leaving questioning behind him.

The vintage moon was rising. It stood over the wall of the pine trees, lighting the crowded city and the silver thread of the river. At night the cold breath of autumn came from the forest. Charlemagne counted the days until he could ride into the forest to rest.

Under the moon Aix resumed its wonted shape. The pavilions were gone from the hills. After sunset few lights showed. In the forest red sparks gleamed where leaves burned. The cattle were turned out to second-crop the garnered fields. Charlemagne summoned his four huntsmen, asking for mastiff dogs and horses to be readied. They were ready.

The physicians begged him not to go forth into the cold. He said he would not fare to the dark Ardennes but to the near preserves of Aix. He told Burchard the things to be done. Walking at night, he felt his way to the candles that burned in the Treasury and Vestiary. For a space he looked at the sealed chests. He sought out the silent Rothaid where she slept apart from other women, and bade her have care of the boy Thierry, born like herself out of wedlock.

One dawn hour he went to the private door of the Mary Church, unshaved and unrobed. He had on the sheepskin jacket and the blue mantle, and he felt at ease. After he had made his prayer, he looked over the vessels on the altar, and the lamps that he had ordered to be kept alight. Then he went out to summon the huntsmen.

"He set out to hunt as usual," Einhard wrote, "although weak from age. From the hunt near Aix the Chapel he returned about the first day of November. There in January

he was seized with a high fever and took to his bed. He prescribed fasting for himself as he usually did with fever. Yet he suffered from a pain in the side that the Greeks call pleurisy; still he persisted in fasting, with only occasional drinks to keep up his strength. On the seventh day after he took to his bed, he died at the third hour of the morning, after partaking of the holy communion, in the seventy-second year of his age."

Charlemagne died in January 814. A few days after that Amalhar, the bishop envoy, arrived from Constantinople with the treaty of peace between the two empires signed. But Charlemagne was no longer there to enforce it and to try to join together the divided halves of Christian rule.

From the first day there was a sense of the unusual in the death of the monarch who had dominated the lives of so many people for nearly forty-six years. Louis, absent in the south, could not take over the direction. Charlemagne had neglected to tell his officers where he wished to be buried. The paladins consulted together and decided to entomb the aged body the next day in royal regalia within a marble sarcophagus beneath the altar of his basilica at Aix, the city he had created. Then, too, only young children led by Rothaid appeared in the mourning procession from the palace.

Stirred by the improvised burial, the people of Aix very quickly remembered portents of the end—how a trembling of the earth had shaken down Charlemagne's colonnade not long before, and a bolt of lightning had struck the dome of the Mary Church, knocking the gilt ball to earth.

In the chapel itself they pointed out to Einhard how the inscription on the cornice above the lower piers had changed mysteriously. In the two words *Karolus Princeps,* the red of the title word had faded away until it could barely be seen. And Einhard thereupon recalled how in the earlier year of the sun's eclipse a flaming light had crossed the sky, to dash Charlemagne's spear from his hand and so forecast the approaching end of his rule.

Such portents could only mean that the hand of the Lord lay upon Frankland. What would follow, if not some change in their world? So, to the widespread sense of loss was joined fear for themselves, deprived of Charlemagne's protection. Out in the villages reassuring rumors sprang up that the great king had not actually died—he slept in his tomb, to waken again if calamity came. Yet fearful throngs of men and women deserted their homes to seek the security of the monasteries—a proceeding that would have drawn an angry tirade from the living Charlemagne.

When Louis arrived at last from Aquitaine, the young emperor proved himself both conscientious and fanatically devout. With care he carried out all his father's directions for the disposal of the palace treasure. At the same time he named four arbiters to comb out of the palace chambers the bevy of privileged women and hangers-on. Beggars and bribe-hungry doorkeepers were driven from the portals, while jugglers and dancing bears were banned as creatures of the Devil.

Louis ordered an arch of gold to be raised over the tomb with the words:

> BENEATH THIS LIES THE BODY
> OF CHARLES, GREAT AND DEVOUT EMPEROR
> WHO NOBLY ENLARGED THE KINGDOM OF THE FRANKS.

Very quickly, however, a change took place. Louis the Pious held himself to be a devout emperor, heir of the Roman emperors. Ruling with beneficial tolerance, he held splendid audiences and assumed the title of Emperor Augustus, which his father had avoided using. At Ingelheim's palace he ordered paintings to show on the walls the victories of Charles the Hammer, the founding of the cities of Rome and Constantinople, and the crowning of his father.

With zeal Louis undertook the duty of caring for the churches, yet he did not ride the width of the provinces and the length of the coasts. The mass of people knew him only by name, and were constrained to seek mercy and aid from their local seigneurs. Without the magic of Charlemagne's name, their loyalty turned more toward the counts and dukes. These also became more independent of the emperor at Aix.

In the family itself Louis conscientiously protected the younglings, the chance-born brood of Charlemagne. (Many of the children became noted in later years, as chroniclers like Nithard, or heads of abbeys like Thierry.) Yet in Italy Bernard, headstrong as his grandfather at that age, revolted against his imperial uncle, and Theodulf, that man of imagination, joined the revolt, which was wiped out in blood.

Lacking force to control the flux of his dominion, Louis the Pious followed the example of his ancestors in partitioning it among three sons. In his case they survived him, and his death began their struggle for mastery. A poet wrote of their battle at Fontenoy in 841:

> The cry of war is here,
> And over there fierce fighting breaks forth,
> Where brother brings down brother . . .
> Their ancient kindness forespent.

Louis had been devout. But religion alone could not hold together this nascent *imperium* of Christians. It had been fostered by the personalities of Charles the Hammer and Pepin the Short. It had been shaped and enlarged by Charlemagne. Without him, lacking racial base or lasting institutions, it ceased to be.

Oddly enough, Louis had been the first to name himself Roman emperor, when the western empire was ending and the chaos of feudal Europe beginning. Suddenly the Rhine ceased to be a mighty arterial and became an embattled barrier between the Germanic-speaking folk to the north and east, and the romance-speaking peoples of West Francia and Aquitaine—between the future Germany and France. Charlemagne's communication corridor from the Lowlands, over the Alps into Italy, was lost in the feudal kaleidoscope—except for a shadowy "Lotharingia"—and the plains of Lombardy became again a road of conquest, while isolated cities fortified themselves with higher walls, ruled by their own dukes of the palace and guilds of the market place, to become a Milan, Florence, Ferrara. And the Venetians on Rialto's isle sought their future on the sea.

Elsewhere, with the shattering of Charlemagne's *imperium,* feudal vassals clung to their fiefs, and the abbeys to their benefices. Soon they would defy the central authority of kings. Papal Rome, unable to summon the armed force of a Pepin or Charlemagne from the outside, would sink into new weakness. Some fragments of the Carolingian frontier zones would develop into new communities, in northern, Christian Spain and along the Danube, where Austria would take shape out of the East March.

But while the brief Carolingian dynasty failed and the nascent empire died, something else survived unnoticed and almost unrecorded. The Carolingian renaissance went on.

It endured through the failure of government and the wars, a fragile heritage of knowledge and hope. Charlemagne's School, Alcuin's fellowship of minds, Angilbert's half-heeded songs, Theodulf's open law courts and strong-ribbed churches were the pioneer efforts of a wider recovery. The chapel of Aix, the palace of Ingelheim, the community of St. Denis gained new, small splendors. Charlemagne's life line of the churches, from Bremen to Tortosa, did not break down entire.

The great Gregorian chants, the sacramentaries and breviaries, Alcuin's new Bible, passed outward in the silence of the monasteries. The copying of books in the clear Carolingian script went on. The verses of Virgil and the vision of St. Augustine reached greater numbers of untaught minds. They went from abbeys and palaces to the parish schools. They escaped destruction in the barbarian invasions because they could not well be looted or burned. They fled with the monks inland to the mountains, to Reichenau and the lake of Constance, where artists gained new skill in illumination.

The Carolingian writing penetrated to Italy, as far as Monte Cassino. In Anglo-Saxon England, a king of Wessex, Alfred the Great, struggling himself to keep culture alive by copying books, sent to Frankland for instructors like John the Saxon.

By then the memory of the real Charlemagne had become obscured. It appeared for the last time in many centuries when Einhard the Dwarfling retired to the Benedictine monastery that he had enriched with relics brought from Rome in his journeys. There Einhard penned his loving portrait of his great king and companion, the *Vita Karoli.* Yet to his human portrait the Dwarfling added nostalgic touches, as well as a few attributes of his other hero of imagination, Augustus Caesar. By that time, a dozen years after his death, the real Charlemagne began to assume the physical likeness of the legendary king.

The remembrance of his lust for women did not vanish without a trace. An obscure monk wrote a *Vision of Charlemagne* relating how the mighty Frank carried away a saintly virgin, one Amalberga, to his palace and in consequence now suffered the torments of purgatory. But this was a lone voice, soon lost in the chorus of *cantilènes,* folk tales, and monastic rewriting of the life and deeds of the son of Pepin the Short.

For, by some alchemy of human imagination, Charlemagne became the hero, not of court chronicles or of his own Franks but of whoever wrote, told, or sang in the new calamities of western Europe. He became, as it were, the heroic monarch of humanity at large.

Soon after Einhard the student poet Walafrid Strabo wrote a foreword to the former's *Vita Karoli.* While Strabo seemed to know the facts about the dead king, his "most glorious Emperor Charles" already showed traces of the remarkable monarch of a golden age. " . . . beyond all kings he was most eager in making search for wise men . . . he rendered his kingdom which was dark and blind (if I may use such an expression) when God put it into his hands, radiant with the blaze of fresh learning, unknown until then in our barbarism. But now once more men turn to other interests, and the light of wisdom, less loved, is dying out in most of them."

It is not, perhaps, surprising that Charlemagne's deeds should be exaggerated in this way. But it is extraordinary that in legend he became what he had never been in life.

The real Arnulfing had been rather tall and unusually forceful, particularly in his determination, as well as shrewd in sizing up people. After three generations his wraith, the legendary Charlemagne, changed in physical semblance. It towered above other men by a head, terrifying pagans and foes by the glance of its piercing eyes. It shed the old Frankish dress for imperial robes, and wore a crown when riding to hunt. By its anger it reduced all listeners to trembling silence. Riding back to stricken Roncesvalles, it holds the sun arrested in the sky to prolong the daylight.

In life the hefty Frank had hardly been a figure of kingly dignity. His legendary self became majestic, all-wise and all-powerful. A long beard added dignity to this *aureus Karolus,* this golden Charles. Naturally the body in the tomb at Aix adjusted itself to the legend. There Charlemagne in his long sleep sat erect, a great Gospel book on his knees, his face toward the portal. Since he was not dead, his beard continued to grow, even into the cracks of the stone flagging.

About this time (885) the worthy monk of St. Gall wrote out his *Gesta Karoli*—Deeds of Charles—to depict with his "stammering and toothless tongue" the mighty events of the "golden empire of the illustrious Charles." After hearing echoes of the *cantilènes* of old soldiers, the good monk gives many a realistic twist to his anecdotes of the real, earthly and "most cunning Charles." Yet by now, in his mind, the great king has become an "iron Charles," whose people, "harder than iron themselves, paid universal honor to his hardness of iron."

So in the memory of the monk an invincible Charlemagne ruled over a warlike people during a golden age of security and peace. This is a startling metamorphosis of the Arnulfing who was no leader in battle but who led an unmilitant people out to campaigns for some two-score years.

The invasions were responsible for it.

Charlemagne had not been in his tomb a dozen years when the Northmen began to break through the sea borders. Up the Rhine and the Seine and the Loire their fleets advanced to devastate the cities. There was no longer an army to hold them off. As early as 845 a grandson of Charlemagne watched helplessly with his seigneurs and levies—who refused to attack the formidable invaders—while the Northmen gathered up eleven hundred captives from the Seine villages.

A second Godfried ascended the Loire with his long ships, to loot and burn Tours. Theodulf's Orléans fell to the sea raiders. At. St. Denis they broke open the tombs of the Arnulfings to get at the regalia on the bodies. Up the Meuse they turned to Aix, burning the Mary Church. Between raids they built themselves winter settlements along the coasts.

While the triumphant Dane-Normans ventured as far as Spain, the Moslem fleets of Andalus and North Africa possessed themselves of the western Middle Sea. From their island bases the aggressive Moslems (Abbasids uniting here with Ommayids) seized the land bridge to Italy. After capturing Malta, they concentrated along the Sicilian coast by Palermo, seizing a bridgehead near Salerno and thrusting up into the Adriatic, and the coast to Rome.

Religious zeal drove the Moslem attack forward, but the Arab admirals made use of organized shipping with high technical skill. One of them, off Sicily in 837, matched the "Greek" fire of a Byzantine fleet with new naphtha flame throwers. They gained their objective, which was to pry the Byzantine navy loose from the sea lanes.

At Rome another Leo built a last-ditch defense wall around St. Peter's. Up the Volturno, Arab horsemen advanced to the rock height of Monte Cassino. Only weak resistance met them. The scattered Carolingian kings lacked ships, the Popes had no army; Benevento sought only to defend itself, Venetian warships undertook little so long as their haven at Rialto was safe; the Byzantine navy fought only to keep open the channels of trade.

Constantinople itself, instead of joining forces with this Christian west, withdrew into new isolation. Flotillas from the Russian rivers, led by Scandinavians, plagued the queen city, while the powerful Bulgars gained mastery in the Balkan hinterland and the Dalmatian coast.

Beyond the Bulgars a greater peril appeared from the "great plain of the east." Savage Magyars drove up the Danube into the Bavarian valleys; their horsemen broke through Charlemagne's East March, skirting the Venetian isles, dividing devastated Aix hopelessly from beleaguered Constantinople. Trade of the outer world no longer penetrated to the remnants of Frankland, which were driven inland as they had been before the rise of the first Arnulfings.

Again the surviving Franks were thrown on their bodily resources. A terrible migration began, away from the coasts, the river routes, and fertile valleys, toward safety in the mountains. It turned east. Fugitives took their herds across the Rhine into the Saxon wilderness. They sought refuge in the hilltop castles of strong, fighting seigneurs. Again they were isolated from the boulevards of the sea.

Inertia set in. Except in northern Italy (the old Lombardy) urban life ceased. In Rome, they say that from the year 870 to 1000 no new building was raised or old one repaired. The island of Paris was besieged and sacked by the methodical and militant Northmen. There was no longer any force to protect the Christian people.

Surviving congregations looked for salvation only after death. In the general despair it seemed as if the familiar world were moving toward its end at the year 1000 of salvation—

Through this breakdown of government and interregnum of thought the memory of Charlemagne lingered, and changed. The image of the "unwearied king" who had never despaired merged into that of the lord of Christianity—*sire de la créstienté*—who preserved his people. By comparison his age seemed to be one of enlightened peace.

More than that, by some transmutation of longing, the name of Charlemagne became the hope of the varied Christian peoples. As their sufferings increased, so grew the poignancy of their lost hope.

Something very unusual happened to the memory of Charlemagne as the ninth century ended. Because the civil strife and barbarian invasions devastated so much of his ancestral Frankland, from the Loire to the Rhine, much of the records, the building, the very objects, and local traditions of his time was lost. Teachers and the "hooded folk" fled from the ancient Roman river towns easterly into the mountains. Ironically, many Frankish nobles migrated across the Rhine into the security of the former Saxonland. Monastic settlements of the old East March, from Fulda to St. Gall, became the new survival centers.

The effect of this exodus on the memory of Charlemagne was decisive. Traces of the actual man largely vanished. Tales of the legendary king went with the migrants into new territory. Precious books and relics salvaged from the menaced Rhine valley became the evidence elsewhere of the idealized lord of Christianity.

During the ensuing catastrophic generations little was written of Charlemagne. His memory went, as it were, underground. But it endured. It passed on by travelers' tales and it crept into songs. Monks of Fulda, observing the stars, called the guide stars of the great Bear the *Karlswagen*. Hostel keepers of the Pyrenees pointed out a cross of stone as Charlemagne's. Hunters in the Alps told how a white hart had appeared, to show Charlemagne the road to the east.

At Venice, which he had attempted to master, he became in memory the inspired prophet of the city's preservation. They said there he passed by, and cast a heavy spear into the deepest green water, declaring, "As surely as no one of us will ever see that spear again, your enemies will always be defeated by God's anger."

Dispersed in this fashion by legend tellers, the memory of Charlemagne took root in many lands. Transplanted, it tended to become the image of a universal benevolent monarch. In Saxonland, now the rallying point of Germanic strength, it went through rather remarkable evolution. Tenth-century Teutons seemed to remember him at first as a maker of laws, and then as the king missionary who had brought Christianity to them. Did not his manifold fine wooden churches prove that beyond a doubt?

Did not the illuminated books, the goldwork, and rare ivory carvings at Fulda and Reichenau testify to the splendor of his day? When these East Germans began to offer real resistance both to Northmen and Magyars, their new kings, the Ottos, arose in Saxony with mixed conceptions of Charlemagne. They could not wholly claim him but they could not manage without him. So they claimed him as the first emperor of their *imperium Teutonici*. The first Otto imitated Charlemagne's festivals and had himself crowned in the rebuilt chapel at Aix. The third Otto sought coronation farther afield in Rome, as restorer, after Charlemagne, of the Roman Empire. (The one thing Charlemagne had not sought to restore.)

After revering him as a missionary monarch, and honoring him as the founder of their "empire" (soon to be entitled the meaningless Holy Roman Empire) the Germans began to conceive of Charlemagne as saintly, keeping in touch with heaven through the services of the Angel Gabriel as messenger.

By then the legendary Charlemagne became a force in the minds of men.

The world, although stricken, did not end in the year 1000. New vitality came to Christian Europe, and the legendary Charlemagne also gained new life.

Like a wraith invisible he accompanied pilgrims journeying to shrines. Along the pilgrim routes, monasteries and hostels naturally desired to gain credit, by miracles and relics. What miracle drew such crowds as that of the *sire de la créstienté* prophesying about the place? What relic would be more coveted than a scrap of writing or shred of cloth "truly of Charlemagne himself?"

The road across the Pyrenees became known as the "road of the Franks." (Actually this pilgrim route did not pass through the rather shallow valley called Roncesvalles.) Each halting place revived feverishly the memory of Charlemagne as the purest of the pilgrims, the mightiest of monarchs. All the way to the edge of the fearful western ocean the memory went, to the shrine of St. James of Compostela. Had not Charlemagne been there when he conquered all of Spain, except Saragossa, from the paynim Saracens? True, that great wayfarer had not been able to cross the barrier of ocean. (The remembrance that his course had been checked by the sea persisted for a long time.)

On the roads of Burgundy, the churches cherished priceless relics, drops of the sacred blood bestowed, they said, upon Charlemagne by the patriarch of Jerusalem. (There was still doubt whether Charlemagne had reached Jerusalem himself, but it seemed that he had fared east to Constantinople to advise the lord emperor of the East how to defend himself against the pagans.)

When the poets of Provence found their songs, they delighted hearers with the deeds of Charlemagne, the king and champion of the Lord. And their audiences demanded still more tales of him. On the island of Paris they sang how he had held his court by the rock of Montparnasse, and had blessed the church of St. Geneviève.

When the songs rose into the great *chansons* of a new France, Charlemagne emerged in them, joyful as the monarch of that sweetest land—*"un roi en France de moult grant seignorie."* Had he not devoted himself to good St. Denis from his boyhood? All his life he had labored for the *dolce France.* In their day they were certain their sweet France had extended far indeed, beyond the dark Ardennes, beyond the Alps of the snowy passes, and the land of the Huns, to far Cathay.

With this beginning of feudal life, the image of Charlemagne assumed the attributes of a feudal monarch. Mighty vassals served him—twenty dukes carried the plates to his table. Four kings attended him, and the Pope chanted the Mass for him. At the crowning of his son, Louis, however something unexpected happened that the psychologists of history might trace back to the reality of the coronation at Aix. To Charlemagne's great anger, Louis was afraid to come forward to take the crown!

With the advent of knighthood and the singing of prowess in single combat, the image of Charlemagne—as the champion of sweet France—fell easily into this new mold.

The man who had been such a consummate strategist and prime mover of peoples in real life became a warrior king in the new style, capable of splitting an armored foeman apart from helm to saddle with one blow of his sword. The man who had tried to keep his Franks out of ranged battle now decided wars by a single triumphant onset and onfray of lances. His iron broadsword—which the records of his time mention only during ceremonies—also gained new personality. *Joyuese* by name, forged of the finest steel, it bore within its hilt the most precious of relics, a fragment of the Sacred Lance. Since minstrels of this later day turned quickly to the love interests of their heroes, Charlemagne also fared forth on behalf of a matchless damsel who was usually the daughter of the Saracen monarch of Spain, converted by Charlemagne from the devil worship of "Mahom" to Christianity. His brood of lusty daughters vanished into the person of a single, virtuous, lily-white and rose-red *Bellisent.*

Nothing that appealed to the popular fancy was denied this "first king of France, crowned by God while the angels sang." Even at the advanced age of two hundred years, he rises from his ivory throne and summons his failing strength to go to their aid, with the cry "Barons of France—to horse and to arms!" Mothers in the cottages consoled their children in hardship by repeating, "When Charlemagne beheld our misery he shed tears from his eyes that ran down his long nose, and all down his white beard and fell to the neck of his horse."

Jealously the imagination of the French nation claimed the Charlemagne of legend as its own. At the same time the aspect of the sleeper in the tomb at Aix changed to conform to the legend. From the diadem of gold, a veil descended over his face. His gloved left hand supported the gold-bound Gospel on his knees, while his right hand held erect his bared sword "drawn for ever against his enemies."

This ghost of the Arnulfin very soon became visible to the eyes of the curious. Illuminators of the manuscripts of his legend painted him aroused from sleep by good St. James, or riding into Constantinople; woven into tapestries, he bore the regalia of later-day majesty, ermine and velvet, on his body, orb and scepter in his hands. Goldworkers shaped reliquaries for his bones or belongings (his body had been exhumed, to be clad in, among other things, a mantle of purple Byzantine silk, adorned with elephants). When stained glass gave splendor to churches, the Charlemagne of fable stood revealed to the congregations.

To these convincing pictures there was soon added a biography. A monk of Châlons wishing to honor his patron saint, James of Compostela, gathered out of the legends a really marvelous life of Charlemagne for the instruction of future generations.

With that the image of Charlemagne became, after more than three centuries, monarch of a world of wish fulfillment in which Normans were driven into the sea, and Saracens expelled from Christendom, and the aid of the Lord brought to sorrowing human beings.

Perhaps only in such an age of growing faith and vitality could a legend leave its imprint on royal courts, national institutions, laws and monastic life, as well as popular literature and arts. But the legendary Charlemagne did that.

A real mystery of his lifetime overshadowed medieval Europe. What, exactly, had been the empire of Charlemagne? Was it the *imperium Christianum?* Men of the churches argued so. Was it the *Imperium Romanorum?* The Papal court maintained so, arguing that it possessed still the authority by which Leo had crowned Charlemagne emperor in Rome. Was it the *imperium Francorum?* The newly risen German monarchs claimed that Charlemagne had founded their Germanic empire. One of them contrived to have him canonized, locally, to begin the cult of Charlemagne. All three concepts were denied by the French, who claimed him as their first king.

So began the long disputation of the powers and principalities of the western, Christian Europe that Charlemagne had tried in vain to gather into a whole. Monarchs of the Holy Roman Empire—which never united Europe—looked back to Charlemagne. Frederick Barbarossa invoked his deeds as precedents for his own ambition; Frederick II staged anew the exhumation of the skeleton, to wrap a new mantle over the elephant shroud, and in our modern age Napoleon Bonaparte, calling himself emperor of the French, invoked the memory of "our predecessor, Charlemagne." But all that lies within the record of history, not of the legend.

It refused to die. It could not be localized. At Aix-la-Chapelle they said that the church bells rang without human touch when Charlemagne died. In the mountains of Bavaria they said that Charlemagne waited there, within a cavern. In the Rhineland they said that when Charlemagne's beard grew three times around his tomb, the end of the world would come.

When the Christians of Spain began their long struggle for freedom with the kalifs of Córdoba, their minstrels told how Charlemagne had gone that way before them, with Roland. The memory of his paladins changed into the Twelve Peers, heroes of other legends, now serving Charlemagne—Oliver, and Ogier the Dane, brave Duke Naimes of Bavaria, and the valiant archbishop Turpin.

When Gascons and Provençals rode to this war they carried the banner of Charlemagne, the standard of Jerusalem, now the oriflamme of France.

Around them the immortal *Song of Roland* took shape, with its burden of courage and death.

When men in the west, from England to the Rhineland, left their homes to journey forth on the first crusade, there was a lifting of spirits, a sense of a new horizon to be found, that had not been felt since the time of Charlemagne.

To the crusaders on ship or shore minstrels sang how Charlemagne had gained Jerusalem before them from the Saracen Harun. He had voyaged to Jerusalem, to the land of the apostles, to guard the Sepulcher itself.

So the image of Charlemagne remained a force in the minds of humanity at large, summoning them forth from their homes. It went with wayfarers as far as the roads led.

The barbarian Arnulfing who built his city in the forest and raised the small gray Mary Church had become a memory jealously possessed, striding over Europe—a memory of a day now vanished when Christians had somehow gathered together to seek their Lord.

Norman Susskind (essay date 1961)

SOURCE: "Humor in the Chansons de Geste," *Symposium* Vol. XV, No. 3 , Fall, 1961, pp. 185-97.

[*In the following essay, Susskind explores the various types of comedy employed in the* chansons de geste, *considers the butts of the jokes and ridicule, and speculates that one of humor's functions was to inject some realism into the depiction of events and characters.*]

The mood of the chanson de geste was never unremittingly sombre. Curtius has remarked that from late antiquity the epic, considered on a level with pleasures of the table and the performance of mimes, contained a mixture of the comic and the serious: "When the medieval Latin, the earliest French, and the earliest Spanish epic conform in this, we may conclude that a comic element had always been part of the stock of medieval epic and was not introduced by corrupt minstrels."[1]

To be sure, instances of humor in the *Chanson de Roland* are few and far between, but from this no generalization should be derived concerning the genre as a whole, for the oldest and finest of Old French epics is also decidedly atypical. Even from the point of view that most of the extant poems represent a corruption of earlier, nobler, more serious works such as the *Roland,* it must be admitted that the chanson de geste, *as we know it,* is much better exemplified by some epics of the Guillaume cycle than by that of Roncevalles. As shown by Hugo Theodor,[2] the dosage of humor increases in the later chansons, but we should remember that it was always prominent in the Guillaume d'Orange epics, the earliest of which may be nearly contemporaneous with the *Chanson de Roland.*

The epic heroes themselves, although dedicated, beset by hardships, and capable of superhuman feats, were not described as maintaining an inhuman severity; a sense of humor was not inconsistent with the image of the ideal knight. In several works there is mention of a customary delight in off-duty joking. In *Girart de Vienne*,[3] Aude, trying to prevent a fight between Olivier and Lanbert, assures the latter that if he surrenders he will have a very comfortable and enjoyable captivity: "Et en mes chanbres le venir et l'aler, / Et avec moi le rire et le gaber" (vv. 3517-18). In the *Pèlerinage*,[4] Charlemagne, explaining to King Hugh the outrageous "gabs" made by himself and the peers, says: "It is the custom in France, in Paris and in Chartres, that when the French are in bed they joke and laugh and speak both wisdom and folly" (vv. 654-56).

So we know that they enjoyed a good laugh, but what was it that aroused the risibilities of the characters and presumably of the audience of a chanson de geste? In attempting to identify passages of comic intent, I have been guided substantially by the occurrence of the verbs "rire" and "gaber," but make no claim to complete objectivity in the application of this method. The vocabulary of mirth in the chansons was extremely limited, and consequently "rire" was richer in nuances than it is today. It appeared in the typical description of a young hero ("le visage riant"), in expressions of affection and good will, and to show enjoyment of diversions other than comic: "Ainçois l'amoient por ce qu'el les fet rire, / Qui chante et note, nus ne la puet desdire, / Lais et biax sons et harpes d'armonie" (*Mort Aymeri*,[5] vv. 3101-03). Some use of subjective judgment was clearly indispensable.

Among the obvious laugh-provoking phenomena are those that fall under the general heading of "démesure." The texts give evidence of a strong sense of propriety regarding not only behavior, but physical attributes as well. Prodigies of size and strength were of course both feared and respected, but there was about their abnormality a ludicrousness that evoked amusement as well as awe. Society, as Bergson stated in *Le Rire,* demands a certain adaptability of its members, and derides all manifestations of inflexibility. An element of comedy is thus inherent in the very nature of the chanson de geste, which presents heroes whose awful stature and prowess make them formidable combatants and at the same time ludicrous civilians: heavy tanks in midtown traffic. In the *Moniage II*,[6] for example, Guillaume bumps his head while entering the house of an average-sized hermit, to whom he complains about the small scale of the building. The hermit replies that he made it for himself, not for someone of Guillaume's proportions. "Lors comenchierent li doi preudome a rire" (v. 2189).

The ambivalent feeling mentioned above is abundantly documented. A characteristic passage occurs in *Renaut de Montauban*[7] when Renaut, penitent, volunteers to carry stones and mortar for masons building the Cologne cathedral. The other workers cannot resist laughing at the incredible strength he displays, even though they realize that he could replace them all and thus take away their livelihood (p. 447, vv. 5-8). At least one of Guillaume's superhuman feats elicits the same sort of reaction. In the *Moniage* I, refused entry into the monastery, he breaks

down the door, which falls on and mortally wounds the "portier." The bourgeois who have witnessed this scene caution each other not to give way to their urge to laugh, for fear that the giant may turn his wrath against them (vv. 1873-79).

Though excessive endowment with the desirable attributes of size and strength had its comical aspect, the redoubtable nature of such abnormality imposed some restraint on the beholder's desire to laugh. On the other hand, in the case of weakness or deformity, ridicule was untrammeled.

In *Aliscans*,[8] Rainouart, in quest of food, forces his way into a monastery and compels a reluctant host to lead him, on the run, to the kitchen: "Rainouart laughed when he saw him limp" (vv. 3621-22). The enemy in *Aspremont*[9] refers to Charlemagne as "li fil au nain." His father, Pepin, they say, was so short that he could roll, and you could play with him as with a ball (vv. 1131-33).

Mutilated enemies were often subjected to cruel jibes. This is particularly evident in the bloodthirsty epic *Raoul de Cambrai*.[10] In one well known passage, Raoul, having cut off the leg of one antagonist and the hand of another, offers them both what he calls marvelous jobs: one will be his watchman, the other his doorkeeper (vv. 2928-30). Later, Raoul's uncle, Guerri, joins in the fun at the expense of the same victims, telling one of them: "By the absence of your left hand you remind me of a jay perched in the tree where I like to shoot. I take off his foot, leaving the rest of his leg intact" (vv. 5031-33).

Among physical peculiarities, the one most generally disapproved and universally derided was obesity, a characteristic still "always good for a laugh" in present-day low comedy. A striking example is found in *Renaut de Montauban*, where Beuves d'Aigremont, haughty, formidable, but alas cruel and intractable, is stripped of a measure of his dignity by the seemingly gratuitous mention of a physical detail. When his life is saved by one of his knights who uses his own body to shield the duke from a sword-thrust, the poet comments: "Dead is the knight, who did not deserve to die, for the love of his lord, who had a fat neck" (p. 17, vv. 26-27). In a more typical passage, this one from the *Chanson de Saisnes*,[11] Baudouin unhorses a Saxon chief. He then gaily assures the latter that he did it in self-defense, and advises him in any case to delay his bid for revenge, saying: "Wait here for your men. Your paunch is so heavy that if you try to remount unaided you will hurt yourself" (vv. 4209-11).

We have hitherto been dealing with deviations from the normal in physical appearance and capabilities. Much more comedy was seen in improprieties of behavior, prominent among which, and linked naturally to the derisible trait of obesity, is overindulgence of the appetites. Of the myriad insults exchanged by allies and enemies alike in the chansons, none is more often repeated than the word "glutton." Indeed, excessive concern with keeping the belly full is the very antithesis of the knightly ideal.[12] This is made quite explicit in several of the texts. In *Girart de Vienne,* young Aymeri, angered by his uncle's knights, tells them they are like the base peasant who can have no joy until he has filled his stomach. "Girart l'antant, si s'en rit volentiers" (v. 1597).

Women are sometimes reminded scornfully of their unmanliness by reference to the restriction of their activities to the satisfaction of their appetites. The violent Raoul de Cambrai, rejecting some excellent advice given him by his mother, says he can have no respect for the nobleman who accepts the counsel of women. "Go to your rooms," he says, "take your ease, and concentrate on eating and drinking to fatten your paunch, for you have no business meddling in other affairs" (vv. 1100-06).

It was possible for a knight to consume great quantities of food, on occasion, without compromising his reputation. He could also drink any amount of wine, provided he stopped short of inebriation. Similarly, his appetite for female companionship could be indulged if it did not detract from his availability or efficiency as a fighting man, but the knight who pursued the ladies to the detriment of his primary mission became a target for ridicule. Even the mighty Guillaume is not entirely blameless in this respect:

> En la Prise d'Orange, el guerrero se pone en gran aprieto con sus dos compañeros, impulsado por su amor hacia Orable, y esta flaqueza sentimental es objeto de las bromas de Guielín, quien, quando los francos y la princesa se encuentran encarcelados y sin esperanza de salir con vida de tan temeraria empresa, zahiere a su tío: "L'en soloit dire Guillelme Fierebrace, or dira l'en Guillelme l'amiable" (vv. 561-62). Esta actitud, que sería inconcebible en un roman courtois, subraya humorísticamente el sentido heroico de la gesta.[13]

The knight who tried to forestall a fight might be disparaged in such terms as: "He would rather kiss a young lady than joust with a warrior" (*Renaut de Montauban,* p. 212, vv. 5-7). The most violent insults include imputations of gluttony and lechery, indulgence in the pleasures of the flesh, and forgetfulness of battles to be fought and pain to be endured by others. Conversely, knightly virtue resides largely in a devotion to duty so great that the joy of battle exceeds those of the table, the bottle, and the boudoir: " . . . plus desirrent bataille et estor fier / Que il ne font a boivre n'a mengier, / Et mout mielz aiment ferir de branc d'acier / Que il ne font an chanbres donoier" (*Les Narbonnais,*[14] vv. 5008-11).

In a society that derided all deviations from its own standards for appearance and behavior, there could be little tolerance or understanding of the peculiarities of outsiders. In fact, just to call someone a foreigner was a form of ridicule. Foreign customs were viewed with condescension and scorn, among others, the silly habit of bathing. Renaut de Montauban, having wounded Ogier, says to him: "I've put holes in your hauberk and your helmet. Your skin is whither than snow on a branch. You Danes get that way

from taking so many baths" (p. 209, v. 38-p. 210, v. 2). The particular virtues of individual foreigners were respected, but only insofar as they coincided with popular ideals. Adherence to customs and beliefs that differed from those of the French was seen as a flaw, sometimes tragic, often merely ludicrous.

No national group was more generally maligned than the Lombards, who were seen as a race of fat, stingy, cowardly buffoons: "Just emperor, who is that old man who by his paunch resembles a Lombard?" (*Girart de Vienne,* vv. 802-03). "He was a Lombard, and full of avarice" (*Les Narbonnais,* v. 1440). "They're so cowardly they have neither strength nor valor" (*Les Narbonnais,* v. 1582). The Germans, too, were treated to more than their share of scorn. A passage in *Aymeri de Narbonne*[15] contains the information that they were dressed foolishly, carried excessively long swords, rode like idiots on unsuitable mounts, and that going into battle they shouted "Godehelpe" like infidels!

As for non-Christians, we have such episodes as the hilarious spectacle of the Jew in the *Pèlerinage* who mistakes Charlemagne and his twelve peers for Christ and the disciples and runs to demand immediate baptism (vv. 130-40). And in *Girart de Vienne* there is some teasing of the rich and respected Jew, Joachin, who gives Olivier arms for his battle with Roland. Olivier slyly promises that if he survives he will see to it that Joachin's son is baptized and knighted. Joachin replies that he would prefer to die and that his son be skinned alive. "Olivier l'ot, volentiers s'en est ris, / Et li baron, li conte et li marchis" (vv. 4915-16).

Humor was seen in the inert impotency of the pagan gods and in their frilly trappings: "The idol was covered with a cloth to protect it from the heat, supported from behind so that it might fall neither forward nor backward, and draped like a woman in accouchement" (*Elie de St. Gille,*[16] cc. 907-10). In defeat, the pagans regularly insult, beat, and discard the erstwhile objects of their devotion: "Es fosez les geterent con autres chiens poriz" (*Floovant,*[17] v. 561).

Much of the comedy in the chansons is directed against the groups that were in general disrepute. In the case of Jews and pagans, customs and beliefs rather than individual characteristics are usually ridiculed. The Jew, Joachin, for example, is laughable only because of his eccentric refusal to accept Christianity, and we have scores of descriptions of pagan knights which include the statement that they would be peerless if only they would abandon their false beliefs.

Anti-monastic feeling, on the other hand, seems to have made no exceptions for worthy individuals. In the *Moniage Guillaume,* the most concentrated expression in epic form of this sentiment, all monks are seen to be lazy, concerned with nothing beyond the satisfaction of their appetites for food and wine, and ready to perpetrate treachery and murder when their comforts are threatened. Evidence of antimonasticism is found in many chansons. There is, in *Renaut de Montauban,* an instance at once funny and terrible that can serve to exemplify the prevalent attitude. When his sons return home after years of forest exile, weakened by malnutrition and seeking food, Aymon mocks them, saying that there was no reason for them to go hungry. If they were really knights and not just boys, they would attack the monasteries and, rather than starve, eat the monks! These Aymon describes at some length and in the most appetizing terms (p. 93, vv. 12-26). Being slothful and overfed, they should be as tender and juicy as so many fatted calves.

Another group subjected to much ridicule is women, although in *Hermenjart, Aude, Guibourc,* and several others we have proof that individual women were not considered incapable of great virtue. The derisible trait attributed to womankind in general was lustfulness. The cuckold's horns were never considered comical by their possessor, but the propensity of women to bestow these appurtenances on their husbands was accepted as a fact of life, and one that could, at least in the abstract, be laughed at: "A woman lets herself be married. Then she sets out to test her husband. If he is found to be a little slow at that task of which I choose not to speak, she has the desires of her body satisfied by someone else" (*Aspremont,* vv. 8975-82). In *Aquin,*[18] the venerable Ohés explains in similar terms his reasons for not taking a new young bride after the death of his first wife, and: "When the French heard him, they were much amused, and laughed and joked heartily among themselves, and answered him: 'That sounds like the truth'" (vv. 921-23).

In addition to all the general standards for appearance and behavior, departure from which was punishable by derision, it was necessary that one remain within a natural or assigned role. A woman's place, for example, was particularly difficult, for, as previously mentioned, she was scorned for the restriction of her activities, but if she performed unwomanly deeds, regardless of their nobility, she might be laughed at. In *Girart de Vienne,* when Aude throws a stone, striking and wounding one of Roland's men, "Rollant s'en rit a la chiere hardie" (v. 4635). In *Aliscans,* Guillaume asks aid at Louis' court. There are no volunteers but his mother, Hermenjart, who offers not only her treasure, but her services in battle: "When I am armed and mounted no pagan within reach of my lance will be able to remain on his charger." And her husband's reaction: "Aimeris l'ot, souef en va riant / Et de pitié en son cuer souspirant" (vv. 2725-30).

The role of the warrior knight was, after a period of training, to fight the enemy with suitable weapons: lance and sword. This is at least partially accountable for the humor in Guillaume's use of his bare hands. Much of the comedy in Rainouart's misadventures stems from the fact that he is a displaced kitchen-boy who has assumed the role of knighthood without adequate preparation. He continues to use his ungentlemanly cudgel; his first equestrian effort (*Aliscans,* vv. 6155 ff.) is a riotous affirmation of the wisdom of keeping one's place. He mounts backwards, ap-

plies his spurs, is promptly thrown, and, holding desperately to his steed's tail, is dragged through the dust. The ride is beneficial to almost all concerned. Rainouart is chastened, the audience is amused, but the poor blameless horse is felled by two blows of the outraged giant's fist.

That there was unquestionably a consciousness of the humor inherent in interchanging roles is evident in a passage from *Moniage* I. Guillaume, entering the monastic order, is asked if he can read. He answers: "Oïl, sire abés, sans regarder en livre. / Vous estes maistres, vos saves bien escrire / En parchemin et en tables de chire" (vv. 131-33). At this, the abbot and all the monks begin to laugh. Guillaume has reminded them that he has been a warrior all his life, not a scholar. That he can read without looking at a book probably means he knows some prayers from memory. As he points out to the monks, reading and writing have been their business, not his.[19]

The knight's proper concern was with action, not words, and one who attempted to sway an enemy with reasoning rather than cold steel exposed himself to a form of ridicule appropriate to such a departure from the rules. In the *Chanson de Saisnes,* Charlemagne's efforts to convert a Saxon are so received: " 'Charles,' said the pagan, 'all you need is a fiddle. You know enough moralizing poetry to be a jongleur'" (vv. 7379-80). And in *Girart de Vienne,* Olivier reacts similarly to the arguments of Roland: "Are you a woman, that you know so well how to bicker?" (v. 4115).

It was also incumbent upon a knight to maintain certain standards of elegance in his accoutrements, and pecuniary disability was viewed with no more indulgence than physical weakness. Aiol[20] sets out for his adventures mounted on the ancient but remarkably well preserved charger Marchegai, and arrayed in the worn and tarnished but indestructible armor of his father, the exiled Elie. Each time he enters a town, his poverty, his failure to live up to the image of a knight in *shining* armor, arouses a veritable storm of mockery. That this was not uncommon is substantiated by Hermenjart in the *Enfances Guillaume.*[21] When her oldest son sets out for Brubant to seek the hand of the duke's daughter, she provides him with three pack animals laden with gold and silver: "So that when you arrive at the city the noble knights do not ridicule you" (vv. 3159-60).

The comic element in much of the foregoing is so elemental as to defy analysis. We might label as grotesque incongruity the frequent appearance of giants among normal men. Perhaps the potentially farcical application of their great strength contributes to their evocation of laughter, for in many instances this potentiality is realized. Guillaume's career in the monastery is almost pure farce. He terrorizes the monks, but they deserve no better treatment; so the proper reaction to his brutality is laughter: "Seeing those monks scatter through the cloister and around the pillars, one could both laugh and feel pity" (*Moniage* II, vv. 1955-57).

In Bergson, laughter is a response to the non-human behavior of human beings, to a mechanical inflexibility and persistence. A perfect example of this is seen in the *Chanson de Guillaume*[22] when Rainouart tries to procure a horse from the enemy by killing its rider. Repeatedly, unable to control his tremendous force, he halves not only the rider, but the horse as well. Frappier has noted that the germ of a similarly farcical scene is found in the *Chanson de Roland:* "Il y a déjà quelque chose de mirifique dans l'exploit semblable que par trois fois Roland accomplit avec Durendal à Roncevaux. Mais tout est une question de dosage et d'atmosphère. . . . "[23]

But the grotesque and the farcical are by no means the only forms of humor in the chansons. Wit is present in a wide range of moods, from gentle criticism to caustic mockery. An early example of the former appears in the *Chanson de Roland.*[24] Olivier, too busy to draw his sword, is fighting the Saracens with the splintered remains of his lance, and Roland points out the incongruity of this weapon by calling it a stick: "Ço dist Rollant: 'Cumpainz, que faites vos? / En tel bataille n'ai cure de bastun: / Fers e acers i deit aveir valor'" (vv. 1360-62).

Some examples of more cutting wit have already been given: the Saxon's appraisal of Charlemagne's talents as a jongleur; Baudouin's comments on the paunch of his fallen enemy. This brings us to what is probably the most widespread use of wit in the chansons: the taunt. We have seen it above in the remarks addressed by Raoul de Cambrai and his uncle to their victims, and throughout the epic literature few single combats end without the victor rubbing some figurative salt in the wounds of the vanquished, living or dead.

The taunt frequently took a somewhat more complex form. The discomfiture of a defeated foe could be increased by asking him if he had succeeded where it was obvious he had failed, or by advising him to do something of which he had been rendered obviously incapable. In *Aliscans,* the king's forester tries to stop Rainouart from cutting down Louis' favorite tree. The giant picks him up, whirls him around, and throws him high into the air. His flight ends in the branches of a tall oak, where he lies with his viscera trailing behind him like the tail of a battered kite. Rainouart then shouts to him, inquiring of his health and suggesting that he now go and tell the king that Rainouart is cutting down his tree (vv. 3415-17).

Discomfiture as a source of mirth was not limited to enemies. The spectacle of a needlessly aroused companion was so well appreciated that teasing, even about the most serious matters, was a regular form of entertainment. In *Renaut de Montauban,* for example, Maugis returns from an espionage mission with information that will save the life of the captured and condemned Richard, but instead of making an immediate report to Renaut, who is frantic with worry about his brother, he tells him that Charlemagne, their enemy, has given him some money, and suggests that they make a fortune by becoming usurers (p. 258, vv. 26-

29). In *Aiol,* when Elie has been returned by his son to a position of wealth and favor, he asks that his cherished horse and armor be given back to him. Aiol, joking, says that the armor is lost or broken and the horse dead and eaten by dogs. Elie, furious, then puts on a fine show for all those present. He vituperates his son, disinherits him, and attacks him with a stick. "Li barnages de France s'en comence a gaber; / Meïsmes Loeÿs en a un ris jeté" (vv. 8276-77).

Much amusement was also provided by cultivation of the well-turned insult, an art that reached a flowering in the chanson de geste. Often, even friends and allies would exchange comments on each other's shortcomings, real or invented. It is in the insult that the epic authors used irony and sarcasm most and to best advantage: " 'Ogier,' said Roland, 'you're very brave; none of your companions is more expert than you at running away'" (*Renaut de Montauban,* p. 214, vv. 35-36). "Quarriaz, my brother, you are an uncommonly good knight: in battle the very first to flee" (*Enfances Guillaume,* vv. 1138-39).

In some long dialogues, the imagination is given free rein, and scandalous insults are exchanged. The participants appear to take delight in their own inventiveness, and a fine time is had by the many spectators usually drawn to witness these verbal jousts. A good example is found in *Aiol,* a chanson precious for its realistic detail of some of the less heroic aspects of medieval life. In the crowd of idlers gathered to ridicule the young protagonist for his poverty, there appears Hersant, the butcher's wife, a slatternly harridan, loathed by all but feared for her sharp tongue. She is, in fact, the local invective champion. "En ranpronant," she suggests that Aiol enter her service. If he does, she promises him "une offrande molt avenant": a great sausage to be placed on his lance so that all will know she is his patroness and will therefore respect him. Aiol's retort not only procures for him the sympathy of the crowd, it establishes him as the new champion, for it is a masterpiece of its genre: "Hideuse estes et laide et mal puant, / Et le vostre serviche pas ne demanc. / Molt vos aiment chez mousques par Dé le grant, / Car vos estes lor mere, mien ensiant: / Entor vos trevent merde, j'en sai itant, / Que a molt grans tropiaus vos vont sivant" (vv. 2508-13).

Scatology, however, is rather rare in the chansons. It is reserved generally for the violent mockery of renegades and cowards, whose debasement provides some comical moments. In the *Chanson de Guillaume,* Thiébaut, fleeing from battle, comes to a crossroads where four thieves have been hanged. As he passes beneath the corpses, a foot strikes his face. Then, as Wilmotte so neatly puts it,[25]" . . . sur la selle du cheval, (Thiébaut) dépose un témoignage mal odorant du trouble intestinal qu'a produit en lui la frousse." In commenting on the desertion of Thiébaut, Frappier[26] remarks, justly I think: " . . . il y a là du comique, à n'en pas douter, mais le réalisme est si appuyé, la trivialité si sarcastique, la satire si violente que la haine, plutôt que le dessein de faire rire semble avoir inspiré cette charge méprisante. . . . "

A comparable episode, and one in which again scorn and hatred seem to overshadow the comic intention, is found in *Aiol,* where the renegade Makaire is put through a vilifying and thoroughly unsanitary ceremony to prove his newly sworn devotion to Mahomet (vv. 9642-55).

More sophisticated humor occurs when, in the forms of parody and burlesque, the epic genre itself is criticized. The best known example of this is the *Pèlerinage de Charlemagne,* a poem in which, among other things, the emperor appears with all the dignity and wisdom of a petulant child, holy relics are distributed as sparingly as campaign buttons on election day, and God's help is piously invoked in the deflowering of a virgin princess. The *Pèlerinage* is unique for its sustained parody, but irreverence toward the epic's form and content is found, in smaller doses, elsewhere.

When common sense is brought into conflict with epic conventions, comedy, at the expense of the formality, usually results. Rainouart, newly knighted, refuses to go through the ritual of demonstrating his prowess by striking the quintain. He says it would be shameful to waste one of his mighty blows on a scarecrow, and that he will prove himself against the enemy instead. "François l'entendent, si en ont ris asses" (*Aliscans,* v. 8059). The supposition that this laughter is directed entirely against Rainouart might be justified, were it not that the quintain ceremony is slighted in other chansons (e.g., *Aymeri de Narbonne,* vv. 157-67).

Laughter is aroused in several cases by ignoble characters who refuse knighthood because of the discomfort and risk it entails. Certainly they are scorned, but just as certainly there is some sympathy for the eminent rationality of their point of view.

In the *Chanson de Guillaume,* the hero is shocked and outraged when his nephew, Guiot, in flagrant violation of the rules of the game, beheads the pagan Derames, who had already lost a leg in combat with Guillaume. Guiot replies to his uncle's reproof with characteristic clear thinking: "I never heard the like! If he lacked a foot to walk on, still he had eyes to see with and the apparatus for engendering children. He would have himself brought back to his country and one day his heirs would return to make trouble for us" (vv. 1968-74). After a few such occurrences, Guillaume is forced to admit that his little nephew is wise beyond his years.

An outstanding burlesque occurs in the *Chanson de Saisnes,* when Charlemagne orders a part of his forces including Lombards and Germans to build a bridge across the Rhone. Their refusal to lower themselves to such a menial job comes in the form of a threat completely out of proportion to the pettiness of the disagreement, but almost interchangeable with any of hundreds of solemn descriptions of battles fought in more consequential causes: "Ainçois en iert perciez maint bons aubers doublier, / Maint escu painturé et maint elme d'acier, / Et mainte

bone espée i feront peçoier, / Maint boël trainer, qasser maint cervelier, / Maint bon destrier de garde sanz signor estraier / Qe par lor genz soit faiz li pons jusq'au planchier" (vv. 4406-11).

Conversely, in many metaphoric references to battle, instead of the completely serious attitude of devotion to a holy cause, we find expressions of comic irony, and even flippancy: "This game isn't suitable recreation for us" (*Raoul de Cambrai,* v. 4622). "Some flee and some give chase. It is customary in this dance that those who fall do not get up again" (*Saisnes,* vv. 5528-29). Swords were said not only to cut, but to teach lessons, preach sermons, confess their victims, and even to serve as musical instruments: "With my sword of steel I'll play you such a song that your heart will never again know joy" (*Raoul de Cambrai,* vv. 5037-38). Finally, there are the frequent references to battle as a commerce in which blows are paid and received, and the rather facetious extension of this to include borrowing and lending: "He fought well against me, returning in full as much as I loaned him" (*Girart de Vienne,* vv. 6043-44). "He paid, received, and borrowed so many blows that his ribs were visible in more than thirty places" (*Saisnes,* vv. 6778-79).

Other comic forms exist in the chansons, but are so rare as to have no place in this paper. The great preponderance of humor in the epics resides in the farcical grotesquerie immanent in the proportions of their characters and in caustic comments on the failings of others, as in taunts. Certainly a large part of this humor is brutal, but even in the earliest chansons, the existence of innocuous joking is undeniable, and it must surely be admitted that there is a substantial qualitative difference between teasing, practical jokes, and the good-natured twitting of a temporarily discomfited friend on the one hand, and on the other, the harsh outbursts of hilarity that followed the maiming or death of an enemy.

Perhaps the most important function of humor in the chansons de geste is its introduction of a note of realism into events and characters. A convincingly life-like ambivalence is present in many of the comic situations, where amusement is part of a reaction that may be complemented by hatred, fear, respect, pity, etc. The figures of most epic heroes are larger than life, but they are magnified without great distortion. Their monumental stature and deeds are balanced by equally grandiose foibles. Their jests are commensurate with their vendettas; their laughter with their tears. They thus appear not as symbols of militant virtue, but as reasonably well rounded human beings best exemplified not by Roland but by Guillaume d'Orange. This warrior, though invincible, is no stranger to fear; relies on his wife for moral, alimentary, and even tactical support; is a connoisseur of horses; has a violent temper; and, what is possibly most significant, has a well developed sense of humor, which enables him to see the lighter side of many predicaments, his own as well as others'. After defeating the giant Corsolt in a battle that has cost him a piece of his nose, Guillaume is able to say: "Well, my nose may be smaller now, but my renown will be larger."[27]

Humor in the chansons de geste is not a corruption and not an afterthought, but an integral element, subordinated of course to the predominantly tragic mood, but often inextricably involved with it. In *Raoul de Cambrai,* the impetuous Guerri disturbs the peace of a royal banquet by clouting Bernier with a leg of venison, but appreciation of the comedy in this ridiculous gesture is cut short by realization of its tragic consequences. Reconciliation of the two warring factions is abandoned, and the poem moves on toward increasingly inevitable catastrophe.

Our conception of the comic differs in some ways from that found in the epics. It is not derisible today even for a professional soldier to confess that he prefers the comforts of the boudoir to those of the foxhole, but obesity is still an invaluable asset to a buffoon, the banana peel underfoot and the custard pie over face have not yet lost all their effectiveness, the use of dialect still enhances a humorous anecdote, and our wars have provided us with disheartening evidence that brutality as a form of entertainment did not disappear with the Carolingian era.

Notes

1. *European Literature and the Latin Middle Ages* (New York, 1953), p. 431.

2. *Die komischen Elemente der altfranzösischen Chansons de Geste* (Halle, 1913).

3. Ed. F. G. Yeandle (New York, 1930).

4. *Karls des Grossen Reise nach Jerusalem und Konstantinopel,* ed. E. Koschwitz (Leipzig, 1895).

5. *La Mort Aymeri de Narbonne,* ed. J. Couraye du Parc (Paris, 1884).

6. *Les deux Rédactions en vers du Moniage Guillaume,* ed. W. Cloetta (Paris, 1906).

7. *Renaus de Montauban, oder Die Haimonskinder,* ed. H. Michelant (Stuttgart, 1862).

8. Ed. Weinbeck, Hartnacke and Rasch (Halle, 1903).

9. *La Chanson d'Aspremont,* ed. L. Brandin (Paris, 1923).

10. Ed. P. Meyer and A. Longnon (Paris, 1882).

11. Ed. F. Menzel and E. Stengel (Marburg, 1906).

12. Ambivalence similar to that evoked by great strength was displayed toward prodigies of ingestion when they were occasional and justifiable, and not to be confused with habitual gluttony. In the *Chanson de Guillaume,* the hero, returned from the rigors of a campaign, eats a stupendous meal: "Guibourc saw this; she shook her head and laughed, but she wept, too" (vv. 1419-20). Any man who can eat so abundantly, she decides, is well qualified to wage war and to uphold the honor of his lineage.

13. Martín de Riquer, *Los Cantares de Gesta franceses* (Madrid, 1952), p. 177.

14. Ed. H. Suchier (Paris, 1898).

15. Ed. L. Demaison (Paris, 1887).

16. Ed. Gaston Reynaud (Paris, 1879).

17. Ed. Andolf (Uppsala, diss., 1941).

18. Ed. F. Joüon des Longrais (Nantes, 1880).

19. This attitude is echoed succinctly in the fabliau of the "Vilain Asnier." Inured to the odor of organic fertilizer, his stock in trade, he is felled, in the market place, by air laden with the perfume of spices. Only a sample of his own wares, waved under his nose, is able to revive him. The fabliau ends with the moral: "Et por ce vos vueil ge monstrer/ Que cil fait ne sens ne mesure/ Qui d'orgueil se desennature:/ Ne se doit nus desnaturer."

20. Ed. J. Normand and G. Reynaud (Paris, 1877).

21. Ed. P. Henry (Paris, 1935).

22. Ed. D. McMillan (Paris, 1949).

23. J. Frappier, *Les Chansons de Geste du cycle de Guillaume d'Orange* (Paris, 1955), I, 270.

24. Ed. Bédier (Paris, 1944).

25. M. Wilmotte, *L'Epopée française* (Paris, 1939), p. 152.

26. Op. cit., I, 199.

27. *Le Couronnement de Louis,* ed. Langlois (Paris, 1925), vv. 1159-60.

Donald Bullough (essay date 1965)

SOURCE: "Epilogue. The Heritage of Charlemagne: Legend and Reality" in *The Age of Charlemagne,* Elek Books Limited, 1965, pp. 201-07.

[*In the following excerpt, Bullough discusses how Charlemagne's legendary status has, at times, threatened to overshadow the reality of his accomplishments.*]

Sometime during the reign of the Emperor Louis—known to posterity as 'the Pious'—a monk of Bobbio, where Irish traditions died hard, wrote a Lament for the dead Charles. *A solis ortu usque ad occidua Littora maris planctus pulsat pectora; Heu mihi misero* 'From the rising of the sun to the shores of the sea where the sun sets breasts are beaten in lamentation; Woe is me', he began. 'Franks, Romans and all Christian folk are plunged into mourning and overwhelmed with sorrow'; 'he was the common father of all orphans, pilgrims, widows and virgins'; 'Francia which has suffered such dread misfortunes, has never borne a sorrow so great as when it committed the august eloquent Charles to earth at Aachen'; 'receive the pious

Charles, O Christ, into thy holy seat with thine apostles'. The idea of a Carolingian Golden Age was already formed.

When Einhard wrote his 'Life of Charles' against whom his successors were being measured and found wanting, this age seemed long past. The quarrels within the Carolingian family had taken a serious turn; the Frankish episcopacy no longer met under the leadership and guidance of the monarch but had achieved independence of action and coherence in opposition to him; magnate families had identified their local and personal rivalries with the cause of one or other claimant to Imperial or royal dignity. The Emperor was failing to display either the *prudentia* or the *virtus* of his father; *inconstantia* had succeeded to *constantia* and *infidelitas* was taking the place of *fidelitas*. A few years later Nithard, the son of Angilbert and Bertha, recorded the tragic history of the quarrels between Louis' three sons that culminated in the terrible 'judgement of God' at the battle of Fontenoy (841). In 843 the once-united Empire was partitioned—irrevocably if not with finality (the struggle over the allegiance of the lands from the Ardennes to the Vosges seems only now to be ending): the re-unification under the west Frankish Charles 'the Bald', shortly before his abdication and death in 887/8, was as short-lived as it was unreal.

The legend of Charlemagne and the idea of Empire long outlived the reality and took possession of their ghosts. Charles' contacts with Jerusalem and the Caliph of Baghdad were transformed into a journey in person to receive the surrender of the Holy Places. The disaster of Roncesvalles became a noble moment in a series of wars against the Infidels in Spain. 'Rise up and remember the manly deeds of your ancestors, the prowess and greatness of Charlemagne' declaimed Pope Urban at Clermont in 1095 when he called on men to liberate the Holy Land from its defilers; and about the same time the portrait of the patriarchal Emperor who was the doughty champion of Christendom received its canonical form in the *Chanson de Roland*. Churches on the pilgrim routes to Spain that were 'remembered' as those once taken by Charles' armies were proud to display treasures which were believed to have been given them by the Emperor or a member of his family, like the *'Chasse* of Pippin' which is partly Carolingian in date or the strange reliquary known as 'the "A" of Charlemagne' which is two centuries younger. In the next generation a place was found in southern French churches for relics of Roland and his companions who died at Roncesvalles (pl. 83); and in the twelfth and thirteenth centuries the widely disseminated literary legend provided those responsible for the decoration of churches with a rich and novel source of visual imagery. The new public for literature in the vernacular was supplied with innumerable accounts of the 'Doings' of the great Emperor. Most of them are tedious today: but they inspired many polished or lively examples of manuscript art in the fourteenth and fifteenth centuries as wealthy laymen too came to regard books as part of the essential furniture of living.

There was a constant interaction between Charlemagne as the universal hero, the monarch who became one of the Nine Worthies along with Abraham and Caesar, and the efforts of particular places and dynasties to claim him for themselves. Each shift of the political spectrum, each adjustment of the mechanism of secular and ecclesiastical government produced its crop of expanded chronicles and falsified or forged diplomas. To the noble and royal dynasties that emerged out of the wreck of the Carolingian Empire there was eventually, however, no finer asset than a lineage that began with the Carolingians themselves. When the Capetians replaced the descendants of Charles on the west Frankish throne in 987, the new king and his supporters and successors insisted that they were merely continuing or renewing the work that had been left undone at his death. It was none the less as much by accident as by design that nearly all the early Capetian kings took wives who had some Carolingian in their ancestry. But by the twelfth century, when—whatever Holinshead and Shakespeare may have believed—women were held capable of transmitting kingdoms, this could be turned into a positive political asset. Both Louis VII and his queen Adela had more than one Carolingian ancestor: when, therefore, their son Philip succeeded in 1180 it was a *reditus regni Francorum ad stirpem Karoli*.

Philip's biographer dubbed him *Augustus*. Another century was to elapse before the courtiers of a French king were to declare him 'Emperor in his own kingdom'. The Imperial dignity was still felt to be superior to that of ordinary kingship and unique: and its possession was for many centuries, like Aachen itself, a priceless asset of the rulers of the eastern or German half of the Frankish Empire. Otto III, grandson of the monarch of Saxon lineage who had revived the Imperial office in the west in 962, demonstrated the source and bias of his own universalist ideas by his actions in the year 1000: returning from Gnesen, where he had tried to create a satellite kingdom of Poland, he proceeded to Aachen to what was believed—probably justifiably, in spite of the uncertainty introduced by Viking destruction in the late ninth century—to be the tomb of the great Frankish Emperor Charles. The ghostly figure of Charles loomed large in the propaganda war over the respective rights of lay rulers and the head of the church in the later eleventh and early twelfth century. When the Emperor Frederick I renewed the struggle later in the century, it was as another Charlemagne—perhaps for the first time the analogy was made specific—destined to triumph over the enemies of the Empire. It was because it seemed to be a symbolic weapon of unique power that at Aachen on 29th December 1165 Frederick and his ecclesiastical supporters proceeded to the proclamation of a new saint, St. Charles.

To justify the cult an appropriate new 'Life of Charles' was prepared. From it were taken the scenes which, with the figures of those who had received Imperial coronation at Aachen, formed the decoration of the splendid reliquary that was to provide a worthy setting for the bones of one in whom the this-worldly and other-worldly heroic virtues were uniquely combined: in July 1215, following his own coronation, the first Frederick's grandson, another Frederick, fittingly completed the process that his grandfather had begun by personally knocking in the last nails that closed the shrine. Yet it proved to be a gesture of honour to a figure of the past rather than a gesture of political significance for the present and the future. Charles the warrior, Charles the leader of European chivalry, even Charles the lawgiver was taking over from Charles the German Emperor. When, in the early sixteenth century, the Emperor Maximilian I planned an elaborate funerary monument to himself in the Court chapel at Innsbruck, Charlemagne stood not among his forebears and ancestors but with Arthur and the other Worthies. Charlemagne as the pattern of supreme political authority, as the apostle of universal dominion, was only to re-emerge in another and radically-transformed Europe.

Was it then Charles' greatest achievement to leave a legend and were the accomplishments of his life-time brought to naught in the unhappy years that followed his death? By no means. Many of the churches that were being built in the early years of the Emperor Louis, although on the grander scale that the activities of his father had encouraged, were in a style that could legitimately be called old-fashioned: in many areas the new architectural ideas established themselves only slowly. At the same time, there was a steady evolution of the decorative details used in buildings of every variety of plan and elevation, and minor as well as major buildings displayed a confidence and technical competence that would have been unthinkable only a few decades earlier. The earliest illustrated Tours Bible and the gold altar of Milan were produced in the very years in which the political troubles of the Empire were at their worst. The middle decades of the century likewise saw some of the most outstanding intellectual and literary achievements that we think of as characteristically Carolingian—and rightly so, because their ultimate inspiration and the resources they exploit stem from the activities of Charles' own life-time. The bishops who opposed, criticized and ultimately also supported Charles' son and grandsons did so in the light of the broader vision, stricter organization and higher standards that his reign had revealed or created.

The impact of the methods and measures of Charles' reign on the rest of the ninth century and beyond are no less evident in the history of secular institutions and of monarchy itself. Itinerant *missi* did not cease to function in 814; the most elaborate set of regulations for the royal control of coinage belongs to the later years of the reign of the Emperor's youngest grandson; the use of a body of men to declare on oath what they knew about a matter in dispute, of which the first tentative beginnings are to be seen in the last years of the eighth century, was enormously extended in the half-century after Charles' death. Even when effective authority shifted away from the person and court of the king or Emperor to local magnates acting without serious restraint, the scope and nature of this authority and the techniques they used to impose it bore the stamp of the changes that had taken place between 768 and 814. The magnate class of western Europe in 850 was not just a mirror-image of its predecessor in 750: and if, as is probably true, one effect of Charles' methods of government had ultimately been to strengthen magnate dominance over other elements in the society of the day, powers had been placed in the hands of monarchs that no subsequent weakness could finally destroy. Not least important, the visual symbols of royal and Imperial authority had been permanently enriched by Charles' endeavours, just as new levels of skill had been reached in giving them material form. Soon no court in western Europe, even when beyond the limits of Carolingian military success, was complete without its palace buildings, ornamental throne and royal insignia and no public occasion possible without its appropriate ceremonial display that corresponded to a functional need. And no ruler who combined energy, a sense of purpose and a measure of luck could fail to draw advantage from these precious assets.

What was the relation of the person of Charles to all this? We do no service either to the man or to the understanding of history by weaving from the legends of the past another legend more appropriate to our own time, nor by creating the image of a super-human being, civilized, far-sighted, in control of his own destinies and of the humblest of his subjects. The harshness and uncertainty of life were not suspended for half a century nor the insuperable problems of communication and the chain of command overcome. For all but a few of the ordinary people in the Frankish kingdom and Empire the period of Charles' rule probably seemed much like any other. The recently reported words of Chinese peasant farmers asked about the dramatic events of the past fifty-five years in their country could surely be put with only slight alteration and without incongruity into the mouths of ninth-century European peasants: 'I have no idea when the dynasty went [a reference to 1911]; we never noticed anything in our village of these revolutions'; 'various armies were fighting each other, bringing misfortune over the land; and landlords plundered and hit and swore and took people for forced labour, and one army was worse than the next; that was all we farmers knew'. In some areas the worst disorders and violence were temporarily checked—thus far the legend may be accepted. Some communities clearly felt the impact of agricultural innovation. Few men, however, can have appreciated the changes that were taking place in the languages they spoke although, where the educational reforms made themselves felt on the ordinary clergy, their parishioners must have been very conscious that the words of the liturgy had become even less intelligible to them.

Charles was a man recognizably of his own period, trained in a hard school; a man of passions, lustful, cruel, ready in his earlier years to exploit any situation that seemed to offer a potential advantage, observant of the externals of the Christian religion but hardly concerned with its deeper implications. What set him apart from other men and other rulers were his extraordinary vigour, both physical and mental; an ability to respond to checks and disasters by even more vigorous efforts and the devising of new measures to overcome recurrent problems; a notable curiosity and a readiness to learn; a perception, however vague, that the human spirit could aspire to something more than carnal pleasure and the thrill of fear; an ability to recognize the latent gifts of others; above all, the quality of impressing them with the strength of his own personality and inspiring them to rise to unanticipated heights. An apparently sudden rise to new levels of human achievement in war or in government, in art or in literature is usually in fact the culmination of a period in which ideas and skills have been slowly maturing: but the quickening of pace, the change from tentativeness to confidence, the acceptance by many of standards that have hitherto seemed beyond the reach even of a few demand the catalytic effect of an event or of a person. It is because he acted as this catalyst that we can properly talk of 'the Age' of Charlemagne. The greatest of its achievements and the noblest of its aspirations, created and proclaimed in a far harsher environment than that of Europe today, still speak to us across more than eleven centuries. For this reason, if for no other, it is an age worth studying.

Notes

Lament: text and transl. in *The Penguin Book of Latin Verse,* ed. F. Brittain (London, 1962), 148 ff.; authorship (?Cadac-Andreas): Bischoff in *Hist. Jahrb,* lxxiv, 97 f. *Iudicium Dei:* Nithard, II 10. Journey to Jerusalem: J. Coulet, *Étude sur le voyage de Charlemagne en Orient* (Paris, 1907). Conques treasures: *Trésors* catalogue, nos. 537, 541. Charles and French monarchy: Folz, *Couronnement impérial,* 243 ff. Charles and Germany: Folz, *Le Souvenir et la Légende de Charlemagne* (Publs. de l'Univ. de Dijon; Paris, 1950). Coinage: MGH *Capit,* ii, no. 273, cc. 8-24. *Inquisitio:* R. C. van Caenegem, *Royal Writs in England* (London, 1959), 51 ff. Chinese peasants: J. Myrdal, *Report from a Chinese Village* (London, 1965).

Jacques Boussard (essay date 1968)

SOURCE: "The Renaissance of Literature" in *The Civilization of Charlemagne,* translated by Frances Partridge, McGraw-Hill Book Company, 1968, pp. 118-56.

[*In the following excerpt, Boussard describes the state of culture at the time Charlemagne began his reign and the educational program he ordered as a remedy. He discusses the results—evident in the Church, civil law, the writing of history and poetry, and the birth of philosophical argument.*]

A GUIDED MOVEMENT

The end of the eighth century and the whole of the ninth saw a remarkable advance in all branches of culture, which has been described as the Carolingian Renaissance. The sovereigns took an active part in this movement, which was inspired and directed by the Church.

It was indeed a kind of renaissance, for the whole of the seventh century and the first half of the eighth had been a

period of almost complete barbarism in the *regnum Francorum.* Of course a few scattered centres of culture still existed and remained active. Without them, and the tradition they preserved, and without certain intellectual currents whose manifestations can now and again be traced, this renaissance would have been impossible. The secrets of ancient culture were not discovered afresh, nor were literature and the arts reinvented all at once. A long period of preparation, in one or two monasteries where a few books had been treasured and an extremely small number of men still devoted themselves to study, led up to the dazzling achievements of the reigns of Charlemagne and Louis the Pious.

When the barbarians conquered the West during the fifth century, culture was already in a deep decline, especially in certain regions such as the northern provinces, the north of Gaul, Germany and Armorica. Here there was a smaller Roman population; intellectual life, less firmly rooted, had offered no resistance to barbarism. The Romans had been submerged by the invasion and the population returned to paganism and a tribal existence. In the neighbourhood of the Mediterranean, on the other hand, Roman culture and thought had in part survived. In Italy and southern Gaul, regions conquered by the Visigoths who had been Christians since the fourth century and whose kings were to some extent Romanised, Latin culture appears to have persisted. The Visigoths were dazzled by the culture they found, and helped preserve it.

But what sort of culture was it that existed at the time of the invasions? Centres of learning and schools were to be found throughout the Roman Empire. At Pavia, Milan, Ravenna and Rome they had been kept going in Theodoric's time, although the authorities had made little attempt to preserve scholastic life. At Arles, Avignon, Vienne and Clermont, flourishing schools still existed in the sixth century; at Narbonne and Barcelona small groups of scholars kept an essentially literary and oratorical culture alive: the principles of eloquence, rhetoric, grammar and poetry were studied, and there was some interest in extending learning, to include subjects such as history, geography and natural history. The civilisation of the ancients seems to have been handed down in this way; but in fact ignorance of Greek, and the consequent impossibility of drawing on the springs of Greek culture and philosophy, led to an impoverishment of knowledge and thought, in spite of the efforts of rare spirits like Boëthius and Cassiodorous. The sciences classified by Boëthius—such as arithmetic, music, geometry and astronomy—had fallen into complete neglect and were only to return to favour after the Carolingian Renaissance, when they would form a basis for education during the Middle Ages. The culture the barbarians had found in the West was thus a mere relic of the true civilisation of the classical period.

In spite of this, the barbarians were greatly impressed by it; but they found it difficult to understand. Their leaders adopted different attitudes towards it. It was encouraged by those who were already Romanised, and had held power under the Emperor, like the first Visigothic and Burgundian kings. Others, such as the Frankish conquerors, or even Euric, a Visigothic king of the end of the fifth century, were uninterested. Later, in the sixth century, the glamour of culture won over the sons and grandsons of Clovis, who were not unresponsive to Latin civilisation. An important event was the adoption of Latin as the cultural language of the aristocracy, and it seems certain that even Roman juridical customs, such as the drafting of acts, began to figure in barbarian law, as also did all practical and scientific skills hitherto unknown to the invaders (surveying, medicine or architecture for instance). Techniques were taking the place of true culture, but Roman educational methods were rejected as of little use to the victorious warrior races. Moreover, if they wanted to earn their living in the barbarian States, Romans of the original stock had to adopt barbarian values and customs. It was therefore left to the Church to preserve the ancient heritage, and an ecclesiastical culture, blending together Christian and classical themes, began to appear.

The growth of monasticism also contributed. The monastic ideal was the pursuit of personal perfection through a life of prayer and study. Consequently, by their assiduous reading of sacred and profane books, the monks helped preserve Latin culture without actually spreading it, and imprinted upon it the blend of classicism and Christianity to be found in the works of the Fathers of the Church, whose writings were often read. Although Latin was the normal language of culture, the form it took in the few works written at the time was incredibly barbarous: phonetics, morphology and syntax were all modified in popular Latin, a simplification and distortion of classical Latin. However, scholars of the middle of the seventh century still conformed to the essential rules of grammar, prosody and rhetoric, and writers such as Virgil were read, as well as the Fathers of the Church.

During the second half of the seventh century the level of culture sank even lower. Neither in Aquitaine, Provence nor Burgundy was it possible to find scholars of the old style. The senatorial families mixed more and more with the Franks, and adopted their way of life; education underwent a complete change. Some degree of culture could still be found at court, where what might be described as a worldly and refined life still existed. But the only real centres were the episcopal and monastic schools. The abbeys following the rule of St Columba were in touch with the Celtic world, which had preserved a very ancient tradition of Latin learning, but this influence affected only a chosen few.

The wars waged by Charles Martel during the first half of the eighth century to crush the movement for independence in Aquitaine, the Lyonnais and Provence, completed the destruction of centres of culture and learning. Ignorance became general. Whereas under the Merovingians influential laymen still knew how to write, it was rare to find one who could even sign his name in the eighth century. A few of the clergy could write, and this had the important result that offices formerly held by educated laymen now passed into their hands, and they became the sole custodians of culture. Anyone who wanted to devote himself to study now retired into a monastery, and these were the only places where manuscripts were copied and texts studied. The *scriptoria* of Corbie, Laon, St Denis, Fleury-sur-Loire and St Martin of Tours, like those of Fulda, St Gall and Bobbio, worked hard at copying ancient texts, and these monasteries also produced some hagiographic works; but they no longer studied the profane authors of antiquity, except in the form of extracts illustrating some moral or grammatical commentary. Culture had sunk to a very elementary level, and its decline had brought with it a dearth of ideas.

This was the state of things at the beginning of Charlemagne's reign. A few men of exceptional intelligence, such as St Chrodegang of Metz, deplored the decadence of learning and enlightenment. Scholarly members of the clergy, like St Boniface, educated in Anglo-Saxon schools where the intellectual level was higher, were disquieted by the effect of the general ignorance of the ministry and clerical life. Realising that a fresh impetus must be given to education, Charlemagne set in motion the great enterprise which was to reach its apogee under Louis the Pious.

This renaissance seems to have been a widespread movement with several definite characteristics. Its inspiration was Christian, and its aim the expansion of the Church; yet although it was addressed principally to the clergy, laymen and even women were urged to profit from it, and schooling was in theory to be provided for everyone. It was exclusively Latin in character, for the Greek world was at this time entirely cut off from the West, and in spite of the influence of certain men who had been affected by Hellenism, such as Paul the Deacon, the sources referred to were purely Latin. Nor was it confined to literature, but embraced all branches of human knowledge, considerable work being done in the fields of canon law, Roman law, theology and science. Finally, it was not a spontaneous movement but a guided one, and Charlemagne's wishes played an extremely important part in it: he gave effect to them by legislation, by collecting scholars around him at court, and by personally stimulating study. The renaissance developed steadily. At the beginning of the reign culture was almost exclusively monastic, but as a result of legislation, other centres opened later on, and schools were to be found close to the royal palace and the cathedrals, and even in country parishes.

The first efforts were directed at producing more books. From about 780 the *scriptoria* were kept hard at work; specialists in calligraphy were employed on the long, arduous and delicate task of reproducing the works of great writers or liturgical books, while as time went on the more valuable of them began to be more and more elaborately and even sumptuously decorated. Papyrus had vanished, parchment was scarce and had to be used sparingly, but the need for books was so great that this activity steadily increased. A real revolution in the art of writing was in progress: instead of the unequal, irregular Merovingian script, cluttered up with confusing flourishes, or the angular writing imported from the British Isles by Irish and Anglo-Saxon scribes, a new style was gradually appearing, with small, separate, rounded and perfectly legible letters; it was called *Caroline minuscule,* and its advantages were so great that it was adopted by virtually all sixteenth-century printers after Gothic type was broken up. It has obvious links with the printed letters of the present day.

Libraries were growing richer. At the beginning of the eighth century there was general neglect in the monasteries, and only the remains of their old collections were left. After about 750, however, conscientious abbots began to add to their possessions and collect new treasures. At St Wandrille, for example, the three abbots who succeeded one another between 747 and 807—Wando, Witluic and Gervold—acquired a hundred volumes for their monastery. At the end of the century, Alcuin realised that his abbey of St Martin of Tours was short of books, and sent emissaries to Britain to get some. Their chief need was for books to copy, and they sent for them to Ireland, Italy and Spain. This practice lasted for a long time, and even at the height of the Carolingian Renaissance, during the first half of the ninth century, books were being searched for everywhere: whether gifts, purchases or loans, they could be copied and so multiplied. We still possess the catalogues of some of these libraries: for the most part they contained sacred books, the works of the Fathers of the Church and the Greek fathers (evidently translated into Latin), but also everything that might help teach young clergy the Latin tongue, now no longer spoken in its pure form, and revive its grammar and literature. In the middle of the eighth century, Corbie certainly possessed a sixth-century copy of Livy; Fleury-sur-Loire some extracts from Sallust; St Amand a manuscript of Pliny the Elder; St Martin of Tours a copy on papyrus of a commentary on Cicero's *Topica;* often there would also be some volumes of ecclesiastical history in these libraries.

In the monasteries or bishoprics where these libraries were to be found, there were also schools for the education of the clergy. The syllabuses were vague and depended entirely on the teachers, but they left great freedom to those who wanted to read, study and educate themselves: thus the Venerable Bede and Alcuin had been taught the elements of science by their masters, and afterwards acquired much wider knowledge in Anglo-Saxon schools. The organisation of schools all over the *regnum Francorum* was in a rudimentary state, and was left in the hands of the clergy and monasteries; the chief object was to train clerics and monks. Charlemagne's contribution consisted in seeking out and bringing to his realm foreign scholars, particularly from countries where schools still flourished like Italy and England, in legislating to provide modest educational foundations as the spearhead of culture, and establishing a centre of science, art and literature at his court. This work was begun in 780.

It was in no way revolutionary; there was no change in the orientation of studies, and the principal aim remained the education of the clergy. But the measures taken by Charlemagne opened vaster horizons, and had results that were felt far outside the educational sphere.

In a capitulary published between 786 and 800, Charlemagne declared: 'Because it is our duty at all times to improve the state of our churches, we are concerned to restore with vigilant zeal the teaching of letters, which has fallen into abeyance through the negligence of our ancestors.' And he gave orders that books whose texts had been corrupted by careless scribes should be corrected, that schools should be opened (the very word had almost been forgotten, he said) all over his realm—restored in Gaul and founded in Germany, where they had never existed. His objects were that divine service should be conducted correctly and with dignity, that monks and clerics should be educated, and Gregorian chant should be properly sung according to the principles laid down by his father. And besides these ecclesiastical aims, he wanted all his subjects to receive the benefits of instruction.

He achieved his end by general measures included in his capitularies, and also by giving personal instructions to bishops and abbots. A mandate addressed to all the archbishops, and to be passed on to their suffragans, ordered that all bishoprics and royal monasteries must be able to provide an education conducive to a regular life and literacy, for all those capable of receiving it. Schools must be available to all for the encouragement of a Christian way of life, although their chief aim must still be to recruit and train the clergy, and the episcopal churches should concentrate on educating those they needed in their own diocese. This was also the drift of a reprimand contained in a letter to an archbishop, probably the Archbishop of Mainz, who was training clerics for other dioceses. A capitulary issued in 789 contained an article on schools. This time it did not deal only with episcopal schools, but was addressed to ordinary priests, advising them to win over as many children as possible to the service of God, and ordering them to open country schools where they could be taught to read, as the first rung in the ladder of education. Charlemagne also gave instructions to the bishops to draw up a course of study for episcopal and monastic schools: the psalms must be read, music, singing, calculation of dates and grammar must be taught.

These measures combined to form a complete educational programme: children were to learn to read, sing, take part in divine service and recite the psalms, as well as to acquire the rudiments of calculation and even of medicine. Some schools gained a special reputation for the high quality of their teaching in one or other of these branches, for example Metz for singing and music. The schools at Lyons, Orleans, Mainz, Trèves, Ferrières, Aniane, St Wandrille, St Riquier, Murbach and St Martin of Tours were becoming famous. At Tours, Alcuin varied the education according to the talents of his pupils; some studied singing, others reading, writing, the liberal arts or Holy Writ.

Charlemagne's directions were often observed and had an undoubted effect. He stimulated the renaissance of study and the opening of schools. Teachers of the next generation, such as Eric of Auxerre or Lupus of Ferrières, praised his efforts, and have handed down to us the respect scholars felt for him. As Lupus wrote: 'Scholars are so greatly in debt to Charles that they will remember him always.'

Charlemagne in fact created an educational structure which lasted for several centuries. Elementary teaching and education in the liberal arts were kept separate. The former could be given in private houses, parish schools and abbey priories, as well as in schools attached to cathedrals, collegiate churches and monasteries (where a more advanced education could also be obtained). It was an elementary course designed for beginners. But we must remember that learning to read involved not only the deciphering of texts, but also the art of reading aloud distinctly; and that singing was a direct preparation for celebrating divine service—one of the main purposes of this basic education; nor were learned men, like Eric of Auxerre, at Laon Cathedral, too proud to teach it to children. The psalms, canticles and hymns that must be learned by heart were normally sung. The technique of writing and the elements of grammar formed the highest grade of this elementary teaching.

A course in the liberal arts was the highest form of education. The programme was fixed in the eighth century and remained the same until the twelfth; it was based on the views of Martianus Capella, Cassiodorus and Isidore of Seville, and included the Seven Arts classified by the ancients. This course was entirely dependent upon the classics, and consisted solely in making commentaries on ancient books; ninth-century teachers seem to have felt unable to add anything to the results produced by scholars of long ago. They held that these arts fell naturally into two separate series: those aiming at developing the intellect alone, and those that could be applied to the physical world and its features, such as number, space, the heavenly bodies and harmony. Alcuin distinguished three aspect of 'logic': grammar, rhetoric and dialectic; next came 'physics', divided into four groups: arithmetic, geometry, music and astronomy. These two great series were given the titles of *trivium* and *quadrivium* two centuries later, and remained the basis of education during the classical Middle Ages. For Alcuin they were the seven pillars of wisdom, or steps by which to ascend to perfect knowledge. He himself wrote treatises on grammar, rhetoric and dialectics, and we know that he taught all branches of 'physics'.

However this complete course was not taken in all schools. In the middle of the tenth century, Gerbert did not start his pupils with grammar, but plunged them straight into dialectics, or the science of reasoning, then into rhetoric, and finally embarked them on studying the style of the classical poets. Each of these sciences needed a special method of teaching: thus grammar included the study of rules and examples taken from writers of antiquity—Virgil, Statius, Terence, Persius, Juvenal, Horace and Lucan; rhetoric studied the art of oratory among the ancients. Dialectics, or the rational method of distinguishing true from false, through definition and discussion, was Alcuin's favourite branch of learning. He knew that Aristotle had thrown light upon it, but was only acquainted with his works indirectly, since no Latin translation existed in the West. The different branches of 'physics' were less commonly taught than 'logic'. Of course it was thought necessary for clerics studying singing to know the rules of musical theory, but in 831 the library at St Riquier contained twenty-six volumes of *libri grammaticorum,* one on medicine and not a single one on physics itself. This course could be followed up by philosophy, that is to say the entire field of learning outside logic and physics, including ethics or the study of the four cardinal virtues. Raban Maur did not hold that the seven liberal arts embraced the whole of learning. It was beginning to be realised that the field of investigation by human intelligence was unlimited.

As for methods of instruction, they all started from one principle: a text must first be read by the teacher or a pupil, this to be accompanied by a grammatical, rhetorical or dialectical explanation, and the study of examples from other branches of learning; next came a dialogue or discussion, carried out according to the methods of dialectical reasoning, the highest form of scholastic exercise. This method was adhered to in all schools throughout the Middle Ages. The influence of the ninth-century teachers who had devised it was therefore a determining factor in the development of the human mind: in spite of the exaggerations and aberrations of scholasticism, this method taught generations of students how to discipline their thoughts; on it was founded the scientific exactitude which made it possible for a chosen few to apply certain accepted facts to science; it formed the minds of several men of outstanding intelligence who flourished in Charlemagne's day, and (in greater number) under Louis the Pious and his sons.

THE INTELLECTUAL ENVIRONMENT

It is not surprising that after a period of such complete barbarism, Charlemagne's work in organising education yielded no brilliant results until the next generation: men who had been students during his reign reached maturity at the time of his death. Nevertheless, several intelligent, and some genuinely learned or talented men, made their mark during his lifetime. The elite among these thinkers were self-educated, having developed a taste for learning after receiving elementary teaching in one of the few surviving intellectual centres. Most of these were to be found outside the Empire, but they contributed greatly to the revival of learning.

As always when a few intelligent men dominate a backward society, they kept in touch with one another, mainly through letter-writing, and so developed ways of thought, a community of interests, and a particular style of literary or scientific production, which had an influence on their contemporaries and successors. This is what is meant by the literary movement of Charlemagne's reign. They took classical writers as their models, and after a return to pure and correct Latin, developed their style in the direction of literary originality. In all their works we can trace the old Germanic background, the influence of Holy Writ and the Fathers of the Church, and lastly the rediscovery of the values of Roman civilisation after centuries of neglect. These different contributions created a way of thinking and a form of original expression peculiar to Carolingian civilisation; like the educational structure it persisted throughout the medieval period, and helped to shape the history of human thought.

By about the year 760, several main currents in literary aesthetics could be distinguished. First, the influence of antiquity, not directly but through more recent authors like Isidore of Seville (560-636). This Spanish bishop and aesthetician left his mark on the Carolingian period by making classical authors available to eighth-century scholars. He introduced them to Latin theories of versification, based on the arrangement of long and short syllables and stress, and also to the rules of rhetoric, grammar and literary creation. He stood for the traditions of classical culture in the latter half of the eighth century, and served as a model for many writers, Theodulf in particular. The influence of the Orient, with its love of brilliance, effect and colour, came from study of the Bible by scholars; it was brought to the West by the works of an Anglo-Saxon, the Venerable Bede (673-735), whose aesthetic theory was based on classical correctness of style enriched by the inspiration of the Bible, to which he was highly responsive. He introduced a new form of rhythmic versification, easier to appreciate than the Latin forms; it gave the unaccented syllables the same value as the short syllables of classical writers. He enriched poetry by Christianising the chief literary forms and taking examples of style from both Virgil and the Bible. Above all, he imitated biblical figures of speech, arrangement of words, and metaphor. He appreciated the beauty of the Bible as literature, and took delight in translating it into the purest Latin possible. He was largely responsible also for the allegoric interpretation of the Bible, and so indirectly for the deplorable popularity of allegory during the Middle Ages, which finally affected aesthetic and even scientific theory. Bede was as important an influence as Isidore of Seville on the writers of the Carolingian period.

Both these men emphasised the importance of writing correct Latin, as close as possible to the classical language. Charlemagne had himself been struck by the decadence of Latin; in a letter to Baugulf, Abbot of Fulda, he insisted that grammatical correctness was necessary so that errors of thought should be avoided: to arrive at the true meaning of Holy Writ one must have a perfect knowledge of the language and of the literary habits of sacred writers. This conviction of Charlemagne's was the basis of his educational reforms. He took lessons himself from Alcuin and Peter of Pisa, the grammarian, and he had a school directed

by eminent teachers close to him in his palace. From a passage in Einhard, and an even more important extract written by an anonymous monk of St Gall, a picture of the Emperor has been reconstructed, as the creator of a palace academy, bringing together fine intellects to discuss rhetoric or philosophy, and taking part himself. This legend is probably based on the fact that Charlemagne certainly did not scorn to take part in such discussions; but there is no evidence that he kept a group of scholars permanently at court, and even if many of them taught at the palace school they took turns to do so. But whatever doubts may be thrown on the existence of this supposed academy, we know for certain that the best scholars were consulted, and that the palace school played an important part in the literary renaissance.

Soon after it was founded, Charlemagne sent for two Italian grammarians, Peter of Pisa and Paul the Deacon. Peter of Pisa, educated in his native town where traditions of Roman culture still survived, had met Alcuin in 767. Charlemagne put him in charge of the grammar department of the palace school. He was imbued with the purest classical doctrines, as we see from the treatise he wrote and dedicated to Charlemagne, in which he goes into the peculiar characteristics of gender and declension. His teaching may be considered as the first step in the reform of Latin scholarship and the return to the pure form of the language. But he was also a poet, and we still have a letter from him to Paul the Deacon, containing a eulogy of Charlemagne. Paul came from a Lombard family of Friuli, and had been educated at Pavia; his high degree of literary culture made him welcome at the Frankish court. After spending four years in the Moselle district, he had to return to Italy. He left behind a large quantity of writings: grammatical treatises, poetry, Roman history, histories of the Lombards and the bishops of Metz, a life of St Gregory the Great and a commentary on the rule of St Benedict. He was of great assistance to Charlemagne. He was a genuine writer, nourished on the classics, and his teaching did much to encourage Latin studies. Grammar went on being treated as a subject of great importance until the end of the reign, when Clement Scotus, author of a treatise on barbarisms, was also teaching at the palace.

But Charlemagne sent for other important scholars as well as grammarians—philosophers and theologians, all of them church-men whose chief interest was in apologetics. At a period when learning was universally regarded as a means of arriving at revealed truth, it is not surprising to find these intellectuals using profane knowledge for the defence of their faith. Paulinus of Aquileia occupied several important positions, such as that of *missus,* and lived at court teaching grammar for several years. He was nominated patriarch of Aquileia in 787, and ruled over his diocese wisely, while still continuing to take part in the affairs of the realm and in theological controversy. He was an adversary of the adoptionist heresy, and attended several councils. He left behind some theological treatises and a *Liber exhortationis,* a moral work addressed to his friend Eric, Duke of Friuli; all were written in fairly correct language inspired by the classics and the Bible.

His friend Alcuin was even more closely connected with educational reform. He was an Anglo-Saxon, educated at the episcopal school of York; Charlemagne met him at Pavia in 781, got him to join him and gave him several abbeys. In 796 he was Abbot of St Martin of Tours, and acted as it were as Charlemagne's minister of cultural affairs. His reputation was due more to charm of character and encyclopedic knowledge than to his creative genius, which was in fact not remarkable. It was he who listed the branches of learning and dictated how they should be taught. We have treatises written by him on all sorts of subjects: grammar, rhetoric, liturgy, philosophy, hagiography, theology and history, as well as poems and literary works. His style is affected, founded on knowledge and imitation of ancient writers; he used classical metres and turns of phrase. Alcuin was the most remarkable of the learned men who came from the British Isles to the West, and represented the combined influence of classical antiquity and biblical tradition originated by Bede.

Theodulf of Orleans exemplified a different branch of culture. Also a theologian, apologist and poet, in love with classical traditions, he had come under the direct influence of the teaching of Isidore of Seville. Finally, a Frankish nobleman called Angilbert, who had a son—the historian Nithard—by Charlemagne's daughter Bertha, had such a great reputation as a poet that the intellectuals of the day gave him the surname of Homer. He too imitated the ancients.

These writers, all of whom were in contact with Charlemagne and often called upon by him to help in his work of reviving culture, were all notable for their eagerness to restore the Latin language and go back to classical texts. From a literary point of view they were purely imitative: their works were modelled on Latin writers and the Bible, and it must be admitted that they often lack inspiration. However, together they produced an original body of work: never had such reminiscences of pagan classicism and of Christianity been so intimately mixed, and the authors of this alliance were many of them of Germanic origin: the Lombard Paul the Deacon, the Anglo-Saxon Alcuin, Theodulf the Visigoth, and Angilbert the Frank. Thus Charlemagne's reign saw the development of new literary forms born of contacts between different civilisations. This fusion is even more plainly seen in the spheres of philosophy, theology and law.

Naturally enough the revival of culture led the clergy to examine problems concerning the Church, particularly the liturgy, theology and canon law. Liturgy laid down rules for the official forms of prayer and religious observance. Its development had been slow, and partly along local lines—there were Roman, Gallic, Celtic, Moorish and Greek rituals—so that, although the essential elements had been made uniform, and Mass always included readings from Holy Writ, singing and sacrificial prayers, marked variations could be observed in the respective importance given to these elements. And, because of the general ignorance of the seventh century, liturgical books were often disgracefully badly copied. With his love of order and unity, Charlemagne took an interest in this question, and instituted reforms bearing on the copying of books, the introduction of Roman customs, and return to the Gregorian chant. He asked the Pope for his advice on this subject.

The revision of liturgical books was very largely the work of Alcuin. First he rewrote the *Comes,* or lector's book of extracts from the Old and New Testaments, to be read aloud to the congregation during services; he made it easier to read, and adapted the text for various different occasions. Thus he composed a lectionary conforming to the liturgical cycle fixed by St Gregory the Great, and so to Roman usage. When it came to reforming the sacramentary—or book of formulas pronounced by the priest when administering the sacrament—he asked Rome what was the official procedure. This too went back to St Gregory the Great, and the Gallic form, founded on an ancient sacramentary dating from Gelasius and not used in Rome since the end of the sixth century, was abandoned. In reply to Charlemagne's request, Pope Hadrian sent him books and a monk to bring the Franks up to date in the matter of Roman usages. Alcuin's Sacramentary was made obligatory by a royal decree in 785. It was the same with the Gregorian, or Roman chant as with the Roman liturgy. Pepin the Short and Chrodegang of Metz had already introduced it in *Francia.* Metz became a centre of Roman music, and clergy were obliged to learn the Gregorian chant by the royal decrees of 789, 802 and 805: Charlemagne was therefore personally involved in this unification and Romanisation of the liturgy.

He was no less interested in theology, and its attempts to discover, by reasoning based on Holy Writ, definite ideas on which to found the Christian faith. At the beginning of the eighth century, the lack of Church councils in Gaul and Germany had led to the decay of theological activity; the religious revival caused by St Columba and his disciples had more effect on piety than on research into dogma. The Carolingian Renaissance brought with it a renewal of theological study, because it was a form of intellectual activity available to scholars who were all churchmen, because the councils were beginning again, and because it led to the study of doctrines coming from countries where culture had persisted, such as the Byzantine East or Moorish Spain. Charlemagne's advisers were asked to make a decision on three questions: adoptionism, iconoclasm and the Procession of the Holy Ghost; and contemporary scholars wrote countless treatises on these subjects. Adoptionism, widely held especially in Spain at the end of the eighth century, was the belief that Jesus Christ was not truly the Son of God and the Word incarnate, but God's adopted son; it had been spread by Elipand, Archbishop of Toledo, and Felix, Bishop of Urgel. The latter was suffragan to the metropolitan of Narbonne, and had propagated this doctrine (condemned by Hadrian 1 in 785) throughout Septimania. In 792 Felix renounced his errors before the council of Ratisbon, but he returned to them later, and Charlemagne encouraged Alcuin to confute the heresy in writing. Alcuin thereupon wrote his *Adversus Felicis haeresim libellus,* in which he treated adoptionism as a form of monophysitism; Felix's reply, in a letter to Charlemagne, was passed on to the Pope and afterwards examined by Paulinus of Aquileia, Theodulf of Orleans and Richbod, Bishop of Trèves. After Paulinus had written his *Libellus sacrosyllabus* and *Contra Felicem Urgellitannum,* Alcuin published another treatise with the same title and followed it up with a letter to Elipand, but the quarrel did not end with the death of the Spanish protagonists, and Agobard, Archbishop of Lyons, evidently thought it necessary to write yet another tract on the same subject after 818. The battle against adoptionism seems therefore to have been inspired by Charlemagne, the Pope and the councils, but the whole doctrinal controversy was set out in writings attacking the heresy by a few well-known scholars. Their intellectual methods of approach to the subject were typical of the Carolingian Renaissance: their arguments were always supported by textual quotations from the Bible or the Fathers. The discussion was philological as well as theological and patristic, often depending on the interpretation of terms used by writers on sacred subjects. This use of philological and grammatical data as a basis for theological argument was the result of the efforts of Charlemagne and his circle to organise studies so that perfect knowledge of the language should lead to mastery of sacred texts. The tone of Alcuin's arguments is no less remarkable: he was neither bitter nor abusive about his adversaries, but full of moderation and charity; he showed an extensive knowledge of the Latin Fathers, some contact with translations of the Greek Fathers, and a talent for subtle reasoning which served as a model for the dialecticians.

The iconoclastic quarrel had begun in the East a long time before Charlemagne's reign, and made a breach between the Churches of Rome and Constantinople. In 754 veneration of images had been forbidden in the Byzantine empire, but the council of Gentilly, convoked in 767 by Pepin the Short, would not accept this decision. Twenty years later the empress Irene convoked an oecumenical council at Nicaea; it was attended by Pope Hadrian's legates, but the Frankish bishops refused to come: the council returned to the question and declared it lawful to venerate images. When the conclusions of this council were conveyed to Charlemagne, he had them studied by theologians, probably headed by Alcuin. They declared that respect should be paid to images of saints, but were careful to distinguish this from the adoration due to God alone; their attitude contained more nuances and reservations than that of the council. Thanks to the action of Charlemagne and his advisers, a more exact definition of the dogmas concerned in this subject was arrived at, and the king of the Franks was recognised as virtually the head of Western Christianity.

Even more important controversies took place over the dogma of the Holy Trinity. The ancient belief of the Church was that the Holy Ghost proceeded from the Father and the Son at the same time. When the council of Nicaea declared in 787 that the Holy Ghost proceeded *through* the Son, this doctrine seemed suspect to Charlemagne, who had a sharp criticism of the council drafted in the *Libri Carolini,* which upheld the view that the Holy Ghost proceeded from the Father *and* the Son: 'ex Patre *Filioque* procedit'. This was the famous controversy of *Filioque,* in which Paulinus of Aquileia, Alcuin and Theodulf all took part. Following the same methods in their writings as they had with adoptionism, and all of them (especially Alcuin) treating their adversaries with consideration, they evolved a doctrine which was approved by the council of Aix-la-Chapelle in 808, and was to become a permanency in the Churches of the West. Here again we see the work of Charlemagne and the chief scholars of the Carolingian Renaissance.

Their influence was just as great in the field of canon law, or in legislation concerning the Church as a social unit. In the barbarism prevailing during the seventh century and at the beginning of the eighth, the canons issued by councils and the papal decretals had been forgotten; these, together with the Bible and the opinions of the Fathers, constituted the sources for Church legislation and the texts used as references. Occasionally some texts would still be collected and summarised, but without checking their authenticity or making them into a proper code. First Carloman and then Charlemagne set out to frame a legislative code founded on ancient usages, and this was revived when the councils began meeting again. In 789, in his *Admonitio generalis,* Charlemagne invited the clergy to observe a tradition that was universal and very old. An official code was sought for among authentic legislative texts. This did in fact exist in the shape of a canonical collection compiled by a sixth-century monk called Denys the Small. Charlemagne received it from Pope Hadrian in 774 and quickly circulated it. It was the collection known as *Dionysio-Hadriana,* and it became the basic text referred to by councils, and to which were added any new texts bearing on the subject and derived from different national sources, such as the Spanish councils. A new collection thus formed, and known today as *Dacheriana* (because it was rediscovered in the eighteenth century by Dom Luc d'Achery) became the source of canon law from about 800 onwards. But in this field, as in other forms of intellectual activity, only a start was made in Charlemagne's lifetime.

Later, under Louis the Pious, experts in canon law exerted themselves to spread authentic texts, and to organise the Church and the customs they wished laymen to adopt, in particular those concerned with penitence and marriage. Although Charlemagne had tried to impose Roman customs in all these matters, his success was very limited. About thirty manuscripts from the *Dionysio-Hadriana* collection, written in the ninth century, have come down to us, and from 845 the interest in canonical collections was so great that forgeries began to be made: the best known are the *False Decretals.* Their very existence proves the importance attached to such texts, but they do not seem to have spread rapidly. We must not forget that in Pepin the

Short's reign ecclesiastical reform had been undertaken by Anglo-Saxon monks, and that the form of monasticism widespread at the time had been inspired by Celtic customs and the religious outlook of St Columba. His influence had established among the clergy certain usages to which he was attached, particularly to do with penances. Books known as penitentials listed possible infringements of the law of the Church, in other words sins, and indicated the required penance for each—prayers, fasting or pilgrimages. Such schedules might be useful to ignorant clergy finding themselves in charge of even more simple-minded worshippers; a good many were to be found in Britain, whence they came to Gaul, but they revealed a tiresome tendency to misunderstand the spirit of canon law and neglect the notions of the sacrament, the grace obtained by the Redeemer, and individual conscience, to which the Roman clergy had always been deeply attached. Specialists in Church law began a campaign against these manuals in the reign of Louis the Pious. In 829 the council of Paris ordered that they should be searched out and burned. Two archbishops, Ebbo of Rheims and Raoul of Bourges, drew up a detailed criticism of these books, and called for a return to Roman unity and regularity. They had to be replaced, because of the widespread ignorance of the clergy. But the new penitentials, particularly the penitential of Halitgar, and the *Quadripartitus,* substituted a system borrowed from the best sources of canon law for Celtic usages, and were preceded by a doctrinal exposition. Raban Maur, who was certainly one of the most intelligent men of his day, composed two penitentials in 841 and 853, based entirely on the *Dionysio-Hadriana* and the *Dacheriana*. It was also necessary to redraft the little manuals used to instruct the clergy in rural districts in their duties and the rules established by the bishops: these were the *capitula episcoporum,* of which the best known were by Theodulf, Haiton, Bishop of Bâle, Gherbald, Bishop of Liège, a bishop of Freising, and later on by Hincmar of Rheims and Raoul of Bourges. All these books were intended to strengthen the hierarchy and the authority of the bishops, to stop laymen interfering in sacred matters, and see that canonical rules concerning penance and marriage were strictly observed. Public penance, and old Church custom for the expiation of serious and notorious offences, had returned to favour in 813, as a reaction against the penitentials. But secret auricular confession was still kept up. An effort was made to condemn and put an end to abuses, such as consanguineous marriages or abductions, by defining the impediments to marriage; in 847 consanguinity in the fourth degree was definitely made an impediment. Thus canon law was made uniform and usages were regularised, all the more effectively because, by the very constitution of the State, legislation was carried out by civil and ecclesiastical authorities in co-operation, with the help of the councils and learned members of the clergy. Roman law was beginning to be studied again, and its influence is often visible in the tendencies that triumphed at this period.

Civil law also benefited from the Carolingian Renaissance. The whole Roman Empire had shared a single legal system, and many thinkers were attracted by this universality, which was based on logical norms very different from those governing Germanic law. In spite of invasions, and the adoption of national laws, Roman law had always been studied in certain centres like Bologna and Pavia, but it only began to have a general influence during the eleventh century. The differences among national laws were attacked in capitularies, and in books by certain broadminded clerics. As with canon law, collections of capitularies were made, for instance that of Ansegis, Abbot of Fontenelle, which dated from 827 and became quasi-official under Louis the Pious and Charles the Bald, and an attempt was made to classify the texts methodically so as to make it easier to consult them. As with canon law, too, texts were faked in order to support some individual pretension. The general purpose behind these compilations, whether authentic or fabricated, was to create a single legal system for the West, and to fight against the particularism of national laws.

Among contemporaries of Louis the Pious, Agobard of Lyons was most forcibly impressed by the absurdity of multiple legislation and the barbarism of some of the national laws. In a treatise addressed to the Emperor, entitled *Adversus Legem Gondobaldi*, he proved himself a high-minded and well educated man, capable of dealing with far-reaching problems. Criticising the Burgundian law which was in force in his diocese, he attacked the principle of separate laws for different nations, showed the abuses it led to, and called for the abolition of national laws and a unified legal code. His object was first and foremost to destroy this system, which was bound to lead to such relics of superstition as trial by ordeal or judicial duel. But Agobard was too much in advance of his time to have a chance of success. Even so distinguished a man as Hincmar, who belonged to a younger generation than Agobard, defended the system of trial by ordeal, and called on his knowledge of the scriptures to prove its excellence. The national laws were eventually replaced by a code with a narrower scope, but the principle survived in some regions until the middle of the tenth century. The reforms started by the contemporaries of Louis the Pious and Charles the Bald in the field of canon and civil law nevertheless continued the work initiated under Charlemagne.

It was the same with theology. The first Carolingian Renaissance produced distinguished intellectuals, who were masters of logical method, able to apply it with all subtlety to the study of difficult problems. But all intellectual advance depends on its framework and surroundings. In the Carolingian period, theology was only studied in abbeys and episcopal schools, where it was taught by the men actively responsible for their administration. It was therefore more inclined to tradition than innovation, and—like philosophy—made no real progress until the eleventh century, when the schools became more independent.

In the reigns of Louis the Pious and his sons, theologians considered problems concerning predestination and the eucharist. The problem of predestination raised an important issue for Christians; it arose in the sixth century, and again at every period when man's future and his relationship with God were subjects for reflection, particularly in the sixteenth century during the Reformation, and in the seventeenth with Jansenism: did God mean to save all men or, on the contrary, to lead a chosen few to eternal life? From the first, three texts from St Paul, relating to divine prescience, man's freedom of will, and grace respectively, were brought to bear on the subject. In the fourth century a Celtic monk called Pelagius rejected the necessity for grace. When attacking his doctrine St Augustine insisted that grace was a free gift from God, and his belief was later distorted to support the conclusion that God did not bestow grace on all men alike, but predestined some to be saved. By a slight further twist, the conclusion was reached that God predestined one part of humanity to eternal life and the rest to damnation. Of course St Augustine did not approach these problems from man's point of view: he was theocentric, and for that very reason left certain aspects of the problem in obscurity. But he had many disciples in Gaul: at the end of the sixth century it was accepted that God predestined man's salvation, but the council of Orange refused to accept that man could be predestined to damnation. At the beginning of the Carolingian period, the problem was again presented. It seemed as if the whole question must be considered afresh. A theological controversy on the subject was initiated by Gottschalk, and led to many theological works, and intervention by several councils. Gottschalk was a learned monk from the monastery of Fulda, who had studied with enthusiasm the works of St Augustine and his disciple St Fulgentius, and collected a whole series of extracts from the Fathers, which often—taken out of context—seemed to support the doctrine of predestination. He was in contact with the most famous writers of the day: Ratramn, Jonas of Orleans, Lupus of Ferrières and Raban Maur, archbishop of the ecclesiastical province in which he lived. Hearing that he had been preaching this doctrine in Friuli, Raban Maur wrote a treatise to refute it, in the form of another collection of extracts, with a moderately Augustinian conclusion. In 848 the council of Mainz condemned Gottschalk, and in 849 this condemnation was renewed by the council of Quierzy, owing to the intervention of Hincmar. Gottschalk was put in prison, but many theologians took up his case. Ratramn of Corbie supported him; Lupus of Ferrières, consulted by Charles the Bald, wrote a treatise on predestination in 850; Prudentius, Bishop of Troyes, was on his side. Hincmar, who supported his condemnation, obtained the advice of one of the most learned contemporary scholars, John Scotus Erigena, a very original thinker, the best and perhaps the only true dialectician of his day. But his reply to Gottschalk's supporters was clumsy, and contained more than one heresy according to several theologians. Prudentius of Troyes replied in a work prefaced by Wenilo of Sens, Hincmar's rival. The quarrel was embittered by personal factors, but it proved that a party wholly dedicated to Augustinianism existed in *Francia Occidentalis.* Prudentius, Lupus, Ratramn and Wenilo believed that the doctrine was threatened not by

Gottschalk but by his adversaries. In Lothar's kingdom the reaction was similar: the entire school of the Church of Lyons, including Amolon, Remi, and above all the scholaster Florus, whose opinion carried great weight, declared that his interpretation of several passages of the Scriptures was correct, attacked John Scotus Erigena, stated that Raban Maur (now dead) had been wrong, and made a bid for appeasement. Between 855 and 860, four councils summoned to consider the doctrine of the council of Orange of 529—it had declared in favour of moderate Augustinianism—attempted to pour oil on the troubled waters; so also did the papal legates at the council of Metz in 863. This quarrel in which the opinion of Raban Maur and Hincmar, two men of action who saw the danger of extreme doctrines, was confronted by that of studious men only interested in logic and pushing their theories to the furthest possible limits, clearly shows the keenness of purely intellectual speculation among these brilliant, learned, subtle minds trained in the art of argument.

Passions just as great were aroused by the eucharistic controversy. One of the essential beliefs of the Church since earliest times had been that the body and blood of Christ was actually present in the bread and wine consecrated during Mass: the members of the congregation who received them in the sacrament of the eucharist were receiving the body of Christ. In every period there had been some who were shocked by this belief, and had questioned the reality of transubstantiation, seeing it purely as a symbolic rite; but the Roman Church always condemned them and held firm on this point. Under Louis the Pious, the desire to understand and explain, born of the revival of learning, led to a controversy concerning the eucharist. In 831, one of Raban Maur's pupils called Paschasius Radbertus, a scholaster of Corbie, humanist, man of letters, hagiographer and theologian, wrote his chief work, *De Corpore et Sanguine Domini,* which he revised in 844 and sent to Charles the Bald. In it he affirmed that the eucharist was both real and symbolic at the same time. As it was thought that the somewhat vague treatment of the subject might give rise to controversy, the King consulted John Scotus Erigena and Ratramn of Corbie. The latter wrote a treatise with the same title as that of Radbertus, in which—without going so far as to make the eucharist purely symbolic — he questioned the identity of the body of Christ (the historical personage), with the body present in the sacrament (which could be taken as the *essential virtue* of Christ). In a letter to the Abbot of Prüm, Raban Maur returned to this question, subtly distinguishing between the essence and the mode of presence, while John Scotus Erigena seems to have tended to a spiritualist and mystical view by speaking of a 'memory' of the body of Christ. These controversies show the revival of speculative reasoning, which had been dormant for two centuries. The method used was literal explanation followed by theological analysis of the Scriptures and the Fathers. Thus Remi of Lyons reproached Pardulus of Laon for having made use of apocryphal texts. But none of this amounted to dialectics, except in the case of John Scotus Erigena, who was justly accused by his contemporaries of using nothing else; he was gravitating towards the dialectics of the eleventh and twelfth centuries, and was already using subtle and exact methods of reasoning. But besides this scientific criticism, a new allegorical form of explanation was beginning to appear, used particularly by Raban Maur; Amalar of Autun pushed it to the extent of symbolism without relation to logic, which was described by Paschasius Radbertus as nonsense. However, the allegories and symbolism originating in the Carolingian period were to remain in favour for a long time, and invade and sterilise medieval science and literature. The religious beliefs of all these men were unshakeable, and they only thought of learning as the foundation of apologetics.

The most remarkable feature of the reigns of Louis the Pious and his sons was the great number of writers who were at work. There were at least forty whose books had some merit. Many of them tried their hands at different forms, and beside the works of scholars and theologians we find history, hagiography, poetry, and encyclopedic works embracing the whole of culture.

History at first took the form of dry and apparently accurate annals, which were simply lists of events in chronological order. Often begun before the new dynasty, they were usually kept going in monasteries, such as Lobbes, St Gall, Fulda, St Vaast of Arras, and Lorsch. But official records were also beginning to be kept at court: the Royal Annals, begun in 741, were still continuing in various centres after 829. There were also works by individual authors who had tried to imitate the great historians of antiquity. Einhard, a friend of Charlemagne's, a learned humanist famous for his knowledge of Latin, and head of the artistic activities at court, set himself to write the Emperor's life modelled on the lives of the Caesars by Suetonius. The *Vita Karoli,* though a sort of pastiche, has undoubted literary value, for its author was faithful to his subject, and envisaged history as a branch of eloquence; its historical value is more dubious, since instead of collecting information from eye-witnesses he was content to follow the text of annals that are still available in a more complete form. Biographies of Louis the Pious were written by Thegan and an anonymous author nicknamed 'the Astronomer' because of his interest in meteorological phenomena. The same subject was treated by a versifier, Ermold the Black, who celebrated his hero's reign in a long poem. Very different qualities are to be found in Nithard's *History of the Sons of Louis the Pious.* This cultivated nobleman, grandson of Charlemagne and lay Abbot of St Riquier, who fought for Charles the Bald and was killed in his service in 844, found time to write a book describing the political and warlike opposition to the sons of Louis the Pious before the Treaty of Verdun. It is a work of the first importance, very carefully thought out and composed. Nithard was not only a man of action, he had a clear and acute mind, and was able to make balanced judgments about men and events. His work bears witness to the solid education received by important laymen during the flowering of the Carolingian Renaissance. Chronicles of world history had been in existence for a long time, for there had always been a few inquisitive minds eager to go back as far as possible into the past; the subject was revived by men like Freculphus, Bishop of Lisieux, who rewrote and completed the ancient chronicles of Eusebius, St Jerome, Prosper of Aquitaine and Orosius; another attempt of a similar sort was made in Charles the Bald's reign, by Adon of Vienne.

A literary form close to history, but more concerned with the edification of readers than with faithfulness to facts, was hagiography. Cultivated even in the Merovingian epoch, it had been revived in Britain by the Venerable Bede. In Charlemagne's day, Paul the Deacon wrote the lives of the bishops of Metz. Under Louis the Pious, Agnellus compiled those of the archbishops of Ravenna—a work remarkable for its careful research into historical sources. The lives of the abbots of Fontenelle by an unknown author, of Sturm, Abbot of Fulda by Eigil, of Wala by Paschasius Radbertus, and many others (quite apart from earlier works rewritten in more polished language) are all examples of hagiography in the reign of Louis the Pious. This interest even led to the creation of legends, such as those invented by Hilduin, Abbot of St Denis, and his followers.

Poetry was also in favour. The collected Latin poems of the Carolingian era take up four fat volumes of the *Monumenta Germaniae historica.* But they are on the whole mediocre. Poets inclined more and more to write in rhythmic verse, better adapted than classical prosody to ears that were unresponsive to the sound of the Latin language. A number of the poets of the period had some talent: Milo of St Amand, Raban Maur, Eric of Auxerre, Ermold the Black, Sedulius Scotus, Walafrid Strabo, Moduin and Prudentius are among the best.

There was also an interest in the didactic exposition of scientific learning. Theologians like Gottschalk, Raban Maur, Paschasius Radbertus, Prudentius, Ratramn and Lupus of Ferrières wrote treatises on philology and scientific subjects as well as theology. John Scotus Erigena was not only a theologian and dialectician; he was also a metaphysician, trying to construct a philosophic system that was neither rationalistic nor pantheistic, but which attempted to analyse such notions as God and Man, using a vocabulary largely borrowed from the neo-Platonists by way of St Augustine. A dozen years after he had written about predestination, he produced his *De divisione naturae,* in which he divided the whole of Nature into four classes (founded upon the creative power of beings and their condition as creatures, and leading to the notion of non-created and almighty God); he was aware of the problem of universals; he distinguished the different departments of theology. It is to his credit that he was not satisfied with merely collecting sources, but combined and transformed them, and evolved his own arguments from them. His works had a great influence throughout the Middle Ages.

In the intellectual intoxication that fermented after the barrenness of the previous period, some writers made inventories and summaries of knowledge. Encyclopedias were compiled, such as Raban Maur's *De rerum naturis,* which is merely an incomplete version of Isidore of Seville's. Lupus of Ferrières, another encyclopedist, was of noble Frankish stock, and showed an eager appetite for every branch of learning, sacred or profane. Theologian, hagiographer, Latinist and humanist, he devoted himself entirely to culture, and his correspondence with princes, prelates and scholars is a monument to the intense intellectual activity of the contemporaries of Louis the Pious and Charles the Bald. But the high quality of the works produced in this period is a function of the habits of thought and the mentality of the elite.

The different currents of ideas during the Carolingian epoch are not easy to study, and the work has hardly begun. One can however glimpse the sources of literary inspiration, and the working techniques used by intellectuals.

Not all the influences orientating the vast movement that began about 780 and went on until the end of the ninth century are yet known, but it is certain that the Irish and the Anglo-Saxons played an important part. Alcuin, John Scotus Erigena, Sedulius Scotus, Dunchad, Dungal and many other writers came from the British Isles and brought the Franks treasures of Latin literature that had been preserved in their country. The exact circumstances of their preservation we know little about, but it is certain that in the seventh and eighth centuries experts in literature like Aldhelm of Malmesbury and Bede were living in Britain, and that books which have since vanished, like Lucan's *Orpheus,* were preserved there. British libraries greatly influenced the Carolingian Renaissance, as did the patronage of important lovers of literature. Charlemagne was the most illustrious of its patrons, but all the sovereigns descended from him followed his example, and Louis the Pious, Charles the Bald and Louis the German counted their books among their most treasured possessions, and were surrounded by brilliant and cultivated courts where intellectuals were in high favour.

The Church was a prime influence because it was open to the world of ideas, because of its power and wealth, and its frequent and easy contact with schools and artists' studios; and of course some intellectual activities were the special domain of ecclesiastics. It was the Church that directed and encouraged the mingling of ideas on a vast scale that went on at this period. And it was the Church's efforts towards educational reform, and a more complete understanding of sacred writings, that led to the writing of so many books on language and grammar. As for the models studied, some of them—especially the poets— were thought to be a danger to faith. However Virgil, and to a lesser extent Horace and Ovid, were avidly read and annotated, in spite of the mythological allusions their works contained. Imitation of them even led to a change in the orientation of the literary renaissance: an artificial style developed, a sort of playful literary paganism, very far from the original aims of the movement. Thus imaginative literature was born of imitation of the ancients.

Hellenism too had a part to play in all this. Some ancient Greek works were preserved and studied in the Byzantine Empire. But Byzantium was still closely connected with Italy, and some works or literary themes were handed on to the Empire of the West through the intermediacy of Greeks from Italy, such as the Neapolitan deacon, Paul. These two sources, Latin poetry and mythology and some relics of Greek culture, influenced the intellectual climate: and side by side with the literature of ideas derived from school teaching, a number of literary forms began to be cultivated for the sake of pure entertainment. But emotional, passionate, or psychological sensibility was virtually non-existent at the time; it was imagination as an intellectual pastime that dominated medieval literature. Legends were accepted, Virgil and Lucan were constantly read and commented on, and an *Ilias latina*—or 'Latin Iliad', a collection of Homeric legends—was compiled. There was a public eager to read of the exploits of heroes and fabulous beings—purely imaginary creations. As for thought with a purely religious content, it was expressed not only in learned works, but also in sermons for Christian audiences. Here we have valuable evidence of the development of a mentality which began in the Carolingian period, for anyone who reads these works can easily see that their main theme is not the New Testament's religion of love, but the vengeful God of the Old; here we see spirituality dominated by an oriental current, hardly tempered by intermediate figures closer to man—the Virgin and the saints.

The most interesting mental development of the time was certainly the birth of philosophical argument, though only a few profound intellects grasped the fact that speculation could lead to two different spheres of thought: philosophy, ruled by pure reason, and theology, which presupposed an initial assumption.

Such were the general intellectual characteristics of our period. The student is struck by its genuine humanism, its eager desire to rediscover and absorb all human knowledge and find a rational method of acquiring it. 'Science', wrote Lupus of Ferrières, 'must be pursued with science'. In these words he expresses the disinterested cult of learning which was the fruit of Charlemagne's educational reforms, though not part of the Emperor's original purpose. The great and admirable impulse he gave to learning, creative activity and method, resulted in a complete revolution in the minds of educated men. The flowering of culture, inspired by Charlemagne's efforts in the middle of the ninth century, changed the direction of men's minds and led to a renaissance of literary invention and methods of thinking, in fact to the formation of a new cultural climate. It was the result of long and patient endeavour and the contributions of outstanding minds, and would probably have led to even more striking progress but for the misfortunes suffered by the West in the ninth and tenth centuries. Nevertheless the two great trends of the movement—the importance of method, and interest in imaginative literature—continued after this troubled period, and directed the course of medieval learning and literature.

The Carolingian Renaissance of learning and literature cannot therefore be considered merely as a brilliant moment in the history of the human mind; it was the fount and origin of an indefinite evolutionary process. This is also true of the revival of the visual arts.

Bernhard Walter Scholz (essay date 1970)

SOURCE: An introduction to *Carolingian Chronicles: Royal Frankish Annals* and *Nithard's Histories,* translated by Bernhard Walter Scholz with Barbara Rogers, The University of Michigan Press, 1970, pp. 1-33.

[*In the following essay Scholz describes and discusses the importance of two Carolingian works: the* Royal Frankish Annals *(740-829), which reflects the King's interest in keeping a record for posterity, and* Nithard's Histories, *a mostly contemporary (840-43) and more objective history which includes an account of Charlemagne's death.*]

One of the perennial obsessions of medieval authors was the suspicion that the past was superior to the present. In the preface to his *Life of Charlemagne,* Einhard of Seligenstadt expressed the fear that his work might offend the minds of those who despise everything modern. Yet he managed to overcome his scruples because he also knew of many "who do not consider everything done today as unworthy of mention and deserving to be given over to silence and oblivion." The vigorous government of the Carolingians and the regeneration of society in their time were indeed a great impulse to historical writing. Charles Martel, Pepin, and Charlemagne and his descendants provided great deeds for the historian. These rulers also dispensed patronage, and their reform of the Church provided a measure of literacy and learning; as a consequence, the number of historical works was large and their variety considerable.[1] Charlemagne himself collected historical poems written in the vernacular, which Einhard called the "barbarous and age-old songs that sing the deeds and battles of the ancient kings." Paul the Deacon wrote the history of his Lombard people, a sort of tribal history (*origo gentis*) in the manner of Gregory of Tours's history of the Franks or Bede's history of the Anglo-Saxons. Freculph of Lisieux and Ado of Vienne followed a familiar pattern of historical literature in their world chronicles. Einhard wrote his celebrated secular biography, the *Life of Charlemagne.* Alcuin was one of many contemporaries who paid homage to the saints by composing their lives. Ermoldus Nigellus recorded the varying fortunes of Louis the Pious in a Latin poetical history, and a monk of St.-Wandrille wrote the history of his monastery, in the tradition of the *Liber Pontificalis,* centered on the lives of its abbots.

The most unassuming works of history written during this age were the Carolingian annals, yet in the *Royal Frankish Annals* they become the most important narrative of this time: the story of the growth and flowering of the empire.

Other works are almost impossible to classify; this is true of Nithard's *Histories,* also called the *History of the Sons of Louis the Pious,* the report of an eyewitness on the internal conflicts which tore the Frankish empire apart. Together, the *Royal Frankish Annals* and Nithard's *Histories* provide a record, contemporary and official, of Carolingian history from the death of Charles Martel to the Treaty of Verdun. Their significance both as sources of the Carolingian age and as examples of medieval historiography has been long recognized. Not surprisingly, much French and German élan and subtlety have gone into the analysis of these works and their authors. The debate on textual problems, value, and viewpoints will certainly go on. But from the studies of these men and a fresh reading of the texts a relatively clear and reliable picture emerges of who these writers were and of what they wished and were able to do.

THE ROYAL FRANKISH ANNALS

The *Royal Frankish Annals* (*Annales regni Francorum,* as they have been called since Ranke) covers the period from 741 to 829. Although the oldest manuscript of the RFA was found in the monastery of Lorsch near Worms, Ranke saw that these annals had not been written there but at the royal court.[2] Of their character and significance M. L. W. Laistner has said:

> The *Royal Annals* provide the reader with a brief, unadorned narrative; but being restricted in scope, they leave him in the dark on many topics connected with the political, diplomatic, and military history with which they deal. Nor must one expect analysis of motives or a deeper understanding of cause and effect in a plain annalistic record of events. Nevertheless the *Royal Annals* must be regarded as the most important single source for the reign of Charlemagne, and must form the basis of any historical reconstruction of that momentous era in European history.[3]

During the Carolingian age annals appeared simultaneously in many places, the result of man's ancient urge to give form to his collective memory.[4] Egyptian and Babylonian rulers had kept annual records, and in Roman days the lists of the consuls had given rise to a similar form of rudimentary historiography. In the centuries when Christian missionaries were carrying the Gospel into the West, the Easter tables provided room for annual entries on the events of the year. Anglo-Saxon monks were apparently the first to record on these lunar calendars noteworthy occurrences around them, and Anglo-Saxon missionaries brought the Easter tables and their casual notations to the Continent. One monastery, then, copied from another, frequently borrowing not only the dates of Easter but the events noted on the margins. Before long the historical records were copied and continued for their own sake and expanded into major works of history by consulting and using other sources of information. Their diversity, varying degree of accuracy, and uncertain relationship to each other make them a difficult source to use. Students of the Carolingian annals have been struck, for example, by the similarity of phrases, which seem to suggest a complicated interdependence; they have assumed that some surviving annals are based on lost works, and with some luck they have even discovered works very similar to those whose existence they had suspected, as was the case with the *Annals of Salzburg* or the *Annals of Metz*. But it has also been made clear more recently that the similarities in many cases may have been due simply to the fact that the language of the annalists was limited and conventional.[5] The earliest continental annals had their origins in monasteries, but soon annals were composed which looked upon the events of their age with a broader view and from a more central perspective; this is particularly true of the *Royal Frankish Annals.*

Among the learned activities which Charlemagne and his court inspired and promoted was the writing of history. Not only was the Frankish king interested, as his biographer reveals, in St. Augustine's theology of history,[6] but he made an effort to preserve records on which the history of his rule could be based. The RFA mentions his archives; he ordered the preservation of his laws, and the compilation in the *Codex Carolinus* of papal and Byzantine letters addressed to himself and his father and grandfather. He probably had the *Liber Pontificalis* copied at his court and apparently gave his approval when Paul the Deacon wrote the *Deeds of the Bishops of Metz,* in which the history of the Carolingian house is given special attention. Whether he ordered the writing of the RFA remains uncertain. But it seems at least likely that Charlemagne encouraged the composition of this work as a record for posterity and an aide-mémoire to the officers of his government.[7]

That the RFA has an official character was convincingly argued by Leopold von Ranke more than a century ago. The historian noted two striking features in the first part (741-95), written evidently by a single author: first, a tendency to keep silent on great disasters in the field and on internal troubles, such as the conspiracies which arose from time to time, and second, his intimate knowledge of the affairs which he chose to record. No monk living in the seclusion of the cloister could have been so well informed on matters of politics and diplomacy. Ranke suggested a comparison of the RFA with the monastic annals of this period. The annals written in monasteries report only the most striking events and then note only their most general features. The first author of the RFA, however, tells in terse and precise terms not only about military campaigns but about the make-up of the armies, their commanders, and the purpose and nature of the individual military actions. He is also well versed in the diplomatic negotiations of the court. No one who was not close to Charlemagne's council could give such detailed information about the operations against Benevento and Bavaria. The combination of these two elements, good information and great reservation, convinced Ranke that the work was an official compilation. Ranke thought that the author was a cleric well acquainted with public affairs and perhaps officially commissioned to do this work. He compiled his notes at the court in a rough style, since he wrote before

the palace school helped polish the Latin of the Frankish clergy; he was a man of the old ways, but he rose above himself because he witnessed and commemorated momentous events.[8]

Ranke's view of the RFA as an official work has now been generally accepted. But its official character does not mean that every single word was examined and approved or that the annals were in any way conceived to have a secret character. On the contrary, their purpose was obviously to influence public opinion and to convey to posterity the Carolingian version of Carolingian history.[9] It was an old custom by the time of Charlemagne, as Smaragdus, the reforming abbot of St.-Mihiel, points out, for the ruler to authorize an official record of his reign. The relatives of Pepin commissioned such a record; Charles the Bald carried with him the annals composed by Prudentius,[10] and Alfred the Great inspired the writings of annals later in the ninth century.[11] Considerations of politics and public opinion occasionally influenced the nature of the information revealed or concealed by the RFA. A Byzantine offer of the imperial title made in 798 has been omitted, obviously for political reasons, since the well-informed annalist could not have been unaware of this extraordinary proposal.[12] The propagandistic character of the work persuaded at least one scholar that more reliable and detailed court annals existed at one time. This hypothesis, however, cannot be upheld, since later annals, in particular the important ninth-century *Annals of St. Bertin,* resume the story in 829, the very year in which the RFA ends.[13]

Even a casual reading of the RFA suggests that more than one author had a hand in this work. Its composite nature is betrayed both by the manuscripts and by its language and style. Friedrich Kurze, who has published the best critical edition of the RFA, attempted to clarify the problem of authorship by an examination of the manuscripts. The results of his effort were unsatisfactory, and more recently scholars have again fallen back on an examination of the linguistic and stylistic peculiarities of the work. It seems certain now that the first author compiled the RFA between 787 and 793 on the basis of older annals and the continuations of Fredegar, and then followed them with contemporary events. The personality of the first author remains an insoluble problem. None of the names suggested, such as Arno, bishop of Salzburg, or Riculf, archbishop of Mainz, have found general acceptance, nor has the thesis that the fall of Duke Tassilo of Bavaria in 788 led to the composition of the annals. The author was probably a member of the royal chapel; he shows familiarity with the language of documents and of the law and made use of official records and notations. Ranke proposed that Angilram of Metz, archchaplain from 784 to 791, inspired the writing of the RFA; it was Angilram who prevailed on Paul the Deacon to write the *Deeds of the Bishops of Metz* and on Donatus to compose a *Life of St. Trudo.* Several authors can be assumed if the work was compiled in the royal chapel, as Monod has pointed out, and the archchaplains would have done no more than supervise the work. The theory of multiple authorship would explain the fact that changes in style do not coincide with the archchaplains' years of death.[14]

The second part of the RFA comprises the years 795 to 807. The entries during these years are obviously contemporaneous with the events, but there is no agreement about the exact year in which authors changed. Different dates, all within the period from 792 to 795, have been suggested. Monod would ascribe the confusion of the annals during these years to the fact that Charles's favorite palace at Worms burned down in 790 and that only in 794 did Aix-la-Chapelle become the new residence of the court. The annals between 795 and 807 are more personal; the narrative remains simple, but the language reveals the author's classical training. Again, the identity of the writer is a mystery and authorship by several members of the chapel is a possibility.[15]

The third part of the RFA begins with the year 808 and extends to the last entries in 829. These annals are also contemporaneous. Their language is characterized by more skillful sentence construction, more extensive use of participles and connectives, a larger vocabulary, a stronger influence of classical models, and an occasional tendency toward bombast. This section of the RFA can be subdivided after the annal for 820. It seems that in the last part, from 818 to 829, the influence of the archchaplain Hilduin, abbot of St.-Denis, is unmistakable; he may have had the cooperation of Helisachar, abbot of St. Maximin in Trier and of other monasteries and chancellor of Louis the Pious (808-19); in any case the composition of these annals in the royal chapel is almost a certainty.[16]

Among the different men who have been suggested as authors of the RFA, the name of Einhard is obviously of special interest. F. Kurze assumed that Einhard wrote the annals from 796 to 819, and B. Simson believed that he could detect Einhard's pen in the annals from 809 to 829. But none of the arguments for ascribing any part of the RFA to the author of the *Life of Charlemagne* has been very convincing. There are similarities in the language of the RFA and in that of the *Life of Charlemagne*. But this is explained by the fact that Einhard knew and used the RFA. The style and the language of the third part of the RFA eliminate Einhard as a possible author. There is a similarity between Einhard's Latin and that of the second part of the RFA, but this is because literary skills improved during the Carolingian Renaissance to the benefit of the authors of both works. The first to claim Einhard as the author of the RFA was Odilo of St.-Médard in his *Translatio S. Sebastiani*. He names Einhard as the author of a work which he entitles *Gesta Caesarum Karoli Magni et filii Hludowici* and which, according to Odilo, has a reference to the translation of St. Sebastian by Hilduin, abbot of St.-Denis. This translation is, indeed, mentioned in the RFA under the year 826; and the *Gesta Caesarum* is obviously identical with the RFA. Odilo's erroneous belief that Einhard was its author probably resulted from the fact that in his, as in most medieval manuscripts, the RFA is preceded by Einhard's *Life of Charlemagne*.[17]

Einhard's relationship to the RFA has been a particular problem with regard to a group of manuscripts of the RFA containing a version of the RFA which has been revised in style and contents. Ranke and others considered Einhard as the author of these revised annals;[18] they appear in print as *Annales qui dicuntur Einhardi*.[19] The revision originally was believed to have been undertaken shortly after 801. But then H. Bloch demonstrated that there are stylistic revisions up to 812, although no change in the material recorded was made after 801. At the present time the consensus among students of the RFA seems to be that the revision was carried out after Charlemagne's death in 814 but before 817; Einhard's *Life of Charlemagne,* which reveals that its author knew the revised RFA, was written after 817. The language of the revised version is similar to that of the third part of the RFA. The revisor apparently belonged to the same court circle as the authors of the RFA, but wished to give the work a form more in keeping with the new style. As far as content is concerned, the revisor attempts to supplement the information of the original RFA by drawing on other sources that were accessible to him at the court. But a different point of view is evident in the revised version; most strikingly, it relates failures and disasters which the original annalist had been careful to omit, for example, the famous debacle of Charles's army at Roncesvalles in 778 which later inspired the *Chanson de Roland*. The revisor adds personal, geographical, and other details, as a comparison of the very first annal in its original and revised forms shows. He is also more inclined to make conjectures and to probe the motivations of the actors. He injects a new element into the RFA by attempting to present Charlemagne as the central figure, who alone plans, decides, and acts. Although he shows a great attachment to the deceased emperor, the revisor betrays that he was further in time from the actual events than the annalists. Apart from Einhard other persons have been suspected of revising the RFA, but no really convincing arguments have been put forward for any one individual.[20]

The authors of the RFA note only the bare outlines of the world in which they live. Military actions, diplomatic missions, and major political events attract their attention first; yet, in their barren record we catch a glimpse of the universe—physical, social, and spiritual—in which the writers breathed and thought.

It is a world in which nature presents a forbidding challenge to man, raising barriers around him and beating down his ambitions. The changes of the season determine the rhythm of life. Summer is the time of action, and campaigns begin when the horses can feed off the land and come to a sudden halt when heavy rains cause rivers to flood. In winter the king settles down in his palace, leaving the annalist little to report. Minor variations in the climate spell disaster. Animals and men are killed by severe cold or by pestilence resulting from mild weather and excessive humidity. Expeditions into foreign lands end with military success and yet lead to calamity when disease carries off the men and horses of the victor. Hail and lack of sunshine spoil the harvest and sour the wine. Famine stays the king's hand and forces him to postpone a campaign. Lightning strikes men and burns villages. Earthquakes cause mountains to tumble on top of cities, and eclipses inspire wonder and apprehension.

While nature threatens man with its spasmodic violence, divinity intervenes mysteriously: a large block of earth is moved without human support; ominous lights appear in the sky at night; a woman for two years abstains from all food except the bread of the Eucharist; a trace of the blood of Christ is found, and the discovery moves the pope to journey from Rome to Mantua; the relics of the saints miraculously heal the sick; the army of Charlemagne when suffering from thirst is marvelously relieved, like the Hebrews in the desert, by a sudden flow of water in a brook; the heathens are unable to burn a church because St. Boniface foretold that it would be proof against fire; and a picture of the Virgin and the infant Christ unaccountably shines with unusual brightness. Although the annalists record the intervention of the supernatural, divine activity is not presented as the immediate cause of political events. Rather it appears as a reminder that the natural order is forever maintained by the divine will and subject to sudden dispensation: the Lord of history ordains the happenings among men. But human decisions and drives—the lofty resolutions of the Frankish monarch and the beastly instincts of the Saxons—and stubborn circumstance cause change and thus make the history which the annalists record.

The annalists live in a world of villages and manors, of camps and castles, of few roads and fixed routes, where the Lombards can keep a single messenger or an entire army from passing across the Alps, and of uncertain frontiers which are difficult to protect. It is a world of simple and unpredictable technology. The Saxon siege machines do more damage to their operators than to the enemy; the gift of an organ from the emperor of Constantinople deserves an entry in the annals of the realm, and an organ-builder from the East is escorted to Aix-la-Chapelle by the treasurer of the emperor. Traveling is hazardous and slow; three men set out for the court of Harun al-Rashid in Bagdad, but only one survives to return after four years. Yet the intrepid main actor of the RFA, the Frankish king, seems as oblivious of physical obstacles as he is impatient with political opponents. In one year he builds two bridges over the Elbe and fortifies one of them by bulwarks of wood and earth at both ends; with a movable bridge of pontoons connected by anchors and ropes he makes the Danube passable. He attempts to construct a canal between Altmühl and Rednitz which would allow him to travel by ship from the Rhine into the Danube. On the coast of the North Sea he builds a fleet and restores a lighthouse. The Danish king Godofrid plans a protective rampart which is to connect the coast of the Baltic with that of the North Sea. These are interesting efforts but they cannot conceal that ambitions and designs far outstripped technical knowledge and expertise. The technological innovations which are made during these centuries naturally

escape the attention of the annalists; they know nothing of the new plough, the harness, the crank, inventions which before long were to revolutionize the European economy, but are fascinated, as the ancients would have been, by a water clock, a marvel from the East, which at the completion of the hour makes a cymbal ring and has twelve tiny horsemen step out of little windows. Craftsmen and merchants are considered a great asset; the provision of builders and bricklayers by the archbishop of Grado is a reason for a diplomatic complaint; the merchants of Reric on the Baltic are resettled by the Danish king in his own kingdom because of the taxes which their town pays. Although this is not a narrow world—the king and his commanders range over the lands from the Ebro to the Elbe and from Schleswig to Salerno—it is a world of poor communication, where the exchange of ambassadors takes years and rumors determine or delay political action.

Since the economic resources are limited, social relations are tense and brutal. Warfare and violence rake Carolingian society. The king embarks on at least one large military campaign a year; his failure to do so he fears might be interpreted as a sign of weakness. Military expeditions aim at the conquest of hostile strongholds and the pacification of provinces, but are regularly accompanied by savage punitive actions designed to ravage and destroy the fields and villages of the enemy. The frontiers of the vast kingdom are fluid and quickly overrun by elusive bands of Saxons, Basques, or Saracens which vanish into their forests or out to the seas before the cumbersome Frankish host appears. Even within the borders of the kingdom, the hold of the Carolingian ruler is precarious; revolt, conspiracy, and sullen opposition force the king into costly and time-consuming operations which frequently end with nothing more than feigned submission. Violence flares where the royal might is a distant menace; the king's emissary is slain and his missionary martyred while preaching the Gospel. Moorish and Viking pirates haunt the coasts, burn villages, seize booty, and carry away the inhabitants, leaving only the old and infirm behind. The Frankish ruler counters the violence of his subjects and enemies with brutal force; rebellious nobles are tonsured and locked up in monasteries; conspirators against the king are blinded or hanged on gibbets; multitudes are slain in battle, and the annalists report proudly the massacres wreaked on foreign tribes; over four thousand Saxon nobles are executed at Verden in 785; countless numbers are forcibly baptized; and entire populations are removed from their homelands and resettled in new regions.

The society of which the annalists write consists of the nobles and the people, *primores* and *populus*, but it is only the former who have a voice in determining the course of affairs. They are the large landowners and feudal warriors who are bound to their lord by bonds of personal loyalty. The RFA refers specifically to the act of homage by which a vassal places his hands in those of the king and becomes the king's man, and to the oath of fidelity sworn on the bodies of the saints. On important issues of the day—a foreign campaign, an expedition to Rome, the trial of a vassal—the king seeks the counsel of his vassals at special meetings or at the annual general assembly of the Franks. Foreign relations and military actions are the major, almost the exclusive, interest of the annalists. This is due in part to the old tradition of political history as first popularized by Thucydides, but it is also a result of the virtual absence from the Carolingian scene of properly organized governmental institutions about which the annalists might have written. The king is the government, an absolute monarch, the supreme commander, the chief legislator, the highest court of appeal. He derives his power from God and is bound to keep the peace on earth and to help his people to be saved in heaven. His despotism is restrained by his scanty resources rather than by the ethics of his political ideology.

There is no central government but only the royal household, and the functions of the officers of the court are primarily domestic. The RFA mentions the officials of the court—the chancellor, the chaplain, the treasurer, the notary, the chamberlain, the seneschal, the marshal, the master of the cupbearers, the master of the doorkeepers. They act as advisers, ambassadors, and military commanders of the king but do not head branches of a central government. The official most frequently mentioned in the RFA is the count, the king's representative who exercises full public authority in one of the several hundred counties into which the realm of the Carolingians is divided. More prestigious and powerful are the positions of the counts or wardens of the marches along the frontiers of the empire or the special posts of command given from time to time to the *missi* of the Frankish king. The most important of these offices are held by relatives of the royal family. An incident which the RFA relates in the revised part of the annals under the year 782 indicates that kinship gives a man higher prestige than any official rank or position. The chamberlain Adalgis, the marshal Gailo, and the count of the palace Worad are defeated by the Saxons because they do not go into battle with a Frankish host under the command of the king's kinsman Theodoric for fear that he would receive all the credit for victory. The king's personal appearance is still the most effective and often the only way of enforcing the royal will, and this is another explanation for the king's ceaseless journeyings through his realm. The Carolingians, under the influence of their clerical advisers, attempt to replace the Merovingian notion that the kingdom is simply the monarch's personal property by the idea that king and community are bound together by mutual obligations. The kings continue to divide the kingdom among their heirs, however, just as they split their booty and distribute their spoils.

Filling the king's treasury, preserved apparently in the royal bed-chamber and guarded by the chamberlain, is one of the unadmitted objectives of Carolingian foreign policy. The incessant conflicts of the Carolingians with their neighbors are a means to provide the king with sufficient funds to reward his vassals and to compensate for the meager resources and inadequate revenues of his kingdom. Tributes, gifts, and booty are therefore constant themes of the RFA. The Saxons have to present three hundred horses every year; Charlemagne carries away the gold and silver stored in the Saxon sanctuary called the Irminsul; he captures the treasure of the Lombard king Desiderius. Duke Eric of Friuli takes the treasure of the Avars, which has been accumulated by centuries of conquest and pillage and is stored in their central fortress, the "ring," and Charlemagne shares it with his vassals and the pope. Similarly, the spoils after the defeat of Ljudovit, duke of Lower Pannonia, are avidly seized and carried home.

The RFA usually fails to reveal the underlying objectives of campaigns and diplomatic missions, but it indicates the direction and the changing thrust of Carolingian foreign policy. In the beginning Pepin and Charles have their hands tied because they are forced to subjugate independently minded powers within the borders of the kingdom, in particular the dukes of Alamannia (742), Aquitaine (742-69), and Bavaria (743-88). These conflicts end with the seizure and submission of the rebels. The annalists make no attempt to determine the deeper causes of these revolts. They are most explicit in the case of Tassilo, duke of Bavaria, who is charged with wickedness, breach of oaths and promises, inconstancy, mendacity, disobedience, treachery, desertion, an attempt on the king's men, lèse majesté, with inciting the Huns against the Frankish king, and with permitting his wife Liutberga, a daughter of deposed King Desiderius of Lombardy, to set him against the Franks. His crime is not that he sought autonomy for his tribe but that he broke his oath of loyalty and deserted his lord.

The alliance of the Frankish kings with the papacy involves the Franks in the affairs of northern Italy, and the ensuing destruction of the Lombard kingdom results in the first great expansion of the Carolingian realm. The annalists describe the conflict from a narrow, self-righteous point of view as a struggle for the pope and the rights of St. Peter and against a wicked and oath-breaking tyrant and his arrogance and oppression. Next, the Saxon war consumes the energy of the Frankish king for more than two decades, ending in the permanent subjugation of the Saxons. Whereas Pepin conducts only occasional retaliatory raids against the pagan Saxon tribes (743, 744, 747, 758), Charles presses the war by annual campaigns (772-85), numerous battles, calculated brutalities, and the systematic depredation of Saxon territory. Charlemagne's determination and at the same time his sense of frustration are indicated by the revisor of the RFA when he writes that the king "decided to attack the treacherous and treaty-breaking tribe of the Saxons and to persist in this war until they were either defeated and forced to accept the Christian religion or entirely exterminated." Although this author is writing long after the Saxons have become part of the Carolingian empire, he does not trust them and maintains, under the year 785, that "the stubborn treachery of the Saxons quieted down for a few years, mainly because they could not find convenient opportunities for revolt." In 793 the Saxons, in fact, rebel again, and even the almost continuous presence of the king and his army between 793 and 799 does not entirely root out all opposition; as late as 804 the emperor has recourse to deportation and resettlement. Whereas the revisor of the RFA explains the bloody campaigns against the Saxons primarily as a consequence of their rebellion, their inroads into Frankish territory, and their stubborn treachery and perfidy, the original annalist sees the conflict above all as a war between Christians and pagans. One of the first acts of Charlemagne in Saxony is the destruction of the Irminsul, the heathen sanctuary; three times Frankish exploits and victories are accompanied by miracles; and phrases like "by the will of God," "with the help of God," "God frustrated their intentions," and "How much the power of God worked against them for the salvation of the Christians, nobody can tell," seem to indicate that to this annalist the Saxon campaign is almost a holy war to increase the kingdom of God.

The conquest of the lands between the Rhine and the Elbe involves the Carolingians with the eastern and northern neighbors of the Saxons. Charles considers the Elbe and the Saale as his eastern frontier and builds castles along these rivers, but the presence of Frankish power easily leads to Frankish interference in the affairs of the Slavs living on the eastern banks of the Elbe and the Saale. Deep inroads into Slavonic territory, like the attack on the Bohemians in 805, however, remain exceptional. The Slavs appear in the RFA for the first time in 780, but from then on Wilzi, Sorbs, Smeldingi, Linones, and especially the Obodrites are of continued interest to the annalists (782, 789, 806, 810, 811, 812, 815, 816, 817, 819, 821, 822, 823, 826). Charles plays the petty Slavonic chieftains against each other and punishes the attacks of the Slavs by expeditions beyond the Elbe, devastating the land and leaving only after hostages have been given. In this way the Slavs are compelled to recognize Frankish overlordship; they remain a potential threat to the Franks because they tend to ally themselves with their northern neighbors, the Danes. The annalists reveal no sympathy or understanding for the interests of these tribes. If the Franks wage war on them it is for breach of faith, or, if the people have at no time been subject to the Franks, because of their arrogance and hatred.

The Danes move within range of the annalists for the first time in 782 when their king Sigifrid sends ambassadors and the Saxon Widukind seeks refuge with them. Their relations with Franks and Slavs and their unending internal squabbles receive much attention in the RFA between 804 and 829. The annalists note that the Vikings infest the North Sea in 800 and are ravaging the Frankish coast in 810 and 820. In later years the RFA is extremely well informed on Danish affairs. The author knows, for example, about their exploits against Scotland and Ireland. Perhaps his information stems from the Frankish ambassadors sent to the Danish kings in 823, Counts Theothari and Hruodmund, who "carefully studied the dispute with the sons of Godofrid as well as the condition of the whole kingdom of the Norsemen and informed the emperor of all they could find out in these lands," or from Archbishop Ebbo of Reims, "who had gone to preach in the land of

the Danes, on the counsel of the emperor and with the approval of the Roman pontiff, and had baptized many converts to the faith during the previous summer." The initial point at issue between Franks and Danes is apparently the question of Saxon fugitives. Later, the factions battling for the Danish throne seek outside support, and Charlemagne sponsors the cause of Heriold, who is baptized in 826 and given a base in Frisia for any emergency that might arise. The Danish kings are represented as haughty and foolhardy potentates who fail to recognize the power and majesty of the Frankish emperor, and references abound to "the mad king," "the arrogance and pride of the Danish king," his being "inflated with the vain hope of victory," his "hypocrisy" and "empty talk." But the concern with the Danes during these years indicates that the authors of the RFA were not only writing with all the frontiers of the wide empire in mind but perceived that the Norsemen constituted a growing threat in their time.

While the annalists frequently complain about the stubborn resistance of Saxons and Slavs, they are equally dissatisfied with the conduct of Basques and Bretons in the west. The Basques inflict a stinging defeat on the Frankish army in 778 in which many officers of the court are killed. The original annalist keeps silent on this episode; the revisor is frank but blames the disaster on "the unfavorable terrain and the unequal method of fighting" and considers the Franks superior to the Basques in arms and valor. Here again the charge of the annalists is that of "customary recklessness," "insolence," and "treachery." The Bretons rebel repeatedly (786, 799, 811, 818, 822, 824, 825), and the revisor as well as the later annalists similarly charge them with "fickleness," "treacherous spirit peculiar to the nation," "senseless obstinacy," and speak of the "arrogance of this faithless tribe," whose opposition, however, quickly collapses under the fierce blows of Frankish counts. Central and southern Italy, in particular the duchies of Spoleto and Benevento, enter the Frankish sphere of influence with the destruction of the Lombard kingdom in 774—and with Charlemagne's growing imperial ambitions. While the dukes of Spoleto are usually Franks appointed by the king, the dukes of Benevento retain a measure of independence but pay tribute. With the exception of the annal for 787 in the original version of the RFA, the affairs of central and southern Italy appear to be of marginal interest to the annalists. In any case, they appear to be of less significance than matters pertaining to Danes or Slavs.

The expansion of the empire and the growing prestige of its ruler bring the Franks into contact with the more distant powers of their world. In 777 a Moslem embassy from Spain is noted for the first time in the RFA; it is followed by a campaign which takes the emperor across the Ebro to Saragossa. Spanish affairs receive much attention between 797 and 828. Repeatedly peace is made with the emirs of Cordova and subsequently broken again. The Frankish kings concentrate their efforts on the areas of Pamplona and Saragossa and create the Spanish March in what later becomes the kingdom of Navarre and the county of Barcelona. But even at the end of the period covered by the RFA the Spanish March is not entirely secured, as the revolt of 827, the ravages of Abumarvan, the failure of the Frankish army, and the punishment of its commanders indicate. In the meantime the Franks are compelled to fight the Moslems on a much more uncertain front, the islands of the Mediterranean—Sardinia, Corsica, the Balearics—and the coasts of Italy which suffer from constant raids of Moslem pirates. The Christians repeatedly suffer severe losses. At one time eight merchant ships are sunk on their way from Corsica to Italy, and at another five hundred prisoners are discovered with a defeated Moslem force. They strike out, however, against the pirates from Italian ports, and Frankish counts fight the Moslems in Sardinia, Corsica, the Balearics, and even in North Africa.

Charles's conflicts with the Umayyard emir of Cordova make him an ally of the Abbasid caliph of Bagdad, the celebrated Harun al-Rashid. The RFA records two embassies sent by Charlemagne to Bagdad and two missions in return from the caliph (797-807). Harun's emissaries carry presents which include an elephant, a clock, and a beautiful tent. Harun al-Rashid even cedes certain rights of the Holy Places in Palestine to Charlemagne. The embassy from the oriental ruler—called the "king of Persia" by the annalists—and his exotic gifts receive much attention in the RFA and seem to confirm in the authors' minds their lofty notion of Charlemagne's place in the world.

For a period of about twenty years (797-817) the RFA gives evidence of close diplomatic relations between Francia and Constantinople. As in the case of Harun al-Rashid the annalists take note of the Byzantine emperor first as the donator of expensive and unwonted presents; in the year 757 the emperor sends an organ to Pepin the Short. The next encounter recorded by the RFA is less friendly; Emperor Constantine V orders his Sicilian governor to attack the Beneventan allies of Charlemagne. He is enraged "because he had been denied the king's daughter," a piece of information contained only in the original version of the RFA. The issues which divide the Frankish and the Byzantine emperors are vaguely identified by the annalists as "the Dalmatian question," the position of Venice, or the role of the archbishop of Grado. The sensitive problem of Charles's imperial title receives only implicit attention. After Venice has been restored to the Byzantines in 810, however, the Greek ambassadors at Aix-la-Chapelle "acclaimed him according to their custom, that is in Greek, and called him Emperor and Basileus." Although there is actual military conflict between Franks and Greeks in the years 806 to 810, the authors of the RFA refer to the Byzantines with respect, note the honorable treatment of Frankish emissaries, and record with interest events in the Byzantine world which have no bearing on the affairs of the West. The hostile and abusive tone which the annalists frequently affect when dealing with the opponents of the Franks is conspicuously absent in their description of Byzantine-Frankish relations.

Two powers complicate the relations between the Franks and the Byzantines in the course of the last ten years covered by the RFA. First the duke of Lower Pannonia, Ljudovit, revolts against Carolingian rule, and the Franks attack him on many campaigns. After Ljudovit's timely death in 823 the Franks encounter a new foe in the Bulgars, whose emissaries appear before Emperor Louis the Pious for the first time in 824. At issue is the border between Franks and Bulgars and the control of the Slavonic tribes living along the Danube in Dacia and in neighboring territories. That the Franks are fighting the Bulgars deep in the Balkans by the time the annalists discontinue the official annals of the realm is a measure of the expansion which the Carolingian empire undergoes over the nine decades of Carolingian history recorded by the RFA.

The RFA assigns a special significance to the contacts between the Frankish kings and the Roman popes. The name of a pope, Zacharias, first appears in the RFA under the year 749, an error for 750, in connection with the famous question of Pepin the Short addressed to the pope: whether the man with the name of king or the one who had the power should rule in Francia. The RFA then becomes the history of the alliance between the Carolingians and the papacy. Under the year 753 it records the unprecedented journey of a pope, Stephen II, across the Alps to Francia; under 754 the anointing of Pepin and his sons by the pope; under 755 the first campaign against the Lombard Aistulf "to seek justice for the blessed apostle Peter"; and under 756 the donation of the exarchate of Ravenna and the Pentapolis to the pope. For the years 773 and 774 the RFA records the renewed intervention of the Frankish king in Italy, stressing the invitation and request of the pope, and the destruction of the Lombard kingdom. In 781 two sons of Charlemagne are crowned kings by the pope. In recording these events the annalists leave no doubt that the pope is the petitioner but at the same time the indispensable mediator of grace when he consecrates kings and princes.

The true nature of Charlemagne's relationship with the pope is revealed by later events. The pope threatens the emissaries of Tassilo of Bavaria "with the sword of his anathema" if they should break fealty to Charlemagne and thus supports with his spiritual power the policy of the Frankish king; the king, on the other hand, when faced with the problem of the Adoptionist heresy, tries the heretical bishop twice before his own synod, relegating the pope and his representatives to a supporting role (792, 794). Councils are convoked and ecclesiastical legislation is initiated by the king and emperor. The pope upon his consecration sends to the emperor the keys of the tomb of St. Peter and the banner of the city of Rome. Popes announce their election to the emperor and have to be confirmed by him; in 827 Pope Gregory is not ordained "until the emperor's ambassadors had come to Rome and examined the character of the election by the people." The annalists record the imperial coronation of both Charlemagne and his son Louis the Pious by the pope, but they are obviously far removed from giving these acts a meaning even remotely similar to later papal interpretations. Instead, there seems to be much implicit criticism of the popes, although the language remains reverential throughout and the charges are reported as hearsay. In 799 Pope Leo III is saved from the fury of his Roman enemies by the agents of the king, but he is forced to purge himself publicly from all charges leveled against him. The emperor is displeased when the pope is reported to be responsible for the execution of some of his opponents (815). He examines carefully and by his own ambassadors the pope's blinding and decapitation of two papal officials whose crime is reported to have been that they always acted loyally toward the emperor's son Lothair, king of Italy. The annalist notes this charge as well as the pope's vigorous defense of the murderers and on another occasion claims that Roman affairs have been "confused due to the wickedness of several popes." As a result the RFA leaves the impression that the annalists think of the emperor very much in terms of the Christian Roman emperors whose foes are guilty of lèse majesté. The emperor is "the Lord's steward," *Dei dispensator,* holding his power from God and responsible alone to the Lord, but assisted in matters divine by a revered and prayerful Roman pope.

Such was the world of the Carolingians as observed and recorded by the nameless royal Frankish annalists, or rather a small part of that world, since the authors in the style of annalists remained indifferent to the complexities of personality and social life. It is a picture of the Carolingian world as viewed by a particular class of men. Although the annalists were men of greatly diverse mind and ability, they shared some common traits. The task, after all, for which they were called required peculiar talents and a special station in society. They were literate men in an age of illiteracy and thus more enlightened than most in their rough environment. They were members of the clergy or had at least attended monastic schools, which would have fostered in them, as it did in Alcuin and Einhard, a deep concern with the religious life and the current issues of theology. As writers they were obviously influenced by the language and thought of the Bible and easily borrowed the polished phrases of classical authors. In spite of their ecclesiastical garb their spirituality was superficial, superstitious, and legalistic, and their devotion to the pope tempered by their loyalty to the king. They were the king's men first, just as were the secular vassals, and cherished above everything the bond which personal fidelity tended to create between lord and faithful followers. They were probably men of aristocratic descent who shared the values and prejudices of their class; who served the king not only as priests and scribes but as emissaries and administrators; who would not wield a sword themselves but appreciated a good bout with plenty of blood and piles of spoils; who were proud of being Franks and contemptuous of their faithless enemies; who knew the court and its intrigues and competed with their peers for the honors and offices dispensed by royal bounty. They were men of limited sophistication who did not usually foresee the consequences of the acts they recorded, but they were also the men who supported Charlemagne's vision of empire and made possible its short-lived realization and the regeneration of Carolingian society.

Regardless of its authors' limitations, the RFA became an important source of information about the Carolingian age and, judging by the number of surviving manuscripts, for centuries was thought to deserve reading and copying.[21] Among the immediate users of the RFA were Einhard in his *Life of Charlemagne* and Nithard in his *Histories,* Poeta Saxo, and the biographers of Louis the Pious.[22] The RFA also served as a direct or indirect source for the other annalistic works of the ninth century, e.g., the *Annales Mettenses Priores* (678-831).[23]

In the revised version the RFA was continued in the ninth century. A copy which contained minor additions for the years 741 to 829 was extended into the *Annales Bertiniani,* named after the location of the first manuscript. The first writer who added to the annals was a native of Belgian Gaul and loyal follower of Emperor Louis the Pious. From 835 on, Prudentius, chaplain of Louis the Pious and later bishop of Troyes (843/46-61), continued these annals. While he wrote at first as the annalist of the empire and with sympathy for the emperor, he identified himself after 840 with the interests of Charles the Bald and the western part of the Carolingian empire. After 853 his attitude towards Charles became more critical and reflected the resolve of the French episcopacy to guide and direct the king. It was, therefore, only natural that after Prudentius' death Hincmar, archbishop of Reims, the most important statesman in the realm of Charles the Bald, took it upon himself to record the events of the kingdom until his death in 882.[24] The *Annales Xantenses* (790-873), whose main author, Gerward, was librarian in the palace of Aix-la-Chapelle and Einhard's successor as supervisor of building, for the years 797-811 incorporates an abridged version of the RFA.[25] The *Annales Fuldenses* (714-902), a source well informed on affairs in the eastern part of the empire, made extensive use of the RFA for the years 771-827. Like the *Annales Bertiniani,* it reflects some sort of official interest or inspiration, perhaps on the part of the archbishop of Mainz.[26] This threefold continuation of the RFA is a fitting symbol of the fate which struck Charlemagne's realm and eventually caused the official annalists to keep their silence.

NITHARD'S HISTORIES

Nithard's *Histories* is the most important source for the wars among the sons of Louis the Pious, which set the stage for the dissolution of the empire. It provides the only evidence for many episodes between the old emperor's death in June 840 and the treaty of Verdun in August 843, which set the seal on the partition. Nithard attached himself to the emperor's youngest son, whose birth in 823 and investment with part of the empire a few years later had been the root of the conflicts between Louis the Pious and his three older sons in the 830's. For this reason, Nithard's work records the fraternal wars from Charles's and a western point of view and with obvious bias against Lothair. Nonetheless, in scope, in deapth, in detail of information, Nithard far surpasses the other historians of the dying empire, such as Prudentius, the annalist of St.-Bertin, who shared Nithard's bias in favor of Charles; Rudolf, the annalist of Fulda, who from a partisan of Lothair gradually changed into a supporter of Louis, or the nameless annalist of Xanten, who favored Lothair but recorded little of relevance about him during these years.[27]

Nithard's *Histories* is not only a significant source of information for a crucial event in the history of medieval Europe but an interesting and rather unusual piece of historical literature. It is contemporary, self-contained, and programmatic history, i.e., Nithard relates the events of his own time and experience, he limits himself to a specific and well-defined theme, and he frankly admits that he writes to prove a point and to forestall a different interpretation. Nithard wrote in this fashion apparently without following a literary model. Tacitus in his *Histories,* however, had written contemporary history. Similarly, Sallust, whom Nithard may have read, in his *Catiline* and *Jugurthine War* had written the histories of significant and self-contained episodes. Hardly a historian, on the other hand, had ever admitted partisanship as candidly before; instead, every writer claimed with Tacitus to be "unmoved . . . by either hatred or partiality." But the open profession of a point of view seems appealing today and did not prevent an upright man from writing an honest work. A further peculiar feature of Nithard's *Histories* is that the author was a layman—"for a long time the last layman to write history, without literary ambition, but with lucidity, insight, and honesty."[28] Like Einhard, also a layman, Nithard benefited from the reform of education and revival of learning in the days of Charlemagne, which improved Latin style, inspired a deeper interest in the knowledge of classical and Christian antiquity, gathered the native memories of the past, and introduced the historical tradition of Anglo-Saxon England. A wide-ranging, realistic, personal, and unparochial historiography was the result; Nithard was an important exponent of this.

Some knowledge of Nithard's family and public life can be gathered from his work. He was a grandson of Charlemagne, his mother being Bertha, the emperor's daughter by Hildegard. His father was the poet Angilbert, nicknamed "Homer" at Charlemagne's court, who received the abbey of St.-Riquier near Amiens and died shortly after his emperor.[29] The illicit relations between Angilbert and Bertha, which produced another son, Hartnid, and may have given rise to the tale of Einhard and Emma, occurred in the 790's, and Nithard thus must have been in his forties when he lived through the fraternal wars.[30] Although Nithard led the life of a soldier and held high public office, he was obviously a man of some learning. His position as Charles's official historian, his careful tracking of a comet which appeared in the winter of 841-42, his biblical quotations and Virgilian reminiscences indicate the breadth of his scholarship.[31] Why Nithard took the side of the young Charles cannot be explained, but he looked upon

him as a ruler appointed by God.[32] In the fall of 840 Charles sent Nithard and another count, Adalgar, as his envoys from Bourges to make peace with Lothair. Because the envoys refused to defect from their lord they lost the fiefs which they had received from Louis the Pious. The author participated in the fratricidal battle of Fontenoy on June 25, 841, and was able to lend crucial support to Adalgar. On October 18, 841, he was in Charles's headquarters at St.-Cloud near Paris, writing his record of the battle. In 842 the historian was chosen as one of twelve magnates representing the western half of the empire to consult with twelve nobles of the eastern half about the proposed division of the entire realm between Louis and Charles.[33]

Little is known about Nithard beyond the data which he provides in his work. Like his father he became lay abbot of the monastery of St.-Riquier or Centulum, apparently in 843. He died in a battle against the Normans on May 15, 845.[34] An epitaph by the monk Mico notes his wisdom and fortitude and bemoans his brief tenure of office and death by the sword.[35] Hariulf's chronicle of St.-Riquier records that Nithard was first buried in the abbey next to his father but after the latter's translation in the eleventh century was placed in Angilbert's sarcophagus. At that time the head wound of which he died could still be seen.[36]

Nithard, as he informs the reader in the preface to the first of his four books, wrote his work at the request of his lord, Charles the Bald, who asked him, before occupying the city of Châlons in May 841, to record the events of their time. Although the author accepted the task as an honor and an obligation which he owed to his lord, he was wary of the difficulties and of possible mistakes. He wondered whether he would have sufficient leisure in such troublesome times; whether he could apply the attention and care necessary and convey the proper meaning of events.[37] At the beginning of the third book Nithard revealed that he would have preferred to end with the second, since he was ashamed of what he had to record about his Frankish people. What alone impelled him to go on was the fear that someone else might produce an improper version of the history of his times.[38] The concern which Nithard voices here indicates the nature of the work: it was an official, partisan piece of history, intended to explain to posterity what Charles and his followers considered the cause and meaning of the fraternal wars. Nithard's main theme was Lothair's unjust persecution of Charles and his party. In Book I he tells why Lothair pursued Charles and his brother Louis after their father's death; in the rest of the work he describes "with how much vigor and zeal" Lothair tried to execute his resolution.[39] Nithard's *Histories* thus consists of two distinct parts: one book of history in the customary sense and three books of contemporary history, the former covering the years from 814 to the depth of Louis the Pious in 840, the latter from the summer of 840 to the spring of 843.

The summary in Book I of the events from the death of Charlemagne to that of Louis the Pious is a concise and necessary prologue to Nithard's topic. It is a more lucid and purposeful survey of the period than the biographies of Louis the Pious and has been called "the best guide to find a way out of the confusions of that time." In the welter of conflicting loyalties and uncertain alliances, Nithard clearly discerned the opposing principles: the unity of the whole versus the autonomy of the parts.[40] The story in Book I is selective; some important events are omitted because they did not seem relevant to Nithard's topic, but even here Nithard is often the only source of essential detail. He alone, for example, reports that Louis the Pious made his illegitimate brothers companions of his table and that it was Bertmund, prefect of the province of Lyons, who blinded Bernard in 818. Since the first book was written from memory and some of the events had occurred more than two decades earlier, Nithard makes some minor mistakes. He fails to mention the widows, orphans, and churches who received a share of Charlemagne's treasure when it was divided after the emperor's death. He erroneously maintains that Charles was held captive with his father at Soissons in the summer of 833, that Pepin met Louis the Pious in St.-Denis instead of Quierzy, that Lothair was told to go to Italy in 834, that Judith's captors in Italy suddenly became her liberators. He underestimates the profound excitement caused by the meeting of the brothers Lothair and Louis at Trent in 838. He is confused in his chronology and refers to Bernard's revolt before the division of the empire in 817, although it was this event which caused the nephew to rise against the emperor; Judith purged herself of charges of adultery in 831 and not in 834; Louis the Pious died at age sixty-two and not sixty-four; he was emperor for twenty-six years and nine months, not twenty-seven years and six months.

The degree of Nithard's objectivity can best be established by an examination of the first book, where only in rare cases is his record the sole source for an event. Nithard proclaims himself a partisan of Charles the Bald at the beginning of his work and his prejudices affect his history. He is silent when the facts might hurt Charles or Louis the Pious; he does not mention Charles's total exclusion at the partition of 833 nor the humiliating act of public penance performed by Louis the Pious at Soissons in October 833.[41] He places Lothair in the worst light, plays down the position of co-emperor which he was given in 817, calls him a breaker of oaths and promises, and makes much of the judgment which Lothair had to pronounce on his own followers when Louis the Pious regained the upper hand over his rebellious son in 831. Lothair is pictured as the lone instigator of the revolt of 830 when, in fact, his presence in Italy at its outbreak precluded his participation; he was, of course, the natural rallying point for all who were disturbed by Judith's influence and the emperor's misgovernment. Nithard permits himself an obvious misrepresentation of the facts when he portrays Counts Hugo and Mathfrid as invidious intriguers, although they opposed Judith solely because they wished to preserve the unity of the empire. On the other hand, he records the granting of Aquitaine to Charles as an incident of no significance when in reality it was highly unfair, made Pepin an open enemy of the empire, and constituted a threat also to the

other brothers. Pope Gregory IV appears as a tool of the conspirators in 833, but Nithard neglects to report that the pope had a genuine interest in the unity and peace of the empire and did not savor the sad role he was forced to play in Lothair's service. The two other brothers of Charles, Louis and Pepin, are also treated unfairly on occasion: Louis' contribution to his father's restoration in 831 and 834 is not sufficiently noted; Nithard exaggerates when he claims that both Louis and Pepin strove for precedence over each other, when their real concern was simply the retention of their respective portions of the empire; the historian looks upon Louis as an inveterate troublemaker when Louis revolted against being deprived of territories he had controlled for many years. In spite of the fact that Nithard viewed events from Charles's perspective, he was not a mindless partisan; his prejudices are those of his environment, the court of Louis the Pious with its hostility to the older sons. This climate, however, did not demoralize the historian, as it did the emotional and deceptive author of the life of Louis the Pious. Nithard believed that Charles's mother Judith had committed adultery with Duke Bernard of Septimania, but was hardly in a position to say so in his book; he nevertheless records the charge and does not dispute its validity. He candidly criticized the same Bernard for abusing his authority, although the man was one of Judith's and Charles's most loyal followers, and toward the end of his work he charges that his lord married the niece of the influential Adalhard "because he believed that with Adalhard he could win a large part of the people for himself."[42]

The three last books of Nithard's *Histories* confirm the impression that the author, though a fervent partisan of Charles and an opponent of the empire, recorded the events of his time with honesty and objectivity. These three books are devoted to the political moves and military campaigns, the diplomatic missions and shifting alliances, the drafts for a division of the empire and the growing weariness of the people, which eventually resulted in the treaty of Verdun.[43] Book II was apparently written from memory, but in Books III and IV Nithard let little time elapse between the event and his record.[44] Charles remains in the center of things throughout the work, but in the later parts a change of method is noticeable. Apparently, Nithard took less pleasure in his task as the war dragged on; in the preface to his last book he not only welcomed a respite from the labor of writing but contemplated a complete withdrawal from the burden of public affairs. Only the prospect that he might dispel the haze of error to the benefit of future generations made him go on. Increasingly, the unity of his theme is disregarded and digressions creep in. Earlier in the work any digression was related to the fate of his hero, as in the story of the royal vestments and insignia which arrived unexpectedly at Troyes on Easter 841.[45] In his last two books, however, the author talks about the weather, a comet, his family, or the war games performed by the soldiers when the forces of Louis and Charles united in 842.[46] In the very last book Nithard's style almost resembles that of the monastic chronicler. Without definite plan and employing awkward connectives, he strings together events in which his hero is involved, but also describes the society of the Saxons, the invasion of the Saracens, an earthquake, and a lunar eclipse.[47] Want and disease and natural disasters abound in the last chapters and induce pessimistic reflections on the selfish and bestial actions of men which provoke the judgment of God.[48] As he started his work with a eulogy to Charlemagne, Nithard ends with a nostalgic glance back at the reign of his grandfather when men were righteous and walked the ways of the Lord and peace and prosperity filled the realm of the Franks.[49] In the later books Lothair emerges again as indecisive, treacherous, and cowardly, Louis on the other hand, as a man of nobility and magnanimity. In both cases Nithard's assessment of the character of the man is generally confirmed by other contemporary sources. Only in his portrait of Charles does Nithard find no corroboration. The later history of his reign reveals Charles II as a spineless coward, greedy, crafty, "timid as a rabbit," in the words of a contemporary, but ruthless enough to have his own son, Carloman, blinded. In Nithard's *Histories* this *novellus Sennacherib* cannot be found; instead Charles, who was in fact a gifted and well-educated man, appears as a cautious diplomat, a resolute leader, a masterly strategist, a humble and charitable prince, almost a martyr. The contrast is striking. Nithard was describing a youth between the ages of seventeen and twenty, however, and his judgment may have been affected not so much by the spirit of party as by the hopes and expectations of a guide and teacher. That he was not an uncritical panegyrist his frank revelation of Charles's failures and defeats makes abundantly clear.[50]

If Nithard was willing to provide an accurate picture of the events of his time, he was also in an excellent position to do so. Only in connection with the battle of Fontenoy does he mention his personal involvement in military action, but he evidently advised and aided Charles in many campaigns of these years. His detailed reports on marches and expeditions, their beginnings and ends, routes and obstacles, on the prevailing weather and the motives and purposes of his lord admit no other conclusion.[51] Similarly, his intimate knowledge of delicate negotiations and deliberations at court, and of the aims and objectives of the main actors, leaves no doubt that he was close to the center of power and belonged to the innermost council of Charles and perhaps previously of Louis the Pious. He knows about the fears which troubled the doting father when Charles was born and of the consultations concerning Charles's future place and safety when the old emperor's days were drawing to an end; he is aware of the rivalries between certain Frankish noblemen as to who was to exercise the greatest influence over Lothair.[52]

Nithard also relied on written evidence; he probably was familiar with Einhard's *Life of Charlemagne,* the *Royal Frankish Annals,* and the *History of the Lombards* by Paul the Deacon. He certainly used numerous documents.[53] He presents verbatim accounts of the speeches made to their troops by Charles and Louis at Strasbourg in February 842 and of the verdict pronounced by the clergy assembled at Aix-la-Chapelle in March of the same year on the partition

of Lothair's share of the empire, and he preserves the German and French texts of the Strasbourg Oaths.[54] In many passages of his work it is obvious that Nithard was using texts of treaties, mandates, letters, and protocols or aide-mémoires and notes which he himself had made on the spot while involved in the business of war and diplomacy. The description of his own and Adalgar's embassy to Lothair, of the treaty of Charles and Lothair at Orléans in the fall of 840, the promises of Bernard of Septimania, Lothair's complaint and Charles's response at Christmas 841, the deliberations of the war council at Attigny, the joint resolution of Charles and Louis after their meeting in the spring of 841 and their mandates to Lothair, the negotiations about the division of the empire before the truce of Ansilla, the truce of Ansilla, all argue heavy reliance on documentary evidence. Similarly, in the first book, the circumscription of the areas assigned to Charles, Lothair's oath to protect Charles, the promise of Louis the Pious in 830 to improve his government, the conditions of peace between Louis and Lothair at Blois in 834, and the last admonitions of Louis the Pious to his son Lothair seem to be derived from written sources.[55]

While Nithard's role as an eyewitness and his reliance on official records inspire confidence in the trustworthiness of his history, his language and style show a marked decline from the high level of literary art in the days of the Carolingian Renaissance. Grammatical errors are rare in the *Histories,* although the author on occasion uses a subjunctive where one would expect an indicative, an adverb instead of an adjective, or a dependent clause instead of an accusative with infinitive, but obscurities and infelicities are more frequent. Nithard's language is artless and unaffected by the influence of ancient historiography; it resembles Alcuin's Latin although it does not imitate the language of the Bible.[56] If Nithard's style sometimes seems pedestrian and repetitious, it must be remembered that his work was that of a soldier and statesman, composed between diplomatic missions and military campaigns. But because Nithard's writing is unsophisticated, he was probably not widely read. The anonymous author of the life of Louis the Pious was familiar with the *Histories;* Mico, who composed Nithard's epitaph, may have known it; Hucbald of St.-Amand in his *Vita Lebuini* copies Nithard's passage on the three classes in Saxon society; excerpts found their way into a manuscript which Abbot Gervinus took from Gorze to St.-Riquier and from which Hariulf extracted his information on Nithard; the thirteenth-century author of a *Historia regum Francorum* refers to Nithard as one of his sources but gives no evidence of really having read him.[57] Nithard's *Histories* consequently survived only in a single tenth-century manuscript of the monastery of St.-Médard in Soissons, of which the monks of St.-Victor in Paris made a copy in the fifteenth century.[58]

Wherever Nithard feels deeply or is personally involved, he can nevertheless write with passion and arouse interest and sympathy, as in the mournful reflections on his grandfather at the beginning and end of the book or in his lively description of the war games conducted by the soldiers of Charles and Louis. By beginning his book with a chapter on Charlemagne, whose work the fraternal wars were to undo, Nithard reveals historical insight as well as a sense of literary artistry.[59] With a few phrases he is able to sum up a complex situation, as when Lothair's bedraggled forces defeated Louis' army in 834 just when the emperor had triumphed over the rebellious son: "The small number of Lothair's men," Nithard says, "put them at a great disadvantage, but at least they moved as one man. Wido's large army made him and his men secure but quarrelsome and disorganized"; or when he speaks of Charlemagne's "tempered severity with which he subdued the fierce and iron hearts of Franks and barbarians."[60]

The simple, direct style mirrors the mind of the author. Nithard's *Histories* is the work of a Frankish noble, a royal vassal engaged in war, administration, and politics and embracing the ideals of his class. Nithard was ready with a light heart to risk his life rather than betray the king and desert his cause; he let Lothair deprive him of the fiefs which Louis the Pious had conferred on him rather than break his oath and join the new emperor, and he likened to slaves those who preferred disloyalty and defection to the temporary loss of their property.[61] To Nithard the supreme wickedness, so it seems, was the breach of one's faith and the flouting of public order and lawful authority. Religion plays a minor role in his writings; they speak the language of the layman, a rare voice in those days. He sees the hand of God move the fortunes of man and decide the battle of Fontenoy in favor of Louis and Charles, but only on two occasions is he bold enough to suggest that divinity supported his hero's cause by a direct miraculous intervention.[62] Although he fought the party which carried the banner of unity and thus helped to destroy the empire of Charlemagne, he was pained by the rising anarchy, the growing autonomy of the nobles, the ever more daring attacks of Vikings and Saracens, the collapse of internal order, and the spreading evidence of want and poverty. He thus shared the pessimism and sense of impending disaster voiced by the poets who supported the party of unity and empire.[63] His stand for the independence of the parts and against the unity of the whole may strike us as perfidious today. It was probably justified in Nithard's mind not only by the idea of personal loyalty to his lord but by a sense of realism. "The natural and inevitable effect of immoderate greatness," as Edward Gibbon said of Rome, is the decline and fall of empires.

The Translation

The translation of the RFA and of Nithard's *Histories* is based on the latest critical editions by F. Kurze and P. Lauer, respectively. These are now considered the standard texts, and their readings or emendations of the manuscripts have been generally followed.

The Latin of the RFA is relatively simple, sometimes archaic and, because of the repetition of the same phrases and formulae, often stereotyped. There is, of course, no unity of style since various authors worked on it and many different sources were mined. But the language of the annalists offers few problems for the translator. Nithard, on the other hand, writes a more difficult Latin, with sometimes long and involved sentences and fuzzy adverbial phrases, which can raise real problems for his readers. This syntactical complexity is compounded by obscurities resulting from the manuscript tradition. Thus, it is easier for the translator to stay close to the text of the RFA than to Nithard's.

A word must be said on the problem of the revised version of the RFA. This is essentially a revision in style. How the revisor modified the original may be seen from a comparison of the annal for the year 749, a famous passage of the RFA:

Original

Burghardus Wirzeburgenses episcopus et Folradus capellanus missi fuerunt ad Zachariam papam, interrogando de regibus in Francia, qui illis temporibus non habentes regalem potestatem, si bene fuisset an non.

Et Zacharias papa mandavit Pippino, ut melius esset illum regem vocari, qui potestatem haberet, quam illum, qui sine regali potestate manebat; ut non conturbaretur ordo, per auctoritatem apostolicam iussit Pippinum regem fieri.

Revision

Burchardus Wirziburgensis episcopus et Folradus presbyter capellanus missi sunt Roman ad Zachariam papam, ut consulerent pontificem de causa regum, qui illo tempore fuerunt in Francia, qui nomen tantum regis, sed nullam potestatem regiam habuerunt; per quos praedictus pontifex mandavit, melius esse illum vocari regem, apud quem summa potestatis consisteret; dataque auctoritate sui iussit Pippinum regem constitui.

It is impossible to reproduce these stylistic revisions in English unless the text of the revised version were to be published with the original. A complete translation of the revision was made, but it seemed advisable to print only those passages which are different from the original not only in style but in content. The revisor occasionally added to, omitted from, and modified in substance the text of the original. His omissions are indicated in the notes, as are phrases and short sentences which he chose to add. Major additions are presented here—indented and marked by R (for revision)—right in the text of the translation. This technique may possibly arouse the wrath of some critics. But the different views of the revisor or the conspicuous omissions of the original annalist seem to provide a worthwhile glimpse into the minds of these authors. This insight would have been lost had the additions all been buried in the notes.

The notes, needless to say, owe much to the French and German scholars, Simson, Mühlbacher, Böhmer, Meyer von Knonau, Lot, Halphen, and others whose works established a solid factual record of Carolingian history, and to the editors of our texts, especially Kurze, Müller, and Lauer. The names of living authorities on Carolingian history have been largely omitted here, because the annotation had to be minimal, not because of indifference.

Notes

1. The best guide to the historians of the Carolingian age is W. Wattenbach, W. Levison, H. Löwe, *Deutschlands Geschichtsquellen im Mittelalter. Vorzeit und Karolinger,* II-IV (Weimar, 1953-63).

2. Kurze, p. ix.

3. M. L. W. Laistner, *Thought and Letters in Western Europe A.D. 500 to 900,* rev. ed. (London, 1957), p. 264.

4. Cf. R. L. Poole, *Chronicles and Annals* (Oxford, 1926), pp. 26-36; C. W. Jones, *Saints' Lives and Chronicles in Early England* (New York, 1947), pp. 7-13, on the origins of the annals. On the earlier Carolingian annals, see Wattenbach-Levison-Löwe, 11, 180-92; H. Hoffmann, *Untersuchungen zur karolingischen Annalistik. Bonner historische Forschungen,* X (Bonn, 1958), where the earlier literature on the subject is mentioned.

5. Hoffmann, *Karolingische Annalistik,* p. 70.

6. Einhard, ch. 24; W. Braunfels and others, eds., *Karl der Grosse; Lebenswerk und Nachleben,* 4 vols. (Düsseldorf, 1965-67), 11, 42-62, 28-41.

7. Wattenbach-Levison-Löwe, 11, 246-47.

8. Quoted ibid.; cf. L. von Ranke, *Gesammelte Werke,* 54 vols. (Leipzig, 1868-90), L 1, 115.

9. I. Bernays, *Zur Kritik karolingischer Annalen* (Strasbourg, 1883), pp. 169-88, argues against the official character of the RFA.

10. Wattenbach-Levison-Löwe, 11, 248, n. 281, 282.

11. *Two of the Saxon Chronicles Paralle,* ed. C. Plummer, 2 vols. (Oxford, 1892-99), 11, civ.

12. Wattenbach-Levison-Löwe, 11, 248, n. 284.

13. Bernays, pp. 184-88; Wattenbach-Levison-Löwe, 11, 249.

14. Wattenbach-Levison-Löwe, 11, 250-51, and notes; G. Monod, *Études critiques sur les sources de l'histoire carolingienne,* 1. *Bibliothèque de l'école des hautes études. Sciences philologiques et historiques,* CXIX (1898), 102-26.

15. Wattenbach-Levison-Löwe, 11, 251-53.

16. Monod, *Études,* pp. 127-42; on Helisachar as author of part of the RFA, see Lina Malbos, "L'Annaliste royal sous Louis le Pieux," *Le Moyen âge,* LXXII (1966), 225-33.

17. Wattenbach-Levison-Löwe, 11, 253-54; MGH, *SS,* x v, pt. 1, 379.

18. M. Manitius, *Geschichte der lateinischen Literatur des Mittelalters,* 1 (Munich, 1910), 646-47; Wattenbach-Levison-Löwe, 11, 254-56.

19. Kurze, pp. 3-115 (facing the unrevised annals).

20. Wattenbach-Levison-Löwe, 11, 255-56.

21. Kurze, pp. ix-xv. The manuscripts of the RFA have been divided into five classes. The two manuscripts of Class A break off in the years 788 and 749, respectively. Manuscripts belonging to Class B, five altogether, are equally defective and seem to derive from a common source which broke off in the middle of the year 813. Manuscripts of Class C have additions in 773 and 776 at a place different from the other manuscripts and an additional sentence in annal 826. The editors have further subdivided the eight manuscripts of this class into two categories with their own distinctive features. The two manuscripts of Class D have additions for the years 785 and 792 on the conspiracies of Hardrad and Penin the Hunchback. Seven manuscripts belonging to Class E contain the revised version of the RFA and seem to have spread first from the monastery of Wissembourg in Alsace.

22. Wattenbach-Levison-Löwe, 11, 276, 255; 111, 337.

23. Ed. B. Simson, MGH, *SrG* (Hanover, 1905); Wattenbach-Levison-Löwe, 11, 260-64; Hoffmann, *Karolingische Annalistik,* passim, esp. pp. 13, 26-27, 12.

24. Ed. G. Waitz, MGH, *SrG* (Hanover, 1883); Wattenbach-Levison-Löwe, 111, 348-49.

25. Ed. B. Simson, MGH, *SrG* (Hanover, 1909); cf. Hoffmann, *Karolingische Annalistik,* pp. 13-16.

26. Ed. F. Kurze, MGH, *SrG* (Hanover, 1891).

27. Meyer, pp. 90-91.

28. *Die deutsche Literatur des Mittelalters: Verfasserlexikon,* ed. W. Stammler and K. Langosch, v (Berlin, 1955), 735.

29. IV, ch. 5

30. Meyer, p. 123, n. 498.

31. Meyer, p. 90; Nithard, 1, Preface; 111, ch. 5; Manitius, *Lat. Literatur,* 1, 660; *NA,* IX (1884), 617-18 (Virgil); XI (1886), 69-70 (Justin and Sallust).

32. 11, ch. 8; 111, ch. 3.

33. 11, ch. 2, 10; IV, ch. 1.

34. Wattenbach-Levison-Löwe, 111, 355-56. His death in a battle against the Normans on May 15, 845, rather than in the battle against Pepin on the Âgout on June 14, 844, was established by F. L. Ganshof, "Note critique sur la biographie de Nithard," *Mélanges Paul Thomas* (Bruges, 1930), pp. 335-44.

35. MGH, *PL,* 111, 310-11, no. 33; Mico's entire work, ibid. 111, 279-368; cf. Manitius, *Lat. Literatur,* 1, 469-76; 11, 806; 111, 1063; *NA,* IV (1879), 515-21.

36. *Hariulf: Chronique de l'abbaye de St. Riquier,* ed. F. Lot (Paris, 1894), pp. 102, 265.

37. Nithard, 1, Preface; 11, Preface.

38. 111, Preface.

39. 11, Preface; Meyer, pp. 81-82.

40. Meyer, pp. 2; 3-18.

41. Nithard, 1, Preface, ch. 2, 4, 6; 11, Preface; Meyer, pp. 3-4, 7, 13-14.

42. Nithard, 1, ch. 2-7; IV, ch. 6; Meyer, pp. 9-13.

43. On these books in general, see Meyer, pp. 18-81.

44. Meyer, p. 79.

45. Nithard, 11, ch. 8.

46. IV, ch. 6, 5; 111, ch. 5, 6.

47. IV, ch. 2, 5, 7.

48. IV, ch. 6, 7.

49. IV, ch. 7.

50. Meyer, pp. 82-85; for Nithard's verdict on Lothair, see ibid., p. 123, n. 491. Nithard records the negative views which Charles and Louis hold of Lothair: 11, ch. 9; 111, ch. 5; IV, ch. 1. Nithard personally attacks Lothair: 11, ch. 5, 8, 1, 2, 10; 111, ch. 3, 7; IV, ch. 3, 4. Nithard comments on Lothair's irresolution: 11, ch. 1, 3, 4; 111, ch. 3.

51. 11, ch. 10; Meyer, p. 89-90; 124, n. 500.

52. 1, ch. 3, 6, 4; Meyer, p. 14.

53. Manitius, *Lat. Literatur,* 1, 660; *Verfasserlexikon,* v, 735. In Nithard, 111, ch. 5, an entire sentence appears almost word for word as in Bk. IV, ch. 37, of Paul the Deacon's *History of the Lombards.*

54. 111, ch. 5; IV, ch. 1; Meyer, p. 126, n. 515.

55. 11, ch. 2, 4, 5, 8, 9; IV, ch. 3, 4; 1, ch. 6, 3, 5, 7; Meyer, pp. 126, n. 515; 95, n. 68.

56. Manitius, *Lat. Literatur,* 1, 659; Meyer, pp. 88-89; 121, n. 474-79.

57. Müiler, pp. ix-x; Manitius, *Lat. Literatur,* 1, 660. Ch. 59-62 of the anonymous life of Louis the Pious are based on Nithard, 1, ch. 6-8; cf. Meyer, pp. 14-18. Mico: MGH, *PL,* 111, 310. Hariulf: *Chronique de St. Riquier,* pp. 79, 102, 265; MGH, *SS,* 11, 361.

58. Paris, Bibliothèque nationale, ms. 9768 (s. X); ms. 14663 (s. XV). Cf. Müller, pp. x-xii.

59. Meyer, p. 2.

60. Nithard, 1, ch. 5, 1; Meyer, pp. 2-3.

61. 11, ch. 4, 2, 3.

62. Meyer, p. 88; 111, ch. 3; 11, ch. 8.

63. Meyer, p. 87; IV, ch. 6, 7; MGH, *PL,* 11, 559-64, 653-54. A summary of the available facts and information about Nithard is contained, along with a full bibliography of all editions and translations, in Lauer, pp. xvii-xx.

Short Titles and Abbreviations

Abel-Simson S. Abel, *Jahrbücher des fränkischen Reiches unter Karl dem Grossen,* I, rev. B. Simson, II by B. Simson. Leipzig, 1888, 1883.

BML J. F. Boehmer, *Regesta Imperii: Die Regesten des Kaiserreichs unter den ersten Karolingern,* rev. E. Mühlbacher, 2d ed. J. Lechner. Innsbruck, 1908.

Einhard *Einhardi vita Caroli Magni,* 6th ed. O. Holder-Egger. MGH, *SrG.* Hanover/Leipzig, 1907.

Kurze *Annales regni Francorum 741-829,* ed. F. Kurze. MGH, *Srg.* Hanover, 1895.

Lauer P. Lauer, ed. and tr., *Nithard: Histoire des fils de Louis le Pieux. Les Classiques de l'histoire de France au moyen âge.* Paris, 1926.

Lot/Halphen F. Lot and L. Halphen, *Le règne de Charles le Chauve.* Paris, 1909.

LP *Le Liber Pontificalis,* ed. L. Duchesne, 2 vols. *Bibliothèque des Écoles françaises d'Athènes et de Rome.* Paris, 1886-92.

Meyer G. Meyer von Knonau, *Über Nithards vier Bücher Geschichten: Der Bruderkrieg der Söhne Ludwigs des Frommen und sein Geschichtsschreiber.* Leipzig, 1866.

Carolingian Chronicles

MGH Monumenta Germaniae historica.

Cap. Legum sectio II: *Capitularia regum Francorum,* 2 vols., ed. A. Boretius and others. Hanover, 1883-90.

EE Epistolae, 8 vols., ed. p. Ewald, L. M. Hartmann, E. Dümmler, E. Perels, E. Caspar, and others. Berlin, 1887-1939.

PL Poetae latini medii aevi: Poetae latini aevi Carolini, 4 vols., ed. E. Dümmler, L. Traube, P. von Winterfeld, K. Strecker. Berlin, 1880-1923.

SrG Scriptores rerum Germanicarum in usum scholarum ex monumentis Germaniae historicis recusi. Hanover, 1840 ff.

SS Scriptores, 32 vols. Hanover/Leipzig, 1826-1928.

Müller *Nithardi historiarum libri IV,* 3d ed. E. Müller, MGH, *SrG.* Hanover Leipzig, 1907.

NA *Neues Archiv der Gesellschaft für ältere deutsche Geschichtskunde*

O Original version of the *Royal Frankish Annals.*

PL J. P. Migne, *Patrologiae cursus completus.* Series Latina, 217 vols. Paris, 1844-55.

R Revised version of the *Royal Frankish Annals.*

RFA *Royal Frankish Annals.*

Simson B. Simson, *Jahrbücher des fränkischen Reichs unter Ludwig dem Frommen.* 2 vols. Leipzig, 1874-76.

Thegan *Thegani vita Hludowici imperatoris.* MGH, *SS,* II, 590-604.

VH *Anonymi vita Hludowici imperatoris.* MGH, *SS,* II, 607-48.

Robert A. Eisner (essay date 1972)

SOURCE: "In Search of the Real Theme of the *Song of Roland*," *Romance Notes*, Vol. XIV, No. 1, Autumn, 1972, pp. 179-83.

[*In the following essay, Eisner contends that inconsistencies in the characterization of Charlemagne in the* Song of Roland *reflect the change of values which occurred between the century of Charlemagne's rule and the century in which the poet who wrote the work lived.*]

The central contention of this essay is that traditional preoccupation with the origin and unity of the *Song of Roland* has obscured the main theme of the poem.[1] The key problem to be considered is the apparent inconsistency in the portrait of Charlemagne: why is he represented as both strong and weak, authoritarian and impotent?

In the first council, which Charles calls to decide what answer should be given to Marsilion's offer of peace, he is decidedly peremptory. Shortly thereafter Roland and Oliver argue about which one of them should go as ambassador to Marsilion; the king tells them in no uncertain terms that neither they nor any others of the twelve peers will go on the mission. Nevertheless, despite his evident power, Charles demands that the council assume the responsibility of choosing an ambassador. When Roland nominates his father-in-law, Ganelon, Charles does not demur. Either he is content with the choice or he is unwilling or unable to alter it.

In the second council, called to decide who will lead the rear-guard as the Franks march out of Spain, Charles again asks, or rather demands, advice. When Ganelon returns the favor by nominating Roland, Charles' sudden outburst of fury seems incomprehensible, especially in the light of his refusal (or inability) to do anything about the choice. Charles' role is admittedly a delicate one: he cannot be blind or impotent, but neither can he be too imperious. A word from him would put an end to Ganelon's machinations. Nevertheless, this powerlessness clashes with features attributed to Charles at other points in the poem. For example, during his struggle with Baligant all the forces of Christianity seem to be epitomized in him.

Erich Auerbach is troubled by the ambivalent portrait of the emperor. He characterizes Charles as "sonambulistically paralyzed"[2] and goes on to develop this disparity: "The important and symbolistic position—almost that of a Prince of God—in which he appears as the head of all Christendom and as the paragon of knightly perfection, is in strange contrast to his impotence."[3]

The ambivalence in the portrait of Charles is, then, a real problem. The historical Charles was, according to historians, an exceptionally strong ruler. He had complete command; he held assemblies and consulted his barons, but the initiative and the decisions were his alone. It should be evident that the historical Charles is equal to only one

dimension of the poetic Charles: the omnipotent, hieratic emperor of the latter part of the poem.

We know that every male over the age of twelve had to swear fealty to Charles.[4] Because of the religious nature of the society, the oath was considered indissoluble. Subsequent to his coronation as emperor, Charles commanded that every man in his kingdom pledge to him the fidelity which he had previously promised to him as king; and all those who had not yet taken any oath should do likewise, down to those who were twelve years old.[5] This second oath, though more specific than the first, nevertheless does not imply a strict bond of obedience to Charles, as a vassal would swear to his lord, but rather only loyalty, and that in mostly negative terms; that is, the subject swears not to interfere with Charles' government.[6] It is thus not to be considered adequate for someone directly in the king's service, who must promise to serve with aid and counsel. This will be an interesting point to consider when we approach the problem of Ganelon's alleged treason, within the context of his relationship to Charles.

Now let us see what aspects of the eleventh century may be detected in the political and social climate of the poem. This will allow us to determine what elements found in the poem are contemporary with the world of the poet. To bridge the gap between the eighth and the eleventh centuries, we should point out that Charles established a strong central government, but himself contributed to its inevitable downfall after him by allowing the aristocracy to distribute benefices to the people, as he did to the aristocracy. Thus, each lord became the protector of a small group of people, all ostensibly faithful to the king. In reality, the nobles' growing authority was confirmed by Charles' order that the men enlist in the army under the command of their lords. Charles hence ensured the future rise of feudalism.[7]

Feudalism was fine in principle, but in practice it usually meant anarchy. Of the reign of Philip I (1060-1108), almost certainly the time during which the *Song of Roland* took its final poetic form, it has been said that "the greater of the king's alleged vassals never came near his court, whether to perform homage or to render any other service. France, obviously, had ceased to be a state in any proper sense of the word. Rather, it had been split into a number of states whose rulers, no matter how they styled themselves, enjoyed the substance of the regal power."[8] Here it is evident that we have a description of the world of the later feudal epics, such as *Raoul de Cambrai, Girart de Roussillon,* and *Renaut de Montauban.* However, the forces that later produce the revolted barons are already at work in the *Song of Roland.* The rise of individuality can be seen here, especially in the person of Ganelon, and the latter's trial illustrates the revolt of a powerful family of barons who do not feel themselves subject to the emperor's will. As Marc Bloch defines the sort of absolutism with strings that prevailed in the eleventh century, it sounds very much like the situation that obtains during the two councils and later in Ganelon's trial: "Selon le code de bon gouvernement alors universellement admis, aucun chef, quel qu'il fût, ne pouvait rien décider de grave sans avoir pris conseil."⁹

Our study of the ambivalence in the portrait of Charles has thus led us to the conclusion that there are elements in the poem that unmistakably reflect the eighth century, as well as others that can only be a reflection of the time when the poet lived—the late eleventh century. This attitude toward the *Song of Roland* leads naturally to a multiple interpretation of the main themes. There is not only a struggle between Christianity and Islam; within the empire there are new forces to contend with: the rise of individuality and the rise of France as an entity. It may be that Charles' mythical age in the poem, his "dous cens anz," is intended to encompass the period of the Carolingian dynasty, from 768 to 987. In this sense, Charles symbolizes the entire dynasty, both its absolutism of the eighth century and its decline in the tenth. He represents the old, authoritarian order, but the action has its setting in the new order. The figure of Charles is equivocal, as if to embody the transition. The central theme of the poem is the decay of the historical Charles' world. Duty in the new order is no longer clear. Roland is an anachronism, an exemplar of the earliest feudal ideal, no longer valid in the realities of the eleventh century. The poet admires him, bestows a beautiful death on him, but makes clear nevertheless the incongruity of his actions. Whereas Roland represents a past age, Ganelon reflects the new, which the poet deplores. The clash of old and new values provides the conflict.

The poet has conceived Roland as the perfect knight, the flower of chivalry. In the portrait of the hero there is a naïveté that gives one the impression that Roland exists within the framework of an early age of innocence, at least in the eyes of the poet. That would be the eighth century, a time that has left its imprint on the poem as being one of simplicity and clearly drawn societal behavior. In the context of the eighth century a perfect knight is, above all, a faithful vassal. The poem abounds with evidence that the poet sees his hero in just that light. There is no question about his sense of loyalty toward his emperor. The personality trait that causes a conflict between his individual objectives and that sense of loyalty is, as every reader must recognize, his desire for fame.

As for Ganelon, though he is assigned the role of villain, he is by no means unattractive. The poet stresses his splendid appearance and the impression he makes. He betrays, but he is in no sense a vile traitor. The treason he commits is unwitting. In his mind, he is doing nothing more than following the dictates of feudal life, marked by war among barons and sworn vengeance against anyone who offends or insults.

We have already seen that the oaths required of a subject in Charles' time were of a negative character, requiring the swearer not to meddle in government affairs. These oaths do not appear to have been adequate for someone directly in the king's service. One is tempted to apply the lessons of history to the fictitious Ganelon and infer from them that he did not feel bound to any extraordinary degree of loyalty to his sovereign. In any case, Ganelon's treason does no harm to the person of Charles; it is avenged because it hurts Charles' *maisnee,* i.e., his lineage. But Ganelon never admits that he has been disloyal to Charles. Thus, what is ultimately tragic in this refusal to see any conflict of interests in his loyalty to his sovereign and his private vendetta against Roland is that it creates a situation that exceeds the confines of Ganelon's person to envelop his entire society. That Ganelon is almost acquitted attests to the disorder of the feudal world. A baron could with impunity destroy another one and with him his men as well, as long as he observed the code of proper challenge. In every respect, Ganelon reflects the mentality of the tenth or eleventh century rather than the time of Charlemagne. He is the incarnation of that later individualism. In the *Song of Roland* this individualism clashes with the old, super-annuated world of the autocratic emperor.

The tragedy of Roncevaux is the result of the breakdown of societal values, and the tragic theme is reflected in the way in which Charles, the representative of the old order, constantly weeps and sighs. As his lamentations become the keynote of the poem, his visions illustrate his inability to check the evolution of the new society; he cannot grasp their details. Charles is still Charles, but the world in which he must function is no longer the authoritarian empire of the eighth century.

Notes

1. This paper was read, in a somewhat longer form, at the Fifth Biennial Conference on Medieval Studies held in May 1970 at Western Michigan University, Kalamazoo, Michigan.

2. *Mimesis,* trans. Willard Trask (Garden City, 1957), p. 87.

3. *Ibid.*

4. Louis Halphen, *Charlemagne et l'Empire Carolingien* (Paris, 1947), p. 165.

5. From a royal capitulary on the *Missi,* quoted by Norman F. Cantor, *The Medieval World: 300-1300* (New York, 1963), p. 154.

6. C. E. Odegaard, "Carolingian Oaths of Fidelity," *Speculum,* 16 (1941), 291.

7. Victor Duruy, *Histoire de France* (Paris, 1905), I, 191.

8. Carl Stephenson, *Medieval Feudalism* (Ithaca, 1942), p. 78.

9. *La Société Féodale* (Paris, 1949), II, 197.

John D. Niles (essay date 1976)

SOURCE: "The Ideal Depiction of Charlemagne in *La Chanson de Roland,"Viator,* Vol. 7, 1976, pp. 123-39.

[*In the following essay, Niles argues that Charlemagne, not Roland, is the chief hero of* La Chanson de Roland *and that Charlemagne's seeming passivity actually "represents power in the pure majesty of its potentiality."*]

The Charlemagne of *La Chanson de Roland* has seemed to many an enigmatic figure. On the one hand he is consistently praised. On the other hand he does fairly little. He seeks out the advice of his lords and accepts it when it is given. He appears to be duped by Marsile and Ganelon. For the greater part of the poem he seems little more than a figurehead, while the attention of the audience is commanded by the high drama of Ganelon's treason and Roland's death. Only once does he enter fully into action, to put Marsile to flight and to crush the army of the Saracen emir Baligant. As soon as his victory is complete he reverts to the relative inactivity which had marked his role from the beginning. The last part of the poem is dominated by the duel between Thierry and Pinable which determines Ganelon's guilt, and when we last see Charlemagne it is in a pose of anguished contemplation:[1]

> "Deus," dist li reis, "si penuse est ma vie!"
> Pluret des oilz, sa barbe blanche tiret.
>
> (lines 4000-4001)

["Lord," says the king, "how burdensome is my life!"
The tears run from his eyes, he rends his white beard.]

In his standard history *The Literature of the Middle Ages* (New York 1960), W. T. H. Jackson summarizes as follows this apparent ambivalence in the poet's depiction of Charlemagne (p. 169):

> The author clearly intends to show the emperor in a favorable light, as the dominating character, the figure on whose behalf all heroic deeds are performed. His appearance is majestic, his manner stern and dignified, his power undoubted. Yet there are some curious discrepancies. It would be possible to argue that it is Charlemagne's weakness as a ruler which is responsible for the tragedy of Roland and the defeat of the Christians. . . . The emperor is great, he personifies the perfect Christian ruler, but he does not control the action. The result is that, in spite of formal eulogy, he often appears weak and vacillating.

Jackson's comments are representative of much critical opinion concerning Charlemagne which has seen print. Equally likely to win general assent is Jackson's assessment of the "Baligant episode" (*ibid.*):

> The second part of the epic shows Charlemagne in a different light. He emerges as the central figure of the story. Roland, Oliver, Turpin are all dead; the Moslems have a new and more powerful leader. There is now a direct conflict between the forces of Christendom and those of the heathen. Charlemagne thus becomes the central figure of the epic, and both the work and the character suffer in the process. The effect is mechanical and, to a modern reader, unsatisfying.

To paraphrase Jackson, when Charlemagne does not act, the poet's words of praise for him ring hollow; when he does act, it is to the detriment of the character and the work as well. In the past such a view has often been accepted by persons who have read Oxford MS Digby 23 as the song of *Roland* and have tended to disregard those elements in the poem which do not directly tend to the glorification of Charlemagne's heroic nephew. Such a view is plausible. It does, however, lead to the consequence that "to a modern reader," in Jackson's words, nearly three-fourths of the poem contains "curious discrepancies" while more than another fourth is "unsatisfying."

In accord with a minority of students of the poem I would like to suggest that there is a way of reading *La Chanson de Roland* which eliminates the apparent anomaly in the poet's depiction of Charlemagne and permits a satisfactory reading of the work as a whole. This way is to accept from the beginning the possibility that Charlemagne, not Roland, is envisioned as the chief hero of the epic which has been given Roland's name. In particular, I would like to suggest (as Karl Heisig has before me)[2] that the internal logic of the poem is clear when one views the emperor against the background of the hieratic Byzantine concept of the ideal ruler. The historical Charles, after all, was not only a Germanic warrior king. When he had himself crowned emperor at Rome on Christmas Day of the year 800 he was initiating in northern Europe an institution long current with its own peculiar mystique in Byzantium. In this respect if in no other the fictive Charlemagne of the poem resembles the historical Charles: not only is he the sword of the realm, but he is meant to embody the serene majesty at its center. Men and women of eleventh- or twelfth-century France listening to the song recited would have had no difficulty comprehending the hierarchy whereby the patriarchal Charlemagne is envisioned throughout as the central figure of the poem, the young Roland as his *destre bras*. In the very tympana of their churches they would daily have been reminded of the immediate source of Charlemagne's power—that Source, in fact, of which Charlemagne was the representative on earth—in the form of the image of Christ in Majesty (*Christus Pantocrator* or *Majestas Domini*) with which many a northern church was adorned in the style which Romanesque art had derived from Byzantium.[3]

Let us then consider certain affinities between the depiction of Charlemagne in *La Chanson de Roland* and the hieratic depiction of the emperor (or by extension the deity) in traditional Byzantine sculpture and painting. Laisse VIII, the laisse in which Charlemagne and his nephew first appear, will provide a convenient point of departure.

As the laisse begins, messengers from the Saracen king Marsile approach the Franks bringing feigned pledges of submission. They find Charlemagne enthroned among his men:

> Li empereres est en un grant verger,
> Ensembl'od lui Rollant e Oliver,
> Sansun li dux e Anseis li fiers,
> Gefreid d'Anjou, le rei gunfanuner,
> E si i furent e Gerin e Gerers;

La u cist furent, des altres i out bien:
De dulce France i ad quinze milliers.
Sur palies blancs siedent cil cevaler,
As tables juent pur els esbaneier
E as eschecs li plus saive e li veill,
E escremissent cil bacheler leger.
Desuz un pin, delez un eglenter,
Un faldestoed i unt, fait tut d'or mer:
La siet li reis ki dulce France tient.
Blanche ad la barbe e tut flurit le chef,
Gent ad le cors e le cuntenant fier:
S'est kil demandet, ne l'estoet enseigner.
E li message descendirent a pied,
Sil saluerent par amur e par bien.

                                        (103-121)

[The Emperor is in a great orchard. With him are Roland and Oliver, Duke Sansun and the fierce Anseïs,
the king's standard-bearer Geoffroi d'Anjou, and Gerin
and Gerier as well. In the same place are many others,
fifteen thousand from lovely France. The knights are
seated on white carpets, they play at backgammon to
amuse themselves while the wise and the elderly play
chess; the quick-blooded young men are fencing.
Beneath a pine tree, by a sweetbriar, is a throne of pure
gold: there sits the king who rules lovely France. White
is his beard and his hair is in full flower, handsome is
his body and his bearing proud: if anyone should ask
for him he needs no pointing out. The messengers
dismount and greet him in the guise of friends and
well-wishers.]

The scene is in near perfect stasis. For the duration of the
laisse time stands still: in his mind's eye the listener creates the entire visual scene detail by detail, each detail fitted into a composition of geometric order and balance. At
the center is a pine. Beneath it is the golden throne on
which sits the king. To his sides stand Roland and Oliver
amid five others of the twelve peers. Beyond are the rest
of the Franks, engaged in various amusements.[4] Before the
throne wait the ambassadors of Marsile. With this last
detail the composition is complete; it can be held in the
mind for a moment while the singer pauses, then at once it
is broken, the actors move in space, and a new laisse
begins.

The scene depicted in this laisse can be recognized as having certain formal affinities with a subject which appears
in Byzantine art as early as the fourth century A.D. and
which in the course of the next few centuries made its
way into northern Europe, the subject of the "Emperor
Enthroned in Majesty."[5] Several early examples of this
subject are to be found on the base of the Obelisk of Theodosius, the late fourth-century monument which still
dominates the Hippodrome in Constantinople. In the relief
on the south face of the monument the emperor Theodosius I is depicted amid his court at the hippodrome. In this
relief he is standing, in others (less well preserved) he is
enthroned. In his right hand he holds the garland which is
to crown the victor of the race. Beside him stand members
of his family, most prominently his two young sons Arca-
dius and Valentinian. To the far sides, separated by a partition, stand the chief members of his court. Behind them is

a row of armed soldiers. Below the platform may be seen
the heads of two rows of spectators, and beneath them a
file of musicians and dancing girls.

A later, more highly stylized sculpture of a similar type is
the tenth-century Byzantine carving known as the Harbaville triptych. In this devotional work the place of honor
is taken by the enthroned Christ. To his sides are John the
Baptist and the Virgin. Below the central trio stand five of
the twelve apostles, while each wing of the triptych is
adorned with the figures of additional saints, martial figures
above and clerical ones below.

The grouping of figures in the Harbaville triptych—*one,*
plus *two,* plus *five,* plus a greater number—corresponds
exactly to that in laisse VIII of *La Chanson de Roland.* . . . [6]

In more significant ways than the simple grouping of
figures, however, these three works may be seen to correspond. First of all is the principle of hierarchy. In the
Harbaville triptych the figures are organized into four
groups: (1) at the top center, the object of adoration; (2) at
the immediate sides, the near-divine, both adoring and
adored; (3) at the bottom, the distinctly human but saintly;
(4) on the wings, lesser saints. In the Obelisk of Theodosius a similar hierarchical progression proceeds from (1)
the emperor, to (2) his sons, to (3) prominent members of
the court, to (4) the assembled crowd. In both of these
sculptures the very size of the figures reinforces the idea
of hierarchy: the most important figures are the largest,
while the others are progressively smaller. One may note
especially the dancing girls, about one third the size of
Theodosius. In laisse VIII from *La Chanson de Roland* a
similar hierarchy proceeds from (1) Charlemagne, to (2)
Roland and Oliver, to (3) five prominent lords, to (4) the
assembled host. Here, as throughout the poem, Roland is
clearly subordinated to Charlemagne.

Second is what might be called the principle of animation.
In each work the artist makes a clear distinction between
the enthroned figure, who is depicted with full austerity
and formality, and his more lively attendants. The
enthroned Christ, like the emperor Theodosius, stares
straight ahead, imperturbable. No individual eccentricities
disturb the generic quality of the portrait: we contemplate
the Son of Man, man raised to his highest level. In like
manner the language used to describe Charlemagne in
laisse VIII, language typical of that used in portraiture
throughout the poem, could scarcely be more general,
more abstract. The poet presents first the title, *li reis,*
second the unmistakable attribute, his *barbe blanche,* and
third a general qualitative statement: he is *gent* and *fier*
(lines 116-119). Only the indispensable is given; we are
left with the quintessential king. Far more lively is the
portrayal of the attendant figures. John the Baptist and the
Virgin, like the chief members of Theodosius's court, seem
endowed with human life and motion. The same is true of
Roland and Oliver in the context of *La Chanson de Roland.* At the same time as the two Franks are raised above

ordinary humanity by their heroism, they partake fully of ordinary existence: they boast, recriminate, make war, and eventually die. While their heroism excites our admiration, their humanity, even their very fallible humanity, endears them to us.

A third principle of correspondence between the three works is what might be called the principle of dependence. The higher an individual's rank, the more intimately he depends on the enthroned figure. John the Baptist and the Virgin are depicted turning toward Christ, their hands raised in a gesture as if of presentation; the figures on the wings of the triptych are shown either facing forward or turning away. The figures closest to Theodosius are shown leaning toward him, intent on his action, while the farthest figures are absorbed in their own dance. A similar principle governs *La Chanson de Roland*. In the feudal world of the poem, the higher a lord's standing, the closer is the bond which ties him to the emperor.[7] Iconographically, though not temporally, Charlemagne's soldiers are gaming and fencing while the council is in progress.

The artists of all three works, then—the Obelisk of Theodosius, the Harbaville triptych, and laisse VIII of *La Chanson de Roland*—have taken a diagrammatic approach to the depiction of reality. In all three works the treatment of the subject is non-illusionistic; it is conceptual. And a large part of the "meaning" of each is simply the expression of the hierarchy itself, in several of its ramifications. Ernst Kitzinger has well summed up the essential style of these works:[8]

> [The artist] disregards the laws of nature; he shows that he is not interested in such things as three-dimensional space and the anatomy of the human body. For these he substitutes other values. His concern is the abstract relationship between things rather than the things themselves. Instead of a realistic scene, he shows us a solemn assemblage of persons with the emperor as the central power. A composition thus arranged like a geometrical pattern on a single plane with a blank background of indefinite depth is removed from the sphere of actual life and has a spiritual meaning, a symbolic and transcendental character.

Kitzinger is discussing a different work of art, a fourth-century Byzantine carving depicting the apotheosis of an unidentified emperor. His words apply with equal force to the three works we have been discussing. At this point in his song the poet of *La Chanson de Roland* is interested in the presentation of ideal order. Although here he is introducing for the first time his two main characters, Charlemagne and Roland, the poet takes no delight in a wealth of physical description. As throughout the poem, he turns his back on the techniques of realism. Instead, he presents a hieratic scene. All characters surround the emperor. The poet's concern is to establish clearly, from the beginning, the abstract relationship between persons which will govern the poem's events.

The Charlemagne of *La Chanson de Roland* thus appears to have about as much to do with the Charles of history as

the enthroned Christ of the harbaville triptych has to do with the historical Jesus. He seems to have stepped out of time into the timeless world of ideas. He is depicted not as he may actually have looked at a particular moment in history—in the year 778, for example, at the time of the battle of Roncevaux—but as he might look in the eye of God, attended by saints and angels. It is thus that by a process of distortion common to the epic process the emperor becomes conspicuous for his flowing white hair and beard: *Blanche ad la barbe cume flur en avrill* (3503). It is thus that Marsile confidently characterizes his enemy as more than two hundred years old—*"Men escientre dous cenz anz ad e mielz!"* (539)—even though at the time of his expedition to Spain *li empereres* was no more than thirty-six and was not to be crowned emperor for another twenty-two years. Nowhere does the perfect fiction of the poem falter. Throughout the poem Charlemagne, patriarch, is imagined with the respect due his rank—a rank which according to the hierarchy of the poem is between that of Roland and that of the angels.[9]

Such an idealized conception of Charlemagne is scarcely explicable without reference to the change in imperial portraiture which occurred in Byzantium over the course of the fourth to eighth centuries.[10] Early in the Byzantine era the emperor is depicted much as if he were a Roman Caesar. He resembles a soldier in the prime of life, close-shaven, muscular. Later he comes to be given the physical appearance of a sage. He is older, at the same time more fierce and more contemplative. He wears a flourishing beard. Instead of military dress he wears richly flowing robes. Above all, he is reverent. One favorite portrait type shows him presenting an offering to Christ or the Virgin.[11] Another shows him attended by a pair of angels, saints, or venerable historical figures. In time, partly through the efforts of the historical Charles to introduce Mediterranean forms of art to the North, this concept of portraiture comes to be typical of the arts of Germany and France as well. It may be seen in the stained glass of the former Romanesque cathedral of Strasbourg. In the ideal world of *La Chanson de Roland* it is supreme.

The commanding importance of Charlemagne in the poem has not been ignored in the critical literature. Albert Pauphilet has strongly urged that the idealized Charlemagne be recognized as the central power of the poem and that he be granted the esteem in the eyes of scholars which he evidently commanded in the eyes of the poet:[12]

> Que le relief extraordinaire du caractère de Roland, que la force dramatique de ses aventures aient attiré sur lui toute l'attention des érudits, il n'en est pas moins vrai que le véritable héros du poème, aux yeux du poète, *c'était Charlemagne.* C'est autour de lui que tournent tous les événements, c'est à lui que sont dévolus les épisodes les plus essentiels ou les plus sublimes. L'humanité imparfaite, énergique, et finalement purifiée par la douleur, de Roland touche plus? Soit, mais Charlemagne est le prince de ce conte.

Recently Albert Lord[13] and Karl Uitti[14] have likewise affirmed the unitary function of Charlemagne in the song of

Roncevaux. With Charlemagne the poem begins in line one; with him it ends four thousand and one lines later. Even when the rearguard is isolated at Roncevaux the poet's frequent references to the absent Charles remind one that the king is absent only in body; his power, or potential power, continues to exert a controlling influence on the action. Every major event of the poem is significant less in itself alone than in its relation to him. To an audience not yet disenchanted with the idea of order, Roland's supreme fealty, like Ganelon's treason, would have no meaning except in relation to its object. Roland's power is human. Like Ganelon's power or Marsile's, it is subject to the limitations of its own nature. Charlemagne's power goes beyond. At the emperor's prayer God causes the sun to stop in mid-sky. Precisely because his power is to such an extent *given,* however, the emperor scarcely has need to act. He has no need to prove himself, as Roland feels he must prove himself at Roncevaux. In a king such a need would be disastrous. Charlemagne need simply *be.* In the legendary world of the poem he represents power incarnate.

What of the one time that Charlemagne does act? Is the Baligant episode to be condemned as an interpolation? Powerful voices have damned it.[15] A more fruitful approach, however, might be to view the Baligant episode as part of a larger movement in the poem, one comprising two loosely connected episodes, a "Marsile episode" (lines 2397-2608) and a "Baligant episode" (lines 2609-3704). In this broad movement, almost a third of the poem, Charlemagne's power is made devastatingly explicit. When the emperor acts he acts with all the force at his command, to avenge his nephew and complete his conquest of Spain. Immediately after Roland's death, it seems, Charlemagne assumes his nephew's function and for some thirteen hundred lines unites in himself the figures of both warrior and king. The mythic element here is strong—witness the halting of the sun in mid-sky—and one is not mistaken in seeing an analogue to the apocalyptic climax of the *Iliad,* when Achilles spreads havoc among the Trojans.[16] The death of Roland, like the death of Patroklos in the *Iliad,* seems to trigger the release of immense energies, energies which in the ordinary course of events are better left undisturbed. Like Patroklos and like Enkidu in the epic of *Gilgamesh,* Roland appears to have the role of a beloved comrade who "goes before" his lord by falling victim to a treacherous attack. His death signals the beginning of the hero's supreme adventure. In the epic of *Gilgamesh* this adventure takes the hero across the waters of death. In the *Iliad* it takes Achilles to the river Scamander and a plain flowing with blood. In *La Chanson de Roland* it takes Charlemagne first to the banks of the river, Ebro, where the pagan host is drowned, then to the field of battle against Baligant and the critical moment when the emir's sword splits Charles's helm and cuts through to the very bone. Here, and not during the earlier battle of the rearguard, the song attains its climax. At this moment, when the emperor staggers under the blow and for an instant the future of Christendom hangs in the balance, the source of Charles's authority makes itself known in the form of the angel Gabriel and he strikes the poem's decisive blow:

> Quant Carles oit la seinte voiz de l'angle,
> N'en ad poür ne de murir dutance;
> Repairet loi vigur e remembrance.
> Fiert l'amiraill de l'espee de France,
> L'elme li freint o li gemme reflambent,
> Trenchet la teste pur la cervele espandre
> E tut le vis tresqu'en la barbe blanche,
> Que mort l'abat senz nule recuvrance.
> "Munjoie!" escriet pur la reconuisance.

(3612-3620)

[When Charles hears the holy voice of the angel he has no fear of death; his consciousness and strength return. He strikes the emir with his French sword, he splits the helm set with flashing gems, he cuts through his skull and face as far as his white beard so that the brains run out; he strikes him dead beyond recall. "Montjoie!" he cries to rally his men.]

With the death of Baligant the main action of the poem draws swiftly toward its close. The pagans flee; Saragossa is taken;[17] and Roland, "sacrificed" before by what seems a kind of mythic necessity, is borne back to France for burial.

The "passivity" shown by Charlemagne throughout the greater part of the poem thus appears on reflection a sign not of weakness but of wise restraint. Charlemagne is not responsible for the tragedy of Roland and the defeat of the rearguard. From a mythic point of view no one is responsible. Roland had to die, and that is that. In terms of the poem's surface motivations, however, it is not Charlemagne who is to blame for the tragedy at Roncevaux. It is Roland. Oliver could not have made the matter more clear in his celebrated address to his brother-in-arms as the two men stand amid the bodies of their dead companions:

> Ço dist Rollant: "Por quei me portez ire?"
> E il respont: "Cumpainz, vos le feïstes,
> Kar vasselage par sens nen est folie;
> Mielz valt mesure que ne fait estulti.
> Franceis sunt morz par vostre legerie.
> Jamais Karlon de nus n'avrat servise.
> Sem creïsez, venuz i fust mi sire;
> Ceste bataille oüsum [faite u prise];
> U pris u mort i fust li reis Marsilie.
> Vostre proecce, Rollant, mar la veïmes!

(1722-1731)

[Roland says: "Why are you angry at me?" Oliver replies: "Comrade, it is your own doing. Courage tempered by intelligence is not a foolish thing; moderation is better than stupid excess. The Franks are dead because of your foolishness. Never again will Charles enjoy our service. If you had believed me, my lord would have returned; we would have [won] this battle; Marsile would have been captured or killed. Your prowess, Roland—would we had never seen it!"]

Oliver's words are uttered in anger. He soon comes to regret them, and the two comrades embrace. Still, the facts are spoken. Out of concern for his own reputation—*En dulce France en perdreie mon los* (1054)—Roland has refused to inform the emperor of the Saracens' attack. Hoping to defeat the pagans on his own, as earlier he had boasted he could do (783-791), he calls down destruction not only on himself but on Oliver and the other Franks as well. His pride in his own courage and might of hand (*vassalage*), grown beyond the control of his moderating intelligence (*sens*), leads to the act of astonishing heroism which results in the death of twenty thousand Franks.

It is precisely in this quality of self-control, so precious to a king, that Charlemagne excels. The emperor is literally *im*passive: that is, he has an active control of his passions. He is *self-possessed,* in the full meaning of that term. Even during the trial of Ganelon, when he wishes nothing more than to see the traitor die, he subordinates his own passion to judgment by the court: that is, to law. Since the court fails him, he is in fact about to have to reconcile himself to Ganelon's release when Thierry steps forward to challenge Ganelon's champion Pinabel.[18] Here is a perfect example of the "passivity" some readers will find in Charlemagne. It is a passivity of which few are capable. Few things are easier than for a strong man to give in to his own violence, in the way of Marsile,[19] especially when he knows himself to be in the right. The hard thing— beautiful as it is rare—is for a man with power voluntarily to forego that power even in the face of his own threatened humiliation.

Does Charlemagne then lack emotions? Hardly. He feels and suffers like any man. His tenderness is one of his most memorable qualities. Yet strong as his emotions are, they never victimize him in a time of action. After the death of Roland the emperor returns to Roncevaux: briefly he stops to look at the bodies, then prays to God that the night not fall, that he have time to avenge his nephew. Only the next day, when the vengeance is complete, does he allow his grief full measure:

> Carles li reis se vint de pasmeisuns;
> Par les mains le tienent IIII de ses barons.
> Guardet a tere, vei gesir sun nevuld.
> Cors ad gaillard, perdue ad sa culur,
> Turnez ses oilz, mult li sunt tenebros.
> Carles le pleint par feid e par amur:
> "Ami Rollant, Deus metet t'anme en flors,
> En pareïs, entre les glorius!
> Cum en Espaigne venis a mal seignur!
> Jamais n'ert jurn de tei n'aie dulur.
> Cum decarrat ma force e ma baldur. . . . "

(2892-2902)

[Charles the King recovers from his swoon; four of his barons hold him by the hands. He looks to the earth, he sees where his nephew is lying. His body is handsome but its has lost its color, the eyes are turned upward and are full of darkness. Charles laments him in faith and in love. "Roland, my friend, may God set your soul in flowers, in paradise, among the glorious! What an ill ruler you followed into Spain! Never will a day pass without my grieving for you. How my strength and my spirits have fallen. . . . "]

Others have spoken of the art of Charles's long *planctus*.[20] Let me only add that nowhere else in the poem is an emo-

tion expressed at greater length, and few if any places with greater depth of feeling.

One has no difficulty understanding why Roland and not the more austerely depicted Charlemagne has captured the imagination of most modern readers of the poem. Roland is a hero who attracts by his very excesses: his impetuosity, his high pride, his refusal to bend his will to the promptings of common sense. To some he must seem the perfect romantic hero: there is something indescribably compelling in the way he extends the principle of loyalty into a sort of suicidal nobility. Whatever a reader's sympathy for Roland, however, one should not be blind to the fact that in the poem as a whole he is not to be conceived of apart from Charlemagne. Charlemagne is the emperor of western Christendom, Roland his right arm. If Roland represents power in the full vividness of its realization, Charles represents power in the pure majesty of its potentiality. Each is part of the other, in the way that the head and hand are part of the same living body. Charlemagne's measured thought in the absence of Roland's impetuosity might seem a pale thing, just as Roland's energy without Charlemagne's restraint would overwhelm. Together the two make up the whole which is the poem and create the balance between complementary ideals which is at its heart.

Like many great works of literature, *La Chanson de Roland* celebrates a defeat. In this case the defeat commemorated is the annihilation of Charlemagne's rearguard and the loss of Roland, with the consequent crippling blow to Charles's imperial dreams. The loss is grievous, and the fact that the hero's adversaries are punished can give only partial comfort. But throughout, the song gives little comfort. Almost the entire world of this poem is war, human suffering at its most intense. Roland, master of this world, is at the same time its victim. Charlemagne alone stands apart. Of all the poem's major characters—Roland, Oliver, Ganelon, Marsile, Baligant—he is the sole survivor. A participant in this world, he seems at the same time an observer. One has no difficulty understanding why in this world of war he seems to walk with extreme reluctance— witness his tears, his hesitations, never more unforgettably expressed than in the poem's final lines.

Doubtless the singer of *La Chanson de Roland* never consciously thought to transform the idea of war into a symbol of the human sphere of action. And yet in this poem, as in the *Iliad*,[21] suffering is the norm, it is what is given; what is significant is human action in the face of suffering and death. Juxtaposed with Charlemagne's magnificent triumph is the loss of Roland and the annihilation of the rearguard. Out of this disaster comes the true triumph celebrated in the poem, the triumph of man over his own weakness in the face of death. This triumph is Roland's, of course, yet in a different way it belongs to Charlemagne as well. The emperor is a hero who seems at home only in the world of ideal perfection, yet who finds himself drawn irresistibly into the tumult of human affairs. In his very reluctance lies a measure of his heroism. Roland acts. Charlemagne waits, thinks, suffers, and acts. In contemplating him the reader cannot help but feel elevated. And is that not the main function of heroic song? To raise people, if only momentarily, to an awareness of the possibility of meaningful action in a world of seemingly aimless brutality? Charlemagne triumphs, yet at the same time he suffers loss more deeply than any other. Of all the poem's characters he is thus the least dispensable, the one closest to the poem's spiritual center: for it is from the simultaneous sensitivity toward great triumph and great loss that *La Chanson de Roland* gains that complex feeling of mixed tragedy and grandeur which we call by the name heroic.

Notes

1. Textual citations are from the commonly available edition of Joseph Bédier (Paris, L'édition d'art H. Piazza, no date but *avant-propos* dated 1937).

2. Karl Heisig, "Das Rolandslied und Byzanz," *Medium aevum romanicum: Festschrift für Hans Rheinfelder* (Munich 1963) 161-178.

3. Helmut Hatzfeld, *Literature through Art: A New Approach to French Literature* (Oxford 1952, Chapel Hill repr. 1969) 3-8, Fern Farnham, "Romanesque Design in the *Chanson de Roland*," *Romance Philology* 18 (1964) 143-164, and Guy R. Mermier, "More About Unity in the *Song of Roland*," *Olifant* 2 (1974) 91-108 have specifically related the poem's treatment of Charlemagne to Romanesque depictions of the deity such as are found on the tympana of the abbey church of Moissac and the church of Conques.

4. One is not to imagine that the gaming and fencing are taking place at the same time as the ambassadors are preparing to speak. As if in a painted panel the poet has juxtaposed two separate times in a single picture.

5. See André Grabar, *L'empereur dans l'art Byzantin* (Paris 1936) 24-30, 54-57, 90-92, 196-198, 207-209, and *Christian Iconography: A Study of Its Origins* (Princeton 1968) 80-82, where he traces the origin of medieval Christian figurations of the deity in Roman and Byzantine figurations of secular authority (emperors and consuls).

6. The analogue between Charles and the twelve peers and Christ and the twelve disciples is made explicit in lines 113-140 of the comic Old French epic poem *Le pèlerinage de Charlemagne*. Charles and the twelve peers take the seats in Jerusalem in which Jesus and the disciples sat to partake of the Last Supper. Thinking the Second Coming is at hand, the Jew who minds the temple rushes to be baptized!

7. Cf. the two types of oath demanded by the historical Charles, the simple oath of fealty and the high oath of vassalage.

8. Ernst Kitzinger, *Early Medieval Art in the British Museum* (London 1955) 14.

9. A clear indication of the poem's hierarchy is given by the account of the genealogy of Roland's sword Durendal (lines 2318-2321). God gave the sword to one of his angels, who entrusted it to Charlemagne, who in turn gave it to Roland. After Roland's death the sword reverts to Charles, who presents it to another lord, Rabel (lines 3014-3018).

10. See Ernst Kitzinger, "Some Reflections on Portraiture in Byzantine Art," *Zbornik Radova Vizantoloskog Instituta* (Belgrade) 8 (1963) 185-193, and (n. 8 above) 4-7.

11. A famous example is the mosaic in Hagia Sophia, Constantinople, which depicts Constantine presenting the City to the Virgin while Justinian presents Hagia Sophia itself: Grabar *L'empereur* (n. 5 above) illustration XXI. Cf. the relief on Charlemagne's tomb at Aix which depicts the emperor offering his chapel to the Virgin: Rita Lejeune and Jacques Stiennon, *La légende de Roland dans l'art du Moyen Age,* 2 vols. (Brussels 1966) vol. 2 illustration 145.

12. Albert Pauphilet, "Sur la Chanson de Roland," *Romania* 59 (1933) 191.

13. Albert Lord, *The Singer of Tales* (Cambridge Massachusetts 1960) 206-207. In Lord's view "although the listeners' attention is occupied mostly with Roland, it is Charlemagne to whom the poem belongs" (207).

14. Karl Uitti, *Story, Myth, and Celebration in Old French Narrative Poetry 1050-1200* (Princeton 1973) 65-127. According to Uitti, "Structurally . . . Charlemagne's role in the poem is unitary: he imposes a logic upon the various events that occur in the work (treason; victory and death of Roland; punishment, vengeance; trial and execution of Ganelon)" (73). "It is Charles who incarnates *auctoritas* in the *Song of Roland*" (102). Note also the remarks of Peter Dembowski at the 1973 annual meeting of the Société Rencesvals, American-Canadian Branch (*Olifant* 1.3 [1974] 8) and of Larry S. Crist at the 1974 annual meeting (*Olifant* 2 [1975] 166-167). Also in *Olifant* 2 is a defense of Charlemagne by Wolfgang G. van Emden, "Pro Karolo Magno: In Response to William W. Kibler, 'Roland and Tierri,'" 175-182: "One might . . . suggest that, 'au-dessus de la mesure humaine,' this patriarch reflects to an extent some of the attributes of God Himself in his holding in tension power, superhuman knowledge of the future, suffering and action, as well as perhaps in the way he allows a large measure of freedom to his men" (180).

15. Among the powerful voices may be numbered Gaston Paris and Ramón Menéndez Pidal. Joseph Bédier defended the poem's unity but his analysis stops before the Baligant episode: *Les légendes épiques,* 3 vols. (Paris 1926-1929) 3,410-453. Paul Aebischer vigorously defends the episode in "Pour

la défense et l'illustration de l'épisode de Baligant," *Mélanges Ernest Hoepffner* (Paris 1949) 173-182. For a general review of the question see Gloria Garrow, *The Baligant Problem: Review of Current Opinion,* Ph. D. diss. (Columbia University 1965).

16. See Lord (n. 13 above) 206.

17. From one point of view the poem might almost be retitled *La Prise de Saragosse.* Charlemagne's previous failure to capture the city, a failure so stressed at the very beginning of the poem (lines 1-6), is an intolerable situation which must be righted. The actual capture of the city, held in suspension until after the Baligant episode, concludes all but the epilogue of the poem.

18. The judgment is thus to be made by trial by combat; that is (in the terms of the poem) it is put directly into the hands of God. For the emperor there could be no surer place.

19. Note Marsile's reaction when he hears Ganelon expound Charles's terms for peace (lines 438-440). He brandishes a javelin and fails to strike down Ganelon only because his men restrain him: *Ferir l'en volt, se n'en fust desturnet* (440). By his act of unbridled wrath Marsile would thus have eliminated his one means of striking a blow at Charles.

20. See Joseph J. Duggan, *The Song of Roland: Formulaic Style and Poetic Craft* (Berkeley 1973) 160-193, and two studies by Paul Zumthor, "Étude typologique des *planctus* contenus dans la Chanson de Roland," *La technique littéraire des chansons de geste, Actes du Colloque de Liège de septembre 1957* (Paris 1959) 219-234 and "Les planctus épiques," *Romania* 84 (1963) 61-69.

21. See the deep essay by Simone Weil, "L'Iliade ou le poème de la force," *Cahiers du Sud* 19 (1940) 561-575 and 20 (1941) 21-34; English translation by Mary McCarthy, *The Iliad or the Poem of Force* (Wallingford Pennsylvania 1956).

Janet H. Caulkins (essay date 1980)

SOURCE: "Narrative Interventions: The Key to the *Jest* of the *Pèlerinage de Charlemagne*" in *Études de Philologie Romane et d'Histoire Littéraire,* edited by Jean Marie D'Heur and Nicoletta Cherubini, Belgium, 1980, pp. 47-55.

[*In the following essay, Caulkins contends that properly interpreting the* Pèlerinage de Charlemagne *requires understanding the interventions of the narrator and recognizing the juxtaposition of the serious and the ludicrous.*]

Nothing makes the Middle Ages more lovable than its humor.

Ronald N. Walpole[1]

The fundamental problem is to recognize signs wherever they are.

Roland Barthes[2]

Seldom in the history of medieval literary criticism has there been such a divergence of opinion over a fundamental interpretation of a work as brief as the *Pèlerinage de Charlemagne,* which numbers less than nine hundred lines. Among the diverse categories in which it has been placed are those of "serious," (Nyrop, etc.)[3], "humorous," (P. Paris, etc.)[4], "Parisian in spirit," (G. Paris, etc.)[5], "English at heart," (Holmes)[6], "a reflection of Celtic Ireland," (Loomis[7], Cross[8], etc.), "a covert political pamphlet," (Heinermann)[9], "a literary parody," (Neuschäfer, etc.)[10], "a moralising sermon," (Coulet)[11], "a pious tale of a conveying of relics," (Bédier, etc.)[12], "a parody, a comical version of the fictitious transferring of relics related in the *Descriptio . . .*" (Knudson)[13], "an outrageous parody from start to finish of the men and adventures of the chansons de geste" (Brians)[14]. Commenting upon the inventory of critical studies of the *Pèlerinage,* Madeleine Tyssens observes that «la critique est au rouet: l'interprétation générale règle l'interprétation des passages ambigus ou obscurcis . . . et celle-ci, en retour, vient étayer le système général.»[15]

Many critics have been perplexed by the text of the *Pèlerinage* and have been led to a diversity of interpretation for two principal reasons: firstly, the treatment of the character of Charlemagne is unusual; in medieval French literature, he is normally represented as an august ruler, and is frequently idealized as the preeminent national hero; in the *Pèlerinage,* Charlemagne is portrayed with considerable human frailty, sometimes humorously[16]: secondly, contrary to common medieval literary convention, the narrator does not furnish an *explicit* either in a prologue, the narrative opens *ex abrupto,* or in an epilogue, the last few lines appear to have been ended hastily.

Horrent, in his monumental study of the *Pèlerinage,* has done much to elucidate the poem's complexities[17]. Concluding his perspicacious analysis of the text, however, Horrent notes: «La source jaillissante de son comique est dans le traitement plaisant qu'il [le poète] impose à son grave sujet politique et dévot; il ne prend pas au sérieux l'histoire qu'il raconte, ne se prend pas au sérieux en la racontant et entend que son public en fasse autant en l'écoutant.»[18] That view has caused problems for scholars who have had difficulty trying to reconcile the dichotomy of a comic treatment of a serious subject. Sturm recognizes the problem, and then takes the position that there is no notion of serious intent. I agree with her analysis of the unifying theme that appears to support the establishment of the superiority of Charlemagne over King Hugon, but I question her conclusion that the supercedence is not a serious subject in the poem, "rather itself the focus of the comic intent"[19]

I take the position that students of this "joyeux 'divertissement'", as Horrent has called it[20], have neglected to examine closely the interventions of the narrator. It is my intention here to demonstrate that a careful analysis of the passages in which the interventions occur, reveals the skillful interweaving of *seria* with *ludicra,* clarifies the poet's attitude towards his characters, particularly Charlemagne and his queen, and underscores the poet's desire to instruct, while entertaining.

It should be recalled that contrary to our customary modern conceptions of boundaries between earnestness and jest, the high middle ages derived much enjoyment from the collocation of *seria* and *ludicra* in all types of literary pieces, including epic and hagiography, in both Latin and in the vernacular[21]. Works were destined to entertain, as well as to teach, hence the importance in medieval literature of the principle *ludicra seriis miscere*[22]

It lies outside the scope of this paper to consider whether the author and narrator of the *Pèlerinage* were one and the same or not. It is not evident from the text of the *Pèlerinage,* as it is, for instance, in the *Continuation-Gauvain,* whence the audience is invited to pray for the repose of the soul of the author *(le Lodonois)* whose work is being told by the narrator *(cil de Lodun)*[23]. However, Gallais has shown that . . . "toute la production littéraire française en vers a été au moins pendant le premier siècle et demi destinée à la récitation"[24] and that as "l'auteur rédige pour un auditoire, il pense constamment à attirer, à retenir, à réveiller son attention"[25]. Consequently the terms "narrator" and "poet" will both be used in the course of the ensuing analysis to refer to the person who recited the *Pèlerinage* in the mid-twelfth century[26] before a Parisian audience which would have included in all probability, King Louis VII and Queen Eleanor, and nobles of the court of Paris[27]

As the opening lines of the *Pèlerinage* are examined in an analysis of the initial episode of the *défi de la reine*[28], during which the narrator intervenes four times[29], it is useful to recall Raymond Jean's observation that «la première phrase d'un récit est toujours une entrée dans un espace linguistique nouveau, l'accés au champ romanesque, l'émergence du signifiant»[30]. By means of familiar outward signs in the *phrase-seuil,* the poet has sown the seeds for genetic intertextuality[31] between the *Pèlerinage* and the vast corpus of heroic tales about Charlemagne and his noble Franks. Conferred automatically on the *Pèlerinage,* is an extraordinary richness and density, which conjures up "une représentation, une histoire, un ensemble idéologique sans qu'on ait besoin de les parler"[32]: "Un jur fut Karlemaine al seint Denis muster: Rout prise sa corune, en croiz seignat sun chef, E ad ceinte s'espee dont li ponz fud d'or mer" (v. 1-3). Resplendently dressed, wearing his crown, with his sword girt at his side, Charlemagne is depicted at the church of saint Denis, making the sign of the cross as he stands before his court of nobles: "Dux i out e demeines, baruns e chevalers" (v. 4). The emperor looks at the queen: "Charles li emperers reguardet sa moillier:

Ele fut corunee al plus bel e al meuz" (v. 5-6). The narrator introduces her to the audience, not in her own right,

but as the wife of Charles the emperor, as his "moillier". We see her as Charlemagne sees her, as an extension of his regality, crowned in a most comely fashion.

The act of leading his wife by the hand to the olive tree, whose branches traditionally symbolise peace and humility, suggests a total, passive submission on the part of the queen to the wishes of her lord: "Il la prist par le poin desuz un oliver" (v. 7). Not only is there an absence of verbal interchange, there is no interaction of gestures.

At this point in the narrative, the dignified tone, typical of French epics about Charlemagne, is exchanged, and the *geste* turns to *jest,* as Charlemagne asks his wife, if she has ever seen a man whose crown and sword become him as well as his: "Dame, veïstes unkes hume dedesuz ceil Tant ben seïst espee, ne la corune el chef?" (v. 9-10), and vaunts " . . . Uncor cunquerrei jo citez ot mun espez!" (v. 11). As William Hazlitt expressed it so poignantly, «the essence of the laughable [. . .] is the incongruous, the disconnecting one idea from another or the jostling of one feeling against another»[33]. Charlemagne's solicitation of such praise, particularly of his wife, rather than of his barons and noble counsellors, "jostles" the sensibilities and provokes laughter, through contrast with the typical portrayal of Charlemagne in French epics, such as that in *la Chanson de Roland.*

Suddenly, however, the lightness gives way to admonition as the narrator intervenes, for the first time, not to comment on Charlemagne's foolish demeanor, but to focus attention on the queen: "Cele ne fud pas sage, folement respondeit" (v. 12). The narrator leaves no room for ambiguity. He passes judgment on the queen, *ex ante,* before the court has heard her response, and condemns her, as a foolish woman who responds without sagacity to the emperor's question[34]: "Emperere, dist ele, trop vus poez priser. Uncore en sai jo un ki plus se fait leger Quant il porte corune entre ses chevalers: Kaunt la met sur sa teste plus belement lui set!" (v. 13-16). An aristocratic audience of the twelfth century must have been jolted back from the stern didacticism into merriment at the audacity of the queen who has the temerity to admonish the emperor for his narcissistic excesses, continuing that she knows another man who is more elegant[35] [than Charlemagne] when he wears his crown at court[36]

Again a dour narrator intervenes, silencing the audience's laughter, and emphasising Charlemagne's reaction to the queen's well aimed humor, as one of great ire: "Quant l'entent Charlemagne, mult en est curecez, Pur Franceis ki l'oïrent mult er est embrunchez" (v. 17-18). The use of the word "Franceis" (v. 18), rather than the earlier "dux", "demeines", "baruns", or "chevalers" (v. 4), adds an element of chauvinism to his appeal. The narrator goes on to elaborate that Charlemagne is troubled because of the Frankish nobility who are present and have heard the impudence of the queen's remarks, which assume the dimension of treasonous utterances. Working himself into a rage, Charlemagne demands to know the name of this king: "E, dame, u est cil reis? E car le m'enseinez! Si porterum ensemble les corunes as cheis! Si i serrunt vos druz e tuz vos cunsilers; Jo maunderai ma court de mes bons chevalers! Si Franceis le me dient, dunc l'otreierai ben; Se vus m'avez mentid, vus le cumperez cher: Trencherai vus la teste od m'espee d'acer!" (v. 19-25). Charlemagne envisions the scene of the two kings for his court: himself and the other, yet to be named, together wearing their crowns, for a comparison, as bulls at a fair. He dichotimizes vividly, by means of "vos", (v. 21), "ma", "mes", (v. 22) the distinction now between himself and the queen. Two separate groups from the court of Charlemagne will be present at the encounter with the other king: some of the queen's friends and counsellors, who formed part of the queen's court, and Charlemagne's own court of knights. If his noble Franks decide that the other king looks more comely than he himself, when each is wearing his crown, he will accede to their judgment, but if the queen has trifled with Charlemagne, she will pay dearly for it: he will cut off her head with his sword of steel.

The queen responds, begging the emperor to temper his anger: "—'Emperere, dist ele, ne vus en curucez! Plus est riche d'aver e d'or e de deners, Mais n'est mie si pruz ne si bon chevalers Pur ferir en bataile ne pur ost encaucer!" (v. 26-29). The queen attempts to meliorate her position by saying that although the other king is wealthier and possesses more gold, he is not as noble or as good a knight as Charlemagne when it comes to battle, or to pursuing the enemy.

Again, the audience is brought to laughter, this time at the queen, who attempts to mollify the enraged emperor. The narrator quickly intervenes, stressing that when the queen realizes the depth of the anger of Charlemagne, she deeply regrets her response to him, and wishes to throw herself at his feet: "Quant ço vit la reïne ke Charles est si iriez, Forment s'en repentit, vuelt li chaïr as pez" (v. 30-31). She has been forced to become the suppliant spouse of the emperor, and as such, begs Charlemagne for mercy: "Emperere, dist ele, mercid pur amur Deu! Ja sui ge vostre femme, si me quidai juer: Jo m'escundirai ja, se vus le cumandez, A jurer serement u juïse a porter: De la plus haulte tur de Paris la citez Me larrai cuntreval par creant devaler, Que pur la vostre hunte ne fud dit ne pensed!" (v. 32-38). She attempts to explain away her remarks by mustering her only defense: she is Charlemagne's wife, and as such, she was only engaging in wifely raillery. It is reminiscent of Quintilian's advice: "For there are certain sayings which are regarded as folly if they slip from us unawares, but as witty, if uttered ironically"[37]. Quintilian's work circulated widely in France in the twelfth century, especially in the Île-de-France[38]. It seems, however, as if the emperor did not draw Quintilian's distinction. The queen offers to exonerate herself, if Charlemagne so allows, by swearing an oath, or undergoing judicial trial, or throwing herself down from the highest tower in Paris to attest to the fact that no offense to Charlemagne was intended. The emperor, however, ignores her entreaties. His sole concern is the name of the king: "—'Nu ferez, ço dist Charle, mais le rei me numez!" (v. 39). The queen then attempts to dissemble: "—'Emperere, dist ele, ja nel puis jo truver" (v. 40). But Charlemagne does not believe that his wife has forgotten the other king's name, and he swears that unless she reveals the identity of this superior monarch, he will have her beheaded:"—'Par mun chef, ço dist Carle, orendreit lem dirrez: U jo vus ferai ja cele teste couper!" (v. 41-42).

Again the narrator intervenes to emphasize the effect on the queen of the emperor's strong reaction and to explicate her fear of Charlemagne's intense anger: "Ore entend la reïne que ne se puet estordre; Volenters la leisast, mais que muër nen osed" (v. 43-44). When the queen's attempt to vindicate herself fails, she realizes that she can no longer conceal the identity of the other king. She would gladly let the matter drop, but for the fact that she dare not gainsay what she has just said. Frightened into revealing the king's name, the queen nevertheless prefaces her admission with a final plea to Charles that he not consider her foolish: "Emperere, dist ele, ne me tenez a fole: Del rei Hugun le Fort ai mult oï parole. Emperere est de Grece e de Costantinoble, E si tent tute Perse tresque en Capadoce. N'at tant bel chevaler de ci en Antioche, Nu fut itel barnez cum le suen, senz le vostre." (v. 46-50). The queen contends that she has heard much about King Hugon the Strong, Emperor of Greece and of Constantinople, who reigns over all of Persia to Cappadocea; further, that there is no finer knight from there to Antioch, no such noble court as his, except that of Charlemagne. Unfortunately for the queen, this argument does not assuage the emperor's wrath. He swears again that he will find out whether or not what she has said is correct and promises her a certain death if she has lied: "—'Par mun chef, ço dist Carle, ço savrai jo uncore! Se mençunge avez dite, a fiance estes morte!" (v. 51-52). Again Charlemagne swears that she has greatly angered him and has lost all his friendship and good will; he is certain that she will lose her head when he verifies her outrageous assertion, and he reprimands her for having entertained such thoughts about his noble person: "Par ma fei, dist li reis, mult m'aveiz irascud, M'amisted e mun gred en avez tut perduz. Uncor quid qu'en perdrez la teste sur le buc: Ne dusez ja penser, dame, de ma vertuz! (v. 53-56). The royal quarrel is charged with emotion and climaxes with a challenge by Charlemagne that he will not stop until he has seen King Hugon: "Ja n'en prendrai mais fin tresque l'avrai veüz!" (v. 57).

The next intervention of the narrator occurs at the end of the section following the royal quarrel, when the emperor, with all his men, is setting out on his quest, bound initially for the Holy Land. The Franks mount their strong, gentle paced mules and spur them as they leave the city: "E munterent as mulz, qu'orent forz e amblanz. De la citez isirent, si s'en turnent brochaunt." (v. 89-90). As the audience is amused at the comic spectacle of Charlemagne and his men spurring not horses, but mules, the narrator intervenes, in all seriousness, to announce that, from now on, wherever Charlemagne goes, he will be protected by God, whereas the queen will stay behind and weep: "Des ore s'en irrat Carles al Damne Deu cumant: La reïne remeint, doloruse e pluraunt." (v. 91-92). The intervention firstly emphasizes the contrary positions of Charlemagne and his queen in the *Pèlerinage,* and secondly, recalls the then well known tales of Charlemagne, the great hero, in which his wife is not even mentioned.

A specific link with the Charlemagne of the *Chanson de Roland,* the most beloved of all tales about the great emperor, is made in the next narrative intervention, after Charlemagne has been in Jerusalem some while. Charlemagne asks permission of the Patriarch of Jerusalem to leave the city. The Patriarch promises to give Charlemagne all his great treasure, in fact, as much as the French wish to carry away, provided that Charlemagne will remain vigilant in the face of the Saracens and pagans who wish to destroy Christianity. The Patriarch specifically asks Charlemagne to slaughter those Saracens who hate them. Charlemagne says that he will do it willingly, and he pledges his faith, saying that he will send for his men, and go into Spain to pursue Saracens. The audience, knowing that Charlemagne is planning to see King Hugon at Constantinople for purely personal reasons, must have been smiling wryly at the emperor's response to the Patriarch when the narrator intervenes in all seriousness: "Si fist il pus encore: ben en guardat sa fei, Quant la fud morz Rollant, li.XII. per od sei" (v. 231-32). The allusion to the *Chanson de Roland* is sufficient to introduce into the text of the *Pèlerinage* what Jenny describes as «un sens, une représentation, une histoire, un ensemble idéologique sans qu'on ait besoin de les parler.»[39] The intervention not only emphasizes the emperor's strength of character by confirming his identification with the great hero of the *Song of Roland,* but also Charlemagne's ability to keep an oath, by announcing to the audience, that he did go into Spain at a later time. An intertextual comparison is thus provided, and with it, "une forte coloration métalangagière".[40]

The narrator's next intervention occurs after the action has moved to Constantinople and King Hugon has called on several of Charlemagne's men to carry out their boasts. When Bernard, one of Charlemagne's barons, is asked to demonstrate his prowess, God works a miracle, causing the water to issue forth from its channels, spread over the fields, enter the city and fill the cellars, thoroughly soaking King Hugon's people. King Hugon himself is obliged to flee to the highest tower on foot. Charles and his twelve peers take shelter at the top of an old pine tree and pray to God to have mercy on them. The French audience must have been amused at the comic spectacle of King Hugon, the great rival of the French King, lamenting in the tower, promising Charlemagne all his treasure if the French King will go back to France, and swearing that he will become Charlemagne's vassal and pledge fealty to him. The French audience must have been further amused when it is learned that the great Emperor Charlemagne feels pity for King Hugon as he hears him crying out to him for mercy. Abruptly, the narrator intervenes, parenthetically, to present a serious moral:—"Envers humilitet se deit eom ben enfraindre" (v. 789)—: that it is indeed right to be inclined to humility. Stierle points out, that according to

Aristotle,"l'exemple possède véritablement un caractère anticipatoire, qui permet à quelqu'un de reconnaître sa propre situation, encore ouverte, à la lumière d'une expérience antérieure".[41] Here, the audience is led to anticipate Charlemagne's eventual forgiveness of the queen upon his return to France.

The last intervention occurs near the end of the *Pèlerinage,* after the episode in which Charlemagne is shown to be one foot three inches taller than King Hugon, when they are both standing wearing their crowns, and the queen is thereby proven incorrect. As Charlemagne and his knights leave Constantinople to return to France, happy that so great a king as Hugon has been conquered without combat, and Charlemagne's superiority has been proven without force, the narrator turns to the audience to ask, rhetorically, what more has he to tell them now: "Que vus en ai jo mès lunc plait a acunter?" (v. 860). The question reveals that, as far as the narrator is concerned, his story has been told. It is an instance of one of the many narrative interventions found in the texts of the period which Gallais has appropriately classified as "auteur en mal de copie".[42] In a matter of only ten lines, the narrator returns Charlemagne and his men to Paris, and has them enter the church of St. Denis where the noble Charlemagne prays to God and places his crown and one of Christ's nails on the altar. Charlemagne has the other relics which have been brought back from Jerusalem, dispersed throughout his kingdom. The queen falls at the king's feet, and Charlemagne pardons her for the love of the holy sepulchre which he had worshipped: "Sun mautalent li ad li reis tut perdunet, Pur l'amur del sepulcre que il ad aüret." (v. 869-70). Charlemagne's arrogance is complete in that he does not forgive the queen because he loves her or because she is a good woman, but because he is a good Christian.

The narrative interventions are the basis for the *jest* of the *Pèlerinage de Charlemagne.* The stand out in stark contrast to the action, which is essentially light and humorous, providing sober and meaningful insight into the psychological interaction between Charlemagne and his queen. They reinforce the patina of male dominance characteristic of early French epics about Charlemagne, in which female characters are rarely mentioned, and never developed, and explicate the way in which, through the threat of brute force, the queen is made to submit to the power of Charlemagne. The queen's criticism of her husband's demeanor is not without foundation, and she is pivotal in causing the undertaking of the "pilgrimage", but she is portrayed, not only as being unwise, but of being incorrect. Charlemagne is infallible, to virtually a pontifical level. He has "God on his side", to quote the old folk song. In a response to the chiding of their leader, Charlemagne, by the queen, the male characters actively engage, throughout the epic, in demonstrating their *macho* and fantasy fulfillment, which could well be expressed as "we'll show that woman who thinks she's so clever." It must have been important to our poet, not only to entertain his audience, through *ludicra,* but to instruct the assembly by inclusion of *seria.* The sober interventions give full thrust to one point of view which suggests an "appel à l'*imitatio*" on the part of the narrator.[43]

In a forthcoming article on the *Pèlerinage*, I examine the particular relevance that the *ludicra/seria* intertexture would have had at the Paris court in the middle of the twelfth century[44]

Notes

1. "Humor and People in Twelfth Century France", *Romance Philology,* 11, 1958, 210.

2. "Une problématique du sens", *Cahiers Média,* 1, 1967, 20.

3. Kristoffer Nyrop, *Storia dell'epopea francese nel medio evo,* trans. E. Gorra (Turin: Loescher, 1888), p. 115.

4. Paulin Paris, "Notice sur la chanson de geste intitulée: 'le Voyage de Charlemagne à Jérusalem et à Constantinople'," *Jahrbuch für romanische und englische Literatur,* 1, 1859, 198.

5. Gaston Paris, "La Chanson du Pèlerinage de Charlemagne", *Romania,* 9, 1880, 1.

6. Urban T. Holmes, "*The Pèlerinage of Charlemagne* and William of Malmesbury", *Symposium,* 1, 1946, 75.

7. Laura H. Loomis, "Observations on the Pèlerinage de Charlemagne", *Modern Philology,* 25, 1927, 331.

8. Tom P. Cross, "The gabs", *Modern Philology,* 25, 1928, 349.

9. Theodor Heinermann, "Zeit und Sinn des Karlsreise", *Zeitschrift für romanische Philologie,* 56, 1936, 497.

10. Hans J. Neuschäfer, "Le Voyage de Charlemagne en Orient als Parodie der Chanson de geste", *Romanistisches Jahrbuch,* 10, 1959, 78.

11. Jules Coulet, *Études sur l'ancien poème français du Voyage de Charlemagne en Orient* (Montpellier: Coulet, 1907), p. 381.

12. Joseph Bédier, *Les Légendes épiques* (Paris: Champion, 1929³), IV, 141.

13. Charles A. Knudson, "A 'Distinctive and Charming Jewel'", *The Romanic Review,* 59, 1968, 1001.

14. Paul Brians, "Paul Aebischer and the gab d'Olivier", *Romance Notes,* 15, 1973, 170.

15. Madeleine Tyssens, *Le Voyage de Charlemagne à Jérusalem et à Constantinople,* trad. crit. *Ktēmata,* 3 (Gand: Éditions Scientifiques E. Story-Scientia, 1978), p. vi.

16. See my forthcoming article "Intertextuality and humor in the portrait of Charlemagne in the *Pèlerinage de Charlemagne*".

17. Jules Horrent, *Le Pèlerinage de Charlemagne. Essai d'explication littéraire* (Paris: Société d'édition "Les Belles Lettres", 1961).

18. Horrent, p. 113. The parenthetical addition is mine.

19. Sara Sturm, "The Stature of Charlemagne in the *Pèlerinage*", *Studies in Philology,* 71, No. 1, 1974, 18.

20. Horrent, p. 166.

21. Ernst R. Curtius, *European Literature and the Latin Middle Ages,* trans. W. R. Trask (New York: Pantheon, 1953), p. 417-35.

22. Curtius, p. 429. In my forthcoming article, on "Intertextuality", I examine the *ludicra* of the *Pèlerinage*. The focus of this paper is on the *seria*.

23. For discussion of "Gauvain au Château du Graal", v. 7035-44, see Pierre Gallais, "Formules de conteur et interventions d'auteur dans les manuscrits de la *Continuation-Gauvain*", *Romania.* 85, 1964, 185-89.

24. Gallais, "Recherches sur la mentalité des romanciers français", *Cahiers de Civilisation Médiévale,* 7, 1964, 483.

25. Gallais, "Recherches", 493.

26. The mid-twelfth century is the date now generally agreed upon, see John W. Davis, "*Le Pèlerinage de Charlemagne* and 'King Arthur and King Cornwall': A Study in the Evolution of a Tale". Diss. Indiana 1974, 62.

27. In my forthcoming article, "*Le Pèlerinage de Charlemagne:* literary and historical perspectives", I develop the thesis that in all probability the audience was Parisian, and comprised of nobles of the court of Paris. I also point to the likelihood of King Louis and Queen Eleanor being in the audience, judging both from the particular relevance the tale would have had for each of them, as well as from the narrator's presentation of the story.

28. The edition used is that of Paul Aebischer, *Le Voyage de Charlemagne à Jérusalem et à Constantinople* (Genève: Droz, 1965).

29. V. 12, 17-18, 30-31, 43-44.

30. Raymond Jean, *Pratique de la littérature* (Paris: Seuil, 1978), 13.

31. For discussion of genetic intertextuality see Laurent Jenny, "La Stratégie de la forme", *Poétique,* 27, 1976, 258-59.

32. Jenny, 267.

33. "On Wit and Humour", in *The Comic in Theory and Practice,* ed. John J. Enck, Elizabeth T. Forter and Alvin Whitley (New York: Appleton-Century-Crofts, 1960), p. 16.

34. Horrent is undoubtedly correct here, "Il est vain de songer ici à de l'ironie", *Essai* p. 18.

35. "leger" = "schmuck", "angenehm", see Tobler-Lommatsch, *Altfranzösisches Wörterbuch,* V, (Wiesbaden: Franz Steiner, 1963), 311.

36. For a discussion of the role expected of a "per", a wife or companion in medieval French literature, see

William C. Calin, *The Old French Epic of Revolt* (Geneva: Droz, 1962), p. 162, and *The Epic Quest, Studies in Four Old French Chansons de Geste* (Baltimore: The Johns Hopkins Press, 1966), p. 144-45.

37. *Institutio Oratoria of Quintilian,* trans. H. E. Butler (London: Heinermann, 1921), 11, 451.

38. A. Mollard, "La diffusion de l'Institution Oratoire au XIIe siècle", *Moyen Âge,* 44, 1934, 161.

39. Jenny, 267.

40. The citation is from Jenny, p. 258.

41. Karlheinz Stierle, "L'histoire comme Exemple, l'Exemple comme Histoire", *Poétique,* 3, 1972, 183.

42. For other examples see Gallais, " . . . la *Continuation-Gauvain*", 208.

43. Stierle, p. 187: "la mise en valeur univoque d'un seul point de vue [. . .] s'explique aisément à partir de l'appelà l'*imitatio*".

44. See my forthcoming article, "*Le Pèlerinage de Charlemagne:* literary and historical perspectives".

Sarah Kay (essay date 1984)

SOURCE: "The Character of Character in the Chansons de Geste" in *The Craft of Fiction: Essays in Medieval Poetics*, edited by Leigh A. Arrathoon, Solaris Press, Inc., 1984, pp. 475-98.

[*In the following essay Kay investigates the interaction of character and plot in various chansons de geste, particularly in* Raoul de Cambrai, *and argues that neither aspect holds a simple priority over the other.*]

The relationship between character and plot confronts the literary critic with a chicken and egg problem of ostrich proportions. How far can we dissociate what a literary character is from what he does, and supposing such dissociation to be operable, which is the proper, primary level of description in any text? Should we say, for instance, that Othello is a character liable to violent jealousy, and so can be set up to kill his ever-loving wife, or do we say that the killing of an unjustly suspected wife leads us to perceive her murderous husband as violently jealous? Do texts differ in this regard? As with Shakespeare plays, some *chansons de geste* are assigned titles featuring a principal character (*Chanson de Roland, Aiol, Gaydon, Chanson de Willame*), others an aspect of the action (*Charroi de Nîmes, Prise d'Orange, Siège de Barbastre, Aliscans*). The prologues of some, like the *Couronnement de Louis,* announce the matter that is to follow as centered primarily on character:

> De Looÿs ne lerai ne vos chant
> Et de Guillelme au cort nes le vaillant,
> Qui tant soffri sor Sarrazine gent;
> De meillor home ne quit que nus vos chant.

[7-10]¹

Others, of which *Girart de Roussillon* is an example, summarize part of the plot:

> Ceste muet de Folcon e de Folchui,
> Et de Girart le conte la vos revui,
> Quant prestrent guere a Charle el e li sui,
> Per quant sunt espandut de sanc mil mui.

[12-15]

Critics of medieval literature writing in a traditional idiom have explored the *chansons de geste* both with an assumption of the primacy of plot, and from the point of view of character; their choice reflects their generation. Among the more senior, this judgement on the *Roland* by Edmond Faral has been much (if incorrectly) cited: "Les idées [. . .] constituent le principe vital de [la *Chanson*], [. . .] mais ce que ces idées ont,à l'application, de force poétique et de beauté morale, c'est dans l'âme des personnages qu'il faut le chercher."² This passage is quoted with approval by Le Gentil in 1955 and 1967,³ and by Misrahi and Hendrickson in 1980.⁴ Le Gentil continues, "Rien de plus exact: dans notre poème, les caractères commandent l'action et les problèmes posés le sont dans et par des 'études d'âmes'" (p. 123). Tony Hunt is representative of the younger school when he asserts, of the same poem, "[the poet] is not interested in motivation but in repercussion [. . .] [His] technique is entirely the result of his interest in tragedy as the product of *action,* not *character*"; and, later in the same article, "Too much emphasis has been placed on the *Roland* as a psychological drama."⁵

There are good reasons why we should not simply turn our backs on this issue.⁶ The gross categories of "actor" and "plot" are those to which the reader reacts first, and beyond which the naïve reader rarely progresses. Through them interest, sympathy, and excitement are elicited in the reader, and ethical and especially political themes conveyed.⁷ They are universals of narrative; to quote the words of Barthes, "the characters [. . .] constitute a necessary plane of the description, outside of which the commonplace 'actions' that are reported cease to be intelligible, so that it may safely be assumed that there is not a single narrative in the world without 'characters' or at least without 'agents'."⁸ They are not far from being universals of criticism, too, to judge by the frequency with which titles on "The hero" continue to appear in bibliographies.⁹ Finally, the relationship between *dramatis persona* and plot in a fiction will relate to (though not necessarily correspond with) contemporary prejudice about the relation between character and action in the real world. This should certainly qualify it as a legitimate concern of literary history; the more so in a genre such as the *chanson de geste* which belongs to a para-historical or even historical mode of discourse.¹⁰

Important though this area of investigation seems to me, it is clear that most literary theorists have their sights trained towards other horizons. Receptional aesthetics with its revalorisation of literary history and concern to explicate reader reaction was an obvious place to look; and indeed an article on "Levels of identification of hero and audience" by Hans Robert Jauss[11] testifies to the recognition accorded to the notion of hero in this critical school. His aim in this article is to revise Northrop Frye's famous modes (mythic, marvellous, high and low mimetic, and ironic)[12] from a receptional standpoint, suggesting modes of reader identification with character ranging from the admiring to the ironic. Comparing the two studies, however, it seemed to me that Jauss was even less interested than Frye to examine how the hero is constituted (through "characterization," authorial intervention, emplotment, or whatever), and while he suggests ways in which the reader can react to character, he says nothing about how he or she perceives it in the first place.

Hard-core structuralist theory also proved a disappointing hunting ground. In *La Sémantique structurale,* Greimas formulates admirably the question which preoccupies me when he acknowledges the possibility of opting between a character-based and a plot-based description of a given corpus of mythological material.[13] The researcher could either (1) identify a series of plots in which the god is active, and so attribute a set of functions to him ("description fonctionnelle"), or else (2) identify a range of descriptions of him ("description qualificative"). The results of these approaches would be, he says, ("dans certaines conditions") complementary and "comme convertibles de l'un à l'autre modèle: le dieu pouvait agir conformément à sa propre morale; ses comportements itératifs, jugés typiques, pouvaient lui être intégrés comme autant de qualités" (pp. 172-3). Sadly the discussion goes no further. Greimas offers no argument for his decision in favour of a functional analysis (one presumes he is merely bowing to the force of the formalist tradition transmitted by Propp),[14] nor does he investigate under what conditions the two descriptive models might cease to be equivalent.

Greimas' approach, then, assumes the primacy of plot and the subordination to it of "character." "Actantial categories" (the term is Greimas'), which are the primary unit of analysis, do not correspond directly with individual surface structure characters but with the roles that underly them. They are held to be reducible to six: Subject (the agent), Object, Adjuvant (the role of any person or element assisting), Obstruant (any element that hinders the activity of the agent), Destinataire (the indirect object or beneficiary) and Destinateur (the role under whose auspices, or with regard to which, the Subject is activated). These actantial categories are identified by reducing successive stages of the plot to minimal narrative units of "deep structure" (that is, to sentences summarizing the surface text), and by reading off the grammatical functions within those sentences as the corresponding category, i.e. grammatical subject = Subject, grammatical Object = object, etc. But as Greimas' conception of deep structure—like that of another discipline one can think of—has got deeper with the years, it is not always easy to determine how the actantial categories are realised by the actual characters in a particular text.[15] Application of his theory to the *chansons de geste* has produced some startling

results. According to one self-confessedly experimental reading of the *Roland,* for example, it appears that God, who is not a "character" at all, is Destinateur and Destinataire, and at times also Adjuvant, namely three out of the total of six categories, whereas Roland is Subject under the modality of will (*vouloir*) only (though with some *savoir*)[16], and as such inferior to Charlemagne who combines *vouloir, pouvoir, faire, savoir,* and *devoir.* Such an analysis, one might pardonably observe, if it lacks an excessive regard for character, is not over-preoccupied with plot either.[17]

More *nouvelle vague* criticism (one is tempted to call it *nouveau vague*), with its diligent glossing of arbitrarily chosen fragments of surface structure text (referred to, since Barthes, as "lexies" or "reading units"), has no interest in crude mimetic categories such as actor and plot which are simply so much noise on its semiotic codes. In an ingenious analysis of a fragment of Chrétien's *Perceval* by Jean-Michel Adam,[18] for instance, the action—Perceval's meeting with the first knights he has ever seen—and his character of naïve persistence, simply disappear down the cracks between the semiotic building-bricks that realise the *"isotopies"* of nature and religion versus chivalry.

This paper—mercifully—does not set out to offer a broad theory of how character and plot should best be defined and integrated into literary criticism. More modestly I investigate some of the ways in which they interact in a body of literature whose exciting narrative stance has always attracted both theoretical and practical criticism—the *chansons de geste* of the twelfth and thirteenth centuries—with particular reference to the text among them best known to me, that of *Raoul de Cambrai.*

. . . . .

It is manifest that one way an author can present his actors as primary, the action as flowing from them, is by serving up slabs of circumstancial and atemporal description of a character, and then offering morsels of incident as being merely illustrative of his or her nature. The example of Balzac leaps to mind. It was to defer consideration of this style of authorial "characterization" that I began with a reference to Othello rather than a narrative hero, since in this respect the *chansons de geste* have always been compared with the theatre. This commonplace of epic criticism is clearly formulated by Misrahi and Hendrickson: "We learn to know and judge epic figures as we do those of medieval theatre, by what we see them do" (p. 360).

The element of portraiture, which is in any case slight, is so traditional in content that its aim can only be to categorize, not individualize. I have pointed out elsewhere that the descriptions of hero and villain in the *Roland* are substantially alike.[19] Attempting a character sketch of Raoul in *Raoul de Cambrai* based on observations *ex persona poetae* and by other characters, I found that nothing was said about Raoul that was not also said of at least one other character. If he is handsome, so are Bernier and Gautier.[20] Did he inherit his clear face from his mother, and his fierceness from Guerri?[21] But then fierceness is found among the Vermandois too.[22] Other people can be wise on occasion, and then carried away on a tide of uncontrollable emotion.[23] Raoul may be a marvellous knight, but so are Bernier, Rocoul, and others;[24] as for the qualities of nobility, valour, rank, and breeding, they are two a penny.[25] He is not alone in his bad qualities either. His tendency to perfidy and immoderateness is shared by the king and even by virtuous Bernier.[26] The poet, in short, makes no attempt to particularize his central character through description. Indeed, a recent series of articles by Moroldo has shown that the descriptive elements which make up the portraits in the *Chanson de Roland* are taken from a common stock which does not differ materially through six other *chansons de geste* of varied tone and date.[27]

This is not to say that epic characters necessarily lack "psychological depth" (though some do), but that perceiving it involves a moral and imaginative effort on the part of the reader/hearer (with perhaps an actor's contribution from the jongleur).[28] While literary characters should not be confused with real people, the fact remains that epic heroes are knowable in a way similar to that in which we know other people in real life; whereas the heroes of a novel whose author is constantly imparting insights about them are known to us more as we know ourselves.[29] This gives epic characters a directness and an otherness which challenge the reader / hearer's imagination along lines which are suggested and guided chiefly by the plot. The descriptive element in the *chansons de geste* is therefore not such as would lead to a distinction between characterization and emplotment; rather one would see them as indissolubly bound up together.

Another feature of the composition of these poems that militates against a dissociation of character from action is repetition. The emplotment of *chansons de geste* is intensive rather than extensive; character and plot are at once reduced in scope, though often with a corresponding gain in intensity: the hero is of such a type that he unrelentingly repeats the same action; the plot is so organized that certain aspects of the hero are insistently brought into play.

In the Loheren cycle, the families of Lorraine and Bordeaux do battle unstintingly through thousands of lines of siege and countersiege, sortie, ambush, and the occasional pitched battle (this clearly perceived as more glamorous). Not surprisingly, then, the character of the Loheren heroes emerges as grim and embattled, as austerely resolute as their unvarying text.[30] The *Couronnement de Louis* reveals a comparable sobriety of invention. William starts by protecting young King Louis at home; then he frees Rome from agressors; then he protects Louis at home; then he frees Rome from agressors (incidentally protecting Louis); and finally he protects Louis at home. In the simplest imaginable way the plot analyses the character of

its hero into two principal facets which it then proceeds to dramatize, viz. feudal competence at home and abroad.[31]

The *Chanson de Guillaume* repeats a single though more extended cycle: feasting, resting, setting out to fight, fighting, returning, feasting, resting, setting out to fight, etc.[32] Only one character, William himself, survives this punishing routine repeatedly; his true grit marks him as the hero. Other characters achieve only part of it. Thiebaut and Esturmi feast and rest to perfection, but when it comes to setting out to fight they turn tail and run away: clearly they have no grit at all. Vivien sets out to fight and fights, but does not return: he is a figure of doomed youth, inspiring but unsuccessful. Girart possesses more of the strength of his uncle, for he sets out to fight, fights, returns, feasts, rests, sets out to fight, and fights, but then fails to return. His score is midway between Vivien and William. Rainouart, finally, completes the cycle successfully but only once, and so lacks the solidity of William's achievements which, in any case, he burlesques. The Frankish warriors are thus all carved of one material. William is the complete man whose nephews are partial copies of himself, and in comparison with whom the cowards are shown to be totally inadequate.

In *Raoul de Cambrai* there are four types of scene in which the hero appears: court scenes (with the king), family scenes (in which I include his meeting with Bernier's mother), council scenes (with his vassals, including Bernier), and fighting scenes. We should not, however, be misled by this apparent diversity. Nearly all the characters whom Raoul meets are subsumed to the role of enemies, and he behaves throughout in a spirit of violent antagonism, threatening the king, insulting his uncle and his own and Bernier's mother, and hitting his vassal with a stick.

This belligerence is invested with ambiguity. As heroic bravery, it is endorsed in Raoul's encounter with the forbidding Vermandois knight, John of Ponthieu, who is almost a giant. Raoul is on the verge of panic when he remembers his father's courage before him and gains the victory through sheer force of character and pride of lineage (ll. 2744-8). In a macabre dissection scene following the death of both knights (l. 3239 ff.), Raoul's heart is found to be as big as that of an ox, while John's is the size of a child's. These scenes present Raoul's warlike temperament *in bono*. For the most part, however, his violence is perceived as excessive and misdirected, an effect largely achieved through the patterning of scenes. Starting at ca. l. 900 the order of events is as follows: (1) Raoul decides to go to war to claim the Vermandois, (2) quarrels with his mother, (3) sets off on the campaign threatening destruction, (4) quarrels with Bernier's mother, (5) destroys Origny, (6) quarrels with Bernier, and finally (7) fights the Vermandois army. This interleaving of scenes connected with actual fighting (1, 3, 5, 7) and scenes of domestic or feudal conflict (2, 4, 6) shows Raoul's aggressivity spilling out into relationships which should be peaceable and supportative.

For much of the text, Bernier is presented as the exact opposite of Raoul. He also appears in the same types of scene but manifests an aversion to violence. He avoids quarrelling with Raoul's mother and his own; he makes only a peaceful protest to the king; he is reluctant to fight; and he endures extraordinary ill-treatment from his overlord before obtaining his release—which he does by proposing himself as victim to Raoul's assault.[33] For both characters, emplotment and characterization are handled with radical simplicity and are in practice impossible to dissociate.

. . . . .

The concatenation of similar scenes is the most obvious compositional principle in the *chansons de geste,* most of which are structurally open-ended: one could devise additional scenes at little cost to the imagination, or else abridge them with no sense of irreparable loss. The episode is their basic unit of composition, just as the *laisse* is of the episode. It is probable that the episode was also the commonest unit of performance: one can imagine an audience clamouring for "the bit where . . . " and certainly the *jongleurs'* catalogue in the romance of *Flamenca* lists many items which are in fact episodes from larger works.[34]

This fragmentation in practical performance no doubt partly accounts for the tendency to invest individual scenes with drama at the expense of overall coherence, which is well attested in the *chansons de geste.* Consistency in the presentation of individual characters may well be sacrificed to heighten the clash between them. When Ganelon is brought before Marsilie in the *Roland,* for instance, he infuriates the Saracen king by demands purported to come from Charlemagne but which formed no part of the Frankish deliberations as reported in the preceding scene, and therefore seem to be Ganelon's own invention. Only a few lines before, Ganelon had seemed fearful even to undertake the embassy, but now he is emboldened to the point of greatly increasing the dangers inherent in it. The payoff of an exciting scene, with Ganelon and Marsilie almost coming to blows, quite eclipses the incoherence of characterization that produced it;[35] as T. Hunt observes, the *Roland* poet is more interested in *interaction* than in *identity.*[36]

In her monumental study of *Huon de Bordeaux,* M. Rossi traces a similar lack of consistency in the central character. Initially Huon demonstrates a lucidity and good sense unusual in an epic hero. Once he is under the magical protection of Auberon, however, the plot risks stagnating: excitement and danger can only be revived when Auberon's friendship is withdrawn, and this has to be engineered by Huon's provoking him with hitherto uncharacteristic *folie.*[37] By adopting a laxer standard of consistency, the poet achieves the double drama of conflict with Auberon and physical risk to his hero. Concern with action as primary has made characterization take second place.

A third example of a text where the personality of a major character is bent to meet the author's conception of the story-line is the *Charroi de Nîmes.*[38] The essentially reduplicative structure whereby in the first half William argues with King Louis and in the second has a battle of wits with the Saracen kings Otran and Harpin sustains the hero in a dramatic conflict of personalities without, however, masking the fact that his own personality undergoes a considerable shift in the process. In the first scene he is all righteous anger as he defends the ideal of an enlightened feudalism that would reward the meritorious while protecting the weak; in the second he emerges as a wily play-actor, a knight disguised as a merchant pretending to be a thief, sardonic manipulator rather than innocent victim, his high-mindedness replaced by bravado and deceit.[39]

In the *laisses similaires* of the better epics, an act is presented from different standpoints which, taken together, are less contradictory than complementary. In the same way, differences in the presentation of a character from one episode to another may be reducible in a creative reading to a coherent presentation of a moral or political theme. In such a case, character is subordinated to a plot conceived not just as a series of acts but as the articulation of an ethical point of view. In the *Charroi de Nîmes,* for instance, the inconsistencies of William's behaviour may be partly neutralised by subsuming them to an apologia for the petite *chevalerie.*

In *Raoul de Cambrai,* the pacific Bernier occasionally rises to Raoul's implacable belligerence, while Raoul declines into moderation and goodwill. After their rupture and Bernier's return to his family with news of the invasion, his prudent father and uncles adopt a policy of appeasement. An ambassador is sent to Raoul's camp who behaves with exemplary decorum (not in the least like an Irishman, l. 2154) and pledges the Vermandois to assist in the reconquest of the Cambrésis from Giboïn. Even Guerri is struck by the generosity of their offer (ll. 2170-73), but Raoul is unbending and accuses him of cowardice. In a second embassy scene, however, the roles are reversed. Bernier is insulting and provocative, calling down a curse on Raoul and enumerating his grievances against him. At first incensed, Raoul is moved by Bernier's message of peace. From *fix a putain* (l. 2252) he switches to addressing him as *ami* (l. 2287), promises to accept the terms and looks forward to renewed friendship (ll. 2286-90, 2296-7). It is because of Guerri's obstinacy and wounded pride that the offer is rejected. Learning this, Bernier is filled with vindictive delight: he thanks God for the war, defies Raoul and at once rushes to attack him, thereby killing an unarmed man who had run to Raoul's defence.

A second diptych, composed of duels, demonstrates a similar changeover of roles between Bernier and Raoul's successor and nephew, Gautier, who is a watered-down version of his uncle. First Gautier, with uncharacteristic moderation, challenges Bernier to single combat in order to avoid further bloodshed. He prepares for the fight by scrupulous attendance at religious services (ll. 4290-5); courteous in word and deed, he ministers at Aliaume's death bed and then actually saves Bernier's life (l. 4715 ff., 4745 ff.). Bernier's pride or folly in insisting that their two seconds, Guerri and Aliaume, should fight as well, is condemned by both of them (ll. 4710, 4731-5). In the events surrounding the second duel, however, Gautier with ruthless intransigeance rejects repeated appeals for peace from the king (l. 5139), Bernier (ll. 5181 ff. and 5267 ff.), the abbé of St. Germain (l. 5295 ff.) and the whole Vermandois family (l. 5346 ff.). His piety shows a marked decline, for he is reluctant to yield to the abbé's offer of absolution, and does so only with a bad grace: "con je le fas dolent" (l. 5360). Bernier, by contrast, has been conciliatory from the start, excusing Gautier to the king on the grounds of his youth (l. 5163), offering him his sword (l. 5256 f.), and prostrating himself on the ground (l. 5365, etc.).

In such scenes the author's conception of character is manifestly subordinate to his desire to expose the psychology of vendetta and reprobate the incessant renewal of strife. This principle of applauding the doves and blackening the hawks—unless, of course, they are engaged in a worthwhile warlike crusade—is constant in the so-called epic of revolt, and applies without regard to the integrity of individual characters. Subrenat comments on the *dénouement* of *Gaydon* that the hero

> "maintient ses exigences certes et, en cela, ne change pas, mais il se rend compte aussi, de lui-même cette fois-ci, que la solution du conflit n'est pas dans les armes. [. . .]
>
> "Et curieusement, à ce moment-là, c'est Riol le sage qui devient plus violent. Ce renversement d'attitude entre les deux personnages souligne le caractère plus conciliant de Gaydon." [40]

In *Girart de Roussillon* the judgments passed on the hero by both author and characters reflect his swings of mood between conciliatoriness and bitter antagonism towards Charles Martel, and it is no coincidence that the extraordinarily long and laudatory description of Foulques occurs shortly after he has condemned Girart's implacability (l. 4832 ff.) and immediately before this line: "E sapçaz d'esta gera mout li desplaz" (l. 5010). [41]

Bertrand de Bar-sur-Aube retained something of this spirit in his often fatuous recasting of the same legendary material in the *chanson de geste Girart de Vienne*. Burlesque though the grounds of Girart's resentment against his sovereign are (he has been tricked into kissing the queen's toe instead of Charlemagne's, and the emperor has refused to punish his wife for this shameful outrage!), he persists in belligerent opposition until he successfully takes Charlemagne's godson, Lambert, prisoner. At once he changes character: hoping to win back Charles's friendship, he offers to waive a ransom demand; and now it is Charlemagne's turn to appear in a bad light. When Oliver, Girart's nephew, comes to his court to sue for peace, the emperor is intent on revenge (ll. 4020-1). He wants to humiliate his opponent, even though legally he himself is in the wrong (ll. 4046-8). Even when accused of treachery by Roland, there is no longer any question of rancour on Girart's part: his moral stock has risen as ineluctably as Charlemagne's has declined. [42]

One means whereby an author can spell out the moral thrust of his tale so that even the dullest wit shall perceive it is by writing in a divine intervention. Since this device deprives the human actors at least temporarily of that agency which is the principal form of expression of character, it again tends to diminish the status of the actors *vis-à-vis* the plot. This is the more true when, as sometimes happens, God is transparently an alias for the author's undistinguished moral prejudices, and the characters dangle puppet-like from unsubtle strings.

An example of such a scene occurs in *Girart de Vienne*. Roland, Charles's champion, and Oliver, Girart's champion, are to fight a duel to determine whether or not Girart has been guilty of irregularity in his feudal obligations. This episode, the most protracted of the text and apparently perceived by the author as its high point, lasts for some thousand lines (from the arming of the heroes, l. 4880 ff., to a conclusion ca. l. 5957), during which the poet spares us nothing of how they vie with each other in prowess and gentility. So many blows, or such nice manners, should, one feels, bring a conclusion to the point at issue: but not a bit of it. God literally brings the curtains down on their efforts by enveloping both combatants in a dense cloud (l. 5891 ff.) while an angel announces that they would be better employed fighting side by side against the Saracens in Spain (ll. 5908-5920). [43] The heroes at once fall in with this way of thinking. The duel is abandoned, and Charlemagne and Girart reach a reconciliation by quite another means. While this divine intervention does facilitate a realisation of the many promptings of mutual affection and esteem between the two young knights, it also deprives their great show of courage and endurance, their eager championship of their respective uncles, and their bitter political arguments of much of their point. The characters, in other words, are sacrificed to the author's concern to express his somewhat banal view of the proper purpose of chivalry (and also, incidentally, to bring them into line for the *Chanson de Roland,* to which his text is a retrospective introduction).

The two redactions of the *Moniage Guillaume* exemplify different approaches to the use of angelic intervention. The shorter first redaction, which proceeds at a *fabliau*-like pace, dispenses with a "psychological" consideration of William's sanctity by assigning an angel to summon him first to the monastery of Genevois-sur-mer (ll. 58-60), then to his hermitage at St. Guillaume le Désert (ll. 820-37), leaving William to a relatively uninhibited exercise of his former, worldly characteristics of pugilism and voracity, with splendid comic effect. The second redaction takes William's holiness much more earnestly. The angel vanishes, to be replaced by much explicit comparison between monasticism and knighthood, and rather too much pious meditation. The result is a far more serious view of character which is not without interest, despite its dampening effect on the cartoon-strip style of comedy of redaction 1.

Even when God is not a direct participant, the ambiance of the Old French epic tends to the religious and moral. In so far as they are "structured" at all, the stories display patterns of reward or punishment measured according to the preoccupations of the author, rather than of success or failure in terms of the desires or intentions of the characters. Heroes and traitors are alike exemplary, and a chief requirement of "realism" is to confer sufficient density on a character for the audience to engage with the type (not an individual) and thereby concur with the author's judgment on it. How characters act will show what they are made of, and elicit audience response; the ultimate test, however, is not what they do, but what happens to them. Thus E. B. Vitz writes of the *Roland* that "religious causation (God's will, revealed or unrevealed) undermines human agency as a narrative force in plot structure," and "men are responsible for their actions, but their actions are not responsible for what occurs."[44] She uses her observations of this and other texts to argue against the validity of a Greimasian notion of "Subject" for medieval literature; certainly I think they confirm that a sense of divine purpose is one way in which characters can be said to be subordinated to plot.

The classic reward for good conduct is a fief and a wife, always beautiful and preferably rich. W. C. Calin has argued that in *Aymeri de Narbonne,* the themes of the conquest of a city and the winning of a bride, which together make up most of the action, are interrelated: with land comes power and position, and with marriage a lineage to maintain it.[45] Aymeri's career in this *chanson de geste* is merely an amplification of that of nearly all his relatives, for his grandfather won the fief of Monglane and the lovely Mabille (*Garin de Monglane*), his son William wins Orange and "la belle Orable" (*Prise d'Orange*), and his grandson becomes king of Andrenas and marries Gaiete (*Guibert d'Andrenas*). Those whose careers involve more danger or excess are rewarded with martyrdom (Renaut de Montauban, Roland (?)), or sainthood (Garin Le Loheren, Girart de Roussillon), or at least with glory. Whoever wrote the second death scene of Vivien in the *Chanson de Guillaume* clearly felt it was less incongruous for the hero to appear to die twice over in very different circumstances than for his efforts to go unacknowledged, and hence rewarded him (l. 1988 ff.) with a touching end, in an odour of sancity, attended with the last rites by his dear uncle, and in a Christian-symbolic setting of fountain and olive tree, even though he had been cut to pieces in a desert landscape some ten to fourteen days before.[46] Conversely punishment usually takes the form of death without honour. Characters like Raoul in *Raoul de Cambrai* and Isembard in *Gormont et Isembard* are "des maudits qui ne sont pas tout à fait des damnés, puisqu'ils se repentent et que Dieu leur laisse une chance de le fléchir, mais des maudits qui n'ont pas droit à un autre sort que la calamité, de la mort subite."[47] Outright traitors are condemned in court (Ganelon in the *Chanson de Roland*), summarily executed (Acelin in the *Couronnement de Louis,* l. 1884 ff., or Makaire in *Aiol,* l. 10900 ff.), or insouciantly killed with a blow from William's tremendous fist (as Aymon le viel in the *Charroi de Nîmes,* l. 678 ff.),[48] all lending their weight to the conviction expressed in *Fierabras*

that "Tous jours vont traïtours à male destinée; U en pres un en loing, jà n'i aront durée."[49]

Happily the hand of Providence is sometimes more discreetly gloved. In the events leading up to the hero's death in *Raoul de Cambrai* there is a conviction of fatality combined with confusion as to its operation. Cursed by his mother, sacrilegious and blasphemous, Raoul seems an obvious target for divine retribution, and yet his actual death is presented in almost wholly secular terms.[50] Is Bernier an agent of the Almighty? The poet spares us this conviction; but then he excels in conveying a sense of the tangibility of moral questions together with the elusiveness of moral answers. A scene which shows a similar, masterly reluctance to dilute the complexity of human problems with an infusion of divine justice is the death scene of Garin in *Garin le Loheren* (ll. 16511-93). It is a martyrdom of a sort: Garin is murdered by the treacherous Bordelais as he kneels at an altar in penitence for the sins of a violent life. Yet before he is dead, a follower with commercial flair and a quick eye to a future saint piously hacks his right arm off for use as a relic: which assault Garin pardons before he dies. Sanctity or burlesque? An air of ambiguity pervades the episode, proof against the easy answer or pat judgment. Two final, and more obvious examples of a sense of the numinous adding to the significance of a human drama without detracting from the alterity and integrity of the characters are the deaths of Roland and Vivien.

．．．．．

I will conclude this paper by considering two features of the composition of the *chansons de geste* which seem to me positively to privilege character *vis-à-vis* the individual events of the plot, and to confer on certain heroes an almost mythic status.

In these poems the distinction between "subject" and "fable" drawn by the Russian formalists and taken over by more recent critics with the terms *"récit"* and *"histoire"*[51] is more than a theoretical construct, it is a vital part of the mechanics of composition and reception. Whereas in modern fiction there tends to be a systematic blurring of the two, the Old French epic poets are quite clear that their narrative (or *"récit"*) is only one possible rendering of a tale (*"histoire"*) from which it is conceptually distinct. Without wanting to go into the subtleties of this distinction here, the devices by which it is most straightforwardly indicated include allusions to sources or other, rival versions; summaries of the *histoire* in prologues and elsewhere; recapitulations and prospections or prophecies which temporarily suspend the flow of the *récit* to reveal at least a partial overview of the *histoire;* and tense usage which opposes an unfolding, present tense *récit* against a complete and known past tense *histoire.*

The "normal" situation is for author and audience to share in this knowledge of the existence of the *histoire* while the characters slog along the line of the *récit,* experiencing and acting as though it were the ultimate reality. At times, however, the characters are received into the complicity of author and audience; they gain insight into the totality of the story in which they figure; and though they continue to enact the roles apportioned to them and to feel the emotions that are their lot, they do so with a curiously enhanced stature which can border on myth.

The commonest device whereby a character learns more about the plot of his text is the prophetic dream. From the structured diversity of dream-lore inherited from Classical Antiquity the authors of *chansons de geste* fixed on one form only: the dream which comes true.[52] It usually forewarns of trouble, conflict, death, or some other disaster. The dreamer is temporarily removed from the flow of the *récit* to perceive some part of the underlying story.[53] In *Raoul de Cambrai,* for instance, Aalais learns of Raoul's death (ll. 3511-20), Beatrice of her husband's (ll. 8467-76). In the *Chevalerie Ogier,* the hero dreams that Charlemagne's army will pursue him (ll. 8213-21). On waking he learns that he has just been betrayed in Castel Fort and that the enemy are upon him. This stock device is amusingly parodied in the *Roman de Renart,* Branche II, ll. 131-60.

Although belonging to a recognizably rhetorical convention, as the *Renart* version shows, these dreams do not utterly conflict with mimetic realism, and do, indeed, reflect contemporary folk belief. More uncanny is when the characters intuit the plot without the need for such mediation. In the *Chanson de Roland,* for instance, Charlemagne receives veiled premonitions of future strife from his angel, but Roland himself appears to have a hotline to foreknowledge.[54] In the opening council scene he is the only one of Charlemagne's barons to discern Marsilie's treachery behind his lavish offers of peace (l. 196 ff.). He seems to divine Ganelon's guilt at the time of his appointment to the rearguard, when he breaks out in violent recrimination of his stepfather and alludes to the earlier scene of Ganelon's being chosen for the embassy—that scene being, of course, the reason for Ganelon's betrayal (ll. 763-65). He expresses no surprise at Oliver's announcement that the Saracens will attack, and quashes his denunciation of Ganelon (ll. 1008, 1026-7), only admitting his guilt later (l. 1457). This admission is accompanied by a prediction of Charlemagne's vengeance (l. 1459). His forecasts of the battle are proved true, though not exactly as he anticipated: fierce blows are struck, great honour won, the Saracens are vanquished or slain, Charles hears the horn and returns. Only as the battle draws towards its close does Roland reckon the full cost of these achievements to himself and his men in the so-called lament:

> Barons franceis, pur mei vos vei murir,
> Jo ne vos pois tenser ne guarantir.
> Aït vos Deus ki unkes ne mentit!
> Oliver frere, vos ne dei jo faillir,
> De doel murra[i], se altre ne m'i ocit.
>
> [1863-68]

Embracing martyrdom, Roland anticipates Charles' arrival on the field to honour their remains (ll. 1922-31), and also

his grief at the irreparable loss to his imperial army (ll. 1985-7). The death scene with the mediating angel sets the seal on Roland's participation in a mythic or quasi-divine level of awareness. As a character, he enjoys an exalted status mysteriously situated above the blow-by-blow unfolding of the action as expounded by the *récit,* a status aligned within the text with God and the angels, and outside it with the foreknowledge granted to author and audience.

Vivien in the *Chanson de Guillaume* presents an interesting mixture of true and false prediction of his future. On the eve of the battle his sober realism is contrasted with the Dutch courage of the inebriates Thibaut and Esturmi: they imagine they can win without reinforcements, but Vivien advises sending for William because "Od poi conpaignie ne veintrun pas Arabiz." (l. 71) The next morning he amplifies this advice: Thibaut should assess the enemy's strength, and then either engage battle or conceal his troops until William can be sent for: with God's help, the victory will be theirs (ll. 171-82). In the course of reconnoitring, Thibaut rashly exposes himself to enemy view and Vivien, feeling the Franks will be dishonoured if they do not at once attack, embarks on a policy of desperation. Though he assures Thibaut they will win, he does so quoting the drunken arrogance of Esturmi (cf. ll. 68 ff. and 207 ff.). A more realistic appraisal of the prospective encounter in ll. 245-51 contains predictions of the deaths of cowards, lesser men, and youngsters, and recognition that only God's power can overcome the heathen. As the battle takes its tragic toll, Vivien is divided between desperate hope that William or Louis will come to bring them victory and realisation that his followers are going to receive a martyr's death (ll. 485-6, 561-2, 573; 502, 538, 545-7). For a moment of terrible misapprehension, he takes Girart's cry of *Monjoie* for the arrival of William or Louis (ll. 453-54); this lack of true perception culminates in two despairing and false predictions, that he himself alone will win the fight, even though all his companions flee (l. 589 "Jo les veinterai ben solunc la merci Deu"), and that William and Louis will arrive in time, on that very day (ll. 751-2). As his last knights are cut down around him, however, Vivien returns to his former lucidity which now, with tragic prescience, encompasses his defeat and death:

> Forz sui jo mult, e hardi sui assez,
> De vasselage puis ben estre sun per; [ie. William's]
> Mais de plus loinz ad sun pris aquité,
> Car s'il fust en l'Archamp sur mer,
> Vencu eust la bataille champel.
> Allas, peccable, n'en puis home gent
> Lunsdi al vespre.
>
> [830-6]

Through this mixture of erroneous belief and terrible lucidity, the author of the *Chanson de Guillaume* gives his hero a stature comparable with Roland's while stressing his greater humanity.

The device of authorial prophecy is used with particular insistence in *Raoul de Cambrai,* making it the more remarkable when certain of the characters suddenly join with the author in announcing what will happen next.[55] From the outset, the audience has been alerted to grief that will follow from Louis's gift of a fief to Raoul (cf. vv. 516-17, 536-37, 639-40, 697-98, 745-46, 778-780, etc.). Quarrelling with her son about his intended campaign, Aalais too predicts that the longed for investiture will in fact bring death to its recipient:

> Qui te donna Peronne et Origni,
> Et S. Quentin, Neele et Falevis,
> [Et] Ham et Roie et la tor de Clari,
> De mort novele, biax fix, te ravesti.

> [987-90; cf. -1004-06]

Asking how he expects to win such a war, she taunts him with an inquiry after Bernier: what will become of him (l. 1077)? Raoul's reply is perhaps unwittingly prophetic: Bernier will help his family if the need arises (l. 1085; contrast the rather different declaration of intent by Bernier in ll. 944-5).[56] In a flash of clairvoyance, Aalais puts her finger on the nub of the whole plot:

> Bien le savoie, a celer nel vos qier,
> Ce est li hom dont avras destorbier,
> C'il en a aise, de la teste trenchier.

> [1089-90]

Again this prophecy echoes, but how much more strikingly, predictions already made by the author (see ll. 6-11, 391, and 741). Raoul therefore proceeds to the war against the Vermandois as the plot and his own logic require, but he does so both as a character enmeshed in the *récit,* and as a participant in a dialogue regarding the *histoire* which exactly parallels a similar dialogue engaged between author and audience. This is a highly effective device for privileging the heroic characters over the action.

My last point concerns discrepancies between *histoire* and *récit* which operate to undermine the credibility of the presentation of events and focus instead on the intensity of character reaction as the only reliable reality. In his highly influential study of *L'art épique des jongleurs,*[57] Jean Rychner established a terminology for classifying the various ways in which *laisses* could be grouped together. *Laisses parallèles* were those in which similar events were presented in similar terms, so that what might be conceived as successive parcels of narrative are in fact presented as "juxtaposed": "à moments similaires successifs correspond une expression similaire répétée" (p. 88). It is relatively easy to find examples of such *laisses;* a typical instance would be the series in *Raoul de Cambrai* where the supporters of the Vermandois arrive one after the other and pledge themselves to kill Raoul (*laisses* 97 [end], 98, 99 + 100, 101, 102, 103) (and cf. Rychner, pp. 83-93). The term *laisses similaires* is initially used to apply to certain groups of laisses in the *Roland* where this lyric "juxtaposition" is particularly marked: *laisses* 40-42 (Ganelon treats with Marsilie), 83-85 (the first horn scene), 133-8 (Roland sounds the horn), etc. Being principally concerned with

formal elaboration (though there is no clear formal distinction drawn between *laisses parallèles* and *laisses similaires*) Rychner prefers to avoid determining the narrative reference of such sequences. Commenting on *laisses* 40-42, for instance, in which Marsilie asks Ganelon when Charlemagne will desist from war and is told, never so long as Roland is alive, he writes:

> Faut-il dire, d'ailleurs, la ou les questions de Marsile? Sous cet ensemble statique, les réponses de Ganelon marquent à chaque fois quelque progrès; ce n'est pas, à vrai dire, un progrès narratif, mais un progrès psychologique et dramatique, dévoilant peu à peu ses pensées secrètes, suggérant, insinuant la trahison. [. . .] Il ne faut donc pas cherchera savoir, sur le plan de l'événement, si Marsile a réellement posé trois fois la même question, car les laisses similaires retiennent le récit dans une halte bien plus lyrique que narrative. (pp. 94-5)

In most of the examples which Rychner goes on to discuss, however, it is clear that the distinguishing feature of *laisses similaires* is the fact that they offer multiple reports of the same event. In *laisses* 174-6 of the *Roland,* for instance, it would not be reasonable to suppose that Roland delivered his glove to a descending angel any more than once; likewise in *laisses* 206-7, we cannot imagine that Charlemagne found Roland's body twice. The examples adduced from other texts (pp. 100-107) confirm that whatever his formal definition, in practice for Rychner *laisses parallèles* are those where different events are described in similar terms and *laisses similaires* are those where the same event is presented more than once in slightly different ways.

This leaves a very considerable number of instances outstanding of which, as in the case of the Marsilie—Ganelon scene, it is impossible to assert whether it is the event or merely the description that is repeated. The narrative becomes unreliable on a quite simple and fundamental issue of plot but supplies instead a very insistent image of a character in the grip of an intense experience or emotion. Since the *laisse* patterns of the *Roland* have attracted so much critical attention, I will illustrate this from *Raoul.*

Nearly all the "lyric" patterns of *laisses* in this text occur in the purportedly older core (up to ca. l. 3740), and focus on the character of the hero. The scene confronting Raoul and his mother, *laisses* 48-54, contains a repeated pattern of maternal admonishment followed by a display of anger from Raoul. In *laisses* 48 and 49 Aalais's warning that the gift of the Vermandois means death is reiterated; in *laisses* 50 and 51 Raoul issues dire threats against the men of Arrouaise if they refuse their support; and in *laisses* 52 and 53 Aalais expatiates on his vassals' faults. Are they both so furious that they keep repeating what they have just said? or is their anger and sense of mutual injury being dwelt on repeatedly by the poet as a technique of amplification (*expolitio*)?

Laisses 77 and 78 create a similar ambiguity around the growing conflict between Raoul and Bernier. In *laisse* 77

Raoul threatens to drive the Vermandois brothers across the sea and seize every penny they own; Bernier replies that this would be outrageous treatment for such worthy knights. In *laisse* 78 Raoul's threats are repeated in more emphatic terms; the penny's worth of land, for instance, becomes:

> . . . le montant d'un denier
> De toute honnor ne de terre a baillier,
> Ou vif remaigne[n]t, ou mort puise[nt] couchier.

> [1633-5]

and "Tant que il soient outre la mer fui" (l. 1621) becomes "Outre la mer les en ferai naigier" (l. 1636). Bernier's reply is likewise amplified. To the defense of Herbert's sons as fine knights is added criticism of Raoul (l. 1639), warning that even if his campaign is successful he will not find it easy to hang on to the Vermandois (l. 1643), and the wish to be revenged on Raoul for his many crimes against him (ll. 1645-51). The descriptions contained in these two *laisses* are different but not incompatible, and so it is impossible to assert whether they record two exchanges, or one. What is, however, unmistakable is the escalation in both provocation and remonstrance, and the consequently sharpened focus on the conflict between the two knights. One cannot be sure exactly what they said on any precise occasion, but one forms a very strong impression of their capacity for emotional antagonism: an impression, that is, of character at the expense of a precisely informed grasp of plot.

The ensuing quarrel between Raoul and Bernier contains further patterns of repetition which create uncertainty about the narrative flow precisely as they emphasize the emotions of the participants.[58] The final phase of this episode is Raoul's offer of reparation for the blow which he has struck Bernier. In the middle of *laisse* 85 he promises a public act of atonement ("Droit t'en ferai voiant maint chevalier," l. 1745), which Bernier angrily rejects: not till the blood flowing down from his head returns there of its own accord, and not till he can obtain revenge (?), will he consider such an offer (ll. 1746-55).[59] In *laisse* 86 Raoul's offer is amplified to occupy nineteen lines (1759-77) and is followed by a murmur of approval among the Franks: "Ceste amendise est bele! Qi ce refuse vos amis ne vieut estre" (1778-9). *Laisse* 87 then combines elements from both these preceding accounts. Raoul urges Bernier to accept reparation; Bernier refuses in almost identical terms to those which he had used before; and Guerri amplifies the reaction of the Franks, condemning Bernier for his obduracy in the face of so splendid an offer (1792-5). Once again details of who says what when are effaced before Raoul's urgent desire to placate, and Bernier's furious implacability.[60]

This study quite explicitly forestalls any temptation to regard it as definitive by the logic-defying concern for symmetry with which it marshalls two arguments in favour of the inseparability of character and plot, and two each for the primacy of the one over the other. Perhaps the whole investigation should be reoriented away from formal relations towards an examination of reference: after all, the fact that in the *chansons de geste* the issues of honour and dishonour, loyalty and treachery, wealth and destitution, life and death are all superimposed and mutually reinforcing is what makes these narratives impressive, their heroes moving even today and clearly far more so to contemporary audiences in a community still strifetorn and in many ways primitive. One framework of reference for this type of study which has already yielded promising results is medieval law; further theoretical approaches are suggested by medieval personality theories and the philosophy of action. My main concern here has been to challenge the easy assumption that either character or plot has a simple, unanalysable priority of status in the economy of a literary text.

Notes

1. Editions cited are as follows:

Aiol: chanson de geste, ed. J. Normand and G. Raynaud (Paris: Didot, Societé des anciens textes français, hereinafter referred to as S. A. T. F., 1877).

Le charroi de Nîmes (. . .), ed. Duncan McMillan (Paris: Klincksieck, 1972).

La chevalerie Ogier de Danemarche, ed. Mario Eusebi (Milan: Istituto Editoriale Cisalpino, 1963).

Les rédactions en vers du "Couronnement de Louis," ed. Yvan G. Lepage (Geneva: Droz, Textes li Héraires français, 1978). The text cited is the *AB* version.

Garin le Loheren (. . .) ed. Josephine E. Vallerie (Ann Arbor: Edwards Bros. Inc., 1947).

Girart de Roussillon, ed. W. Mary Hackett (Paris: Picard, S. A. T. F., 1953-55).

"Girard de Vienne" de Bertrand de Bar-sur-Aube, ed. Wolfgang van Emden (Paris: Picard, S.A.T.F., 1977).

La chanson de Guillaume, ed. Duncan McMillan (Paris: Picard, S. A. T. F., 1949-50).

Les deux rédactions en vers du "Moniage Guillaume," ed. Wilhelm Cloetta (Paris: Didot, S.A.T.F., 1906, 1911).

Raoul de Cambrai, ed. P. Meyer and A. Longnon (Paris: Didot, S.A.T.F., 1882).

Le roman de Renart, ed. Jean Dufournet (Paris: Garnier-Flammarion, 1970).

La chanson de Roland, ed. Frederick Whitehead, 2nd ed. (Oxford: Blackwell, 1946).

I would like to take this opportunity to thank my colleagues Dr. G. S. Burgess and Dr. O. A. C. Waite for their helpful and learned advice with this paper.

2. Edmond Faral, *La Chanson de Roland, étude et analyse* (Paris: Mellottée, Collection Chefs d'oeuvre de la littérature expliqués, 1933), p. 261.

3. Pierre Le Gentil, *La Chanson de Roland,* first printed 1955; 2nd ed. rev. (Paris: Hatier, Collection Connaissance des Lettres, 1967), p. 123.

4. Jean Misrahi and William Lee Hendrickson, "Roland and Oliver: Prowess and Wisdom, the Ideal of the Epic Hero," *Romance Philology* 33 (1979-80), 357-72, p. 359.

5. Tony Hunt, "Character and Causality in the Oxford Roland," *Medioevo Romanzo* 5 (1978), 3-33, pp. 12-13. See also his article "The Tragedy of Roland: an Aristotelian View," *Modern Language Review,* 74 (1979), 791-805; Sarah Kay, "Ethics and Heroics in the Song of Roland," *Neophilologus,* 62 (1978), 480-91; and François Suard, "Le personnage épique," in *Proceedings of the 5th Conference of the Société Rencesvals, Oxford 1970* (Salford: University of Salford Press, 1977), 167-76.

6. Cf. the defence of character study by Marguerite Rossi, *Huon de Bordeaux,* (Paris: Champion, Collection Nouvelle Bibliothèque du Moyen Age, 1975), 463-67.

7. See for example John Bayley, "Character and Consciousness," *New Literary History* 5 (1973-4), 225-35.

8. Roland Barthes, "An Introduction to the Structural Analysis of Narrative," *New Literary History* 6 (1974-5), 237-72, pp. 256-57 (translation, with additional material, of an essay originally published in *Communications* 8 [1966]).

9. E.g. Norman T. Burns and Christopher J. Reagan, eds., *Concepts of the Hero in the Middle Ages and the Renaissance* (Albany: State University of New York Press, 1975); Micheline de Combarieu du Grès, *L'idéal humain et l'expérience morale chez les héros des chansons de geste, des origines à 1250* (Aix-en-Provence: Publications de l'Université de Provence, 1979).

10. See D. J. A. Ross, "Old French," in A. T. Hatto, ed., *Traditions of Heroic and Epic Poetry,* 1, *The Traditions* (London: Modern Humanities Research Association, 1980), 79-113, pp. 90-91: "In the Middle Ages the *chansons de geste* seem generally to have been accepted as having a basis of valid historical fact."

11. Hans Robert Jauss, "Levels of Identification of Hero and Audience," *New Literary History* 5 (1973-4), 283-317.

12. Northrop Frye, *Anatomy of Criticism: Four Essays* (Princeton: Princeton University Press, first published 1957, p.b. 1966), pp. 33-4 (1966 edition).

13. A. J. Greimas, *Sémantique structurale: recherche de méthode,* (Paris: Seuil, 1966). It has been pointed out to me that by trying to integrate a theory of narrative within a theory of poetry, Greimas risked losing sight of the specificity of either.

14. "Dans l'étude du conte, la question de savoir *ce que* font les personnages est seule importance; *qui* fait quelque chose [est une] question qui ne se pose qu'accessoirement," V. Propp, *Morphologie du conte* (Paris: Seuil, 1970), p. 29, cited by Michel Mathieu, "Les acteurs du récit," *Poétique* 5 (1974), 357-67, p. 357, who endorses this bias.

15. A. J. Greimas, "Les actants, les acteurs et les figures," ed. Claude Chabrol *et al., Sémiotique narrative et textuelle* (Paris: Larousse, Collection Université, 1973), 161-76.

16. A further refinement to the theory is the introduction of modality permitting the nature of the Subject's agency to be analysed according to whether its "deep structure" action implies the presence of a modal verb.

17. Larry S. Crist, "Roland, héros du vouloir: contribution à l'analyse structurale de la *Chanson de Roland,*" in *Mélanges de Philologie et de Littératures Romanes offerts à Jeanne Wathelet-Willem, Marche Romane* No. spécial (1978), 77-101. See also Patricia Harris Stablein, "The Structure of the Hero in the Chanson de Roland: Being and Becoming," *Olifant* 5 (2) (Dec. 1977), 105-19, which suggests that the role of hero is divided between Roland, Oliver, and Charles. Recent studies of other medieval genres influenced by a functionalist approach include Pierre Gallais, "L'hexagone logique et le roman médiéval," *Cahiers de Civilisation Médiévale* 18 (1975), 1-14, 133-48; Donald M. Maddox, *Structure and Sacring: The Systematic Kingdom in Chrétien's "Erec and Enide,"* French Forum Monographs 8 (Lexington: French Forum, 1978); and several studies by Evelyn Birge Vitz including "Narrative Analysis of Medieval Texts: *La fille du comte de Pontieu,*" *Modern Language Notes* 92 (1977), 645-75. Vitz is critical of Greimas' concept of the Subject which, however, she seeks always to equate with a single surface structure character.

18. Jean-Michel Adam et Jean-Pierre Goldenstein, *Linguistique et discours littéraire: Théorie et pratique des textes* (Paris: Larousse, Collection Université, 1976), pp. 108-120.

19. Sarah Kay, "The Nature of Rhetoric in the Chanson de Geste," *Zeitschrift für Romanische Philologie* 94 (1978), 305-20, p. 316.

20. Cf. *Raoul de Cambrai,* ll. 347, 515, 625, 1549, 1555 (Raoul) with ll. 395, 591, 5596 (Bernier) and 3824, 4326, (Gautier).

21. Cf. ll. 392, 399, 831, etc. (*Raoul o le vis cler* and variants) with ll. 30, 364, 1217, etc. (*Aalais . . . o le vis cler,* and variants); ll. 506 (Raoul's *fier contenant*) with l. 3579 (Guerri's *fiere contenance*). Guerri has a *fier vis* and *fiere veüe* in ll. 2534, 1208; Raoul's *coraige* is *fier* in ll. 1629, 1728, etc.

22. Cf. ll. 1365 (Marsent), 2024 (Wedon), 4501 (Bernier) and 5385 (Ybert).

23. Raoul is *saige,* l. 781, as also Guerri, ll. 1045, 2012, and Gautier, l. 3998, but of all three is it repeatedly

said that *le sens quide / quida changier* (e.g. ll. 3081, 3402, 4505).

24. Cf. l. 2819 (Raoul) with l. 2906 (Rocoul), and also, though the formula is a slightly different one, with ll. 146 (Giboïn), 790 (the hostage Wedon de Borbone), and 1316 (Bernier).

25. Raoul is frequently *ber* (e.g. l. 836), as are Giboïn (e.g. l. 116), Guerri (e.g. l. 295), Louis (e.g. l. 844), and Gautier (e.g. l. 4946); the term *gentis,* used of Raoul (e.g. l. 372), is also used of Wedon (e.g. l. 1980), Bernier (e.g. l. 4264), and the abbé (l. 5310); Raoul is *preu* in ll. 534, 5170, as are Gautier (e.g. l. 4794), Guerri (e.g. l. 3221), Bernier (e.g. l. 3436). The qualificatives *au coraige vaillant* and *cortois* are likewise shared: cf. ll. 338, 2408, 2658, 4916, 4917, and 372, 5386, 5514, 5553.

26. Cf. ll. 2010, 881, 5169 and 2883, 778. This consistency of characterisation in the poem is commented on by Italo Siciliano, *Les chansons de geste et l'épopée. Mythes—Histoires—Poèmes,* Biblioteca di Studi Francesi 3 (Turin: Società Editrice Internazionale, 1968), 399: "Tout divers qu'ils soient, les preux et les sages du *Raoul* ont sensiblement la même taille, tous sont coupés dans la coulée d'une larve ardente et mouvante. Exception faite pour la triste Marsent, ils s'assemblent et se ressemblent. Toute porportion gardée, Aalais, Raoul, Guerri le Sor, Bernier, Garnier [Siciliano means Gautier], Aliaume sont de la même race et de la même force. Ici c'est le choeur qui chante la chanson et qui en fait l'unité, et c'est un choeur inquiet et inquiétant qui s'agite, court d'un bout à l'autre de la pièce, tourne en rond, s'épuise en interminables disputes, vit et périt de sa violence."

27. Arnaldo Moroldo, "Le portrait dans la chanson de geste," *Le Moyen Age* 86 (1980), 387-419 and 87 (1981), 5-44.

28. Cf. Barthes' assertion, in "The Structural Analysis of Narrative," p. 263, that the creation of "psychology" in a fiction presupposes mobility of stance from 3rd to 1st person and back again, which is transparently based on post-medieval narrative.

29. Cf. Jean Frappier, *Les chansons de geste du cycle de Guillaume d'Orange,* 1 (Paris: Société d'édition de l'enseignement supérieur, 1955), pp. 173-4: "les personnages existent de l'intérieur, ils ne révèlent pourtant leur nature morale que de l'extérieur, par leurs gestes, leurs paroles et leurs actes [. . .] Sans chercher à rendre nos héros plus complexes qu'ils ne sont, sachons goûter une simplicité expressive et franche qui parvient à montrer ou à suggérer la qualité des âmes."

30. The treacherous Bordelais, with whom for the most part the initiative lies, are more obviously imbued with "personality." In a sensitive study aimed at differentiating Garin from his brother Begon, Anne

Iker Gittleman notes that often it is the absence of a descriptive element or motif that characterises Garin, to whom she attributes "une grandeur dépouillée": see *Le style épique dans "Garin le Loheren,"* (Geneva: Droz, 1967), p. 215.

31. Cf. W. W. Ryding, *The Structure of Medieval Narrative* (The Hague: Mouton, 1971), pp. 45-6.

32. Cf. Beate Schmolke-Hasselmann, *Boire et mengier: essai d'une analyse structurale de la "Chanson de Guillaume,"* paper read at the 17th International Congress on Medieval Studies, Kalamazoo, May 1982. I would like to thank Dr. Schmolke-Hasselmann for kindly sending me a copy of this as yet unpublished paper.

33. See Pauline Matarasso, *Recherches historiques et littéraires sur "Raoul de Cambrai"* (Paris: Nizet, 1962), p. 146.

34. *Le Roman de Flamenca,* ed. Ulrich Gschwind (Berne: Francke, 1976), vol. 1, 621 ff., and vol. 2, notes to ll. 630-1, 641-2, 677-8.

35. Cf. Suard, "Le personnage épique" (cited in fn. 5), p. 168, for another example of possible inconsistency in Ganelon.

36. Hunt, "Character and Causality in the Oxford Roland" (cited in fn. 5), p. 11.

37. Rossi, *Huon de Bordeaux,* p. 484.

38. ———Pace D. D. R. Owen, "Structural Artistry in the *Charroi de Nîmes,*" *Forum for Modern Language Studies* 14 (1978), 47-60.

39. In a fascinating article "Type et individu dans l'autobiographie' médiévale," *Poétique,* 6 (1975), 426-45, Evelyn Birge Vitz attempts a study of the medieval concept of personality based on Abelard's *Historia Calamitatum*. A part of her exposition deals with the question of consistency: concerned to present his experiences more from the point of view of their intensity (and of his own superiority, or extreme sensibility) than of their fundamental unity, Abelard allowed various parts of his career to appear completely compartmentalised one from another.

40. Jean Subrenat, *Etude sur "Gaydon", chanson de geste du XIIIᵉ siècle,* Etudes Littéraires. (Aix-en-Provence: Editions de l'Université de Provence, 1974), pp. 210-11.

41. For a study of the pacific ethos of *Girart de Roussillon,* see René Louis, *De l'histoire à la légende: 2, Girart, comte de Vienne, dans les chansons de geste* (Auxerre: Imprimerie Moderne, 1947), 1: 405-16. Cf. also the remarks under the heading *Condamnation de l'attitude belliqueuse* in vol. I of Micheline de Combarieu's *L'idéal humain,* p. 147 ff.

42. For further inconsequences in *Girart de Vienne,* see Ryding, *Structure of medieval narrative,* pp. 51-2.

43. There is a similar scene in *La Chevalerie d'Ogier de Danemarche,* ll. 10454-70. A more successful analogue is the supernatural fire which consumes the standards of Girart and Charles Martel in *Girart de Roussillon,* thus forcing an end to their battle at Vaubeton (l. 2874 ff.), since it operates as an effective metaphor of the violence and irascibility of the two antagonists, as also of the cauterising process of self-examination in the two camps following this disturbing experience. Charles Martel is pronounced to be accursed of God (ll. 2906-26); despite a rehearsal of his grievances, Girart is condemned by his uncle for not seeking peace (ll. 3018-30). God's intervention is in harmony with, but does not cause, the signal act of personal abnegation which actually finalises the peace negotiations, namely Tierri's voluntary exile (ll. 3122-35, especially ll. 3123-4: "Ne place a Damlideu, au manne rei, Que ja mais per mon cors nus on gerrei!"). In this case, the credibility and integrity of the characters seem to me to have been maintained alongside the expression of God's will.

44. Evelyn Birge Vitz, "Desire and Causality in Medieval Narrative," *Romanic Review,* 71 (1980), 213-43, pp. 223-24.

45. W. C. Calin, *The Epic Quest: Studies in Four Old French Chansons de Geste* (Baltimore: John Hopkins University Press, 1966), especially pp. 5-31. Calin stresses the hero's representative character, p. 23: "All of society participates in Aymeri's quest."

46. See Minette Grunman, "Temporal Patterns in the *Chanson de Guillaume,*" *Olifant,* 4 (1) (Oct. 1976), 49-62, p. 56.

47. Jean-Charles Payen, *Le motif du repentir dans la littérature française médiévale (des origines à 1230)* (Geneva: Droz, 1967), p. 180.

48. For remarks on William's celebrated rabbit punch, consult Frappier, *Guillaume d'Orange,* 1:94-96. On the *post mortem* prospects of traitors, see Payen, *Le motif du repentir,* p. 158 and notes.

49. Quoted by William Wistar Comfort, "The Character Types in the Old French *Chansons de Geste,*" *Publications of the Modern Language Society of America* 21 (1906), 279-461, p. 356. Cf. also *Garin le Loheren,* l. 6357, "Hom desloiax ne puet longues garir," cited by Micheline de Combarieu, *L'idéal humain,* 1:98.

50. See my article *La composition de "Raoul de Cambrai,"* forthcoming in the *Revue Belge de Philogie et d'Histoire.*

51. See Sarah Kay, "The Contrasting Use of Time in the Romances of *Jaufre* and *Flamenca,*" *Medioevo Romanzo* 6 (1979), 37-62, especially pp. 39-40 and notes.

52. See Herman Braet, *Le songe dans la chanson de geste au XIIe siècle, Romanica Gardensia,* 15 (Gent: Romanica Gandensia, 1975), 198.

53. On the integration of the dream to other forms of *annonce,* see Braet, *Le songe,* p. 103 ff.

54. Thus E. Vance writes in "Roland et la poétique de la mémoire," *Cahiers d'Etudes Médiévales* 1 (1975), 103-115, p. 106: "Les héros du *Roland* non seulement parlent-ils dans les mêmes formules métriques que le poète, mais ils ont recours aux mêmes épithètes, aux mêmes listes, voire à la même pré-science que le poète." This article has appeared in English as "Roland and the Poetics of Memory," in *Textual Strategies: Perspectives in Post-Structural Criticism,* ed. Josué Harari (Ithaca: Cornell University Press, 1979), 374-403.

55. For some other, less convincing examples of the characters of *Raoul* predicting their own future, see Carlo Pica, "*Raoul de Cambrai:* crisi di un sistema," *Cultura Neolatina* 40 (1980), 67-77, pp. 71-72.

56. The Brussels fragment of *Raoul de Cambrai* adds after the passage corresponding to ll. 944-945 "Mais tant vous di que ie lor aiderai; Se pooir ai, sachiez ie vous nuirai," which would, of course, deprive Raoul's words of their prophetic force. See A. Bayot, "*Raoul de Cambrai* (Brüsseler Fragmente)," *Revue des Bibliothèques et Archives de Belgique,* 4 (1906), 412-29.

57. Jean Rychner, *La chanson de geste: essai sur l'art épique des jongleurs* (Geneva: Droz, and Lille: Giard, 1955).

58. *Laisses* 82-83 repeat in very similar terms Bernier's account of his mother's forcible abduction by Ybert; the mention of his mother's nobility in the very short *laisse* 80 is amplified in *laisse* 81.

59. The text is not very clear; Meyer suggests the possibility of a lacuna between ll. 1754 and 1755. I would punctuate and translate as follows:

> Ja enver vos ne me verres paier
> Jusqe li sans qe ci voi rougoier
> Puist de son gre en mon chief repairier.
> Qant gel verai, lor porrai esclairier
> La grant vengance qe vers ton cors reqier—
> Je nel laroie por l'or de Monpeslier.

[1750-55]

"You will not see me reconciled with you until the blood that I see running red returns to my head of its own accord. When I see that, then I shall give vent to the terrible vengeance I desire against you—not for all the gold of Montpellier would I forego it!"

60. A further example of ambiguity is presented by *laisses* 143, 144, 147, and 151 describing Ernaut's flight from Raoul on the battlefield.

W. R. J. Barron (essay date 1987)

SOURCE: "The Matter of France" in *English Medieval Romance,* Longman Group UK Limited, 1987, pp. 89-108.

[In the following excerpt, Barron considers the relationship between the French and the English romance through the exploration of key works including the Chanson de Roland, Otuel and Roland, The Sege of Melayne, The Sowdon of Babylon, *and* Fierabras.]

The dual effect of the Norman Conquest in severing the Germanic roots of English culture and importing a dialect of *romanz* which exposed England to the cultural influence of France in the age of its ascendancy was ultimately to have profound consequences. The Matter of England romances show how slow the roots were to wither and how readily they became entwined with elements of the imported culture to produce narrative literature equally appealing to English and Anglo-Norman audiences. Not all such elements were equally assimilable: the dominant form of secular literature in the century following the Conquest, the epics of the Matter of France, might have been expected to appeal to a society whose native tradition had long included heroic poetry of a similar character, yet they are represented in English by only a handful of texts, late in date and largely unrepresentative of the genre. There is evidence that the *chansons de geste* were popular with the French-speaking rulers of England, where three of the earliest texts have been preserved, but none that epics were ever composed in Anglo-Norman.[1] While the ruling class could understand the originals, there was no need for English adaptations; they came mostly in the fourteenth century when the form was already in decay and sufficiently adulterated with elements of romance to appeal to the tastes of ordinary men. As a result, the true epic of the *geste du roi,* of Charlemagne and his *douzepers,* the twelve peers of France, embattled against the forces of paganism for the defence of Christendom, is represented only by a single fragmentary text.

THE SONG OF ROLAND

This version of the *Chanson de Roland* (see above, pp. 15-19), made somewhere in the east Midlands about 1400, survives as a fragment of 1049 lines, about a quarter of the French original. It represents no known text of the *Roland,* combining details from the oldest manuscript with others from later rhymed versions, probably already conflated in its source. To this have been added some elements from the *Pseudo-Turpin Chronicle,* a Latin prose compilation of the first half of the twelfth century designed to do for the Matter of France what Geoffrey of Monmouth's *Historia* did for the Matter of Britain by weaving the material of the epics into a supposedly historical account attributed to Charlemagne's clerical lieutenant, Archbishop Turpin. The real clerical authorship of the *Pseudo-Turpin* is apparent in the occasional moral interpolations such as the incident with which the English fragment opens: Ganelon, returning from his mission to Saragossa, brings a present of wine and women from the Sultan with which Charlemagne's men indulge themselves on the journey back to France, suggesting a moral cause for the coming disaster, just as elsewhere Ganelon's greed is stressed as the motive for his betrayal. But if the English

adapter too was a cleric, he made no thematic use of these importations; the morality of his version like the original is feudal and the root cause of the disaster is Ganelon's treason. How well he appreciated the underlying issues is difficult to judge from the surviving fragment, but the coverage of two key elements is sufficient to form some impression of his understanding:

In the original (ll. 737-73), when Ganelon nominates Roland to command the rearguard, Charles rages against him as a fiend of hell, but Roland first responds calmly that France will suffer no loss through him; then, in the variant *laisse,* with violence, mockingly reminding him how he let fall the Emperor's glove which was the emblem of his mission to Saragossa and claiming Charles's bow as the sign of his own charge. In the English version (ll. 134-77), the poet adds his own curses to Charlemagne's accusation that Ganelon desires Roland's death and Ganelon makes his self-interest more obvious by nominating himself to command the van, yet Roland accepts the charge eagerly without mentioning his stepfather, fear of whose treason is so widespread that no other *douzeper* will volunteer for the mission. By casting Ganelon so openly in the role of villain the redactor has removed the element of ambivalence from his character and much of the tension from the plot; substitution of simple malice on his part for the original conflict between his desire for chivalric reputation and his rivalry with his stepson has turned the mixture of open defiance and ironic acceptance of the implied challenge with which Roland originally responds into something like culpable blindness on his part. When, in the French (ll. 1017-90), the Saracen hordes fall upon the rearguard, Oliver immediately attributes the attack to Ganelon's treachery but Roland silences him, reminding him that he is speaking of his stepfather; the rebuke has gone from the English version (ll. 511-44) along with Oliver's triple call for the blowing of the horn, while Roland's repeated refusals for the sake of his own reputation, the fame of his kinsmen, the honour of France are reduced to a single denial that there is any need while they still remain uninjured. In fact the horn is never blown, though Ganelon's assurance to Charles that Roland is merely hunting pointlessly survives; instead, Roland finally proposes to send a messenger to the Emperor to prevent further loss of life, to which Oliver angrily replies: "'Broder, let be all siche sawes!'" (*speeches*) (l. 1049).[2]

The English fragment ends at that point, leaving in doubt whether anything further was to have been made of the contrast between valiant Roland and prudent Oliver. There is no indication that the poet understood the original significance of Roland's *demesure* any more than Ganelon's ambivalent motivation; everyone seems wholly convinced of the latter's treachery and Charlemagne is criticized for not trusting those who tell him of it just as Roland is openly blamed (ll. 633-41) for his failure to blow the horn. In each case, the original supplies some warrant for what is said, but the redactor has not, apparently, appreciated the significance of the pattern of repetition with variation. What survives in his version are black and white issues of loyalty and treason, of Christian solidarity in resistance to overwhelming pagan forces. Two-thirds of the surviving section are concerned with battle, faithful to the original in general outline but largely independent in the detailed description of action.

Though the English changes scene with the French, moving from the battlefield to Charles's camp and back again, it does not reproduce the isolated tableaux of the original, moments of frozen action in which the variant *laisses* present different aspects of the same situation. The narrative moves swiftly and competently, with obvious pleasure in the description of violence effectively conveyed by the irregular but persistent alliteration in the four-stress line—though both alliteration and rhyme have obviously suffered in transmission. The poet lingers for a moment over some of the familiar topics of the alliterative tradition: wild and desolate scenery (ll. 305-09), a fierce storm among mountain peaks (ll. 845-62), speeches of battlefield defiance (ll. 570-77), the splendour of armour (ll. 702-11), above all, the violence of hand-to-hand fighting:

> Roulond rod furthe, he wold not rest, I wene;
> He sawe wher a Sairsyn seche hym wold,
> Kinge was of Criklond, crounyd with gold.
> In he ridithe ful fast hym againste;
> He smot throughe sheld and man almost,
> That man and horse on the hethe fell.
> Then he nemythe 'MonJoy!' full still,
> He drawithe out his swerd and swappithe hym about.
> Helmes and hedes he hewithe of stout,
> He hewithe doun hethy men full many.
> There ys no man alyf may say southly
> That euer eny man sley so many.
>
> (ll. 740-51)

Little of the alliterative tradition other than its rhetorical manner survives here. Even at this late date there were poets, such as the author of the alliterative *Morte Arthure* (see below, pp. 138-42), who inherited its epic spirit; had one of them undertaken this redaction, we might have had a version which showed more understanding of the *Roland* than this somewhat superficial, external account.

THE MATTER OF FRANCE AS PIOUS LEGEND: "OTUEL AND ROLAND" AND "THE SEGE OF MELAYNE"

Whatever part churchmen may have played in the transmission of the legends which gathered round the names of Charlemagne and Roland and in the composition of the *chansons de geste,* once the Matter of France had established itself the Church was not slow to exploit its claim upon the imagination of the ruling class in the interests of faith and feudal solidarity. Propaganda was more to its purpose than poetry and what the early *chansons* demonstrated in action, without commentary, clerics made explicit in prose as well as verse. Characteristic is the Latin prose *Descriptio* which describes how the Emperor of Constantinople, finding himself unable to protect the Christian community in the East from a Sa-

racen attack, calls for aid from Charlemagne as Emperor of the West and, when he has freed the Holy Land from their threat, rewards him with the only treasure he will accept, relics of Christ's passion to be revered in Western shrines. Sober historians recognized the improbability of such a campaign but, written early in the twelfth century, the chronicle caught the imagination of the age of the crusades by turning Charlemagne, whose struggle with Islam had been fought on his own doorstep, into a prototype crusader. The *Pseudo-Turpin Chronicle* (c. 1140) extended the same process to the Emperor's campaigns in Spain, using his legendary military exploits as a thread on which to hang numerous moral and didactic episodes in which Charles figures as a saint of the Church Militant. Both accounts were used in the *Vita Karoli Magni* complied on the occasion of Charles's canonization in 1165, were translated into French in the early thirteenth century and finally conflated in 1206 as the *Estoire de Charlemagne* which proclaimed its academic respectability by denouncing the *chansons* as mendacious rhymes, with every success to judge from the numerous manuscripts which survive.[3] Now that the legends of Charlemagne had assumed the character of a saint's life, converts to the true faith were required to complete the analogy. Poets engaged on romanticizing the *chansons de geste* supplied them from among the Saracen ranks, converting them by force of arms or mystical experiences modelled on the Grail romances, and attaching them to the *geste du roi* in defiance of historical probability. The historicity of the Matter of France meant even less to fourteenth-century English audiences, but the flavour of the saint's life apparently appealed to them.

Two further fragments of the *geste du roi* in Middle English apparently represent detached portions of a lost tail-rhyme romance, referred to as *Charlemagne and Roland,* based on the *Estoire de Charlemagne* into which the redactor has inserted a version of *Otinel,* the romance of a Saracen convert which, in its Anglo-Norman version, was a popular source of other redactions in English, Welsh, and Icelandic. From *Charlemagne and Roland* the compilers of the Auchinleck MS (c. 1330) quarried the romance of *Roland and Vernagu* whose preoccupation with the miracles which demonstrate the genuineness of the relics of the Passion and assist Charles's triumphal conquest of Spain may have appealed to the pious tastes of the intended bourgeois readership. It ends with a combat between Roland and the giant Vernagu, who is so impressed by the courtesy of the Christian champion that he submits to instruction in his faith before resuming the fight to determine whether it is superior to his own Muslim code—and proves it by his death! The last lines announce that Vernagu's death was reported to his fellow-Saracen Otuel who vowed to avenge him, and the following item in the Auchinleck is a romance in short couplets headed *Otuel a Knight;* but, unexpectedly, it is not the continuation of the *Charlemagne and Roland*—that is found in another manuscript, the Fillingham (1475-1500), where *Otuel and Roland,* using a variation of its tail-rhyme stanza, gives a version of the *Otinel* and completes the *Estoire de Charle-*

magne context. Neither *Otuel* text seems derived from the other, but there are sufficient verbal parallels between them to suggest that both derive from a lost English original presumably in couplet form. There is yet another version, *Duke Roland and Sir Otuel of Spain,* made in the North about 1400, using a tail-rhyme scheme so complicated that the poet has chosen to abbreviate and simplify the original story.[4]

What was there in this part of the Matter of France to appeal repeatedly to English tastes? *Otuel and Roland* begins with stanzas, apparently paraphrased from the original opening of *Charlemagne and Roland,* listing the overall content, divided between the pious legends of Charles's lightning conquest of the Holy Land and the parallel mission in Spain to which he was summoned by a vision of St James of Compostela who urged him to free his burial-place from pagan hands. The action opens as Otuel arrives at the court at St Denis demanding in the name of Garcy, Saracen King of Spain, that Charles turn Muhammadan; Roland challenges him and, as they fight, the Holy Ghost as a dove alights on Otuel's helmet, he surrenders, is christened and betrothed to the Emperor's daughter Belisent, and joins her father in a campaign against Garcy's capital of Utaly in Lombardy. His fidelity to his new faith and allegiance is repeatedly demonstrated as he rescues Roland and Oliver from overpowering numbers, defeats the Saracen champion Clarel in single combat, and assists in the overthrow of Garcy who is led prisoner to Paris and baptized by Archbishop Turpin. The narrative then returns to the sequence of the *Estoire de Charlemagne;* the Emperor wins one Saracen kingdom after another in Spain, until the Sultan pretends submission, Ganelon turns traitor and events are set in train for the triumphant disaster of Roncevaux.

The poet's interests are indicated by the fact that, though he gives some 1700 lines to the adventures of Otuel, the whole Spanish campaign occupies him for only 1100. Many of them are taken up with the extraneous material, largely pietistic, of the *Pseudo-Turpin:* when Charles prays for a sign to distinguish those who will fall in the next day's battle and finds a thousand of his men marked with a red cross, he leaves them at home in his chapel but, returning after a bloodless victory, finds them all dead; Turpin, saying mass in Charles's camp, hears devils bearing the soul of a Saracen leader to hell and learns from them that Roland's soul is already in paradise; Charles is ruthless in hanging Saracen prisoners and christening the inhabitants of captured cities, but shows his piety by making Compostela the seat of an archbishopric and building a church at Roncevaux. Turpin is absent from the battle there, since he must survive to write the *Pseudo-Turpin;* so is Charles, yet he remains the focus of interest in this part of the poem, described in an elaborate set-piece portrait as of great size and strength, wearing the crown of thorns at the chief feasts of the Christian year and guarded as he sleeps by a hundred knights with drawn swords. Little is left for Roland to do but die; there is no personal conflict with Ganelon, no struggle over the command of

the rearguard, no issue concerning the sounding of the horn. The pace is such that the poet has little time for theme, still less for ambivalence as he skips from one famous set piece to the next: the bursting of Roland's temples as he sounds the horn (which he has blown quite casually just before), his struggle to break his sword, his final prayer. The emphasis is upon sentiment which slips all too easily into bathos: Oliver, blinded by wounds, strikes out at Roland who asks him if he has become a paynim; Roland himself escapes from a tight corner by hiding in a ditch! The minstrel ineptitudes of the tail-rhyme stanza echo the degradation of the *Chanson de Roland:*

> With dwele and muche crye,
> Charlys went in hye,
> Roulond for to se;
> And fond hym there ded,
> And thus to hym he sayde,
> As y schal telle the:
> 'O Roulond, the good conqueror,
> And the noblyst warryour,
> That euermore schal be!
> Now y haue the forlore,
> Dey y wylle the before,
> But God wyl saue!'

> (ll. 2499-2510)[5]

An even more complex variation of this stanza-form serves comparatively well for the Otuel section where only the superficial values of the Matter of France are evoked, given an added interest by being exemplified in a pagan convert. Initially, Otuel demonstrates all the defects of the unenlightened: arrogance in boasting of Garcy's power and demanding Charles's apostasy, anger at the celebration of mass which delays his combat with Roland, obduracy in resisting conversion even when he is close to defeat. The French respond with Christian magnanimity: Belisent arms him with her own hands, warns him to beware of Roland's famous sword, and wishes him luck. Once converted by divine intervention he displays the same Christian spirit, refusing to marry Belisent until he has proved himself worthy, aiding Roland and other *douzepers* when they are hard pressed, rescuing from them a fellow-Saracen who responds with equal generosity of nature until he learns of Otuel's conversion when his defiance forces Otuel to remember where his Christian duty lies and he kills him—at which the Saracens break their idols in bitterness.

Charlemagne's Lombardy campaign is no more than a backdrop to this demonstration of the power of Christian chivalry to transform an alien nature. But the romance is fractured at the heart; just when Otuel's virtues might have found fuller expression in the Spanish campaign he has to disappear from the action in order not to detract from Roland's essential central role. Much of the spirit of the poem, born of the poet's interest in his vigorous personality, exemplifying Christianity in effective action without pietism, goes with him. The fullness of the narration, allowing space for convincing detail, lively exchanges of dialogue, and effective management of the minstrel stanza, gives the character a chance to live, even, when he cleaves his Saracen opponent to the teeth, for ironic humour:

> Tho lowe Otuel and sayd:
> 'Y sawe neuer, so God me rede,
> Sythe that y was bore,
> Neuer man in knygtys wede,
> Also fer as y haue rede,
> A berd so clene yshore.
> So God me saue and Sent Sauour,
> Now ys Cursins a good rasour!'
>
> (ll. 1464-71)

Without Otuel the Roncevaux episode seems lifeless and perfunctory.

The tendency of the *chansons de geste,* after the earliest period of literary texts, to form themselves into cycles is not truly represented by the related versions of a limited range of subject-matter presented in the English romances. They seem designed for audiences whose attention span was strictly limited but who welcomed sequels from the same 'historical' context and dealing with similar themes. This is perhaps why the manuscript containing the abbreviated *Duke Roland and Sir Otuel* precedes it with a separate romance, also written in the North about 1400, *The Sege of Melayne* which, like *Otuel,* deals with the war against Garcy in Lombardy. No French origin for the episode is known, though references to 'the Cronekill', 'our rearguard', and 'our Bretons' imply such a source. Whether it can have served there as introduction to an *Otuel* version is uncertain. The text breaks off as the climactic battle is approaching; Garcy's death or baptism seem the inevitable conclusion to a detached romance, yet he is still at liberty to defy Christendom in the *Otuel* texts. Perhaps, like the carbon-copy movies made as sequels to a box-office success today, the compiler, French or English, was merely imitating a proven formula, reusing familiar situations and locations and an established hate-figure whose improbable survival need not be plausibly explained.

Certainly the well-tried motifs of the *Pseudo-Turpin* are apparent in the plot. When an angel in a dream warns Charles that the Lord of Milan has lost his city to the Saracen Arabas, Ganelon nominates Roland for the rescue mission which goes badly for him; he and other *douzepers* are imprisoned until their captors are blinded in a blasphemous attempt to set fire to a cross, when they escape, kill Arabas, and return to France as sole survivors. Turpin recruits 100,000 priestly warriors for a second mission, which Ganelon persuades Charles to ban until Turpin is forced to excommunicate the Emperor. Turpin then besieges Garcy, the new Sultan, in Milan, and by a combination of heroic feats and saintly fasts and self-sacrifice is about to overwhelm him when the poem breaks off. The vague outline of the *geste du roi* still supplies the background to action; Charles is still the champion to whom all Christendom turns for aid against the power of Islam, Roland his chief lieutenant in the field, Ganelon the traitor motivated by hatred of his stepson. But the focus of interest has shifted so that the religious theme of defence of the faith dominates almost to exclusion the feudal theme of conflicting loyalties, while the rare miraculous interventions of the early *chansons* now rival the military action in importance.

The established characters play out their formulaic roles, but much reduced in status and significance. Roland is still strong of arm, capable of killing sixty Saracens single-handed (statistically aided by a facile alliteration), but liable also to the humiliation of being captured and bound. He is now a missionary as much as a military figure, preaching conversion to his captors and being laughed at for his pains; he and his companions are rescued by divine intervention when the burning cross blinds their captors and provided with miraculous horses which vanish once they reach St Denis, where the bells ring of their own accord to greet them. He is still the object of Ganelon's malice not from any conflict of feudal idealism but for the sake of the inheritance which his stepfather might gain by his death, and not to a greater degree than the rest of the French whose morale the traitor undermines, advising submission to the Sultan until Turpin publicly curses him. He shares that fate with the Emperor himself, excommunicated for his reluctance to renew the attack on Milan after the loss of an army of 40,000 men and finally goaded into laying violent hands on his archbishop. Charles's zeal is never sufficient for Turpin, and even when he takes the field in single combat against a Saracen leader, the Archbishop stands on the sidelines urging him on.

In Turpin the *geste du roi* has a new hero, moral and military, who dominates the action for the later two-thirds of the poem's 1600 lines. Faced with the massive defeat of Roland's mission, he reproaches the Virgin Mary for deserting the French, much as the Saracens abuse their gods when they suffer a reverse. But he immediately preaches a crusade, leads an army of militant clerics to Milan, and himself performs prodigies in the field. God shows himself on the side of the French—Roland sees a vision of his slaughtered companions led to paradise—and specifically on Turpin's side: when he celebrates mass for the dead, the bread and wine are sent down from heaven! On the battlefield he eclipses even Roland in skill and courage; with chivalric propriety he rebukes his squire for wishing to strip a fallen Saracen and when Charles hesitates to attack overwhelming numbers reproves him with: "'The more powers that they be,/The more honour wyn shall we'" (ll. 1510-11).[6] But there is as much of the saint as of the soldier in his nature: he vows not to eat or drink until Milan is captured and his example inspires the French to be satisfied with bloodstained water from a ditch; repeatedly wounded he three times refuses medical aid until the city falls; and if the spear-thrust and wound in his side suggest comparison with the sufferings of Christ, Turpin himself acknowledges the association:

> 'What! wenys þou, Charls,' he said, 'Þat I faynte bee
> For a spere was in my thee,
>   A glace thorowte my syde.
> Criste for me sufferde mare;

He askede no salue to his sare,
    No no more sall I this tyde.'

                            (ll. 1345-50)

His emphatic personality, domineering with men, demanding of God, gives coherence to a routine collection of
incidents typical of the spiritualized Matter of France. The
poet's interest in him may be reflected in the technical
competence of the romance, forcefully narrated in short
scenes whose point is chiefly made in dramatic dialogue.
Despite its complex rhyme-scheme, the minstrel stanza is
made to serve the various needs of the narrative with ease
and occasionally with effective emphasis.

THE DECADENCE OF THE MATTER OF FRANCE

The change in the relative importance of the twin concerns
of the Matter of France, feudal and spiritual, was followed
by a slow decline which was eventually to rob it of any
real thematic interest and reduce the *chansons* to random
sequences of stereotyped incidents often indistinguishable
from those of the *roman d'aventure*. Their focus was most
often external, concerned with the continuing Muslim
threat which compelled the cohesion of feudal Christendom and overrode its internal tensions. They expressed an
ambivalent attitude towards the Saracens who were made
to represent the Islamic enemy in general: recognition of a
social system and military ethos very similar to those of
feudal Europe and rejection of pagan beliefs and practices
which challenged the true faith. Constant commercial and
military contacts with Islam in Spain and the Holy Land
gave both poets and public every opportunity to know the
true nature of that culture. In military matters the poets
pay it grudging admiration; Saracens make excellent
knights if only they can be won or forced to Christian
conversion.

In two respects they traduce it with all the self-delusion of
blind prejudice: the Muslim faith is polytheistic, idolatrous,
its adherents superstitious, treacherous, polygamous;
Muslim women are, in consequence, lascivious, seductive,
irresistibly attracted to Christian knights, and, after willing
conversion, faithful only to them. The adventures of the
romanticized epic in which European readers could project
themselves into such a fantasy of Islamic society allowed
them both to indulge their prejudices and to father upon
their traditional opponents an exotic version of their own
idealism: Saracens who offended against their codes illustrated them by inversion like the various Black Knights
of chivalric romance, those who adopted them upon
conversion acknowledged their superiority, while the
compliant Saracen maidens promised sensual fulfilment
without the restraints imposed by Christian society. This
was fertile ground for romance, combining a dominant
preoccupation of contemporary reality, the Muslim threat,
with the wish-fulfilment made possible by projecting ideals upon exotic but often chivalrous opponents in distant
lands where forms of magic unknown in Christendom
made possible the most fantastic adventures.[7]

THE "FIRUMBRAS" GROUP: "THE SOWDON OF BABYLON" AND THE FILLINGHAM "FIRUMBRAS"

The degraded form of the *chanson de geste,* in which the
original ideals were parodied and mocked, does not seem
to have appealed to English audiences. But some compilations of exotic adventures largely devoid of thematic coherence which did were reworked in several versions, perhaps
suggesting that the range of French texts available to those,
such as the compilers of the Auchinleck MS, who catered
for a popular readership, was not large. That the English
texts which exemplify such random collections of
adventures, those of the *Firumbras* group, were likely to
appeal to such an audience is suggested by an odd detail
which may connect them with the bookshop where the
Auchinleck compilation was made. None of the French
works dealing with Charlemagne's acquisition of relics
from the Holy Land includes the lance of the Passion
among them, but some English accounts of Athelstan,
whose defeat of the Norsemen at the Battle of Brunanburh
(937) led chroniclers to see him as the first true King of
England, a national champion to rival Charlemagne, say
that relics he received as a gift from France included the
sacred lance once owned by the Emperor. The reference
occurs twice in the Auchimnleck MS, in its metrical
Shorter Chronicle and again in the *Roland and Vernagu*
account of the Passion relics. A similar reference figures in
the Fillingham MS of *Firumbras,* though the lance is not
among the relics mentioned in its French source. Just as
the Fillingham *Otuel* may have derived from a version
included in the Auchinleck MS, so its *Firumbras* text may
originate from one of the thirteen items now lost from that
compilation and have derived its knowledge of the lance
from the reference to it there.[8] The persistence of this
small detail, which other texts such as the alliterative *Morte
Arthure* and Barbour's *Bruce* derived from their knowledge
of the *Firumbras* tradition, shows the interest of English
readers in anything which could associate the Matter of
France with their own culture and the readiness of such
popularizers as the Auchinleck editors to cater to that
interest.

The *Firumbras* group derives from a lost twelfth-century
chanson celebrating the role of the French in relieving
Rome from the Saracen conquest of 846, the content of
which is known from a summary in the *Chronique rimée*
of Philippe Mouskés (*c.* 1243) who treated it as sober history. One of its romanticized episodes, dealing with
Oliver's defeat of the Saracen champion Fierabras had
been used already (*c.* 1170) as the starting-point of a
compilation of stock motives and incidents by a poet who
wished incidentally to explain how the relics of the Passion came to be in France. The mixture of elements in his
Fierabras caught the interest of audiences all over Europe,
and England produced at least four redactions based on
various forms of the original. To replace the 'historical'
context from which the Fierabras episode had been
detached, a poet who knew the original *chanson* produced
a prefatory poem, the *Destruction of Rome* which, in a Hanover manuscript, is followed by a copy of *Fierabras* not

modified to take account of the introductory material. There is also an Anglo-Norman version in which the two components have been radically abbreviated and to some extent unified.

Of the English versions, *The Sowdon of Babylon* shares so many details with the Anglo-Norman text as to suggest that both derive from a common original now lost.[9] The triple division of the English poem, produced in the east Midlands about 1400-50, reflects the composite nature of the original. The opening section (ll. 1-938), derived from the *Destruction of Rome,* describes how the Sultan of Babylon and his son Ferumbras plunder the city and carry off the relics from St Peter's; Charlemagne, summoned by the Pope, arrives too late but pursues them to the Saracen capital in Spain. A linking passage (ll. 939-1050), compiled by the English redactor, makes apparent use of a passage from *Piers Plowman* in a conventional invocation to Spring, of Chaucer's 'Knight's Tale' in a Saracen prayer for victory addressed to Mars, and of much information not found in the French texts on their pagan rites and the tribes of many origins who compose their army. In the third section (ll. 1051-3274), derived from *Fierabras,* the Sultan's son challenges Roland and his companions, fights all day with Oliver, and finally accepts baptism; Roland and Oliver, captured by the Sultan, are freed from prison by his daughter Floripas who, when the other *douzepers* arrive to rescue them, falls in love with their leader Guy of Burgundy; with her help they seize the Sultan's castle and hold him at bay until Charles, whom Ganelon has tried to persuade that they are already dead, comes to their aid; Floripas gives the relics to Charles who marries her to Guy, divides Spain between him and Ferumbras, and orders Ganelon's execution.

The redactor's additions in the linking passage, however derivative, suggest some wish to treat his material creatively; but it was not strong enough elsewhere to give him more than limited independence in paraphrasing the French, though with such looseness and haphazard disregard for inconsistencies as to suggest that he was working, in part at least, from memory. He freely omits whole episodes in the siege of Rome, then, as if realizing that he has scamped an important event, tacks them on later, out of sequence and mingled with incidents of his own invention. His additions suggest a taste for grotesque comedy and a tendency to repeat effects: twice the curses of an insulting Saracen are cut off by an arrow and twice a pursuing infidel is cut in half by a falling portcullis! He shows as little regard for thematic consistency as for the factual contradictions introduced by his omissions and transpositions. Though his version opens with a blessing on all who read the tale, he virtually ignores the spiritual theme in the original. The relics are mentioned from time to time, but as trophies in the Christian-Muslim conflict rather than for their sacred significance. Christian knights may pray for aid in a tight corner, but it is the Muslim faith which receives most attention as a focus for prejudice and picturesque detail. Each time Saracen forces suffer a set-back the Sultan tries to destroy his gods and is only

with difficulty dissuaded by the priests. Yet when finally captured and led to the font for baptism, he spits in it and is beheaded on the spot; his soul goes to hell to dance with the devils there. Ganelon still hovers in the background ready for any treason, but his feud with his stepson has gone and only a shadow of the old feudal tensions survives in Roland's resentment when Charles praises younger knights, which causes his uncle to strike him and call him traitor. Roland is little more than a cipher, robbed of the honour of defeating and converting Ferumbras by Oliver and unfitted by his 'historical' association to be loved by Floripas. Even her love for Guy, unexplained in origin, is a narrative convenience rather than a thematic element to be developed; the advances come from her, Guy can barely be persuaded by his companions to go through a kind of Saracen betrothal ceremony with her and thereafter she serves them all and the cause of France for his sake until, after her baptism, he accepts her from the Emperor's hands.

The real interest of the *Sowdon* is neither religion, love, nor even war, but adventure, a mass of incident, exotic in setting and varied in kind, to be enjoyed for its own sake. Like some minor epic of the modern cinema, made with the costumes, props, and surplus footage of an earlier success and a script which seems to have been extemporized during shooting, it capitalizes shamelessly on all the clichés of its kind: the band of companions holding out against superior numbers, the worthy foe whose defeat in fair fight converts him into a loyal partisan, the solitary woman who combines sexual promise with all the courage and resource of a good comrade, the massed cavalry riding to the rescue at the last moment. But just as such a film can succeed by sheer variety and rapidity of action, the clarity of its situations in which good and evil are opposed in black and white terms requiring only physical effort for their solution, the shamelessness with which it ignores manifest improbabilities of situation and motivation, so the *Sowdon* disarms criticism of its improbable events by the sweep of its narrative, the primary nature of its values—unabashed violence, crusading indignation, mutual loyalty between comrades in arms—the zest with which it piles up picturesque detail.

It revels in such exotic solutions to plot impasses as Floripas's magic girdle which quenches the hunger and thirst of her imprisoned companions while they wear it by turns, the dauntless spirit which leads her to push her duenna out of the window when she proves uncooperative and brain the prison warder with his own key, showing herself worthy of a Christian company whose wit and courage overcome such monsters as the giant Saracen bridge-guard and his scythe-wielding wife. The already abbreviated source is sometimes reduced to incoherence by the redactor, yet he finds space for such colourful incidentals as the giantess's twins, four feet tall at seven months old, the Sultan's treasure which Floripas uses to pelt his besieging forces much to his distress, and the feast with which the Saracens celebrate the fall of Rome:

    Thai blewe hornes of bras,

Thai dronke beestes bloode.
Milke and hony ther was,
That was roial and goode.
Serpentes in oyle were fryed
To serve Þe Sowdon with alle,
'Antrarian, Antrarian' thai lowde cryed
That signyfied 'Ioye generalle'.

(ll. 683-90)[10]

Another treatment of the same scenario shows what a little art can do with indifferent material. *Fierabras* attracted at least two other English redactors: one whose version survives in the Ashmole MS worked in the Exeter district about 1380, producing a full if rather pedestrian account which changes metre at a point which may represent a switch from an abbreviated text of the original to one containing the fuller standard version; and one who, working apparently in the east Midlands about 1375-1400, left a fragmentary version of the standard text in the Fillingham MS.[11] Beginning about mid-point it completes the story in 1842 lines rhyming in couplets, each line of six stresses divided by a medial caesura. A more limited selection of episodes from a fuller version gives the redactor space to treat the narrative individually. The pace is still rapid but more coherent, with more of the spirit of epic in the numerous combats and a more genuine sense of the conflict of faiths: the Saracens still abuse their gods in moments of defeat but even Floripas, faint with hunger during the siege, thinks of praying to them for help and is only persuaded by the mockery of the French to admit that they are merely metal idols; the Saracens come to blows among themselves on the merits of the two faiths; when they set fire to the tower in which the Christians are besieged, Floripas uses her magic arts to turn the flames against them; the relics which she ultimately surrenders to Charles prove their authenticity by the miracles they perform.

It is not only this greater respect for the values of the original which distinguishes the Fillingham *Firumbras* from the *Sowdon*. Though equally fascinated by action, its author outlines the incidents with clarity and economy, setting scenes with a minimum of descriptive detail, allowing the characters to speak for themselves in a way which reveals them as youthful, impulsive, full of zest for life, largely independent of codes and conventions. A characteristic episode (ll. 554-732): when Guy, captured by the Saracens, is led to the gallows within sight of his besieged comrades, Floripas falls on her knees to Roland:

'The best knygt on lyue, y crye yow mercy!
Schulde ye suffre my lord byfore yowre sygt
To haue suche a deth—why wyl ye nougt fygt?—
Hit ne schal neuer be in no maner wyse,
But alle thys world schal speke of yowre cowrdyse.'

(ll. 578-82)[12]

The rescue is carried out in proper chivalric fashion: Roland kills one paynim to provide Guy with a horse and another for his armour and, while Floripas, rosy red and bathed in tears, watches from the tower, they cover the plain with Saracen dead. Then, seizing a passing supply train, they relieve the famished garrison. The incident has been given movement combining action and emotion resolved in victory and the lovers' reunion; the pedestrian but servicable verse caters adequately for a variety of moods.

THE LATE PROSE VERSIONS

As surprising as the repeated treatment in the verse romances of subjects from the same limited range is the absence of major categories of the Matter of France which might have been expected to appeal to English audiences. There is nothing from the *barons revoltés* tradition of the rebellion of his vassals against Charlemagne's autocracy, potentially attractive to a nation under foreign rule, or from the cycles of the crusades in which English forces had played a major role. But the surviving texts belong to an age when the rulers of England had long ceased to be regarded as foreign oppressors and were, to all appearances, intended for an audience beneath the social level at which feudal relationships or patriotic sentiment were likely to operate.[13]

Major treatments of those themes were to appear in English in the late fifteenth and early sixteenth century, but in prose and based on originals in which their true nature had already been radically altered. Caxton produced versions of the three major divisions of the Matter of France: of the *geste du roi* in his *Charles the Grete* (1485) in which the legendary history of France from the Trojan founding-father Francus to the Emperor's conquests in Spain is only a frame for the Fierabras story; of the *barons revoltés* in his *Foure Sonnes of Aymon* (1489) in which the epic struggle of Renaud de Montauban and his three brothers in resistance to their oppressive overlord Charlemagne, facing their father Aymon with a conflict of loyalties, has been elaborated by French prose redactors into a farrago of adventures involving their magician cousin, Renaud's marvellous horse who covers thirty feet at a stride, his pilgrimage to free Jerusalem from the Saracens and eventual 'martyrdom' while working as a labourer on the building of St Peter's at Cologne; and of the crusades in his *Siege of Jerusalem* (1481) whose history of how chance brought Godfrey of Bouillon, youngest son of an ancient but modest house, to the throne of Jerusalem at the end of the First Crusade (1099), reads like the stuff of romance. As his original prologues suggest, Caxton saw them all as chivalric propaganda expressing the belief of his noble patrons in the inspirational value of history, in the need to seek honour by emulating the positive code, uncomplicated by ambiguity, exemplified by his one-dimensional heroes, and to stem the tide of Turkish conquest after the fall of Constantinople in 1453. These ideas were current in the Burgundian courts which strongly influenced the England of Edward IV and from whose libraries many of Caxton's sources seem to have come. They were equally propagated by his manuals of courtesy and his versions of *romans courtois* on other matters; his full and faithful translation added little of his own except the gloss of his admirable style.[14]

He had his imitators in Robert Copeland, whose *Helyas, the Knight of the Swan,* printed by Wynkyn de Worde in 1512, also deals with Godfrey of Bouillon, but in a version which derives from the epic cycle where his crusade adventures are preceded by those of his legendary ancestor, the swan-knight; and in Lord Berners whose, *Duke Huon of Burdeux,* in which the hero, unjustly deprived of his lands by Charlemagne, rehabilitates himself by winning trophies from Babylon with the help of Oberon, King of the Fairies, was printed by de Worde about 1534. The romantic associations of Oberon in Shakespeare and in Weber's opera suggest how far the Matter of France has evolved from its roots in the *chansons de geste.* It was in these late prose redactions that it penetrated the imaginations of Spenser and the writers of Elizabethan romance, indistinguishable from other chivalric matters, largely devoid of nationalistic or religious significance. In an age when gunpowder was steadily devaluing individual initiative and courage in war, but when the nobility still wore the trappings of chivalry, played at jousting, mimicked the *douzepers* in their orders of knighthood, these unquestioning celebrations of the virtues of a golden age had all the allure of high romance.

The Character of the Matter of France Romances

The process by which the ideals of one age, though originally presented as problematic, in conflict with each other or with contemporary reality, become, with the passage of time, the unquestioned achievements of heroes of old, is characteristic of the romance mode. The way in which it allows the imagination to project the ideal from the actual, conjuring what might be out of what is, often (as in science fiction) invoking powers beyond present possibility, makes it vulnerable to social change. Even in the age which produced it the relationship between ideal and reality may not have been precisely perceived, the element of wish-fulfilment in romance inhibiting objective judgement. The passage of time, obliterating knowledge of social circumstances and blurring the distinction between the real and the ideal, encourages the belief that once upon a time, in the age of gold, men were capable of heroism, idealism, fidelity to codes and values of which, in the age of iron, they seem incapable. If the golden age can be historically located and its heroes identified with revered ancestors, so much the more potent its romantic aura.

The age of Charlemagne, associated in men's minds with fundamental values of feudal solidity, individual heroism, and militant Christianity, exercised a fascination which gave the Matter of France currency throughout Europe and established its heroes in the order of the Nine Worthies, Ganelon as one of the archetypal villains of all time. Their charisma outlived precise memory of the qualities for which they were originally celebrated and their epoch served, like the Regency for modern romantic novelists or the two world wars for film-makers, as a highly coloured backdrop to adventures which had increasingly little to do with them or their values. It has become conventional to

dignify the earliest treatment of the Matter of France as epic, distinguished by seriousness of purpose, solidarity, and worth of values from the fantasy and escapism of romance. The distinction may owe more to modern preconceptions than to any absolute difference of intention on the authors' part; the makers of the *chansons* may have been striving to subdefine and celebrate social codes already current, the *roman courtois* poets to project ideals to which their patrons might learn to aspire, but both acknowledged the challenge of reality in the characteristic manner of the romance mode. Since the values of the latter refined and supplemented rather than displaced those of the former, the Matter of France retained its general validity long after its specific idealism had faded to a romantic afterglow.[15]

In the English examples that process is already far advanced. The fascination of such key events as Roncevaux, the charisma of the archetypal figures linger still, lip-service is paid to the basic ethical values, but the ambiguities and internal conflicts to which they gave rise are no longer deeply felt, even in the surviving fragment of the *Roland.* They have been replaced by cruder, more generalized values—belief in might as right, comradeship rather than unique heroic virtues, a simplistic faith bordering on bigotry—celebrated not so much for their own sake than as a focus for martial adventure. Religion is treated with more commitment than chivalry, but it is a narrower, more prejudiced creed than the frank convictions of the *chansons de geste* that 'paien unt tort et chrestiens unt dreit'; love is a one-way process, loving women a prize or a battle trophy for successful warriors. Both are less significant in themselves than as furnishers of exotic incident, of warrior-priests, champion converts, and adoring girl Fridays. Action replaces theme, the remnants of history increasingly yield place to fantasy; Otuel disappears to leave the field clear for Roland at Roncevaux, but Ferumbras reduces him to one among many in the ranks of France. An occasional flicker of the old epic spirit recalls the origins of the legends, as when the *Foure Sonnes of Aymon* and *Huon of Burdeux* raise the old ghost of the tyrannous overlord; but when a rebellious vassal enlists the King of Fairy against his emperor the sun is setting for the Matter of France.

Notes

1. See D. J. A. Ross, 'Old French' in *Traditions of Heroic and Epic Poetry,* 1 *The Traditions,* edited by A. T. Hatto, Publications of the Modern Humanities Research Association, IX (London, 1980), pp. 79-133 (p. 82), a useful introduction to the *chansons de geste* for non-specialists, and M. D. Legge, *Anglo-Norman Literature and its Background* (Oxford, 1963), pp. 3-5.

2. Text from British Library MS Lansdowne 388, edited by S. J. Herrtage, *The Sege off Melayne, The Romance of Duke Rowland and Sir Otuell of Spayne, together with a Fragment of the Song of Roland,* EETS, ES, 35 (London, 1880).

3. See R. N. Walpole, *Charlemagne and Roland: A Study of the Source of Two Middle English Metrical Romances, 'Roland and Vernagu' and 'Otuel and Roland'*, University of California Publications in Modern Philology, xxvi, No. 6 (Berkeley, California, 1944), pp. 387-400.

4. See Walpole, pp. 400-33.

5. Text from British Library MS Add. 37492, edited by M. I. O'Sullivan, *Firumbras and Otuel and Roland*, EETS, 198 (London, 1935).

6. Text from British Library MS Add. 31042, edited by S. J. Herrtage, *The Sege off Melayne*, EETS, ES, 35 (London, 1880).

7. See C. Meredith Jones, 'The Conventional Saracen of the Songs of Geste', *Speculum*, 17 (1942), 201-25, and Dorothee Metlitzki, *The Matter of Araby in Medieval England* (New Haven, Connecticut, 1977), pp. 160-210.

8. See L. H. Loomis, 'The Athelstan Gift Story: Its Influence on English Chronicles and Carolingian Romances', *PMLA*, 67 (1952), 521-37.

9. See H. M. Smyser, '*The Sowdon of Babylon* and its Author', *Harvard Studies and Notes in Philology and Literature*, 13 (1931), 185-218.

10. Text from MS Garrett 140 (formerly Phillips 8357) edited by E. Hausknecht, *The Sowdone of Babylone*, EETS, ES, 38 (London, 1881).

11. That yet another version once existed is indicated by the episode in John Barbour's *Bruce* in which Robert the Bruce reads a romance of Ferumbras to his men on the shores of Loch Lomond.

12. Text from British Library MS Add. 37492, edited by M. I. O'Sullivan, *Firumbras and Otuel and Roland*, EETS, 198 (London, 1935).

13. Poets occasionally selected from the traditional categories characteristic folk-tales which had been caught up in it or themselves attached such folk-tales to the Matter of France. This seems to have been so even from an early period; in 1287 Baron Bjarni Erlingsson took back to Norway an English romance, now referred to as *Olive and Landres*, which, judging from the version incorporated in the *Karlamagnussaga*, was on the old folklore theme of the caluminated wife and the cruel mother-in-law casually attached to the Matter of France (see R. M. Wilson, *Early Middle English Literature*, second edition (London, 1951), p. 201). These adventitious elements are to be treated separately (see below, pp. 181-82).

14. See Diane Bornstein, 'William Caxton's Chivalric Romances and the Burgundian Renaissance in England', *English Studies*, 57 (1976), 1-10.

15. On the changing perception of epic and romance as related expressions of the romance mode see D. M. Hill, 'Romance as Epic', *English Studies*, 44 (1962), 95-107, and on the implications for the classification of English romances on the Matter of France see John Finlayson, 'Definitions of Middle English Romance', *Chaucer Review*, 15 (1980), 44-62, 168-81.

List of Abbreviations

In addition to the standard abbreviations used as titles of periodicals:

AUMLA: Journal of Australasian Universities Modern Language and Literature Association

ELH: Journal of English Literary History

PMLA: Publications of the Modern Language Association of America

the following abbreviations are employed throughout the Notes and Bibliography:

EETS: Early English Text Society

EETS, ES: Early English Text Society, Extra Series

STS: Scottish Text Society

Anne Elizabeth Cobby (essay date 1988)

SOURCE: Introduction to *The Pilgrimage of Charlemagne (Le Pèlerinage de Charlemagne)*, edited and translated by Glyn S. Burgess, Garland Publishing, Inc., 1988, pp. 1-27.

[*In the following essay, Cobby discusses* The Pilgrimage of Charlemagne, *including arguments regarding the date of the text; difficulties in classifying the work; its artistic merit and use of humor; and its sources and influences.*]

AUTHOR AND DATE

Few medieval works have given rise to as much disagreement as the *Pèlerinage de Charlemagne*. The difficulties begin with the question of its origin and date. The text is known from a single manuscript (Royal 16 E VIII of the British Library) which went missing on 7 June 1879 (see George F. Warner and Julius P. Gilson. *Catalogue of Western Manuscripts in the Old Royal and King's Collections*. 4 vols, London: British Museum, 1921, II, p. 196). The manuscript probably dates from the thirteenth century (Warner and Gilson, p. 196, Michel, p. xxii, Koschwitz, 1875-77, p. 2, I. de Riquer, p. 23), though the fourteenth has also been suggested (Koschwitz, 1907, p. i, Favati, p. 120, Picherit, 1984, p. ix).

If the date of the manuscript is relatively uncontentious, the same cannot be said for that of the text it contains. Suggestions have ranged from the late eleventh century (e.g. Koschwitz, 1875-77, p. 60) to the late thirteenth (Favati, p. 124), with most critics assigning it to the early or mid-twelfth century. The latitude is due to several factors: the manuscript is lost, the text is an Anglo-Norman copy of a continental French poem, it presents unusual linguistic forms and is metrically irregular, and its subject matter lends itself to the identification of all manner of historical parallels. The linguistic evidence is inconclusive as far as the date of the text is concerned; there appears to be a chronological mixture of forms, and it has been suggested that the poet deliberately used archaisms (Heinermann, p. 561, Bates, p. 24, Favati, p. 125).

The impossibility of dating the text on linguistic grounds leaves the field free for an approach based on contemporary history, and this has been much favoured. The peaceful Middle Eastern situation depicted in the poem led Gaston Paris (p. 36), for example, to claim it could only have been written before the First Crusade of 1095. Heinermann on the other hand saw a detailed allusion to the marital and military affairs of Louis VII and dated it to the mid-twelfth century. According to Süpek Louis VII's grandfather, Philip I, was being admonished by the poet; he based this view on an equation between the Charlemagne of the poem and the kings of England in the period around 1100. No such approach can give an incontrovertible date; poets can use their imagination to depict circumstances other than those of their own age, and the identification of contemporary allusions cannot be a source of proof in its own right when a number of mutually contradictory references can be identified.

A third approach, based on literary criteria, is more fruitful, and gives a date rather later than those of the majority of scholars. The poem cannot have been written later than the translation into Old Norse, unanimously dated in the thirteenth century, which derives from something very close to, if not identical with, the extant *Pèlerinage* (see below, p. 13). A starting date, on the other hand, is given by the poem's clear reference to the conventions and language of courtly literature. The poet relies on his audience's knowing that tradition in order to achieve his effects; his work must therefore necessarily have been composed after the first romances, maybe some considerable time later, when the courtly style was well established and familiar to all. The *Pèlerinage* thus cannot be earlier than 1150, and was in fact more probably written well into the second half of the twelfth century.

The poem is also more likely to be a product of France than of England (though Holmes, and Aebischer, 1965, pp. 22-23, disagree). Though the language of the manuscript shows many Anglo-Norman features, the content of the text, with its French setting, French heroes, frequent references to places in France both in narrative and in conversation, clearly suggests a continental origin. Of himself, however, the author gives no hint. Like the author of *Aucassin et Nicolette*, he had an excellent knowledge of the various literary traditions of his day and a keen awareness of their weaknesses. He was also a highly skilled craftsman able to produce fine and complex comic effects. But of his name, life, station, or home we know nothing at all.

ARTISTIC ACHIEVEMENT

The complexity and subtlety of the anonymous author's writing have led to much discussion about his meaning, and often to underestimation of his work. The poem has affinities with several medieval traditions, and its message can be interpreted in various ways. Some have seen it as serious in intent, magnifying Charlemagne or the abbey of Saint-Denis (Koschwitz, 1907, p. xxxi, Adler, Panvini, pp. 65-78, Caulkins, Gosman) or satirising contemporary politics (Heinermann, Süpek). Others view it as a humorous work, either a light-hearted comedy (Horrent, e.g. 1961, pp. 115-22, 1981, I, pp. 43-44, Aebischer, "Versions norroises," p. 9), or a parody, with or without satirical intent (Aebischer, "Versions norroises," pp. 161-62, Neuschäfer, Walpole, 1963-64, pp. 141-43, Favati, pp. 39, 78-79, 92-93, Owen). Such divergence of opinion is fostered by the tendency of scholars to study the *Pèlerinage* primarily as an example of one medieval genre or another: as a *chanson de geste* (e.g. G. Paris, Coulet, pp. 294-315, Panvini, pp. 78-80, I. de Riquer, pp. 9-17), a folktale (Scheludko, Niles, Bonafin, 1984), or a pious story (Coulet, pp. 266-75). The poem's originality is that all these traditions indeed form part of its background, but none of them, taken alone, accounts for it adequately. A number of critics over the years (Bédier, IV, p. 153, Favati, pp. 79-80, Aebischer, "Versions norroises," pp. 9, 161, 1965, p. 15) have accordingly characterised it as something different again, namely a "gab;" two scholars have recently developed this idea, showing how the poem's structure of boast or jest, challenge, test, justification, and pardon corresponds to the evolution of the jesting boasts or *gabs* which form part of its plot (Grigsby, "A Note," Ceron; see also Torrini-Roblin). Certainly the *Pèlerinage* is much more than the incoherent mixture of events, themes, and tones which it might seem to be at first sight.

The poem can be divided into four sections. An opening passage, set in France (vv. 1-97), prepares for a journey to two destinations, first Jerusalem (vv. 98-258) and then Constantinople (vv. 259-857). The final laisse (vv. 858-70) recalls the achievements of both visits and returns the scene to France. This structure of departure, travel, and homecoming is the framework for a tale telling of the destruction and re-establishment of personal and interpersonal harmony. Piqued by a taunt of his queen, who claims to know a king superior to him, Charlemagne resolves to go to find this king, Hugo the Strong of Constantinople (vv. 1-57). He tells his men, however, that they are going on pilgrimage to Jerusalem. They duly arrive there, are mistaken for Christ and the apostles, and are given relics (vv. 112-203). After staying in Jerusalem some time, Charles remembers his original aim and sets off for Constantinople (vv. 233-58). There the queen's scorn is justified. Charles and his men cut poor figures in contrast with the magnificence of Hugo and his court (vv. 259-414). After being feasted, they make wild, boastful jests (vv. 448-617) which Hugo later obliges them to make good; this they do, with God's help (vv. 679-801). In this way Charles's superiority over Hugo is affirmed, but he too is humiliated in the final test, for the flood which forces Hugo to capitulate threatens Charles and the Franks as well (vv. 771-801). Charles's victory is formally recognised in a procession in which the authority he has travelled so far to establish is reduced to a mere physical greatness, for he is described as being one foot three inches taller than Hugo (vv. 802-30). Nonetheless he returns to France in triumph, distributes the relics he has received, and is reconciled with the queen (vv. 858-70).

The symmetry of the text's circular movement is, however, offset by a number of imbalances. The two destinations of Charles's journey are linked by nothing stronger than a rough geographical proximity: his purposes in seeking them are entirely different. The amount of space given to each also differs greatly (160 lines to Jerusalem, 598 to Constantinople). And, as even its bare outline shows, the story does indeed derive to some degree from all the genres to which it has been assimilated. Thus, in many respects it belongs to the epic tradition: Charlemagne and his twelve peers, the supreme heroes of the *chanson de geste,* confront and conquer a great rival. They are, moreover, supported and helped by God, just as the Charlemagne of the epic tradition is. At the same time the journey of a king to measure himself against a rival has parallels in Celtic folktale, as have various aspects of the description of Constantinople and its customs (L. H. Loomis, Cross, Krappe). Constantinople shares many themes with the courtly romance: beauty, splendour, leisure, love, and it is portrayed in courtly language. Lastly, the poem tells of the acquisition of relics and shows Charles as God's protégé, so that it could be seen as a pious, even a hagiographic, tale. In fact it is the tensions which the poet establishes between these diverse backgrounds that give the *Pèlerinage* its rich texture.

The poem's epic qualities are immediately evident. The opening scene places us in an epic atmosphere by depicting Charlemagne as the traditional emperor, wearing his crown and gold-pommelled sword, in the midst of his lords, under an olive tree at Saint-Denis (vv. 1-7). He then sets off against his enemies, with a great band of men and an inner circle, the "twelve peers," which consists of the greatest names of the *chanson de geste* (vv. 61-66). These latter are drawn from two epic cycles (the royal cycle and that of William of Orange) and so represent the essence of the epic world (cf. Favati, pp. 37-39). They and their king are described in standard epic formulae ("Karles od le fer vis," v. 623 etc., "les feres cumpainies," v. 111 etc., "ruiste barnét," v. 254 etc., "l'adurez," vv. 62, 65). They talk of epic deeds, especially Charles who boasts that he will slice one of Hugo's men in two, together with his horse, a feat achieved on many an epic battlefield (vv. 453-64; cf. *The Song of Roland: An Analytical Edition,* ed. Gerard J. Brault. 2 vols, University Park: Pennsylvania State University Press, 1978, II, laisses 104, 107). Though the Franks do not in fact come to blows with Hugo and the Greeks, the theme of hostility and eventual conquest is a fundamental one. Finally, the form of the poem is that of a *chanson de geste,* for it is composed in assonating laisses.

It is, therefore, not surprising that the *Pèlerinage* has most often been classified as a *chanson de geste.*

But it is no ordinary *chanson de geste.* The opening scene is full of epic details, yet its matter is not some lofty council but a domestic quarrel, which appears the more ignominious by contrast with its noble setting. The great emperor demonstrates violent and disproportionate anger, which is reminiscent of nothing so much as a tantrum, as he repeatedly threatens to decapitate his wife (vv. 25, 42, 52, 55). His journey is no defence of his kingdom or of Christendom, but a voyage of curiosity born of wounded pride. The epic language applied to Charles and his men does not in fact praise them but rather mocks them, for it is used above all at times when they are unworthy of it, frightened or humiliated or at the very least in situations which are not epic (e.g. vv. 400, 623, 649, 662, 699, 780, 781, 784). Epic deeds feature in the poem only as drunken jests; and Charles's victory over Hugo is not only ambiguous but utterly unwarlike. So while from one point of view the *Pèlerinage* belongs to the epic tradition, to which it is linked by characters, themes, and language, its spirit is quite different; and this divergence in essentials is highlighted by the many points of contact which do exist between our poem and the *chanson de geste.*

No more wholeheartedly is the *Pèlerinage* a pious tale. Charles does, it is true, visit Jerusalem and receive honour and gifts there; he is explicitly assured of God's support in Constantinople (vv. 674-77); and he does distribute relics through his kingdom (v. 867). But none of these facts works unambiguously to glorify him. Charles's true purpose in going to the East is neither pilgrimage nor the acquisition of relics, but his own aggrandisement. The relics are not even treated with total respect. Either they produce effects which upstage the miracles of the Bible (every cripple is cured, every river parted through their agency, vv. 255-58), or they extract the Franks from the scrapes into which their drunken boasts have put them (vv. 667-73), and that through achievements which are far from charitable or moral: the daughter of the Franks' host is seduced, his palace demolished, his city inundated (vv. 683-801). Nor can the theme of pilgrimage be taken fully seriously. Charles claims to have been told in three dreams to visit Jerusalem (v. 71), but the timing of his statement, and the fact that these dreams are heard of neither before nor afterwards, make it very hard to see them as anything other than an excuse designed to get Charles's men on the road. When the idea of pilgrimage is recalled in the last line of the poem, it has a similar flavour: if Charles forgives his wife it is surely not, as the poet maintains, because he has adored the Holy Sepulchre in Jerusalem, but because his pride has been restored in Constantinople.

Even the most explicit hagiographical elements in the poem, Charles's being mistaken for Christ in Jerusalem and his presentation as God's protégé in Constantinople, do not make of it a work of piety. Neither episode shows Charles in an altogether good light. In Jerusalem, though he is likened to God and honoured, he himself seems insensible to the dignity of his position, but casually admires his surroundings (vv. 119-28) and then uses the opportunity of being renamed Charles the Great (v. 158, see note) to ask for souvenirs in the form of relics (vv. 159-61). In Constantinople the deeds "done by God for love of Charlemagne" (vv. 751-52, 791), in response to the prayers he makes before the relics, are unworthy of either of them. Yet this love of God for Charles is a complex matter. The Charlemagne of the *chanson de geste* has a special relationship with God: he is the defender of Christendom and God works marvels for him, just as He does in the *Pèlerinage* (cf. *The Song of Roland*, vv. 2458-59). So the religious status of Charles in the *Pèlerinage*, ambivalent as it is, is part of his depiction as an epic hero. Yet, just as he is not a true epic hero, so too his religious status is flawed. Charles, the warrior, does not seek victory for God's cause but uses God's support for his own ends; and the unworthiness of these ends shows how little Charles deserves to be treated as God's friend. So the religious theme, like the epic reference, serves not to magnify but to criticise Charles; at the same time a tension between the hagiographical and the epic threads is set up which adds depth to the poem.

The *Pèlerinage*, then, is neither a true *chanson de geste* nor an authentically pious tale, but the poet uses its links with these two traditions for purposes of comparison and contrast. The same is true of the poem's relation to the courtly romance and, through that genre, to Celtic folktale. The most striking borrowings from the romance are concentrated in the Constantinople episode, which takes place in a courtly world. There the Franks find themselves in a garden full of sophisticated people who lead a leisured life (vv. 262-74). King Hugo is ploughing nearby with a golden plough; later he feasts the visitors splendidly in his magnificent, even magical, palace (vv. 283-97, 342-414). The exotic world of Constantinople is cut off from the more or less realistic world of Jerusalem, for the Franks' itinerary between the two seems deliberately vague (vv. 259-61, see note below, p. 80). Its isolation, its marvels, and its strange customs all make of Constantinople a world apart. Its fantastic aspects are partly to be explained by the fact that it belongs to the mysterious and magnificent Orient, but more important are its literary ancestors: like the destinations of many romance heroes, the Constantinople of the *Pèlerinage* is descended from the Celtic otherworld (see Webster, pp. 355-66, Howard Rollin Patch, *The Other World according to Descriptions in Medieval Literature*. Cambridge, Mass.: Harvard University Press, 1950, pp. 277-82), and its description makes clear reference to the romance tradition and so contrasts with the representatives of the epic, namely the Franks.

Though the links between the *Pèlerinage* and the courtly romance are most evident in this scene, they are not confined to it, nor even to the Constantinople section, but inform the whole poem. The plot, which can be read as epic and as pious, can also be seen as a courtly quest, and the Franks, would-be epic heroes, are thus in a sense heroes of romance as well (cf. Bennett, pp. 483-87). Like

many a courtly knight, Charlemagne sets out to seek, meet, and measure himself against a distant hero of whom he has heard. The origin of this quest, as of courtly ones, lies in a relationship with a woman, in this case the queen; and a second such motif (the love of Oliver for Hugo's daughter) plays a considerable part in the later development of the poem. In both description and narrative the *Pèlerinage* can be viewed as a romance.

Yet it is no more a straight romance than a straight *chanson de geste*. First, the courtly elements do not account for the whole poem: its epic qualities, and especially its heroes, cannot be disregarded. Secondly, the courtly, like the epic, elements are distorted. Constantinople is indeed a courtly enclave, but its values survive only until the arrival of the Franks, whose behaviour there challenges the courtly conventions. Faced with magnificence, the Franks would vandalise or destroy it (vv. 326-28); the marvels of Hugo's rotating palace terrify them (vv. 385-96); Oliver's "love" for Hugo's daughter is nothing more than lust (vv. 404-08). These are less cultivated, more realistic responses than those which are assumed in the heroes and audiences of courtly literature; they show up the Franks as boors, but at the same time they reveal the unreality of the courtly conventions. The quest theme too is distorted; though Charles's quest originates in a relationship between the sexes, the relationship and the purpose of the quest are quite different from those normal in the romance. Far from trying to prove his worth for a lady he wishes to win and serve, Charles sets out to prove himself right against the wife he already has and whom he bullies. Once more the comparison diminishes the hero of the *Pèlerinage;* yet we may reflect that the relationship depicted in the poem is more true to life than one based upon courtly love.

Just as the poem's religious elements are played off against its epic ones, so too the poet sets up a fruitful tension between his epic and his courtly themes. The personal rivalry between Charles and Hugo is reflected in a contest between the epic world of the one and the courtly world of the other, and beyond that in an opposition between the established tradition of the *chanson de geste* and the new genre, romance. On no level is victory given unequivocally to one side or the other. The interpersonal conflict ends in a fine balance: Hugo flees to his highest tower to escape the flood caused by Charles, but the Franks with their emperor are obliged to scurry up a pine tree to avoid being drowned themselves (vv. 771-801). In a broader perspective, each king succeeds in his own terms and fares badly in those of the other. Hugo cannot withstand Charles's force, which is epic even though it is expressed not in a battle but through a miracle; nor can Charles, engaged as he is on a courtly quest, rise to the standards expected of him in the courtly world. He is boorish from his first appearance on an ambling mule (vv. 275, 298) to his final gloating over Hugo's discomfiture (v. 799). The practical victory, even so, is his: Charles, the hero of feudal literature, the literature of war, is acknowledged as lord by the emperor of Constantinople, which glitters and dazzles, full of splendour and marvels and courtliness. So on one level the epic conquers the courtly; but at the same time we are invited to admire the sophistication of courtly life, characteristic of the literature which, for the poem's first audience, was new and fashionable. And there is yet another level of ambiguity in the audience's response: while on the one hand we admire the splendid world of Constantinople, on the other (viewing the text with the eyes of a twelfth-century Frenchman) we applaud our national heroes and deride foreigners, in this case Greeks who were renowned for their effeminacy and untrustworthiness.

So the *Pèlerinage* is very far from being the confused conglomeration of elements, taken from different traditions, which it might seem to be on a superficial reading. Rather, the poet's skilful weaving of his varying threads is crucial to his artistic aim. For the purpose of the text is comedy, and its comedy rests in large measure on effects of juxtaposition and contrast, effects which these multiple literary references are well suited to providing. To this end the construction of the poem is tightly controlled, with themes and echoes linking the different episodes and underpinning a carefully established unity.

The opening scene at Saint-Denis lays the foundations for many aspects of the poem. It establishes the relationship between Charles and the queen which will be recalled at each turning-point in the plot (vv. 234-35, 364, 813-20) and restored to harmony in the closing lines (vv. 868-70). This is also reflected in the other important and evolving relationship in the poem, that between Charles and Hugo, a reflection which is stressed by verbal echo. At the beginning Charles's arrogance and violence towards his queen are expressed in a series of threats to decapitate her (vv. 25, 42, 52, 55). These threats are echoed later when Hugo vows the Franks will die if any should fail in his boast (vv. 647, 698, 742). Such echoing is comic as well as unifying, for it points up the reversal of Charles's fortunes and the degree to which he brings disaster upon himself: in his determination to prove the queen wrong in her claim that Hugo is greater than he—and, if she is wrong, he swears she will lose her head—he comes to the brink of losing his own at Hugo's hands. In the event he escapes this fate, and so does she: harmony is restored first between Hugo and Charles and then between Charles and his queen. The circularity of the plot, reflected in this apparently small detail, indicates a carefully thought out construction and a keen eye for comic irony.

The Jerusalem episode too is linked to the opening scene, through the notion of greatness. This theme is fundamental to the entire poem, and appears in different forms in each of its chief sections (cf. Sturm). At Saint-Denis Charles demands of his queen recognition of his superiority to all men. She says that Hugo of Constantinople wears his crown better than Charles: an expression of greatness which stops at superficialities, though we do not yet notice how literally her phrase "belement lui set" (v. 16) is to be taken. In Jerusalem Charles is recognised as a great king and given the title of "Charlemagne, crowned above all

kings" (v. 158, see note); yet he does not act in keeping with his greatness (cf. above, p. 6). The name Charles the Great and the phrase "sur tuz reis curunez" set the scene for the dénouement in Constantinople, where Charles and Hugo wear their crowns together, thus making tangible the queen's comparison. Charles is indeed the greater king—by one foot three inches (v. 811). His superiority, challenged at Saint-Denis and seemingly confirmed in Jerusalem, is destroyed by this reduction to a matter of physical size, and the superficiality of its original expression is fulfilled in the extreme. Here too a recurring detail ties the different sections together, from the establishment through to the resolution of the conflict; it also provides comedy through literalism, through deflation, and through the pointing of contrasts between the different stages of the evolving narrative.

Such comedy is only one instance of the humour of the *Pèlerinage de Charlemagne*. The plot is full of stock comic devices: incongruities, reversals, deflations, repetitions, surprises, instances of the biter being bit. The heroes are figures of fun in their own right: the Franks brag (vv. 448-617) and panic (vv. 385-96, 648-71), Charles ingenuously admires himself (vv. 95-97) and lumbers into Constantinople on his mule (vv. 275, 298), Hugo is depicted with a prosaic hat upon his head (v. 292) as he sits on his golden plough. They are also the source of a deeper comedy, for we perceive incongruous contrasts between the heroes of the *Pèlerinage* and the characters who share their names in other, more serious, poems. It is Charlemagne, the great national hero, who is touchy and who throws a tantrum (vv. 19-57), who when confronted with the splendour of Constantinople asks pathetically when things will return to normal (v. 396); it is God's anointed emperor who prays in terror to be rescued from his rashness (vv. 664-71) and who perches with his court in a pine tree (vv. 780-84). It is the twelve peers of France, the heroes of the *chanson de geste,* who make rash boasts and express mean sentiments; the contrast with the valour and nobility we know they have in the *chanson de geste* adds depth and piquancy to their ignominy, and renders it not merely critical but comic.

The Franks' jests, the *gabs,* have a particular place in the comedy of the *Pèlerinage.* In the poem as a whole humour is diffuse: while it is the work's guiding principle, its rôle in individual scenes is usually to add colour to passages whose own primary purpose is to advance the plot. The long scene of the *gabs* (vv. 448-617) is different. It does contribute to the plot, for it leads to Hugo's demanding that the jests be fulfilled and so to his defeat. But its length is out of all proportion to this function. In this scene the poet devotes himself to comedy: peer after peer boasts that he will perform some extraordinary feat (often, but not always, at Hugo's expense), and each time Hugo's spy, who is listening, makes a comment (vv. 465-68, 482-83, 490-92, etc.). These comments are highly repetitious and have their own humour of predictability (see especially vv. 482-83, 562-64, 589-90). The *gabs* themselves are comic too in their extravagance: Roland will blow his horn so violently that metal doors will clash and whiskers will be burnt off (vv. 470-81); Oliver will possess Hugo's daughter a hundred times in one night (vv. 485-89); Turpin will juggle on horseback (vv. 494-504), and so on. There is a comedy of sheer spectacle here, but even this has a deeper humour based on the poem's literary background. The horn that Roland says he will blow is the one associated with him since his sublime exploits at Roncevaux told by the *Song of Roland* (laisses 133-35). Turpin is no court jester but the archbishop who, again at Roncevaux, blessed the dead and dying of Charlemagne's army (laisses 162-63). Other *gabs* are less tuned to the literary history of individuals, but they may still depend on epic or religious associations for comic effect: see for example Berenger's *gab* (vv. 541-50) with its epic battle-sounds produced by a daredevil stunt, or Ogier's imitation of Samson (vv. 520-27). Reminiscent in this way or not, each *gab* is comic as a piece of fantasy; the poet has let his imagination run in this scene, embroidering his theme for the sake of sheer entertainment. So much the greater are the surprise, the dismay (for the audience as for the Franks), and so the irony, when Hugo takes the jests at face value and forces them to play a part in the plot.

The *Pèlerinage* thus draws on many sources of humour which are internal to itself: extravagance in the *gabs,* details of character, reversal, surprise, predictability, and the like in the narrative. But at the same time the poet produces rich comic and ironic effects from his poem's relationship to other literature, particularly the *chanson de geste* but also religious and courtly literature. He takes familiar elements from elsewhere and uses them to set up contrasts, both between aspects of his own work and between the latter and its sources. He at once relates the poem to, and sets it apart from, contemporary genres; and the divergences thus established both provide comic contrast and direct ridicule at some aspect of the poem.

Is the *Pèlerinage,* then, a parody? If we take parody in a broad sense, allowing it to embrace all those techniques which depend on a contrast or interplay between a literary model, familiar to the audience, and the text in hand, then the poem is parodic. It depends for its richest effects on such interplay, and so well calculated are they that it is implausible that they were not deliberately created by the author. It is, however, not a parody in the sense of criticising its models. Wherever a contrast is established between a literary tradition and the *Pèlerinage,* it is the element in the *Pèlerinage,* and above all its heroes, which fall short of the model. Not that the author is in any way defeated by his ambitions; he achieves his aim, which is to amuse his audience by causing it to laugh at his heroes and with his work. The background to which he refers as a means to this end is the ideal they cannot reach; it is not itself attacked.

The same, by and large, is true of *Aucassin et Nicolette.* Fifty to a hundred years later another skilful author followed the poet of the *Pèlerinage;* he too knew the various literary traditions of his age well, was clearsighted about their foibles, and was able to draw out their comic potential. Like the author of the *Pèlerinage,* the man who composed *Aucassin* uses the themes and language of contemporary literature as a prime source of amusement. Each of them relies on his audience's familiarity with this literary background, and its appreciation of his manipulation of it; they each borrow, juxtapose, contrast, exaggerate, and distort. But neither of them attacks his literary sources; rather they are the means by which the ridiculous elements in the new works are shown up. The two texts can thus very fruitfully be read in conjunction with each other: they show similar mentalities at work in successive ages, using an evolving literary context in comparable ways and for the same essential purpose, namely entertainment.

SOURCES AND INFLUENCE

The *Pèlerinage de Charlemagne* is not the first narration of a journey by Charlemagne to the East or of his acquiring relics. Already in the late tenth century Benedictus de Sancto Andrea, a monk of Monte Soracte in Italy, tells how Charlemagne travelled peaceably to Jerusalem and to Constantinople, making an alliance with the emperors of the latter and receiving from them a relic which he gave to the chronicler's monastery (ed. *Monumenta Germaniae Historica, Scriptores,* in folio, tomus III. Hanover: Hahn, 1839, pp. 708-11; III, p. 708; see Aebischer, "Versions norroises," pp. 107-25). In inventing or repeating this tale Benedict uses elements which have recognisable historical origins. Charlemagne maintained good relations with the Patriarch of Jerusalem and with the Caliph of Baghdad, Harun al-Rashid, from both of whom he received gifts, including relics from Jerusalem; that knowledge of embassies should have been transformed into a belief that Charlemagne made a personal journey to the East is not surprising. Another witness to the same tradition is the belief of the first crusaders, in 1095, that they were following the example and route of the great emperor. (See Robert Folz, *Le Souvenir et la légende de Charlemagne dans l'empire germanique médiéval.* Paris: Les Belles Lettres, 1950, pp. 134-38).

Much closer to the *Pèlerinage*—so close, indeed, that it has been seen as the latter's direct inspiration (Walpole, 1963-64, pp. 141-43)—is the *Descriptio qualiter Karolus magnus clavum et coronam Domini a Constantinopoli Aquisgrani detulerit qualiterque Karolus calvus hec ad sanctum Dyonisium retulerit* (ed. Rauschen, pp. 103-25). This recounts a military expedition by Charlemagne to the East, where he first liberates Jerusalem from the Saracens at the request of the Patriarch, and then visits Constantinople; here he is rewarded with relics of the Passion and of the saints, which overlap with those listed in the *Pèlerinage.* These perform miracles as Charlemagne brings them back to Aix-la-Chapelle; three (the crown of thorns, a nail, and wood from the cross) are later given to Saint-Denis. The *Descriptio* is a work from Saint-Denis, written to authenticate its relics and its great fair known as the Lendit; it is usually assigned to the late eleventh or early twelfth century (Aebischer, "Versions norroises," pp. 182-83, Picherit, 1984, p. vi).

It is probable that other versions of the tale of Charlemagne's pilgrimage existed, and notably a serious epic account preserved by an abbreviated translation in the Old Norse *Karlamagnús saga,* Branch I (see Aebischer, "Versions norroises," pp. 74-106). This thirteenth-century compilation also includes (in Branch VII) a version very close indeed to that of our *Pèlerinage,* and a third version in Branch X which derives from the *Speculum Historiale* of Vincent of Beauvais (Aebischer, "Versions norroises," pp. 126-51; for the texts see *Karlamagnús Saga: The Saga of Charlemagne and his Heroes,* trans. Constance B. Hieatt. 3 vols, Toronto: Pontifical Institute of Medieval Studies, 1975-80, and *Karlamagnús saga, branches I, III, VII et IX,* eds Knud Togeby, Pierre Helleux, Agnete Loth, trans. Annette Patron-Godefroit. Copenhagen: Reitzels, 1980). In addition there are translations into other Scandinavian languages and into Welsh, and French versions from the late Middle Ages: *Galien le Restoré,* the cyclical *Garin de Monglane,* the *Charlemagne* of Girart d'Amiens (see Horrent, 1981, II, pp. 58-60, 106-08, Koschwitz, "Sechs Bearbeitungen," pp. 73-133).

A few scholars have seen the heart and origin of the *Pèlerinage* as lying not in Charlemagne's legendary visit to the East, but in a Celtic tale, either of a journey to the other-world or of an expedition by one king to seek another (Webster, Cross, L.H. Loomis, Krappe, R.S. Loomis, pp. 134-38); for them, the pilgrimage theme, the Jerusalem section, and the very figure of Charlemagne are intrusions. The poem has especially been related to the ballad of *King Arthur and King Cornwall,* a tale of a journey undertaken out of rivalry (Webster). While Celtic elements are to be expected in a text showing a clear relation to courtly romance and so to the latter's Arthurian forebears, none of the specific narrative parallels adduced has found general acceptance. The poet uses themes, motifs, and language from all the literary traditions of his age, but the centre of his tale, which his use of such borrowings turns into literature, comes squarely from the legendary history of Charlemagne. It is his ability to fuse, to exploit, and to manipulate with such control these divergent elements that reveals him as a master of the art of comic writing.

· · · · ·

Finally a word on the title of the poem. In 1836 Michel gave the work the title *Charlemagne,* but on the opening page of the text he provides the title *The Travels of Charlemagne to Jerusalem and Constantinople.* Later editors have tended to prefer the concept of a "voyage" for their titles (Koschwitz uses "Reise") with or without the addition of the names of the cities of Jerusalem and Constantinople (Aebischer, Favati, Tyssens, Picherit). Anna J. Cooper and Isabel de Riquer, on the other hand, use the title *Pèlerinage de Charlemagne,* and a majority of critics have also preferred this title. Since the poem does not present a genuine pilgrimage, it might seem that the term "voyage," which corresponds to the form *voiet* found in the incipit ("cumment Charles de Fraunce voiet in Jerusalem"), is preferable to "pèlerinage." We adopt, however, the title "Pilgrimate of Charlemagne" and so pay

tribute to the comic dimension of the text. At the outset Charles claims to be making a pilgrimage ("La croix et le sepulcre voil aler aurer," v. 70) and at the end of the text he abandons his anger against his wife "because of the sepulchre which he has adored" (v. 870). Though his real reason for leaving France was a selfish one, and the core of the poem is the visit to Constantinople, the notion of a pseudo-pilgrimage suits well the poet's purpose of poking fun at the antics of Charles and his men.

Bibliography

I. Editions And Translations

Charlemagne: An Anglo-Norman Poem of the Twelfth Century. Now first published with an introduction and a glossarial index by Francisque Michel. London: Pickering, Paris: Techener, 1836.

Karls des Grossen Reise nach Jerusalem und Constantinopel: ein altfranzösisches Gedicht des XI. Jahrhunderts. Ed. Eduard Koschwitz. Altfranzösische Bibliothek, 2. Heilbronn: Henninger, 1880 [or rather, 1879].

Karls des Grossen Reise nach Jerusalem und Constantinopel: ein altfranzösisches Heldengedicht. Ed. Eduard Koschwitz. 2., völlig umgearbeitete und vermehrte Auflage. Altfranzösische Bibliothek, 2. Heilbronn: Henninger, 1883. (3rd ed. 1895, 4th ed. 1900.) The text of the 2nd and all later editions differs greatly from that of the 1st, being much less conservative.

Karls des Grossen Reise nach Jerusalem und Constantinopel: ein altfranzösisches Heldengedicht. Ed. Eduard Koschwitz. 5., verbesserte Auflage, besorgt von Gustav Thurau. Altfranzösische Bibliothek, 2. Leipzig: Reisland, 1907. Later editions reproduce the 5th.

Le Pèlerinage de Charlemagne. Ed. and trans. Anna J. Cooper. Paris: Lahure, 1925. With modern French translation and English glossary.

Medieval Narrative: A Book of Translations. Trans. Margaret Schlauch. New York: Prentice-Hall, 1928; rpt., New York: Gordian Press, 1969. Includes an English translation of the *Pèlerinage* (pp. 77-101).

Il Pellegrinaggio di Carlomagno a Gerusalemme e a Costantinopoli. Ed. and trans. Alfredo Cavaliere. Venezia: Libreria Universitaria, 1965. With Italian translation.

Le Voyage de Charlemagne à Jérusalem et à Constantinople: texte publié avec une introduction, des notes et un glossaire. Ed. Paul Aebischer. Textes Littéraires Français, 115. Geneva: Droz, Paris: Minard, 1965. A 2nd edition, also dated 1965 but in reality published in 1971, differs in a number of readings from the 1st, and adds material to the introduction.

Il "Voyage de Charlemagne": edizione critica. Ed. and trans. Guido Favati. Biblioteca degli *Studi Mediolatini e Volgari,* 4. Bologna: Palmaverde, 1965. With Italian translation.

Le Voyage de Charlemagne à Jérusalem et à Constantinople: traduction critique. Trans. Madeleine Tyssens. Ktēmata, 3. Ghent: Story-Scientia, 1978. A modern French translation with extensive critical notes.

The Journey of Charlemagne to Jerusalem and Constantinople (Le Voyage de Charlemagne à Jérusalem et à Constantinople). Ed. and trans. Jean-Louis G. Picherit. Birmingham, Alabama: Summa Publications, 1984. With English translation.

Le Pèlerinage de Charlemagne / La Peregrinación de Carlomagno. Ed. and trans. Isabel de Riquer. Biblioteca Filológica, 3. Barcelona: El Festín de Esopo, 1984. With Spanish translation.

II. Critical Studies

Adler, Alfred. "The *Pèlerinage de Charlemagne* in New Light on Saint-Denis." *Speculum,* 22 (1947), 550-61.

Aebischer, Paul. "Le Gab d'Olivier." *Revue Belge de Philologie et d'Histoire,* 34 (1956), 659-79.

———. "Sur quelques passages du *Voyage de Charlemagne à Jérusalem et à Constantinople:* à propos d'un livre récent." *Revue Belge de Philologie et d'Histoire,* 40 (1962), 815-43.

———. *Les Versions norroises du "Voyage de Charlemagne en Orient": leurs sources.* Bibliothèque de la Faculté de Philosophie et Lettres de l'Université de Liège, 140. Paris: Les Belles Lettres, 1956.

Bancourt, Paul. "La Décoration des intérieurs sarrasins dans les chansons de geste du XIIe siècle et l'art musulman." In *Mélanges de langue et littérature françaises du moyen-âge offerts à Pierre Jonin.* Senefiance, 7. Aix-en-Provence: Université de Provence, Paris: Champion, 1979, pp. 63-88.

Bates, Robert C. "*Le Pèlerinage de Charlemagne:* A Baroque Epic." *Yale Romanic Studies,* 18 (1941), 1-47.

Beckmann, Gustav Adolf. "Hugue li Forz - zur Genesis einer literarischen Gestalt." *Zeitschrift für französische Sprache und Literatur,* 81 (1971), 289-307.

Bédier, Joseph. *Les Legendes épiques: recherches sur la formation des chansons de geste.* 4 vols, Paris: Champion, 1908-13; 3e éd. 1926-29 (vol. IV, pp. 121-56).

Bennett, Philip E. "*Le Pèlerinage de Charlemagne:* le sens de l'aventure." In *Essor et fortune de la chanson de geste dans l'Europe et l'Orient latin: actes du IXe congrès international de la Société Rencesvals pour l'étude des épopées romanes, Padoue - Venise, 29 août - 4 septembre 1982.* Modena: Mucchi, 1984, pp. 475-87.

Bonafin, Massimo. "Fiaba e *chanson de geste:* note in margine a una lettura del *Voyage de Charlemagne.*" *Medioevo Romanzo,* 9 (1984), 3-16.

———. "Tre note sul testo del *Voyage de Charlemagne.*" *Medioevo Romanzo,* 11 (1986), 171-74.

Braet, Herman. *Le Songe dans la chanson de geste au XIIe siècle.* Romanica Gandensia, 15. Ghent: Rijksuniversiteit te Gent, 1975.

Brians, Paul. "Paul Aebischer and the 'Gab d'Olivier'." *Romance Notes,* 15 (1973-74), 164-71.

Burgess, Glyn S. "Old French *Contenance* and *Contenant.*" In Raymond J. Cormier, ed., *Voices of Conscience: Essays on Medieval and Modern French Literature in Memory of James D. Powell and Rosemary Hodgins.* Philadelphia: Temple University Press, 1977, pp. 21-41.

Burns, E. Jane. "Portraits of Kingship in the *Pèlerinage de Charlemagne.*" *Olifant,* 10 (1982-85), 161-81.

Carmody, Francis J. *Le Pèlerinage de Charlemagne: sources et parallèles.* Greenbrae, California: author, 1976.

Caulkins, Janet H. "Narrative Interventions: The Key to the *Jest* of the *Pèlerinage de Charlemagne.*" In Jean Marie d'Heur and Nicoletta Cherubini, eds, *Etudes de philologie romane et d'histoire littéraire offertes à Jules Horrent à l'occasion de son soixantième anniversaire.* Liège: s.n., 1980, pp. 47-55.

Cavaliere, Alfredo. "Per il testo critico del *Pèlerinage Charlemagne.*" In *Studi in onore di Italo Siciliano.* Biblioteca dell'*Archivum Romanicum,* serie 1, 86. 2 vols, Florence: Olschki, 1966, I, pp. 213-23.

Ceron, Sandra. "Un *Gap* épique: *Le Pèlerinage de Charlemagne.*" *Medioevo Romanzo,* 11 (1986), 175-91.

Cobby, Anne. "Religious Elements in *Le Voyage de Charlemagne à Jérusalem et à Constantinople*" In *Au Carrefour des routes d'Europe: la chanson de geste. X^e congrès international de la Société Rencesvals pour l'étude des épopées romanes (Strasbourg, 1985).* Senefiance, 20-21. 2 vols, Aix-en-Provence: Université de Provence, 1987, I, pp. 367-82.

Coulet, Jules. *Etudes sur l'ancien poème français du "Voyage de Charlemagne en Orient".* Publications de la Société pour l'étude des langues romances, 19. Montpellier: Coulet et Fils, 1907.

Cromie, Maureen. "Le Style formulaire dans *Le Voyage de Charlemagne à Jérusalem et à Constantinople (Le Pèlerinage de Charlemagne).*" *Revue des Langues Romanes,* 77 (1967), 31-54.

Cross, Tom Peete. "The Gabs." *Modern Philology,* 25 (1927-28), 349-54.

Densusianu, O. "Aymeri de Narbonne dans la chanson du *Pèlerinage de Charlemagne.*" *Romania,* 25 (1896), 481-96.

Deroy, Jean. "Respect du code de l'amour dans le gab d'Olivier." In *Société Rencesvals pour l'étude des épopées romanes, VIe congrès international (Aix-en-Provence, 29 août - 4 septembre 1973): actes.* Aix-en-Provence: Université de Provence, 1974, pp. 241-51.

Drašković, Vlado. "L'assonance transitoire dans le *Pèlerinage de Charlemagne* et dans le *Cantar de mio Cid.*" *Linguistica,* 12 (1972), 61-66.

Duggan, Joseph J. *The Song of Roland: Formulaic Style and Poetic Craft.* Publications of the Center for Medieval and Renaissance Studies, U.C.L.A., 6. Berkeley: University of California Press, 1973.

Duval, Amaury. "Anonyme auteur du *Voyage de Charlemagne à Jérusalem et à Constantinople.*" In *Histoire littéraire de la France,* ouvrage commencé par des religieux bénédictins de la Congrégation de Saint-Maur et continué par des membres de l'Institut. Paris: various publishers, 1733-date, XVIII, pp. 704-14.

Foerster, W. "Der Pflug in Frankreich und Vers 296 in *Karl des Grossen Wallfahrt nach Jerusalem.*" *Zeitschrift für romanische Philologie,* 29 (1905), 1-18.

Gänssle-Pfeuffer, Cäcilie. "*Majestez* und *vertut* in der *Karlsreise:* zur Problematik der Deutung der Dichtung." *Zeitschrift für romanische Philologie,* 83 (1967), 257-67.

Gosman, Martin. "La Propagande politique dans *Le Voyage de Charlemagne à Jérusalem et à Constantinople.*" *Zeitschrift für romanische Philologie,* 102 (1986), 53-66.

Grégoire, Henri. "De Marsile à Andernas; ou, l'Islam et Byzance dans l'épopée française." In *Miscellanea Giovanni Mercati.* Studi e Testi, 121-26. 6 vols, Vatican City: Biblioteca Apostolica Vaticana, 1946, III, pp. 431-63.

Grigsby, John L. "A Note on the Genre of the *Voyage de Charlemagne.*" In Norris J. Lacy and Jerry C. Nash, eds, *Essays in Early French Literature presented to Barbara M. Craig.* York, South Carolina: French Literature Publications Co., 1982, pp. 1-8.

———. "The Relics' Rôle in the *Voyage de Charlemagne.*" *Olifant,* 9 (1981-82), 20-34.

———. "*Le Voyage de Charlemagne,* pèlerinage ou parodie?" In *Au Carrefour des routes d'Europe: la chanson de geste. X^e congrès international de la Société Rencesvals pour l'étude des épopées romanes (Strasbourg, 1985).* Senefiance, 20-21. 2 vols, Aix-en-Provence: Université de Provence, 1987, I, pp. 567-84.

Hatcher, Anna Granville. "Contributions to the *Pèlerinage de Charlemagne.*" *Studies in Philology,* 44 (1947), 4-25.

Heinermann, Theodor. "Zeit und Sinn der *Karlsreise.*" *Zeitschrift für romanische Philologie,* 56 (1936), 497-562.

Heisig, Karl. "Ein phrygisch-skythisches Sagenmotiv in der *Karlsreise.*" *Germanisch-Romanische Monatsschrift,* 15 (1965), 194-95.

Holmes, Urban T. "The *Pèlerinage de Charlemagne* and William of Malmesbury." *Symposium,* 1 (1946-47), 75-81.

Horrent, Jules. "Chanson de Roland et geste de Charlemagne." In Hans Robert Jauss and Erich Köhler, eds, *Grundriss der romanischen Literaturen des Mittelalters.* Vol. III, *Les Epopées romanes,* ed. Rita Lejeune. Heidelberg: Winter, 1981-date, I, pp. 1-51, II, pp. 5-111.

———. "La Chanson du *Pèlerinage de Charlemagne:* problèmes de composition." In *La Technique littéraire des chansons de geste: actes du colloque de Liège (Septembre 1957).* Bibliothèque de la Faculté de Philosophie et Lettres de l'Université de Liège, 150. Paris: Les Belles Lettres, 1959, pp. 409-28.

———. "La Chanson du *Pèlerinage de Charlemagne* et la réalité historique contemporaine." In *Mélanges de langue et de littérature du moyen âge et de la Renaissance offerts à Jean Frappier par ses collègues, ses élèves et ses amis.* Publications Romanes et Françaises, 112. 2 vols, Geneva: Droz, 1970, I, pp. 411-17.

———. "Contribution à l'établissement du texte perdu du *Pèlerinage de Charlemagne.*" In *Studi in onore di Italo Siciliano.* Biblioteca dell'*Archivum Romanicum,* serie 1, 86. 2 vols, Florence: Olschki, 1966, I, pp. 557-79.

———. "*Pèlerinage de Charlemagne.*" In Georges Grente, ed., *Dictionnaire des lettres françaises. Le Moyen Age.* Paris: Fayard, 1964, pp. 578-80.

Horrent, Jules. *Le Pèlerinage de Charlemagne: essai d'explication littéraire avec des notes de critique textuelle.* Bibliothèque de la Faculté de Philosophie et Lettres de l'Université de Liège, 158. Paris: Les Belles Lettres, 1961.

———. "Sur les sources épiques du *Pèlerinage de Charlemagne.*" *Revue Belge de Philologie et d'Histoire,* 38 (1960), 750-64.

Knudson, Charles A. "A 'Distinctive and Charming Jewel': *Le Voyage de Charlemagne à Jérusalem et à Constantinople.*" *Romanic Review,* 59 (1968), 98-105.

———. "Serments téméraires et gabs: notes sur un thème littéraire." In *Société Rencesvals, IVe congrès international, Heidelberg, 28 août - 2 septembre 1967: actes et mémoires.* Studia Romanica, 14. Heidelberg: Winter, 1969, pp. 254-59.

Koschwitz, Eduard. *Sechs Bearbeitungen des altfranzösischen Gedichts von Karls des Grossen Reise nach Jerusalem und Constantinopel.* Heilbronn: Henninger, 1879.

———. *Überlieferung und Sprache der "Chanson du Voyage de Charlemagne à Jérusalem et à Constantinople": eine kritische Untersuchung.* Heilbronn: Henninger, 1876.

———. "Ueber das Alter und die Herkunft der *Chanson du Voyage de Charlemagne à Jérusalem et à Constantinople.*" *Romanische Studien,* 2 (1875-77), 1-60.

Krappe, Alexander Haggerty. "Hugo von Byzanz, der Pflügerkönig." *Zeitschrift für französische Sprache und Literatur,* 59 (1935), 361-66.

Leupin, Alexandre. "La Compromission (sur *Le Voyage de Charlemagne à Jérusalem et à Constantinople*)." *Romance Notes,* 25 (1984-85), 222-38.

Levy, Raphael. "Sur le vers 384 du *Pèlerinage de Charlemagne*." *Romania*, 64 (1938), 102-04.

———. "The Term 'Language' in *Le Pèlerinage de Charlemagne*." *Modern Language Notes*, 62 (1947), 125-27.

Loomis, Laura Hibbard. "Observations on the *Pèlerinage Charlemagne*." *Modern Philology*, 25 (1927-28), 331-49.

Loomis, Roger Sherman. *Arthurian Tradition & Chrétien de Troyes*. New York: Columbia University Press, 1949 (pp. 133-38).

Ménard, Philippe. *Le Rire et le sourire dans le roman courtois en France au moyen âge (1150-1250)*. Publications Romanes et Françaises, 105. Geneva: Droz, 1969.

Moland, Louis. *Origines littéraires de la France*. Paris: Didier, 1862; nouvelle éd. 1863 (pp. 100-18).

Morf, H. "Etude sur la date, le caractère et l'origine de la chanson du *Pèlerinage de Charlemagne*." *Romania*, 13 (1884), 185-232.

Moroldo, Arnaldo. "Le Portrait dans la chanson de geste." *Le Moyen Age*, 86 (1980), 387-419, and 87 (1981), 5-44.

Neuschäfer, Hans-Jörg. "*Le Voyage de Charlemagne en Orient* als Parodie der Chanson de geste: Untersuchungen zur Epenparodie im Mittelalter (I)." *Romanistisches Jahrbuch*, 10 (1959), 78-102.

Nicholls, J. A. "The *Voyage de Charlemagne*: A Suggested Reading of Lines 100-108." *Australian Journal of French Studies*, 16 (1979), 270-77.

Niles, John D. "On the Logic of *Le Pèlerinage de Charlemagne*." *Neuphilologische Mitteilungen*, 81 (1980), 208-16.

Owen, D. D. Roy. "*Voyage de Charlemagne* and *Chanson de Roland*." *Studi Francesi*, 11 (1967), 468-72.

Panvini, Bruno. "Ancora sul *Pèlerinage Charlemagne*." *Siculorum Gymnasium*, nuova serie, 13 (1960), 17-80.

———. *Il "Pèlerinage Charlemagne"*. Quaderni di Filologia Medievale, 7. Catania: C.U.E.C.M., 1983.

Paris, Gaston. "La Chanson du *Pèlerinage de Charlemagne*." *Romania*, 9 (1880), 1-50.

Paris, Paulin. "Notice sur la chanson de geste intitulée: *Le Voyage de Charlemagne à Jérusalem et à Constantinople*." *Jahrbuch für romanische und englische Literatur*, 1 (1859), 198-211.

Picherit, Jean-Louis. "Sur le vers 288 du *Voyage de Charlemagne à Jérusalem et à Constantinople*." *Zeitschrift für romanische Philologie*, 99 (1983), 512-13.

Pinson, M. "Un Nouvel Essai d'explication: *Pèlerinage de Charlemagne* vv. 100-108." *Romanische Forschungen*, 89 (1977), 266-68.

Polak, Lucie. "Charlemagne and the Marvels of Constantinople." In Peter Noble, Lucie Polak and Claire

Isoz, eds, *The Medieval Alexander Legend and Romance Epic: Essays in Honour of David J. A. Ross*. Millwood: Kraus International, 1982, pp. 159-71.

Rauschen, Gerhard. *Die Legende Karls des Grossen im 11. und 12. Jahrhundert*. Publikationen der Gesellschaft für Rheinische Geschichtskunde, 7. Leipzig: Duncker & Humblot, 1890.

Richard, Jean. "Sur un passage du *Pèlerinage de Charlemagne*: le marché de Jérusalem." *Revue Belge de Philologie et d'Histoire*, 43 (1965), 552-55.

Riquer, Martín de. *Les Chansons de geste françaises*. 2ᵉ éd. entièrement refondue, traduction française par Irénée Cluzel. Paris: Nizet, 1957 (pp. 194-207).

Rossman, Vladimir R. *Perspectives of Irony in Medieval French Literature*. De Proprietatibus Litterarum, series maior, 35. The Hague: Mouton, 1975 (pp. 71-77).

Rychner, Jean. *La Chanson de geste: essai sur l'art épique des jongleurs*. Publications Romanes et Françaises, 53. Geneva: Droz, Lille: Giard, 1955.

Scheludko, D. "Zur Komposition der *Karlsreise*." *Zeitschrift für romanische Philologie*, 53 (1933), 317-25.

Schlauch, Margaret. "The Palace of Hugon de Constantinople." *Speculum*, 7 (1932), 500-14.

Spitzer, Leo. "*Lenguages* dans *Pèlerinage de Charlemagne*, v. 209." *Modern Language Notes*, 53 (1938), 20-21 and 553.

Sturm, Sara. "The Stature of Charlemagne in the *Pèlerinage*." *Studies in Philology*, 71 (1974), 1-18.

Suchier, Hermann. "La XIVᵉ Laisse du *Voyage de Charlemagne*." *Le Moyen Age*, 1 (1888), 10-11.

Sullivan, Penny. "Medieval Automata: The 'Chambre de Beautés' in Benoît's *Roman de Troie*." *Romance Studies*, 6 (1985), 1-20.

Süpek, Otto. "Une Parodie royale du moyen âge." *Annales Universitatis Scientiarum Budapestinensis de Rolando Eötvös Nominatae, Sectio Philologica Moderna*, 8 (1977), 3-25.

Susskind, Norman, "Humor in the *Chansons de Geste*." *Symposium*, 15 (1961), 185-97.

Thomas, A. "Sur un vers du *Pèlerinage de Charlemagne*." *Romania*, 32 (1903), 442-44.

Torrini-Roblin, Gloria. "*Gomen* and *Gab*: Two Models for Play in Medieval Literature." *Romance Philology*, 38 (1984-85), 32-40.

Tyssens, Madeleine. "Encore les 'neiles de paile' (*Karlsreise* v. 746)." *Marche Romane*, 26 (1976), 19-30.

Van Belle, G. "*Le Voyage de Charlemagne à Jérusalem et à Constantinople*: pour une approche narratologique." *Revue Belge de Philologie et d'Histoire*, 64 (1986), 465-72.

Vigneras, L.-A. "L'Abbaye de Charroux et la légende du pèlerinage de Charlemagne." *Romanic Review,* 32 (1941), 121-28.

Walpole, Ronald N. "*Le Pèlerinage de Charlemagne:* Jules Horrent and its 'réalité cachée'." *Romance Philology,* (1963-64), 133-45.

————. "The *Pèlerinage de Charlemagne:* Poem, Legend, and Problem." *Romance Philology,* 8 (1954-55), 173-86.

Walton, Edward. "The Palace of Hugon: Historical Allusion and Literary Reality in the *Pèlerinage de Charlemagne.*" *Les Bonnes Feuilles,* 1 (1972), 26-33.

Webster, K. G. T. "Arthur and Charlemagne: Notes on the *Ballad of King Arthur and King Cornwall* and on the *Pilgrimage of Charlemagne.*" *Englische Studien,* 36 (1906), 337-69.

Mary Garrison (essay date 1994)

SOURCE: "The Emergence of Carolingian Latin Literature and the Court of Charlemagne (780-814)" in *Carolingian Culture: Emulation and Innovation*, edited by Rosamond McKitterick, Cambridge University Press, 1994, pp. 111-40.

[*In the following essay, Garrison considers factors that enabled the creation and survival of Carolingian verse. She also contrasts the perspectives of genteel coterie poetry, written by the court elite, with those of less-censured contemporary victory poems.*]

> Inter caenandum aut aliquod acroama aut lectorem audiebat. Legabantur ei historiae et antiquorum res gestae.[1]

> While dining he used to listen to some entertainment or to a reader; stories and the deeds of the ancients were read to him.

If history has traditionally belonged to those who tell the stories, or leave records, then literary history has, even more problematically, been the domain of those whose tales and poetry were written down and survived. For the early Middle Ages, the implications of this fact are far-reaching. Thus we learn about the enemies of the Carolingian Empire chiefly through Carolingian historical sources; the extant Carolingian literature records the concerns and diversions of a small elite. Other types of composition (such as songs and stories in the vernacular or texts expressing the viewpoint of the people conquered by Charlemagne) did not make the transition from oral circulation to parchment. Indeed, despite Charlemagne's interest in the *barbara et antiquissima carmina* which told of ancient kings' heroic exploits, no manuscripts preserving such tales survive which can be traced directly or indirectly to Charlemagne's initiative.[2] Latin compositions had better chances of survival since the Latin language was primarily the medium of literate men working in stable

institutions, such as cathedrals and monasteries, where texts could be copied and preserved. Nonetheless, many Latin poems can be shown to have perished while others survive in unique manuscripts or fragments only.

The survival of a poem or manuscript from the ninth century to the twentieth therefore reflects the complex interaction of chance and intention. The original composition and copying, however, required not only intention, but also a significant investment of effort and material resources. Accordingly, any significant increase in the creation and copying of literature, particularly when it is associated with the wealth and power of a secular court, demands investigation. An increase in literary activity raises questions for the historian which extend beyond literary history to a more abstract level of speculation about the relationship between wealth and power on the one hand, and artistic creation and the ideology which it incorporates, on the other. One might wish to speculate on the way material, political and social circumstances foster the circulation and later transmission of literature and even how these same factors may influence the genre, contents and arguments of compositions. For example, what effect do kings and courts have on the production and preservation of literature? What are the respective roles of wealth, absolute power and personal charisma in inspiring literary creation? How do rulers elicit panegyric? Conversely, what factors limit the scope for expressions of dissent? When and by whom can a king be criticised? Finally, can the language and form of a poem offer clues about the audience or occasion for which it was written?[3] In this connection, it is important to know that Latin poetry written according to the classical rules of prosody, that is, where vowel length rather than stress determined the metrical pattern, was an increasingly artificial, backward-looking form, removed from the stress-patterns and rhythms of the language spoken every day.[4] Although speakers of the languages descended from Latin, which are usually called the emergent Romance vernaculars, might understand such verse fairly easily, rhythmical verse in fact corresponded more closely to the stress system of the spoken language and would probably have been both easier to compose and to understand.[5]

Some of these questions will be addressed in this chapter with reference to the first generation of writers associated with the court of Charlemagne. First, however, a brief characterisation of the Carolingian literary revival will be necessary. In order to explain the sudden emergence of a lively interest in verse-writing at Charlemagne's court from the 780s, I shall discuss the interplay between the literary inspiration derived from earlier poetry and from the poets' immediate circumstances—their careers, their other activities and the nature of their shared life at court. I shall then analyse their perception of themselves and their claims for the status of their craft. Finally, the representation of current events will be considered and the opportunities for literary expressions of dissent will be assessed.

From the time of Charlemagne onwards there is evidence both for a proliferation in the copying of classical and late-antique Latin literature and also for a dramatic increase in the composition of new texts, especially Latin verse, in an unprecedented range of forms and genres. There are also signs of a new standard of correctness.[6] These developments can be witnessed most dramatically in the king's immediate entourage from the late 770s, although there is some scattered evidence for literary activity in the preceding decades.[7] This increase in the production and survival of verse is especially striking because the evidence for Latin verse-composition anywhere else in the immediately preceding period is sparse. In some areas, verse-composition may have almost died out; in others, the verse that was written simply did not survive. In Spain, for example, no verse survives from the eighth century.[8] For England, the situation is more favourable. Despite the renown of the school and library at York, however, only two or three of Alcuin's poems can be shown to have been written in England.[9] Extant verse from Francia in the first half of the eighth century is no more abundant. For all areas, the very low survival rates for pre-ninth-century manuscripts are partly to blame, although in Francia (and perhaps elsewhere) declining standards of education and Latinity are also implicated, as the low standard of Merovingian charters might seem to indicate. Although it is not possible to trace a continuous tradition of Latin poetry in any region, we can be sure that the skill retained its prestige and continued to be taught, for most of the foreign scholars who assembled at Charlemagne's court would have been trained to write verse in their homelands. The Carolingian achievement in Latin verse-composition therefore results from an increase in production as well as from a significant improvement in the chances for survival. The implementation of *De litteris colendis* and the *Admonitio generalis* must have contributed to the survival of verse by promoting the establishment of scriptoria (albeit for the multiplication of liturgical and doctrinal texts).

The scholars responsible for this verse are referred to as poets in accounts of the literature of the period, but in most cases, verse comprises only a small part of their surviving writings, and they would have thought of themselves primarily not as poets, but as ambassadors, teachers of grammar, experts on time-reckoning and biblical exegesis, advisers to the king or theologians. Thus when Charlemagne eventually rewarded these members of his entourage with bishoprics and abbacies, he did so for their political, administrative and educational services rather than for their verse. Indeed, most of the authors who belong to the first generation of Carolingian scholars wrote many other prose works, and apparently did not concern themselves with the compilation or publication of their poems after they had been performed or sent to an addressee.[10] In striking contrast to classical authors and to one of the best-known early medieval poets, Venantius Fortunatus, Carolingian poets did not issue collections of their verse.[11] (There are only two known exceptions: for the verse of two authors, Alcuin and Theodulf, such assemblages existed in a single manuscript, but were prob-

ably not authorial, and in both cases the manuscript disappeared after its use by a seventeenth-century editor.) In the Carolingian world, the ability to write verse in Latin according to the rules of classical prosody did not make a man a professional poet; that skill was seen simply as the final phase of a thorough education. The challenge of composing Latin verse was naturally greatest for native speakers of a Celtic or Germanic vernacular. Hence it was an Anglo-Saxon, Aldhelm (d. 709), who had created the first *gradus,* or metrical dictionary, to assist non-Latin speakers.[12] Even for native speakers of the languages closely related to Latin, however, special instruction was necessary and this training continued to be regarded as an important goal of Latin education. In other words, the art of writing quantitative Latin verse seems to have been regarded as a prestigious acquisition, but neither such competence nor the careers of the early Carolingian writers qualify them as professional poets. It is therefore all the more significant that they elaborated a discourse about the value of poetry and the importance of the poet—claims which are contradicted by their apparent disregard for the preservation of their verse and by their careers.

These claims, along with the expanded range of forms and genres of Carolingian verse, reflect the availability of influential literary models. Equally important as a stimulus to poetic activity were the new occasions (mainly provided by the court) where verse was required for communication, celebration, entertainment and display. Although few scholars would wish to argue for the enduring literary quality of most of the verse that resulted, all would agree that it emerged in a burst of energy and innovation. Of course, writers continued to turn out poems in the standard genres (such as inscriptions for churches, dedicatory poems and epitaphs—all in demand throughout the Middle Ages), but alongside this predictable trend, important new developments can be traced. Secular epic re-emerged, apparently for the first time in centuries. Similarly, pastoral poems were composed after a centuries-long gap, modelled on Vergil's Eclogues and on the works of the later pastoralists: Calpurnius and Nemesianus. (The latter two authors seem to have been unread for centuries.)[13] There was a new vogue for acrostic poems based, like the pastoral, on late-antique models. The importation of the works of Ennodius of Pavia (d. 521) inspired the use of epistolary adonics[14] and the reintroduction by Alcuin of Boethius' *De consolatione philosophiae* would stimulate new directions in poetry and speculative thought in writers of the ninth century.[15] Finally, perhaps for the first time since Classical Antiquity, there begins to be an appreciable number of poems evoking biographical circumstances and the inner life—homesickness, longing for absent friends, dismay at finding a welcome denied—with striking freshness and poignancy. Beast-fable also returns, but love-lyric is conspicuously absent.

Perhaps the most important single model for Carolingian poets was the life and work of Venantius Fortunatus (*ca* 530-*ca* 600).[16] A prolific writer of epitaphs, panegyrics, poems of consolation or congratulation and other *pièces d'occasion,* Fortunatus had been a true professional poet. He had been able to make his living as an itinerant poet and courtier at several Merovingian royal and episcopal courts before becoming bishop of Poitiers. The eleven-book collection of his verse circulated widely and was closely studied in the early Middle Ages.[17] It decisively influenced the diction and generic range of Carolingian poetry. And it was from their knowledge of Fortunatus that Carolingian writers adopted the conceits of the professional poet. If the first generation of Carolingian authors managed to invent literary personae for themselves as 'court poets', their success certainly owed at least as much to Fortunatus as it did to the example of any classical poet. For in contrast to poets in the ancient world and to Venantius Fortunatus, Carolingian writers of verse could not make a living with their verse and yet nonetheless adopted their predecessors' lofty notions about poetry and even wrote about themselves as if they were professional poets.[18]

Despite the importance of classical and late-antique literary models, the novelty, profusion and survival of Carolingian verse are at least equally indebted to the role of Charlemagne's court in fostering poetic endeavour. Although various earlier medieval rulers had had learned men in attendance and received panegyrics, there are no obvious parallels to the number (and far-flung origins) of the scholars Charlemagne had gathered around him by the 780s.[19] For example, Theodoric the Ostrogoth had employed both Boethius and Cassiodorus in administrative capacities, but had eventually executed the former, while the latter's most important literary work was accomplished after he had given up his official duties for monastic retirement. The Merovingian king Chilperic (d. 584) was remembered as a writer of verse by Fortunatus and Gregory of Tours and, indeed, a single poem by him survives, a rhythmical hymn.[20] The Merovingian courts of Chlotar and Dagobert II had attracted literate men including St Audoin (Audoenus or Dado, bishop of Rouen), St Eligius (bishop of Noyon, d. 660) and St Desiderius (bishop of Cahors, d. 655); their correspondence after each had left court for his bishopric might lead one to suspect that they would have been engaged in some literary sport while in the royal entourage, but if they were, no evidence of it survives and none of these bishops is remembered as a writer of verse. Most significantly, the court of the Lombard kingdom in Pavia had maintained an impressive interest in Latin culture, grammar and secular history, but that tradition was fatally interrupted by the fall of the kingdom in 774 and then by the punishments for the revolt of 776. In Francia before the 770s, during the reign of Pippin and the first decade of Charlemagne's rule, the limited evidence for a concern with learning reflects practical and ecclesiastical needs exclusively; the manuscript evidence is legal, liturgical and grammatical,[21] and the associated dedicatory verses are undistinguished, and in one case, largely derivative.[22] In the decade following Charlemagne's conquest of the Lombard kingdom, however, poetry for entertainment and display is associated with the Carolingian court for the first time.

To understand how what had been a peripatetic warrior-court became the setting for the performance and exchange of poetry, we need to consider two developments. First, Charlemagne's itinerant court had become larger and increasingly sedentary. Between the late 770s and the time of the court's final settlement in Aachen in 794, Charlemagne usually spent the whole winter in a small group of favoured palaces—perhaps six.[23] This extended sojourn enabled the king to gather an enlarged retinue and to eat, drink and plan with it for an extended interval of up to four months. If these conditions hardly seem conducive to study and writing, they were nonetheless an improvement over the old routine of continuous movement from one residence to the next throughout the Frankish realm. In the palace, poetry provided entertainment and an outlet for competition, while for courtiers absent on official business, the composition of poetic epistles was one way to stay in touch.

The second and more important factor was the influx of scholars (and their books) from all corners of Europe; their arrival was a consequence of Charlemagne's conquests, administrative and ecclesiastical aspirations and ability to reward talent.[24] The overthrow of the Lombard kingdom brought at least four new men: the first to arrive were probably Fardulf (*ca* 774) and the grammarian Peter of Pisa (by 769). Fardulf came as a captive or hostage, but eventually transferred his allegiance to Charlemagne and was rewarded for exposing the conspiracy of 792 by being appointed to the abbacy of St Denis; he also served as a *missus*. Only four poems by him survive. Peter had been at the Lombard court and was remembered by Einhard as Charlemagne's teacher. He wrote several poetic epistles in Charlemagne's name; these and his other verse show a streak of mocking humour. At approximately the same time, Paulinus joined the court and remained there until 787 when he became patriarch of Aquileia. His works include a versified account of the Trinity, several rhythmical poems, and a book of moral advice for Eric of Friuli, for whom he later wrote a lament (799). Charlemagne rewarded Paulinus' loyalty during the 776 Lombard uprising by granting him land that had belonged to one of the rebels.

That rebellion also led to the arrival of Paul the Deacon, the last of the Lombard scholars to reach Francia. He came to Charlemagne in 782 as a suppliant, begging for the release of his brother who had been taken into captivity in Francia for his part in the uprising seven years earlier. Paul had been educated in Latin and some Greek at the Lombard court in Pavia. Unlike the other members of the court circle, a significant portion of his extant work, prose and verse, predates his move north. His early works give some idea of the range of his interests and the cultivation of his Lombard royal patrons, for they include verse-epitaphs and praise poems for members of the royal family, and in prose, an abbreviated and extended version of the Roman historian Eutropius. The pre-Carolingian corpus of Paul's verse also includes a hymn in praise of St Benedict, and a rhythmical poem relating the history of the world. Paul's poems and letters illustrate his accommodation to the circumstances of his troubled times: while a monk in Italy he complained that his muse disliked the limits of the cloister; from Charlemagne's court he wrote back to his abbot at Monte Cassino, homesick for the monastery, and protesting that no promise of gold, only physical weakness kept him abroad.[25] Charlemagne initially seems to have detained Paul at court by his refusal to release the captive brother. Gradually, however, the conqueror of the Lombards won Paul's loyalty, as the sequence of riddling verse-epistles and greetings exchanged in the early 780s demonstrates (Peter served as Charlemagne's poetic amanuensis). Paul went on to write various works while in Francia: a history of the bishops of Metz (influential as a model for all subsequent episcopal histories and itself based on the *Liber pontificalis*),[26] epitaphs for members of the royal family, a grammatical work consisting of extracts from Pompeius Festus, and a commentary on the Benedictine Rule. Eventually Charlemagne permitted Paul to return to Monte Cassino (probably in 786 or 787). From there he remained in touch with the king by letter and assembled a homiliary at his request. Although Paul had at first been virtually a hostage because of his need to appease his brother's captor, by the time of his departure Charlemagne had clearly succeeded in inspiring him with enthusiasm for his projects.

The Anglo-Saxon Alcuin joined this group sometime after 782 and remained at court until 796 when he became abbot of Tours. Unlike the Lombards, he seems to have left his native land voluntarily, invited by Charlemagne after a meeting in 781 in Parma. On several occasions Alcuin would feel compelled to defend his decision to leave the community in York where he had been raised; to his friends there, he insisted that his service to the Church, rather than the rewards proffered by Charlemagne, were keeping him abroad; in a letter to a Frankish colleague he explained that a holy man with the gift of prophecy had foretold his continental mission.[27] Charlemagne's teacher in rhetoric, dialectic and astronomy, Alcuin was remembered by Einhard as the 'most learned man anywhere to be found'. A host of students followed Alcuin to the continent, and some, also to Tours, including Frithugils (Fredegisus), Joseph Scottus, Hwita (Candidus or in German, Wizo). Alcuin himself was a prolific poet as well as an outstanding teacher; in addition to his theological and didactic works, he wrote verse for every possible occasion. Through his letters one can trace his reactions to Charlemagne's activities and to the political turmoil in late eighth-century Northumbria; his loyalty to his native York and his need to remain in touch with his former colleagues and students are also evident.

Theodulf, a Goth from Spain, joined the royal entourage probably sometime in the early 780s after he had been forced from his homeland, perhaps through exile or banishment.[28] He experienced banishment again in 817 when he was suspected of complicity in the revolt against Louis the Pious led by Bernhard of Italy. During the intervening years, he served as a *missus* on a judicial investigation in the south of France in 798 and as bishop of Orleans from 800. As a poet, Theodulf was perhaps the most versatile and accomplished of his generation; his verse bears the stamp of his familiarity with Ovid and Prudentius, as well as of his satirical temperament and his penchant for literary feuds.

Although native Franks undoubtedly played an important role in Charlemagne's administration, the Frankish contribution to the literature of the 780s and 790s was small—in part, no doubt, because Charlemagne recruited his Frankish helpers primarily from among the laity, in part, perhaps, because educational standards in Francia had sunk to a low level, as the very earliest Carolingian dedicatory verses imply.[29] Angilbert, courtier, *missus*, emissary to Rome and later lay-abbot of Saint-Riquier, was educated at court and given the by-name Homer by Alcuin. Contemporaries (Modoin and Fiducia) praised his poetic skill, but only two significant poems by him survive. Less than half a dozen compositions can be securely attributed to him and another group of his poems was rewritten and passed off as the work of a late ninth-century bishop.[30] Angilbert's poems and prose letters together reveal a shaky grasp of grammar and prosody not up to the standards of his teachers. Another Frank, Einhard, was educated at the monastery of Fulda and sent to court by his abbot in, or shortly after, 794. Although contemporaries regarded him as an accomplished poet, not a line of his verse survives; instead, he is remembered for his biography of Charlemagne. The Frankish contribution to Carolingian Latin literature increased in later decades as students in monastic schools began to reap the fruits of the revived interest in learning and the newly advertised prestige of poetry.[31]

Charlemagne's court was international and the scholars there were animated by feuds and one-upmanship as well as by a sense of common purpose and an awareness of their status as a new elite. On the basis of surviving evidence, Alcuin was excluded from the literary sport of Peter and Paul although he and Paulinus got along well. Theodulf despised several Irish scholars and was never given a nickname by Alcuin, although the jocular tone of some of Alcuin's letters to him indicates that he did not remain an outsider. The shared life at court therefore provided all of these learned expatriates with opportunities for collaboration as well as rivalry, and even invective, and these possibilities are dramatised in some entertaining poems associated with the court, which range in date from the early 780s to the mid-790s.[32] These poems are the chief evidence for the mentality and diversions of a versatile and extraordinarily lively and energetic group. The designation 'coterie poetry' signals an important common feature: the compositions are destined for the amusement of a limited contemporary audience of the author's learned friends and colleagues. Accordingly, they are characterised by insider jokes, allusions to earlier verse, the use of by-names—all traits that indicate their shared literary and social background.

The earliest example in this category is a verse epistle composed by Alcuin and sent from England probably in 781, before Alcuin joined the royal entourage.[33] The poem uses the literary device of a personified letter which is instructed to bring greetings and even a supply of grammar books to Alcuin's scattered continental acquaintances, emigrés from England and contacts from Alcuin's own previous voyages abroad. Presumably the poem itself and the books would have been conveyed by a single messenger. When the letter reaches the court it is instructed to greet Charlemagne and some of his attendants in terms which demonstrate that the criticism of others' verse by members of the court was already a routine peril:

> Hic proceres patres fratres percurre, saluta
> Ante pedes regis totas expande camenas,
> Dicto multoties: 'Salve, rex optime, salve.
> Tu mihi protector, tutor, defensor adesto,
> Invida ne valeat me carpere lingua nocendo
> Paulini, Petri, Albrici, Samuelis, Ione,
> Vel quicumque velit mea rodere viscera mursu [sic];
> Te terrente procul fugiat, discedat inanis.'[34]
> Run round to the great men, fathers, and monks, and greet them;
> Before the feet of the king, sing out all the songs you know,
> Many times over say to him: 'Greetings best King, hail.
> Be a protector to me, a guardian, and stand by as my defender
> Lest someone's envious tongue should harm me with its carping—
> Paulinus' or Peter's, Alberic's, Samuel's or Jonas'—
> Or whoever else might want to bite me to the quick.
> With you to terrify them, let them run off and depart without
> accomplishing any harm.

Additional evidence for the censure of verse comes from a poem addressed to Angelram of Metz (d. 791) by an otherwise unidentifiable figure called 'Fiducia'. In this text, Fiducia claims that Charlemagne himself had corrected Fiducia's faulty composition. The personified poem concludes:

> Me tetigit Carulus dominus de cuspide pinnae
> Errore confect [a] scriptio nostra fuit.[35]
> Lord Charles touched me with the tip of his quill-pen
> For our composition was confected with error.

More competent poets also feared back-biting; thus Peter to Paul the Deacon:

> Dentibus egregium tu desine rodere fratrem
> Iratus regis qui numquam cernitur aula.[36]
> You, hold off from gnawing the good brother [Alcuin or Peter?] with
> your teeth,
> Who never is seen to be angry by the king's court.

Ermold to Pippin:

> Carmina nostra tuo, princeps, tutamine posco
> Ante tuos vultus sint recitata, pie;

> Quisquis cupit nostros molimine rodere versus,
> Audiat a vobis: 'Parce Nigellus abest.'[37]
> I beg, good king, that with your protection
> Our poems may be recited in your presence;
> Whoever wants to gnaw our poetry violently
> Let him hear from you: 'Hold off! Nigellus is not here.'

Modoin of Autun:

> Forsan et obiciet crimina lingua nocens,
> Livor edax tacito sic secum murmure dicat.[38]
> And perhaps a hurtful tongue will bring accusations
> Just as gnawing envy should mutter to himself under his breath.

Another early example of Carolingian coterie poetry consists of a spirited sequence of riddle poems and challenges exchanged between 782 and 786 by Peter of Pisa, Paul the Deacon and Charlemagne. Two poems in this group illustrate the tenor of their poetic sparring vividly. First Peter writes to Paul on Charlemagne's behalf, welcoming him to court and extravagantly praising his learning and knowledge of Greek.[39] Paul's crisp reply reveals that he knows Peter to be the author of the first poem. He rejects the outrageous praise but belies his assertions of modesty by appending a Latin translation of a Greek epigram.[40] Other poems in the series show Charlemagne challenging Paul to figure out a riddle overnight, and Paul stalling for time by replying with additional riddles. One of the riddles indicates that Charlemagne had already begun to be referred to as David.[41]

Two slightly later ventures show how a similar spirit of competition and collaboration animated other members of the court. Although the 'coterie' provides the circumstantial background for these poems, they are not, strictly speaking, 'coterie poetry', but epitaphs and acrostic panegyrics. Both projects also illustrate the role of classical models and the rivalry between Theodulf on the one hand, and Alcuin and his students on the other.

The earlier example consists of a group of seven elaborate acrostic poems dedicated to Charlemagne and transmitted together in a ninth-century manuscript (s. ix[1] Bern Burgerbibliothek 212).[42] On the basis of internal evidence, the compositions can be dated to the decade 780-90. They contain acrostics, telestichs and mesostichs which form separate messages. For the Carolingian authors, as for their late antique model, acrostic poems (*carmina figurata*, they would have called them) are primarily a medium for visual display and pious commonplaces. Of the seven poems, one is by Theodulf, two are by Alcuin and four are by Joseph Scottus, one of Alcuin's Irish pupils. All seven poems are directly inspired by the similar compositions of Publilius Optatianus Porfyrius, a fourth-century court poet who wrote a series of such poems devoted to Christian themes and to the praise of the emperor Constantine. Dieter Schaller's exhaustive investigation of these Carolingian acrostic poems, the manuscript and the text history of Porfyrius suggests that it was Alcuin who brought the text of

Porfyrius to the continent and assembled his imitations and Joseph's for presentation to Charlemagne in this order: poem by Alcuin—four poems by Joseph—another poem by Alcuin. Soon afterwards Theodulf was invited to take up the challenging assignment and his poem was appended to the group. Surprisingly for a poem in a form that is constraining and derivative, Theodulf includes a poignant autobiographical allusion which indicates that he had only recently arrived at court: 'Since I am an exile from catastrophes without measure . . . '[43] Alcuin prefaced the new compositions with a copy of the old Porfyrian models, revealing that he did not fear comparison. This compilation was subsequently recopied at Saint-Amand to produce the manuscript Bern Bürgerbibliothek 212, the sole surviving witness to these Carolingian experiments.

The contest to write an epitaph for Pope Hadrian had higher stakes.[44] After Hadrian's death on Christmas Day 795, Charlemagne apparently wanted to offer a special commemoration to the pope who had been a personal friend, and so in 796 both Alcuin and Theodulf composed appropriate epitaphs. Eventually a magnificently inscribed marble slab was sent to Rome.[45] Its perfectly executed square capital lettering was inspired by classical models and qualifies as the finest epigraphy made north of the Alps for centuries. As it turned out, it was Alcuin's text, not Theodulf's which was chosen for this impressive monument.

There is some evidence for an earlier instance of poetic emulation connected with the writing of epitaphs, for two commemorative epitaphs of the sixth-century poet Venantius Fortunatus survive, one by Alcuin, and the other by Paul the Deacon.[46] Paul's poem was composed sometime before 786. Years later in the *Historia langobardorum* he would explain how, when he came to pray at the grave of Fortunatus, he had been invited to write an epitaph by the abbot of Saint-Hilarius, Poitiers.[47] The occasion which prompted Alcuin to supply an epitaph for his most influential poetic forebear is unknown, but the wording indicates that this epitaph, too, was intended for display near Fortunatus' burial place; moreover, tenuous but undeniable similarities of diction suggest that either Alcuin or Paul was familiar with the other's work before undertaking his own; unfortunately the direction of influence cannot be established.

The latest and most entertaining examples of true coterie poetry are known as *Zirkulardichtungen* or circulating verse epistles.[48] Most extant examples date from after the time of the court's settlement in Aachen. Internal evidence from these poems shows that they were sent to court by their absent authors; the text was passed around for private reading by a select group before a public recitation. Representatives of this genre supply incidental information about court hierarchy, ceremonial and diet, and combine worshipful greetings and panegyric to Charlemagne with humorous and even, in Theodulf's poems, aggressive allusions to other members of the court. In 794 or 795 Angilbert used this form to send his effusive greetings to Char-

lemagne, the royal family, and their attendants.[49] His poem includes several lofty-sounding refrains. The use of a refrain is indebted to the intercalary verses in Vergil's eighth eclogue; the words of the refrain, however, echo Psalm 107:3. Thus the poem begins with the line '*Surge, meo domno dulces fac, fistula, versus,*' ('Arise, shepherd's pipe, make sweet verses for my Lord'), and that line recurs, with variations, eight more times. In addition, the line '*David amat vates, vatorum est gloria David*' ('David [i.e. Charlemagne] loves poets, David is the glory of the poets') is repeated ten times in the space of 108-line poem, celebrating the close relationship between the king and his 'poets' and perpetuating the fiction that a king who never learned to write was a connoisseur of Latin verse.

In 796 Alcuin and Theodulf each sent poems of this genre to the court. Alcuin's poem, which is fragmentary, contains the elaborate greetings, hyperbolic praise of Charlemagne and catalogue of court personnel which one would expect, and also shares with Angilbert's poem a concern with the status of poetry. Alcuin's anxiety however is more practical than ideological, for he is writing to complain about the lack of proper instruction in poetry since his retirement from the court to Tours. His poem also contains two characteristically Alcuinian features. The first of these is a reference to porridge, apparently a favourite food:

> Ipse Menalca coquos nigra castiget in aula,
> Ut calidos habeat Flaccus per fercula pultes.[50]
> And let Menalcas reprove the cooks in the dark hall
> So that Flaccus can have his warm porridge in courses.

In an earlier poem, the circular letter of pre-781, Alcuin had fondly recalled a meal of porridge with butter and honey.[51]

The second Alcuinian element is some criticism of the curriculum of the school at Aachen, to which I shall refer later when discussing the literature of dissent. Alcuin protests that all the other branches of learning have their representatives at the palace, but not poetry:

> Quid Maro versificus solus peccavit in aula?
> Non fuit ille pater iam dignus habere magistrum,
> Qui daret egregias pueris per tecta camenas?
> Quid faciet Beleel Hiliacis doctus in odis?
> Cur, rogo, non tenuit scolam sub nomine patris?[52]
> Was Maro the poet the only one who committed some
> sin at court?
> Or did that father not deserve to have a teacher
> Who would give choice verses to the students at court?
> What will Besaleel [i.e. Einhard], who knows the
> Iliadic odes do?
> Why, I ask, did he not keep the school in place of his
> father [i.e. Alcuin]?

Such open criticism of Charlemagne's policy is unparalleled in the verse of Alcuin's contemporaries.[53] Although the unwritten code of deference at court permitted poets to compete and even to carp at each other, praise and respectful familiarity were the only registers available for addressing or describing the king. These literary conventions may reflect the social and ceremonial conduct of the king's retinue.

Theodulf's verse-epistle to the court outdoes its precursors in several respects. The praise of Charlemagne is extravagant:

> Te totus laudesque tuas, rex, personat orbis[54]
> The entire world sounds forth your praises
> O facies, facies ter cocto clarior auro,
> Felix qui potis est semper adesse tibi[55]
> O countenance, countenance more splendid than thrice-purified gold,
> Blessed the one who can always be near you

The hyperbole continues: the king's intellect, strength and beauty are derived respectively from David, Solomon and Joseph. The magnitude of his cleverness and prudence exceed the size of the largest rivers in the world. In contrast to Angilbert and Alcuin who had provided static images of the other members of the royal family, Theodulf animates his catalogue by recounting how obediently the king's sons take their father's gloves and sword, how charmingly the daughters bring flowers and fruits and then entertain their father with conversation, jokes and laughter. For Theodulf's antagonists outside the royal family, however, there is satire. Alcuin is a target twice when his pedantic riddling sessions with Charlemagne and his meal of porridge accompanied by wine or beer—or both—are caricatured.[56] Then abruptly Theodulf interjects: 'Good riddance, porridge and heaps of curds!'[57] Theodulf's next victim, a fat and stupid warrior, is depicted in a comic interlude. This character, Wibod, is apparently unable to understand the poem. He reveals his irritation, cursing at the absent Theodulf. When the king calls to him he makes his loud and clumsy way across the hall.[58] His discontent is mild compared to the tantrum of Theodulf's arch-enemy, a short irascible and competitive Irishman.

> Haec ita dum fiunt, dum carmina nostra leguntur,
> Stet Scotellus ibi, res sine lege furens,
> Res dira, hostis atrox, hebes horror, pestis acerba.[59]
> While these things are going on, while our poem is read aloud,
> Let the Irish twerp stand there, a thing raging without law
> A dire thing, a savage foe, a sluggish horror, a bitter plague.
> Nunc gemitus tantum, nunc fera verba sonet,
> Nunc ad lectorem, nunc se convertat ad omnes
> Adstantes proceres nil ratione gerens.[60]
> By turns he utters groans, by turns, uncultivated words,
> Now let him face the reader, now, all the assembled magnates,
> Behaving with no rhyme or reason.

The poem concludes with the end of the banquet and a much needed apology:

> At tu posce pio reditum mea fistula regi,
> Et cunctis veniam, quos ciet iste iocus.[61]
> But you my pipe, ask the good king for your return
> And beg indulgence from all whom this jest incited.

Despite the differences in their background and training and their potentially divisive rivalries, many authors of Carolingian court poetry share certain distinctive claims about the significance of their learned activities. Firstly, they make lofty-sounding statements about the value of poetry and the poet's craft and secondly, they articulate the perception that they are engaged in a renewal of Antiquity a number of times. Neither discourse can be taken at its face-value, but some discussion of each may be helpful in order to show what these claims reveal about the writers' self-awareness and their relationship to their literary heritage and contemporary circumstances.

Claims about the value of poetry are often associated with the representation of Charlemagne as a connoisseur of poetry and learning. Angilbert's poem on the court (discussed above, pp. 123-4) repeated the line 'David [i.e. Charlemagne] loves poets, David is the poets' glory' nine times in a poem barely over one hundred lines in length, simultaneously flattering the king and exalting the importance of poetry at court.[62] An Irish poet at Charlemagne's court (*Hibernicus Exul*) asked his muse what poetry was worth and composed a reply for the muse which linked poetry's eternity with royal magnificence:

> Regumque obrizo candor dum fulminat auro,
> Munera Musarum saeclis aeterna manebunt.
> His regum veterum clarescunt inclita gesta,
> Praesentum et saeclis narrantur facta futuris.[63]
> As long as the splendour of kings flashes out in pure gold,
> The everlasting gifts of the Muses [i.e. poetry] will endure through the ages.
> With verse, the glorious deeds of ancient kings are celebrated
> And the accomplishments of men of the present age are related to future centuries.

Modoin, probably less than ten years later, composed a similar debate about the value of poetry; this time a young poet-narrator champions his own cause against the discouraging counsels of a grouchy old poet.

> Spreta adeo domino non sunt mea carmina magno:
> Ille solet calamo silvestri ludere saepe,
> Nec vilem tantus iudex me iudicat esse.[64]
> My songs [i.e. pastoral, low style] are not so despised by the great lord,
> He has a habit of often playing the woodland flute,
> Nor does that great judge deem me to be so vile
> Crede, satis gratas dominis consistere Musas
> Praecipuis meritis hinc esse memento poetas.[65]
> Believe me, poetry remains pleasing to the masters,
> Remember that there are poets with outstanding rewards for that.

Theodulf insisted that his poetry could influence, not just please:

> . . . sonet Theodulfica Musa,
> Quae foveat reges, mulceat et proceres.[66]
> Let Theodulf's Muse sing,
> In order to cheer kings and charm magnates.

What is the material basis for these claims? From the point of view of text-history, statements about the eternity of verse seem to be a literary conceit divorced from reality. The transmission of Carolingian verse is poor and unsystematic; poems often travel individually or in miscellanies, rather than in authorial compilations; they are often transmitted without attributions; many survive in one manuscript only, and it is not unusual to find poems crammed into left-over space in codices devoted to other topics.[67] For example, the statement by *Hibernicus Exul* quoted above, Alcuin's verse-epistle to his continental colleagues (above, p. 120) and the Rhythm on the Avars (discussed below, pp. 132-3) all survive in single manuscripts only. In short, even if we allow for the ravages of time, the manuscript transmission of Carolingian verse implies a nonchalance about the value of poetry and its survival directly contradicted by certain of the poets' claims. Apparently verse was intended to address and entertain contemporaries, not posterity.[68]

The internal references to patronage do nothing to contradict the impression that court poetry was ephemeral and occasional; they also reveal the gradual emergence of a discourse about poetry as an autonomous activity of professionals. The first court poets make few assertions about the value of their verse and rarely mention rewards for verse overtly, although poetry and hospitality from the king may be part of an exchange and poetry may serve as a tribute gift to the king. Thus Paul the Deacon implies that poetry is no match for riches:

> Nulla mihi aut flaventis est metalli copia
> aut argenti sive opum, desunt et marsuppia.
> Vitam litteris ni emam, nihil est, quod tribaum.
> Pretiosa quaeque vobis dona ferant divites . . .
> meo pura tribuetur voluntas in munere.[69]
> I have no heap of golden metal
> Nor of silver, nor of riches; I do not even have any money-bags,
> Unless I buy my keep with letters, there is nothing I could give.
> Let wealthy men bring all sorts of precious gifts to you, . . .
> From me, pure (good) will is bestowed as a present.

In the early 780s, both Theodulf and Paul implied that their willingness to compose verse depended upon their happiness at court. That scholars received rewards is evident from Einhard's and Notker's stories about the king's willingness to support learning, but poetry does not seem to have held a special place. Both Alcuin and Paul the Deacon wrote letters to the monastic communities they had left, protesting that it was not Charlemagne's wealth which detained them in Francia—but with no specific reference to poetry.

The students of the first court poets, though still conscious of the novelty of their role, were less reticent; in their verse, explicit references to remuneration from verse, and to verse as an annual gift to the king emerge.[70] Thus Modoin's Eclogue triumphantly likens Carolingian patronage to the patronage system of the Roman world; after recalling the rewards received by Vergil, Lucan and Ennius, Modoin announces:

> . . . haec etiam nostro nunc tempore cerne:
> nam meus ecce solet magno facundus Homerus
> Carminibus Carolo studiosis sepe placere.
> Ni Flaccus calamo modulari carmina nosset,
> Non tot praesentis teniusset premia vitae.
> Theodulfus gracili iam dudum lusit avena:
> Plurima cantando meruit commertia rerum.[71]
> See once again things are thus even in our age today
> For my eloquent Homer [i.e. Angilbert] is accustomed
> To please great Charles often with accomplished songs;
> If Flaccus [i.e. Alcuin] had not known how to play songs on his flute
> He would not have had so many of the rewards of this present life;
> Now for a long time Theodulf has played a graceful pipe,
> By singing he has earned great gains of affairs.

The catalogue of poets rewarded is an established literary commonplace.[72] To graft the Carolingian poets on to a list comprising Lucan, Vergil and Ennius, as Modoin has done, is to assert the prestige of contemporary verse with extraordinary confidence, a confidence which other writers of verse seem to share. Verse is no longer a poor substitute for riches as it had been for Paul, but a possible tribute-gift in its own right. *Hibernicus Exul* in the Tassilo-poem[73] and later, the Irish Dicuil, in an extended astronomical work, both present their compositions as tribute-gifts to the king with none of the diffidence evinced earlier by Paul.[74] Together with the quotations above, their statements indicate that the verse-writers succeeded in promoting their notion of poetry (or panegyric at least) as a prestige commodity. Or, more cynically, taking the king's point of view, one might conclude that the Carolingian capacity to exact poetry is a literary corollary to their improved ability to monopolise the plunder gained in battle.[75]

Statements about the *renovatio* of learning and the revival of Antiquity occur in prose and verse alike and evoke an exuberant sense of possibility and new beginnings. The classical by-names of many members of the court seem to reflect their cultural aspirations most directly. Alcuin, apparently the originator of this custom, called himself Flaccus (after the poet Horace), and occasionally Publius Albinus; Angilbert was Homer and Audulf, the cup-bearer, Menalcas; Pippin was Julius, Riculf of Mainz, Flavius Damoetas; Charlemagne was addressed on one occasion as Flavius Anicius Carlus and had other designations as well. Although many of the original court poets had already dispersed by the time of the court's transfer to Aachen in 794, the building activities there seem to have made a great impression on the writers who were present. In Modoin's poetic transformation, Charlemagne becomes Palaemon and Aachen a new Rome:

> Prospicit alta novae Romae meus arce Palemon
> Cuncta suo imperio consistere regna triumpho
> Rursus in antiquos mutata secula mores,
> Aurea Roma iterum renovata renascitur orbi.[76]
> From the high citadel of a new Rome my Palemon

sees
That all the regna are joined in his empire through victory,
That the age has been changed back into the culture of Antiquity,
Golden Rome is restored and reborn to the world.[77]

Similarly, in the anonymous text known as the Paderborn Epic (composed in or after 799),[78] Charlemagne is likened to Aeneas and a retrospective account of the building of Aachen likens it to Rome: 'second Rome', 'Rome-to-be', or just 'Rome' are the designations employed.[79] With more intellectual than architectural concerns, Alcuin wrote to Charlemagne in 799: 'For if many men pursue the excellent subject of your wish, perhaps a new Athens may be established in Francia—indeed, one better by far; for this one, ennobled by the teaching of the Lord Christ, surpasses all the wisdom of academic striving . . . '[80]

Finally in his prologue to Einhard's *Vita Karoli*, Walahfrid Strabo looked back nostalgically to the revival of learning sponsored by Charlemagne as a Golden Age:

> Of all kings, Charlemagne was the most eager in his search for wise men and in his determination to provide them with living conditions in which they could pursue knowledge in all reasonable comfort. In this way Charlemagne was able to offer to the cultureless, and I might say, almost completely unenlightened territory of the realm which God had entrusted to him, a new enthusiasm for all human knowledge. In its earlier state of barbarousness, his kingdom had hardly been touched by any such zeal, but now it had opened its eyes to God's illumination. In our own time the thirst for knowledge is disappearing again: the light of wisdom is less and less sought after and is now becoming rare again in most men's minds.[81]

A critical evaluation of these statements about poetry and renewal shows that they are not part of a single coherent ideology, and are far less programmatic than one might assume. For example, the characteristic renaissance-claims only occur in poems and letters addressed to Charlemagne[82] and might be seen as a special idiom for the flattery of a cultivated king. The designation 'second Rome' had been used in earlier panegyric poetry (of Constantinople)[83] and the image of the rebirth of Rome had occurred in royal panegyrics by Venantius Fortunatus.[84] As for Aachen, the New Rome and Athens: no form of the names for Aachen current in the eighth century could be accommodated in a Latin hexameter. Furthermore, the proliferation of by-names introduced by Alcuin included far more nicknames derived from the Old Testament, the animal world, and early Christian times than from Classical Antiquity. The nicknaming, then was just one part of a search for models and images from the past intended not to recreate another era, but rather as part of a search for transhistorical models which would express otherwise unarticulated dimensions of present circumstances. Some scholars have suggested that the names were meant to add a tone of informality to the court and classroom and indeed, Alcuin himself stated that they were given for familiarity. At the same time, the names might also be seen as the trappings of a new elite.

These strictures on the interpretation of the examples suggest that the poets' claims must be taken with a grain of salt. In other words, their lofty pronouncements are significant, but do not articulate any unified theory of Rome, Poetry and Greatness. Nonetheless, even if we dismiss some statements as a special type of panegyric and reject the notion that the poets were consciously trying to revive Antiquity, the novelty of the Carolingian literary revival is striking and stands out all the more when viewed in historical perspective. As the brief survey of its antecedents should have demonstrated, the awareness of new beginnings was fully justified.

The poetry so far surveyed sheds light on poets' presentation of themselves, the court and their high claims for the status of poetry. Charlemagne was represented as learned, but genial, and even in Theodulf's circular poem on the court, intended for recitation after the victory over the Avars, the harsh realities of warfare were bypassed for a splendid imaginary scene of Charlemagne receiving tribute from as yet unconquered peoples. In other words, despite the literary feuds, coterie poetry offers a genteel dinner-party image of the court in which the fiercest disputes were personal or intellectual.

Some contemporary historical poems can offer an alternative perspective on current affairs and on Charlemagne's rulership. The most important of these are: a poem on the 777 conversion of the Saxons;[85] a fragment attributed to *Hibernicus Exul* on the overthrow of Tassilo of Bavaria in 787;[86] a rhythmical poem on Pippin's victory over the Avars in 796;[87] and finally, the *Paderborn Epic* (also known as *Karolus Magnus et Leo Papa*) which describes events of 799.[88]

Almost without exception, these texts present difficult problems of dating, attribution and generic classification. All share an astonishing lack of interest in historical specificity. For example, the background of Tassilo's revolt is nowhere explained and his disobedience is accounted for by diabolical intervention. The Avar Rhythm presents a dramatic, ballad-like account of the way the cowardly Avar Kagan, or king, is intimidated by someone on his own side into surrendering; Pippin's success is credited to the intervention of St Peter. Extravagant praise for the Franks and a concern to demonstrate the Christian legitimation of their conquests were more important to these authors than journalistic detail. In any case, if the intended audience consisted of participants in these various expeditions, they would not need to be told what they had done, but would want to hear a celebration of their achievement. So, for example, the poem on the conversion of the Saxons wanders into an extended series of epic similes devoid of concrete information when it evokes Charlemagne's forced baptism of these enemies: he has turned wolves into sheep, crows into doves and so on, providing the poet with a chance to display his zoological knowledge while glorifying the conversion.[89]

The Saxon poem and the Avar poem both offer grotesque accounts of non-Christian practices. The Saxons' holy offerings are described as sordid gifts, and they are said to sacrifice bulls on gore-covered altars; barbarous frenzy (*barbarica rabie*) is the motive for their devotions.[90] The Avars are accused of desecrating Christian holy places:

> Multa mala iam fecerunt ab antico tempore,
> fana dei destruxerunt atque monasteria,
> vasa aurea sacrata, argentea, fictilia.
> Vestem sanctam polluerunt de ara sacratissima,
> linteamina levitae et sanctaemonialium
> muliebris tradita suadente demone.[91]
> From ancient times they have done many evil deeds,
> they have destroyed the monasteries and shrines of God,
> their holy vessels of gold, silver and clay.
> They have fouled the holy cloth of the most sacred altars;
> At the persuasion of the Devil, they have given over
> The linen vestments of deacons and nuns to their women.

In three of the poems, the political use of terror is depicted, even glorified. In both the *Paderborn Epic* and the poem on the conversion of the Saxons, terror as an instrument of religious and political coercion is presented in heroic terms. Unlike Alcuin, who had expressed doubts about the efficacy of forced conversion, the author of the Paderborn Epic had no such qualms:

> Quod mens laeva vetat suadendo animusque sinister,
> Hoc saltim cupiant implere timore coacti;
> Quod non sponte prius miseri fecere rebelles,
> Exercere student avide instimulante timore.
> Qui pius esse fero iam dudum more repugnat,
> fitque timore pio pius impius ille coactus.[92]
> What the contrary mind and perverse soul refuse to do with persuasion,
> Let them leap to accomplish when compelled by fear,
> What wretched rebels at first did not do of their own accord,
> They eagerly rush to accomplish, with fright goading them.
> The one who in savage fashion for a long time refused to be pious,
> That impious one, is made pious when coerced by holy fear.

In the poem on the conversion of the Saxons, a scattering of phrases borrowed from the *Aeneid* adds epic colouring. Here again, victory is achieved through intimidation and divine favour:

> Hanc Carolus princeps gentem fulgentibus armis
> Fortiter adcinctus, galeis cristatus acutis,
> Arbitri aeterni mira virtute iuvatus,
> Per varios casus domuit, per mille triumphos,
> Perque cruoriferos unbos, per tela duelli,
> Per vim virtutum, per spicula lita cruore
> Contrivit, sibimet gladio vibrante subegit.[93]
> Charles the Chief [subdued] this nation with weapons glittering,
> Stoutly armed, crested with sharp helmets,
> Assisted by the miraculous strength of the Eternal Judge,
> He subdued [them] with various destructions, with a thousand triumphs
> With gore-spattered shields, with spears of combat,
> With the might of virtues, with blood-smeared javelins,
> He ground (them) down and subjugated (them) to himself with his sword flashing.

Finally, in the Avar Rhythm, terror is the motive for all of the poem's limited action and the Avars are portrayed as laughable cowards. The Avar king's adviser is '*satis pavens*', 'panicking quite a lot'; and the king himself, '*undique perterritus*', thoroughly terrified.[94] If the celebration of might and terror seems sinister from our contemporary perspective, it may be worth stressing that the Carolingian writers were merely applying to Charlemagne an earthly version of the terror and majesty of some representations of God in the Old Testament.[95]

Alfred Ebenbauer's recent study of Carolingian historical poetry has suggested that these poems attempt in various ways to transpose secular Frankish history to the level of *Heilsgeschichte*.[96] (*Heilsgeschichte* is the one-word term which encapsulates the aims of much medieval historical writing: it means salvation history, the interpretation of history stressing God's saving grace.) Ebenbauer's suggestion is persuasive.[97] From a comparative perspective, however, it may also be illuminating to consider these poems as a type of 'frontier literature'. Just as the participants in the American westward expansion believed in 'Manifest Destiny' and their divine right to the land,[98] so too, the Franks, from the 750s onwards, had encountered and eventually espoused the notion that they were the Chosen People.[99] Both groups misunderstood the behaviour of the peoples whose land they were expanding into and demonised their adversaries in songs. And finally Western songs and stories about Daniel Boone, Davy Crockett, Kit Carson and other frontier heroes, like these Frankish texts, see the conflict between settlers and natives in unambiguously heroic dimensions: a complex historical process is distilled into a simple conflict between adversaries: heroes with supernatural attributes and enemies of exaggerated treachery and iniquity, whether Saxon or Native American. In both instances, 'frontier literature' transmits stories from the perspective of the victors only. Curiously, the conquering Franks and the North American homesteaders also expressed similar cultural aspirations: just as Aachen was a new Rome or Athens, so too, Americans in their westward expansion established numerous Troys, Athenses, and Spartas, Arcadias and Carthages, and even went one step farther than Alcuin's circle in using Seneca, Vergil, Homer and Euclid as first names, rather than merely as by-names.[100]

Because these Carolingian historical poems bear a superficial resemblance to battle and victory poems from other cultures, medieval and modern, their role may seem less alien than, say, the custom of reciting circular letters to the court after a feast. Nonetheless, it may be worth looking for more explicit testimonies about their original diffusion or performance. What was their function? The

Tassilo-poem poet begins with a description of the annual tribute-giving ceremony[101]. The leading men of the world approach the king with great loads of gold and jewels; the poet, at a loss, asks his Muse what he can give and she suggests that he should sing poetry. To dispel his doubts, she makes grandiose claims for the eternity of poetry and its capacity to celebrate the deeds of ancient kings and to transmit the accomplishments of the present age to future centuries (a nice irony in a poem that has survived in one manuscript only).[102] From this reference and from the one by Dicuil mentioned earlier, we can assume that poems might be offered to the king and performed at great assemblies such as the one for the collection of tribute in May. These were occasions for the king to dramatise his special status by festive crown-wearing, and the recitation of a victory poem would certainly have been appropriate. There is no incontrovertible proof that any of these poems was performed, but most seem to have been intended for recitation. Recall Einhard's comments about Charlemagne's fondness for reading and story-telling at meals. The fact that Theodulf's court poem (discussed above, pp. 125-6) was intended for performance after the Avar victory and that it depicted the occurrence during a feast of an imaginary tribute-giving ceremony supports the theory. Moreover, the colloquial language of the Avar Rhythm suggests that it was destined for a wider audience than just the court scholars. Finally, some evidence for liturgical commemoration of Carolingian battles has been discovered in two calendars from the eighth and ninth centuries, but the extent and precise nature of this practice have yet to be elucidated before its possible relationship with the performance of these poems can be a subject of speculation.[103]

The probable function and performance of these historical poems make it likely that they would have been composed and declaimed not long after the events they recount, for they would lose their relevance if too many seasons (and other exploits) had elapsed. There would be no point in celebrating Charlemagne's third-to-last victory when the story of a more recent triumph was waiting to be told. And a poem on the glorious 777 conversion of the Saxons would not be welcome after the Saxons' subsequent uprisings. In whatever way the poems were performed, we might imagine that they had a function analogous to someone's slide show of a recent trip—an excuse for participants and their friends to recall their adventures while confirming the solidarity of the group.

To judge from their transmission, these compositions were of relatively little interest to others. The Tassilo poem survives in one manuscript only (s. x or xi); the Avar Rhythm is also transmitted in a single manuscript—the nearly contemporary grammatical compilation, Berlin, Staatsbibliothek Diez. B. Sant. 66, where the text is scrawled on an empty leaf.[104] The Paderborn Epic too exists today in one manuscript dated to the end of the ninth century; but it was evidently available for study at court since Ermold the Black made extensive use of it in a poem in honour of Louis the Pious. The poem on the conversion

of the Saxons survives in two manuscripts only. Additional manuscript witnesses for these poems may have perished or may await discovery, but the overall impression to be gained from the text histories of these court-poems is unlikely to be significantly revised: they were apparently ephemeral compositions destined for performance on a particular occasion. In contrast, evidence from medieval library catalogues shows that more extensive circulation was possible for at least one Latin heroic poem on a theme of more general and enduring interest, since versions of another (probably) Carolingian poem, the secular heroic epic known as the Waltharius, can be shown to have been available in several monastic centres.[105] The Waltharius is based on legendary material which enjoyed an almost pan-European diffusion in the Middle Ages; it tells the story of the escape-journey of Walter of Aquitaine from the court of Attila and the fights that ensue. Walter travels with Hiltgunt, a Burgundian princess, who had also been a hostage at the court of Attila. The poem concludes with a series of bloody combats in a mountain pass; Walter is wounded but survives to marry Hiltgunt and rule his own people.

The historical poems surveyed, all in different ways, present a smug and exultant portrait of Charlemagne's activities, and the view of poetry promoted by writers associated with Charlemagne implies that verse is the appropriately ostentatious gold frame for the portrait. The quantity of hyberbolic praise in this literature combined with the scarcity of criticism suggests that perhaps it was Charlemagne's might which both inspired poetry and excluded the possibility for dissent.

To find any criticism of the Carolingians, we must look farther afield, to later generations, to prose, and to other genres.[106] Even though it is not always easy to specify the genre of medieval Latin texts, the occasions for which they were composed exerted a decisive influence on the contents. Disagreement was usually confined to prose, or to texts not, as far as we can determine, intended for public recitation. The genre of Fürstenspiegel, or 'Mirrors for princes', which enjoyed a vogue at this time was one place for moral instruction.[107] Writers of a later generation discovered that laments and allegory offered safe poetic channels for expressing discontent: hence the otherwise unknown poet Angelbert's grim account of the Battle of Fontenoy in 841, fought by the sons of Louis the Pious: Lothar I and Pippin II against Louis the German and Charles the Bald,[108] or Florus of Lyons' apocalyptic complaint, disguised in the form of a lament, on the ensuing division of the empire in the 840s.[109]

When we look for earlier evidence of dissent, Alcuin stands out immediately—not only for his threatening letters to contemporary kings of Northumbria, written when he was safely separated from them by sea, but also for his confidence in disagreeing with Charlemagne in discussion, as Notker reports, as well as in prose letters. Notker (chapter 9), who had never met Alcuin, reported that Alcuin alone dared disagree with the emperor. Alcuin's occasionally assertive tone in letters to Charlemagne corroborates the report. For example, Alcuin argued emphatically against imposing the tithe too soon on the newly converted Saxons and dared advise against an expedition into Benevento in 800-801.[110] His advice was cautiously but firmly phrased; he nonetheless felt compelled to justify his presumption: 'perhaps somebody (may) comment: "Why does that man meddle in other people's business?" But he does not know that nothing concerning your prosperity is foreign to me, which I declare that I prize above the health of my body or the length of my life.'[111] After his retirement to Tours, Alcuin had complained to Charlemagne about the curriculum at Aachen in both prose and verse. For Alcuin, then, the capacity to criticise the king seems to have been a result of personal standing. In the Carolingian verse of Paul the Deacon, who might have harboured real bitterness against a king who had crushed the Lombard kingdom and imprisoned his brother, anti-Frankish sentiment is absent— and not surprisingly, for Paul came to court as a suppliant. In a prose letter written from court to his former monastic community, and in his *Historia langobardorum* (written for an Italian audience) however, Paul's true feelings can be detected,[112] and the contrast between those two texts and his court poetry signals the ambivalence which could be evoked by Charlemagne's might and charisma.

If any of the authors discussed in this chapter could be invited to participate in the historiographical debate about the Carolingian Renaissance, they would surely defend the term. For as we have seen, the perception that these authors are participating in a renewal of Classical Antiquity was articulated a number of times in Carolingian poetry. Yet the emulation of classical models is neither the most important inspiration for the first generation of Carolingian poets, nor the source of what is most lively and distinctive about that verse, for its vitality results from the picture that emerges of strong personalities responding to the challenges of each other's verse, and to the stimulus of their unique historical situation—rather than from enduring literary quality. To be sure, some critics have found little enough to admire. As Laistner commented, 'the first impression made on the mind of the reader who peruses the four massive volumes of Carolingian poetry in the *Monumenta germaniae historica* is inevitably one of fatigued disappointment . . . '[113] But as a lens through which to view figures and events which we encounter otherwise only in prose and documentary sources, Carolingian verse can offer unique insights into the aspirations, self-understanding and squabbles of a talented, influential and international coterie, for the Carolingian verse that survives refracts their concerns into an extraordinarily vivid—if narrow—spectrum. At the same time, the emergence of this verse as well as its circulation and transmission to our own century—all must be explained as consequences of Charlemagne's wealth, absolute power and concern for religion and education.[114]

Notes

1. Einhard, *Vita Karoli*, c. 24, ed. O. Holder-Egger, MGH SRG (Hanover, 1911) p. 29, lines 6-8. The account of after dinner entertainment is ultimately inspired by a similar passage in c. 74 of Suetonius' biography of Augustus in his *Vitae Caesarum*, but Einhard has made several significant omissions which indicate that he is attempting to provide an accurate portrait of his subject.

2. Einhard, c. 29, p. 33, lines 11-12. On Old High German literature, see chapter 5 below.

3. On the audience of Carolingian Latin verse, see the discussion by McKitterick, *Carolingians,* pp. 227-32.

4. On the Latin/Romance debate, see the essays in *Latin and the Romance Languages in the Early Middle Ages,* ed. R. Wright (London, 1991).

5. On rhythmical verse, see D. Norberg, *La Poésie latine rythmique du haut moyen âge,* Studia Latina Holmiensia 2 (Stockholm, 1954).

6. On book production and copying, see chapter 8 below.

7. M. Manitius, *Geschichte der lateinischen Literatur des Mittelalters* I (Munich, 1911) pp. 243-248; W. von den Steinen, 'Der Neubeginn', in: *Karl der Grosse* II, pp. 9-27; D. Bullough, *The Age of Charlemagne* (1965; reprinted London, 1973) pp. 99-101 and 'Aula Renovata: the Carolingian court before the Aachen palace', *Proceedings of the British Academy* 71 (1985) pp. 267-301 at pp. 269-77, reprinted in D. Bullough *Carolingian Renewal: Sources and Heritage* (Manchester, 1991) pp. 123-60.

8. See R. Collins, 'Poetry in ninth century Spain', *Papers of the Liverpool Latin Seminar,* 4 (1983) pp. 181-95.

9. For a discussion of literary activity at York in the later eighth century, see M. Lapidge, 'Aediluf and the School of York', in: *Lateinische Kultur im VIII. Jahrhundert. Traube-Gedenkschrift,* ed. A Lehner and W. Berschin (St Ottilien, 1990) pp. 161-78, at pp. 163-5. Godman, *Poetry,* pp. 1-4.

10. On evidence for the performance of Carolingian verse, see below, p. 135.

11. On the transmission of Carolingian verse, see below, nn. 104 and 105; P. Godman, 'Latin poetry under Charles the Bald and Carolingian poetry,' in: *Charles the Bald: Court and Kingdom,* BAR International Series 101, ed. M. T. Gibson and J. L. Nelson (London, 1981) pp. 293-309 at pp. 294-295 provides the most useful and incisive summary of the issues, but note that Modoin's *Egloga* survives in two manuscripts, not one: E. Dümmler, ed. 'Nasos (Modoins) Gedichte an Karl den Grossen,' *Neues Archiv* 11 (1896) pp. 77-91.

12. 'Aldhelm's prose writings on metrics', translated by N. Wright, appendix to M. Lapidge and J. Rosier, *Aldhelm: The Poetic Works* (Woodbridge, 1985) pp. 181-219, at pp. 188-9.

13. On the probable reintroduction of these two authors from Italy by Paul the Deacon see Manitius, pp. 270-1, n.5; see also K. Neff, *Die Gedichte des Paulus Diaconus, kritische und erklärende Ausgabe*, Quellen und Untersuchungen zur lateinischen Philologie des Mittelalters III (Munich, 1908) p. 92, poem 19 (note on lines 7-14).

14. On the probable introduction of the works of Ennodius to the Carolingian court by Paul the Deacon, see M. Lapidge, 'The authorship of the Adonic verses "ad Fidolium" attributed to Columbanus', *Studi medievali* 3rd ser. 18 (1977) pp. 815-80, at p. 823.

15. See M. Gibson, 'Boethius in the Carolingian schools', *TRHS* 5th ser. 32 (1982) pp. 43-56 and P. Courcelle, *La Consolation de philosophie dans la tradition littéraire: antécédents et posterité de Boèce* (Paris, 1967) p. 335 and chapter 2: 'Alcuin et la tradition littéraire du IXe au XIIe siècle sur philosophie', pp. 29-66.

16. See Manitius, pp. 171-81 and P. Godman, *Poets and Emperors: Frankish Politics and Carolingian Poetry* (Oxford, 1987) pp. 1-37.

17. On the manuscripts and circulation of Fortunatus see W. Meyer, 'Über Handschriften der Gedichte Fortunats', *Nachrichten von der kgl. Gesellschaft der Wissenschaften zu Göttingen, philol.-hist. Kl.* (1908) pp. 82-114; R. Koebner, *Venantius Fortunatus, Beiträge zur Kulturgeschichte des mittelalters und der Renaissance* 22 (Leipzig, 1915) pp. 125-43; G. Glauche, *Schüllekture im Mittelalter, Münchener Beiträge zur Mediävistik und Renaissance-Forschung* 5 (Munich, 1970) pp. 5-6; M. Lapidge, 'Appendix: knowledge of the poems in the earlier period', *Anglo-Saxon England* 8 (1979) pp. 287-95 at pp. 287-88 (including notes) and Godman, 'Latin poetry under Charles the Bald', p. 294.

18. I have in preparation a study of the patronage of Carolingian verse.

19. On literature produced at courts, see R. R. Bezzola, *Les Origines et la formation de la littérature courtoise en Occident (500-1200)* i, Bibliothèque de l'École des Hautes Etudes 286 (Paris, 1944); P. Riché, 'Le Renouveau culturel à la cour de Pepin III', *Francia* 2 (1974) pp. 59-70 and G. Chiri, *Poesia cortese latina: profilo storico dal V al XII secolo* (Rome, 1954).

20. Norberg, *La Poésie latine rhythmique*, pp. 31-40.

21. MGH Poet. I, pp. 89-90; Bullough, *Age of Charlemagne*, p. 79; pp. 99-101; see also Bullough, 'Aula renovata,' pp. 269-270 and Manitius, pp. 245-7.

22. MGH Poet. I, p. 97 with borrowings from Eugenius of Toledo.

23. J. Fleckenstein, 'Karl der Grosse und sein Hof', *Karl der Grosse* I, pp. 24-50 at pp. 29-30: Herstal, Worms, Quierzy, Thionville, Attigny, Nijmegen.

24. See the discussion by G. Brown, chapter 1 above.

25. K. Neff, *Die Gedichte des Paulus Diaconus*, pp. 71-2.

26. L. Duchesne (ed.), *Liber pontificalis* (2 vols. Paris, 1886-92; vol. 3 with Duchesne's corrections and additions, ed. C. Vogel, Paris, 1957); trans. Raymond Davis, *The Book of Pontiffs. Liber Pontificalis*. Translated Texts for Historians: Latin Series 5 (Liverpool, 1989) and 13 (Liverpool, 1992).

27. MGH Epp. IV, Alcuin letters nos. 43, 47 and 200 (pp. 87-9; 91-2; 330-3).

28. E. Dahlhaus-Berg, *Nova Antiquitas et Antiqua Novitas: typologische Exegese und Isidorianisches Geschichtsbild bei Theodulf von Orléans*, Kölner historische Abhandlungen 23 (Cologne, 1975); D. Schaller, 'Philologische Untersuchungen zu den Gedichten Theodulfs von Orléans', *DA* 18 (1962) pp. 13-91; K. Liersch, 'Die Gedichte Theodulfs, Bischofs von Orléans', diss. phil. Halle-Wittenberg (Halle, 1880); L. Nees, *The Tainted Mantle* (Philadelphia, 1991).

29. MGH Poet. I, pp. 89-90.

30. Manitius, pp. 545-6; L. Traube, 'karolingische Dichtungen', in *Schriften zur Germanischen Philologie* I, ed. M. Roediger (Berlin, 1888) pp. 46-109 at pp. 57-60.

31. For an account of later developments, see P. Godman, 'Louis the Pious and his poets', *Frühmittelalterliche Studien* 19 (1985) pp. 239-89.

32. See K. Liersch, *Die Gedichte Theodulfs Bischofs von Orleans* (Halle, 1880) p. 13; D. Schaller, 'Vortrags- und Zirkulardichtungen am Hof Karls des Grossen,' *Mittellateinisches Jahrbuch* 6 (1970) pp. 14-36 and his 'Poetic rivalries at the court of Charlemagne', in *Classical Influences on European Culture, 500-1500*, ed. R. R. Bolgar (Cambridge, 1973) pp. 151-7; Godman, *Poetry*, pp. 9-13.

33. Alcuin, poem 4, MGH Poet. I, pp. 220-23; trans. H. Waddell, *More Latin Lyrics from Vergil to Milton* (London, 1976) pp. 150-5. For the precise generic description, *Stationsgedicht*, see D. Schaller, 'Vortragsund Zirkulardichtung', pp. 19-20. The poem survives in a manuscript copied at St Denis, the location of its final addressee (Schaller, p. 19, no. 18).

34. MGH Poet. I, p. 222, Alcuin poem 4, lines 37-44.

35. Neff, pp. 181-3 and MGH Poet. I, p. 77, poem 44, lines 21-2; I have emended *confectus* to *confecta*.

36. Neff, p. 86, poem 17, lines 29-30, with discussion in the notes about the identity of the *egregium fratrem*.

37. Ermoldus to Pippin, lines 215-18 of 'Ad eundem Pippinum', ed. with Fr. trans., E. Faral, *Ermold le Noir, poème sur Louis le Pieux et épîtres au Roi Pépin*, Classiques de l'histoire de France au moyen age 14, 2nd edn (Paris, 1964), pp. 218-33 at p. 232, lines 215-18.

38. Modoin's *Ecloga,* prologue, lines 10-11; MGH Poet. I, pp. 384-91; the text was re-edited by Dümmler after the discovery of a new manuscript: 'Nasos (Modoins) Gedichte an Karl den Grossen', *Neues Archiv* 11 (1896), pp. 77-91; ed. R. P. H. Green, *Seven Versions of Carolingian Pastoral,* Reading University Medieval and Renaissance Latin Texts (Reading, 1979) pp. 14-20 and pp. 62-9; D. Korzeniewski, ed., trans., *Hirtengedichte aus Späträmischer und Karolingischer Zeit: Marcus Aurelius Nemesianus, Severus Sanctus Endelechius, Modoinus, Hirtengedicht aus dem Codex Gaddianus* (Darmstadt, 1976) pp. 74-101. Quotation here from prologue, lines 10-11 and see Green, p. 69, for note on line 10. Subsequent references to citations from this poem will be given from the text of Dümmler's *Neues Archiv* edition (unless otherwise specified) in the form 'Ecloga, lines . . . ' Partial text and translation in Godman, *Poetry,* pp. 190-6.

39. Neff, pp. 60-2, poem 12; Godman, *Poetry,* pp. 9-10 and pp. 82-6.

40. Neff, pp. 64-8, poem 13; Schaller, 'Vortrags- und Zirkulardichtungen', Godman, *Poetry,* pp. 9-10 and pp. 86-9.

41. Neff, p. 105, poem 22.

42. D. Schaller, 'Die karolingischen Figurengedichte des Cod. Bern. 212', in: *Medium Aevum Vivum, Festschrift für Walter Bulst,* ed. D. Schaller and H. R. Jauss (Heidelberg, 1960), pp. 22-47 and R. McKitterick, *The Frankish Kingdoms under the Carolingians* (London, 1983) pp. 212-13. On Alcuin's figure-poems, see also H. B. Meyer, 'Crux, Decus es Mundi: Alkuin's Kreuz- und Osterfrömmigkeit', in: *Paschatis Sollemnia: Studien zur Osterfeier und Osterfrömmigkeit,* ed. B. Fischer and J. Wagner (Freiburg, 1959) pp. 96-107.

43. *quia sum inmensis casibus exul:* MGH Poet. I, pp. 480-2, Theodulf, poem 23, line 28. As an additional example of parallel literary endeavour, note that Alcuin and Theodulf both also wrote versions of the fable of the cock and the fox: MGH Poet. I, p. 262 (Alcuin poem 49) and p. 550 (Theodulf, poem 50).

44. The epitaphs written for Hadrian are published in MGH Poet. I, pp. 489-90 and pp. 113-14. Schaller, 'Vortrags- und Zirkulardichtungen'. p. 28 proposed the competition theory; Liersch discussed the two epitaphs and the Theodulf-Alcuin rivalry at pp. 21-2. See also L. Wallach, *Alcuin and Charlemagne* (Ithaca, N.Y., 1959), pp. 178-97.

45. For illustrations of the inscription, see D. Bullough, *The Age of Charlemagne* (1965; 2nd edn, London, 1973), plate 19, facing p. 67 and S. Morison, *Politics and Script: Aspects of Authority and Freedom in the Development of Graeco-Latin Script from the Sixth Century B.C. to the Twentieth Century A.D.* (The Lyell Lectures, Oxford, 1957) ed. N. Barker, (Oxford, 1972) pp. 143-4, pp. 170-2 and illustration at p. 172 (plate 104). The slab itself can still be seen in Rome.

46. Alcuin, MGH Poet. I, p. 326, poem 99 section 17 and Paulus, poem 29, Neff, pp. 121-2; also printed in MGH Poet. I, pp. 56-7, poem 19.

47. *Historia langobardorum,* ed. L. Bethmann and G. Waitz, MGH SRL (Hanover, 1878), section II.xiii, p. 80.

48. D. Schaller, 'Poetic rivalries at the court of Charlemagne', pp. 151-7 and 'Vortrags- und Zirkulardichtung', pp. 14-36; Liersch, pp. 34-46; Godman, *Poetry,* pp. 10-13 and trans. at pp. 118-21, pp. 112-19, and pp. 150-63.

49. MGH Poet. I, Angilbert poem 2, pp. 360-3; text, translation in Godman, *Poetry,* pp. 112-19.

50. MGH Poet. I, Alcuin poem 26, pp. 245-6, lines 48-9. Porridge (or a poultice) as a medicinal preparation is also mentioned earlier in this poem, at line 14.

51. See discussion of this poem above, p. 120. MGH Poet. I, pp. 220-3, Alcuin poem 4, lines 9-10: *In Traiect mel compultim buturque ministrat: / Utpute non oeleum nec vinum Fresia fundit.*' 'In Utrecht he [Hadda] serves you honey with porridge and butter, / Since Frisia doesn't pour forth wine or oil.'

52. MGH Poet. I, p. 245, Alcuin poem 26, lines 18-22 — an excerpt which contradicts the view expressed in the *Vita Alcuini* and followed by some modern scholars that Alcuin grew hostile to secular verse in his old age.

53. P. Lehmann, 'Das literarische Bild Karls des Grossen vornehmlich im lateinischen Schrifttum des Mittelalters', in P. Lehmann, *Erforschung des Mittelalters; ausgewählte Abhandlungen und Aufsätze,* vol. 1 (Stuttgart, 1959), pp. 154-207 at pp. 155-6, observes that absolutely all contemporary Latin historical and occasional poetry depicts Charlemagne panegyrically and that critical characterisation is entirely absent.

54. MGH Poet. I, pp. 483-90, Theodulf poem 25, line 1; trans. Godman, *Poetry,* pp. 150-63.

55. Ibid., lines 13-14.

56. Ibid., lines 131-41 and 191-9.

57. Ibid., line 197; on *Speisemetaphorik,* compare Schaller, 'Vortrags- und Zirkulardichtung', p. 29.

58. MGH Poet. I, pp. 483-90, Theodulf poem 25, lines 205-12.

59. Ibid., lines 213-15.

60. Ibid., lines 224-5.

61. Ibid., lines 237-8, interpreting *reditum* as a discreet reference to patronage; I am grateful to Neil Wright for this point.

62. MGH Poet. I, pp. 360-3; Godman, *Poetry,* pp. 112-19.

63. MGH Poet. I, pp. 396-9, lines 32-5 with a debt to Vergil and Ovid in line 33; Godman, *Poetry,* pp. 174-9.

64. Modoin *Ecloga,* I, lines 45-7.

65. Ibid., lines 95-6.

66. MGH Poet. I, p. 488, Theodulf poem 25, lines 204-5; Godman, *Poetry,* pp. 160-2.

67. The transmission and circulation of Carolingian verse require further investigation. Some studies are: E. Dümmler, 'Die handschriftliche Ueberlieferung der lateinischen Dichtungen aus der Zeit der Karolinger', *Neues Archiv* 4 (1878/9) pp. 87-159; 239-322; 511-582; Traube, 'Karolingische Dichtungen', *Schriften zur Germanischen Philologie* I, ed. M. Roediger (Berlin, 1888); Godman, 'Latin poetry under Charles the Bald,' pp. 293-309 at pp. 294-5.

68. These observations apply primarily to occasional and historical verse rather than to compositions intended to be inscribed in stone.

69. Neff, poem 13, pp. 64-8, stanza 7 and stanza 8 (excerpted); text, trans., Godman, *Poetry,* pp. 88-9.

70. Contrast *Hibernicus Exul's* claims for the golden splendour of verse with Joseph Scottus' *carmen figuratum* where the thing brighter than gold is the four virtues, *Sapientia, Spes, Fides, Veritas:* MGH Poet. I, p. 154, Joseph poem 4, acrostic verses.

71. Modoin, *Ecloga* I, lines 84-90.

72. Green, p. 77, in a note on line 71 of Modoin's poem, cites Ovid, *Tristia* 4.10.41 and Venantius Fortunatus, *Vita Martini,* 1.14; to these I would add Ovid, *Amores* 1.15.9ff. and compare *Versus Fiduciae* (Neff, pp. 182-3), lines 16-19.

73. On Hibernicus Exul, see below, p. 132.

74. On Dicuil, see Manitius, pp. 647-53; and M. Esposito, 'An Irish teacher at the Carolingian court: Dicuil', *Studies* 3 (Dublin, 1914) pp. 651-76; 'An unpublished astronomical treatise by the Irish monk Dicuil', *Proc. Royal Irish Academy,* 26 C (1907) pp. 378-446 and 'A ninth-century astronomical treatise,' *Modern Philology* 18 (1920-21) pp. 177-188, with the reference to the annual tribute at p. 182. These articles have been reprinted in: *Irish Books and Learning in Mediaeval Europe* ed. M. Lapidge (Aldershot, 1990) as article VI, article VII (the text) and article VIII.

75. T. Reuter, 'Plunder and tribute in the Carolingian Empire', *TRHS* 5th ser., 35 (1985) pp. 75-94 at p. 79.

76. Modoin, *Ecloga* I, lines 24-8.

77. Godman, *Poets and Emperors,* p. 85; the theme of new or restored Rome had been a commonplace in earlier panegyrics; see below, notes 83 and 84.

78. *The Paderborn Epic,* also known as 'Karolus Magnus et Leo Papa' has been edited by Dümmler, MGH Poet. I, pp. 366-79 and by H. Beumann, F. Brunhölzl, W. Winkelmann, *Karolus Magnus et Leo Papa, Ein Paderborner Epos vom Jahre 799* (Paderborn, 1966); partial text and translation in Godman, *Poetry,* pp. 197-207.

79. See O. Zwierlein, 'Karolus Magnus — alter Aeneas?' in *Literatur und Sprache im Europaische Mittelalter: Festschrift für Karl Langosch,* ed. A. Önnerfors, J. Rathofer, F. Wagner (Darmstadt, 1973) pp. 44-52.

80. MGH Epp. IV, p. 279, letter 170, lines 22-6, addressed to Charlemagne in 799: 'si, plurimis inclitum vestrae intentionis studium sequentibus, forsan Athenae nova perficeretur in Francia, immo multo excellentior. Quia haec Christi domini nobilitata magisterio omnem achademicae exercitationis superat sapientiam.'

81. Einhard, *Vita Karoli,* ed. O. Holder-Egger MGH SRG (Hanover, 1911); Walahfrid's pref. at pp. xxviii-xxix; Eng. trans. L. Thorpe, *Two Lives of Charlemagne* (Harmondsworth, 1969) pp. 49-50.

82. H. Frederichs made this shrewd observation in *Die Gelehrtenkreis um Karl den Grossen in ihren Schriften, Briefen und Gedichten (Teildruck)* (printed extract of an otherwise unpublished Berlin dissertation) (Berlin, 1931) p. 36.

83. W. Hammer, 'The concept of the New or Second Rome in the Middle Ages', *Speculum* 19 (1944) pp. 50-62; Corippus' use of the phrase in his *In laudem Justini* discussed at p. 52.

84. Godman, *Poets and Emperors,* pp. 20 and 85.

85. Saxons: MGH Poet. I, pp. 380-1.

86. Tassilo: MGH Poet. I, pp. 396-9; partial trans., Godman, *Poetry,* pp. 174-9.

87. Avars: MGH Poet. I, pp. 116-17; text, trans., Godman, *Poetry,* pp. 187-91; trans., H. M. Jones in P. S. Allen, *The Romanesque Lyric: Studies in its Background and Development from Petronius to the Cambridge Songs* (New York, 1928), pp. 231-3.

88. Paderborn Epic: MGH Poet. I, pp. 366-79; *Karolus Magnus et Leo Papa, Ein Paderborner Epos vom Jahre 799,* ed., trans. H. Beumann, F. Brunhölzl, et al. (Paderborn, 1966); partial text, trans. Godman, pp. 197-207 and contrast Alcuin poem 45 (MGH Poet. I, pp. 257-9) and Theodulf, poem 32 (MGH Poet. I, pp. 523-4) which concern the same events.

89. MGH Poet. I, p. 380, lines 48-54 — i.e. seven lines out of the poem's seventy-five.

90. Saxons: MGH Poet. I, p. 380, lines 30-4.

91. MGH Poet. I, p. 116, stanzas 2 and 3; Godman, *Poetry,* pp. 186-9. Following Godman's text, I have emended *tradata* to *tradita.*

92. MGH Poet. I, p. 367, lines 41-6; Godman, *Poetry,* pp. 200-201.

93. MGH Poet. I, p. 381, lines 40-6; with echo of *Aen.* I.204 in line 43.

94. MGH Poet. I, p. 116-17, stanzas 6 and 10; Godman, *Poetry,* p. 188.

95. On the Carolingian appropriation of the Old Testament image of God as the terrifying Lord of Hosts, see E. Rieber, 'Die Bedeutung alttestamentlicher Vorstellungen für das Herrscherbild Karls des Grossen und seines Hof', unpublished Ph.D. dissertation (Tübingen, 1949), p. 105.

96. A. Ebenbauer, *Carmen Historicum: Untersuchungen zur historischen Dichtung im Karolingischen Europa* I, Philologica Germanica 4 (Vienna, 1978).

97. In a review of Ebenbauer's book, T. M. Andersson objected: 'Carolingian verse is chiefly remarkable as a burst of literary energy, not as an arm of sacred history', *Speculum* 55 (1980) p. 115.

98. For an attitude to land apparently similar to the American notion of 'Manifest Destiny', note that the author of the Tassilo-fragment refers to the Bavarian territory as if it was already Frankish: MGH Poet. I, p. 398, line 92: *'nostris arvis.'* Compare the sentiment expressed in Robert Frost's poem 'The Gift Outright' which begins: 'The land was ours before we were the land's / She was our land more than a hundred years / Before we were her people . . . ' and ends with the lines: 'But still unstoried, artless, unenhanced, / Such as she was, such as she would become', *The Poetry of Robert Frost,* ed. E. C. Lathem (1969; reprinted London, 1971) p. 348.

99. On the identification of the Franks with the Chosen People of the Old Testament, see H. H. Anton, *Fürstenspiegel und Herrscherethos in der Karolingerzeit,* Bonner Historische Forschungen 32 (Bonn, 1968) p. 419 and note 266. The comparison emerges in the papal letters of the *Codex Carolinus* and the prologue of the *Lex Salica.* See also J. L. Nelson, 'The Lord's anointed and the people's choice: Carolingian royal ritual', in: *Rituals of Royalty: Power and Ceremonial in Traditional Societies,* ed. D. Cannadine and S. Price (Cambridge, 1987) pp. 137-80 at p. 149.

100. Perhaps the significance of this is just that one harks back to origins at the beginning of any new undertaking. On the use of classical names for people and places during the westward expansion of the US, see W. A. Agard, 'Classics on the midwest frontier', in: *The Frontier in Perspective,* ed. W. D. Wyman and C. B. Kroeber (Madison, Wis., 1957) pp. 165-83 at pp. 166-72.

101. MGH Poet. I, p. 396 and Godman, *Poetry,* pp. 174-7. See Reuter, 'Plunder and Tribute', and Nelson, 'The Lord's anointed', p. 166. Also M. Esposito, 'A ninth-century astronomical treatise', *Modern Philology* 18 (1920-1) pp. 177-88, with the reference to the annual tribute at p. 182.

102. MGH Poet. I, p. 397, lines 34 to 40; Godman, *Poetry,* p. 178.

103. M. McCormick, *Eternal Victory: Triumphal Rulership in Late Antiquity, Byzantium, and the Early Medieval West* (Cambridge, 1986) pp. 360-2. The manuscripts are Willibrord's Calender (BN lat. 10837) from Echternach and a Lorsch calendar from the second half of the ninth century (Vat. pal. lat. 485).

104. There is a facsimile of the manuscript edited by B. Bischoff: *Sammelhandschrift Diez B. Sant. 66, Grammatici latini et catalogus librorum,* Codices selecti phototypice impressi, vol. XLII (Graz, 1973); the Avar Rhythm occurs on fols. 127-8.

105. For the text of the poem: MGH Poet. VI, i, pp. 24-85; *Walter of Aquitaine, Materials for the Study of his Legend,* translations, F. P. Magoun and H. M. Smyser (New London, 1950) at pp. 5-37; also *Waltharius and Ruodlieb,* ed., trans. D. M. Kratz (London, 1984). On the poem's tradition, P. and U. Dronke, *Barbara et antiquissima carmina* (Barcelona, 1977). For the date, see P. Dronke, 'Waltharius and the "Vita Waltharii" ', *Beiträge zur Geschichte der deutschen Sprache und Literatur* 106.3 (1984) pp. 390-402 and *Barbara et antiquissima carmina,* pp. 66-79.

106. On the universally positive depiction of Charlemagne by contemporaries, see Lehmann, 'Das literarische Bild Karls des Grossen vornehmlich im lateinischen Schrifttum des Mittelalters', pp. 155-6; on positive and negative literary depictions of Louis the Pious, see H. Siemes, 'Beiträge zum literarischen Bild Kaiser Ludwigs des Frommen in der Karolingerzeit', unpublished Ph.D. dissertation (Freiburg-in-Breisgau, 1966) and Godman, 'Louis the Pious and his Poets'.

107. Anton, *Fürstenspiegel und Herrscherethos in der Karolingerzeit;* L. K. Born, 'The *specula principis* of the Carolingian Renaissance,' *Revue belge de philologie et d'histoire* 12 (1933) pp. 583-612.

108. MGH Poet. II, pp. 138-9; trans. Godman, *Poetry,* pp. 262-4; H. Waddell, *Mediaeval Latin Lyrics* (1929; reprinted New York, 1948) pp. 102-5 and trans., H. M. Jones in P. S. Allen, *The Romanesque Lyric,* pp. 231-3.

109. MGH Poet. II, p. 559-64; trans., Godman, *Poetry,* pp. 264-73.

110. On the tithe, MGH Epp. IV, p. 289, letter 174; for Alcuin's disapproval of the expedition to Benevento, ibid., letter 211.

111. MGH Epp. IV, p. 352, letter 211: 'Forte quislibet dicit: "Quid ille homo alienis se ingerit rebus"? Non agnoscit nihil mihi alienum vestrae prosperitatis esse debere; quam super salutem corporis mei vel vitae meae longaevitatem diligere me testor.'

112. See D. Bullough, 'Ethnic history and the Carolingians: an alternative reading of Paul the

Deacon's *Historia langobardorum'*, in: *The Inheritance of Historiography 350-900,* ed. C. Holdsworth and T. P. Wiseman, Exeter Studies in History 12 (Exeter, 1986) pp. 85-105 at pp. 96-7, reprinted in D. Bullough, *Carolingian Renewal: Sources and Heritage* (Manchester, 1991) pp. 97-122.

113. M. L. W. Laistner, *Thought and Letters in Western Europe AD 500 to 900,* revised edition (London, 1957) p. 330. P. S. Allen was no more enthusiastic: 'I may not speak for another, but I believe the inevitable sensation which comes from first reading in the volumes of the *Poetae aevi Karolini* is one of bitter disappointment. It is perhaps as if one's hand had reached out half unconsciously for a book of poems and had picked up a table of logarithms instead For the purpose of appreciative comment and aesthetic criticism, the poetry of AD 580-880 is still an insoluble mess.' P. S. Allen, *The Romanesque Lyric* (North Carolina, 1928), p. 214.

114. Acknowledgements: I should like to thank Julia Crick, Matthias Kahl, Michael Lapidge, Rosamond McKitterick, Andy Orchard, Julia Smith and Neil Wright for suggestions and criticisms; of course, I am responsible for all errors that remain. I am also deeply indebted to the work of Dieter Schaller.

Select bibliography

Reference Works

D. Schaller and E. Könsgen, *Initia carminum latinorum saeculo undecimo antiquiorum* (Göttingen, 1977)—this gives an alphabetical list of the *incipits* of Latin verse written before the eleventh century; for each text there is bibliographical information about manuscripts, editions, translations and recent scholarly discussions. For fuller information about the lives, works, printed editions and textual transmission of individual authors, see the articles in *Die deutsche Literatur des Mittelalters: Verfasserlexikon,* ed. K. Ruh, et al. (Berlin, 1978-). Extremely brief, but also useful as a guide to editions and translations is the *Tusculum Lexikon griechischer und lateinischer Autoren des Altertums und des Mittelalters* ed. W. Buchwald, A. Hohlweg and O. Prinz (Munich, 1982). For a concise survey of Charlemagne in medieval Latin verse, see D. Schaller, 'Karl der Grosse in der Dichtung, i. Mittellateinische Literatur', in *Lexikon des Mittelalters* V (Munich, 1991) cols. 961-2.

Primary texts

Most Carolingian Latin verse can be found in the volumes of the MGH Poetae latini medii aevii series: MGH Poet. vols. I (1881) and II (1884), ed. E. Dümmler; vol. III (1886-96), ed. L. Traube, vol. IV.i (1899) ed. P. von Winterfeld; IV.ii (1914), ed. K. Strecker; IV.iii, (1923), ed. K. Strecker; *Nachträge zu den Poetae aevi carolini,* I (1951), ed. K. Strecker and O. Schumann; II (forthcoming), ed. G. Silagi and B. Bischoff. For some texts, more recent editions have superseded those of the

MGH but the volumes of the MGH still provide the most convenient collection for browsing through the whole range of Carolingian Latin verse. Note however K. Neff, *Die Gedichte des Paulus Diaconus, kritische und erklärende Ausgabe,* Quellen und Untersuchungen zur lateinischen Philologie des Mittalalters, III (Munich, 1908) (with interpretation and German translations). For pastoral see: R. P. H. Green, *Seven Versions of Carolingian Pastoral,* Reading University Medieval and Renaissance Latin Texts (Reading, 1979), pp. 14-20, 62-69; also two books by D. Korzeniewski: ed., trans., *Hirtengedichte aus Spätrömischer und Karolingischer Zeit: Marcus Aurelius Nemesianus, Severus Sanctus Endelechius, Modoinus, Hirtengedicht aus dem Codex Gaddianus* (Darmstadt, 1976) and *Hirtengedichte aus Neronischer Zeit: Titus Calpurnius Siculus und die Einsiedler Gedichte* (Darmstadt, 1971).

Literary histories and guides

R. R. Bezzola, *Les Origines et la formation de la littérature courtoise en Occident (500-1200),* I, Bibliothèque de l'Ecole des Hautes Etudes 286 (Paris, 1944)

F. Brunhölzl, *Geschichte der lateinischen Literatur des Mittelalters* I (Munich, 1975)

E. R. Curtius, *European Literature and the Latin Middle Ages,* Eng. trans. W. Trask (London, 1953)

K. Hauck, *Kirchengeschichte Deutschlands,* vol. II, 3rd/4th edn (Leipzig, 1912)

M. Hélin, *A History of Medieval Latin Literature,* revised edn trans. J. C. Snow (N.Y., 1949)

M. L. W. Laistner, *Thought and Letters in Western Europe AD 500-900* (1931, revised edn London, 1957)

M. Manitius, *Geschichte der lateinischen Literatur des Mittelalters,* vol. I (Munich, 1911)

M. R. P. McGuire and H. Dressler, *Introduction to Medieval Latin Studies: A Syllabus and Bibliographical Guide,* 2nd edn (Washington, 1977)

D. Norberg, *Manuel pratique de latin médiéval* (Paris, 1968)

F. J. E. Raby, *A History of Christian-Latin Poetry from the Beginnings to the Close of the Middle Ages.* 2nd edn (Oxford, 1953)

————. *A History of Secular Latin Poetry in the Middle Ages,* 2 vols, vol. I, 2nd edn (Oxford, 1967)

L. D. Reynolds, et al., *Texts and Transmission: A Survey of the Latin Classics,* 3rd edn (Oxford, 1991)

K. Strecker, *Introduction to Medieval Latin,* trans., revised by R. B. Palmer (Berlin, 1957)

H. Waddell, *The Wandering Scholars* (1927, revised, reprinted London, 1958)

Some Carolingian verse available in English translation

P. S. Allen, *The Romanesque Lyric,* with translations by H. M. Jones (1928, reprinted N.Y., 1969) [To be read with caution]

P. Goodman, *Poetry of the Carolingian Renaissance* (London, 1985) [The fullest selection]

H. Waddell, *Mediaeval Latin Lyrics* (1929; reprinted N.Y., 1948)

————. *More Latin Lyrics from Vergil to Milton* (London, 1976)

Discussions

R. Collins, 'Poetry in ninth-century Spain', *Papers of the Liverpool Latin Seminar* 4 (ARCA Classical and Medieval Texts, Papers and Monographs, 11) pp. 181-95

H. Cooper, *Pastoral: Mediaeval into Renaissance* (Ipswich, 1972)

P. Dronke, *Women Writers of the Middle Ages: A Critical Study of Texts from Perpetua (d. 203) to Marguerite Porete (d. 1310)* (Cambridge, 1984)

P. and U. Dronke, *Barbara et antiquissima carmina* (Barcelona, 1977) [On *Waltharius*]

R. Folz, *Le Souvenir et la légende de Charlemagne dans l'empire germanique mediéval* (Paris, 1950)

P. Godman, 'Latin poetry under Charles the Bald and Carolingian poetry', in: *Charles the Bald: Court and Kingdom,* ed. M. T. Gibson and J. L. Nelson, BAR International Series 101 (London, 1981) pp. 293-309

————. 'Louis the Pious and his Poets', *Frühmittelalterliche Studien* 19 (1985) pp. 239-89

————. *Poets and Emperors: Frankish Politics and Carolingian Poetry* (Oxford, 1987)

M. Lapidge, 'The authorship of the adonic verses "ad Fidolium" attributed to Columbanus', *Studi medievali* 3rd ser. 18 (1977) pp. 815-80

P. Lehmann, 'Das literarische Bild Karls des Grossen vornehmlich im lateinischen Schrifttum des Mittelalters', in his *Erforschung des Mittelalters: ausgewählte Abhandlungen und Aufsätze,* vol. I (Stuttgart, 1959) pp. 154-207

F. P. Magoun and H. M. Smyser (trans.), *Walter of Aquitaine, Materials for the Study of his Legend* (New London, 1950)

L. Nees, *The Tainted Mantle* (Philadelphia, 1991) [On Theodulf]

D. Schaller, 'Poetic Rivalries at the Court of Charlemagne', in: *Classical Influences on European Culture 500-1500,* ed. R. R. Bolgar (Cambridge, 1973)

——————

FURTHER READING

Bibliographies

Farrier, Susan E. *The Medieval Charlemagne Legend: An Annotated Bibliography,* New York: Garland Publishing, Inc., 1993, 646 p.

Divides its study into three broad groupings: The Historical Charlemagne, Between History and Legend (Medieval Biography and Chronicle), and Charlemagne Literature, and further into twenty-seven subcategories to aid scholars.

Biographies

Almedingen, E. M. *Charlemagne: A Study,* London: The Bodley Head, 1968, 252 p.

Biography considers Frankish history, the country as Charlemagne found it, and Charlemagne's faith in God and allegiance to Christ's Church.

Cabaniss, Allen. *Charlemagne.* New York: Twayne Publishers, 1972, 176 p.

Biography incorporates many Latin sources.

Chamberlin, Russell. *Charlemagne: Emperor of the Western World.* London: Grafton Books, 1986, 245 p.

Biography in three parts: "The Cauldron of Europe," "The Road to Rome," and "Imperium."

Einhard. *The Life of Charlemagne, Circa 830-33.* Ann Arbor: The University of Michigan Press, 1960, 74 p.

Classic work is the first medieval biography of a lay figure; originally written in Latin.

Ganshof, François L. "Charlemagne," *Speculum* XXIV, No. 4 (October 1949): 520-28.

Describes the different phases of Charlemagne's reign and evaluates him as a statesman.

Halphen, Louis. *Charlemagne and the Carolingian Empire.* 1947. Translated by Giselle de Nie. Amsterdam: North-Holland Publishing Company, 1977, 366 p.

Biography includes detailed account of the Carolingian empire in the ninth century.

Loyn, H. R. and John Percival. *The Reign of Charlemagne: Documents on Carolingian Government and Administration.* London: Edward Arnold, 1975, 164 p.

Provides translations of original source material divided into four categories: Biographies and Annals, Capitularies, Letters, and Charters and Allied Material.

Notker the Stammerer. *Charlemagne.* Circa 884-87. In *Two Lives of Charlemagne.* Translated by Lewis Thorpe. Baltimore: Penguin Books, 1969, 227 p.

Classic work treats Charlemagne's life in a series of anecdotes.

Criticism

Fleischman, Suzanne. "A Linguistic Perspective on the *Laisses Similaires*: Orality and the Pragmatics of Narrative Discourse," *Romance Philology* XLIII, No. 1 (August 1989): 70-89.

> Linguistic study of the Song of Roland analyzes the discourse-pragmatic functions of its repetitive overlay structure.

Grigsby, John L. "A Note On the Genre of the *Voyage de Charlemagne*," in *Essays In Early French Literature Presented To Barbara M. Craig*, pp. 1-8. Edited by Norris J. Lacy and Jerry C. Nash. York, S.C.: French Literature Publications Company, 1982.

> Explores the nature of genres, and declares that the *Voyage de Charlemagne* created a new genre, that of the *gab*.

Heinemann, Edward A. "Network of Narrative Details: The Motif of the Journey in the *Chanson de Geste*," in *The Epic in Medieval Society: Aesthetic and Moral Values*, pp. 178-92. Edited by Harald Scholler. Tübingen, Germany: Max Niemeyer Verlag, 1977.

> Outlines the components of the motif of the *chanson de geste*.

Kay, Sarah. "The Nature of Rhetoric in the *Chanson de Geste*," *Zeitschrift für Romanische Philologie* 94, No. 3/4 (1978): 305-20.

> Explores the distinctive character of the rhetoric used in some Old French epic poems.

Sturm, Sara. "The Stature of Charlemagne in the *Pèlerinage*," *Studies in Philology* LXXI, No. 1 (January 1974): 1-18.

> Contends that the question of stature in the *Pèlerinage* concerns physical height and not spiritual or moral stature.

Cnaeus Naevius
c. 270 B.C.-c. 201 B.C.

Latin dramatist and epic poet.

INTRODUCTION

The inventor of the Roman historical play and the writer of the first truly Roman epic, the *Bellum Punicum*, Naevius was a politically outspoken author of both tragedies and comedies. His work is extant only in fragments, but based on what remains, critics consider him an original and independent writer. He is credited with breaking away from Greek subjects in drama, practicing *contaminatio,* (combining two plots from other works into a single new piece), advancing the use of musical accompaniment on stage, and for aiming his stinging satire and sarcasm at, among others, the leaders of Rome.

BIOGRAPHICAL INFORMATION

It is uncertain whether or not the Latin poet was a native of Rome. A remark by Aulus Gellius about Naevius's epitaph demonstrating "Campanian pride" is ambiguous, as the term could be proverbial or factual, but Henry T. Rowell has argued convincingly that Naevius was indeed born in the city of Capua in Campania. Little is known of Naevius's life. It is known that he was born into a plebeian family and soldiered towards the end of the first Punic War, which lasted from 264 B.C. to 241 B.C. Naevius first began presenting plays around 235-31 B.C. Not long after 222 B.C. he originated the *fabula praetexta* or Roman historical play, with *Clastidium,* which concerned Marcus Claudius Marcellus's victory in 222 B.C. over the Gallic Viridomarus. The *Bellum Punicum* was written when Naevius was fairly old, possibly around 210 B.C. Naevius used his plays as opportunities to systematically abuse prominent Roman statesmen. A remark, now infamous, offended the house of Metelli: *"Fato Metelli Romai fiunt consules."* Tenney Frank, among others, explains that the line can be understood in either of two different ways, or more likely both at the same time: "The Metelli became consuls at Rome by chance" or "The Metelli became consuls to Rome's sorrow." The reply by Lucius Caecilius Metellus, the Metullus in charge in 206 B.C., threatened: *"Debunt malum Metelli Naeuio poetae"* ("The Metelli will give misfortune to the poet Naevius"). Naevius was imprisoned about 204 B.C. and, while held captive, wrote two plays, *Ariolus* and *Leon,* apologizing in each work for his hurtful remarks. Seemingly repentant and with the help of his peer Plautus, Naevius was released by the *tribuni plebis.* Soon, however, he offended the aristocracy again and was banished from Rome and Italy. He settled in Utica, in northern Africa, where he died around 201 B.C.

MAJOR WORKS

Naevius's many works exist only in fragments. Seven titles of his tragedies are known, and from them only about sixty lines remain. The titles are *Aesiona* or *Hesione, Andromache, Danaë, Equos Troianus, Hector Proficiscens, Iphigenia,* and *Lycurgus.* Most of the surviving fragments seem to come from the *Lycurgus.* Little can be ascertained except they appear to be adaptations of Greek dramas. Naevius used Roman history in writing his *Clastidium* and *Romulus,* or *Alimonium Romuli et Remi.* Not enough of the latter survives to comment upon except that it likely dealt with the legendary origins of Rome. Thirty-four titles of comedies by Naevius are known, comprising about one hundred and thirty lines. Nothing in the line of narrative or plot can be determined from their scarce remains, but J. Wight Duff has written that "there is enough to illustrate that observation of character which, combined with a fondness for mordant innuendos and unwelcome exposures, made his plays amusing to the plebeian and sometimes too spicy for the noble." The titles—which are all that exist for the majority of them—are *Acontizomenos, Agitatoria, Agryphontes, Appella, Ariolus, Astiologa, Carbonaria, Colax, Commotria, Corollaria, Dementes, Demetrius, Dolus, Figulus, Glaucoma, Gymnasticus, Hariolus, Lampadio, Leon, Ludus, Nagido, Nautae, Nervolaria, Paelex, Personata, Projectus, Quadrigemini, Stalagmonissa, Stigmatias, Tarentilla, Technicus, Tribacelus, Triphallus,* and *Tunicularia.* Naevius drew from his experiences in the Punic War while composing the *Bellum Punicum,* an epic in Saturnian verse (a native Italian meter) that traces the history of Rome. Less than eighty lines of it survive. Originally written as one piece, the book was divided into seven by C. Octavius Lampadio sometime in the second century B.C.

CRITICAL RECEPTION

Naevius appears to have been regarded rather highly in his time and influenced Ennius. The Roman critic Volcatius Sedigitus considered him, circa 100 B.C., third best in his list of authors of comedy. While some scholars balk at this assessment, determining the true merits of Naevius's verse is not possible due to its fragmentary state. Many of his lines have been preserved only by virtue of being quoted in the texts of grammarians as examples; critics have pointed out that it is highly unlikely that the cited examples are typical Naevius. Thelma B. De Graff, however, believes there is sufficient material to render judgment. In examining his most famous line, *"Fato Metelli Romae fiunt consules,"* she writes that "there is a sting more deadly than the sting which lurks at the close of Martial's most bitter epigram. Only a man whose pride and self-assurance were boundless would have been capable of such an utterance against a member of the aristocracy in the Roman oligarchy of the third century B.C." She adds that Naevius had a glorious spirit and the gift of vigorous expression. The value of the *Bellum Punicum* is reflected in the fact that it strongly influenced the poet Vergil. In addition to debating Naevius's overall merit as a writer, scholars argue over the proper assignation of fragments to the *Bellum Punicum*. Rowell, for example, has taken issue with earlier reconstruction attempts and advocates a method employing rigorous testing with due consideration of both the textual tradition and the implications of a new order.

PRINCIPAL WORKS

Principal English Translations

Remains of Old Latin, Vol. II (translated by E. H. Warmington) 1936

Bronze and Iron: Old Latin Poetry from Its Beginnings to 100 B.C. (translated by Janet Lembke) 1973

CRITICISM

Leonhard Schmitz (essay date 1877)

SOURCE: "Cn. Naevius" in *A History of Latin Literature*, William Collins, Sons, & Company, 1877, pp. 24-5.

[*In the following excerpt, Schmitz provides a brief summary of Naevius's life and importance.*]

I

. . . Cn. Nævius was a native of Campania, but probably a Latin, though not a Roman citizen, as in this case he could hardly have been treated by his enemies with the severity he had to submit to. He produced his first plays on the Roman stage in B.C. 235. He had served as a soldier in the first Punic war. As a poet he followed, on the whole, the example of Livius Andronicus, but preferred comedy to tragedy; and as a Campanian he seems to have been of a somewhat fiery and independent disposition, and unconcerned as to whom he might offend by the sallies of his wit. He thus drew upon himself the enmity of the proud Roman aristocrats, especially of the Metelli, whom he offended by the line—

"Fato Metelli Romai fiunt consules."

In consequence of this he was thrown into prison and afterwards sent into exile. He died at Utica, in Africa, about B.C. 199, or, according to Cicero, somewhat earlier.

Nævius was a man animated by a truly national spirit, and introduced into dramatic literature the kind of comedy known by the name *prætextatæ* or *togatæ,* that is, comedies in which the chief characters were Romans, in short national characters, as opposed to *palliatæ, i.e.,* comedies of which the characters were Greek, and which were either translations or adaptations from the Greek. This national spirit of the poet gained for his works a popularity which lasted several centuries, and which, if we may judge from the few fragments that have reached our time, was well deserved. We know the titles of about seven tragedies and of about thirty-six comedies that are ascribed to him.

In his later years, Nævius wrote an epic poem on the first Punic war, in the old Saturnian metre, which was subsequently divided by grammarians into seven books; the first two contained the early history of Rome, and the remaining five gave an account of the Punic war. The style of the work was plain and simple, somewhat resembling that of our rhyming chronicles. . . .

W. Y. Sellar (essay date 1881)

SOURCE: "The Beginning of Roman Literature—Livius Andronicus—Cn. Naevius, B.C. 240-202" in *The Roman Poets of the Republic*, Clarendon Press, 1881, pp. 47-61.

[*In the following excerpt, Sellar discusses the importance of Greek literature as the model for early Roman literature and praises Naevius's Latin for its vigor and purity.*]

The historical event which first brought the Romans into familiar contact with the Greeks, was the war with Pyrrhus and with Tarentum, the most powerful and flourishing among the famous Greek colonies in lower Italy. In earlier times, indeed, through their occasional communication with the Greeks of Cumae, and the other colonies in Italy, they had obtained a vague knowledge of some of the legends of Greek poetry. The worship of Aesculapius was introduced at Rome from Epidaurus in B.C. 293, and the oracle of Delphi had been consulted by the Romans in still earlier times. As the Sibylline verses appear to have been composed in Greek, their interpreters must have been either Greeks or men acquainted with that language.[1] The identification of the Greek with the Roman mythology had probably commenced before Greek literature was known to the Romans, although the works of Naevius and Ennius must have had an influence in completing this process. Greek civilisation had come, however, at an earlier period into close relation with the south of Italy; and the natives of that district, such as Ennius and Pacuvius, who first settled at Rome, were spoken of by the Romans as 'Semi Graeci.' But, until after the fall of Tarentum, there appears to have been no familiar intercourse between the two great representatives of ancient civilisation. Till the war with Pyrrhus, the knowledge that the two nations had of one another was slight and vague. But, immediately after that time, the affairs of Rome began to attract the attention of Greek historians[2], and the Romans, though very slowly, began to obtain some acquaintance with the language and literature of Greece.

Tarentum was taken in B.C. 272, but more than thirty years elapsed before Livius Andronicus represented his first drama before a Roman audience. Twenty years of this intervening period, from B.C. 261 to B.C. 241, were occupied with the First Punic War; and it was not till the successful close of that war, and the commencement of the following years of peace, that this new kind of recreation and instruction was made familiar to the Romans.

> Serus enim Graecis admovit acumina chartis;
> Et post Punica bella quietus, quaerere coepit
> Quid Sophocles et Thespis et Aeschylus utile ferrent[3].

Two circumstances, however, must in the meantime have prepared the minds of the Romans for the reception of the new literature. Sicily had been the chief battle-field of the contending powers. In their intercourse with the Sicilian Greeks, the Romans had great facilities for becoming acquainted with the Greek language, and frequent opportunities of being present at dramatic representations. Many Greeks also had been brought to Rome as slaves after the capture of Tarentum, and were employed in educating the young among the higher classes. Thus many Roman citizens were prepared, by their circumstances and education, to take interest in the legends and in the dramatic form of literature introduced from Greece; while the previous existence of the saturae, and other scenic exhibitions at Rome, tended to make the new drama acceptable to the great mass of the population.

The earliest period of Roman poetry extends from the close of the First Punic War till the beginning of the first century B.C. During this period of about a century and a half, in which Roman oratory, history, and comedy, were also actively cultivated, we hear only of five or six names as eminent in different kinds of serious poetry. The whole labour of introducing and of keeping alive, among an unlettered people, some taste for the graver forms of literature thus devolved upon a few men of ardent temperament, vigorous understanding, and great productive energy; but with little sense of art, and endowed with faculties seemingly more adapted to the practical business of life than to the idealising efforts of genius. They had to struggle against the difficulties incidental to the first beginnings of art and to the rudeness of the Latin language. They were exposed, also, to other disadvantages, arising from the natural indifference of the mass of the people to all works of imagination, and from the preference of the educated class for the more finished works already existing in Greek literature.

Yet this long period, in which poetry, with so much difficulty and such scanty resources, struggled into existence at Rome, is connected with the age of Cicero by an unbroken line of literary continuity. Naevius, the younger contemporary of Livius, and the first native poet, was actively engaged in the composition of his poems till the time of his death; about which period his greater successor first appeared at Rome. For about thirty years, Ennius shone alone in epic and tragic poetry. The poetic successor of Ennius was his nephew, Pacuvius. He, in the later years of his life, lived in friendly intercourse with his younger rival Accius, who, again, in his old age, had frequently conversed with Cicero[4]. The torch, which was first lighted by Livius Andronicus from the decaying fires of Greece, was thus handed down by these few men, through this long period, until it was extinguished during the stormy times which fell in the youth of the great orator and prose writer of the Republic.

The forms of serious poetry, prevailing during this period, were the tragic drama, the annalistic epic, and satire. Tragedy was earliest introduced, was received with most favour, and was cultivated by all the poets of the period, with the exception of Lucilius and the comic writers. The epic poetry of the age was the work of Naevius and Ennius. It has greater claims to originality and national spirit, both in form and substance, and it exercised a more powerful influence on the later poetry of Rome, than either the tragedy or comedy of the time. The invention of satire, the most purely original of the three, is generally attributed to Lucilius; but the satiric spirit was shown earlier in some of the dramas of Naevius; and the first modification of the primitive satura to a literary shape was the work of Ennius, who was followed in the same style by his nephew Pacuvius.

No complete work of any of these poets has been preserved to modern times. Our knowledge of the epic, tragic, and satiric poetry of this long period is derived partly from ancient testimony, but chiefly from the examination of numerous fragments. Most of these have been preserved, not by critics on account of their beauty and worth, but by grammarians on account of the obsolete words and forms of speech contained in them,—a fact, which probably leads us to attribute to the earlier literature a more abnormal and ruder style than that which really belonged to it. A few of the longest and most interesting fragments have come down in the works of the admirers of those ancient poets, especially of Cicero and Aulus Gellius. The notion that can be formed of the early Roman literature must thus, of necessity, be incomplete. Yet these fragments are sufficient to produce a consistent impression of certain prevailing characteristics of thought and sentiment. Many of them are valuable from their own intrinsic worth; others again from the grave associations connected with their antiquity, and from the authentic evidence they afford of the moral and intellectual qualities, the prevailing ideas and sympathies of the strongest race of the ancient world, about, or shortly after, the time when they attained the acme of their moral and political greatness.

The two earliest authors who fill a period of forty years in the literary history of Rome, extending from the end of the

First to the end of the Second Punic War, are Livius Andronicus and Cn. Naevius. Of the first very little is known. The fragments of his works are scanty and unimportant, and have been preserved by grammarians merely as illustrative of old forms of the language. The admirers of Naevius and Ennius, in ancient times, awarded only scanty honours to the older dramatist. Cicero, for instance, says of his plays 'that they are not worth reading a second time[5].' There is no ground for believing that Livius was a man of original genius. The importance which attaches to him consists in his being the accidental medium through which literary art was first introduced to the Romans. He was a Greek, and, as is generally supposed, a native of Tarentum. If he was among the captives taken after the fall of that city, he must have resided thirty years at Rome before he ventured to reproduce a Greek drama in the Latin language. He educated the sons of his master, M. Livius Salinator, from whom he afterwards received his freedom. The last thirty years of his life were devoted to literature, and chiefly to the reproduction of the Greek drama in a Latin dress. His tragedies appear all to have been founded on Greek subjects; most of them, probably, were translations. Among the titles, we hear of the *Aegisthus, Ajax, Equus Trojanus, Tereus, Hermione,* etc.—all of them subjects which continued to be popular with the later tragedians of Rome. No fragment is preserved sufficient to give any idea of his treatment of the subjects, or of his general mode of thought and feeling. Little can be gathered from the scanty remains of his works, except some idea of the harshness and inelegance of his diction.

In addition to his dramas, he translated the Odyssey into Saturnian verse. This work long retained its place as a school-book, and is spoken of by Horace as forming part of his own early lessons under the rod of Orbilius[6]. One or two lines of the translation still remain, and exemplify its bald and prosaic diction, and the extreme irregularity of the Saturnian metre. The lines of the Odyssey . . . [7]

are thus rendered:—

> Namque nilum pejus
> Macerat hemonem, quamde mare saevom, viris quoi
> Sunt magnae, topper confringent importunae undae.

He was appointed also, on one occasion, near the end of the Second Punic War, to compose a hymn to be sung by 'virgines ter novenae,' which is described by Livy, the historian, as rugged and unpolished.[8]

Livius was the schoolmaster of the Roman people rather than the father of their literature. To accomplish what he did required no original genius, but only the industry, knowledge, and tastes of an educated man. If his long residence among his grave and stern masters, and the hardships and constraint of slavery, had subdued in him the levity and gaiety of a Tarentine Greek, they did not extinguish his love of his native literature and the intellectual cultivation peculiar to his race. In spite of the disadvantage of writing in a foreign language, and of addressing an unlettered people, he was able to give the direction which Roman poetry long followed, and to awaken a new interest in the legends and heroes of his race. It was necessary that the Romans should be educated before they could either produce or appreciate an original poet. Livius performed a useful, if not a brilliant service, by directing those who followed him to the study and imitation of the great masters who combined, with an unattainable grace and art, a masculine strength and heroism of sentiment congenial to the better side of Roman character.

Cn. Naevius is really the first in the line of Roman poets, and the first writer in the Latin language whose fragments give indication of original power. He is believed to have been a Campanian by birth, on the authority of Aulus Gellius, who characterised his famous epitaph as 'plenum superbiae Campanae.' Though the arrogance of Campania may have been proverbial, yet the expression could scarcely with propriety have been applied, except to a native of that district. If not a Roman by birth, he at least belonged to a district which had become thoroughly Latinised long before his time, and he showed himself to be, like his successor Ennius, thoroughly Roman in his sympathies. He served as a soldier in the First Punic War, and recorded his services in his epic poem on that subject. The earliest drama of Naevius was brought out in B.C. 235, five years after the first representation of Livius Andronicus. The number of dramas which he is known to have composed affords proof of great industry and activity, from that time till the time of his banishment from Rome. He was more successful in comedy than in tragedy, and he used the stage, as it had been used by the writers of the old Attic comedy, as an arena of popular invective and political warfare. A keen partisan of the commonalty, he attacked with vehemence some of the chiefs of the great senatorian party. A line, which had passed into a proverb in the time of Cicero, is attributed to him,—

> Fato Metelli Romae Fiunt consules;

to which the Metelli are said to have replied in the pithy Saturnian,

> Dabunt malum Metelli Naevio poetae.

It is, however, doubted whether the first of these lines was really written by Naevius, as the Metelli did not enjoy their rapid succession of consulships till nearly a century after his death; but even at the time of the Second Punic War they were powerful enough to procure the imprisonment of the poet, in consequence of some offence which he had given them. Plautus[9] alludes to this event, in one of the few passages in which Latin comedy deviates from the conventional life of Athenian manners to notice the actual circumstances of the time. While in prison, he composed two plays (the **Hariolus** and **Leon**), which contained some retractation of his former attacks, and he was liberated through the interference of the Tribunes of the Commons. Being afterwards banished, he took up his residence at

Utica, where he is said by Cicero, on the authority of ancient records, to have died, in B.C. 204,[10] though the same author adds that Varro, 'diligentissimus investigator antiquitatis,' believed that he was still alive for some time after that date.[11] It is inferred, from a passage in Cicero,[12] that his poem on the First Punic War was composed in his old age. Probably it was written in his exile, when removed from the sphere of his active literary efforts. As he served in that war, some time between B.C. 261 and B.C. 241, he must have been well advanced in years at the time of his death.

The best known of all the fragments of Naevius, and the most favourable specimen of his style, is his epitaph:—

> Mortales immortales flere si foret fas,
> Flerent divae Camenae Naevium poetam,
> Itaque postquam est Orcino traditus thesauro,
> Obliti sunt Romae loquier Latina lingua.

It has been supposed that this epitaph was written as a dying protest against the Hellenising influence of Ennius; but as Ennius came to Rome for the first time about B.C. 204, it is not likely, even if the life of Naevius was prolonged somewhat beyond that date, that the fame and influence of his younger rival could have spread so rapidly as to disturb the peace of the old poet in his exile. It might as fairly be regarded as proceeding from a jealousy of the merits of Plautus, as from hostility to the innovating tendency of Ennius. The words of the epitaph are simply expressive of the strong self-assertion and independence which Naevius maintained till the end of his active and somewhat turbulent career.

He wrote a few tragedies, of which scarcely anything is known except the titles,—such as the ***Andromache, Equus Trojanus, Hector Proficiscens, Lycurgus,***—the last founded on the same subject as the Bacchae of Euripides. The titles of nearly all these plays, as well as of the plays of Livius, imply the prevailing interest taken in the Homeric poems, and in all the events connected with the Trojan War. The following passage from the Lycurgus has some value as containing the germs of poetical diction:—

> Vos, qui regalis corporis custodias
> Agitatis, ite actutum in frundiferos locos,
> Ingenio arbusta ubi nata sunt, non obsita.[13]

He composed a number of comedies, and also some original plays, founded on events in Roman history,—one of them called ***Romulus,*** or ***Alimonia Romuli et Remi.*** The longest of the fragments attributed to him is a passage from a comedy, which has been, with less probability, attributed to Ennius. It is a description of a coquette, and shows considerable power of close satiric observation:—

> Quasi pila
> In choro ludens dadatim dat se, et communem facit:
> Alii adnutat, alii adnictat, alium amat, alium tenet;
> Alibi manus est occupata, alii percellit pedem;
> Alii spectandum dat annulum; a labris alium invocat;
> Cum alio cantat, attamen dat alii digito literas.[14]

The chief characteristic illustrated by the scanty fragments of his dramas is the political spirit with which they were animated. Thus Cicero[15] refers to a passage in one of his plays (*ut est in Naevii ludo*) where, to the question, 'Who had, within so short a time, destroyed your great commonwealth?' the pregnant answer is given,

> Proveniebant oratores novi, stulti adolescentuli.

The nobles, whose enmity he provoked, were probably attacked by him in his comedies. One passage is quoted by Aulus Gellius, in which a failing of the great Scipio is exposed.[16] Other fragments are found indicative of his freedom of speech and bold independence of character:—

> Quae ego in theatro hic meis probavi plausibus,
> Ea nunc audere quemquam regem rumpere?
> Quanto libertatem hanc hic superat servitus?[17]

and this also[18]:—

> Semper pluris feci potioremque ego
> Libertatem habui multo quam pecuniam.

He is placed in the canon of Volcatius Sedigitus immediately after Plautus in the rank of comic poets. He has more of the stamp of Lucilius than of his immediate successor Ennius. By his censorious and aggressive vehemence, by boldness and freedom of speech, and by his strong political feeling, Naevius in his dramas represents the spirit of Roman satire rather than of Roman tragedy. He holds the same place in Roman literature as the Tribune of the Commons in Roman politics. He expressed the vigorous independence of spirit that supported the Commons in their long struggle with the patricians, while Ennius may be regarded as expressing the majesty and authority with which the Roman Senate ruled the world.

But the work on which his fame as a national and original poet chiefly rested was his epic or historical poem on the First Punic War. The poem was originally one continuous work, written in the Saturnian metre; though, at a later time, it was divided into seven books. The earlier part of the work dealt with the mythical origin of Rome and of Carthage, the flight of Aeneas from Troy, his sojourn at the court of Dido, and his settlement in Latium. The mythical background of the poem afforded scope for imaginative treatment and invention. Its main substance, however, appears to have been composed in the spirit and tone of a contemporary chronicle. The few fragments that remain from the longer and later portion of the work, evidently express a bare and literal adherence to fact, without any poetical colouring or romantic representation.

Ennius and Virgil are both known to have borrowed much from this poem of Naevius. There are many passages in the Aeneid in which Virgil followed, with slight deviations, the track of the older poet. Naevius (as quoted by Servius) introduced the wives of Aeneas and of Anchises, leaving Troy in the night-time,—

> Amborum
> Uxores noctu Troiade exibant capitibus
> Opertis, flentes abeuntes lacrimis cum multis.

He represents Aeneas as having only one ship, built by Mercury,—a limitation which did not suit Virgil's account of the scale on which the war was carried on, after the landing in Italy. The account of the storm in the first Aeneid, of Aeneas consoling his followers, of Venus complaining to Jupiter, and of his comforting her with the promise of the future greatness of Rome (one of the cardinal passages in Virgil's epic), were all taken from the old Saturnian poem of Naevius. He speaks also of Anna and Dido, as daughters of Agenor, though there is no direct evidence that he anticipated Virgil in telling the tale of Dido's unhappy love. He mentioned also the Italian Sibyl and the worship of the Penates—materials which Virgil fused into his great national and religious poem. Ennius followed Naevius in representing Romulus as the grandson of Aeneas. The exigencies of his chronology compelled Virgil to fill a blank space of three hundred years with the shadowy forms of a line of Alban kings.

Whatever may have been the origin of the belief in the connexion of Rome with Troy, it certainly prevailed before the poem of Naevius was composed, as at the beginning of the First Punic War the inhabitants of Egesta opened their gates to Rome, in acknowledgment of their common descent from Troy. But the story of the old connexion of Aeneas and Dido, symbolising the former league and the later enmity between Romans and Carthaginians, most probably first assumed shape in the time of the Punic Wars. The belief, as shadowed forth in Naevius, that the triumph of Rome had been decreed from of old by Jupiter, and promised to the mythical ancestress of Aeneas, proves that the Romans were possessed already with the idea of their national destiny. How much of the tale of Aeneas and Dido is due to the imagination of Naevius it is impossible to say; but his treatment of the mythical part of his story,—his introduction of the storm, the complaint of Venus, etc.,—merits the praise of happy and suggestive invention, and of a real adaptation to his main subject. There was more meaning in the mythical foreshadowing of the deadly strife between Romans and Carthaginians, at a time when the two nations were fighting for their very existence, and for the ultimate prize of the empire of the world, than in the age of Virgil, when the power of Carthage was only a memory of the past, and the immediate danger from which Rome had escaped had arisen not so much from any foreign enemy, as from the fierce passions of her own sons.

The mythical part of the poem was a prelude to the main subject, the events of the First Punic War. Naevius and Ennius, like others among the Roman poets of a later date, allowed the provinces of poetry and of history to run into one another. They composed poetical chronicles without any attempt to adhere to the principles and practice of the Greek epic. The work of Naevius differed from that of Ennius in this respect, that it treated of one particular portion of Roman history, and did not profess to unfold the whole annals of the State. The slight and scanty fragments that remain from the latter part of the poem, are expressed with all the bareness, and, apparently, with the fidelity of a chronicle. They have the merit of being direct and vigorous, but are entirely without poetic grace and ornament. Rapid and graphic condensation is their chief merit. There is a dash of impetuosity in some of them, suggestive of the bold, impatient, and energetic temperament of the poet; as for instance in the lines

> Transit-Melitam Romanus exercitus, insulam integram
> Urit, populatur, vastat, rem hostium concinnat[19].

But the fragments of the poem are really too unimportant to afford ground for a true estimate of its general merit. They supply some evidence in regard to the irregularity of the metre in which it was written. The uncertainty which prevails as to its structure may be inferred from the fact that different conjectural readings of every fragment are proposed by different commentators. A saying of an old grammarian, Atilius Fortunatianus, is quoted to the effect that he could not adduce from the whole poem of Naevius any single line, as a normal specimen of the pure Saturnian verse. Cicero bears strong testimony to the merits of the poem in point of style. He says in one place, 'the Punic War delights us like a work of Myron[20].' In the dialogue 'De Oratore,' he represents Crassus as comparing the idiomatic purity which distinguished the conversation of his mother-in-law, Laelia, and other ladies of rank, with the style of Plautus and Naevius, 'Equidem quum audio socrum meam Laeliam (facilius enim mulieres incorruptam antiquitatem conservant, quod, multorum sermonis expertes, ea tenent semper, quae prima didicerunt); sed eam sic audio, ut Plautum mihi aut Naevium videar audire. Sono ipso vocis ita recto et simplici est, ut nihil ostentationis aut imitationis afferre videatur; ex quo sic locutum ejus patrem judico, sic majores[21].' Expressions from his plays were, from their weight and compact brevity, quoted familiarly in the days of Cicero; and one of them 'laudari a laudato viro,' like so many other pithy Latin sayings, is still in use to express a distinction that could not be characterised in happier or shorter terms. It is to be remarked also that the merit, which he assumes to himself in his epitaph, is the purity with which he wrote the Latin language.

Our knowledge of Naevius is thus, of necessity, very limited and fragmentary. From the testimony of later authors it may, however, be gathered that he was a remarkable and original man. He represented the boldness, freedom, and energy, which formed one side of the Roman character. Like some of our own early dramatists, he had served as a soldier before becoming an author. He was ardent in his national feeling; and, both in his life and in his writings, he manifested a strong spirit of political partisanship. As an author, he showed great productive energy, which continued unabated through a long and vigorous lifetime. His high self-confident spirit and impetuous temper have left their impress on the few fragments of his dramas and of his epic poem. Probably his most important service to Roman literature consisted in the vigour and purity with which he used the Latin language. But the conception of his epic poem seems to imply some share of the higher gift of poetical invention. He stands at the head of the line of Roman poets, distinguished by that force of speech and vehemence of temper, which appeared again in Lucilius, Catullus, and Juvenal; distinguished also by that national spirit which moved Ennius and, after him, Virgil, to employ their poetical faculty in raising a monument to commemorate the power and glory of Rome.

Notes

1. Cf. Lewis, Credibility of Early Roman History, vol. i. chap. ii. 14.

2. Cf. Lewis, Credibility of Early Roman History, vol. i. chap. ii. 14, 15.

3. Horace, Epist. ii. I. 161 3.

4. Cic. Brutus, ch. 28.

5. Brutus, 18.

6. Epist. ii. 1. 71.

7. viii. 138.

8. xxvii. 17.

9. Miles Gloriosus, ii. 2. 27.

10. Brutus, 15.

11. Mommsen remarks that he could not have retired to Utica till after it fell into the possession of the Romans.

12. De Senectute, 14.

13. 'Ye who keep watch over the person of the king, hasten straightway to the leafy places, where the copsewood is of nature's growth, not planted by man.'

14. 'Like one playing at ball in a ring, she tosses about from one to another, and is at home with all. To one she nods, to another winks; she makes love to one, clings to another. Her hand is busy here, her foot there. To one she gives a ring to look at, to another blows a kiss; with one she sings, with another corresponds by sings.'

   The reading of the passage here adopted is that given by Munk.

15. De Senectute, 6.

   > Etiam qui res magnas manu saepe gessit gloriose,
   > Cujus facta viva nunc vigent, qui apud gentes solus praestat,
   > Eum suus pater cum pallio ab amica abduxit uno.

17. 'What I in the theatre here have made good by the applause given to me, to think that any of these great people should now dare to interfere with! How much better thing is the slavery *here*' (*i.e.* represented in this play), 'than the liberty we actually enjoy?'

18. I have always held liberty to be of more value and a better thing than money.' The reading is that given by Munk.

19. Mommsen remarks that, in the fragments of this poem, the action is generally represented in the *present tense*.

20. Brutus, 19.

21. 'I, for my part, as I listed to my mother-in-law, Laelia (for women more easily preserve the pure idiom of antiquity, because, from their limited intercourse with the world, they retain always their earlier impressions), in listening, I say to her, I fancy that I am listening to Plautus or Naevius. The very tones of her voice are so natural and simple, that she seems absolutely free from affectation or imitation; from this I gather that her father spoke, and her ancestors all spoke, in the very same way.'—Cicero, De Oratore iii. 12.

George Augustus Simcox (essay date 1883)

SOURCE: An introduction to *A History of Latin Literature from Ennius to Boethius*, Vol. 1, Harper & Brothers, 1883, pp. 1-21.

[*In the following excerpt, Simcox ventures that "a superb and reckless character served [Naevius] instead of literary talent."*]

. . . The first Latin playwright, the first schoolmaster who taught Greek literature, was Titus Livius Andronicus. He was a native of Tarentum: he came to Rome as a slave, and employed himself after his emancipation as a schoolmaster and an actor. In the latter capacity he originated the curious division of labor whereby one actor, commonly himself, danced and acted, while another, whom the audience were not supposed to see, sang the words which he would have sung himself if the exertion of singing and dancing at once had not been too overwhelming. Such a device implies that the public came for the spectacle, and held the pantomime more important than the song; so it is not strange that the plays of Livius Andronicus should have been very meagre, and that the dialogue should have been very little above the level of stage directions, just serving to explain to the audience what was going on. Besides plays of mythology, plays of Greek life, plays of contemporary Roman history, he wrote an official thanksgiving for a happy turn in the war with Hannibal. Perhaps his most considerable work was a school-book, an abridgment of the "Odyssey" in the saturnian metre, which served as a class-book and to give some notion of the story, though hardly any of the poetry. The fragments that we have of it are like the explanations that an impatient teacher might give to an impatient pupil. For instance, "Homer" enumerates the provisions with which Circe furnishes Ulysses for his voyage, while Livius tells us that they (Circe's handmaidens, whom "Homer" names) brought good things to the ships, and ten thousand things else were put aboard the same. Perhaps his choice of metre may be taken to imply that the saturnian was a hexameter pure and simple, neither dactylic nor trochaic, nor anaæstic nor iambic, though more nearly trochaic than anything. Still, it is curious to find a very smooth quatrain ascribed to him by Terentianus Maurus, who gives a specimen of his own in the same very elaborate metre;[1] especially as Terentianus tells us that he quotes later writers by choice, because they were more accurate in their versification; and it is not easy to see why Terentianus or any one else should have been at the pains to modernize a quatrain of Livius.[2]

His successor, Nævius, wrote in saturnian verse as a matter of national pride. Latin was his mother tongue: he was a native of Campania, then thoroughly Latinized, and he resented the progress of Greek at Rome with all the pride of a Campanian. One might almost gather from his remains that a superb and reckless character served him instead of literary talent, as it afterwards served Alfieri; though he, with a great literature behind him, had opportunities for cultivating fastidiousness which Nævius had not. Nævius was fastidious by nature: he despised everything, from the Metelli to the starveling Greeks who were weaning his countrymen from their native speech; yet his great poem was addressed to Greeks. It was an epic on the origin of Rome and her recent achievements in the first Punic war: it told exactly the two things that foreigners would most want to know who were becoming curious about the city which had conquered Sicily. Cicero has preserved a specimen of his narrative, which deals with the battle of Ægusæ, and probably does him full justice, as Cicero, who undervalued nothing in Latin literature, ventures to compare it with Ennius. We find plenty of fire and fulness in the fragment, no relief or climax—in a word, nothing artistic in execution or intention. To judge by the fragments, the national epic was not superior, if it was equal, to the spirited adaptations of Greek plays, of which Nævius produced several. His true glory is not to be the last surviving representative of an imaginary popular literature uncorrupted by Greek, but to be the precursor of Ennius and Accius, of Varius and Vergil.

Notes

1. The miurus, consisting of hexameters, with every other line ending in an iambus instead of a spondee.

2. Consequently, the reading or the good faith of Terentianus has been called in question.

Tenney Frank (essay date 1927)

SOURCE: "Naevius and Free Speech," *American Journal of Philology*, Vol. XLVIII, No. 2, 1927, pp. 105-10.

[*In the following essay Frank offers his interpretation of Naevius's most famous line, "Fato Metelli Romae fiunt consules," and explains why it held a "double sting" for Metellus.*]

The famous senarius of Naevius *Fato Metelli Romae fiunt consules* was preserved only by Pseudo-Asconius[1] in commenting upon Cicero's thrust at Metellus Creticus in the first Verrine oration, but it is clearly assumed as known by Caesius Bassus[2] who quotes the answer of Metellus. Wis-

sowa[3] following Zumpt attempted to prove the line much later than Naevius, on the ground that *fato* in the sense of "fatal necessity" could apply to the Metelli only in the post-Gracchan period when several Metelli became consuls in close succession. Marx[4] rightly rejected Wissowa's argument, pointing out that the Stoic use of the word *fato* was unnecessary and unlikely in this passage. Marx in turn understood *fato* in the sense of oracular prediction, referring to Plautus, *Bacch.* 953 ff. (Ilio tria fuisse audivi fata), and argued that the friends of Metellus had probably secured the aid of an oracle in order to procure his election to the consulship.

That the line is authentic I think few will doubt despite the authority of Wissowa and Leo. However, Marx's interpretation of it is not compelling. The sense of oracular prediction does not seem to fit the circumstances, and that meaning for *fatum,* though common in classical Latin, is found in early Latin only in translations[5] from the Greek, which do not necessarily reveal the earlier native tone of the word. In point of fact the old Romans had no respectable oracles. They knew of Etruscan and Greek soothsayers, sortes, and haruspices, but they hardly took them seriously except in times of great nervous anxiety. I doubt whether we have a right to interpret *fatum* in a line of Naevius with meanings that grew up later in connection with Stoic ideas and after Greek respect for oracular divination had become prevalent.

In searching for the real meaning of the Naevian line I believe that we may get some aid from another passage in Cicero which—so far as I can find—has not yet been brought into the discussion. In the year 62 B.C. when Cicero had his clash of wits with Metellus Celer (a relative of Metellus Creticus), in a very carefully phrased letter[6] which steers guardedly between formal courtesy and half-concealed sarcasm he says: Had I not resisted your brother, men would have concluded that during my consulship I had been courageous *casu potiusquam consilio.* I believe that this phrase was meant to remind Metellus Celer of the line which Cicero had brought to the memory of Metellus Creticus, a line which no Metellus was ever allowed to forget. Cicero knew the setting of the original, its context and its occasion. His interpretation of it is therefore a safer guide than the few early instances of *fato* that have survived to us with Greek connotations. If the phrase in this letter to Metellus Celer is a reference to the old epigram, *fato* originally suggested a meaning akin to *casu.*[7] And this meaning will fit into the line of Naevius as well as into Cicero's allusion to it in the Verrine passage.

It will be remembered that Q. Metellus had actually reached the consulship by a happy chance.[8] He had been fortunate enough to be chosen as one of the three messengers to carry to Rome the news of the brilliant victory at Metaurus in 207. It was in the autumn and shortly before the elections. The people were so elated over the good news that they elected to the next consulship two of the three messengers. Metellus was one of these, though he had not yet held the praetorship. There is not the slightest reason to suppose that he would even have been considered for the high office if he had not been the fortunate herald of a startling victory. In fact he had no success in the field as consul and proconsul in the following years, and was later known chiefly for his support of Scipio—a course which probably accounts for the enmity of Naevius. What Naevius meant therefore was apparently that Metellus had become consul by mere chance. This meaning also fits well into the passage of the Verrine orations in which Cicero attacked Metellus Creticus in the year 70. There, turning upon Metellus who was supporting Verres, he says: Verres has been saying that you became consul *non fato ut ceteros ex vestra familia sed opera sua.* In all the passages I believe that the contrast between *casu* and *consilio* were intended.

It is of course apparent to anyone who reads Cicero and Vergil that the word *fatum* is used with all deference by them and not as a synonym of *casu.* Stoic philosophy was then in vogue and Latin had no other term with which to convey the doctrine of determinism; and since the Stoics also defended orderly divination, *fatum* in the sense of oracular responses also won respect. But if the word (*fari* is evidently a very old word) was used in the pre-Greek period for predictions obtained by use of *sortes* and *haruspicina* it must have been as humble in its connotations as those words were. When Cicero (*De Div.* II, 52) repeats Cato's saying that the haruspices must have smiled knowingly when they met, he adds: Quota enim quaeque res evenit praedicta ab istis? Aut si evenit quippiam quid adferri potest cur non *casu* id evenerit? He had the same scorn for *sortes* (ibid. II, 85); quibus in rebus temeritas et *casus,* non ratio nec *consilium* valet. And in these utterances he was reflecting the attitude of the earlier Rome. More than once the senate had ordered the books of soothsayers burned and the fortune-tellers banished. Only at old Etruscan sites like Veii, Caere, Falerii and Praeneste were such things respected. If indeed *fatum* was once used for predictions the word must have had about the same standing as *hariolatio,* and like the equally sordid word *vates* gained respect only by a literary accident. Some term had to supply the need occasioned by the invasion of new ideas.

It is probable, therefore, that Naevius used the word in the sense of *fortuito.* However, the line probably had a double sting, for it was meant to convey not only the idea that Metellus had become consul by chance (taking *fato* as an ablative) but also that his consulship was a misfortune to Rome (a double dative). The mind was invited to hesitate between two possible constructions and to accept both. The use of *fatum=malum* is not actually vouched for before Pacuvius (Trag. 377), but the answer of Metellus— Malum dabunt Metelli Naevio poetae—would seem rather pointless unless we assume that this meaning was also contained in the attack.

Those who have rejected these lines as spurious or late have also been prone to reject the story of Naevius' imprisonment and exile. In fact they have argued against the authenticity of the lines on the ground that early Roman law could not have recognized libel as a capital offense. The question leads further than we can go here, but a few words are necessary for the sake of the preceding argument. The large question which we need not discuss in detail is whether Naevius could have been punished by imprisonment and exile for inserting caustic criticism of magistrates in his comedies. The chief point at issue is whether the twelve tables contained both of the clauses which St. Augustine claims to cite from Cicero: *si quis occentavisset* and *sive carmen condidisset quod infamiam faceret flagitiumve alteri.* The first clause probably refers to incantation, but the latter seems to refer to libel. Mommsen thought both belonged to the twelve tables and that Naevius had incurred the death penalty[9] (i. e., loss of civil rights) under the latter. Huvelin[10] and others, including Beckmann,[11] hold that Cicero or some one before him misunderstood the first clause and explained it by the second in order to define the crime as libel. Fränkel[12] has unfortunately reverted to Mommsen's view. Fränkel is right in holding that the language of the second clause is pre-Ciceronian, but that does not prove it a part of the decemviral code. It is difficult to see how any recent historian who has read deeply into Roman institutions can believe that libel or slander was included among capital offenses in the early code, especially as the code allowed settlements on the basis of talion for corporal injuries. We cannot afford to forget that liberty to criticize was very highly valued during the republic. Lucilius for many years ridiculed men high and low,

> Primores populi arripuit, populumque tributim,

without fear. Catullus, Calvus, Furius and Memmius published unquotable epigrams mentioning Caesar and Pompey by name, and the political pamphlets in prose of Cicero's day were sparing neither in names nor epithets. We have mention of only two cases[13] during the republic in which suits for damages were brought on charges of verbal injury, and in both cases the culprit was a mimus, doubtless a slave. Both these instances seem to belong to the post-Gracchan period, and Huvelin is doubtless right in holding that the law which included verbal abuse in the scope of *injuria* was then recent. There is no instance on record except that of Naevius of a citizen brought to punishment because of criticism of political personages.

How, then, are we to explain the misfortune of Naevius if the accounts of his penalties are to be accepted? It would hardly have been under the revised laws regarding *injuria* because these laws specified fines as damages; they did not recognize loss of civil rights. I think we must assume that the penalties of the twelve tables were invoked in his case, and that the most reasonable explanation is that under the severe strain of war-nervousness during the last years of the Punic war some praetor of the Scipionic party deliberately stretched the meaning of the decemviral prohibition against "carmina," adding an interpretative clause, and thus found a plausible basis for a judgment. Every war will provide parallels in which overzealous judges have strengthened the machinery of war-censorship by questionable interpretations. I cannot point to an exact parallel in early Rome, but a review of the legislation passed during the stress of the Punic war will show that restrictive measures, meant chiefly for war-times, were carried to the extreme. For example, in order to save resources for public purposes a number of drastic sumptuary laws were passed.[14] Women were forbidden to wear jewelry by the Oppian law (repealed after the war), the lex Metilia regulated the fabric that could be used in clothing (disregarded later if not repealed), expensive gifts were forbidden at the Saturnalia (later a dead letter), lawyers' fees were forbidden (apparently observed afterwards), games of chance were outlawed, and finally expenditures at festivals were regulated.

My suggestion is that a strict censorship was also applied temporarily by some praetor in the same spirit. The Metelli were supporting Scipio's invasion of Africa to end the war. Scipio was vigorously opposed by the older conservative nobles and Naevius was writing in the interest of the latter. The younger group were ready to resort to extreme measures to remove the offensive satirist. It is probable that the praetor, finding no law to cover the case, knowingly stretched the interpretation of the phrase *si quis occentavisset* for the purpose and in his edict added as an interpretative gloss the second phrase *sive carmen condidisset*, etc., and on that basis pronounced his sentence and ordered the III viri to proceed. Since the twelve tables were commented by Aelius Paetus a few years later in a book which Cicero knew well, we may suppose that that book was the source of Cicero's citation. After the war the praetors must have omitted this interpretation from their edicts since we hear of no more judgments of the kind.

We may, therefore, accept the stories of Naevius' punishment as we do the authenticity of the lines that passed between him and Metellus, even if we find it impossible to believe that the twelve tables imposed the death penalty for libellous verses.

Notes

1. Cicero, *Verr. Act.* I, 28, hoc Verrem dicere aiebant te non fato ut ceteros ex vestra familia sed opera sua consulem factum; on which the scholiast remarks; dictum facete et contumeliose in Metellos antiquum Naevi est: Fato Metelli Romae fiunt consules. Cui tune Metellus consul iratus versu responderat senario hypercatalecto, qui et Saturnius dicitur: Dabunt malum Metelli Naevio poetae. De qua parodia subtiliter Cicero dixit: Te non, etc.

2. Caes. Bass. (G. L. VI, p. 265), Optimus est quem Metelli proposuerunt de Naevio *aliquotiens ab eo versu lacessiti*, Malum dabunt Metelli Naevio poetae.

3. *Genethliakon für C. Robert*, 1910, 51 ff.

4. Naevius, Sitz. Sächs. Ges. (1911) 69 ff. Despite this article, Leo in his *Gesch. d. Röm. Lit.*, p. 78, n. 5 (1913) agreed with Wissowa.

5. Plaut. *Bacch.* 951-59 (where it is an obvious makeshift); Enn. *Scaen.* 58; Acc., 451, 481.

6. Cic. Ad Fam. V, 2, 9, si virtute et animo non restitissem, quis esset qui me in consulatu non casu potius existimaret quam consilio fortem fuisse?

7. Wende, *De Caeciliis Metellis* (1875) p. 32, without knowledge of the allusion in Cicero's letter, interpreted *fato* as *fortuito*.

8. Livy XXVII, 50, 9-11, and 51, XXVIII, 10.

9. Gell. 3, 3, 15, ob assiduam maledicentiam et probra in principes civitatis dicta in vincula a triumviris conjectus esset. Hieron. (p. 126 Sch.) pulsus Roma factione nobilium ac praecipue Metelli.

10. *La notion de l'iniuria* (Lyons, 1903).

11. Zauberei und Recht, Diss. 1923.

12. In *Gnomon,* 1925, pp. 180 ff.

13. Auct. ad Her. II, 19 and I, 24.

14. See Botsford, *Roman Assemblies,* ch. XV.

Tenney Frank (essay date 1930)

SOURCE: "Early Tragedy and Epic" in *Life and Literature in the Roman Republic*, University of California Press, 1930, pp. 30-64.

[*In the following excerpt, Frank notes Naevius's innovations in drama, which include disregarding time and place and increasing the use of musical accompaniment; he also discusses the role of Naevius and his fellow dramatists in the development and eventual failure of Roman tragedy.*]

Browning has recalled the story of how Greek war captives taken at Syracuse in the Peloponnesian war earned their release by reciting snatches from the plays of Euripides. It was a century and a half after that seige that the Romans came to Sicily in the First Punic War, and the city was still interested in the old drama, indeed was now taking its part in producing tragedies. One of the last of the dramatists, one of the so-called "Pleiad," was a Syracusan of Hiero's time, and King Hiero was himself so devoted to the drama that he even built a theater for Agyrion, a petty village on the border of his small kingdom. We have noticed how the Roman youth who campaigned year after year in Sicily learned something of the arts of civilization and on their return home created a demand for the things they had come to enjoy while abroad. The year after the victorious troops returned from Sicily, Livius, a schoolmaster of Greek origin, staged a translation of a Greek tragedy as a supplement to the annual chariot race. This production marks the beginning of Rome's education in letters. There must be some close connection between this homecoming of the army, and the performance of Livius' play, for the change in character of a great religious festival could not have been suggested by a freedman. The magistrates responsible for the performance were senators and the senate had of course requested the play. In all likelihood it was also the senate that invited King Hiero of Syracuse to Rome to see the games; for he, if any one, would have been asked to supply some actor to help stage the first play, and it was only appropriate that he should come to inaugurate the new era of culture.

From that time on plays were produced every year. Five years after the first performance, Naevius, who had served in the Sicilian campaigns (and had perhaps learned Greek there), began to help in the work of adapting Greek plays for the Roman stage. Only brief fragments of those early plays have survived and in reviewing the list of titles we might wonder at the enthusiasm they reveal for plays shaped on the old Greek mythology. But the predominance of titles derived from the Trojan cycle explains this enthusiasm. It was in Sicily that the Roman soldiers had learned the Greek story of how Rome had been founded by Trojan refugees. The stories of Hector, of the Trojan horse, Achilles, Ajax, Iphigenia, and the rest were therefore not without personal interest in the barbaric city. The unlettered shoemakers, smiths, and carpenters at Rome, men whose modern equals could hardly be expected to sit patiently through a performance of Gilbert Murray's *Trojan Women,* eagerly listened to the half-comprehended lines of Livius' translation. They had been told that these were the stories of their long-lost ancestors.

Livius is merely a name, which is unfortunate, since we know that he deserved well of Roman civilization. Naevius is less shadowy, a personality whose creative work left an impress on such powerful men as Cicero and Vergil two centuries later. He wrote not only plays, but an epic, condensing Rome's history in an annalistic poem, the climax of which was the great victory over Carthage in which he had had a share. From the sixty scattered lines of this epic rescued by late lexicographers we do not quite find the justification for Vergil's high regard. There is no poetry in them. But grammarians pick their lines to illustrate linguistic usage and not for effective phrasing. Even Shakespeare becomes prose if judged by the citations found in Webster. However, for the preservation of the metrical schemes employed by Naevius we are grateful. Though he had used a large variety of Greek meters for his drama, he did not in his epic. Here he preserves the native Saturnian line that had been used in religious songs, and apparently in ballads. That he did not adopt a standard Greek meter for his epic, as he did for his tragedies and comedies, is proof enough that the old native narrative verse was fully established in a well-known body of poetry which we have lost.

In many respects this verse resembles the old English line that relies upon alliteration and rhythmic ictuses which balance each other in the two severed parts of the line:

> In a sómer séson when sóft was the sónne.

But the Saturnian had six ictuses instead of four, and as Latin verse was more aware of its quantities and less of its word stress than English the ictuses, while somewhat regardful of word accent, were more attentive to quantity. Finally, since alliteration is more effective when the ictus falls on the first syllable, and since the Latin accent had to a large extent shifted away from the first syllable by the time of Naevius, the use of alliteration was somewhat less frequent in Naevius than in *Beowulf.* In Vergil's day the effect of this verse must have been somewhat like that of Langland's poems upon the Elizabethans. The shift of the Latin word accent toward the penult was already destroying the effectiveness of the verse even when Naevius wrote; and the break of the line in the center rendered it ineffective for sustained narration. Its halting movement may be somewhat inadequately illustrated by a paraphrase of Naevius' own epitaph:

> If death of any mortal sadden hearts immortal,
> The heavenly Muses surely Naevius' death bemoan;
> For after he departed to the shades of Orcus
> The voice of Rome is silent music is forgotten.

Ennius abandoned the line, and it was eventually doomed, just as the Anglo-Saxon meters in England began to disappear when the richer rhythms of French poetry came to be appreciated.

It was Naevius also who broke away from Greek subjects in the drama, though with what success we cannot say. He made what we may call a "chronicle play" of the Romulus legend which disregarded the conventional unities, and he also wrote a pageantry play to commemorate the heroic single combat of Marcellus with a Celtic chieftain. He is therefore among the first to stage contemporary drama and to disregard the restrictions of time and place. That he made the same innovations in comedies like his **Hariolus** is probable but cannot be proved from the few lines that remain.

An independent creator he was and might have carried progress far had not so large a part of his activity fallen in the restraining period of the Second Punic War. His end was in character. Accustomed to speak his mind freely in his comedies, he vigorously supported the Fabian policy when it was unpopular, and after the group supporting Scipio, which demanded a more aggressive conduct of the war, came into power, he continued his sarcastic criticism of the Scipionic group. Rome had always tolerated free speech, but even at Rome patience was short in war time. War censorship discovered an old law which, with a little imaginative interpretation, could be stretched to cover the case of this satirist.[1] Only one line has survived of the satiric comedy which referred to the fact that Metellus, a friend of Scipio's, had taken advantage of a fortuitous circumstance to stand for the consulship. He was elected through no desert of his own. The point of the line—Fato Metelli Romae fiunt consules—rests on a *double entendre,* because *fato* may be construed either as ablative or as dative, while *Romae* may be genitive or locative. The line therefore may mean either:

> "The Metelli became consuls at Rome by chance,"

which is hardly a flattering remark, or what is even less flattering:

"The Metelli became consuls to Rome's sorrow."

The Metelli apparently thought Naevius meant to suggest both, which is likely enough, and they succeeded in having him imprisoned, and eventually banished. He seems to have found a home in Carthage, the land of the enemy against whom he had once fought.

These two dramatists, for reasons which must be discussed later, increased the use of musical accompaniment in tragedy and comedy. In Euripides the body of the drama had been in recited trimeters. The choral parts were of course sung to the accompaniment of rhythmical movements called dance, and there was also music when the actors engaged in dialogue with the chorus, as well as in some of their monologues. But the musical element had been reduced very much during the century that followed Euripides when the drama had gradually dispensed with the chorus even in the staging of Euripides. Rome was then too primitive to provide the twelve or more trained singers and dancers that even the later Greeks had found beyond their resources. Livius indeed had experienced such difficulty in securing actors with good voices that he himself took the leading rôle, and, not adequately gifted for the singing parts, he tried, we are told, the inartistic device (not unknown on our comic stage) of placing a singer beside the musician to carry the melody of the lyric parts while he acted and presumably recited the lines of the songs. That was, of course, only a temporary makeshift, but it shows how difficult it was to provide satisfactory artists at the time. It would seem then that since these early writers found it impossible to produce choruses adequately because these required the elaborate training of many singers in intricate musical compositions, they compensated as best they could by increasing the number of monodies in their plays, writing them in a few well-defined meters, such as the septenarii, cretics, and bacchiacs,[2] which were not too difficult to learn. Thus it was that Roman tragedy became even more like modern opera than the tragedy of the Greek stage had been. these early men of Rome, who mean so little to us, had developed a form which was capable of carrying on the work of Greek tragedy on a primitive stage, and capable also of growing into a richer drama as soon as the resources of the small city should permit. They made the drama possible for Rome.

As a composer of tragedies and epic verse, Ennius succeeded Naevius, but, writing in an era of enthusiastic phil-hellenism, he came near yielding too much to a great foreign influence. Had he not been a man of remarkable poetic powers his example might well have quenched the spirit of Rome in the rising literature. One of the first Latin authors that we would ask the excavators of Herculaneum to restore to us is Ennius. No single work of his has survived. Of his twenty-five or more tragedies we possess only about four hundred lines; of the eighteen books

of *Annals* a little over five hundred complete lines; of his satires, his *Euhemerus* and his *Epicharmus,* not enough fragments have survived to give us a very clear idea of the scope of each. All in all we have about three per cent of his work in scraps, but here at least there are several connected passages cited in appreciation of something else than the grammatical usages they illustrate.

Ennius too, like Naevius, told Rome's story in verse. One's impulse is to discount the accuracy of any history that employs artifice. And one must grant of course that a poet will select his incidents with a view to their dramatic values and picturesqueness. One must remember, however, that poetry had a serious place in all early literature for the reason that, before the day of much writing, all teachable things, even history and philosophy, were put into verse for mnemonic purposes. The works of Solon and Heracleitus would not have contained different matter if they had been put into prose. In Ennius' day many national histories that purported to be accurate were composed in verse. And Ennius probably did not permit himself to include fictive incidents in his *Annals,* nor has he been proved incorrect at any point.[3] Cicero cited him for the gist of the famous speech of Appius Claudius, and added as a matter of indifference that the original of the speech was in existence. Apparently Ennius' summary was accurate enough so that it was not necessary to refer to the original text.

The influence of his *Annals* was in its field comparable to that of Homer. From Ennius all school-boys got their first impressions of what Rome's great heroes had accomplished. He was unsurpassed as a painter of character. With a few telling strokes he revealed the essential traits of those strong, bold, tireless heroes who made the old Republic irresistible in power, magnificent in tradition, and a saving inspiration in the days of decadence. He was near to these men, and it was as he saw them that they lived on in memory and still live on. He made Roman character memorable in the two lines on Fabius Maximus:

Unus homo nobis cunctando restituit rem:
Noenum rumores ponebat ante salutem.

and in the single line on Curius:

Quem nemo ferro potuit superare nec auro.

His epic was an exposition of the text he himself devised so effectively:

Moribus antiquis res stat Romana virisque:

And it was Ennius who more than any one else kept Roman society upon that foundation.

We happen to be able to test his influence by what he did with the portrait of Pyrrhus. Only a generation before Ennius was born this picturesque enemy of Rome had had a friendly alliance with the Messapian tribe to which Ennius himself belonged. The poet, therefore, had heard much about the king. Pyrrhus, in fact, had some very sympathetic traits of character, a remarkable chivalry, and a certain sense of honor and loyalty such as is often found in the chieftains of primitive folk. These qualities stand out in the characterization of him that Ennius has left us; and these are the outstanding traits that we find in all the later Roman references to Pyrrhus. That Ennius should have responded to these qualities is not strange, but that all the rest of the Romans should thus enthusiastically have lauded an enemy who nearly wrecked Rome is less to be expected. The explanation is of course that what Ennius wrote colored the historic conceptions of all who followed. This becomes evident when we read Plutarch, a Greek, and his biography of Pyrrhus. When drawing upon Roman sources for the Italian campaign of the king, Plutarch paints the same picture as Ennius, but when he draws upon Greek authors in describing the Greek campaigns, he reveals the fact that the knightly hero of the Roman historians had a less charming side which certain close observers at home were well aware of. Like all historians Ennius had his enthusiasms, and he had such power of portraiture that not a trait blurred.

He was also fair. Pyrrhus got his meed of praise, but the opponents of Pyrrhus, Fabricius and Appius Claudius, were characterized with equal sympathy. Of his own contemporaries, Fabius the Slow-goer was effectively portrayed as we have seen, and Cato "in caelum tollitur," as Cicero affirms, although Scipio Africanus, who was bitterly opposed by these conservatives, became, as he deserved to be, the outstanding hero of the book.

It was entirely appropriate that, for his heroic narrative, Ennius borrowed the dactylic hexameter of the Greeks, but it was after all a daring thing to do, since meters seldom transplant with success. However, Naevius' use of the native Saturnian had demonstrated its inability to carry heroic narrative. Imagine *Paradise Lost* crammed into the primitive English rhythms of Langland! The dactylic hexameter was in Greek regularly associated with the epic. It had one disadvantage in its requirement of a larger proportion of short syllables than normal Latin writing contained, but that was overcome by simply permitting more spondees than Homeric custom had enjoyed. This resulted in a reduction of tempo which after all suited Roman military movement. There was another difficulty which was more serious. While Greek verse needed to give little attention to word accent, the Latin word accent was jealous of attention. With the relative fixity of the accent, it was impossible to write Latin dactyls based both upon quantity and word-accent. Ennius nevertheless ventured upon an experiment. That he had a very delicate ear for the demands of the Latin language is proved by the careful adjustments in his dramatic senarii, where adjustments were not easy to make. He would not have foisted impossible dactyls upon Rome. The fact that he wrote quantitative dactyls and continued to write them, and that his *Annals* lived for centuries is proof that he did not overstep the bounds of good taste. The explanation of his success is probably that the word stress in the Latin of his day was so moderate that a conflict with the ictus was not fatal to aesthetic

pleasure if only it fell upon long syllables, and also that during the forty years of dramatic performances at Rome, the ears of the audiences had become trained under the influence of music to disregard such conflicts in the many lyric rhythms, including dactyls. By his sensible modification of the Homeric line, Ennius created as great a resource for Latin poetry as Chaucer did for English poetry, and shaped for Vergil's use "the stateliest measure ever moulded by the lips of man."

Ennius began to write tragedies about 200 B.C. at the very time when philhellenism was at its height. Being a man of wide culture who knew his Greek well he readily responded to the general demand for things Greek. Though he produced one play (*The Rape of the Sabine Women*) on a Roman theme, and a pageantry play called the *Ambracia* to commemorate the victory of a friend during the war with Aetolia, he seems to have striven chiefly to reproduce on the Roman stage the effects of Euripides' tragedies. And now that the restraints of poverty had become somewhat relaxed, and the drama had continued long enough to foster a certain amount of skilful talent for its interpretation, he was freer to present his tragedies more nearly in the old Greek manner. It has accordingly been plausibly conjectured[4] that it was Ennius who reintroduced the chorus so that the Greek plays might be given without cutting. There is no reason for supposing that the choral song in the *Thyestes* (written in bacchiacs) or the one in the *Medea* (octonarii) or the one in the *Iphigenia* (septenarii) were recited by a single singer. It is clear from the fragments that in several of his plays, notably in the *Achilles*, the *Eumenides*, the *Hector*, and the *Hecuba*, choral groups were actually participants in the plays as they had been in the Greek originals. And since in the plays of his successor, Accius, it can be demonstrated that a chorus sang, we ought to accept the reasonable interpretation of the Ennian fragments and attribute to this philhellenist the importation of choral song into Roman tragedy. Ennius, however, deferred to Roman taste so far as the rhythms were concerned. He adhered largely to the lyric meters which Livius and Naevius had popularized, and seldom attempted to employ the more intricate systems of the Greeks.[5] That Ennius was as successful in his tragedies as in his epic is adequately proved by the fact that many of his plays were still being produced a century after his death and were avidly read by men like Cicero.

Pacuvius, the nephew and successor of Ennius, did not write many plays. From the little that remains of his work we should judge that he preferred themes somewhat off the beaten track and that in choosing plays that contained heterodox discussions of ethical themes, he, too, felt the influence of the new Greek learning and kept in mind the interests of the intellectualist at Rome. The grammarians have also noticed the fact that his lyric meters paid more attention to Latin word stress than those of his predecessors.[6] They cite particularly his care in composing anapaests with caesuras in such a way that long initial syllables fell under the ictus. These anapaests in fact read like dactyls with an anacrusis of two shorts at the beginning.

This innovation decidedly proves that the poet had a precise ear and desired to attain harmonious effects. His successors showed that they appreciated his innovation, but they occasionally used the old turbid lines to express emotional excitement.

The most successful of the writers of tragedy was Accius, a poet who spanned the era between the Gracchans and the Social War. We have fragments of more than forty tragedies from his busy pen, and many of his plays were re-staged in Cicero's day. He was the favorite of the great actors, Aesopus and Roscius. He did not depart far from the customs laid down by Ennius in respect to meters, music, and chorus, but the fact that he freely readapted the Greek plays which furnished themes to his predecessors can only mean that he used the same liberty in giving his own interpretation to old plots that Euripides had used in treating anew the myths that had been staged by Aeschylus and Sophocles. We happen to know from the remarks of Terence that convention did not permit the staging of more than one paraphrase of any given Greek play. When, therefore, Accius writes plays upon familiar themes we must assume that he is offering something essentially original in his interpretation of the old plot. In fact we find good evidence of his original treatment in the fragments. So, for instance, in his *Antigone* he changed the personnel of the chorus (as Ennius had done in the *Iphigenia*), which implies that the purpose of the play was altered. It is also clear that Accius made free to disregard the conventional unities of place and time, for in the *Brutus* there are scenes laid in Gabii, in Ardea, and in Rome.

All these dramatists apparently altered their originals freely in order to make the story and its meaning more plausible to a Roman audience. The *Medea* of Ennius reveals many changes of this kind. For instance, the Latin author felt that he must prepare the audience early in the play for the gruesome death of the children,[7] a detail unnecessary in Euripides, who wrote for an audience that knew the plot. This kind of thing must have occurred frequently. Again, Ennius had to alter Medea's long monologue, since before a Roman audience accustomed to seeing a matron in public, there was no point in making her apologize for appearing outside of the palace.[8] Ennius has here been needlessly accused of misunderstanding the Greek original! Ennius knew his Greek; he had learned it at school in Tarentum. His alterations were introduced to suit the psychology of his own audience. Similar changes are numerous and need not be dwelt upon.

The alteration of the very purport of the plays is of more importance to us. For instance, Atreus, the old Greek tyrant of primitive brutality, was calculated to offend Roman taste. It is apparent from the fragments of Accius that it was the sufferings of Thyestes rather than the daring of Atreus which received sympathetic attention—a fact not surprising in a city where the word *rex* was feared and hated. Euripides' story of Andromeda had a matter-of-fact plot in which Andromeda's father begged Perseus to slay the dragon and to rescue his daughter. This plot followed the myth and was expected in Athens. But not so at Rome. In Accius' play Perseus is rather the chivalrous knight; he rescues the lady first and then pleads for her hand. Similarly, in the *Clytemestra* of Accius one also finds a very modern note, for Accius suggests that if Agamemnon's inconstancy could be excused because of his long separation from his wife, Clytemestra might possibly have the benefit of the same argument. In the *Andromache* of Ennius and the *Astyanax* of Accius there is an intense note of sorrow for the child of Hector and Andromache that reminds one of Vergil's lines in the third book of the Aeneid. This is a Roman strain deriving from the Romans' claim to be descended from the Trojans. In the *Phoenissae* of Accius the motivation of the whole play is changed by representing Eteocles breaking a command rather than a personal pledge. In the *Eurysaces* of Accius we have a slightly different reason for the use of Roman motive. This play was re-staged by the great actor Aesopus when Cicero was in exile, because of its picture of the unjust banishment of Telamon. The Roman audience appreciated the possible allusion to Cicero's suffering and cheered Aesopus' lines to the echo. Accius may well have written it originally and introduced the changes in order to influence his audience and obtain the recall of some political exile like Popilius, about 130 B.C. The lines have a genuine Roman ring.

In our own day when every dramatist is compelled to create a new plot it is easy to underestimate the originality of men like the Greek Euripides, the Roman Accius, the French Racine, the English Shakespeare, who all in varying degrees were satisfied to use old plots, even old plays, and to give all their attention to a personal and original interpretation of the inner meaning of a familiar story and of the motives that impelled the characters. We may illustrate the old method of procedure by examining Seneca's *Medea,* since here we have a complete Latin play which shows what even an uninspired Roman dramatist might do by way of re-reading an ancient legend. Medea in the old unvarnished myth of the barbaric age was apparently a bundle of natural passions, a savage creature gifted with superhuman powers. Jason owed her his life, but since a Greek prince could hardly wed a barbarian and make her his queen, he might reasonably, according to Greek standards, abandon her when his "higher" duties to state and position demanded it. In a rage of jealous hate, the creature might then wreak her vengeance upon Jason and Jason's children. Such action was quite comprehensible to the semibarbarous age that shaped the myth, but not to the more humane Athenians of Euripides' day. The Greek dramatist, accordingly, had offered a new explanation of the problem. In his version Jason has disregarded the higher demands of humanity for a selfish passion or a more selfish ambition. Medea, the woman, has been infinitely wronged, and in her helplessness—it is not all jealousy and hate—she slays her children to save them from a worse fate. But to the Roman even this interpretation seems impossible, and the character of Jason least comprehensible of all. A Roman nobleman could not so abandon his sons, and the woman, if she was indeed human, could not slay her children either in hate or in love. Seneca, therefore, while keeping the main plot, seeks a new explanation for the woman's act. Medea is again painted as the barbaric witch that she was before Euripides transformed her. Jason marries Creusa for the sake of his children—a wholly comprehensible act to a Roman of Nero's day—and the uncontrollable Medea is driven into a rage that does not hesitate to commit murder. But, however jealous she might have been, Seneca feels that she could not have laid hands upon her own offspring. Yet the tale said that she did. Seneca's solution of the dilemma is simple. Woe has driven Medea insane and the ghost of her brother hovers before her, a symbol of that insanity. Accordingly, it is in a fit of madness that she does the deed. In Seneca, as in Euripides, the action follows the ancient myth, but the interpretation of that myth varies with the author, and in both cases this reinterpretation is not so much an invention of the dramatist as a reflection of the changed point of view of the society of his time. The moderns have, of course, felt the same need for a re-reading of the story as the widely differing versions of Grillparzer and Catulle Mendéz demonstrate. This is but one simple illustration of how the Roman dramatists could re-stage old myths and yet constantly invite the audience to something new. The emphasis upon the interpretation rather than upon the plot is precisely the same as it was in the days of Racine and Shakespeare.

How far the Roman dramatists were indebted to predecessors for their very striking employment of song is still a moot problem. Leo,[9] following a suggestion of Crusius, held that the Plautine cantica followed the manner of the contemporary music-hall lyrics of Greece as illustrated by the then recently discovered "Grenfell song." This theory was rejected by Fraenkel[10] because he found no vital similarity between the Grenfell fragment and the Plautine cantica. In his view the Roman predecessors of Plautus—Livius and Naevius—who paraphrased both tragedy and comedy, had probably developed the cantica in tragedy from Euripidean models and then employed them in comedy as well. This theory has a certain plausibility but cannot yet be tested because the cogent examples of cantica in tragedy must be drawn from Ennius, who was not a predecessor but rather a tardy contemporary of Plautus. The view of Leo has received some little support from a brief and peculiar mime-fragment of the British Museum recently published by Milne.[11] However this fragment is so late that it may represent post-Plautine developments, and therefore cannot be pressed into decisive service. It must also be added that recent studies tend to show that Greek New Comedy of the time of Menander had not wholly given up the use of strophic lyrics,[12] and that the Plautine and Ennian cantica themselves seem to have retained not a few traces of strophic structure.[13]

Without attempting to solve a problem for which too many of the quantities are still unknown, I would only wish to suggest the need of considering the practical factors of Roman experience and of Roman exigencies when we try to explain the Roman trend toward an operatic form. In the first place it is well to keep in mind that Naevius, who dominated the Roman theater for thirty years of its formative period, had campaigned in Sicily long enough to become the first annalist of the Punic war. Practically every city of Sicily where Roman troops were stationed had a theater, and in the days of Hiero the demand for dramatic entertainment in Sicily was so vigorous that new theaters were being built. We still have evidence[14] of Hellenistic theaters at Syracuse, Tauromenium, Segesta, Tyndaris, Akrae, Catania, and Agyrion. It is agreed that the Greek tragedies and comedies that were then being produced—the plays that Naevius probably saw—were generally devoid of choruses. The elaborate choruses of the tragedies had fallen away, partly because of the cost of staging them, and partly doubtless because new musical fashions had grown impatient of the somewhat academic formalism of the strophic songs.[15] In comedy, considerations of the expense and a desire for scope and freedom in choosing theme and form in song worked toward the same end. There can be little doubt that in Sicily Naevius saw performances of post-classical tragedies and comedies, not to mention music-hall performances of mimes and farces, that gave him good suggestions as to how the plays of Euripides could be staged without a chorus, and how a paraphrase of a Menandrian comedy that had lost its *entr'acte* songs could be turned into something like light opera. And a genius as inventive and independent as Naevius would soon break through the limitations of the Roman stage and shape, with the help of such suggestions, a performance suited to Roman needs.

But even if the Sicilian performances offered suggestions of how to stage comedies and tragedies without choruses it seems to have been the Romans who made the old classics conform to the new method and in doing so greatly enlarged rather than diminished the scope of the musical accompaniment. The second reason for this increase in songs seems to me, therefore, to lie in the need for music to help carry the new meters which dramatic writing demanded. Latin had been as poor in meters as early English was later. The chief drudge of all work had been the Saturnian verse, a form unfit for either sustained narrative or for realistic dialogue. Its line was slow and reflective. it had been used for ritual song, for funeral elegy, for lullabies, for gnomic poetry, and apparently also for lampoons; but it was as unfit for the drama as Ennius had found it to be for epic narration. There was also apparently a lively marching verse, the quadratus, the meter with which we are familiar from the trochaic tetrameters of the Greeks and from the lines of Tennyson's *Locksley Hall:*

> With the standards of the peoples plunging through the thunder storm.

At least critics are now ready to accept the remark of Horace that lines like

> Rex erit qui recte faciet, qui non faciet, non erit,

were sung in the days of old Camillus. Whenever we happen to have a fragment of a soldier's song quoted in Latin it is in this quick step:

Ecce Caesar nunc triumphat, qui subegit Gallias.

That meter had possibilities in the drama, and it was very freely used, though it doubtless had to be weaned away from its boisterous military associations. For rapid action and excitement it served well. It appears that early tragedy felt that it belonged to music and used it in lyric passages, in recitative chants as well as in dramatic speeches. Naevius was very fond of it.

Tragedy, however, needed an easy line of moderate length for its ordinary dialogues, and several meters in different moods to carry the monologues, songs, and emotional dialogues. For these Livius and Naevius, as we have noticed, had taken over and adapted a large number of Greek verse-forms. Now the adaptation of a foreign meter is a very serious matter. It took English poetry hundreds of years to merge French and old English rhythms, as it took France centuries to find a satisfactory adaptation of the medieval Latin systems. The labor of reshaping Greek meters for use in Latin was all the more difficult at the time because the Latin language happened to be just then at a critical point in its accentual development. The Greek word-accent had but very slight stress, so that quantity was permitted to determine verse-rhythm. In Latin, also, the quantity of the vowel and the syllable was still the dominant element at this time, indeed determined the position of the word accent, and was responsible for the penultimate accent rule that prevailed in most words during the century in which Naevius wrote. Latin must have been nearly as precise in the observance of longs and shorts as Greek. But the difficulty was that the stress of the word accent had also been a marked factor in Latin pronunciation for some time. Now in forming or introducing new rhythms the Latin poets would have to choose either stress or quantity as the decisive element on which to build and force the other element to comply. This is a choice that very few languages have imposed upon their poets. In English there was of course no such decision necessary since our accent remained a strong stress while our syllabic quantities, in the mingling of Germanic and French, became so completely confused that the values of half of them are hardly determinable by ear. This difference between Latin and English has not always been given due weight. When, for instance, the late Poet Laureate of England assumed that the quantitative meters of Ennius and Vergil resemble in effect the quantitative meters that he composed in English, he disregarded the vital difference between the two languages.[16] While in Latin quantities were readily distinguished even by the rabble, a fact that is shown by the emergence of the penultimate law before there were any teachers, in English it requires a laboratory apparatus to decide what really is the length of certain syllables. On the other hand, stress is dominant in English and unmistakable in all colloquial speech, whereas in Latin it was so moderate in the new position it had recently acquired that for many centuries after Plautus it had very little effect upon the morphology of the language. Apparently the first Roman poets chose as wisely as could be expected in determining to base their meters upon quantity rather than upon word-stress. But in doing so they had to face a serious dilemma: a stress-accent does not like to be disregarded, and ultimately (six centuries later) it asserted itself and insisted upon dominance. The quadratus, or trochaic tetrameter, which apparently grew up before the Romans knew Greek or grammar, had made a compromise that satisfied the ear. It looked to quantity as the dominant element, placing the verse-beat invariably upon a long (or its equivalent), but it by no means wholly disregarded word accent. In the lines of soldiers' songs that survived, it is not often that word accent is slighted more than once in a line, and Ennius, Naevius, and Plautus in their plays seldom permitted themselves to neglect it more often than twice in a spoken line.

In "Rex erit qui recte faciet, qui non faciet, non erit," aside from the last syllable which of course is hidden in a falling cadence, only *erit* at the beginning, an unemphatic word, gets what may be called a mechanical accent. But this smoothness is natural chiefly in the trochaic meter and it occurs here because the normal penultimate accent of Latin, which stresses a long syllable next to the final, is by nature adapted to a trochaic quantitative rhythm. Obviously an iambic line can take advantage of all the qualities of the trochaic line if the poet will so adapt the first word as to secure a trochaic swing in the rest of the line. Livius was very skilful in adapting the Greek trimeter to the spirit of the Latin trochaic. He increased the caesuras—that is he freely cut the iambic foot in two—not for the sake of caesuras but in order that by cutting iambic feet he could create a trochaic rhythm which would operate easily with a penultimate accent; he permitted resolved longs in any position except the last foot, because when the penult is short the antepenult receives the accent, and a fair coincidence of accent and ictus is again secured; finally, since there was no way of avoiding a slight clash in the sixth iambic foot, he frequently tempered the fifth foot by insisting that when it contained a single word, this word must be spondaic. That is, by dwelling upon the first syllable of the fifth foot he reduced the ictus on the second.[17] The result of this exceedingly delicate modulation of the line by Livius—a modulation revealing an astonishingly keen ear—was that the dramatic senarius in Latin had a rhythm in which quantitative and accentual beats usually coincided, and this rhythm served its purpose in Latin drama quite as effectively as did the trimeter in Greek. Considering the gentleness of the accent in Latin we may surmise Latin dramatic senarii, when thus treated, ran at least as smoothly as Browning's blank verse despite the fact that they had to give heed to accent as well as to quantity.

In teaching the rules of the Latin senarius it is a pedagogical mistake to compare it with the Greek trimeter as Lindsay does in his brilliant book, *Early Latin Verse;* indeed I am persuaded that it distorts historical facts to do so. If Livius was the man who shaped this line for Latin needs, we must remember that he had reached Rome as a mere child and had as a youth grown accustomed to the swing of verse pronounced in the Saturnian and the quadratus meters and that he would not have had any occasion at Rome to learn to comprehend the amazing precision of the Menandrian trmeter. And Naevius, the Campanian soldier, must have had much the same experience. To such men the Greek trimeter could only have suggested the possibility of writing a six-foot iambic line which would carry through to the end, with the lightness of the quadratus, the opening rhythm of the Saturnian. And the rules of the first hemistich of the Saturnian must have been the determining regulations of the senarius. Those rules had all to do with the purely Latin problem of writing quantitative verse that should not overmuch offend the demands of an accentual stress. Indeed it is fair to say that if Livius had never seen a Greek trimeter but had undertaken to adapt a six-foot iambic line on suggestions taken only from the Saturnian and the quadratus, he would have arrived at precisely what he did. By failing to see this simple historical sequence we have, from Bentley to the elaborate but misleading statistics of Klotz, followed Horace in misconceiving the spirit of the very worthy Latin senarius.

But there was more for the early dramatists to do than to shape a line suitable for dialogue, for Greek drama had taught these poets that a great variety of meters must be used to give the mood and tempo of emotional scenes. The Roman writers of tragedy did not attempt to reproduce the intricate polymetric and antistrophic Greek songs. However, they adopted several very effective meters (perhaps also creating some) which they used for massed effects, such rhythms as the cretic, bacchiac, anapaestic, glyconic, and the longer iambic and trochaic lines, not to mention various rarer forms. In a fragment of Ennius quoted by Cicero, Andromache in distress runs from senarii through a passage of pleading cretics:

(Quid petam praesidi aut exequar quove nunc etc.)

then through excited narration in excellent alliterative septenarii:

(Fana flamma deflagrata tosti alti stant parietes)

into turgid and wild anapaests:

(Priamo vi vitam evitari etc.).

And Cassandra's mad scene runs similarly from septenarii through dactylic tetrameters, trochaic octonarii, and anapaests into iambic octonarii. The tone of such cretics has been caught fairly well in Tennyson's *The Oak,*

All his leaves, fall'n at length,

while the bacchiac rhythm is, if pronounced with care, conveyed by Arnold's

Ye storm-winds, of autumn

These brief experiments on the part of English poets, which show an observance of word-stress and also of quantity, will indicate the nature of the difficult task which Latin poetry had to face in taking over meters native to the Greek language, except that the Latin poet, conversely, must place his verse ictus on a long syllable and secondarily, if possible, observe the word stress as well. That was a difficulty with which classical Greek did not have to contend, since its word accent was musical and could easily be slighted. German and English poetry—except in learned experiments—has refused to face the double task, a task which has fortunately never been compulsory.

If we keep these facts in mind I think we may be willing to concede that the Latin poets of the early time may have called in the extended aid of the flute and of melody partly in order to obscure the occasionally inevitable conflict between the word accent and verse ictus. The point can be illustrated by a simple example. In Tennyson's song "Blow, bugle, blow," the line

And the wild cataract leaps in glory,

which falls unrhythmically in the midst of an iambic system, hides its confusion when sung in regular three-fourths time. The flute or violin, unlike any of the percussion instruments, does not convey a stressing tone, it measures notes and carries a quantitative rhythm readily, thereby obscuring any word accents that fall irregularly.

It is my belief that when the drama came into Rome and found the language just at the point where the quantitative principle was having its conflict for dominance with the accentual factor, a moment when the task of shaping adequate rhythms for new forms would be very difficult, it did the natural thing, accepted quantity as dominant, attempted at the same time to observe the word stress, and then hid occasional discrepancies by using song and recitative freely. And this, it seems to me, is one of the reasons why Roman tragedy was the more willing to go in the direction of modern opera.

If a recent theory concerning French verse be true, we may find there an instructive parallel. It has been suggested that when medieval Latin verse floundered between quantity and accent, early French verse, unable to find usable quantitative distinctions and hampered by a monotonous word accent, hesitated for a dominant principle, and allowed the singing line with its counted notes to assume control. Whether or not this is the reason, at any rate the French lyric emerged with its isosyllabic lines and fluid ictus, and in so far provides a partial parallel to what happened in Latin verse.

It is not improbable that, if the Romans had come in contact with culture a century later than they did, so that the Latin accent might have affected colloquial morphology unhindered by literature and sophistication for another century, native poetry might have abandoned its quantitative basis and frankly accepted word accent as the most vital factor of its rhythm. It would perhaps have been a liberating influence had this happened. As it was, by their use of music and by their reasonable compromise with Greek meters, the early poets accustomed the Roman ear to slight the claims of accent, and Ennius was able to compose spoken lines in hexameters which almost entirely followed the dictates of quantity. Once completely naturalized, this method was no longer questioned, and Lucretius, Horace, and Vergil—except at line ends—could safely disregard the word accents. It was the musical part of the drama that had naturalized such principles of rhythm.

After Accius the writing of tragedy fell off as rapidly at Rome as it had in Greece after the conquests of Alexander. How is this to be explained? Why did not England produce great tragedies after the successes of the Elizabethan stage, or France for a long time after the classical period, or why did not America during the two centuries of play-writing before 1900 beget a single great dramatist? Recently there was published a list of the American plays copyrighted in Washington between 1870 and 1920; it contains over 60,000 titles. How many of these have become a part of the world's literature? Probably not one in 10,000. Can we explain why?

It is not well to be dogmatic in discussing the reasons for such a phenomenon as the decline of tragedy at Rome, but we may be permitted perhaps to repeat some conjectures. We have already remarked[18] that the second century B.C. was a period of striking social changes, of a decrease in the middle class native stock and a very remarkable increase in the slave population, and from this slave population there grew up at Rome the new generation of proletariat citizens that had to be amused at festival seasons. It was a population that was probably as intelligent as the old, but it had hitherto been brought up in slavery and in the devotion to material advancement that slavery implies. These new Romans could hardly be expected to concern themselves with the quality of the entertainment provided, with civic ideals and artistic standards. In Cicero's day the games at festivals were more frequently gladiatorial shows and wild beast hunts. To freedmen and freedmen's sons these seemed to provide what Aristotle called tragic purgation somewhat more effectively than did representations of the *Medea, Orestes,* and *Oedipus.* It is apparent that if society was to continue in its course of degeneration the exacting tragedy of the old type was doomed.

Nevertheless, the old plays were being revived by men who were interested in high standards, and when a famous actor played a part he would draw large audiences. Aesopus and Roscius, the best actors of Cicero's day, were in great demand and both grew rich at their profession. Though references to dramatic performances in Cicero's day are casual, we hear of not a few. We know, for instance, that there were reproductions of Ennius' plays a century after his death, and we find in the list his *Andromache, Telamo, Thyestes,* the *Alcumeo,* the *Iphigenia* and the *Hector.* Of Pacuvius' plays Cicero had seen the *Antiope,* the *Iliona,* and a play about Orestes which he describes as a favorite of the gallery. Accius was even

more popular. Aesopus produced his *Atreus* repeatedly. His *Eurysaces* was given in 57 B.C., the *Clytemestra* in 55, and the *Tereus* in 44 after the authorities had suppressed the *Brutus* because of its political significance. And there were many more.

This success of the old plays—artificial though it may have been in some instances—shows that respectable audiences could still be reckoned on so long as the Republic lasted, and that the plays were attractive enough to justify the aediles in presenting them. With the Empire, however, the decline was rapid; the populace found the tragedies tedious, and when in Horace's day a popular actor discovered a way of cutting the plays and presenting the more effective scenes in pantomime, with a lavish amount of music and a gorgeous setting, legitimate tragedy gave way to something resembling a Russian ballet. Old tragedies were cut and adapted for this new kind of presentation and new ones were written that consisted chiefly of scenarios and monologues. Even closet plays, like Seneca's, were shaped into a succession of recitations in the hope that they might sell to the new industry. Literary tragedy, however, had come to its end at Rome.

This process of decay was natural enough and was only to be expected, given the changes in Rome's society and with them the decline of Roman ideals. But it is still somewhat of a riddle why at Rome as well as at Athens good playwrights ceased to write a hundred years before tragedy ceased to attract respectable audiences. It would seem as if the art of writing plays lost its stimulus even before the plays themselves ceased to please. The reason for this may well be that tragedy kept too long to its convention of interpreting sacred myths. The themes were outworn, and each myth had had every human interest exploited by the time that several writers had given it their several interpretations.

Today it would seem quite the obvious thing to have dramatized fictitious experience, even as comedy had long ago learned to do. But a moment's reflection will show that to assume that this might have been done involves an anachronism. Greece did not take this step after Euripides, for Agathon's experiment was not followed, nor France for some time after the classical period, nor England after the Elizabethan successes, and conditions at Rome in the days of Accius were in many respects analogous to those in the countries named. Though the dramatic instinct seems always to be presumable, the drama depends upon social conditions and must draw its life from that which society provides. Its evolution has accordingly been a fairly consistent story. Early tragedy assumes the rôle of interpreting the most sacred and time-honored of a nation's stories. The sufferings, thoughts, emotions of the great—heroes, demigods, and kings—are worthy of presentation, and these alone. At first the tale must not be altered, it must be told as nearly as possible in the way that tradition has hallowed. As time goes on, however, and men have changed, the tale thus told will seem inconsonant with human nature; then the dramatist may re-tell it, suppressing what has grown obsolete, emphasizing the elements that still seem true to experience. A very daring realist will venture to present Telephus in tatters, but the critics will be upon his heels immediately. For the hero will remind you of a beggar, and it would be desecration to set mere man upon the stage made for the demigods. Common man belongs in comedy; you may laugh at him and with him, but life's great lessons are illustrated only in the characters of the great. And that is where Euripides stopped—was doubtless compelled to stop. And it is nearly where Shakespeare found the outward boundary of his tragedies. His tragic plots derive from old Chronicles or from Ancient Rome, or from foreign lands sufficiently removed from his audience by mists of unknown space to make them suitably heroic. His tragic characters never represent the men of contemporary England. They are as real and human as the man of the street, to be sure; but that is after all not the same thing. Try to imagine the heroines of Ibsen or Pinero or O'Neill upon the stage of the Globe Theatre in Shakespeare's day! The Elizabethan conception of the function of tragedy makes such heroines unthinkable except in comic rôles.

Realistic tragedy is of course a thing of slow growth, or perhaps we should say that a nation fits itself slowly for the reception of it. Comedy paves the way somewhat. When the great may not be laughed at, it is well that comedy should present the foibles and deformities of the common man, if it be merely for ridicule. Slaves served the purpose of comedy for Menander and Plautus, though they were careful not to compromise the dignity of their art by giving title rôles to such humble fellows. Yet as a matter of fact the study of mean subjects contributed directly and very largely to the understanding of the ordinary character as material for tragedy. Shakespeare's portraiture of Shylock, for example, carried him so far that modern critics do not know where comedy ends and tragedy begins. In the *Andria,* the *Hecyra,* and the *Heauton* of Terence the emotion shifts more than once from laughter to deep sympathy. But something more was needed than the dramatist's study of the man of the street. Human society must itself change. It is not an accident that genuine realistic tragedy failed to find its fully accepted place upon the stage till the nineteenth century, in a word not till thoroughgoing democracy, by preaching the equality of men, had persuaded us of the dignity of the mere human being, and through the prose novel taught the man on the street to concern himself with his fellows as worthy themes of art. That was a stage of democratic realism which Rome did not reach while the literary art was still creative. And therein probably lies the final explanation of the slow failure of Roman tragedy.

Notes

1. *Am. Four. Phil.,* 1927, 105.

2. Livius and Naevius were both very fond of the septenarii; the iambic tetrameter appears in the tragic fragments of Naevius once; cretics are found in the *Equos Trojanus,* and bacchiacs apparently in Naevius' *Danae* and in his *Lycurgus.* Fraenkel,

Hermes (1927), 357 ff., has shown that the trochaic septenarius (quadratus) was an old Latin meter. We need not, however, assume with him that it was derived from the Greek. As a marching rhythm it is too natural to require explanation. The assumption of an Indo-European *Urvers* needs to be exiled from our books. Song and dance are very old.

3. See *Cambridge Ancient History,* VII, 644.

4. See Duckett, *Studies in Ennius,* 56, who revises the views of Leo, *De Tragoedia Romana* (Göttingen, 1910).

5. For a strophic system in Ennius, see Crusius, *Philologus,* Supp. XXI, 114.

6. *Gram. Lat. Keil,* VI, 77, 7; Vollmer, *Röm, Metrik,* in Gercke's *Einleitung,* I, 8, p. 6; however among the preserved fragments of Pacuvius there are several anapaests that resemble those of Ennius.

7. Ennius, ed. Vahlen, *Scaenica,* 272.

8. See *Am. Four. Phil.* 1913, 326.

9. Leo, *Die plautinischen Cantica* (1897).

10. Fraenkel, *Plautinisches im Plautus* (1922), criticized by Immisch, *Sitz. Heid. Akad.* 1923.

11. Milne, *Cat. of lit. pap. in British Mus.* 1927 (no. 52); cf. Wuest and Croenert, *Philol.* 1928, 153 ff.

12. See Marx's ed. of *Rudens,* 254 ff.

13. Crusius, *Die Responsion in den plaut. Cantica* (1929).

14. See Bieber, *Denkmäler d. Theaterwesen* and Bulle, *Abh. Bayer. Akad.* 1928.

15. If Horace's strictures on the new music of the drama in the *Ars Poet.* 200-15 took a hint from Neoptolemus, we may suppose that Hellenistic critics had objected to this change.

16. Robert Bridges, *Ibant Obscuri.* Such hexameters as

> They were amid the shadows by night in loneliness obscure
> Walking forth i' the void and vasty dominyon of Ades:
> As by an uncertain moonray secretly illumin'd

do not represent what happened to Latin in Ennius, for the reason that in Latin pronunciation the quantity was the dominant element controlling event the accent. In English the reverse is true. Fraenkel, *Iktus und Akzent,* has recently committed a similar mistake in judgment, influenced apparently by the high respect that speakers of German must necessarily have for stress. He has resorted to daring hypotheses in trying to prove that Plautus always correctly observes a species of stress (see Sonnenschein in *Class. Quart.,* 1929, 81). It is significant that the French, who feel little stress in their diction, go to the other extreme and find stress insignificant in Latin. Latin in fact was like neither; it resembled Hungarian in being primarily quantitative, and in its word accent had a moderate stress not without a rather noticeable pitch such as is found in some parts of Sweden.

17. See Lindsay, *Early Latin Verse,* Leo, *Geschichte Lat. Lit.,* p. 68. Fraenkel, *Iktus und Akzent,* seems to me only to have confused the results that have been summarized with consummate skill and good sense by Lindsay.

18. In chap. I.

Thelma B. De Graff (essay date 1931)

SOURCE: "Some Remarks on Naevius as Poet and as Man" in *Naevian Studies: A Dissertation*, W. F. Humphrey, 1931, pp. 58-66.

[*In the following excerpt, De Graff explains why it is so difficult to evaluate Naevius's merit as a writer and points out that many fragments of his work are extant solely because they were used as examples in grammar texts.*]

There are certain great names in the world of letters which are immortal[1] Upon them has been impressed the stamp *omnium temporum et aetatum et locorum*[2], which marks them as classic. In the chorus of universal approval which greets them there is scarcely a discordant note. To estimate their value there is no need to read innumerable tomes compiled in exegesis of them by the *literati* of many generations. But there are other authors who have not made so general an appeal. Their reading public has been limited to a small group of specialists whose interest is preeminently historical or linguistic. Their works have not made their way into the Schools and the Colleges as textbooks. Were it not for a strong antiquarian interest inherent in them, these writers would probably sink into oblivion. Outstanding in this number is the Roman poet Gnaeus Naevius.

The would-be interpreter of Naevius is thrown almost exclusively upon his own resources in his endeavor to estimate Naevius's place in the world of letters. Such an interpreter has at his disposal isolated fragments which are in no case clearly illuminated by the light of the context.

The first Roman epic[3] poet seems to have won considerable respect from his compatriots, but not to have stirred them to much comment upon him or his work. In the field of comedy, where his fearless outspokenness and mordant satire had the freest scope, he was ranked third by Volcatius Sedigitus[4]. Ennius, his successor, wrote scornfully of his verse form[5],

scripsere alii rem
versibus quos olim Fauni vatesque canebant,

not even deigning to mention him by name. Yet it is noteworthy that Ennius, for all his superb confidence in himself as the possessor of the soul of Homer[6] considered

Naevius's treatment of the First Punic War adequate, for he did not treat it himself[7]. Cicero[8], who rebuked the father of Latin poetry for his characterization of Naevius, quem in vatibus et Faunis annumerat Ennius, was even more stinging in the words that follow: et luculente quidem scripserunt, etiam si minus quam tu polite, nec vero tibi aliter videri debet, qui a Naevio vel sumpsisti multa, si fateris, vel, si negas, surripuisti. Naevius's **Bellum Punicum** Cicero likens to the work of the great Myron[9], that famous sculptor, whose statue of the Discobolos is renowned the world over. As Gardner[10] said of Myron, "we find that the life of his statues is what most impressed later writers" so may we say of Naevius that his virile genius gave his successors an epic "von eigenem Fleisch und Blut" for a model[11]. But as the peaceful expression on the face of the Discobolos belies his flexed muscles, and the archaic treatment of his hair is surprising, when we glance at the lifelikeness of the toes of his left foot, so are we astonished by the prosaic quality of some of the fragments of the inventor of the *fabula praetextata,* when we read his matchless description of a coquette[12]. However, it is no more fair to censure Naevius because he lacks "the oceanroll of rhythm" of Vergil than it would be to minimize Myron's excellent points because he was not a Phidias or a Praxiteles.

Horace complains that the conservatism of the people of his day made them extravagant in the praise of everything ancient[13]:

Si veteres ita miratur laudatque poetas
ut nihil anteferat, nihil illis comparet, errat;
si quaedam nimis antique, si pleraque dure
dicere credit eos, ignave multa fatetur,
et sapit et mecum facit et Iove iudicat aequo.

In these verses he urges a proper evaluation of the writers of old and condemns indiscriminate praise of such writers. Scoring that spirit which made the practical Romans live so much, intellectually and spiritually, in the past, and gave the aura of sanctity to the venerated *mos maiorum,* he contrasts that spirit with the more progressive spirit of the Greeks[14]:

Quod si tam Graiis novitas invisa fuisset
quam nobis, quid nunc esset vetus?

How likely it is that Naevius would hold a high place in a Rome that[15]

habet hos numeratque poetas
ad nostrum tempus Livi scriptoris ab aevo,

seeing that Livius Andronicus's Latin version of the Odyssey was still a textbook in the school where the youthful Horace and his classmates were taught by the stern Orbilius[16].

Naevius in manibus non est et mentibus haeret paene recens?,

asks Horace[17], indicating that Naevius still had his public[18].

It is difficult for us to judge Naevius fairly. When we consider that the fragments which remain to us were, in the majority of cases, quoted only to illustrate obsolete words and archaic forms, we realize that we must not be severe in our judgment concerning him. "Poetische Schönheit zeichnet keines der wenigen Fragmenten ausrdquo;, writes Hosius[19] of the pitifully few fragments of the **Bellum Punicum** that are left to us. But what is "poetische Schönheit?" Does Hosius mean the noble grandeur of the Iliad? Yet even in that poem, which contains, *mea quidem sententia,* the most exquisite scene[20] in all literature, there are moments when the great Homer nods, when he follows too slavishly the epic convention, and when, despite his own obvious joy in the conflict, we weary a little of the dauntless heroes who display such extraordinary efficiency in sending their less fortunate opponents down to the house of Hades[21].

Or is "poetische Schönheit" that haunting, brooding sense of *lacrimae rerum* that made the peace-loving Mantuan look far beyond "the tumult and the shouting" of the fray to the bitter tragedy, e.g. of the boy Troilus who met an untimely death because he was *impar congressus Achilli?* But Vergil, who was his own severest critic and had set so high a standard for himself that, if we may believe the well-known story, after eleven years of inspired and conscientious work he wished to have his masterpiece consigned to the flames, would suffer greatly if he were quoted for grammatical reasons only. Let us suppose, for the sake of argument, that the words[22]

> Sic tota passim regione vagantur

were quoted only to illustrate the use of the ablative without a preposition to denote the place where something is (was) done. Who would conceive of the rare beauty of[23]

> Manibus date lilia plenis
> purpureos spargam flores, animamque nepotis
> his saltem accumulem donis, et fungar inani munere,

the passage which immediately precedes *Sic vagantur?* Or suppose that some grammarian interested in word-formation quoted the words[24]

> Talia dicta dabat, sed viribus ensis adactus transabiit
> costas

to illustrate the addition of the prefix *trans-* to a verb already compounded with a prefix. Who would know that just two lines below this physiological description of a fatal wound there occurred the lines in which grim death is so finely described[25]?

> purpureus veluti cum flos, succisus aratro,
> languescit, moriens, lassove papavera collo
> demisere caput, pluvia cum forte gravantur.

The pathos of[26]

> quod patrio princeps donarat nomine regem

would not be nearly so poignant if some commentator on Lucretius had quoted this line alone without the context of the whole pitiful tale of Iphigenia.

Even the lyric poets, who more than all others are inspired by the love of beauty, would suffer were they quoted for grammatical reasons only. There have never been written two other lines which bare so completely the tragedy of a soul torn by conflicting emotions as Catullus's verses[27],

> Odie et amo. Quare id faciam fortasse requiris.
> Nescio. Sed fieri sentio et excrucior.

But suppose that some Priscianus or some Nonius had left us just a part of this couplet, which he had quoted to illustrate the use of *quare* for *cur* in an indirect question. If that fragment happened to be *Quare id faciam fortasse requiris,* never should we, who lack the divine fire and the emotional fervor of a Catullus, be able to appreciate our loss. Shelley, the apostle of beauty, does not always walk on the heights of inspiration.

> Go home,
> Henry, and play with Lilla till I come[28],

sounds like Robert Louis Stevenson in one of his less inspired moments. But let us assume that two thousand years hence, by some unthinkable catastrophe, all the complete copies of Shelley shall have been lost, and that there shall remain of his work only a few fragments which have survived for antiquarian reasons. Under such circumstances the two proper names, Henry and Lilla, might well have saved for posterity such a fragment as this, which had better have been consigned to oblivion.

It is a curious thing that our totally inadequate sources of information with regard to Naevius[29] give us after all so clear a picture of his vivid personality. At certain stages of the world's history there is born a Socrates, a Naevius, a Voltaire, a Heine, or a Shaw. Their methods and their temperaments are typical of the nations they represent. Naevius's function at Rome may be likened to Socrates's at Athens. Different as they were in many ways, there is a certain similarity between the Roman and the Athenian. Both men were patriots, both had fought for their country; they would both have been entirely unmolested had they remained silent about the faults of those around them. The one paid for his frankness by drinking the hemlock, the other by imprisonment and exile.

The Athenians could appreciate the incomparable wit of Aristophanes, and join in the general chorus of mirth at his brilliant sallies against specific personalities, famous or notorious. But the dialectic of the patient Socrates, who pursued his eternal quest for truth, in the search for which he considered[30] omnes cruciatus corporis, omnia pericula mortis atque exsilii parvi esse ducenda, was more than the sensitive Athenians could endure. Hence they put to death the greatest Athenian of them all, a man who was the apotheosis of the immortal spirit of Greek thought, because he was merciless in his exposure of sham and sophistry and hypocrisy, faults of which each individual has his share. The crowd could laugh with Aristophanes at his victims, for it has always been true that[31]

> quae sibi quisque timebat
> unius in miseri exitium conversa tulere.

At Rome, however, things were different. If we *can* conceive of the Roman genius as producing a Socrates, we may easily imagine the scorn which the Romans of the Punic War days would have felt toward one who spent all his time asking questions. Not a Socrates, but a Naevius was needed in Rome, a man whose patriotism was unassailable, but whose temerity in pointing out the faults of the elect, upon whose prestige the Roman State was founded, was salutary, if inexcusable. The fact that the Romans respected Naevius's originality and realized that the power of the pen, in some fields, was mightier than that of the sword accounts for the intolerance of the patricians toward the first great Roman poet, whose genius was marred by his faculty, to the patrician mind so unhappy, of scoring the faults of prominent members of the aristocracy. Unlike the satirists of the Empire, he attacked not the dead, but the living; he dealt not only in generalities, but also in personalities.

But we must not give the impression that Naevius's sole claim to fame was his gift for satire. His comedies[32] must have been his best vehicle for that side of his nature; he does not seem to have worn the buskin with overwhelming success. Therefore, we should expect to find his most dignified and noble poetic expression in the ***Bellum Punicum.*** Nor are we surprised by the epic fullness of expression in the fragments, though we know that Naevius possessed the Roman gift of compact and pithy utterance. Publilius Syrus himself could not improve upon[33]

> male parta male dilabuntur,

while the famous verse[34]

> Fato Metelli Romae fiunt consules,

wrote a chapter in Roman literary history. When we examine[35]

> amborum uxores
> noctu Troiad exibant capitibus opertis,
> flentes ambae, abeuntes lacrimis cum multis,

we find *exibant flentes* repeated in *abeuntes lacrimis cum multis.* The repetition, however, is exceedingly effective, for these women are leaving their homes forever. In the fragment that has been critized for its prosaic quality[36],

> transit Melitam
> Romanus exercitus, insulam integram urit,
> populatur, vastat, rem hostium concinnat,

the use of expressions practically synonymous, *urit, populatur, vastat,* and *rem concinnat,* indicates a fate for Malta that is appalling in its thoroughness. In the verse[37]

> superbiter contemptim conterit legiones,

we have the same cumulative effect in the use of the two adverbs.

Sometimes this fullness of expression indicates lavish wealth or display. We read[38] of an *auream victimam pulcram,* and[39] of *pulchras creterras, aureas lepistas*[40], *vestemque citrosam*[41], and *magnam domum decoremque ditem*[42]. At other times it pictures the dignity and the majesty of the gods. Surely the fragment[43],

> senex fretus pietati deum adlocutus
> summi deum regis fratrem Neptunum
> regnatorem marum,

is impressive and stately. One gets clearly from it a sense of the vast realm over which Neptune rules as well as of the high rank and noble connections of the god of the sea. No less dignified is the fragment[44],

> patrem suom supremum optumum appellat.

The mighty Apollo is described as[45]

> pollens sagittis, inclutus arquitenens,
> sanctus Iove prognatus, Pythius Apollo,

and his graceful sister Diana is[46]

> Arquitenens sagittis pollens dea.

Moreover, in these isolated fragments, we see many a clear picture. We see the aged Anchises, who has just interpreted the divine will by the omen of a bird's flight, sacrificing a beautiful victim to the gods[47]. We see an aged man *fretus pietati* calling upon the god of the sea[48]. That is a noble phrase, *fretus pietati,* by no means lacking in "poetische Schönheit"[49]. We are introduced to a peace-loving race[50], *silvicolae homines bellique inertes,* who dwell, perhaps, *regnata per arva Saturno.* In one picture, the youthful Proserpina, daughter of Ceres, advances with a step that marks her every inch a goddess[51]; in another picture brave men have decided that honorable death is to be preferred to living disgrace[52]. Now we are watching the toiling, sweating oarsmen strain their way across the *liquidum mare*[53]. The sea may be calm and the rowers may be enthusiastic, yet, like young Jean in Daudet's[54] famous story, they find that the constant strain on their muscles ultimately outweighs their enthusiasm.

Each of these fragments is complete and eloquent. Others[55] are less eloquent. Yet they are all fragments. It is as if a series of stereopticon slides had been carelessly rifled and most of the slides had been irretrievably lost. To attempt to reconstruct a coherent whole from the few remaining slides would be well-nigh impossible. But, if the slides extant were sufficiently stimulating and the story of which they told a part was sufficiently famous, we should be greatly tempted to reconstruct them in the light of what we might assume to be their context and to fit them into their proper places in the whole series. That would be a fascinating, yet dangerous, process.

Notes

1. The length of the introduction to this chapter may be pardoned when it is explained that an attempt to estimate Naevius's place in the literary world would seem to justify a discussion of this type.

2. My expression here is based on Cicero, Pro Archia 7.

3. See note 87 to Chapter I, above.

4. Compare Gellius 15.24 Sedigitus in libro quem scripsit de poetis quid de his sentiat qui comoedias fecerunt, et quem ex omnibus praestare ceteris putet ac deinceps quo quemque in loco et honore ponat his versibus suis demonstrat. Line 7 of a thirteen-line fragment of Sedigitus gave third place to Naevius: Dein Naevius, qui fervet, pretio in tertiost.

5. Varro, De Lingua Latina 7.36; Cicero, Brutus 76, Orator 171, De Divinatione 1.114; Quintilian 9.4.115.

6. Lucretius 1.124-126; Horace, Epistulae 2.1.50; Cicero, De Re Publica 6.10. Porphyrio, on Horace, Epistulae 2.1.51, says, Ennius in principio Annalium suorum somnio se scripsit admonitum quod secundum Pythagorae dogma anima Homeri in suum corpus venisset.

7. Cicero, Brutus 76 qui <= Ennius> si illum <= Naevium> ut simulat contemneret, non omnia bella persequens primum illud Punicum acerrimum bellum reliquisset.

8. *Ibidem.*

9. *Ibidem:* tamen illius quem in vatibus et Faunis annumerat Ennius bellum Punicum quasi Myronis opus delectat.

10. 274.

11. See Leo, Plautinische Forschungen, 93.

12. Diehl, Fragment 104:

> quasi in choro ludens datatim dat se et communem facit.
> Alii adnutat, alii adnictat, alium amat, alium tenet.
> Alibi manus est occupata, alii percellit pedem,
> anulum dat alii spectandum, a labris alium invocat,
> cum alio cantat, at tamen alii s<uo> dat digito litteras.

13. Horace, Epistulae 2.1.64-68.

14. *Ibidem,* 2.1.90-91.

15. *Ibidem,* 2.1.61-62.

16. *Ibidem,* 2.1.69-71.

17. *Ibidem,* 2.1.53-54.

18. He had his public still in Gellius's day. See passages listed by Hosius in his edition of Gellius, in the Index Auctorum, 2.317.

19. Schanz-Hosius, 53. Hosius proceeds thus: "es klingt wie eine versifizierte Chronik, wo nur die Taten reden, oder wie die ersten Scipionengrabschriften wenn es im Fragment 37 heisst" (the reference is to Baehrens 37 = Diehl 22).

20. I refer to the parting of Hector and Andromache, described in Iliad 6.392-493.

21. Compare, for example, such a passage as Iliad 4.457-538, or Iliad 6.5-28.

22. Aeneid 6.886.

23. *Ibidem,* 6.884-886.

24. *Ibidem,* 9.431-432.

25. *Ibidem,* 9.435-437.

26. Lucretius 1.94.

27. Catullus 85.

28. From the poem Rosalind and Helen (page 233 in the edition by Thomas Y. Crowell Co., New York).

29. In Rheinisches Museum 37 (1882), 485-491, R. Förster discusses the question, Gab es wirklich noch einen Naevius und Ennius im Mittelalter? On page 485 he quotes Friedrich Haase as saying, "Es scheint dass Ennius noch im Mittelalter vorhanden gewesen ist. Alanus ab Insulis hat nach seinem Anticlaudianus 5.165 die Annales noch vollständig gekannt, und Cramer (Hauschronik S. 233) hat in der Dombibliothek zu Prag eine Handschrift gesehen, in welcher sich hinter Statius ein Bücherverzeichniss einer Bibliothek des 13. Jahrhunderts befindet, in dem noch Ennius und Naevius vorkommen". Compare Alanus ab Insulis, Anticlaudianus 1.326 A:

> Illic pannoso plebescit carmine noster
> Ennius, et Priami fortunas intonat; illic
> *Maevius,* in caelos audens os ponere mutum,
> gesta ducis Macedum tenebrosi carminis umbra
> pingere dum tentat, in primo limine fessus
> haeret, et ignavam queritur torpescere Musam.

The reference to Naevius is, however, by no means certain. The reading in the text is *Maevius,* instead of *Naevius.* On pages 488-491 Förster refutes the words of Haase quoted above by showing that, to Alanus, Ennius and Naevius were merely names, and that the manuscript referred to (by Cramer) was by no means infallible, or even clear. Compare Vahlen, Praefatio, CXXX.

30. Compare Cicero, Pro Archia 6.

31. Vergil, Aeneid 2.130-131.

32. His type of genius was better suited to comedy. In number his comedies far exceed his tragedies.

33. Diehl, Fragment 70.

34. *Ibidem,* Fragment 47.

35. *Ibidem,* Fragment 3.

36. *Ibidem,* Fragment 22.

37. *Ibidem,* Fragment 31.

38. *Ibidem,* Fragment 2.

39. *Ibidem,* Fragment 5.

40. *Ibidem,* Fragment 5.

41. *Ibidem,* Fragment 6.

42. *Ibidem,* Fragment 35.

43. *Ibidem,* Fragment 7.

44. *Ibidem,* Fragment 8.

45. *Ibidem,* Fragment 18.

46. *Ibidem,* Fragment 43.

47. *Ibidem,* Fragment 2:

> postquam avem aspexit in templo Anchisa,
> sacra in mensa penatium ordine ponuntur,
> immolabat auream victimam pulcram.

48. See note 42, above.

49. When one reads the fragments, one gets the sense of a lavish use of adjectives on Naevius's part. His compound adjectives, such as *silvicolae, arquitenens,* and *bicorpores,* his frequent superlatives, such as *supremum, summi,* and *fortissimos* his words of color, such as *auream* and *purpureus,* and the frequent use of *pulcher,* indicate how effective his adjectives are. I find no fragment that describes beauty in terms of the effect it has upon the beholder, as e. g. Homer describes Helen's beauty in Iliad 3.156-158. But that is being unfair, perhaps, because the context is missing in the case of fragments of Naevius and, besides, Naevius was not a Homer.

50. Diehl, Fragment 13.

51. *Ibidem,* Fragment 17, prima incedit Cereris Proserpina puer. For *incedo* compare e.g. Vergil, Aeneid 1.46.

52. *Ibidem,* Fragment 24:

> seseque ei perire mavolunt ibidem,
> quam cum stupro redire ad suos populares.

> For the same noble sentiment see Fragment 23 also.

53. *Ibidem,* Fragment 21:

> conferreque aut ratem aeratam
> qui per liquidum mare sudantes
> eunt atque sedantes.

54. Compare Alphonse Daudet, Sapho, Chapter I,, where Jean Gaussin carries Fanny Legrand upstairs.

55. As, for example, Diehl, Fragments 27, 29.

Henry T. Rowell (essay date 1947)

SOURCE: "The Original Form of Naevius's *Bellum Punicum,*"*American Journal of Philology,* Vol. LXVIII, No. 1, January 1947, pp. 21-46.

[*In the following essay Rowell contends that the common distribution and assignment of fragments of the* Bellum Punicum *is faulty and he offers suggestions for a different arrangement of particular segments.*]

From statements of Suetonius and Santra, it is known that Cn. Naevius wrote his **Bellum Punicum** in the form of a single unbroken narrative which was later divided into seven books by C. Octavius Lampadio, probably in the second half of the second century B.C.[1] That this edition of Lampadio was used either directly or indirectly by some of the later writers who refer to the **Bellum Punicum** is indicated by their identification of specific books as the sources of their quotations and references.[2] Consequently scholars who have compiled and edited the fragments, since the revival of learning, have distributed them among seven separate books[3] and there can be no quarrel with this arrangement.

The method, however, which has been followed in assigning specific fragments to specific books has long needed to be challenged. From 1595, when Merula first expressed an opinion regarding the contents of the first books of the **Bellum Punicum,**[4] until the near present, certain fragments have been assigned to certain books in flagrant violation of the testimony of the ancient authors by whom they are preserved. These dislocations have not only affected our views regarding the continuity which Naevius observed in describing the first Punic War. They have also created the prevailing concept of the place within the opening books occupied by the legendary material which Naevius also treated and the relation of that material to the historical account of the war.

The manner in which this occurred deserves to be noted. First of all, certain fragments were arbitrarily dislocated in order to fit them into a preconceived notion of the original order of contents of the poem. This can be clearly seen in the early reconstructions of Spangenberg[5] and Klussmann[6] which influenced Vahlen's arrangement[7] in which those fragments alone which seem to pertain to legendary events are assigned to the first two books. Subsequently, as this notion of the order of contents was passed on unaltered in its essentials from scholar to scholar, it acquired an independent authority and began to enjoy the respect due to an established fact. It then either caused the precarious base on which it rested to be ignored or was adduced as a reason for accepting the dislocations which made its existence possible. So great is the power of repetition.

Now the traditional reconstruction—for so we shall call it henceforth for convenience—of the **Bellum Punicum** is reproduced in recent works of scholarship substantially as follows:

Naevius began his epic with the Fall of Troy and the wanderings of Aeneas. These events together with the founding of Rome and possibly that of Carthage occupied the first two books. The main theme of the poem, the first Punic War, began with Book III and continued through

Book VII, that is, to the end of the poem.[8] Roman history between the founding of Rome and the first Punic War was not included.[9]

The reason for this arrangement, however, was not easily explained. The omission of events between the founding of the city and the first Punic War did not allow the material of the first two books to be interpreted as the opening part of an annalistic account of Roman history in verse similar in plan and purpose to the *Annales* of Ennius. Since Dido and Anna appeared in the **Bellum Punicum** (frg. 6) and the main theme of the poem was a war between Rome and Carthage, many scholars found it reasonable to assume, especially in the light of Virgil, that Dido and Aeneas were made responsible in some way for the enmity between the states which they had founded[10]—an enmity which flared into open warfare in 264 B.C. Those who declined to accept this theory were compelled to assume another link between the legendary and historical parts of the poem. As stated by Leo, whom Fränkel cites in this connection, "Also war es nur die Entstehung Roms um deren willen Naevius die Einleitung vorausgeschickt hat."[11]

This, then, is the traditional reconstruction. But it has been finally challenged by Ladislaus Strzelecki, who published his monograph, *De Naeviano Belli Punici Carmine Quaestiones Selectae*, in 1935.[12] Part of this work is of capital importance since it contains a new concept of the original form of the first three books of the **Bellum Punicum** based on a new arrangement of the fragments. The approach is new, to be sure, only in so far as it breaks with the traditional method of reassigning certain fragments arbitrarily. In principle it is hardly radical since it consists in following the evidence of the manuscripts.[13] Without anticipating the general plan which Naevius might or should have followed in composing his epic, Strzelecki advocates placing the fragments where they are said to belong by the ancient authors in whose works they are preserved and not where they have to be placed to support the traditional reconstruction of contents.

Unfortunately, Strzelecki's monograph does not appear to have received the consideration which it deserved before the Second World War[14] and no one, to my knowledge, has yet made full use of its conclusions.[15] Part of this neglect, at least, is probably due to the author's greater interest in tracing reflections of the **Bellum Punicum** in Virgil's *Aeneid* than in working out his reconstruction in more than a cursory manner. I wish to give Strzelecki full credit for his accomplishment which is the work of a pioneer. But I believe that it can be stated in all fairness that he is content to show us in a few bold strokes the way which we must travel in the future, but does not concern himself with many details of the departure or accompany us for any distance on the way.

My purpose, therefore, in writing this article is to follow the way indicated by Strzelecki as far as it will take us in regard to the original form of the entire poem. The fragments which the traditional reconstruction has displaced are the foundation stones of any reconstruction and their position in the work as a whole must be tested far more rigorously than Strzelecki cared to test them. This can be done only by examining them separately in the light of the textual tradition. Next, when the evidence for their position has been established, their contents must be analyzed for what they can tell us about the order and contents of the first three books of the poem. Finally, when this step has been completed, we shall be in a position to investigate the order and form of the remaining four books in the light of our new conclusions.

If the technical investigation which has been proposed succeeds in creating a new concept of the poem's original form, it will have created a new problem simultaneously. Many of the fragments which have not been displaced or have been assigned by conjecture will have to be rearranged and a new and detailed reconstruction of the entire contents, especially of the legendary part, will have to be undertaken. Such a reconstruction must lead eventually to questions regarding the genesis of the poem: What did Naevius know of the Trojan Legend? How did he select and transform material already at hand? What did he add which was peculiarly his own creation? Why did he choose a particular form in preference to others? In time these questions must be answered, in so far as the evidence permits.

For the present, however, the task must be the laying of a firm foundation for future investigation along the lines just indicated. For only after it has been laid and its flaws detected can further work be carried out with profit. It therefore seemed advisable to conduct an investigation which attempted no more than to furnish a new conception of the original form of the poem as a whole and to develop its implications and consequences in other studies.

As has been indicated above, the evidence of a seven book edition of the **Bellum Punicum** and the fact that certain fragments are attributed to specific books in our sources make any reconstruction of the poem depend on the relative order of the fragments and notices. The following fragments are assigned expressly to the first three books:

> Nos. 5, 13, 19, 21, and 32 to Book I
> Nos. 22, 23, 29, and 30 to Book II
> Nos. 3 and 24 to Book III

Yet, of these fragments, Nos. 3, 24, and 32 have been assigned arbitrarily to other books by modern scholars. Let us now see to what extent such displacements can be justified.

Fragment 32 which has been reassigned to Book III (Vahlen, Baehrens, Morel) reads as follows in Morel's edition (p. 23):

> Manius Valerius
> consul partem exerciti in expeditionem
> ducit

The verses are preserved by Charisius (p. 163 Barwick; p. 128 Keil) with the notice: **Gn. Naevius Belli Punici** I. In the *Codex Neapolitanus* from which this passage in other sources is ultimately derived, the *praenomen* of Valerius is given in abbreviation as *M*. Hence Barwick and Keil read *Marcus*. But since the only Valerii who were consuls during the first Punic War are known to have borne the praenomina *Manius* and *Lucius,* we must accept the emendation, as old as Merula's edition, of M' for M and identify the consul of the passage with Manius Valerius Maximus, consul in 263 B.C. who conducted military operations in Sicily in the course of the same year.[16]

Emending the number of the book, however, from I to II with Spangenberg and Klussmann or from I to III with later scholars is quite a different matter. Baehrens and Cichorius alone, so far as I have been able to ascertain, have sought paleographic grounds for assuming a corruption in the text.[17] They found them in the fact that the *praenomen* of the consul in abbreviation follows directly upon the number of the book. Hence confusion between an original III and the M' of *Manius* is assumed. But this common assumption did not lead to common results. For Baehrens suggests that the manuscript I *M* represents an original IIII followed by *Valerius,* while Cichorius conjectures an original III *M'*.

Yet, the facts of the matter are these. The *Neapolitanus* and all its derivatives, that is, the sum total of existing evidence, give the reading I according to Keil and Barwick, who made thorough studies of them. This is the only firm evidence which we have. Behind it we cannot go except in conjecture and such conjecture must be properly justified. Its only justification in this instance is the assumption which has become powerful by repetition but is actually devoid of any supporting evidence that Naevius did not begin the **Bellum Punicum** with the war which gave it its title but with the fall of Troy. Hence this fragment which refers to the Punic War had to be assigned to Book II or III or even IV according to the opinions of the several editors regarding the place in the poem where the legendary account ended and the historical account began. Paleography was then called upon by a few to furnish questionable support for a desired emendation. The rest simply made the emendation without the slightest regard for the textual tradition.

Fragment 24, which has been reassigned to Book II (Vahlen, Baehrens, Morel), reads as follows in Morel's edition (p. 21):

> Manusque susum ad caelum sustulit suas rex
> Amulius divis < que > gratulabatur

The verses are preserved by Nonius under *gratulari: gratias agere* (p. 165 Mueller, p. 167 Lindsay) with the notice: **Naevius Belli Punici** III. The emendations *manusque* for *isque* (Merula) and *rex* for *res* (Stephanus) are also accepted by Mueller and Leo.[18] Lindsay retains the manuscript readings. In the second line, the emendation *Amu-*

lius for *Amullus* has been accepted by all editors since Bentinus. Given the part played by Amulius in the legend of Rome's foundation, it is reasonably certain. The manuscript *gratulabatur divis* (retained by Lindsay) has been rearranged in various ways to accord with the several editors' opinions of what a Saturnian verse should be. Morel, as indicated by his reference *ad loc.,* adopted Leo's version, which is as satisfactory as any other.

But there is no reason to emend the number of the book from which the passage was taken except to make it support the traditional reconstruction. Since Naevius was believed to have begun his account of the first Punic War with Book III, there could be no place in Book III for the mention of an event which was so clearly connected with the legendary history of Rome. Hence, editors reassigned the fragment to Book II in spite of the fact that all manuscripts give Book III as its source.

The last of the dislocated fragments is Number 3, which has been reassigned to Book I (Vahlen, Baehrens, Morel). In Morel's edition (p. 17) it reads as follows:

> Postquam avem aspexit in templo Anchisa,
> sacra in mensa penatium ordine ponuntur;
> immolabat auream victimam pulchram.

The fragment is preserved by Probus (*ad* Verg. *Ecl.,* 6, 31 [p. 336 Hagen; p. 14 Keil]) with the notice: **Naevius Belli Punici** *libro tertio sic* (the *Monacensis* gives: 3 *libro*). The *Anchises* of the *Vaticanus* was emended to *Anchisa* by Keil, an emendation later adopted by Hagen and Leo.[19] The rest of the text is based on a uniform manuscript tradition. Furthermore, it is confirmed from *templo* to *ponuntur* by Cynthius Cenetensis,[20] a scholar of the fifteenth century who in composing a commentary on Virgil's *Aeneid* appears to have used the now lost Bobbio manuscript of Probus which was the archetype of all existing manuscripts and of the *editio princeps*.[21] But for our present purpose, the words with which Cynthius introduces his citation are of greater importance. They read, as reproduced by Mai: **Et Naevius belli punici** *lib.* III .

Thus, the original position of the fragment is well attested by the sum total of our evidence. But this evidence has been consistently ignored in favor of the traditional reconstruction. Obviously a fragment which mentions Anchises could not find an appropriate place in a book (III) which was believed to have begun with the opening events of the first Punic War. On the other hand, its contents could be interpreted conveniently as a sacrifice undertaken by Anchises in connection with the fall of Troy or the setting forth of the Trojans to seek a new home. Hence reassignment of the fragment from Book III to Book I.

These, then, are the fragments of the **Bellum Punicum** which have been dislocated by scholars in order to give them new positions in the contents of the poem as a whole. The analysis of the sources in which they are preserved has shown that the dislocations, so far as the manuscript tradition is concerned, are thoroughly unjustified. We shall therefore follow the order of the fragments attested by the sources in examining what the fragments have to tell about the original form and contents of the poem. In a way, this will be a second testing of the sources in regard to the fragments' position. For if intolerable difficulties are placed in the way of understanding the contents by returning the fragments to where they are said to belong, we shall have to suspect again that the sources are in error.

In establishing the text of fragment 32 above, we also established a firm date for the historical event to which it refers. This was the year 263 B.C. when Manius Valerius Maximus was consul and conducted military operations in Sicily.[22] After Valerius and his consular colleague had raised the siege of Messena, which was being besieged by a Carthaginian and a Greek army, the latter under the command of Hiero, Valerius pursued Hiero to Syracuse. There he forced him to come to terms which included an alliance with the Romans.[23]

De Sanctis suggests that our Naevian fragment refers to Valerius' first invasion of Syracusan territory, an event in which he sees the beginning of Roman imperialism.[24] Cichorius does little more in his commentary than restate what Naevius tells us except that he assumes that the military operation in question was a sally into the interior which took place during the siege of Messina.[25] Since the Latin phrase *expeditionem ducere* means no more than to lead out troops on a military operation,[26] we know for certain only that Naevius is referring to a march, sally, or campaign undertaken by Valerius.

Little as this fragment may add to our historical knowledge of the first Punic War, it is of capital importance for our understanding of the original form of Naevius' **Bellum Punicum.** Both its position in Book I and its reference to an event of the year 263 B.C. indicate beyond reasonable doubt that Naevius did not begin his poem with the fall of Troy and the legend of Aeneas, but with the historical subject which gave the poem its name. Moreover, Naevius' method of handling the events of the war in chronological order, as attested by the fragments of the last four books, allows us to assume that the part of the war which preceded the military operation mentioned in the fragment was also described in the same Book I and preceded the fragment in the order of the text. It would be absurd to assume that Naevius could have omitted the crossing into Sicily and the military operations of 264. It is unlikely that he would not have touched, at least, upon the war's immediate causes.[27] These causes and events must have furnished the contents of the opening part of the poem.

On the other hand, it is certain that episodes from the fall of Troy and the legend of Aeneas were also included in Book I.[28] This legendary material continued to be treated in Book II and, as we shall demonstrate below, in Book III. Since Naevius used the same chronological method of ordering his legendary material as he used in describing historical events, we have no grounds to assume any interruption of the legendary account by historical digressions

of which no traces have survived. On the contrary, all the evidence points to a continuous presentation of the Trojan legend from the fall of Troy to the founding of Rome on the soil of Latium.

The point has now been reached where we must ask whether the order of contents or the contents themselves, as we have just analyzed them, present difficulties such as to compel us to question the correctness of the source which assigned the basis of our reconstruction, Fragment 32, to Book I. By following the evidence so far we have reached the conclusion that the legendary part of the poem was inserted within the body of the main narrative, that is, the account of the first Punic War. In other words, we have a story within a story, the former relating events which precede in time the events contained in the latter. If such a device did not occur elsewhere in ancient literature, we might be entitled to doubt the evidence which produced it. But, indeed, the opposite is the truth, for we have a precedent of the greatest authority: Odysseus' account of his wanderings contained in Books IX-XII of the *Odyssey.* The differences in purpose and treatment in the inserted narratives of Homer and Naevius are obvious. They can best be analyzed in connection with the purely literary problems which, as I have said above, do not lie within the scope of this article. Here, I shall simply emphasize that Homer set the example for the formal device and that it had already been made known to the Latin reader through the version of Livius Andronicus. It could have struck but very few literate persons of the period as something entirely new.

If, then, we have no right to displace Fragment 32 because it has created something unprecedented in a literary form, we must now attempt to estimate how far down Naevius carried his account of the first Punic War in Book I before beginning his account of the legendary material.

As we have seen, Fragment 32 refers to an event of the year 263. Two fragments (33 and 34) which are not assigned to any book in our sources, have been referred to the siege of Agrigentum in 262 by Cichorius with some probability.[29] Even without them we would have to assume that Naevius described this important event. The question is where? Was it before or after the insertion of the legendary material?

Fortunately three lines of the **Bellum Punicum** (frg. 19) preserved by Priscian (I, p. 198 Hertz) and assigned expressly to Book I furnish the means of approach. They read as follows:

> Inerant signa expressa quomodo Titani
> bicorpores Gigantes magnique Atlantes
> Runcus ac Purpureus filii Terras

It is obvious that this passage was originally part of a description of a monument or object which either was itself figured or contained statues. Consequently, since the time of Spangenberg many identifications have been proposed.[30] About them it can only be said that they are not convincing because of the manner in which they are made. A monument or work of art which Naevius mentioned or might well have mentioned in the course of his poem is taken as the object of identification. Then, without further evidence, it is assumed that the figures which are expressly mentioned by Naevius in Fragment 19 were contained in the object in question.

There is, however, an identification which is an exception to the rule and recommends itself as resting on a reasonably firm foundation. In 1935, Hermann Fränkel called attention to the passage in the *De Architectura* in which Vitruvius describes the architectural figures which the Romans [called] *telemones*.[31] The function of these male figures was to support *mutuli* or *coronae*, or to put it more generally, they served as male counterparts, architecturally speaking, of female Caryatids. Fränkel then pointed out that the oldest and most famous monument known to us which contained *magni Atlantes* was the temple of Zeus at Agrigentum in Sicily; further, that a description of this temple has been preserved by Diodorus;[32] finally, that mentioned therein were sculptured representations of a gigantomachy and the fall of Troy. Hence the fragment of Naevius in question would belong to a description of the temple of Zeus at Agrigentum.

This was all pure gain. But confidence in the traditional reconstruction of contents prevented Fränkel apparently from following his valuable discovery to its logical conclusion. Although he was aware of the part played by Agrigentum in the first Punic War and although he could assume reasonably that Naevius himself had seen the temple in the course of his campaigns, nevertheless he connected Naevius' description of the temple with a hypothetical visit of Aeneas to Agrigentum. In other words, he assumed a retrojection of the historical temple known to Naevius into the legendary past, because the fragment describing the temple belonged in Book I and that book was considered by all to have dealt exclusively with legendary events.

If we turn now to the remains of the temple of Zeus at Agrigentum, we find ample evidence for the existence of the *Atlantes* although archaeologists cannot agree on the position which they occupied in the structure of the temple.[33] Of the Giants and Titans mentioned by Naevius in the same passage we have no certain remains.[34] But the express statement of Diodorus that a Gigantomachy stood in the east part of the temple[35] and the evidence of the *Atlantes* compel us to agree with Fränkel that Naevius' Giants and Titans are to be identified with the figures which stood in the Gigantomachy. The mention of Titans does not militate against the identification. In classical antiquity, Giants and Titans were often confused or brought together in a single group,[36] and, whereas Diodorus was giving a generic indication, Naevius was describing the several kinds of figures.

We may therefore conclude that Naevius described the siege and fall of Agrigentum in Book I before beginning his account of the fall of Troy in the same book. Furthermore, as we shall see below (pp. 43 ff.), the historical events which are described directly after the legendary material make it unlikely that Naevius could have carried his historical account in Book I much beyond the end of the year 262. To these considerations, we must add the following reasons for concluding that the last historical event described by Naevius in Book I was in fact the fall of Agrigentum.

The first reason is that the fall of Agrigentum was an appropriate point at which to abandon the historical for the legendary, to turn from Rome's present to Rome's past. This event meant more to the Romans than the completion of a tedious and difficult military operation. As Polybius tells us,[37] it was then that the Romans became aware of their power and began to entertain hopes of driving the Carthaginians out of Sicily. No longer were they content to have saved the Mamertines and to enjoy the profits which they had already reaped from the war. They now perceived the advantages of a total victory and set their minds on it. The hesitant step of 264 had become a determined march toward the acquisition of an empire.

From the vantage point of time Polybius saw this clearly. But I do not believe that we would be expecting too much of the Latin poet who had himself fought in that war[38] if we assumed that he too, when he came to write his poem recognized the same turning point as Polybius. If the past was to be considered, here was the appropriate place to begin, the place whose fall had determined the deadly struggle which was destined to endure for the next hundred years.

The second reason is that the Temple of Zeus at Agrigentum furnished material which the poet could use to effect a transition between actual events and the legendary past. It has already been noted that the counterpart of the Gigantomachy in the east part of the temple described by Naevius was a representation of the fall of Troy. That the latter might be connected with Naevius' account of the legendary material occurred to Alfred Klotz, who having accepted Strzelecki's new arrangement of the fragments, attempted to find an historical event which would lead naturally to the legendary insertion.[39] Having failed in his attempt, he added the following suggestion, apparently an afterthought since it appears in the form of a K (orrecktur N(ote) to his completed article: "Oder sollte die Erzählung von Aeneas vielleicht mit dem Giebelschmuck des Zeustempels zusammenhängen und an die Eroberung dieser Stadt angeschlossen sein, die doch einen Wendepunkt des Krieges bezeichnete?"

The "Giebelschmuck" to which he refers is obviously the sculptured representation of the fall of Troy which according to Diodorus was in the west part of the temple.[40] But that it, or the Gigantomachy, which was its counterpart on the east, stood in a pediment is pure assumption. Neither the language of Diodorus nor archaeological remains permit more than hypotheses with regard to their places in the structure of the temple.[41] Comparisons may be made with other temples of the same century[42] which had sculptured representations of the same two subjects, but they will produce little profit. Scholars agree substantially that the fall of Troy assigned by Pausanias to a place above the columns of the second temple of Hera in the Argive Heraeum occupied the west pediment.[43] On the other hand, the Gigantomachy mentioned in the same passage is assigned to metopes.[44] On the Parthenon, scenes from a Gigantomachy and from the fall of Troy occupied metopes.[45] So far as I know, the fall of Troy is not represented elsewhere in a pediment, on a series of metopes, or on a frieze.[46] But the numerous Gigantomachies which can be added to those just mentioned appear in all three positions.[47] In view of this comparable material, it is safe to assume only that the Gigantomachy and Fall of Troy of the temple of Zeus at Agrigentum were represented on pediments or on metopes.

We may therefore conceive of a group of figures, each of which had been given the attitude and attributes of the part which had been assigned to it in the scene as a whole. Fortunately, we have a strong parallel to support this concept. Four of the metopes on the north side of the Parthenon are sufficiently well preserved not only to place their subject matter beyond doubt but also to provide a fair idea of the way in which it was presented. Metopes XXIV and XXV represent Menelaus' first meeting with Helen after the fall of Troy; XXVII and XXVIII the flight of Aeneas, Anchises, Ascanius, and probably Creusa from the fallen city.[48] I refer the reader to the descriptions given by competent archaeologists for the details. Here, I would only state that the episodes are executed dramatically, that the gestures of the figures befit the persons whom they represent in the situations where they find themselves, that material attributes such as armor, garments, and statues are appropriately provided.

To return now to Naevius, it was such a dramatic representation of the fall of Troy which he must have seen on the temple of Zeus at Agrigentum. It has already been noted that he described its counterpart, the Gigantomachy, in some detail. We can well ask ourselves if he would have done so if it had not belonged to a building which in another part offered him material suitable to his literary purpose. Naevius, after all, was not writing a description of the monuments of Sicily. But more important is this: the earliest fragments of the *Bellum Punicum* which refer to the Trojan legend, one of which is expressly assigned to Book I, describe Aeneas, Anchises, their wives, and their followers escaping from Troy.[49] We do not know to what extent the poet may or may not have described preceding events, but the fragments which we have represent a motif which we found on the Parthenon metopes and can reasonably assume to have been included in the group at Agrigentum.

We have then an event which was a turning point not only in the first Punic War but in Roman history as a whole. At such a moment before the next irrevocable step was taken,

it would have been appropriate to pause for consideration of the contestants and their antecedents. In regard to the Romans, the ultimate causes of Rome's existence, the fall of Troy and the departure of Aeneas, were there to see, the first certainly, the second very probably, on the most important temple of the city where the historical event took place. In the present condition of our evidence, I believe that we are justified in assuming that Naevius used the fall of Troy represented on the temple of Zeus at Agrigentum as a point of departure for his legendary account.

From this point on—and we are, I would recall, within Book I—the *Bellum Punicum* was devoted to legend. That this legendary part extended at least as far as the founding of Rome is indicated by Naevius' identification of Romulus, the founder of Rome, as the grandson of Aeneas by a daughter (frg. 25) and his mention of the Palatine (frg. 27). In the traditional reconstruction, the founding of Rome is assigned to Book II on the grounds that Naevius began his account of the first Punic War at the beginning of Book III. But here again what we have learned from our examination of Fragments 3, 24, and 32 in relation to their proper position in the poem will lead us to a different conclusion.

First of all, we have seen that Naevius began his account of the first Punic War not at the beginning of Book III but at the beginning of Book I. In the second place, it has been demonstrated that Fragments 3 and 24 are assigned to Book III in our sources and have been dislocated in direct violation of the evidence in order to make them fit into the traditional reconstruction. Let us now see what their contents teach us regarding the place where Naevius ended his legendary account to return to the first Punic War.

Fragment 24 mentions King Amulius. In the account of Livy[50] and Dionysius of Halicarnassus[51] he appears together with his brother Numitor as the last of the long line of Alban Kings, whose literary existence can be traced as far back as the History of Fabius Pictor.[52] In the same authors it is also Amulius who orders Romulus and Remus, the sons of his brother Numitor's daughter, Ilia or Rea Silvia, to be drowned.[53]

Since Naevius made Romulus the grandson of Aeneas,[54] there was no place in his account for the line of Alban Kings who fill in the period of time between the fall of Troy as dated by the Greeks and the founding of Rome as dated by the Romans. As noted already by others, Naevius ignored Roman chronology in composing the legendary part of his poem and drew on one or several versions of the founding of Rome which were earlier than that of Fabius.[55]

On the other hand, although the Amulius of Naevius could not have occupied the same position among the Alban Kings which he occupied in the works of Fabius and later historians, there are unmistakable indications that his part was played in Latium and that it was connected with the legend of Romulus. First of all, Amulius is called *rex* in the fragment from the **Bellum Punicum** (24), while he appears in the *praetexta Lupus,* also by Naevius, as *rex Albanus.*[56] The title of the play alone would suggest that it dealt with the story of Romulus and Remus, and Leo's correct interpretation of a passage of Donatus has placed the matter beyond reasonable doubt.[57] We may reason, then, that Naevius would not have been likely to use two different versions of the same events, one in his play and the other in his epic. Differences in treatment and detail we must of course assume, but not to the extent of changing the basic rôles and relations of the principal characters.[58]

In the second place, we have the testimony of Ennius. He, too, made Romulus the grandson of Aeneas by a daughter and Amulius a king of Alba.[59] In these elements of the legend, there is complete correspondence with Naevius and if Ennius was not following him directly, he at least was drawing upon a common source. Whether we may assume with Mesk that Ennius continued to follow this common source in handling other parts of the legend[60] is uncertain and need not concern us here. For our purpose we have learned that the Amulius of Fragment 24 of the **Bellum Punicum** was king of Alba and as such played a part in the events in Latium after the arrival of the Trojans which led to the founding of Rome. And since Fragment 24 belonged to Book III, part of Book III, at least, contained a part of the legendary account.

We now come to the last of the dislocated fragments, Fragment 3. In it, Anchises is performing a sacrifice. The ritual is Roman (*auspicia, templum, penates*),[61] but this does not allow us to assume anything about the place where the sacrifice was performed. Naevius might well have used a Roman ritual in describing a sacrifice performed by Anchises in Troy. But the fact that the fragment in question belongs to Book III and the knowledge which we now have that legendary events in Latium were described in that book make it very likely that the sacrifice took place in Latium.

Hence, Naevius would have brought Anchises to Latium. This is contrary to the Virgilian account and, apart from the influence exercised by the traditional reconstruction, this discrepancy has played no small part in moving scholars to reassign the fragment to Book I. But if we dismiss Virgil from our minds for the moment, there is no good reason to believe against the evidence that Naevius could not have brought Anchises to Italy with Aeneas.

In the first place, Anchises' presence in Latium is not peculiar to Naevius' account. Cato brought Anchises to Latium in his *Origines*[62] and his death there is mentioned expressly by Strabo.[63] Dionysius, we may assume, had this version in mind, when he reports that there were authors who said that the tomb of Aeneas in Latium was built originally for Anchises by Aeneas.[64]

In the second place, so far as our evidence permits us to judge, there was no fixed tradition about Anchises, at the time when Naevius was writing the **Bellum Punicum,** which would prevent him from being brought to Latium. Naevius knew from Greek authors that Anchises had escaped the destruction of Troy and so he portrayed him.[65] Naevius may have known of Anchises' departure for the West with Aeneas. From that point on, the poet was free to do what he wished with the character of Anchises. What could be more natural, then, than to have him accompany his son to the end of his voyage, especially if the prophetic books which Venus had given to Anchises[66] could be used to advantage in Latium?

Where, then, did Naevius return to his account of the first Punic War? We have no fragments dealing with the War assigned to Book III in our sources. Fragment 39 which describes a Roman raid on Malta is assigned to Book IV in our source. It is the earliest event in Book IV which we can identify with complete certainty and it took place in 258 or 257, more probably in the latter year.[67] Fragment 36, however, which is also assigned to Book IV, has been identified by Cichorius as referring to an event of 260. It reads:

> virum praetor advenit auspicat auspicium
> prosperum.

Cichorius points out that only three occasions are attested on which a praetor commanded an army outside of Rome during the first Punic War: in 260, 248, and 242 B.C.[68] Inasmuch as the last two dates would be too late for Book IV, he chooses the event of the year 260 when the *praetor urbanus* was sent out from Rome to take over the command of Scipio who had been captured by the enemy.

The reasoning is sound and the conclusion attractive. But before we come to a final conclusion regarding the place where Naevius resumed his account of the first Punic War, we must see if the evidence furnished by subsequent fragments can help us.

There are no fragments assigned to Book V in our sources. As to Book VI, Fragment 45 is assigned to that book by Nonius. It has been identified by Cichorius with great probability as referring to the arrogant attitude toward his troops of P. Claudius Pulcher, consul in 249.[69] Fragment 48, also assigned to Book VI by Nonius, mentions the seventeenth year of the war. Although the event to which it refers must remain a matter of conjecture, the date of the event is certain: 248-247. In Fragment 50, assigned to Book VII, the terms of the peace which brought the war to an end in 241 are mentioned.[70]

This evidence has been carefully selected in order to furnish the firmest possible foundation for a concept of the order and contents of the later books. Only such fragments as were assigned to specific books in their sources were considered and among these, only those were discussed which could be referred to datable historical events either with complete certainty or great probability. In several cases attractive and reasonable identifications made by Cichorius were discarded as falling short of the established criteria.

We have here four Books (IV-VII) covering a period of nineteen years. It is certain that events of 258 or 257, 248 or 247, and 241 were mentioned in books IV, VI, and VII respectively. It is probable that events of 260 and 249 were mentioned in Books IV and VI. Thus, the order of the probable fragments fits in nicely with that of the certain fragments. The conclusion is obvious: in Lampadio's seven book edition, the last four books seem to have been divided so that each book contained the events of about five years of the war. We cannot assume that the divisions were absolutely even, since the number and importance of the events to be described varied from year to year. Also Lampadio, as shown by his inclusion of historical and legendary material in Book I, was dividing by quantity[71] rather than contents. Nevertheless, the evidence indicates a reasonably uniform proportion between the various books and the periods which they covered.

Returning now to the place where Naevius abandoned his legendary account to resume that of the first Punic War, we may reason as follows. If Fragment 36 of Book IV is correctly identified as referring to the year 260—and I think it is—, the legendary part of the poem must have run at least as far as the end or the beginning of the end of Book III. For there was only a single year of the war to be treated, 261, between the fall of Agrigentum at the end of 262[72] where the legendary part began within Book I and the arrival of the *praetor urbanus* in 260 in Book IV. We cannot assume, of course, that Lampadio made the end of the legendary account coincide with the end of Book III, for, as we have seen above, he did not work in this way. In view of this, he may have included the events of 261 at the end of Book III, or even extended the end of the legendary account into Book IV. But it could not have gone far into Book IV since this book had to contain certainly the historical events from 261 to 258 or 257 and probably those down to 256 or 255.

On the other hand, if we discard the evidence of Fragment 36 as uncertain, we still must distribute the events of 261 to 258 or 257 between Books III and IV. In this case the reasonable assumption is again that Book IV contained approximately the events of 260 to 255 and that consequently the legendary part ended somewhere in the vicinity of the end of Book III.

The conclusions which have been attained in the course of this study may now be summarized: Naevius began his **Bellum Punicum** with an account of the opening years of the first Punic War. He carried this account down to the fall of Agrigentum in 262 B.C. where he abandoned the historical narrative in order to begin an account of Rome's origins from the fall of Troy and the setting forth of Aeneas. The fall of Troy represented in the sculptures of the temple of Zeus at Agrigentum afforded him a means of transition. The legendary account was extended without interruption to the founding of Rome. At this point, Naevius returned to the first Punic War with the historical events of the year 261. The rest of the poem was devoted to a chronological account of the war down to its end.

Lampadio divided Naevius' continuous narrative into seven books approximately as follows: Book I contained the account of the war as far as the fall of Agrigentum in 262 as well as the beginning of the legendary account of Rome's origins from the fall of Troy. Book II and all or the greater part of Book III contained the continuation of the legend. If Book III was not entirely devoted to the legend, it also contained the historical events of the year 261. It is possible, however, that the very end of the legendary account was contained in the beginning of Book IV. If this was so, Book IV, like Book I, contained both a legendary and an historical part. The rest of Book IV and Books V, VI, and VII continued the narrative of the war, each of them covering a period of about five years.

Notes

1. Suetonius, *De Grammaticis,* 2; Santra *ap.* Nonius, *s. v. septemfariam,* I, p. 250 Lindsay; cf. Buecheler, *Rh. Mus.,* XL (1885), p. 148. That Lampadio was influenced by Crates of Mallos in undertaking this division is not unlikely (cf. Hendrickson, *A. J. P.,* XIX [1898], p. 286), but the words of Suetonius (*ibid.*) do not permit the certainty with which the matter is treated by Birt (*Das antike Buchwesen,* p. 481) and Hillscher (*Jahrb. f. d. class. Phil.,* Suppl. XVIII [1892], p. 359).

2. Of the 61 fragments cited by Morel (*Fragmenta Poetarum Latinorum,* pp. 17 ff.) which can be attributed to the *Bellum Punicum,* 24 are assigned to specific books by the ancient sources. The authors who cite entirely or chiefly by Lampadio's edition are Charisius, Macrobius, Nonius, and the authors of the commentaries on Virgil which pass under the names of Probus and Servius Danielis. Priscian cites with and without book number which indicates the use of both ancient editions. Verrius Flaccus (as the source of Festus) and Varro seem to have used Naevius' original edition exclusively. For a detailed discussion, see L. Strzelecki, *De Naeviano Belli Punici Carmine Quaestiones Selectae* (Polska Akademja Umiejętności, Rozprawy Wydzialu Filologicznego, T. LXV, 2 [Krakow, 1935]), pp. 1-5.

3. They are so distributed in the following editions: Ernst Spangenberg, *Quinti Ennii Annalium Libb. XVIII Fragmenta. Accedunt Cn. Naevii Librorum De Bello Punico Fragmenta Collecta,* etc. (Leipzig, 1825); Ernst Klussmann, *Cn. Naevii Poetae Romani Vitam Descripsit,* etc. (Jena, 1843); Johannes Vahlen, *Cn. Naevi De Bello Punico Reliquiae* (Leipzig, 1854); Emil Baehrens, *Fragmenta Poetarum Romanorum* (Teubner, 1886); and Willy Morel, *Fragmenta Poetarum Latinorum* (Teubner, 1927). In this article, fragments of Naevius will be given the numbers which they have in Morel's edition unless otherwise stated.

4. Paul Merula, *Q. Enni, Poetae cum Primis Censendi, Annalium Libb. XIIX quae apud Varios Auctores Supersunt Fragmenta Collecta,* etc. (Leyden, 1595). Merula's observations on the *Bellum Punicum* begin

on p. 49 of his commentary and are made chiefly to illustrate the text of Ennius. Nevertheless, it is there for the first time, so far as I can ascertain, that we find the germ of a reconstruction of contents.

5. *Op. cit.,* p. 188.

6. *Op. cit.,* pp. 29 f., 216 f.

7. *Op. cit.,* pp. 9-14.

8. This reconstruction appears in Schanz-Hosius, *Gesch. d. röm. Lit.,* I[4] (1927), p. 53; Cichorius, *Röm. Studien* (1922), p. 25; Fränkel, *R.-E.,* Suppl. VI (1935), col. 638; Enk, *Handboek der Latijnse Letterkunde,* II, 1 (1937), p. 73. Leo (*Gesch. d. röm. Lit.,* p. 81), who is also inclined to accept it, suggests, nevertheless, that the historical account may have begun early in Book II, a suggestion that is condemned by Fränkel (*loc. cit.*). In the literary histories of Klotz, Ussani, and Wight Duff, the prevailing view is stated as an established fact which needs no further discussion.

9. Lucian Mueller alone, so far as I know, attempts to prove by detailed arguments that Naevius treated the entire history of Rome down to the first Punic War (*Q. Ennii Carminum Reliquae* [1884], pp. XX-XXXII). His conclusions are repeated without discussion of evidence by Marchesi (*Storia della letteratura latina,* p. 46) while Terzaghi (*Storia della letteratura latina,* p. 53) implies their adoption. Plessis (*La poésie latine,* p. 13) is noncommittal. But the evidence against Muller's conclusions is overwhelming; cf. Strzelecki, *op. cit.,* p. 6, note 2; Leo, *op. cit.,* p. 82, and Fränkel, *loc. cit.*

10. Whether Naevius brought Dido and Aeneas together and if so, how fully his account is reflected in Book IV of Virgil's *Aeneid,* has been debated for over a century; see the exhaustive lists of proponents and opponents in A. S. Pease, *Publi Vergili Maronis Aeneidos Liber Quartus,* pp. 18-19, notes 120 and 121. Strzelecki (*op. cit.,* pp. 12-24) is now to be added to the list of proponents.

11. Leo, *op. cit.,* p. 82; Fränkel, *loc. cit.,* col. 638.

12. See note 2 above.

13. Strzelecki, *op. cit.,* pp. 5-11; 36-38.

14. The only critical review known to me which attempts to do justice to Strzelecki's treatment of the order of contents is that of Haffter (*Deut. Lit. Zeit.,* LVIII [1937], pp. 659-663). Haffter does not accept Strzelecki's proposed rearrangement of the fragments explicitly, but sees no obstacle to its acceptance. Of the writers of short notices who do not discuss the details, Amatucci (*Boll. Fil. Class.,* XLII [1936-37], p. 133) accepts the rearrangement as logical and soundly based on existing evidence; Ernout (*Rev. Phil.,* XI [1937], p. 182) and Constans (*Rev. Ét. Anc.,* XXXVIII [1936], p. 241) are noncommittal; the reviewers for the *Rivista di Filologia* (XV [1937], p. 431) and the *Bulletin Budé*

(suppl. crit., VIII [1936], p. 113) do not touch upon the rearrangement; Skutsch (*C. R.,* L [1936], p. 149) devotes thirteen lines to it and concludes flatly that it fails. I have been unable to find any mention of Strzelecki's work in American learned journals.

15. Klotz, who accepts the rearrangement, used it only in connection with a single point; cf. *Rh. Mus.,* LXXXVII (1938), p. 190, and p. 36 below.

16. Consulship and *praenomen* of Manius are expressly attested by the *Fasti Consulares, C. I. L.,* I[2], 1, p. 22; *Fasti Triumphales, ibid.,* p. 46; Polybius, I, 16; cf. Pliny, *H. N.,* VII, 214, and *Ineditum Vaticanum,* 4 (Drachmann, *Diodors röm. Annalen,* p. 69). Morel (*ad loc.*) assigns Valerius' consulship incorrectly to the year 262, an error which he apparently took from Cichorius to whom he refers in his notes; cf. *Römische Studien,* p. 27.

17. Cichorius, *loc. cit.;* Baehrens, *F. P. R., ap. crit.* on frg. 35, p. 48.

18. *Der Saturnische Vers* (*Abh. Gött.,* VIII [1905]), 5, p. 33, note 4; p. 52, note 5.

19. *Op. cit.,* p. 44, note 1.

20. Mai, *Class. Auct.,* VII, p. 386.

21. On Cynthius' use of Probus, see Keil's edition of Probus' *Commentary,* pp. VIII-IX. The descent of all existing manuscripts and the *editio princeps* from the lost *Bobbiensis* is maintained by Keil (*op. cit.,* pp. V-IX), Hagen (Thilo-Hagen edition of Servius, III, 2, p. VIII), and F. M. Wheelock (*Harv. Stud. Class. Phil.,* XLIV [1933], pp. 247 ff.). Wheelock, however, who adduces new material, argues for a less direct descent than was assumed by his predecessors. See his stemma on p. 248 where X[1] represents the *Bobbiensis.*

22. See note 16 above.

23. I am here following De Sanctis' interpretation of the sources (*Storia dei Romani,* III, 1, pp. 114ff.) as best explaining why a triumph was accorded to Valerius alone of the two consuls (cf. *C. I. L.,* I[2], 1, p. 46). Frank (*C. A. H.,* p. 675), apparently accepting the statement of Diodorus (XXIII, 4), has both consuls pursue Hiero. But even if it was a joint pursuit, the *Ineditum Vaticanum* (4) mentions Valerius alone as making the treaty with Hiero; cf. De Sanctis, *op. cit.,* p. 116, note 37.

24. *Ibid.,* p. 114.

25. *Op. cit.,* p. 27.

26. *Expeditio* in the general sense of a military operation is well attested by Sallust (*Jug.,* 37; 103; *Hist.,* frg. 98, 6 Maurenbrecher), Caesar (*B. G.,* V, 10), Hirtius (*B. G.,* VIII, 6 and 8), and Cicero (*Div.,* I, 33, 72; II, 30, 65). The precise nature of the operation is sometimes added *expressis verbis* or can be inferred from the context. That the meaning of *expeditio* in the military terminology of the Empire

is generally "campaign" (a military operation of some magnitude) can be ascertained from a glance at Dessau's *Index* (*I. L. S.,* III, p. 509).

27. Frg. 31 appears to refer to the formal declaration of war by the Romans; cf. Cichorius, *op. cit.,* pp. 26 f.

28. Fragments 5, 13, and 17, dealing with the fall of Troy and the wanderings of Aeneas, are all assigned specifically to Book I in our sources.

29. *Op. cit.,* pp. 28 ff.

30. Spangenberg, *op. cit.* (see note 3 above), p. 196: figureheads or figures on Roman warships; Baehrens, *F. P. R.,* p. 46: temple at Cumae; Waser, *R. E.,* Suppl. III, col. 701: shield.

31. Fränkel, *Hermes,* LXX (1935), pp. 59 ff.; Vitruvius, VI, 7, 6.

32. XIII, 82.

33. On the temple in general, the following important studies have appeared since the work of Koldewey and Puchstein (*Die Griechischen Tempel in Unteritalien und Sicilien,* pp. 153 ff.); Pace, *Mon. Ant.,* XXVIII (1922), pp. 174 ff., and Marconi, *Agrigento* (1929), pp. 57 ff. There is also a brief description in Robertson, *Greek and Roman Architecture* (2nd ed., 1943), pp. 122 ff. On the *Atlantes* the most thorough study is that of Marconi (*Bollettino d'Arte,* VI [1927], pp. 33-45), restated briefly in his *Agrigento,* pp. 168-170. Earlier hypotheses regarding the position of these figures in the structure of the temple are summarized by Pace, *loc. cit.,* pp. 185 ff. The hypothesis of Koldewey and Puchstein (*op. cit.,* pp. 160 ff.) that the *Atlantes* were situated in the intercolumniations on the outside of the temple to provide additional support for the architrave has been strengthened by Marconi's investigations.

34. It is possible, though far from certain, that a fragment of sculpture depicting a lion's tail comes from the Gigantomachy. Otherwise, the sculptural remains are too few and fragmentary to be identified.

35. (XIII, 82, 4).

36. On the confusion of Giants and Titans in ancient authors, see Maximilian Meyer, *Die Giganten und Titanen in der antiken Sage und Kunst,* pp. 144 f., especially note 211; cf. pp. 1 ff. Additions to Meyer's evidence have been made by Wüst, *R.-E.,* VI (A), col. 1503.

37. I, 20.

38. Naevius, frg. 2.

39. *Rh. Mus.,* LXXXVII (1938), pp. 190-192.

40. See note 35 above.

41. Jahn (*Annali,* XXXV [1863], p. 245, note 1) and Pace (*loc. cit.,* pp. 244 ff.), who do not believe that the temple had pediments, distribute the two groups over metopes. Koldewey and Puchstein (*op. cit.,* p. 164) and Marconi (*Agrigento,* pp. 171 f.) assign them to pediments. But the fact remains that neither Diodorus nor the remains permit certain attribution.

42. The temple of Zeus at Agrigentum had not been completed by 409 B.C. (Diodorus, XIII, 82, 2), although it is clear from the same passage that it already then contained the Gigantomachy and the fall of Troy. Pace conjectures reasonably that the temple was begun shortly after the battle of Himera in 480 B.C. when the Agrigentines set their prisoners to work quarrying marble from which to build their greatest temples (*loc. cit.,* pp. 178 f.; cf. Diodorus, XI, 25). On stylistic grounds, Marconi assigns the *Atlantes* to the decade 480-470 B.C. and the fragments of sculpture to 450-440 (*Agrigento,* p. 66). If Marconi is correct, these sculptures are not far removed in time from those with which they are now compared.

43. Pausanias, II, 17, 3. On the temple in general, see Waldstein, *The Argive Heraeum,* pp. 117 ff. On the position of the sculptured groups, the following are in substantial agreement: Jahn, *loc. cit.* (see note 41 above); Curtius, *Peloponnesus,* II, p. 570; Heydemann, *Iliupersis,* pp. 8 f.; Frazer, *Pausanias,* III, p. 182; Waldstein, *op. cit.,* pp. 148 ff.

44. See references cited in the preceding note.

45. The latest and most detailed study of these metopes is that of Praschniker in which appropriate reference is made to earlier discussions (*Parthenonstudien* [Wien, 1928]). For the east metopes (Gigantomachy), see pp. 186 ff.; for the north metopes (Fall of Troy), see pp. 87 ff. We shall return to the north metopes in more detail below.

46. In speaking of the Fall in this connection, I mean those events alone which are part of the capture of the city. Such scenes from the Trojan War as are represented on the west pediment of the Temple of Aphaia at Aegina or on the east frieze of the Treasury of the Siphnians at Delphi do not concern us here.

47. The evidence has been collected by Waser, *R.-E.,* Suppl. III, cols. 670 ff.

48. Michaelis first recognized that metopes XXIV and XXV represented the episode of Menelaus and Helen (*Der Parthenon,* p. 139). His view, which was generally accepted, has been confirmed most recently by Praschniker's careful reëxamination of the metopes themselves and his comparative study of the same episode as represented on vases (*op. cit.,* pp. 98 ff.). The identification of the Aeneas episode (XXVII and XXVIII) is the work of Praschniker (*op. cit.,* pp. 107 ff.) and is accepted by Studniczka (*Neue Jahrb.,* V [1929], p. 645). Here we need not discuss other metopes of the north side, the interpretation of which is uncertain in regard to their place in the Fall, or the still unsettled question

whether all the metopes of this side were devoted to the Trojan legend.

49. Frgs. 4 and 5. The latter is assigned to Book I by Servius Danielis on *Aeneid,* II, 797 (II, p. 506 Rand).

50. I, 3, 10.

51. I, 71, 4.

52. Frg. 5ᵃ, *H. R. R.,* Peter; cf. Leuze, *Die röm, Jahrzählung,* pp. 86 ff.

53. Livy I, 4, 3; Dionysius, I, 79, 4 = Fabius, frg. 5ᵇ.

54. Frg. 25.

55. Cf. Leo, *Gesch. d. röm. Lit.,* pp. 83 f.; Mesk, *Wien. Stud.,* XXXVI (1914), p. 22.

56. Frg. 1, *T. R. F.*³, p. 322 Ribbeck.

57. Donatus on Terence, *Ad.* 537. Leo's views (*op. cit.,* p. 90, note 1) have been accepted by Fränkel (*R.-E.,* Suppl. VI, col. 627).

58. Cf. Mesk, *loc. cit.,* pp. 28 f.

59. See the *testimonia* collected by Vahlen on Ennius, *Ann.,* frgs. 28 and 30.

60. Mesk, *loc. cit.,* p. 29.

61. Cf. Weinstock, *R.-E.,* XIX, col. 420.

62. Frg. 9, Peter.

63. V, 3, 2, p. 229.

64. I, 64, 5.

65. Frgs. 4 and 5.

66. Naevius, frg. 13a.

67. Cichorius, *op. cit.,* p. 39.

68. *Op. cit.,* p. 32.

69. *Op. cit.,* p. 45.

70. That Fragments 49 and 50 do not belong together in context, although they both derive from the same passage of Nonius, was first observed by Buecheler (*Kleine Schriften,* I, pp. 387 f.). The division is accepted by Lindsay in his edition of Nonius (pp. 760-761) and Morel has given the fragment the numbers cited above. Cichorius (*op. cit.,* pp. 50 ff.) has shown that Fragment 49 probably refers to an event of 248 and belonged to Book VI. This does not affect Nonius' statement that the lines composing Fragment 50 came from Book VII.

71. On the basis of the average length of seven books of the *Iliad,* Leo estimates that the *Bellum Punicum* contained between 4000 and 5000 verses (*op. cit.,* p. 81), Birt about 7000 verses (*Buchwesen,* p. 462). Both these estimates are reasonable, but the evidence allows them to be no more than conjectures.

72. In December according to De Sanctis (*op. cit.,* III, 1, p. 211) on the basis of Polybius, I, 18, 6, and I, 19, 5.

Henry T. Rowell (essay date 1949)

SOURCE: "The 'Campanian' Origin of C. Naevius and Its Literary Attestation" in *Memoirs of the American Academy in Rome,* Vol. XIX, Yale University Press, 1949, pp. 15-34.

[*In the following essay, Rowell examines the earliest source material, particularly the efforts of Varro, for compiling biographical information concerning Naevius, with emphasis on the question of whether or not Naevius came from the city of Capua.*]

The only indication which we have of the origin and nationality of the poet Naevius appears in a chapter of the *Attic Nights* in which Aulus Gellius records the epitaphs of Naevius, Plautus, and Pacuvius.[1] In introducing the epitaph of Naevius, Gellius makes the following comment: *Epigramma Naevii plenum superbiae Campanae quod testimonium esse iustum potuisset nisi ab ipso dictum esset.* Here the word *Campanae* is our indication. But the information which it contains remains, unfortunately, rather uncertain for so important a fact until we establish the precise sense in which Gellius used it and the source of information which permitted him its use. Although this subject has often been touched upon, I believe that there is still much to be learned from a methodical investigation of all its aspects and it is such an investigation which I propose to carry out in these pages. Apart from any conclusions regarding Naevius' origin, it will also have the value, I hope, of being the first complete study of our sources of information for Naevius' life.

Now it has long been recognized that the epitaph proper which Gellius cites directly after the comment given above was taken from the first book of Varro's *De Poetis.*[2] Gellius mentions this book expressly as his source for the epitaph of Plautus which follows that of Naevius and no reasonable doubt can be raised that all three epitaphs, coming together in the same small chapter in which only a single source appropriate to all of them is mentioned, go back to the same Varronian treatise.

For the moment, however, we cannot extend our certainty regarding the source of the epitaph to the comment upon it. Marx[3] and Marmorale[4] apparently consider the latter's Varronian origin to be self-evident; Fränkel[5] holds it probable; others[6] accept the crucial word *Campanae* more or less at face value and ignore its source. But on the whole these various views are casual opinions rather than results of methodical investigation. The basic problem still remains unsolved: what is the source of the information which permitted Gellius to speak of *superbia Campana* and exactly what did he mean by it?

In attempting a solution of this problem, let us first see what Gellius believed about the source of the epitaph. As he tells us in the opening words of his chapter, he believed that it had been composed by Naevius himself: *Trium poetarum inlustrium epigrammata, Cn. Naevii, Plauti, M.*

*Pacuvii quae ipsi fecerunt et incidenda sepulchro suo reli-
querunt.*[7] This belief appears again in the statement that
the epitaph could have been a *iustum testimonium,* if it
had not been composed by Naevius himself.

Here we learn where the *superbia* of the epitaph lay in the
eyes of Gellius. The lines

> *itaque postquam est Orchi traditus thesauro*
> *obliti sunt Romae loquier lingua Latina*

are in themselves open to the charge of arrogance. But
Gellius concedes that they, together with the two preceding lines concerning the sorrow of the Muses at Naevius'
death, could have been a fair attestation (of Naevius' poetic
genius) had he not written them himself. To Gellius, then,
the arrogance did not lie so much in the contents of the
epitaph as in the fact that Naevius had composed it about
himself. In other words, the epitaph is full of arrogance in
relation to its author and the "Campanian" quality of its
arrogance must hence be connected with the "Campanian"
quality of its author.

Now it has long been established that it is impossible to
understand *superbia Campana* as a proverbial phrase
denoting an arrogance of a particularly offensive or excessive kind, regardless of its "provenance." Whenever these
words or their equivalent are used by Cicero in his first
two orations, *De Lege Agraria* (I, 18-22; II, 76-98) or by
Livy (IX, 6, 5; XXIII, 5, 1) they always refer to the city of
Capua (I include the *ager* in this designation) and its
citizens and to the kind of arrogance which was found
there and among them. But Cicero and Livy have more to
teach us than this. They tell us something indirectly about
the mental environment of the concept which is worth
knowing.

To Livy the arrogance of the Capuans culminated in their
defection from Rome during the Second Punic War. After
Cannae they began to scorn the Roman *imperium* and the
defeated consul whom their envoys approached at Venusia
is *quam poterat maxime miserabilem bonis sociis, super-
bis atque infidelibus, ut erant Campani, spernendum*
(XXIII, 4, 6; 5, 1). This trait was, of course, nothing new
in them, for it is mentioned by Livy in an earlier connection. As the Romans approached Capua after passing under
the Samnite yoke, pity for their plight overcame the *superbiam ingenitam Campanis* (IX, 6, 5). But we must note the
use of the past tense (*erant*) in Livy, XXIII, 5, 1. The
historian knew of the punishment which awaited the
Capuans for their defection, a punishment which would
take the arrogance out of them (see the description of
Capua in XXXI, 29, 11). After this punishment, there is no
further mention of Capuan arrogance in Livy.

Coming now to Cicero, there is no mention of this trait in
all his works except in the first two orations of the *De
Lege Agraria.* In them Cicero was attempting to deter the
senate and the people from supporting the bill of Rullus
by painting a terrifying picture of its consequences. Part of

the bill provided for the planting of a colony at Capua. Cicero proclaims this provision to be most dangerous. He
speaks of *illam Campanam adrogantiam atque intoleran-
dam ferociam (Leg. Agr.,* II, 91) which the *maiores* reduced
to impotence by the measures which they imposed upon
Capua after its surrender. *Campani semper superbi boni-
tate agrorum et fructuum magnitudine, urbis salubritate,
descriptione, pulchritudine* (95). Hence the arrogance
which made the Capuans demand that one consul should
come from Capua; hence the luxury which enervated Hannibal. What, then, would be the effect of these natural
riches, of this splendid city, on the new colonists? Obviously to make them arrogant in turn and a danger to Rome.

It is quite clear what Cicero was doing. He was resurrect-
ing a well remembered chapter from Capua's past and
turning it to the immediate purpose of frightening his audience. There can be little doubt that sending a colony to
Capua in 63 B.C. would have been no more dangerous to
Rome than sending it to any other part of Italy. In fact, a
colony was sent out to Capua in 59 B.C. and again in 43
B.C. with no dire results. But Cicero was attempting to
present all of Rullus' bill in the darkest light possible and
a colony at Capua was one of its provisions. It was not the
only time that he argued a weak point skillfully.

We need not therefore be surprised that we do not hear of
Capuan arrogance after Livy except in Gellius. This Roman estimate of the Capuan character was connected
primarily with the events of the Second Punic War and
with Capua before its fall except in so far as Cicero
brought it down to his own time for the purpose which we
have noted above. If we find it, then, in Gellius, a writer
of the second century A.D., it appears likely that it there
represents a reflection of an earlier period.

In this connection, I would here submit the hypothesis that
Gellius was influenced by Cicero. We know that he was
familiar with the first two orations *De Lege Agraria.* He
cites a fragment from that part of the first oration which is
now lost (Gellius, XIII, 25, 6 = Cicero, frag. 4, Oxford
edition) and two fragments of the second (XIII, 25, 6 = II,
59; VII, 16, 7 = II, 100). The fact that he makes Favorinus
the speaker in XIII, 25 will not deceive anyone who is
familiar with Gellius' methods of presentation regarding
Gellius' firsthand knowledge of the Ciceronian text. And
in VII, 16, he cites Cicero directly.

I would, therefore, reconstruct as follows. Gellius found
the epitaph of Naevius at the end of Varro's biography of
Naevius in the *De Poetis.* It was accompanied by the statement that it was composed by Naevius himself. He copied
it down as something which pricked his curiosity and
added to it the epitaphs of Plautus and Pacuvius which he
also found at the ends of their respective biographies in
the same book.

When he came to write the chapter in which he presents
the three epitaphs, that of Naevius seemed to him to
deserve a word of comment. As an admirer of Naevius'

dramatic works, he was forced to concede the justice of the contents, but the fact that Naevius had written thus about himself struck him as a piece of arrogance. He knew that Naevius had been a Capuan. In the back of his mind were Cicero's words about the city and its citizens: *superbia nata inibi* (*Leg. Agr.,* I, 20), *quantam locus ipse adferat superbiam* (II, 92), *Campani semper superbi* (II, 95) *in domicilio superbiae* (II, 97). Here was the *mot juste* sanctioned by the use of the master. It would recall to the reader its Ciceronian associations. Furthermore, it was completely appropriate since Naevius was born a Capuan in the proud days before the city's fall. What neater way could there be to characterize Naevius' arrogance than with the words *superbia Campana?*

I claim for this hypothesis a fair degree of probability. But it is also quite possible that Gellius found the comment on the epitaph in Varro. Of one thing, however, we can be certain. If the comment was original with Gellius, he knew that Naevius was a *Campanus* in the sense in which the word was used by Cicero; that is, a native of Capua. For otherwise his *superbia Campana* would have no reminiscence or point. On the other hand, if the comment came from Varro, the word *Campanus,* as we shall see below, gives us again a clear indication of Naevius' Capuan origin. In view of what I have said above, I am inclined to think that the comment is original with Gellius and that he found the statement that Naevius was a *Campanus* at the beginning of Varro's biography of the poet. For where, if not in Varro, could Gellius have learned that Naevius was a Capuan?

In the well-known passage in which Gellius recapitulates the chronology established by Varro for the beginnings of Latin literature,[8] we are informed that Naevius began to produce plays in 235 B.C. and that Varro stated in the first book of the *De Poetis* that Naevius had campaigned in the First Punic War and had stated this fact himself in the poem which he composed about it (the **Bellum Punicum**). Here again, we find Varro furnishing Gellius with an important biographical fact. But we may not assume that Gellius was not familiar with the **Bellum Punicum** at first hand because he cites a piece of information which it contained from Varro. A few lines above, in the same discussion, Gellius cites the same book of Varro in a very similar manner, but this time in connection with Ennius. "Varro writes," he says, "that Ennius was in his sixty-seventh year when he was writing the twelfth book of the *Annals* and that Ennius himself so stated in that very same book." There can be no doubt, however, that Gellius had not only read the *Annals* but knew them extremely well.[9] He was simply working from Varro at the moment and was honest enough to say so.[10]

On the other hand, Gellius mentions the **Bellum Punicum** only once again.[11] This he does in connection with an explanation of the word *Diovis: Idcircoque simili nomine Iovis 'Diovis' dictus est et 'Lucetius,' quod nos die et luce quasi vita ipsa afficeret et iuvaret. 'Lucetium' autem Iovem Cn. Naevius in libris belli Poenici appellat.* Gellius does not mention his source. But in view of his dependence on Varro in the discussion of such matters,[12] and the fact noted above that Varro was familiar with the **Bellum Punicum,** I am inclined to agree with Hosius[13] that we have here an excerpt from the *Res Divinae*. Be that as it may, it is a fact of greater importance that Gellius does not cite a single verse from the **Bellum Punicum.** When we compare this silence with his frequent citations from the *Annals,* it is reasonable to believe that Gellius had not read the **Bellum Punicum** and hence could not draw on it for biographical data.

Gellius has two more notices regarding Naevius' life. One tells us of his incarceration and forms the counterpart to a notice about Plautus' literary activity while working in a mill.[14] Gellius states expressly that he has been using Varro's *De Comoediis Plautinis* in writing this chapter and it is generally assumed—and rightly, I believe—that the information concerning Naevius comes from the same source.[15]

The second contains the famous verses of Naevius which, according to Gellius, were almost certainly directed against Scipio (*et propemodum constitisse, hosce versus a Cn. Naevio poeta in eum scriptos esse*).[16] Again the source is not mentioned but we have some indication of its nature. Gellius states that what he is telling us is historical (*ex historia*); secondly, the story revolves around Scipio's *continentia* and the verses of Naevius are introduced merely as proof that Scipio's reputation in his youth was far from stainless. We are therefore led to think of some source which dealt with Scipio's life. Leo (*Geschichte*, p. 78, n. 2) thinks it probable that Gellius found the verses in Valerius Antias, who is mentioned in the same chapter as a writer who was hostile to Scipio's reputation. Valerius is certainly a more likely source than Oppius, Hyginus, or the unnamed others mentioned by Gellius (VII, 1), who appear to have stressed Scipio's *admiranda*. But whoever furnished the notice, he was clearly more occupied with Scipio than with Naevius.

To summarize the first step in our investigation, it has been demonstrated that where the source can be ascertained with reasonable accuracy, Gellius was indebted to Varro for everything which he knew about Naevius' life with the exception of the attack upon Scipio. It would therefore be logical to assume that the knowledge that Naevius was a *Campanus* came also to Gellius from the same author. This assumption will be strengthened if we examine the biographical information concerning Naevius which is not contained in the *Attic Nights*.

Under the year 01. 144, 3 = 202 B.C. in his revision of the *Chronicle* of Eusebius, St. Jerome places the following notice: *Naevius comicus Uticae moritur pulsus Roma factione nobilium ac praecipue Metelli.* We need not dwell on St. Jerome's immediate source here, for it has already been demonstrated beyond reasonable doubt that he was indebted to the *De Viris Illustribus* of Suetonius for this and similar information regarding Latin writers.[17] We must rather go back beyond Suetonius and attempt to establish his source.

Fortunately, the desired information can be attained through a passage of Cicero. In the *Brutus* (60) he writes: *His consulibus* (Cethegus and Tuditanus, 204 B.C.) *ut in veteribus commentariis scriptum est, Naevius est mortuus; quamquam Varro noster diligentissimus investigator antiquitatis putat in hoc erratum vitamque Naevi producit longius.*

In commenting on this passage, Leo[18] expresses the opinion that the *veteres commentarii* were probably the records of the magistrates who were in charge of the public games and that the last production of a play of Naevius was there entered under the year 204. From this others concluded that Naevius died in that year, but Varro knew of reasons other than death why his plays then ceased to be produced at Rome. Consequently he gave him a longer span of life.

Helm[19] has carried the investigation further with good results. Varro must have perceived, he points out, that if Naevius had died in Utica in 204, he would have died in a city which was in the possession of the Carthaginian enemy. But as indicated by Cicero's vague phrase *producit longius,* he could not have known the exact date of death. Hence in discussing Naevius, Varro would have shown the impossibility of placing his death in Utica in 204, stating that it could not have occurred in that city until the end of the Second Punic War. Inasmuch as Helm equates 01. 144, 3, the date given by Jerome, with 201 B.C., he further suggests that Varro may have chosen the year 201 because it was the date when the peace was ratified and Naevius could have visited Utica. St. Jerome, finding in Suetonius' version of Varro no exact date for the death, would have taken the latest one mentioned therein. The same assumption, of course, could be maintained in regard to the more correct equation 01. 144, 3 = 202 B.C., since it was in 202 that Zama was fought and the war ended to all intents and purposes.

In recapitualting Helm's arguments, the question of Suetonius' relation to Varro in regard to the notice in question has been somewhat anticipated. Let me return to it here. First of all, Suetonius' dependence on Varro for certain biographical information has been proved.[20] In the second place, St. Jerome, repeating Suetonius, shows that the latter did not accept the traditional date of 204 B.C. for Naevius' death but like Varro extended his life beyond it. Finally, the fact that St. Jerome gives the year of death, which was apparently unknown to Varro, does not mean that Suetonius obtained it from some other source. Helm's fine study[21] has taught us how St. Jerome used his source material and what little faith we can place in the exactitude of his chronological data. We are now justified in believing that the exact year of death was not given by Suetonius who was following Varro and that St. Jerome devised it quite possibly in the manner suggested by Helm above.

To return now to the passage in the *Brutus* which enabled us to trace St. Jerome's notice back to Varro, Cicero speaks in it as if he had consulted Varro at first hand. Yet we are now well aware of Cicero's dependence in the *Brutus* on

the *Liber Annalis* of Atticus which was dedicated to Cicero in 47 B.C. and furnished him with a convenient chronological table of important events, both historical and literary.[22] Comparison, however, of the chronology of early Latin literature as established by Varro (preserved in Gellius) and Atticus (preserved in Cicero) has demonstrated that Atticus chose to adopt Varro's dates in preference to those which had earlier been established by Accius.[23] It is therefore possible that in speaking of Varro in the passage in the *Brutus* which now holds our attention, Cicero was speaking of him as Atticus' source and actually had the *Liber Annalis* before his eyes. I cannot believe, however, that Cicero did not often turn from the summary notices of Atticus to the more detailed accounts which lay behind them. But be that as it may, Varro in this instance was the ultimate source of Cicero's knowledge.

In the *Cato Maior* (14, 50) Cicero tells us that Naevius wrote his **Bellum Punicum** as a *senex*. Since the same chapter contains a similar notice on Plautus and the Varronian date for the first production of a play by Livius Andronicus, he may again have been following Varro through Atticus.[24] On the other hand, Cicero speaks in the *Brutus* (19, 75) as if he were familiar at first hand with the **Bellum Punicum** of Naevius. This is curious in view of the fact that he does not cite a single verse from it. Possibly he did not find this work which pleased him *quasi Myronis opus,* suitable for citation. At any rate, when he says in the *Brutus* (60) that Latin as spoken in the time of Cethegus could be found in the works of Naevius, he was probably thinking of the plays which he had read.[25] We must therefore confess that we do not know whether Cicero had ever read the **Bellum Punicum.** But if he had, he might have found within it the information that Naevius had written it as a *senex*. For as we have seen above on the authority of Varro, the epic contained biographical data.

Mention of Cicero's familiarity with some of Naevius' plays brings us to the latter's famous quarrel with the Metelli. We know of it chiefly by virtue of the commentary of Pseudo-Asconius on Cicero's first Verrine oration.[26] In attacking Metellus Creticus (*Cos.* 69) for the support whhich he received from Verres at the time of his election, Cicero states: *Nam hoc Verrem dicere aiebant, te non fato, ut ceteros ex vestra familia sed opera sua consulem factum.* On which the commentator writes: *Dictum facete et contumeliose in Metellos antiquum Naevii est:*

Fato Metelli Romae fiunt consules.

Cui tunc Metellus consul iratus versu responderet senario hypercatalecto, qui et Saturnius dicitur

Dabunt malum Metelli Naevio poetae.

De qua parodia subtiliter Cicero dixit: Te non fato, ut ceteros ex vestra familia.

Since Jachmann[27] and Frank[28] have presented valid reasons for believing in the authenticity of the quarrel, I shall not discuss here the earlier doubts of Wissowa[29] and Leo.[30] But inasmuch as the proponents of authenticity have concentrated their attention on the historical circumstances which could have given rise to the verses and the interpretation of the verses themselves, a few words regarding the way by which Pseudo-Asconius obtained his information remain to be said. They will, I believe, not only strengthen the thesis of authenticity, but also serve the purpose of ascertaining the ancient sources of Naevius' biography.

To begin with Cicero, who furnished the occasion for the comment, it is quite clear that he had the verse *Fato Metelli Romae fiunt consules* in mind when making the remark directed against Metellus Creticus in the first Verrine oration. A reflection of the same verse, as Frank has pointed out,[31] occurs in a letter written by Cicero to another Metellus (Metellus Celer) in 62 B.C.[32]

The verse is clearly a senarius and hence comes from some play of Naevius.[33] Cicero may have read the play himself for, as we have seen, he was familiar with some of Naevius' dramatic works. On the other hand, it is equally possible that it was circulating in Rome as part of the anecdote which was later repeated in full by Pseudo-Asconius and that Cicero lifted it from its context as a verse which could be easily paraphrased for use against the Metelli of his own time and would be readily recognized together with its political implications.

Turning now to the anecdote as it appears in Pseudo-Asconius, let us first note that the verse *dabunt malum Metelli Naevio Poetae* was known to Caesius Bassus, who lived under Nero. Bassus characterizes the verse as follows:[34] *optimus (saturnius) est quem Metelli proposuerunt de Naevio aliquotiens ab eo versu lacessiti:*

      Malum dabunt Metelli Naevio Poetae.

Hic enim saturnius constat ex hipponactei quadrati iambici posteriore commate et phallico metro.

If we now compare the notices of Bassus and Pseudo-Asconius regarding this verse, we find substantial agreement in the matter of context. That the verse begins with *malum dabunt* in one and with *dabunt malum* in the other, a reverse in order of the same words which affects neither sense nor meter, can hardly be considered more than a copyist's error which need not concern us here. Rather, the important thing is that both authors knew that the verse was composed by a Metellus in answer to an attack on him or his family by the poet Naevius. From the verse itself Bassus could have inferred that the Metelli had written it about Naevius and indeed his use of the plural *Metelli* in his comment *quem (versum) Metelli proposuerunt de Naevio* indicates that this comment had been influenced by the contents of the verse. Pseudo-Asconius is more exact in speaking of a *Metellus Consul*. But it would have been impossible for Bassus to infer from the verse alone that it was a reply to an attack by Naevius and, what is more, an attack in verse (*Metelli aliquotiens ab eo [Naevio] versu lacessiti*). This is one of several cogent reasons

why Wissowa's hypothesis that this Saturnian was invented by Bassus must be abandoned.[35]

On the other hand, the word *aliquotiens* is significant. Pseudo-Asconius states expressly that the Saturnian *dabunt malum* was a reply to the insulting verse *fato Metelli*. Bassus' *aliquotiens* ("on several occasions") thus indicates a vaguer knowledge of the background. Bassus knew that Naevius had attacked the Metelli in verse and that the Metelli had answered in a Saturnian. He doesn't appear to have known just how Naevius took the first provocative steps, but it seemed reasonable to him to assume that there had been a number of attacks.

All this is consistent with the purpose and plan of his work. Bassus was not writing a commentary on Cicero but a work on meters. He was interested in Naevius only in so far as Naevius could furnish him with examples of Saturnians for his chapter on the Saturnian verse. In citing two of Naevius' Saturnians (1 and 7 Morel), he states simply *apud Naevium poetam hos repperi idoneos,* or when speaking of the difficulty of finding correct Saturnians, *ut vix invenerim apud Naevium quos pro exemplo ponerem.*[36] On the other hand, the Saturnian of the Metelli needed fuller identification than *apud Naevium poetam*. It was not evidently contained in any work which could be briefly indicated by the name of the author as the **Bellum Punicum** was indicated by the name of Naevius; nor could the document in which it stood be cited as in the case of the two Saturnians quoted *ex Regilli tabula* and in *Acilii Glabrionis tabula.*[37] To indicate the origin of the Saturnian of the Metelli, to identify it for the reader, a few words regarding its background were necessary. They or something very much like them must have been in Bassus source. They represent part of the anecdote told in full by Pseudo-Asconius, but they were made to serve another purpose.

What, then, was Bassus' source? Surely a work on metrics. But whose? Let us see what we can now learn from an analysis of his entire chapter.

In demonstrating that the Saturnian *Malum dabunt* was composed *ex hipponactei quadrati iambici posteriore commate et phallico metro,* Bassus cites as an example of a *hipponacteus quadratus* the following verse without indication of author: *quid immerentibus noces quid invides amicis.*[38] The *quid invides amicis* is made the equivalent of *malum dabunt Metelli,* while with the removal of the first syllable (*detracta syllaba prima*) it becomes *invides amicis* or the equivalent of *Naevio Poetae.*

In spite of Bassus' silence, the origin of the verse *quid immerentibus* has been ascertained. In an important article on ancient metrical systems, Leo[39] called attention to the fact that the same verse is cited by Diomedes from Varro: *septenarium versum Varro fieri dicit hoc modo cum ad iambicum trisyllabus pes additur et fit tale: quid immerentibus,* etc.[40]

Wissowa was inclined to believe that this verse is a post-Varronian invention reflecting Horace, *Epod.* 6, 1: *quid immerentis hospites vexas canis.*[41] In view of Diomedes' express testimony, such a view can hardly be accepted. Thus we have learned that Bassus was indebted to Varro for one example, at least, in his discussion of the Latin Saturnian. Is there other Varronian material to be found therein?

Bassus begins his chapter by saying that *nostri* (Latin writers on metrics) considered the Saturnian peculiar to Italy, but that they were in error since it had been used by the Greeks.[42] The *nostri* are not difficult to identify since Varro indicates clearly in the *De Lingua Latina* (VII, 36) that he considers the Saturnian a native Italic verse form. Bassus then proceeds to give three examples in Latin of some Greek Saturnians. As Leo observed,[43] we have in these Greek Saturnians no more than Latin verses which are the metrical equivalents of three Greek verse forms: the *Euripedeum, Archilocheum* and *Eupolideum.* To explain the fact that Bassus presented these forms as Greek Saturnians, Leo assumed—and rightly, I believe—that Bassus knew of genuine Latin Saturnians which had these same forms. He then found their Greek metrical equivalents in a manual of Greek meters and thus classified these meters as Greek Saturnians. The final step was to compose verses in Latin which would illustrate them.[44] Since Varro did not believe in a Greek Saturnian, it follows that this part of Bassus' chapter could not have come from Varro.

On the other hand, Bassus might well have found in Varro the genuine Latin Saturnians, the metrical forms of which allowed him to find exact Greek equivalents (his Greek Saturnians). He naturally had to give new Latin versions of these Greek forms since otherwise he would have been presenting genuine Latin Saturnians which would have been recognized as such. But had he presented his examples in Greek, they would have been quickly recognized as the Greek verse forms which they were: not Saturnians, but a *Euripedeum,* etc. Bassus was striving to prove the existence of a Greek Saturnian at any cost.

But when we come to the Latin Saturnians which follow in Bassus' discussion, we come to actual verses, not verses manufactured to serve as metrical illustrations. Two of them, as we have noted above, are taken from *tabulae triumphales* and two from Naevius' **Bellum Punicum.** Bassus cites them as if at first hand. But the fact is that he otherwise cites no author older than Terence[45] and it is not likely that he consulted the *tabulae* or the epic directly. Leo and Wissowa both believe that he found these verses reproduced in Varro[46] and I agree. But if this is so, why should he not have found there also the Saturnian *malum dabunt,* which is an integral part of the same section?

The apparent reason is this: his metrical analysis of *malum dabunt* is not the analysis which we should expect of Varro. As we know from its vestiges preserved in the grammarians, Varro propounded a metrical system based on the theory that all meters were derived from two original forms, the dactylic hexameter or the iambic trimeter, by means of *adiectio, detractio, concinnatio* or *permutatio.*[47]

To Varro, for example, an octonarius is formed *cum duo iambi pedes iambico metro praeponuntur,* a septenarius *cum ad iambicum trisyllabus pes additur*[48] (both examples of *adiectio*). We would therefore expect a less complex analysis of the Saturnian than that given by Bassus and, in fact, this is what we have.

In his brief definition of the Saturnian verse, Diomedes writes as follows: *Saturnium in honorem die Naevius invenit addita una syllaba ad iambicum versum sic: summas opes qui regum regias refregit. Huic si demas ultimam syllabam, erit iambicus de quo saepe memoratum est.*[49]

Although Diomedes does not cite his source, his analysis obviously rests on the principle of *adiectio* and must go back ultimately to Varro.[50] Bassus, however, as we have noted above, gave a far different analysis, although there seems to be a trace there of general Varronian theory (*cui detracta syllaba prima facit phallicon metrum;* clearly *detractio*). Yet in doing so, he used a verse of Varro as the basis of his analysis (the *quid immerentibus noces*) which Varro defined as a septenarius formed by the addition of a three-syllable foot to an iambicus while Bassus defined it as an *hipponacteus quadratus.*

With this evidence before us, we can see how Bassus worked in composing his chapter *De Saturnio Versu.* In the belief that Greek Saturnians existed, he discovered Greek verses which were the metrical equivalents of some Saturnians and composed Latin counterparts to illustrate their metrical structure. Coming to the Latin Saturnian, he cited genuine examples including that of the Metelli from Varro. When he came, however, to the analysis of the Saturnian verse form, he had a theory which differed from that of Varro. This was natural since he did not agree with Varro also on the origin of the verse. But he found in Varro a *septenarius* which would serve to illustrate his theory and he used it. It was one thing to draw his genuine Saturnians from Varro; another to explain their composition.

The thesis which has just been presented on the evidence of Bassus alone that he took the verse *malum dabunt* and what he knew of its historical background from a metrical work of Varro receives welcome support from Pseudo-Asconius. As a commentator, Pseudo-Asconius was primarily concerned with explaining a remark of Cicero. But curiously enough he adds to the factual material which serves his immediate purpose, a metrical comment: *cui tunc Metellus Consul responderat senario hypercatalecto qui et Saturnius dicitur.* This must have stood almost certainly in his source and gives us a slight indication of its nature. It was not the kind of glossary or grammatical work from which he seems to have drawn most of his quotations from the older poets, for such works, as we know from Festus-Paulus, were rarely concerned with metrical problems. The author of this source was primarily interested in an event in Naevius' life; but he was also interested enough in metrical matters to offer an analysis of a Saturnian in passing. To him a Saturnian was a *senarius hypercatalectus.*

I hardly need to point out that this is merely a more succinct way of saying that a Saturnian was a verse formed *addita una syllaba ad iambicum versum* or Varro's definition of a Saturnian. Howsoever the collection of scholia which passes under the name of Pseudo-Asconius may have grown up, we have a part of it at least which indicates Varro as the ultimate source. We cannot tell, of course, through how many hands it passed before reaching the Verrine scholia but of one thing we can be certain: it did not pass through Bassus. On the other hand, the similarity of the accounts of Bassus (as far as he goes) and Pseudo-Asconius in everything but metrical analysis (and we have seen why and how the difference arose in Bassus) points to common Varronian origin for the material held in common but does not point to the same work. The source of Bassus was a discussion of the Saturnian meter, that of Pseudo-Asconius a biographical notice.

Where was this notice contained? Varro knew of Naevius' imprisonment *ob assiduam maledicentiam et probra in principes de Graecorum poetarum more dicta* (Gellius, III, 3). The words *de Graecorum poetarum more* indicate that Varro was thinking of attacks by Naevius from the stage on the chief men of the state. We have one such attack preserved in the verse *sato Metelli*. Moreover, it is rightly believed by almost all scholars that part, at least, of the *malum* which the Metelli promised to inflict on Naevius took the form of the imprisonment to which Plautus refers.[51]

Gellius took the notice of this imprisonment, as we have seen above, from the *De Comoediis Plautinis*. But we can hardly believe that such an important event in Naevius' life, together with its attendant circumstances, was not recounted in some detail in the biography of Naevius contained in the *De Poetis*. That Varro indulged in such natural repetition is proved by the notice of Plautus' labor in a mill. It appeared both in the *De Comoediis Plautinis*, as attested by Gellius (III, 3) and in the *De Poetis* as attested by St. Jerome (01. 145, 1, p. 24 Reiffersheid).

As for the metrical definition of the verse *dabunt malum* which Pseudo-Asconius reproduces, it seems most likely that Varro, whose interest in the Saturnian we have observed, took the occurrence of this verse in his biographical anecdote as an occasion to express his opinion in passing regarding its formation. His contemporaries needed no explanation of the preceding senarius and did not receive one; a Saturnian in the time of Varro was something that merited particular comment.

Our study, therefore, of the sources of information regarding Naevius' life in authors other than Gellius has led us time and again back to the works of Varro, in general, and to his *De Poetis* in particular.[52] If we add the sum total of this evidence to what we earlier ascertained about Gellius' dependence on Varro for his knowledge of other aspects of Naevius' life, we shall have to conclude that Gellius learned also from Varro that Naevius was a Capuan. Whether he found it in some such form as *Cnaeus Naevius Capuae natus est* (cf. the Suetonian life of Terence, 1.1) or

Naevius Campanus (cf. Jerome's *Pacuvius Brundisinus*) makes little difference. As we have seen above, if Gellius wrote the comment on the *superbia Campana* of Naevius' epitaph, he understood the word Campanus in the sense of Capuan. If, on the other hand, the comment is repeated from Varro, we arrive at the same result, for we know that to Varro *Campanus* also meant Capuan and would have been used in this sense anywhere in his biography of Naevius.

The instances of the word *Campanus* in Latin literature have been collected in the *Thesaurus*.[53] There it can be seen that it was used in literature, until Livy, solely in reference to the city of Capua and its *ager*.[54] In Livy, it usually retains its old, circumscribed meaning, but in one passage this meaning has been extended to cover the natives or inhabitants of other cities situated in Campania.[55] Because the term had thus begun to lose its precise meaning, it was evidently felt that a new term should be used to designate the "Capuan" in contradistinction to the "Campanian." Although *Capuanus* is not attested in literature until Symmachus, its popular use was as old as Varro. In the *De Lingua Latina* he writes (X, 16): *quare proinde ac simile conferri non oportet ac dicere, ut sit ab Roma Romanus, sic ex Capua dici oportere Capuanus quod in consuetudine vehementer natat.*

Varro, then, stood against the use of *Capuanus* for Capuan. Clearly, then, he must have used the traditional *Campanus*. Both in *R.R.,* I, 2, 10 and in the fragment of the *Res Humanae* cited by Macrobius (III, 16, 12) where he uses *Campanus,* he is obviously thinking of Capua. His use of *Campanus* in *R.R.,* I, 2, 6 is classed as *dubiae interpretationis* in the *Thesaurus* but a comparison of the context with the fragment cited by Macrobius makes it clear that we again have the meaning Capuan. (The reference in the *Thesaurus* to Varro, *rust.,* 2, 3, 14 is a mistake for Horace, *Sat.* II, 3, 143-144). In view of this evidence, especially the express statement in the *De Lingua Latina,* I cannot attribute much importance to the statement of Servius Danielis on *Aen.* X, 145 (p. 404 Thilo-Hagen) that *Varro dicit— campum eundem Capuanum cratera dictum.* Here Varro may have reproduced a popular designation of his time (*Capuanus crater*) which contained a form of the adjective of which he disapproved or the author of the scholium may have slipped unwittingly into the terminology of his own time while transcribing.

We may have seemed to have taken a long path to arrive at the conclusion that Naevius was a Capuan and that Varro said so. But for our understanding of much in Naevius' life it was essential that his origin be placed on the firmest possible basis. I plan elsewhere to use this Capuan origin of Naevius to restudy parts of his life about which too much has already been written without due reference to his civil status. It was worth while too, I believe, to learn how deeply indebted we are to the great Roman polymath for our knowledge of the life of the first Latin poet. With Varro as our authority, we may be certain that what we know about Naevius is true in so far as Varro could attain the facts. And we know that Varro worked well and wisely to attain them.

Notes

1. I, 24.

2. Cf. Funaioli, *GRF,* pp. 210 ff. where some of the older literature is cited; also, Schanz-Hosius, *Gesch. d. röm. Lit.,* I⁴ (1927), p. 563; Fränkel, *RE,* Suppl. VI (1935), col. 622, and Enzo V. Marmorale, *Naevius Poeta* (Catania, 1945), pp. 9 f.

3. *Sitzb. Sächs. Akad.,* LXIII (1911), 49 f.

4. *Op. cit.,* p. 40.

5. *Op. cit., loc. cit.*

6. Leo, *Gesch. d. röm. Lit.,* p. 76, n. 1; Schanz-Hosius, *op. cit.,* p. 50.

7. The epitaphs of Naevius and Plautus were probably not true epitaphs but epideictic epigrams, while that of Pacuvius was a true epitaph; cf. Buechler, *Rh. Mus.,* XXXVII (1882), 521, n. 1 = *Kleine Schriften,* II, 466, n. 1, and Leo, *op. cit.,* 438, n. 1. But this doubtful authenticity does not affect our immediate problem.

8. XVII, 21, 42 ff. = Funaioli, *op. cit.,* pp. 209 f.; cf. Leo, *Plautinische Forschungen*², pp. 66 ff.

9. In this connection, I did not find O. Froehde's "Römische Dichtercitate bei Gellius" (*Festschrift Johannes Vahlen,* pp. 525 ff.) very helpful. Consequently, I examined all of Gellius' citations from the *Annals* and assured myself that in at least seven passages Gellius states or indicates that he is citing the *Annals* either by memory or from the text (I, 22, 16; X, 29, 2; XII, 4, 5; XIII, 21, 13; XVI, 10, 1; XVIII, 2, 16; XX, 10, 4).

10. He does this again in X, 1, 6.

11. V, 12.

12. On this dependence, see J. Kretzschmer, *De Auctoribus A. Gellii Grammaticis*² (Berlin, 1866), pp. 44 ff.

13. In the preface to his Teubner edition of Gellius, pp. xxxiv f.

14. III, 3.

15. Cf. Funaioli, *op. cit.,* pp. 220 ff.

16. VII, 8.

17. First perceived by Joseph Justus Scaliger. The most complete discussion of the problem is still that of Reifferscheid, *Suetoni Reliquiae,* pp. 363 ff. The notice on Naevius appears there on p. 23. For a recent estimate of the nature and extent of the section of the *De Viris Illustribus* which dealt with the Latin poets, the section from which St. Jerome took his information on Naevius, see Rostagni, *Suetonio de poetis e biografi minori* (Torino, 1944), pp. v-xxiv.

18. *Plautinische Forschungen*², p. 69.

19. *Philologus,* Suppl. XXI (1929), Heft II, 13 ff.

20. Ritschl, *Parerga,* pp. 621 ff.; Reifferscheid, *op. cit.,* p. 423.

21. *Op. cit.* (n. 19 above). See particularly the conclusions, pp. 92 ff.

22. The most satisfactory discussion of the *Liber Annalis* and its relation to Cicero's later works is that of Münzer, *Hermes,* XL (1905), 50 ff. For the date of composition and dedication, see *idem,* pp. 50 f.

23. Leo, *op. cit.,* pp. 66 ff.; Münzer, *op. cit.,* pp. 55 ff.

24. Münzer has also shown that many other parts of the chronology of the *Cato Maior* were taken from the *Liber Annalis; op. cit.,* pp. 61 ff.

25. The passages in which Cicero discusses or cites Naevius have been collected by W. Zillinger, *Cicero und die altrömischen Dichter* (Erlangen Diss., 1911), pp. 91 ff.

26. Pseudo-Asconius, p. 215 Stangl., on Cicero, *Verr., Act.* I, 10, 29.

27. ANTIδωPON (*Festschrift Jacob Wackernagel*), pp. 181 ff.

28. *AJP,* XLVIII (1927), 105 ff.

29. *Genethliacon für Carl Robert,* pp. 51 ff.

30. *Gesch. d. röm. Lit.,* p. 78, n. 5.

31. *Op. cit.,* p. 106.

32. *Ad Fam.,* V, 2, 8: *Huius* (Metelli) *ego temeritati si virtute atque animo non restitissem, quis esset qui me in consulatu non casu potius existimaret quam consilio fortem fuisse?*

33. Marmorale (*op. cit.,* pp. 57 ff.) not ony considers this verse a Saturnian and assigns it therefore to the *Bellum Punicum* but holds also that it was written to honor L. Caecilius Metellus (*Cos.* 251).

34. *GL,* VI, 266, 5 Keil.

35. Wissowa, *op. cit.,* p. 61.

36. *GL,* VI, 265, 30; 14.

37. *Idem,* p. 265, 24; 28.

38. *Idem,* p. 266, 10.

39. *Hermes,* XXIV (1889), 280 ff., especially n. 2, p. 281. The parts dealing with Bassus and the Saturnian have been expanded in the same author's *Der Saturnische Vers, Abh. Gött.,* VIII (1905), 7 ff.

40. *GL,* I, 515, 5.

41. *Op. cit.,* p. 60.

42. *GL,* VI, 265, 8.

43. *Sat. Vers,* p. 10.

44. Wissowa, *op. cit.,* p. 59.

45. Cf. Rufinus, *GL,* VI, 555, 22.

46. Leo, *Hermes*, p. 281, note; somewhat modified in *Sat. Vers.*, p. 10; Wissowa, *op. cit., loc. cit.*

47. Cf. Bassus, *GL*, VI, 271, 5; Leo, *Hermes*, p. 289, especially 5.

48. Cf. Diomedes, who cites Varro expressly as his source for both definitions; *GL*, I, 515, 8; 3.

49. *Idem*, p. 512, 18.

50. In his first article (*Hermes*, p. 281, n. 1), Leo was certain of this. Later (*Sat. Vers*, p. 9, n. 2; cf. p. 7, n. 2) he still admitted the possibility of Varronian origin but considered Diomedes' example *summas opes qui regum regias refregit* very doubtful as a genuine Saturnian. In view of Varro's metrical system as illustrated above and what I shall later say about the source of Pseudo-Asconius, I believe that all the evidence still points to Varro.

51. *Miles*, 211 f.; cf. Festus-Paulus, *s. v. Barbari*, p. 23, Lindsay. The exact interpretation of Plautus' allusion has caused much discussion (cf. Marmorale. *op. cit.*, pp. 107 ff., who deals with earlier theories). But Leo (*Geschichte*, p. 78, n. 5), Fränkel (*op. cit.*) and others are undoubtedly correct in referring it to Naevius' imprisonment.

52. The only piece of information the source of which I have not discussed is the one of Plautus and Festus-Paulus mentioned in the preceding note. As a contemporary of Naevius, Plautus, to say nothing of his audience, had heard of Naevius' imprisonment at first hand. There is no question here of a literary source. As for the notice in Paulus (Festus is lost here) which identifies the *poeta barbarus* of Plautus as Naevius, it probably goes back to a glossary of Plautus, for it appears within a list of Plautine glosses (cf. Reitzenstein, *Verrianische Forschungen*, pp. 58-67). There is no way, however, of identifying its author.

53. *TLL, Onomasticon* II, cols. 129 ff.

54. An exception to this statement may be contained in Horace's *morbus Campanus* (*Sat.*, I, 5, 62) if this meant the Campanian rather than the Capuan disease.

55. This can be seen in XXVI, 34. In section 6, we find *Campani* used to designate "Capuans" in contradistinction to *Atellani, Calatini* and *Sabatini* (cf. 33, 12); in 8, we find *qui nec Capuae nec in urbe Campana quae a populo Romano defecisset.* Here the *urbs Campana* would be Atella or Cales.

J. Wight Duff (essay date 1960)

SOURCE: "The Pioneers of Roman Poetry" in *A Literary History of Rome: From the Origins to the Close of the Golden Age*, Ernest Benn Limited, 1960, pp. 87-113.

[*In the following excerpt, Duff examines some examples of what he considers inspired verses of Naevius.*]

In Cn. Naevius (*circ.* 270-*circ.* 199) greater independence and originality are recognisable.[1] He may be called home-born, and the native spirit is strong in him. Especially in the historical plays (*fabulae praetextae* or *praetextatae*) invented by him, and in his epic, he proves himself inspired by the greatness of the national life. His truly Latin genius is testified to by the epitaph in Saturnians (according to Gellius, of his own composition[2]) in which he pitches his claims at their highest, as a poet to be mourned by the divine *Camenae*, one after whose passing men 'forgat to speake the Latin tongue at Rome':

> *Immortales mortales si foret fas flere,*
> *Flerent diuae Camenae Naeuiom poetam:*
> *Itaque postquam est Orchi traditus thensauro,*
> *Oblitei sunt Romai loquier lingua Latina.*

When Gellius remarks that this epitaph is 'full of Campanian pride' (*plenum superbiae Campanae*), he does not necessarily mean that Naevius was born in Campania. Campanian vainglory was as proverbial as that of the Castilian or the Gascon in later times. So, too, a display of 'Hielan' pride' is conceivable in one who is no Kelt. Naevius bore a plebeian name common in Rome, and was most likely Roman;[3] otherwise the aid of the tribunes might not have been available to release him from the durance vile to which his dramatic outspokenness subjected him. Gellius[4] quotes Varro *de Poetis* to show that Naevius served in the first Punic War. From the same passage in Gellius we learn that his first plays were given in 235 B.C. His comic abilities brought him into trouble; systematic abuse (*assidua maledicentia*) of men in high place led to his incarceration. Roman aristocratic government had no tolerance for the political criticism which had animated the Old Comedy in democratic Athens. So the less caustic Plautus is moved to refer to the misfortunes of his brother-dramatist:

> I have heard a Roman poet has to pillar head on hand,
> While two pair of fetters guard him all his weary prison hours.[5]

In time, something like an apology or recantation in his plays, *Hariolus* and *Leo,* written in prison, brought about the intervention of the tribunes and his liberation.[6] His ambiguous gibe at the house of the Metelli:

> *Fato Metelli Romai fiunt consules—*

is only less notorious than the menacing retort by the Metellus who was consul in 206:

> *Dabunt malum Metelli Naeuio poetae.*[7]

Neither prison nor threats could silence him. In the end he was exiled, and died at Utica. As the siege of that city by Scipio ended only in 202, Naevius could not have died there in 204, the date deduced by Cicero from 'ancient commentaries.'[8] Cicero, however, mentions that Varro, *diligentissimus inuestigator antiquitatis*, thinks the traditional date of death an error, and extends Naevius's life. Jerome's date, 'year of Abraham 1816,' that is, 201 B.C., is therefore nearly right; and some have conjectured 199.

It is only necessary to give the seven remaining titles of his tragedies—*Aesiona (Hesione), Andromache, Danaë, Equos Troianus, Hector Proficiscens, Iphigenia, Lycurgus*—to mark the predominating interest in the Trojan cycle of legend. Of some forty surviving tragic lines the bulk may be referred to the *Lycurgus,* which is on the lines of the *Bacchae* of Euripides. To Naevius's talent for pithy expression we owe the preservation by Cicero of thoughts like

> Ill-gotten gain is lost in pain,[9]

and that on the height of commendation,

> Praise from thee is precious, father; all the people praiseth thee.[10]

His iambic trimeters too evince, with all their quaint diction, a nascent feeling for beauty, as in the *Lycurgus:*

> Ye trusty guardians of the royal life,
> Hie straight into the forest leaf-yclad,
> Where trees by taking thought do grow unsown.[11]

Inward stirrings of individuality and nationality combined to prompt Naevius's excursions into the domain of Roman history in quest of themes for his *Clastidium,* and *Romulus* or *Alimonium Remi et Romuli.* The former dramatised contemporary events. Its hero was the victor of 222 B.C. and winner of the *spolia opima* from the Keltic chieftain Virdumarus. He was the same Marcellus whom—perhaps with reminiscences of Naevius—Virgil, towards the close of the pageant of souls shown to Aeneas, so affectingly introduces as attended by his youthful descendant, once the centre of imperial hopes.[12] On several occasions such a play might appropriately have been acted—at Marcellus's triumph, or at the funeral games in his honour, or at the dedication of the Temple of Virtus in fulfilment of a paternal vow. In any case, the occasion was like the theme—national. What lustre or interest the other *praetexta* on **The Nurture of Remus and Romulus** shed upon the foundation of Rome, the morsels left are insufficient to show. The example thus set in *praetextae* was bequeathed to Ennius and Pacuvius, but enjoyed no great career. Historical dramas, after long desuetude, were resuscitated in the first century A.D., not for acting, but as a literary expression of hostility to the imperial *régime.* Such were the efforts composed in the time of Nero and Vespasian by Curiatius Maternus, familiar to readers of Tacitus's *Dialogus.* One of those later productions is the sole survivor of the *praetextae.* This is *Octavia,* a dramatisation of the death of Nero's wife. Traditionally coupled with Seneca's tragedies, which it resembles in manner, it is on internal evidence of later date.

But it must have been in comedy that Naevius's varied genius most fully expressed itself. A list of thirty-four *pal-*liatae—or about five comedies to every tragedy—certifies his fertility. Though the fragments amount only to about 130 lines, and though there has been confusion with the records of Laevius, Livius, and Novius, there is enough to illustrate that observation of character which, combined with a fondness for mordant innuendos and unwelcome exposures, made his plays amusing to the plebeian and sometimes too spicy for the noble. The vivid picture of a coquette is now generally considered to belong to his *Tarentilla,* or *The Girl from Tarentum,* herself perhaps the very damsel who

> as if playing ball in a ring, skips from one to another,
> and is all things to all men, with her nods and winks,
> her caresses and embraces, now a squeeze of the hand
> or a pressure on the foot, her ring to look at, her lips to
> blow an inviting kiss, here a song and there the
> language of signs.[13]

There was no knowing on what seamy side of politics or morals such a command of realism might throw awkward light. It was not pleasant to have a scandalous episode in the life of a Scipio thus antithetically set before the public:

> *Etiam qui res magnas manu saepe gessit gloriose,*
> *Cuius facta uiua nunc uigent, qui apud gentes solus praestat,*
> *Eum suus pater cum pallio ab amica abduxit uno.*

He was equally scathing when he attacked a whole class, say of spend-thrift youths, or of those who brought such rapid ruin on the state, 'the crop of new-fangled speakers, silly young fools!'[14] A more positive note, as if from a moral censor, seems to echo in the advice:

> If you would return to virtue, you must shun depravity—
> Fatherland and father follow, more than foreign infamy.[15]

His butts were to be found outside Rome also; for he had jokes at the expense of the favourite fare of provincial towns like Praeneste and Lanuvium. It is a plausible suggestion that the fun of his *Apella* centres in the mockery meted out to an Apulian woman and her lumpish compatriots.[16] Titles like *Testicularia* and *Triphallus* plainly indicate the coarse nature of some of the plots. Other features of his comedies connect themselves with his treatment of his Greek originals. Already in Naevius, we know from Terence, had begun the process of *contaminatio,* or weaving together of plots from two separate originals.[17] Already, too, we also learn from Terence, the parasite had cringed and the braggadocio swaggered on the Naevian stage, as they had done on the Menandrian and were now about to do on the Plautine.[18]

The dramatic talents of Naevius cannot be said to have obtained absolutely free play. His comic genius was hampered by the indignant opposition of the great families, while his historical plays were eclipsed by the superior attractions of Greek tragedy. Through the epic of his old age[19] he was destined to exert a far more powerful influence on literature. The **Bellum Punicum,** of which less than eighty lines survive, was in the main a narrative in Saturnian verse of the first war between Rome and Carthage, in which the poet had played a part. But it was more than personal and historical: it drew upon legend. Naevius did not plunge *in medias res.*[20] Preferring to hark back to the origins of the hostile cities, and, possibly in consequence of his campaigns, acquainted with the manner in which the Sicilian Timaeus connected Rome and Troy, he was enabled to decorate his poem with myths of heroes and gods. The paramount interest, then, of the first and second books—for the work was arranged into its seven books by Lampadio[21]—is that they provided sketches in the rough of what became polished scenes in Virgil. The influence of the poem on Ennius must have been immediate: it may well have appeared about 204 B.C., when that author first came to Rome.

The connexion of Rome with Troy had become a familiar idea before Naevius wrote. This is implied in the historic instance from the period of the first Punic War, when the Acarnanians appealed to Rome for help on the ground that they had not assisted the Greeks against Troy.[22] While Naevius makes use of this idea, it is by no means likely, though often alleged, that he introduced the episode of Aeneas's visit to Dido's court, which adds so vital a human interest to the *Aeneid.* Apparently both Naevius and Ennius push the foundation of Rome back to a period contemporaneous with that of Carthage, and they make Romulus, the founder of Rome, a grandson of Aeneas.[23] Aeneas, then, must have reached Italy before the foundation of Carthage; and the words of Naevius,

> *Blande et docte perconctat Aenea quo pacto*
> *Troiam urbem liquisset,*

in which some have impulsively seen Dido's request that he should, as in Virgil, recount the 'unutterable woe' of the downfall of Troy, may be more appropriately, if less romantically, referred to old King Latinus.

Ample proof of Naevius's employment of legendary episodes and of their influence on Virgil is afforded by the fragments themselves, by comments on Virgil by Servius—or his interpolator—as well as by Macrobius. Embryonic forms of things familiar in the *Aeneid* emerge, such as the flight of Anchises and Aeneas with their wives from blazing Troy, the storm sent by Juno to harass the voyage, Aeneas's words of heartening to his men, the complaints of Venus to Jove, and Jove's promises of a high future for Rome. Naevius secures his rights again in the records of literature when one notes the Servian comment on Aeneas's speech of encouragement in *Aeneid* I as 'entirely taken over' from the **Punic War**[24] and the similar remarks of Macrobius where, discussing the debt of Virgil to his predecessors, he declares the 'whole passage' of the storm and Venus's subsequent complaints to be 'taken' from Naevius.[25] The saturnians could at best make rough material for Virgil's noble lines; yet it is something to be a hod-man when princes build.

There are, of course, Hellenic echoes in Naevius like his Invocation to the Muses, and like the piece which may be a description of figures upon Aeneas's shield modelled on the Homeric Shield of Achilles.[26] But the total effect of a poem in the native metre and on a native theme is Roman. So Roman is he in details that Naevius significantly hastens to explain his Invocation—with a touch of that prosaic prolixity which so easily beset him—that the 'Nine harmonious sisters, daughters of Jove' are they whom 'Greeks name Musae and whom we name Casmenae.' It is doubtful how much actual history he covered before the Punic War begins in his third book. Did he leap straight to the third century from the mythical lore attending the foundation, or did he rapidly recount the story of the city up to the war with Pyrrhus?[27] In any case, for the historical portions Naevius doubtless borrowed in both matter and expression from the *tituli triumphales* set up in the Capitol by victorious generals and composed in Saturnians. For exploits by individuals he could also draw upon oral tradition as well as family memorials in prose or verse.

In the matter of style there is a risk of doing less than justice to Naevius. Of his diction it is so easy to say that it shares the faults of early Latin poets, creeps oftener than it soars, and mistakes the baldest annalistic for the poetic. No one will say there is poetry in

> *Manius Valerius consul*
> *Partem exerciti in expeditionem*
> *Ducit.*

Yet there are pieces in our own Wordsworth no better than this simple condescension upon such details as 'a section of an army' led out 'for an expedition'! Of his metre, if one approaches his Saturnians from the standpoint of strictly regular verse, it is hardly possible to form anything but a low opinion. There is a passage formerly referred to Atilius Fortunatianus, but now assigned to Caesius Bassus, a contemporary of Nero, in which the writer, recognising the lawless nature of the lines in the **Bellum Punicum,** confesses that he can hardly find a normal example of Saturnians in Naevius.[28] He does eventually quote a few, but it is evident he is judging by the anachronistic standard of Greek measures. There is no more illuminating criticism on Naevius than that put by Cicero in the mouth of Brutus.[29] He likens the charm of the **Bellum Punicum** to a sculpture by Myron. He admirably weighs the relative merits of Ennius and his forerunner—Ennius, of course, was more polished (*sane, ut certe est, perfectior*), but his disdain for Naevius was merely an affectation. Ennius knew he must reckon with Naevius when he left out of his *Annales* the first Punic War, because 'others have versified it' (*scripsere alii rem uersibu'*). 'Yes,' the passage proceeds, 'versified it with clearness, if with less elegance, Ennius, than your own. This cannot fail to be plain to you, for you borrowed, if you will only acknowledge it, many a thing from Naevius; if you don't acknowledge it, I say you pilfered (*surripuisti*)'. Cicero's judicial attitude prepares one for the place occupied by Naevius in the list in which Volcatius Sedigitus with complacent dogmatism awards their order of merit to ten authors of comedy.[30] Therein

Naevius is third. Caecilius Statius heads the list, and Plautus makes a good second. Whatever may be said about Naevius's rustic saturnians, he has in Comedy his revenge—Ennius is at the bottom! 'I add a tenth,' says Sedigitus, 'because he is old—Ennius.' The honour is explicitly conferred *antiquitatis causa*.

Notes

1. For fragments of *Bell. Pun.*, Bährens, *F.P.R.*; L. Müller, *Enni Carm. Reliq.; Accedunt Naeui Belli Poenici Quae Supersunt*, 1884; for dramatic fragments, Ribbeck, *Scaen. Rom. Poes. Frag.*; selections in W. W. Merry, *Fragments of Roman Poetry*, ed. 2, 1898; L. Müller (*op. cit.*, pp. xx-xlvii) discusses contents and versification of *Bell. Pun.*: cf. Lamarre, *Hist. d. l. litt. romaine*, vol. i., pp. 208-217.

2. *Noct. Att.*, I. xxiv. But it may be from Vatro's *Imagines*.

3. For this view see *Cn. Naeuii poetae Romani uitam descripsit, carminum reliquias collegit*, etc. E. Klussmann, 1843; *De Naeuii poetae uita et scriptis disseruit*, M. J. Berchem, 1861.

4. *Noct. Att.*, XVII. xxi.

5. *Mil. Glor.*, 211-12:

   'Nam os columnatum poetae esse indaudiui barbaro,
   Quoi bini custodes semper totis horis occubant.'

   The 'foreign poet' is so called from the Greek standpoint of the play. The reference is probably contemporary.

6. Gellius, *N.A.*, III. iii.

7. Pseud-Ascon. on Cic., *In Verr. act. pr.* 29.

8. Cic., *Brut.*, xv. 60.

9. 'Male parta male dilabuntur.' *apud* Cic. *Phil.* ii. 65.

10. 'Laetus sum laudari me abs te, pater, a laudato uiro,' *apud* Cic. *Ad Fam.* XV. vi. 1.

    'Vos qui regalis corporis custodias
    Agitatis, ite actutum in frundiferos locos,
    Ingenio arbusta ubi nata sunt, non obsita.'

11. The compound epithet *frundifer* had in later Latin a more obsolete ring than 'leaf-bearing' has in English. Some Middle-English word is analogous; perhaps the Chaucerian 'y-corouned' (with leaves).

12. *Aen.* vi. 854 *sqq.*

13. Or is it 'a *billet-doux* from her own hand?' This passage cited by Isid., *Orig.*, 1. 25, as from Ennius, is given by Ribbeck and others to the *Tarentilla* (see *Com. Rom. Frag.*):

    ' Quasi pila
    In choro ludens datatim dat se et communem facit.
    Alii adnutat, alii adnictat, alium amat, alium tenet.
    Alibi manus est occupata, alii percellit pedem,
    Anulum dat alii spectandum, a labris alium inuocat,
    Cum alio cantat, at tamen alii suo dat digito literas.'

14. 'Proueniebant oratores noui, stulti adulescentuli.'

15. 'Primum ad uirtutem ut redeatis, abeatis ab ignauia, Domi patres patriam ut colatis potius quam peregri probra.'

16. Berchem, *op. cit.*, pp. 68-69, quoted by Lamarre, *op. cit.*, p. 203.

17. Ter., *Andr.*, prol. 18. Attacked for blending different plots, Terence retorts:

    'quom hunc accusant, Naeuium, Plautum, Ennium Accusant.'

    For a different view of *contaminatio* see W. Beare in O.C.D. (s.v. *Contaminatio*) and articles there cited.

18. Ter., *Eun.*, prol. 25, where reference is made to these personages in the *Colax* of Naevius and *Colax* of Plautus.

19. Cic., *De Sen.*, xiv: 'Quam gaudebat *Bello* suo *Punico* Naeuius! Eos omnes quos commemoraui his studiis flagrantes senes uidimus.'

20. But see Suppl. Bibl. under Naevius.

21. Suet., *Gramm.*, ii.

22. Justinus, xxxviii. 1.

23. Servius on *Aen.*, i. 273.

24. *Aen.*, i. 198-207. The comment is 'totus hic locus de Naeuio (? Naeuii primo) belli Punici libro translatus est.'

25. Macrob., *Saturn.*, VI. ii: 'In principio Aeneidos tempestas describitur et Venus apud Iouem queritur. Hic locus totus sumptus a Naeuio est ex primo libro *Belli Punici*.'

26. Bährens, *F.P.R.*, p. 46, § 20. L. Müller (*Enni carm. rel.*, p. xxviii) thinks the figures belong to a ship taken at Mylae.

27. L. Müller maintains that he covered the longer period, for reasons ingeniously argued out (*op. cit.*, pp. xxv-xxvii).

28. 'Ut uix inuenerim apud Naeuium quos pro exemplo ponerem,' Keil, *Gramm. Lat.*, vi. 255 *sqq.*

29. Cic., *Brut.*, xix. 75, 'Illius quem in uatibus et faunis enumerat Ennius *Bellum Punicum* quasi Myronis opus delectat.'

30. Gellius, *Noct. Att.*, XV. xxiv, quotes the list from Sedigitus's book on the poets:

    'Caecilio palmam Statio do mimico;
    Plautus secundus facile exsuperat ceteros;
    Dein Naeuius qui feruet pretio in tertiost;
    Si erit quod quarto detur dabitur Licinio.
    Post insequi Licinium facio Atilium;
    In sexto consequetur hos Terentius;
    Turpilius septimum, Trabea octauum optinet;
    Nono loco esse facile facio Luscium;
    Decimum addo causa antiquitatis Ennium.'

FURTHER READING

Duckworth, George E. "The Golden Age of Drama at

Rome," in *The Nature of Roman Comedy: A Study in Popular Entertainment*. 1952. London: Bristol Classical Press, 1994, pp. 39-72.

Brief profile describes Naevius as original, independent, outspoken, and the inventor of the Roman historical play; mentions Plautus's borrowing various passages from him.

Warmington, E. H. Introduction to *Remains of Old Latin,* Vol. II. Edited and translated by E. H. Warmington. 1936. Cambridge: Harvard University Press, 1982, pp. vii-xxx.

Examines Naevius's accomplishments, including the *Punic War,* termed the first national or really Roman epic, and originating the historical Roman play.

Strabo

c. 63 B.C.-c. 21 A.D.

Greek historian and geographer.

INTRODUCTION

Strabo is the author of the seventeen-book *Geography,* the only study of its kind from antiquity that survives. The *Geography,* conceived as a philosophical and political work as well as a physical description of the world then known, was meant to educate and inform intelligent citizens and high-ranking officials and rulers of Rome. Strabo wrote the *Geography* as a complement to his now-lost *Historical Sketches* and used the same criteria in selecting what to write about; in keeping with Strabo's aim of recording what is "noble and great, . . . what is of social importance, or memorable, or entertaining," the work displays an encyclopedic wealth of knowledge and intriguing observations concerning both past and present, presented in what critics have deemed an excellent style. Though its cartography is outdated today, the *Geography* remains an important source of information about the development of ancient geography. Its many digressions constitute an invaluable, engaging repository of a large amount of historical, ethnographical, and geological information.

BIOGRAPHICAL INFORMATION

Most of what is known of Strabo's life originates with or can be extrapolated from the *Geography.* He was born to a wealthy, prominent family in Amasia, Pontos, near the Black Sea, circa 63 B.C. In Caria he studied under Aristodemus; in Rome, under the geographer and grammarian Tyrannion. First an Aristotelian, Strabo later became a subscriber to the practices and beliefs of the Stoics. He traveled extensively to many countries, including Ethiopia and Armenia, as well as Egypt in 25/4 B.C. with his patron, the Roman governor of Egypt, Aelius Gallus. Strabo returned to Amasia for perhaps as long as twenty-seven years. There he wrote his *Historical Sketches.* Some critics have argued that Strabo did not write his final work, the *Geography,* in Amasia because there appear to be gaps in his knowledge that would not have been present if he had resided there at the time. The bulk of the *Geography* appears to have been written circa 7 B.C., with final touches made circa 2 B.C. Strabo made minor additions up until his death circa 21 A.D.

MAJOR WORKS

Nearly the entire forty-three-book *Historical Sketches* is lost—a work which started at the point that Polybius's his-

tory stopped, 146 B.C. The *Geography,* however, is almost wholly extant—an extremely unusual situation for books of antiquity—except for the greater part of book seven. The first two books of the *Geography* concern the tradition of geography and offer extensive, detailed criticism of Strabo's predecessors. In them Strabo sets forth his philosophy of geography, a view that challenges in its scope much of the work that preceded him, and, indeed, is more broad than many modern studies. Books three through ten cover Europe and the mythology of Greece; eleven through sixteen deal with Asia; and seventeen considers Egypt, Ethiopia, and northern Africa.

CRITICAL RECEPTION

The *Geography* seems to have had remarkably little influence in Strabo's time. It took five centuries, when Stephanus of Byzantium would take note, until scholars began to give him due credit and the work became a standard. Milton V. Anastos writes of Strabo's importance to Columbus, who used his writings to back up the arguments he presented to his critics. Scholars debate the extent of Strabo's travels. He sometimes makes erroneous statements that seem odd if he had personally witnessed what he was describing. He makes no secret that much of what he writes is based on others' experiences; indeed, he credits dozens of other authors and often quotes their work. However, because Strabo is not always explicit concerning whether or not he actually visited a place himself, scholars argue over the source of some of his accounts. Advancing the case that Strabo did or did not visit Greece, for example, is a point of contention for scholars. Charles Heald Weller surveyed the situation in 1906, pointing out that sometimes Strabo's interest was "to determine whether this or that town was under the sway of Nestor or Menelaus or Achilles, rather than to portray the condition of the country in his own day." This runs counter to the view of scholars who believe that when Strabo gives short shrift to a description of a locale, it is likely he did not visit it. But, Weller goes on: "In a thoroughly scientific manner he verifies and supplements the statements of his authorities. But when to an author's general literary dependence are added quotations from others concerning matters which an eyewitness must know personally, or when an author makes palpable blunders regarding things that a visitor must have seen, belief in his autopsy becomes doubtful. If such quotations and strange statements are frequent, doubt approaches certainty." Another often-disputed area is the date of composition of the *Geography*. Some believe it is the work of an aged man, finished near his death. Others hotly dispute this, emphasizing that with its vitality the work can be only that of a man in his prime, and noting that descriptions reliably dated to later years are simply minor revisions. Strabo's manuscripts, with their many variants, have been the source of much scholarly research. Acclaimed Strabo scholar Walter Leaf writes: "There is no sort of textual corruption which cannot be abundantly illustrated from the MSS. of Strabo; but they stand alone in one characteristic—the multitude of lacunae."

PRINCIPAL WORKS

Historical Sketches. 43 Books. (history) first century B.C.

Geography. 17 Books. (geography and history) circa 7 B.C.

Principal English Translations

Selections from Strabo (translated by H. F. Tozer) 1893

Geography. 8 Vols. (translated by Horace Leonard Jones and J. R. S. Sterrett) 1917-33

Strabo on the Troad; book XIII, cap. I (translated by Walter Leaf) 1923

*Now lost.

CRITICISM

E. H. Bunbury (essay date 1883)

SOURCE: "Strabo" in *A History of Ancient Geography among the Greeks and Romans from the Earliest Ages till the Fall of the Roman Empire*, J. Murray, 1883, pp. 209-75.

[*In the following excerpt, Bunbury surveys and critiques Strabo's description of Europe, revealing errors and noteworthy oversights as well as pointing out sections which are accurate, detailed, and engaging.*]

DESCRIPTIVE GEOGRAPHY.—EUROPE.

. . . 1. In his third book Strabo commences the particular description of the different countries of Europe, beginning with Spain, to which the whole of this third book is devoted. His description of the Iberian peninsula is marked at once by the chief merits as well as the chief defects that characterize his work in general. We have already seen how imperfect was his idea of its geographical form and position, and how distorted his conception of its appearance on a map. But he was well acquainted with its leading geographical features: the great rivers that traversed it from east to west, the Bætis (Guadalquivir), the Anas (Guadiana), the Tagus, the Durius (Douro), and the Minius (Minho): as well as the Iberus or Ebro, which however he considered as having its course parallel with the chain of the Pyrenees, and consequently flowing from N. to S. On the other side of the valley of the Ebro, and parallel with the Pyrenees, was a chain of mountains to which he gives the name of Idubeda, and which he describes as containing the sources of the Tagus and Durius. From the middle of this range branches off another called Orospeda which trends to the westward, and ultimately takes a turn to the south. Beginning at first with hills of moderate elevation, it gradually rises in height till it joins the range that separates the valley of the Bætis from the coast near Malaca (the Sierra Nevada), which he regarded as the main continuation of this central chain, while other parallel ridges on the north side of the Bætis contained the mines for which Spain was so famous. The Anas and the Bætis had their sources near one another in the range of Orospeda: they are correctly described as flowing at first to the west and then turning off more towards the south. Imperfect as is this outline of the physical geography of Spain, it shows a general acquaintance with the leading features of the country, and a correct appreciation of the manner in which those features determine the character and conformation of its different regions.

2. The whole of the northern part of the peninsula, adjoining the Ocean, he correctly describes as occupied by a tract of mountainous country, extending from the headland of Nerium (Cape Finisterre) to the extremity of the Pyreness: and the nations inhabiting this quarter, the Callaïci, Astures and Cantabri, which had but lately been brought under the dominion of Rome, were still lawless and preda-

tory tribes, living in a semi-barbarous condition. The account given of their habits of life and customs, which must have been taken by Strabo from previous writers, may probably refer to a period somewhat earlier than that at which he wrote, but it is at all events curious and interesting. Some of their peculiarities were indeed, as he himself remarks, common also to the Gauls as well as to the Thracians and Scythians,[1] and were probably inherent in their mode of life and the stage of semi-civilization in which they found themselves, rather than belonging to them as a race. The Lusitanians on the west, from the promontory of the Artabri to the mouth of the Tagus, partook to a great extent of the same characteristics, even the inhabitants of the plains and fertile districts having gradually been compelled by the continued incursions of their ruder neighbours to adopt their warlike and desultory habits: but the inhabitants of the Hither province, as it had long been called,[2] occupying the eastern portion of the peninsula, were in a much more civilized state, and even the Celtiberian tribes of the interior, which had cost the Romans such repeated and long continued efforts to subdue them, were gradually settling down under the influence of Roman civilization and of the numerous Roman colonies that had been established among them. The province of Bætica on the other hand, which was occupied principally by the Turdetani in the valley of the Bætis, and the Bastelani between them and the sea coast, was not only completely tranquil and civilized, but had become *Romanized* to such an extent as to have almost entirely laid aside the use of the native language, and adopted Latin in its stead.[3]

This result was mainly owing to the great natural fertility of the country. Strabo can indeed hardly find words to express his admiration of the richness of Turdetania, the modern Andalusia, which had from the earliest times been proverbial for its wealth, under the name of Tartessus,[4] and had continued to enjoy the same pre-eminence under the Phœnicians, Carthaginians, and Romans. It not only produced corn, wine, and oil in great abundance, but wool of first-rate excellence,[5] honey, wax, pitch, kermes, and vermilion (cinnabar); while the sea-coast furnished salt-fish in quantities equal to that of the Euxine. The mouths of the rivers and the estuaries formed by the action of the tides gave peculiar advantage for the export of these various commodities: hence an active and constant trade was carried on, and the ships of Turdetania that sailed from thence to Dicæarchia and Ostia—the two ports of Rome— were the largest of all that were seen in those great centres of commerce.[6]

But in addition to all these varied sources of wealth, Strabo dwells above all upon the extraordinary mineral riches of this favoured tract. In this respect indeed the south of Spain enjoyed a reputation in ancient times similar to that of Mexico or Peru down to our own day. Gold, silver, brass (copper), and iron were found in quantities, as well as of a quality, unsurpassed in any other part of the world. Gold was not only obtained by digging, but by simple washing. The other metals were all derived from mines;

and these were worked principally in the mountains near the sources of the Bætis, and extending from thence towards New Carthage: the most valuable of all the silver mines being in the immediate neighbourhood of that city. In the time of Polybius these had given employment to 40,000 workmen, and were said to have yielded 25,000 drachms (about £900) a day; but in Strabo's time the mines had passed into the hands of private persons, and the produce had apparently fallen off.[7]

3. It is remarkable, that throughout his description both of the natural productions and physical peculiarities of Spain, and of the manners and customs of its inhabitants, Strabo appears to have relied almost exclusively upon Greek authorities, his statements being derived principally from Polybius, Artemidorus, and Posidonius. He indeed speaks in one passage[8] in very disparaging terms of the Roman writers in general, whom he accuses of doing little but copy the Greeks; but it seems impossible that their historians, in relating their long-continued wars with the Spaniards, should not have contributed many facts to the geography of the country. The construction of roads in all directions through Spain, and the itineraries which must certainly have existed in his day of the stations and distances along these, would also have furnished most valuable materials to a geographer that was able to appreciate them. But no attempt is made by Strabo to turn to account these sources of information. The only instance in which he especially refers to the Roman campaigns is that of D. Brutus Callaïcus against the Lusitanians, and the particulars of this he probably learnt from Polybius.[9] Even where he adverts to the construction by the Romans of a great highway from the Pyrenees through Tarraco and Saguntum to the frontiers of Bætica, and thence on to Corduba and Gades, he gives no account of the distances; and contents himself with telling us that Julius Cæsar accomplished the journey from Rome to his camp at Obulco on his way to Munda in twenty-seven days.[10]

In his enumeration of the names of towns and of the native tribes in Spain, Strabo has made a judicious selection, and must have followed good authorities, as almost all the names he mentions are well known from other sources, and must have been places of some importance. At the same time he avoids the error into which Pliny and Ptolemy subsequently fell, of loading their pages with obscure and insignificant names. He indeed adds some judicious remarks[11] on the proneness of geographical as well as historical writers to bestow the title of towns and cities on places that were, in fact, mere villages. It was thus that some writers asserted that there were more than a thousand *cities* in Spain; and even Polybius affirmed that Tiberius Gracchus took or destroyed three hundred *cities* in Celtiberia alone. This exaggeration, as he points out, was the more inexcusable in the case of Spain, as the inhabitants of the interior for the most part lived wholly in villages, and the barren and rugged character of the country was ill adapted to the formation of towns.[12]

4. In the last section of the third book Strabo treats of the islands adjacent to Spain, and describes at some length the

Balearic Islands, as well as the neighbouring Pityusæ, both of which were in his day well known: the former especially having received two Roman colonies. He then gives a long account of Gadeira (Gades), which was still at this period one of the most important emporia of commerce in the world; and enters into somewhat idle disquisitions as to its relations with the fabulous island of Erytheia, the abode of king Geryones. In conclusion, he mentions the celebrated Cassiterides, which he describes as ten in number, lying close together, but far out to sea to the north of the port of the Artabri, from which they were separated by a wider extent of sea than that between Gaul and Britain.[13] The inhabitants are described as wearing long black garments, and walking about with long wands in their hands, looking like the Furies of tragedy. They traded in tin and lead, in exchange for which they received pottery, salt, and bronze vessels. The trade with these islands had for a long time been confined to the Phœnicians from Gades, but had been opened out to the Romans by P. Crassus, who visited them in person, and from that time the intercourse was carried on briskly.[14]

It is remarkable that he says nothing, either here or elsewhere, of the proximity of the Tin Islands to Britain:[15] he seems to have regarded them only with reference to Spain, and in connexion with Gades, from whence the trade with them had originally been carried on.

5. The fourth book is devoted to Gaul, Britain and the Alps. His ideas concerning the form and position of Gaul have already been explained, and we have seen how widely they departed from the truth. But erroneous as were his notions in a strictly geographical sense, he was, as in the case of Spain, well acquainted with the general character of the country, the nations that inhabited it, and the main geographical features that determined its conformation. Besides the Alps and Pyrenees he describes the Cemmenus (Cevennes) as a chain of mountains, branching off from the Pyrenees, at right angles, and extending to the centre of Gaul, where it gradually sank into the plain. He mentions also the Jura, under the name of Iourasios, and describes it as separating the Helvetii from the Sequani, who inhabited the region known in modern times as Franche Comté.[16] With the Rhone and its tributaries he was well acquainted, and describes very correctly the confluence of the Dubis (Doubs) with the Arar (Saône), and that of the latter river with the Rhone, but he erroneously supposed both the Arar and the Dubis—as well as the Sequana (Seine)—to take their rise in the Alps—showing how vague was his knowledge of the relations of the different mountain-chains in this part of Gaul.[17] He was familiar also, as already mentioned, with the great rivers that flowed into the Ocean—the Garonne, Loire, and Seine—all of which he conceived to flow, in a general way, from south to north, parallel with the Rhine and the Pyreness. And he was fully alive to the remarkable advantages derived by Gaul from the facilities of internal communication afforded by these rivers, which approached so near to each other that a very short passage over land was needed from the Saône to the Seine on the one hand,

and from the Rhone to the Loire on the other.[18] These facilities were in his time turned extensively to account: and a flourishing transit trade was carried on from the ports on the Ocean to those of Narbo and Massilia on the Mediterranean. Burdigala (Bordeaux) at the mouth of the Garonne was already an important emporium of trade. The names of the sea ports at the mouths of the other two great rivers, the Loire and the Seine, Strabo has unfortunately omitted to mention. Corbilo, which had formerly been the chief port on the Loire,[19] had in his time ceased to exist.

6. His description of the Roman Province, or Gallia Narbonensis, as it was now beginning to be called, is minute and accurate, and he clearly points out the difference of its climate, which distinguished it from other parts of Gaul, and more nearly approached to that of Italy.[20] With the rest of Gaul his acquaintance was comparatively superficial, but he had here an excellent authority before him in Cæsar, of whose Commentaries he made great use, and whom he generally follows in regard to the names and divisions of the Gaulish tribes. A more recent authority was indeed available in his time in the inscription on the altar at Lyons erected in honour of Augustus by the combined nations of Gaul, and which bore the names of sixty tribes or states (civitates).[21] But Strabo does not appear to have derived any assistance from the materials furnished by this document. Nor do we find him making any use, for the purposes of his geographical description, of the lines of road which the Romans had already constructed through the country: though he himself tells us that Agrippa had made four such lines of highway, all proceeding from Lugdunum (Lyons) as a centre. The first of these proceeded through the Cevennes to the Santones and Aquitania; the second led to the Rhine; the third to the shores of the Ocean, adjoining the territory of the Bellovaci and Ambiani; and the fourth to the Narbonitis and the neighbourhood of Massilia.[22] From thence another line branched off by Tarasco to Nemausus and Narbo, and thence to the passage of the Pyrenees. This last he describes minutely, as well as another branch proceeding from Tarasco through the land of the Vocontii to Ebrodunum (Embrun), and thence over the Mont Genèvre to Ocelum in Italy.[23] This was in his day one of the most frequented passes over the Alps. But his accurate details concerning these roads through the Roman province, which had existed long before, render the absence of them in regard to the great central lines the more striking.

There can be no doubt that his knowledge of the parts of Gaul adjoining the Ocean was very imperfect: the vagueness and generality of his notices of this part of the country contrasts strongly with the detailed accuracy of his description of the regions adjacent to the Mediterranean and the Pyrenees. The only exception is with regard to the Veneti, of whose naval power and the construction of their ships he gives a full account; but this is taken directly from Cæsar.[24] Of the other Armorican tribes he mentions only the Osismii, whom he identifies with the Ostimii of Pytheas, and states that they dwelt upon a promontory projecting a considerable distance into the sea, but not to the extent maintained by that writer, and those who followed him. It is evident that Strabo had here no correct information, and had no idea of the real extent and magnitude of the Armorican promontory. He apparently conceived the Veneti, who, as he learned from Cæsar, carried on an extensive trade with Britain, to be situated opposite to that island.[25]

7. With regard to the division of Gaul he begins by stating in accordance with Cæsar that it was divided into three nations, the Aquitanians, the Celts or Gauls properly so called, and the Belgæ. The Aquitanians were, as he justly observes, a wholly distinct people from the Celts, and more nearly resembled the Iberians. In this ethnographical sense they were bounded by the Garonne to the north: but in the reorganization of Gaul by Augustus, that emperor had extended the limits of Aquitania to the Loire, thus uniting fourteen tribes of Celtic origin with the Aquitanians properly so called. The rest of Gaul was divided into the provinces of Gallia Lugdunensis and Belgica: but Strabo differs from all other writers in extending the latter province along the shores of the Ocean from the mouths of the Rhine to those of the Loire, so as to include the Veneti and Osismii among the Belgic tribes.[26] This is probably an error, but Strabo himself remarks that the geographer does not require to take much pains with regard to the merely political and administrative divisions of countries where these do not coincide with natural boundaries.

His account of the manners and customs of the Gauls, as well as of their religous rites and ceremonies, is taken almost entirely from Cæsar, but with the addition of some circumstances of more dubious authenticity, which he derived from Posidonius, Artemidorus, and other Greek authorities. He adds however that the Gauls were rapidly becoming civilized, and imitating the Roman manners, as well as adopting their language. This change had already taken place to a great extent in the Roman province, or Narbonitis, where the native tribes had been stimulated by the example of the Massaliots, and begun even to devote their attention to literature and study: and it was from thence extending itself by degrees into the neighbouring parts of Gaul.[27]

8. Of Britain he had very little knowledge beyond what he derived from Cæsar. We have already seen that he erroneously conceived the south coast of Britain to extend opposite to that of Gaul, from the mouths of the Rhine to the Pyrenees, and that the interval was throughout much the same, so that the distance was not much greater from the mouths of the Garonne and the Loire than from those of the Seine and Rhine. But the nearest point, he correctly adds, was from the Portus Itius, in the land of the Morini, from whence Cæsar sailed on his expedition to the island: the distance at this point being only 320 stadia. It is strange however that he altogether rejects the statements of Cæsar with regard to the dimensions of the island, and regards the side opposite to Gaul—the length of which he estimates at the utmost at 5000 stadia—as the longest side

of Britain, instead of being, as Cæsar had described it, and as it really is, by much the shortest.[28] He consequently gave to the island a very inconsiderable extension towards the north, so as to bring its most northerly portions into the same latitude as the mouths of the Borysthenes, and only 8700 stadia, or 14½ degrees of latitude north of the Strait of the Columns.[29]

No attempt had been made since the time of Cæsar to subjugate Britain, but the native princes had entered into friendly relations with the Roman Emperors, and a considerable commerce was carried on with the island. Among the products exported from thence Strabo enumerates gold and silver as well as iron, but makes no mention of tin: besides these, he says, it furnished corn, cattle, hides and slaves, and dogs for the chase of a very fine breed. The climate was milder than that of Gaul, but very subject to mists, so that even in bright weather the sun was only visible for three or four hours in the day.[30]

Ierne or Ireland he conceived, as has been already mentioned, and as he himself repeatedly states, to be situated *to the north* of Britain. Its length was greater than its breadth, but he does not give an estimate of either: nor does he in this place say anything of its distance from Britain. But he elsewhere states that the interval was not known with any certainty.[31] He however regarded it as the most northern of all known lands, and as barely habitable on account of the cold.[32] Of its inhabitants little was known: they were said to be mere savages, addicted to cannibalism, and holding promiscuous intercourse with their women. But Strabo himself adds that he had no trustworthy authorities for these facts. The other islands around Britain he treats as unworthy of notice, and mentions Thule only to repeat his disbelief of the account of it that had been given by Pytheas.[33]

9. He next returns to speak of the Alps, his knowledge of which shows, as might be expected, a great advance upon that of Polybius. Indeed the recent subjugation of the Alpine tribes under Augustus, and the frequent communication held by the Romans with their Transalpine provinces, had necessarily led to a much more familiar acquaintance with these mountains. Hence Strabo is not only able to give us many interesting particulars concerning the different nations inhabiting the Alps and a correct description of their localities, but his account of the mountain chain itself shows a clear idea of its general form and configuration, and of the rivers that flowed from it. Thus he describes the Alps as forming a great curve having its concave side turned towards the plains of Italy, its centre in the land of the Salassians, and its two extremities bending round, the one by Mount Ocra, and the head of the Adriatic, the other along the sea coast of Liguria to Genoa, where they join the Apennines.[34] In another passage[35] he fixes the termination of the Maritime Alps with more precision at Vada Sabbata (*Vado*), 260 stadia from Genoa, which almost exactly coincides with the view generally adopted by modern geographers. The highest summits of the whole range he supposes to be those in the

land of the Medulli (between the Mont Genèvre and the Petit St. Bernard), where the direct ascent of the mountains was said to be not less than 100 stadia and the descent on the other side into Italy the same distance. Here among the hollows of the mountains was a lake, and two sources, from one of which flowed the Druentia (Durance) into Gaul to join the Rhone; from the other the Durias (Dora) to join the Po.[36] That river itself had its sources in the same neighbourhood, but at a lower level, and was swelled in its course by the junction of many tributaries.[37] In like manner he tells us correctly that the Rhone and the Rhine had their sources near to one another in the Mount Adula;[38]—the only distinctive appellation of any particular group which he mentions—and that they each formed a large lake in their course lower down.[39] He was also aware of the true source of the Danube, which he well describes as lying in a detached ridge of mountains, beyond the Rhine and its lake, adjoining the Suevi and the Hercynian Forest.[40]

With the eastern extremity of the Alps, where the chain sweeps round the head of the Adriatic he was also well acquainted, and gives a curious account of the commerce that was carried on in his day over the Mount Ocra— which he correctly describes as the lowest part of the Alps—from Aquileia to a place called Nauportus or Pamportus on the Save. It was by this route that Italian goods were conveyed into Pannonia and the other countries on the banks of the Danube.[41] The other mountaineers of the Alps also carried on some trade with Italy, bringing down resin, pitch, wax, honey, and cheese. In his time they were become tranquil subjects of Rome, and had laid aside the predatory habits which they had practised for centuries.

10. Augustus, who had completed the subjugation of the mountain tribes, had also, he tells us, bestowed great pains upon the construction of roads through their country: and had rendered these practicable for carriages, wherever the natural difficulties were not too great.[42] Still the number of high roads thus opened was but small. Of the two passes leading from the valley of the Salassi to Lugdunum, the one through the Centrones (the Little St. Bernard) which was the longer and more circuitous was available for carriages, the other across the Pennine Alps (the Great St. Bernard) was more direct, but narrow and steep, and not practicable for carriages. The road through the Graian Alps, and the petty kingdom of Cottius (the Mont Genèvre)[43] was apparently also open to carriages, and was one of the most frequented passes in the Roman times. No mention is found of any other pass between the Great St. Bernard and that through the Rhætians (the Brenner pass in the Tyrol) which from its comparative facility must have been frequented in all times. But Strabo, with a want of method often found in his work, while censuring Polybius for noticing only four passes across the Alps, has omitted to give us any regular enumeration of those known and frequented in his own day. He describes in strong terms the natural difficulties of these passes, the frightful chasms and giddy precipices along which the narrow roads had to be carried, as well as the avalanches of snow, which

were capable of carrying away whole companies of travellers at once. These he ascribes with remarkable precision to the sliding of great masses of snow, congealed by successive frosts, one over the other.[44]

11. The fifth and sixth books are devoted to the description of Italy and the adjoining islands, with which he was of course well acquainted, and for the topography of which he had abundant materials at his command. We have already seen how erroneous was his conception of the true position and configuration of the peninsula, as it would be represented on a map; but with its general features he was naturally familiar, and his outline of its physical geography is on the whole clear and satisfactory. The leading natural features of Italy are indeed so strongly marked by nature that it would be difficult not to seize them correctly. Such is in the first place the broad valley, or rather plain, of the Po, bounded by the great chain of the Alps on the north and by the inferior, but scarcely less marked, range of the Apennines to the south, and gradually passing into the lagunes and marshes of Venetia and the low country near Ravenna. The Apennines also are well described by Strabo as extending directly across the whole breadth of the land, from the frontiers of Liguria and Tyrrhenia on the one sea to the neighbourhood of Ariminum and Ancona on the other, and then turning inland so as to divide the peninsula into two through its whole length, but keeping nearer to the Adriatic till they turn off again in Lucania, and after passing through Lucania and Bruttium end in the promontory of Leucopetra not far from Rhegium.[45] He compares the peninsular portion of Italy—excluding the two projecting spurs or promontories of Iapygia and Bruttium—with that of the Adriatic Sea adjoining it:[46] rather a singular comparison and rendered more so by his adding that the length of each is not much less than 6000 stadia (600 G. miles), a great exaggeration, as the distance from Ariminum to the extremity of the Iapygian peninsula (thus *including* the latter, which Strabo *excludes*) is little more, as measured on the map, than 360 G. miles.[47]

This last statement is probably copied from some of his earlier Greek authorities: and indeed throughout this portion of his work we find him fluctuating between two sets of authorities—the earlier Greek writers, to whose statements he clings with a strange tenacity, even in regard to matters on which much better sources of information were open to him, and the more recent statements of Roman writers, based upon more accurate measurements and itineraries. Among the latter especially we find him repeatedly citing an anonymous author whom he calls "the chorographer," and of whom all that we know is that from his giving the distances in miles it may be fairly inferred that he was a Latin, not a Greek, author.[48] Whether this anonymous work was based mainly on the itineraries and consequently confined chiefly to distances, cannot be affirmed with certainty, nor do we know from what sources Strabo derived his knowledge of the topography of those parts of Italy which he had not himself visited, but it is certain that these topographical details are for the most part very correct, and the order in which the numerous towns mentioned are enumerated is generally systematic and well chosen. It is clear indeed, as has been already shown, that maps of Italy were well known, and probably not uncommon, in the time of Strabo, and the clear and methodical character of his description certainly gives the impression of having been written with such a representation before him. At the same time the more lively and graphic manner in which he describes particular localities—as for instance the Port of Luna, Volterra, Populonium, and the greater part of Campania—points clearly to being the result of personal observation. His account of Northern Italy on the other hand, in which he gives many interesting details concerning the marshes and lagunes of Venetia and the coast of the Adriatic from Altinum to Ravenna, and his description of the site of the latter city—a position almost exactly resembling that of Venice at the present day[49]—must probably have been derived at secondhand from some other writer. He follows the popular Roman notion that the Padus was the largest river in Europe except the Danube:[50] but rejects without hesitation its identification with the famous Eridanus, which he treats as a wholly fabulous stream.[51]

In describing Campania he takes occasion to give us some curious particulars concerning the volcanic eruptions of which it had been the scene, particularly of one of Mount Epomeus in the island of Pithecusa (Ischia), which had been described by the historian Timæus, having happened not long before his time.[52] On the other hand he has recorded his sagacious observation of Mount Vesuvius, that it had every appearance of having once been a burning mountain, but which had gone out for want of fuel.[53] It was little suspected by any one how soon it was destined to resume its activity.

The account of the south of Italy—Lucania, Bruttium, Iapygia, and Apulia, which occupies the greater part of the sixth book, is mainly derived from Greek authorities, and taken up to a great extent with historical particulars concerning the Greek colonies which bordered the whole of these shores. Many of these are of much interest and would be otherwise unknown to us, but not strictly of a geographical character. In describing the Apulian coast he treats of the distances along the Adriatic generally, and points out the discrepancy between "the chorographer" and his Greek authorities, Artemidorus especially; and takes the opportunity of commenting on the diversity frequently found in this respect among different authors.[54] When he has no means of determining between them, he adds, he contents himself with repeating the conflicting statements: but it does not seem to have occurred to him that the Roman authorities, having the advantage of measured roads, were in most cases, if not in all, entitled to the greater credit.[55] In describing Brundusium he notices briefly the course of the Appian Way—the great highway from Rome to the provinces of the East, which in his day consisted of two main branches, the one, practicable for carriages, leading from Brundusium to Tarentum, and thence direct through Venusia to Beneventum: the other, practicable for mules only, proceeding through Egnatia,

Canusium, and Herdonea, and rejoining the main line at Beneventum.[56] He gives the whole distance from Rome to Brundusium as 360 miles, which is almost precisely correct, the distance by the first of the two roads described being 358 miles according to the Antonine Itinerary.[57]

12. He describes Sicily at considerable length, and on this occasion gives us the distances furnished him by "the chorographer" in detail, showing the nature of the materials on which that author relied. Nor does his estimate of the dimensions of the island differ widely from the truth; though, as we have already seen, he had such a distorted idea of its position, and the bearings and directions of its three sides. But he had never himself visited the island and his description is neither very complete nor very accurate. He draws indeed a lamentable picture of the state of decay to which it was reduced in his time, notwithstanding its great natural fertility, so that many of the towns had altogether disappeared, while the interior was abandoned almost entirely to shepherds;[58] and on this account he dwells the less carefully upon topographical details.

Of the physical geography of the island he does not attempt to give any general view, but dwells at considerable length upon the peculiar characters of Ætna, and the volcanic phenomena to which it was subject. Of the streams of lava especially he gives an accurate and philosophical account, pointing out how the burning matter that overflows from the crater in a liquid state gradually hardens into a compact and hard rock, like a millstone.[59] He notices also the great fertility of the soil produced by the volcanic ashes for the growth of vines: a circumstance that he had already observed in regard to Vesuvius.[60] Much of this description appears to be taken from Posidonius: but Strabo adds an account of the appearance of the summit and the actual condition of the crater, as he had heard it from persons who had recently made the ascent.[61] It is evident therefore that in his time it was not uncommon for inquisitive travellers to make the ascent, which really offers no difficulties. He gives us also many interesting particulars concerning the volcanic phenomena of the Æolian Islands, especially of the remarkable eruption that had thrown up a small islet or rock out of the sea in the neighbourhood of the island called by the Greeks Hiera, as being above all others sacred to Vulcan, and the scene of his subterranean operations.[62] Both this island and that of Strongyle (Stromboli) seem to have been at this period in a state of constant volcanic activity.

13. Of the other two great islands of the Mediterranean, Sardinia and Corsica, Strabo has given but a very brief and imperfect account.[63] Both of them indeed were in ancient times, as they have continued almost to our own day, in a state of semi-barbarism little corresponding with their size and their natural resources; and though they had long been brought under the direct authority of Rome, the mountaineers of the interior continued in both islands to lead a lawless and barbarous life, plundering their neighbours in the plains, and only checked from time to time by the Roman governors, who would make a *razzia* for the

purpose of carrying off slaves, but never attempted to exercise any permanent authority over these wild districts.[64] Some parts of Sardinia, however, as Strabo observes, were fertile and produced abundance of corn, but they suffered much from unhealthiness, as well as from the depredations of their neighbours in the mountains. The only towns of any importance were Caralis and Sulci.[65]

It has already been pointed out that Strabo committed a strange error with regard to the geographical position of Sardinia and Corsica, as well as that of Sicily: and it is a striking instance of his disregard for real geographical accuracy, that he repeats the measurements given by the anonymous chorographer, both for the length and breadth of the two islands, and for the distance from Sardinia to Africa, without perceiving, or at least without noticing, how entirely they were at variance with his own system and arrangement.

14. Returning to the north of Europe, Strabo proceeds, in the seventh book, to give a brief general account of the countries extending from the Rhine eastwards to the Borysthenes and the Tanaïs, and situated to the north of the Danube, which he describes as cutting the whole of this eastern half of Europe into two divisions. No part of his work is more defective than this. Imperfect as was the knowledge actually possessed of these regions, he was far from turning to account all the information concerning them that was really available in his day. In regard to Germany, indeed, he did not fail to make use of the new discoveries that had been opened out by the campaigns of Drusus and Germanicus, which had extended, as he observes, the knowledge of Germany from the Rhine to the Elbe.[66] He mentions also the intermediate rivers; the Amisia (Ems), and the Visurgis (Weser), as well as the minor confluents the Lupia (Lippe) and the Salas (Saale). All these streams, as we have seen, had attracted attention in the Roman wars. He mentions also the principal names of German tribes and nations, with which the same wars had rendered his contemporaries familiar, though with very little attempt to explain their topographical relations, of which he had probably very imperfect knowledge. He describes at some length the Hercynian Forest, which according to his conception constituted one of the main physical features of the country, extending from the Lake of Constance and the sources of the Danube[67] to the northern frontier of Bohemia and Moravia, including within it (*i.e.* between it and the Danube) a tract of fertile country, occupied in part by the Quadi and Marcomanni, who had recently taken possession of the district previously known as Boiohemum (Bohemia).[68]

But beyond the Elbe he tells us that everything was entirely unknown; an ignorance which he ascribes in great part to the policy of Augustus in preventing his generals from carrying their arms beyond that river:[69] and while he rejects as fables the tales that were related by Greek writers of the Cimbri, who had long been known by a kind of vague tradition as dwelling on the northern Ocean,[70] he has nothing to substitute in their place. Even of their geographical

position he had no clear notion, and would have led us to imagine that they dwelt on the west side of the Elbe; he only notices the belief that they inhabited a peninsula in connection with the tradition (which he rejects as a fable) that they had been expelled from it by an irruption of the sea.[71] Of the great Cimbric Chersonese or Promontory, as a geographical feature, he had evidently no idea, or of the bay beyond it (the Codanus Sinus of Latin writers), though some vague accounts of both had certainly reached the Roman authorities in his day.[72] Nor does he condescend to notice the tradition adopted by some earlier authors of the existence of a great island in this part of the northern Ocean—the Basilia of Timæus and the Abalus of Pytheas. Even the name of the Vistula, which was certainly known to the Romans in his day, finds no place in his geography, and it is strange that he does not even allude to the trade with these regions for amber, which attracted so much attention both among Greeks and Romans.

The whole coast of the Ocean beyond the Elbe, he expressly tells us,[73] was utterly unknown, nor had any one made the journey by land, so that it was only by geographical inference from the comparison of parallels of latitude that one could arrive at the conclusion that proceeding eastward from the Elbe would bring one to the Borysthenes, and the regions north of the Euxine. But who were the nations inhabiting this extensive tract, whether Bastarnæ, Iazyges, Roxolani, or other Scythian tribes, no one could say: nor whether any of these tribes extended to the northern Ocean, or there was a space beyond, uninhabitable from cold or other causes. On one point alone he was correctly informed: for he tells us that the whole country eastward from the frontiers of Germany to the Caspian was one vast plain:[74] thus discarding altogether the vague notions as to the Rhipæan Mountains in the north, which had so long lingered among Greek geographers, and which still retained a hold on popular belief down to a later period.

15. It is remarkable that Strabo's acquaintance with the regions to the north and north-west of the Euxine was almost as imperfect as with those on the Baltic. Regarding Herodotus as altogether unworthy of confidence, he evidently neglected to avail himself of the interesting materials collected by that historian, and he had no means of supplying the deficiency. It would appear that the increasing pressure of the northern barbarians upon the Greek cities of the Euxine had limited their commercial relations with the interior: and though Strabo himself tells us that the campaigns of the generals of Mithridates had been the means of opening out a more accurate knowledge of these countries, it is certain that these did not carry their arms far from the coast, and the interior seems to have remained virtually unknown. Thus he tells us that the sources of the Tanaïs, like those of the Nile, were wholly unknown:[75] and the same was the case with those of the Borysthenes, Hypanis and Tyras.[76] The Borysthenes he describes as navigable for 600 stadia,[77] and he apparently regarded it as not known any higher up. The most northerly people known to our geographer in this part were the Rox-

olani, who in his time dwelt between the Tanaïs and the Borysthenes, and were known in history from their having taken part in war against Diophantus, the general of Mithridates.[78] They were regarded by Strabo as a Sarmatian tribe, as were also the Iazyges; while the Bastarnæ, a powerful nation who at this time occupied the tract between the Tyras (Dniester) and the Carpathians, so as to adjoin the Germans on the west, are described as pretty nearly of German race themselves.[79]

The Tyras had formed the limits of the conquests of Mithridates on the west, which was marked by the erection of a fort at the mouth of that river bearing the name of his general Neoptolemus.[80] The Romans in the days of Strabo had not attempted to extend their power beyond the mouths of the Danube. The interval between the two was occupied by an unpeopled tract, called by Strabo "the desert of the Getæ," and which he describes as the scene of the expedition of Darius, of which Herodotus has left us so exaggerated an account. But it is difficult to adopt Strabo's suggestion literally, and suppose that the Persian king never even reached the Dniester, a distance of less than a hundred miles from the Danube.[81]

The accurate and detailed account which Strabo gives us of the Tauric Chersonese forms a striking contrast with the vague and unsatisfactory knowledge he possessed of the countries to the north. Here he was in a land which had long been occupied by Greek colonies, to whom it had thus become known in detail. It had more recently passed under the dominion of Mithridates, and it was probably from the historians of that monarch that Strabo derived his particulars. His statement that the peninsula as a whole resembled the Peloponnesus both in form and size is more correct than such general comparisons usually are:[82] he was aware that it was really joined to the mainland only by a narrow isthmus, and has given a correct and curious account of the peculiar character of the Putrid Sea which separates it from the Palus Mæotis.[83]

16. Of the Getæ or Dacians, who at this time occupied the extensive tract north of the Danube, Strabo had very little real knowledge, and the greatest part of the section devoted to this people is in fact occupied with a very unsatisfactory discussion as to the ethnographical relations of the people called by Homer Mysians, and the "illustrious mare-milking" tribes of the same poet. As already mentioned, he describes the Getæ and Dacians as two distinct nations, or at least distinct branches of the same nation, for he adds that they speak the same language, which was the case also with the Getæ and the Thracians.[84] He appears not to have noticed or comprehended the fact that the one name was originally applied to them by the Romans, the other by the Greeks. Yet he recognized a similar fact with regard to the Danube, which as he points out was called by the Romans Danubius *down to the cataracts,* while below that point they adopted the Greek appellation of Ister.[85]

With regard to the regions south of the Danube, Illyricum, Pannonia and Mæsia, which as we have already seen had

been lately brought under the dominion of Rome, Strabo had not much that was new to relate, though by availing himself of the results of the Roman wars and conquests in these parts, he was doubtless enabled to bring together a more complete and consistent view of these nations, than had been presented by any previous Greek writer. But their ethnological relations were then, as they have always continued to be, extremely obscure, and his notices with regard to them, though not without value, show but an imperfect insight into the subject, while he has unfortunately neglected in almost all cases to cite the authorities from whom he has derived them. In respect to the geography of this part of Europe he has correctly seized the main fact of the chain of Mount Hæmus (the Balkan) branching off from the great Illyrian ranges which descend in a continous mass from the Alps along the east coast of the Adriatic, and extending in a line parallel with the Danube (from west to east) to the shore of the Euxine.[86] He has indeed an exaggerated notion of its importance, both in height and extent, but this was the case even with modern geographers down to a very recent period; and he justly rejects the statement of Polybius that from the summit both the Euxine and the Adriatic Seas were visible at the same time.[87]

17. His account of Macedonia and Thrace is preserved only in a fragmentary form, this part of his work being wanting in all the extant manuscripts, but the deficiency is in great part supplied by the two Epitomes, and it is not probable that we have lost much that is really valuable. In regard to both countries, his minute and accurate account of the portions adjoining the coasts of the Ægean contrasts strongly with his vague and general information concerning the mountain ditricts of the interior, and the wild tribes that inhabited them. The latter were still very imperfectly subdued, and their relations with the Romans were chiefly those of mutual hostility.[88] This portion of the Turkish Empire was even down to the present day one of the least known parts of Europe, and the same thing appears to have been the case in the time of Strabo. The geographer had however here the great advantage of the Roman military highway, the Via Egnatia, which traversed the whole country from west to east: the importance of which, with its measured distances, had been already recognized and pointed out by Polybius; from whom indeed Strabo's account of it is almost entirely derived.[89]

18. Three books are devoted by Strabo to the geography of Greece and the neighbouring islands. Here of course nothing new was to be expected, while materials for the topographical description of the country could not fail to be forth-coming in profusion. Yet there is hardly any part of his work which in a geographical point of view is more unsatisfactory. That tendency to digression upon mythological and poetical topics, which, as we have already pointed out, is one of the leading defects of Strabo's whole work, is here developed to the greatest extent, and has had the effect of converting all these three books into a desultory and rambling commentary upon the Homeric Catalogue of the Ships, together with some other passages of

the ancient poets, rather than a systematic geographical treatise. Nor is this commentary illustrated with local details and topographical identifications, which would have had some real interest, and conveyed much information to the modern student. He had himself visited only a few points of Greece,[90] and was therefore compelled to collect his information at second hand: and unfortunately he sought this more in the works of the logographers and grammarians, than in those of the topographers and local historians. It is but justice to him to remark on the contrast which his account of Corinth—which he *had* seen—presents with the rest of this portion of his work.[91] Here his description—though not very full or detailed—is clear, intelligent and characteristic. Of Sparta and Argos on the contrary he gives us no description at all—or nothing worthy of the name—contenting himself with remarking that they were too well known to require it: and the reader would gather from his pages no idea of the striking character and natural features of the plain of Argos, or the valley of the Eurotas. Nor does he anywhere give us a clear outline of the grouping and connexion of the mountain chains, which in so remarkable a manner constitute as it were the skeleton of the Peloponnese, and determine the physical geography of the country.

One circumstance that appears to have contributed to prevent him from dwelling more fully upon the actual geography of Greece in his own time was the state of decay to which it was then reduced: a circumstance to which he recurs again and again. Even the fertile district of Messenia was in great part desolate and abandoned: Laconia retained a few towns which were tolerably flourishing, though its population had much declined: but the upland plains of Arcadia were almost wholly depopulated, the towns had ceased to exist or were lying in ruins, and even the agricultural labourers had quitted the country, leaving the fertile arable lands to support nothing but herds of cattle, horses, and asses.[92] The case was little better, if at all, with Northern Greece. Bæotia especially had never recovered from the ravages of the Mithridatic War: Thebes was reduced to a mere village,[93] and Tanagra and Thespiæ alone could still claim the appellation of towns.[94] In other passages he points out the state of depopulation and decay of Acarnania, Ætolia, Locris and the adjoining territory of the Ænianes.[95] The new colonies founded by Augustus—Nicopolis, Patræ, and Corinth—were indeed flourishing settlements, but their prosperity was to a great degree at the cost of the neighbouring districts. Such a state of things might be some excuse for not entering minutely into topographical details, but it is none for going back to the heroic ages, and wasting time in idle discussions on the obscure towns mentioned only by Homer, whose names and sites were alike unknown in the flourishing ages of Greece, as well as in the days of Strabo.[96]

This unfortunate mode of treating his subject appears to have arisen in great measure from his following the example of the writers who had composed professed commentaries upon the Homeric Catalogues, Apollodorus and Demetrius of Scepsis, rather than the authors of strictly geographical or topographical works, which were certainly not wanting in his day.[97] But his blind reverence for the great poet, whom he regarded as the first and best of authorities,[98] was the original source of this defective method. Besides the two writers already cited, his principal, and by far his most valuable, authority was Ephorus, from whom he derived the greater part of his information in regard to the historical facts which he relates concerning the foundation of cities, the changes of population, &c.; much of which is really valuable and interesting. But though Ephorus, like Polybius, had devoted a portion of his work to a separate and regular geographical treatise, it is remarkable that he is hardly ever cited by Strabo for any statement of a distinctly geographical character.

19. In this respect indeed, strange as it may appear to us, the knowledge of Greece possessed by Strabo was scarcely less defective than that of the more western portions of Europe. Familiar as was the general notion of the Peloponnese, as resembling a leaf of the plane-tree, as well as the leading promontories and bays that determined its configuration, it will be found that its *orientation* (if the word may be allowed) was wholly erroneous: and when Strabo tells us that its length and breadth were about equal (1400 stadia in each direction), he adds that its greatest length was from Cape Malea to Ægium, and its greatest breadth from west to east from Cape Chalonatas in Elis to the Isthmus.[99] He must therefore have regarded the Isthmus as nearly, if not quite, the most eastern point of the Peloponnese, ignoring the extent to which the coast of Argolis runs out in an easterly direction to Cape Seyllæum, or rather supposing the great promontory thus formed to have a southerly instead of a south-easterly direction. The effect of this is to give to the whole map of the Peloponnese a *slew* round which greatly distorts its general appearance. At the same time this brings Cape Malea much to the west of its true position, and explains why Strabo, in measuring the length of the peninsula from north to south, drew his line from Cape Malea to the Corinthian Gulf, instead of from Cape Tænarum.

Still more erroneous was his conception of the configuration and position of Northern Greece. We have already seen that he considered Cape Sunium, the extremity of Attica, as *but little* farther north than Cape Malea,[100] so that a line drawn from thence to the Isthmus of Corinth would present but a slight curve, while a straight line (or nearly so) might be drawn from the Isthmus through the Gulf of Corinth to the straits at its entrance, and thence to the Acroceraunian Promontory.[101] This conclusion he derived from Eudoxus of Cnidus, a man (as he justly observes) of mathematical knowledge, and acquainted with the observations of latitude, as well as familiar with the countries in question; and whose authority he consequently accepts as unexceptionable.[102] That such a man should have arrived at conclusions so wide of the truth in regard to countries so well known, is indeed a striking proof how little geography could yet be regarded as based upon any sound and satisfactory foundation. Yet we shall find—as in so many similar cases—the influence of this error once introduced into systematic geography continuing to pervade the works of successive writers, and even materially affecting the Ptolemaic map of Greece.

Again, while he points out correctly the manner in which continental Greece is cut into by a succession of deep bays and inlets, so as to constitute in a manner a series of successive peninsulas, his notions of the distances between these bays and their relative position to one another, are often strangely erroneous, and it is not always easy to reconcile his statements with one another.[103]

20. Concerning the physical geography of Greece he gives us very little information. He notices indeed, as he could hardly fail to do, the remarkable formation of parts of Arcadia and Bæotia, and the manner in which the streams found subterranean channels, and the lakes were discharged by similar outlets, the stoppage of which from time to time gave occasion to great inundations or to the extension of the lake-waters far beyond their ordinary limits. In regard to the Lake Copaïs in particular he gives us some curious details, based apparently on good authority. He adopts also the popular notion that the river Erasinus in Argolis derived its sources from the Lake of Stymphalus,[104] and that the Alpheius and Eurotas had their origin from two fountains close together, the waters of which pursued their course for some distance underground, and then issued forth again, the one in Laconia, the other in the Pisatis.[105] Neither of these facts has been verified by modern observers, but the last is certainly not without a foundation of truth; and that the rivers of Greece frequently pursue a subterranean course for considerable distances is undoubtedly true: the same phenomenon occurs in other countries composed of similar cavernous limestones, such as Carniola and Dalmatia.

The mountains of Greece were of course familiar by name to all men of letters in the days of Strabo, whether geographers or not. But no attempt is found in his description of the country to arrange them in groups or point out the geographical relations of the different ranges. He states, in accordance with the generally received notion in his day, that Cyllene was the highest mountain in the Peloponnese, but adds that "some said" it was 20 stadia (12,000 feet) in perpendicular height, and others only fifteen.[106] This is the only instance in which he attempts to give the height of any of the mountains mentioned: he does not even allude to the different estimates or alleged measurements that had been made of Mount Olympus and its neighbours Ossa and Pelion.

21. Of the islands in the Ægean his account is very meagre, and their geographical positions are but obscurely indicated. They were for the most part in a state of great poverty and decay:[107] even Delos having never recovered from the blow it sustained in the Mithridatic War. His description of Crete is fuller and more interesting than usual; and he correctly points out in this instance the distinct character of the White Mountains, the most

westerly group in the island, forming a ridge 300 stadia in length, and not inferior to Taygetus in height, and the isolated mass of Mount Ida, of still greater elevation, and having a circumference of not less than 600 stadia.[108] Yet we have already seen how imperfect was his notion of the position or dimensions of the island, and how erroneous and conflicting are his statements concerning its distance from the nearest points of the mainland.

The chorographer reckoned Corsica as 160 Roman miles in length and 70 in breadth: and Sardinia as 220 miles long by 98 broad. (Strab. p. 224.) The measurements of modern geographers give to the former island 116 English miles (124 Roman) by 51 in its greatest breadth: while Sardinia measures about 140 G. miles by 60, or 175 Roman miles by 75. The distances given by the chorographer are therefore largely in excess: but this is still more the case with his statement that the shortest interval from the African coast to Sardinia amounted to 300 miles, an estimate more than double the truth, as the southernmost point of Sardinia, Cape Spartivento, is really little more than 100 G. miles or 125 Roman miles from Cape Serrat in Africa. So enormous an error, in regard to a distance that might be supposed so well known, is very difficult to account for. Some of the editors of Strabo have proposed to read 200 for 300, which would accord with the estimate of Pliny (*H. N.* iii. 13, § 84), but in any case the distance is greatly over-stated: and it is hazardous to make such arbitrary changes without authority. It may be added that the distances cited by Strabo from the chorographer do not in general agree with those of Pliny.

Notes

1. iii. 4, p. 165.

2. The distinction between the two provinces had been established from an early period, and still subsisted in the time of Strabo (iii. 4, p. 166), though, as he observes, the political limits of the divisions fluctuated from time to time.

3. Strabo, iii. 2, p. 151.

4. See the well-known passage of Herodotus (i. 163), and those quoted from other writers by Strabo (iii. 2, § 13, pp. 150, 151). In Strabo's time the name had become quite obsolete, and he himself points out its fluctuating and uncertain use by earlier writers, some of whom applied it to the whole country, some to a town, some to a river. The last was unquestionably the same with the Bætis or Guadalquivir.

5. So highly was the wool of this part of Spain valued, that, as he assures us, rams for breeding purposes had been known to fetch as much as a talent each.

6. iii. 2, § 6, p. 145.

7. Strabo, iii. 2, §§ 8-10, p. 146. It is amusing to find him noticing among other advantages of Turdetania, its freedom from all destructive wild beasts, *except rabbits* (!), which abounded so much in all parts of Spain as to do great damage to the crops. They were

killed by means of ferrets, the use of which he describes exactly as it is practised at the present day (Ib. § 6). He relates on this occasion the well-known story of the inhabitants of the Gymnesian Islands (Iviza and Formentera), having sent a deputation to the Roman government to represent that they were absolutely driven out of their homes by the multitude of these animals. What happened in the island of Porto Santo after its discovery by the Portuguese shows that this may have been no exaggeration.

8. Ibid. 4, p. 166.

9. iii. 3, p. 152. The campaigns of D. Brutus against the Lusitanians and Callaïci or Gallæcians, by which he earned the surname of Callaïcus, took place in B.C. 138-135, a few years only before Polybius was in Spain with his friend Scipio during the Numantine War.

10. iii. 4, § 9, p. 160.

11. Strabo, iii. 4, § 13, p. 163.

12. It seems strange to us at first to find the broad corn-growing plains of Old and New Castile included in this character, as wild and barren regions, supporting but a scanty population. But their inclement climate was alone sufficient to produce this impression to a Greek or Italian, and even at the present day a recent writer speaks of "the trackless, lonely, wind-blown plains" of Castile as much exposed to drought, notwithstanding the fertility of the soil, and thinly-peopled in consequence.

13. iii. 5, § 11, p. 175.

14. Ibid. p. 176. It can scarcely be doubted that this Publius Crassus is the same as the lieutenant of Cæsar, who subdued the Armorican tribes in Gaul, and visited the shores of the Western Ocean (Cæsar, *B. G.* ii. 34); but it is strange that if Strabo had access to the information which he collected, he should still connect the Cassiterides with Spain, instead of Gaul or Britain.

15. It may be remembered that no mention of the Cassiterides is found in Cæsar. In another passage indeed (ii. 5, p. 120), Strabo speaks of them as lying in the open sea north of the Artabri, "in about the same latitude as Britain:" the south-western angle of which he regarded as facing the Pyrenees! But this very phrase evidently excludes the supposition that they were in its immediate vicinity.

16. iv. 3, § 4, p. 193.

17. iv. 3, § 2, p. 192.

18. iv. 1, § 14, p. 189.

19. Polyb. ap. Strab. iv. 2, § 1, p. 190. See Chapter XVII. p. 19.

20. iv. p. 178. The whole of the Narbonitis (he says) produces the same fruits as Italy. But as you advance to the north, and to Mount Cemmenus, the country ceases to produce olives and figs, though other things still grow. As you advance farther, the vine also does not readily ripen its fruit. But the whole country bears corn, millet, acorns, and all kinds of cattle.

21. Strabo, iv. 3, § 2, p. 192. This altar is again referred to by Dion Cassius (liv. 32), by Suetonius (*Claud.* 2), and by Juvenal (*Sat.* i. v. 44). Unfortunately no record has been preserved to us of the inscribed names.

22. iv. 6, § 11, p. 208.

23. iv. 1, § 3, pp. 178, 179.

24. iv. 4, § 1, p. 194. Compare Cæsar, *B. G.* v. 13.

25. Strabo, iv. 4, § 1. He may in part have been misled by Cæsar's expression, where, after enumerating the maritime nations that sent auxiliary forces to the Veneti, including the Osismii and Lexovii, as well as the Morini and Menapii, he adds, "auxilia ex Britannia, *quæ contra eas regiones posita est,* arcessunt" (*B. G.* iii. 9). There is nothing in Cæsar to show whether he was acquainted with the configuration of the coasts of Brittany and Normandy; he twice mentions the name of the Osimii among the Armorican tribes, but with no further indication of their position (*B. G.* ii. 34; vii. 75).

26. Strabo, *l. c.*

27. iv. 1, § 12, p. 186.

28. Strabo, i. 4, § 3, p. 63; iv. 5, § 1, p. 199. See Chapter XIX. p. 127.

29. Id. ii. 5, § 78, pp. 114, 115.

30. Id. iv. 5, § 2, 3. In another passage (ii. 5, p. 115) he tells us that the Romans purposely refrained from conquering the island, in order to avoid the expense of maintaining it.

31. ii. 5, § 8, p. 115. . . . Again, in another passage (ii. p. 72), he tells us that Ierne was not more than 5000 stadia distant *from Gaul:* a statement that he must have found some difficulty in reconciling with his own system.

32. See the passages cited in note to p. 232.

33. Strabo, iv. 5, § 5, p. 201. Of the Cassiterides he had already spoken, in connection with Spain, and evidently did not regard them as belonging to the group of the Britannic Islands (see above, p. 245).

34. v. 1, § 3, p. 211.

35. iv. 6, § 1, p. 202.

36. iv. 6, § 5, pp. 203, 204.

37. Ibid. p. 204.

38. Ibid. § 6, p. 204. He adds that the Aduas (Adda), which formed the Lake Larius, had its sources in the same mountain group.

39. Of these he was well acquainted with the name of the Lake Lemanus, through which the Rhone flowed; but apparently knew no name for the lake formed by the Rhine, though it had recently attracted attention during the campaign of Tiberius against the Vindelici, who had actually established a naval station on the only island it contains (Strabo, vii. 1, § 5, p. 292).

40. iv. 6, § 9; vii. 1, § 5.

41. iv. 6, § 10, p. 208.

42. iv. 6, § 6, p. 204.

43. This route is described in detail, iv. 1, § 3, p. 179.

44. iv. 6, § 6, p. 204.

45. v. 1, § 3, p. 211.

46. Ibid.

47. Strabo had apparently, in common with the earlier geographers, an exaggerated notion of the length of the Adriatic, and adapted his ideas of Italy to it. The Antonine Itinerary gives the distance (by road) from Ariminum to Brundisium at 524 Roman miles, or 420 G. miles.

48. On this subject see the note to p. 177, Chapter XX.

49. v. 1, § 7, p. 213. It is remarkable also that he notices the *tides* in this part of the Adriatic, which is, as he observes, the only part of "our sea," which is affected in this respect like the Ocean. Ibid. § 5, p. 212.

50. iv. 6, § 5, p. 204.

51. v. 1, § 9, p. 215.

52. v. 4, § 9, p. 248.

53. v. 4, § 8, p. 247.

54. vi. 3, § 10, p. 285.

55. In this instance the chorographer gave the distance from Brundusium to the Garganus at 165 (Roman) miles, and from thence to Ancona at 254 miles. The first distance is almost precisely correct, according to the Itineraries, which give 167 miles from Brundusium to Sipontum (Manfredonia); but the second falls considerably short of that given in the Itineraries, which amounts to 281 miles. It is probable, however, that in this instance the latter exceed the truth.

56. vi. 3, § 7. It would seem that in his time the name of the Appian Way was confined to the portion from Beneventum to Rome, after the junction of the two branches.

57. Itin. Ant. pp. 107-111, 120.

58. vi. 2, § 6, p. 272.

59. vi. 2, § 3, p. 269.

60. v. 4, § 8, p. 247.

61. . . . vi. 2, § 8, p. 274.

62. vi. 2, § 11, p. 277. This outbreak, which was related by Posidonius as occurring within his own memory, was almost certainly the same event as that mentioned by Pliny, and referred by him to the 3rd year of the 163rd Olympiad (B.C. 126). It is noticed also by Orosius and Julius Obsequens; but Orosius describes a similar phenomenon, the emergence from the sea of an island not previously existing, as taking place 60 years earlier (B.C. 186). It is probable that the small island, now called Vulcanello, is due to one or other of these eruptions.

63. v. 2, § 7, pp. 224, 225.

64. v. 2, § 7, p. 225.

65. Ibid.

66. vii. 1, § 4, p. 291.

67. vii. 1, § 5.

68. Ibid. § 3. . . .

69. Ibid. § 4. p. 291.

70. The Cimbri were certainly known to Posidonius (ap. Strab. vii. 2, p. 293) and apparently at an earlier period, as that author found fault with the fables related concerning them. The irruption of the Cimbri and Teutones into Gaul and Italy (about 100 B.C.), must have made the Romans familiar with the *name*, and would naturally excite curiosity as to their original abodes.

71. Strabo, vii. 2, § 1, p. 292.

72. See Chapter XX. p. 191.

73. Id. vii. 2, § 4, p. 294.

74. . . . vii. 3, § 17, p. 306.

75. xi. 2, § 2, p. 493. He, however, justly maintains that the Tanaïs falls into the Palus Mæotis from the north; and rejects the wild hypotheses which derived it either from the east and the Caucasus, or from the far west, near the sources of the Danube (!)

76. ii. 4, § 6, p. 107.

77. vii. 3, § 16, p. 306.

78. vii. 3, § 17, p. 306.

79. Ibid.

80. vii. 3, § 16. See Chapter XVIII. p. 84.

81. vii. 3, § 14, p. 305. The same tract was, according to Strabo, also the scene of the expedition of Lysimachus, in which that monarch was defeated and taken prisoner by Dromichætes, king of the Getæ, but this may more probably be placed farther west, between the Danube and the Carpathians.

82. . . . vii. 4, § 5, p. 310.

83. Ibid. § 1, p. 308. The precise agreement of Strabo's account of this curious natural feature of the country with its present condition is a striking proof that no considerable physical changes have taken place in this part of the Euxine since the time of the

geographer; as a depression or elevation of a few feet would suffice entirely to change the character of the Putrid Sea.

84. . . . vii. 3, § 13, p. 305.

85. Strabo, vii. 3, § 13, p. 304. This is the first mention in any ancient author of the cataracts or rapids, popularly known as the Iron Gates, which constitute so serious an impediment to the navigation of the Danube.

86. vii. 5, § 1, p. 313.

87. This had indeed been an article of the popular creed long before the time of Polybius. It was already asserted by Theopompus, and the expedition of Philip V., king of Macedonia, to the summit, was evidently originated in consequence of this belief. The detailed account of that expedition, given by Livy (xl. 21, 22), is doubtless derived from Polybius, but the Roman historian shares in the doubts so reasonably expressed by Strabo. Pomponius Mela at a later period repeats the ordinary story (ii. 2).

It is impossible to determine what was the particular summit actually ascended by Philip; we are told only that he marched thither from Stobi through the country of the Mædi. Leake supposes him to have selected one of the lofty group near the head waters of the Strymon, between Sofia and Kiüstendil, but the orography of this part of Turkey is still too imperfectly known to enable us to form even a plausible conjecture.

It is strange that Strabo, who shows on this occasion a very reasonable scepticism, should accept without hesitation the popular story that the rising sun was visible from the summit of Mount Athos *three hours* before it made its appearance to those at the foot of the mountain! (vii. Fr. 33, 35).

88. The account given by Tacitus (*Annal.* iv. 46-51) of the outbreak of the Thracian tribes in A.D. 26, some years after the death of Strabo, shows how far these wild mountaineers were from being effectually reduced to subjection.

89. Strabo, vii. 7, § 4, pp. 322, 323. See Chapter XVII. p. 27.

90. Athens, Megara, and Corinth, are the only points in continental Greece, which he can be proved to have actually visited. Groskurd adds Argos, but I can see no evidence of this.

91. viii. 6, § 21, p. 379.

92. vii. 8, § 1.

93. ix. 2, § 5, p. 403.

94. Ibid. § 25, p. 410.

95. ix. 4, § 11; x. 2, § 23.

96. At the same time he took so little interest in tracing the remains of these extinct cities, that he does not even notice the gigantic ruins of Tiryns and Mycenæ, but adds with regard to the last that not a trace of it was visible! (viii. 6, § 10, p. 372.)

97. The fragment of a *Description of Greece,* commonly ascribed to Dicæarchus, whether or not it be justly attributed to that author, shows that such topographical works were in existence long before the time of Strabo, and we can hardly doubt that there were many such. (See Chapter XVI. p. 617.)

98. See especially viii. pp. 337, 349.

99. viii. 2, § 1, p. 335.

100. ii. 1, § 40, p. 92.

101. ix. 1, § 1, p. 390.

102. Ibid. § 2, p. 391.

103. See viii. 1, § 3. His description of Greece as constituting four successive peninsulas is in great measure fanciful, though his conception of the largest of these, as bounded by a line drawn from the Ambracian Gulf on the west, to the Maliac Gulf on the east, corresponds to a natural division, which has been taken as the basis in the limitation of the modern kingdom of Greece. His estimate of the width of this so-called isthmus between the two gulfs at 800 stadia (80 G. miles) is not greatly in excess of the truth; the direct distance in a straight line being just about 70 G. miles.

104. viii. 8, § 4, p. 389.

105. viii. 3, § 12, p. 343.

106. viii. 8, § 1 . . . the lofty mountain group in the north-east of that region was generally regarded as the highest in the Peloponnese; no one apparently suspecting that it was exceeded in elevation by Taygetus. The real height of Cyllene, according to the French commission, is 7788 feet.

It is singular that Strabo does not refer to the more moderate estimate of Apollodorus, an author of whom he made such frequent use. (See Chapter XVI. p. 618.)

107. The only one of which Strabo distinctly speaks from personal observation is the rocky islet of Gyaros, where he found only a fishing village, whose inhabitants were so poor that they deputed one of their number to represent to the emperor Augustus their inability to pay a tribute of 150 drachms! (Strabo, x. p. 485.) But Gyaros is one of the smallest and poorest of the islands, and when visited by Dr. Ross in 1841 had no permanent inhabitants (Ross, *Reise auf den Griechischen Inseln,* vol. ii. p. 171). Yet it was frequently used under the Roman Empire as a place of banishment or confinement for criminals. (See Juvenal, i. 73; Tacit. *Ann.* iii. 68, &c.)

108. x. 4, § 4. According to the recent measurements of Captain Spratt, the highest summit of the White Mountains and Mount Ida are very nearly of the

same height, both of them exceeding 8000 feet, and thus somewhat higher than Taygetus, which is in reality the highest mountain in the Peloponnese, but does not exceed 7900 feet.

H. F. Tozer (essay date 1893)

SOURCE: An introduction to *Selections from Strabo*, Clarendon Press, 1893, 1-53.

[*In the following essay, Tozer provides an overview of Strabo, his life and death, teachers and influences, political views, travels, and the* Geography—*discussing its intended audience, style, and critical reception.*]

ON STRABO'S LIFE AND WORKS.

As the events of Strabo's life are almost entirely unnoticed by other writers, we are obliged, in endeavouring to trace them, to have recourse to statements incidentally introduced into his *Geography.* He was born at Amasia in Pontus, of which place . . . he has left us a succinct but graphic description in his Twelfth Book (Extract No. 58). That city—the remarkable position of which, and its rock-hewn sepulchres, 'the tombs of the kings,' as they were called, excite the admiration of the modern traveller—was at one time the residence of the sovereigns of Pontus, and became a considerable centre of Greek culture. Of his father and his father's ancestry the Geographer tells us nothing, but his mother's family produced several persons of distinction, whose names occur in the course of his work. The earliest in date of these that he mentions, Dorylaus Tacticus, lived in the latter half of the second century B.C., and was intimate with Mithridates Euergetes. At the time of that monarch's death, in 120, he happened to be absent at Cnossus in Crete, whither he had been sent to enlist mercenaries; and having risen to a high position in that place, owing to the services which he had rendered as general to the Cnossians in a war with Gortyna, he settled there with his family. At the commencement of the first century B.C. his son Lagetas, Strabo's great-grandfather, returned to Pontus at the invitation of Mithridates the Great, who subsequently patronized both him and his children, until after a time they fell into disgrace in consequence of a plot to betray the kingdom to the Romans, which was set on foot by a member of another branch of the family[1]. We also hear of a great-uncle of Strabo, called Moaphernes, being made governor of Colchis by Mithridates the Great[2]. The name of this person betrays an Asiatic origin, as also does that of another relation, Tibius, who is mentioned in the same passage; for Strabo tells us elsewhere[3] that Tibius was a familiar Paphlagonian name. From these facts we learn that the Geographer was of mixed lineage, but by language and education he was thoroughly Greek. His family also held a good position in society, and he must have inherited considerable wealth, for his studies and his residence in foreign countries imply that he had ample means at his command, and he nowhere makes mention of any occupation by which he could have obtained a livelihood.

Among the many perplexing questions connected with the biography of Strabo, perhaps the one which has been most elaborately discussed is that of the date of his birth. Various arguments—deduced from such points as the period to be assigned to his successive ancestors, the duration of his own life, and the persons whom he mentions that he had seen—though more or less uncertain, seem to point to a time not earlier than 68 or later than 54 B.C.; but, by carefully estimating certain expressions which Strabo employs, it seems possible to arrive at a more definite conclusion than this. . . . The time-marks thus obtained are corroborated by other passages, and thus we are led to the conclusion that Strabo was probably born in 63 B.C., the year of Cicero's consulate. It may be well to remember, as an answer to any objections to a calculation of this sort that may arise in our minds on the ground of its being too subtle, that all these events took place in Asia Minor, and must therefore have been familiar to Strabo, since he was brought up in that country. Indeed, the soundness of this mode of argument seems to be generally recognized, though some objections have been raised against the application of it in these particular instances.

Of the date of Strabo's death we know thus much for certain, that it could not have taken place earlier than 21 A.D., for he mentions the death of Juba, king of Mauretania[4], which took place in that year, or, as some writers maintain on the authority of coins, two years later. It is further argued, with the view of fixing an ulterior limit, that, as he states that Cyzicus at the time when he wrote was still a free city . . . [5], whereas we know from Tacitus[6] that that place lost its independence in 25 A.D., he could not, even if he was alive, have been engaged on his Geography as late as that period. This, however, may be equally well explained by supposing that in revising his work Strabo did not in all points bring it up to date—a fact which is sufficiently evident from other passages. Thus he speaks of Arminius, who died in 19 A.D., as continuing the war . . . [7] ; and in the Sixth Book he not only regards Germanicus, who also died in that year, as still alive, but Juba as well[8]. No doubt, the supposition that the Geographer did not live long after 21 A.D. is probable enough because of his advanced age, for if he was born in 63 B.C. he would then have reached his eighty-fourth year; and it may be remarked in passing, that this is an argument against placing his birth much further back than the date we have assigned to it.

Strabo mentions three prominent teachers of that period as having taken part in his education. The first of these in order of date was Aristodemus, the same who gave instruction to Pompey's sons at Rome; his lectures in grammar and rhetoric, Strabo tells us, he had attended when quite a youth, at Nysa on the Maeander[9]. The next was Tyrannion the grammarian, who superintended the education of Cicero's two sons, Marcus and Quintus. As Strabo mentions having been his pupil in his account of Amisus in

Pontus, of which city Tyrannion was a native[10], it has been thought by some that he received instruction from him at that place, which was within easy reach of Amasia, before going to Nysa: this, however, is impossible, for we are expressly told by Suidas . . . that Tyrannion was carried as a captive to Rome by Lucullus after his campaign against Mithridates. This took place in the year 70 B.C., and consequently it must have been in Rome that Strabo was his pupil. It is not an unreasonable supposition that Strabo imbibed a taste for geography from Tyrannion, for we learn from Cicero that he was an authority on that subject[11]. It was at Rome also that he attended the lectures of his third teacher, the Peripatetic philosopher Xenarchus, of whom Strabo says that he devoted himself to education in that city[12]. Perhaps it was at this time that he was a fellow-student with Boëthus, the Stoic philosopher, for he remarks in connexion with Sidon, the birth-place of Boëthus, that they had studied the system of Aristotle together[13]. To these three instructors some authorities would add a fourth, Posidonius. The only support for this statement is found in a passage of Athenaeus[14], where that writer quotes Strabo as saying in the Seventh Book of his *Geography*—apparently in the part of that book which is now lost—that he was acquainted with that philosopher. As Posidonius lived till 45 B.C., it is possible, no doubt, that Strabo may have met him; but even so there is nothing to show that he became his pupil.

It is somewhat surprising to find that, while two of Strabo's instructors, Tyrannion and Xenarchus, were Peripatetic philosophers, he himself professed the Stoic tenets. About the fact there can be no question. . . . By Stephanus he is called without qualification 'Strabo the Stoic philosopher.' At what period of his life, and owing to what influences, he attached himself to this school of philosophy, we have no means of ascertaining; but since he informs us that he was intimate with the Stoic Athenodorus[15], who resided for some time at Rome, and was first the instructor and afterwards the adviser of Augustus, it is possible that the change may have been in some measure attributable to him. As to the effect of this on Strabo's work, it would be too much to say that his method, or the treatment of his subject in general, was influenced by Stoic or any other philosophical tenets; but here and there his views come to the surface in special passages. Thus his belief in a divinity or in the gods, as far as he possesses any, is pantheistic, and he treats popular religion and the observances of public worship as unworthy of a philosopher[16]. With him the primal agency which caused the organization of the world was Providence . . . and by this impersonal force that interconnexion of all the parts was produced, from which its unity and perfection proceeded. The passage in which this principle is most definitely set forth occurs in the Seventeenth Book[17], where Strabo is speaking of the formation of the ground in Egypt. . . .

In politics Strabo was a hearty advocate of the Roman government, and especially of its concentration in the hands of a single ruler. This admiration of the power of Rome he inherited from Polybius, whose views of history

he in so many ways adopted; but in this respect he even outstripped his predecessor, for, in describing the destruction of Corinth by Mummius, while he mentions in passing the terms of compassion in which Polybius refers to that event . . . [18], he himself regards the inhabitants as having paid the penalty of their misdeeds. . . . Similarly he mentions the conquest of his own fatherland, Pontus, by the Romans with a singular absence of feeling[19]. Elsewhere he constantly betrays his sympathy with the ruling power, both as maintaining the *pax Romana,* and as being the primary agent in advancing civilization. At the beginning of his work he extols those leaders, who by obtaining the command of land and sea succeed in bringing all nations and states under one political administration[20]; and, in particular, he refers to the security afforded to commerce by the tranquillity arising from the extinction of piracy[21], and to the safety of life and property in districts formerly disturbed, such as Lycia and Syria, owing to the cessation of brigandage in consequence of the Roman system of government[22]. In Spain, he says, the well-being of the country was in proportion to the advance of the Roman arms[23], and elsewhere that power had succeeded in introducing communication among hostile tribes[24]. Similarly, the prosperity of Gades and Massilia was in great measure due to their friendship and alliance with the Romans[25], and the people of Tarentum were better off after they had received a Roman colony[26]. Indeed, throughout the work the conquests and administrative measures of the Romans are spoken of in the highest terms, and even their harsh treatment of revolted provinces is represented as a form of necessary discipline.[27] . . . And, as regards the imperial power, he remarks that the administration of an empire of such magnitude could hardly be carried on except under the paternal rule of a single governor[28]. The impression made on him by the solicitude of the emperors for the welfare of the provincials is shown by his referring more than once to the assistance afforded by Augustus and Tiberius to the cities of Asia Minor which had been ruined by earthquakes[29].

In endeavouring to trace the course of Strabo's life after he quitted Asia Minor, which is in most respects obscure, we have at least one definite date to start from. In his description of the Cyclades he tells us that he was at the island of Gyaros at the time when Augustus was at Corinth, returning from Egypt, on his way to celebrate his triumph for the victory at Actium[30]. This was in 29 B.C.; and as the Geographer says that one of his fellow-passengers, when he left the island, was a delegate from that place, commissioned by the inhabitants to obtain from Augustus a diminution of the tribute which they paid, he was evidently on his way to Europe; and it has reasonably been assumed that he was journeying from Asia by way of Corinth to Rome. From another passage, however, we gather that this was not his first visit to the capital. When speaking of the works of art that were carried to Rome after the capture of Corinth, he states that he had himself seen the famous picture of Dionysus by Aristides, which was taken from that place, and set up in the temple of Ceres at Rome, and that it had subsequently perished, when that building was consumed by fire[31]. Now we learn from Dion Cassius that this conflagration took place in 31 B.C., that is to say, two years before the date given above[32]. It is not improbable also that he stayed at Corinth on the occasion of his earlier voyage to Rome, for he mentions having seen the place shortly after it was restored by the Romans, referring to the establishment of a Roman colony there, after it had been deserted for a century, by Julius Caesar in 44 B.C.[33] Certainly his description of the devastation wrought by the new colonists in the necropolis of Corinth, and of their finds of works of art, seems to proceed from one who was on the spot at the time when this occurred, or shortly after. The date, 44 B.C., for his first visit to Rome would further correspond to another occurrence, which on any other supposition cannot easily be reconciled with the facts of Strabo's life, viz., his having seen Publius Servilius Isauricus, a circumstance which he mentions in his account of Isauria[34]. Servilius died in 44; and, though it is possible that Strabo may have seen him elsewhere than at Rome, yet the advanced age of that commander—he was probably about eighty years old at the time of his death—renders it highly improbable that for some time before this he should have been absent from the capital. If the date which has been given above for Strabo's birth, 63 B.C., is accepted, he would have been at this time nineteen years of age. There is no evidence to show how long was the duration of these sojourns in Rome, or where the intervening or the subsequent period was passed; but it is clear—as will appear when we come to speak of Strabo's travels—that some part of his life after he had reached maturity was spent in his native country. Not only does he allude to his having resided in certain cities in Asia Minor, but his exact and observant descriptions of places in Cappadocia, Pontus, and elsewhere in that region, imply that he had seen them as a grown-up man. That he was in Asia during the interval between his two visits to Italy is evident from our finding him journeying from east to west in 29 B.C.

Subsequently to this, as we know from his own testimony, Strabo resided for a long period in Alexandria[35] . . . ; and it was then that he made the expedition through Egypt, in the company of his friend and patron, Aelius Gallus, which was the most considerable of his journeys. Gallus was appointed praefect of Egypt in 26 B.C., and returned to Rome in 22 B.C., when his office came to an end; but whether Strabo accompanied him from Rome, and returned thither along with him, we have no means of deciding. The expedition on the Nile seems to have taken place in 25-24 B.C. One of the latest and best critics of Strabo[36] holds it to be probable that he continued to reside at Alexandria until 12 B.C.—relying, among other evidences that seem to point in that direction, on an inscription[37], which states that the Caesareium in that city, the position of which Strabo mentions[38], was dedicated in the year 13-12. It should be remarked, however, that it is so habitual with Strabo to supplement the information which he acquired at an earlier period, either through his own observation or from the testimony of others, by the addition of facts subsequently obtained, that no great stress can be laid on such a mode of proof. In any case, there can be no doubt that after leaving Egypt he revisited Rome, though it is a much disputed point how long he remained there. This question must mainly be solved, as far as it admits of solution, by noticing his descriptions of buildings which were erected in Rome, and of objects that were brought thither, during the remainder of his life, together with his accounts of events that happened within that period, and then seeing whether they give clear evidence of personal observation and inquiry on the spot. The facts themselves may in some cases be of slight importance; but in estimating the work of a geographer everything is of value which enables us to appreciate aright his opportunities of gathering information.

The following circumstance renders it probable that Strabo was in Rome in or after the year 20 B.C. In his account of India he tells us that Porus, an Indian prince, sent an embassy to Augustus, bearing a friendly letter to him, and accompanied by a number of presents, one of which was a living man without arms, or, as he is called in the Greek, a Hermes[39]. This object the Geographer had inspected, but the same was not the case with the embassy and the other objects, for he describes them on the authority of Nicolaus of Damascus, who was at Antioch in Syria when they passed that way. It follows that the Hermes, when Strabo saw him, was not *en route*, and in that case he must almost certainly have seen him at Rome, which was his natural destination. Now we learn from Dion Cassius that the date of the arrival of this embassy w 20 B.C.[40]. A further reason renders it likely that Strabo was in Rome subsequently to 12 B.C. In various parts of his *Geography* he quotes an authority . . . and speaks of his work. . . . Now it has been conjectured with much probability that this was none other than the great survey of Agrippa, who caused a map of the Roman empire and the countries adjacent to it to be set up in the Porticus Octaviae at Rome, and accompanied it with a detailed commentary, stating the distances from one important point to another, and the length and breadth of the different provinces. This work was not completed until after Agrippa's death, which took place in 12 B.C.[41] Again, when in his description of Rome he speaks of the splendour of the objects to be seen in the Porticus Liviae, we may gather that he was in Rome later than 7 B.C., the year in which that building was erected. The passage no doubt is rhetorical in tone, but it is evidently intended to convey the impression that the writer had himself viewed them[42]. On the other hand, he could hardly have lived in Rome without intermission during the next few years, for he states in his account of Germany that the Romans had never passed the Elbe[43], whereas we know from Tacitus[44] that Domitius Ahenobarbus crossed that river and received the triumphal *insignia* in consequence; and this expedition took place between 1 B.C. and 1 A.D. Had Strabo been in Rome at the time when this occurred, he could not have failed to hear of so important an event. In 6 A.D., however, it seems not unlikely that he was there, for he mentions the appointment of the *vigiles* as a provision against the frequent conflagrations in the capital, and the restriction on the height of the houses to prevent the fall of buildings, both which measures were carried out in that year[45]; and he also notices the vase sent by the Cimbri to Augustus[46], the presentation of which was probably a result of the expedition of Tiberius in 5 A.D.: but statements like these cannot be regarded as certain evidence, for the writer may have obtained information concerning them when at a distance from Rome. The question of Strabo's place of residence during the remainder of his life is still more difficult to determine. As it is closely connected with another point, viz., the place where he composed his *Geography,* it may be well to defer the consideration of it until we reach that part of our discussion.

Let us now turn to the subject of Strabo's travels. To these he himself attached great importance, for he boasts that he had journeyed in different directions as far as any other writer on geography—that is to say, from Armenia to the western part of Etruria, and from the Euxine to the confines of Aethiopia; whereas other travellers, who had reached a further limit towards the west, had not proceeded so far eastward, and vice versa; and the case was the same with those who had travelled towards the north and the south[47]. This may very well have been literally true, but it does not therefore follow that Strabo was a great traveller, any more than visits to Japan and Australia justify the excursionist of the present day in claiming that title; indeed, a boast of this kind is liable to raise a presumption adverse to the claims of him who makes it. Everything must depend on the extensiveness of the travels that were carried out within the given area, and on the scientific spirit of research in which they were undertaken. In investigating these points there is great need of caution, to avoid being led away, on the one hand by insufficient evidence, on the other by unreasonable scepticism. The Geographer is fond of mentioning the places which he visited, and the objects which he saw in them. There are thirty notices of this kind in the course of his work, relating to twenty different localities[48]; and he seems to go out of his way to introduce these, as if he desired by this means to confirm his statements, and to produce in his readers' minds the impression that he was an independent inquirer. This does not prove that he did not see other places about which he makes no such remark; indeed, in some cases we can demonstrate that he did so. For instance, though he nowhere tells us that he visited Puteoli, yet the account which he gives of the unlading of Egyptian merchant ships at that port in his description of Alexandria is a sufficient proof that he had been on the spot when this was being done[49]; and many similar passages might be named. But it suggests that we should require tolerably clear evidence of his having seen them; and to establish this the accurate description of a city or an object is not sufficient, for that might be obtained at second-hand from other writers; what is wanted is the mention of such details as imply personal observation. Thus, when he describes the view of, and still more the view from, a place—when we read of the vast caves in the rocks between Terracina and Formiae, which are occupied by handsomely furnished dwellings, and look out upon the islands of Pandataria and Pontia[50]; or of the Plutonium at Hierapolis, where the spectator can hardly see the bottom for the exhalations

that are emitted from it[51]; or when he speaks of the Paneium at Alexandria as commanding from its summit a panorama of the city[52]—we should feel a strong presumption that he is speaking as an eye-witness, even if in some of these instances he had not actually stated it. Yet in other cases not unlike these we know that the descriptions were borrowed from other writers. Thus in his account of Spain, a country which he certainly did not visit, he remarks on the lofty position of Hemeroscopeium, a colony of Massilia, which causes it to be visible from afar when approached from the sea[53]; and on the charming scenery . . . on the banks of the Baetis, which is due to the ground being laid out in plantations and well cultivated fields[54]. Bearing these cautions in mind, we may proceed to inquire, within such limits as our space allows, what parts of the world Strabo had visited, and with what completeness he had explored them.

In Africa the only country with which he was acquainted was Egypt, though he mentions that he saw Cyrene from the sea[55]; this may easily have occurred when he was sailing from Rome to Alexandria, or in the opposite direction. His knowledge of Egypt was very thorough, as might be expected from his long residence in Alexandria, and from his having ascended the Nile along with Aelius Gallus as far as the First Cataract. The results of this are traceable, not only in his elaborate sketch of the topography of Alexandria and the account which he has given of the chief cities on the banks of the river, but in his descriptions of the Lake Moeris, the Labyrinth, and the Nilometer at Elephantine; and in addition to this his narrative contains graphic notices of a variety of curious episodes—his inspection of the bull Apis at Memphis[56], his feeding the sacred crocodile at Arsinoë[57], his listening in a critical spirit to the sound emitted from the statue of Memnon[58], and his fears of drowning, at which he himself laughs, when he crossed on a frail native craft to the island of Philae[59]. In consequence of this the Seventeenth Book is one of the most interesting parts of Strabo's *Geography.*

In Asia again he seems hardly to have visited any country except Asia Minor. The regions further to the east, Mesopotamia and Babylonia, are excluded from the area of his travels by his own statement that he had not advanced beyond Armenia in that direction: and by Armenia is here meant the western boundary of that land, for he does not appear to have set foot in it. Nor can I find any evidence that he travelled in Syria, or even coasted along it. Tyre, in particular, which he would hardly have left unvisited if he had been in that neighbourhood, he certainly did not see, for in describing its many-storied houses, which, he says, exceeded in height those in Rome, he quotes from other authorities[60] On the other hand, he was well acquainted with his native land of Asia Minor, especially with its extreme eastern and western districts—with Cilicia, Cappadocia, and Pontus, and with western Phrygia, Lydia, Ionia, and Caria. In Cilicia his descriptions of the city of Tarsus[61] and of the Corycian cave[62]—the latter a very remarkable account, the accuracy of which has been recently established by Mr. Bent's interesting discovery of the site[63]—bear all the marks of personal observation, and the presumption thus raised is confirmed by our discovering that Strabo was familiar with the neighbouring province of Cappadocia. There he tells us that he visited the gorge of the river Pyramus in Cataonia, the appearance of which he has strikingly delineated[64]; there also he was present at the Magian rites, which he says were still celebrated in his time in numerous Persian shrines in that country[65]; at the Cappadocian Comana, which was one of the greatest centres of the native worship in those parts, he resided for some time[66]; and Mazaca (afterwards called Caesareia), the capital of this province, together with the imposing mass of Mount Argaeus in its neighbourhood, he had evidently seen[67]. With Pontus he was of course well acquainted, and his narrative proves his familiarity, not only with the cities of the interior, like Comana, another religious centre[68], and his birthplace Amasia[69], but also with those on the sea-coast, especially Sinope, his account of which contains highly interesting details[70]. In western Asia Minor, we know that as a boy he resided at Nysa, and he mentions having been at Ephesus and Hierapolis— the former in connexion with the works of art which he saw in the temple of Artemis[71], the latter, as having tested the overpowering force of the vapours in the Plutonium at that place by letting loose some sparrows into it, which immediately fell dead[72]. His notices also of Philadelphia, with the walls of its houses cracked by earthquakes[73], of Sardis[74], and of Mylasa[75] and Alabanda in Caria, the latter of which he compares, on account of its position at the foot of two hills, to a crouching mule[76], are very graphic; and from his having seen these places, which lie at a considerable distance from one another, we may conclude that he was acquainted with much of the intervening district. Similarly, his appreciative description of the city of Rhodes[77] would lead us to think that he had visited that island; and the same thing may be true also of Cos[78] and Samos[79]. Perhaps it is safe to conclude that once at least— that is, on the occasion when he passed by Gyaros—he made Trogilium his starting-point for a voyage to Europe, for he says that that port offered the shortest passage by sea to Sunium, and he describes the first part of the route between it and the Cyclades[80]. We cannot speak with equal confidence of Strabo's visits to other places in Asia Minor, but with some at least he could hardly fail to become acquainted in journeying to and from Amasia. His descriptions of Selge in Pisidia[81], of Pessinus in Galatia[82], and of Cyzicus on the Propontis[83], are all striking, and still more so is that of Nicaea in Bithynia[84], though none of these necessarily imply personal observation. But I fail to discover any evidence that he had seen the Plain of Troy, notwithstanding that he has written at great length about it in his Thirteenth Book. Probably all his details on this subject are borrowed from the work of Demetrius of Scepsis, who, from living close by, had ample opportunities of collecting information about it; and if Strabo himself had visited the Troad, he might have been saved from the unfortunate mistake of fixing the site of Troy at . . . —a position which is neither strong, nor conspicuous, nor suitable to the Homeric descriptions.

This brings us to Greece. And here at starting I must plainly say that, with the exception of Corinth, about which he has written with a fullness that contrasts strongly with his treatment of the other cities, I hardly think he visited any place in that country. An exception may be made in favour of the porttown of Munychia and the pass of the Scironian rocks, his descriptions of which are certainly vivid[85]; he probably touched at the former of these, and sailed within sight of the latter, on his way to Corinth. Professor Ernst Curtius puts in a claim also for Olympia and the coast of Elis in its neighbourhood[86]; but it is doubtful whether in Strabo's notices of these there is anything that might not have been borrowed. He certainly had not been on the site of Mycenae, for he remarks that not even a trace of that city was preserved[87]; whereas its ruins were subsequently seen by Pausanias[88], and are not unknown at the present day. Nor had he visited Delphi, as is shown by his erroneous statement about the position of Crisa; for, while that town was situated on a spur of Mount Parnassus, in the vicinity of Delphi, he places it on the sea-coast[89]. Finally, though it may seem almost incredible that he should have omitted to see Athens, yet the evidence points strongly in that direction. The apologies which he makes for omitting all details respecting it, as being superfluous in the case of so world-renowned a place, excite our suspicions; and on the one point which he singles out for criticism, viz., the question whether the water of the stream of the Eridanus near the Lyceum was pure or impure, about which the authorities differed, he has to refer to the statements of others, thus making it clear that he had not himself inspected it[90]. Possibly he may have paid a hurried visit to Athens from Munychia, but of any real acquaintance with the city itself or with its environs there is no trace in his work.

With Italy the case is altogether different. Here we find clear proof that he had turned to account his sojourns in Rome by exploring the neighbouring country in various directions. This is especially true of Latium, where—to cite only two from among a great number of instances— his account of the Pomptine Marshes[91], and that of the Lacus Nemorensis near Aricia[92], are remarkably graphic. He had visited also the coast-towns of Etruria; this he definitely mentions in the case of Populonium, where he saw the iron being worked, which was brought across from the island of Aethalia[93] (Ilva); and his remarks also about the Bay of Luna and the quarries of white marble in its vicinity (the modern Carrara), and about Pisae, imply personal observation[94]. Again, he shows an intimate acquaintance with the whole district that bordered on the Bay of Naples—with the cities of Cumae and Neapolis, in which he was struck by the survival of Greek customs and culture[95]; with the lake Avernus[96], and with the harbour-works of Puteoli[97]—and he descants with evident enthusiasm, both on the volcanic features of this region, and on the aspect presented by the dwelling-houses and plantations which fringed the shore of the bay in every direction[98]. With the line of the Appian Way he seems to have become acquainted in journeying from Asia to Rome, for he remarks that every one who proceeded to the capital from Greece and the East travels by way of Brundisium[99]; and his description of that port[100], and still more that of Tarentum[101], are singularly accurate. But the remainder of the Adriatic coast of Italy was an unknown land to him. In the case of Ravenna, which from its great importance we should expect to have had especial attraction for him, this is unquestionable, for his account of that city represents it as it appeared at an earlier date, and omits all notice of the great works which were carried out there by the orders of Augustus[102]. Of Sicily he would naturally see something when on his way from Rome to Alexandria, for which place Puteoli formed his natural point of embarkation. That he did so is rendered probable by his saying in his description of the crater of Etna, that his information was derived from persons who had recently ascended the mountain[103]; and his narrative leaves little doubt that he had communicated with them on the spot.

The conclusion which seems to follow from the preceding review is this—that, though Strabo was led by the circumstances of his life to visit countries widely distant from one another, yet he was not a great traveller, and his journeys were not undertaken with the object of research, or in order to verify the statements of former writers. Except in Asia Minor, in Egypt, and in Central Italy, he had not deviated far from the route which he would naturally take in passing to and from his home and the great centres of civilization in which he resided at different intervals. To compare him to an eminent explorer like Posidonius, who traversed a great part of Europe, including some of the remotest districts of Spain and Gaul, and collected original information in those countries on numerous subjects, is absurd. But it would be equally far from the truth, if we were to regard Strabo's travels as having been of slight importance to him as a writer on geography. In reality, he learnt from them what was most important for him to learn, to take a comprehensive view of his subject, to interest himself in a variety of topics and in different races of men, and to get that power of vividly realizing and forcibly representing to others the matters he treats of, which can only be obtained from ocular inspection, or at least from familiarity with similar objects. Being an intelligent and keen-sighted man, he kept his eyes open wherever he went, and the result is that he writes, not as a student in his closet, but as one who was trained to observe and to criticize. This practical view is conspicuous throughout his work, and greatly enhances its usefulness. . . .

Turning now to Strabo's **Geography,** we have first to consider three points of some difficulty relating to it, all of which have been much debated; namely the period of the author's life to which this work is to be ascribed, the place at which it was written, and the class of readers for whom it was intended. These are naturally important, because the view which we take of them cannot fail in some measure to influence, not only the interpretation of various details, but also our estimate of the scope and purpose of the treatise at large. As regards the first of these questions, the time of writing—until recently it has been generally as-

sumed that Strabo was far advanced in years when he commenced it; indeed, until the year 1879, when Dr. Paul Meyer published his *Quaestiones Strabonianae,* almost every one who had written on the subject was agreed that the period of its composition lay between the years 17 and 23 A.D. The support of this view was found mainly in the numerous passages in different parts of the work, in which occurrences are mentioned that took place during that interval; and these were thought to imply that the work could not have been begun earlier than the year 17. It may, however, fairly be asked—and it is to Dr. Meyer's credit that he has brought this point prominently forward— whether it is necessary to suppose, either that Strabo composed the whole of his **Geography** at one time, or that he did not afterwards revise it, and introduce the mention of subsequent occurrences. It is surely unreasonable to argue from the incidental mention of an event, that the book in which it is found, and still more that the whole work, must have been compiled after that event occurred. Indeed, the opposite supposition, viz. that the execution of the work extended over a great number of years, not only involves no antecedent improbability, but in the case of a subject of such magnitude appears only natural. In this way also we escape from the necessity of believing that a treatise, which is characterized in a high degree by freshness and vigour, was produced by an old man—for, if we have rightly fixed 63 B.C. as the year of Strabo's birth, he would have been 80 years of age in 17 A.D. Moreover, the view that it was not written at a stretch, but at different periods of the author's life, may serve to some extent to account for the marked inequality in style and treatment which is traceable in various parts. Episodes too, which otherwise appear out of place in the connexion in which they occur—such as the description of the triumph of Germanicus in Book VII[104], which stands out as it were from a strange setting in the account of Germany in which it is found—are easily explained as having been of later introduction. In saying this much, however, we would not deny that this task occupied the later rather than the earlier portion of Strabo's life; this indeed would naturally follow from his having been previously engaged on his historical work. With regard to the time at which particular portions of the Geography were composed, the evidence is too slight to enable us to speak with confidence; but the period of revision we can fix with some certainty as having fallen in the years 18 and 19 A.D., because the latest events that are introduced—and they are somewhat numerous—occurred about that date. This was the case with Germanicus' triumph, which was celebrated in 17 A.D.; with the death of Archelaus king of Cappadocia in the same year[105], concerning which event Strabo says, that his kingdom had been reduced to a Roman province, but that its organization was not yet known[106]; with the appointment of a son of Pythodoris and Polemo as king of Armenia[107]; with the conversion of Commagene into a Roman province[108]; and with the great earthquakes in Asia Minor, and the measures which Tiberius took for restoring the cities then injured. Still more conclusive is the evidence afforded by the passage in Book IV relating to the final pacification of Rhaetia—the only event in his whole work to which Strabo assigns a definite date. It is there stated that the Noricans and Carnians had paid tribute regularly for thirty-three years; and as the date of their subjugation by Tiberius and Drusus was the summer of 15 B.C., the date at which this was written would be the latter half of 18 A.D. That Strabo did not altogether cease from making additions to his work after that time is clear from his mentioning the death of Juba; and we have already noticed that he did not in all points bring it up to date, e. g. in omitting to record the deaths of Germanicus and Arminius. This is hardly a matter for surprise, when we take into account his advanced age. . . .

As regards the class of readers for whom Strabo's work was intended, it has been maintained with equal confidence that he wrote specially for Romans, and that he wrote specially for Greeks. In favour of the former view his own statement at the commencement of his treatise is quoted, that the object of geographical study is that it should be of service to men in high position. By these he clearly means the generals and statesmen, to whom were assigned the conquest and administration of provinces. Thus, when speaking of astronomy and mathematical geography, as subjects subsidiary to general geography, he says that they ought to be studied so far as they are useful to the statesman and the general[109]; and to prove the serviceableness of geography to the latter of these two classes, he notices various instances of campaigns which had been seriously affected by ignorance of the features of the country— notably, the recent reverses which had befallen the Roman arms in Parthia, and the difficulties which they had experienced in carrying on the war in Germany[110]. There can be no doubt that the persons here referred to were Romans. Besides this, those critics who support the view that Strabo's *Geography* was composed at Rome suggest, that his purpose in writing was affected by his residence in that city, and by the influence of Roman dignitaries, whose confidence he enjoyed. The sketch of the Roman empire, and of its division into provinces, with which he concludes his work, is thought to point in the same direction. On the other side it is contended that, however much the writer may have professed the desire to be of service to Roman officials, there is very small trace in his work of his having kept this in view. His elaborate disquisitions on mythology, his long historical notices, his enumerations of philosophers and literary men produced by different cities, and these too in almost every instance Greeks, his descriptions of remarkable physical phenomena, and the other topics which he introduces in rich profusion, while they would render his work acceptable to his own countrymen, could hardly serve the purposes of Roman statesmen and generals. It is also remarked that here and there he gives evidence of writing for persons unacquainted with Latin, by explaining the meaning of Latin words. . . . Again, if his work was intended to win the ears of Romans, his depreciation of Roman in comparison of Greek authors, and the want of originality which he attributes to them, would certainly be strange. 'Roman writers,' he says, when speaking of Spain, 'imitate the Greeks, but not with much success; for they borrow their statements from them, and

do not for themselves bring to the subject much love of enquiry; so that where the Greeks fail us, these do not greatly help to supplement them[111]. The number of Roman writers whom he quotes by name is, no doubt, remarkably small; besides Cicero, whom he cites twice[112], the only others are Caesar[113], Asinius Pollio[114], and Fabius Pictor[115].

It cannot be denied that the arguments thus adduced on both sides have considerable weight; but a third view has now to be mentioned, which, if established, may serve to neutralize the apparent antagonism between them. It has been suggested that Strabo wrote, neither for Greeks nor for Romans exclusively, but for cultivated men in general without reference to their nationality[116]. He seems, indeed, to imply as much as this, when he says that he intends his treatise to be popular . . . and defines . . . for whom it was intended as 'one who is not wholly uneducated, but has gone through the general course of study which is pursued by free-born and cultured men[117].' In other words, he expects his readers to be educated gentlemen; but beyond this he does not appeal exclusively to any particular class or body of men. He would naturally assign the foremost position among them to Roman statesmen, for it was reasonable that he should wish to instruct the masters of the world, especially as they were extremely ignorant of geography; at the same time, the thought suggests itself, that some of Strabo's introductory remarks on this point may partake of the nature of an advertisement, the object of which was to attract Roman readers. The contents of the *Geography* fully bear out this larger view of the public to which it was addressed, for it is congenial both to the scientific spirit of the Greeks and to the practical ideas of the Romans, and the information which is found in it would be interesting to persons of both those races. Yet, after all has been said, it is not perhaps far from the truth, that Strabo, while he *wished* to be read by Romans, *expected* to be read by Greeks.

The object then which Strabo had in view in writing his *Geography* was a practical one, to instruct and interest intelligent readers. Thus he himself says, that the criterion of such a study is its usefulness[118]; and applying this principle in another passage, where he is speaking of his accounts of modes of life and political constitutions that had become extinct, he explains that these were introduced as lessons for the instruction of others, either for imitation or for avoidance[119]. It is important that we should bear this in mind in estimating his work, because it explains his comparative neglect of mathematical geography. This no doubt is the weakest side of his treatise, for he deals with this part of his subject only in his Introduction, and there unsystematically in the form of controversy with his predecessors in that study. The excuse for this is to be found in his considering that this branch was sufficiently represented in works already existing, especially in the writings of Eratosthenes, Hipparchus, and Posidonius, so that he felt it to be sufficient if he corrected what he supposed to be their mistakes. This would satisfy his contemporaries, who had those works in their hands, though to us who have lost them the omission is a matter for serious regret. At the same time, there can be no doubt that Strabo was in this respect greatly inferior to those eminent writers, and that sometimes, when he criticizes them, he either misunderstands them, or is himself in error. But the point of view from which he regarded geography was a different one from theirs. For the globe at large, or even for the northern temperate zone, which alone he believed to be the dwelling-place of man, he cares nothing, except in so far as a knowledge of it serves for a preliminary to the study of the inhabited world. Hence, when discussing the use of such aids to geography as globes and maps, he professes himself contented with a simple sketch . . . which, without any attempt at scientific delineation, supplies a general idea of the features of a country[120].

The greatness of Strabo's work consists in its encyclopaedic character. His aim was to bring together, and to exhibit in a readable form, all that it was important to know about the different countries of the world and their occupants. No treatise of this kind had been produced before, and nowhere else can be found so comprehensive a view. . . . The modern book to which it can best be compared is Ritter's *Erdkunde,* in which almost all the information which a reader can desire, about Asia at all events, is contained. In both these works the conformation of the ground in each district, the nature of the products, the character and condition of the inhabitants, and similar topics, are dealt with; in both cases also the most prominent element is historical geography. In Strabo this is especially conspicuous. Not only does he everywhere introduce the history of a country side by side with its geography, but he endeavours to show the intimate connexion that existed between the two. Thus in describing the lines of Roman roads through eastern Spain he refers to Caesar's march along them before the battle of Munda[121]; in his account of the passes that lead from Upper Italy into Etruria he distinguishes the one by which Hannibal crossed[122]; the mention of the condition of the Samnite towns in the Augustan age introduces a sketch of Sulla's campaign by which they were finally subjugated[123]; the pass of the Climax on the coast of Lycia recalls the danger to which Alexander's troops were exposed in traversing it[124]; and so on throughout the whole work. Still more striking is the way in which he traces the influence of the features of a land on the character and history of its inhabitants. On a large scale this is noticeable in his comparison of Europe with the other great continents in its effect on the races that occupied it[125], and in his discussion of the influence exercised by the physical features of Italy on the development of the power of Rome[126]; and in a more restricted area the same thing appears in his remarks on the advantages enjoyed by Corinth for purposes of commerce owing to its position between two seas and on the line of road between Northern Greece and the Peloponnese[127], and on the effect produced on the inhabitants of Aegina by the barrenness of its soil, which forced them to betake themselves to the sea and became a naval power[128]. Nowhere is Strabo's originality more clearly seen than here. He is in fact the only writer in antiquity who

has systematically treated of the influence in this respect of nature on man. Both here and in the general conception of his work a tendency towards generalization is apparent which is highly philosophical. As M. Dubois epigrammatically expresses it;—if the title of *Philosophy of History* is rightly assigned to treatises which generalize on that subject, then on the same principle Strabo's book might be called the *Philosophy of Geography*[129].

While such, however, was the Geographer's conception of what his work should be, and while his execution of his plan has in many ways been so successful, we cannot but feel that not unfrequently he fails to reach his ideal. There is indeed a strange inequality in his treatment of his subject, so that from time to time the feebleness of his criticism, and a want of exactness and method in the arrangement of his facts, impress us with the idea that we are not listening to one who possessed a powerful grasp of mind. Often, too, we perceive that he is too much disposed to make the geographical portion subservient to the historical, and still more to the mythological. There is an almost comical instance of this in his account of the district Adiabene in Babylonia, which he commences by saying, 'Adiabene is for the most part level;' and then, after giving an account of its historical relations to the neighbouring peoples, he concludes it with the words, 'such is Adiabene[130].' The long-protracted discussion, also, about the Curetes in Book X shows how far the writer could be carried in his enthusiasm for mythology. Inquiries such as these were no doubt acceptable to the Greeks of his time, who took a special interest in such questions, but they mar the unity of his work. Again, it is a distinct drawback to the usefulness of such a treatise that it cannot be regarded as a picture of the known world, as it existed at the time when the author wrote—a point which the student requires to bear constantly in mind, when employing it as an authority. In his account of India, for instance, Strabo has to follow the narratives of persons who wrote some centuries before his age; and the same thing is true in a lesser degree of Spain, Gaul, and other lands. The deficiencies which arise from this cause, however, cannot to any great extent be attributed to the author, who could but avail himself of such information as was forthcoming in his day. And, whatever deductions have to be made on these grounds, we cannot but feel that the wide range of Strabo's interests, the judgement with which he selects the facts that were most important and most attractive, and the literary skill by which he renders a geographical work at once readable and of permanent value, entitle him to a high position among authors.

There is, indeed, both in the method and the execution of the ***Geography***, a thoroughly Greek feeling for the due proportion of things, and for the need of considering the form as well as the matter in combining so great a variety of materials. In entering on such a work the author feels that he is an artist, and that it must be executed in an artistic spirit. This becomes at once apparent, when we compare the skilful grouping of the facts which make up Strabo's compact and well-arranged chapters, with the lists of names and catalogues of objects which are crowded together in Pliny's *Natural History,* or with the dry details that compose the work of Ptolemy. To say this is not to depreciate the work of those authors, but to point out that the object with which they wrote was different from Strabo's. He speaks of a geographical treatise as a colossal work . . . in which, as in a colossal statue, the general effect should be studied, and insignificant minutiae, which would detract from this, should be omitted[131]. This is especially conspicuous in the dislike he expresses for superfluous and cacophonous names. Thus, in speaking of the mountain tribes of Spain, he says, 'I shrink from accumulating their names, odious as they are to write—unless any of my readers are gratified by hearing such names as Pleutauri and Bardyetae and Allotriges, and others even worse and more unimportant[132].' The same remark he applies to the names of some of the Arabian tribes, which he omits on account of the vulgarity and clumsiness of their pronunciation[133]. The exclusion of some of these we at the present day may regret, because the knowledge of them would have assisted our researches, but they would have rendered his work less readable: nor can he be accused of sacrificing his scientific to his literary aims, for in reading his accounts of countries historically famous, such as Italy and Greece, our pleasure is often marred by the lists of towns which he feels it his duty to introduce. In the main, also, notwithstanding what has just been said about the preponderance that he assigns to the historical element, he shows tact in combining a number of subjects in such a manner as not to allow any one of them to overbalance the rest. Besides this, he endeavours in many ways to vary and enliven his narrative, with the view of interesting his readers as well as instructing them. He enables them to realize geographical features by comparing them to familiar objects. Thus he likens Spain to a bull's hide[134], the Peloponnese to the leaf of a plane-tree[135], the Oases in the Lybian desert to the spots on a leopard's skin[136], the harbour of Brundisium and the Golden Horn at Byzantium with their winding inlets to a stag's head and horns[137], Mesopotamia to a cock-boat[138], the Trojan Ida, with its long range and numerous spurs, to a milleped[139]; and other comparisons of the same kind might be mentioned[140]. Many of these, no doubt, were borrowed, especially from Eratosthenes, but Strabo's skill is shown by the way in which he utilizes them. In the same manner he enlarges his reader's view by noticing the similarities between places, districts, and features of the ground in different countries. He compares the height of the houses in Tyre and Rome[141], the healthiness of Ravenna and Alexandria notwithstanding the shallows in their neighbourhood[142], the size and shape of the Peloponnese and the Tauric Chersonete[143], the intermittent streams by which the Lacus Fucinus in Latium and the river Amenanus in Sicily were fed[144], and the periodical inundations of the Nile and the rivers of India[145]; and he also quotes the saying, in which the Acro-corinth and the acropolis of Messene on Ithome were spoken of as the two horns by which the cow (the Peloponnese) might be held[146]. Nor does he consider it below the dignity of his subject to introduce a humorous, and sometimes even a comical element. Of this nature are

the admirable story of the musician and the deaf man[147], the riddle about the unprofitableness of the mines in Attica[148], the mention of the mistake of the Vettones, who when they saw Roman centurions walking up and down for the sake of exercise, treated them as madmen[149], and the narrative of the Salassi, who, after rolling down boulders on Caesar's army, excused themselves on the ground that they were constructing roads or bridges[150]. The proverbs and proverbial expressions that are scattered over the work are very numerous; more than thirty such have been collected by Dr. Paul Meyer in his *Straboniana*[151]. Two of the best known of them, which occur in the same chapter of the Eighth Book[152], are 'Double Malea and forget your home,' . . . with reference to the danger to which sailors were exposed in rounding that promontory; and 'Not every one can afford a trip to Corinth, . . . which turns on the extravagant rate of living in that luxurious city.

The most characteristic feature of Strabo, however, as an author is his manysidedness. His work is a mine of information on subjects connected with the ancient world—to use that term in a much wider sense than that of classical antiquity; and in consequence of the extent of its range it is referred to more than any other ancient treatise by students of various subjects; indeed, in some instances it is our only source of information about them. To put aside for the moment the themes which form the staple of the book—geography proper, history and sociology, together with the reflexions and general deductions which these give birth to—let us notice a few of the topics, which occupy a secondary place in it, and are in many cases introduced incidentally. Strabo's interest in peculiarities in the physical conformation of the earth, especially in volcanic phenomena, is very marked, and for these he possessed a rich store from which to draw in the work of his predecessor Posidonius. Hence his accounts of the chief volcanic centres, whether extinct or still active, which were known in his age—Vesuvius, the Lipari islands, Etna, Thera (*Santorin*), the Catacecaumene in western Asia Minor, and Mount Argaeus in Cappadocia—as well as of the most important eruptions and earthquake movements that were on record, are of extreme value both for geologists and others. Nor does he ever miss an opportunity of noticing other strange features of the ground, such as the rolled stones of the Plaine de la Crau (Campi Lapidei) in Southern France, or the subterranean passages that are of frequent occurrence in the limestone soil of Greece, by which rivers are engulfed and lakes are drained. Climate also has an especial attraction for him; he does not fail, for instance, to notice the cloudy, sunless atmosphere of Britain[153], and the monsoons and the rainy season in India[154]; and he remarks that the amount of snow that falls is greater, and the snow-line is lower, on the northern side of a range of mountains than on the southern[155]. And in innumerable passages he draws attention to the effect of varieties of climate on the vegetation, on the animals, both wild and domesticated, on the physical characteristics of the inhabitants, on the food and clothing of various tribes, and on the rapid development of civilization in regions which, like

Baetica in southern Spain, are especially favoured in this respect[156]. On the subject of trees and plants he furnishes a great variety of information: the banyan-tree in India, with its self-formed layers, the papyrus and the Egyptian bean, the palm-groves and balsam-gardens of Jericho, the iris (orrice-root) and gum-producing storax, for both of which Selge in Pisidia was famous, the trees which supplied the finest of the precious woods that were used for the furniture of the wealthy Romans, and many others, are described, together with their mode of growth and the purposes which they were made to serve. Again, to turn to subjects more immediately connected with man, he gives detailed accounts of engineering works, like the mines in Spain and the canal-system by which the inundations of the Euphrates were checked and its waters utilized; of inventions, such as that of glass by the Phoenicians; and of scientific discoveries, e.g. that of the true calendar by the priests of Heliopolis, and those of arithmetic and astronomy by the Sidonians. The ethnologist and the anthropologist will find in the *Geography* an ample store of facts in the observations it contains on the early history and traditions of numerous peoples, on their dress, their character, their dwellings and mode of life, and their manner of fighting. Finally, the history of religion is largely illustrated by what is there recorded concerning the opinions and forms of worship of castes in all respects widely removed from one another, as of the Druids in Gaul, and of the Brahmans in India, and concerning the great centres of religious observance and ceremonial, such as the two Comanas, and others hardly less important, in Asia Minor, with their orgiastic rites and organized system of temple votaries. Most of the points here referred to will be found illustrated in the following extracts.

Another source of unfailing interest in Strabo's work is found in his love of curiosities. Owing to this a large amount of information has been preserved, which, while it may possibly have only amused his contemporaries, yet to us, with our partial acquaintance with antiquity, is an important source of knowledge. No gazetteer was ever more on the look-out for every thing that could minister to the taste of the general reader. A number of these notices may be grouped under the heading of what at the present day would be called 'sport,' though Strabo himself would hardly have classified them under that title. In the account of Spain we find a description of ferreting, which was largely employed as a remedy for a plague of rabbits that infested the country.[157] In connexion with the Straits of Messina we have a graphic and exciting account, derived from Polybius, of the capture of the sword-fish in that neighbourhood;[158] and elsewhere there are interesting details of the migrations of tunnies between the Mediterranean and the Palus Maeotis. In the Fifteenth Book we read of the methods of hunting and decoying elephants in India, which closely correspond to those that are observed in that country at the present day.[159] The use of crampons in mountain climbing, and tobogganing on the snow-slopes, are described as being familiarly practised in the Caucasus;[160] and the ascents of high summits, like Etna and Argaeus, are noticed, together with the experiences of

those who made them.[161] Other points are of a nature to engage the attention of naturalists—the fish that live embedded in the ice of the Palus Maeotis,[162] the red rock-salt which turns white when pounded,[163] and tidal peculiarities, such as the occurrence of tides at the head of the Adriatic,[164] and the constantly shifting currents of the Euripus at Chalcis.[165] Other students again may be interested in the curious customs which from time to time are noticed, such as the habit of tattooing among the Illyrians and Thracians,[166] the practice of casting malefactors over precipices, with which the story of the Lover's Leap seems to have been connected,[167] the custom of widow-burning in India,[168] and numerous observances in connexion with death and burial.

It is hardly necessary to review in detail the accounts which Strabo has given of the various countries of the then known world, but for the sake of clearness it may be well to notice briefly the contents of the seventeen books which compose his treatise. The first two of these are devoted to the Introduction, in which he states the aim and scope of his work, and the principles on which he conceives that it ought to be composed, and draws attention to the general features which characterize both the entire area and the several continents; he also sets forth his views on mathematical and physical geography, and criticizes at some length the opinions of former geographers on those subjects. After these preliminaries he commences his survey, and in the remaining fifteen books, starting from the west, conducts his readers over the [oik-oumenē], with the Mediterranean Sea for his central point; so that at last, after reviewing successively Europe, Asia, and Africa, he finds himself once more at the western limit of the world. The third book deals with the Iberian peninsula, the fourth with Gaul, including Britain on the one side and the Ligurian sea-coast on the other; the fourth and fifth with Italy and Sicily. Then, before proceeding to Hellenic lands, Strabo retraces his steps, and gives an account in Book VII, as far as his scanty information allows, of the northern and eastern districts of Europe—Germany and the lands which lie between it and the Euxine, the countries to the north of that sea and about the Palus Maeotis, and the region to the south of the Danube, comprising Illyricum, Epirus, Macedonia, and Thrace. The end of this book, which deals with the two last-named countries, is unfortunately lost, and all our knowledge of its contents is derived from epitomes. The three next books (VIII-X) describe respectively the Peloponnese, Northern and Central Greece, and the Greek islands. With the eleventh book we enter Asia, the boundary between which and Europe, according to Strabo, is the Tanais; and here, after noticing the main divisions of that continent, and the chain of the Taurus as its determining geographical feature—including under that name the Himalaya and other mountains which run through it from west to east—he surveys, first the lands which lie between the Euxine and the Caspian and to the eastward of the last-named sea, and afterwards the more central regions of Parthia, Media, and Armenia. Then follow three books (XII-XIV) on Asia Minor, about which, as might be expected in the case of the Geographer's native country, the information given is very full. India and Persia form the subject of the fifteenth book, while the sixteenth comprises the remaining portions of Asia—Assyria, Babylonia, Syria, and Arabia. The seventeenth, which concludes the work, treats of Egypt and of the remainder of Africa.

The Greek of Strabo is usually clear and intelligible, especially in the descriptive portion of his work, for his sentences are seldom long or complicated, and his diction is simple and, as befits the subject, devoid of ornament. But when he comes to discuss disputed questions and investigate doubtful points, he is often involved and obscure, so that it is no easy task to make sure of his meaning, as is shown by the great divergence that is found in the interpretation of such passages by his translators. A further difficulty will be found in the wide range of his vocabulary, which arises from the great variety of subjects of which he treats; and owing to the same cause, and partly also to the change that had passed over the language in the transition from earlier to later Greek, the words are frequently employed in unfamiliar senses—a fact which accounts for the constant recurrence of Strabo's name in Greek lexicons, though notwithstanding this not a few of his meanings are left unexplained.

The fortunes of Strabo's work, in respect of the attention which it has attracted, and the estimates which have been formed of it at different periods, have been strangely chequered. The neglect from which it suffered in antiquity has been already noticed. On this subject a first-rate authority says—'It was certainly in the hands of the learned as early as the time of Athenaeus (about the beginning of the third century), who refers to it in two passages, neither of them having any direct bearing on geography:[169] but its geographical importance is for the first time recognized by Marcianus of Heraclea—a writer who cannot be placed earlier than the third century—who mentions Strabo, in conjunction with Artemidorus and Menippus of Pergamus, as one of the authorities most to be relied on with respect to distances. With this exception we find hardly any reference to it till the time of Stephanus of Byzantium, towards the end of the fifth century, by whom it is frequently cited.'[170] Possibly Harpocration also should be noticed, by whom the *Geography* is twice named. . . . Perhaps Strabo's contemporaries, who possessed works such as those of Artemidorus and Posidonius, from which he largely borrowed, may not have estimated his work as highly as we do. Perhaps also the voluminous nature of the treatise, and the consequent expense involved in copying it, may have restricted the sale; and its publication at Amasia, if this supposition is a true one, would have been unfavourable to its circulation. But the fact remains that it was almost ignored. In the middle ages, however, the case was quite different. To the writers of that period he was known as the geographer *par excellence,* and Eustathius in particular frequently calls him by that name. His popularity at that time is attested by the formation of two chrestomathies of his work. In like manner in modern times Strabo's treatise has been very variously appreciated. To

some writers—notably to Müllenhoff[171]—he seems to be a dull unintelligent compiler; and others, who judge him somewhat more dispassionately, regard his *Geography* as little more than a new edition of the treatise of Eratosthenes. That it was not this is sufficiently proved by a comparison of the size of the two works; for, whereas Strabo's, as we have seen, extended to seventeen books, that of Eratosthenes was comprised in three, and the greater part of these must have been devoted to general views of the subject and technical details of mathematical geography, so that but small space could have been left for minute description, or for the miscellaneous information which Strabo so bountifully supplies. Nor will any one be ready to regard Strabo as a mere compiler, who observes how careful he is to cast his materials into a shape of his own, and to give the result of his comparison of various authorities. In answer to such views it may be sufficient to quote the judgment of some of the greatest authorities of the present century. To pass by our own Lyell, whose opinion will be cited later on in the present volume, Alexander von Humboldt says, 'The gifted geographer of Amasia does not possess the numerical accuracy of Hipparchus, or the mathematical and geographical information of Ptolemy; but his work surpassed all other geographical labours of antiquity by the diversity of the subjects, and the grandeur of the composition.'[172] Lassen also, the great Indian authority, remarks, 'Strabo's work holds a very conspicuous position among the creations of the Greek intellect, both in respect of the fullness of its contents and the thoroughness of its investigations, and of the well-considered arrangement of the matter, and the clearness and gracefulness of its descriptions.'[173] Nor should it be overlooked, as evidencing the judgement of one who never failed to recognize genius, that it was the admiration felt by Napoleon I for this ancient writer, which caused him to authorize the French translation of Strabo by Gossellin, La Porte du Theil, Coray and Letronne (Par. 1805-1819), which, with its introductions, notes and appendices, is the greatest work which has been accomplished for the elucidation of the *Geography.*

In considering the use which Strabo made of the authorities from whom his materials are derived, we are struck both by his sympathies and his antipathies. His devotion to Homer as a source of geographical information was unbounded, so that his judgement is frequently hampered by it in a prejudicial manner. In this, it is true, he was only following the example of most of his predecessors in scientific geography, especially Hipparchus, Polybius, and Posidonius, to whom the Homeric poems had become a sort of Sacred Book, the statements contained in which might not be questioned. Possibly in Strabo's case two other influences may have been at work in increasing his bias in that direction; the first, his Stoic views, for an exaggerated devotion to Homer had become one of the tenets of that sect; the second, his relation to the literary schools of Pergamus and Alexandria, which were at variance as to the extent of the authority to be attributed to the poet, the former maintaining, the latter opposing, his claims to decide questions of general geography. On this subject Strabo ranged himself on the side of the Pergamene school[174], and in consequence of this we find him attacking the statements of Eratosthenes, who had ventured to advance the opposite opinion[175]. But the veneration which he felt for these ancient poems seriously interfered with the execution of parts of his work, especially with the section of it which is devoted to Greece (Books VIII-X). Here the Iliad and the Odyssey are his text books, and his narrative is almost as much a justification of the poet's statements as a description of the country. Indeed it is highly probable that much of what is there introduced is derived from the commentary of Apollodorus on the Homeric catalogue, and that that work, and the similar treatise of Demetrius of Scepsis, were drawn upon, though to a less extent, for his account of Asia Minor (Books XII-XIV). On the other hand, his depreciation of Herodotus as an authority both on geography and history is equally unqualified. Refusing to distinguish the results of observation and inquiry from what was derived from hearsay in his history, he regards him as a mere retailer of fables, in whom no confidence can be reposed[176]. He classes him with Ctesias and Hellanicus, as writers whose statements are less deserving of credence than those of Hesiod and the tragic poets, and who wrote, like them, simply for the amusement of their readers. Tempted by the success of the professed myth-writers, they thought to render their compositions agreeable by putting into the form of history things which they had neither seen nor heard, at least from reliable informants[177]. In the same spirit he pours contempt on the narrative of the early traveller, Pytheas of Massilia, who professed to have visited the north-western shores of the continent of Europe, and described the tribes that inhabited them. In this case there was more excuse for Strabo's disbelief, since in this he was only following Polybius, and the facts retailed by that explorer often appear extravagant; but, notwithstanding this, the tendency of modern opinion is to restore to Pytheas the credit for truthfulness, which the Geographer and the majority of subsequent writers have denied him. Strabo's neglect of Roman authors has already been adverted to, and is certainly remarkable. It has sometimes been explained by the supposition that he was not thoroughly conversant with the Latin language[178], but in the case of one who had spent many years of his life at Rome this seems highly improbable. The reason may with more likelihood be found in the deficiency of Roman literature, not only in the production of systematic treatises on geography, but also in the intelligent description of the natural features of countries. His sense of this may have discouraged him from further investigation of works in that language from which valuable facts might have been gleaned.

Of the authorities whom Strabo used, by far the most important is Eratosthenes; he cites him continually, and from him he derived both the plan of his work, and the greater part of his scientific views. After him come Hipparchus, Polybius, Ephorus, Artemidorus, and Posidonius, all of whom contributed extensive materials for the treatment of various sides of his subject. In particular, it was from Polybius that he derived his interest in historical

geography, and learnt to take a comprehensive view of the history of mankind, and of the earth's surface as the sphere of its operation and as modifying its development. Posidonius furnished him with a large store of observations about the phenomena of physical geography, together with miscellaneous information on numerous subjects, which he had collected in the course of his extensive travels. Of this latter kind also were the valuable contributions of Artemidorus. Besides these, there were numerous other writers on geography, of whose compilations and narratives Strabo availed himself for special countries, and additional details were supplied from local sources. To discuss their merits and the debt which Strabo owed to them respectively is a task beyond the scope of this Introduction, but for the convenience of the reader a list of those who are mentioned in the following extracts is appended. On the general subject of the sources of the *Geography* I may refer to the work of M. Dubois[179], who has treated it more fully than any previous writer.

LIST OF WRITERS ON GEOGRAPHY, WHO ARE
MENTIONED IN THE FOLLOWING EXTRACTS.

1. Anaximander, of Miletus, b. 610 B.C.; philosopher of the Ionian school, and pupil of Thales. He introduced the use of the gnomon into Greece, and was said to have invented geographical maps.

2. Aristobulus; one of the companions of Alexander the Great in his campaigns in Asia, of which he composed a history.

3. Artemidorus, of Ephesus, *circ.* 100 B.C. He travelled extensively, especially about the shores of the Mediterranean, and wrote a treatise on geography, containing much general information, which is frequently quoted by Strabo.

4. Cleitarchus; companion of Alexander, and author of a history of his Asiatic campaigns, which ancient writers did not highly estimate.

5. Demetrius Callatianus, of Callatia in Moesia, date uncertain; wrote a geographical treatise on Europe and Asia in twenty books.

6. Demetrius, of Scepsis, about the middle of the second century B.C.; a Greek grammarian, who wrote a disquisition, historical and geographical, in thirty books, on the Trojan allies mentioned in the Homeric catalogue.

7. Democritus, the philosopher of Abdera, b. *circ.* 460 B.C.; he was an extensive traveller and observer.

8. Dicaearchus, a pupil of Aristotle, *circ.* 320 B.C.; wrote a treatise on general geography, and a topographical description of Greece. He was the first person who attempted to measure the altitude of mountains.

9. Ephorus, of Cume in Aeolis, *circ.* 400 B.C.; wrote a general history in thirty books, two of which were specially

devoted to the geography of Europe, Asia and Africa. Strabo often quotes him, especially with regard to Greece.

10. Eratosthenes, of Cyrene, b. 276 B.C.; the greatest mathematical geographer of antiquity before Ptolemy. His work on geography was comprised in three books, the first of which was introductory, while the second was devoted to mathematical, and the third to political and descriptive geography.

11. Eudoxus, of Cnidos, *circ.* 366 B.C.; a famous astronomer, who also wrote a geographical work, which Strabo several times quotes. The same writer mentions that the observatory of Eudoxus in Cnidos was still shown in his time (17. 1. 30; cp. 2. 5. 14).

12. Hecataeus, of Miletus, *circ.* 520 B.C.; historian and geographer. Herodotus mentions him in connexion with the Ionian revolt against the Persians. He appears to have travelled extensively both in Asia and about the shores of the Mediterranean. His geographical work, which was called [*Gēs periodos*] or [*Periēgēsis*]seems to have embodied all the information on that subject which the Greeks of his time possessed.

13. Hipparchus, *circ.* 150 B.C., the famous astronomer. He divided the known world into *climata,* or zones of latitude.

14. Megasthenes, *circ.* 290 B.C. He was sent by Seleucus Nicator as ambassador to Chandragupta (Sandrocottus) at Pataliputra (Palibothra) on the Ganges. His writings were the chief source from which the knowledge of India which the Greeks and Romans possessed was drawn.

15. Nearchus, one of Alexander's companions in his Eastern expedition. He was appointed in 326 B.C. to command the fleet of that monarch, which descended the Indus, and proceeded from the mouth of that river to the mouth of the Euphrates. His narrative of this expedition has been preserved for us in substance in Arrian's *Indica.* Strabo also borrowed from it, though he censures Nearchus as a retailer of fables (2. 1. 9).

16. Onesicritus, another companion of Alexander and historian of his campaigns. He accompanied Nearchus as second in command on the voyage down the Indus to the Persian Gulf. He was also sent by Alexander to communicate with the Indian Gymnosophists. Strabo severely criticizes his exaggerations.

17. Polybius, the historian, b. *circ.* 204 B.C. He travelled in Spain, Gaul and Africa, and recognized the importance of geography as an aid to history, interspersing his historical narrative with geographical remarks, and devoting one entire book (now lost) to that subject.

18. Posidonius, of Apamea in Syria, b. *circ.* 135 B.C.; a Stoic philosopher who taught at Rhodes. He wrote a continuation of the history of Polybius, and, like that writer, introduced into it numerous geographical notices, accounts of the manners and customs of the peoples whom he had visited, and especially observations on physical phenomena. For all these subjects Strabo was largely indebted to him, especially in connexion with Spain and Gaul, in which countries he had travelled extensively; and from the information which can thus be traced to him we gather that he was one of the most intelligent observers in all antiquity.

19. Pytheas, of Massilia, a navigator and author of travels, of uncertain date, but probably contemporary with Alexander the Great. The scene of his voyages was the western and northwestern coasts of Europe. Strabo treats his statements as unworthy of credit, and his alleged discoveries have often been regarded as fictitious; but the tendency of modern investigation is to rehabilitate him.

20. Straton, of Lampsacus, a Peripatetic philosopher, who became head of that school in 287 B.C. He received the surname of [*ho physikos*] on account of the attention he devoted to the physical branches of philosophy.

21. Theophanes, of Mytilene, *circ.* 60 B.C.; a friend and companion of Pompey, who accompanied him on many of his campaigns, and wrote a history of them. Strabo uses his work especially for the region between the Euxine and the Caspian.

22. Timosthenes, of Rhodes, *circ.* 280 B.C.; admiral of the Egyptian fleet under Ptolemy Philadelphus. He wrote a work on Harbours in ten books, which was apparently designed as a practical guide to the navigator.

23. Xanthus, a Lydian historian, *circ.* 480 B.C.. Strabo quotes him more than once in reference to changes that have taken place on the earth's surface.

A few words may be added as to the text of Strabo. Hardly any other ancient author has suffered so much in respect of the condition in which his writings have been handed down to posterity—a misfortune which is due, we may suppose, in the first instance to the neglect of his work in antiquity, and the rarity of its transcription at an early period, which would be the necessary result of that neglect. In consequence of the limited number of copies that were in circulation, there were hardly any means of checking errors by comparison. As it is, all the existing MSS. are known to be derived from one archetype, for—not to mention other lacunae which universally occur—the latter part of the seventh book is wanting in all of them, though that portion of the work was complete in the MS. from which the Palatine Epitome was made in the tenth or eleventh century. The text has suffered severely also at the hands of unintelligent copyists, as is shown by the frequent recurrence of certain classes of errors, such as the transposition of passages, and the omission or insertion of pronouns, conjunctions, and prepositions, involving a hopeless confusion of syntax. The archetype just mentioned is proved to have been itself exceedingly corrupt by the correspondence in error which prevails in the manuscripts that are derived from it[180]. A further mischance, the ill effects of which were not counteracted until the present century, was the adoption of a singularly bad MS.—Par. No. 1395—for the text of the Aldine edition of 1516, the first that was printed. The mistakes and imperfections which originated in this manner were modified, but only partially remedied, by means of revision and the comparison of other MSS., by Casaubon and subsequent editors. It may be noticed in passing, that it is to Casaubon's edition (C) that reference is always made at the present day, when Strabo's work is quoted by pages. It was reserved for the famous Modern Greek scholar, Coray, at the beginning of the present century, to purge the text of Strabo of its chief errors, and to restore to soundness innumerable corrupt passages. To the extraordinary acuteness of perception and critical insight, which are displayed in his edition of the **Geography** (Par. 1815-19), a high tribute has been paid, both by Groskurd in the Preface to his German translation (vol. 1. p. lviii), and by Dr. C. Müller in the prefatory remarks to his *Index Variae Lectionis* in the Didot edition of Strabo. The latter of these two authorities (p. 940) speaks of him as 'Corayus, vir nunquam satis laudandus, quem unum, modicis licet copiis instructum, plus quam ceteros omnes et praedecessores et successores in Strabone pristino nitori restituendo praestitisse sincerus quisque ingenue profitebitur.' What was wanting to Coray's work was a complete examination of the MSS. of Strabo, with the view of determining their family affinities, and their relative value in the constitution of the text. This task was executed with devoted industry and excellent judgement by Dr. G. Kramer, of Berlin, whose edition in three volumes (1844-52), with its *apparatus criticus* and preface containing an account of the MSS., at once became the groundwork of all future study of the subject. Through him we know that the Paris MS. No. 1397 is the chief authority for the first nine books, which are all that it contains; and that for the remaining books we have mainly to depend on Vat. No. 1329, on the *Epitome Vaticana*, and on Venet. No. 640. The one defect which is traceable in Kramer as an editor is his timidity, or, as it may more correctly be termed, his too great modesty. In consequence of this he has relegated to the notes numerous emendations, which might with advantage have been introduced into the text. Meineke, in his edition, subsequently published (1866-77), has largely occupied himself in embodying these; indeed, if we were to trust his own account of the matter, we should be led to believe that this was the sum of his work, for he says (Pref. p. iv), 'si quid in hac Strabonis editione ad meliorem rationem revocasse judicabor, id totum Kramero deberi lubens fatebor.' But in reality he did much more than this, for he suggested not a few important corrections of his own, and his greater boldness formed an excellent corrective to Kramer's caution—a quality which is of the highest value in textual criticism generally, but is somewhat out of place in dealing with so corrupt a text as that of Strabo. On this subject Meineke remarks (ibid. p. iii)—'cum corruptissimi sint Strabonis codices, in refingenda scriptoris oratione paulo plus libertatis mihi concessum putavi.' In the following selections the text of Meineke's edition has been adopted. At the same time it was impossible to ignore what has been ac-

complished in the way of emendation since it was published; and I have therefore occasionally introduced new readings, though in all such cases the variation from Meineke's text has been noticed. The chief sources of these have been Madvig's *Adversaria Critica*, Cobet's *Miscellanea Critica*, and the selection of recent emendations which is given by Dr. Vogel in vols. 39 and 41 of the *Philologus*. On the general subject of various readings and emendations of Strabo's text, Dr. C. Müller's *Index Var. Lect.* is of the utmost value for the information which it contains up to the time of its publication in 1857; some of his own emendations also, which occur there, are excellent, and will be mentioned from time to time in the following pages.

. . . . .

In writing this Introduction I have made use of the following works:—

Bunbury, *History of Ancient Geography*, vol. 2, chs. 21, 22.

Butzer, *Ueber Strabos Geographica.*

Dubois, *Examen de la Géographie de Strabon.*

Groskurd, *Introduction to German Translation of Strabo.*

Häbler, *Hat Strabo seine Geographie in Rom verfasst?* in *Hermes*, vol. 19.

Hasenmüller, *De Strabonis Geographi Vita.*

Meyer, *Quaestiones Strabonianae.*

————.*Straboniana.*

Niese, *Beiträge zur Biographie Strabos*, in *Hermes*, vol. 13.

————.*Straboniana*, in the *Rheinisches Museum*, Neue Folge, vol. 38.

Otto, *Strabonis . . . Fragmenta*, and *Quaestiones Strabonianae*, in the *Leipziger Studien zur classischen Philologie* vol. 11 (supplement).

Pais, *Straboniana*, in the *Rivista di Filologia classica*, vol. 15.

Ridgeway, art. *Strabo* in *Encyclopaedia Britannica.*

————.*Contributions to Strabo's Biography*, in *Classical Review*, vol. 2. p. 84.

Schröter, *De Strabonis Itineribus.*

————.*Bemerkungen zu Strabo.*

Vogel, *Literaturhistorisches über Strabon*, in *Philologus*, vol. 41. pp. 508-531.

Notes

1. 10. 4. 10.

2. 11. 2. 18.

3. 7. 3. 12.

4. 17. 3. 7 and 25.

5. 12. 8. 11.

6. *Ann.* 4. 36.

7. 7. 1. 4.

8. 6. 4. 2.

9. 14. 1. 48.

10. 12. 3. 16.

11. *Ad Att.* 2. 6. 1.

12. 14. 5. 4.

13. 16. 2. 24.

14. Athen. 14. 75, p. 657.

15. 16. 4. 21.

16. 1. 2. 8; 7. 3. 4.

17. 17. 1. 36.

18. 8. 6. 23.

19. 12. 3. 33.

20. 1. 1. 16.

21. 3. 2. 5.

22. 14. 3. 3; 16. 2. 20.

23. 3. 3. 8.

24. 2. 5. 26.

25. 3. 1. 8; 4. 1. 5.

26. 6. 3. 4.

27. 5. 4. 13.

28. 6. 4. 2.

29. 12. 8. 18; 13. 4. 8; cp. Tac. *Ann.* 2. 47.

30. 10. 5. 3.

31. 8. 6. 23.

32. Dion Cass. 50. 10.

33. 8. 6. 21.

34. 12. 6. 2.

35. 2. 5. 8.

36. Pais, *Straboniana,* in the *Rivista di Filologia classica,* vol. 15, pp. 229, 230.

37. *Ephemeris Epigr.,* vol. 4, p. 34; vol. 5, p. 8; it is bilingual, in Greek and Latin.

38. 17. 1. 9.

39. 15. 1. 73.

40. Dion Cass. 54. 9.

41. Ridgeway in *Class. Review,* vol. 2. p. 84; Bunbury, *Hist. of Anc. Geogr.,* vol. 2. p. 177.

42. 5. 3. 8.

43. 7. 2. 4.

44. *Ann.* 4. 44.

45. 5. 3. 7.

46. 7. 2. 1.

47. 2. 5. 11.

48. These are the following: in Africa ten—Cyrene, Egypt generally, Alexandria, Arsinoë, Heliopolis, Memphis, the Pyramids, Thebes, Syene, Philae; in Asia Minor six—Cappadocia generally, the river Pyramus, Comana, Hierapolis, Ephesus, Nysa; in Europe four—Gyaros, Corinth, Rome, Populonium. See Schröter, *De Strabonis Itineribus* (Leipz. 1874), p. 13, where the references are given. This excellent dissertation has brought together all the information that is obtainable on the subject, but I find myself obliged to differ somewhat widely from the writer in respect of the extent which he assigns to Strabo's travels.

49. 17. 1. 7.

50. 5. 3. 6.

51. 13. 4. 14.

52. 17. 1. 10.

53. 3. 4. 6.

54. 3. 2. 3.

55. 17. 3. 20.

56. 17. 1. 31.

57. 17. 1. 38.

58. 17. 1. 46.

59. 17. 1. 50.

60. 16. 2. 23. . . .

61. 14. 5. 12.

62. 14. 5. 5.

63. See *Hellenic Journal,* vol. 12, pp. 212 foll.

64. 12. 2. 4.

65. 15. 3. 15.

66. 12. 2. 3.

67. 12. 2. 7, 8.

68. 12. 3. 36.

69. 12. 3. 39.

70. 12. 3. 11.

71. 14. 1. 23.

72. 13. 4. 14.

73. 13. 4. 10.

74. 13. 4. 5.

75. 14. 2. 23.

76. 14. 2. 26.

77. 14. 2. 5.

78. 14. 2. 19.

79. 14. 1. 14.

80. 14. 1. 13.

81. 12. 7. 3.

82. 12. 5. 3.

83. 12. 8. 11.

84. 12. 4. 7.

85. 9. 1. 15; 9. 1. 4.

86. 8. 3. 30; Curtius, *Peloponnesos,* vol. 2, p. 114.

87. 8. 6. 10.

88. Pausan. 2. 16. 5-7.

89. 9. 3. 1.

90. 9. 1. 19. The opinion here advanced with regard to Strabo's not having visited Athens is shared by Dr. Vogel (*Philologus,* vol. 41, p. 516) and Professor Mahaffy (*Greek World under Roman sway,* p. 192).

91. 5. 3. 6.

92. 5. 3. 12.

93. 5. 2. 6.

94. 5. 2. 5.

95. 5. 4. 4; 5. 4. 7.

96. 5. 4. 5.

97. 5. 4. 6.

98. 5. 4. 8.

99. 6. 3. 7.

100. 6. 3. 6.

101. 6. 3. 1.

102. 5. 1. 7.

103. 6. 2. 8.

104. 7. 1. 4.

105. Tac. *Ann.* 2. 42.

106. 12. 1. 4.

107. 12. 3. 29.

108. 16. 2. 3; these events, which were the result of Germanicus' progress through those countries, took place in 18 A.D.: see Tac. *Ann.* 2. 56.

109. 1. 1. 21.

110. 1. 1. 17.

111. 3. 4. 19.

112. The Brutus in 14. 2. 25, and a speech now lost in 17. 1. 13.

113. 4. 1. 1.

114. 4. 3. 3.

115. 5. 3. 1.

116. Bunbury, *Hist. of Anc. Geogr.,* vol. 2, p. 217; Dubois, *Examen,* p. 104.

117. 1. 1. 22; cp. 2. 5. 1.

118. 1. 1. 16.

119. 2. 5. 17.

120. 2. 1. 23 and 30.

121. 3. 4. 9.

122. 5. 2. 9.

123. 5. 4. 11.

124. 14. 3. 9.

125. 2. 5. 26.

126. 6. 4. 1.

127. 8. 6. 20.

128. 8. 6. 16.

129. Dubois, *op. cit.,* p. 121.

130. 16. 1. 19; see Butzer, *Ueber Strabo's Geographica,* p. 25.

131. 1. 1. 3.

132. 3. 3. 7.

133. 16. 4. 18.

134. 3. 1. 3.

135. 8. 2. 1.

136. 2. 5. 33.

137. 6. 3. 6; 7. 6. 2.

138. 2. 1. 23.

139. 13. 1. 5.

140. See Butzer, *op. cit.,* pp. 16, 17.

141. 16. 2. 23.

142. 5. 1. 7.

143. 7. 4. 5.

144. 5. 3. 13.

145. 15. 1. 19.

146. 8. 4. 8; Butzer, pp. 17, 18.

147. 14. 2. 21, Extract No. 66.

148. 3. 2. 9, Extract No. 10.

149. 3. 4. 16.

150. 4. 6. 7; Butzer, p. 8.

151. p. 8, note 1.

152. 8. 6. 20.

153. 4. 5. 2.

154. 15. 1. 13.

155. 16. 1. 13.

156. Butzer, pp. 23, 24.

157. 3. 2. 6.

158. 1. 2. 16.

159. 15. 1. 42.

160. 11. 5. 6.

161. 6. 2. 8; 12. 2. 7.

162. 7. 3. 18.

163. 3. 3. 7.

164. 5. 1. 5.

165. 9. 2. 8.

166. 7. 5. 4.

167. 10. 2. 9.

168. 15. 1. 62.

169. Athen, 3, p. 121; 14, p. 657.

170. Bunbury, *Hist. of Anc. Geogr.,* vol. 2, pp. 334, 335.

171. *Deutsche Alterthumskunde,* vol. 1, p. 315.

172. *Cosmos* (Otté's translation), vol. 2, p. 555.

173. *Indische Alterthumskunde,* vol. 2, p. 744.

174. Dubois, *op. cit.,* pp. 176-179.

175. 1. 2. 17, 20.

176. 12. 3. 21; 17. 1. 52.

177. 11. 6. 3.

178. Groskurd, vol. 1, Introd. p. xxxv.

179. *Examen de la Géographie de Strabon,* pp. 153 foll.

180. See Kramer's Preface to his 3 vol. edition, p. lxxxiv.

H. F. Tozer (essay date 1897)

SOURCE: "Strabo" in *A History of Ancient Geography*, Cambridge University Press, 1897, pp. 238-60.

[*In the following essay, Tozer provides an overview of Strabo's life and of the* Geography, *explaining the work's importance and its distinguishing features, and providing an outline of its seventeen books.*]

It may be regarded as a piece of extraordinary good fortune that the most important work on geography which was produced in antiquity should have coincided in date with the Augustan age. The knowledge of the world which the ancients possessed had then almost reached its furthest limits, while the interest which had been awakened by Greek enquirers in the scientific side of the subject had not yet been neutralised, as it was destined soon to be, by utilitarian views of geographical study. At various preceding periods, as we have seen, the different branches of the enquiry had occupied, each in its turn, the most prominent position. In the latter half of the third century before Christ, mathematical geography reached its culminating point at Alexandria under Eratosthenes. The following century saw the rise of historical geography under Roman influences in the hands of Polybius. Later still, the scientific explora-

tions of Posidonius caused the study of physical geography to predominate. It remained that some one should arise, who could sum up the work that had been accomplished in these different lines; and such a writer was found in Strabo. His *Geography,* whatever its defects, is our great repertory of information concerning the knowledge of these subjects which the ancients possessed, and the wide range of his interests guaranteed that none of them should be neglected. In estimating its importance from a modern point of view, we have to take into account not merely its intrinsic merits, but also the greatness of the loss which we should have suffered if it had perished. It is the one complete treatise on geography which has survived from antiquity, and, moreover, we are chiefly indebted to it for our acquaintance with the writings of his predecessors. These are so entirely lost, that they are only known through quotations preserved in other authors, and it is in Strabo that the majority of such passages are found.

Strabo was a native of Amasia in Pontus, a city which was at one time the residence of the sovereigns of that country, and became a considerable centre of Greek culture. The date of his birth has been much disputed, but it was probably 63 B.C., the year of Cicero's consulate[1] The events of his life are almost entirely unnoticed by other writers, and in endeavouring to trace them we are forced to have recourse to statements incidentally introduced in his *Geography.* We find that three prominent teachers of that time took part in his education. When quite a youth, he attended at Nysa on the Maeander the lectures in grammar and rhetoric of Aristodemus, the same who gave instruction to the sons of Pompey. Afterwards he proceeded to Rome, where he was the pupil, first of Tyrannion the grammarian, who superintended the education of Cicero's two sons, Marcus and Quintus, and afterwards of the Peripatetic philosopher Xenarchus. As Tyrannion was an authority on geography, it is not improbable that Strabo imbibed a taste for that subject from him. The remainder of his long life—he seems to have been 84 years of age at the time of his death, or even older—was passed for the most part either in Rome or in Asia Minor. The duration of these sojourns we have no means of determining; but his mention of buildings of recent erection in Rome, and of objects newly introduced there, which he had himself seen, proves that he visited the capital at intervals; and, on the other hand, he is shewn to have returned to Asia Minor, both by his allusions to periods of residence in certain of its cities, and by his exact and observant descriptions of places in various provinces of that region, which imply that he was acquainted with them as a grown-up man. We also know from his own testimony that he dwelt for a long period in Alexandria; and the date of this can be approximately fixed, for it was then that he made the expedition through Egypt, which was the most considerable of his journeys, in the company of his friend and patron Aelius Gallus, who was prefect of the country, and this expedition seems to have taken place in 25–24 B.C.

Widely different opinions have been held as to the extent of Strabo's travels. He claimed for himself that he had journeyed in different directions as far as any other writer on geography—that is to say, from Armenia to the western part of Etruria, and from the Euxine to the confines of Aethiopia[2]; and this may have been literally true. But before we concede to a person the title of a great traveller, it is necessary to estimate the extensiveness of the journeys which were carried out by him within a certain area, and the scientific spirit of research in which they were undertaken. In Strabo's case the conclusion to which we are brought by an examination of the evidence which his work affords as to the places which he visited is that, except in Asia Minor, in Egypt, and in Central Italy, he did not deviate far from the route which he would naturally take in passing to and from his home and the great centres of civilisation in which he resided at different intervals. His journeys into distant lands were determined by the circumstances of his life, rather than by any desire on his part to prosecute researches, or to verify the statements of former writers. In Asia Minor he was well acquainted with the extreme eastern and western districts of the country— with Pontus, Cappadocia, and Cilicia, which were within easy reach of his home at Amasia; and with Western Phrygia, Lydia, Ionia, and Caria, which he had visited either at the time of his education at Nysa or on subsequent occasions. Egypt he had explored at his leisure and thoroughly, as might be expected from the opportunities offered by his residence at Alexandria, and from his having ascended the Nile as far as the First Cataract with Aelius Gallus. In Italy he had become acquainted with the coast-towns of Etruria as far north as the Bay of Luna, and was familiar with Latium and the neighbourhood of the Bay of Naples: he knew also the line of the Appian Way with the ports of Brundisium and Tarentum, and part of the eastern coast of Sicily, of which he would see something when on his way from Rome to Alexandria. Of the rest of the world, however, he had very little knowledge from personal observation. He could hardly have visited even the coast of Syria, otherwise he would not have failed to touch at Tyre; yet, in describing the many-storeyed houses of that city, which, he says, exceeded in height those in Rome, he quotes from other authorities[3]. In Greece there is no clear proof that he stopped at any place except Corinth; and the fulness of detail with which he has delineated that town contrasts strongly with his notices of the rest of the country[4]. The Adriatic coast of Italy was also a *terra incognita* to him; and in consequence of this his account of Ravenna, in particular, is defective, for he relies on earlier authorities, and omits all notice of the great works which were carried out there by the orders of Augustus[5]. The remoter regions of the world, such as Spain or Babylonia, he does not profess to have visited. Still, though Strabo cannot be spoken of as a great traveller in the same sense as Posidonius, it would be a mistake to suppose that his journeys were of small importance to him as a writer on geography. In reality he learnt from them to take a wide view of his subject, to interest himself in a variety of topics and in different peoples, and to get that power of vividly realising and forcibly representing to others the matters he treats of, which can only be obtained from ocular inspection, or at least from familiarity with similar objects. At the same time his mind was trained in the art of observation; and the result of this is that he writes, not as a student in his closet, but as one who was accustomed to notice and to criticise.

A word or two must be added concerning Strabo's philosophical and political opinions, because these make themselves felt from time to time in the course of his work. In philosophy, as two of his instructors, Tyrannion and Xenarchus, were Peripatetic philosophers, it is somewhat surprising to find that he was himself a Stoic. At what period of his life he became an adherent of that school we have no means of ascertaining, but perhaps the change may have been in part due to his intimacy with the Stoic Athenodorus, who was first the teacher, and afterwards the adviser, of Augustus. In consequence of this, his belief in a divinity or in the gods, as far as he possessed any, was pantheistic, and with him the primal agency which caused the organisation of the world was Providence—an impersonal force, which produced the interconnexion of all the parts, and caused its unity and perfection[6]. Accordingly, when the natural features of a country are found to be adapted to the needs of its inhabitants, and to contribute to their development, this is characterised as 'conformity to nature' . . . and is regarded as the 'work of Providence' . . . [7]. The views here expressed, and the terms by which they are represented, are definitely those professed by the Stoics. In politics Strabo was a hearty advocate of the Roman government. He was strongly impressed by the influence of the *pax Romana*—by the safety of life and property in districts formerly disturbed, the security afforded to commerce by the extinction of piracy, and the advantages to civilisation which arose from a central political administration[8]. The same feeling caused him to look favourably on the concentration of the power in the hands of a single ruler; indeed he remarks that an empire of such magnitude could hardly be carried on except under the paternal supervision of one person[9]. So far did these opinions carry him, that he not only regarded the harsh treatment of revolted provinces by the Romans as a form of necessary discipline[10], but he mentions the conquest of his own fatherland, Pontus, by that people with a singular absence of feeling[11].

A considerable part of Strabo's literary life was occupied in writing a work on history, which he called *Historical Memoirs*. . . . This treatise, which seems to have been a continuation of the history of the world from the point where the History of Polybius ended, 146 B.C., is referred to by name by the author himself in his *Geography* and by Plutarch[12]; and it was extensively used both by Josephus and Arrian. Though it no longer exists, it is highly probable that many of the historical notices, which so frequently occur in the *Geography,* are summaries of portions of it. The last-named work was the product of the later period of Strabo's life, but there is no need to assign it, as many writers have done, to a date as far advanced as from 17 to 23 A.D.—a conclusion from which we would gladly escape, because it involves the necessity of believing that a treatise, which is characterised in a high degree by freshness and vigour, was produced by an old man. If we have rightly fixed 63 B.C. as the year of Strabo's birth, he would have been 80 years of age in 17 A.D. The chief argument in favour of the late date is found in the numerous passages in which events are mentioned which took place in the interval between 17 and 23 A.D.; but the occurrence of these does not necessitate the conclusion that the work at large was composed at that time. It seems more probable, especially when we consider the magnitude of the task, that its execution extended over a long period, and that it was brought up to date by the insertion of subsequent incidents at a later period. This supposition also may serve to some extent to account for the marked inequality of style and treatment which is traceable in various parts of the *Geography.* A more difficult question arises when we attempt to determine the place at which it was written. The alternative here lies between Rome on the one hand, and on the other some provincial residence, such as Strabo's native city Amasia. The arguments in favour of the former of these turn mainly on the intimate acquaintance which the writer shews, until quite the end of his life, with events that were passing at the capital, and with occurrences affecting the Roman empire, which might not be expected to reach the ears of provincials. His knowledge of these is very striking; and, however much allowance we may make for the rapid circulation of news at this time and the consequent facility of obtaining information, it might turn the scale in favour of Rome as the place where the work was composed, or at least completed, were it not for one overpowering argument on the other side. This is derived from the extraordinarily slight recognition which it met with in antiquity, so that it is not even named by so diligent a compiler as Pliny. Considering the merits and importance of the work, this would seem almost impossible if it had been published in a great literary centre such as Rome; whereas the difficulty disappears, if we suppose it to have seen the light in a remote place like Amasia.

Another point which calls for consideration as affecting our estimate of the *Geography,* is the class of readers for whom it was intended. On this subject Strabo's own statements appear to be somewhat misleading. He says at the commencement of his treatise that the object of geographical study is that it should be of service to men in high position—in other words, to the Roman generals and statesmen, to whom were assigned the conquest and administration of provinces[13]; and this view he confirms by other remarks to the same effect. A perusal of his work, however, suggests the idea that these introductory observations are of the nature of an advertisement, intended to attract Roman readers. Its contents are by no means of such a character as specially to suit the needs of imperial officials. His elaborate disquisitions on mythology, his long historical notices, his enumerations of philosophers and literary men produced by different cities, and his descriptions of physical phenomena, seem intended to interest a very different class of persons. The truth of the matter seems to be that Strabo, while he wished to be read by Romans, expected rather to be read by Greeks; but he wrote neither for the one nor for the other exclusively, but for cultivated men without reference to their nationality. His treatise as a whole is congenial both to the practical ideas of the one people, and to the scientific spirit of the other; and he says himself that he intends it to be popular, and adapted to 'the general course of study which is pursued by free-born and cultured men[14].'

The conspicuous merit of Strabo's work is its comprehensiveness. He aimed at bringing together, and exhibiting in a readable form, all that it was important to know about the different countries of the earth and their inhabitants, and in this respect his *Geography* was unique in antiquity. All the four branches, into which, as we have seen in our first chapter, the subject divides—mathematical, physical, descriptive, and historical geography—are represented in his pages. In speaking of each district, he deals with the conformation of the ground, the nature of the products, the character and condition of the inhabitants, their history, and similar topics: and in doing this he does not confine himself within the range of what we call classical antiquity, for he includes in his review the whole of the ancient world and its occupants, whether barbarous or civilised. The variety of the subjects which he incidentally introduces greatly enhances the interest of his survey. Geological peculiarities have an especial attraction for him. Not only has he furnished us with a large collection of facts relating to volcanoes and earthquake movements, but he notices other strange features of the ground, such as the rolled stones of the Plaine de la Crau (Campi Lapidei) in southern France[15]. Climate also is a topic to which he often refers. He dwells on the cloudy, sunless atmosphere of Britain[16], and the monsoons and the rainy season in India[17]; and he remarks that the amount of snow that falls is greater, and the snow-line is lower, on the northern side of a range of mountains than on the southern[18]. On the subject of trees and plants he contributes a great variety of information; thus he describes the palm-groves and balsam-gardens of Jericho, the papyrus and the Egyptian bean, and the trees which supplied the precious woods that were used for furniture at Rome. He also paid great attention to the mode of life, the habitations and dress, and the traditions of numerous half-civilised peoples; and to the religious beliefs and rites which prevailed in various parts of the world—as, for instance, at the two Comanas in Eastern Asia Minor, and among the Druids in Gaul, and the Brahmans in India. On matters, too, which belong to a higher sphere of intelligence his work furnishes interesting observations; such as works of art, the opinions of philosophic schools, and scientific discoveries, *e.g.* that of the true calendar by the priests of Heliopolis in Egypt.

Among these various departments of geographical study the one which predominates in Strabo's work is undoubtedly the historical. Not only does he everywhere introduce the history of a country side by side with its geography, but he illustrates the one by the other, and endeavours to point out the intimate connexion that existed between the two. In describing the pass of the Climax on the coast of Lycia he refers to the danger to which Alexander's troops were exposed in traversing it[19]. The mention of the lines of Roman roads through eastern Spain recalls Caesar's march along them before the battle of Munda[20]; and so on throughout the entire work. Besides this he is fond of tracing the influence of the features of a land on the character and history of its inhabitants. A noticeable instance of this is his discussion of the manner in which the physical peculiarities of Italy contributed to the development of the power of Rome. In this he dwells on the advantages which that country derived in respect of safety from its peninsular character, which secured it against attack, and in respect of commerce from its excellent harbours; on its varied and temperate climate, and the difference of elevation in different parts, which caused it to enjoy the products both of the mountains and the plains; on its plentiful water-supply, and ample provision of the necessaries of life; and finally, on its central position among the great races of the ancient world[21]. Remarks such as these, in which the modifying power exercised by external nature over the history of man is traced, are the most original feature in Strabo's work, and go far to justify the title of 'The Philosophy of Geography,' which has been applied to it. Though similar notices occur from time to time, as we have seen, both in Ephorus and Polybius, yet no ancient writer except Strabo has systematically followed out and generalised on the working of these influences.

Another feature of the *Geography* which distinguishes it from other works on the same subject, besides its many-sidedness, is the artistic spirit in which it was composed. This becomes most apparent, if we compare it with the lists of names which are crowded together in the geographical section of Pliny's *Natural History,* or with the dry details which make up the treatise of Ptolemy. In contrast with these, the facts which are brought together in Strabo's well-arranged chapters are skilfully grouped, in a manner which clearly shews that in combining so great a variety of materials the form as well as the matter has been considered. With a view to this, the accumulation of names which appeared to the author to be either superfluous or barbarous in sound is avoided, as for instance in the case of the Arabian tribes, some of which he purposely omits on account of the vulgarity and clumsiness of their pronunciation[22]. A treatise on general geography, he says, is a colossal work, and in this, as in a colossal statue, insignificant minutiæ, which would detract from the general effect, should be neglected[23]. For the same reason Strabo endeavours to lighten the reader's task by enlivening his narrative in various ways. Ascents of high mountains, such as Etna and Mount Argaeus in Cappadocia, are noticed, together with the observations of those who made them. Sporting experiences are recorded; thus ferreting is mentioned as having been employed in Spain as a remedy for a plague of rabbits[24], and the methods of hunting and decoying elephants in India are described[25]. No opportunity is missed of introducing a good story, and the proverbs and proverbial expressions that occur are very numerous. Comparisons, again, some of which are remarkably apposite, are used to illustrate geographical features. The Peloponnese is likened in shape to the leaf of a plane-tree[26]; the Oases in the Libyan desert to the spots on a leopard's skin[27]; the Trojan Ida, with its long range and numerous spurs, to a millepede[28]. Many of these, no doubt, were borrowed from other writers, but Strabo's skill is shewn by the way in which he makes use of them. He also enlarges the reader's view by drawing attention to the resemblances which are traceable between districts and features of the ground in different countries. Ravenna and Alexandria are compared in respect of their healthiness, notwithstanding the shallow water in their neighbourhood[29]; the intermittent streams are noticed by which the Lacus Fucinus in Latium and the river Amenanus in Sicily were fed[30]; and the saying is quoted, in which the Acrocorinth and the acropolis of Messene on Mount Ithome were spoken of as the two horns by which the cow (the Peloponnese) might be held[31]. In these and other ways the texture of the work is diversified, and the materials of which it is made up are enriched, and thus the composition at large is raised to a higher level.

The estimates which have been formed of Strabo's work, and the attention which it attracted, have varied greatly at different periods. We have already noticed the neglect from which it suffered in antiquity, as shewn by the absence of any mention of it by the writers of the succeeding age. Athenaeus (about the beginning of the third century) refers to it in two passages, but neither of these has any direct bearing on geography: its geographical importance is first recognised by Marcianus of Heraclea—a writer who cannot be placed earlier than the third century—who mentions Strabo as one of the authorities most to be relied on with respect to distances. With this exception we hardly find any reference to it till the time of Stephanus of Byzantium, towards the end of the fifth century, by whom it is frequently cited[32]. During the middle ages, however, exactly the opposite of this was the case. To the writers of that time he was known as *the* geographer, and Eustathius in particular frequently quotes him by that title. Again, in modern days a great discrepancy of opinion has existed with regard to Strabo's merits. Some authorities, among whom Müllenhoff is the most conspicuous, have treated him as a dull, unintelligent compiler. Others, who refrain from passing so sweeping a condemnation, regard his *Geography* as little more than a new edition of the work of Eratosthenes. This view, however, is sufficiently disproved by a comparison of the size of the two treatises, for whereas Strabo's ran to the length of seventeen books, that of Eratosthenes was comprised in three, and only a portion of the last of these was devoted to descriptive geography. Indeed, however much Strabo may have been indebted to others for his materials, his independence of judgment is shewn by his carefulness in comparing his authorities and balancing their statements, and by the trouble which he takes to cast the facts which he collects in a mould of his own. A more impartial, though at the same time a laudatory, estimate is furnished by one whose encyclopædic studies specially qualified him to pass judgment on such a subject—Alexander von Humboldt. "The gifted geographer of Amasia," he says, "does not possess the numerical accuracy of Hipparchus, or the mathematical and geographical information of Ptolemy; but his work surpassed all other geographical labours of antiquity by the diversity of the subjects, and the grandeur of the composition[33]."

As the object of Strabo's work was to furnish a survey of the whole of the habitable world that was known in his day, the extent of the area which it included and the limits within which it was restricted can be sufficiently inferred from what we have already seen of the knowledge of the subject which was possessed by the Greeks under the successors of Alexander, and of the additions which were made to it by the advance of the Roman arms. In western Europe, Spain and Gaul as far as the coast of the Atlantic, and the south-eastern part of Britain, were fairly well known; but towards the north the Elbe and the Danube still marked the limit of accurate geographical knowledge. Something more might have been added concerning the lands and seas in that direction from the narrative of Pytheas, had not Strabo been strongly impressed with the untruthfulness of that writer; and a similar mistrust of Herodotus, whom he regarded as a mere retailer of fiction, caused the same thing to happen with regard to the countries northward of the Euxine, from Strabo's account of which the valuable information furnished by the old historian is excluded. The lands on the further side of the Palus Maeotis were also unexplored, but the chain of the Caucasus and the regions to the southward of it between the Black Sea and the Caspian had become known through the narrative of Theophanes. The Caspian was still believed to communicate with the Northern Ocean, and beyond it the Jaxartes remained, as it was in the days of Alexander, the limit of discovery. In India the peninsula of Hindostan continued to be unknown, and the Ganges was regarded as flowing into the eastern ocean. The Cinnamon country and the territory of the Sembritae about the upper Nile were the southernmost points that Strabo was acquainted with in Africa, and no one had penetrated into the interior of that continent beyond the land of the Garamantes. The student of the geography of the Augustan age requires further to be reminded, that not a little of the information contained in Strabo's work dates from a period earlier than that era. In some instances, as notably in that of Ravenna, which we have already mentioned, this arises from the author not having availed himself of the latest sources of evidence; but to a great extent it was unavoidable. In writing of India, for instance, he was obliged to follow the narrative of persons who wrote some centuries before his age; and the same thing was the case in a lesser degree with regard to various other countries. Under such circumstances the writer is not in fault, for he can but make the best of the materials that are available; but his work cannot fail to suffer from a certain amount of anachronism.

We may now proceed to consider briefly the contents of Strabo's work. The two first books are devoted to an Introduction, in which he states the aim and scope of his treatise and the principles on which he conceives that it ought to be composed, and draws attention to the general features which characterise both the entire area of the world and the several continents. In this part also he sets forth his views on mathematical and physical geography. His treatment of the former of these is the least satisfactory portion of his book, for he deals with it unsystematically in the form of controversy with Eratosthenes, Hipparchus, and others who had preceded him in that study. In criticising them, however, he betrays his own inferiority, so that not infrequently he either misunderstands their views, or is himself in error. On the other hand, his remarks on physical geography are of great value. He has brought together a large amount of material to throw light on the changes which have passed over the face of the earth owing to the retirement of the sea, and to earthquakes and volcanic eruptions; and he discusses the causes which have brought these to pass. The two main principles which he enunciates as his own are mentioned with high praise by Sir Charles Lyell, as being anticipations of the latest conclusions of modern science. These are (1) the importance of drawing inferences with regard to the more extensive physical changes from those which take place on a lesser scale under our own eyes; and (2) the theory of the alternate elevation and depression of extensive areas[34]. With regard to the shape of the inhabited world he followed the view of Eratosthenes, who described it as forming an irregular oblong with tapering extremities towards the east and west. This figure Strabo compares to the chlamys, or Greek mantle, which was rectangular in outline, and usually about twice as long as it was broad, with a gore, or triangular piece, attached to either extremity[35]. For geographical purposes this oblong area was supposed to be inscribed within a parallelogram, the sides of which were drawn so as to pass through its extreme limits. He also introduces a number of remarks, of great interest from the point of view of historical geography, on the shape of the three continents into which this area was divided, and the superiority of Europe to the other two as a habitation for man. Europe, he remarks, is very varied in its outline, and Africa forms a contrast to it from its uniformity, while Asia in this respect holds an intermediate position between them. The advantage of this multiplicity of form consists in the facilities of communication which it affords to the inhabitants, and from this the historical interest of such countries arises. Europe is also more favourable to the development of character from its temperate climate, its equal distribution into mountains and plains, which supply respectively a warlike and a peaceful element to the population, and its furnishing its occupants with the necessaries of life rather than superfluities and luxuries[36].

The second and third books treat of the western countries of Europe—Spain, Gaul, and Britain. For Spain the principal authorities on whom Strabo relies are Polybius, Artemidorus, and Posidonius, all of whom had visited that country, but Posidonius' information was far the most valuable, on account of his intimate acquaintance with the remote parts of the interior. The same traveller furnished him with the chief materials for his account of Gaul and Britain, but these he was able to supplement from the writings of Cæsar. The geographer's idea of the coast-line of these countries was in several respects faulty, for he regarded the Sacrum Promontorium (Cape St. Vincent), instead of the Magnum Promontorium (Cabo da Roca) near the mouth of the Tagus, as the westernmost point of Spain, and he ignored the deep recess in the coast formed by the Bay of Biscay, and the projection of the Armorican peninsula, so that he conceived of the coast of Gaul in this part as stretching along almost in a continuous line, with that of Britain opposite to it. He also erroneously supposed, like the other geographers of his time, that the direction followed by the Pyrenees was from north to south; but in other respects his general idea of the geographical features of these countries was accurate. He was acquainted with the five great rivers of Spain which flow towards the Atlantic—the Baetis (Guadalquivir), the Anas (Guadiana), the Tagus, the Durius (Douro), and the Minius (Minho)—and with the Iberus (Ebro), which reaches the Mediterranean. He knew also the watershed which divides these, and which gradually rises as it advances southward, until it joins the Sierra Nevada; and he was aware that along the northern coast there was a mountain region between the Pyrenees and Cape Finisterre. In Gaul he draws especial attention to the completeness of the river system, in which respect that country has greater advantages than any other in Europe, and to the easy communication which existed between one river-basin and another, and the consequent facilities which were provided for trade routes[37]. Very effective, too, is the contrast here presented by the advanced civilisation of the province of Baetica, which at this time was completely Romanised, and the primitive condition of the tribes in the centre and north of Spain; and the leading features of character of the Iberian race in that land, and of the Celtic tribes in Gaul, are interestingly delineated. We find here also a striking description of the two famous cities of Gades and Massilia, both in respect of their sites and of the condition of their inhabitants. It gives us an impressive idea of the commerce of Gades, when we are told that the greater part of its population was to be found, not in the place itself, but on the sea[38]: and in the account of Massilia we find a sketch of its political constitution, to which Aristotle had devoted a treatise, and a notice of its learning and its schools, which caused it to become a Greek university for southern Gaul[39].

Italy and Sicily are the subject of the fifth and sixth books. Here again Strabo is greatly indebted to Posidonius, though no small part of his material was derived from his own observation and researches, or from Agrippa's wall-map and its accompanying commentary—for this seems to be what is meant by the 'Chorography,' to which he frequently refers. He commences with a true conception of the Alps, which formed the northern boundary of this area, for he describes them as starting from the same neighbourhood as the Apennines, at Vada Sabatia (Vado) to the westward of Genoa, and extending thence to the head of the Adriatic in a great curve, the concave side of which is turned towards Italy[40]. He traces the lines of the chief Roman roads, with the cities that lay in their neighbourhood; and

in consequence this portion of his work is somewhat overcrowded with names—an unavoidable result, since their importance forbade their omission. Owing to the prevalence of volcanic action in this part of Europe, numerous references are here introduced to this class of phenomenon. The islands in the Bay of Naples, and Vesuvius, which, though quiescent at that time, gave evidence in its appearance of its former activity; the Aeolian (Lipari) islands and Etna; and other features, such as the jets of volcanic gas in the lake of the Palici in the interior of Sicily, are described[41]; and many interesting details are communicated, especially about Etna, the formation of the lava beds of which, and the changes in the form of its crater, are noticed[42]. As might be expected from Strabo's lengthened residence in Rome, full details are furnished about Latium and Campania; and his graphic descriptions of Tibur, Praeneste, and the Alban Hills, of the Pomptine marshes, of the Lake Avernus and the Lucrine Lake, and of the artificial harbours of Puteoli, which was at that time the most important city of Italy after Rome, give clear evidence of personal observation. Not less valuable is the account of Naples as a place of literary leisure, and of the traditional Hellenic culture which survived there; elsewhere also he tells us that that city was the only place in South Italy besides Tarentum and Rhegium where Greek was spoken in his age[43]. It was no part of his plan to enter into elaborate details about the famous edifices of Rome, and the only building there which is delineated with any minuteness is the Mausoleum of Augustus, which would seem to have been the sight of the day. But his general remarks on the public works in the capital—the roads, aqueducts and sewers—are excellent; and the same thing may be said of his sketch of the Campus Martius, with the bright scene afforded by the races and other sports to which it was devoted, the works of art in its neighbourhood, and the handsome structures which were beginning to encroach upon it[44]. They enable us forcibly to realise the impression made on an intelligent stranger by Rome in the Augustan age.

From Italy, before proceeding to Greece, Strabo retraces his steps northward, and in his seventh book gives an account, as far as his scanty information allows, of the northern and eastern districts of Europe—Germany and the lands between it and the Euxine, the countries to the north of that sea and about the Palus Maeotis, and the region to the south of the Danube, comprising Illyricum, Epirus, Macedonia, and Thrace. In treating of the northern part of this area he availed himself of the intelligence which had been recently obtained through the campaigns of Drusus and Germanicus, and he remarks in an interesting manner on the nearness of the upper waters of the Danube and the Rhine[45]: but, as we have already seen, his knowledge of the north of Europe was unnecessarily limited, owing to his mistrust of Pytheas and Herodotus. All the more striking in consequence of this is the accurate account which he has given of the Tauric Chersonese[46] (Crimea); his acquaintance with this was due in great measure to the narratives which existed of the expeditions of Mithridates in those parts, and of his ultimate occupation of the country. In the latter part of this book there is a sketch of the topography of Actium, Nicopolis, and the entrance of the strait, which was the scene of the famous battle[47]; and also of that of the Thracian Bosporus and the Golden Horn, together with a graphic account of the tunny-fishing which took place there[48]. The concluding chapters, which dealt with Macedonia and Thrace, are unfortunately lost, and our knowledge of their contents is derived from epitomes; this, however, is the only portion of the entire treatise which is wanting.

Strabo's next three books are devoted to Greece; the eighth to the Peloponnese, the ninth to northern Greece, the tenth to the islands, both those to the west, and those to the east of the continent. There is a want of thoroughness in this part, which causes it to be the least satisfactory section of the *Geography.* The chief reason for this is to be found in Strabo's extravagant veneration for Homer as a geographical authority. In this he was only following the example of most of his predecessors, especially Hipparchus, Polybius, and Posidonius, to whom the Homeric poems had become a sort of Sacred Book, the statements contained in which might not be questioned; and Eratosthenes, who opposed the view that points in general geography were to be determined in accordance with the poet's expressions, became the object of attacks in consequence. In Strabo's case two other influences tended to increase his bias in that direction—one his Stoic opinions, for an excessive devotion to Homer had become one of the tenets of that sect: the other his connexion with the literary school of Pergamus, which was now at feud with that of Alexandria on this very question, and maintained the more advanced estimate of the Homeric claims. In consequence of this Strabo's judgment was hampered in a prejudicial manner, and in describing Greece he makes Homer his text-book, and employs himself chiefly with the examination of his geographical statements. Even his general information seems to have been to a great extent derived from commentators, such as Apollodorus and Demetrius of Scepsis, rather than from writers on topography. He made use, however, of the geographical treatise of Ephorus, to which he refers in several passages. Fortunately, the remarkable physical geography of Greece attracted his attention, and he has left us interesting notices, not only of the striking conformation of land and sea which distinguishes its coasts, but also of the subterranean drainage of particular districts, especially the Arcadian valleys and the basin of the Copaic lake. His principal error in this part relates to the position of the promontory of Sunium, which he supposed to extend nearly as far south as that of Malea[49].

In his eleventh book Strabo conducts us into Asia, the boundary between which and Europe according to him is the Tanais. He first notices the main divisions of that continent, and the chain of the Taurus as its leading geographical feature, including under that name the Himalaya and other mountains which run through it from west to east; and then surveys, first the lands which lie between the Euxine and the Caspian and to the eastward of the last-named sea, and afterwards the more central regions of Parthia, Media, and Armenia. In his general geography of Asia he adopts Eratosthenes as his authority, while for the western part of the area which is specially treated in this book he relies on the historians of the Mithridatic wars, and for the eastern on Patrocles and the companions of Alexander. We have already noticed the fulness of his account of the districts of Iberia and Albania, and of the tribes inhabiting them, which is borrowed from Theophanes; and we are also indebted to him for an accurate description both of the mountain system of Western Asia, and of the upper courses of the Euphrates and Tigris. He represents the Taurus—here using that term in its more restricted sense—as running through the south of Asia Minor, and at the eastern extremity of that country throwing off the Anti-Taurus to the north, and the Amanus, the commencement of the chains of Syria and Palestine, to the south; then, as it pursues its course towards the east, forming a marked boundary between Armenia and Mesopotamia, into both which countries it ramifies, and increasing in elevation until it culminates in Mount Niphates, near the brackish lake Arsene[50] (Lake of Van). As regards the rivers—Strabo was not aware of the fact, which modern geography has taught us, that both the Euphrates and the Tigris have two sources, and flow for a considerable distance in two separate streams[51]: he confines the name Euphrates to the western branch of that river, the modern Frat, which rises near Erzeroum; and the only stream which he recognises as the Tigris is its eastern branch, the river of Bitlis, with which Xenophon also had identified it. But he rightly remarks, that the Euphrates rises in the north, the Tigris in the south of the Taurus, *i.e.* of Armenia; and he carefully distinguishes the provinces—Sophene, Commagene and others—between which the Euphrates flows in this part of its course[52].

As the geographer was a native of Asia Minor, it is only natural that he should pay especial attention to that part of the world, and accordingly we find that he devotes to it three books—the twelfth, thirteenth, and fourteenth. The contents of these are of great value, both because the writer is frequently drawing on his own observation, and also on account of the rich store of information which they provide about the physical geography and products of the country, and the religious and political condition of the people. These points may best be illustrated by a few examples. Strabo notices the absence of trees in Cappadocia, a feature of which he furnishes the explanation when he says that this country, though lying further south than Pontus, is the colder of the two[53]. He also enlarges on the volcanic activity which at that period still existed about the sides and base of Mount Argaeus in that province, and on the strange craters of the Katakekaumene, or Burnt Country, in Western Phrygia[54]. He mentions the valuable red earth, which was called 'Sinopic earth,' because it was brought down from the interior to Sinope for export[55]; and the gum of the storax-tree and the 'orris-root,' which were found at Selge in Pisidia[56]. Observations, also, are frequently introduced on the strange religious worship that prevailed in Asia Minor, with its orgiastic rites, the numerous votaries that were attached to the temples, and the elaborate festival processions[57]. Finally, the study of political constitutions is illustrated by the descriptions that are given of the federation which was known as the Lycian League[58], of the tetrarchies of the Galatae with their elaborate system of government[59], and of the municipal organisation that was established at Ephesus[60].

The remainder of Asia—that is, in the main, the lands which lie to the southward of the dividing mountain chain—is treated of in the fifteenth and sixteenth books; the former embracing the eastern portion—India, Persia, and the intervening districts; the latter the countries to the west of these—Assyria, Syria, and Arabia. His account of India, which is very interesting, is compiled from the only authorities that existed at that time—the narratives of Nearchus, Aristobulus, Onesicritus, and others, who accompanied Alexander on his eastern expedition, and the treatise of Megasthenes—and its contents have already been noticed in connexion with them. For Ariana and Persia, too, sufficient materials were forthcoming from the writings of Alexander's contemporaries and successors, and these had already been reduced to a geographical form by Eratosthenes. In describing Persia, Strabo rightly distinguishes according to their climates the three regions into which that country is divided between the coast of the Persian Gulf and the Median uplands: the first being a parched and sandy tract, where only the datepalm flourished; the next a well-watered and fertile district of the interior, abounding in plains and lakes; while the northernmost was mountainous and cold[61]. In the section which is devoted to Babylonia there is an elaborate account of the system of canals by which that country was intersected[62]. These were rendered necessary by the periodical inundations of the Euphrates, which were caused by the melting of the snows on the Armenian highlands; and they served, not only to divert the surplus water from the river, but also as reservoirs in which the water could be stored, so as to be used for irrigation during the dry season. Accordingly, they were not mere channels cut in the soil, but capacious water-courses, elevated on huge embankments to a considerable height above the surface of the ground; and the methods are here described by which they were cleared from the silt which accumulated in them, and were also closed by raising a dam, when they were to be used as reservoirs. As we approach nearer to the Mediterranean, the historical interest of the narrative increases. The cities of Phoenicia, from their remarkable sites, their famous commerce, and the scientific discoveries and inventions which proceeded from them, naturally attracted the geographer's attention; and he also notices the peculiar features of the Dead Sea[63], and the palm-groves and balsam-gardens of Jericho[64], which were presented to Cleopatra by Antony, and were first farmed for her, and then redeemed for himself, by Herod the Great. To judge from the accounts of Palestine which are given by Pliny and Tacitus, as well as by Strabo, the balsam-tree and the Dead Sea seem to have been the objects in that country which chiefly attracted the attention of the Roman world in ancient times. The description of Arabia, with which this part of the work concludes, is as complete as the knowledge of that age allowed, and embodies the additional information on the subject which Agatharchides had collected. Strabo also relates the events of the campaign which Aelius Gallus prosecuted in that country at the command of Augustus, but in respect of geography that expedition did not add much to what was already known.

The last book of the *Geography* is devoted to Africa, and the larger portion of it is occupied with an account of Egypt, of which country, as we have seen, Strabo had personal knowledge. He commences with a description of Alexandria, which is the most elaborate notice of any city that is found in his work[65]—an honour which it fully deserved from its importance as a commercial, geographical, and scientific centre. The other famous places in Egypt are briefly depicted, in accordance with the author's rule of confining his work within the limits which he originally assigned to it; but his narrative in these parts is sometimes enlivened by personal experiences, such as his inspection of the bull Apis at Memphis[66], his witnessing the feeding of the sacred crocodile at Arsinoë[67], and his own trepidation, when being ferried across on a frail raft to the island of Philae[68]. Concerning the course of the Nile to the southward of that place he is able to furnish some fresh information from the expedition of C. Petronius in Aethiopia[69]. The remainder of Africa is somewhat briefly treated, and Strabo was not aware of the marked projection formed by the northern coast near Carthage opposite Sicily. About Mauretania he might have had more to say, if he had used the treatise of his contemporary Juba, but with that work he does not seem to have been acquainted.

Notes

1. For the evidence which bears on this and similar points relating to Strabo reference may be made to the Introduction to the author's *Selections from Strabo*.

2. Strabo, 2. 5. 11.

3. 16. 2. 23.

4. 8. 6. 20-23.

5. 5. 1. 7.

6. 17. 1. 36.

7. 4. 1. 14.

8. 1. 1. 16.

9. 6. 4. 2.

10. 5. 4. 13.

11. 12. 3. 33.

12. 1. 1. 23; 11. 9. 3; Plutarch, *Lucull.* 28.

13. 1. 1. 18.

14. 1. 1. 22; cp. 2. 5. 1.

15. 4. 1. 7.

16. 4. 5. 2.

17. 15. 1. 13.

18. 16. 1. 13.

19. 14. 3. 9.

20. 3. 4. 9.

21. 6. 4. 1.

22. 16. 4. 18.

23. 1. 1. 3.

24. 3. 2. 6.

25. 15. 1. 42.

26. 8. 2. 1.

27. 2. 5. 33.

28. 13. 1. 5.

29. 5. 1. 7.

30. 5. 3. 13.

31. 8. 4. 8.

32. Bunbury, *Hist. of Anc. Geogr.,* 2, pp. 334, 335.

33. *Cosmos* (Otte's trans.), vol. 2. p. 555.

34. Lyell, *Principles of Geology,* vol. I. pp. 24, 25; Strabo, 1. 3. 5, 10.

35. 2. 5. 14.

36. 2. 5. 18, 26.

37. 4. 1. 14.

38. 3. 5. 3.

39. 4. 1. 5.

40. 4. 6. 1; 5. 1. 3.

41. 6. 2. 9.

42. 6. 2. 3, 8.

43. 6. 1. 2.

44. 5. 3. 8.

45. 7. 1. 5.

46. 7. 4.

47. 7. 7. 6.

48. 7. 6. 1, 2.

49. 2. 1. 40.

50. 11. 12. 2; 11. 14. 8.

51. *v. supra,* p. 114.

52. 11. 12. 3.

53. 12. 2. 7, 10.

54. 12. 2. 7; 13. 4. 11.

55. 12. 2. 10.

56. 12. 7. 3.

57. 12. 2. 3; 12. 3. 31, 32, 36, 37.

58. 14. 3. 3.

59. 12. 5. 1.

60. 14. 1. 21.

61. 15. 3. 1.

62. 16. 1. 9, 10.

63. 16. 2. 44.

64. 16. 2. 41.

65. 17. 1. 6-10, 13.

66. 17. 1. 31.

67. 17. 1. 38.

68. 17. 1. 50.

69. 17. 1. 54.

John Robert Sitlington Sterrett (essay date 1917)

SOURCE: An introduction to *The Geography of Strabo,* Vol. I, G. P. Putnam's Sons, 1917, pp. xi-xviii.

[*In the following essay, Sterrett discusses Strabo's ancestors, education, political views, and the scope and purpose of his travels.*]

What is known about Strabo must be gleaned from his own statements seattered up and down the pages of his *Geography;* this is true not merely of his lineage, for we also learn much by inference concerning his career and writings. Dorylaus, surnamed Tacticus or the General, is the first of the maternal ancestors of Strabo to be mentioned by him, in connexion with his account of Cnossus (10. 4. 10). This Dorylaus was one of the officers and friends of Mithridates Euergetes, who sent him on frequent journeys to Thrace and Greece to enlist mercenary troops for the royal army. At that time the Romans had not yet occupied Crete, and Dorylaus happened to put in at Cnossus at the outbreak of a war between Cnossus and Gortyna. His prestige as a general caused him to be placed in command of the Cnossian army; his operations resulted in a sweeping victory for Cnossus, and great honours were heaped upon him in consequence. At that juncture Euergetes was assassinated at Sinope, and as Dorylaus had nothing to hope for from the widowed queen and young children of the dead king, he cast in his lot permanently with the Cnossians. He married at Cnossus, where were born his one daughter and two sons, Lagetas and Stratarchas. Their very names indicate the martial proclivities of the family. Stratarchas was already an aged man when Strabo saw him. Mithridates, surnamed Eupator and the Great, succeeded to the throne of Euergetes at the early age of eleven years. He had been brought up with another Dorylaus, who was the nephew of Dorylaus the general. When Mithridates had become king, he showed his affection for his playmate Dorylaus, by showering honours upon him, and by making him priest of Ma at Comana Pontica—a dignity which caused Dorylaus to rank immediately after the king. But not content with that, Mithridates was desirous of conferring benefactions upon the other members of his friend's family. Dorylaus, the general, was dead, but Lagetas and Stratarchas, his sons, now grown to manhood, were summoned to the court of Mithridates. "The daughter of Lagetas was the mother of my mother," says Strabo. As long as fortune smiled on Dorylaus, Lagetas and Stratarchas continued to fare well; but ambition led Dorylaus to become a traitor to his royal master; he was convicted of plotting to surrender the kingdom to the Romans, who, it seems, had agreed to make him king in return for his treasonable service. The details of the sequel are not known; for all that Strabo thinks it worth while to say is that the two men went down into obscurity and discredit along with Dorylaus (10. 4. 10). These ancestors of Strabo were Greeks, but Asiatic blood also flowed in his veins. When Mithridates annexed Colchis, he realized the importance of appointing as governors of the province only his most faithful officials and friends. One of these governors was Moaphernes, the uncle of Strabo's mother on her father's side (11. 2. 18). Moaphernes did not attain to this exalted station until towards the close of the reign of Mithridates, and he shared in the ruin of his royal master. But other members of the family of Strabo escaped that ruin; for they foresaw the downfall of Mithridates, and sought cover from the impending storm. One of them was Strabo's paternal grandfather, Aeniates by name (if the conjecture of Ettore Pais be accepted). Aeniates had private reasons for hating Mithridates, and, besides that, Mithridates had put to death Tibius, the nephew of Aeniates, and Tibius' son Theophilus. Aeniates therefore sought to avenge both them and himself; he treasonably surrendered fifteen fortresses to Lucullus, who made him promises of great advancement in return for this service to the Roman cause. But at this juncture Lucullus was superseded by Pompey, who hated Lucullus and regarded as his own personal enemies all those who had rendered noteworthy service to his predecessor. Pompey's hostility to Aeniates was not confined to the persecution of him in Asia Minor; for, when he had returned to Rome after the termination of the war, he prevented the Senate from conferring the honours promised by Lucullus to certain men in Pontus, on the ground that the spoils and honours should not be awarded by Lucullus, but by himself, the real victor. And so it came about that Strabo's grandfather failed of the reward of his treason (12. 3. 13). A further proof of the existence of Asiatic blood in the veins of Strabo is the name of his kinsman Tibius; for, says Strabo, the Athenians gave to their slaves the names of the nations from which they came, or else the names that were most current in the countries from which they came; for instance, if the slave were a Paphlagonian, the Athenians would call him tibius (7. 3. 12). Thus it appears that Strabo was of mixed lineage, and that he was descended from illustrious Greeks and Asiatics who had served the kings of Pontus as generals, satraps, and priests of Ma. But by language and education he was thoroughly Greek.

Strabo was born in Amasia in Pontus in 64 or 63 B.C. (the later date being the year of Cicero's consulate). It is plain that his family had managed to amass property, and Strabo must have inherited considerable wealth; for his fortune was sufficient to enable him to devote his life to scholarly pursuits and to travel somewhat extensively. His education was elaborate, and Greek in character. When he was still a very young man he studied under Aristodemus in Nysa near Tralles in Carla (14. 1. 48). His parents may have removed from Amasia to Nysa in consequence of the embarrassing conditions brought about by the victories of Pompey, the enemy of their house; but the boy may have been sent to study in Nysa before the overthrow of Mithridates the Great; and, if so, he was probably sent thither because one of his kinsmen held high office in the neighbouring Tralles. Ettore Pais points out that, when Mithridates the Great ordered the killing of the Roman citizens in Asia, Theophilus, a Captain in service in Tralles, was employed by the Trallians to do the killing. It seems probable that this Theophilus was the kinsman of Strabo, and the same person who was afterwards executed by Mithridates, an execution that caused Strabo's paternal grandfather to betray the king and desert to Lucullus.

In 44 B.C. Strabo went to Rome by way of Corinth. It was at Rome that he met Publius Servilius, surnamed Isauricus, and that general died in 44 B.C. (This was also the year of the death of Caesar.) Strabo was nineteen or twenty years old at the time of his first visit to Rome. In connexion with his account of Amisus (12. 3. 16) we read that Strabo studied under Tyrannion. That instruction must have been received at Rome; for in 66 B.C. Lucullus had taken Tyrannion as a captive to Rome, where he gave instruction, among others, to the two sons of Cicero. It is Cicero (*Ad Att.* 2. 6. 1) who tells us that Tyrannion was also a distinguished geographer, and he may have guided Strabo into the paths of geographical study. It was probably also at Rome that Strabo had the good fortune to attend the lectures of Xenarchus (14. 5. 4), the Peripatetic philosopher; for he tells us that Xenarchus abandoned Seleucia, his native place, and lived in Alexandria, Athens, and Rome, where he followed the profession of teacher. He also tells us that he "Aristotelized" along with Boëthus (the Stoic philosopher of Sidon), or, in other words, under Xenarchus in Rome (16. 2. 24). Strabo knew Poseidonius (7. fr. 98, quoted from Athenaeus 14. 75. p. 657), and it has been argued from that statement that Poseidonius, too, was one of Strabo's teachers. But in spite of the fact that his teachers were Peripatetics, there can be no doubt that he was himself an adherent of Stoicism. He confesses himself a Stoic (7. 3. 4); he speaks of "our Zeno" (1. 2. 34); again, he says: "For in Poseidonius there is much inquiry into causes and much imitating of Aristotle—precisely what our School avoids, on account of the obscurity of the causes" (2. 3. 8). Stephanus Byzantius calls him "the Stoic philosopher." Strabo lets his adherence to Stoicism appear on many occasions, and he even contrasts the doctrines of Stoicism with those of the Peripatetic School. What had brought about his conversion cannot be ascertained. It may have been due to Athenodorus; for in his account of Petra he says that it is well-governed, and "my friend Athenodorus, the philosopher, has spoken to me of that fact with admiration" (16, 4. 21). This philosopher-friend was the Stoic Athenodorus, the teacher and friend of Augustus. Strabo makes his position in regard to the popular religion quite clear in several passages; he insists that while such religion is necessary in order to hold the illiterate in check, it is unworthy of the scholar. "For in dealing with a crowd of women, at least, or with any promiscuous mob, a philosopher cannot influence them byreason or exhort them to reverence, piety, and faith; nay, there is need of religious fear also, and this cannot be aroused without myths and marvels. For thunderbolt, aegis, trident, torches, snakes, thyrsus-lances,—arms of the gods—are myths, and so is the entire ancient theology" (1. 2. 8). In speaking of the supposed religiosity of the Getans (7. 3. 4) he quotes Menander to the effect that the observances of public worship are ruining the world financially, and he gives a somewhat gleeful picture of the absence of real religion behind those same observances of public worship. Yet Strabo had a religion, and even though he believed that causes are past finding out, he nevertheless believed in Providence as the great First Cause. He sets forth the Stoic doctrine of "conformity to nature" at some length in speaking of Egypt (17. 1. 36), and he also adverts to it in his account of the river-system of France (4. 1. 14).

As for his political opinions, he seems to have followed Polybius in his profound respect for the Romans, with whom, apparently, he is in entire sympathy; he never fails to show great admiration, not only for the political grandeur of the Roman Empire, but for its wise administration as well; he is convinced of the necessity of a central monarchial power: "The excellence of the government and of the Roman Emperors has prevented Italy (which has often been torn by civil war from the very time when it became subject to Rome), and even Rome itself, from proceeding further in the ways of error and corruption. But it would be difficult for the Romans to govern so vast an empire in any other way than by entrusting it to one person—as it were, to a father. And certainly at no other period have the Romans and their allies enjoyed such perfect peace and prosperity as that which the Emperor Augustus gave them from the very moment when he was clothed with autocratic power, a peace which Tiberius, his son and successor, continues to give them at the present moment; for he makes Augustus the pattern in his policy and administration; and Germanicus and Drusus, the sons of Tiberius, who are now serving in the government of their father, also make Augustus their pattern" (6. 4. 2). And he constantly takes the Roman point of view. For instance, in leading up to his account of the destruction of Corinth by Mummius, he tells us that the Corinthians had perpetrated manifold outrages on the Romans; he does indeed mention the feeling of pity to which Polybius gave expression in telling of the sack of Corinth, and says that Polybius was horrified at the contempt shown by the Roman soldiery for the sacred offerings and the masterpieces of art; "for Polybius says he personally saw how paintings had been thrown to the ground and saw the soldiers playing dice on them." But Strabo gives us to understand that his own private feeling is that the Corinthians were merely paying for the many insults they had heaped on the Romans (8. 6. 23). He is equally dispassionate in telling of

the Roman conquest of his own native country (12. 3. 33). He seems to be thoroughly Roman at heart; for theRomans have united the world under one beneficent administration (1. 1. 16); by the extinction of the pirates the Roman peace has brought prosperity, tranquillity, security to commerce, and safety of travel (3. 2. 5; 14. 3. 3; 16. 2. 20); a country becomes prosperous just as soon as it comes under the Roman sway (3. 3. 8), which opens up means of intercommunication (2. 5. 26); friendship and alliance with Rome mean prosperity to the people possessing them (3. 1. 8; 4. 1. 5); so does the establishment of a Roman colony in any place (6. 3. 4).

We have seen that Strabo went to Rome in 44 B.C., and that he was nineteen or twenty years old at that time. He made several other journeys to Rome: we find him there in 35 B.C.; for that is the date of the execution of Selurus (6. 2. 6), which Strabo witnessed. He was then twenty-nine years old. He was in Rome about 31 B.C.; for he saw the painting of Dionysus by Aristeides (one of those paintings seen by Polybius at the sack of Corinth) in the temple of Ceres in Rome, and he adds: "But recently the temple was destroyed by fire, and the painting perished" (8. 6. 23). It is known from Dio Cassius (50. 10) that the temple of Ceres was burned in 31 B.C. He was thirty-two or thirty-three years old at that time. We know of still another journey to Rome: "I landed on the island of Gyaros, where I found a small village inhabited by fishermen; when we sailed from the island, we took on board one of those fishermen who had been sent on a mission to Augustus (who was then at Corinth, on his way [from Egypt] to celebrate his triumph after his victory at Actium). On the voyage we questioned this fisherman, and he told us that he had been sent to ask for a diminution of the tribute" (10. 5. 3). Here we find Strabo journeying from Asia Minor, by way of the island of Gyaros and Corinth, and the clear inference is that he was on his way to Rome at the time. This was in 29 B.C., and Strabo was thirty-four or thirty-five years old. Augustus had just founded Nicopolis in honour of his victory at Actium (7. 7. 6), and it is not unlikely that Strabo visited the new city on that voyage. In 25 and 24 B.C. he is in Egypt, and accompanies Aelius Gallus up the Nile, proceeding as far as Syene and the frontiers of Ethiopia (2. 5. 12). At that time he was thirty-nine years old. He was still in Egypt when Augustus was in Samos in 20 B.C. (14. 1. 14). He was then forty-four years old. Accordingly he lived for more than five years in Alexandria, and we may infer that it was in the Alexandrian library that he made from the works of his predecessors those numerous excerpts with which his book is filled. We find him again in Rome about 7 B.C.; for in his description of Rome he mentions buildings that were erected after 20 B.C., the last of them being the portico of Livia, which was dedicated in 7 B.C. (5. 3. 8). This was perhaps his final visit to Rome, and he was then fifty-six or fifty-seven years old. It seems that he lived to be eighty-four years old, for he chronicles the death of Juba in 21 A.D., but the last twenty-six or twenty-seven years of his life were spent far from Rome, and probably in his native Amasia. His residence at this remote place made it impossible for him to follow the course of recent political events and to incorporate them in the revised edition of his book.

Strabo thought that he had travelled much. He says: "Now I shall tell what part of the land and sea I have myself visited and concerning what part I have trusted to accounts given by others by word of mouth or in writing. I have travelled westward from Armenia as far as the coasts of Tyrrhenia opposite Sardinia, and in the direction of the South I have travelled from the Euxine Sea as far as the frontiers of Ethiopia. And you could not find another person among the writers on Geography who has travelled over much more of the distances just mentioned than I; indeed, those who have travelled more than I in the western regions have not covered as much ground in the east, and those who have travelled more in the eastern countries are behind me in the western countries; and the same holds true in regard to the regions towards the South and North" (2. 5. 11). And yet it cannot be said that he was a great traveller; nor can it be said that he travelled for the purpose of scientific research—the real reason for his journeys will presently appear. He saw little even of Italy, where he seems to have followed without much deviation the roads Brindisi-Rome, Rome-Naples-Puteoli, and Rome-Populonia. It does not appear that he lived for any very long stretch of time at Rome; and it cannot be maintained with positiveness that in Greece he saw any place other than Corinth—not even Athens, strange as this may seem. In the South and the East his travels were more extensive: in the South he visited the Nile valley as far as the frontiers of Ethiopia; he was at Comana Aurea for some time; he saw the river Pyramus, Hierapolis in Phrygia, Nysa in Caria, and Ephesus; he was acquainted with Pontus; he visited Sinope, Cyzicus, and Nicaea; he travelled over Cilicia and much of Caria, visiting Mylasa, Alabanda, Tralles, and probably also Synnada, Magnesia, Smyrna, the shores of the Euxine, and Beirut in Syria. Though we may not limit the places he saw to the places actually mentioned as having been seen by him, still it is clear that his journeys were not so wide as we should have expected in the case of a man who was travelling in the interest of science.

Ettore Pais seems to make good his contention that the work of Strabo was not written by a man who was travelling on his own account and for scientific reasons, but by one who seized every occasion to study what circumstances and the pleasure of others gave him an opportunity of knowing. He contends, further, that it was for the sake of others that Strabo made his journeys; that he was instructor and politician, travelling perhaps with, and certainly in the interest of, persons of the most exalted rank; that he was the teacher and guide of eminent men. Strabo never fails to mention the famous scholars and teachers who were born in the East—the list is a long one; and we are fain to believe that he occupied a similar social position. He insists that his *Geography* is political: The greater part of *Geography* subserves the uses of states and their rulers; *Geography* as a whole is intimately connected with the functions of persons in positions of political leadership (1.

1. 16); *Geography* is particularly useful in the conduct of great military undertakings (1. 1. 17); it serves to regulate the conduct and answer the needs of ruling princes (1. 1. 18). Presumably it was with just such people that he travelled. But Pais joins issue with Niese and others in their contention that the men with whom and in whose interest he travelled were Romans, and he makes out a good case when he argues that Strabo wrote his *Geography* in the interest of Pythodoris, Queen of Pontus. Even the great respect shown by Strabo for Augustus, Rome, and Tiberius is to be explained by the circumstances in which he found himself; for subject-princes had to be obsequious to Rome, and as for Pythodoris, she owed her throne to Augustus fully as much as to Polemon. It was good business, therefore, that necessitated the retouching of the book and the insertion in it of the many compliments to Tiberius—all of which were added after the accession of that prince, and for fear of him, rather than out of respect for him.

The question as to when and where Strabo wrote his geographical work has long been a burning one in circles interested in Strabo criticism. Niese seemed to settle the question, when he maintained that Strabo wrote his *Historical Geography* at Rome, at the instigation of Roman friends who occupied exalted positions in the political world of Rome; and that he acted as the companion of those friends, accompanying one of them, Aelius Gallus, from Rome to Egypt, and returning with him to Rome; and further that it was at Rome that he wrote his *Geography,* between the years 18 and 19 A.D. In the main, scholars had accepted the views of Niese, until Pais entered the field with his thesis that Strabo wrote his work, not at the instigation of politicians at Rome, but from the point of view of a Greek from Asia Minor, and in the interest of Greeks of that region; that the material for the *Geography* was collected at Alexandria and Rome, but that the actual writing of the book and the retouching of it at a later period were done at Amasia, far from Rome—a fact which accounts for his omissions of events, his errors, his misstatements, his lack of information concerning, and his failure to mention, occurrences that would surely have found a place in his book if it had been written in Rome; it accounts, too, for the surprising fact that Strabo's *Geography* was not known to the Romans—not even to Pliny—although it was well-known in the East, for Josephus quotes from it.

To go somewhat more minutely into this question, it may be stated that Strabo mentions Tiberius more than twenty times, but the events he describes are all connected with the civil wars that occurred after the death of Caesar and with the period in the life of Augustus that falls between the Battle of Actium (in 31 B.C.) and 7 B.C. He rarely mentions events in the life of Augustus between 6 B.C. and 14 A.D., and, as he takes every opportunity to praise Augustus and Tiberius, such omissions could not be accounted for if he wrote his Geography about 18 A.D. The conclusion reached by Pais is that Strabo wrote the book before 5 B.C. and shortly after 9 B.C., or, in other words, about 7 B.C.

Such matters as the defeat of Varus and the triumph of Germanicus were not contained in the original publication of the work, and were inserted in the revised edition, which was made about the year 18 A.D. The list of the Roman provinces governed by the Roman Senate, on the last page of the book, was written between 22 B.C. and 11 B.C., and Strabo himself says that it was antiquated; it was retouched about 7 B.C., not at Rome, but far from Rome. The facts are similar in the mention he makes of the liberality of Tiberius to the cities of Asia Minor that had been destroyed by earthquakes; in the case of the coronation of Zeno as king of Armenia Major (18 A.D.), and in the case of the death of Juba, which occurred not later than 23 A.D., Strabo made no use of the map of Agrippa—an omission with which he has been reproached—for the very good reason that the map of Agrippa had not been completed in 7 B.C.

If Strabo first published his *Geography* in 7 B.C., it appeared when he was fifty-six or fifty-seven years old, at a time when he was still in full possession of all his physical and mental powers. But if we say, with Niese and his followers, that the work was written between 18 and 19 A.D., we thereby maintain that Strabo began to write his *Geography* when he had passed the eighth decade of his life. He himself compares his book to a colossal statue, and it is incredible that he could have carried out such a stupendous work after having passed his eightieth year.

Strabo is so well-known as a geographer that it is often forgotten that he was a historian before he was a geographer. Indeed it may be believed that he is a geographer because he had been a historian, and that the material for his *Geography* was collected along with that for his *Historical Sketches,* which comprised forty-seven books (see 1. 1. 22-23, and 2. 1. 9, and footnotes). But his *Geography* alone has come down to us. In this connexion it will be useful to read Strabo's own account of his *Historical Sketches* and his *Geography:* "In short, this book of mine should be generally useful—useful alike to the statesman and to the public at large—as was my work on *History.* In this work, as in that, I mean by 'statesman,' not the man who is wholly uneducated, but the man who has taken the round of courses usual in the case of freemen or of students of philosophy. For the man who has given no thought to virtue and to practical wisdom, and to what has been written about them, would not be able even to form a valid opinion either in censure or in praise; nor yet to pass judgment upon the matters of historical fact that are worthy of being recorded in this treatise. And so, after I had written my *Historical Sketches,* which have been useful, I suppose, for moral and political philosophy, I determined to write the present treatise also; for this work itself is based on the same plan, and is addressed to the same class of readers, and particularly to men of exalted stations in life. Furthermore, just as in my *Historical Sketches* only the incidents in the lives of distinguished men are recorded, while deeds that are petty and ignoble are omitted, so in this work also I must leave untouched what is petty and inconspicuous, and devote my attention to what is noble and great, and to what contains the practi-cally useful, or memorable, or entertaining. Now just as in judging of the merits of colossal statues we do not examine each individual part with minute care, but rather consider the general effect and endeavour to see if the statue as a whole is pleasing, so should this book of mine be judged. For it, too, is a colossal work, in that it deals with the facts about large things only, and wholes, except as some petty thing may stir the interest of the studious or the practical man. I have said thus much to show that the present work is a serious one and one worthy of a philosopher" (1. 1. 22-23).

The *Geography* of Strabo is far more than a mere geography. It is an encyclopaedia of information concerning the various countries of the Inhabited World as known at the beginning of the Christian era; it is an historical geography; and, as Dubois and Tozer point out, it is a philosophy of geography.

J. G. C. Anderson (essay date 1923)

SOURCE: "Some Questions Bearing on the Date and Place of Composition of Strabo's *Geography*" in *Anatolian Studies Presented to Sir William Mitchell Ramsay*, edited by W. H. Buckler & W. M. Calder, Cambridge University Press, 1923, 1-13.

[*In the following essay, Anderson presents his case that the bulk of the* Geography *was completed by 2 B.C. and that it was written in "some provincial city in the eastern Mediterranean."*]

I.

Nine or ten years ago I began to prepare a commentary on Strabo's description of Pontus for a projected edition of the books dealing with Asia Minor, which, in the present state of the world, is not likely to see the light—a fact to be deplored, if only because we lose the valuable information and well-pondered ideas which would have been contributed by the scholar in whose honour this volume is written. In preparing the commentary, I had to review afresh some old problems, and the renewed study of them led me to examine, more carefully than I had done, the question of the date of Strabo's *Geography.* Life is too short, and leisure too scanty, to permit of the independent examination of every question which arises in the course of one's work, and many have too readily accepted Niese's view that the first part of the *Geography* was written in the second half of A.D. 18, and the second part in the first half of A.D. 19, before the death of Germanicus in October. For speed of composition that would surely be a record; Strabo himself compares his work to a colossal statue. Book XVII, indeed, points to a later date, since it mentions the death of King Juba, which appears to be fixed with fair certainty to A.D. 23 by the combination of literary and numismatic evidence, and Niese's effort to disprove this conclusion was unsuccessful. But even if the period of writing be extended to A.D. 23, difficulties arise. In A.D. 18

Strabo would be in his eighty-first year,[1] and it is not likely either that he would have deferred his task till he reached that great age, or that he could produce at that time of life such a voluminous work, full of freshness and vigour. It was no light task for one who had travelled comparatively so little as Strabo, and depended on written and oral sources for the bulk of his information.[2] It required long years of preliminary work in collecting materials; much was probably collected in Alexandria, where he stayed a long time (II, 3, 5), possibly before he returned to Rome about B.C. 20.[3] There is another weighty consideration, which cannot escape the notice of any careful reader, viz. the quite extraordinary dearth of allusions to facts belonging to the latter half of Augustus' reign, a strange silence about events of the first importance and about other facts which Strabo is specially fond of mentioning.

It was such considerations that led Prof. E. Pais, in 1886, to put forward his view about the date of composition, a view which he re-stated in 1908, and reinforced by new arguments.[4] Briefly, he holds that the *Geography* was begun not long after the completion of the *Historical Memoirs* (i.e. soon after B.C. 27), and was completed by B.C. 7; afterwards it was hastily touched up by the insertion of references to Tiberius and to some recent events, particularly events concerning the eastern provinces. The accession of Tiberius and Germanicus' visit to the East were both very important events. There was good reason, therefore, for revision.[5]

It seems difficult to disagree with the conclusion that there was an incomplete revision, in or about A.D. 18, of a text which had been written many years before. There can be no doubt about the almos unbroken gap that extends over the second half of Augustus' reign. Clearly, so far as this period is concerned, it is hazardous to argue from Strabo's silence, or to infer that his statements always represent facts as they were at the apparent date of composition, about A.D. 18-23.

The nature of the difficulties raised by his narrative may be illustrated by two instances from Book XII, which are not utilized by Pais.[6] The first concerns Garsaoura, a Cappadocian town lying on the great trade route from Ephesus to the Euphrates, close to the border of Lycaonia. It is mentioned three times in Book XII,[7] and once in Book XIV, where he is quoting from Artemidoros (c. 2, 29). The first passage describes it as a *komopolis,* which was once the metropolis of the district. The second does not define it. The third calls it a *polichnion* and a *phrourion,* and the fourth a *polichnion.* These terms, though not identical in meaning, are all differentiated by Strabo from *polis,* an "autonomous" city-state more or less fully organized on the Hellenistic model.[8] Now, as Leake showed, Garsaoura was identical with Archelais, a foundation of the last king of Cappadocia.[9] The town, therefore, had been organized as a [polis] some time before Archelaos was summoned to Rome by Tiberius.[10] As the summons followed soon after Tiberius' accession, there is little doubt that the re-foundation of the town dated from the time of Augustus.

The change of status and the change of name are facts which Strabo would certainly have recorded, had he known of them when he was writing Books XII-XIV. As he is in general well informed about Cappadocia under Archelaos, they probably occurred after the time when he wrote, and were overlooked on revision, if, indeed, they ever became known to him (see below). In any case, his statement was not true in A.D. 18.

The second instance is furnished by the chapter in which the third mention of Garsaoura occurs (XII, 6). One cannot fail to be struck by the omissions in the account of the subjugation of the Pisidian-Cilician mountaineers of the Taurus region. Strabo describes in detail the operations of King Amyntas against these wild tribes, and narrates how, after capturing Kremna and other fortresses, the king lost his life in his campaign against the Homonadeis (or rather Homanadeis, as Sir W. Ramsay has shown),[11] and how he was subsequently avenged by Quirinius, the governor of Syria. We now know that the operations of Quirinius took place in the years following B.C. 11/10, and that they were succeeded by a systematic reorganization of the whole region, in the course of which Augustus planted no fewer than five Roman colonies to act as garrisons, connecting them with the older military centre Colonia Caesarea (Antioch) by a great system of roads, the *Viae Sebastae,* which were under construction in B.C. 6. This carefully-planned work of pacification would take some years to complete.[12]

Strabo's account breaks off with Quirinius' victory, and the removal of the population from their mountain fastnesses to the neighbouring cities. His sole reference to the subsequent settlement—the most important piece of work done by Augustus in Asia Minor during the latter part of his reign—is contained in a single clause stating that "Kremna is now occupied by Roman colonists." How are we to account for Strabo's failure even to name the other four *coloniae?* The establishment of a *colonia* is a type of fact which he constantly mentions, and the planting of four simultaneously in a single inland district was a notable event. The quality of his account of the country concerned, and his outline of the operations, have led Sir W. Ramsay to think that his information was derived from an officer who served in the war. It would seem that his information about the reorganization following the war was extremely limited, and we shall find other evidence that for the years following B.C. 6 the information which he had was insufficient to enable him to comprehend its full significance. It might, indeed, be argued that such knowledge as he possessed of Augustus' work in Pisidia reached him after the completion of his account, and that the mention of the colony at Kreman was inserted later; certainly it is somewhat oddly inserted in the middle of the account of Amyntas' operations, and the occurrence of Kremna in the original narrative would naturally suggest a reference here to the colonization scheme. But Strabo knows of other events that occurred not only in B.C. 6/5, but also in B.C. 3/2 (below) and we can hardly suppose that they are all later additions.

Still more noteworthy is Strabo's want of full and accurate knowledge about events affecting his native land and the immediately adjoining districts which were included by him (as they were at one period) in the region of Pontus. His definition of Pontus as a territorial designation is based on the arrangements of Pompey, who included under it all the lands held by Mithradates in Asia Minor, except Lesser Armenia and Colchis, and joined it with Bithynia, to form a dual province. So it remained until Antony partitioned the whole of it, except the littoral west of the Halys, the *ora Pontica,* among "kings and dynasts," and this system of principalities continued till B.C. 6, when Augustus began to re-incorporate the more westerly districts in the Empire. In his opening sentences (XII, 3, 1), Strabo notes these later developments, in general language, and adds: "As we go through the details, we shall describe things as they now are, making a few references to older facts, where it is useful to do so." It is natural, then, that his description should have been regarded as an authoritative statement of the conditions existing at the apparent date of composition (A.D. 18 foll.).

Now, Mithradates' realm included not only the Paphlagonian coast-land, but also two valleys of inland Paphlagonia, running parallel to the coast range, the valley of the Amnias west of the Halys (in which Pompeiopolis lay) and the rolling district of Phazimonitis (which continues that depression east of the Halys, and contained Pompey's city Neapolis). In Strabo's earlier life these two districts were separated from the province of Pontus, and separated permanently. The separation took place in B.C. 40, when Antony bestowed them (together with the rest of inland Paphlagonia and the kingdom of Galatia) on Kastor II, who ruled till B.C. 36. He was succeeded in Paphlagonia by his son Deiotaros Philadelphos, who died in B.C. 6/5. Augustus then annexed the principality, and added it to the province of Galatia, in which it remained till the time of Diocletian.[13] The date of annexation is proved by inscriptions, which also show that the Paphlagonian principality included Pompeiopolis and Neapolis.[14]

What is Strabo's account? In § 9 he tells us that "Mithridates held the nearest portion of inland Paphlagonia, which extended in part even beyond (east of) the Halys (i.e. the districts of Pompeiopolis and Neapolis), and this is the limit which the Romans have drawn for the province of Pontus; the rest remained even after the fall of Mithridates under the rule of princes." That is to say, thenceforward the districts of the two cities formed part of the province of Pontus. The perfect tense "have drawn" . . . would naturally be interpreted as implying that Pompey's arrangement still existed when Strabo wrote.[15] This is in such complete conflict with ascertained facts that formerly I sought to save Strabo's repute for accuracy.[16] In vain. Section 40 reveals clearly that Strabo was totally unaware that Pompeiopolis had ever ceased to belong to the province of Pontus, . . . that it had passed into the hands of "dynasts," that it had been finally annexed only in B.C. 6, and that it was then added to the province, not of Pontus, but of Galatia. Here there is no question of the date of

composition. Strabo's statement is false. His knowledge was defective, and his information about the change of B.C. 6/5, following on the death of Deiotaros (which he mentions in the very next section), was too incomplete to enable him to detect and correct his mistake.

Next, as regards Neapolis and its territory (§ 38). After describing Pompey's arrangements here, he merely adds: "But his successors assigned this district also [like Zela and Megalopolis] to kings," and there he stops. He is unaware that the last king had died in B.C. 6, and that the district was then annexed and added to Galatia;[17] he is also unaware that it had formed part of the principality of Deiotaros, whose death he records in § 41 as the occasion of the annexation of inland Paphlagonia. He did not realise that the prince's death had any bearing on his narrative in § 38. He failed to appreciate the full meaning of reports which reached him about the political changes of the year B.C. 6/5, even though the districts affected immediately adjoined the territory of his native city Amaseia.[18] In consequence, his account is not true to the facts as they were after B.C. 6/5.

Our discussion appears to throw light on the vexed problems connected with Karana and Megalopolis which arise out of § 37. There has been general unanimity until recently among scholars that Pompey's city Megalopolis is identical with Sebasteia, the modern Sivas, and this view carried conviction. According to Strabo, Pompey transformed what had been a native village or town into a [*polis*] which he named Megalopolis, and to which he assigned the districts of Kouloupene and Kamisene. . . . Both districts can be identified with certainty. Kamisene is the district round Kamisa, and Kamisa, "an ancient fortress now in ruins" (says Strabo), is the modern Kemis, in the upper Halys valley. Kouloupene contained the towns of Sebasteia and Sebastopolis (Sulu Serai, SSE. of Zela), as we learn from Pliny (*N.H.,* VI, 3, 8) who is the first author to mention them under these names.

When Antony, in pursuance of his Eastern policy, suppressed the municipal autonomy of Zela and Megalopolis, he divided their territory between Lykomedes, priest-king of Komana, the priest of Zela (who recovered his autonomous position), and a Keltic prince Ateporix. On the death of the last, proceeds Strabo, his fief, which was not large, . . . was incorporated in the province of Galatia, and the town of Karana was formed into a [*polis*] by concentrating the population there. . . . The other territories "are still held" by Pythodoris, queen of Pontus, and Dyteutos, priest of Komana. Now the era of Sebastopolis is shown by inscriptions to have begun in October, B.C. 3, and so the town was annexed (like Amaseia) in the year Oct., B.C. 3-2.[19] The conclusion followed that Sebastopolis and its territory formed part (and probably the greater part) of the fief of Ateporix. Karana therefore was apparently the earlier name of Sebastopolis.[20] On the other hand, the era of Zela and the rest of Pontus Polemoniacus dates from A.D. 64, and Sebasteia is assigned by Ptolemy to Pontus Polemoniacus. So it seemed clear that Sebasteia was the later name of Megalopolis.

But a difficulty arose when Imhoof-Blumer identified as belonging to Sebasteia certain coins which used an era dating from B.C. 2/1-A.D. 1/2. As this attribution has been accepted by numismatists, we are faced with the difficulty that Sebasteia was annexed by Augustus, and probably (since it was in the same district of Kouloupene as Sebastopolis) in B.C. 2, though apparently later than October, when the local year in Asia Minor began.[21] On the other hand, Strabo affirms more than once that Megalopolitis was still ruled by queen Pythodoris (§§ 31, 37).

How is this contradiction to be resolved? One solution is to deny the identification of Megalopolis with Sebasteia, as M. Th. Reinach does, and to seek for a site elsewhere. But it appears impossible to find a site that will satisfy the conditions. Reinach's suggestion that it may have lain in *haut Halys*, i.e. east of Sivas, is a counsel of despair; he suggests no possible site there, and a situation at the extreme east end of a vast territory would be a very unlikely choice for Pompey to have made. Nor can it be sought in the hill country north of Sivas, where natural roads and modern towns are alike lacking. All Pompey's cities were founded at important points on great natural lines of communication, and the strategic and commercial importance of Sivas is (now at least) too well-known to need emphasizing. Further, the fact that Ptolemy assigns Sebasteia to Polemon's Pontus shows that Sivas was originally included in the realm of that king; and there is no reason to doubt his accuracy.[22] Indeed, he is corroborated by two coins of Neocaesareia belonging to the period when the two Pontic districts, Polemoniacus and Galaticus, were conjoined as *Pontus Mediterraneus*. These coins, dated A.D. 209/10, represent the cities of the *Koinon* as five goddesses (*Tychai*), grouped around the standing or sitting *Tyche* of the metropolis Neocaesareia. In each case they are arranged in groups of three and two, the three standing in front of the *Tyche* of the metropolis on her right, and the two behind on her left. The three are to be identified[23] as Amaseia, Komana, Sebastopolis (Pontus Gal.) and the two as Zela and Sebasteia (Pontus Pol.). Though merged officially, the two districts retained their separate individuality, a characteristic trait of provincial life in the East. Till A.D. 64 Sebasteia must have been attached to Pontus Galaticus. On the annexation of Polemoniacus it was restored to its old connexion.

The true solution appears to me to be that Strabo's narrative reflects a state of things which ceased to exist in B.C. 2. The territory of Megalopolis was withdrawn from queen Pythodoris, in whole or part, when the town was annexed by Augustus. It is to be noted that Strabo does not mention the new names Sebastopolis and Sebasteia, fond as he is of mentioning such things. Yet the form of the names and the era show beyond reasonable doubt that they were adopted in honour of Augustus, in gratitude for the dignity conferred on the cities by admission within the pale of the civilized world of the Roman Empire. Strabo's narrative about Karana and Megalopolis seems explicable only on the view that it was completed before the re-naming of the former, and before the annexation and re-naming of the latter. If the later facts ever came to his knowledge, he did not make the necessary corrections in §§ 31 and 37, although he describes the fortunes of queen Pythodoris' family in A.D. 18-19 (§ 29). Perhaps they never came to his knowledge. It is obvious that the appointments of a king of Armenia and a prince of Thrace were events which would come to Strabo's ear, wherever he was residing, but that he might remain ignorant of the minor matters with which we have been dealing.

We have seen that Strabo's knowledge about Eastern affairs was becoming meagre by B.C. 6/5, but that it extends to B.C. 3/2. The latter year seems to mark the beginning of the great lacuna, which appears to admit of no satisfactory explanation, except that the work of composition was then drawing to an end, to be followed many years later by a superficial revision which took note of some important events that had happened recently. . . . [24] But however the gap is explained, it is clear that the *Geography* cannot be regarded as giving an authoritative statement of conditions as they were in the later years of Augustus or in A.D. 18.

II.

While the above discussion lends support to Pais' view about the date of composition, it does not tell in favour of the theory which he has put forward concerning the place where Strabo wrote, and the readers whom he had specially in view. He rejects Niese's view that Strabo wrote at the instigation of Roman friends, and for a Roman public, and holds that he wrote from the point of view of a Greek of Asia Minor, and in the interests of Greeks, who probably belonged to Asiatic dynasties. He believes that it was events in Pontus and Cappadocia that gave occasion for the first and second redactions of his work. "It seems most probable," he says, "that just as the death of Polemon (B.C. 8) and the incorporation of Amaseia in the Roman Empire marked the end of the first redaction and first definite arrangement of the text, so the arrival and sojourn of Germanicus in Asia Minor (A.D. 18/19) caused Strabo to take up the work which he had written twenty-five years earlier,[25] and to bring it down to date by inserting recent events" (p. 408); at the same time he took the opportunity of paying homage to the new emperor, Tiberius.

Further, he rejects Niese's view that Strabo wrote in Rome. Niese's arguments are indeed invalid,[26] and Pais adduces very strong evidence against the theory.[27] His own belief is that the *Geography* was composed, from materials collected at Alexandria and Rome, in some distant city of Asia Minor, possibly (as some older scholars thought) at Amaseia, and that it was written in the interests of Pythodoris and her family. Strabo, he suggests, may have held a social and political position at her court, similar to that of Nicolaus at the court of Herod; he used the historical works of Nicolaus freely, and may have known him personally. In support of this view he points to Strabo's lack of knowledge of western events during the later years of Augustus, to the special interest which he displays in the fortunes of Polemon and his house, to the striking warmth of his eulogy of queen Pythodoris as a capable ruler, and to the frequent allusions in various places to her and her family. Apart from Augustus, Tiberius, and the governors of Egypt, she is the only ruler whom Strabo compliments and eulogizes; and none other is so frequently mentioned in the entire ***Geography.*** He also points out the opportunities which Strabo had of becoming acquainted with Pythodoris' family before she became queen of Pontus, and reminds us that he belonged to a family which had held the highest offices under Mithradates, and that Polemon was, perhaps, one of the kings to whom Amaseia was handed over by Pompey's successors.

This theory is at first sight attractive, and it has won some acceptance. Its author frankly admits that it is necessarily problematical. The suggestion that Strabo held an official position is, of course, purely conjectural. The evidence may be thought to suggest a personal acquaintance with the royal house. Certainly it indicates a lively interest in its fortunes. But such interest was natural. The Polemonian house played a highly importart part in the history of north-eastern Asia Minor, Bosporus, and Cilicia. Its rulers were outstanding figures in the public life of the country, and, by the marriage of Pythodoris and Archelaos, the dynasty became closely connected with the Cappadocian kingdom. But our discussion does not favour the view that Strabo was, in later time at least, in close relations with the Polemonian court, or that he was writing at Amaseia. If he had been, we should have expected fuller and more recent knowledge about political and administrative changes in districts adjoining his native city, and more accurate information about the geography of some parts of the kingdom of Pythodoris, a subject which we cannot enter into here. Nor do Pais' arguments lend adequate support to the supposition that the work was composed for Pythodoris. It is clear that Strabo regarded himself as the successor of the Hellenistic geographers, carrying on the study in the spirit of Polybius and Poseidonius, who insisted strongly on the intimate connexion between geography and history. For him geography is a description of the world as the scene on which human history is enacted (I, 1, 16). It is a part of philosophy, it is the hand-maid of . . . the science which directs the system of life in civilized states, it furthers scientific knowledge and serves the needs of states . . . the geographer is the philosopher who is concerned with the art of life. . . . His geography is to be both scientific and practical. Like his history, it is addressed to the . . . educated man who has taken the course of study usually pursued by free men and students of philosophy. It is intended for such readers, and especially, he adds, for those concerned with the government of states. . . . The mention of this class of readers accords with the political conditions of his time. No doubt his frequent insistence on the utility of geography for rulers suggests a purpose, but he seems to be thinking primarily of Roman rulers and generals. His treatise was certainly not very suitable for a Roman public. The frequent lengthy discussions of mythological and historical matters, the tedious excursuses on Homeric geography, the

notices of notable men produced by various cities, men distinguished in literature, science, and art—all these were much more likely to appeal to Greeks than to Romans. But the introductory chapters give the impression that he is attempting to enlist the interest of Roman readers also, especially Roman public men. If so, he signally failed. The omnivorous Pliny knew nothing of his work.

If we reject the view that Strabo wrote at Amaseia, and the view that he wrote at Rome, we are left with the alternative that his work was composed in some provincial city in the eastern Mediterranean, where he would be out of touch with western affairs, and not in close touch with the progress of events in his own country.

Notes

1. He was born probably in B.C. 63, as Niese showed by an ingenious argument.

2. II, 5, 11, p. 117.

3. Strabo (I, 1, 23) tells us that he resolved to write the work after he had finished his 47 books of *Historical Memoirs,* the last 43 of which continued Polybius' history down (apparently) to the beginning of the Empire. This work Niese assigned to the period B.C. 22-A.D. 18.

4. Opinions differing from Niese's had already been expressed by several writers. Pais' view was adopted by the late Prof. Sterrett in the *Introduction* to his translation in the Loeb series.

5. *Riv. di filol. class.,* XV (1886), pp. 97 ff., and *Ancient Italy,* translated by C. D. Curtis, Chicago, 1908, pp. 379 ff.

6. The second is mentioned, but the date and the facts were not then properly known.

7. XII, 2, 6; 2, 10; 6, 1.

8. The term is, however, sometimes used loosely of cities which were not organized in that manner, e.g. Pessinous and the two Komanas.

9. Ramsay, *H.G.A.M.,* p. 284, who concludes that "probably Strabo's information was not up to date." Under Claudius the town became a *colonia.*

10. Tac., *Ann.* II, 42.

11. *J.R.S.,* VII (1917), pp. 263 ff.

12. Cheesman, *J.R.S.,* III (1913), pp. 253 ff.; Ramsay, *Bearing of Recent Discovery,* 1915, pp. 275 ff.; *J.R.S.,* VI (1916), pp. 83 ff., and especially VII, pp. 229-283. Cp. Bleckmann, *Klio,* XVII (1920), pp. 104 ff.; and Dessau, *ibid.,* pp. 252 ff.

13. This is proved by the evidence of Roman milestones *C.I.L.,* III, *Suppl.,* 14184, 25, 27, 30. Ptolemy also states the fact correctly.

14. *Stud. Pont.,* I, p. 91 ff., III, no. 67 = *I.G.R.P.,* III, 139; and *I.G.R.P.,* III, 135, with Ramsay, *Rev. Et. gr.,* 1893, p. 251 f.

15. J. A. R. Munro, in *J.H.S.*, XX (1900), p. 160 f., and XXI (1901), p. 61, *note* 1.

16. *Stud. Pont.*, I, pp. 95 ff.

17. . . . Amaseia was annexed in B.C. 3/2, Dessau, *Zft. f. Numism.*, XXV (1906), pp. 339 ff., *Stud. Pont.*, III, p. 109 f.

18. Neapolis is only forty miles in an air-line north-west of Amaseia. In view of the fact that Strabo mentions events of B.C. 3/2, it would be an improbable hypothesis that § 41 was re-written or added at a later date, while § 38 was left uncorrected.

19. Dessau proposes to dissociate the era of Sebastopolis and Amaseia from the date of their annexation (*Zft. f. Numism.*, 25 (1906), pp. 339 ff.), but this is contrary to many analogous cases, and appears wholly unacceptable. Cp. *Stud. Pont.*, III, p. 73 f. and the commentary to No. 66, ll. 1-3, which give a simple explanation of the peculiar dating of this inscription, on which Dessau's argument rests. The particular date, and the manner of stating it, were affairs of the Roman Government; the cities had no voice in the matter.

20. Ramsay in *Rev. Ét. gr.*, 1893, p. 252.

21. Dessau's argument (*op. cit.*, p. 342, n. 3), that the era is consistent with annexation at a much later date, is based on the same grounds as in the previous cases, and seems to me to fail for the same reasons. The name Sebasteia coupled with the era is surely conclusive.

22. Cp. Ramsay, *H.G.A.M.*, p. 69, on the general accuracy of his description of Pontus Polem. and Pontus Galaticus. There are some bad blunders in his account, but they appear to be confined to the coast districts, where he had other sources, such as *Peripli*, to confuse him.

23. This suggestion, made in *J.H.S.*, XX (1900), p. 155, is adopted by Babelon-Reinach, *Recueil*, p. 25.

24. On Strabo's use of [*recently*] which betrays various dates of composition extending over a great number of years, see Pais, *Anc. Italy*, pp. 383 ff. He uses it in reference to Jul. Caesar's re-foundation of Corinth in B.C. 44, sixty-one years before A.D. 18, when he uses it of Zeno's accession to the throne of Armenia. . . .

25. He assumes the old date (B.C. 7) for the annexation of Amaseia (see above, p. 7, note 1).

26. Two of them are based on the use of . . . adverbs . . . often used by Strabo, not in the sense of "the place where I am," but in the sense of "the place of which I am speaking." The third is drawn from the reference in XIII, 1, 19, p. 590, to Agrippa's removal of the lion of Lysippus to Rome, but the passage points so definitely to Rome that even a more careful stylist than Strabo might regard the express mention of the city as unnecessary. Cp. Haebler in *Hermes*, XIX (1884), pp. 235 ff.

27. The evidence, of course, is cumulative, but the strongest arguments are:—

(i) Strabo's complete silence about the German and Illyrian wars of A.D. 4-11 (the latter being regarded by Romans as the most serious war since the wars with Carthage, Suet., *Tib.*, 16).

(ii) His lack of knowledge of such an important geographical document as the map of Agrippa, or of recent works, like that of Isidoros of Charax on Parthia (written for C. Caesar, and therefore before B.C. 1) or those of King Juba on Libya and Arabia (the latter written for the use of C. Caesar).

(iii) His statement that the temple of Ceres at Rome had been burnt "recently" (i.e. in B.C. 31), without any allusion to the fact that a new temple had been dedicated by Tiberius in A.D. 17 (VIII, 6, 23; Dio., L, 10, 3; Tac., *Ann.*, II, 49).

(iv) His silence about the great monument to Augustus above Monte Carlo, with its inscription (B.C. 7-6) preserved by Pliny, commemorating the reduction of the Alpine tribes.

(v) The fact that Strabo's work was entirely unknown to the elder Pliny. . . .

Abbreviations

H.G.A.M. The Historical Geography of Asia Minor, by W. M. Ramsay.

I.G.R.P. Inscriptiones Græcæ ad res Romanas pertinentes.

J.H.S. Journal of Hellenic Studies.

J.R.S. Journal of Roman Studies.

Rev. Ét. gr. Revue des Études grecques.

Studia Pontica (Anderson, Cumont, Grégoire).

Zft. f. Numism. Zeitschrift für Numismatik.

T. R. Glover (essay date 1932)

SOURCE: "Strabo: The Greek in the World of Caesar" in *Greek Byways*, The Macmillan Company, 1932, pp. 223-59.

[*In the following essay, Glover examines Strabo's family history and his views on religion, philosophy, history, geography, and science.*]

His book is the swan-song of Hellenism.

W. W. TARN.

Amaseia was a city of Asia Minor, in the kingdom of Pontus, a very strong city (c. 547).[1] It stood in a deep broad gulley through which flowed the river Iris. A high precipitous rock, with the river at the foot of the precipice, on the one side, and twin cliffs rising sheer above it on the other "towering magnificently"—the site seemed designed by Nature and by Providence[2] for a fortress and a city; and it was both. Walls linked the river to the peaks, there was an abundant natural water-supply, and the city was adorned with the palaces and monuments of kings (c. 561).[3] The country was fertile (c. 547) and not quite without fame in literature. Xenophon with his Ten Thousand had made his way along the shore and had described the native savages, the Mossynoeci; and utterly savage the mountaineers remained after three and a half centuries, a danger to travellers. Pompey himself had lost troops there, drugged with the poison-honey (of which Xenophon spoke[4]) and, while unconscious, attacked and killed (c. 549). Another tribe was more famous still; the Chaldaeans, as men now called them, were the Chalybes of the poets, the inventors of iron and swords and other forms of trouble for mankind—

Juppiter ut Chalybon omne genus pereat!

and there was a thrilling question whether, if Chalybes could be altered in modern days, they might not really be the Alybes of Homer. The Halizones came "from afar from Alybe where is the birthplace of silver";[5] and, says the geographer, there were silver mines there in early days. Names undergo many changes, especially among barbarians, he adds (c. 549)—and the story of North America confirms him, where whole tribes were duplicated by the vagaries of spelling; who would guess the Chippewas and Ojibways to be one and the same? What need then to alter Homer's text, as so many do—Ephorus for instance making the Halizones into Amazons with an unusually long Ō, and changing Alybe into Alope, to get them into the neighbourhood of Cyme, his own native place? Not that Alope is so easily found after all. And Apollodorus, who wrote a book on the forces at Troy, is as bad; he will allow no allies to cross the Halys to help Priam. Altogether these emendators take a lot of refutation; but as the iron-founders do not concern us at present, we will leave them, only echoing the geographer's bitter cry that it is rather superfluous . . . (to alter a text accepted for so many years (c. 296). The great ports of the country were Amisus and the more famous Trebizond on the Black Sea; inland was a holy city, to which we must return.

Our geographer does not give the account of the climate which we find in Tertullian. Marcion the heretic came from that country in the second century A.D., and his early environment helps to explain him. To the South the country is full of high mountains, sloping Northward to the sea; and across the sea[6] are the huge plains of Russia reaching to the Arctic; so "the day is never open, the sun is never glad, all the air is fog, every breath of wind comes from the North Pole;[7] all is torpid, all is rigid, nothing is ever hot there, except savagery". Tertullian is not altogether wrong here, but human life was sustained with some variety and some culture in spite of Aquilo and Alybes.

About the famous year of Cicero's consulship there lived at Amaseia a family of some distinction. A hundred years before two boys had been born into it, Dorylaos and Philetairos. Dorylaos became a notable general . . . , and, wandering as such people did in that age, he was employed, on behalf of his King Mithridates Euergetes, in gathering mercenary soldiers . . . through Thrace and Greece as far as Crete. That island was full of Greeks, glad to serve as mercenaries or pirates, for Rome was not yet mistress of the Eastern Mediterranean. On one of his visits to Crete, war broke out between the two cities of Cnossos and Gortyn. Cnossos enlisted Dorylaos with the happiest results; for Cnossos won the war, and the general found a home. To any one who has seen Cnossos among its lonely hills and carries away in his mind a picture of excavations, with thoughts of a strange city of pre-historic times, it comes oddly to think of Cnossos engaging in a war in the days of the Gracchi and hiring a general. King Mithridates was very shortly afterwards murdered by his friends at Sinope. So Dorylaos' occupation was gone; he married a Macedonian, called Sterope, and begot two sons, with names as soldier-like as his own, Lagetas and Stratarches.

We need not follow Pontic politics too closely, but every schoolboy used to know how Mithridates Eupator, the Mithridates of history, became king at the age when normal boys may be in the fourth form, founded an empire, lived largely on antidotes (we used to think), and fought the Romans off and on for a generation, taxing their best— Sulla, Lucullus and Pompey. The great Mithridates, then, had a fosterbrother, the son of Philetairos, a second Dorylaos (c. 477). Growing up with him, he was very fond of him, and when the chance came, he made him High Priest of the Pontic Comana (c. 557). The High Priests of these Asian holy cities were "almost dynasts" (c. 567), Prince-Bishops we might say, lords of temple lands and revenues, and of temple serfs innumerable (whom, however, they might not sell (c. 558)); they ranked next to the king (c. 535, 557), if they did not actually belong to the royal family (c. 535). So Dorylaos, the foster-brother, wore a diadem (c. 557), and enjoyed the greatest honours (c. 478). He remembered his cousins in Crete, and sent for them; and the king included them also in his patronage and care (c. 478).

But they were not a very lucky family; perhaps few families were very lucky for long in those days, or in any days among Eastern dynasties. Mithridates' ambition overleaped itself, and he became embroiled with the Romans, who were stronger than he thought in spite of their civil wars. Lagetas had lived in Crete, a good deal nearer the sphere of Roman influence and the province of Achaia, and he made the opposite mistake; he overestimated the immediate prospects of Roman success. "He was caught in the attempt to make the kingdom revolt to the Romans, on the understanding that he should rule it himself"; and he came to grief and (naturally) his kindred with him. In the meantime Cnossos had fallen on evil days, "ten thousand changes"; so that retreat was cut off, and they were brought very low . . . (c. 478). Dorylaos was in the plot and shared the disaster (c. 557).

Then somehow fortune smiled again. The daughter of La-getas was married, probably before this, to an unnamed man, who was brother to a friend of the king. Moaphernes (his name hardly suggests pure Greek descent, nor does his nephew's[8]) was a satrap . . . of Mithridates in the region of Colchis, from which the king drew most of the supplies for his navy (c. 499)—timber,[9] linen, hemp, wax and pitch (c. 498). But once again trouble came. The king put a nephew and great-nephew of his satrap to death. Moaphernes saw his chance of revenge. The king was again at war with Rome, and Lucullus was making a suc-cessful campaign. So Moaphernes revolted and brought over fifteen garrisons to the Romans. Lucullus made him large promises; and then disaster came yet again. The Ma-nilian Law (66 B.C.) transferred the control of the war from Lucullus to Pompey; the two generals hated each other, and Pompey had a mean streak in him. He would have nothing to say to the friends of Lucullus, and meantime he was all-powerful from the Bosporus to Jerusalem.

In the year 63, then, in Ciccro's consulship—or it might have been in 64, the year when Augustus was born—the niece of Moaphernes gave birth to a son, whom we know as Strabo. The name implies Roman citizenship, but we are not told how, or when, or by whom the citizenship was acquired. The family, as we have seen, and as Strabo makes quite clear, owed most of its misfortunes to its adhesion to Rome. It is a little odd, however, to find the name Strabo, more often associated with Pompeys, in a group related so closely to Lucullus. If guessing is legitimate, one wonders whether Pompey relented, or found an adherent in the father of Strabo; but by now it is not of much importance. The question has also been raised as to whether once again the family rejoiced in royal goodwill, and whether the Geographer in later life was at-tached in some capacity to Queen Pythodoris, whom he praises as a woman of prudence and well fitted to rule, as she did in part at least of Pontus, including (it would seem) Amaseia (c. 555, 649). It is a modern conjecture of an Italian scholar,[10] certainly pleasing in its way. What does signify in this story of five generations is the view it gives us of Hellenized Asia—half Greek, with settlers and mercenaries in its towns; savages in its mountains; dubi-ously Hellenized barbarians on its thrones; and more or less Greek High Priests in its very oriental temple princedoms. "More or less", as Strabo says in one of his half-humorous asides, is a trick of speech much found in kings and geographers (c. 9); neither class can be quite certain of everything, he says, nor can we. In all these researches we have

> The mingled charm of not too much,
> Part seen, imagined part.

The education of Strabo, no reader will fail to see, was very much along the ordinary lines of Greek culture. No really readable writer of his period has less rhetoric, though he must have studied it in due course. His writing is gener-ally simple and direct, and equal to its purpose. Once or twice, when he has to speak of masters of rhetoric, a slight inflection of tone shows his mind on the matter. Thus,

when he writes of the outstanding men of Pergamum, he lumps in with a dubiously royal pretender another who "has been thought worthy of a great name," to wit, "Apol-lodorus the rhetorician, who wrote the treatise on *Rhetoric* and was the founder of the Apollodorean school, whatever it may be; for there were many fashions, some of them beyond my power of judgment, and among them was the Apollodorean school and the Theodorean. What chiefly exalted Apollodorus was the friendship of Caesar Augus-tus". Still the man had a capable pupil, a real man of note, Strabo adds with his usual fairness (c. 625). Again, he touches off Hegesias of Magnesia, "who above all started the so-called 'Asian' affectation . . . and corrupted the standard Attic style" (c. 648); and he quizzes the Tarsians for their universal readiness to improvise oratory and never stop (c. 674).[11] There are no speeches in Strabo's book. Modern readers might not expect them in a Geography; but they know little of ancient rhetoric who think anything impossible for its true addicts. Strabo also wrote a History, where speeches might have been more in keeping, but one remembers his admiration for Polybius, and will not as-sume that a lost work might have glittered with irrelevance. Strabo is never irrelevant unless Homer gives him an excuse; and Homer was not irrelevant to a Greek geogra-pher or to a Stoic.

Homer was in fact still a large part of a liberal education. What is more, Homer was the chosen author of the Stoics, their Bible, one might almost say, whose virtual infallibil-ity they upheld against the world, by means of a lavish use of allegory, the traditional weapon of the orthodox. The editors of the Homeric Hymns remark that in one respect Strabo's orthodoxy is more than scholastic; he never refers to those Hymns at all—a silence which implies that they are outside the canon.[12] Of course this might be accident, but those who know Strabo well will not think so. Once he pauses for a half apology, which every human heart will surely accept—"I might perhaps not be examining the old stories at such length; it might suffice perhaps to tell in each case how things are now; if one had not grown up from boyhood with the tradition. Amid so many differing voices, a man must make his own choice" (c. 348). If his taste for legend began in boyhood, there will be the less wonder at the wealth of legend that he knows. He does not believe it all, as we shall see, but he rescues a good deal for us. He has a Herodotean instinct for a story, old or new, though he rations himself severely in telling them. Still he lets us see that he knew them and liked them, and often gives us a good outline. "All these are names of places, deserted or scantily peopled, or of winter torrents; but they are often mentioned because of their ancient his-tory" (c. 614). And they were in this instance, in Northern Asia Minor. When he starts upon the Troad, he hopes his readers will forgive him; the country is in ruins and desola-tion, but its fame! That prompts a writer to "no ordinary prolixity." . . . Let his readers put the blame not all on him but some of it on those who have a passion for antiquity, a glorious antiquity (c. 581). Had not Demetrius of Skepsis in the Troy region written a commentary of thirty books on sixty lines of Homer? (c. 603). It is remarked to-day that, great as his interest was in Homer and the Homeric scene, his investigations were made in books and commentaries; he does not appear to have visited the Troad himself; it was not nearly as ruinous as he supposed.[13]

Growing up in Pontus and coming of a family connected with holy places, it is not surprising that he is interested in religion. Here is his picture of the Pontic Comana, where his kinsman Dorylaos had been Prince-Bishop. He does not in so many words say he had been there, as he does about the Cappadocian Comana; but he says the Pontic temple was founded from the other in honour of the same goddess, and that in the rituals, the dignity of the priests and the divine possession (or inspiration or frenzy . . . the places are much alike. Comana, then, is a populous town, and a notable centre of trade for Armenia,[14] and when the processions of the goddess are held, people throng from every quarter, town and country, men and women alike, for the festival. Others permanently reside in the place, bound by vows, and doing continual sacrifices to the goddess. There is a great deal of luxury, the estates are covered with vines, and the town is thronged by women who live by their persons, most of them sacred to the goddess. In a way, the city is a little Corinth; for there too, on account of the swarms of courtesans sacred to Aphrodite, outsiders resorted in great numbers for holidays; merchants and soldiers would waste their money to the last coin, so that the proverb arose regarding them: "Not every man to Corinth may set sail". Such then is Comana. He names four other similar holy places, beside Corinth and the Sicilian Eryx.[15] Only a Hindu could to-day think of such a scene and such a profession as religion; but it was then an act of piety to dedicate slaves and slave-girls to the goddess (c. 532). Pindar—at least it is attributed to him by Athenaeus[16]—wrote a poem for a man who dedicated a hundred slave-girls to Aphrodite at Corinth. But to a thinking man, bred on literature and philosophy, and moving toward the Stoics, it must have raised questions about religion.

Questions were raised by other aspects of popular religion. . . . [God-possession,] "enthusiasm", for instance—it interests him very much, and in a long passage (c. 466-473) he discusses it with its adjuncts and varieties. The varieties are many, but there are common features about the god-possessed, . . . whether it be Bacchic frenzy or Samothracian; they are ministrants, and the rites are sacred; terror is roused by war-dance, cymbal, drum, flute, arms and shouting. Yes, he says, any discussion of this sort might be said to belong to theology, but it is not alien to the speculations of philosophy; and with great wealth of tradition he discusses it. . . . But "every discussion about the gods must examine ancient opinions and myths; for the men of old would speak their thoughts of nature and reality in riddles, and would ever add myth to their arguments. All these riddles it is not easy to solve with precision; but, if the great mass of what is told as myth be set out, some of it harmonizing and some not, one might be able more easily to guess the truth" (c. 474).

Greeks and barbarians alike perform their sacred rites with the relaxation of a festival; in some cases there is "enthusiasm", god-possession, but not in all; music is used in some, but not in other rituals. Some of the ceremonies are done in the mystic way, others openly. And so Nature bids. (Here we catch a Stoic accent.) For the relaxation draws the mind away from human cares, and turns the true mind to the divine. The "enthusiasm" appears to imply some sort of divine inspiration and to approach in kind the prophetic spirit.[17] The mystic concealment of the holy things (or rites) induces reverence for the divine; it copies the nature of the divine which seeks to avoid our perception. "Music, involving dance, rhythm and song, by the pleasure it gives and by its artistic beauty links us to the divine; and this is the reason. For it has been well said that men best imitate the gods, when they are doing good to others—better still it would be, when they are happy; and joy and festival, philosophy and music, are of that nature. . . . For this reason Plato, and, still earlier, the Pythagoreans, called philosophy music, and tell us that the universe is constituted in harmony, assuming every kind of music to be the work of gods" (c. 468).

Daemons and gods in his age are becoming two classes,[18] but, though he alludes to the daemons a little below, he draws no sharp distinction; both groups are called gods (c. 471); here he just touches on the main dogma with which Plutarch defends polytheism—the distinction is vital for Plutarch who traces it to Hesiod. Elsewhere he quotes Polybius to the effect that each of the gods is honoured as the discoverer of something useful (c. 24); Aeolus, for instance, for having taught men the art of steering in the Straits of Messina with their changing currents (c. 23). Here again is a line of thought used a good deal by pagans who reflected on polytheism, used still more and with more drastic effect against the gods by Tertullian and the Christians. Once more he anticipates what we find in Plutarch. "Great Pan is dead", says the mystic voice in Plutarch's story,[19] and the good man writes a tract to explain why the oracles are failing. Strabo, a hundred years before him, chronicles so much; "Dodona like others is in eclipse, has failed" (c. 327); Delphi, in earlier times held in extraordinary honour, has fallen into much neglect (c. 419); and, "after saying much of Ammon, so much I must add that among the ancients prophecy generally and oracles were more in honour, but nowadays there is much disregard for them. The Romans are content with the utterances of the Sibyl, and the divinations of the Etruscans from entrails and birds and signs in the sky. So the oracle of Ammon also has been abandoned" (c. 813).

But old rituals are kept up. The goddess Feronia is still honoured in the town of that name under Soracte, and a remarkable ceremony is performed in her honour; "for those who are possessed by this goddess . . . walk with bare feet over a great heap of embers and ash unscathed; and crowds of people come both on account of the annual festival and to see the sight I have mentioned" (c. 226). Virgil also speaks of the fire-walking at this place.[20] At Castabala, not far from Tyana in Asia Minor, in the temple of Artemis, "they say the priestesses walk with bare feet over hot embers unscathed" (c. 537). It is still to be seen done in Japan, as a friend told me who saw it. People still sleep in temples on their own account, and for others, to learn the cure of diseases; sometimes it is better that an experienced priest should do the sleeping for you in the sacred cave.[21] He appears to imply that it is also a regular part of Judaism (c. 761).

Strabo gives a curiously interesting account of Judaism (c. 760). The Jews, as they are now called, are, according to the best accounts obtainable at the Jerusalem temple, of Egyptian descent. For one Moses, from among the Egyptian priests, vexed with things in Egypt, migrated, and took with him a great many people "honouring the divine" . . . "for Moses said, and taught, that the Egyptians had a wrong idea in making the divine like to beasts and cattle,[22] and the Greeks too were wrong in modelling gods in human form. For, he urged, God would be this one thing only, this thing that encompasses us all and land and sea as well, the thing we call sky and Cosmos and Nature. Who with any sense would dare to fashion a likeness of this, like to any thing among us? No, men ought to drop all making of images, and, setting apart a precinct and a grove . . . worthy of the purpose, worship without [and here a word fails us in the text]"; and then he ascribes the practice mentioned of [enkoimēsis] to Moses—men who are good at dreams . . . should sleep in the sanctuary for themselves and for others; and, finally, Moses taught that those who live soberly and with righteousness should always expect some gift or sign from God, but others should not.

Judaism has become amazingly Stoic. This identification of God with Nature and the universe meets us in one of the most spirited and eloquent passages of Seneca;[23] but it is not quite Jewish. God as the first author of beauty is the doctrine of the hellenized Jew who wrote *The Wisdom of Solomon;*[24] but that is very far from the sheer Stoicism which Strabo finds in Moses—or attributes to Moses. But the passage is an interesting one, in striking contrast with the story of the ass's head which even Tacitus thought worth telling a century later.[25]

It has been made more and more clear as we have gone on that Strabo leant to Stoicism, that he identified himself with the school. The first person in his sentence "which we call sky, etc." implies that the Stoic position is his own; and he makes no secret of it. But his teachers, whom he names, were not Stoics. One of them, Tyrannion (c. 548), taught in Rome—whether Starbo heard him there or in Asia—and was, as we learn from Cicero, one of the unfortunate instructors of the young Marcus and the young Quintus; and he was interested in Geography. Aristodemos would lecture on Rhetoric in the morning and Grammar in the evening (c. 650). Xenarchus was a Peripatetic (c. 670). Strabo does not definitely say that he went to lectures of the Stoic Athenodorus, but he says "he was a companion of mine", and we learn from other sources that he was also the friend of Augustus.

As for popular religion, Strabo makes his position quite clear; it is very much the view of Polybius[26]—"let it alone". We have to look, says Strabo (c. 19), at the emotional nature of the reasoning animal, man. Man is a creature that loves knowledge, and the prelude to knowledge is love of story. . . . It is that love of story that prompts children to listen and learn, and to inquire. Novelty is the thing; but add to it the marvel and the portent, and you increase the pleasure and the appeal. (It sounds like the story of his own boyhood.) Now the illiterate and uneducated are in a sense still children, and like stories; and so with the half-educated . . . —a class not often so directly named. The tale of portent can be terrible as well as pleasing; witness the bogeys children are told about, Lamia, Gorgo, Ephialtes, Mormolyce. In the same way, grown persons of the types described can be scared from evil ways when they are told—or are given to understand— that punishments, terrors and threats are used by the gods. "For in dealing with a crowd of women, for instance, or any promiscuous multitude, a philosopher cannot lead them by reason and so exhort them to reverence, piety and faith. No, there is need of superstition, too . . . and that requires tales and marvels. Thunderbolt, aegis, trident, torches, snakes or thyrsus, the weapons of the gods are all myths; and so is all ancient theology. . . . " The founders of states knew all about this—Numa, for instance, in Plutarch.[27] History and philosophy are later growths, but "philosophy is for the few, while poetry is more serviceable for the people and can fill the theatres". And of course he touches on Homer—he generally does; for Homer gave much thought to truth, but "therein he set" (like Hephaistos making the armour) falsehood also—the one he accepted, the other he used as a demagogue might to outmanoeuvre the masses. . . . Let us quote here once for all the great sentence of Polybius which is ever in Strabo's mind, and say Goodbye, if we can, to the Homeric question—"to invent everything is neither convincing nor Homeric" (c. 25).[28]

But now for his own belief, which he sets out in a very curious passage (c. 809, 810). Nature and Providence both contribute to the world we see. Nature provides the spheric earth, solid and central, with a spherical covering of water all over it. Then Providence takes a hand, "being herself all full of cunning devices and artificer of ten thousand things." . . . It is her will to beget . . . living creatures, and, chief among them, gods and men, for whom really the rest exist. But the earth is covered with water, and man is not a water creature but a being of dry land and air and light; so she devises sea and mountain, thus varying the surface of the globe, and providing for further variety in earth hard or crumbling or full of iron ore, and water sweet and salt, medicinal and deadly, cold and hot; and, still further, for future changes of level and surface. (We shall hear of this again.[29]) Thus the configuration of Southern France moves him to reflect on the harmonious arrangement . . . of the country with river and sea, Mediterranean and Atlantic; that is its virtue . . . —so wonderfully adapted to ideal human life—especially nowadays, when, under the influence of Rome, they have taken in earnest to farming, and live civilized. "In such cases, one must believe there is evidence confirming the view that it is the doing of Providence, since the regions are laid out not in a fortuitous way but, as it were, with re-flexion, or reason" (c. 188, 189). Perhaps he wavers a little, as a man may, when, in arguing against Posidonius, he maintains that the distribution of animals, plants and climates is *not* the work of Providence, nor the differences of race and dialect; arts and institutions do not depend on latitude, but some on nature and some on training—contrast the Athenians and the Boeotians (c. 102, 103).

Thus with a background of history—the family fortunes visibly linked to the fates of kings—of popular religion, of Greek education and Stoic philosophy, Strabo steps out into the world. So far his literature has only been hinted at, but his book is full of it—not obtrusively at all, when he is not arguing about Homer; but for a well-read man places have associations. Halicarnassus means Herodotus for every human being; and Strabo adds Heraclitus, who has come into English literature in a beautiful epitaph exquisitely rendered; and he does not forget to conclude "and in our own times Dionysius the historian". And here a personal digression may be forgiven. Let a man read Strabo and Dionysius in one long vacation, and he will realize how men of learning may differ, and, without an unkind thought for *ce bon Denys,* as Sainte-Beuve calls him, prefer Strabo.

For, letting the kings and captains pass, and the Prince-Bishops and professors with them, one finds Strabo very good company when once he is done with latitudes and equators, which, interesting and valuable as they are, still are not things of joy but must come into Geography. He is a human being and lets you know on his first page, quite quietly, that he is interested in the animals, plants and fruits of land and sea; they are a part of any real knowledge of the world; and we shall return to them. Timaeus, we read in another author,[30] fancied that, from the number of meals mentioned in the *Illiad* and the *Odyssey,* Homer must have been a good trencher-man—a view very properly denounced. But, even so, it is at least a human trait, and a pleasant one, that the Geographer pauses to tell us whence the best fish-sauce comes (c. 159), that the hams cured in the glens of the Pyrenees are excellent, and rival those of Cantabria (c. 162), that Lyons sends the best bacon to Rome (c. 192); . . . that Caecuban and Faler-nian are exceedingly good, too (c. 234), as we learn from others; but Samian wine is *not* good, he warns us (c. 637). When he tells of Indian ascetics, "it all tends to sobriety", he admits, "but those other habits of theirs nobody could approve of—solitary feeding on all occasions and no com-mon hour for all to have dinner and breakfast, but each as he pleases. The opposite way is the thing for social life and civilized people" (c. 709); and we can agree with him, and reprobate "the bestial practice of solitary feeding".[31] In one of the many discussions of Homer's tribes, this time about the Abioi, he quotes Posidonius as saying they may well be called so, a race of celibates—Homer obviously thinking life without women only half-life (c. 296).[32] He

drifts on into quoting Menander, however, on woman's way of wasting substance in sacrifices—

> Five times a day we had to sacrifice,
> Seven slave-girls with their cymbals in a ring,
> Others a-shrieking to the gods.

Irrelevant to scientific Geography, perhaps, and a digres-sion? But some digressions help the reader, and illustrate the writer's mind. Iasos is an island of poor soil, and depends on fishing; and people, says Strabo, invent stories about it, thus: A musician was giving a recital there, sing-ing to his own accompaniment on the lyre. But a bell rang, and everybody at once got up and went out, except one man. The lyrist thanked him for his courtesy, and for his love of music; everybody else had gone when the bell rang. "What's that?" says the man, a little deaf, "the fish-bell rang? Goodbye" (c. 568). He pauses to allude to the wicked slander against Cyme that the people there did not know enough to come in out of the rain (c. 622), and how Magnesia's repute suffers for the omission of an *iota* in a prominent inscription, like Selwyn College (c. 648). A good quotation (c. 670), a happy misquotation (c. 655), will light up the page from time to time, or a proverb about a place—"he put the Colophon on it" (c. 643), as we might say "as sure as God's in Gloucestershire", or "all ship-shape and Bristol fashion". Dealing with Spanish tribes, he writes "I shrink from overflowing with names—they are so unpleasant to write, unless anybody can really enjoy hearing Pleutauroi and Bardyetai and Allotriges, and others still worse and more insignificant" (c. 155). Later on he omits some Arab names for the same reason—they are "so odd to pronounce" (c. 777). When he tells how he and his friends were ferried over the Nile from Syene to the island of Philae[33] in the most terribly primitive contriv-ances, "we crossed easily", he says, "and all our fears were in vain . . . for there is no danger—if they don't overload the boat" (c. 818). Why does he tell us of Posidonius' discovery that crows are black in Spain? (c. 163).

This brings us to his travels, of which he was rather proud; few geographers have been much farther; if they have seen more of the West, they have not been so far in the East; for Strabo has travelled from Armenia to Etruria, and from the Black Sea to the frontiers of Ethiopia (c. 117). Polybius and Posidonius appear to have ranged much farther afield; and there are critics who think that Strabo travelled generally in a straight line to his terminus. He tells us he stood on Acrocorinthos[34] and saw "Parnassus and Helicon, lofty mountains and snow-clad", and the gulf of Corinth (as we call it) below (c. 379); and he describes the city shortly after its restoration by the Romans (c. 379), when Caesar had Corinth and Carthage both rebuilt (c. 833). But he did not visit Mycene, or he could hardly have said there was not a trace of it left (c. 372);[35] and critics think he did not leave his route so far as to go to Athens.[36] If that is right, it was his loss, not ours; for oth-ers have described Athens to us, and there are a hundred places, of which all we know we owe to Strabo. It is, however, characteristic that he notices the view from the citadel of Corinth; he seems to have been sensitive to scenery. He pauses to speak of the waterfall at Tibur[37] "plunging from a great height into a deep gorge" (c. 238).

. . . The region we know as Venetia, with its lagoons, where alone "our sea" has tides like the Ocean, reminds him of Lower Egypt with its dikes and canals; and it is a wonderful voyage up the Po (c. 212). Sinope, like Amaseia, is "beautifully equipped by Nature and Providence", set on its peninsula, guarded by shoals, and splendidly adorned by its inhabitants (c. 545). Vesuvius, save for its summit, is covered with farms of great beauty . . . ; the summit is a flat plain, sterile and ash-coloured, with great cracks in the scorched rock, as if eaten by fire— "one might conjecture that in former days it was on fire, and had had craters of fire, quenched for want of anything to burn" (c. 247). There is later evidence that this conjecture was only too sound. Then he discusses the relation of the fruitfulness of the country round, comparing it with the vineyards that flourish under Etna (c. 247, 273). One of his most interesting pages describes an ascent of Etna given to him by some acquaintances who had recently made it, with some difficulty and courage (c. 274).

Strabo went to Rome, they tell us, in 44 B.C., deducing the date from his statement that he saw Publius Servilius Isauricus (c. 568), who died there in that year. But the most dreadful event of the century, that fell on the Ides of March, he does not mention as within the period of any visit of his. He records the ends of two of the murderers (c. 331, 646). He made other visits to Rome, which readers have tried to date, not always convincingly. Rome he evidently studied with the attention of a geographer, an historian and a lover of art. The site, he thinks, was not so much suitable as inevitable; it was not a strong position to defend and it had not at first much land (c. 230). He gives in outline "the most generally believed" account of early Rome—the coming of Aeneas (not precisely as Virgil does, quite apart from Virgil's art), the older and mythical Arcadian foundation of Evander, the twins (some myth in the narrative here, he thinks), the kings, and the incorporation of Aikouoi and Ouolskoi and other familiar people (c. 231). All Latium is fertile (c. 231)—here pause to note this recurrent term . . . which brings the shore of Arabia quite out of the class of the islands of the Blessed into the category of ordinary fertility, which indeed is something. The Sabines, again, are a very ancient race, with fine old-fashioned ways . . . —courage, at any rate, and a quality that has kept them to this day (c. 228). One phrase might tempt the reader, but for the variant tale of Aeneas, to think that Strabo knew something of Virgil—"all Italy most excellent nurse of herds and crops" (c. 228)[38]—but one dare not say so. Greeks did not read Latin poetry, and it is with surprise that we find one allusion to it in Strabo—no Horace at Tibur, no Virgil at Mantua, but at Rudiae Ennius (c. 281).

Italy has changed a good deal since the days of Romulus. The Samnites were all but wiped out by Sulla, who had said that "he had realized from experience that no Roman at all could have any peace as long as the Samnites existed as a nation" (c. 249); their towns are reduced to mere villages. The Oscans are a people no longer, though their dialect still lingers and is used on the stage in mimes (c. 233). Romans are intermingled with Umbrians and Etruscans; these old names are kept but the people are all Romans—and so are the Gauls and Ligurians of the North (c. 216). Even the people of Naples, the resort of retired teachers, are Romans now, though much of the Greek way of life . . . survives (c. 246). The old *Magna Graecia* has been "barbarized"; Campanians have occupied some of it, and all is Roman (c. 253).

The city of Rome, capital of Italy, as we should say, and capital of the world, obviously impressed Strabo, and called forth one of his significant comments. The Greeks, he said, had the repute of being happy in the foundation of cities, largely in this that they aimed at beauty and strength of position, and thought of harbours and fruitful soil. The Roman mind turned to what the Greeks neglected—the paving of the streets, the water-supply and sewers that could wash the filth of the city into the Tiber. They levelled their roads through the land with cuttings and embankments. The sewers were vaulted with close-fitting stone, and some of them were big enough to let a cartload of hay through. The aqueducts brought such a supply of water to Rome, that "rivers" flow through the city and the sewers; and every house, you might say, has cisterns and pipes and fountains in plenty. This was largely the work of Marcus Agrippa, though he had also adorned the city with many fine structures. The early Romans made little account of beauty; they had other things to do; but to-day everything is done to make Rome beautiful. The Campus Martius, with its wonderful space and its grass, its chariots and its games, and the works of art all round it, appeals to him; and he lifts up his eyes to the hills whose crowns he sees surrounding the city—it is such a sight that it is hard to turn from it. And much more. Such is Rome, he concludes (c. 235, 236).

But Strabo looks at the place not solely as a tourist. Rome is being ceaselessly rebuitl—like modern New York. Houses fall, are burnt, are sold and torn down; and the rivers of Western Italy, and chiefly the Tiber, are constantly bringing from the forests and quarries of Italy the stone and lumber to rebuild it all (c. 235). From Luna comes marble, white and bluish grey, the best of marbles and quarried close to the sea (c. 222); Pisa has quarries and timber for ship-building (c. 223); Tibur and Gabii send a fine stone for the better work (c. 238). Augustus has laid down new laws, regulating the height of buildings (70 ft.) and establishing a fire brigade of freedmen. And merchandise of all sorts[39] pours in—from the countryside down the Anio, the Nar, the Teneas (c. 235), and up the great roads that span the land, the Appian Way that goes as far as Brindisi (c. 233), the Latin Way and the Valerian (c. 237). The harbourage is poor; with all those tributary streams the Tiber carries a lot of silt, *multa flavus arena*—how much of all this Virgil has told us!—and the merchantmen of the world cannot come in to Ostia unless it is light ship, when the efficient tender system has brought the goods ashore (c. 231, 232). The ships had been bringing things for a long time.

For, as this Greek walked Rome, he noted—and it goes down in his *Geography*—how many famous masterpieces of ancient Greek art had come to Rome. Lucullus had brought the Apollo of Calamis (c. 319), Agrippa the Fallen Lion of Lysippus (c. 590), and Mummius endless art from Corinth; and he pauses to speak more kindly of Mummius than one would expect—a man "more generous than skilled in art" (c. 381). There is a bitter tone in Polybius[40] when he speaks of all this pillage; easy, he might say, to be generous with other people's treasures; for it was bitterly resented. Strabo quotes Polybius' account of what he saw with his own eyes at the sack of Corinth—the Roman soldiers dicing on the Dionysos of Aristides, one of the most famous of Greek pictures. Strabo saw the picture hanging in honour in the temple of Ceres in Rome, and tells us that it perished when the temple was burnt not very long ago. This happened in 31 B.C., we are told, which may help us to the dating of his visit or visits, and of the earlier parts of his book.[41] Pillage of Antony's Augustus restored to Samos (c. 637) and to Egypt (c. 595); but he took from Cos the statue of Venus Anadyomene, and dedicated it as the foundress of their family to "the deified Caesar", Julius; and it is said he remitted a hundred talents of tribute to the Coans in exchange (c. 657). Rome has thus another likeness to New York in being adorned with the art of another world and another age.

So Strabo saw the world's centre, and we have a hint as to the beginning of his work; and to that work we must now turn. It was not his only book. "He looked on himself primarily not as a geographer", writes Mr Leaf, "but as a philosophical historian. It was to History that he had given his life; the *Geography* was the work of his old age, destined to be an appendix to his histories."[42] But the [*Historical Sketches*] (c. 13), which were used by Plutarch, Josephus and Arrian, and are supposed to have been a continuation of Polybius—not the only one, by the way— have perished. The fact that his first work was on History explains the richness of historical matter in the book that happily survives. A Geography—to English ears it does not promise half what it gives us. Mr H. F. Tozer calls its composition in the Augustan age "a piece of extraordinary good fortune", not merely for its intrinsic merits but for the fact that we are chiefly indebted to it for our acquaintance with his predecessors.[43] "No more picturesque book", writes Mr W. W. Tarn,[44] "remains since Herodotus."

Geography, he says, is a sphere of Philosophy as much as any other science; indeed to treat of it aright the geographer needs philosophy as well as knowledge of facts, history, natural history and what we nowadays call economics— with a preference, as in duty bound, for the world as it exists (c. 574), but a love (as we have seen) for antiquity. He should not be tied down too closely to delimit frontiers—he is not a land-surveyor (c. 629); he is allowed the "more or less" of which he spoke; and he need not really go outside the inhabited world (c. 131, 132). He must inevitably bor-

row a good deal of his material, and there may be errors in it, which may be forgiven, if his treatment is on the whole better or fuller (c. 465)—the spread of the Roman and Parthian empires, like that of Alexander, has added immensely to knowledge (c. 14). But, of course, there are what Polybius criticized in other writers . . . as "popular notions", e.g. hearsay statements or estimates of distances (c. 317), though Polybius did not quite always avoid them himself (c. 465), to say nothing of the opposite fault of that great man, . . . abstruseness and stiffness in matters really simple (c. 107). Strabo means his book to be useful to the statesman, to men in high station,[45] and also to people of ordinary culture, who have had the usual round of letters and philosophy (c. 13). His task, he says, anticipating a phrase of Dr Johnson's, is "carving a colossus" . . . he has to think of the general effect of the thing on the scale planned, and minutiae are of very minor importance (c. 13, 14). Like Homer who never mentioned his native land (c. 30), he has to learn to omit; and omission is not proof of ignorance—though he gives himself away a little perhaps by saying that, if Homer had known about India, he must surely have mentioned it (c. 39).

Every geography has to be in some measure a compilation, to depend on authorities. It is needless here to make a list of Strabo's authorities. It is obvious that they are not all his contemporaries; they hardly could have been; and he has to depend for India on men who combined what is recognized to-day to be true with what no one outside medieval and Mandeville circles could have believed (c. 711). In two cases, however, he refuses to look at very interesting figures. Following Polybius, he dismisses Pytheas, the explorer of Britain and the North Sea shores about 320 B.C., as a liar of the most portentous type—a "Bergaean" (c. 47). Modern critics who know more of Britain and the shores of the North Sea, even than Polybius (who explored the Atlantic coast of Africa), recognize from the fragments of Pytheas which Strabo gives us that he really had been where he claimed.[46] The other man's case is rather different. The voyages of Eudoxus to discover the extent of Africa Southward Strabo sums up in a most attractive page; it is a first-rate tale, and the reader would wish it to be true; but this Strabo will not allow, and he points out improbabilities and tears it to shreds, though the great Posidonius had accepted it (c. 98-102). Mr Tozer and Mr Warmington lean to a friendly opinion about it; "it has often been treated with scepticism", says Mr Tozer, but "he must have contributed largely to the stock of knowledge"[47]

From time to time Strabo comments on the historical sources available for his work, with some generalizations. "The ancient historians tell us a great deal that is not true; they became accustomed to falsehood, through writing myths; and the result is that they contradict one another" (c. 341). Olympia is the centre of stories told in many ways, and not very credible (c. 355), and we can neglect matters which merely lead to controversies about myths (c. 596). Old Persian history, too, is unreliable for the same reason—an excessive love of myth (c. 507). Some stories are repeated suspiciously often—so many images are brought from Troy, and the captive Trojan women so often burn their captors' fleets on the voyage from Troy (c. 264)—at the mouth of the river Neaethus in Southern Italy (c. 262), the very name being suggestive of blazing ships, and in the neighbourhood of Potidaea, where the name Phlegra has the same temptations (VII, fragm. 25). Many rivers in many parts of the world flow underground—and he chronicles a good many of these *katavothra*—but that does not warrant such nonsense as Alpheius flowing under the sea and coming up again at Syracuse, or the absurdities of the great Sophocles about the Inachus, and of Ibycus about the Asopus (c. 271). There are still regions unknown (c. 294, 493), and there were in the past; and where peoples were barbarian and remote, cut up into small kingdoms, etc., their records are few and unsafe; and the farther from Greece, the greater our ignorance. Greeks have come to be the most talkative of men; but the Roman historians imitate them, they translate from the Greek, but they have not much love of knowledge, so, where the Greeks leave a gap, there is very little done by the Romans to fill it; most of the most distinguished names are Greek (c. 166). And then a shrewder comment; how many migrations have there been since the Trojan War—of Greeks, Trêres, Cimmerians, Lydians, and so on to the Galatians? These migrations have disturbed and confused everything, and not these only; for the historians have used different names for the same people, calling the Trojans Phrygians as in tragedy, and the Lycians Carians, and so on (c. 572, 573); and the Macedonians too have changed the names of places (c. 518). History has been tampered with to glorify Alexander—the Caucasus, Prometheus and all, shifted into India (c. 505). There was indeed great confusion about the names of the mountain ranges even without the design of flattery. Names undergo many changes among barbarians (c. 549); and the civilized peoples lump the natives of a little-known region together—the tribes are all Scythians in Russia, all Celts or Iberians in the West, or, worse still, are compounded and become Celtiberians and Celtiscythians; and probably Ethiopian was as vague a term in the past (c. 33). We know the wild use that the West has made of "Indian" since the Renaissance, and the East of "Frank", and the dreadful profanity of American purists who, to avoid confusions with Hiawatha's kindred, will talk of a Mohammedan Hindu. After all this, it seems an almost lovable vanity that would emend the text of Homer to connect a pedigree with Nestor (c. 339).

Still, with all these difficulties, it is remarkable how much History his book carries with it, like the many streams he tells of that wash down the gold dust, with the chance every now and then of a nugget . . . (c. 778). But the gold comes as naturally as in the river; he does not, like the modern poet, try to cram every rift with gold. His wide range of interest, reading and observation allows endless variety, and whether it is art or nature, or both, his story moves easily. There must be many a reader who takes some time to realize how gracefully it is written, and how well the author handles an immense amount of learning that in another's hands might have been unsufferable.

The Greek world preserved his book without abridgement, and well it might. I shall not attempt an analysis of the work, beyond saying that, after a discussion of longitudes and latitudes very proper for a prelude, and some argument on Homer as a geographer—how could a Stoic pass the flippant suggestions of Eratosthenes that the aim of every poet is to charm . . . not to instruct[48] (c. 7), and that we shall find the lands Odysseus saw when we have caught the cobbler who stitched the bag in which the winds were tied up? (c. 24)—he proceeds to describe the various lands from West to East, gives us a mass of collectanea about India, tells of Egypt as he saw it himself from end to end with Aelius Gallus, makes a brief survey of North Africa, and concludes with some paragraphs on the Roman Empire. It will be generally felt by his readers, as I have already hinted, that he gives us less on Greece than on any land—perhaps because we know more of Greece than of the rest of the ancient world. Here I propose to consider very briefly certain lines of observation which one finds in every part of his work. To the student of Geography it will be important to weigh the facts presented to him, but even he, like ourselves, must study the geographer. What is the geographer looking for in this broad world he writes about, what does he see, what does he think significant? If we can answer these questions, we shall have a better idea of the man, and be more able to understand the value of his work.

He begins with a long section on scientific Geography, familiar to every student of ancient science, but with surprises for those who have confined themselves to the great central Classics and not wandered much upon byways. "The reader of this book ought not to be so simple-minded (or so lazy) as never to have looked at a globe or the circles drawn upon it, some parallel, others at right angles to the parallels, and others again oblique to them; or, again, not to have observed the position of tropics, equator . . . and zodiac—through which the sun is borne on his course and by his turning determines the differences of zones . . . and winds. Anyone who has learnt so much, and about horizons and arctic circles, and what else belongs to elementary mathematics—even in a general way—will be able to follow what is said here" (c. 13). So much for a beginning, and the modern reader will notice at once that Strabo, here as elsewhere, holds fast to a geocentric universe. He does not, I think, so much as mention Aristarchus of Samos, who propounded that the sun is the real centre for us; his Aristarchus is the other, the Homeric critic (c. 103). Another vestige of ancient astronomy, held by the Stoics and used by Lucan,[49] is the notion that the stars were fed by evaporation from the sea (c. 6). The astronomy and the mathematics I will leave to the better informed reader, who may wish to pursue them; but one or two outstanding points, of great significance, may be noted before we pass on.

First, then, Strabo starts and continues, as Aristotle did, with a spherical world. In the decline of learning in the middle ages this was lost;[50] and Theology for the time being, on the assurance of Hebrew poets, decided for a flat earth. It was the recovery of the ancient Greek geographers that gave the impulse to fresh speculation and at last to the voyaging of Columbus.[51] Strabo's prime argument is from the senses—from what anybody knows who has made even a very short voyage; "it is obviously the curvature of the sea that prevents people on ships from seeing distant lights that are set on a level with their eyes. At any rate, if the lights are raised above the level of the eye, they are visible, even though at a greater distance; or, if the observer is at a higher point, he sees what before was hidden"; and he clinches it by a quotation from Homer—how Odysseus "with a quick glance, as a mighty wave heaved him high", saw the land (c. 12; *Od.* v, 393). Aristotle—I may interpolate this, for, while I was at work on this essay, there was a total eclipse of the moon—Aristotle added the argument that the shadow of the earth on the moon during an eclipse proves the rotundity of the earth. Strabo was convinced that the Ocean covered the globe, except where the land stood out above it; that was the work of Providence, as we saw (c. 810); the habitable world is surrounded by water (c. 5, 6) and is in fact an island of immense size (c. 6). The highest mountains will be negligible on the surface (c. 112).[52]

Now, he suggests,[53] make yourself a globe (c. 109)—he recommends a ten-foot diameter for it (c. 116), or the habitable part will show too small; mark on it Iberia (Spain) and India—they will be, as measured partly by land travel, partly by seafaring from West to East, 70,000 stades apart (c. 116). There will obviously be a great deal of Ocean. One mistake, by the way, not made by Herodotus, is made by Strabo, his Caspian is open to the Ocean on the North (c. 507); but that is a minor point. But look at your globe the other way, and then turn to an earlier page of Strabo, where he quotes Eratosthenes in a most significant sentence which we should never forget—"if the size of the Atlantic Ocean did not make it impossible, we could sail over the rest of the circle along one parallel from Iberia to India" (c. 64). How much of human history has been made by definitely trying the experiment of Eratosthenes! and how strange to find in a geographer of Alexandria two centuries before Christ the actual plan of Columbus! And Eratosthenes was called *Beta*, because he was nowhere quite first class.[54] The "rest of the circle" added to the length of the habitable part made, according to Eratosthenes, the circumference of the globe roughly 252,000 stades (c. 113), or 24,662 miles, which implies a diameter of 7850 miles or 50 miles less than the value of the polar diameter.[55] That it should have been calculated at all, and a result so amazing reached, is worth consideration. Ptolemy afterwards gave the measurement as 180,000 stades; and, Ptolemy being the standard, it prevailed. Perhaps we may be glad that it did; it reduced the prospective voyage of Columbus by a good half or more, and it was terrible enough at that.

Certain homely suggestions for our globe are added by Strabo. We habitually think of Italy as shapped like a boot; in a memorable phrase the Marquis d'Azeglio said, about 1830, of the divided Italy that "the railways would stitch

the boot"—as the Roman roads had done. Strabo suggests that our habitable world will be the shape of a Greek *chlamys* or sleeveless cloak (c. 113, 118); he is helped to this view by an immense error as to the Southern extension of Africa which he makes far too small. The city of Alexandria is another *chlamys* (c. 793). Another section of the world is like a cook's knife (c. 519), and the Nile's course is like the letter N (c. 786).

Nature and Providence, as we saw, left the globe fit for man's habitation and well-being, but with possibilities of changes between land and sea (c. 810)—changes brought about by the action of water and fire, earthquakes and volcanoes (c. 49). How else is it that mussels, oysters and scallopshells are found in masses sometimes as far as 3000 stades from the sea—and salt marshes, too? (c. 49). The modern perhaps does not class these together; but, from Xenophanes onward (*c.* 500 B.C.), the ancients were familiar with the idea of great changes of level at one period or another in the earth's surface (c. 49-51; 102). There are minor changes, easier to note; the Achelous is the standard instance of a river bringing down silt and linking islands to the mainland (c. 458),[56] while the delta of the Nile is, as Herodotus said,[57] the gift of the river. "Then," says Strabo, "there are Bura and Helice [towns of Achaia]; Bura disappeared in a chasm of the earth, Helice in a wave of the sea" (c. 59).[58] The country all about the river Maeander is "well-earthquaked"—a most ingenious adjective (. . . . c. 578); there is fire below and water—witness the hot springs of Hierapolis with their quick deposit of stone, and the strange cave near by, the Plutonion with its deadly vapour ("we threw in sparrows and they dropped dead", and so will a bull) (c. 629, 630), and the constant disasters to cities throughout the region, which Augustus and Tiberius helped to rebuild (c. 579). The Straits of Messina are evidence, he says, and many other Classical writers also hold the view, that Sicily was ripped[59] off by earthquake from Italy; and there are islands that have risen in the open sea (c. 258). He records the belief that wind has something to do with volcanic eruption; wind at least accompanies it and ceases with it; and winds are begotten by evaporation from the sea and fed by it (c. 275, 276).

But turning to the solider earth, on which we can more or less rely, and to man's life on that earth, he remarks with Ephorus how much the sea is the decisive factor for the Greek world (. . . . c. 334). Living in a region of gulfs and headlands and peninsulas, with the Peloponnese as a sort of acropolis (c. 334), "we are in a way amphibious . . . and belong no more to the dry land than to the sea" (c. 8). Havens and rivers naturally interest a Greek; even if he comes from the continent, Trapezus and Sinope are household words. He pauses to describe the mouths of the Rhone (c. 186) and the Nile; and it may be noted that he knows the cause of the Nile's summer overflow which so much perplexed Herodotus and the men of his time.[60] Alexander's admiral, Nearchus, had announced the explanation in the summer monsoon rains (c. 696); the ancients guessed, but in later days the cause was plain enough to those who went to the cinnamon country[61] and were engaged in elephant-catching—the overflow depended on the rains in the mountains of Ethiopia or Abyssinia (c. 789). Strabo pauses to pay a tribute to the scientific interests of Ptolemy Philadelphos which ancient kings had not shared (c. 790). And before we leave this region and forget about harbours, there is Myos Hormos to be thought of, the port on the Red Sea as we call it—Herodotus' Arabian gulf—whence in Strabo's day some hundred and twenty ships might sail in a season for the Malabar coast (c. 118; 815), though few would go as far as the Ganges (c. 686). He does not actually mention the monsoon, the Hippalos, so-called (they say) after the Greek mariner who taught sailors to trust it, but the numbers of the vessels surely suggest that it was already known, as it certainly was a very little time after Strabo's writing.[62] All this Indian traffic used Alexandria as its junction with the Mediterranean, a city brought near ruin by the later Ptolemies but restored by the Romans, and the greatest *emporion* of the world (c. 797, 798).

Strabo saw a good deal for himself, and he borrowed a great deal, borrowed wisely, and wisely owns it; what he saw developed in him the instinct to know what to borrow. He is interested to give the general sense of a countryside, to seize the significant features—the great alluvial plain of the Po (c. 212, 218), the Russian steppes (c. 307, 493), the swamps of Boeotia (c. 406-7), and the Galatian plateau nearer home (c. 568). He takes note of climate; the tide washes out the water-ways of Ravenna and saves it . . . as the Nile purifies the lake behind Alexandria in summer, and both cities escape the bad effects common where there are lagoons (c. 213, 793). South Russia is little known because of the cold and poverty of the country; the natives can bear it, living on flesh and milk, but other people cannot (c. 493). Ierne—or Erin, as some have since spelled it—again, away to the North of Britain, is a miserable place to live in because of the cold (c. 72), the abode of utter savages (. . . c. 115), gluttons, cannibals, indecent—"though we have not indeed reliable witnesses for all this", there are parallels that make it probable (c. 201). It may be the humidity of India that prevents Indian hair from curling (c. 690). But fertile though North India may be (c. 73), the Nile productive above all other rivers (c. 695), and Arabia "happy", it is Europe and especially the Mediterranean basin that are most favourable to the development of men and politics (c. 126). Europe is most independent of other lands, whether in peace or war; her fields are safely tilled, her cities are secure, she produces the best of fruits and crops, she has all the most useful minerals, she has abundance of cattle and is largely free from wild beasts. All she needs to import is spices and precious stones, "and life is no worse for those who lack these things than for those who have plenty of them" (c. 127). For history, culture, arts and government, the Mediterranean lands are well ahead of all others (c. 122). And so they were.

The natural products of these lands interest him—timber for building Rome, as we have seen, ship-timber in Cy-

prus (c. 681), cedars in Cilicia (c. 669), finer woods for furniture (c. 546, 826),[63] ebony from Ethiopia (c. 822); and he pauses to tell us of the Persian "Song of the Palm" and its three hundred and sixty uses (c. 742-3); of lucerne or Medica (c. 525), of which Servius tells us Virgil's country was full; of the medicinal drugs of Cyprus (c. 684), and Indian cotton and cotton seed (c. 693, 694). Earth has other products, and we have seen his interest in the quarries of Italy; and there are others on Scyros (c. 437) and at Mylasa (c. 658). He speaks of oil-boring in Asia near the Ochus river (c. 518), and of asphalt Eastward and elsewhere (VII, fr. 55; 743, 763-4, 830). But to anyone interested in mining his book is a revelation. I have collected more than a score of references to goldmining alone,[64] and I resist with regret the desire to quote at length his accounts of various processes, from the primitive fleeces of Colchis (c. 499) to the joyous page on Spain (c. 146)—but I must not imitate "the flowery style of Posidonius, who drew his language as it were from the mine", even if Posidonius was, as is probable, Strabo's authority here. There are also the silver mines of Attica—exhausted, he is told, with piles of mining rubble round them (c. 399, 447), copper mines in Africa (c. 830), and plenty more; and he does not ignore the bad conditions of labourers in some of the mines (c. 561). Ruddle (c. 540), potash (c. 529), and the topaz (c. 770)[65] may conclude a sadly truncated paragraph.

At the beginning of his book Strabo states his view that, in addition to all other multifarious knowledge, "polymathy", the geographer must take account of the natural history of animals, sea-beasts and land-beasts (c. 8). He fulfils the implied promise; and a very interesting thing he makes of it. Take his account of the animals of Spain (c. 163)—Spain is one of his best sections—or of Egypt (c. 823). He is perhaps the first to tell us what a plague rabbits may become—a Spanish animal; "Spain has hardly any destructive animals except the burrowing hares, which some call *lebêrides;* for they damage both plants and seeds by eating the roots". This pest covers Spain and spreads to Marseilles. Some one brought a couple to the Balearic islands, with the result that the inhabitants at last called on the Roman government to find them a new home, where there would be no rabbits. Ferrets from Africa, well muzzled, are put down the burrows, and drive the rabbits before them to be caught and killed as they come out (c. 144, 168). He notices plague spread by field-mice, and the ruin of crops, and the necessity for the government offering a bounty for the killing of the mice (c. 165, cf. 604, 613). Spain has many deer and wild horses; its marshes team with swans and other waterfowl, and the beaver builds in the rivers—though luckily for the beaver its Black Sea cousin is more useful medicinally (c. 163). So he goes on, noting the big cetaceans in both Oceans, Atlantic and Indian (c. 145, 725) and perhaps the narwhal, if it ever came so far South and if it is the oryx; the habits of the tunny, its life in the Black Sea (c. 320), its fancy for an acorn abundant on the shore of Spain (c. 145), and plenty of places where the fishermen have look-outs for it; seals in the Caspian (c. 513, 776)—the square-faced animals of Herodotus;[66] the little dogs of Malta[67] (c. 277); the horses of Arcadia (c. 388), of Media (c. 525), of Cyrene (c. 837). And to all this, and the natural history of the Black Sea (c. 312), we have to add of course the elephant in India and Africa, and how he is hunted (c. 710), with some dubious stories about the Indian being larger than the African (c. 705) as Polybius also said, and about the wells he digs with his tusks (c. 773), and how he sleeps standing because his legs have no joints (c. 772), which Aristotle had already refuted;[68] but he refuses the mere fables of Artemidorus about the olive branch, etc. (c. 829). He speaks of the giraffe (c. 775, 827) and tells us how he saw a rhinoceros, but apparently not of the biggest (c. 774), and how the Egyptians feed the sacred crocodile at Arsinoe (c. 811). Perhaps he ought not to have brought up the gold-mining ants again (c. 702, 706, 718, 782), though they may come from some Sanskrit literature; but he is surely right in reprobating Megasthenes for his dwarfs and mouthless men, the folk who sleep in their own ears and the notorious dog-headed (c. 711); but national associations may make one glad to read of Indian "horses with one horn and the head of a deer",[69] coupled with the wondrous bamboo (c. 710). The big crabs and the pearls of the Persian Gulf must end an incomplete list.

The primitive peoples of Europe from Gibraltar to Moscow claim his attention, and he makes a great contribution to Anthropology. The migrations of the races, Cimbric, Spanish and others (c. 102, 166, 305) are noted as imperfectly known, and the shrewd observation is made that, where a tribe remains stationary to the point of being *autochthonous,* as in Attica, it means differentiation in speech and custom (c. 333). His treatment of Spanish ways is a capital passage (c. 154, 163); and the Celts match it—a tall race, . . . mad on war,[70] . . . especially good as cavalry, honest and not ill-mannered but quite . . . (the type that calls a spade a spade, as Philip of Macedon almost put it[71]), keen on education and culture, especially on Greek— "they even write their contracts in Greek" (c. 195, 180). The Greek influence came from Marseilles, and lasted for centuries; Greek names abound in Christian Gaul, and even the British heretic Pelagius must turn Morgan (they say) into Greek. The Germans are savages, and treacherous (c. 291)—he came too early to be able to read Tacitus' *Germania;* but he writes something of the kind of his own about the Scythians, using them with their primitive virtue (c. 300, 302) as a foil to the luxury of the Roman world. Savages sleep on the ground like the Selloi of Homer (. . . . c. 164[72]), and allow much influence to their women; the rule of women, . . . is not civilization (c. 165). Nomads clearly interest him, and he notes how the Ethiopians watch over their flocks by night, "singing a song of a sort by the fire" (c. 776). The cowboy in Canada and the States has to ride round his bunch by night and, if they begin to rise, he has to sing to them till they settle down, for otherwise there is the risk of a panic rush. Arab polyandry (c. 783) and African polygamy (c. 835), the Nabataean plan of fining a man who reduces his property (c. 783), and a great mass of information about India with its castes, its *suttee,* its Brahmans and its ascetics, show the range he traverses and how thoroughly he fulfils the promises of his opening pages.

But by now the civilized world, at least the world of the Mediterranean, is Roman; and, as we survey land after land, we see what the change means. Piracy with its atrocious slave trade is put down. The kings of Syria and Cyprus, who countenanced the pirates, have ceased to be (c. 669); and Delos is no longer the horrible market, where ten thousand captives would be landed from the slave-ships in a day (c. 668). It is once again the possession of Athens (c. 486), and it is forbidden to keep dogs there— happy isle! Bandits and brigands, East and West, are stamped out by the Romans. Strabo tells of one bandit chief, Selurus, who called himself "son of Etna", and harried Eastern Sicily, but was caught, and publicly torn to pieces by beasts in Rome— . . . "I saw it", he says (c. 273). He has a more amusing story of another, Cleon by name, whose headquarters were on Mount Olympus in the Troy country, who had better opportunities and used them aptly. In Antony's interests he countered the extortion of money from the district for the renegade Labienus, and was duly rewarded; but at the time of the battle of Actium he was discreet enough to choose the winning side. Augustus made him Prince-Bishop of the Mysian god. Zeus Abrettenus—a change from being a brigand, says Strabo drily. But whether the goddess of the temple did not like him eating swine's flesh, which was taboo in her precinct, as the temple people said, or whether it were mere ordinary over-eating, he died in a month (c. 574, 575). There is no longer a sanctuary at Ephesus, it had become a nuisance, and Augustus stopped it (c. 641, 642). Roads and *emporia,* centres of distribution, were taken care of by the Romans, suitable places strengthened with "colonies"; and all is noted in due course by Strabo. Athens and Sparta are free cities (c. 398, 365); but the helots of Sparta are also free now (c. 364). Fifty thousand Getae from over the frontiers are settled in Thrace (c. 303); the Allobroges are turned farmers (c. 186); the Britons are left to themselves. There was nothing to fear from Britain, and nothing to be gained by annexation; it seemed that more revenue was to be drawn from duties on imports from Britain and exports to it than from any tribute the country could yield, when the cost of occupation should be deducted (c. 116). His account of Britain is in our English history books, but one may note that among other taxed exports to the barbarous isle were ivory necklaces (c. 200).[73]

Side by side with all this civilization and prosperity Strabo brings to our notice a great amount of desolation—Sicily, Southern Italy, and, above all, Greece are empty and forsaken as compared with the days of old. No doubt there was great emigration from old Greece to the cities and camps of the Hellenistic kings, and perhaps there still was emigration. But Strabo reminds us of Polybius' statement that Aemilius Paullus sold one hundred and fifty thousand of the people of Epirus into slavery[74] (c. 322). That was nearly two hundred years ago, but there is no creation of population *ex nihilo.* The barbarian in Tacitus may well say *solitudinem faciunt, pacem appellant.* Most of the old languages of Asia Minor have disappeared (c. 565); not a trace of Lydian is left (c. 631).[75]

But it was peace, and that Strabo emphasizes along with the Emperor's care for the well-being of the Empire. The Roman citizenship is being gradually extended; it reaches to the Alps in Italy (c. 210). Prosperity is found in friendship with Rome (c. 140). "The Romans took over many nations savage by nature on account of the regions they inhabited, regions rugged, harbourless or cold, or otherwise little suited for human life; and races that had been isolated they interwove with one another, and taught the wilder kinds to live like citizens"; and each sort helps the other, one supplies arms, the other food, arts and culture (c. 127). The movement, as in the Rhone region, is toward the Roman *type*, . . . in speech, in habits of life, and in some cases in city life (c. 186). The cost has been great; the Empire was initially won by force (c. 401[76]). "Italy was long torn by factions, but since it came under Roman rule, it has been saved, like Rome herself, from utter ruin and destruction by the excellence of Rome's polity and the excellence of her rulers. But it would be a difficult thing to administer an Empire so great, except by entrusting it to one man as to a father. Never in fact have the Romans and their allies had such abundance of peace and prosperity as Caesar Augustus gave them, from the time when he assumed absolute rule, and as Tiberius, his son and successor, gives them now, making Augustus the model of his administration and decrees, as his sons Germanicus and Drusus make their father their model and work with him" (c. 288).

Notes

1. The references in brackets, thus (c. 547), are to the pages of Strabo. The description of Amaseia is his.

2. The translators want to render [*pronoia*] "art" here; they may be right; but cf. page 235.

3. The tombs are still to be seen; H. F. Tozer, *Geography of Greece*, p. 23.

4. Xenophon, *Anabasis*, IV, 8, 20; the plant which produces the honey is said to be a rose-laurel, *Nerium oleander*, of the family Apocynaceae.

5. *Iliad*, II, 857.

6. *Euxinus natura negatur nomine illuditur; adv. Marcionem*, I, 1.

7. *Dies nunquam patens, sol nunquam libens, omnis aer nebula, omne quod flaverit Aquilo est.*

8. Strabo, c. 304, says that Athenians call their slaves by the names of their races, Gela and Daos for example, Lydus and Syrus, while a Phrygian will be called Manes or Midas, and a Cappadocian Tibius. Tibius was the name of the murdered cousin, and his son was Theophilus.

9. See Robert Curzon, *Armenia*, p. 3, on the forests of the shore-lands east of Sinope.

10. Ettore Pais. J. G. C. Anderson in *Anatolian Studies*, p. 12, finds the theory "at first sight attractive", but far from proven, and at last unlikely.

11. The aim of History is truth, he says; that of rhetoric is vigour, (c. 25).

12. Sikes and Allen, *Homeric Hymns*, Intr. p. liv.

13. See Walter Leaf, *Strabo on the Troad*, Intr. pp. xxviii-xxxi.

14. Mahaffy, *Silver Age of Greek World*, p. 264, sums it up—these sanctuaries "promoted trade and injured morals".

15. Alexandria had its popular and disorderly religious centre at Canopus (c. 801).

16. Athenaeus, XIII, 573[e].

17. See page 267.

18. See page 263.

19. Plutarch, *de defectu oraculorum*, 17, 419c.

20. *Aeneid*, XI, 785-8.

21. c. 649; cf. also c. 801, the temple of Serapis at Canopus. For the same practice in Islam, see Snouck Hurgronje, *Mekka* (trn), p. 37.

22. Cf. Strabo, c. 805.

23. Seneca, *Nat. Quaest.* II, 45.

24. *Wisdom*, xiii, 3.

25. Tacitus, *Hist.* V, 4.

26. Polybius, VI, 56. See page 200.

27. Plutarch, *Numa*, 8.

28. On Strabo's views of Homer and of poetry, see E. E. Sikes, *The Greek View of Poetry*, p. 171.

29. See page 250.

30. Polybius, XII, 24; see page 41.

31. R. L. Stevenson, *St Ives*, chapter 25.

32. The Abioi, whom Homer praised, send envoys to Alexander (Arrian, *Anabasis*, IV, 1, 1).

33. The reader may be glad to be reminded of Robert Curzon's visit to this island, described in his delightful *Monasteries of the Levant*.

34. William Mure, *Journal of a Tour in Greece*, II, p. 137, says that neither the Athenian Acropolis, nor Gibraltar, can enter into the remotest competition with this gigantic citadel; but time forbade his ascending it. Mahaffy, *Rambles in Greece*, p. 324, supposes the view to be the finest in Greece. So W. Macneile Dixon, *Hellas Revisited*, p. 69.

35. Pausanias, II, 16, 5, speaks of the walls, the lion-gate, and other remains, familiar to modern travellers.

36. He is very brief on the Parthenon (c. 395). Note in passing that Polybius seems not to have visited Athens. J. P. Mahaffy, *Silver Age of the Greek World*, p. 225, believes most of Strabo's account of Greece is borrowed material.

37. Cf. Horace, *Odes*, I, 7, 14; III, 29, 6; IV, 2, 31.

38. I Virgil, *Georgic,* II, 173, *slave magna parens frugum, Saturnia tellus.*

39. He mentions Patavium as making clothing for the Roman market (c. 213).

40. Polybius, IX, 10, 8.

41. On the dates of the book's composition, see J. G. C. Anderson in *Anatolian Studies Presented to Sir W. M. Ramsay,* a shrewd examination of the text in the light of epigraphy, which brings out some errors of the geographer.

42. Walter Leaf, *Strabo on the Troad,* p. xxx.

43. H. F. Tozer, *History of Ancient Geography,* ch. XII.

44. W. W. Tarn, *Hellenistic Civilization,* p. 236.

45. This passage to some seems to hint at his relations with Queen Pythodoris and her government.

46. On Pytheas, see c. II, 45, 63, 104, 201. See also H. F. Tozer, *History of Ancient Geography,* ch. VIII; and T. Rice Holmes, *Ancient Britain,* ch. IV.

47. H. F. Tozer, *Hist. Anc. Geogr.,* pp. 189-190; E. H. Warmington, *Commerce between Roman Empire and India,* pp. 49, 61, 74; G. F. Hudson, *Europe and China,* p. 177.

48. On this see E. E. Sikes, *Greek View of Poetry,* pp. 31, 175.

49. 1 *Pharsalia,* VII, 5.

50. 2 Cf. Sir Raymond Beazley, *Dawn of Modern Geography,* 1, 39f.

51. Cf. Justin Winsor, *Christopher Columbus,* p. 107, who specially notes the printing of Strabo in a Latin version in 1469, several times reprinted in the next few years. See also Sir Clements Markham, *Columbus,* pp. 33-35.

52. Polybius (cited in c. 209) had told the Greeks that the Alps were vastly higher than anything they knew.

53. On this globe of Strabo's see E. L. Stevenson, *Terrestrial and Celestial Globes,* 1, p. 8; Crates is credited with the first globe.

54. 1 W.G. de Burgh, *Legacy of Ancient World,* p. 165; but perhaps it was jealousy, he adds. Mahaffy, *Ptolemies,* p. 249, calls him "the best man of his time".

55. 2 J.L.E. Dreyer, *Planetary Systems,* pp. 174-178; cf. also H. F. Tozer, *History of Ancient Geography,* p. 172; and Sir T. Heath, *Aristarchus of Samos,* p. 339, following Dreyer. See Pliny, *N.H.* 11, 247, who gives Eratosthenes' figure, *improbum ausum verum ita subtili argumentatione comprehensum ut pudeat non credere.*

56. Herodotus, 11, 10; Thucydides, 11, 102.

57. Herodotus, 11, 5.

58. Cf. Pausanias, VII, 24; and H. F. Tozer, *Geography of Greece,* pp. 130ff., on Greek earthquakes.

59. He wavers as to the derivation of Rhegium from the Greek . . . or the Latin *regium,* which the Samnites might have given it (c. 258).

60. Herodotus, II, 20-24. . . .

61. But cf. G. F. Hudson, *Europe and China,* p. 94.

62. On Hippalos, see E. H. Warmington, *The Commerce between the Roman Empire and India,* pp. 44-48; H. G. Rawlinson, *Intercourse between India and the Western World,* pp. 109-112.

63. "Mauretania supplies the Romans with the one-piece tables of the greatest size and most beautiful grain."

64. Let me at least copy my list in a note: c. 142, 146, 156, 187-8, 190, 205, 208, 214, 218, VII, fr. 34, c. 499, 506, 509, 511, 529, 625, 680, 700, 711, 718, 726, 778. See pages 75-77.

65. Cf. Job xxviii, 19, the topaz of Ethiopia.

66. Herodotus, IV, 109.

67. Cf. page 173.

68. Cf. page 143.

69. Cf. page 147.

70. Cf. Polybius, II, 20, 7. . . .

71. Plutarch, *Apophthegm. Reg.* 15, 178B, says that, when certain Olynthians complained to Philip that some of his friends called them traitors, the king rejoined that the Macedonians are a rude and rustic people. . . . Cf. Lucian, . . . *Hist. Conscr.* 41, 54. . . .

72. Cf. *Iliad,* XVI, 235.

73. 1 It is interesting to learn that in crossing to Britain you embark at night on an ebb-tide and land next day at 2 P.M. (c. 193; cf. c. 199, and Caesar, *Bell. Gall.* IV, 23; v, 8). The ships are flat-bottomed, high-prowed, high-sterned (c. 195).

74. 2 To understand this, see Sir Edwin Pears, *Turkey and its People,* p. 108, on the Turkish massacre and enslavement of the Chiots in 1822; or Finlay, *History of Greece,* VI, pp. 255-260.

75. 3 It is very odd to find Rostovtzeff, *History of Ancient World,* 1, p. 378, saying that "we have the express evidence of Paul the Apostle that the natives of Asia Minor still spoke Phrygian and Galatian". St Luke (Acts xiv, 11) says the priests at Lystra spoke [*Lykaonisti*]. Sir William Ramsay has shown us that this town was in the Roman province of Galatia. Strabo does not allude to any Lycaonian dialect.

76. Some simple reflections on the relations of power and finance (c. 415).

Glanville Downey (essay date 1941)

SOURCE: "Strabo on Antioch: Notes on His Method," *Transactions and Proceedings of the American Philological Association,* Vol. LXXII, 1941, pp. 85-95.

[In the following essay, Downey examines some problems and difficulties with Strabo's account of Antioch and argues that it should be read as a stylized literary passage.]

I

Strabo's account of the foundation and growth of Antioch has given trouble to modern scholars for a variety of reasons. An important part of his account disagrees with a statement of Malalas, whose information should carry weight. Strabo does not mention the island, which formed a part of the city, and that part of his account which might be taken to apply to it disagrees with what Libanius says about the island. Again, scholars have sometimes been led, by a natural eagerness to obtain as much information as possible from the passage, to attempt to utilize it for the information which they would like to find in it, and have not always taken into account the nature and extent of the limitations as a source of topographical and historical material to which it might inherently be subject. As a result, scholars have debated the information which the passage ought to give, instead of studying its background and context and determining whether these have any bearing on the amount and kind of information which can actually be recovered from what Strabo says.[1] Points which were self-evident to Strabo and his contemporaries are no longer clear to us; and if we can sift out these points, and try to see what is really at stake in them, there will be some gain, even if we cannot settle all the difficulties which the passage of time and the loss of knowledge have created for us.

Strabo purports to describe very briefly the foundation of Antioch and its enlargement by a succession of its rulers. He writes:[2]

> Antioch is likewise a tetrapolis, since it consists of four parts; and each of the four settlements is fortified both by a common wall and by a wall of its own. Now Nicator founded the first of the settlements, transferring thither the settlers from Antigonia, which had been built near it a short time before by Antigonus; the second was founded by the multitude of settlers; the third by Seleucus Callinicus; and the fourth by Antiochus Epiphanes.

Malalas declares in two places (in his account of Epiphanes' reign, and in his description of the work of Tiberius at Antioch), that Epiphanes did not build a wall about the quarter which he founded, but that this was done by Tiberius.[3] And Libanius says that the island (which Strabo does not mention) was founded by Antiochus the Great, who built a wall about it; he does not mention Seleucus Callinicus as the founder of a part of the city.[4]

Carl Otfried Müller[5] followed Strabo and thought that his account proved that Malalas was wrong, since Strabo says that already before the time of Tiberius, Antioch was a tetrapolis, surrounded by a common wall, with each of its parts, in addition, enclosed by its own wall. This is the opinion also of Wilhelm Weber[6] and Alexander Schenk von Stauffenberg.[7]

The disagreement with Libanius has been as easily disposed of. Droysen, for example, rejected Libanius out of hand and followed Strabo, who he considered had greater authority in such a matter.[8] The alternative, adopted by Müller,[9] is to combine the accounts and conclude that the settlement of the island was begun by Seleucus and finished by Antiochus.

Students have had to be content with these solutions, and have had to suppose that either our information or our understanding of it is deficient. If one studies the passage in its context, however, a much more satisfactory view of it can be found. The passage on Antioch follows a description of the Seleucis, the region of Syria in which Antioch lay. Here Strabo writes as follows:[10]

> Seleucis is not only the best of the above-mentioned portions of Syria, but also is called, and is, a tetrapolis, owing to the outstanding cities in it, for it has several. But the largest are four, Antiocheia near Daphne, Seleuceia in Pieria, and also Apameia and Laodiceia; and these cities, all founded by Seleucus Nicator, used to be called sisters, because of their concord with one another. Now the largest of these cities was named after his father and the most strongly fortified by nature after himself, and one of the other two, Apameia, after his wife Apama, and the other, Laodiceia, after his mother. Appropriately to the Tetrapolis, Seleucis was also divided into four satrapies, as Poseidonius says, the same number into which Coele-Syria was divided, though Mesopotamia formed only one satrapy. Antioch is likewise a tetrapolis, since it consists of four parts; and each of the four settlements is fortified both by a common wall and by a wall of its own. Now Nicator founded the first of the settlements, transferring thither the settlers from Antigonia, which had been built near it a short time before by Antigonus; the second was founded by the multitude of settlers; the third by Seleucus Callinicus; and the fourth by Antiochus Epiphanes.

This sounds well enough, in fact it is very neat; and if the passage is examined, it will be found that it is rather too neat. A. H. M. Jones has at last placed this account in its proper perspective; he writes as follows:[11]

> Strabo, on the authority of Poseidonius, who should have known the facts seeing that he was born in Apamea and lived there during the last days of the Seleucid dynasty, states that correspondingly to the tetrapolis—of Antioch, Seleucia, Apamea, and Laodicea—the Seleucis was divided into four satrapies. An examination of the map, however, shows that it cannot have been true, for all the four cities of the tetrapolis are crowded into one corner of the Seleucis. The explanation probably is that the words 'correspondingly to the tetrapolis' are not quoted from Poseidonius, but are an inference by Strabo—the Seleucis was often known as the tetrapolis from its four great cities, Poseidonius says it was divided into four satrapies, therefore each of the four cities was the capital of a satrapy. All that we know from Poseidonius is, then, that Seleucid Syria was divided into four satrapies. An inscription shows that one of these had its capital at Apamea. It is *a priori* highly probable that Antioch was

the capital of another. The other two probably comprised the eastern part of Syria.

It seems plain that one of the major difficulties in Strabo's account of Antioch—his failure to mention the island, and his statement that the whole city was surrounded by a common wall (which could hardly have included the island as well as the remainder of the city)—shows that what Strabo writes about Antioch is an equally rhetorical complement to his rhetorical statements about the tetrapolis of Seleucis and its four satrapies. . . . Antioch, Strabo had read (possibly in Poseidonius), had four quarters, or four foundations; therefore it was a tetrapolis; and therefore (in view of the nature of a *polis*) each of its quarters had its own wall. Plainly Strabo was not attempting to give a strictly factual account of the development of the city, but rather was anxious to fit his account into the literary scheme which he had hit upon in describing the Seleucis. If Strabo thus viewed what he had to say about Antioch simply as a pendant to what he had already written about the Seleucis, we have no right to attribute to his statements any authority except in so far as they can be shown to be independent of their rhetorical coloring; and if his statements disagree with those of other sources, they must be examined from the point of view of the literary purpose with which Strabo wrote them. . . .

The disagreement between Strabo's statement that Seleucus Callinicus was one of the royal founders and Libanius' attribution of the island quarter to Antiochus the Great could likewise be characteristic of Strabo's literary method as it has been emerging from this examination. Beyond the passages in Libanius and Strabo we have no record of the ancient tradition with regard to the settlement of the island. A statement by Libanius on a matter such as this has great authority, but there must have been some basis for Strabo's assertion that Callinicus "founded" a quarter of the city. There is good reason to believe, from the history of the period, that Callinicus had occasion to develop the island as a quarter of the city; and since in addition Antiochus the Great had settlers whom he may well have wished to establish in the city, it seems reasonable to conclude, with Müller and Förster, that Antiochus continued the development which had been begun by Callinicus. Antiochus' work in this respect was evidently so important that he was regarded (at least in the tradition which Libanius represents) as the founder of this quarter.[12] Callinicus could at the same time, however, be technically called the founder, since he had inaugurated the work. If the island was first settled under Callinicus, who laid out a plan and began to build public buildings there, and then was enclosed in a wall by Antiochus, either ruler could be regarded as the founder. Strabo and Libanius followed different traditions, or had different sources which adopted divergent points of view. Or if two founders were reported in the tradition, Strabo would choose the earlier—after all a logical procedure—since all that he wanted was to give the name of *a* founder for the third quarter.

Strabo's account may now be examined in the light of Malalas' statements that Epiphanes did not build a wall about the section of the city which he founded, but that this was first done by Tiberius. It is at least very possible, as has been seen above, that Strabo's statement that Epiphania was walled represents an inference from the tradition that Epiphanes founded this quarter, or from the circumstance that it was called a *polis*. Malalas' polemical tone suggests that there was a controversy on this point; he may well have been combatting a tradition such as that represented by Strabo.[13] On the other hand several considerations make it impossible to judge between the two authors at once and to accept Malalas' assertions without hesitation. One immediately becomes suspicious in a case like this because of the characteristic understanding and use by Malalas and other chroniclers of the term "to build."[14] According to this usage the "builder" of a work was not necessarily the man who first constructed it, but might be only a man who rebuilt or repaired or completed it. Thus Strabo and Malalas may each have been right, according to his own light, and Tiberius may have completed or extended a wall which had been begun or built by Epiphanes. Malalas evidently did not have, for the Seleucid period at Antioch, as complete or detailed material as he did for the Roman period.[15] Thus he may have had no evidence that Epiphanes built a wall about his quarter, but he may have had a statement, in a source which was primarily concerned with the Roman period, that Tiberius "built" a wall, and he may have had reason to believe that this was the original construction. The rest of the work at Antioch which is attributed (by Malalas) to Tiberius is so extensive that a Roman source would naturally regard him as the initiator and guiding force of everything with which his name was associated, while a Greek source (especially if it were written with an anti-Roman bias) would as naturally be anxious to vindicate the work for the Seleucid ruler.

A final resort is to try to discover whether there is anything in the history of Epiphanes' reign which gives reason to think that he did or did not build a wall about Epiphania. It would seem unlikely that Epiphanes would develop a new quarter of Antioch, and adorn it with costly public buildings, and then leave it unprotected by a wall. The logical procedure would seem to be to build the wall first, and then erect the buildings. But Epiphanes' plans and undertakings were not distinguished by their logic. Moreover, his reign was an unbroken story of frenzied finance in which display in festivals, luxurious living and magnificent building undertakings reached giddy proportions. He brought back much treasure from his triumph in Egypt in 169,[16] and he confiscated large amounts of wealth from various temples.[17] He spent much money in truly regal manner, as Livy says, in urbium donis et deorum cultu.[18] But it is characteristic that some of his building projects remained unfinished. The most notable example of course is his work on the temple of Olympian Zeus at Athens. At Megalopolis he began, but did not finish, the construction of a wall about the city, and a marble theatre which he began to build at Tegea likewise remained uncompleted.[19] These undertakings, it is true, all lay outside his own domain, and one would perhaps expect that in his capital city at least Antiochus would leave nothing unfinished, and indeed would not undertake any major project for which complete provision was not made. With Epiphanes, however, one cannot assume that such a sober and prosaic scheme would have been followed. The spendthrift king may well have begun his new quarter at Antioch with the public buildings and temples—which were so much more interesting, and so much more impressive, than a mere wall—and may have left the wall to the last. Then he might have been unable to build the wall, or possibly he died before the work could be started; and his successors were all so poor that the completion of such a project may well have been beyond their means. In any case they all had more pressing affairs to concern them.[20]

Tiberius' work at Antioch, on the other hand, following as it did upon the important building operations which the Romans inaugurated as soon as they occupied Syria, seems to have constituted a veritable transformation of Epiphania. His operations may well have been such that they entailed, if not a new wall, at least an extension or a rebuilding of an old one if such existed.[21]

While it is apparent that the evidence is not enough to furnish a decisive answer to the question of the authorship of the wall of Epiphania, the present investigation has tended to show that Epiphanes did not necessarily build a wall about his quarter of the city. Certainly it has become plain that it is difficult to attribute to Strabo's account any value beyond that which it can reasonably claim as a brief and palpably stylized account of a long process which (as Strabo himself would no doubt have recognized) was not really to be described completely and accurately in a few words. Strabo certainly had no intention of falsification, but his account must not be taken for more than it was intended to be—a literary passage in which only a certain amount of information, of a not too specific nature, needed to be given.[22]

II

There remains to be considered Diodorus' reference to Antioch as a tetrapolis. This is preserved in the scholia on Strabo's description of Syracuse, in which Strabo says that the city was a pentapolis "in olden times." . . .

One might be inclined to suppose that Diodorus' statement serves to support Strabo's description of Antioch as a tetrapolis, and to lend authority to Strabo's belief concerning Epiphanes' wall. In the light of what has already been seen concerning Strabo's information about Antioch, however, it seems difficult to assign all of this value to this fragment of Diodorus. The chief point is that there is no indication that Diodorus believed or had any information that Epiphanes' quarter was walled. It would have been perfectly possible for Diodorus or his source to say that Antioch was a tetrapolis simply because they had read that it contained four principal quarters. All that one can safely and reasonably conclude from this fragment of Diodorus is that it is evidence that there were four principal quarters at Antioch—and of this, of course, there can be no dispute. While Evagrius' reference to Diodorus makes it possible that his remark about Antioch being a tetrapolis was made in an account of the colonization of the city, there is no proof, and indeed no necessary reason to believe, that this was actually the case; he might very well have made a remark like this in some other connection.

It is worth noting, finally, that this fragment of Diodorus does not furnish any evidence that Strabo, instead of being governed, in composing his description of Antioch as a tetrapolis, by the rhetorical scheme which has been suggested above, took his information, and his rhetorical pattern, from a source (the same which Diodorus would have used). The principal result of Strabo's procedure as it has been reconstructed here was the statement that Epiphania was walled, and no suggestion or implication to this effect can be found, or need be found, in what the scholiast says about Diodorus' statement. . . .

Notes

1. Almost exactly the same thing has happened with Procopius' passage on Antioch, with resulting misinterpretation and confusion; see G. Downey, "Procopius on Antioch: A Study of Method in the *De Aedificiis*," *Byz.* 14 (1939) 361-378. For recent maps of the city, see C. R. Morey, "The Excavation of Antioch-on-the-Orontes," *Proceedings of the American Philosophical Society* 76 (1936) 638, and *Antioch-on-the-Orontes, 11: The Excavations, 1933-1936*, ed. by R. Stillwell (Princeton, 1938), 215.

2. 16.2.4, p. 750, transl. of H. L. Jones in the Loeb Classical Library.

3. 205.21; 233.22, Bonn ed.

4. *Or.* 11.119.

5. *Antiquitates Antiochenae* (Göttingen, 1839) 54.

6. "Studien zur Chronik des Malalas," *Festgabe für Adolf Deissmann* (Tübingen, 1927) 28, note 1.

7. *Die römische Kaisergeschichte bei Malalas* (Stuttgart, 1931) 455-456.

8. J. G. Droysen, *Gesch. des Hellenismus*, ed. 2 (Gotha, 1877-1878), 3.2.15, note 4.

9. *Op. cit.*, 51, followed by R. Förster, "Antiochia am Orontes," *JDAI* 12 (1897) 120.

10. *Loc. cit.* (note 2).

11. *The Cities of the Eastern Roman Provinces* (Oxford, 1937) 242-243.

12. On the history of this period at Antioch, see the present writer's article, "Seleucid Chronology in Malalas," *AJA* 42 (1938) 109, and the studies cited there. Consult also A. H. M. Jones, *The Greek City from Alexander to Justinian* (Oxford, 1940) 16.

13. That Malalas knew Strabo directly seems unlikely, but the question is not of vital importance.

14. See G. Downey, "Imperial Building Records in Malalas," *ByzZ* 38 (1938) 1-15, 299-311.

15. See Downey, *op. cit.,* and in *AJA* 42 (1938) 106-120.

16. E. R. Bevan, *The House of Seleucus* (London, 1902) 2.141.

17. *Ibid.,* 156-157, 160; cf. also A. Bouché-Leclercq, *Histoirc des Séleucides* (Paris, 1913-1914) 281.

18. 41.20; the information comes from Polybius.

19. Livy, *loc. cit.;* cf. Bevan, *op. cit.* 2., 148-149.

20. There is no evidence to show at what time during Epiphanes' reign the work at Antioch was carried out. Livy (*loc. cit.*) does not mention a wall built at Antioch by Epiphanes; but this cannot be taken as evidence that he did not build a wall, for Livy is listing only a few notable examples of the king's work. He does not in fact even mention that Antiochus enlarged his capital; in any case he would regard the construction of a wall in a place such as Antioch as a purely utilitarian work to be taken as a matter of course. Livy evidently mentions the wall at Megalopolis only because it was unfinished and because it lay outside the Seleucid territory. Antioch received few public buildings from the kings who followed Epiphanes, and the work attributed to the Romans makes it evident that the city's public buildings had fallen into grave neglect and disrepair in the last years of the dynasty. See Müller's account of this period, *op. cit.* 62-70, 75-77, also G. Downey, "Q. Marcius Rex at Antioch," *CPh* 32 (1937) 144-151.

21. See above, note 18.

22. For a recent evaluation of the *Geography,* see E. Honigmann, *op. cit.* 92. A new bit of evidence concerning Strabo's veracity has recently emerged from a Latin inscription of Seleucia published in *Antioch-on-the-Orontes, III: The Excavations, 1937-1939,* ed. by R. Stillwell (Princeton, 1941), p. 107, no. 231. . . .

Milton V. Anastos (essay date 1953)

SOURCE: "Pletho, Strabo and Columbus" in *Annuaire de l'Institut de Philologie et d'Histoire Orientales et Slaves,* Secrétariat des Éditions de l'Institut, 1953, pp. 1-18.

[*In the following essay, Anastos credits George Gemistus Pletho with the fifteenth-century introduction of the Geography to the Latin West and examines its popularity during the Renaissance, including its use by Christopher Columbus.*]

I hope to show in the course of this paper[1] that the geographical encyclopaedia of Strabo, designated *infra* as the **Geographika** . . . to distinguish it from Ptolemy's

Cosmographia came into prominence when it did because of the efforts of George Gemistus Pletho, the famous Byzantine humanist, who was almost one hundred years old at the time of his death in 1452[2]. He was a man of prodigious learning and considerable versatility, and wrote on theology, history, government, philosophy, geometry, rhetoric, poetry, music, grammar, astronomy, and geography. Many of his works are in the form of excerpts which he made from ancient authors both for his own divertissement and for the use of his students[3].

One of the writers of whom he was especially fond was Strabo, the geographer. Pletho filled one hundred and eight folia with excerpts from Strabo's **Geographika** and added a brief critical essay entitled . . . (*A correction of certain errors made by Strabo*)[4]. The *Excerpts from Strabo* and the *Diorthosis* were both written around 1439, or shortly thereafter, as we can tell from a reference in the *Diorthosis* to Paolo Toscanelli, whom Pletho met while he was attending the Council of Florence. It is with these two works that I propose to deal in this paper.

The discussion is divided into four sections. First, there is a critical analysis of the *Excerpts* and the *Diorthosis.* Second, a survey is made of the facts which indicate that Pletho was the first to introduce Strabo to Western Europe at the end of the Middle Ages. Third, it is demonstrated that Pletho's introduction of Strabo to the West is all the more significant when it is recalled that the chief theoretical principles and a large number of the geographical coordinates recorded in Ptolemy's *Cosmographia* were available in Latin from the middle of the twelfth century, if not before. Fourth, it is then concluded that, in calling attention to Strabo, Pletho performed a service noteworthy not merely in the history of the transmission of an ancient text but also in the history of the geographical theory of the renaissance.

I.—THE *EXCERPTS FROM STRABO* AND THE *DIORTHOSIS.*

Of the twenty-nine manuscripts known to me[5] containing various portions of the Plethonic *Excerpts from Strabo,* twenty include the *Diorthosis* and nineteen, *Excerpt I.* The popularity of these two parts of the work is easily explained, for they both deal with the shape and extent of the inhabited world. This is a subject which interested Pletho very much; and he often speculates on the habitability of unknown lands lying beyond the sea. The other *Excerpts from Strabo* treat of a great variety of subjects, but in the *Diorthosis* Pletho confines his attention almost exclusively to the sections that concern mathematical geography and the extent of the *oikumene.*

Free use of Pletho's text of Strabo has been made by various editors from Casaubon to Jones. In the absence of a printed edition, however, it is impossible to determine whether Pletho's emendations of the corrupt Strabonic text are of real value and reflect the niceties of textual criticism to be expected from one who spoke and wrote virtually pure Attic Greek, or whether they merely afford additional examples of the looseness and informality characterizing the attitude of renaissance scholars to the texts which they copied and excerpted.

The Diorthosis itself, though very short, is an intensely interesting document. Pletho here criticizes the views held by Strabo that the Caspian Sea is a gulf of the Ocean, that there is a torrid zone which is wholly uninhabitable on account of heat, that meridians may be represented satisfactorily on a plane surface by straight lines, and that the Nile is the boundary between Libya and Asia. He then goes on to recount what he had heard from reliable observers about the Island of Dateia (Scandinavia) and about the White Sea. Next he discusses the easternmost limits of the *oikumene* and expresses belief in the existence of an eastern sea and unknown lands east of India. Finally, after raising the question whether the Indian Ocean is a land-locked sea or not, he concludes with a few words of praise for Strabo, whose authority he does not regard as seriously impaired by a few errors.

A few points in this brief tractate call for attention. At first thought, it is strange that Pletho should have been ignorant of the voyages of renowned travelers like Marco Polo and Odorico da Pordenone. But this apparently singular lapse is the less remarkable when one reflects that Aeneas Sylvius Piccolomini, known during his pontificate (1458-64) as Pope Pius II, in the section on Asia in his *Historia rerum ubique gestarum locorumque descriptio* seems to have made no use of the voyages of Marco Polo, despite the fact that the papal library had owned a copy of *Il Milione* at least as early as the pontificate of Eugene IV (1431-47)[6].

As for Pletho's knowledge of Strabo, it can be shown that he had studied Strabo with care and did not limit himself altogether to the sections excerpted. In finding fault with certain aspects of Strabo, he did not ignore passages in which the statements reprehended might have been qualified or amended. Six of the ten paragraphs of the *Diorthosis* contain criticisms of Strabo. In regard to at least five of these, Pletho's judgment withstands analysis in every particular. Only once does he falter, although the case against him is far from clear. But even were we to resolve every question of doubt against Pletho and grant him no quarter whatsoever, he comes off with an average of 83.3, which, all things considered, if not excellent, is more than ordinarily tolerable in an age innocent of the printing press and the encyclopaedic concordance.

So much, then, for Pletho's use of Strabo. But what is to be said about his competence as a geographer? It is quite true that Pletho greatly exaggerated the merits of Strabo, if we are to apply the canons evolved in the course of the past five hundred years. But we must not make the mistake of judging Pletho's capacity as a critic from the point of view of modern geography. We cannot hold a scholar of the early fifteenth century to the standards and criteria of geographical research which obtain in the twentieth. The

truth is that, when compared with his contemporaries, Pletho does not fare badly. Consider, for example, the world maps of Andreas Walsperger and Fra Mauro, dated in 1448 and 1459 respectively[7]. In spite of some slight use of empirical data based on the voyages of de' Conti to the extreme Orient, they are, from many points of view, inferior to Pletho.

All in all, considering his times, we must admit that Pletho had a fair knowledge of geography. Like most of the enlightened men of the Middle Ages, he knew the world was round, and abjured the fanciful geographical conceptions of the superstitious. He does not deal in weird monsters like the Sciapodes, nor does he harbor any delusions as to the realm of the mythical Prester John, whose curious history haunted the imaginations of men even later than the fifteenth century. On the contrary, he accepts enthusiastically the latest geographical information available. And, if he is behind the times in some respects, as for example in his ignorance of the exploits of Marco Polo, he outstrips the majority of his contemporaries in others (with regard to Dateia and Russia, concerning the latter of which, as previous investigators have failed to realize, he was probably informed by Isidore of Kiev, Russian delegate at the Council of Florence, and by Isidore's Russian companions). Moreover, to judge from his empirical approach to the authorities upon whom he relies, it is clear that, although he knew nothing of Niccolò de' Conti, he would not have taken Pope Pius II's skeptical attitude towards the account of de' Conti's far eastern voyages published by Poggio Bracciolini[8]. It might, perhaps, be too much to conclude that Pletho would not suffer in comparison with the leading scientists of his day. But in having an open mind, he was already in possession of the prime requisite of all scientific research, and could take his place with the most fearless and most enterprising intellects of the fifteenth century.

II.—Pletho's Introduction of Strabo to the West.

In the *Diorthosis,* the principal emphasis is on Strabo. Indeed, in making the *Excerpts from Strabo* Pletho was undoubtedly seeking to introduce Strabo to a wider public. He recognized the merits of Ptolemy, but when confronted at the Council of Florence with the new cult of Ptolemy and with the humanists' unawareness of Strabo, he must have observed both to himself and to others that he could advance the study of geography by bringing forward a few of the more interesting sections of Strabo in handy form. For Ptolemy, it will be remembered, had been available in the Latin translation by Jacobus Angelus (Jacopo d'Angelo da Scarperia) dating from 1406; and Ptolemaic maps had been used as early as 1427 in a Latin version[9]. The importance of Ptolemy was universally recognized, and the great influence which Ptolemy's *Cosmographia* was to exert upon the renaissance was already assured. What was necessary, Pletho felt, was to rejuvenate Strabo, whose geographical treatise had never really been given the attention it deserved, even in the lands in which Greek was read and understood.

It was in pursuit of this purpose, therefore, that Pletho composed the *Excerpts* and the *Diorthosis.* We may be sure, too, that he made the best of his opportunities at Florence to initiate the geographers and classicists within his sphere of influence into the mysteries of the Strabonic geography. He says himself that he met in Florence men like Ugo Benzi and the famous Paolo Toscanelli, whose letter to the Portuguese canon, Fernão Martins, and correspondence with Christopher Columbus are important literary monuments in the history of the discovery of America[10]. Nor could he have failed to have associated at the same time with Nicholas of Cusa and Guarino da Verona, the latter of whom possibly first conceived the project (completed in 1458) of translating Strabo into Latin as a result of the stimulation and inspiration provided by Pletho.

Pletho would have inevitably pointed out in the course of the learned symposia he attended during his residence in Florence that Ptolemy, admirable as he was, should be compared with his predecessor Strabo, whose ***Geographika*** supplemented and complemented Ptolemy's work on the same subject at many points. Among other things, he would certainly have observed, as he does in the *Diorthosis,* that Ptolemy's view of the Indian Ocean as landlocked was open to serious question and that Africa, as Strabo taught, was probably circumnavigable. This latter fact was of unusual significance and may have exerted influence on the great African voyages of the Portuguese in the third quarter of the fifteenth century.

We must now inquire into the nature of the evidence for the view just asserted, that before Pletho's sojourn in Italy the Latin West had had no previous knowledge of Strabo. I have found support for this proposition in three quarters: a) in the history of medieval libraries, b) in the history of the use of Strabo by Latin writers, and c) in the history of the medieval tradition of the text of Strabo.

A) MEDIEVAL LIBRARIES.

It has not been possible to examine all of the many hundreds of catalogues now available in print containing lists of books found in various medieval collections. But is is clear from the standard manuals on the contents of the libraries of the Middle Ages and from the very considerable number of catalogues of individual medieval libraries which I have consulted that no manuscript of Strabo found its way to the west before the fifteenth century[11]. The only exception, which is more apparent than real, is that of a Constantinopolitan palimpsest of the sixth century, which was preserved for many years at the library of the monastery at Grottaferrata. But this codex cannot be taken as representing a western tradition of the text. For, to say nothing of its Constantinopolitan origin, its entire occidental history is confined to the Greek monasteries of Southern Italy and Tusculum. Moreover, at some early date in the Middle Ages, the text of Strabo was erased and replaced by a Latin version of the Pentateuch[12].

B) USE OF STRABO BY LATIN WRITERS IN THE MIDDLE AGES.

In a field so vast, only a few preliminary tests could be made at the points which seemed most promising. Accordingly, a study was undertaken of those authors in whom it was thought on *a priori* grounds (their knowledge of Greek, e. g., or their interest in geography, or the encyclopaedic character of their work) that a reference to Strabo might possibly be expected.

According to some, Orosius' geographical introduction to the *Historiae adversum paganos* (*ca.* 419) shows the influence of Strabo, although Strabo is never actually mentioned. But there is no evidence whatever that the superficial similarities between Strabo and Orosius are not to be explained by the use of some other source. Strabo is named thrice in the ninth century (?) Latin translation (*Solutiones eorum de quibus dubitavit Chosroes Persarum Rex*)[13] of a lost work written in Greek by Priscian Lydus, one of the scholars who fled to Persia with Damascius, Simplicius, and others after the closing of the Platonic Academy of Athens by Justinian in 529. Though none of these three passages (one of which lists Strabo among Priscian's authorities, and the other two of which allude to matters of local geography) deals with geography in a broad sense, it is conceivable that they may, nevertheless, have served to keep the memory of Strabo alive in the later Middle Ages. Charles Gidel very guardedly gives the impression that Strabo is cited in Eriugena's *De divisione naturae;* but I can find no proof of this, and Cappuyns does not include Strabo in his careful catalogue of the authors cited by Eriugena[14].

Jordanes (*ca.* 551), borrowing no doubt from Cassiodorus, actually uses Strabo in dealing with some meteorological matters. But the references to Strabo in the *Memoria Seculorum* of Godfrey of Viterbo (*ca.* 1185), in the *De proprietatibus rerum* of Bartholomaeus Anglicus (*ca.* 1230), and in the *Imago* mundi of Pierre d'Ailly (1350-1420), who merely reproduces Bartholomaeus Anglicus, are unimportant geographically and may in point of fact refer, not to Strabo the geographer, but to Walafrid Strabo, the grammarian . . .[15].

Enough has been said to prove that the cosmography of Strabo was not known in the West during the Middle Ages. The most we can find is a very few miscellaneous scraps of unconnected and unsystematic information on small points of detail. The main outlines and the general principles of geography enunciated by Strabo were wholly and completely inaccessible.

C) THE MEDIEVAL TRADITION OF THE TEXT OF STRABO.

At the outset, it is to be observed that there was no translation of Strabo previous to that completed in 1458 by Guarino da Verona. The translation by Gregory Tiphernas was begun after Guarino's[16].

The facts concerning the principal Ms. can be summarized as follows[17]:

1) None of the eight codices of Strabo which were transcribed between the tenth and the fourteenth centuries had any occidental circulation whatsoever before the beginning of the fifteenth century.

2) Three codices of Strabo had been imported from Greece during the first third of the fifteenth century, two by Giovanni Aurispa, and one by Francesco Filelfo[18]. But they were bought in large lots together with a number of other classical texts, not separately for their own sakes, and none of them had borne progeny even as late as *ca.* 1459, the date of the first Greek manuscript of Strabo copied in the West that was not definitely related to Pletho's *Excerpts* and their earliest descendants.

3) None of the Greek manuscripts transcribed in the West can be dated before 1439; and a number of manuscripts exhibit a type of text that reproduces peculiarities found only in Pletho's *Excerpts*. These codices, therefore, may be regarded as part of the result of the impetus given Strabonic studies by Pletho and by Guarino's Latin translation.

On the basis of this evidence, we can only conclude that the *Geographika* of Strabo as such was not available in the Latin West until soon after 1439, when a demand arose for reproductions of the Greek text. As we have seen, this new interest in Strabo is directly associated with Pletho and his zeal in persuading his friends to make a study of the *Geographika.*

III.—Knowledge of Ptolemy in the West.

It is usually maintained that the geography of Ptolemy was unknown in the West during the Middle Ages. This is quite true of the strictly cartographical sections of the treatise, that is to say, of the maps and the formulation of the fundamentals of map projection set forth in the first book. But in other respects, it can be shown, the *Cosmographia* could claim some medieval circulation. An outline of Ptolemy's chief theoretical principles and a not inconsiderable part of his tables of latitude and longitude, often with marked improvements and rectifications, were accessible to all who cared to use them. This is not to say that Ptolemy's theories and figures were widely or correctly adopted for geographical purposes. But they were available, and could have formed the basis for plotting a fairly adequate map, in spite of the fact that the Arabic and Latin versions are often inconsistent in their use of Ptolemaic data[19].

Among the Latins who were acquainted with Ptolemy's geography in one form or another were Ammianus Marcellinus, Martianus Capella, Priscian Lydus (in the Latin version), Cassiodorus, Jordanes, Eriugena, Alfred the Great, and Adam of Bremen. In addition, there is a record in the twelfth century of a request for a copy of *Ptolomaeum de cosmographia*[20]. The texts cited in the previous note show in varying degree that the tradition of Ptolemy's geography had not altogether perished in the West. But the greater part of what was known of Ptolemy in the Occident during the Middle Ages was derived from Arabic cosmographical and astronomical texts based upon Ptolemy, and made available in Latin by the translations of Gerard of Cremona, Plato of Tivoli, Robert of Chester, John of Seville, and John of Hollywood. Strabo, however, was not known by the Arabs, nor was any use made of his *Geographika* by Syriac writers.

IV.—Strabo and the Renaissance.

Pletho's judgment in preferring Strabo to Ptolemy was vindicated during the course of the renaissance. Strabo even beat Polemy to press and went through three editions (1469-73) before the appearance of the first printed version of Ptolemy in 1475[21]. Pius II definitely rejected the Ptolemaic conception of Africa in favor of the Strabonic[22]; and, somewhat before, Pierre d'Ailly (1350-1420) had asserted, against what he took to be the view of Ptolemy, that perhaps as little as one seventh of the world is covered with water, not so much as three fourths or five sixths[23]. Christopher Columbus followed d'Ailly enthusiastically on this point and regarded Bartholomew Diaz's accomplishment (1488) in rounding the Cape of Good Hope as involving a repudiation of the Ptolemaic description of the limits of the inhabited world[24].

Columbus cites Strabo in support of a belief in the existence of other and as yet unknown inhabitable lands, and frequently refers to his name in commenting upon Pius II's *Historia rerum ubique gestarum locorumque descriptio*[25]. But the clearest and most definite statement of the use Columbus made of Strabo is recorded in the biography of Columbus by his son Fernando. According to Fernando, Strabo was one of the chief authorities for the cosmography of Columbus. There were, he tells us, two principal lines of documentary evidence which led his father to believe that he could reach the Indies by a new route. The first gave assurance that the sea to be crossed was not inordinately wide, the second that it was possible to reach the East by sailing due West. The quotations from Strabo on both of these points are unambiguous and were, therefore, highly esteemed by Columbus.

Strabo is first mentioned by Fernando in a chapter entitled *La principal cagione che mosse l'Ammiraglio a credere di poter discoprir dette Indie,* to illuminate the discussion of the distance between the Azores and India:

> Alla qual ragione s'aggiunge quel che dice Strabone nel xv libro della sua Cosmografia, niuno esser giunto con esercito al fine Orientale dell' India: il quale Ctesia scrive esser tanto grande, quanto tutta l'altra parte dell' Asia; e Onesicrito afferma esser la terza parte della sfera; e Nearco aver quattro mesi di cammino per pianura[26].

The passage of Strabo Fernando had in mind here attributes a great eastward extension to India[27]. This was a matter of the highest significance for the Admiral. Indeed, it was his confidence in the projection of India into the east (and the consequent diminution of the distance to be traversed by sea from the western terminus of *terra firma*) that gave Columbus courage to undertake his hazardous enterprise into the unknown.

Strabo is named again in the seventh chapter (*La seconda causa che mosse l'Ammiraglio a scoprire l'Indie*), along with Aristotle, Seneca, Marco Polo, and others, as one who maintained that it was possible to sail from Africa and Spain to the Eastern terminus of India, and that the unknown ocean was not of great extent:

> che dal fine occidentale dell' Africa e della Spagna potrebbe navigarsi per l'Occidente al fine orientale dell' India; e che non era gran mare quello che in mezzo giaceva.

Appeal is made to both the first and the second Books of Strabo's **Geographia:**

> E Strabone nel primo libro della sua Cosmografia dice, che l'Oceano circonda tutta la terra: e che all' Oriente bagna l'India, e nell' Occidente la Spagna e la Mauritania: e che, se la grandezza dell' Atlantico non impedisse, si potrebbe navigare dall' uno all' altro luogo per uno istesso parallelo. E il medesimo torna a dire nel secondo libro[28].

The first[29] of these contains Strabo's summary of the section in which Eratosthenes discusses the great extension of the inhabitable world longitudinally (i.e., from east to west) and expresses the opinion that the inhabited world

> forms a complete circle, itself meeting itself; so that, if the immensity of the Atlantic Ocean did not prevent, we could sail from Iberia to India along one and the same parallel over the remainder of the circle.

Strabo quibbles over details but adds:

> It is possible that in the same temperate zone (*sc.* which we inhabit) there are actually two inhabited worlds, or even more, and particularly in the proximity of the parallel through Athens in the region of the Atlantic Ocean.

The second[30] is equally striking. There Strabo remarks that Poseidonius did well to quote Plato's statement that there was a possibility that the island of Atlantis had once actually existed. He then goes on to say:

> And he (*sc.* Poseidonius) suspects that the length of the inhabited world, being about seventy thousand stadia, is half of the entire circle on which it has been taken, so that, says he, if you sail from the west in a straight course you will reach India within the seventy thousand stadia.

None of these texts is quoted in the works of the other authors studied and annotated by Christopher Columbus[31], who must, therefore, have found them in the **Geographika** of Strabo itself. At this point mention should be made of the view of Henry Vignaud that all the cosmographical

knowledge and ancient lore displayed by Columbus in his writings and recapitulated by his son and others were manufactured *post eventum*. Vignaud contends that when Columbus set out in 1492 he had no intention of sailing to India. He was only following the course, the secret of which had been bequeathed to him by an «unknown pilot.» All the learned apparatus, Vignaud argues,—the Strabo, the *Imago Mundi* of Pierre d'Ailly and the rest,—were fabricated by Columbus after his return from the first voyage in order to avoid recording his debt to the «unknown pilot» and so as to create the impression that his expedition across the Atlantic was the logical conclusion of long and arduous research in both theoretical cosmography and practical navigation[32]. But the mass of evidence admirably summarized by Professor Samuel E. Morison in his important book on Columbus[33], a great thesaurus of Columbian learning, renders Vignaud's hypothesis untenable.

Of course, it is possible that Columbus may have laid his plans for an Atlantic crossing before reading Strabo, for he was a man of action and leaned heavily upon actual nautical experience. Nevertheless, the texts from Strabo offered him not only confirmation and support to strenghten his own resolution and purpose but also a welcome learned authority to flaunt before the pedants appointed to scrutinize and report upon the feasibility of his scheme.

In conclusion, therefore, although no one would venture to credit Pletho with a share in the actual discovery of America, we must recognize that, in interesting the scholars of the West in the **Geographika** of Strabo, he made an important contribution to the development of the geographical theory of the renaissance, which reached its supreme fulfilment in the great achievement of Columbus.

Notes

1. This communication is a brief summary of a chapter taken from my doctoral dissertation (Harvard, 1940); a much longer version, containing many additional details together with full documentation and analysis, is now being prepared.

2. On the date of Pletho's death see Martin Jugie, 'La date de la mort de Gémistos Pléthon,' *Échos d'Orient,* 34 (1935), 160 f.; A. Dain, 'Sur un manuscrit grec de Salamanque,' *Emerita,* 10 (Madrid, 1942), 8 ff.

3. For the bibliography on Pletho, see my *Pletho's Calendara and Liturgy* (*Dumbarton Oaks Papers,* Number 4 [Cambridge, Mass., 1948]), 183 ff., 190 f.

4. The latest and best edition of the Greek text is that of Aubrey Diller, 'A geographical treatise by Georgius Gemistus Pletho,' *Isis,* 37 (1937), 441-51, which is based upon *Codex Marcianus Graecus,* 379. Diller's text supplants that of I. A. Goez, *Anecdota Graeca* (Nuremberg, 1798), 90-96.

5. Not having a modern critical text of Strabo, I have had to rely upon the edition of Horace L. Jones (Loeb Library, 8 vols., 1917-32), and those of G.

Kramer (3 vols., Berlin, 1844-52) and A. Meineke (3 vols., Leipzig, 1852-53). Important work on the text of Strabo has been done by Professor Aubrey Diller of the University of Indiana, and by Professor Francesco Sbordone of the University of Naples, the latter of whom hopes eventually to publish a scientific edition of the text. What I know of the *Excerpts from Strabo I* have learned from Kramer's introduction and the various catalogues of manuscripts.

6. Eugène Müntz and Paul Fabre, *La bibliothèque du Vatican au XVe siècle* (*Bibliothèque des écoles françaises d'Athènes et de Rome,* 48 [Paris, 1887]), 6, 20; See Alfred Berg, *op. cit.* (p. 5 *infra*), 31. The *Il Milione* is not listed among the books owned by Pius II: Aeneas Piccolomini, 'De codicibus Pii II et Pii III deque Bibliotheca ecclesiae cathedralis Senensis,' *Bullettino Senese di Storia Patria,* 6 (1899), 483-96; Josephus Cugnoni, 'Aeneae Silvii Piccolomini Senensis qui postea fuit Pius II Pont. Max. opera inedita,' *Atti della R. Accademia dei Lincei,* anno CCLXXX, S. 3a, *Memorie della classe di scienze morali, storiche e filologiche,* 8 (Rome, 1882-83), 333 ff.

7. G. H. T. Kimble, *Geography in the Middle Ages* (London, 1938), 117-19, 198-200, pl. 12 and 16.

8. On Isidore, etc., see Giovanni Mercati, *Scritti d'Isidoro, il Cardinale Ruteno* (*Studi e testi,* 46 [Vat. C, 1926]); Ludwig Mohler, *Kardinal Bessarion als Theologe, Humanist u. Staatsmann,* 1 (Paderborn, 1923), 117 f.; C. F. Hefele - H. Leclercq, *Histoire des conciles,* 7, 2. (Paris, 1916), 1080 f.; Pierling, *La Russie et le Saint-Siège,* 1 (Paris, 1896), 7 ff., 16 ff.; Henri Vast, *Le Cardinal Bessarion* (1403-72), *étude sur la chrétienté et la renaissance vers le milieu du XVe siècle* (Paris, 1878), 107.

On Pius II, see *Pii. II. Pon. Max. Asiae Europaeque elegantissima descriptio, mira festiuitate tum veterum, tum recentium res memoratu dignas complectens. . . . Accessit Henrici Glareani . . . compendiaria . . .* (Paris, 1534), 18 f.; cf. 28 f. See also Alfred Berg, *Enea Silvio de' Piccolomini* (*Papst Pius II.*) *in seiner Bedeutung als Geograph. Ein Beitrag zur Erdkunde im Quattrocento* (Halle a. S., 1901); Georg Voigt, *Enea Silvio de' Piccolomini, als Papst Pius d. Zweite, u. sein Zeitalter,* 2 (Berlin, 1862), 336. Cf. Waldemar Sensburg, *Poggio Bracciolini u. Nicolò de Conti in ihrer Bedeutung für die Geographie des Renaissance-Zeitalters* (Vienna, 1906).

9. Joseph Fischer, *Claudii Ptolemaei Geographiae Codex Urbinas Graecus 82 phototypice depictus,* 1, 1 (Leiden-Leipzig, 1932), 183 ff., 191, 201 ff., 213, 301 ff.; Fischer's book, including 3 volumes and a large atlas, is the standard work on Ptolemy.

10. *Diorthosis,* ed. Diller, *Isis,* 27 (1937), 443, 447 f.; MPG, 160, 982B. On Toscanelli, see Morison, *op. cit.* (p. 17 *infra*), vol. 1, 45-7, 56-8, 85-7, 102;

Vignaud, *op. cit.* (p. 17 *infra*); Norbert Sumien, *La correspondance du savant florentin Paolo dal Pozzo Toscanelli avec Christophe Colomb* (Paris, 1927).

11. My results are based upon the following works and upon a study of a great many of the lists of the contents of medieval libraries there cited: Theodor Gottlieb, *Ueber mittelalterliche Bibliotheken* (Leipzig, 1890); Gustav Becker, *Catalogi bibliothecarum antiqui* (Bonn, 1885); B. Altaner, 'Griechische codices in abendländischen Bibliotheken des XIII. u. XIV. Jahrhunderts,' *BZ,* 36 (1936), 32-5; J. S. Beddie, 'The ancient classics in the mediaeval libraries,' *Speculum,* 5 (1930), 1-20. See also Pearl Kibre, 'The intellectual interests reflected in the libraries of the fourteenth and fifteenth centuries,' *Journal of the history of ideas,* 7 (1946), 257-97.

12. On this see Wolf Aly, *Der Strabon-Palimpsest, Vat. Gr. 2061A* (*Sitzungsberichte d. Heidelberger Ak. d. Wiss., Philos-hist. Kl.,* 19 [1928-29]); *idem, Neue Beiträge zur Strabon-Ueberlieferung, ibid.,* 22 (1931-32).

13. Kimble, *op. cit.,* 20. Strabo is not listed by Karl Zangemeister in his *index scriptorum quibus Orosius usus est: Pauli Orosii Historiarum adversum paganos libri vii,* CSEL, 5 (Vienna, 1882). Cf. Friedrich Wotke, *s. v.* Orosius, Pauly-Wissowa-Kroll, *Real-Encyclopädie,* 18. 1 (1939), 1185-95; D. Detlefsen, *Ursprung, Einrichtung u. Bedeutung d. Erdkarte Agrippas* (*Quellen u. Forschungen zur alten Geschichte u. Geographie,* herausg. v. W. Sieglin, Heft 13 [Berlin, 1906]), 18, 21. *Prisciani Lydi quae extant,* ed. I. Bywater (*Supplementum Aristotelicum,* 1, pars 2 [Berlin, 1886]), 42. 8 f., 71. 4, 91. 6, 11; Maïeul Cappuyns, *Jean Scot Érigène, sa vie, son oeuvre, sa pensée* (Louvain-Paris, 1933), 148 f.

14. Gidel, *Nouvelles études sur la littérature grecque moderne* (Paris, 1878), 179; Cappuyns, *op. cit.*

15. Jordanes, *Getica,* 2, 12, 14, ed. T. Mommsen, *Monumenta Germaniae Historica, Auctores Antiquissimi,* 5.1 (Berlin, 1882), XXX, XL ff., 56. 19-57. 2, 12 (Strabo, 4. 5. 2); Gotifredus Viterbiensis, MGH, *Scriptores,* 22 (Hanover, 1872), 95; Bartholomaeus Anglicus (Nuremberg, 1492), Liber 15, c. 112 (*De paradiso*); Edmond Buron, ed., *Ymago mundi de Pierre d'Ailly texte latin et traduction française des quatres traités cosmographiques de d'Ailly et des notes marginales de Christophe Colomb,* 2 (Paris, 1930), 458 ff. and n. 342. Christopher Columbus found the passage from Bartholomaeus in Pierre d'Ailly, *loc. cit.,* and paraphrases it in the journal of his Third Voyage (August 11, 1498), *Raccolta* (p. 14 *infra*), 37.20 ff.

16. Remigio Sabbadini, 'La traduzione guariniana di Strabone,' *Il libro e la stampa,* N. S. 3 (1909), 5-16: Tiphernas, who translated only Books 11-17, did not collaborate with Guarino, and finished his translation

in 1456. Cf. R. Sabbadini, ed. *Epistolario di Guarino Veronese raccolto, ordinato, illustrato,* 3 (*R. Deputazione di Storia Patria, Miscellanea di Storia Veneta,* Serie III, vol. 14 [1919]), 483-7.

17. The manuscripts are for the most part those listed by the various editors in their editions. See also the valuable articles of Aubrey Diller, 'Codex B of Strabo,' *American Journal of Philology,* 56(1935), 97-102; 'The Vatopedi manuscript of Ptolemy and Strabo,' *ibid.,* 58 (1937), 174-84. I hope, with the aid of Professors Diller and Sbordone (see p. 2 *supra*), to base my final results upon a complete list of the extant manuscripts. At present, of course, the conclusions here summarized are of a tentative nature.

18. See Remigio Sabbadini, *Le scoperte dei codici latini e greci ne' secoli XIV e XV,* (Florence, 1905), 46 ff.; *idem,* ed., *Carteggio di Giovanni Aurispa* (*Fonti per la Storia d'Italia,* 70, [Rome, 1931]), IX, XV ff., 10 ff., 13.4 f. and n. 2, 73. 5-12, 97. 19-24, 127 n. 4; P. A. Revilla, *Catálogo de los códices griegos de la Biblioteca de El Escorial,* 1 (Madrid, 1936), 471 ff.; Aristide Calderini, 'Ricerche intorno alla biblioteca e alla cultura greca di Francesco Filelfo,' *Studi italiani di filologia classica,* 20 (1913), 393-7.

19. See Dana B. Durand, *The Vienna-Klosterneuburg map corpus of the fifteenth century* (Leiden, 1939), a book of great value, the publication of which has been delayed by the war; John K. Wright, *The geographical lore of the time of the Crusades* (N. Y., 1925); George Sarton, *Introduction to the history of science,* 3 vols. in 5 (Baltimore, 1927-48); J. H. Kramers, s. v. Djughrāfiyā, *Encyclopaedia of Islam, Supplement* (Leiden-London, 1934-6), 61-73.

20. Martianus Capella, *De nuptiis Philologiae et Mercurii,* ed. A. Dicks (Leipzig, 1925), Sec. 610, p. 301. 2-16, cf. Sec. 813, p. 430. 5, on which cf. Ptolemy, *Geographia,* ed. C.F.A. Nobbe, 1 (Leipzig, 1843), Liber 1, c. 3, 7, and 11; Priscianus Lydus, *Solutiones eorum de quibus dubitavit Chosroes Persarum Rex, ed. cit.* (p. 9 *supra*), 42. 11 f.; *Cassiodori Senatoris institutiones,* ed. R.A.B. Mynors (Oxford, 1937), 66. 22 ff., cf. 184, 192; Jordanes, *Getica,* 3, 16-19, *ed. cit.* (p. 10 *supra*), 57. 17-58. 16; Eriugena, *De divisione naturae* (MPL, 122, 719A), ed. C. B. Schlüter (Münster, 1838), 279 (from Martianus Capella, *loc.cit.;* M. Cappuyns, *op. cit.* [p. 9 *supra*], 213, 215); G. Becker, *Catalogi bibliothecarum,* 228, n° 111, 1 (12th c.). C. R. Beazley, *Dawn of modern geography,* 2 (London, 1901), 523, claims that Alfred the Great and Adam of Bremen had some acquaintance with Ptolemy. For Ammianus Marcellinus' knowledge of Ptolemy, see Fischer, *op. cit.* (p. 6, n. 1 *supra*), 483 ff.

On the Arab use of Ptolemy's *Cosmographia* and on the transmission of Ptolemaic materials to the Latin West, chiefly in the form of astronomical tables containing Ptolemaic geographical data, see previous note.

21. Arnold C. Klebs, 'Incunabula scientifica et medica,' *Osiris,* 4 (1938), 265 f., 311.

22. Pii. II. Pont. (p. 5, n. 2 *supra*), pp. 6, 10 f.

23. *Ymago mundi,* ed. Buron, 1, 206 ff.

Note, however, that in the *Cosmographia* Ptolemy makes no statement on the percentage of the surface of the earth covered by water. The passages on this subject attacked by d'Ailly and Columbus are cited from other writings of Ptolemy. On medieval theories concerning the relative proportion of water and dry land, something, but not very much, is to be found in Arnold Norlind, *Das Problem des gegenseitigen Verhältnisses von Land u. Wasser u. seine Behandlungen im Mittelalter* (*Lunds Universitets Årsskrift,* N. F., Avd. 1, Bd. 14, Nr. 12 [Lund, 1918]).

24. *Ymago mundi,* ed. Buron, 1, 206 ff.; Cesare de Lollis, *Scritti di Cristoforo Colombo* (*Raccolta di documenti e studi pubblicati dalla R. Commissione Colombiana pel quarto centenario della scoperta dell' America,* Parte 1, vol. 2 [Rome, 1894]), 376 f.; cf. 38. 30 ff., 39.4 ff. Columbus' annotation is one of the many (898 on the *Ymago mundi,* 861 on Pius II's *Historia rerum ubique gestarum locorumque descriptio,* 366 on Marco Polo, 24 on the elder Pliny's *Naturalis historia,* and 437 on Plutarch's *Vitae*) that he wrote in the margins of his favorite books. All of these marginalia have been published by de Lollis, *op. cit.* Cf. Buron, *loc. cit.,* 27.

25. Ed. Caddeo, 1, 96 (see following note); *Raccolta* (see previous note), Parte 1, vol. 2, 291 n. 5, 292 n. 11, 306 n. 144, 307 nn. 150 f., 308 n. 162, 309 n. 173, 310 n. 184, 313 n. 216, 316 n. 258, 324 n. 348, 328 n. 395, 332 n. 441, 336 n. 490, 345 n. 623, 360 n. 816.

26. *Le Historie della vita e dei fatti di Cristoforo Colombo per D. Fernando Colombo, suo figlio,* ed. Rinaldo Caddeo, 1 (*Viaggi e scoperte di navigatori ed esploratori italiani,* 11 [Milan, 1930]), 41 ff. The only witness to the no longer extant Spanish text of Fernando Colón is the Italian translation by Alfonso Ulloa (Venice, 1571).

27. 1. 4. 6; 15. 1. 5 f., 10-12 (Casaubon, pp. 64 f., 686 f., 688-90).

28. *Op. cit.,* 47, 50; n. b. Caddeo's analysis of the sources. Christopher Columbus' use of Strabo is attested also by Fray Bartolomé de Las Casas, who, like Fernando Colón, had had access to the Admiral's log-book, letters, and papers, and made use of them in his *Historia de las Indias* (Madrid, 1875, the *editio princeps;* a new critical text is now being prepared by Dr. Lewis Hanke, Chief of the Hispanic Division of the Library of Congress, and Professor Agustín Millares Carlo of the Colegio de México). Las Casas refers to Columbus's use of Strabo in Book 1, c. 5, vol. 1, 55 ff.

29. Strabo, 1. 4. 6 (Casaubon, pp. 64 f.); here and *infra* I have used the translation of Horace L. Jones with a few minor variations.

30. Strabo, 2. 3. 6 (Casaubon, p. 102).

31. On Columbus's *postille,* see p. 14, nn. 2 f. *supra.*

32. Henry Vignaud, *Histoire critique de la grande entreprise de Christophe Colomb* (Paris, 1911), espec. 1, 211-50, 347 f.; 2, 481-97; Idem, *Toscanelli and Columbus. The letter and chart of Toscanelli on the route to the Indies by way of the west* (London, 1902), 99 ff., 267 ff.

33. *Admiral of the Ocean Sea, a life of Christopher Columbus,* 2 vols. (Boston, 1942). In the longer version of this article, which I am now preparing, I hope to include a detailed criticism of Vignaud.

Lawrence Waddy (essay date 1963)

SOURCE: "Did Strabo Visit Athens?," *American Journal of Archaeology,* Vol. 67, No. 3, July, 1963, pp. 296-300.

[*In the following essay, Waddy notes Strabo's decidedly modest use of his own eyewitness accounts in the Geography and, rejecting arguments made by other scholars, contends that it is virtually certain that Strabo visited Athens.*]

This is a question which has often been discussed; but no clear answer has been reached. C. H. Weller, in an article entitled "The extent of Strabo's travels in Greece," summed up the opinions of scholars who had gone before him. There is no need to quote these again at length; but it can briefly be said that at one extreme came the early opinion of Leake: "As his account of the sea-coast is generally more accurate and detailed than that of the inland districts, we are tempted to believe that few parts of the interior were visited by him, but that his travels were principally performed by sea." This would credit Strabo at least with careful observation of the cost. At the other extreme Niese stated that Corinth was the only place in Greece which Strabo knew from personal observation, and Tozer and Frazer agreed that the contrary could not be proved.[1]

Since Weller's article appeared, H. L. Jones, in the introduction to the Loeb edition of the *Geography,* has expressed the same view as Tozer and Frazer: "It cannot be maintained with positiveness that in Greece he saw any place other than Corinth—not even Athens, strange as this may seem."[2] And Aly, in his thorough study of Strabo's sources, has put it even more strongly: "Strabon hat von Hellas kaum etwas gesehen. In Patras, das er passiert haben muss, blitzt vielleicht eine Spur von Autopsie auf (8.7.5), aber weder in Athen noch in Olympia ist dies der Fall."[3]

Weller pointed out that the evidence on which the question has to be decided is all internal. He went on to say that it

"must be gleaned principally from books VIII, IX and X."[4] In this I believe him to have been mistaken. Statements in Strabo have always tended to be considered too much in isolation. What neither Weller nor any other writer on the subject has done is to consider the question as it were through Strabo's eyes. We do not simply need to know what were the sources for his Books on Greece, and where in these Books he shows signs of having been an eyewitness. We need rather to ask a wider question: what place do eyewitness accounts take in the *Geography* as a whole? How important did Strabo think that it was to say whether he had visited a place about which he writes?

It is, of course, Strabo's boast that he was a great traveller, and the passage in which he says so deserves careful consideration. He writes: "I shall describe then what parts of the land and sea I have visited myself, and for what parts I trust to the verbal or written evidence of others. I have travelled westwards to the parts of Tyrrhenia opposite Sardinia, and southward from the Euxine to the borders of Ethiopia. Nor could any of the geographers be found who has covered much more of the distances which I have described; but those who have travelled more in the west have done less in the east, and the opposite is also true. And the same thing holds good for the south and the north. But both they and I receive the greater part of our material by hearsay, and then put together the shape and size and other features of what we describe." And, later in the same section: "For Generals also carry out everything themselves, but are not present everywhere in person; they order most things through others, relying on despatches and sending out their instructions in accordance with what they hear. But the man who claims that only eyewitnesses have knowledge takes away the criterion of 'understanding through hearing', which for scientific knowledge is much more important than sight."[5]

Strabo was an honest man, and he knew and admitted that his books were mainly compiled out of other people's books. He quotes from about 110 Greek prose authors, 43 Greek poets, and a small number of Latin prose sources. Even though some of these authors were certainly not quoted at first hand, but found by him in the works of others such as Posidonius or Demetrius of Scepsis, he was by the standards of his age a painstaking student; and so, even when he makes his claim to have travelled extensively, he acknowledges that it is [understanding through hearing] which really counts.

Many writers have given theri opinions about the number of eyewitness references in his work, and the lists differ according to the interpretation of the evidence. Sometimes, of course, there is no question about it: he says plainly that he has seen a place or an incident. At other times there is only a greater or lesser possibility that he did so. What seems to me to be neglected is his persistent *failure* to give any personal reference in places where he must have been, and this is important for the question of Athens. Perhaps "failure" is the wrong word. I believe rather that he did not think personal reminiscences to be important enough to mention unless a particular reason made them significant.

Let us see what he does record. There are four places in which he is known to have lived; it two of them for long periods, Amaia in Pontus and Alexandria; in one of them, Rome, on a number of occasions, and perhaps for long periods; and in the fourth, Nysa in Caria, as a student who "took a whole course."[6] Without going into the chronology of his life, we can say with confidence that he spent his early years in Amasia, and probably returned there for the last part of his life; that his visits to Rome came at intervals between 44 B.C. and 7 B.C., with the possibility of another in A.D. 6; that he spent years at Alexandria, using the Library for his reference work; and that he worked under Aristodemus at Nysa.

Strabo made a real attempt (not always successful, but genuine) to weigh his sources and to reject evidence which seemed to him to be flimsy or unreliable. He comes back repeatedly to his main authorities, Eratosthenes, Artemidorus, Polybius, Posidonius and, in a different sense, Homer. He is critical even of them, but they form the acknowledged framework of his writing. For a particular area he may also rely heavily on an author with special knowledge: Demetrius of Scepsis for the Troad, Megasthenes and others for India. He likes to have first-hand information, and frequently tells us that he is using an eyewitnes source. In fact, his reading and experience taught him to rely mainly on a few books written by men whoe travels and critical ability made them worthy guides and sources. He did not trust casual, isolated pieces of information.

I believe that he treated his own observations in much the same way. If he had lived in a place, and become throughly acquainted with it, his experience and observation became for him reliable evidence, and he used them. Obviously he was his own best source for Amasia, his birthplace; and he seems to write with assurance and a command of detail which betokens personal observation about other places in this area. Sinope, with the strange round holes on its prickly rock shore, and the market-gardens in its suburbs; the types of trees that grew in Sinopitis, and their uses; the plain of Themiscyra, with an unusual amount of detail about crops, fruits, wild animals and water supplies; all these are described with authenticity and confidence.[7] In Rome he sometimes gives eyewitness descriptions. The size of the Campus Martius impressed him, with space available for chariotraces, riding, ball-games, hoop-rolling and wrestling, and a view like a stage set, from which it was hard to look away. . . . He saw Selurus, the Sicilian brigand, executed in an elaborate manner in the Forum.[8] Turning to Alexandria, we find him giving ample details about the climate, the street plan, the Pharos, the life of scholars at the Museum, which tell the same story of authenticity.[9] And when he travelled in Egypt with Aelius Gallus, the Governor, he was in a party which was carefully guided and given full information; so that his ac-counts of Memphis, Arsinoe and Thebes are also personal and detailed.[10] (Was he a rather parasitic observer? When he was one of a party, treated as an important visitor, he remembered what he saw. Alone, he perhaps saw much less.) Finally, his period of residence at Nysa left its mark on his description of that part of Asia Minor, but less decisively. There is no question of a boast that he knew the district well. He only tells us that he was there at all because he mentions Aristodemus as one of the well-known natives of Nysa. However, he writes a vivid description of the Plutonium at Hierapolis, where he threw sparrows into the vapours and saw them fall and die; and the details which he gives about Smyrna (its Library and porticoes, its streets, beautifully planned and paved, except that the architects forgot to put in proper drainage) seem to betray familiarity with the place. At Tralleis, not far from Nysa, he may have had relations living. There is no clear sign of eyewitness writing in his account of the place; but he calls the site of the city "trapeze-shaped," and it is interesting to compare this with his description of Cyrene, as he himself saw it from the sea, "lying in a trapeze-shaped plain."[11]

More evidence could be given, from each of these four areas, to show that Strabo trusted his eyes when he had had time to see places carefully. He was cautious as an observer, and unenterprising, in spite of his overall claim which has been quoted. He recorded remarkably little about Italy after his many visits, and he never took the trouble to go and see the Troad despite his veneration for Homer. He digested thoroughly what was near at hand, and perhaps what his friends or employers took him to see. He may have worked for other Romans as he did for Aelius Gallus in Egypt. (If he had held a position as a tutor it would account for his rather strange reference to the retired tutors who lived at Naples and "gave it a more distinctive Greek flavour.")[12] But our conclusion so far is that he trusted his eyes if he had had ample opportunity to use them.

A second conclusion follows from a study of the *Geography;* namely, that in all areas other than these four, eyewitness references are astonishingly rare. Not only are they rare, they are haphazard. Strabo happens to say that he was at the island of Gyaros in 29 B.C., but only because an interesting incident occurred there.[13] The mention of Cyrene, quoted above, is casually introduced. His visit to Poplonium in Etruria leads to a good description of the view of Elba, Corsica and Sardinia.[14] But why Poplonium in particular? Why tell us about this one place in Italy, when even the Naples area is so described that we cannot be *certain* that he went there? What of Brindisi, Bari and all the places on the way from Southern Italy to Rome? Or from Rome to Poplonium? Moving to Asia Minor, we find mystery surrounding his journeys to and from Amasia. What route did he take to Nysa, as a student? How did he return home later in life? There are a very few clues which we must notice, but the general conclusion is quite clear: that in the great majority of cases Strabo did not think it worthwhile to say that he had visited a place, when he discussed it in the *Geography.*

Hence the differing lists given by different scholars. They have to act on hints, subjectively interpreted. Bunbury included Megara among the points which Strabo had certainly visited in Greece. It is true that his description of the Scironian Rocks, and of the narrow road which runs past them, is careful and vivid; and he speaks of Tripodes as being "now called Tripodiscium, near which the market-place of the Megarians now lies."[15] However, there is no certain proof here of a visit. He was using at least one "Periplus" from which these observations could be quoted. The same is true of Bari and Brindisi. There is an unusual amount of detail such as a traveller might notice and record: an ill-smelling spring at Bari, and the alternative means of transport from thence to Brindisi according to the state of the sea; and the merits of the two roads from Brindisi, one a mule-road, the other better for carriages. But you would never guess that he had travelled by this route a number of times.[16] His short, tame reference to the canal journey from Tarracina, where the travellers prefer a night passage and the barges are pulled by mules, opens with the impersonal verb . . . "people sail."[17] This restraint shows, no doubt, a creditable desire to avoid mere tourist chatter, but we could wish that he had allowed his eye a freer range. Digressions, when they came from his source-books, were meat and drink to him; but personal observation was kept under very severe control.

In Asia Minor, the travels which he made in his youth came long before he began to write a *Geography;* but even so they leave surprisingly little trace. Jones thinks that he visited Cyzicus and Nicaea.[18] The evidence is similar to that which Bunbury used for Megara. Cyzicus is well described: its bridges, its fertility, its beauty and good government. Of Nicaea he writes that "from one stone which is set in the centre of the Gymnasium all four gates are visible." This is slender proof of a voyage through the Black Sea and a coastal journey down to Ephesus. We know that he crossed Asia Minor from north to south, or the reverse, for he gives a description of the river Pyramus rushing through an underground passage in Cataonia;[19] and he can hardly have been as far from Amasia as this unless his purpose was to cross from coast to coast. He could well have been at Tarsus, from his description of it, and Aly sees traces of a voyage along the Cilician coast in the references to the Corycian Cave (its uneven floor, the shrubs and saffron crops) and to Seleucia.[20]

I conclude from these passages, and from the much more frequent omissions of any mention of personal examination, that Strabo was not so much a slovenly as a very modest eyewitness. Only a remarkable occurrence (Selurus' execution), a natural phenomenon (the Pyramus gorge or the size of a rhinoceros), or a personal meeting (with Servilius Isauricus) deserves recording. [Understanding through hearing] is his regular source, and if his own memories are added it is hard to discern their presence.

But what about Athens? *Could* a Mediterranean traveller have visited that city, and yet not say so when he described it? We must try to answer this in the light of Strabo's usual practice.

There is a marked contrast in his treatment of Athens and Corinth. At the latter, which he visited in 44 B.C. and presumably on other occasions, his experience was significant. He was there just after Julius Caesar had decided to refound the city, and he therefore saw with his own eyes something which no book could tell him. Moreover, he climbed the Acrocorinth, and looked carefully at the magnificent view from the top. (I cannot help feeling that he did this as a member of some Roman party, as he did when he went sightseeing in Egypt; but there is no proof of this.) He made one mistake in describing what he saw, confusing Mount Gerania, which lay between Corinth and Megara, with the Oneian Mountains; but he knew that his description was authentic and careful, and so he used it.[21]

He approaches Attica from the north. In his picture of the route from Nisaea to Piraeus there are no sure marks of personal experience. The city of Salamis, he notes, has been moved, since the time of Aeschylus' description of the area, to a position by a gulf, on an isthmus facing Attica. The chapel built by Ictinus at Eleusis is large enough to contain a crowd of spectators. The tomb of Circe is visible on the larger of the two Pharmacussae islands. All this *might* come from personal observation—that which concerns the chapel perhaps more than the others; but there is no sort of proof. Then there is the question of the quarry at Amphiale, overlooking Salamis. Meyer rightly pointed out that Strabo was always interested in quarries and in types of building stone. He distinguishes between many different kinds of marble, and tells us of quarries at places as far distant from each other as, for example, Mazaca in Cappadocia and Gabii (these he might have seen), Proconnesus and Tunis. Even the making of millstones on the island of Nisyros earns a mention. In spite of this known interest, I cannot feel that a three-word mention of the Amphiale quarry . . . has any real bearing on the question whether Strabo was using his eyes rather than somebody else's book. There is, sad to say, no sign that he looked hard at the waters over which the battle of Salamis was fought. He was not using his own observation as a serious source. His mind was turned far too much towards Homer and his commentators, and his usual rule applied: stick to the book sources unless personal experience is of definite significance.[22]

And so we arrive at Athens, Piraeus and Munychia. Apart from any internal evidence in Book 9, there is a strong probability that Strabo travelled in ships which called at one of the Athenian harbours. Merchant ships in the Mediterranean hopped from port to port, only making long open-sea voyages when they had to do so. We have to account for about a dozen voyages made by Strabo to or from Asia Minor (or Egypt) and Rome. Unless he came by one of the Alexandrian corn ships, he passed up or down the Saronic Gulf on each of these journeys. It is possible that he used the corn ships on occasions, but if so he has left very little trace of it, even for him. These ships could sometimes be picked up in southern Asia Minor (St. Paul's party joined one at Myra); they then voyaged south of

Crete and across open sea to the Straits of Messina, and on to Puteoli. Sometimes they stopped at Malta for refuge from the weather. Strabo might be describing a voyage he made himself when he refers to Leucopetra and Heracleum (the toe of Italy), and notes the southwest wind which carries the ship on to Cape Iapygia, and the windswept harbour of Zephyrium. And there could be an oblique reference to such a voyage in his very interesting comment on the Italian trade with Egypt: "The exports from Alexandria are greater than the imports; and an observer could notice, at Alexandria and Dicaearchia (Puteoli), seeing the vessels at their arrival and departure, how much heavier or lighter they sailed to or from either port."[23]

No one can be sure whether, or how often, Strabo went this way. I can only say that it seems more likely that he preferred the local ships which formed the bulk of the eastern Mediterranean traffic. We know that he was travelling on one of these when he visited Gyaros and Corinth. We can only infer that he did so on most of his other voyages, with slender, unsatisfactory hints of familiarity with some of the islands as our evidence. For example, the temple of Poseidon on Tenos, . . . "worth seeing" (no proof that he had seen it); and the geographically muddled, but interesting, short passage about Patmos, the Corassiae islands and Icaria. At a conservative estimate, I should say that he passed near to Athens, in ships which normally called there because they went into harbour every night, six times or more. Bearing in mind that we shall not expect personal traces unless Strabo experienced something unusual or significant, let us now return to Weller's case against a visit to Piraeus and Athens.[24]

At first sight it looks a strong case, but on closer examination it largely falls to the ground. It divides into two parts, concerned with the harbour area and the city.

Weller points out that according to Strabo wars have "reduced . . . the Piraeus to a small settlement round the harbours and the temple of Zeus the Saviour"; while Pausanias "was able to name not only the Temple of Zeus, but also (1.1) the Long Colonnade, two markets, the ship-sheds, sanctuaries of Artemis, Demeter, Athena and Zeus, together with various altars and images." "It is hard, therefore," he concludes, "to believe that Strabo saw the city at all—and if not Piraeus, not Athens."[25]

In all this he seems to me to disregard totally the amount of devastation which went on in Athens, as in many parts of Greece, in the first century B.C. For Piraeus alone there is abundant evidence. Plutarch describes Sulla's treatment of the area in 87-6. . . . Appian says that Sulla undermined the walls of Piraeus and burned it, because it gave him so much more trouble than Athens. . . . But much more important for our purposes is the letter sent by Servius Sulpicius Rufus to Cicero from Athens in March 45. . . . [26]

In view of this, can we be surprised at Strabo's impression? His description fits in far better with what he himself would have seen in 44 or later than with what a writer like Apollodorus or Artemidorus would have seen in the previous century. Of course by Pausanias' day the picture was completely changed. Greece under the Antonines was a very different place from the depressed and depopulated land which Strabo described, at a time when Thebes was hardly worth calling a village and many former towns had disappeared altogether.[27]

I should say that Strabo's description of Piraeus, short though it is, is given at first hand; and there is a small detail which should be noticed in support of this. In describing the temple of Zeus Soter he says: "The small colonnades contain wonderful paintings, the works of famous artists. The open court . . . on the other hand contains statues." There is an almost exact parallel in his account of Samos. There he speaks of the Heraeum. . . . "Apart from the large number of pictures kept in it, there are other galleries, and some chapels full of ancient works of art. And the open court . . . is likewise filled with excellent statues." As he says that Antony had taken some of the best statues away, but Augustus had restored them, his knowledge of Samos is up-to-date. It is one of the places which he describes well and in quite full detail, and he probably visited it.

So much for Piraeus. No sooner does he reach Athens than he specifically refuses to give any but a perfunctory picture of it. Two lines about the Parthenon are followed by the disappointing, but understandable, apology: "But if I plunge into the mass of things concerning Athens which are so often praised and celebrated, I am frightened of going too far." . . . He then quotes, rather feebly, the third century historian Hegesias, who had likewise excused himself from describing Attica. But, feebly expressed or not, Strabo's decision is reasonable. He could not describe Athens as he did, say, Ephesus or Rhodes. They were in some ways comparable to Athens, but the main points in their history, and their most famous citizens, could be enumerated without the balance of the narrative being lost. . . . The "famous citizens of Tarsus," of whom he noted nine, led him into quite a long enough discussion. If he were to start on the Athenian statesmen from Solon to Demosthenes, the poets, philosophers, orators and architects, there would be no end to it. It was not laziness but common sense which led him to cut the account short.

Admittedly he was clumsy and confused over the Hegesias quotation. . . . [Did] he really mean Eleusis, seventeen miles away? Or did he mean the Eleusinion, which is now known to have been on the edge of the Agora, and visible from the Acropolis. We do not know; and it was slipshod of Strabo to use such an unsatisfactory quotation. But he *had already decided not to try* to give a full description. For critical purposes, he was not acting as an eyewitness. Therefore I do not think that there is much in Weller's additional point, that Strabo calls both Hymettus and Pentelicus "near to the city," when Pentelicus is much further away. How many well-informed Romans would have known more than that these were the quarries of Athens, somewhere near to it? Strabo would have made the distinction if he had looked at Athens as he did at Corinth or Alexandria; but this he deliberately decided not to do.[28]

Nevertheless, I believe that one little regarded passage from Book 1 makes it virtually certain that he went to the city. He is discussing the reliability of Eratosthenes, and writes: "He is neither so open to attack . . . that we can assert that he never even set eyes on Athens, as Polemo tries to show, nor so reliable as some people have been taught to believe." This means that, in Strabo's opinion, to write about the Mediterranean world without having seen Athens would be to lay oneself open to severe criticism. *Could* he have written this, if he himself had crossed the Aegean several times and never been to the city?[29]

My conclusion is that Strabo was a sound eyewitness, but a very limited one. As far as Greece is concerned, it is true that he can only be proved to have visited Corinth; but it is extremely probable that he went to Athens also. An argument from silence has no validity for the **Geography,** since personal reminiscence is with Strabo the exception rather than the rule.

Notes

1. *CP* (1906) 339-56. He there quotes Leake, *Athens and the Demi of Attica* I 32; Tozer, *History of Ancient Geography* 241; and Frazer, *Pausanias* I xci.

2. Loeb Strabo, I xxii.

3. *Strabonis Geographica,* Band 4, 331-32.

4. *op.cit.* 340.

5. 2.5.11.

6. . . . 14.1.48.

7. Amasia 12.3.39. Sinope 12.3.11. Sinopitis 12.3.12. Themiscyra 12.3.15.

8. 5.3.8, 6.2.6.

9. 17.1.6-9.

10. Memphis 17.1.24. Arsinoe 17.1.38. Thebes 17.1.46.

11. Plutonium 13.4.14. Smyrna 14.1.37. Tralleis 14.1.42. (The description of Larisa, near Tralleis, also has details which suggest that Strabo knew it.) Cyrene 17.3.20. For Strabo's relatives, see Jones in Loeb edition, I xv, where he quotes Pais' probable conjecture about the identity of Theophilus. I cannot understand Jones' statement that "the boy may have been sent to study in Nysa before the overthrow of Mithridates the Great." Mithridates was "overthrown" before Strabo was born, and died in 63, the almost certain date of the geographer's birth.

12. 5.4.7.

13. 10.5.3.

14. 5.2.6.

15. 9.1.9-10.

16. 6.3.5-7.

17. 5.3.6.

18. Loeb edition, I xxii. Cyzicus 12.8.11. Nicaea 12.4.7.

19. 12.2.4.

20. Tarsus 14.5.12-15. Aly, *op.cit.* 29-34 on 14.5.5.

21. 8.6.19-23.

22. 9.1.9-14. Cf. Pritchett in *AJA* 63:3 (1959) 253.

23. Acts 27 (Myra and Malta) and 17.1.7. See also Lionel Casson in *APA* 81 and 85 for corn ships. Leucopetra 6.1.7. I am assuming, as seems certain, that Strabo never went overland by the Via Egnatia.

24. Tenos etc. 10.5.11-13. Cf. 14.1.13 on the island route west from Samos. . . .

25. Weller, *op.cit.* 351-52.

26. 9.1.15. Plut. *Sulla* 14. App. *Mithridatica* 30-41. Cic. *ad Fam.* 4.5.4.

27. Thebes 9.2.5; cf. Rostovtzeff, *Social and Economic History of the Hellenistic World* 942.

28. Hegesias 9.1.16.

29. 1.2.2.

FURTHER READING

Bibliographies

Allen, T. W. "MSS. Of Strabo at Paris and Eton," in *The Classical Quarterly* IX, No. 1 (January 1915): 15-26 and No. 2 (April 1915): 86-96.

Detailed description of the Paris manuscripts of Book IX and additional information on the Eton manuscript.

Cook, J. M. "On Stephanus Byzantius' Text of Strabo," in *The Journal of Hellenic Studies* LXXIX (1959): 19-26.

Analysis of a manuscript dated circa 500 A.D. explains why it deserves more scholarly attention than usually afforded it.

Diller, Aubrey. "Codex *B* of Strabo," in *American Journal of Philology* LVI, No. 2 (1935): 97-102.

Presents conclusions as to the scholarly value of the *B* Codex.

———. "The Scholia on Strabo," in *Traditio* X (1954): 29-50.

Analysis of the earliest scholia in the manuscripts of Strabo.

———. *The Textual Tradition of Strabo's Geography,* Amsterdam: Adolf M. Hakkert, 1975, 222p.

Comprehensive history of manuscripts of Strabo.

Leaf, Walter. "Notes on the Text of Strabo XIII.1," in *The Journal of Hellenic Studies* XXXVII (1917): 19-30.

Examines arguments concerning the textual corruptions found in Book XIII.

Pritchard, J. P. "Fragments of the *Geography* of Strabo in the Commentaries of Eustathius," Classical Philology XXIX, No. 1 (January 1934): 63-65.

Describes how some previously unattributed fragments have been identified as the work of Strabo.

Sarton, George. "Roman, Hellenistic, and Chinese Geography and Geology," in *Introduction to the History of Science: Volume I: From Homer to Omar Khayyam,* pp. 227-30. Baltimore: The Williams & Wilkins Company, 1927.

Extensive bibliography includes texts, translations, and general and specialized studies.

Criticism

Leaf, Walter. "Strabo and Demetrios of Skepsis," in *The Annual of the British School at Athens* XXII (1916-1917; 1917-1918): 23-47.

Account of the relationship between the scholar Demetrios and Strabo.

Paassen, Christiaan van. "The Heritage of Classical Greek Geography: Ptolemy and Strabo," in *The Classical Tradition of Geography,* pp. 1-32. Groningen, Djakarta: J. B. Wolters, 1957.

Analyzes Strabo's aim for his *Geography* as a political and philosophical work.

Sherwin-White, A. N. "The Northern Barbarians in Strabo and Caesar," in *Racial Prejudice in Imperial Rome,* pp. 1-32. Cambridge: Cambridge University Press, 1967.

Examines Strabo's description of foreign barbarians.

Weller, Charles Heald. "The Extent of Strabo's Travel in Greece" in *Classical Philology* I, No. 4 (October 1906): 339-56.

Examines the arguments concerning whether or not Strabo visited Greece.

Johannes Tauler
c. 1300-1361

German author of sermons.

INTRODUCTION

Tauler was one of the most important religious figures of late-Medieval Germany. During this time, the Black Death ravaged Europe, and many believed that the Apocalypse was at hand. His influential sermons circulated widely throughout Germany and the Low Countries and were well-received in the Western world for centuries. Luther's promotion of Tauler's sermons helped lead to their acceptance among Protestants in the 1500s, when they rejected much of the Catholic tradition. Tauler, a member of the Dominicans, is the most celebrated disciple of the mystic Meister Eckhart. Avoiding much of the controversy surrounding mystics and the charge of heresy that eventually was leveled against Eckhart, Tauler made Eckhart's mysterious message more practical and easily graspable by the common people, trying to inspire his listeners to realize their own true, religious natures. Tauler was one of the leaders of the very loose-knit, spiritual movement known as the Friends of God. He stressed turning inward, citing Christ's statement that the kingdom of God is within us. Tauler urged his listeners to try to attain the union of the human and the divine by rooting out all sinful desires and accepting personal suffering, by practicing faith, hope, love, humility, gentleness, and patience.

BIOGRAPHICAL INFORMATION

Less is known of Tauler's life than was seemingly known in previous centuries. When *The History and Life of the Reverend Doctor John Tauler* was revealed as almost certainly spurious in the late nineteenth century, much of Tauler's biography went with it; precious little remains except conjecture. Tauler was born in Strasbourg circa 1300 into a well-off burgher family. Virtually nothing else is known about his family save that his sister became a Dominican nun and was present at Tauler's death. In 1314 or 1315 Tauler joined the Dominican Order. Although this was the same time that Eckhart visited the Dominicans in Strasbourg, there is no evidence that Eckhart and Tauler ever actually met, although Tauler would certainly have heard the master preach. After one year of introductory studies, Tauler would have spent six to eight years on logic, natural and moral philosophy, and theology. He then would have received more preparation in order to serve as a preacher, which he would not have become before age twenty-five at the earliest. Tauler probably preached in

Basel from 1339 to 1343 and also in Cologne, but most of his life was spent in Strasbourg. The Dominicans were entrusted with the pastoral care of nuns and Beguines; Tauler's sermons are chiefly addressed to them. The sermons began to create interest outside Strasbourg and Tauler's reputation also grew with his involvement with the Friends of God. The Friends of God stressed inward reflection and praying. As their spiritual director, Tauler appears to have kept the members from becoming overzealous in their mysticism and thus falling victim to the forces who banned and charged Eckhart. Tauler died in 1361.

MAJOR WORKS

Between sixty and eighty of the many known sermons credited to Tauler are accepted as genuine; many others are in dispute or deemed fraudulent. Tauler wrote exclusively in German; the belief that he wrote in Latin is a mistaken one. The sermons, which were delivered mostly to Dominican nuns, generally explore biblical texts used for Sundays and feast days. Practical rather than speculative, Tauler's sermons are generally straightforward and sometimes include examples from ordinary life. The message is to turn inward, away from outward practices and outward things, to become detached and empty so that God may fill the void. Although this way is fraught with pain, suffering, and self-doubt, it is the way to eternity with God. It is thought that Tauler did not write out any of the sermons in the form they now exist. Most likely they were transcribed by the nuns to whom Tauler delivered the sermons, and perhaps were later given final polish or approval by Tauler. As many were published during Tauler's lifetime, it seems probable that those particular sermons were in authorized form. There are serious scholarly arguments concerning the authenticity of many other sermons sometimes attributed to Tauler. One of the chief unanswered questions is whether the widely differing writings reflect an equally wide range in their author or whether they indicate the sermons were written by more than one author. The problem is further aggravated by the fact that many of the sermons were written down simply by those who heard Tauler preach, and they may have lacked the level of skills and memory necessary to create an accurate transcription. Scribes no doubt added and subtracted over the years as they saw fit. The existing sermons, some incomplete, are scattered throughout the world in libraries and private collections; a critical edition is yet to be realized. Although Luther had edited the *Theologia Germanica* and highly praised Tauler as the author, this was one of several works that scholars determined in the nineteenth century to have been misattributed to Tauler. *The Book of the Poor of Spirit,* a highly influential book probably written by a fellow Friend of God, is also now considered not to be the work of Tauler. In like fashion, the treatises *The Book of Spiritual Poverty* (also known as *Imitation of the Poor Life of Christ*), *The Marrow of the Soul,* the *Divine Institutions,* the *Exercises on the Life and Passion of our Saviour Jesus Christ,* and the *Prophecies of the Enlightened Dr. John Tauler* have all been rejected as authentic Tauler.

CRITICAL RECEPTION

Although Tauler's sermons have been highly acclaimed for centuries, interest in them has diminished somewhat in the twentieth century with a corresponding rise in interest in the works of the long-neglected Eckhart. Tauler's work, however, benefits from the lack of contentiousness that surrounds Eckhart's. Some critics admit frustration at how little they know of the man himself and others bemoan the lack of definitive texts with which to work. Interestingly, when so many texts once thought to be Tauler's were rejected as such, this did not hurt his reputation. James M. Clark states: "As a result of this clearance of the literary field, Tauler has gained in stature rather than lost. He is more impressive than the banal 'Master' of the 'Life' and a truer representation of his Order and his age." The use of language in authentic Tauler is widely admired. Josef Schmidt, writing in 1985, praises Tauler and his fellow German mystics for raising medieval German vernacular to heights surpassing scholarly Latin: "They expanded the horizons of the vernacular as a social code in theological and psychological dimensions that even today inspire awe in the modern reader. Their heritage is still a living force in German intellectual discourse, whether in theology or in philosophy." Critics note that Tauler's true concern for his audience always comes through vividly. Evelyn Underhill writes: "Without the hard intellectualism occasionally noticeable in Eckhart, or the tendency to introspection and the excessive artistic sensibility of Suso, Tauler is the most virile of the German mystics. The breadth of his spirituality is only equalled by the depth of his spirituality."

PRINCIPAL WORKS

Principal English Translations

The History and Life of the Reverend Doctor John Tauler of Strasbourg (translated by Susanna Winkworth) 1857.
The Inner Way: Being Thirty-Six Sermons for Festivals, by John Tauler (translated by Arthur Wollaston Hutton) 1901.
The Sermons and Conferences of J. Tauler (translated by W. Elliot) 1910.
Signposts to Perfection: A Selection from the Sermons of Johann Tauler (translated by Elizabeth Strakosch) 1958.

Spiritual Conferences (translated by Eric Colledge and M. Jane) 1961.
Johannes Tauler: Sermons (translated by Maria Shrady) 1985.
The Rhineland Mystics (translated by Oliver Davies) 1989.

CRITICISM

"A layman" (essay date c. 1340)

SOURCE: "The History and Life of the Reverend Doctor John Tauler" in *The History and Life of the Reverend Doctor John Tauler of Strasbourg,* translated by Susanna Winkworth, Smith, Elder, and Co., 1857, pp. 1-71.

[*The following excerpt, written circa 1340, is from a history first printed in the 1498 edition of Tauler's sermons. Believed to be genuine by Winkworth when she translated it, the history was shown by Heinrich S. Denifle in 1879 to have grave problems and, although the work is still controversial, scholars now consider it spurious, possibly the work of Rulman Merswin, and treat it as a legend.*]

In the year of Our Lord 1340, it came to pass, that a Master in Holy Scripture preached ofttimes in a certain city, and the people loved to hear him, and his teaching were the talk of the country for many leagues round. Now this came to the ears of a layman who was rich in God's grace, and he was warned three times in his sleep that he should go to the city where the Master dwelt, and hear him preach. Now that city was in another country, more than thirty leagues distant. Then the man thought within himself, "I will go thither and wait to see what God is purposed to do or bring to pass there." So he came to that city and heard the Master preach five times. Then God gave this man to perceive that the Master was a very loving, gentle, good-hearted man by nature, and had a good understanding of the Holy Scripture, but was dark as to the light of grace; and the man's heart did yearn over him, and he went to the Master and said, "Dear and honoured Sir, I have travelled a good thirty leagues on your account, to hear your teaching. Now I have heard you preach five times, and I pray you in God's name to let me make my confession to you." The Master answered, "With all my heart." Then the man confessed to the Master in all simplicity, and when he desired to receive the Lord's Body, the Master gave it him. When this had lasted twelve weeks, the man said to the Master, "Dear Sir, I beg you for God's sake to preach us a sermon, showing us how a man may attain to the highest and utmost point it is given to us to reach in this present time." The Master answered, "Ah! dear son, what dost thou ask for? how shall I tell thee of such high things? for I ween thou wouldst understand but little thereof." But the man said, "Ah! dear Master, even though I should understand little or nothing thereof, yet I cannot but thirst after it. Multitudes flock to hear you; if there were only one among them all who could understand you, your labour were well bestowed." Then said the Master, "Dear son, if I am to do as thou sayest, I must needs give some study and labour to the matter before I can put such a sermon together." But the man would not cease from his prayers and entreaties till the Master promised him that he should have his desire.

So, when the Master had finished his sermon, he announced to the people that in three days they should come together again, for he had been requested to teach how a man could attain to the Highest and Best and nearest to God that might be reached in this present time. And when the day was come, much people came to the church, and the man sat down in a place where he could hear well; and the Master came, and thus began his discourse, and said:

Dear children, I have much to say to you in this sermon concerning those things of which I have promised to speak; wherefore I cannot for this time expound the gospel of the day to you as is my wont, neither shall I speak much Latin in this sermon; for what I have to say, I will prove with Holy Scripture [and he said]: "Dear children, I would have you to know that there be many men, who indeed attain to a clear understanding and reasonable judgment, but who do this by means of images and forms through the help of other men, and without the Scriptures. Further, there be found many who, when they mark that something is known to them through the Scriptures, are not therewith content. Such a man is still far from his highest and greatest good. Dear children, if a man had broken through these things, and was become dead to them, and had got above forty stages of contemplation, and above the conceptions of our reason, whether they come to us through images or forms of speech—if there were a man who had come to this, he would be dearer and more precious in God's fight than a hundred thousand men who never get out of their own self, and live after the way of their own choosing; for to such God cannot find entrance, nor work in their souls. This all comes of their own will, and their self-glorifying folly, which takes delight in the dexterity of their own reason, in framing and handling conceptions. But those men who while on earth have broken through these things, and have given themselves to God in such sort that they have died unto themselves, and have both made themselves free from all outward forms, and the use of sensible images in their exercises of contemplation, and humbly toiled and pressed onwards above the images of mere reason, as Dionysius says, "the light of faith requires that a man should be raised above the apprehensions of reason;"— know, dear children, that in such souls God doth find rest, and a place wherein to dwell and to work when He chooseth. Now when God findeth thus no hindrance in such a man, He works His own works in him, and draweth him truly to Himself in Himself. Now know that such a man is rare, for his life and ways are hidden from others, and unknown to them, except to such as have a like life, of whom, alas! I fear there be but few. To this state, and this noble perfectness, none can come except through boundless humility, an unclouded understanding, and a clear

reason; for it has happened ere now that some great doctors and priests have fallen; and a multitude of rational spirits belonging to the angelic hosts, who perceived nothing else in their nature and essence but mere reason, have erred hence, and fallen everlastingly away from eternal truth. And this is what happens still to all those who look to their own reason, and want to be and do as God by the light of their self-willed understanding. For which reason it is profitable and needful to know who are the proper, truly reasonable, enlightened, contemplative men. Now as far as I can find from Scripture, there are four-and-twenty tokens which such a man must possess.

The First is given us by the highest Master of all doctors, arts and wisdom, namely, our Lord Jesus Christ, when he says: "Hereby shall ye know whether ye be my disciples, if ye have love one to another even as I have loved you." As much as to say, 'Though ye should possess arts and wisdom, and high understanding, it is all in vain if ye have not withal fidelity and love.' We believe that Balaam was so replete with understanding, that he perceived what things God purposed to do or reveal hundreds of years after his day; but it availed him nothing, forasmuch as he did not cleave with love and loyalty to the things which he understood.

The Second mark appertaining to a truly reasonable, enlightened man is that he must become empty of self; and this must not make him proud, but he shall consider how he may ever more attain to this freedom, and sit loose by all creatures.

The Third Article: He shall resign himself utterly to God, that God may work His own works in him, and he shall not glory in the works as being his own, but always think himself too mean to have done them.

The Fourth Article: He shall go out from himself in all the things in which he is wont to seek and find himself, whether belonging to time or to eternity, and by so doing he shall win a true increase.

Fifth Article: He shall not seek his own ends in any creature, whether temporal or eternal, and hereby he shall attain to perfect satisfaction and content.

The Sixth Article: He shall always wait on that which God will have him to do, and shall try, with the help of God, to fulfil that to the uttermost, and shall take no glory to himself therefor.

The Seventh Article: He shall daily, without ceasing, give up his will to the will of God, and endeavour to will nothing but what God willeth.

The Eighth Article: He shall bend all his powers into submission to God, and exercise them so constantly and so strenuously in God, and with such power and love, that God may work nothing in him without his active concurrence, and he may do nothing without God.

The Ninth Article: He shall have the sense of the presence of God in all His works, at all times, and in all places, whatever it please God to appoint, whether it be sweet or bitter.

The Tenth Article: All his pleasure and pain he shall receive, not as from the creature, but from God; howbeit God ofttimes works through the creature, yet he shall receive all things as from God alone.

Eleventh Article: He shall not be led captive by any lusting or desire after the creatures without due necessity.

The Twelfth Article: No contradiction or mishap shall have power to move or constrain him so that it separate him from the truth; therefore hold fast always and entirely by the same.

Thirteenth Article: He shall not be deceived by the glory of the creature, nor yet by any false light, but in a spirit of kindness and love he shall confess all things to be what they are, and from all things draw out what is best, and use it to his own improvement, and in no wise to his own detriment; for such a course is a certain sign of the presence of the Holy Spirit.

Fourteenth Article: He shall at all times be equipped and armed with all virtue, and ready to fight against all vice and sin, and with his good weapons he shall obtain the victory and the prize in all conflicts.

Fifteenth Article: He shall confess the truth in simplicity, and he shall mark what it is in itself, what God requireth of us, and what is possible to man, and then order his life accordingly, and act up to what he confesses.

The Sixteenth Article: He shall be a man of few words and much inward life.

The Seventeenth Article: He shall be blameless and righteous, but in no wise be puffed up by reason of the same.

The Eighteenth Article: His conversation shall be in all uprightness and sincerity; thus he shall let his light shine before men, and he shall preach more with his life than with his lips.

The Nineteenth Article: He shall seek the glory of God before all things, and have no other aim in view.

The Twentieth Article: He shall be willing to take reproof; and when he striveth with any he shall give way if the matter concern himself alone, and not God.

The Twenty-first Article: He shall not desire or seek his own advantage, but think himself unworthy of the least thing that falls to his lot.

The Twenty-second Article: He shall look upon himself as the least wise and worthy man upon earth, yet find in himself great faith; and above all he shall take no account of his own wisdom and the works of his own reason, but humble himself beneath all men. For the Author of all truth will not work a supernatural work in the soul, unless He find a thorough humility in a man, and go before his doings with his perfect grace, as he did with St. Paul. But I fear, alas! that little heed is taken to this in these our days.

The Twenty-third Article: He shall set the life and precepts of our Lord Jesus Christ before him for a pattern to his life, words, and works, and without ceasing look at himself therein as in a mirror, that, in so far as he is able, he may put off everything unbecoming the honoured image of our Lord.

The Twenty-fourth and last Article is: He shall comport himself as a man of small account,—as nothing more than a beginner in a good life; and though he should therefore be despised by many, it shall be more welcome to him than all the favour of the world.

Now, dear children, these are the signs that the ground of a man's soul is truly reasonable, so that the image of all truth shineth and teacheth therein; and he who does not bear in himself these signs, may not and must not set any store by his own reason, either in his own eyes or those of others. That we all may become such a true image, in thorough sincerity and perfect humility, may He help us who is the Eternal Truth, the Father, Son, and Holy Ghost. Amen!

When this sermon was ended, the man went home to his lodging, and wrote it down word for word as the Master had spoken it. And when he had finished he went to the Master, and said, "I have written out your sermon, and if it be not troublesome I should like to read it to you." The Master replied, "I shall be glad to hear it." Thereupon the man read the sermon over, and then said to the Master, "Dear sir, pray tell me if there be a word wanting, that if so I may set it down." The Master said, "Dear son, thou hast written every word and phrase just as it came out of my mouth. I tell thee, if any one would give me much money for it, I could not write down every word so exactly as thou hast done it here, unless I set to afresh to draw it from the Scripture. I confess that I am greatly astonished at thee to think that thou hast been concealed from me so long, and I should never have perceived how full of wit thou art, and so often as thou hast confessed to me, thou shouldst so have hidden thy talent that I have never perceived it in thee." Then the man made as though he would depart, and said, "Dear Master, if God will I am purposed to go home again." But the Master said, "Dear son, what shouldst thou do at home? Thou hast neither wife nor child to provide for; thou must eat there as well as here: for if God will, I am minded to preach again of a perfect life." Then said the man, "Dear Master, you must know that I have not come hither for the sake of your preaching, but because I thought, with God's help, to give you some good counsel." Quoth the Master, "How shouldst thou give counsel, who art but a layman, and understandest not the Scriptures; and it is, moreover, not thy place to preach if thou wouldst. Stay here a little longer; perchance God will give me to preach such a sermon as thou wouldst care to hear." Then the man said, "Dear Master, I would fain say somewhat to you, but I fear that you would be displeased to hear it." But the Master answered, "Dear son, say what thou wilt; I can answer for it that I shall take it in good part." Hereupon the man said, "You are a great clerk, and have taught us a good lesson in this sermon, but you yourself do not live according to it; yet you try to persuade me to stay here that you may preach me yet another sermon. Sir, I give you to know that neither your sermons, nor any outward words that man can speak, have power to work any good in me, for man's words have in many ways hindered me much more than they have helped me. And this is the reason: it often happened that when I came away from the sermon, I brought certain false notions away with me, which I hardly got rid of in a long while with great toil; but if the highest Teacher of all truth shall come to a man, he must be empty and quit of all the things of time. Know ye that when this same Master cometh to me, He teaches me more in an hour than you or all the doctors from Adam to the Judgment Day will ever do." Then said the Master, "Dear son, stay here, I pray thee, and celebrate the Lord's Death with me." Whereon the man answered, "Seeing that you adjure me so solemnly, it may be that, in obedience to God, I ought to stay with you; but I will not do it unless you promise to receive all that I have said to you, and all I may yet say to you, as under the seal of confession, so that none may know of it." Quoth the Master: "Dear son, that I willingly promise, if only that thou wilt stay here." Then said the man, "Sir, ye must know, that though you have taught us many good things in this sermon, the image came into my mind while you were preaching, that it was as if one should take good wine and mix it with lees, so that it grew muddy." Quoth the Master: "Dear son, what dost thou mean by this?" The man said, "I mean that your vessel is unclean, and much lees are cleaving to it, and the cause is, that you have suffered yourself to be killed by the letter, and are killing yourself still every day and hour, albeit you yourself know full well that the Scripture faith, 'The letter killeth, but the Spirit giveth life.' Know, that same letter which now killeth you will make you alive again, if so be you are willing; but in the life you are now living, know that you have no light, but you are in the night, in which you are indeed able to understand the letter, but have not yet tasted the sweetness of the Holy Ghost; and, withal, you are yet a Pharisee." Then said the Master, "Dear son, I would have thee to know that, old as I am, I have never been spoken to in such fashion all my life." The man said, "Where is your preaching now? Do you see now what you are when you are brought to the proof? And although you think that I have spoken too hardly to you, you are in truth guilty of all I have said, and I will prove to you from your own self that it is true." Then said the Master, "I ask for no more, for I have ever been an enemy to all Pharisees." Quoth the man, "I will first tell you how it is that the letter is killing you. Dear sir, as you know yourself, when you were arrived at the age to understand good and evil, you began to learn the letter, and in so doing you sought your own welfare, and to this day you are in the same mind; that is to say, you are trusting to your learning and parts, and you do not love and intend God alone, but you are in the letter, and intend and seek yourself, and not the glory of God, as the Scripture teacheth us to do. You have a leaning towards the creatures, and specially towards one creature, and love that creature with your whole heart above measure, and that is, moreover, the cause why the letter killeth you. And whereas I said that your vessel is unclean; that is also true, inasmuch as you have not in all things a single eye to God. If you look into yourself, you will, for one thing, find it out by the vanity and love of carnal ease whereby your vessel is spoiled and filled with lees; wherefore, when the pure unmixed wine of godly doctrine has gone through this unclean vessel, it comes to pass that your teaching is without favour, and brings no grace to pure, loving hearts. And whereas I further said that you were still in darkness, and had not the true light; this is also true, and it may be seen hereby that so few receive the grace of the Holy Spirit through your teaching. And whereas I said that you were a Pharisee, that is also true; but you are not one of the hypocritical Pharisees. Was it not a mark of the Pharisees that they loved and sought themselves in all things, and not the glory of God? Now examine yourself, dear sir, and see if you are not a proper Pharisee in the eyes of God. Know, dear Master, that there are many people in the world who are all called Pharisees in God's sight, be they great or small, according to what their hearts or lives are bent upon."

As the man spoke these words the Master fell on his neck and kissed him, and said: "A likeness has come into my mind. It has happened to me as it did to the heathen woman at the well. For know, dear son, that thou hast laid bare all my faults before my eyes; thou hast told me what I had hidden up within me, and specially that I have an affection for one creature; but I tell thee of a truth that I knew it not myself, nor do I believe that any human being in the world can know of it. I wonder greatly who can have told thee this of me? But doubt not that thou hast it from God. Now, therefore, I pray thee, dear son, that thou celebrate our Lord's Death, and be thou my ghostly father, and let me be thy poor sinful son." Then said the man, "Dear sir, if you speak so contrary to ordinances, I will not stay with you, but ride home again; that I assure you." Hereupon said the Master, "Ah, no! I pray thee, for God's sake, do not so; stay awhile with me; I promise thee readily not to speak thus any more. I am minded, with God's help, to begin a better course, and I will gladly follow thy counsel, whatsoever thou deemest best, if I may but amend my life." Then said the man, "I tell you of a truth, that the letter and learning lead many great doctors astray, and bring some into purgatory and some into hell, according as their life here hath been,—I tell you of a truth, it is no light matter that God should give a man such great understanding and skill, and mastery in the Scripture, and he should not put it in practice in his life."

Then said the Master, "I pray thee, for God's sake, to tell me how it is that thou hast attained to such a life, and how thou didst begin thy spiritual life, and what have been thy exercises and thy history." The man said, "That is, indeed, a simple request: for I tell you truly, if I should recount, or write, all the wondrous dealings of God with me, a poor sinner, for the last twelve years, I verily believe that you have not a book large enough to contain it if it were all written; however, I will tell you somewhat thereof for this time.

"The first thing that helped me was, that God found in me a sincere and utterly self-surrendering humility. Now I do not think there is any need to tell you the bodily exercises by which I brought my flesh into subjection: for men's natures and dispositions are very unlike; but whenever a man has given himself up to God with utter humility, God will not fail to give him such exercises, by temptations and other trials, as He perceives to be profitable to the man, and such as he is well able to bear and endure if he be willing. But this you ought to know: he who asks counsel of many people will be apt to go often astray; for each one will point him to his own experience. But oft-times a man may exercise himself in a certain practice which is good and profitable to himself; while, if another did the same, it might very likely be useless, or even hurtful to him. The Devil often stirs up a man to practise great austerities, with the intent that the man may grow sick and infirm thereby, or weak in his brain, or do himself some other injury.

"I will tell you how it befel me in the beginning. I was reading the German books about the lives of the Saints, when I thought to myself, 'These were men who lived on this earth as well as I, and perhaps, too, had not sinned as I have.' And when these thoughts came into my head, I began to exercise myself in the life of the Saints with some severities, but grew so sick thereby that I was brought to death's door. And it came to pass one morning at break of day, that I had exercised myself so that my eyelids closed from very weakness, and I fell asleep. And in my sleep it was as though a voice spoke to me and said, 'Thou foolish man, if thou art bent upon killing thyself before thy time, thou wilt have to bear a heavy punishment; but if thou didst suffer God to exercise thee, He could exercise thee better than thou by thyself, or with the Devil's counsel.' When I heard speak of the Devil I awoke in a great fright, rose up, and walked out into a wood nigh to the town. Then I thought within myself, I had begun these exercises without counsel: I will go and tell the old hermit all that has happened to me. And I did so, and told him the words that I had heard in my sleep, and besought him in God's name to give me the best counsel he could. So the hermit said, 'Thou must know that if I am to advise, thou must first tell me all about thy exercises.' So I did, and he said, 'By whose counsel hast thou done these things?' and I answered, 'Of my own will.' Then the hermit said, 'Then know that it has been the Devil's counsel, and thou must not obey him any more as long as thou livest, but thou must utterly give thyself up to God; He can

exercise thee much better than thou thyself, or the Devil.' Behold, dear Master, thereupon I ceased from these exercises, and yielded myself and my doings altogether up to God. For the rest, dear sir, you must know that by nature I was a very ingenious, clever, good-hearted man; but I had not the Scriptures in my hand, like you, but could only learn to know myself by my natural intelligence; and with this sometimes I got so far that I was surprised at myself. And once upon a time, I thought in my reason, 'Thou hast such good parts, may be, if thou shouldst give thy mind to it with all earnestness, thou couldst attain to comprehend somewhat of divine things.' But as this thought came into my head I marked straightway that it was the Devil's counsel, and saw that it was all false. So I said, 'O thou Evil Spirit, what an impure false counsel hast thou put in my heart, thou bad, false counsellor! If we had such a God I would not give a berry for him.' After that, another night, when I was saying my matins, [Three o'clock in the morning.] an ardent longing came over me, so that I said, 'O eternal and merciful God, that it were thy will to give me to discover something that should be above all our sensual reason!' As soon as I had said it I was sorely affrighted at this great longing, and said with great fervour, 'Ah, my God and my Lord, forgive me of thy boundless mercy for having done this, and that it should have entered into the heart of a poor worm like me to desire such a great gift of such rich grace, and I confess indeed that I have not always lived as I ought of right to do. I confess, moreover, dear Lord, that I have been un-thankful to Thee in all things, so that methinks I am not worthy that the earth should bear me, still less that such an ardent, gracious desire should spring up in me; wherefore my body must be punished for my sin.' With that I threw off my garments and scourged myself till the blood ran down my shoulders. And as these words remained in my heart and on my lips till the day broke, and the blood was flowing down, in that same hour God showed His mercy on me, so that my mind was filled with a clear understanding. And in that same hour I was deprived of all my natural reason; but the time seemed all too short to me. And when I was left to myself again I saw a supernatural mighty wonder and sign, insomuch that I could have cried with St. Peter, 'Lord, it is good for me to be here!' Now know, dear sir, that in that self-same short hour I received more truth and more illumination in my understanding than all the teachers could ever teach me from now till the Judgment Day by word of mouth, and with all their natural learning and science. Now, dear Master, I have said enough for this time, as to how it stands with you."

Then said the Master, "If God give thee grace to say still more, I should heartily rejoice in it, for I tell thee in all sincerity that I have listened to thee gladly, dear son: now I beg thee for God's sake do not leave me, but stay here, and if thou lack money I will not let thee want for anything, if I have to pledge a book for it." Then said the man, "God reward you, dear sir: know that I need not your kindness, for God hath made me a steward of His goods, so that I have of earthly wealth five thousand florins, which are God's, and if I knew where there was need of them, or where God would have them bestowed, I would give them away." Then said the Master, "Then, dear son, thou art indeed the steward of a rich man and a great Lord! I am in great wonderment about that thou saidst, that I and all teachers could not teach thee as much by the Day of Judgment as thou hast been taught in an hour. Now tell me, for I wish to hear, has the Scripture proceeded from the Holy Ghost?" Then said the man, "Sir, methinks it seems impossible that after I have said so much to you, you should talk in such a childish fashion! Look here, dear Master! I will ask you a question, and if with all your reason you can explain it to me, either by the Scriptures, or without the Scriptures, I will give you ten thousand florins." Then said the Master, "What is that?" The man said, "Can you instruct me how I should write a letter to a heathen far away in a heathen land, in such fashion and language that the heathen should be able to read and understand it; and make the letter such that the heathen should come to the Christian faith?" Then said the Master, "Dear son, these are the works of the Holy Ghost; tell me where has this happened? If thou know anything of the matter, tell me in what way this came to pass, and whether it happened to thyself?" Then said the man, "Albeit I am unworthy of it, yet did the Holy Spirit work through me, a poor sinner; and how it came to pass would take long to tell, and make such a long story that one might write a large book about it: The heathen was a very good-hearted man, and often cried to Heaven, and called upon Him who had made him and all the world, and said: 'O Creator of all creatures, I have been born in this land: now the Jews have another faith, the Christians another. O Lord, who art over all, and hast made all creatures, if there be now any faith better than that in which I have been born, or if there be any other better still, show it to me in what wise Thou wilt, so that I may believe it, and I will gladly obey Thee and believe: but if it should be that Thou dost not show it me, and I should die in my faith, since I knew no better, if there were a better faith, but Thou hadst not shown it nor revealed it to me, Thou wouldst have done me a grievous injustice.' Now, behold, dear sir, a letter was sent to that heathen, written by me, a poor sinner, in such sort that he came to the Christian faith; and he wrote me a letter back again, telling what had befallen him, the which stood written in a good German tongue, that I could read it quite well. Dear sir, there were much to be said on this matter, but for this time it is enough; you are well able to mark the meaning thereof." Then said the Master, "God is wonderful in all His works and gifts! Dear son, thou hast told me very strange things."

The man said, "Dear sir, I fear that I have said some things to you which have vexed you greatly in your mind; it is because I am a layman, and you are a great doctor of Holy Scripture, and yet I have said so much to you after the manner of a teacher. But that I have meant it well and kindly, and sought your soul's salvation in it, and simply the glory of God, and nothing else, of that God is my witness." Then said the Master, "Dear son, if it will not make thee angry, I will tell thee what vexes me." Then said the man, "Yea, dear sir, speak without fear; I promise not to take it amiss." The Master said, "It amazes me greatly, and is very hard to receive, that thou being a layman, and I a priest, I am to take instruction from thee; and it also troubles me much that thou calledst me a Pharisee." Then said the man, "Is there nothing else that you cannot take in?" The Master answered, "No, I know of nothing else." Then said the man, "Shall I also explain to you these two things?" He answered, "Yes, dear son, I pray thee in all kindness to do so, for God's sake." Then said the man, "Now tell me, dear Master, how it was, or whose work it was, that the blessed Saint Katharine, who was but a young virgin barely fourteen years old, overcame some fifty of the great masters, and moreover so prevailed over them that they willingly went to martyrdom? Who wrought this?" Then said the Master, "The Holy Ghost did this." Qouth the man, "Do you not believe that the Holy Ghost has still the same power?" The Master, "Yes, I believe it fully." The man, "Wherefore then do you not believe that the Holy Ghost is speaking to you at this moment through me, a poor sinner and unworthy man, and is minded to speak to you? He spoke the truth through Caiaphas, who was also a sinner; and know, that since you take what I have said to you so much amiss, I will refrain from saying anything to you for the future." Then said the Master, "Dear son, do not do that: I hope, if God will, to be the better for thy words." The man said, "Ah, dear sir, it vexes you also that I should have called you a Pharisee, and yet I gave you such full proof of it that you could not deny it. This should have been enough to content you, but since it is not, I must say still more, and prove to you once again, that I am right, and that you are what I said. Dear Master, you know very well that Our Lord Jesus Christ said himself, 'Beware of the Pharisees, for they bind heavy burdens, and grievous to be borne, and lay them on men's shoulders; but they themselves will not move them with one of their fingers.' Now, dear sir, look at yourself; in this sermon of yours you have bound and laid upon us twenty-four articles, and you keep few enough of them yourself. Again: Our Lord said, 'Beware of the Pharisees: whatsoever they bid you observe, that observe and do, but do not yet after their works, for they say and do not.' " Quoth the Master, "Our Blessed Lord spoke these words to the men of his own day." The man said, "He speaks them still, now and evermore, to all men. Dear Master, look at yourself; whether you touch these burdens and bear them in your life is known to God and also to yourself; but I confess that as far as I can judge of your present condition, I would rather follow your words than your life. Only look at yourself, and see if you are not a Pharisee in the eyes of God; though not one of those false hypocritical Pharisees whose portion is in hell-fire." The Master said, "I know not what I shall say; this I see plainly, that I am a sinner, and am resolved to better my life, if I die for it. Dear son, I cannot wait longer; I pray thee, simply for God's sake, to counsel me how I shall set about this work, and show me and teach me how I may attain to the highest perfection that a man may reach on earth." Then said the man, "Dear sir, do not be wroth with me; but I tell you of a truth that such counsel is scarcely to be given you; for if you are to be converted, all your wonted habits must be broken through with great pain; because you must altogether change your old way of life: and besides I take you to be near fifty years old." Then said the Master, "It may be so; but O dear son, to him who came into the vineyard at the eleventh hour was given his penny the same as to him who came in at the first. I tell thee, dear son, I have well considered the matter, and my heart is so firmly set that if I knew this moment that I must die for it, I would yet, with the help of God, cease from my carnal life, and my earthly reasonings, and live according to thy counsel. I beseech thee for God's sake not to keep me longer waiting, but to tell me this moment how I must begin." Then said the man, "Dear sir, because you have received grace from God, and are willing to humble yourself and submit, and to bow down before a poor, mean, unworthy creature; for all this let us give the glory to God, to whom it is due, for this grace proceeds from Him, and flows back to Him. Since then, dear sir, I am to instruct you, and counsel you in God's name, I will look to Him for help, and do so in love to Him, and set you a task such as they give children to begin with at school,—namely, the four-and-twenty letters of the alphabet, beginning with A:

After a manly and not a childish sort, ye shall, with thorough earnestness, begin a good life.

Bad ways ye shall eschew, and practise all goodness with diligence and full purpose of mind.

Carefully endeavour to keep the middle path in all things, with seemliness and moderation.

Demean yourself humbly in word and work, from the inward holiness of your heart.

Entirely give up your own will; evermore cleave earnestly to God, and forsake Him not.

Forward and ready shall ye be to all good works, without murmuring, whatever be commanded you.

Give heed to exercise yourself in all godly works of mercy toward the body or the spirit.

Have no backward glances after the world, or the creatures, or their doings.

Inwardly in your heart ponder over your past life with honesty, sincere repentance in the bitterness of your heart, and tears in your eyes.

Knightly and resolutely withstand the assaults of the Devil, the Flesh, and the World.

Learn to conquer long-cherished sloth with vigour, together with all effeminacy of the body, and subservience to the Devil.

Make your abode in God, with fervent love, in certain hope, with strong faith, and be towards your neighbour as towards yourself.

No other man's good things shall ye desire, be they what they may, corporeal or spiritual.

Order all things so that you make the best and not the worst of them.

Penance, that is, suffering for your sin, you shall take willingly, whether it come from God or the creatures.

Quittance, remission, and absolution, you shall give to all who have ever done you wrong in thought, word, or deed.

Receive all things that befal you with meekness, and draw improvement from them.

Soul and body, estate and reputation, keep undefiled with all care and diligence.

Truthful and upright shall ye be[1]

towards all, without guile or cunning.

Wantonness and excess, of whatsoever kind it may be, ye shall learn to lay aside, and turn from it with all your heart.

Xt., our Blessed Lord's life and death, shall ye follow, and wholly conform yourself thereunto with all your might.

Ye shall evermore, without ceasing, beseech our blessed Lady that she help you to learn this our lesson well.

Zealously keep a rein over your will and your senses, that they may be at peace with all that God doth, and also with all His creatures.

All this lesson must be learnt of a free heart and will, without cavilling.

Now, dear sir, take kindly as from God, without cavilling, this child's task, which He sets you by the mouth of me, a poor and unworthy human being."

Then said the Master, "However thou mayst call this a child's task, methinks it needs a man's strength to attack it. Now tell me, dear son, how long a time wilt thou give me to learn this lesson?" The man answered, "We will take five weeks, in honour of the five wounds of Christ, that you may learn it well. You shall be your own schoolmaster; and when you are not perfect in any one of these letters, and think yourself hardly able to learn it, then cast aside your garment and chastise your body, that it may be brought into subjection to your soul and reason." Then said the Master, "I will gladly be obedient."

Now when this discipline had lasted three weeks, the man said to the Master, "Dear sir, how goes it with you?" The Master said, "Dear son, thou must know that I have received more stripes in these three weeks about your lesson than I ever did in all my days before." Then said the man, "Sir, you well know that no man giveth his pupil a new task before he have learnt the first lines." Then said the Master, "If I said that I knew them, I should say what is not true." Then said the man, "Dear sir, go on as you are doing till you know your lesson right well."

But at the end of another three weeks the Master sent for the man, and said to him, "Dear son, rejoice with me, for I think, with God's help, I could say the first line; and if thou art willing, I will repeat over the whole lesson to thee." "No, dear sir," said the man, "I will gladly rejoice with you, and take your word for it that you know it." Then said the Master, "I tell thee of a truth it has gone hard with me. And now, dear son, I pray thee give me further instruction." Then said the man, "I can for myself teach you nothing further; but if so be that God willeth to teach you through me, I will gladly do my part, and be an instrument in the Lord's hand by which He may work out His purposes.

"Hearken, dear Master: I will counsel you in godly love and brotherly faithfulness. If it should happen to you as to the young man in the Gospel, to whom our Lord said, 'Go and sell all that thou hast and give to the poor, and come and follow Me,' I will not be answerable." Then said the Master, "Dear son, have no fears on that score, for I have already left all that I have, and, with God's help, am resolved to go forward, and be obedient unto God and to thee." Then said the man, "Since your heart is steadfastly fixed to commit yourself wholly unto God, I counsel you in all faithfulness that ye be obedient to your Order and your superiors; as it may be that you may be brought into great perplexity if you be minded to go the strait and narrow way, and that you will be hard pressed and assailed, and most of all by your brethren. And if this should come to pass, your earthly feelings will seek everywhere for help, and make you call to mind the words in which you pledged yourself to God, and also other things, with the intent that, if possible, they might break away from the cross; and that must not be, but you must yield a willing obedience to suffer all that is appointed you, from whatsoever it may proceed. For know that you must needs walk in that same path of which our Lord spoke to that young man;—you must take up your cross and follow our Lord Jesus Christ and His example, in utter sincerity, humility, and patience, and must let go all your proud, ingenious reason, which you have through your learning in the Scripture. You shall also for a time neither study nor preach, and you shall demean yourself with great simplicity towards your penitents; for when they have ended their confession, you shall give them no further counsel than to say to them, 'I will learn how to counsel myself, and when I can do that I will also counsel you.' And if you are asked when you will preach, say, as you can with truth, that you have not time at present, and so you will get rid of the people." Then said the Master, "Dear son, I will willingly do so; but how then shall I occupy myself?" The man replied, "You shall enter into your cell, and read your Hours, and also chant in the choir if you feel inclined, and shall say mass every day. And what time is left, you shall set before you the sufferings of our Lord, and contemplate your own life in the mirror of His, and meditate on your wasted time in which you have been living for yourself, and how small has been your love compared to His love. In all lowliness ye shall study these things, whereby in some measure ye may be brought to true humility, and also wean yourself from your old habits, and cease from them. And then, when our Lord sees that the time is come, He will make of you a new man, so that you shall be born again of God.

"Nevertheless, you must know that before this can come to pass, you must sell all that you have, and humbly yield it up to God, that you may truly make Him your end, and give up to Him all that you possess in your carnal pride, whether through the Scriptures or without; or whatever it be, whereby you might reap honour in this world, or in the which you may aforetime have taken pleasure or delight, you must let it all go, and, with Mary Magdalene, fall down at Christ's feet, and earnestly strive to enter on a new course. And so doing, without doubt, the Eternal Heavenly Prince will look down on you with the eye of His good pleasure, and He will not leave His work undone in you, but will urge you still further, that you may be tried and purified as gold in the fire; and it may even come to pass, that He shall give you to drink of the bitter cup that He gave to His only-begotten Son. For it is my belief that one bitter drop which God will pour out for you will be that your good works and all your refraining from evil, yea your whole life will be despised and turned to nought in the eyes of the people; and all your spiritual children will forsake you and think you are gone out of your mind, and all your good friends and your brothers in the convent will be offended at your life, and say that you have taken to strange ways.

"But when these things come upon you, be not in any wise dismayed, but rejoice, for then your salvation draweth nigh; howbeit, no doubt, your human weakness will shrink back in terror, and give way. Therefore, dear Master, you must not be faint-hearted, but trust firmly in God, for He forsakes none of His servants, as you know well from the examples of the blessed saints. Now, dear sir, if so be that you are minded to take these things in hand, know that there is nothing better or more profitable for you at this present than an entire, hearty, humble self-surrender in all things, whether sweet or bitter, painful or pleasant, so that you may be able to say with truth, 'Ah, my Lord and my God, if it were thy will that I should remain till the Day of Judgment in this suffering and tribulation, yet would I not fall away from thee, but would desire ever to be constant in thy service.' Dear sir, I see well, by God's grace, how you are thinking in your heart, that I have said very hard things to you, and this is why I begged you beforehand to let me go, and told you that if you went back like that young man, I would not have it laid to my charge." Then said the Master, "Thou sayest truly; I confess it does seem to me a hard thing to follow your counsel." The man answered, "Yet you begged me to show you the shortest way to the highest perfectness. Now I know no shorter nor surer way than to follow in the footsteps of our Lord Jesus

Christ. But, dear sir, I counsel you in all faithfulness, to take a certain space of time to consider these matters, and then in God's name do as God gives you grace to do." Then said the Master, "That will I do, and wait and see whether, with the help of God, I may prevail."

On the eleventh day after this, the Master sent for the man, and said to him, "Ah, dear son, what agony and struggle and fighting have I not had within me day and night, before I was able to overcome the Devil and my own flesh. But now by God's grace I have gathered myself together with all my powers inward and outward, and set my hand to this work with good courage, and am purposed to remain steadfast therein, come weal come woe." Then said the man, "Dear sir, do you remember still all I said to you when you asked me how you should begin?" The Master answered, "Yes, the moment thou didst depart I wrote down all thou hadst said to me, word for word." Then said the man, "Dear sir, that through God you have found this bold heart, rejoices me from the bottom of my soul, and I am as well pleased as if it had happened to myself, so God be my witness. And now in the name of our Lord Jesus Christ, set forward." Then the man took his leave, and the Master did as he had been bidden.

Now it came to pass that before a year was out the Master grew to be despised of all his familiar friends in the convent, and his spiritual children all forsook him as entirely as if they had never seen him. And this he found very hard to bear, and it caused him such grief that his head was like to turn. Then he sent for the man and told him how it fared with him; how he was ill in his whole body, and especially in his head. Then said the man, "Sir, you must not be dismayed, but you must humbly cleave to God, and put your firm trust in Him. Know that this account of yours pleases me well, and it stands well with your life, and will grow better every day.

"Dear sir, you know well that he who will walk in the right way, and tread this path, must be made a partaker of the sufferings of our Lord Jesus Christ; therefore be not afraid, but commit yourself wholly to God. For know that the same thing happened to me also. Meanwhile you must take some remedies while you are in this state, and treat your body well with good food which may strengthen it. A box of spices was made for me, and I will have such an one prepared for you to strengthen your head. But you must know that I always gave myself up body and soul to God, that He might do with them what he pleased."

Then said the Master, "But thou didst tell me before that I must shun good eating and drinking." The man answered, "Yes, sir, that was in the first beginning, when the flesh was yet wanton, but now that it is tamed and obedient to the spirit, we may come to its help with remedies, else we should tempt God. So long as you are in this sickness, you will be serving God to cherish your body by allowable means, but not to live disorderly; that must not be. Dear sir, make God your help, and go forward with cheerful mind, and commit yourself to God with true and thorough

resignation, and put your trust in His boundless mercy, and wait for His grace to show you what He will have you to do, and then with His help strive to fulfil that to the uttermost, whether it be bitter or sweet. Further, I beseech you for God's sake not to take it amiss of me, but I must go home on account of a very important matter, which I assure you in all earnestness I have much at heart; but if so be that you could not or would not do without me, send into the town for me, and I will gladly come; but if you can bear up without the aid of any creature, that would be best of all for you." Then said the Master, "Dear son, say not so, for I cannot and would not do without thee for any length of time; it would be hard indeed if thou didst forsake me, for then I should have no consolation left in the world." The man said, "Dear sir, I will show you a better Comforter, that is the Holy Ghost, who has called and invited and brought you to this point, by means of me His poor creature, but it is His work which has been wrought in you, and not mine; I have been merely His instrument, and served Him therein, and have done so right willingly, for the glory of God and the salvation of your soul." Then said the Master, "Dear son, may God be thine eternal reward! Since it is so weighty a matter, I will commit myself to God, and bear this suffering as best I may." The man said, "Dear sir, since you are now under the yoke, and have entered on a spiritual life and obedience to God, and have voluntarily devoted yourself thereto, you should know how to live discreetly and wisely, and to govern yourself aright; and do not let it repent you because you are forsaken of the creatures, but if it should happen that you lack money, or have need of some, put a part of your books in pawn, and do not suffer yourself to want for anything, but by no means sell the books, for a time will come when good books will be very useful, and you will have need of them." Then the man took his leave and departed from that place, but the Master's eyes filled with tears, and he began to weep.

Now when the Master had suffered thus for two years, from sore assaults and temptations of the Devil, and great contempt from all his friends, and also great poverty, so that he was obliged to pledge a part of his books, and withal fell into great weakness of the body, and he had demeaned himself with great humility throughout;— behold, it came to pass on the Feast of St. Paul's Conversion, that in the night he was overtaken by the most grievous assault that may be imagined, whereby all his natural powers were so overcome with weakness that when the time for matins came he could not go in to chapel, but remained in his cell, and commended himself to God in great humility, without help or consolation from any creature. And as he lay in this state of weakness, he thought of the sufferings of our Lord Jesus Christ, and His great love that He had for us, and considered his own life, how poor his life had been compared to the love of God. Whereupon he was overwhelmed with contrition for all his sins and all his wasted time, and exclaimed with tongue and heart: "O merciful God! have mercy upon me a poor sinner, for thy boundless mercy's sake, for I am not worthy that the earth should bear me." And as he was lying in this weakness and great sadness, but fully awake, he heard with his bodily ears a voice saying: "Stand fast in thy peace, and trust God, and know that when He was on earth in human nature, He made the sick whom He healed in body sound also in soul." Straightway when these words were uttered, he lost his senses and reason, and knew not how or where he was. But when he came to himself again, he felt within himself that he was possessed of a new strength and might in all powers outward and inward, and had also a clear understanding in those things which aforetime were dark to him, and he wondered greatly whence this came, and thought to himself, "I cannot come to the bottom of this matter. I will send for my friend and tell him all that has happened." So he sent for the man; and when he was come, the Master told him all that had befallen him. Then the man said, "It rejoices me from the bottom of my heart to hear all that you have told me. Dear sir, you must know that you have now for the first time received the true and mighty gift of God's grace; and I tell you of a truth that now, for the first time, your soul has been touched by the Most High; and know that, as the letter hath in some measure slain you, so it shall likewise make you alive again, for your doctrine will come now from the Holy Ghost, which before came from the flesh; for you have now received the light of the Holy Spirit by the grace of God, and you already know the Holy Scriptures. Therefore you have now a great advantage, and you will henceforward have a much clearer insight into the Scripture than you had before. For, as you know, the Scripture sounds in many places as if it contradicted itself, but since that you have now, by the grace of God, received the Holy Scriptures into your own heart through the illumination of the Holy Spirit, you will perceive that all Scripture has the same intent, and does not contradict itself, and you will also be able rightly to follow the pattern left us by the Lord Jesus Christ. You ought also to begin to preach again, and to teach your fellow-Christians, and show them the right path to eternal life. The time is come now when good books will be profitable to you; for know that one of your sermons will be more profitable now, and the people will receive more fruit therefrom, than from a hundred aforetime, for the words that you say now, coming from a pure soul, will have a pure and simple savour. Wherefore, just as much as you have been despised by the people, so shall you now be esteemed and beloved by them. But it will be most especially needful that you keep yourself humble, for you know well that he who carries a great treasure exposed to view must ever be on his guard against thieves. I tell you truly the Devil is in great terror when he perceives that God has bestowed on any man such a noble and precious treasure, and the devils will set all their arts and wisdom, and their lusts too, to work, to rob and bereave you of this costly treasure; wherefore look wisely to your goings, for nothing will so greatly help you to preserve it as utter humility. Now, dear sir, it is no longer needful for me to speak to you as a teacher, as I have done hitherto, for you have now the right and true Master, whose instrument I have been: to Him give ear, and obey His commands; this is my most faithful counsel. And now, in all godly love, I desire to receive instruction from you, for I have, with God's help, accomplished the good work for which I was sent and came hither. I would fain, if God will, sojourn here a good while and hear you preach. If God give you to do so, methinks it were well that you should now begin to preach again." Then said the Master, "Dear son, what had I better do; I have pledged a great many good books, as many as come to thirty florins?" The man answered, "Look! I will give you that sum, for God's sake, and if you have any of it left over, give it back to God, for all that we have is His, whether temporal or spiritual." So the Master redeemed his books, and ordered notice to be given that he would preach three days after. The people wondered much thereat, because it was so long since he had preached, and a great crowd gathered together to hear him. And when the Master came and saw that there was such a multitude, he went up into a pulpit in a high place, that they might hear him all the better. Then he held his hood before his eyes, and said, "O merciful, Eternal God, if it be Thy will, give me so to speak that it may be to the praise and glory of Thy name and the good of this people." As he said these words, his eyes overflowed with tears of tenderness, so that he could not speak a word for weeping, and this lasted so long that the people grew angry. At last a man spoke out of the crowd, "Sir, how long are we to stand here? It is getting late; if you do not mean to preach, let us go home." But the Master remained in earnest prayer, and said again to God, "Oh, my Lord and my God, if it be Thy divine will, take this weeping from my eyes, and give me to deliver this sermon to Thy praise and glory. But, if Thou dost not do it, I take it as a sign that Thou judgest I have not yet been enough put to shame. Now fulfil, dear Lord, Thy divine will on me Thy poor creature, to Thy praise and my necessities." This all availed nothing; he wept yet more and more. Then he saw that God would have it so, and said, with weeping eyes, "Dear children, I am sorry from my heart that I have kept you here so long, for I cannot speak a word to-day for weeping; pray God for me, that He may help me, and then I will make amends to you, if God give me grace, another time, as soon as ever I am able." So the people departed, and this tale was spread abroad and resounded through the whole city, so that he became a public laughing-stock, despised by all; and the people said, "Now we all see that he has become a downright fool." And his own brethren strictly forbade him to preach any more, because he did the convent great injury thereby, and disgraced the order with the senseless practices that he had taken up, and which had disordered his brain.

Then the Master sent for the man, and told him all that had happened. The man said, "Dear Master, be of good cheer, and be not dismayed at these things. The Bridegroom is wont to behave so to all His best and dearest friends, and it is a certain sign that God is your good friend, for, without a doubt, He has seen some speck of pride concealed within you that you have not perceived, nor been conscious of yourself, and therefore it is that you have been put to shame. You may have received some great gifts of God, which you yourself do not know or perceive, that have been given you by means of the patience with which you have endured this assault; therefore be of good cheer, and be joyful and humble. Neither should you think this a strange thing, for I have seen many such instances in other people. You shall not despise this pressure of the cross which God has sent you, but count it a great blessing and favour from God. I counsel you that you remain alone for the next five days, and endure without speaking to any, to the praise and glory of the five wounds of our Lord Jesus Christ. And when the five days are ended, beg your Prior to give you permission to deliver a sermon in Latin. If he refuse, beg him to let you try in the school and read a lecture to the brethren." And he did so; and read to his brethren such an excellent lecture as they had never heard in their lives before, so grand and deep and godly was his doctrine. Then they gave him permission to preach a sermon; and after one of their breathren had preached in the church where the Master was wont to preach, he gave notice to the people, and said, "I am ordered to announce that to-morrow the Master intends to preach in this place; but if it should befal him as it did lately, I will not be answerable for it. So much I can say with truth, that in our school he has read us a lecture containing such great and profound instruction, with high and divine wisdom, as we have not heard for a long time. But what he will do this time I know not; God only knoweth." The next day after, the Master came to the convent (it was a convent of ladies), and began to preach, and said.

"Dear children, it may be now two years or more since I last preached. I spoke to you then of four-and-twenty Articles, and it was then my custom to speak much Latin, and to make many quotations; but I intend to do so no more, but if I wish to talk Latin, I will do so when the learned are present, who can understand it. For this time repeat only an Ave Maria to begin with, and pray for God's grace.

Dear children, I have taken a text on which I mean to preach this sermon, and not to go beyond it: in the vulgar tongue it runs thus,—*"Behold the Bridegroom cometh, go ye out to meet him."*

The Bridegroom is our Lord Jesus Christ, and the Bride is the Holy Church and Christendom. Now we are all called brides of Christ, wherefore we ought to be willing to go forth and meet our Bridegroom; but, alas! we are not so. The true paths and straight highways by which to go out to meet the Bridegroom are, alas! now-a-days quite deserted and falling into decay, till we have come hardly to perceive where they are; nay, this highway is to many quite strange and unknown, so that they do not go out to meet the Bridegroom, as they are in duty bound to do, of which I will speak another time, with God's help; but now, since we hear that we are all called brides, I will tell you somewhat concerning what the Bride must do in order to go and meet the Bridegroom.

It is seemly that a faithful Bride should avoid everything that is displeasing to the Bridegroom, such as vain-glory, pride, envy, and all the other sins of this world, and all the delights of the body and the flesh, whether it be the ease and indulgence of the body, or other things which are beyond the necessaries of life. Further, it beseems a faithful Bride to be shame-faced. When this comes to pass, and the Bride, for her Bridegroom's sake, has despised and given up all these things, then she begins to be somewhat well-pleasing to the Bridegroom.

But, if she desires to be yet more well-pleasing in His sight, she must humbly bow down before Him, and say with heart and lips, "Ah! my dear Lord and Bridegroom, Thou knowest all hearts. I have said to Thee, with my whole heart, that I desire to do all that I can and may, and to do it willingly, as far as Thou givest me to perceive through my conscience what is agreeable and well-pleasing to Thee." When the Bride makes this vow to the Bridegroom, He turneth himself and begins to look upon her. Then she beseeches Him to bestow upon her some gift as a token of love. What is the gift? It is that she is inwardly and outwardly beset with divers assaults, with which He is wont to endow his special friends.

But if the Bride be as yet unaccustomed to suffer, she will say, "Ah! dear Lord and Bridegroom, this is very hard upon me; I fear greatly that I shall scarcely be able to endure it. Therefore, dear Lord and Bridegroom, I pray Thee to make my burden somewhat more tolerable, or else to take a part of it away." Then the Bridegroom answers, "Tell me then, dear Bride, should the Bride fare better than the Bridegroom has fared? If thou desirest to meet the Bridegroom, thou must imitate Him in some sort, and it is, moreover, reasonable that a faithful Bride should suffer somewhat with Him for her Bridegroom's sake." Now when the Bride heareth what is the will of her Bridegroom, and how grave a matter it is, she is sore affrighted, and says, "Dear Lord and Bridegroom, be not wroth with me, for I will gladly hearken unto Thee: appoint unto me what Thou wilt; I am willing to suffer all things with Thy help and in Thy love." When the Bridegroom heareth this, He loveth the Bride yet better than He did before, and giveth her to drink of a still better cup. This cup is that she is to cease from all her own thoughts, and all her works and refrainings will give her no content, for she can take pleasure in nothing that is her own. However good the actions may be in themselves, she is always thinking how she shall anger her Bridegroom therewith, and feareth much that she will, perhaps, have to suffer a great punishment for them hereafter. Moreover, she is derided by all, and these things are accounted her folly.

Now, children, by reason of all these things, her natural powers become wearied out and grow feeble, insomuch that she is constantly in fear lest she should not hold out to the end, but must die at last; and hereupon she is greatly terrified, for she is yet somewhat timorous and faint-hearted. Then she cries earnestly unto the Bridegroom, and says, "Ah! dear Lord and Bridegroom, how great are Thy terrors; know that I cannot endure them long: I must die." But the Bridegroom answers, "If thou wilt in truth go out to meet thy Bridegroom, it is fitting that thou should first tread some portion of the path that He has travelled. Now whereas the Bridegroom has suffered shame, hunger, cold, thirst, heat, and bitter pains, for three and thirty years, and at last a bitter death, for the Bride's sake, out of pure love, is it not just and right that the Bride should venture even her life for the Bridegroom's sake, out of love, and with all her heart? Verily, if thou hadst the right sort of love and true faithfulness unto thy Bridegroom, all thy fear would vanish."

Then when she hears these words of the Bridegroom her whole heart is moved with fear, and she says, "Ah! dear Lord, I acknowledge in all sincerity that I have done wrong, and I am out of all measure terrified at it; I grieve from the bottom of my heart that I have not with a faithful heart yielded myself up unto Thee, even unto death. Dear Lord and Bridegroom, I here vow and promise to Thee surely that all which Thou willest I also will. Come sickness, come health, come pleasure or pain, sweet or bitter, cold or heat, wet or dry, whatever Thou willest, that do I also will; and desire altogether to come out from my own will, and to yield a whole and willing obedience unto Thee, and never to desire aught else either in will or thought: only let Thy will be accomplished in me, Thy poor unworthy creature, in time and in eternity. For, dear Lord, when I look at what I am, I am not worthy that the earth should bear me."

Now when the Bridegroom seeth this entire and faithful will in the Bride, and her deep and thorough humility, what does He then do? His heart yearns over the Bride, and giveth her a very costly, noble, sweet cup to drink. What is this cup? It is that she suffers yet far more from all manner of temptations and tribulation than she has ever suffered before. And when the Bride perceiveth this, and seeth the Bridegroom's earnestness and good pleasure concerning her, she suffereth all these things willingly and gladly for the Bridegroom's sake, and boweth herself down humbly before Him, and saith, "Ah! dear Lord and Bridegroom, it is just and right that Thou shouldest not will as I will, but I desire and ought to will as Thou wilt; I receive this gift right willingly and gladly for Thy love from Thy divine hand, whether it be pleasant or painful to the flesh, I acquiesce wholly in it for love of Thee."

Now when the Bridegroom, in His eternal wisdom, perceives this disposition within His humble Bride, and her thorough earnestness, she begins to grow precious to Him, and from hearty love He giveth her to suffer in all her nature, until the Bride is wholly purified from all faults and stain of sin, and become perfectly fair and unspotted. Then He says, "Now rise up, my beloved, my pleasant, my beautiful Bride, for Thou art pure and without spot, and altogether lovely in my eyes." Then He looks upon her with infinite, mighty, divine love. To this joyful high-tide cometh the Father of the Eternal Bridegroom, and saith to the Bride, "Rise up, my lovely, chosen beloved, it is time to go to Church," and He taketh the Bridegroom and the Bride, and leadeth them to the Church, and mar-

ries them to each other, and binds them together with divine love; yea, God doth bind them together in bonds so fast that they can never be parted again, either in time or eternity. And when, in these divine espousals, they have been made one, the Bridegroom saith, "O, beloved and Eternal Father, what shall be our wedding-gift?" And the Father saith, "The Holy Ghost, for that it is His office to be in the Father's stead." And He sheds forth upon the Bride the torrent of divine love, and this love flows out unto the Bridegroom, insomuch that the Bride loseth herself, and is intoxicated with love, so that she forgets herself and all creatures, in time or eternity, together with herself.

Now he only who is bidden to such a spiritual, glorious marriage-feast, and has obeyed the call, does for the first time perceive and taste the real, true, blessed, gracious sweetness of the Holy Spirit. Now is this Bride a true worshipper, for she worshippeth the Father in the Holy Spirit. In this marriage-feast is joy upon joy, and therein is more peace and joy in one hour than all the creatures can yield in time or in eternity. The joy that the Bride hath with the Bridegroom is so vast that no senses or reason can apprehend or attain unto it."

As the Doctor spoke these words a man cried out with a loud voice, "It is true!" and fell down as if he were dead. Then a woman called out from the crowd and said, "Master, leave off, or this man will die on our hands."

Then the Master said, "Ah, dear children, and if the Bridegroom take the Bride and lead her home with Him, we will gladly yield her to Him; nevertheless, I will make an end and leave off. Dear children, let us all cry unto the Lord our God in Heaven. For verily we have all need so to do, seeing that, alas! we have grown so dull of hearing and foolish of heart that none of us has compassion on his fellow, although we confess that we are all called brothers and sisters. There be also few who are willing to fight their way against their own flesh, and follow the Bridegroom, in order to reach a nobler joy and a glorious wedding-feast.

I give you to know that in these days those be few and far between who do truly go out to meet the Bridegroom, such as there were many in the olden time. Therefore it behoveth each one to look at himself and consider his ways with great earnestness. For the time is at hand—nay, it is already come—when it may be said of most who are now living here, that "they have eyes and fee not, and ears that hear not." Dear children, let us all strive to enter into this wedding-feast, most rich in joy, and honour, and blessedness.

But when the Bride departs from this marriage-feast and is left to herself, and beholds that she has come back again to this miserable earthly state, she says within herself, "O! poor miserable creature that I am, am I here again?" And she is sad in herself; nevertheless, she is so utterly resigned in boundless humility to her Bridegroom, that she in no wise may think of or desire His presence, because she deems herself wholly unworthy thereof. But the Bridegroom does not therefore forsake her, but looketh upon His Bride from time to time, because He well knoweth that none will or can comfort her, but He alone.

And now that you have heard this, let it not surprise you that I have not told you how lovingly the Bridegroom talketh with the Bride. It might well happen that none would believe me (except such a one as had tried and tasted it himself), should I tell you what strange words the Bride saith to her Bridegroom. We find, too, in the Scriptures, that the loving soul ofttimes holds such converse with her Beloved as words cannot perfectly express. Nay, does it not happen every day with earthly lovers, that a bride and bridegroom talk together in such wise that if others heard it they would declare them mad or drunk?

Now, dear children, I fear that I have kept you too long; but the time has not seemed long to me: also, I have said it all for your good, and could not well this time make my sermon shorter if I were rightly to explain my meaning; therefore receive it kindly.

That we may all become real, true, perfect brides of our Lord Jesus Christ, and that we may in sincere, true, utter humility and resignation, go out to meet our glorious Bridegroom, and abide with Him for ever, may God help us, the Father, the Son, and the Holy Ghost. Amen."

Notes

1. [The letters R and S have been transposed; the rest follow the order of the original, in which, as in the translation, the important word of the sentence is by no means always the one with which it commences. The letters V and W are wanting in the original.—Tr]

Arthur Wollaston Hutton (essay date 1901)

SOURCE: An introduction to *The Inner Way: Being Thirty-Six Sermons for Festivals by John Tauler*, Methuen & Co., 1901, pp. ix-xliii.

[*In the following excerpt, Hutton portrays Tauler as both mystical and practical, as more than an allegorist, and as a man influenced by his time. Hutton debunks common misconceptions of mysticism and distinguishes between its different varieties.*]

III

NOTES ON TAULER'S TEACHING

Only to Tauler's Sermons must recourse be had to ascertain his teaching; and even of these, as has been noted, a critical edition is desirable. The other works once attributed to him, and printed as his in the Latin version of Surius, are now accounted doubtful, if not certainly spurious. These works are:—(1) "The Following of the Poor Life of Christ"; (2) "Exercises on the Life and Passion of our Saviour Jesus Christ"; and (3) "Divine Institutions," also called "The Marrow of the Soul." All these are spiritual works of high value, and they deserve a place in any library of devotion; but, as attributed to Tauler, they are not authentic. Such at least is the present verdict of the critics.

Judged then solely by his Sermons, Tauler is described by Von Loë, his latest biographer, as "one of the foremost among the mediæval German mystics and preachers, uniting the intellectual depth of Eckhart with the interior spirituality of Suso and the fervour of Berthold of Ratisbon." The first-named was mystical; the last-named was practical; Suso was both; but he was rather a director than a preacher. Tauler also was both, and, like Berthold, he preached for his times. Herder criticises him, saying that to have read two of his sermons is to have read them all; but this is hardly a verdict to be accepted; for his method varies largely, and the Sermon numbered xi. in this volume, for the most part so dull and in places barely intelligible, would strike a critic as not the work of the same author as the Sermon numbered xv. which the German editors have described as "a most precious and thoughtful exhortation," and perhaps the best example of Tauler's method. Sometimes moreover he expounds a text like a homilist; sometimes his text is barely referred to, and becomes a mere peg on which to hang a discourse on a subject of which he was full. No doubt there are readers to whom his allegorical interpretation of Scripture will be distasteful. Kingsley admits that it is "fantastic and arbitrary"; and the method is, of course, one that can easily be abused, especially when the interpretation of numbers is in question. But it has its justification, both in the fact that it is in accordance with Christian tradition—it is found in St Paul, in the early Fathers (as Keble's Tract lxxxix. made abundantly clear), and in the offices of the Church, whether those for the choir or those for the altar, and traces of it are left in the Anglican Prayer-Book—and also in the experience of sympathetic souls, who find light and consolation in its use. But Tauler's mysticism (of which more is said below) by no means exhausted itself in the allegorical interpretation of Scripture. To him, as to Keble and to Kingsley, the book of Nature was full of parables of things spiritual; and, beyond that again, he clearly enjoyed (for he was no hypocrite) an intuition of things divine, wherein he found more light and certitude than in mere submission to the dogmatic *magisterium* of the Church.

Further, as to his manner, he is eager and earnest in his presentation of his subject; he uses homely illustrations from daily life, yet without loss of dignity, and when he disparages, as he often does, "outward works," he is saying nothing against the performance of the duties, even the humblest, of ordinary life; he is merely protesting against reliance on ecclesiastical routine, such as fasting, self-discipline, long prayers, and such-like; and this protest is of course quite compatible with Catholic orthodoxy; nor is it unnecessary for these times any more than for his own. But the manner of his sermons, as they have come down to us, is sometimes hard and even menacing; and readers may not always find it easy to reconcile his frequent use of the words "dear children" with such an apparent lack of tenderness and sympathy. But, likely enough, this defect of manner was less noticeable in the discourses as delivered, than it is in the reports as now read.

Readers will also find it necessary to bear in mind that the mystical standpoint in religion does not by itself free a man from contemporary views and prepossessions. The mystic is of his own age and race; and it is amply evident that the articles of Tauler's creed were just those of any other Catholic believer of his time. There is throughout a spiritual element in his teaching; but it does not exclude the use of what we should now account popular and conventional language about the fall of man, the pains of hell, and so forth. True, he says in one place, what indeed any Catholic preacher may say, that the chief pain of hell is the consciousness of being excluded from the Presence of God; but he does not go on to suggest, as a spiritually-minded teacher might now, that all other language about the pains of hell, "the worm that dieth not and the fire that is not quenched," is merely figurative of that one pain, and that such language was and is necessary to bring home to men,—to all men in different degrees,—the exceeding greatness of that pain or penalty, as it will hereafter be realised. He is liberal indeed in extending to the spiritually-minded heathen a sufficient knowledge of things divine. He holds that in the "inner ground"[1] Plato and Proclus apprehended the Holy Trinity; he thinks that in Plato can be found the whole meaning of the opening verses of St John's Gospel, though in veiled words. He teaches that a king, remaining such, may yet rise to the height of "interior poverty," if there is nothing that he is not ready cheerfully to resign to God's Fatherly love. He extols the "evangelical counsels"; but teaches also that the highest perfection is attainable by a married cobbler working to maintain his family. His doctrine of Purgatory does not differ from that usually held by Catholics; but he regards it more as a place for the purging away of self-will than for the expiation of sin. In his sermon for the second Sunday in Lent there is a passage somewhat in disparagement of the invocation of Saints. A good soul, he says, once prayed to the Saints; but they were so lost in God that they did not heed her. Then she betook herself humbly to God direct, and straightway she was lifted far above all *media* into the loving abyss of the Godhead. But perhaps he comes nearest to the Protestant position in his language about the "Friends of God." They are, he teaches, the true pillars of the Church, and without them the world could not stand. In his sermon for *Latare* Sunday he bids his hearers "beg the dear Friends of God to help them [in the way of perfection], and to attach themselves simply and solely to God and to his chosen Friends." And there is a similar passage in the sermon for All Saints (see pp. 218-222, and *cf.* pp. 93 and 174). But, in his teaching, the "Friends of God" do not form, as they would have formed for the later Puritans,

"the Church invisible"; they constitute rather a second visible Church, to which the hierarchical Church is in some respects inferior. Some thirty years after Tauler's death the Inquisition at Cologne condemned as heretical certain propositions of Martin of Mayence; one of which was that these "Friends of God" (who were laymen) understood the Gospel better than some of the Apostles, even better than St Paul; and another was that submission to their teaching was necessary to perfection. But Tauler never went so far as this.

It may be added that, from the modern Christian social point of view, Tauler's limitations are obvious. True, that in his sermon for Septuagesima he exhorts his hearers to use "natural gifts" for God. But his conception of "nature" is a very narrow one. Rightly it should include, besides those natural gifts which constitute personal character, such social virtues as patriotism, love for the community and for the family, a desire to master the earth and to make it the seat of a well-ordered Christian society, a realisation of the Kingdom of God on earth. But Tauler manifests no conception of anything of this. For the social elevation of mankind, here and now, he has nothing whatever to say.

Nevertheless, whatever were our author's limitations, Preger's judgment on the value of Tauler's sermons is one to command general assent:—"Their strength lies in the fact that Tauler knew how to put into them his whole heart, the fulness of his moral being. So utterly and completely is he penetrated by love of God and of Christ, so happily is the sublime and unworldly zeal of the orator blended with gentleness and freedom, that he masters the will unawares, and lays the heart open to the demands he makes upon it. . . . His sermons will never cease to hold their place among the most perfect examples of pure German speech, of fervid German faith, and of German spirituality in all its depths."

IV

TAULER AND MYSTICISM

It may be convenient to some of those into whose hands this little volume will come, if a brief account is here given of that "Mysticism" to which repeated reference has been made, and to which reference must be made, when the significance of Tauler's teaching is under consideration. Although the subject is now much better understood than it was in 1856, when Robert Vaughan published his "Hours with the Mystics," a notable book, queerly put together, interesting in its facts, but irritating in its manner, and one that was sympathetically reviewed by Kingsley in "Fraser's Magazine,"[2] there is still need to point out what mystics are not, more perhaps than what they are. Mystics are not dreamers; they are not fanatics; they are not fools; they are not a sect; and mysticism is not a religion. As a rule, mystics are so termed by others; they do not use the term of themselves. But thousands and millions of Christian believers have been and are mystics, without themselves knowing the word. In fact, as Dr Bigg says, "mysticism is an element in all religion that is not mere formalism"; and it is confined to no one form of Christianity. A Carthusian hermit, prostrate on the floor of his cell in meditation, may or may not be a mystic; but so may also be a grocer's assistant who occasionally attends a Methodist chapel. When Cardinal Newman taught that in the act of faith the conclusion is more certain than the premises, he (perhaps inadvertently) proclaimed himself a mystic; and so, I think, did Ritschl, in spite of himself, when he affirmed the certitude of the "value-judgment" by which a man lays hold on the historic Christ; for mysticism is such a way of apprehending spiritual truth; it is a way that is neither purely intellectual, nor purely emotional; but one that employs, in one act, all the powers of a man's soul. The mystical attitude towards truth is thus in harmony with Matthew Arnold's lines:—

> "Affections, Instincts, Principles and Powers,
> Impulse and Reason, Freedom and Control—
> So men, unravelling God's harmonious whole,
> Rend in a thousand shreds this life of ours.
> Vain labour! Deep and broad, where none may see,
> Spring the foundations of that shadowy throne,
> Where man's One Nature, queen-like, sits alone,
> Centred in a majestic unity."

It is true that mysticism has to do with mystery; and that is why the term is popularly held in disrepute. But the mysteries with which mysticism chiefly has to do are neither numerous nor fantastic: they are *God,* and the *Soul,* and *Revelation;* the last being the making known of the One to the other: and, beyond this, Christian mysticism views the Eternal as approached through Jesus Christ, the Door; a few texts from St Paul and St John sufficing to state the whole case. Individual mystical writers have, no doubt, gone far beyond this, and have said extravagant things; but the essence of the whole lies herein; and (again to quote Dr Bigg), "the Church can never get rid of the mystic spirit; nor should she attempt to do so, for it is, in fact, her life. It is another name for conscience, for freedom, for the rights of the individual soul, for the grace and privilege of direct access to the Redeemer, for the presence of the Divine Spirit in the heart."[3]

And further, most people are now familiar with the distinction between the dreamy, unpractical mysticism of the East and the vigorous variety of the same mode of thought in the West. In both cases it produces the same consciousness of certitude and of interior peace; but in the one case that tends to mere contemplation and self-introspection, while in the other it inspires a Tauler or a Cromwell or a Coleridge; and from the latter's mysticism, movements that are vigorous to-day have derived their spiritual energy, though but few of those whom the movements affect may be aware of the fact. It is also necessary to distinguish between mysticism as a way of holding spiritual truth, and mysticism as an interpretation, sometimes fantastic, of the world and of man; and again between this interpretation and the mystical interpretation of Scripture, already referred to, which is apt, indeed, to allegorise wantonly, though its fancies are almost always of service in securing

a broader and more edifying interpretation for texts which, if regarded as mere history or legend, would lack religious significance. The evolution of these other aspects of the subject from that first mysticism, which is the apprehension of spiritual things by the soul, a few moments reflection will make clear. The mystic, who sees God in all things and all things in God, recognises more in nature than mere natural phenomena, and more in the Word of God than its first literal significance. To him every thing, every event, every person, is a vision from the Unseen, a voice from the Inaudible. He lives in a world of parables, full of spiritual significance; and, while for him there is a Real Presence everywhere, he finds it also most truly and effectively where it is most clearly discerned by faith. Nothing that might be accounted magical is required to produce it, for it is there and everywhere already. So too, in his interpretation of the Book, which contains, with whatever admixture, the fullest record of that which has been revealed to man as necessary for the salvation of his soul, he sees more than the mere student of the letter. In God's dealings with man from first to last he perceives a harmony that implies a foreshadowing of the last in the first, of the whole in the part; and in this way he can find an interpretation of spiritual value even in the thoughts of good men, who have pictured to themselves, inaccurately, it may be, as to matters of fact, God's earlier work in the creation of the world and of man. And, thus broadly understood, mysticism is now "in the air," and is becoming recognised as a force that makes for unity among Christians, who differ somewhat as to dogma, and more as to their methods of its external expression. Happily however, its interior and reserved character will always hinder mysticism from being degraded, as external religion can be and is, to the position of a mere badge or cry of an ecclesiastical party.[4]

Not to know anything about mysticism is, according to Professor Royce, not to know anything about a large part of human nature; for mysticism is the philosophy of experience; the mystics are the only thorough-going empiricists in the whole history of philosophy; and the realm of experience is that which is decisive of truth. A complete history of mysticism would cover a very large field in the history of the world; and that not only of the world of thought; for, in the West at any rate, the mystics have repeatedly built the platform on which great dramas have been played; and in this sense (but in this sense only) Tauler and the "Friends of God" were "precursors of the Reformation," much as the Puritans were the precursors of the modern Revolution. It may be quite possible to show that Tauler was an orthodox Catholic friar, and that his obedience to the Church was throughout irreproachable; but, none the less, his mystical doctrine of the inner and the outer, of the letter and the spirit, tended irresistibly towards the overthrow of Catholicism, so far as in his day it consisted in mere formalism and obedience to external rule. The same doctrine in the teaching of St Paul made short work of the Jewish Law; and again in our own day (for there are symptoms of its revival) it will either destroy or will newly inspire modern Catholicism, whether Roman or Anglican, which, without the mystic spirit, must inevitably degenerate into mere Byzantinism, the religion of credulity and of ceremonial routine.

The earliest home of mysticism was in the East; but before the Christian era it had passed over into Europe, or had an independent origin there. So at least is the alternative stated by Professor Royce. But its independent origin in the West, in the mystical teaching of Jesus Christ, as we recognise it in the language used by St Paul and St John, must surely be acknowledged as beyond question, save by those who hold that the Prophet of Nazareth acquired mystical doctrines in the farther East, perhaps by residence there; and of this there is at present absolutely no evidence that can be termed historical. According to Professor Seth, it is a mode of thought or of feeling, from its very nature insusceptible of exact definition, in which reliance is placed on spiritual intuition or illumination, believed to transcend the ordinary powers of the human understanding. In this sense Plato (whom Eckhart quaintly describes as "the great Parson"—*der grosse Pfaffe*), was a mystic. It is the endeavour of the human soul (in its own judgment successful) to grasp the Divine Essence, or the ultimate Reality of things, and to enjoy the blessedness of actual communion with the Highest. Thus, mystical theology is that knowledge of God and of things divine, which is derived, not from observation or from argument, but from conscious spiritual experience; and, being thus based, it possesses, for the individual who holds it, an irrefragable certainty.

From Plato and from Aristotle's account of God's inner life, the Greek mysticism, as a stream distinct from the mysticism of the New Testament (*i.e.* of St Paul, and of the writings attributed to St John), passed into Plotinus, and so, through Philo and the neo-Platonists, it became an element in Christian theology; and the writer known as "pseudo-Dionysius" was its chief prophet in the early Church. It would take long to trace, so far as it can be traced, the filiation of the doctrine from the age of the neo-Platonists to the fourteenth century; and it must suffice to say that there existed in Tauler's day at least four Latin versions of the works of Dionysius, that of Scotus Erigena being the one with which he was most likely to be familiar. Dionysius was also commented on by the greatest scholastics, incidentally even by St Thomas Aquinas, who sought to deal justly with the mystics without endangering orthodoxy. Eckhart, whose disciple Tauler in some sense was, had been trained in the school of St Thomas; but he gradually emancipated himself from the scholastic yoke; and he is commonly reckoned the spiritual ancestor of Kant and Hegel. Indeed, in other ways and by a more direct descent, mysticism at this day largely affects multitudes to whom its very name is unknown. The favourite devotional books of all the churches, and many of our most popular hymns, are essentially mystical. It has been defined above as philosophical empiricism; but it is more than that, and much more than mere sentimentality. Again to quote Professor Royce:—"It is the conception of men whose piety has been won after long conflict, whose thoughts have been dissected by a very keen inner scepticism, whose single-minded devotion to an abstraction has resulted from a vast experience of painful complications of life. . . . It has been the ferment of the faiths, the forerunner of spiritual liberty, the inaccessible refuge of the nobler heretics, the inspirer, through poetry, of countless youth who know no metaphysics, the teacher, through the devotional books, of the despairing, the comforter of those who are weary of finitude; it has determined directly or indirectly, more than half of the technical theology of the Church."[5]

With the above eloquent passage, written only the other day, may be compared Kingsley's lament, written in 1856, that mysticism was a form of thought and feeling then all but extinct in England. The Anglican divines, he said, looked on it with utter disfavour; they used the word always as a term of reproach; and they interpreted the mystical expressions in the Prayer-book (chiefly to be found in the collects) in accordance with the philosophy of Locke, being ignorant that these collects were really the work of Platonist mystics. But meanwhile, he pointed out, it was the mysticism of Coleridge "the fakir of Highgate," that had originated both the Oxford Movement and Emersonian free-thought; while Carlyle, "the only contemporary mystic of any real genius," was exercising more practical influence, and was infusing more vigorous life into the minds of thousands of men and women, than all the other teachers of England put together. If he had also mentioned Words-worth, Tennyson, Browning and Ruskin, he would have made still clearer how immense has been the power of our latter-day mysticism; while the names of Neale and of Keble, of Faber and of Newman, can speak for the same potent influence among those who were ecclesiastics by profession.

This perhaps may suffice, if any need there was, to secure for those who read Tauler's sermons now for the first time, sympathy with him instead of suspicion on account of his reputation as a mystic. There is no need to follow him when he becomes subtle or extravagant; but of his generally broad and spiritual teaching no one can doubt the wholesome influence. Ritschl, in his zeal for his new rational Lutheranism, is bitter against the mystics; yet even he admits that Tauler did good service in inculcating interior as compared with mere ceremonial religion, and in lessening the great mediæval distinction between clergy and laity. There was in Tauler's day a great need for a revival of the religion of the heart—when is there not such a need?—but it was also necessary that the established methods of religion should be respected and remain intact; for there existed no other social bond equally fitted to hold men together. And this was the secret of Tauler's influence. He was able to fill the old bottles with new wine from an ancient vineyard without bursting them. Recent historical criticism may have destroyed some of the romance with which his name was associated. But if, as it now appears—and Harnack as well as Ritschl agree with Denifle in this—he was not a "Reformer before the Reformation," and was not the subject of a singular conversion in the midst of his successful career as preacher, he still remains, and will always remain, a striking and venerable figure in the mediæval Church, a reformer at any rate of practical abuses, and a prophet of righteousness in days that were corrupt as well as stormy. . . .

Notes

1. See the note on this word *Grund,* on p. 94.

2. The review was reprinted in Kingsley's "Miscellanies," Vol. I.; and with it should be read his Prefaces to Miss Winkworth's edition of the *Theologia Germanica* (1854, and now reprinted in the "Golden Treasury" series) and of Tauler (1857).

3. "Unity in Diversity," p. 93.

4. Those who are interested in this subject may be referred to Bigg's "Christian Platonists of Alexandria" (1886), and to Inge's Bampton Lectures on "Christian Mysticism" (1899), as also to Professor Royce's Gifford Lectures on "The World and the Individual," whence are taken some of the thoughts and phrases in the paragraphs which follow.

5. "The World and the Individual," pp. 81, 85.

Rufus M. Jones (essay date 1909)

SOURCE: "The Friends of God" in *Studies in Mystical Religion*, Macmillan and Co., Limited, 1909, pp. 242-97.

[*In the following excerpt, Jones sketches the troubled times in which the Friends of God lived; describes their literature with its vision of Apocalypse and emphasis on renunciation; and profiles Tauler—particularly his insistence on the inner Light.*]

I

One of the most important and remarkable expressions of mystical religion in the history of the Christian Church is that which flowered out in Germany in the fourteenth century, and whose exponents are known under the name of "Friends of God." The title does not cover a sect, nor even a "Society," in the strict sense of the word. It, rather, names a fairly definite type of Christianity, which found its best expression in persons of the prophet-class in that century, both men and women, who powerfully moved large groups of Christians by their preaching, their writings, and their extraordinary lives. All the leaders of the movement were profoundly influenced by the teaching of that luminous figure of German mysticism, Meister Eckhart, but they were hardly less definitely influenced by the apocalyptic writings of the great German "prophetesses" of the two preceding centuries—St. Hildegarde, St. Elizabeth of Schoenau, and St. Matilda of Magdeburg. The writings of these famous women are full of incidents, phrases, and images which formed "suggestion material"

for the experiences and ideas of the Friends of God. In fact, they have very similar conceptions of the Church and the world, and of the impending catastrophes that are about to break upon both the world and the Church. I shall give illustrations of this influence later.

The period covered by the movement which we are now studying was one of the most troublous epochs in medieval history. Woes and disasters came thickly one after the other, and they produced a "psychological climate," which partly accounts for the morbid features which characterize the movement, and which partly explains the abnormal occurrences in the lives of many of the "Friends of God." Every sensitive person was over-wrought and strained. There was a widespread expectation that apocalyptic prophecies were soon to be fulfilled; this visible world was believed to be the sport of supernatural powers, both good and bad, and men and women everywhere were in "hair-trigger condition" of response to any captivating suggestion, as the terrible outbreak of flagellation which swept many of the Rhine cities plainly indicates. A few of the events which helped to produce this "mental climate" may be mentioned here. From 1309 to 1377 occurred the so-called "Babylonish Captivity" of the Church, when the papal seat was changed to Avignon, and when the popes were more or less puppets of France. To many of the faithful this "captivity" was a supreme woe—the reward and result of sin and apostasy. A still greater misfortune followed hard after the period of "captivity." Upon the death of Gregory XI., in 1378, there occurred a double election, resulting in two rival popes, and during the next forty years the Church was torn and almost wrecked by what is known as the "Great Schism," which lasted from 1378 to 1417.

More important for our distinct period, and carrying with it more serious practical consequences for the common people of the German cities, was the "Great Civil War," which resulted from a double election of emperors. Louis of Bavaria was chosen Emperor in 1314, by one party of electors, and Frederick of Austria by another party. The Pope took sides against Louis, excommunicated him, and laid an interdict upon all cities which supported him. By the interdict, all public religious services were prohibited, and all consolation of religion suspended, through the section of the country covered by the interdict. Infants were unbaptized, the Mass was not celebrated, the sacred offices for the dead ceased. In many cities of Germany where the citizens were loyal to Louis, the priests were forced to go on with their religious functions in spite of the interdict, or to go into banishment.

While Europe was thus suffering through the wrath of man, a veritable scourge, which in that age seemed traceable directly to the wrath of God, fell upon the German cities. It was a pestilence known in history as the "Black Death." It first struck the west of Europe in 1347, and raged for two years, returning again in less virulent form in 1358 and in 1363. In some places the mortality was so great that it is estimated that only one-tenth of the population survived. There were, too, many earthquakes through the Rhine valley about the middle of the century, one of which, "the great earthquake," left the city of Basle a heap of ruins, and wrought similar havoc in many small towns.

The Friends of God formed small groups, or local societies, gathered about some spiritual leader or counsellor. There was little or no organization. The type of each particular group was largely determined by the personality of the "leader," while the whole movement was unified and moulded by the work of itinerant "prophets," and by the production of a very remarkable literature. These mystic circles, or groups, were widespread, and were formed in far-sundered places, stretching from Bavaria, possibly from Bohemia, to the low countries, with the most important groups in Strasbourg, Cologne, and Basle.[1]

There was a voluminous exchange of letters among the leaders, and frequent personal visits. The visits and the itinerant missions were generally prompted by some direct revelation. In fact, the whole plan and direction of the movement, as well as the preparation of the most important pieces of their religious literature, are ascribed to direct revelation granted to the leaders.

Some of the societies had retreats in which the members lived—"quiet nests" Tauler calls them. They were "brotherhood houses," modelled on the plan of the Beghards. In many respects the Friends of God were like the Beghards—there is no sharp line of differentiation between them, though the former are always radically opposed to the loose and antinomian tendencies which affected many groups of Beghards and Beguines. The Friends of God were inclined, rather, to err in the opposite direction. Their failing lies in the direction of extreme asceticism and self-renunciation. All the leading Friends of God, both in sermons and in writings, speak vigorously against the negative freedom and licence of the "Brethren of Free Spirit."

The leading figures of the group are Rulman Merswin of Strasbourg; his friend and secretary, Nikolaus von Löwen; John Tauler; Henry Suso; Jan Ruysbroek; Margaret and Christina Ebner; Henry of Nördlingen, and the great unknown, who wrote the little book called *German Theology.* The most important literature for the purposes of this study are the writings attributed to Rulman Merswin and to "The Friend of God of the Oberland"; the sermons of Tauler; the writings of Suso and Ruysbroek; the *German Theology,* and the correspondence between Margaret Ebner and her friends.[2]

As I shall often refer in this chapter to Rulman Merswin and his "double," the so-called "Friend of God from the Oberland," it will be well to consider here who they were. There is no more difficult problem in the history and literature of mysticism than that of the identity and personality of this "Friend of God"—everywhere treated as a somewhat supernatural "character"—who figures so prominently in the great collection of mystical literature ascribed to him and to Rulman Merswin.[3]

It was assumed in the fifteenth century that this mysterious "Friend of God from the Oberland" was a certain Nicholas of Basle,[4] and this tradition came down with little challenge until recent times. It was adopted and given wide currency by the valuable publications of the famous Strasbourg historian, Karl Schmidt. It is a view, however, now everywhere discredited by scholars. Preger believes that he was a great unknown who lived in or near the city of Chur (Coire), in Switzerland, and Jundt held this view when he wrote his valuable book, *Les Amis de Dieu* (1879). But since Denifle's important studies in the mystical literature of the fourteenth century, the belief has been growing that the "Friend of God of the Oberland" is not an historical personage at all.[5] All his movements are wrapped in profound mystery. There is no historical evidence of his existence outside the evidence furnished by this collection of literature, ascribed to him and Merswin. The accounts of his life say that sometime about 1343 he was forbidden to reveal his identity to any one whatever, except to Rulman Merswin. In the correspondence, supposedly between the "Friend of God" and John of Schaftholsheim, a prominent Church official at Strasbourg, the latter, writing about 1363, urges his unknown correspondent to reveal himself to him. The answer comes back that he cannot do it: "I should like to grant your request, but it is impossible. Cease to ask it, for the love of God. More than twenty years ago God forbade me to reveal myself to any man except one." Every effort is made to destroy all traces of his personal identity, and there is an evident purpose, both in the correspondence and the books ascribed to him, to leave the impression that whatever he does is done by the Holy Spirit. The human medium is, for this very purpose, made as mysterious and shadowy as possible. This entire collection of writings betrays the marks of a single hand. There is a striking similarity in the experiences which occur both to Merswin and the "Friend of God," though there is a boldness of tone and a sureness of direction in the utterances ascribed to the latter which are missing in the former. The same expressions and the same phrases appear and reappear in the writings ascribed to both.

Before, however, undertaking to account for his mysterious "double," we must endeavour from the literature at hand to get some biographical details concerning Rulman Merswin. He was born in Strasbourg in 1307. As a young man he became a banker, and amassed a large fortune. He was "a man of watchful conscience and of great fear of God," and he belonged to a very important family of the city. When he was forty years of age he gave up business, "took leave of the world," and devoted himself entirely to divine things, after the manner of the Franciscan Tertiaries, or the Waldensian brothers. He, however, did not give away his money; he kept it "to use for God," as He might direct from time to time. His wife, Gertrude of Bietenheim, though a pious woman, had not yet attained what the Friends of God call "the light of grace." With Waldensian rigour he resolved to live henceforth as celibate.

His first experience of ecstasy came to him at the time of his resolve to devote all his money to the service of

God—as the first step in his "new life." Suddenly he felt himself raised from the earth and carried through the air all about the garden. At the same time he felt unutterable joy and spiritual illumination unknown before. He passed through the usual "stages of spiritual experience" that were expected at this epoch. He had terrible inward temptations and struggles; he endeavoured to conquer his evil nature and his "hated body" by extreme ascetic practices. John Tauler became his confessor in 1348, and he wisely told him to stop his macerations. Merswin was next called to pass through an absolutely joyless period when he felt himself destined to burn in hell for ever; then, at length, all sufferings left him, and he came into "the joy and peace of the Holy Spirit."[6]

The Story of the First Four Years of a New Life, which is a remarkable piece of biographical literature, was, according to Merswin's friend, Nikolaus von Löwen, found after his death in a sealed cupboard. This document gives an account of the first appearance of the mysterious "Friend of God." Merswin says:

> "Of all the wonderful works which God had wrought in me I was not allowed to tell a single word to anybody *until the time when it should please God to reveal to a man in the Oberland to come to me.* When he came to me, God gave me the power to tell him everything. He became my intimate friend; I submitted myself to him in the place of God, and I told him all the secrets of those four years as God inspired me to do. Then he said: 'My dear, beloved friend, take this book;[7] thou wilt find in it the story of the five years of *my* conversion, and now give me in writing the story of thy four years of conversion.'"

Merswin stoutly resisted the request to write his experiences, but finally the unnamed friend "commanded me to write, in the name of the obedience which I had promised him, and I was compelled to submit. He knew very well that my refusal came entirely from my humility."

The sentence above in italics, which intimates that Merswin had a subjective idea of the "Friend of God" sometime before he had ever seen him or even heard of him, is certainly suspicious, and would, on the face of it, make us inclined to question the historicity of the narrative. Even more suspicious is the account given of the most important event in Merswin's life—the purchase of Grünenwörth, or the "Convent of the Green Isle." This was purchased, according to the narrative, by Merswin, and fitted up as a quiet retreat—"a mystic nest"—for the Strasbourg circle of the Friends of God, a sort of "school of prophets" for which the most important books of this mystical collection were written. Merswin himself is *supposed* to be the author of the account of the founding of the retreat. He brings in his mysterious "Friend," and gives the entire transaction a miraculous colouring. He says that during the night of October 9, 1364, the "Friend of God," in his Oberland home—"six days' journey" from Strasbourg—dreamed that he was ordered by God to go to his friend Rulman Merswin, and help him to found a "nest" in

Strasbourg for the Friends of God. The same night, in a dream, Rulman Merswin himself had a revelation that *he* ought to found such a retreat in Strasbourg!

Both men were opposed to the idea of founding such a retreat, and they refused to follow the suggestion made in their dreams. The night of the following Christmas they both simultaneously in their respective homes fell seriously ill at midnight; the illness increased until they were at the point of death; suddenly, at precisely the same time, they were told in indescribable visions to found the retreat! The "joint" illness lasted for nearly two years, when a general paralysis of their limbs rendered them both helpless! They were now told that this condition would last until they followed the will of God. At length they yielded, and immediately they were both restored to health! Confirmed by such miraculous signs, the two friends now set to work to carry out the plan which had been revealed to them.[8]

The later accounts, which describe the last years of Merswin and the "Friend of God," throw even more suspicion on the historicity of the narratives, and force us to question the existence of this mysterious "Friend of God." Shortly before his death, which occurred in 1382, Merswin and the "Friend of God," with eleven other Friends of God, met miraculously for a "divine diet" to intercede for Christianity. On Good Friday, 1380, as they were praying, a letter fell from the sky in their midst, and an angel told them that God had granted to Christianity a reprieve of Judgment for three years, on condition that they—these thirteen Friends of God—would, according to the contents of the Divine letter, become "the captives of the Lord," *i.e.* die absolutely to self and the world, giving their lives "as a continual sacrifice for the salvation of Christianity"—and so they did! The last word that came from the "Friend of God," now grown even more mysterious than ever, was an *instruction* on how to begin and end the day with prayer, during the pestilence of 1381, and Rulman Merswin, still "the captive of the Lord," died in 1382.

Everybody who has worked over this collection of Friends of God literature has been impressed with the difficulties of the problems involved in it. It seems well-nigh certain that "the Friend of God from the Oberland" was not a historical person, but, if not, who "created" him?

It has been assumed, especially by Denifle, that "the Friend of God" is a literary creation of Rulman Merswin. This entire collection of mystical treatises, it is assumed, was written by Merswin, with the assistance, perhaps, of a school of prophets, and it is all *tendency-literature,* composed to express and develop the ideals of the great religious movement to which Merswin's life was devoted.

The "great unknown" from the Oberland is the ideal character—the "Christian" of a fourteenth-century *Pilgrim's Progress*—who illustrates how God does His work for the world and for the Church through a divinely-trained and spiritually-illuminated layman. On this hypothesis Rulman Merswin as the creator of this ideal Christian of the fourteenth century, as the author of this remarkable autobiographical literature, and as the writer of the great *Book of the Nine Rocks,* would take rank as a genius of uncommon order and as one of the foremost exponents of mysticism in any age, though, as Denifle points out, he would have to be regarded as an arch-deceiver who wilfully misled all his associates and be-fooled all his readers for four centuries.

In order to clear Merswin from the charge of deceit, Auguste Jundt has proposed a very bold and ingenious hypothesis to solve the mystery. He suggests that Rulman Merswin was a "double personality," of a pathological type now well known to all students of psychology.[9] In his *primary state* he wrote the books ascribed to him and experienced the events recorded in his autobiography; while in his *secondary state* he became the person known as "the Friend of God from the Oberland," and in this state he wrote the books, treatises, and letters ascribed to "the Friend of God." This view, if proved sound, would surely make Rulman Merswin one of the most interesting psychological "subjects" in the entire range of history.

There is a third hypothesis which rests on solider ground than either of the two preceding views. It is presented with sound learning and minute and accurate scholarship by Karl Rieder.[10] He holds that Rulman Merswin is neither a deceiver nor "a double personality," and, with the iconoclasm characteristic of modern German scholarship, he concludes that Merswin is not the author of any of these mystical treatises, and that none of them furnish reliable biographical facts bearing on Merswin's life.

What he finds is that this entire collection of literature has gone through the hands of Nikolaus of Löwen and been transformed by him. Nikolaus was a friend and trusted secretary of Rulman Merswin, his associate in the foundation and development of the Religious House of Grünenwörth, afterwards the House of St. John, and the first local head of the House of St. John during the life-time and after the death of Merswin.

There came into the hands of Nikolaus, possibly as part of the library of Grünenwörth, a rich collection of mystical treatises, the creation of different members of the group of Friends of God, but with no definite authorship attached to them or ascribed to them.[11] In order to glorify the Religious House to which he belonged, and to give a weighty influence and authority to its founder, Nikolaus attached Merswin's name to some of these anonymous treatises, and finally created out of his own imagination the mysterious and somewhat supernatural adviser, "the Friend of God from the Oberland," to whom he ascribed the origin of most of the remaining mystical treatises. As the plan grew, Nikolaus expanded the anonymous narratives relating extraordinary experiences, and inserted the names of Merswin and "the Friend of God," and passed them off as autobiographical, inventing a concrete setting for narratives which in their original form had been purely ficti-

tious, and written to illustrate principles which were dear to the Friends of God. The arch-deceiver, therefore, was Nikolaus von Löwen, and his was the genius that created "the Friend of God from the Oberland."

Rieder's main contention that this mystical literature has received a transformation and a local setting at the hands of Nikolaus von Löwen, and that he has woven in much fictitious material to glorify the House of St. John, and its founder, Merswin, seems to me sound; but I see, however, no good reason for the conclusion that Rulman Merswin is not the author of any of these mystical treatises. It now becomes difficult, if not impossible, to *prove* that he wrote, for example, *The Banner of Christ* and *The Book of the Nine Rocks,* but if he were known to Nikolaus and to others of the religious circle to be the actual author of some of these important treatises, it makes it much easier to understand how Nikolaus could have conceived his bold scheme of enlarging the scope of his friend's activity, and how he was able to deceive so successfully his contemporaries.

We shall, however, in any case be compelled to give up using any of this collection of mystical literature as genuine biographical and historical material. It is all *tendency-literature,* full of fictitious situations, and, until more light is thrown upon it, it must be treated as anonymous. It does, nevertheless, furnish us material for discovering the prevailing ideas and ideals of these mystical groups of the period, known to us as Friends of God, and I shall now endeavour to gather up the trend and characteristics of the movement.

Their religion was extremely simple and practical. They humbly claim that they "have drunk at the heavenly fountain," and have had their "inner eyes opened." They were not primarily speculative, like Eckhart, but were rather concerned with the concrete matters of actual life, though they evidently put undue emphasis on "experiences" and on visions, and they shared the tendency of the times to drift into exuberant apocalyptic fancies. But, however deep and intense their piety was, it always conformed to the medieval type rather than to the spirit of the Reformation period. Some writers have tried to find in these Friends of God Protestants before the Reformation, but a careful historical study gives little ground for such a view. Even the most spiritual of them were scrupulous in their obedience to the rules of the Church; they were the children of their age, and they were loyal to Roman Catholic ideals. Even during the terrible period of the interdict there is little indication of a revolt, though some of the Friends of God rose to the discovery that it is possible to have spiritual life without the mediation of the Church.

It was distinctly a *laymen's* movement, and there is an evident purpose in the literature of the Friends of God to exalt the ordinary lay Christian, and to show how the Church can be saved and the ministry purified by unordained persons; but these men do not show any spirit of revolt from the ancient system, they have not gained the Protestant temper, and they never dreamed of dispensing with the mediation of the Church, though they occasionally admit that spiritual life is possible without such mediation. The nearest approach to a religion purely of the Spirit is found in *The Book of the Nine Rocks,* where it is said that even Jews and pious pagans, who are hampered only by *ignorance,* will be saved at the moment of death by ways known only to the Holy Spirit. Here is the passage:

> If a Jew or Mohammedan fears God from the depth of his heart, and leads a good and simple life; if he does not know any better religion than the one in which he was born; if he is ready to obey God in case He reveals to him a better faith than his own, why should not such a man be dearer to God than wicked and impious 'Christians' who, though having received baptism, wilfully disobey the commands of God? When God finds a good Jew or Mohammedan of pure life He feels a thrill of love and infinite pity for him, no matter in what part of the earth he lives, and *God will find some way of saving him unknown to us*! If baptism cannot be conferred upon him, though he has a desire for it, *God can baptize him in the holy desire of his will,* and there are in the eternal world many good pagans who have been received in this way.[12]

One of the utterances which sounds most like a spirit of revolt came from Christina Ebner, who, beholding the miseries of the unshepherded people, cried out: "The actions of the Pope toward the clergy make groans and cries rise to heaven."

It is not possible to decide whether Tauler obeyed the interdict or not, but it is at least certain that he said in one of his powerful sermons: "While the Holy Church is able to take from us the external Sacrament, no one can take from us the spiritual joy which comes from union with God, *i.e.* inward joy from the free partaking of the body and blood of Christ."[13]

During the period of the interdict and the "Black Death," when the religious services were suspended in Strasbourg, a plan of life, ascribed to Rulman Merswin, was drawn up by which a Christian layman could dispense with the services of the priest. This proved so valuable that it was copied and spread broadcast, not only throughout the city of Strasbourg, but far beyond its limits. This "Advice" well illustrates the simple, practical, spiritual religion of the "Society." It reads as follows:—

> All those in whom the love of God, or the terror created by the terrible calamities of the present, arouses a desire to begin a new and spiritual life, will find great profit in a withdrawal into themselves every morning when they rise, to consider what they will undertake during the day. If they find in themselves any evil thought, any intention contrary to the Divine will, let them renounce it for the glory of God. Likewise, in the evening, on going to bed, let them collect themselves and consider how they have spent the day; what acts they have done, and in what spirit they have done them. If they find that they have done any good, let them

thank God and give Him the glory. If they find they have committed any sin, let them attribute the fault of it to themselves, and to nobody else, and let them show to God a deep repentance, saying to Him:

> 'Oh! Lord, be merciful to me—poor, unworthy sinner, and forgive me all the sins of this day, for I seriously repent, and I have a firm purpose henceforth with Thy help to avoid sinning.'

But, notwithstanding the fact that they often caught a glimpse of a spiritual religion far in advance of the prevailing ideals of their time, they shared for the most part the theology of their age, and in some instances they were grossly superstitious, like their unmystical countrymen.

They had not yet outgrown a naive faith in the efficacy of "holy relics." Henry of Nördlingen is one of the leading "expects" of his time in the efficacious *values* of different relics, and we frequently hear of him in some remote region, searching for the holy bone of a saint which is to work wonders among the faithful. He carries his superstitious worship to such an extreme that he even believes that there is a supernatural power in objects which have touched the body of his saintly friend, Margaret Ebner, the Friend of God, who was head of the "circle" at Medingen in Bavaria.

There is, too, an excessive love of supernatural manifestations apparent in all the literature of the movement. In the earlier stages of what they called their "commencement," the Friends of God subjected themselves to terrible bodily tortures, self-inflicted, often of the most ingenious sort, and they generally emerged from this aberration with enfeebled constitutions and wrecked nervous systems. Certain typical "experiences" were expected, and sooner or later they generally occurred. The stress and strain of the troublous epoch produced a mental type of person easily affected by suggestion, and thus the ideas and experiences of the leaders spread in this responsive material. We find in the literature of the movement accounts of almost every known form of *psychic experience.* There are accounts of hallucinations of every sense—sight, touch, smell, taste, and hearing. I give one instance from the *Imprisoned Knight.* This knight had been taken prisoner, and was thrust into a dungeon under a tower, where, loaded with chains, he had passed six months. Feeling himself about to die, he wished to take communion, but his request was harshly denied. At midnight he saw a "radiant light," and heard a voice saying that the mother of God had come to his aid. "She has prayed her Son," the voice continued, "to divide between the chaplain of the castle and thee the wafer which will be used to-morrow in the consecration of the Mass. The wafer will be divided into two parts, but the Lord will be entirely present without division in both parts." The next morning the knight *saw,* surrounded with a dazzling light, a half water enter his prison! It went directly into his mouth, and at once revived his strength, so that for the entire day he took none of the food which was brought to him. This miracle was repeated for six consecutive days, and after the first day the jailer also saw both the light and the wafer.[14] Reports of collective hallucination are frequent in the literature of the "Society." Christina Ebner, head of the circle at Engelthal, in Bavaria, many times heard the Divine Voice say that Tauler was of all men the one whom God most loved. She also was *told* that there were two names written in heaven—those of John Tauler and Henry of Nördlingen. The voice said that God dwelt in Tauler like melodious music. The members of the group were *telepathic* and often felt what was happening to some other Friend of God far away.

They all looked upon the state of ecstasy as a supreme divine favour. In these moments of "unspeakable ecstasy" they believed that God was talking with them face to face, and the uprushes of intimation which came at such times were counted as veritable "revelations" from the Holy Spirit. These revelations were considered by them as authoritative as the Holy Scriptures. Henry of Nördlingen calls the revelations which come through Margaret Ebner "a holy scripture." He allows the Friends of God in Basle to have communion during the interdict, and he explains in a letter that he granted the privilege to the *spiritual circle* on the strength of a personal revelation given to Margaret Ebner. In an ecstasy, Margaret was called into the presence of the Saviour Himself, and in tender love He invited her to take His holy body, and Henry adds: "I dare not oppose myself to Thee." In the *Book of the Master of Holy Scripture,* "the Friend of God," speaking as an oracle of the Holy Spirit, says to the Master: "If you are to receive the words I speak as though they come from *me,* I shall say no more to you." Their writings everywhere imply or assert that God speaks through them in the same way that He spoke through "His Friends in the Old and New Testament"; in both dispensations the "counsel" of a Friend of God is "the counsel of God Himself."

They never question the authority of the Scriptures, nor undervalue their teaching; in fact, they were in no other respect so like the Protestants of the sixteenth century as in their devotion to the Bible—but at the same time they insisted on the reality of present inspiration and continuous revelation. Those who receive "the luminous grace of the Holy Spirit" are granted immediate revelations bearing upon both inner experience and outer events. They talk of two stages of truth. To the *lower stage* belong the interpretations of Scripture which the learned doctors of the Church give. It is their function to tell what has been revealed in past ages. The higher stage is the truth of immediate revelation. "God has a few whom He whispers in the ear!" They have the privilege of being the bearers of a first-hand word from Him. "They hear," as one of them says, "in their own souls what they are to speak." This stage they call "the upper school of the Holy Spirit." This distinction between the "lower school" of those who have only "knowledge about" and the "higher school" of those who have also "knowledge of experience" is well illustrated by a passage from the *Book of the Two Men.*

> If two men gave thee a description of the city of Rome, one by mere hearsay, and the other by experience after he had been there, thou wouldst give thy attention

mainly to the second. So also, if a man who has been touched inwardly by divine grace hears the preaching of a doctor who still loves himself, he feels that the preaching of such a doctor does not come from pure and unadulterated love of God. The soul that is filled with divine love is not touched by such a sermon. Such a preacher is speaking only by hearsay of the heavenly Rome, and of the roads which lead to it. He knows only what he has learned from Scripture. But if the same man hears the preaching of a master who knows both from Scripture and through his own spiritual experience, a master who has renounced all self-love and self-advantage, who knows the heavenly Rome, not only by hearsay, but because he has travelled the road to it, and because he has seen the form of its buildings, he rejoices to hear his message, because it proceeds from the Divine Love itself.

Those who have had this first-hand experience, and belong to this "upper school of the Holy Spirit," are the true teachers and guides of the rest.[15] For this reason the Friends of God insisted, as a matter of first importance, that all who were in the stage of "preparation" should submit themselves entirely to the counsel and direction of some holy man of the "Society."

By far the most famous account of submission and direction is that recorded in the *Book of the Master.* This book relates that in 1346 there was "a great doctor, a master of Holy Scripture," who preached in a certain city, and multitudes flocked to hear him—"his preaching was talked about for miles around." "A certain *layman,* a man full of divine grace, the beloved Friend of God from the Oberland, came by command of God" ten days' journey, and heard five sermons by the master. He perceived that the "master," though "a man of good heart," was "still in the dark and without the full light of grace." At the end of the fifth sermon the "Friend of God" asked "the doctor" if he would preach a sermon on "The way to attain the highest degree of spiritual life." The preacher demurred for a time on the ground that the layman could not understand it if he should preach it, as it would be beyond his experience and comprehension. He, however, finally assented and preached the sermon. In this sermon the great preacher pointed out, in mystical fashion, that the highest state of spiritual life is found in an experience beyond "intellectual comprehension," beyond ideas and images. Quoting from Dionysius, he says that the light of faith takes man above the sphere of intellectual conceptions. The perfect man must rise above everything sensible and intellectual, must empty himself of all content, and then God will come in and dwell in him. He must absolutely renounce self, selfwill, self-love, and the pursuit of all personal advantage either in this world or in the next.

After a day of consideration the "Friend of God" came back to the preacher and passed severe criticism on the sermon and on the preacher himself. He told him that he was preaching what he had not yet experienced, and even went to the length of calling "the doctor" a Pharisee, and an imitator of the work of the Pharisees. The preacher showed great offence at this freedom on the part of a mere layman, but as the layman went on to reveal the height and depth of his own spiritual experience, the master of Holy Scripture perceived that he was in the presence of one who had attained something which he himself had not at all reached, and in great humility he asked the layman how he had gained such a degree of spiritual experience. The layman answered that God had brought him into complete humility and abandonment of self, and so had taught him directly by the Holy Spirit. "The Holy Spirit," he says, "has the same power to-day as ever. He is as able to speak through me, a poor sinner, as He did through the mouth of the sinner Caiaphas. In truth, if you think that these words which I speak come through me, I will not speak another word to you."

Under this criticism and instruction, the preacher, seeing his own inner poverty revealed, asks how he can begin for himself a new course of life so as to attain to the highest degree of spiritual life, saying that even if he must die for it he will follow "the counsel." Thereupon, the layman gives him first of all the A B C of religion to study, which was a series of twenty-three sentences bearing upon the rudiments of religious experience. At the end of six weeks he set before "the great doctor" the conditions upon which he can advance to a higher life. He is to go into his cell, and separate himself from all his old life and occupations. He is to say Mass every day, and spend the rest of the day in solitary meditation, comparing his life with that of the Saviour, and thinking of what he has lost by self-love, until he shall arrive to complete humility. He is told that he will be called a fool, will lose his best friends, and will be the laughing-stock of all his companions, but this will be to him a blessing, for it will bring him to the point of having confidence in none but God Himself.

For two years "the doctor" underwent a life of this rigid regime, exposed to ridicule and scorn, and then there came upon him a wonderful experience. He lost all consciousness, and was carried he knew not whither. When at last he awoke and came to himself, he felt new forces throughout his whole being, and immeasurable joy filled him, such as he had never known before. His mind was illuminated with a light from above.

On hearing of this experience the layman said to him: "Thou hast been touched by God with spiritual knowledge, in the very highest part of thy soul, and now," he adds, "thou wilt have the Holy Spirit added to thy knowledge of Scripture, and one of thy sermons will do more good than a hundred of thy former discourses did."

Before leaving him the "Friend of God" told him that henceforth he must live in the Spirit, and not in the letter which kills. Instead of wasting his time in the study of the letter of holy books and writings of great doctors, he should penetrate to the spirit and the wisdom which the books contain. Many of the passages, he says, which formerly seemed obscure and contradictory, will now become clear. "You will discover that all Scripture is one, and now you may commence again to preach and instruct

your fellows; henceforth your words will come from a pure vessel, and will be received with joy by all who love the Lord. I shall give you no more instruction. It is now for you to instruct me, and I shall stay until I have heard many of your sermons. As much as you have been scorned, so much you will now be esteemed by those about you. Continue in humility, and do not lose what you have gained."

The master announced that in three days he would preach to the people. A crowd gathered, and he began his sermon, but was overcome with emotion, and found it impossible to speak. The news spread rapidly that the master had failed to meet their expectation, and more than ever he was the laughing-stock of the people, and it was even believed that he had lost his mind. Once again he gained permission to attempt a sermon, and this time he preached with great power on the text, "Behold the Bridegroom cometh, go ye out to meet Him." With extraordinary power he worked out the allegory of the Lord coming to meet His bride. Suddenly one of the listeners cried: "It is true," and fell to the ground in a swoon. When the sermon was over, fully forty persons lay on the floor incapable of movement. From this time to his death, nine years later, "the master" increased in power and reputation. He fearlessly attacked the evils and corruptions of the Church, leaving no class of the clergy untouched by his vigorous criticism, and though the offended monks made a strenuous effort to stop him from preaching, the common people of the city implicitly trusted him and obeyed him, so that he enjoyed almost unlimited influence, and was consulted on all the affairs of Church and city.

This book has for centuries been taken as actual history, and "the master of Holy Scripture" has generally been identified with John Tauler. The identification with Tauler, however, rests wholly on tradition. In his searching critical study of this episode, Denifle first showed what slender historical basis there is for the Tauler tradition.[16] The question has been hotly debated since the appearance of Denifle's investigation, and good scholars like Karl Schmidt and Preger and Jundt continued to stand by the historicity of the *Book of the Master of Holy Scripture*, and to see in it an important chapter in the life of the famous Strasbourg preacher.[17] The historical view has, however, lost ground, and is untenable.

The *Book of the Master of Holy Scripture* is in the main fictitious—a piece of tendency-literature, written to set forth a special religious truth. The central idea embodied in the book is the extraordinary influence of a holy layman when he has been illuminated by the Divine Spirit. He is able to become the infallible counsellor to the greatest preacher in the country, and his instruction is sufficient to bring "the master" from his stage of mere head-knowledge to the stage of first-hand spiritual experience, so that he can rise to a wholly new level of power. It is a telling, concrete illustration of the ruling idea of the Friends of God that a divinely-instructed layman, who has attained the highest stage of mystical experience, "speaks in the place of God," and has an apostolic authority which puts him above any priest or doctor who has only the authority of ordination or of scholarship. For a comprehension of the views of the Friends of God this book is most important, but it must not be treated as furnishing the account of an historical event in the life of Tauler.

II

There is a powerful apocalyptic strain in all the literature of the Friends of God. In this particular they show a close affiliation and relationship with the German prophetesses, St. Hildegarde, St. Elizabeth of Schoenau, and St. Matilda of Magdeburg, who were granted "visions" of the corrupt condition of Christianity and of the speedy judgments of God.

> "The Church has lost its state of purity," cries St. Hildegarde; "its crown is tarnished by schism and heresy. Its servants, its priests, who ought to make its face shine like the morning and its garment like the light, have by their simony, their avarice, their dissolute morals, covered its face with dirt and soiled and rent its garments. Their wickedness is as habitual as if it were commanded; they enjoy sin as the worm does earth. Deaf and dumb, they no longer hear the Scriptures, and they no longer teach others. All classes of Christianity are corrupt. The Church no longer has any staff to sustain it. All its commandments are ready to disappear; each one takes his own will for rule."

St. Elizabeth of Schoenau speaks with the boldness of a Hebrew prophet:

> Cry with a loud voice! cry to all the nations! Woe, for the whole world is covered with darkness. The vineyard of the Lord has perished; there is no one to cultivate it. The Lord has sent labourers into it, but they have all proved idle. The head of the Church is sick, and its members are dead. Each one wishes to govern himself, and to live according to his own caprice. Very rare are those in the Church who follow the commands of the Lord. But I swear by My right hand and by My throne, says the Eternal One, this condition shall not continue. To all you who are in authority on the earth—kings, princes, bishops, abbots, priests—I order you to purify My Church, otherwise you will be smitten with the sword of My mouth. Miserable hypocrites, you appear religious and innocent in the eyes of men, but inwardly you are full of the spirit of wickedness. Shepherds of My Church, you are asleep, but I will wake you.

In similar strain, Matilda of Magdeburg takes up her prophecy:

> Oh, holy Christianity, glorious crown, how thy splendour has vanished! Thy precious stones are fallen, thy gold is tarnished by impurities. Oh, bride of God, thy face once so pure and chaste is blackened by the fire of guilty passions; on thy lips are lies and hypocrisy; the flowers of thy virtues are faded! Oh, holy clergy, shining crown, how thy glory is dimmed; thy beauty is gone; thy strength is weakened; thy ruin comes on! He who is ignorant of the road to hell has only to watch

the debauched and corrupted clergy! The road they follow leads straight into it! Therefore God has decided to humiliate them. His vengeance will break upon them in a day when they do not expect it.[18]

The fallen condition of Christianity is constantly on the lips of the prophets of the movement we are now studying, and they paint its future in very sombre colours. The apocalyptic element is not wild and excessive, but they all announce that the Church is far out of the way, that Christianity is sadly sunk in the ways of the world, and that Divine judgment is fast approaching. As the woes and disturbances of the period increased, especially in the middle decade of the fourteenth century, the sombre tone of apocalyptic prophecy increased in the writings of the Friends of God. They have "revelations" that the evil condition is to go on from bad to worse, until God will be compelled to chastise Christendom with pestilence, earthquake, famine, divisions, wars, and heresies, and that many will lose both body and soul in this time of testing.

In 1356 a catastrophic earthquake, already mentioned, occurred throughout the Rhine valley, with its most disastrous central point at Basle; the city was turned into a heap of ruins, and a terrible fear struck all hearts, the echo of which appears in all the mystical writings of the time. The mystical prophets saw in this awful catastrophe warning signs of the approaching end of the world, and of a reconstruction of the universe.[19] "God," they say, "is about to winnow the whole of Christendom, and those only who bear the seal of God on their foreheads will be preserved through these calamities."[20]

Through the tribulations of the present age they see signs of the coming of new heavens and new earth, and they declare that out of the "saints of the earth" God will select for blessedness an equal number with that of the fallen angels, so that the population of the new heaven will be the same as the population of the primitive celestial city before there was a fall!

Even Tauler, in the sermons of this period, occasionally speaks in apocalyptic imagery. In one of his sermons he says:

> It is written in the Apocalypse that calamities, hardly less terrible than the last judgment, will come upon the earth. The time which according to the prophecy, is to pass before these calamities, is now fulfilled. We expect their appearance every year, every day, every moment, and nobody who is not sealed with the Divine seal can come through them and endure.

The writings ascribed to Rulman Merswin and to "the Friend of God from the Oberland" tell how they, after having passed through terrible suffering and temptations in the various stages of their conversion, are promised that henceforth they will have *"no other trials to pass through, except to see the evil state of Christianity—that will be their cross."* In the book entitled *Revelation Addressed to the Friend of God from the Oberland during Christmas*

Night, at the time when great and terrible earthquakes oc-curred,[21] the writer sees the end drawing near, and he tells how he experiences in his own body the sufferings which are due for the sins of the Church. He hears Divine Mercy tell Divine Wisdom to forbid the Friends of God to intercede any longer for the wicked world, and thereupon he addresses *a last warning.* As has happened so often before and since, the event miscarried, and the Divine judgment was postponed! But, as new "signs" appeared (desolations of war in 1375; the papal schism in 1378; Christianity divided into hostile camps), again the fatal moment seemed near, and there were new prophecies of impending doom uttered. The Friends of God, under the inspiration of Merswin, again intercede for the world, and as "God could not remain deaf to the prayers of His Friends," a "suspension" of judgment was granted. This extraordinary spiritual drama, with God, on the one hand, holding the doom of the world in His hand, and the Friends of God keeping back the phials wrath by their prayers, goes on for years, until there comes a final command to pray no more for Christianity.[22]

One of the greatest mystical apocalypses of the middle ages is the *Book of the Nine Rocks*—and it may, I think, be called the greatest literary creation of the Friends of God. It is the best illustration there is of the ideas current among these mystical Christians on the state of Christianity and on the expected "tempest of God," and it is also the best account we have of the "stages" of spiritual experience by which the soul rises to its goal. The book contains a series of "visions" which the author of it *saw* about 1351. He was commanded to write them down. He long resisted the command, saying: "Are there not books enough by great doctors, who can write much better than I can?" and protesting that his book "will carry no conviction, because it is not proved by the Scriptures." The Divine Voice answered: "Without doubt the Scriptures came from the Holy Spirit, but why cannot God still write such a book? Thou art not the first person through whom the waters of Divine Grace have come. Is not the power of God the same as in Scripture times? Whoever does not believe that God can work His wonderful works through His 'Friends' to-day, as He did in the times of the Old and New Testament, *that man is not a Christian, for he does not believe that the Divine power remains the same throughout the centuries.*" "I will obey," cries the author; "thou hast uttered the truth through Caiaphas; speak as thou wilt through me, poor sinner."[23]

The theme of the early part of the book is the terrible decadence of Christianity as compared with the pristine glory of the primitive Church. In a series of stern judgments the various orders of Christianity are passed in review and condemned. For example, here is the "vision" of the state of the papacy:

> Open thy eyes and see how popes live to-day! All respect for the commandments of religion is extinct in them. They are ambitious for worldly goods; more zealous for their own honour than for that of God; they think only of *places* for their relatives and friends.

Once popes chose awful deaths before they would swerve for an instant from the will of God. Now no pope for a long time has been sainted.

After seeing doleful "visions" of the ecclesiastics of the Church from the top down, he is told that "God has now conferred His grace on *other men* [these are, of course, Friends of God], whom He has richly endowed with spiritual gifts. These men are, alas! few in number, but if they wholly disappeared from the world, Christianity would utterly come to an end."[24]

In the second part of the book is described the *vision* of the nine rocks. The writer *sees* an immense net which covers the entire earth, except one mountain in which nine great platforms in ascending stages are cut in rock. These nine platform-ledges rise like the stages of Dante's Purgatory from the level plain, where stands a terrible figure, stretching his net over men and catching them in it. The seer opens his eyes and sees men running away from the net and beginning to climb the mountain. Those on the *first rock* receive the colour of health, and, by sincere confession, are delivered from the mortal sins with which their hearts were stained. But, unfortunately, persons keep falling off this rock back into the net again.

On the *second rock* are those who have made a solid resolution to give up their own will, and to submit to an illuminated Friend of God, who shall be their guide and counsellor in the place of God. The *third rock* is the abode of those who are practising severe mortifications of the body, and are doing it for the purpose of gaining heaven. They are still in the state of a religion of self-interest. Those on the *fourth rock* are still practising self-mortification, but have the purpose of doing it solely to please and glorify God. Unfortunately, they are still animated by self-will, and have themselves chosen mortification without discovering the Divine will for them. The dwellers on the *fifth rock* have entered upon the sacrifice of their own will, though they have not yet attained to a complete and final *death* to self-will and self-pleasing. Those on the *sixth rock* have completed the sacrifice begun on the rock below. They have burned their bridges, and have entirely abandoned themselves to their Lord. Their only imperfection is that they desire the supernatural revelations which they see others enjoy. Those who have reached the *seventh rock* have got beyond this desire for supernatural revelations, but they take an excessive joy in such revelations when they are granted to them. Those on the *eighth rock* have nearly conquered the enjoyment of anything that concerns self. They have renounced earthly possessions except to use them for God; they have given up counting on heaven. They are ready to accept what God gives them, both in time and in eternity. Their only imperfection is that they not attained the state where they can have perfect peace, even when God hides His face from them and leaves them no tokens of His grace.

The *ninth rock* is the top of the mountain. The number of the denizens on each rock decreases as the stages go up, until finally on this summit there are only three dwellers to be seen. In them, all personal desire is destroyed. They are crucified to the world, and the world to them. They enjoy whatever God does. They have attained an absolutely disinterested state. They seek no "signs"; they wish for no "manifestations." They have lost all fear. They have arrived at the full stature of a man, and they love all men in God with an equal love. Here on the top is granted the supreme experience, dimly felt sometimes on the lower levels, *the experience of beholding the Divine Origin.* "The man," the voice says, "who beholds the Divine Origin, loses his own name and no longer bears an earthly name. He has now become God by grace, as God is God by nature!"

There comes at last to the writer of the book himself this supreme vision of the Divine Origin, and when the indescribable glory passes he hears a voice saying: "Thou hast been in the upper school where the Holy Spirit teaches directly within the man himself. This august Master of the school has taken thy soul and filled it with such an overflowing love that it has flooded even thy body and transfigured it." "My beloved!" cries the man in a transport of Divine love, "thou hast become so dear to me that with all thy power thou couldst not do anything that would be disagreeable to me. Do toward me whatever thou wilt; whatever thou givest, whatever thou takest away, I shall rejoice in it."

Here we have drawn for us by a leader of the movement the ideal Friend of God.

It has already become apparent that the Friends of God put a heavy stress on *renunciation.* They often pushed it to the extreme of annihilation of will altogether. "The true Christian who wishes to follow the mystical life," says the "Friend of God," in the *Book of the Two Men,* "must renounce all self-pleasure and all self-will; he must destroy all will that aims at anything for self; he must give up all selfish joys and *all self-imposed sufferings.* He must be wholly directed by God, ready to receive from Him with equal submission either pain or joy, temptation or ecstasy, sickness or health."

There is an extraordinary case of a Friend of God who got to the indifference-point to such a degree that he, "through the power of love, became without love," and in this state of perfect surrender, he heard a voice say to him: "Permit Me, My beloved child, to share in thee and with thee all the riches of My divinity; all the passionate love of My humanity; all the joys of the Holy Spirit," and the "Friend of God" replied: "Yes, Lord, I permit Thee, on condition that Thou alone shalt enjoy it, and not I!"

There is also the case of Ellina of Crevelsheim, called the "Holy child of God," who, in an ecstasy of the marvellous love of God, remains seven years without uttering a word, and at the end of this period God touched her with His hand, so that she fell into an ecstasy which lasted five days, and in this ecstasy the *pure truth* was revealed to

her, and she was given the privilege of entering the holy interior of the Father's heart. She was raised to an experience of God and the Supreme Unity; she was bound with the chains of love; enveloped in light; filled with peace and joy; her soul carried above all earthly sufferings; and she attained a complete submission to the will of Christ, whatever it might be.[25]

Throughout this literature the ideal Friend of God endeavours to hide his life, to be anonymous, to efface himself by becoming "a captive of the Lord," "a hidden child of God." There was in this tendency much that was morbid and misdirected. It was often a waste of noble powers, and often a mock humility. The strained introspection of inward spiritual states; the constant analysis of themselves to see whether they had "a disinterested love of God"; whether they were "ready to go through the eternal sufferings and pains of hell for the love of God"; whether they had reached a complete annihilation of will—all this is unhealthy enough, as we now know. But we must judge men in the light of their age, and when we do that we must pronounce these Friends of God the noblest representatives of popular mystical religion in the middle ages. The best of them attained to an *unconscious* holiness, *"shining within like angels of light, without knowing that they were shining."* "Dost thou not know," says the heavenly voice to one of these Friends of God, "that thy earthly marrow and blood have been consumed, and that thou hast received a new blood of perfect purity?" "No, I know nothing of it," answers the unconscious saint. "That is precisely it," replied the heavenly voice; "thou hast forgotten it, and it is just this forgetfulness of self that makes the willing, glowing, Divine love come to birth in thee and possess thee!"[26]

Then, when we remember that these men bore their sufferings and strove to annihilate self-will, and even accepted the hiding of all self "as captives of God," in order to be vicarious offerings on behalf of the corrupt Christianity of their time, we find a touch of real sublimity in their saintly lives which does much to atone for their errors of judgment.

Tauler gives this touching incident in one of his sermons:

> One day the Lord offered to kiss a Friend of God with a kiss of divine love. The Friend replied: 'I do not want to have it, for the joy of it would flood my heart so that I should lose consciousness, and *then I could no longer serve thee!*'[27]

They succeeded as well as any mystics have done in avoiding the *pitfalls* of perfectionism. They taught, no doubt, that a man may attain even here below to a life with God, may even become through grace what God is by nature, may achieve perfect peace, may come into the very presence of the Divine Origin. Tauler says that "the Divine and heavenly man enters by God's grace even in this present life into life eternal. He already has one foot in Heaven. He lives attached to his Origin, and God can no more abandon him than He can abandon Himself. The heavenly life has begun in such a man, and will go on for ever." But they held that, with all his attainments, it always remains possible for a man to fall away into sin. Until the end he may never intermit his vigils and watchfulness. Tauler says that the evil basis of our human nature is never completely annihilated in this earthly life. To the very end—on the highest heights of spiritual experience—these Friends of God are examples of humility; they still speak of themselves as "poor sinners"—"poor unworthy creatures." The "Friend of God from the Oberland" teaches his friends these prayers, which are good for all stages and steps of the spiritual ladder:

> In the morning say, 'Oh Lord, I wish, for the love of Thee, to keep from all sin to-day. Help me this day to do all I do to Thy glory and according to Thy dear will, whether my *nature* likes it or not'; and in the evening say, 'Oh Lord, I am a great sinner, a poor and unworthy creature. Be merciful to me and forgive me to-day all my sins, for I repent of them, and sincerely wish by Thy help to commit no more.'

They do not teach a fixed and final *state* of perfection. There is no "Olympian calm" where progress ends. To *stop* on the "road of perfection" is to *go back,* as one of their wise men says. The "spiritual ladder" in reality has no last round on which the completed saint may sit in moveless felicity! *The Book of the Five Men* urges its readers to expect no gifts of grace from the Holy Spirit if they are living in the "holy inactivity" of absolute quietism.

There can be no question that these Friends of God took themselves very seriously, and thought themselves to be the spiritual "remnant" that was to save Christianity from the utter wreck into which they believed it to be drifting—they were in their own estimation the true Church of God within the visible Church. "If a Friend of God," says the *Book of the Nine Rocks,* "were put at the head of Christianity, he could transform it, because he would have the counsel of the Holy Spirit. If any city in the world would submit to the direction of a holy Friend of God, it would be saved from the woes and plagues that are falling on the world." John Tauler fully shared this view, and in many of his sermons he puts the highest estimate on their spiritual service. Here are a few examples:

> Those whom God has drawn into the unity of the Godhead are the persons on whom the Church rests. They are divine, supernatural men, and they hold up the world and the pillars of it: *If they were not in Christendom it would not last an hour.*"[28]

> Without the help of the Friends of God, God could give no blessing to sinners, for His justice demands satisfaction, and here is precisely the service of the Friends of God—they intercede in favour of Christendom, and their prayer is heard.[29]

> In case of need, these men (the Friends of God) could govern the country, by the help of the Divine gift and the light of eternal wisdom with which their souls are filled.[30]

> Get the Friends of god to help you return into the Divine Origin, where the true light shines. Attach yourself to those who are attached to God—for they can take you with them to Him.[31]

> If it were not for the Friends of God—who are in the world—we should indeed be badly off.[32]

III

I have already referred often to John Tauler, and have frequently quoted from his sermons to illustrate principles and tendencies of the Friends of God. I must now bring together the most important characteristics of his teaching, for he was one of the purest and noblest leaders of this religious movement, and, with all his imperfections, one of the best exponents of spiritual religion in his century. He was undoubtedly regarded by the Friends of God themselves as their greatest man, and he was best loved by the people because his sermons helped them most to find the door of hope and comfort and joy. Tauler "is passing through deep suffering," writes Henry of Nördlingen in 1347, "because he is teaching *the whole truth* as nobody else teaches it, and furthermore his whole life conforms to it."[33]

There is very little to tell of his outward life. He was born in Strasbourg, about 1300. In his early youth he entered a Dominican convent, and after the proper steps of training he was ordained a priest in that Order. He had already come under the powerful influence of Meister Eckhart, and was deeply versed in the writings of the great Christian mystics, who were always his most intimate outward guides. In 1338-39 he was in the city of Basle, where he was the central figure of a mystical group of Friends of God. His friend, Henry of Nördlingen, writes that "God is daily working a great and marvellous work, through Tauler, in the hearts of men at Basle."

It is a much-debated question whether Tauler obeyed the interdict, or whether he continued in defiance of it to perform religious services for the people. It has been the delight of Protestant writers to show Tauler as a fearless reformer before the Reformation, defying the Pope, claiming a direct authority from the Holy Spirit, and to represent him as speaking words which have the ring of Luther's spirit in them.[34] There are, however, no *well-authenticated facts* to support this position. It is more than probable that he obeyed the interdict. These words, from one of his sermons, at least do not indicate that he would be likely to lead a revolt from the authority of his Church:

> I received the privilege of belonging to my Order from the grace of God and from the holy Church. It is from both that I have this hat, this coat, my dignity as priest, my right to preach and to hear confession. If the Pope and the holy Church, from whom I have received these privileges, wish to take them from me, I ought to obey them without reply; to put on another coat if I have one; leave the convent; cease to be a priest, and stop preaching and hearing confession. I should have no right to ask the wherefore of such a decision. . . . If

the holy Church wishes to deprive us of the external sacrament, we must submit. *But nobody can take from us the privilege of taking the sacrament spiritually (Aber geistlich zuo nemende, das mag uns nieman genemmen)*, although everything which the Church has given us it can take from us, and we ought to obey without a murmur.[35]

If he *did* obey the order of the Pope as a faithful churchman of his time, he rose far above a merely external religion which could be given or taken away at the caprice of a pope, and he found the secret of eternal religion in a direct spiritual intercourse with the Saviour; and, moved with tender sympathy for the common people, he tried to turn them to spiritual religion. The importance of this inwardness and directness of religion comes out again in another sermon, where he says: "Great doctors of Paris read ponderous books and turn over many pages. *The Friends of God read the living Book where everything is life*"[36], and he tells us that one of the greatest Friends of God he had ever known was a simple day labourer, a cobbler, who had no magic of ordination and no wisdom of scholarship.

I have already discussed the question of the historicity of the narrative which records the conversion and discipline of "the master of Holy Scripture," by "the Friend of God from the Oberland." I am convinced that this cannot be used as material for the life of Tauler. This conclusion takes away a most dramatic incident from his biography, and we are left with very little material indeed with which to draw the figure of the popular preacher of Strasbourg, who did a great work there six hundred years ago. We only know that from 1340, until his death in 1361, he comforted multitudes of souls with as pure an evangel as his century heard, and he showed many devout spirits the inward, secret way to the Father of Light and Love.

Tauler, like all true mystics, insists on the fact of an *inner Light*—the master light of all the soul's seeing. He says that the Friends of God have "an inward, divine knowledge, a Divine Light which illuminates them and raises them into union with God." "God illumines His true Friends," again he says, "and shines within them with power, purity, and truth, so that such men become divine and supernatural persons."[37] Again: "This Light gives man *all truth (alle warheit)*—a wonderful discernment, more perfect than can be gained in any other manner here below." "These divine men" [the Friends of God], Tauler says in another sermon, "enjoy an enlightened understanding."[38] When they have been disciplined by temptations, they possess the gift of discerning spirits; by merely looking at their neighbour they can tell his inward state; they know whether he belongs to God or not, and what hinders him from spiritual progress.[39] "The vision of the eternal Light makes their souls so luminous that they could teach all men if the occasion for it came."[40] "They become endowed [by this Divine Light] with a perfect conscience in respect to what they ought to do and what leave undone."[41] "They gain [from their inner illumination] an inward peace and joy in the Holy Spirit."[42] "The Divine illumination gives a man a

marvellous discernment, more perfect than he is able to acquire on earth in any other manner."[43] In his sermon "On the Feast of St. Mary Magdalene," he says: "In one short hour you can learn more from the inward voice than you could learn from man in a thousand years."

None of these passages indicate that Tauler believed that this illumination belonged to man as man—he is here speaking of the "gifts" which belong to a special class of men, whom he calls "divine and supernatural men."[44] He does, however, sometimes speak in his sermons of "the uncreated ground of the soul"; "the apex of the soul"; "the kingdom of God in the innermost recesses of the spirit"; "the unseen depths of the spirit, where lies the image of God," as though there were something of God in the very structure of the soul, unlost by the fall, or the sin, or the stupidity of man. This is vigorously said in a striking sentence from Tauler: "As a sculptor is said to have exclaimed on seeing a rude block of marble, 'What a god-like beauty thou hidest!' so God looks upon man *in whom His own* image is hidden." But this "Divine soul centre" does not become an operative power, *a dynamic possession,* until "the outward man is converted into this inward, reasonable [intelligible] man, and the two are gathered up into the very centre of the man's being—the unseen depths of his spirit, where the image of God dwelleth—and thus he flings himself into the Divine Abyss in which he dwelt eternally before he was created; then when God finds the man thus solidly grounded and turned towards Him, the Godhead bends and nakedly descends into the depths of the pure, waiting soul, drawing it up into the uncreated essence, so that the spirit becomes one with Him."[45]

He is much less speculative than his master, Eckhart. In the language of simple experience he tells his listeners that "there is nothing so near the inmost heart of man as God," but he can also on occasion use the language of speculation, and talk with his great mystical teacher of "the Hidden God"—"the calm waste of the Godhead"; "the necessity of withdrawing into the bosom of the Divine Dark." There are passages in his sermons where, by the road of negation, he takes us up to the same empty abstraction which we have so often found in speculative mysticism.

> "God is," he says in his *Third Instruction,* "a pure Being [that is, a Being with no attributes], a waste of calm seclusion—as Isaiah says, He is a hidden God—He is much nearer than anything is to itself in the depth of the heart, but He is hidden from all our senses. He is far above every outward thing and every thought, and is found only *where thou hidest thyself in the secret place of thy heart,* in the quiet solitude where no word is spoken, where is neither creature nor image nor fancy. This is the quiet Desert of the Godhead, the Divine Darkness—dark from His own surpassing brightness, as the shining of the sun is darkness to weak eyes, for in the presence of its brightness our eyes are like the eyes of the swallow in the bright sunlight—this Abyss is our salvation!"

In harmony with this conception of a God *above* all attributes and distinctions, he makes much of the *negative road* to Him, *i.e.* the way of self-dying and renunciation. There are three stages of self-dying.[46]

The first stage is found in those who practise acts of self-denial through fear of hell and for the hope of heaven. At this "half-way stage" they believe that what is painful to the flesh is highly prized by God. The person at this stage is self-centred, unloving, harsh in judgment; what he does is from constraint of fear rather than from love.

The second stage of self-death is found in the person who endures insult, contempt, and such-like depths; who learns in humility and patience to pass through spiritual destitution, and to be bereft even of the gracious sense of the Divine Presence. These "barren seasons" are for discipline to bring the man by inward poverty to a dissatisfaction with himself and to carry him to a state where he shall cease to be occupied with himself. The third stage is one of perfect union of the human will with the Divine will—entire resignation and perfect denial of self and self-love. All delight in having one's own will is overmastered and quenched, because the Holy Spirit has supplanted the man's will and love, and he wills nothing on his own account—though he cannot fathom the Abyss of God, he feels perfect joy in the *experience of God.*

In another sermon,[47] Tauler says that those who wish to be Friends of God *must rid themselves of all that pertains to the "creature";* must especially free themselves from all that is called "necessary"; must avoid being blinded by "transitory things," and look alone to the source and Origin. "Divine Love can brook no rival," therefore all unnecessary conversation, all outward delight in human beings, all images external and internal that merely please the natural man, must be cut off so that God can work His work freely—even external works of love may blind us and prevent us from perceiving the Divine Voice. "We shall never find God anywhere so perfectly, so fruitfully, and so truly as in retirement and in the wilderness." In a beautiful sermon on the temple within man,[48] he points out that as man is meant to be a temple—"a clean, pure house of prayer"—he must first drive out all "traders," *i.e.* all human fancies and imaginations; all delight in the creature and all self-willing thoughts of pleasure, aims at self-gratification, ideas of temporal things. These are the "traders" that keep God out of His house.

But Tauler does not stop with negations, and he does not make the attainment of a state of "barren wilderness" his spiritual terminus. In this same sermon he goes on to say that after the inner mind has become "free of traders," there must come a *positive devotion* of spirit, an inner *consecration* of self toward the attainment of union and communion of the man with God; and finally there comes the experience—again a positive experience—that the soul in its inmost deeps actually is a temple where God eternally reveals "His Father Heart" and begets His Son, "a temple where is the true, pure presence of God, in whom all things live and move, and where all suffering is done away!" But even this life in the inner temple is not wholly an end in itself. We cannot expect a devout Catholic of the fourteenth century to enter fully into the spirit of service, which is the very breath of our best modern Christianity, but Tauler often rises to an insight which carries him far beyond contemplation and joy in inward states, however exalted. "Works of love," he says, "are more acceptable than contemplation"; "spiritual enjoyments are the food of the soul, but they are to be taken only for nourishment and support *to help us in our active work*"; "sloth often makes men eager to get free from work and set to contemplation, but *no virtue is to be trusted until it has been put into practice*"[49] One of the finest passages in his sermons—in fact, one of the finest words that any mystic has given us—is the well-known and often-quoted passage, which has the true note of social service:

> One man can spin, another can make shoes, and *all these are gifts of the Holy Ghost.* I tell you, if I were not a priest, I should esteem it a great gift that I was able to make shoes, and I would try to make them so well as to be a pattern to all.

The most important feature of Tauler's teaching—a feature which allies him with all the great prophets of the soul—is his constant insistence on *a religion of experience.* There are long passages in his sermons which are too scholastic to be of any permanent value; there are other passages which are too much bound up with the conceptions of the medieval Church to touch our lives to-day; there are still other passages—even whole sermons—which are commonplace and devoid of inspiration, but again and again the reader finds in the writings of this pre-Reformation prophet words which are laden with a living message, good for all men, and quick and powerful for any century. "The man who truly experiences the pure presence of God in his own soul," he tells his "dear children,"[50] "knows well that there can be no doubt about it"—by "devout prayer and the uplifting of the mind to God" there is "an entrance into union of the created spirit with the uncreated Spirit of God," so that all the human is "poured forth into God and becomes *one spirit* with Him." But this knowledge is not something to be learned from "the Masters of Paris"; it can come only through *experience* of "entering in and dwelling in the Inner Kingdom of God, where pure truth and the sweetness of God are found." "What this is and how it comes to pass is easier to experience than to describe. *All that I have said of it is as poor and unlike it as a point of a needle is to the heavens above us!*" . . .

Notes

1. Lady Frick, a close friend of Henry of Nördlingen, on her return to Basle after an absence, writes that she is "filled with joy to be again in the holy and spiritual society at Basle," which she says is "large," and she feels as though she had come from purgatory to paradise. She declares that she would not change her home in Basle for any other, unless it were for one in Medingen, in Bavaria, where there was a group of Friends of God, with Margaret Ebner as its head.

2. The letters are published in Heumann's *Opuscula* (Nürnberg, 1747), pp. 331-404.

3. The great religious books, or treatises, which have been in part or in whole ascribed to "The Friend of God from the Oberland" or to Rulman Merswin, are as follows: First a collection of sixteen treatises which are preserved in the "Great German Memorial" (Das grosse deutsche Memorial). They are:

(1) *Two Fifteen-year-old Boys.*

(2) *The Imprisoned Knight.*

(3) *The Story of Ursula and Adelaide.*

(4) *Two Holy Nuns in Bavaria.*

(5) *The Spiritual Stairway.*

(6) *The Spiritual Ladder.*

(7) *The Spark* (Fünklein) *in the Soul.*

(8) *A Lesson for a Young Brother of the Order.*

(9) *Story of a Man Endowed with Worldly Wisdom.*

(10) *A Revelation given to "the Friend of God" on Christmas Night.*

(11) *A Young Man of the World.*

(12) *Warnings which "the Friend of God" sent to the People.*

(13) *The Book of the Banner of Christ.*

(14) *The Three Halting-places* (Durchbrüche).

(15) *The Seven Works of Mercy.*

(16) *Book on Prevenient Grace.*

The MS. of *Das grosse deutsche Memorial* is in the Universitäts- und Landes-bibliothek at Strasbourg. The Treatises numbered 1, 2, 10, and 12 have been published in Karl Schmidt's *Nikolaus von Basel* (Wien, 1866). Those numbered 5 and 6 have been printed in Jundt's *Rulman Merswin* (Paris, 1890). In the collection known as *Pflegermemorial* the following Treatises are preserved:—

The Book of the First Four Years of Rulman Merswin's New Life, and the *Book of the Five Men,* which is the story of "the Friend of God" and his companions. There is a fifteenth-century manuscript of this in the Bezirksarchiv of Strasbourg. "The Book of the Five Men" is published in Schmidt's *Nikolaus von Basel.*

Besides these the most important Treatises for the Religious ideas of the Friends of God are the *Book of the Master of Holy Scripture,* the *Book of the Two Men,* and the *Book of the Nine Rocks.* "The Book of the Two Men" is published in Schmidt's *Nikolaus von Basel,* and it has also been edited and published by Lauchert, *Des Gottesfreundes in Oberland* [= *Rulman Merswin*], *Buch von den Zwei Mannen* (Bonn, 1896).

There is an autograph MS. of the *Nine Rocks* in the Universitäts- und Landes-bibliothek at Strasbourg [L. germ 665; Neun Felsen: Rulmanni Merschwin,

Fundatoris domus St. Johannis de 9 Rupibus autographus]. This was edited and published by Schmidt, *Das Buch von den Neun Felsen* (Leipzig, 1859). *Das Meisterbuch* [Book of the Master of Holy Scripture] is in the collection known as *Das erste übriggebliebene Lateinbuch.* It has been published by Schmidt under the title: *Nikolaus von Basel, Bericht von der Bekehrung Taulers* (Strasbourg, 1875).

There is also an important collection of Letters (*Briefbuch*) professing to be Letters to and from the "Friend of God." There is a MS. of this *Briefbuch* in the Bezirksarchiv [H 2185]. The Letters are printed in Karl Schmidt's *Nikolaus von Basel.*

4. This Nicholas of Basle was a Beghard, and was burned at the stake in Vienna, as a heretic.

5. See especially Denifle's *Der Gottesfreund im Oberlande und Nikolaus von Basel* (1870).

6. During the years of his "commencement," as they termed the period of preparation, he underwent, according to the accounts, almost unbelievable transformations and psychic experiences. For example, whenever he saw blood, as, for instance, when he was bled by the physicians, the thought of the sacrifice of Christ would so fill his mind that he would swoon away into an ecstasy. He was the frequent recipient of "Divine voices," and many important situations were revealed to him.

7. *The Book of the Two Men,* containing the story of the conversion of the "Friend of God."

8. Merswin bought the Isle with its ruined convent in the autumn of 1366, and put it in complete condition for a retreat of peace and calm, suited to the mystical life. As the result of another "joint revelation," the retreat was turned over to the Order of Saint John in 1371. The important documents for the story of Merswin's connection with Grünenwörth, or "the Convent of the Green Isle," are the collections known as *Das grosse deutsche Memorial, Erstes lateinische Memorial und Pflegermemorial,* and *Johanniter Chronik,* all of which are in the Universitäts- und Landesbibliothek; and the collection known as *Das Pfleger-memorial* and *Erweitertes Pflegermemorial* and *Das Briefbuch* in the Bezirksarchiv. The reader who wishes to study the actual *history* of Grünenwörth, freed from the colouring of fiction, should read Karl Rieder's *Der Gottesfreund vom Oberland* (Innsbrück, 1905).

9. A. Jundt, *Rulman Merswin et l' Ami de Dieu* (Paris, 1890). It is a very interesting piece of work, and the theory is ably presented.

10. *Der Gottesfreund vom Oberland: eine Erfindung des Strassburger Johanniterbruders Nikolaus von Löwen,* von Karl Rieder (Innsbrück, 1905).

11. This modesty of authorship appears to be a characteristic of many writers among the Friends of God.

12. *Book of the Nine Rocks.*

13. Tauler, Sermon No. LXXI.

14. It is true that this narration is fictitious, but the writer is not creating *mere fiction.* He is writing for edification, and he gives what he believes is *possible* experience for the group.

15. This phrase, "upper school of the Holy Spirit," had already been used by Matilda of Magdeburg.

16. Denifle, *Taulers Bekehrung,* Strasbourg, 1879.

17. See Preger, *Geschichte der deutschen Mystik* (Leipzig, 1893), vol. iii. pp. 116-139. Jundt, *Les Amis de Dieu.*

18. These passages are translated from Jundt, *Rulman Merswin,* pp. 4-6.

19. The "Black Death," it will be remembered, fell upon Germany in 1347, and returned again in 1358 and in 1363.

20. These "sealed ones" are evidently the Friends of God.

21. This book contains the famous "Epistle to Christianity"; or "The Lament of a German Layman of the Fourteenth Century on the Decline of Christianity," printed by Karl Schmidt, in his *Nikolaus von Basel.*

22. There is a curious account which relates how, in the year 1379, eight Friends of God from different countries met in a "Divine Diet," on a mountain top, to pray God to postpone His judgment. On the eighth day they were surrounded by darkness, assailed by demons, and heard groans coming from the forest. Suddenly the darkness disappeared, a radiant light broke forth, and an angel stood before them and announced that *judgment was delayed for one year,* but they must not pray for any further postponement, for Christianity must be chastised.

23. This resistance against the command to put revelations into writing is almost universal with mystics. It appears in quite similar form in the writings of Hildegarde, Elizabeth of Schoenau, and Matilda of Magdeburg.

24. They thus devoutly believed that they were the true Church.

25. Jundt, *Les Amis de Dieu,* p. 59.

26. *Book of the Nine Rocks.*

27. Sermon XXXIV. (Frankfort edition, 1825).

28. Sermon LXI.

29. Sermon XXXIV.

30. Sermon LXIX.

31. Sermon XLIV.

32. Sermon XLIII

33. Jundt, *Les Amis de Dieu,* p. 53.

34. There is no historical evidence to establish as genuine the following words, frequently quoted as though spoken by Tauler: "Those who hold the true Christian faith and sin only against the person of the Pope, are no heretics. Those, rather, are real heretics who refuse to repent and forsake their sins; for let a man have been what he may, if he will do so, he cannot be cast out of the Church."

35. Tauler, Sermon No. LXXI.

36. Sermon LIX.

37. Sermon VII.

38. Sermon XLVI.

39. Sermon XLVIII.

40. Sermon LXXXI.

41. Sermon LXXXIV.

42. Sermon LII.

43. Sermon XV.

44. In his sermon "On the Conception of Our Lady," he says: "There is nothing so near the inmost heart as God. He who will seek there shall find Him. Thus, every day we find Him in the Blessed Sacrament and *in all the Friends of God.*"

45. Tauler's "Sermon for the Fifteenth Sunday after Trinity," Hutton's *The Inner Way, being Tauler's Sermons for Festivals.*

46. See Sermon IV., "On the Feast of St. Stephen," *The Inner Way.*

47. Sermon XV., "On the Feast of St. Mary Magdalene." *The Inner Way.*

48. Sermon XXXVI., "Second Sermon at the Dedication of a Church," *The Inner Way.*

49. Those three passages are taken from Inge, *Christian Mysticism,* p. 188.

50. Sermon XXXVI., "Second Sermon at the Dedication of a Church.'

James M. Clark (essay date 1949)

SOURCE: "Johann Tauler" in *The Great German Mystics: Eckhart, Tauler, and Suso,* Basil Blackwell, 1949, pp. 36-54.

[*In the following essay, Clark offers an overview of Tauler's life and works, describes his use of language, and traces his varying critical reception over the centuries.*]

The ascertained facts about Tauler's life are not as numerous as one could wish, but there is no doubt about his birthplace. He was a native of Strasbourg and was born about 1300. There are various references to the Tauler family in Strasbourg charters between 1312 and 1349, from which it appears that they were prominent citizens and property owners in that city. It has been conjectured that Nikolaus Tauler, described as a citizen and magistrate, who witnessed a deed of gift to the Dominicans in 1319, was the father of Johann. This at least is certain, our friar was the son of a wealthy man; for he tells us himself that he could have lived on his patrimony if he had so desired. The family was evidently religious; Tauler joined the Order of Preachers and his sister became a nun in the Dominican convent of St. Nikolaus in undis, in Strasbourg. He was not forced into the cloisters against his will, but had a genuine sense of vocation. 'Once when I saw the holy brethren who keep the rules of the Order strictly, I would gladly have done likewise,' he wrote many years later to Margareta Ebner.

There is every reason to suppose that after the close of his novitiate Tauler followed the prescribed course of instruction, which normally lasted for eight years. If he entered the Strasbourg convent at the usual age he would be a novice about 1314, in which year Eckhart was prior. Whether Tauler was Eckhart's pupil in the technical sense or not, he was certainly his pupil in the wider sense of knowing the master through his writings and teachings, and he was profoundly influenced by them. He was evidently a youth of promise and was sent to the *studium generale* at Cologne to complete his studies.

Karl Schmidt maintained that he was also sent to Paris, and alleged in support of this statement, first the references in his sermons to the masters of Paris, and secondly an inscription in a book by Friar Johann von Dambach. Neither of these arguments is convincing. In the sermons contained in Vetter's edition the masters of Paris are mentioned three times.[1] In the first there is a comparison between a child of six and a master of Paris. Here the phrase simply means 'learned man.' In the other two passages the masters of Paris are mentioned together with those who follow the mystic way, very much to the advantage of the latter: 'The masters of Paris read big books and turn over the leaves: it is well, but these (the mystics) read the living book wherein everything lives.' This is scarcely the language of a former student speaking of his *alma mater.*

The inscription cited by Schmidt runs as follows: 'Friars Magister Johannes de Tambacho and Johannes Taulerii of the convent of Strasbourg in the Province of Germany, presented this book *De Sensibilibus Deliciis Paradisi* to the convent of Paris;'[2] the word 'presented' (contulerunt) does not necessarily imply that the book was handed over in person; it may have been sent by a messenger. It was natural that Johann von Tambach (or Dambach), who was a doctor of Paris, should give a copy of one of his own works to his old university, the convent of St. Jacques. It is not quite so clear why Tauler should have been associated with the gift, but one could think of many possible reasons. Only those Friars were sent to Paris who were intended for the doctorate, but Tauler's name is not to be found in the very accurate and complete list of doctors of the university. In short, there is no evidence that Tauler studied in Paris or that he ever visited that city.

In a list of eminent Dominicans in an old Basel manuscript,[3] Tauler is described as a 'lector'; presumably he lectured in his own convent of Strasbourg. For it was with his native town that he was most closely associated; there he found an active religious life and a great tradition of preaching in the vast cathedral. But it was there that Tauler had to undergo stern ordeals and trials, including voluntary exile for conscience' sake.

The Strasbourg Dominicans became involved in the struggle between the Emperor Ludwig and the Pope. In 1325 Lewis had been excommunicated by the Pope, and his lands were laid under an interdict. Four years later the ban was renewed and more rigorously enforced. In the imperial cities opinion was on the side of the Emperor, but the Dominican friars were loyal to the papacy. The inmates of the Strasbourg convent were allowed to continue preaching and saying mass for a time, but the anti-papal authorities finally insisted on the strict observance of the interdict, and hence the friars were forced into exile. They went to Basel, where they were allowed to celebrate mass and preach unmolested. This was in 1339. Tauler was already in Basel when his brethren arrived; it is not quite clear why he had preceded them, but it has been suggested that the Provincial *studium* or school removed first and that Tauler, as one of the teachers, accompanied the pupils.

An entirely different version of the events that led up to Tauler's exile is given by the Strasbourg chronicler Speckle, who died in 1598.[4] He asserts that in 1341 a Dominican friar by name of Johannes Taulerus began to preach in Strasbourg and continued to do so for some twenty years. He vigorously condemned the interdict, as a result of which great numbers of poor ignorant people died unshriven. Together with a Carthusian prior named Ludolf of Saxony and Thomas, an Austin friar, he wrote many anti-papal works, in consequence of which all three were banished. Two articles extracted from their writings were condemned as heretical. The first dealt with the interdict and neglect of the dying on the part of the clergy, the second maintained the independence of the secular power from the spiritual.

Speckle's story is vague and contradictory, but he is so notoriously unreliable that no credence can be given to him. Writing as he did at the time of the Reformation, he was extremely prejudiced, and moreover he wrote two centuries after the events he professed to describe. The silence of other Strasbourg chroniclers and total absence of confirmation from any other source must be noticed. It is in the highest degree unlikely that Tauler, a Dominican friar, should oppose the papal instructions. For him obedience to the see of Rome was axiomatic. His friend Johann von Dambach had written a treatise on the legality of interdicts, urging submission to the Pope. On the other hand Tauler expressed himself on occasion very disrespectfully about secular rulers. Denifle has pointed out that it was permissible to give the last sacraments to the dying even at a time of interdict.

In 1343 the Dominicans returned to Strasbourg and Tauler followed them in 1347-8. It is not known why he stayed at

Basel after the other friars had left. He paid a visit to Margareta Ebner at Maria Medingen late in 1347 or early in 1348. Shortly after his return to Strasbourg he became the confessor of Rulman Merswin, a wealthy local merchant who had retired from business to devote himself to religion. But apparently this relationship was not of long duration.

In some passages of Tauler's writings there is a kind of apocalyptic atmosphere. The sufferings of the age, the interdict and excommunication of the Emperor, the civil war, the Black Death, and the earthquake at Basel in 1356, produced a feeling of impending doom . Well might people believe that the end of the world was at hand, Many sought refuge in vice, and conventual discipline suffered much. Both Tauler and Suso testify to the decline in morals. 'If I had known what I now know,' said the former, 'I should have lived on my inheritance and not on alms.'[5] There is a note of disillusionment here. The holy life that had attracted him as a boy no longer prevailed.

There is little information about the last decade of Tauler's life. According to Surius, the biographer of Ruysbroeck, he often went to Groenendal near Waterloo to see the great Flemish mystic, but there is no indication of the date of these journeys.[6] From the correspondence of Tauler's friends two facts emerge: the last Strasbourg period was one of great activity in preaching and at the same time one of great sorrow and distress for the preacher. 'They (Tauler and Heinrich von Nördlingen) have set the world ablaze with their fiery tongues,' wrote Christina Ebner in the Dominican nunnery of Engeltal near Nürnberg about 1350.

The call to repentance and stern condemnation of evil that resound in Tauler's sermons did not make for popularity with the general public. 'Pray for our dear father Tauler,' wrote Heinrich von Nördlingen to Margareta Ebner, 'he is generally in great distress because he teaches the truth as whole-heartedly as any teacher I know.' One suspects that Tauler was speaking from actual experience when he said: 'If anyone comes and warns them of the dreadful peril in which they live and how anxiously they should meet death, they mock him and say he is a Beghard and call us visionaries. They jeer and sneer at us as neither Jews nor pagans ever did to Christians.'[7]

We know that Tauler was in Cologne in his student days and again in 1339, but this second stay seems to have been short. Did he revisit Cologne between 1350 and 1360? Preger was at great pains to show that he did, and that he spent over a year there. It is true that Preger was anxious to make the facts fit in with his erroneous theories about Tauler's life, but we must take his views seriously. His argument is ingenious and intricate. Put briefly, it amounts to this: As the rubric indicates, one of Tauler's sermons was preached on St. Cordula's Day, which was October 23rd. At that time this saint was venerated only in Cologne. The gospel from which the text was taken is that of the twentieth Sunday after Trinity. The only year in Tauler's life in which this particular Sunday fell on October 23rd was 1357. Therefore Tauler was in Cologne in that year.

It is not possible to check all Preger's statements. One of the manuscripts he quotes was destroyed in 1870, and another, in the Munich library, may not have survived the last war. His argument rests on a series of assumptions, such as that the gospel pericopes of the fourteenth century were unchanged in the sixteenth, and that the table of festivals he used is absolutely reliable. But even if the date 1357 is wrong, one cannot help thinking that a residence in Cologne of a year or two certainly took place either before or after 1339. It may have been an extension of the years of theological study. It would follow his ordination, for which the earliest possible date is approximately 1325.

A considerable number of his sermons were found in Cologne, and an old local manuscript tells us that they were preached at St. Gertrud's convent there. There is also strong internal evidence.[8] In one of the sermons in question Tauler commends the Cologne custom of frequent communion, but complains that the sacraments are not always taken in the right spirit. In another he says that he has been in countries where the people are so manly and pious that God's word brings forth more fruit in one year than in ten in Cologne. This suggests a close knowledge of local conditions. A third sermon was preached on the dedication festival of the cathedral, as the opening sentence shows. In a fourth there is a detailed description of the building of a vast church. This could not refer to Strasbourg or Basel, where the cathedrals were completed, but would be quite appropriate to Cologne, where extensive building operations were in progress at the time. The sermon preached on St. Cordula's Day has already been mentioned.

Tauler died on June 16th, 1361, according to the inscription on his tombstone.[9] Quétif's date, 1379, is due to a wrong reading of the inscription. An old tradition affirms that he died after a ten weeks' illness in the garden of the convent of St. Nikolaus de undis, where his sister was a nun. He was buried in the cloisters of the Dominican friary. His tombstone is now in the new Protestant Church, which was built on the same site. These are the authenticated facts of Tauler's life, but a mass of legend has accumulated round them.

There is a Latin *Life of Tauler* that was often bound together with his sermons and was therefore regarded as genuine. It relates that in the year 1346 a Master of Theology preached in a certain city and people thronged to hear him from far and near. A pious layman heard of him, and after being summoned three times in a dream to do so, he set out to the city, which was thirty leagues away. Five times he heard the master preach and found that he was a kind, good-natured man and learned in the Scriptures, but 'without grace.' Accordingly he went to the master, told him that he had heard five sermons preached by him, and asked if he might make his confession. This the preacher allowed; the layman confessed his sins and received the sacrament.

After twelve weeks had passed, the layman asked the priest to preach a sermon showing how a man might attain the greatest heights that can be attained in this life. The master objected that the layman would not understand such lofty matters. The visitor pleaded, and finally the master acceded to his request. He announced to his congregation that in three days he would teach them how a man could attain the highest point of perfection and nearness to God. A large congregation assembled to hear him on the appointed day.

The sermon contained twenty-four articles or points which were essential for true holiness of life. After hearing the preacher, the layman went to his lodgings and wrote down the sermon word for word as it was preached. Then he went to the priest and read it aloud to him. The priest agreed that he could not have done it better himself. The layman told the priest that he did not practise what he preached, that he was a Pharisee. After some discussion he convinced the priest that this judgment was correct. The master said that, like the Samaritan woman at the well, he had been 'illuminated,' and that his faults had been revealed to him as never before. He promised to submit in everything to the layman as his spiritual adviser.

The layman told the story of his own conversion, how he gave up practising bodily austerities as an inspiration of the devil, and devoted himself entirely to God. He also related that he had converted a heathen in a far country by writing him a letter, which the heathen had answered in good German.

The priest asked to be instructed how to live according to the counsels of his friend, and to this end he was given an alphabet or manual, in the form of twenty-four sentences, each beginning with a different letter of the alphabet. The master spent six weeks in making himself perfect in these matters, even chastising himself repeatedly at the behest of his instructor as a punishment for his laxity. He then received further instruction. He was told to stop preaching and studying for a time, not to give his penitents any advice after they had confessed, but to spend his time in his cell reading his breviary, or in the choir singing or saying mass and contemplating the sufferings of Christ and his own misspent life, waiting humbly till he was regenerated.

When he attempted to put these counsels into practice the master suffered acutely, and in addition, his friends in the convent all despised him and thought him mad, his penitents deserted him and finally he fell ill. The layman comforted him and give him some delicacies to restore his strength. After two years of this life, in which he suffered much pain, grief and poverty, as a result of which he pawned many of his books, the master heard a voice assuring him of deliverance. He fell into a swoon and when he came to himself he felt a new strength and a clear understanding of things which had hitherto been obscure to him. He sent for the layman who explained that now he would receive from the Holy Spirit true doctrine and the power to expound the scriptures aright; that he must begin to preach again; that the people who had despised him

would now love him, but he must keep himself humble or the devil would rob him of the gift of grace. The layman gave the master thirty florins to redeem his books which were in pawn.

Three days later the master preached once more and a great crowd of people came to hear him; but when he stood in the pulpit he could do nothing but weep, and although he prayed for help his tongue was tied and it was of no avail. He became a laughing-stock and his brethren of the convent forbade him to preach again because of the scandal to their order. The layman consoled him and said that these afflictions were a sign of divine grace. He finally obtained permission to preach again in the convent, which was a convent of nuns, and spoke of Christ the heavenly Bridegroom. At the beginning of the sermon he said that two years or more had passed since he preached to them and the sermon was then on the twenty-four articles necessary to perfect godliness.

After this the master said Mass and gave Communion to the people. Twelve persons who had been in the church fell into a trance in the churchyard and were as dead. The master attained great fame in the city and was highly respected by the citizens. After eight years he fell grievously ill and died in great torment. Before he died he exhorted the layman not to mention his name nor his own in the book he was going to write nor to allow anyone in the city to read it lest his identity be discovered. After his death he appeared to the layman and assured him that his painful death was inflicted on him as a purgatory and that he was taken by angels straight up to heaven, where for five days he suffered no pain, but was deprived of the beatific vision. He was then permitted to enjoy the bliss of paradise. The layman also came to a blessed end.

Quétif-Echard and other scholars have pointed out various suspicious circumstances about this story. In fact it will not stand critical examination. How does it come about that a layman had to travel thirty leagues, that is to say some 150 miles, to hear good sermons? Surely he would have found eloquent friars in his own town or in the nearest city. As we have seen, Tauler had never studied at Paris and was not entitled to the prefix 'Master' or 'Magister.' Is it likely that a man of his learning and distinction should have to accept the teaching of a layman, however pious he may have been?

Quite apart from these points, there are plenty of other reasons for being sceptical about this story. It belongs to a special type of devotional tale, in which the characters are usually a priest and a layman, the latter gets the better of the former and shows him the way to true religion. It is all part of what we might call propaganda; the anti-clerical bias betrays the layman-author. It will be remembered that such a story grew up round the figure of Eckhart.

Denifle proved that Tauler and the Master of the story could not be the same person. He did more, he showed how the legend had grown up, step by step. It was not until the sixteenth century that it was associated with the name of Tauler. In a series of masterly articles Denifle revealed Rulman Merswin as the author of the fictitious narrative. The 'layman' is an invention on the part of Merswin, just as the 'Master' is.

We have dealt with the spurious *Vita* or *Historie,* as it is also called, in some detail because of its importance. For centuries this inferior production has coloured the personality of Tauler as seen by scholars. Long after Denifle had exploded the myth in 1880, it reappeared and even in our own day it is not forgotten. An English translation of the *Vita* by Susannah Winkworth appeared in 1857, together with an English version of some of Tauler's sermons and a preface by Charles Kingsley. In 1887 the *Life of Tauler* was reprinted at Philadelphia. Even eminent scholars continue to treat it as gospel, because they have not made themselves sufficiently familiar with the literature of the subject.

After the *Life* had been proved spurious, all the treatises attributed to Tauler were similarly deprived of their claim to genuineness. First *The Book of Spiritual Poverty,* also known as *Imitation of the Poor Life of Christ,* was eliminated.[10] Then *The Marrow of the Soul (Medulla Animae),* the *Divine Institutions,* the *Exercises on the Life and Passion of our Saviour Jesus Christ,*[11] and finally the *Prophecies of the Enlightened Dr. John Tauler,* were disposed of. As a result of this clearance of the literary field, Tauler has gained in stature rather than lost. He is more impressive than the banal 'Master' of the 'Life' and a truer representative of his Order and his age.

It was thought at one time that Tauler wrote in Latin, but this view is mistaken. All his works are in German. They consist of the sermons and one single letter to Margareta Ebner. The first printed volume, which appeared at Leipzig in 1488, was entitled **'Sermons, pointing out the nearest true way, translated into German for the salvation of many.'** This was taken to mean that they were translated from Latin into German, but the original was in Low German, in the dialect of Cologne, and this was rendered into High German. The second edition[12] perpetuated the error: **'Sermons, turned from Latin into German.'** Tauler had no occasion for using Latin. His sermons were mainly or exclusively preached to nuns and laymen, and he wrote no learned works, as far as we know.

As a preacher Tauler is usually easy to understand, homely and simple. There is occasional obscurity, but it is not quite clear to what extent this is due to the recorder of the sermons or the scribe who copied them. It is chiefly in the more mystical passages that the obscurities occur. He uses either short sentences or long periods of the Latin type. His language is often very picturesque and vivid, rising to real heights of eloquence when the subject demands it. He knows how to deal with questions of dogma or abstract thought by popular analogies and examples, and draws upon a rich store of observation and knowledge of ordinary life. He is well versed in proverbial lore and does not despise alliteration, antithesis and metaphor, though he is no rhetorician. He uses dialogue very effectively to expound a doctrine or to meet possible objections.[13] His imagery is derived from hunting, war, sea-faring, viniculture, farming, trade and natural history. But he makes a more restrained use of these devices than the Franciscans were wont to do.

He adapts himself much more to his congregation than Eckhart does. The latter is much more unconventional than Tauler; in fact it might almost be said that Eckhart's sermons are monologues, bold flights of imagination which too often leave his hearers stupefied and uncomprehending. He was a poet and a genius, and was not free from the limitations of such men. If the two mystics differ in the form of their work, they also differ with regard to the matter. Eckhart sees only the goal of the mystic way: the union of the soul with God, or as he puts it, the birth of the Divine Word in man. This is to him something so near and so real; it is the one all-important reality. Tauler stresses the way itself, the method by which the soul can be made ready for this great consummation. We are speaking, of course, of Tauler the mystic, but that is not the whole Tauler. He has two different moods, the practical and ascetic on one hand, the lyrical and mystical on the other. The former predominates.

He had been trained in the art of preaching. He could deliver a set piece on occasion, dividing the theme in the scholastic manner, but this is not his usual procedure. The majority of his sermons were addressed to nuns, so that a more homely approach was required. There is usually the threefold division into introduction (*exordium*), development (*tractatio*) and conclusion (*conclusio*). He often proceeds on the lines of the old-fashioned homily, taking the gospel of the day and expounding it phrase by phrase; or he selects a single text from the gospel pericope and works it out in detail. Sometimes he seems to have no fixed plan at all, but digresses freely, even losing the thread of his thought at times.

So loose is the construction that Strauch assumed that the texts we possess are only summaries. This is not a satisfactory explanation, nor can we accept the theory that the apparent formlessness of the text is entirely the fault of the scribe. The sudden changes in the trend of ideas, the interruptions and digressions belong to the very texture of the sermon, and we are compelled to the conclusion that Tauler was accustomed to improvise. These are the impromptu utterances of a busy man, with the typical illogical breaks and sudden transitions of popular speech. They were suitable for the time, place and audience.

The condemnation of Eckhart had put an end to speculation. Henceforth mysticism was confined to safer channels. It is not surprising that Tauler is practical in tendency. He eschews the metaphysical and fixes his attention on the needs of everyday life. There is in his writings more exegesis than imaginative treatment. To expound the scriptures in the traditional manner is a safe policy. As a general rule, Tauler avoids the semblance of heresy. When dangerous ground is to be trod, he defines his terms and keeps well within the limits of the strictest orthodoxy. Unlike his great master, he rarely speaks of the 'spark of the soul,' but often of the 'ground of the soul.' It means very much the same thing, but has no pantheistic implications. He is never weary of repeating Eckhart's injunction that God must be born in the soul, but he is careful to add that the soul is not God, that the Creator and creature are distinct, that they are of a different nature, that in this life we can only be united with God as a result of divine grace. Eckhart also held these views and said the same thing on occasion but he did not always qualify his remarks to the same extent. If Tauler omits to add the saving clause at times, it is generally understood or implied in the context.

Only once does Tauler mention Eckhart by name, and that is in the famous 64th Sermon,[14] which is so strongly mystical in tendency that some writers doubt its authenticity. Eckhart is mentioned third in the list of teachers: 'Of this inner nobility of the soul which lies hidden in the ground, many masters have spoken, both old and new, Bishop Albrecht,[15] Master Dietrich,[16] Master Eckhart. The one calls it a spark of the soul, the other a ground or peak (*tolde*), one calls it a beginning, and Bishop Albrecht calls it an image in which the Holy Trinity is formed and contained.'

There is another passage which is generally supposed to allude to Eckhart: 'Concerning this (the mystic union with God) a beloved master has written and spoken to you and you do not understand it. He spoke in terms of eternity, and you understood according to time. Dear children, if I have said too much of this, it is not too much for God, but you must forgive me; I will gladly make amends. A sublime master spoke of the perception that knows no way or form. Many people grasp this with their sensual minds and become sinful men, and therefore it is a hundred times better that one should come to it by ways and forms (by the usual method).'[17] Paraphrased this means: 'The master spoke of the mystic union of the human with the divine, but fanatical persons were led astray and understood this in a pantheistic sense, that is, they claimed that they had become divine and were incapable of sin.'

Many mystics are willing enough to speak of their own spiritual experiences but not so Tauler. He resembles Eckhart in his reticence, his impersonal treatment of religion, which accords well with the austerely intellectual attitude of the Dominicans, their dignity and lack of sentimentality. How little do we know of the inner life of these two men! It is true that there are occasional hints, but we must beware of reading too much into what they say. Tauler's emphatic references to a change in spiritual outlook at the age of forty may well be due to his own experiences. He speaks of it no less than three times. It is, however, dangerous to jump at conclusions. In this way legends and fables arise. So little do we really know about Tauler as an individual that some writers have gone so far as to deny that he was a mystic at all! I cannot share this view: that he speaks of things he has himself seen, heard and felt

cannot be doubted if we pay due attention to the note of strong conviction with which he always speaks of the union of the human and the divine; here is the unmistakable autobiographical touch.

Quite apart from his reticence, there is another barrier to the full understanding of the man. His writings are not free from contradictions and inconsistencies. In sermon after sermon we hear the friar preaching on orthodox scholastic lines, carefully avoiding pitfalls, warning his congregation of the dangers that beset those who seek after the ultimate reality. But we also come across passages, even sermons, which have quite a different trend. We seem to be hearing the voice of his beloved master Eckhart, the authentic and unmistakable note of the real mystic. How does it come about that the man who can express himself with such caution, such scrupulous care, can, on occasion, let himself go, and indulge in the boldest flights of fancy? One solution of the problem that has been suggested is that these passages are not genuine. If this is so, whole sermons are not Tauler's work at all.[18] But there is another explanation that has the advantage of reconciling the apparent contradiction.

One cannot help thinking that the master's tragic fate had opened the mind of his disciple to the dangers of discussing the profounder mysteries of theology in the presence of untrained minds. The persistent growth of error had revealed the consequences of stimulating or permitting emotional religion in the cloister or among pious laymen. Tauler had seen what havoc had been wrought in the minds of Beghards and Brethren of the Free Spirit by the ill-considered teachings of an intellectual giant. He was torn in two directions. On one hand he did not wish to transgress the law he was in duty bound to obey; on the other hand he longed to speak of the inner secrets of the soul, which were to him an overwhelming reality. He felt the urge to pour out as his great predecessor had done in the same place, probably in the same pulpit, the story of the darkness of the Godhead, of the divine emanations, of the birth of the Word in the soul. Those who had felt the impact of the vast personality of Eckhart in their formative student years could never forget what they had heard.

Does not this account for the different reactions of later writers to Tauler's teachings? Some laid the emphasis on the practical side of his writings, others stress the Neoplatonic trend and considered it to be his real message to the world. Thus Louis de Blois, Denifle and Gottfried Fischer are stout champions of his orthodoxy, while Johann Eck (1523) and Petrus Noviomagus (1543) took the opposite view.

Tauler did not suffer such vicissitudes of fortune as did Eckhart. His works were widely read in his lifetime, copied throughout the Middle Ages and then printed in the late fifteenth and early sixteenth century. He was never forgotten and his fame never suffered eclipse. But the conception which succeeding generations had of Tauler varied with the age. Much apocryphal matter collected round his name and the process of rediscovery had to be made. Legend had to be stripped away and the truth sought out.

At first sight it may seem strange that Tauler, who was undoubtedly inferior to Eckhart in learning and force of personality, should have been such a powerful and enduring force in later ages.[19] There are various reasons for this. The ban on Eckhart suppressed his writings to a considerable extent and forced his influence underground, so to speak. In any case his works are more difficult to understand than Tauler's, which are admirably suited for use as devotional manuals. Tauler's practical tendency helped his fame; and the story of his conversion, which usually accompanied the sermons, made a strong appeal to Protestant sentiments. Finally the recommendation of Luther gave the Dominican mystic additional prestige.

In the critical years 1515-1518 Luther read Tauler with enthusiasm and not without profit.[20] The simple eloquent style of the mediaeval writer helped Luther in his approach to the general public in his pamphlets and sermons. He also gained as a theologian: he was enabled to acquire a new sense of the sacramental in worship and a deeper insight into personal religion. Doubtless Luther read his own ideas into Tauler and misunderstood him. He selected what fitted in with his own beliefs and ignored or minimized the rest. This was not unnatural. The Reformation was a period of savage controversy and acrimonious dissension; impartiality was scarcely possible. Neither side erred in the direction of sweet reasonableness or tolerance. Quite apart from this, we must bear in mind the fact that Luther regarded the *Imitation of the Poor Life of Christ* as genuine.

Luther believed he saw in Tauler a kindred spirit and saw in his doctrines support for his own. He claimed that Tauler stood for 'evangelical Christianity' without any admixture of 'popery.' Four aspects of Tauler's doctrines attracted him above all: the idea of complete resignation to the divine will; the attacks on outer works as useless in themselves; the descriptions of the sufferings of the devout soul, its sense of being forsaken by God; and finally the attitude to Scholasticism.

It is true that Tauler on occasion commands the renunciation of outer works, if they stand in the way of communion with God, but he is not in favour of mere passivity or quietism, as some readers have supposed. He holds that even the sinner can do good and thus prepare for the grace of sanctification, whereas Luther's view is that man is in a state of spiritual death, from which he cannot be released by his own efforts. The mystics, and Tauler among them, are more prone to stress the natural good in man than the natural evil or original sin. They are incurable optimists in their own characteristic moods, however gloomy they may be in phases of depression.

Luther identified his feeling of alienation from God with Tauler's description of spiritual loneliness, but there is an important difference. With Luther the sense of isolation was permanent; with the mystics the 'dark night of the soul' was a passing phase, an interval between moments of intense bliss and exaltation. Luther detested Scholasticism and aspired to liberate religion from the shackles of philosophy, that is to say, of the philosophy of Aristotle. Tauler had no antipathy to Scholasticism. He often quoted Thomas Aquinas and other Scholastics, and always as unquestionable authorities.[21] He does deviate from Thomist doctrines at times, but not on fundamental questions. It was not Tauler, but Pseudo-Tauler, who spoke disrespectfully about learning. As we have seen, Luther did not know of the existence of Pseudo-Tauler.

As a result of Luther's championship, both Churches became interested in Luther. They contended, as it were, for the possession of his writings; each side claimed him in turn as one of themselves. But there were strange crosscurrents in the polemical stream. In 1523 Johann Eck published a work in three volumes denouncing Luther and including Tauler in his condemnation, declaring that he could not be regarded as a representative of true orthodoxy. Eck did not know Tauler; he was led astray by the Dutch Jesuit Lessius, who is better known as the main object of Pascal's attacks on the casuists in his *Provenciales*. 'Pour sauver la foi catholique, Jean Eck avait sacrifié l'orthodoxie de Tauler,' writes Father Hugueny.[22]

The opposite procedure was adopted by another famous Jesuit, Peter Canisius (Petrus Noviomagus), who tried to save Tauler's orthodoxy by sacrificing the text of his writings. Canisius edited Tauler in drastic fashion, suppressing whole sermons, missing out compromising passages, such as those which might seem to restrict the authority of the Pope, or which were in any way liable to be interpreted in a heterodox manner. Phrases too reminiscent of Eckhart were toned down.

Another powerful apologist was the Carthusian monk Surius, who zealously strove to separate Tauler's name from that of Luther, whom he abhorred. With this end in view he translated Tauler into Latin. It would, however, be more correct to speak of a paraphrase, because Surius' aim was to produce a version in polished Latin prose, making omissions or additions as he thought fit. His work appeared at Cologne in 1543 and there were twelve subsequent editions (Cologne, Venice, Lyons and Paris). Surius' Tauler was twice translated into German for Protestants by Sudermann (1621) and for Catholics by Carolus a S. Anastasio (1660). There are also Dutch and Italian versions.

The Dutch translation of 1565 was intended for the use of Protestants, which involved alterations, and for this reason, it was put on the papal index in 1667, which explains the often repeated assertion that Tauler's works were forbidden by the Pope. Nevertheless in Catholic circles, in spite of the efforts of Canisius and Surius, prejudice and suspicion clung to Tauler's name. The effects of Eck's animadversions were slow to disappear and the belief that Tauler's doctrines promoted Quietism caused the Jesuits to put Tauler on the index in 1578. In 1595 the Capucins, for reasons connected with the movement in their own Order, followed suit, including the writings of Ruysbroeck, Suso and others in the ban. It was not until the seventeenth century that Tauler's name was completely cleared.

Apart from Surius and works derived from him, there were many other French, Italian and Spanish translations of the treatises that bore Tauler's name, but none of the sermons.

In the Quietist controversy in France both sides appealed to Tauler in support of their views. He was popular in Pietist circles in Germany, but from the beginning of the eighteenth century there was a decline in interest. No new editions appeared for a century and such references as we come across in historians are superficial. Herder knew Tauler and read some at least of his sermons but strangely enough without being impressed. He admired his 'nervous language,' but dismissed his mysticism in a few words. 'He who has read one sermon by him has read all.'[23]

In the early nineteenth century Tauler came into his own again. The Protestants revived the Pietist tradition in which the love of mysticism was still strong and the Catholics re-edited his works as devotional reading to counteract the effects of the Age of Enlightenment.

The Romanticists were naturally attracted by Tauler. One of the founders of the movement, Friedrich Schlegel, drew attention to the numerous mystics in Germany in the Middle Ages; he stated that they were connected with each other and formed a kind of school. 'I will only quote one out of their number,' he continues, 'who is very important for the history of the language. This is the preacher or philosopher Tauler, who long after the Reformation was admired and enjoyed by both Protestants and Catholics alike until oblivion fell to his lot.'[24] He then comments upon the fact that the Alsatians, after their political allegiance was transferred to France, still retained the German qualities of thorough historical and linguistic scholarship. He praises the contribution of the mystics to German prose. 'If we compare their language with that used in Luther's time, or even a century later for such purposes, we find it is just as superior as the melodious verse of the thirteenth century is superior to the rough doggerel (Knittelverse) of the sixteenth.' There is a good deal of truth in these remarks, though it is an error to call Tauler a philosopher in the strict sense of the term.

Schlegel rightly attributed the revival of Tauler to Alsatian scholarship. Jeremias Jacob Oberlin, who was Professor of Logic and Metaphysics at Strasbourg University, read Tauler and in 1786 he wrote an appreciation of him as a writer; this was one of the first attempts at literary criticism of the German mystics. It was another Alsatian, Carl Schmidt, who later inaugurated the learned research on Tauler's life.

Other Romanticists continued Schlegel's work in popularizing Tauler. Brentano read his works between 1817 and 1824 with Katharina Emmerich, at the time when his energies were entirely devoted to religion. Görres, the historian of the movement, devoted several pages to the life of Tauler in his introduction to Suso's works. His observations are a mass of errors, but his enthusiasm is evident. The philosopher Franz von Baader was reading Tauler in 1810 and four years later he called for a new edition of his works. Hegel quoted him in his lectures.

Until 1836 the attitude to Tauler was uncritical. No distinction was made between genuine and spurious works; there was no attempt to investigate the facts of his life. The Romantic poets and philosophers quoted Tauler without troubling to find out either what he actually said or what he meant by it. At the same time mystical authors and especially Tauler were reprinted and came on the market as popular devotional reading. This work was almost entirely in Catholic hands. Reprints, not critical texts, were required.

In 1836 scholars began to turn their attention to the matter: Pischon edited three fragments by Tauler and called for a critical edition of the sermons. In the same year Carl Schmidt's first book on mysticism appeared and in 1841 his life of Tauler. These works led to the rediscovery of Tauler in the world of learning, which for a generation was almost a Protestant monopoly. Schmidt, Jundt and Preger discovered new facts and discarded errors, but their theories were often hasty and ill-considered. Their method was faulty; they are given to making sweeping assertions on scanty evidence, of trying to make facts fit their preconceived notions.

It was the merit of Schmidt to assemble everything that was known about Tauler and add many new details. He was the first to undertake to divide the work of Eckhart and Tauler in the Basel edition. He clarified the relation between these writers and their relationship with Suso, though not fully. For Schmidt thought he could detect in the two pupils the pantheism of the master. He showed that three of the treatises ascribed to Tauler were not genuine. His biography of Tauler offers a mass of material, but it is not sufficiently sifted. Schmidt accepted the story of Tauler's conversion by a layman with all that it involved, in spite of the well-founded objections of Echard and Pischon. He followed Görres in retelling Speckle's remarks about Tauler and the interdict, without suspecting their falsity. He regarded Tauler as a Protestant before his time, as Luther had done, stressing particularly the doctrines concerning outer works. These views long persisted among Protestants and have not yet died out.

Milman[25] called Tauler a 'harbinger' of the Reformation, and thought he was considerably influenced by the Waldensians, John Dobree Dalgairns, a convert to Catholicism and collaborator of Newman, wrote a book in 1858 which was far in advance of the research of the time, and was in the main a defence of the Catholic orthodoxy of Tauler.[26] He rejected Speckle's statements as a 'myth' and cast serious doubts on the identification of the 'layman' of the *Life* with Nikolaus of Basel. But he regarded Eckhart as a heretic. Dalgairns occupies an isolated place in the scholarship of mysticism. No one in Germany took any notice of him and very few in Britain.

A new phase opened in 1875, when Denifle appeared on the scene. Hitherto the Catholics had been very much on the defensive in the field of scholarship, as a result of the onslaught of the idealist philosophers. Now the Catholics pass over to the attack and the Protestants, more particularly Preger, beat a rearguard action. The end of this phase was that the story of Tauler's conversion was relegated to legend, and all the *Gottesfreund* literature exposed as fictitious. The idea of Tauler as a precursor of the Reformation was rudely shaken. Discerning and well-informed Protestant critics have very largely abandoned the claims of Preger. With commendable caution the Lutheran theologian Ferdinand Cohrs observes: 'Yet Tauler is fundamentally mediaeval and non-evangelical and the Reformation elements that are to be found in him do not really belong to his system.'[27] Catholic writers would go still further and reject the idea of Protestant ideas in Tauler root and branch.

From about 1880 onwards interest in Tauler has waned somewhat owing to the lack of new sources of information and to various other reasons. As he has receded, Eckhart has gained in popularity. The one important event that still needs recording is the publication of Vetter's standard edition in 1911. It is defective in many respects, being based on five manuscripts only out of eighty or so. Of these five manuscripts two, those of Engelberg and Freiburg, are no doubt excellent, but the three Strasbourg versions were never seen by Vetter, who had to depend on very unreliable transcripts made by Schmidt.[28] Two of these Strasbourg manuscripts were destroyed during the bombardment of Strasbourg in 1870, a fact which German writers pass over rather lightly, and French scholars duly stress. The third Strasbourg manuscript, which was believed to have been burnt in 1870, turned up in Berlin and was finally returned to Strasbourg.

Of the eighty-one sermons in Vetter's edition, two are doubtful.[29] Two others are parts of the same sermon for Epiphany and seem to have been transposed.[30] No. 9 is a formula for general confession; Nos. 58 and 79 are short treatises not sermons. No. 79 is an excerpt from Ruysbroeck's *Vanden vier bekoryngen.*[31] Vetter omitted from his edition two sermons from the Strasbourg manuscript A89, which were printed later by Helander. Other genuine pieces, either complete or fragmentary, are to be found in German, Dutch or Swiss libraries, in manuscript form or in early printed books. It will be a task for the future to sift this material and prepare the way for a new edition. The first step was taken by Strauch in 1920.[32] The difficulties are enormous: much of Tauler's work was written down by his hearers and suffered in the process. These texts then passed through the hands of various scribes who added or took away as they thought fit, hence discrepancies arose. But when all reservations have been made, Vetter's version is very useful and it has furthered the study of Tauler immensely.

Notes

1. Page 366, line 17; p. 421, 1. 1; p. 432, 1. 2.

2. *Quétif-Echard,* 1, p. 667.

3. University Library, D IV 9, fo. 2.

4. The original manuscript was burnt in 1870. See *Suso,* edited Diepenbrock, pp. 35-39; Schmidt, *Tauler,* pp. 53-55.

5. Théry's interpretation of this passage (*Sermons de Tauler,* t. 1, p. 12) strikes me as unconvincing.

6. A. Wautier d'Aygalliers suggests c. 1350.

7. *Predigten,* ed. Vetter, p. 138, lines 1-5.

8. Vetter, p. 125, line 30; p. 130, 1. 7; p. 377, 1. 3.

9. See the very full account in Corin, *La Tombe de Tauler.*

10. See *Das Buch von geistlicher Armut, herausg.,* Denifle; Ritschl, *Untersuchung.*

11. Translated into English in 1904 by A. P. J. Cruikshank.

12. Augsburg, 1508.

13. E.g. Sermon 72, Vetter, pp. 391-394.

14. Vetter, pp. 346-353.

15. Albertus Magnus.

16. Dietrich von Freiberg.

17. Vetter, p. 69.

18. E.g., Nos. 1 and 64; see Müller, *Scholastikerzitate,* p. 418.

19. See Gottfried Fischer, *Geschichte der Entdeckung der deutschen Mystiker,* p. 5.

20. References in Grisar, *Luther;* and Köstlin, *Luthers Theologie.*

21. See Günther Müller, *Scholastikerzitate bei Tauler.*

22. *Sermons de Tauler,* p. 51.

23. *Briefe das Studium der Theologie betreffend,* 41. Brief. Carlsruhe, 1829.

24. *Sämmtliche Werke,* I. Band, 68-69, Wien, 1822.

25. *History of Latin Christianity,* London, 1855, Vol. VI, p. 560.

26. *The German Mystics of the Fourteenth Century.*

27. p. 456.

28. See Rieder, 1912.

29. Nos. 1 and 64. Some scholars attribute No. 1 to Eckhart.

30. Nos. 3 and 4.

31. *Lieftinck,* pp. 207-208.

32. *Zu Taulers Predigten.*

C. F. Kelley (essay date 1954)

SOURCE: An introduction to *The Book of the Poor in Spirit, by a Friend of God,* Longmans Green and Co, 1954, pp. 1-50.

[In the following excerpt, Kelley provides an overview of the Friends of God and discusses factors that led to their formation and rapid disappearance.]

It is an accepted maxim that the more a particular age becomes secular and dead to religious truth, the more marked becomes the line of demarcation between the indifferent and the concerned. The concerned person finds himself bound to abstain from occupations and pleasures which, though not injurious in themselves, have become corrupt. Furthermore, the perils of enthusiasm, the mistaking one's own natural emotions for divine influence, are greatest when that influence, known by the concerned to be real, is ignored, even denied by the world in general. Yet the world in general always claims to be preoccupied with truth.

When we counsel others: "Know the truth, and the truth shall make you free," what kind of truth do we mean? How often do we confuse truth with a collection of undigested facts, a mere recording of events? We concern ourselves with what has taken place but too frequently fail to ask why. Because no "scientific proof" is possible we tend to ignore real issues. We become indifferent to the realm of opinion and speculation. But intellectuals without conviction are little more than irresponsible disciples of objectivity, and their disciples in turn become a clan of spectators, not actors. For without real purpose there can be no real action.

The pursuit of truth is certainly not synonymous with objective research. It is not an examination of the different sides of a question and then refraining from adopting a conviction. It concerns itself with meaning and purpose, first principles and ultimate reality. It also concerns itself with belief and commitment. And belief and commitment imply concerned action. The more a man commits himself to the pursuit of God's truth, which is inseparable from His beauty and goodness, the more receptive he becomes to the divine influence.

The truly concerned man—one might even call him a mystic—recognizes more in nature than mere natural phenomena, more in the word of God than its verbal meaning. Every person, thing or event is for him a vision from the Unseen. Viewing God in all things and all things in God, he lives in a world of parables full of spiritual meaning. And though the presence of God is for him everywhere, he finds it most where it is perceived through the eyes of faith. He requires nothing mysterious to produce it, for it is already there and everywhere. And when he turns to the Scriptures he finds far more than the mere student of the letter. Regardless of all else that the Scriptures may contain, he also finds in them the clearest recording of that which has been revealed to man as indispensable for his soul's pursuit.

Certain members of the concerned have in each age endeavoured to pass on to others what they have found to be the spirit behind the letter of Scripture. Their exaltation of eternal views, with a life centred in them, springs primarily from a personal inward experience. Yet their findings are most sound and most helpful to others when they are supported by philosophical common sense, the witness of other concerned seekers as well as the revealed Word itself.

In presenting to English readers a modern edition of *The Book of the Poor in Spirit* I am presenting what all who are familiar with the text agree is one of the most "concerned" works of Christian literature. Taking for his theme "Blessed are the poor in spirit, for theirs is the kingdom of heaven,"[1] this unknown fourteenth-century writer has composed a treatise of such high spirituality and balanced intellectual power that it ranks with the leading writings of the school of Rhineland mysticism. When all sides of its teachings are considered, it is seen to be perhaps most representative of those Friends of God whose leaders were David von Augsburg, Meister Eckhart, Nicholas von Strassburg, Johann Tauler, Heinrich Suso and Marcus von Lindau. Moreover, its author accomplished what some of his colleagues failed to accomplish—a preservation of their mystical doctrine, coupled with practical counselling, within the sound framework of scholastic thought and the authority of Christian tradition.

1

Until the latter half of the nineteenth century, *The Book of the Poor in Spirit* was thought to have been written by Johann Tauler. Many aspects of its doctrine are akin to the teachings of this great exponent of German spirituality. But only Tauler's **Sermons,** and not more than eighty per cent of these can, according to the critics, be said to be truly his.[2] Even those who now believe that Tauler could not have composed this book agree that it was written about 1350 by a Dominican Friend of God—one of that large group of concerned seekers who formed the nucleus of the Rhineland school of mysticism. Nevertheless, the author has taken pains, not only to conceal his own identity, but to construct a treatise (or set of four treatises) compact, complete and individual in itself, yet full of the basic teachings which guided the mystic spirit of that time. (See Addendum A, p. 287.)

It is a book which has had great influence on Christian thought since Marcus von Lindau, who died in 1392, quoted so extensively from it in his treatise on the *Ten Commandments.*[3] Those who admire it consider it not only an outstanding spiritual classic, but also a summary of the teachings of fourteenth-century German spirituality. In other words, here is what not a few have taken to calling the text-book of the Rhineland school, a compact instruction which is clearer and more precise than that to be found in the actual sermons of Eckhart, Nicholas von Strassburg or Tauler himself.

Surius, the famous Carthusian monk from Cologne, translated it into Latin in 1548 and through this translation it played a part in the rise of the Carmelite mystics in Spain; it was on the shelves of St. François de Sales; both sides of the Quietest controversy referred to it; even the English Benedictine, Father Augustine Baker, had frequent access to it. All, of course, attributed it to Tauler and even regarded it as his most important work.

Since it is a religious book which is almost entirely free of any dogmatic and formal questions, it has always commended itself to a large number of Christians. Lutherans have praised it highly,[4] though some of its teachings, especially those placing a stress on charity, were naturally criticized by some followers of Melanchthon and the Calvinist Beza. When one learns about the influence the book exerted on Abbot Blosius, it is easy to understand how he confuted their objections.[5] For one of the features of the book is that its views are those shared not only with the orthodox Rhineland teachers, but with the most eminent saints and doctors of Christendom and the Plotinian thinkers of earlier times. Obviously influenced by the philosophical groundwork of St. Thomas Aquinas, the author moves on into the realm of pure spirituality and at once joins hands with Richard or St. Victor, St. Bernard, St. Augustine and the Pseudo-Dionysius.

As early as 1250 the Rhineland became a centre of interest for the Franciscan and Dominican Orders of the Church. It was they who were mostly instrumental in causing the sudden development of German prose, elevating it to a level equal to, if not above, the wonderful poetry of the old Minnesingers and Nibelungen-Lieder. The Franciscans and Dominicans more and more came to the front and soon proved, through their admirable treatises and sermons, that the German language of their time was adequate to cope with their most profound and lofty themes. Most of the Rhineland mystics came from these Orders and their impact throughout the Upper and Lower Rhine became so great that they have always been known as the fathers of German speculation.

It is in these men that the beginnings of German philosophy, the origins of well-known systems of Western thought,[6] and even the seeds of later spiritual movements may be traced. Apart from the men mentioned above—the popular leaders—there were a host of lesser known men and women, each caught up in the rapid growth of this religious movement, a movement, what is more, which lessened the gap between the clergy and the laity. It was one of those wonderful yet strange periods of spiritual flowering, perhaps one unequalled by any other in Western tradition. How are we to account for such a sudden bursting forth into the realms of mysticism and speculative thought, a flower which bloomed for a few generations and then withered and died? More puzzling still is how such a flower could bloom in the midst of the brambles of fourteenth-century society. For it was a society which remained preoccupied with the unholy feuds of peasants, princes, bishops and monks, a society which lay burdened by unbelievable sufferings, plagues and wars. Or is it only a weak human eye which creates this paradox?

Yet in times of religious, political and economic conflict—in times like our own—the good people of this world always cry out: "Stop this madness!" But how can we expect anything but a certain degree of insanity in this world of time and space which by the very nature of its existence is schizoid—split between hell and heaven, evil and good? It is then that our mystics and saints tell the merely good people that love is still the only virtue that counts, that the only real sin is not to love. As our author says: "God prefers any kind of love to no love at all" (Part IV, Chapter iv, Section 3).

But a period of crime and natural calamity does not alone explain the rise of the Rhineland mystic spirit. There have been other dark ages which failed to produce it. Furthermore, that spirit has sometimes flourished, as in sixteenth-century Spain, when the local culture was at its peak. Nor can one say that Rhineland mysticism was merely a reaction against the theological schools. After all, most of its leaders were products of scholasticism and, in fact, incorporated scholastic traditions into the very core of their teachings. Neither Eckhart, Nicholas von Strassburg nor Tauler are ever found in opposition to St. Thomas or Albertus Magnus in an essential point of doctrine.[7] For them theology was of the utmost importance.

To say that the ascendancy of the Rhineland school was a protest against institutional religion is at best a fragmentary truth. Here again it must be remembered that its leaders were all members of the Church hierarchy. These Friends of God did not rebel against the established order of the Church as it existed in those hectic days of the early fourteenth century. They were in their beginnings a result of the indifferent conditions of the times. If some of their descendants later went off on particular heretical tangents, that was certainly due to other causes and was in no way connected with the origins of the movement.

Perhaps the most plausible explanation is that this sudden development of the mystic spirit was due to the introduction of scholastic philosophy to educated women in the convents.[8] Continual wars and conflicts had killed many men and caused a surplus of women. Many unmarried women of the educated class entered the cloistral life, and, as a result, religious houses, especially those of the Dominicans, greatly increased in number and importance. The duty to administer these nunneries and maintain their spiritual discipline fell, of course, to the friars, and those chosen to undertake this pastoral care were learned teachers. Hence it happened that in these religious houses of women there was an active intellectual life and many writings in prose and verse give evidence of it. Take, for example, Mechtild von Magdeburg, Margaret and Kristina Ebner, Elsbeth von Begenhofen, Adelheid Langmann, Elsbeth Stagel.

The task of the friars, then, was to express theological and philosophical ideas in a guise that would make them understood by these women. The result of all this was that many of the finest spiritual writings were sermons, conferences or treatises designed for nuns. Most of Tauler's Sermons, the Conferences of Nicholas von Strassburg and

Heinrich von Nördlingen, Suso's wonderful *Little Book of Eternal Wisdom* and, perhaps *The Book of the Poor in Spirit* belong to this category. Scholasticism provided a philosophy of mysticism. Sermons and treatises of a devotional nature were composed in the vernacular; and where technical terms suitable to the Latin were lacking, they had to be invented; abstract ideas were simplified and a more personal tone was introduced so that the true seeker became passionately aware of the immediate presence and accessibility of God. Thus the eloquence of these early Friends of God kindled a flame that long survived their death.

2

In the Rhineland of the fourteenth century, the Dominican Order held a position somewhat similar to that of the Society of Jesus three centuries later. It was the academy of great theologians, preachers and confessors. Originally bound together to combat heresy, these sons of St. Dominic soon realized the necessity of providing a teaching which could purify the streams of European thought at their source. In the first half of the thirteenth century they surmounted the opposition of University heads at Paris and succeeded in founding chairs of theology from which they challenged the paganizing philosophers of Christendom with their own weapons of reason. In St. Albertus Magnus of Cologne and St. Thomas Aquinas they in a sense reconquered philosophy for the Church and christianized Aristotle who soon took Plato's place as the Master of Philosophy.

Some of our Rhineland mystics had spent their student days at Paris, and most of them were thorough-going scholastics, that is, they thought it supremely important to give reason the noble respect due to it and to establish an intellectual expression for belief. Eckhart, Nicholas von Strassburg and Tauler, for instance, were reckoned among the most intellectual men of their day, but by the time they reached their prime, especially Tauler in the second quarter of the fourteenth century, many of the French Schoolmen had let themselves be taken prisoner by this wonderful gift of reason which St. Thomas had found so liberating. As our author says: "True wisdom is not studied in Paris but in the Passion,"[9] which echoes St. Bonaventure who wrote: "The divine Word teaches one more in real wisdom than all study,"[10] a statement with which St. Thomas certainly agreed. Tauler says in one of his sermons: "Those great teachers at Paris read enormous books and turn over the pages with great diligence, which is a very good thing. But spiritually enlightened men read the true living book, wherein all things live. They turn over the pages of the heavens and the earth and study the admirable wonders of God."[11]

Though recognizing the study of God's wonders to be the best that a man can choose, Tauler and his colleagues always hold that the study of philosophy is a "very good thing", that reason, like form, like the body, is a good if not necessary vehicle to God. This sound position,

however, was not favoured by all. There were some people in the Rhine provinces who advocated the denial of reason and form, the doctrine of absolute freedom of the spirit, the abolition of all distinctions between the creature and the Creator. Called Beghards and Brethren of the Free Spirit they were quite energetic in their proselytizing work among the clergy as well as the laity. In Cologne they were very numerous, and in spite of—or because of?— frequent persecutions, they continued to grow. That some of the Rhineland mystics were connected with them is certain, but they do not seem to have exercised any influence on men like Eckhart, Tauler, Suso or our author, who preached and wrote against them, and whose position is clear enough: "The Free Spirits, striving after a false freedom, and on the pretext of following the interior light, follow only the inclination of their own nature."[12]

The following selection of passages from Tauler is also worth noting, for it furnishes a complete refutation of the charge of these tendencies sometimes brought against his own sermons, and it serves as a fitting prelude to *The Book of the Poor in Spirit:*

> From these two errors proceeds the third, which is the worst of all. The persons who are thus confused call themselves beholders of God. . . . They think that they are free from sin, united to God without any means whatsoever, and that they have risen above all subjection to the Holy Church, above the Commandments of God and above all works of virtue. For they believe this emptiness to be so noble a thing that it should in no way be hindered. Hence they remain empty of all subjection and do no works either toward them who are above or below them. They believe that if they work it hinders the work of God, and therefore they empty themselves of all virtue. And they would be so empty that they would not give praise or thanks to God nor pray, for they have already, as they suppose, all that they could pray for and think that they are without self-will. . . . For the sake of this emptiness of spirit they desire to be free, and obedient to none, neither the Pope, nor the Bishop, nor the Pastor; and though they seem outwardly to be so at times, yet they are inwardly obedient to none, neither in will nor action. . . . They believe themselves to be exalted above the angels, and above all human merit and faith, so that they can neither increase in virtue nor commit sin. For they live, as they suppose, without will, and possess their spirits in peace and emptiness, and have become nothing in themselves and one with God. They believe that they may do freely, without sin, whatsoever nature desires, because they have attained to the highest innocence, and there is no law or commandment for them, and therefore they follow all the lusts of the flesh in order that the emptiness of the spirit may remain unharmed. They care neither for fasts, nor feasts, nor precepts, because they live without conscience in all things. Let each man examine himself whether he be not one of these![13]

The fanatical Beghards were by no means the only promoters of heresy under the guise of mysticism. The Catharists, Waldeneses, Albigenses, the Jochamists and a host of others were still making their presence felt. In fact, the fourteenth-century Rhinelanders were almost engulfed in religious anarchy. And little wonder! The whole German race was riddled with political dissension and warfare. These battles were in turn mixed up with the religious controversies then flourishing. Moreover, there was discord between the heads of the Church and its most diligent servants. Bishops clashed with the Pope, pastors with their bishops; Franciscans clashed with Dominicans and these with their Provincial Superiors.

On 25 November, 1314, at Aix-la-Chapelle, both Ludwig of Bavaria and Frederick of Austria were crowned head of the Holy Roman Empire. The result, of course, was a war which lasted until 1322. The whole Rhineland was divided between the rival Emperors and when Frederick marched up the great river in 1315 and entered Strasbourg, most of the burghers received him, not as their sovereign, but merely as a distinguished guest. The Bishop of Strasbourg and the clergy, on the other hand, gave him regal honours. When Ludwig heard of this he immediately confirmed the privileges and liberties of the city. Five years later when he arrived with his army and was offered the allegiance of the people in the great cathedral, he again confirmed their privileges. Public worship, however, had been suspended by the clerics who still recognized Frederick as Emperor and on whose side most of the nobles took their stand.

When Ludwig finally took Frederick prisoner, the hot war ceased, and when many of the noble families and some of the clergy came over to his side, it seemed that peace might be restored. But Pope John XXII, fearing that Ludwig's power, popularity and conceited temperament might make him too independent of the Papal Chair, decided to intervene in the affairs of the Empire. He refused to acknowledge Ludwig and placed all who did (this finally included whole cities!) under the famous interdict of 1324. Not only did this action create new and dreadful calamities throughout Europe, it stirred up the people to a resistance which was bound to weaken their reverence for the Holy See.

The clash between temporal and spiritual authority became more marked. Again Ludwig countered. He published a manifesto in which he refuted all the accusations brought against him and tried to prove that the Pope lacked authority to judge the Emperor. And to display his own sense of unchallengeable authority, he ordered that no one should observe the papal interdict. In fact he sentenced all who did, individuals, communities or cities, to be deprived of their citizen rights and privileges. In many places the churches had long been closed, and when the clergy did not obey the Emperor's edict to open them, the impatient citizens forced all priests who refused to perform services to leave.

This split the clergy into two parties. The larger number obeyed the Pope and removed themselves to other provinces. Some remained, particularly the Dominicans and Franciscans, who had availed themselves of the special privilege granted to their Orders of celebrating Mass dur-

ing the time of the interdict. They did not cling to this out-dated privilege very long, however, for, as the Emperor continued in his open opposition to the Holy See, the fear of excommunication weighed more heavily upon them and all but a few left. In some places churches, monasteries and schools stood empty for nearly three years.

How this affected our author we do not know. But Johann Tauler was in the midst of it all and the question has often been raised as to the part he played. Most of the evidence indicates that he, along with the Dominican house at Strasbourg, submitted to the Holy See. If this meant the giving up of important duties in that city where he lived with the mystic Johann von Sterngassen and the theologian Johann von Dambach, it certainly increased his field of labour elsewhere. Most of the free cities from Cologne to Basle heard his sermons and lectures, and he became quite as well known as his teacher Eckhart of the preceding generation.

There was a time during the interdict when Tauler lived with his Carthusian friends at their monastery near Strasbourg. Neither Tauler in his sermons nor our author makes precise comments on current events or on political and religious problems; but the tone of their writings certainly evinces an utter disappointment in the conduct of their temporal and spiritual leaders. Tauler says: "Now the Apostle tells us to contend against princes and powers, and the rulers of the darkness of this world. This means the devils. But it also means the princes of this world, who ought to be the best of all, and are nevertheless the very horses on which the devils ride to sow discord and treason, and who torment their subjects by their pride and unjust tyranny and manifold oppressions, as we now see throughout the world."[14]

And to all these political and ecclesiastical disturbances even greater miseries were added. The upper Rhineland was successively laid waste by violent tempests, earthquakes and famine, culminating in the Black Death of 1348. In some places two-thirds of the population perished, causing a state of terror and the complete disruption of social bonds. Popular fanaticism frequently accused the Jews of causing the plague by poisoning the wells, and the furious mobs, setting fire to the ghettoes, burnt thousands of men and women and children in their homes. It was not uncommon to find among the masses a hope for a Messiah in the person of the great "priest-hater", Frederick II, who was to rise from the dead, redeem the poorer classes, punish the priests, force nuns and monks to marry, and then crusade to the Holy Land and place his crown on the Mount of Olives. Nor was it uncommon to find people turning to another fanaticism, to the extravagant penance which developed into the ghastly processions of the Flagellants.

All these convulsions of the natural and social world struck terror in the depths of men's hearts. But, as often happens in an age of fierce violence and suffering, the fourteenth-century Rhineland culture was distinguished by restless and energetic productivity. A general level of excellence was not to be expected in a land so broken and disordered, but the soil of German human nature was nevertheless rich in capacities. From its confused and retarded vegetation, rare plants emerged—inventors, architects and craftsmen of great capabilities. These people, who were unable to produce a great statesman or a Dante, did put into use two implements which have done most to revolutionize Western society—gunpowder and the printing press. But more than this, it produced men like Eckhart, Suso and Tauler who, with the earnestness of profound conviction, began to discourse to the people in their native tongue on lofty philosophical and spiritual themes, till then only thought fit to be treated in Latin before learned assemblies. And because virtue has no publicity, it is unlikely that we shall ever discover how many saints it produced.

3

The need for a revival of the religion of the heart was, in the fourteenth-century Rhineland, quite obvious. But it was equally necessary that such a revival should preserve as well as respect the established order of religion, for there was no other social bond able to hold men together. Keeping this order intact when so many forces were tending towards schism was one of the secrets of the Dominicans and Franciscans.

Now, in spite of all the scandals of that age, most of the people were far from being "wicked". In that age, as in ours, there were many men and women who possessed clean, calm and affectionate natures. Being schooled in conscientious habits, so many of their desires were for quite harmless or even good things that it was frequently difficult to see why or how they should be renounced. They were good people—just, kind, finding much of their personal happiness in the happiness of others. And for the most part they lived in pleasant relations with their neighbours and had little to trouble their conscience beyond the fear of neglecting the path upon which duty had called them.

But the dangers to which such people were exposed were more insidious (because less obvious) than those which faced others who were sorely tempted. Their greatest danger perhaps was their tendency to depend too much on the respect and affection which others gave them. They were in danger of measuring themselves according to a standard of virtue which had come to be, not one of spiritual combat, but one of placing intellectual clarity above moral strength and insight; of mistaking the comfort they felt in the performance of duty for submission to God's will; and perhaps most important, of recoiling from new perceptions of truth which might temporarily disorientate their faith and disturb the even-going pattern of their lives.

The spiritual welfare of such people as these (and we have seen that a great number of them were nuns) became the chief responsibility of the friars. In lifting a few of them

out of their groove, they did not turn them into mystics or saints; but they filled them with a concern for truth and the spiritual life, and out of the concern mysticism and sanctity were the logical developments. Now when the concern is genuine it produces a genuine mysticism, not a magical pseudo-mysticism based on the assumption that demons, superhuman powers, angels, even God, can be compelled to do whatever the ego may want them to do. There is a pseudo-mysticism—all too natural and human—which seeks mastership over God; there is a genuine mysticism—supernatural and divine—which seeks friendship with God.

The term "Friend of God" is one which is frequently observed in the writings of the Rhineland mystics. It is a title which seems to have two different connections.[15] On the one hand it indicates those who habitually practise a spiritual, rather than a mere formalistic devotion. On the other hand, "Friends of God" denoted an actual group of individuals who formed more or less a nucleus to this religious revival. They differed widely from each other in station, opinion and vocation, counting among their members Franciscans and Dominicans, married and single tertiaries, nobles, craftsmen and servants, a great flock of nuns like Margaret and Kristina Ebner, many Beguines, a Queen like Agnes of Hungary, a banker like that strange and dubious Rulman Merswin, then Ludolf the Carthusian, Konrad von Kaiserheim, Deitrich von Köln—even the Flemish Ruysbroeck, even Johann von Schönhofen of the Netherlands, for the *Pfaffengasse* or "Parson's alley", the highway of the Rhine which led to Rome, had its northern extension into the heart of the Low Countries.

The title *Gottesfreunde* or Friends of God, which also applied to many others less known, was undoubtedly used among themselves to indicate those who gave evidence of being more truly concerned about the realities of religion than the great majority of their neighbours. In John 15:15, we read: "I will not now call you servants: for the servant knoweth not what his lord doeth. But I have called you friends: because all things, whatsoever I have heard of My Father, I have made known to you." It was an inevitable process that those filled with such common concerns should instinctively seek out each other. By clinging to and relying upon each other, an association without precise plans naturally developed. And if one reads the writings of men like Tauler, Suso and Ruysbroeck it would appear that the main distinction and bond of the *Gottesfreunde* was the sense of having entered into a personal cooperation with God. And this friendship with God was accompanied by a compassion for those who had fallen, either into wickedness or into mere respectable goodness, and a desire to assist them in their efforts to raise themselves to where the reality of God became more real than the realities of time and place.

The Friends of God did not form a sect. In fact they rejected any tendency in that direction. As Tauler himself says: "The prince of this world has in our time been sowing everywhere brambles among the roses so that the roses are frequently suffocated, or seriously torn by the brambles. Dear Children, there needs to be a flight or a distinction, some sort of divergence, whether within the cloisters or without, and that such friends of God should profess to be unlike the friends of the world does not make them into a sect."[16] And these friends of God became friends of the friars. Many of them were lay people, some continued with their professions, introducing into them a godlike direction. Others—women particularly, the famous Beguines—without entering any of the established Orders, withdrew from society and formed little communities. And though they lived together without monastic rules, they differed little from the regular religious. References to these communities are often found in the friars' sermons, and a great number of their members attached themselves to the leaders of this religious movement.

The Friends of God aimed at becoming saints and at giving edification in Catholic devotion, not heterodox enthusiasm; at affective contemplation, not mystical brain-work. And that leaders like Tauler had full confidence in them is shown when he says: "For those who want to live for the truth, it is a great assistance to have a Friend of God who may guide them by the spirit of God. It would be well worth one's while to travel a hundred leagues to seek out an experienced Friend of God."[17] Similar affirmation can be found in Suso's *Briefbuchlein.*

As long as the *Gottesfreunde* remained under the guidance of men like Tauler and Suso, they were preserved from defect. In an age that was witnessing the sterility of scientific theology, Heinrich Suso was founding the Children of Mary. As his *Little Book of Eternal Wisdom* was composed for spiritual reading, so was his *The Book of Truth*[18] written to refute the errors of the Beghards. Nicholas von Strassburg, himself a great mystic, placed more emphasis on ascetical devotion than on metaphysical speculation. And Tauler, as we have seen, opposed the pseudo-mysticism of the Free Spirits and the schismatical tendencies of Ludwig of Bavaria while directing his followers towards a full co-operation with God's grace. But the glory of the Friends of God was not to last.

It is very easy to show that the leaders of Rhineland mysticism were orthodox in all their principal teachings and that their obedience to the Church was throughout irreproachable. But it must also be recognized that their mystical doctrine of the inner and outer life, of the spirit and the letter, gave lesser minds an excuse for a disregard of many aspects of Catholicism, so far as in their century and land it consisted largely in formalism and obedience to external rule. For instance, the influence of Meister Eckhart's boldness is strongly felt in Tauler and Suso, in the mysticism of Ruysbroeck, and later in the synthesis of Nicholas von Cues, in Thomas à Kempis and Angelus Selesius.[19] But it was also felt no less in persons not nearly as astute.

Professor J. M. Clark in his *The Great German Mystics,*[20] has been the first to point out to English readers how the unorthodox have often tried to claim Eckhart for their son, disregarding his overwhelmingly orthodox teachings and his unswerving fidelity to order and the Church. They endeavoured to establish their claim on a few exceptional passages which he later modified or corrected; but does not the exceptional always gain the most publicity? The Meister's occasional failure to clarify his views resulted in the condemnation of some of his statements. Though he recanted, the blow to mystical speculation was felt. And after his death in 1328, mysticism became more practical and less speculative. Of the three stages in the mystic way—purgative, illuminative and unitive, it was the first two, the preparatory stages, in which the will played the more decisive role, that received importance. No doubt the tragic fate of Eckhart opened the minds of men like Tauler and Suso to the dangers of discussing the profounder mysteries of theology in the presence of untrained minds. As Tauler says in one of his sermons:

> A well-loved Master [Eckhart] has written and preached to you concerning this mystic union with God and you did not understand him. He spoke in terms of eternity and you understood in terms of time. Dear Children, if I myself have talked too much about this, it is not too much for God, but you must forgive me; I will make amends gladly. This wonderful Master once spoke of that rare perception that knows no way or form. Many people seize upon this with their sensual minds and become sinful men, and for that reason it is a hundred times better that one should arrive at it by ways and forms.[21]

There is always a danger of institutionalism and of hardened systems of thought, whether scholastic or otherwise, in the touch of the living God on the heart of man. But Tauler, Suso and the other leaders did accomplish the unique task of upholding the law they were in duty bound to obey while at the same time speaking of the inner secrets of the soul, which became for them a profound reality. It meant the adoption of a *via media,* and as long as this middle course was kept, the Friends of God grew in spiritual and numerical strength. The association, however, did not long remain under the guidance of wise men.

One of the happy aspects of this movement was that it did not confine itself to priests and nuns, and in one sense the merchant Rulman Merswin represented its lay genius. But Merswin, probably through ignorance and excessive zeal, played a large part in bringing the whole movement of Rhineland mysticism into disrepute. By founding a religious house which was to be a great centre for the Friends of God, and by writing a book about his alleged spiritual master—a mysterious layman of the upper Rhine (*Der Gottesfreund vom Oberland*),[22] he became very popular and after Tauler's (1361) and Suso's (1366) death, the favourite leader of the movement. It was then, and towards the turn of the fifteenth century, that certain exaggerated and erroneous doctrines began to creep into the Friends of God.[23] In a posthumous work, *The Book of the Nine Rocks,* Merswin ascribes to his unknown *Gottesfre-*

und (the Friend of God *par excellence*) counsellings in favour of violent discipline, all sorts of revelations, prophecies of impending chastisement and a divine mission to expurgate the Church. All of this is diametrically opposed to the teachings of Tauler, Suso and the author of *The Book of the Poor in Spirit.*

The story of Merswin and those who looked upon him as their spiritual leader is certainly one of the greatest puzzles of the fourteenth-century spiritual revival. Most of the critics have now concluded that his famous *Gottesfreund,* the anonymous spiritual director, was quite fictitious. Even in his own day the true descendants of Tauler and Suso refrained from association with these pseudo-Friends of God, and they gave still less attention to Nicholas von Basel who, upon Merswin's death, became the recognized leader of the heterodox wing. He, however, was eventually condemned as a Beghard and from 1410 the Friends of God, whether true or false, disappear. Either because of the general decline of the mystic spirit and the terminology connected with it, or because the term itself fell into disrepute as a result of Merswin and heretical associations, the word *Gottesfreund* fails to appear in the spiritual writings of the fifteenth century. Here, perhaps, is another example of how the death of true mysticism is the inevitable result of vicious attacks on the false mystics. . . .

Notes

1. Matthew 5.3.

2. See *Vorwort, Die Predigten Taulers, Deutsche Texte der Mittelalters,* by F. Vetter. Vol. XI, 1910. See note 110.

3. Marcus von Lindau was Franciscan Superior of the Strasbourg Province. See Bishop Greith in note 105.

4. Luther himself was familiar with the book and even enthusiastic about those aspects which grant a deeper insight into personal religion. He seems, however, to have forgotten these when he came to construct his rigid theology of a "completely other God". See *Luther's Theologie,* by Köstlin, and also note 100.

5. *Geschichte der Entdeckung der deutschen Mystiker,* G. Fischer, and also note 100.

6. It should be mentioned that the references made to Eckhart by Hegel and Schopenhauer are from writings falsely attributed to him, hence it is inaccurate for them to regard him as a kindred spirit. See *Das Göttliche in der Seele,* O. Karrer, Würzburg, 1928.

7. Hugueny, P., *Sermons de Tauler,* Paris, 1927, I, p. 73. Furthermore: "A disciple of Eckhart, Tauler is, as his master, wholly penetrated with Scholasticism." F. Vernet says: "These Rhineland mystics are, after all, theologians trained in the scholastic discipline, formed by the school of St. Thomas and in complete accord with him." (*Dictionnaire de Spiritualité,* I, col. 325.) See also:

E. Gilson—*La Philosophie au moyen âge,* Paris, 1922, II, pp. 142-143; X. de Hornstein—*Les Grands mystiques allemands,* Lucerne, 1922, p. 228; M. Grabmann—*Die Lehre des heiligen Thomas von Aquin der Scintilla Animae in Ihrer Bedautung für die deutsche Mystik im Predigeorden,* in *Jahrbuch für Philosophie und spekulative Theologie,* 1899, p. 413.

8. Grundmann, J., *Religiöse Bewegungen,* Berlin, 1935, p. 276.

9. IV, ii, 7.

10. *Itinerarium Mentis ad Deum,* C. VII.

11. Lehmann W., *Johann Tauler Predigten,* Vol. II, p. 235, Jena, 1913. (A translation of Vetter.)

12. Büttner, H., *Meister Eckharts Schriften und Predigten,* Vol. II, p. 196, Jena, 1912. See also Suso's *Buchlein von der Wahrheit,* ch. VII; *Theologia Germanica,* Ch. XXV; and our author's section on "Spiritual Misdirected Freedom," I, iv, 3.

13. Sermon on the Fifth Sunday in Lent, No. 31, Frankfort Ed., 1836. See also Lehmann, *op. cit.,* Nos. 36 and 40, and his Introduction, for a good life of Tauler based on the genuine available data.

14. Lehmann, *op. cit.,* Vol. II, p. 216.

15. Jundt, A., *Les Amis de Dieu au quatorzième siècle,* Paris, 1879; E. Peterson—*Der Gottesfreund* (*Beiträge zur Geschichte eines religiösen Terminus*), in *Zeitschrift für Kirchengeschichte,* Gotha, 1923, V, pp. 161-202; K. Egenter—*Gottesfreundschaft,* Augsberg, 1928; M. Grabmann—*Idee der Gottesfreund* (*Beiträge zur Geschichte der Philosophie des Mittelalters*), II, p. 1021; B. Schoemann—*Die Rede von den XV Graden, Rheinische Gottesfreundmystik, "ein characteristik Texte",* Berlin, 1930.

16. For the use which the *Gottesfreunde* made of Psalm 138.17, see *Speculum Ecclesiae,* by Kelle, p. 94; also *Kirchengeschichte Deutschlands,* I, p. 70. Prof. Chiquot says: "In this sense referred to by Tauler, so St. Augustine, St. Bernard, St. Albert the Great, St. Thomas, St. Bonaventure were proclaimed Friends of God." (*Amis de Dieu, Dictionnaire de Spiritualité,* I, col. 493.) The Rhineland Friends of God were known to quote St. Thomas's *Caritas amicitia quaedam est hominis ad Deum,* 2. 2. qu.23, a.1.

17. Sermon on the Birth of Our Lady, No. 127, Frankfurt Ed.

18. These two books may now be had in one volume in Prof. J. M. Clark's splendid translation. (Faber and Faber, London, 1953.) *The Book of Truth* is published in English for the first time.

19. Karrer, Otto, *Meister Eckhart,* Das system seiner religiösen Lehre und seiner Lebensweisheit, Munich, 1926.

20. *The Great German Mystics, Eckhart, Tauler and Suso* (Oxford, 1949).

21. Lehmann, *op. cit.,* Vol. I, p. 71.

22. Strauch, P., *Schriften aus der Gottesfreundliteratur,* Halle, 1927. See also: A. Chiquot—*Histoire ou légende? Jean Tauler et le 'Meisters Buoch',* Strasbourg, 1922, with review in *Revue D'Histoire Ecclésiastique,* XXI, p. 428.

23. Denifle, H. S., *Die Dichtungen Gottesfreundes im Oberlande, Zeitschrift für deutsches Altertum,* 1880. Perhaps had Rufus Jones, for his *Flowering of Mysticism,* and Evelyn Underhill, for her *Mysticism,* studied this and other more current works they would not have written so favourably of Merswin. . . .

Eric Colledge (essay date 1961)

SOURCE: An introduction to *Spiritual Conferences,* by John Tauler, edited by Eric Colledge and M. Jane, B. Herder Book Co., 1961, pp. 1-32.

[*In the following essay, Colledge describes some of fourteenth-century Christendom's scandalous and divisive elements and explains how Tauler advocated dealing with them through the practice of true simplicity and true humility.*]

Three great figures dominated German spirituality in the fourteenth century, and all three were members of the Order of Preachers: Eckhart, Tauler and Suso. We cannot rightly appreciate any one of them without knowing and understanding the other two; and although Eckhart and Suso appear to us across the centuries as mysterious and tragic personalities, utterly unlike the genial, sanguine, equable Tauler, we are made to realize, as we learn to know him better, that he had not escaped the mortal sorrows which had afflicted his brethren. He speaks of these sorrows, not with Suso's violence and self-pity, but with his own characteristic tranquil simplicity, when he says, "What then remains to the man formed after God's image? There remain to him a soul full of God and a body full of suffering."

In his Sermon XVI, for the Sunday after Easter, expounding the theme that "sorrow shall be turned into joy" by the Paraclete and Comforter, he shows us, without any special reference to himself, how utterly he had been possessed by sorrow and how wholly Christ-like had been his bearing of it. "What does Christ mean when He says, 'I must leave you,' except that we shall be abandoned, comfortless, indifferent; that we shall be weary and cold and heavy and sad? When this happens to us, then He has left us. Those who would ponder these things and turn them to their profit could find here great riches, which could bring them much happiness, for everything that had been broken up in them would become one whole; their sorrows would turn into comfort and their mourning into joy, and all their bitterness would be truly sweet."

Here we have one of the great lessons which Tauler has to teach, the lesson of the mystery which Job expounded: for man without sorrow there can be no joy, because sorrow is its price. Tauler does not speak of forgetting sorrow or of compensating for it; he says that it is sorrow itself which leads to and becomes joy. Again and again he tells us that this happens as we turn from God's creatures to Him and do His will.

We cannot attempt here to solve the many problems which are presented by Eckhart: his personality, his teaching, his condemnation and his posthumous fame; but we shall not understand the depths of Tauler's tribulations and the greatness of his triumph over them until we at least see what those problems are. They raise questions which do not merely stir the arid dust of a dead and bygone age, but which are as pertinent to the twentieth century as to the Middle Ages. And we shall see that the answers which Tauler in his simplicity found for them will lead us, by the straight and plain road of faith, to conclusions which are being confirmed more and more as valid by the discoveries and the judgments of modern scholarship. The afflictions and the grief to which the lives and works of Tauler and his contemporaries testify are in part the common lot of humanity and in part the additional burden which must be carried by all those to whom God has chosen to reveal Himself in all the fullness of His being, but the times in which they lived and the age to which they were heirs laid their own burdens upon them.

The fourteenth century was from first to last an epoch of scandal and division in Christendom. We can feel the whole weight of the tragedy as we read Suso's *Horologium Sapientiae,* but with Tauler, as with St. Bernardine of Siena and St. Vincent Ferrer later, we often can only marvel that a man living in the midst of such fearful conflicts could achieve and maintain such perfect serenity. Very occasionally he will allude to the times—"Children, the grievous ways of life which so enraged the Heavenly Father that He wished to destroy all the world in the days of our father St. Dominic, who then by his prayers dissuaded Him, these same sinful ways have reappeared, and we cannot tell how it shall go with us"—but it is not necessary here to describe how, during Tauler's life-time, Germany was divided in the conflict between Pope and Emperor and how different members of his Order took opposing sides. But there were other, less open but more bitter, struggles being fought, in which Tauler was deeply involved, and of them we must take some little account.

When we think of thirteenth-century religious life in Western Europe, most of us will first remember the two great religious leaders who so influenced it: the little Poor Man of Assisi, whose entire way of life seems to us at first so startlingly unlike anything which medieval Christianity had so far produced, and, in great contrast to his dazzling personality, the self-effacing yet finally all-pervasive influence of St. Dominic. Historians are assembling more and more evidence to convince us that the emergence of these two men was indeed amazing, but not for the reasons which have hitherto been given. In addition to being the first to suffer in ecstasy the dolors of the Passion, St. Francis, we are now learning, embodied and personified a new method of devotion to those dolors which was springing up everywhere in the West, a devotion whose roots we cannot yet trace, but of which he seems to be not the root but the flower. So too with St. Dominic, who shared St. Francis's intense love for that poverty which he saw most perfectly exemplified in Christ Himself. Today we are coming to realize that the wonder in the lives of these two saints is that they were able to grasp, to purify and to direct a devotion to Christ's poverty as an antidote to priestly worldliness which, had it not been for them, might have brought anarchy and ruin into every Christian land. St. Francis and St. Dominic, with the aid of Pope Innocent III, were able to close the gap between the hierarchical Church and the growing religious movement, hitherto suspected and repressed everywhere by the bishops, which sought to promote "apostolic" itinerant preaching and "evangelical" poverty. One of the results of this effort was that Pope Innocent was able to enroll in the war upon heresy and in the operations of the Inquisition precisely those elements which hitherto had been, potentially at least, disaffected.

Those of us who are chiefly concerned or familiar with English religious history in the Middle Ages will find ourselves on unfamiliar ground here. The author of the English rule for anchoresses, the *Ancrene Riwle,* writing early in the thirteenth century, is able to remark, with as much truth as complacency: "Heresy, thanks be to God, does not prevail among us." But when we look (as the author of the *Riwle* undoubtedly was looking) across the North Sea at what was happening in Europe, we are bound to suspect that the real reason why there was so little heresy in England was because there was so little religious enthusiasm.

One of the most able of recent historians, Professor Herbert Grundmann, has remarked that in the Middle Ages every religious movement was faced with the choice either of becoming a monastic order or of separating from the Church and becoming a heretical sect. Like most generalizations, this statement seeks to include and to simplify too much, but it is nevertheless of deep significance for the early history of the Dominican Order. Further, when we seek to understand Eckhart's place in the Order and his influence upon Tauler, we shall do well to remember, although with reservations, the same scholar's remark that the great weakness that prevails in historical studies of the heretical sects is that their authors, whatever their religious beliefs, are too interested in the differences between heretics and the orthodox. The great Dominican historian of the last century, Denifle, arrived by very different ways at a similar conclusion: if today we think of Eckhart as an opponent and destroyer of Catholic orthodoxy, it is chiefly because we have always allowed the opponents of such orthodoxy to claim him for their own.

The earliest days of the first mendicant missions to Germany prepare us for the later troubles in which Eckhart and his followers were to be involved. The Franciscans arrived in 1219. After arrest and imprisonment they were glad to be able to return to Italy, suspected as they were of heresy and not having sufficient facility in German to defend themselves. Their second expedition, two years later, was led by German brethren, but even then, like the Dominicans before them, they were accused of being the "wandering men" and "false prophets" against whom earlier prophecies had warned the Germans. It is significant that the center of their troubles seems to have been in Cologne and among its clergy.

Yet, from the earliest days in Germany the mendicants, and especially the Dominicans, attracted to themselves groups and houses of religious women who were seeking a way of life which would give scope and direction to their spiritual aspirations. Professor Grundmann is the historian of this astonishing outburst of piety among the laity of Germany, and Fr. Stephanus Axters, O.P., has produced a comparable history for the Low Countries, where many such communities, rejected in their attempts to seek incorporation with the Cistercian and other orders, formed the houses and sororities of charity and devotion whose inhabitants were given the name of "Beguines."

In the Rhineland and elsewhere in Germany the many communities who wished to be affiliated with the Dominicans met great difficulties at the beginning. At the time of the death of St. Dominic, the Order's policy was to reject all such proposals, and many years were to pass before established communities of religious women were admitted, partly under continued pressure from such women and partly because of a change of legislation by the Holy See.

In 1245 many such affiliations were allowed, and in Tauler's days, as he and his brethren travelled through their Province of Teutonia (erected in 1303, together with the Province of Saxony, when it was at last conceded that the old German province contained so many houses that it could no longer be administered, extending as it did from Schwyz, Neuenkirch and Brunnadern in Switzerland, to Cologne and Auderghem), a Dominican nunnery was never far away. Many of them were situated in the vast and wealthy dioceses of Constance and Strasbourg. In the city of Strasbourg there were no fewer than seven convents of the Order, and throughout Teutonia in 1303 there were approximately seventy convents, more than half the total number in the Order and more by far than the friaries, of which in 1277 there were fifty-three in Germany. We need not wonder that a man of Tauler's gifts seems to have devoted his entire life in the Order to the "care of women," and if we are to understand the background to his life, we must always remember that the Dominican nuns to whom he preached were the heiresses of that great movement of lay piety and popular devotion which had marked the previous century.

One of the chief difficulties in the way of any assessment of these popular devotions has always been a comparative lack of textual evidence, although it has for long been agreed that it is inconceivable that some of the earliest surviving mystical works written in German or Dutch, such as *The Flowing Light of the Godhead* by Mechtild of Magdeburg and the letters, visions and poems of Hadewijch, are not the products of a long tradition of such vernacular writing. Further diligent search may well produce traces of such early works, and recently the possible discovery of a later link in the chain has been announced.

Writing in 1935, Professor Grundmann observed that there was a close connection between the doctrines of the heretics who were apprehended in Swabia in the early 1270's and the book of Margaret Porette, which was condemned as heretical by the bishop of Cambrai in 1305. Margaret herself, who persisted in publishing the book and in teaching its doctrines, was condemned and burned in Paris five years later. The evidence on which Grundmann based his opinion consisted, so far as the Swabian heresies are concerned, of various Dominican records, and principally of a series of notes made by St. Albert the Great, whose opinion seems to have been sought by those who had interrogated the suspects. It appears that they met and taught in conventicles; that some of them were women; that some of these women averred that Christ had had carnal knowledge of them (another had said that she had suckled the Holy Infant, and St. Albert noted that this was not a heresy to be confuted but a folly to be cured with a sound thrashing); most of all, they taught *deificatio* or *Vergottung*. "Man can become God," the heretics say, "and in union with God the soul can become divine."

The suspects were asked if they believed that this "deification" came about as the experience of grace, as a supernatural operation of the Godhead which draws man toward God and into God (a doctrine common to all mysticism), or whether they believe that man is able to become deified by his own natural powers, or whether deification refers to man's likeness to God. The suspects' evasive answers concerning grace led St. Albert to brand them as Pelagians.

Grundmann goes on to point out that in *The Flowing Light of the Godhead* we shall find sentiments not unlike these. Mechtild makes God say to the soul: "My lady soul, your nature has become so much My nature (*ir sint so sere genaturt in mich*) that nothing can be left between you and Me." Because of these and similar utterances, Mechtild was accused of heresy, and we have her own account of how she answered her accusers: "In one place in the book I said that the Godhead was my Father by nature, but that you would not allow, and you said that all that God has worked in us is of grace and not of nature. You are right; and I too am right." She goes on to explain in the form of a simile what the illumined soul may understand of the Godhead; how God by His nature has worked upon the soul, reformed her, planted the soul within Himself and has "united Himself with the soul more than with any other creature, and has encompassed the soul within

Himself, and has poured His divine nature so much into her that the soul cannot say other than that the Godhead is in every sense her Father."

Grundmann observes that from the point of view of dogma this may be incontestable, but it is not unambiguous, and if we had merely an inquisitor's notes of this answer, it might sound very much like that of the Swabian heretic who asserted that "a good man may say that he has grace and that he has not grace." But Professor Grundmann goes on to make the very just observation that there is one other essential difference: Mechtild consciously associated herself with those who were obedient to the law and the rule of the Church, whereas St. Albert records that the Swabian heretics taught that "good men ought not to reveal their goodness and their grace to scholars, because scholars do not understand these things."

The next point which Grundmann made was that similar doctrines can be discerned in what little evidence was available, in 1935, concerning the contents of Margaret Porette's book. When he wrote, none of her writings had survived, it was believed, except two articles of her doctrine which were quoted by the inquisitors who had condemned her: "The soul brought to nothing (*anima adnichilata*) no longer cares for the virtues and is no longer in their service, for the soul no longer exercises virtues, but they obey her command"; and: "Such a soul no longer cares for God's consolations or gifts, nor ought to care for them nor can, since all her intention is toward God, and such cares would impede her." It is true that a contemporary chronicler, reporting Margaret's condemnation, says that she taught that "the soul brought to nothing in the love of her Creator can and should permit to nature whatever it longs for and wants, without any twinge of conscience or remorse." If Margaret had taught this, it would make her no better than any of the Brethren of the Free Spirit, those unhappy souls against whose vile doctrines Ruysbroek was to preach so unremittingly, and whose miserable exaltation of carnal promiscuity into the service of God is so horribly portrayed for us at the close of the Middle Ages in Jerome Bosch's terrible allegorical paintings.

Fortunately, we have recently acquired further information which indicates that this second report is the chronicler's own invention and a baseless libel. In 1946 Dr. Romana Guarnieri announced the sensational conclusions of her study of the evidence concerning Margaret. Her book, far from having disappeared, is none other than *The Mirror of Simple Souls,* a text constantly studied by pious souls throughout Europe in the fourteenth and fifteenth centuries with little suspicion that it had once been condemned as heretical. One must not seek here to anticipate events; our judgment must be suspended until we have before us the edition of the medieval Latin and Italian texts which Dr. Guarnieri promises and also a text of the French version, which may prove to be derived from Margaret's original work, hitherto presumed to be lost, but which has recently been discovered at Chantilly in the Condy Museum. Until then we can only judge from the partial evidence of the single printed text available, that made from the medieval English version. We see in this text that the author of *The Mirror* had submitted it for approval to three censors, one of whom we know to have died in 1306 (and we know that in 1310 Margaret was accused of seeking approval for her book after it had been condemned in 1305). Another of the censors, while giving it approval, had said that he thought its language dangerous and that few people should see it. We also learn from several scholars that *The Mirror* was deeply influenced throughout by a work of the early twelfth-century writer, William of St. Thierry: *Letter to the Brethren of the Mount of God,* and particularly by his teaching that the soul has a likeness to God which is "above virtues." But nowhere in *The Mirror* shall we find any hint of the doctrine which states that because the soul has become like to God and "above virtues," it is indifferent whether the body practice virtue or vice.

If Dr. Guarnieri's thesis be proved true, the justice of Margaret Porette's condemnation as a heretic will have to be reconsidered. Many persons of her own time, themselves of unimpeachable orthodoxy, questioned other such condemnations. The Beguine Hadewijch, in one of her "visions," includes a list of the holy men and women throughout Christendom known to have vowed themselves to the perfect service of God. One such woman is now dead, she says, because "Master Robert put her to death because of her true love." "Master Robert" is undoubtedly the notorious exheretic and inquisitor, called "le Bougre," who finally had to be withdrawn from the Low Countries and France because of the indignation which his ferocity aroused. We know little of the victim of his whom Hadewijch mourns, but Hadewijch must have known that her own "true love" might easily lead her to the same fate. As Margaret Porette and *The Mirror* speak of a soul "brought to nothing" in the love of God, so Hadewijch, in one of her great songs of divine love, sings:

> "To be brought all to nought in love,
> That is the best thing that I know,"

and then continues:

> "Press on to joy, press on to woe;
> If you know how to storm love's citadel
> There is no hiding-place for love to go;
> She must take you with her to dwell."

The most recent commentator on her poems shows that it is impossible to convey in any language but Hadewijch's Dutch the play between "to nought" (*te niete*) and "by storm" (*met niede*), a play which she might well have expected her hearers to appreciate.

The same commentator, who has concealed his identity behind his initials, "Fr. J.-B. P.," goes on to make the same point with respect to these verses as Professor Grundmann made concerning the extant articles of Margaret Porette's doctrine: either might have been Eckhart (although Eckhart (although it is essential that we

remember that both women wrote before his works were known). "The treatise, *Of the Passing-Over of the God-head,"* writes Fr. J.-B. P., "which is of the school of Eckhart, is devoted precisely to this being brought to nothing of the soul; and in it the author tells us that 'when man enters that state which is beyond rational analysis . . . in which he is led to the mysterious power of the Father, . . . his heart becomes without depths, his soul without love, his spirit without shape and his nature without manner!' "

Presently we shall see that this "unfathomable shapelessness," without and beyond love and manner, appears also in the doctrine of Tauler, who had learned it from Eckhart. These are the terms in which they sought to describe something of the nature of "the mysterious union with God to which not all men are called, which consists in the soul's being raised through the special operations of grace to a higher contemplation of heavenly things, and even of God Himself, so that the soul by such means comprehends that supernatural community with the being of God which sanctifying grace grants to the just, comprehending it no longer merely through faith but learning to recognize it through experience." (This definition is that of the nineteenth-century theologian, Kleutgen, and Denifle quotes it with approval, as part of his demonstration that the way of mystical union is an "extraordinary way" and that Tauler and his masters cannot be shown to have taught otherwise.)

If one had space enough and learning, it would be rewarding to take each item of the Eckhart-Suso-Tauler body of teaching and examine its ancestry, but perhaps enough has been said here to show that the thirteenth century was marked by great popular outbursts of piety, especially in the Netherlands and the German-speaking lands of the Empire; that such piety and mystical devotion were common among the communities of women who attached themselves to various religious movements and orders, notably the German Dominicans and the Netherlands houses of the Beguines; that in such pious communities the composition of devout treatises in the vernacular probably began even earlier than the oldest extant records; that such treatises and records manifest certain trends of thought which only with difficulty can be distinguished from the heresies which were being taught by contemporary groups of the devout who had separated themselves knowingly from the faith and rule of the Church; and that among some orthodox mystics certain persons were privately venerated as martyrs who had taught the mystical way of union with God and whose teachings, it was believed, had been misunderstood and misinterpreted by the witch-hunters of the time.

We must keep these things in mind if we wish to understand why Eckhart taught as he did, and why his disciples continued to venerate him after his condemnation. Tauler tells us in so many words that he knows Eckhart to have been misinterpreted, but characteristically unlike Suso, he does not lay the blame upon Eckhart's professed enemies. In his Sermon XV, for the eve of Palm Sunday, on the Scriptural text: *Clarifica me Pater claritate quam habui prius,* Tauler speaks of the "extraordinary way" to God along which mere intellect and spiritual exercise will never lead us, and then he continues: "There was one great teacher who taught you and told you about these things, but you did not understand him. He talked about eternity, but you took it as referring to time." Here Tauler puts his finger upon one of the dangers in so subtle a doctrine as Eckhart's: few will understand him aright, and those who do not, will distort his teaching. To such pupils, and also to their teachers, one of the remedies which Tauler often recommends is humility and simplicity. In his Sermon XLII, on *Duc in altum,* he contrasts various mystical theologians: "Many masters, both old and new, have spoken of this inward excellence which lies hidden in the depths of the soul—Bishop Albert, Master Dietrich, Master Eckhart. One of them calls it a 'spark of the soul,' another a 'plain' or a 'peak,' another a 'principle.'" It is certainly not fortuitous that Tauler then goes on to say that the way to true blessedness is the way of humility, and quotes our Lord's words: "Learn of Me, for I am meek and humble of heart," and says again that the Father has revealed His mysteries to little children and has hidden them from the wise.

It was true simplicity, never to be achieved without true humility, which Tauler taught, and not the rash simplification by which foolish men believe that the truth can be known without effort. Every man, however simple, may well ask: "If God made all things, and He is good, who made evil?" Throughout history two most tempting answers to this eternal problem have been that of the Monist ("God made it, and therefore it is not evil") and that of the Dualist ("Another made it, the creator and prince of evil"). These are the answers of men blinded and deceived, trusting in mere intellectual subtlety and lacking that knowledge of truth which only the Holy Spirit can give. In Sermon XXXII, on *Caro mea vere cibus est,* Tauler says: "[Mystical union] is something unfathomable; so stop chattering about it, trying to explain it, arguing around it. It takes place in the illuminated soul, within, in its depths, hidden in God." This same thought, that intellectual progress must go hand in hand with spiritual experience, underlies Sermon XXVIII, the First Sermon for the Trinity. The best exposition in this world of the mystery of the Trinity "is more like a lie than the truth," and Tauler's nuns are to leave such matters to scholars, the best of whom can do no more than "stammer something for the sake of Holy Church." (Some of his hearers might be expected to recognize this allusion to St. Thomas' *De potentia,* q. 9, art. 5.)

We are here getting close to the cult of "learned ignorance," but we must not attribute too much to Tauler. When he goes on to say in this same sermon, "You should treat this as forbidden ground," it is pretentious sermonizing on the refinements of the doctrine of the Trinity to which he is referring, not at all to meditation on the mystery itself. Again, in Sermon LIII, on *Beati oculi qui vident,* he is

making the same point: "[On the Day of Judgment] there will be many who will wish that they had never achieved the semblance of monastic life, that they had never heard tell of all these high-flown clever ideas, that they had never occupied themselves with them and gained great reputations. They will wish then that they had driven cattle all their lives and earned a pittance by their sweat." It would be surprising if this remark has never been quoted to show Tauler as an enemy of the religious life to which he was vowed, but that is not at all what he means. It is not religion which he is attacking here, but the empty, hypocritical religiosity of the "Scribes and Pharisees," eager for their own advancement; not the proper use of all man's intellectual abilities, but a false and presumptuous intellectuality founded upon no experience of life or of eternity.

That this is so is made very plain elsewhere, for example, in Sermon LXI, for the Fourteenth Sunday after Trinity, where he discusses "ignorance," "not knowing" and "unknowing." He begins by quoting from the Book of Job: "A man whose way is hidden, and God has surrounded him with darkness," and from St. Gregory's exposition of this verse in the *Moralia,* where he says that as man goes to God he is in ignorance, in unknowing. Tauler tells us that man's road to God must pass between two places between which he must squeeze his way: the one, knowing, the other, unknowing. Had he written a thousand years earlier or a hundred years later, he would probably have told us that the intellect is a Scylla, ignorance is a Charybdis, and that we must not be shipwrecked upon either.

In all his pronouncements upon such topics we shall find, if we scrutinize them carefully, that Tauler is most circumspect, and there was every need that he should be so. We have already seen the antithesis which the Swabian heretics fabricated between "good men" and "scholars." This contempt for theology reappears in every century, with every fresh wave of religious enthusiasm. Tauler knew well how dangerous it would be to encourage ideas in his hearers which, however well-founded, experience had shown to have unhappy consequences when taken up and pressed too hard by the uncritical. At times we must be surprised at the boldness of his approach to such topics, and always we must admire the skill with which he himself squeezes his way along the narrow path of truth.

His boldness and skill are nowhere more apparent than in his treatment of one of the most disputed and dangerous topics of the times: the comparative merits of activity and passivity. Margaret Porette, we have seen, had taught that the "soul brought to nothing" would pass beyond the exercise and the need of virtues into a state of pure passivity, and it was soutbless such language as this which even the censors who first approved her book, if indeed she wrote the *Mirror,* deplored as dangerous. In this respect, as in so many others, we can see today how wrong was the old-fashioned view of Eckhart as an over-subtle Scholastic whose doctrines became virtually unintelligible to all but himself. When he taught, for example, that "God is glorified in men who do not seek honors nor profit nor inward devotion nor sanctity nor rewards nor the kingdom of heaven, but have renounced all such things," his thought and language are those of the many devotees of previous decades. He is not speaking of the active life of the Christian, but of the secret, "extraordinary" life of the *anima adnichilata*. Once the soul has been so "brought to nothing," it will have achieved its highest goal; and it is of that goal that he teaches in averring that all God's creatures are "a pure nothing." In that "pure nothing" is perfection. He also teaches that perfection excludes all memories of the world, including contrition for sins committed. (Of all Eckhart's doctrine, perhaps this article gave greatest scandal.) Finally, we can see that even his most daring hyperbole, when he teaches that the glory of God is shown forth and shines out equally in all works, even evil works which merit punishment and blame, can be paralleled from the writings of the mystics whom he succeeded.

In *The Flowing Light of the Godhead* we have Mechtild's tender expressions of her unbounded love for all God's creatures, even, she is not afraid to say, for the souls whom He has damned and who are in His hell. In one of her *Letters,* Hadewijch writes thus on the theme of the benefits of the soul's afflictions: "For I tell you truly that all the desolation which we suffer with a good will toward God is pleasing to Him in His whole nature. But it would not be profitable for us to know how acceptable this is to God, for if we did, there would be no desolation for us, for if anyone could know that that were acceptable to the will of God, he would gladly and willingly be in the depths of hell, never wanting to escape nor to come to any place where he might be free from torment. The man who could know that what he did was pleasing to God would never care what became of him."

Just as Eckhart's hyperbole is based upon the subtle and ingenious use of verbal nuance taught in the schools, so Hadewijch here uses, for divine ends, the rhetoric and forms of thought common to the poets of earthly, courtly love, the rhetoric which had found its extremest form in Aucassin's cry of despair when he is counselled to forget his love for Nicolette and join those who forsake sin that they may win heaven: "They will go to paradise, but I have nothing to do with them, for I wish to go to hell, where the fine scholars are, and the fair knights, and the lovely ladies of the courts. With them will I go, and I shall have Nicolette my sweetest love with me." Hadewijch sees herself as an Aucassin, an Orpheus, and her hunger for God, to which she is as much enslaved as any earthly knight ever was to the all-demanding service of love, will lead her to hell or to whatever other place God has prepared for her.

None the less, we need hardly wonder that the secular clergy of Cologne in Eckhart's day, suspicious of the religious enthusiasm which he represented, fearful of the spread of heresy to which such enthusiasm often had led, and antagonistic to the intellectual discipline evolved and practiced by his Order, complained of his influence and

his teaching. It would be difficult and tedious to attempt to trace the long story of Eckhart's struggles to defend himself against the charges of heresy brought against him. It had its culmination on March 27, 1329, in the Bull of John XXII, *In agro dominico*. Twenty-six articles defended by Eckhart, with an additional two put in by him in his objections, had been examined, first by the Archbishop of Cologne's commissioners, then by a commission of theologians at the Curia, and finally by the Pope himself and the Sacred College. Of the articles, the first fifteen and the additional two were condemned as heretical, both in their sense and their form of words. The remaining eleven (including, of those which we have quoted, the statement that "all creatures are a pure nothing"), although by means of exposition and addition they could be made to conform to true doctrine, are unfortunately worded, invite suspicion of heresy, and ought not to have been preached to the simple faithful. The Bull ends with an exhortation that all those to whom this is to be made known are also to be told that Eckhart, at the end of his life, made a profession of faith, recanted and deplored any of these articles or other of his teaching and sermons which might have given rise to error in the minds of the faithful, and submitted himself and his teachings to the Apostolic See.

Tauler may well have been present at Eckhart's final profession of faith. Tauler was born about the year 1300 and was a contemporary of Suso. As students in the Dominican Order, they both had probably been pupils of Eckhart. We know that Tauler was with Suso in the *studium generale* at Cologne, when he would have been about twenty-five years old, having then completed the novitiate and the eight years of preliminary studies, which he seems to have followed in his native city of Strasbourg. Eckhart had taught and preached there for some eight years, until about 1320, so that they may have known each other even before the Cologne days.

About the time when Tauler had entered the Order at Strasbourg, there had been a most cruel persecution in that city of members of the heretical sect known as the Brethren of the Free Spirit, and many of them fled to Cologne, where, however, they found no peace. The Archbishop of Cologne continued their persecution and one of their leaders, Walter, was burned in 1324. Heresy-hunting was in the air, and although to be sent to the *studium generale* was a sign that one's teachers of Scripture and dogma thought highly of one's promise as a future teacher, the years in Cologne, always darkened by the protracted process against Eckhart, could not have been happy years for the young Tauler and Suso. In *The Little Book of Eternal Truth* and in the *Horologium Sapientiae* Suso wrote a catalogue of those woes. It is not always easy to tell whose sorrows he is bewailing, St. Thomas', Eckhart's, or his own, and he gives us fairly clearly to understand that all three of them had experienced enmity and hostility within their Order as well as from without. One of Suso's own griefs was that he had been cheated of the academic laurels which he had thought his by right. It was this disappointment which helped to turn him to a life of self-mortification and penance.

From what Tauler says in sermons of his later life, he too for a time wished to live according to a strictly ascetic way, until he found his bodily strength unequal to it. About 1329 he returned to Strasbourg, but because of the troubles of the times he seems soon to have been sent to Basel. In 1339 Henry of Nördlingen writes of him as having been there for a long time and having given Henry great help. Basel by this time was a center for that great devotional movement whose members, some of them religious, others secular priests, others lay men and women, were known in the Netherlands and in all German-speaking territories simply as the "Friends of God." Tauler and Henry of Nördlingen seem to have been their leaders in Basel, and Tauler is known to have communicated with other leaders of the movement. He was, however, constantly on the move at the behest of his superiors. He revisited Cologne often, spending a considerable time there. It is from this period that many of his recorded sermons date, and most of them seem to have been preached for the Dominican nuns of St. Gertrude's in that city. He died on June 16, 1361, in Strasbourg, where his body is buried.

There is no doubt that Tauler preached Sermon XXXIII, the Fourth Sermon on the Eucharist, to the Cologne nuns. In it, treating of the theme of conversion, he alludes to his many journeys and to his relations with the Friends of God, saying: "I have been in countries where they act like men, showing great strength in their conversion and great steadfastness. The word of God produces greater and finer fruits there in one year than in ten whole years with us. Miracles and great grace are to be seen there among such blessed people."

Is Tauler here referring to the Friends of God in his own native highlands or to his contemporary, John Ruysbroek, and his circle in the Low Countries? One cannot be sure. Pomerius, the later chronicler of Groenendael, the house of Augustinian canons which Ruysbroek founded and in which he died, says that many Friends of God from Basel and Strasbourg came there to visit Ruysbroek, and among them he names "Canclaer," which has often been explained as a mistranscription of "Tauelaer."

This is, however, a minor matter which can safely be disregarded, as can several alleged quotations from Ruysbroek's works in Tauler's sermons, since the sermons themselves prove to be falsely ascribed to Tauler and, indeed, not to be sermons at all. But Tauler could well have known the other's works, for Ruysbroek himself told the Carthusian, Gerard of Saintes, that *The Spiritual Espousals* "had been multiplied at the foot of the mountain," by which plainly he refers to the frequent copying of one or other of the two High German recensions of the *Espousals* which were made in his lifetime. At times, as we read Tauler's sermons, we are reminded very strongly of the *Espousals:* in what he writes, in Sermon X, on *Ego sum lux mundi,* of "flowing and flowing back again" (the simile constantly used by Ruysbroek to describe the relations between the Persons of the Trinity and between God and the soul); in much of Sermon XI, on *Si quis sitit,* especially

what Tauler says of "jubilation" and "discretion"; and in his exposition, in Sermon XIV, for the Friday before Palm Sunday, of Christ's inconceivable sufferings in His higher and lower faculties. When, in Sermon XXIII, on *Estote prudentes,* Tauler speaks of remedies in times of acute depression, he says that some have recourse to learned men and to Friends of God, but that this is not the best remedy. "The best thing to do when a storm of this kind breaks on the soul is to behave like people who have been caught in a thunderstorm. They hurry to take shelter under a roof and there they stay until the storm is past." This is almost exactly Ruysbroek's similitude of the bee's sagacity in the *Espousals.*

Nevertheless, great discretion and caution should be observed in suggesting that either Tauler or Ruysbroek borrowed from one another or that either writer directly affected the other. We lack much knowledge which would be indispensable to such statements. It is impossible, for example, to assign any date, even within ten years, to most of Tauler's sermons. Furthermore, so to insist on these particular relations and influences is to ignore the more important characteristic which their works share. They resemble one another because they had alike inherited, from the religious movements of the thirteenth century, certain fundamental ideas about the relations of man to God, and they are both concerned in their works to preserve all that is best and untainted of the teachings of the great master, Eckhart.

Again, we must be slow in comparing Ruysbroek and Tauler to the advantage of either. We must not seek in Tauler's sermons for absolute consistency; they are not an ordered and considered exposition of a philosophical system. He affects to prefer an untutored simplicity to that intellectual orderliness of the philosophers of which Ruysbroek was master. More than that, Tauler's sermons were preached on various occasions, and some of them to different kinds of audiences. His sermons may also reflect different stages in the growth of his own spiritual life. For instance, at times he is manifestly impatient of the way of devotion which follows the popular medieval exercise known as "The Hours of the Passion," yet elsewhere he comes very near to advocating such devotions. There is no real conflict between what he says in Sermon XLIII, on *Johannes est nomen eius,* to disparage the "Hours," and in Sermon LV, on *Transite ad me omnes,* about constant recollection of the Passion and the Sacred Wounds. They seem to have been written in different frames of mind and at different epochs.

Then, too, Tauler seems in general to have lacked Ruysbroek's gift for precise exposition. For example, although both wish to teach us that the passive life of contemplation and the active life of virtuous works do not hinder one another and must be pursued together (and such teaching is vitally necessary if Eckhart's apparent Quietism is to be avoided and his real doctrine of "the soul brought to nothing" is to be of profit to souls), we find this very clearly set out in *The Spiritual Espousals,* whereas Tauler's various statements seem to contradict each other. Yet at times Tauler can surpass Ruysbroek in saying, simply for simple people, what is the truth in these deep matters. Thus, in *Caro mea vere cibus est,* referring to that "emptiness" and lack of activity which "the soul brought to nothing" shall achieve, he says merely: "If we would truly know the unutterable and incomprehensible splendor of the Blessed Sacrament, we must live a life cut off from the world and from ourselves, suffering God's working in us, at unity with Him, living a life in God." They must be "cut off" (*abescheidelich*); they must renounce all that is not God. They must be "suffering God's working" (*lidelich*); they must suffer and endure, they must not act. They must be "at unity with Him" (*eineklich*); they must be one within themselves and one with God. They must live "a life in God" (*innerlich*); they must seek God in the depths of their soul.

Tauler explains more in detail what he means by these terms in the First Sermon for Pentecost, Sermon XXV, to the study of which this one sentence may serve as a prologue, and we must observe, bearing Eckhart's sad story in mind, how in the Third Sermon for Corpus Christi Tauler goes on: "We must not understand this to mean what many people suppose, that we cannot attain to this life without abandoning everything, being completely passive, living an extraordinary life, being different from other people. Some people, finding that they cannot do all this . . . lose heart completely." The rest of this sermon tells us, in terms clearer than we shall find even in the *Espousals,* that it is not activity as such which must be renounced, but activity which comes between the soul and God.

Very often Tauler shows us, when he deals with this problem of true and false passivity, that he never forgot the lessons learned through Eckhart's fall. Unfortunately, one of the places in which he most plainly deals with the disputed question of contribution for past sins is exceedingly difficult to interpret, because the manuscripts all seem corrupt. This is in Sermon XXXVI, the Second Sermon for the Third Sunday after Trinity, where, as Vetter's edition of the German text reads, Tauler is made to say: "If you wish to be this lamb (whom the Shepherd will seek when it is lost), establish yourself in a true peace in all things which may happen to you, however they may come. When you have done your part, then do not be afraid of anything, whatever it may be, but be at peace, and confide all things to God, and abandon yourself utterly to Him, even in your sins; that is, so far as your senses are concerned, not in your reason; that is, in your aversion from them, your hatred for them. You cannot do this too much, although in the senses it would be a great hindrance to one. So in all things be at peace."

Obviously something has gone wrong here, and it is significant that Vetter reports that at this point the now destroyed Strasbourg manuscript omitted most of the passage, because the scribe's eye had jumped from one "be at peace" to the other, so that he had left out the intervening words (a common source of error in manuscripts). It may be that a similar omission, made good by some conjectural restoration by a later scribe, lies behind the reading, translated here, from the other two manuscripts used by Vetter.

Hugueney, in his modern French translation, quite unjustifiably transposes a "not" to give "not so far as your senses are concerned, but in your reason." But it is clear that what Tauler is trying to insist is that his hearers are not to fall into Eckhart's condemned error of believing that true passivity would exclude even repenting one's past sins. Probably what Tauler means is: "So far as your senses are concerned, leave your past sins and their future punishment to God, and forgot them. But so far as your reason is concerned, you must always be mindful of them, so that you may keep a firm resolve never to sin again."

Elsewhere, Hugueney himself helps us to see that such is Tauler's meaning. In Sermon LIX, the Fourth Sermon for the Exaltation of the Holy Cross, the text according to Vetter reads: "St. Paul says *Diligentibus Deum omnia cooperant in bonum;* and the Gloss especially adds, 'Be silent and flee to God.' " Hugueney has been able to correct this and to show that what Tauler said was: "St. Paul says 'All things work for good to those who love God'; and the Gloss especially adds, 'Even their sins.' Be silent, and flee to God."

We should note Denifle's remarks on this point: "It is as if Tauler had the author of *The Book of Spiritual Poverty* in mind when he observed (in Sermon LXXVII, on *Vigilate quia nescitis horam*) that in some lands one finds people who practice a false passivity, holding themselves apart from all activity, even refraining from pious meditation, and they say that in this way they have attained peace and that they have advanced beyond the exercise of virtues. But they are obsessed by the devil." Here, it is plain, we have what Tauler meant when he said that Eckhart had spoken to pious souls of the things of eternity, but they had thought he was talking about this life. Here, too, we have Denifle's reasons for refusing to accept *The Book of Spiritual Poverty* as Tauler's, reasons which are still valid, in spite of recent attempts to discredit them.

But Tauler never ceases to insist that this passivity is false only because it is unlike the true passivity which God's lovers should exercise. He is prepared to make many allowances, for those who are young, for those endowed with great physical or mental vigor which must be worked off, for those not called to the highest life; but he rests firm upon his contention that this highest life consists not in doing, but in true passivity, in turning inward to the depths of the soul, and in waiting there upon God. "When our Lord blamed Martha, it was not because she was working. What she was doing was good and holy. What He blamed her for was her overanxiety" (Sermon XLVII, *Divisiones ministrationum sunt*).

Often, too, Tauler shows an impatience with the pious practices, characteristic of the religious enthusiasm of the times, which he knows to be a hindrance to true passivity. Such impatience has already been observed in his criticism of the "Hours of the Passion," and in Sermon I for Christmas Day (a sermon, incidentally, which some critics believe to be not by Tauler but by Eckhart himself), there is this praise of the virtue of silence: "So you must be silent. Then God will be born in you, utter His word in you, and you shall hear it. But be very sure that if you speak, the word will have to be silent. The best way to serve the word is to keep silence and listen." Later, in this same sermon, the preacher continues: "Yet furthermore, Mary was enclosed; so too ought the handmaiden of God to keep herself apart, . . . abstaining not only from those earthly activities which may seem of their nature to be harmful, but even from the merely sensory practices of virtues. She should very often be silent and at peace with herself, inwardly enclosed, hidden within the spirit, so that she may withdraw herself and escape from the senses and make for herself a place of silence and inward repose."

This silence and repose Tauler contrasts with what he finds among his nuns. In Sermon XLI, on *Ascendit Jesus in naviculam,* speaking about the afflictions inseparable from the mystical way, he says: "Stay alone within yourself; do not run outside; suffer it through; do not try to escape! Some people, when they find themselves in this distress of spirit, run off, always seeking some fresh way out, to avoid this affliction, and that does them harm. Or they go off to complain and to ask their teachers, and so they are worse off than before. There is nothing else for it; stay where you are. After the darkness comes the bright day, the light of the sun."

We find a similar complaint of these pious colloquies and constant analyzings in Sermon LV, on *Transite ad me omnes:* "And then people complain: 'But I feel no love for God, no longing for Him!' How could they possibly feel love and longing for God when they put such obstacles (love and desire for the things of this world) between themselves and Him? Each of us must look into his own heart. No one can tell you better than yourself what comes between you and God; ask yourself. You want it both ways; you want to have God and His creatures both together, and that is impossible."

Sometimes this impatience and dissatisfaction seem to extend to the organization of religious life as he found it in his day, but it would be wrong to give his words more weight than Tauler meant them to carry. In *Caro mea vere cibus est,* preaching on devotion to the Blessed Sacrament, he says: "Alas, nowadays we find far too many people in religion who live all their days, from youth to old age, occupied with themselves." Clearly he does not mean here that this deplorable lack of true devotion is peculiar to religious orders. He is preaching to a convent, and naturally he points out to his hearers that they, professed religious, should be even more on their guard against such worldly preoccupations (though it is more than mere concern with secular affairs which he is reprehending) than other people.

Again, in a famous passage in *Divisiones ministrationum sunt,* he says: "I know one of the greatest of the Friends of God who has been a farmer all his life, for more than forty years, as he still is now. And once he asked our Lord if He would have him abandon this way of life and go into the church and sit still. But our Lord said, No, he should not do so, but he should earn his bread with the sweat of his brow to the honor of His Precious Blood."

As a modern critic has observed, there is more than a flavor of anti-clericalism here; and it is repeated, perhaps referring to the same Friend of God, in *Littera occidit,* where Tauler observes: "The holiest man on whom I ever set eyes . . . had not heard more than five sermons in all the days of his life. Once he had found out what it was all about, he thought that that would do, and he died to all to which he should die and lived for that for which he ought to live." But we shall be wrong if we use such observations in an attempt to prove that Tauler was an enemy of his own Order, of monastic religion, or of any of the Church's institutions. What he is disparaging is the shortcomings of the men and women for whom religion and institutions were made, and who fall so far short of their ideals. He is reminding the religious to whom he preached that there are men and women in the world, lacking their aids to sanctity, who are yet holier than they, but for them and for himself, he always makes it clear, perfection is to be striven for within their own cloisters.

Nowhere is the perfect harmony and balance of Tauler's attitude better demonstrated than in his counsels on prayer, in *Carissimi estote unanimes,* where he says: "True prayer is not a lot of babbling with the lips, so many psalms and so many vigils, clattering your beads and letting your hearts wander up and down. Believe me, if you find that reciting prayers and performing acts of devotion hinder you in the spirit of prayer, you should not hesitate to give them up, however efficacious they are supposed to be, however holy they seem. This does not apply to your Office, of course; you are obliged to this by the laws of Holy Church. But except for the Office, give up anything that keeps you from true and living prayer."

Here, in simple form and treating of simple matters, Tauler is putting into practice the mysterious doctrines of "with means" and "without means," of "likeness" and "unlikeness," which he and Ruysbroek alike had learned from Eckhart. True, real prayer will use the means ordained by the Church, but it will transcend those means, to lead the soul up to where it will achieve "likeness," in union with God, and at times Tauler does speak of what that union itself is.

Occasionally he allows us a glimpse of his own interior life. "There was once someone who loved our Lord very dearly, and to him our Lord offered His divine kiss. But this soul said: 'No, truly, dear Lord, this is not what I want at all. If I were to be so taken out of myself in rapture, I could not be of any more use to You'" (Sermon LX, *Carissimi estote unanimes*). We need hardly doubt that he is here speaking of himself, but usually he professes that such matters are hidden from him.

In the First Sermon for the Exaltation of the Holy Cross he devotes a little time to the physical phenomena of mysticism, prefacing what he has to say with the remark: "To speak and hear about these exalted matters which are outside our own experiences may well cause us some trepidation, poor, sinful mortals as we are. Even people who have experienced these things, and therefore know something about them, do not know how to tell properly what they are." In spite of the deprecating remarks of some of his modern commentators, in what follows, Tauler undoubtedly is talking of the physical sensations and symptoms which have been known to accompany ecstasy, but he utters a warning that such experiences are neither mystical union with God nor the peace of God. They are merely the dispensable preliminaries to it. This whole sermon is filled with nuances, disguised warnings, subtle reservations. Perhaps the most striking and original is the passage in which, after using the Crucifixion both as a metaphor and a simile to describe such phenomena, he quotes Job, *Elegit suspendium anima mea,* and comments: "He chose that for all the good which God had done to him: to hang upon the cross in the greatest of torments, because his God has hung upon the cross for his sake. And then God sends to man the most horrible darkness and the deepest woe, which is to be altogether forsaken." He may well say that this "does not concern everyone."

On a merely intellectual level his thought here is almost impossible to analyze. Job's words are treated primarily as prophetic of the Crucifixion, yet at the same time Tauler wishes us to recall the literal sense: Job's own sufferings of body and spirit as well as those of Christ. Then, in the allusion to the great darkness which followed the Crucifixion, we are to remember the words of Job and the words of our Lord when they believed that they were abandoned by the Father. So too will the loving soul believe, yet it will choose this way of affliction as Job and Christ chose it, knowing that which is beyond telling, that such sufferings are not only the threshold, the "means" to joy and peace, but are themselves greater than joy and peace. It must be that Tauler so uncharacteristically launched himself upon this sea of imagery because he knew that among his hearers there were those who could follow him.

But whatever the depths and heights of his own interior life may have been, Tauler speaks to us today with the same living voice as his German audiences heard, because he himself never ceased to exemplify perfectly that threefold life of action in the world through holy works, of mounting toward God above works, and of union with God beyond works; that threefold life like to the Blessed Trinity, since no one of its ways may be perfected without the other two.

Man's holy works are means: "All the exercises we perform, all the gifts and graces we receive, are a road by which we come to God, so that man by means of them

may come to God; they prepare us for union with Him. They are means by which we may come to God and enter into Him. But this gift . . . is God Himself and no intermediary" (Sermon XXXII, *Caro mea vere cibus est*). God will be found without means in the depths of man's soul: "We must go into our own souls, into the very depths, and seek the Lord there, as He counselled us when He said: 'The kingdom of God is within you!' Anyone who wants to find this kingdom—that is, to find God, with all His riches and in His own being and nature—must look for it where it is, in the very depths of his soul, where God is infinitely closer to the soul and more integral to it than is the soul to itself" (Sermon XXXVII, *Quae mulier habens dragmas decem*). In this closeness to God the soul will lose its own likeness and will become like to God, "just as fire acts upon wood to deprive it of all its moistness and greenness and coarseness, and makes it hotter, more heat-giving, more like" (Sermon XXXII, *Caro mea vere cibus est*).[1] Yet always, while scaling these heights of contemplation, man must still practice the life of action in the world, truly active as was our Blessed Lord Himself; and this Tauler says perhaps most simply and movingly in Sermon XXV, the First Sermon for Pentecost: "It is not activity, but disordered activity, that can hinder you. . . . Always act with the sincere intention of pleasing God, and nothing else. . . . In this way all your activities will bring you only contentment, and the Holy Ghost will come to you and fill you, live in you, and work marvels in you, if you are true to His teaching. May all this happen to us with God's help. Amen."

Notes

1. Here the play upon this last word, *gelicher,* cannot be translated. In unity with God, the soul is consumed, loses all "likeness," all its own marks of created personality, as wood loses its natural characteristics. Both the soul and the wood kindle and give out heat and become *gelicher;* the soul, more like to God, and the wood, more like to the fire, its consuming element.

Josef Schmidt (essay date 1985)

SOURCE: An introduction to *Sermons,* by Johannes Tauler, translated by Maria Shrady, Paulist Press, 1985, pp. 1-34.

[*In the following essay, Schmidt discusses Tauler's life, distinctive features of his sermons, and his complex, connotative use of language.*]

References to "German medieval mysticism" usually involve a particular triad in this rich and extensive spiritual tradition: Meister Eckhart (around 1260-1328), Henry Suso (Seuse; 1295-1366), and John Tauler (around 1300-1361), all members of a young and dynamic mendicant order, the Dominicans. Tauler and Seuse were disciples of Meister Eckhart, who died in Avignon facing charges of heresy.

Although they were spared the calamity of papal accusation, they did have their share of tribulations in a time unsettled and uprooted by ecclesiastical schism, political upheaval, and profound social change.

Before situating John Tauler in this particular context, however, a few distinguishing points should be mentioned, for each one of these three mystics is distinct in his experiences, his teaching, and what tradition made of him and his works. It can safely be said that Tauler's work—apart from a series of nonauthentic treatises, a collection of some eighty sermons—has found the widest, the most consistent and most continuous favorable reception in Western spirituality. While Eckhart undoubtedly holds the central position in terms of innovative fundamental theology and comprehensive formulation of mystical concepts, Tauler and Seuse were responsible for propagating, and expanding on, a collection of religious insights that, because they had been adversely touched by the odor of heresy, were in danger of becoming obliterated and systematically expurgated, or pushed into the sectarian underground by the persistent suspicions of the institutional Church. Seuse and Tauler were not simply testators of their master's legacy; they developed from disciples into masters in their own right. Tauler's main merit lies in elucidating and transforming mystical concepts of the *vita contemplativa* into the domain of the *vita activa* and *publica*. Seuse, on the other hand, translated Eckhart's mysticism into devotional piety and practice.

The power of Tauler's message in the following centuries is best documented by his reception during the Reformation. In his formative stage, Luther edited three times (1516-1518) what at first he mistakenly believed to be the work of John Tauler (*Theologia Germanical/Deutsch*), heaping effusive praise on this "German Church-father." The first German Jesuit, Petrus Canisius (1521-1597), author of the *Catechism,* was a young man when he edited Tauler's sermons in 1543. And in the course of the Counter-Reformation, one of Canisius's friends, Laurentius Surius (1523-1578), produced a Latin rendition of the medieval mystic's sermons that finally ensured his recognition as the most influential medieval German mystic.[1] Tauler's role, then, must be seen as equal to that of other great spiritual authors of the fourteenth century such as Richard Rolle or the anonymous author of *The Cloud of Unknowing*. But before we enter a discussion of Tauler's sermons and theology, we will have a brief sketch of his life; even though it is poor in established fact, it is rich in posthumous invention and legend.

LIFE

Very few facts are known about Tauler's life. However, the two major disruptions of fourteenth-century Europe both directly and markedly touched his career and development.[2] The political conflict between state and Church, which resulted in the Avignon exile of the Pope, forced Tauler to spend an extended and formative period of his life away from his native city of Strasbourg. Momentous

positive and negative change, disasters such as the outbreak of the plague in 1348-1349 or the famine during the second decade of the century, led members of the emerging burgher class to change their collective attitudes and to turn to a life of spirituality. In Tauler's case it was a regional movement, the "Friends of God," that became the major collective audience of his message. But it is not just the scarcity of factual biographical information that makes it advisable for us to consider his life in the context of general history of the period.

In her colorful historical study *A Distant Mirror: The Calamitous 14th Century,* Barbara W. Tuchman states that the analogies of disaster between the late medieval times and our century are dazzling. The complex disorders "were the hoofprints of more than the four horsemen of St. John's vision, which had now become seven—plague, war, taxes, brigandage, bad government, insurrection, and schism in the Church."[3] But the profound differences between our perceptions and those of that century have to be kept in mind when trying to understand Tauler's spirituality and mysticism:

> Much of the medieval life was supportive because it was lived collectively in infinite numbers of groups, orders, associations, brotherhoods. Never was man less alone. Even in bedrooms married couples often slept in company with their servants and children. Except for hermits and recluses, privacy was unknown.[4]

Tauler was not a hermit; in fact, he lived for most of his life as a mendicant preacher and spiritual director (*lebmeister*) in two very busy towns, Strasbourg and Basle. How then should his mysticism be understood in its historical context? For mystical teaching by its very nature seems to be a private and individualistic undertaking and very inimical to communal settings unless they are of a monastic nature.

John Tauler was born around 1300 into a well-to-do burgher family in Strasbourg, a town of about 20,000 inhabitants.[5] The town played a very important role in its region for centuries both as a seat of learning and a center of commerce and trade. The only fact known about Tauler's family is from the circumstances of his death in 1361, during the outbreak of the second (of four) incidents of the plague. He died in the monastery of Saint Nicholas in Undis with his sister, who had become a Dominican nun, at his side. Tauler had begun the normal training of the Dominican Order in 1314, the year of Meister Eckhart's visitation of the Dominicans in Strasbourg; whether he came to know Eckhart in person at that time is unclear. It appears that his status as a disciple of the master's theology and mysticism came through study rather than personal acquaintance. After a one-year novitiate, three years of studying logic, and two years of doing "naturalia" (probably not in Strasbourg, perhaps in Cologne), he returned to his native town for his last two years of studies. During this time he learned Peter Lombard's (d. 1164) *Sentences,* then the standard text for theological studies. His familiarity with Saint Augustine came through the study of Lombard, as is evidenced by numerous references in his sermons. He then was further trained for the preacher's office. The Order's chronicle of the *Scriptores Ordinis Praedicatorum Recensiti*[6] proudly mentions his three main roles as those of a "sublimis et illuminatus theologus, vitaeque magister spiritualis" (spiritual director/*lebmeister*), and preacher of excellence.

The German Dominican Order counted among its members at that time a number of scholars of European renown who were active in the places where Tauler studied. Besides Eckhart the two most prominent ones were Nicholas of Strasbourg (*Sermon on the Golden Hill,* 1324) and John of Sterngassen (d. after 1327). Both followed a more traditional scholastic line of spirituality. All three were exemplary in combining Latin erudition with a thorough knowledge of popular devotion in the vernacular.

Strasbourg had seven Dominican nunneries (each having up to one hundred members) and several small communities of Beguins totaling between two hundred and three hundred women. They were, however, not the exclusive audience for Tauler. Given the rhetorical strategy of the sermons, many of them unmistakably reveal Tauler's appeal to several kinds of secular audiences. Through some of the monastic members of his flock, however, we have a few authentic epistolary references. The most notable was the mystic Margareta Ebner (d. 1353), a Dominican nun in the monastery of Medingen (near Dillingen), whom Tauler visted several times. Through the remarks of Ebner's spiritual director, Henry of Nordlingen (d. 1350), we can infer that Tauler soon became widely known outside the narrow confines of Strasbourg and its vicinity.[7]

Tauler was also a friend of the other famous disciple of Eckhart, Henry Suso. Together they established growing reputations as leaders of a group known as the Friends of God, a spiritual movement that evolved in Bavaria, Switzerland, the Rhineland, and the Low Countries. It was comprised of men and women from all ranks of society.[8] They cultivated a life of interior devotion and intense prayer because they felt a need to draw closer together in times of social upheaval. The name, Friends of God, was conceived in accordance with biblical tradition (Epistle of Saint James 2:23 and Saint John 15:14f.; *amicus Dei*). The movement also included a sizable number of Dominican nuns, many of whom enjoyed an intimate union with God in prayer and experienced states of ecstasy. They were instructed by Dominicans. Religiously, the movement of the Friends of God has to be regarded as "an unorganized corporate experience in mystical religion, fed on the intellectual side by Eckhart, on the prophetic visionary side by the older German mysticism."[9]

There is, of course, also a social dimension to this phenomenon. It was centered in towns, villages, and nunneries. Many of its proponents actually hailed from the emerging burgher class. Tauler seems to have become "the greatest personality" of this movement, "saving it from degenerating into the fanatical extravagancies of many

contemporary sects" by maintaining contact with mainstream spiritual Christianity.[10] It is important to keep in mind this role when reading Tauler's sermons, especially when he makes references of this sort (e.g., in the Sermon on the fifth Sunday in Lent, Hofmann [herafter H] 10; see notes for full reference). Repeatedly he stresses his function as a spiritual director (*lebmeister*). He does this to the point of warning against certain intellectual excesses of the academically oriented *lesmeister,* the member responsible for the education of novices.[11]

Tauler often traveled in the vicinity of Strasbourg. But, again, it is hard to discern fact from fiction. Visitations to friends (like Margareta Ebner) seem to have preceded his move to Basle in 1339, which was caused by the struggle between Louis of Bavaria and Pope John XXII. The Pope had placed under Interdict (interdiction to carry on normal sacramental practices) the cities loyal to the secular Emperor, and the Dominicans (and Augustinians), because they sided with the Pope, were obliged to leave the towns that disobeyed the Interdict. During the same year Tauler visited Cologne for unknown reasons, and this seems to have revitalized his study of Eckhartian mysticism. In Basle, where he spent the next four or five years, a period of intensive study and spiritual guidance led to his ever-growing influence among the Friends of God.

Two references make this period significant for his biography. The first is found in his Second Sermon on the Feast of Ascension (H 19), where he refers to human age: "Until a man has reached his fortieth year, he will never attain lasting peace, never be truly formed into God, try as he may. . . . Before the proper time has arrived, he cannot achieve true and perfect peace, nor can he enter into a God- seeing life." Why he would place such emphasis on a period of life that, in the historical context, amounts to very late middle age can be inferred in terms of attaining ascetic tranquillity and harmony or true indifference and detachment. Legend and life, however, illustrate what this meant concretely in his experience. The most beautiful legendary attribution to his life, *The History and Life of the Reverend Doctor John Tauler,*[12] recalls how a mysterious "layman who was rich in God's grace" taught the "Master in Holy Scripture" and true preaching. The layman did this by imposing upon him a prolonged retreat (two years), which enabled him henceforth to dispense divine wisdom to "both the clergy and laity" and become a much sought-after arbiter "in spiritual and temporal affairs." One documented fact throws light on this legendary illumination. The legend was probably inspired—perhaps even written—by a famous spiritual protégé of Tauler's, Rulman Merswin, a wealthy Strasbourg merchant who, in the middle of his life and with the consent of his wife, divested himself of most of his earthly possessions in order to enter truly into the state of a "Friend of God." The record of this conversion seems a good point at which to summarize and characterize the significance of spirituality in Tauler's life from a modern historical perspective.

Tauler's development contained two dynamic components that reflected the dialectics of collective spirituality: the contradiction between humble Christian self-denial and the social individuation that was its inevitable "by-product," and the tension between lay piety and a monastically originated form of ascetic spirituality. One of our most prominent experts on that period, Steven E. Ozment, pointed out the first dilemma in a wider historical context in his study *Mysticism and Dissent: Religious Ideology and Social Protest in the Sixteenth Century;* Tauler and Eckhart are cited as representative figures at the historical root of the problem that fully erupted with the Reformation.[13] But out of historical concern one could also ask in what way Tauler's spirituality was anti-institutional by inextricable logical force, or in fact by an immediate effect of the cause of the disreputable and decrepit state of the institutional Church as revealed by the highest representative. Mystical movements can be regarded as true counter-cultures in that, like official institutions, "they bridge the barriers of sex, age, social class, education and heresy" and as such produce, in relative terms, "democratization" and "egalitarianism."[14]

Undoubtedly, one of the reasons for Tauler's success in propagating German mysticism is his social origin. Firmly rooted in a prosperous municipality, the imagery of his sermons shows loving respect for artisans, craftsmen, and farmers without excluding the aristocracy and its values. And this is surely one of the reasons for his growing influence through the Renaissance and the Reformation, and later centuries. His native town was to excel in humanistic learning in a later period (Sebastian Brant, d. 1521) and became the arena for the most powerful pre-Reformation preacher, Geiler von Kaisersberg (d. 1510). The homiletic imagery can also highlight the aforementioned dilemma of individual piety and monastically based spirituality.

Daniel R. Lesnick, citing the example of the Dominican preacher Giordano da Pisa in the context of "Religion and Social Transformation: Popular Preaching in Late-Medieval Florence," shows that at the beginning of the fourteenth century Dominicans

> were in fact created by St. Dominic and welcomed by the higher orders of urban society as a religious order with the specific aim of serving the needs of a newly pre-eminent, mercantile-capitalist class . . . a major intention of the Dominicans was to help this class as it worked to consolidate its hegemony in the economic, social and political worlds—albeit within the context of medieval hierarchy—by elaborating an individualistic ideology and formulating parallel and compelling behavior.[15]

Tauler's sermons, as we will see, are not "mainstream" like those of Giordano da Pisa. Moreover, this is not the place for generalizations such as the one above. But the speed with which and the social network through which Tauler's contemporaries adopted his preaching and his mysticism—the Friends of God exchanged devotional writings in the form of letter references and transcripts—demonstrate that part of his impact has to be attributed to the social dimensions of his various roles. As a spiritual director, as a teacher of both his Order and his town and class, he represented the new spirituality that developed dialectically parallel to or even away from the monastically based asceticism. It ran parallel to early forms of social individualism while at the same time transcending community-based aspirations and attitudes of a late medieval town and its population.

Of Tauler's many voyages, the most important would have been the visit to John Ruusbroec in Groenendael (Belgium), but we are certain only that another trip, to Cologne in 1346 and to friends in the closer vicinity, interrupted his activity as a spiritual director and preacher. During the first wave of the Black Death he must have lived in Strasbourg. The onslaught of this dramatic event was accompanied by unbalancing social side-effects. The town had its share of flagellant processions—and things worse than that. Even before the plague had reached the town, in early 1549, the Jews of Strasbourg, numbering close to two thousand, were taken to the public burial ground and, if unwilling to convert, burnt at the stake. The town council, which had opposed this measure, was deposed by the guilds and another one elected.[16]

The tombstone of Tauler's grave has been preserved. It shows a slender figure with an open and pensive face.[17] It seems to incorporate the essential features of the actual person: intellectual depth, warmth, moderation, clarity, and mystical spirituality.

Sermons and Preaching

Tauler's legacy, but also his main activity and office, was that of a preacher. There is a social as well as a spiritual dimension to the cultural context out of which his sermons grew.

Probably the most important social factor for German medieval mysticism as a whole was the necessity of providing instruction for the many convents of Dominican nuns. What was essentially an attempt to instill control and order in this constituency, which the institutional Church regarded with suspicion and distrust, resulted in action brought about by the nuns. In 1267, Clement IV officially commanded the Order to provide preachers and confessors for the spiritual welfare of these women. The German province (later divided in 1303) received the practical directive from the provincial Herman Minden (1286-1290) stating that

> the word of God should be preached to the sisters "by learned friars in a manner suited to the training of sisters." Consequently the province entrusted its professors with the task of guiding the nuns. These lectors and masters of theology visited the monasteries at regular intervals and, in their conferences and sermons, imparted to the nuns the doctrine that they themselves had learned and expounded in the schools.[18]

The combination of spiritual supervision and instructive preaching is probably best embodied in the person of Humbert of Romans, who served as master general from 1254-1263. During his stewardship, he stabilized the relationship of the Order with Dominican nuns, gave the latter Constitutions, and fended off impositions of the secular clergy. During the last decade of his life, he wrote an important and programmatic homiletic work, *De eruditione praedicatorum* (1266).[19] It is one of a small number of major treatises demonstrating the innovative techniques of preaching in the thirteenth and fourteenth centuries.[20] The innovations consisted of new ways of indexing the materials (e.g., alphabetical or numerical lists of key terms and biblical terms and passages).[21] Also in Humbert's case we have the first systematic listing of different kinds of audiences—a fact indicating the new social reality and awareness the Dominican preacher was facing in late medieval times. Humbert gives clear descriptions and even definitions of the relevant target groups. The Beguines are, for instance, defined as follows:

> (Dicuntur Beguinae) quae timore Domini conceperunt spiritum salutarem, et in medio perversae nationis ducunt vitam sanctissimam. (p. 483).

> (Beguines are women who, out of fear of God, embrace the spirit of salvation, and in the midst of the misfortune of their nation, they lead very holy lives.)

The first part of *De eruditione praedicatorum* is devoted to practical rhetorical advice while the second part (published as *De modo promate cudendi sermones*) provides one hundred skeleton-dispositions of sermons for all classes of listeners, one hundred sketches for all kinds of rhetorical settings and occasions. The thirty-three sermons for liturgical seasons and the twenty-five for feasts of saints are unfortunately appended to only one known manuscript and have not been included in printed versions of the work. It would be wrong, however, to assume that such manuals provided the first real instruction for the medieval preacher. In fact, the sermon in the (German) vernacular was flourishing at that time. Again, one figure may stand for this rich and extensive tradition: Berthold von Regensburg (d. 1272), a Franciscan, whose fame in Southern Germany is widely documented. He practiced a popular kind of homily, addressed straight to the populace at large, and he skillfully married theological instruction with popular forms of devotion.

Tauler's sermons are very often instructions on mysticism; they were not preached exclusively to monastic groups but often show strategies clearly targeted at the secular urban audience of his native city, Basel, or one of the smaller settlements he used to visit.

A more complex dimension of Tauler's sermons lies strictly within the rhetorical realm of the homiletic tradition, for a closer look reveals that Tauler artfully blended the two main forms of sermon prevalent in his day: the homily and the thematic sermon, sometimes preferring one, often mixing them together. Both forms use the biblical quotation as a point of departure. But whereas the *homily* leans toward a loosely structured exegesis of the

readings of the particular day's Mass (pericopes), the *thematic sermon* is more a

> systematic, logical form of preaching, as opposed to the informality and lack of structure of the homily or of the simple preaching of St. Francis. The theme takes the form of a quotation from Scripture. The preacher then divides the theme into a series of questions which may be as numerous as the number of words in the quotation. He takes up each of these divisions in turn, interpreting them with other quotations from Scripture and applying them to his congregation.[22]

There is an important underlying feature separating the thematic sermon from the more open homily: "Thematic preaching is not missionary preaching. The congregation is assumed to believe in Christ; the preacher instructs them about the meaning of the Bible, with particular emphasis on moral action."[23]

Preaching manuals drew on a variety of ancillary techniques in addition to biblical commentary and scholastic distinctions. The ancient rhetorical tradition as known from Saint Augustine, Boethius, and Saint Gregory was supplemented by practice used in grammar and other liberal arts disciplines; the figures of "dilation" and "amplification" used in this development deserve particular mention.[24] The *thematic sermon* was traditionally associated with the university. This academic feature expressed itself in the slightly more refined *disposition* of the sermon of which Tauler made use in his weightier statements. The "thema," announced in Latin, was immediately rendered into German. Often a "prothema" was introduced, amplifying the biblical phrase with parallels from a concordant Scriptural passage. The "introductio" then save the key concept for the sermon. This was the place for traditional and catechetic clarifications demonstrating the utility and truth of the thema, if necessary in dialectical form. The divisions used were not necessarily exclusively intellectual indices; often they served a clearly recognizable mnemotechnic function so that especially the layperson could understand and retain the form and substance of a given sermon and reconstruct it for further study. The most widely used amplification was that of scholastic "distinctions"—these were indications about the plurality or quality of the material under discussion. Unlike the division, they did not explain the whole in terms of its various parts. The "clausio," a summary of both divisions and distinctions, led to a brief closing prayer or simple supplication. Thus the division (with its own system of subdivisions) and the introduction were the chief persuasive strategies of the preacher.[25] He enjoyed a considerable amount of freedom in leaving out part of this structure or he could use these figures (tropes) to abandon the initial biblical passage and choose a new point of departure—as Tauler frequently did—in the form of a reference from a Church Father or even secular proverbs and statements.

The important status of the mind's disposition versus the rhetorical disposition of the sermon in the eyes of the contemporaries can be deduced from the legendary *His-*

tory and Life of the Reverend Doctor John Tauler mentioned earlier. In addition to stressing the conversion aspect of the preacher, the legend also contains in Chapter 4 a "Golden Alphabet," twenty-three programmatic sentences reflecting the systematic refinement in homiletic practice of the past few generations. If one tries theologically to anchor this devout concern about the holy office of preaching, the example of the venerated model, Meister Eckhart, is an obvious choice. The master—some sixty sermons of the many more preserved are judged authentic—had indeed postulated precepts of preaching that would form the framework of the spiritual world he wanted to reveal to his audience:

> Whenever I preach, I usually exhort detachment and that man should free himself of himself and of everything. Secondly, that one should become embedded (*eingebildet*) into the one-fold good that is God. And thirdly, that one should contemplate the great nobility that God has implanted into the soul so that man comes in mysterious ways into God. And fourthly, of the purity of divine nature—of which light be in divine nature, this is truly ineffable.[26]

This is more than a programmatic statement on preaching. Actually it is Eckhart's spiritual doctrine. In order to see that, one just has to compare it with the sober and forthright statement of Alan of Lille whose treatise *The Art of Preaching* was penned a good century earlier and served as a role model for later treatises of this kind. He states in the introduction that "preaching is an open and public instruction in faith and behavior whose purpose is the forming of men; it derives from the path of reason and from the fountainhead of 'the authorities.'"[27]

When one tries to situate Tauler's sermons in relation to the master's precepts, parallels with especially the first two points—combining the pastoral concern with the spiritual initiation—are obvious. Tauler's first sermon (H 1, Christmas) is a beautiful example of how Eckhart's first point, detachment, is developed by the disciple into catechetic spirituality. The *Introitus* to the third Mass on Christmas, "Puer natus est" (Is 9:6), starts out as an allegorical interpretation of the threefold birth in which every Christian should rejoice: as a reflection of the Holy Trinity, the true virginity of Mary, and the rebirth in Christ of every Christian. The sermon seems to follow a clear three-point division that is directly related to the theme. But several distinctions lead off the ordinary path of homiletic argumentation into the typical mystical impetus of Eckhart as developed by Tauler. First, the order of points is shifted during the sermon. Second, they are not given equal treatment. And third and most important, the sermon ends in a notion that is not directly related to the biblical theme it purports to teach. Instead, it offers a description of the meaning of silence as a precondition and existential basis for achieving the highest aim that Eckhart considered the first homiletic precept: silence, detachment.

A very astute reader of Tauler's sermons, Martin Luther, was an eager listener for this particular message. Of the few marginal notes on Tauler's sermons, the ones dealing with this particular homily are fairly extensive. This Augustinian monk of the sixteenth century reconstructs without difficulty the distinctions, and he shows familiarity with an Eckhartian counter-theme to the *vita contemplativa,* the position of Martha as opposed to that of Mary (for the medieval master had, in opposition to tradition, favorably compared the industrious Martha to the passive Mary). Luther adds a fairly traditional interpretation according to the four meanings of the Scriptures (literal, allegorical, moral, and anagogical). With uncanny affinity his meditation lets him recognize the principal message of Tauler (the notes are scribbled in German and Latin):

> Aug.—got muoss das als ervollen: Vacuum naturale non est possibile, multo minus spirituale est.—Und daumb solt tu schweigen: Silentium Anagogicum . . . Unde totus iste sermo procedit ex theologia mystica, quae est sapientia experimentalis et non doctrinalis. Quia nemo novit nisi qui accipit hoc negotium absconditum.
>
> (According to St. Augustine, God has to fulfill everything: but since natural emptiness is not possible, spiritual emptiness is even less so.—And for this reason you shall be silent: for the ultimate silence. . . . And from this follows that this whole sermon evolves from mystical theology which draws its knowledge from experience and not from doctrine. Nobody comprehends this unless he accepts this hidden detachment.)[28]

This example should also demonstrate how key notions of Tauler's could be directly and accurately heard in later centuries, fermenting new ideas.

Tauler's Christmas sermon is also an illustration for the second point of Eckhart's programmatic statement: the return into the Godhead. Indeed, it is given the major part in the homily. Recent commentators of this Eckhartian notion have stressed how different his understanding is from the tradition of gradual approachment, namely purification-illumination-union. Matthew Fox even named his collection of Eckhartian sermons according to a key notion and neologism of the master: *Breakthrough.*[29] This concept does not easily lend itself to the catechetic function of the sermon as does the traditional schema of three (or more) stages leading to spiritual perfection and mystical union. For at the very center of Eckhart's understanding of experiencing God is the presupposition that ultimately any way can be the way, and every way is also a nonway, because man can break through by detaching himself and being completely open to God. In his Christmas sermon Tauler attempts to communicate this intellectual radicalism by balancing it against two traditional ways of relating the birth of Christ to the essence of the Holy Trinity and the image of the virgin birth. These two points provide the rhetorical framework for the major idea of the sermon, which, in general terms, corresponds to Eckhart's second precept in his programmatic statement: to become embedded in God.

There is a sermon by Eckhart on the same theme in which he takes the occasion of the Christmas night liturgy to speak of the threefold birth and silence.[30] In other words, the main theme is that to which Tauler alludes in the conclusion of his first sermon. It would be inappropriate to press a comparison of the two sermons to the point of parallel exegesis, but the difference between the two preachers is eloquent. While both Eckhart and Tauler insert numerous concordant passages from Scripture, move along a very clear threefold structure, and use their mystical stratagem of concepts and subconcepts to depict spiritual perfection and union, there are noticeable differences at many points, which distinguish the intellectual master from the pastoral-mystic disciple. Whereas Tauler refers to Saint Augustine several times in well-distributed pacing, Eckhart draws from a wider circle of references, including Dionysius. Tauler skillfully blends mystical notions with popular images, popular proverbs, and even down-to-earth exhortations in order to admonish his audience to observe proper behavior. Eckhart dwells in a world of biblical references and theological abstractions. It is moving to watch how both mystics perceptibly gravitate toward the same main concept in the context of Christmas. For Eckhart and Tauler, spiritual perfection means becoming free of sensual imagery—a true counter-theme to the event of the incarnation of Christ. At a central point in their divisions, they both quote Matthew 19:29: "Whoever leaves father and mother and all possessions for my sake shall receive a hundredfold and eternal life." They then develop the thought of abandonment of one's own free will as a precondition to truly experiencing the birth of Christ within us. Eckhart assembles a bold series of biblical quotations toward the closing and climactic prayer: "May the God who was reborn today as a human being help us in this birth! May he eternally help us weak human beings so that we may be born in him in a divine way. Amen."[31] Tauler, in a more laconic but also more concrete manner, ends with: "May God help us prepare a dwelling-place for this noble birth, so that we may all attain spiritual motherhood. Amen." I think these two supplications aptly illustrate the common foundation and the different attitudes of the two mystics. While Eckhart moves toward abstraction by way of translating Christ's birth into some reflections on human perception, Tauler stays much closer to biblical images, to pastoral immediacy, and to maintaining, in a metonymic form, part of the biblical event in order to move his audience.

The rhetorical context of the Dominican sermon as preached by Tauler has two features that, in practical terms, are of importance: the liturgical connotation and the manner of reception and preservation. The sermons were given to (predominantly female) monastic audiences and addressed people whose education did not match that of the preacher in terms of scholastic training. The audience, however, was literate and educated in general terms. The sermon is thus not to be mistaken for the ordinary popular homily delivered to public parishes.[32] The preacher was usually available for Sundays and feast days, and he combined his homiletic office with other duties such as that of confessor. Only in exceptional circumstances did he form a personal and close bond to the communities as

did Tauler—if we are to believe historical record, the duty was considered a burden and assigned to the younger priests.[33] But before the question is raised of how these sermons were recorded, collated, and handed down to a wider audience and later generations, a specific sermon will be used to exemplify how we can deduce the direct interaction between the preacher Tauler and his listeners.

A recent study analyzing the styles of Eckhart, Tauler, and Suso by means of computer-aided programming of syntactic patterns and idiosyncracies has led the author, Gabriele von Siegroth Nellessen, to an of conclusions.[34] She found Tauler the most spontaneous and audience-oriented preacher of the three. Since her syntactic method relies on the Middle High German and is accessible only to the specialist, I restrict myself to the rhetorical part of her argumentation, amplifying it from other sources and viewing it in a wider framework. She chooses the sermon on a text from the Epistle for the Fifth Sunday after Trinity (H 40); the sermon thematizes prayer, but it is also an example of how Tauler perceptibly distances himself from radical Eckhartian notions.[35] However, Tauler also deviates from the traditional understanding by offering at least three, if not more, of his own key notions. While Eckhart prefers to follow the pattern of the treatise even while preaching, Tauler relates to the everyday context of the audience. He presents points of reflection that are almost self-contained units without caring too much for a strict logical disposition. Sentences are comparatively short and reflect an oral pattern. In rhetorical terms, he follows one of the eight precepts of Humbert of Romans: the topic of religious experience (*scientia experimentalis*).[36] This requires that the preacher know the appropriate language (*aptum*) and have insight into the disposition of the target audience (*status animarum*). He can thus rely on a host of enthymemes (presuppositions that are either impossible or unnecessary to prove because they are commonly shared by the preacher and his listeners).

Tauler opens the sermon with a thematic three-point division: nature, essence and method, locality (third of twenty-eight paragraphs in the American translation). This partition is introduced in the form of a direct address to his audience. He then seems to make a traditional scholastic distinction regarding the essence of prayer. Here, "traditional" means according to John of Damascene, Saint Anselm, and Saint Augustine: Prayer is the ascent of mind and heart to God (*ascensus mentis in Deum*). But Tauler dispenses of it in one sentence and immediately turns to the other main points of his division. In fact, it soon becomes obvious that he is developing only the third point, and this in a most unusual fashion: when and where to pray. The fifth paragraph opens with another direct address to the audience ("Now I would like to talk briefly about the nature and method of prayer") but steers right off in the direction of the old mystical schema of three stages of perfection as evidenced in proficiency in praying: neophytes, practitioners, and those who have attained excellence (*incipientes, proficientes, perfecti*). This is soon followed by another mystical tradition, firmly established since Dionysius: the external and the inner eye. From this example, it follows that Tauler was not observing the rules that apply to a harmonious rhetorical argumentation according to his stated partition; instead, he anchors these underlying concepts without specific transitions in the practical life of ordinary vices and vanities ("all kinds of frivolities"). In the next direct address (seventh paragraph; "Beloved . . . "), he ventures into a totally new idea and a favorite theme of his: detachment in order to be totally immersed in God. The following paragraph (again in the form of reiterating direct appeals) is a harsh condemnation of institutional forms of devotion if they are hindering spiritual progress, and a whole series of prayers are mentioned by name. It offers a beautiful example of how Tauler prefers the ad hoc image to any kind of logical rigor ("This prayer in spirit . . . "). At first sight, the analogy of sacred communal effort and stages and contexts of spiritual prayer seems to flow naturally. However, when one ponders where the combining element of the analogy actually lies, and what the traditional simile-formula "And so it is with spiritual prayer . . . " transcendingly translates, one realizes that Tauler has not outlined this in any clear or concise fashion. One may contemplate such an analogy, but it is certainly not spelled out. When he reaches the meditation on the Holy Trinity (paragraph 11, "The Heavenly Father . . . ") he has moved away from the Epistle, his partition, and the previous points—only an audience accustomed to such a texture of mystical meditation could follow the train of thought of this preacher.[37] For Christian unanimity in praying as set out in the theme of the biblical passage has become almost totally reoriented to mystical "single-mindedness in prayer" (penultimate paragraph).

One objection to such an analysis might be that many jumps and turns of a loose structure could be interpreted as effects of oral tradition and that since preservation and collation of manuscripts literally involved many hands, "corrupt" texts are to be expected. Many obscure and distorted passages are due to such causes in the history of reception. But one has to remind oneself that these sermons were given by a mendicant preacher who was trained to prepare carefully. He surely exercised control over most transcriptions done by one or more listeners. We can safely assume that usually the preacher provided the general disposition in written form, that nuns or other religious persons composed a transcription, and that the preacher then approved the medieval equivalent of a modern final version. The role of later scribes and copyists has, of course, to be remembered when analyzing the finer points of language with arguments concerning devotional texts of that time.

Another distinctive feature of Tauler's preserved work is that it is written exclusively in Middle High German. This has to be kept in mind when entering a discussion of how medieval mysticism raised the vernacular to the level of the substance and flexibility of Latin in the course of a few decades. Subtlety of argumentation, as in the case of Meister Eckhart, often surpassed that of Latin works by

the very same person. Furthermore, there was a dynamic force inherent in the training of a preacher who was steeped in Latin scholastic tradition, but was also thoroughly familiar with popular culture in the vernacular—and who expressed himself to an audience that had no direct access to the Latin tradition.

Tauler's sermons do not show signs of systematic or direct use of popular ancillary manuals (in manuscript form) such as Caesarius of Heisterbach's *Dialogus miraculorum* (ca. 1222), a collection of miraculous anecdotes; the *Gesta romanorum* (around 1300); or the *Physiologus,* the most popular collection of animal-allegories dating back to antiquity. The reason is fairly evident: Tauler was interested in conveying a mystic message, and his sermons are not directed at the broad masses even though they are public in character.[38] Another form of model was, of course, collections of sermons of famous preachers of that time, usually arranged according to moral categories (vices and virtues), occasions (on death, etc.), and, less often, according to the liturgical year.

Tauler's distinctive orientation toward mystical spirituality in preaching shines through when one compares his texts with those of great spiritual masters who must have been part of his theological education. He learned from them, as was remarked above, in the form of medieval textbooks that contained excerpts or "sentences" organized according to various themes. I shall conclude this section on preaching by comparing two of his sermons, selected at random, with equivalent texts of theologians of the first order who were great preachers and mystics, Saint Augustine and Saint Bernard of Clairvaux (1091-1153).

Saint Augustine's thirty-fourth treatise of his *Admonitio de sequentibus in Ioannem tractatibus* deals with John 8:12,[39] "*Ego sum lux mundi*/I am the light of the world," the textual basis of Tauler's Sermon on the Fifth Sunday in Lent (H 10). As is to be expected, the Church Father and master rhetorician presents in his treatise a point-by-point development of distinctions of the concert of light. Although Tauler quotes Augustine toward the end of his sermon, a comparison yields just this reference but hardly any other points of the conceptual framework of the treatise.[40] Analogies or parallels are coincidental and not set in any parallel system of points of reference. In the case of Saint Bernard's *Sermo in Ascensione Domini,* the same thema (Mk 16:14: "When the eleven disciples were sitting together") serves as a point of departure.[41] But the directions taken already begin to differ in the prothema. Saint Bernard states it as an extension of *"benignitas et humanitas Salvatoris."* He then expands on the notion that we can learn goodness by aiding faith with good works. Numerous biblical references structure the short and concise exhortation. Tauler, on the contrary, after having briefly dealt with the thema of hardheartedness, quickly develops two mystical prothemes: living water and true love. He builds the former into an illustrative and extended allegory of the cistern (containing only putrid water) and reiterates the second notion of true love. After two concluding metaphors—the ship in the storm and the wounded knight—all is condensed into the supplication "let waters of pure love be poured into us," a rather remarkable move away from the homiletic entrance on Mark 16:14.

Tauler does occupy a very specific place in the history of medieval preaching mainly on account of his mystic spirituality. His sermons are part of a rich and dynamic tradition that flowed in a broad stream. It is impossible to locate precisely all the feeding sources, rivers, and inlets from which they emerged. But clearly he embodied in his work a spiritual quality that was eagerly perceived by his contemporaries and Christians of all denominations in the centuries to come.

MYSTICAL LANGUAGE

Saying the ineffable entails a dilemma inherent in all mystical expression. The ultimate impossibility of appropriate verbal expression is an intrinsic quality of the mystical relation between creature and Creator. The Christian tradition on this topic is rich and varied. Dionysios, an early exponent of the *via negativa,* noted at the end of his treatise:

> . . . he has no name; we cannot know him. . . . When we attribute something to him, or deny any or all of the things which he is not, we do not describe him or abolish him, nor in any way that we can understand do we affirm him or deny him. For the perfect and unique cause of all is of necessity beyond comparison with the highest of all imaginable heights, whether by affirmation or denial.[42]

Tauler echoes this perception when he expands on the theme in his Sermon II on the Feast of Blessed Trinity (H 29). He describes the Holy Trinity with such a powerful paradox as "imageless Image" or transposes a colloquialism to mystical depths: "When we come to speak of the Most Blessed Trinity, we are at a loss for words." This sermon thematizes the superiority of experience over articulation, parallels silence with self-denial, and transforms this problem into a description of the mystical process itself.

Our contention that any form of mysticism happens in a very specific cultural context makes it necessary to dwell on Tauler's language in the form of a few short observations on the medieval German vernacular in its relation to mystical language of that time—this in order to show both the limitations and the possibilities of Middle High German and its partial formation by the mystical authors who employed it. They expanded the horizons of the vernacular as a social code in theological and psychological dimensions that even today inspire awe in the modern reader. Their heritage is still a living force in German intellectual discourse, whether in theology or in philosophy. In the nineteenth century, philosophers tried to do justice to this achievement by ascribing it to the idiosyncrasy of individual genius, especially that of Eckhart. But modern research has convincingly demonstrated that the collective achievement of German mystics was not so much the creation and invention of myriads of neologisms; rather they were able, in the span of a few decades, to raise the vernacular to the level—and often beyond—of the scholarly Latin of their day.[43] The limitations stem from a fact directly accessible to the American reader, whose language contains many Germanic words whose meanings remain in part identical with the German ones (cognate). Middle High German, like the English language of that day, however, possessed some properties absent from the modern language, and had a range of connotations not spontaneously accessible to the reader of our day. Let us, therefore, exemplify these general conditions in concrete semantic terms. This will then be used to trace one of Tauler's most beautiful passages in a particular train of thought of that generally considered his central mystical conception and intellectual creation: the ground of the soul.

Middle High German, like the English language of that period, was fluid and in a state of transition. The mystic was an essential part of the dynamics of the process in that he or she had specific linguistic requirements that came directly from their predicament, for example, their need for apophatic language. To say the ineffable in appropriate terms entailed the prolific use of negative morphemes with verbs, nouns, and adjectives. Some are still alive (*entziehen* = to withdraw), others are virtually untranslatable even into modern German (*entwerden* = *zu Nichts werden* = to become nothing). There are morphemes that can no longer be used in compositions but that were possible in the older language. When Tauler bursts into a description of the divine dimension of the soul and has her become *"gotvar, gotlich, gottig"* (V 37;146,21) only the second epithet can be rendered into high German without loss (*güottlich* = godly, divine)—the first and the third do not exist any more (they would be: *gottbar, gottig*), and hence the problem arises as to how to translate this threefold differentiation of "divine."[44] In the case of abstract nouns (*Gottheit* = Godhead) the distinction often lies in a partially changed meaning of a lexem (*arbeit* = work; but in Middle High German it also means the travails of a knight on his quest). The considerable linguistic distance from Middle High German, therefore, causes serious difficulties even at the level of intertranslatability within its own language tradition.[45] The condition becomes more complex, of course, when translation into another language—even into one that is a linguistic relative—takes place.

The word *grunt* is of Germanic origin and had many connotations, some of which are still present in their modern from (*der Grund* = ground, reason, etc.). Etymologically, the first meaning (lower part of a physical entity, topographical or human) is still visible in the modern notion of "buildings and grounds." This notion became configurative by acquiring the intellectual meaning of "fundamental, basic." Tauler successfully combined literal and figurative meaning in a mystical context by describing the innermost dwelling-place of mystical union with this word, and by signifying that this is also a dynamic process, he transferred yet another connotation into the concept. But before its actual usage is demonstrated, some medieval connotations have to be reviewed. The word was not simply an equivalent of one particular Latin term like *fundus* or a string of terms.[46] It did, however, have a pre-coined elective affinity in that the description of chivalresque love poetry put the center of tender feelings at the *herzens grunt* (= bottom of the heart). Another important derivation is word formations that, in part, are common to German and English: *grundelôs* (groundless), *gruntlich* (thorough), *gründen* (to base something upon something, etc.)—their modern usage still reflects some of the literal and figurative meanings confluent in the root word *grunt*. The matter becomes more complex when Tauler, by way of standard German (and English) word transformation—the addition of a preposition—changes the basic lexem into a composite when using the biblical image of "abyss" (unfortunately, at this stage the cognate character to the English semantic equivalent is lost): *abgrunt*. But the semantic incorporation of the most fundamental meaning of "ground" into one of the principal lexical markers for infinity and the relationship between man and God has reached a density, and at the same time diversity, of connotation such that all these underlying significations become accessible only to the contemplative mind versed in this kind of reflection.[47]

Sermon 24 on 1 Peter 4:8 ("Live wisely, and keep your senses awake to greet the hours of prayer") is an example of how Tauler adapts the biblical notion to his terminology, and of how he, by means of traceable amplification, enriches the ground of the soul, which then becomes the concluding expression of union and divinization. Tauler's theme is the division of prayer (= spirit of discernment; given in the second of sixteen paragraphs) into "detachment, abandonment, inwardness, and single-mindedness." The sermon is unusually rich in the development of concrete images from everyday life, in particular the change of seasons for the farmer and the tilling of the "ground." Tauler even includes the observation that the preparation for a feast day is the time when "the kitchen abounds in sweet fragrances of rich and rare dishes" (fifth paragraph). A prothema, restated in paragraph twelve (*"Fratres, sobrii estote et vigilate"* is a very familiar Psalm verse from the prayer of the hours), is translated as "For true prayer is a direct raising of the mind and heart to God, without intermediary (MHG *unmittelichen*). This and nothing else is the essence of prayer."

I would now like to list the distinctions of this particular amplification of prayer (traditionally it is the seventh, expounding the property of things) and point out where and how Tauler switches his mystical code from "prayer" to "achieving the state of discernment" in the mystical union of, and in, the "innermost ground." Toward the end of paragraph thirteen, Tauler specifies that through "essential," "true," and eventually "heavenly" prayer, God may enter the soul's "deepest ground" (MHG *innerlichsten*

grunt) where alone there is "undifferentiated unity." In the next paragraph, he introduces (following Saint Augustine) the etymological/biblical amplification that the core of the soul really is a "hidden abyss" (MHG *verborgen appetgrunde*) which is also an "abyss of love" ("Into this noble and wondrous ground" = MHG *"In dem edlen minneclichen abgrunde"*). In the next (penultimate or fifteenth) paragraph, the abyss changes its connotation in that it is God whom all truly praying men embrace in "this same abyss" (MHG *daz selbe abgrunde*). They "gaze back to this loving abyss" (MHG *der minnen abgrunde*), "until they return to the loving, dark, silent rest of the abyss" (MHG *in das minnenkliche dunster stille rasten in dem abgrunde*). The conclusion: "Thus they go in and out, and yet remain at all times within, in the sweet silent ground (MHG *minneclichen stillen abgrunde*) in which they have their substance and life." A description of the divinization that arises from such a contemplative state follows. The enumeration of identical attributes for "prayer" and "ground" are meant to initiate the listener into the notion of elective affinity between man and God. The transformation of a state of praying into a state of actual being is expressed as mystical oration; for the etymological derivation of "ground" as the core of man becoming totally immersed in the "derivation" (*Abgrund* = God) verbally parallels the course of spiritual transformation. This, then, would be one of the more sublime examples of how Tauler the mystic preacher develops the conceptual understanding of the "imageless Image," saying the ineffable.

THE MYSTIC WAY

So far, the mystic pattern has been shown to be interwoven within the threads of the the social and intellectual life of the fourteenth century. Let us now consider the actuality of Tauler's mystical message, and try to decipher the specificity of his way as articulated in our collection of sermons and as lived out by the Dominican nuns, the Friends of God, and others. Besides the devotees of Eckhart, Tauler, and Suso, a variety of other movements, groups, and communities exerted a far-reaching influence and appeal:

> . . . the relationship between the sanctity of the fourteenth century and the normal Christian piety was complex. . . . mystical experiences were dramatic manifestations of a devotional trend which, translated into the vernacular idiom and transformed for a secular milieu by writers such as Eckhart, was increasingly popular in the later Middle Ages.[48]

There was, for example, the Franciscan tradition, beautifully enshrined in one of its basic texts, *The Soul's Journey into God* by Saint Bonaventure (1217-1274), which is in the form of a lucid and poetic treatise.[49] The Modern Devotion also emerged at this time. Its founder, Gert Groote (1340-1384), was actually a lay preacher. In his youth, he was deeply influenced by the German and Dutch mystics, particularly Meister Eckhart and John Ruusbroec.[50] There were many other spiritual movements that were essentially mystical. In the case of Tauler, the foremost question is less what kind of movement he joined, or represented, than his relation to his spiritual mentor, Meister Eckhart.

This question can be better answered when one keeps in mind the broader spiritual context of the age. Steven Ozment has summarized the three central features of medieval Christian mysticism, of which Tauler is both an heir and an integral factor, as follows.[51] A first feature was the dichotomy of traditions. The Latin tradition drew heavily on a traditional monastic spirituality, which was rooted firmly in the writings of Dionysius the Areopagite, prejudiced toward will, and emphasized practical piety, while remaining Christocentric in nature. Another tradition, emerging from the Dominican Order, tended to be more intellectual, striving for a merger with the divine abyss rather than the imitation of Christ and conformity with Him, while remaining decidedly Neoplatonist in theology. A second feature was the belief common to nearly all medieval mystics that "the religious realities in faith can actually be experienced." The Germanic mystical tradition furnished the two most widely popular elements in this notion of the intrinsically divine nature of man: Eckhart's spark of the soul (*scintilla animae* or *synteresis*) and Tauler's ground of the soul (*Seelengrund*) encompass a vision of the soul returning into God by returning into itself. A third notion of the German mystics is closely related to this essential condition: Withdrawal from the world enables man to become "like God" again by transcending the physical limitations of human existence. These three features are not necessarily separable entities; however, they will be used to follow Tauler's mystic way.

From our introduction we know that Tauler's general position in the broad tradition tended toward an intellectual conciliation of the more abstract German mysticism with the Latin tradition.[52]

1. With regard to the Neoplatonic heritage, Tauler saw himself as a disciple of Eckhart, a master to whom he refers several times in his sermons in a loving and respectful way. In the Sermon on the Eve before Palm Sunday, for example, he concludes a description of divine union with this remark:

> That was the teaching and these were the words of a most lovable master, but you did not comprehend. For he spoke about eternity, and you understood it in temporal terms. Beloved, if I have said too much, forgive me, I shall gladly restrain myself; but for God there can never be too much.[53]

This passage should also remind one of an important condition of Tauler's absorption of Eckhartian mysticism: Eckhart's trial for heresy had ended in a posthumous condemnation of some of the master's more controversial and enigmatic (Latin and German) statements.[54] The disciple must have been conscious that too bold a formulation might lead to something similar. But Tauler maintains like Eckhart that man, before emanating from God, was "one essential being" with, and in, God. A central aim of his mystic thrust is, therefore, the articulation of the desire

to reenter into this precreated purity. It is not surprising, then, that Tauler utilizes a host of well-known Neoplatonic imagery when preaching homilies on the Gospel of Saint John (III, H 10; XIV, H 44; XVI, H 59). However, Tauler's inclusion of more traditional mystical precepts was less out of cautious deference than from his role as a spiritual director (*lebmeister*); pastoral practice was directed toward very specific individuals and communities. This must explain his seemingly effortless transition from moral admonition to mystical exhortation, as demonstrated in the following conclusion of the Sermon on the Sunday after Ascension:

> All I have preached to you in this sermon is addressed to the spiritual man; let him bear the counsels continually in mind, and let him regulate his conduct accordingly. It will be quite possible for him to do so when the tranquillity of his soul is rooted and grounded in God; when his desire is directed wholly toward God. In this light he will know and understand all virtues for what they are, sloughing them off by the help of Christ. This is the way of all those who are born anew and are strengthened interiorly in true detachment. The more this interior process increases, the more richly the Holy Spirit is given, the more gloriously received. (H 23)

The ascent from virtuous conduct of life to illuminated detachment in God is clearly visible. In this Tauler differs from Eckhart. A good example is their differing attitudes toward the main object of pious devotion of the time, the veneration of the Passion (which often led to quite ostentatious behavior). In the last sermon of our collection, the commemoration of the Exaltation of the Cross, Tauler gradually interiorizes the gesture of ascent into a description of the soul in what to him is the highest ascent: the return of the created spirit into God. Eckhart, in a comparable homily, does not differ from Tauler, but he moves directly into the significance of the event, without including the more traditional stepping up of levels of meaning.[55] Tauler's sermons abound in practical spiritual advice: how to avoid mechanical prayer, habitual sins (X, H 33), exalted enthusiasms (II, H 2), and the positive benefits of sacramental life (III, H 10). In fact, in one sermon (XV, H 55), the expected mystical theme of divinization (Feast of Our Lady's Nativity) is quickly redirected into down-to-earth advice on detachment from earthly possessions.

Tauler often has harsh words for higher learning not directly linked with spirituality. Such utterances have to be read in context, and not construed as an overt or covert criticism of the Church Fathers from whom Tauler derived his spiritual knowledge. A rather moving example of this attitude is the second interpretation of the Feast of the Blessed Trinity (H 29). Note how Tauler affirms the authority of Saint Thomas in relation to the problem at hand, a description of the Holy Trinity:

> Scholars discuss this image a great deal, trying to express in various ways its nature and essence. They all assert that it belongs to the highest faculties of our soul, which are memory, intellect, and will; that these

faculties enable us to receive and enjoy the Blessed Trinity. This is indeed true, but it is the lowest degree of perception, leaving the mystery in the natural order. Saint Thomas says that the perfection of the image lies in its activity, in the exercise of the faculties; that is, in the active memory, in the active intellect, and the active will. Further than that, Saint Thomas will not go.

A bit further on in the sermon, Tauler cites Christ's statement "The kingdom of God is within us," and he comments: "It is to be found in the inmost depth, beyond the activities of our faculties." This shows how Tauler very consciously distinguished between the doctrine and the mystical way. The homilist prefaces the above reference to Saint Thomas with a reflection on a central image of Neoplatonic tradition: rebirth.

> You, however, should allow the Holy Trinity to be born in the center of your soul, not by the use of human reason, but in essence and truth; not in words but in reality. It is the divine mystery we seek, and how we are truly its image; for this divine image certainly dwells in our souls by nature, actually, truly, and distinctly, though of course not in as lofty a manner as it is in Itself.

However, it is not so much the traditional aspect I would like to emphasize as the opposition of word/reality. For Tauler, if we read him correctly, did not experience that ultimate union which so many of his contemporaries professed to have achieved. Why, then, the incessant homiletic attempt to transmit what the spiritual counsellor himself has not seen: union with and in God? It is here that Tauler moves beyond Eckhart along his own path. He justifies and explains his spiritual activities by anchoring them in concrete pastoral concerns and catechetic advice.[56] By clearly designating the ultimate state of being into an eschatological time and an infinite space, Tauler develops the concept of faith as nonexperience, as the recognition and acceptance of human limitation. In many of his sermons he refers to a traditional stage of mystical experience: the night of desolation, isolation, and utter desertedness. He then goes on to assert that because he and others do not come into this experience during earthly life, their faith carries the Church. Nonexperience is thus thematized as mystic faith expressed in faithful preaching.

2. Steven Ozment's second assertion concerns the creation and formulation of basic conceptions of German mysticism that became distinguishable elements of the medieval tradition. In the case of Tauler, judging from the influence of his legacy, two conceptual formulations have drawn particular attention: the formula *grunt und gemuete* and his understanding of the abandonment of one's will and submission to God's: detachment or *Gelassenheit*.[57]

Meister Eckhart left a treatise, *On Detachment*, which charts in a short and concise form the function of the virtue of detachment for the mystical way.[58] By freeing himself from earthly things, man prepares the soul to receive God, to become uniform with God, and to become "susceptible" to divine inflowing. The spiritual context is that of ultimate humility. Tauler uses the concept of detachment in many forms: as a preparatory stage that varies in different people (VI, H 23), or as the decisive, all-embracing act enabling one to become immersed in the ground of the soul, the divine abyss (VII, 24). The two sermons of the present collection provide an excellent sense of how Tauler understands and uses the concept. As in Eckhart, the soul readies itself for divinization by achieving true detachment. However, Tauler instills a strong sense of self-denial and abandonment of self-will, a volitional dimension into the terms describing this disposition that had not been there before. This remains noticeable in the mystical tradition, especially in the highly influential *Theologia Germanica,* a tract written about ten years after Tauler's death by the anonymous Franckforter around 1370.[59] Again, it is almost impossible to render directly into English the semantic associograms the medieval author used. Detachment entails, for instance, the notion of active passivity, a condition poignantly mirrored in the verb *leiden* where various meanings (to suffer, to like, to pass through, etc.) are matched by the functional duality of expressing something both transitively and intransitively and becoming an almost matching expression of "striving for perfect self-surrender."[60]

The *gemuete* and the "ground" of the soul have received extensive and penetrating treatment by Ozment.[61] After the short linguistic commentary on the word *Grund* in the preceding section of this introduction, we might quote Ozment's conceptual summary in which he identifies the two terms as anthropological motifs belonging to the Neoplatonic and Augustinian traditions. From a multiple usage characteristic of Tauler, the "ground of the soul" emerges as a "naturally given and firmly established dwelling-place in the soul where God is present and from which he neither can, nor desires to, separate Himself." The *gemuete* (the High German *Geist* is a pale translation) resembles most closely the Latin *mens* (mind) and is "an active power, grounded in and emerging from this 'ground,' which embraces the powers of the soul (i.e., reason and will) and directs and draws the creature back to his origin in uncreatedness by first drawing him into the created and subsequently into the uncreated ground of the soul." The two terms very closely resemble Eckhart's "spark of the soul"; the conclusion of Sermon 5 (H 19; Ascension II) uses the central image of the master in this very context.

3. Of all the notions used by medieval German mystics, *vergottung* (divinization) caused the greatest misunderstanding and error—on the part of the medieval inquisitor, or, for that matter, the nineteenth-century romantic or philosopher.[62] What Ozment described above as a medieval mystic's insistence on "becoming 'like God' " is indeed a complex theological area describing innumerable aspects of the relationship between Creator and creation. Another cause for confusion lies in the fact that mystical union as the ultimate aim of any spiritual activity was "conventionally" seen in the spousal imagery of the Song of Songs. Tauler naturally knew this (cf. IV, H18); he not only refers to the biblical book but also its treatment by one of the

great medieval commentators, Richard of Saint Victor. John Ruusbroec, a contemporary and student of Tauler's sermons, also made bridal imagery the central point of reference for his presentation of the mystic way. Tauler's decision to use other imagery in order to arrive at an apt description of seeing the ineffable, the imageless Image, the unfathomable abyss, therefore, warrants a final hypothesis.

Hans Urs von Balthasar, in describing Tauler's distinctive mystical way, points out how Tauler uses, almost in conflict with Eckhart's perception, the images of the noble and Godlike soul to set forth the image of man's will to empty itself for the Godhead.[63] Haas, too, stresses Tauler's firm and unwavering tendency toward a spirituality of the Passion of Christ and the Holy Trinity.[64] We may assume that the imagery from the Song of Songs merits only occasional mention since it is not part of the union as Tauler describes it in the traditional pattern of saying the ineffable, the paradox. As the imageless Image, the prayer transformed into divine silence, the search, having found ultimate tranquillity in the unfathomable abyss of the ground of the soul—Tauler's mystic way was one of genuine prostration. He was preaching in the context of an everyday medieval reality that he tried to make translucent for men of good will, enabling them to return to what he perceived to be the ultimate union: the return into God.

Notes

I wish to acknowledge with gratitude the helpful criticism of John Hellman and Robert Sullivan.

The following abbreviations will be used with regard to the different editions:

V = Ferdinand Vetter, *Die Predigten Taulers* (Deutsche Texte des Mittelalters XI; Berlin 1910)—the authoritative critical Middle High German edition.

H = Georg Hofmann, *Johannes Tauler, Predigten I, Vollständige Ausgabe,* übertragen von G. H., Einführung von Alois M. Haas (Einsiedeln 1979; 1. Ausg. 1961)—the authoritative translation of the complete sermons into modern German.

(A French translation was done by A. L. Corin, *Sermons de J. Tauler et autres écrits mystiques* . . . (Bibliothèque de la Faculté Philosophie et Lettres de l'université de Liège XXXIII/XLII; Paris 1924/29).

1. Hans Urs von Balthasar, *Herrlichkeit, Eine theologische Aesthetik* (III, 1; Einsiedeln, 1965), 411.

2. For major sources of reference, cf. Bernard McGinn's "Medieval Christianity; An Introduction to the Literature," *Anglican Theological Review* LX, 3 (1978), 278ff., particularly IV, History of Theology, 292-299. The same author, together with Edmund Colledge, has translated and introduced the *Meister Eckhart* volume in this Classics of Western Spirituality series (1981); both the introduction and the bibliography contain material directly relevant to this volume.

3. (New York, 1979), xiii.

4. Ibid., 39.

5. The most concise recent biographical portrait (with a very informative bibliography) is to be found in Alois M. Haas's introduction to the re-edition of Georg Hofmann's translation of the complete sermons into modern German (1961). Cf. also F.-W. Wentz-laff- Eggebert, *Deutsche Mystik zwischen Mittelalter und Neuzeit: Einbeit und Wandlungen ibrer Erscheinungsformen* (3. Aufl.; Berlin, 1969), Kap. III,2, "Tauler," 102-118. Kurt Ruh's article on Tauler in *Dizionario Critico della Letteratura Tedescha,* diretto da Sergio Lupi (vol. 2; Torino, 1976), 1147-1150, is an excellent concise depiction of the man and his work. There is a biographical introduction in English with emphasis on theological questions in the English *Spiritual Conferences by John Tauler o.p.,* translated and edited by Eric Colledge and Sister Mary Jane, o.p. (1961; reprinted Rockford, 1978). For information on the Dominican aspect, cf. William A. Hinnebusch, o.p., *The History of the Dominican Order, Intellectual and Cultural Life to 1500* (vol. 2, New York 1973).

6. I cite the old edition (ed. by Jacob Quetif and Jacob Echard, Paris 1719, 678) since the last volume (T-Z) of Thomas Kaeppeli's modern and annotated edition has not yet appeared.

7. Haas, IV, V.

8. Hinnebusch, 320f.

9. Jeanne Ancelet-Hustache, *Master Eckhart and the Rhineland Mystics* (London, 1957), 139.

10. Underhill, 140.

11. Haas, IIf.

12. Trans. by Susanna Winkworth (same title, London, 1925); preface by Charles Kingsley—in addition to twenty-five sermons.

13. (New Haven and London, 1973).

14. Steven E. Ozment, *The Age of Reform 1250-1550: An Intellectual and Religious History of late Medieval and Reformation Europe* (New Haven and London, 1980), 115.

15. *Europe, Revue d'etudes interdiscialinaires,* tome 3, 1 (1979/80), 19-59; 19.

16. Tuchman, 113f.

17. A small reproduction is shown in vol. XIII of the *New Catholic Encyclopedia,* illustrating E. Colledge's article on Tauler on pp. 1944-1945.

18. Hinnebusch, 298.

19. Ibid., 288-292. For a comprehensive survey, cf. Edward Tracy Brett, *Humbert of Romans: His Life and Views of 13th-Century Society* (Studies and Texts 67; Toronto, 1984), chapter 9, 151-166. The *Maxima bibliotheca veterum patrum vol. XXV* (ed. by Margarinus de la Bigne, Lyon 1677) was used

since the modern edition by Joseph J. Berthier (Rome, 1898-1899, 2 vols.) does not contain Book II, which is of particular interest in this context.

20. For a representative survey and analysis cf. James J. Murphy, *Rhetoric in the Middle Ages: A History of Rhetorical Theory from St. Augustine to the Renaissance* (Berkeley, Los Angeles, London, 1974). The analysis of key authors of the thirteenth century (like Alan of Lille) commences on p. 310.

21. Richard H. Rouse and Mary A. Rouse, *Preachers, Elorilegia and Sermons: Studies on the "Maniaulus Elorum" of Thomas of Ireland* (Toronto, 1979), provide an excellent historical survey in their first chapter, "13th-Century Sermon Aids," 3-42.

22. George A. Kennedy, *Classical Rhetoric and Its Christian and Secular Tradition from Ancient to Modern Times* (Chapel Hill, 1980), 191.

23. Ibid.

24. Lesnick, 34f., gives a concise summary of the standard article on the subject: "Artes Praedicandi: Contribution a l'histoire de la rhétorique au moyen age," in *Publications de l'Institut d'Études Medievales d'Ottawa* (vol. VII, Paris & Ottawa, 1936), 111-74.

25. Besides Murphy, who reviews Richard of Thetford's eight ways of amplification, 326 ff., cf. also Rudolf Cruel, *Geschichte der deutschen Predigt im Mittelalter* (Darmstadt, 1966; 1. Aufl. 1879), 279 and *passim.*

26. I translate directly from the Middle High German quotation in Alois Haas, "Meister Eckharts geistliches Predigtprogramm," in *Freiburger Zeitschrift für Philosophie und Theologie* 29 (1982), 192f.

27. Trans. and introduced by Gillian R. Evans (Cistercian Studies 23; Kalamazoo 1981), 16f.

28. The marginal notes were probably written in 1516; cf. *Weimarer Ausgahe,* vol. 9, 96f.

29. Matthew Fox, *Breakthrough: Meister Eckhart's Creation Spirituality in New Translation;* with introduction and commentaries (Garden City, N.Y., 1980). Cf. also Haas, loc. cit. 194ff.

30. Fox edition, 293-301; the thematic verse is Ws 18:14, "Dum silentium . . . /When peaceful silence lay all over" (Introitus for the Sunday of Christmas Week).

31. Fox edition, 301.

32. Herbert Grundmann, "Geschichtliche Grundlagen der deutschen Mystik," in Kurt Ruh, Hrsg., *Altdeutsche und Altniederländische Mystik* (Wege der Forschung XXIII; Darmstadt, 1964), 82ff.

33. Heribert Christian Scheeben, "Über die Predigtweise der deutschen Mystiker"; ibid., 101ff.

34. *Versuch einer exakten Stilbeschreibung für Meister Eckhart, Johannes Tauler und Heinrich Seuse* (Medium Aevum 38; München, 1979). The analysis of the sermon discussed is to be found on pp. 221-251.

35. See Alois M. Haas, "Wege und Grenzen mystischer Erfahrung"; in *Sermo Mysticus, Studien zu Theologie und Sprache der deutschen Mystik* (Dokimion 4; Freiburg, 1979), 147ff.

36. Haas, ibid., 147.

37. Siegroth-Nelleson, at the end of her analysis of this sermon, sees the "inconsequential" structure of Tauler in slightly negative terms.

38. Alan of Lille, 19, points out that one of the most telling signs of hereticism is the sermon preached in secrecy.

39. Migne, *Patrologiae Latinae,* tom. XXXV, 1652-1657.

40. The quotation as given by Tauler: "The great sun has created for itself a lesser sun, and veiled it in a cloud, not to render it invisible, but to temper its brightness so that we should be able to glance at it." Distinction 4 (1653/4) of St. Augustine goes as follows: "(Deum de Deo, lumen de lumine.) Per hoc lumen factum est solis lumen: et lumen quod fecit solem, sub quo fecit et nos, factum est sub sole propter nos. Factum est, inquam, propter nos sub sole lumen quod fecit solem. Noli contemnere nubem carnis: nube tegitur, non ut obscuretur, sed ut temperetur."

41. Migne, *Patrologiae Latinae,* CLXXXIII, 299-301.

42. Cf. *The Cloud of Unknowing and Other Works,* trans. and introduced by Clifton Wolters (Harmondsworth, 1978), 217/18.

43. Alois M. Haas, "Meister Eckhart und die Sprache, Sprachgeschichtliche und sprachtheologische Aspekte seines Werks," in *Geistliches Mittelalter* (Dokimion 8; Freiburg 1984), 199ff. A systematic view of the problem is given in B. Q. Morgan and F. W. Strothman, eds., *Middle High German Translation of the Summa Theologica by Thomas Aquinas* (New York, 1967; 1st ed. 1950).

44. This passage is not contained in E. Colledge's and Sister M. Jane's partial translation of this particular sermon; but their excerpt does include a highly instructive statement by Tauler, reflecting on his use of the vernacular: "Not everyone will understand what I am saying, though I always speak plain German" (p. 77).

45. The problem is briefly discussed (with references) by Alois M. Haas in his introduction to HXIV.

46. For this possibility, cf. the excellent article by Paul Wyser, o.p., "Taulers Terminologie vom Seelengrund," in Kurt Ruh, 324-352, where he carefully delineates this and other possible Latin roots, 328ff. He revises some earlier observations of Hermann Kunisch, *Das Wort 'Grund' in der Sprache der deutschen Mystik* (Münster, 1929).

47. Cf. Josef Quint, "Mystik und Sprache: Ihr Verhältnis zueinander, insbesondere in der spekulativen Mystik Meister Eckharts," in Kurt Ruh, 113-151, where a rich selection of material (in a German context) is presented by an authority in the field.

48. Richar Kieckhefer, *Unquiet Souls: Fourteenth Century Saints and Their Religious Milieu* (Chicago and London, 1984), 165.

49. In Ewert Cousins, trans. and ed., *Bonaventure* (Classics of Western Spirituality; New York, Ramsey, Toronto, 1978), 51-116.

50. R. R. Post, *The Modern Devotion: Confrontation with Reformation Humanism* (Leiden, 1968). The author points out, however, that apart from exceptions (like Gerlach Peters, 338f.), the movement itself quickly turned against mysticism, cf. especially chapter 8.

51. Steven E. Ozment, *The Age of Reform,* 115-117.

52. Steven E. Ozment implied this in *Homo Spiritualis: A Comparative Study of the Anthropology of Johannes Tauler, Jean Gerson and Martin Luther (1509-16) in the Context of Their Theological Thought* (Leiden, 1969), 13-26.

53. H 15b, 103.

54. Cf. E. Colledge's presentation of the trial and the resulting circumstances in *Meister Eckbart,* 11ff.

55. Bernard McGinn, *Meister Eckhart,* 46.

56. Alois M. Haas, "Sprache und mystische Erfahrung nach Tauler und Seuse," in *Geistliches Mittelalter,* 240-242. He draws his examples mainly from V 40 and 41.

57. Cf. Alois Haas, "Johannes Tauler," in *Sermo mysticus,* 255-295, where he incorporated findings in condensed form from an earlier study, *Nim dîn selbes war: Studien zur Selbsterkenntnibei Meister Eckhart, Johann Tauler und Heinrich Seuse* (Freiburg, 1971).

58. E. Colledge and B. McGinn, *Meister Eckhart,* 285-297. Cf. also McGinn's commentary on p. 47.

59. Bengt Hoffmann, ed., *The Theologia Germanica of Martin Luther;* preface by Bengt Häglund (Classics of Western Spirituality; New York, Ramsey, Toronto, 1980).

60. Kieckhefer, 71.

61. Ozment, *Homo Spiritualis,* 22.

62. A highly instructive study of why and how the modern age could read its own theorems into the work of medieval mystics—a question of reading truly out of context—is given in Wolfram Malte Fues, *Mystik als Erkenntnis; Kritische Studien zur Meister Eckhart Forschung* (Studien zur Germanistik, Anglistik und Komparatistik, Bd. 102; Bonn 1981).

63. Loc. cit., 413.

64. Haas, "Johannes Tauler," 289-295.

FURTHER READING

Inge, William Ralph. Introduction to *Light, Life and Love: Selections from the German Mystics of the Middle Ages.* 1904. London: Methuen & Co., 1935 (third ed.), pp. ix-lxiv.

> Provides background on Meister Eckhart; his teachings; and the writers of his school, particularly Henry Suso, John of Ruysbroek, and the author of the *Theologia Germanica.*

———. "Lecture V: Practical and Devotional Mysticism," in *Christian Mysticism.* 1899. New York: Meridian Books, 1956, pp. 167-209.

> Summarizes Eckhart's teachings and the beliefs of his chief followers.

Ozment, Steven E. "Johannes Tauler," in *Home Spiritualis: A Comparative Study of the Anthropology of Johannes Tauler, Jean Gerson and Martin Luther (1509-16) in the Context of Their Theological Thought,* Leiden, The Netherlands: E. J. Brill, 1969, pp. 11-46.

> Explores Tauler's beliefs on the nature of the soul, particularly the distinctions he made between *gemuete* and *grunt*; the natural covenant; and man's ultimate reunion with God.

Underhill, Evelyn. *Mysticism: A Study in the Nature and Development of Man's Spiritual Consciousness.* 1910. New York: E. P. Dutton and Company, 1930 (twelfth ed.), 519 p.

> Introduces the general subject of mysticism and analyzes the development of mystical or spiritual consciousness.

How to Use This Index

The main references

> **Calvino, Italo**
> 1923-1985 .... CLC 5, 8, 11, 22, 33, 39,
> 73; SSC 3

list all author entries in the following Gale Literary Criticism series:

BLC = *Black Literature Criticism*
CLC = *Contemporary Literary Criticism*
CLR = *Children's Literature Review*
CMLC = *Classical and Medieval Literature Criticism*
DA = *DISCovering Authors*
DAB = *DISCovering Authors: British*
DAC = *DISCovering Authors: Canadian*
DAM = *DISCovering Authors: Modules*
      DRAM: *Dramatists Module;* *MST:* *Most-Studied Authors Module;*
      MULT: *Multicultural Authors Module;* *NOV:* *Novelists Module;*
      POET: *Poets Module;* *POP:* *Popular Fiction and Genre Authors Module*
DC = *Drama Criticism*
HLC = *Hispanic Literature Criticism*
LC = *Literature Criticism from 1400 to 1800*
NCLC = *Nineteenth-Century Literature Criticism*
NNAL = *Native North American Literature*
PC = *Poetry Criticism*
SSC = *Short Story Criticism*
TCLC = *Twentieth-Century Literary Criticism*
WLC = *World Literature Criticism, 1500 to the Present*

The cross-references

> See also CANR 23; CA 85-88;
> obituary CA116

list all author entries in the following Gale biographical and literary sources:

AAYA = *Authors & Artists for Young Adults*
AITN = *Authors in the News*
BEST = *Bestsellers*
BW = *Black Writers*
CA = *Contemporary Authors*
CAAS = *Contemporary Authors Autobiography Series*
CABS = *Contemporary Authors Bibliographical Series*
CANR = *Contemporary Authors New Revision Series*
CAP = *Contemporary Authors Permanent Series*
CDALB = *Concise Dictionary of American Literary Biography*
CDBLB = *Concise Dictionary of British Literary Biography*
DLB = *Dictionary of Literary Biography*
DLBD = *Dictionary of Literary Biography Documentary Series*
DLBY = *Dictionary of Literary Biography Yearbook*
HW = *Hispanic Writers*
JRDA = *Junior DISCovering Authors*
MAICYA = *Major Authors and Illustrators for Children and Young Adults*
MTCW = *Major 20th-Century Writers*
SAAS = *Something about the Author Autobiography Series*
SATA = *Something about the Author*
YABC = *Yesterday's Authors of Books for Children*

Literary Criticism Series
Cumulative Author Index

Anderson, Jessica (Margaret) Queale 1916-
.... **CLC 37**
See See also CA 9-12R; CANR 4, 62

Anderson, Jon (Victor) 1940- . **CLC 9; DAM POET**
See See also CA 25-28R; CANR 20

Anderson, Lindsay (Gordon) 1923-1994 .....
CLC 20
See See also CA 125; 128; 146; CANR 77

Anderson, Maxwell 1888-1959 ...... **TCLC 2; DAM DRAM**
See See also CA 105; 152; DLB 7; MTCW 2

Anderson, Poul (William) 1926- ..... **CLC 15**
See See also AAYA 5; CA 1-4R, 181; CAAE 181; CAAS 2; CANR 2, 15, 34, 64; CLR 58; DLB 8; INT CANR-15; MTCW 1, 2; SATA 90; SATA-Brief 39; SATA-Essay 106

Anderson, Robert (Woodruff) 1917- .... **CLC 23; DAM DRAM**
See See also AITN 1; CA 21-24R; CANR 32; DLB 7

Anderson, Sherwood 1876-1941 .... **TCLC 1, 10, 24; DA; DAB; DAC; DAM MST, NOV; SSC 1; WLC**
See See also AAYA 30; CA 104; 121; CANR 61; CDALB 1917-1929; DA3; DLB 4, 9, 86; DLBD 1; MTCW 1, 2

Andier, Pierre
See See Desnos, Robert

Andouard
See See Giraudoux, (Hippolyte) Jean

Andrade, Carlos Drummond de ..... **CLC 18**
See See Drummond de Andrade, Carlos

Andrade, Mario de 1893-1945 ...... **TCLC 43**

Andreae, Johann V(alentin) 1586-1654 .. **LC 32**
See See also DLB 164

Andreas-Salome, Lou 1861-1937 .. **TCLC 56**
See See also CA 178; DLB 66

Andress, Lesley
See See Sanders, Lawrence

Andrewes, Lancelot 1555-1626 .... **LC 5**
See See also DLB 151, 172

Andrews, Cicily Fairfield
See See West, Rebecca

Andrews, Elton V.
See See Pohl, Frederik

Andreyev, Leonid (Nikolaevich) 1871-1919 .
TCLC 3
See See also CA 104

Andric, Ivo 1892-1975 .... **CLC 8; SSC 36**
See See also CA 81-84; 57-60; CANR 43, 60; DLB 147; MTCW 1

Androvar
See See Prado (Calvo), Pedro

Angelique, Pierre
See See Bataille, Georges

Angell, Roger 1920- .... **CLC 26**
See See also CA 57-60; CANR 13, 44, 70; DLB 171, 185

Angelou, Maya 1928- ... **CLC 12, 35, 64, 77; BLC 1; DA; DAB; DAC; DAM MST, MULT, POET, POP; WLCS**
See See also AAYA 7, 20; BW 2, 3; CA 65-68; CANR 19, 42, 65; CDALBS; CLR 53; DA3; DLB 38; MTCW 1, 2; SATA 49

Anna Comnena 1083-1153 .... **CMLC 25**

Annensky, Innokenty (Fyodorovich) 1856-1909 .... **TCLC 14**
See See also CA 110; 155

Annunzio, Gabriele d'
See See D'Annunzio, Gabriele

Anodos
See See Coleridge, Mary E(lizabeth)

Anon, Charles Robert
See See Pessoa, Fernando (Antonio Nogueira)

Anouilh, Jean (Marie Lucien Pierre) 1910-1987 .... **CLC 1, 3, 8, 13, 40, 50; DAM DRAM; DC 8**
See See also CA 17-20R; 123; CANR 32; MTCW 1, 2

Anthony, Florence
See See Ai

Anthony, John
See See Ciardi, John (Anthony)

Anthony, Peter
See See Shaffer, Anthony (Joshua); Shaffer, Peter (Levin)

Anthony, Piers 1934- ... **CLC 35; DAM POP**
See See also AAYA 11; CA 21-24R; CANR 28, 56, 73; DLB 8; MTCW 1, 2; SAAS 22; SATA 84

Anthony, Susan B(rownell) 1916-1991 ....
TCLC 84
See See also CA 89-92; 134

Antoine, Marc
See See Proust, (Valentin-Louis-George-Eugene-) Marcel

Antoninus, Brother
See See Everson, William (Oliver)

Antonioni, Michelangelo 1912- .... **CLC 20**
See See also CA 73-76; CANR 45, 77

Antschel, Paul 1920-1970
See See Celan, Paul
See See also CA 85-88; CANR 33, 61; MTCW 1

Anwar, Chairil 1922-1949 .... **TCLC 22**
See See also CA 121

Anzaldua, Gloria 1942-
See See also CA 175; DLB 122; HLCS 1

Apess, William 1798-1839(?) .... **NCLC 73; DAM MULT**
See See also DLB 175; NNAL

Apollinaire, Guillaume 1880-1918 . **TCLC 3, 8, 51; DAM POET; PC 7**
See See also Kostrowitzki, Wilhelm Apollinaris de
See See also CA 152; MTCW 1

Appelfeld, Aharon 1932- .... **CLC 23, 47**
See See also CA 112; 133; CANR 86

Apple, Max (Isaac) 1941- .... **CLC 9, 33**
See See also CA 81-84; CANR 19, 54; DLB 130

Appleman, Philip (Dean) 1926- .... **CLC 51**
See See also CA 13-16R; CAAS 18; CANR 6, 29, 56

Appleton, Lawrence
See See Lovecraft, H(oward) P(hillips)

Apteryx
See See Eliot, T(homas) S(tearns)

Apuleius, (Lucius Madaurensis) 125(?)-175(?) .... **CMLC 1**
See See also DLB 211

Aquin, Hubert 1929-1977 .... **CLC 15**
See See also CA 105; DLB 53

Aquinas, Thomas 1224(?)-1274 ... **CMLC 33**
See See also DLB 115

Aragon, Louis 1897-1982 . **CLC 3, 22; DAM NOV, POET**
See See also CA 69-72; 108; CANR 28, 71; DLB 72; MTCW 1, 2

Arany, Janos 1817-1882 .... **NCLC 34**

Aranyos, Kakay
See See Mikszath, Kalman

Arbuthnot, John 1667-1735 .... **LC 1**
See See also DLB 101

Archer, Herbert Winslow
See See Mencken, H(enry) L(ouis)

Archer, Jeffrey (Howard) 1940- ..... **CLC 28; DAM POP**
See See also AAYA 16; BEST 89:3; CA 77-80; CANR 22, 52; DA3; INT CANR-22

Archer, Jules 1915- .... **CLC 12**
See See also CA 9-12R; CANR 6, 69; SAAS 5; SATA 4, 85

Archer, Lee
See See Ellison, Harlan (Jay)

Arden, John 1930- ..... **CLC 6, 13, 15; DAM DRAM**
See See also CA 13-16R; CAAS 4; CANR 31, 65, 67; DLB 13; MTCW 1

Arenas, Reinaldo 1943-1990 . **CLC 41; DAM MULT; HLC 1**
See See also CA 124; 128; 133; CANR 73; DLB 145; HW 1; MTCW 1

Arendt, Hannah 1906-1975 .... **CLC 66, 98**
See See also CA 17-20R; 61-64; CANR 26, 60; MTCW 1, 2

Aretino, Pietro 1492-1556 .... **LC 12**

Arghezi, Tudor 1880-1967 .... **CLC 80**
See See also Theodorescu, Ion N.
See See also CA 167

Arguedas, Jose Maria 1911-1969 ... **CLC 10, 18; HLCS 1**
See See also CA 89-92; CANR 73; DLB 113; HW 1

Argueta, Manlio 1936- .... **CLC 31**
See See also CA 131; CANR 73; DLB 145; HW 1

Arias, Ron(ald Francis) 1941-
See See also CA 131; CANR 81; DAM MULT; DLB 82; HLC 1; HW 1, 2; MTCW 2

Ariosto, Ludovico 1474-1533 .... **LC 6**

Aristides
See See Epstein, Joseph

Aristophanes 450B.C.-385B.C. ..... **CMLC 4; DA; DAB; DAC; DAM DRAM, MST; DC 2; WLCS**
See See also DA3; DLB 176

Aristotle 384B.C.-322B.C. ... **CMLC 31; DA; DAB; DAC; DAM MST; WLCS**
See See also DA3; DLB 176

Arlt, Roberto (Godofredo Christophersen) 1900-1942 ..... **TCLC 29; DAM MULT; HLC 1**
See See also CA 123; 131; CANR 67; HW 1, 2

Armah, Ayi Kwei 1939- . **CLC 5, 33; BLC 1; DAM MULT, POET**
See See also BW 1; CA 61-64; CANR 21, 64; DLB 117; MTCW 1

Armatrading, Joan 1950- .... **CLC 17**
See See also CA 114

Arnette, Robert
See See Silverberg, Robert

Arnim, Achim von (Ludwig Joachim von Arnim) 1781-1831 .... **NCLC 5; SSC 29**
See See also DLB 90

Arnim, Bettina von 1785-1859 ..... **NCLC 38**
See See also DLB 90

Arnold, Matthew 1822-1888 ... **NCLC 6, 29; DA; DAB; DAC; DAM MST, POET; PC 5; WLC**
See See also CDBLB 1832-1890; DLB 32, 57

Arnold, Thomas 1795-1842 .... **NCLC 18**
See See also DLB 55

Arnow, Harriette (Louisa) Simpson 1908-1986 .... **CLC 2, 7, 18**
See See also CA 9-12R; 118; CANR 14; DLB 6; MTCW 1, 2; SATA 42; SATA-Obit 47

Arouet, Francois-Marie
See See Voltaire

Arp, Hans
See See Arp, Jean

Arp, Jean 1887-1966 .... **CLC 5**
See See also CA 81-84; 25-28R; CANR 42, 77

Bauchart
See See Camus, Albert

Baudelaire, Charles 1821-1867 ...... **NCLC 6, 29, 55; DA; DAB; DAC; DAM MST, POET; PC 1; SSC 18; WLC**
See See also DA3

Baudrillard, Jean 1929- .... **CLC 60**

Baum, L(yman) Frank 1856-1919 .. **TCLC 7**
See See also CA 108; 133; CLR 15; DLB 22; JRDA; MAICYA; MTCW 1, 2; SATA 18, 100

Baum, Louis F.
See See Baum, L(yman) Frank

Baumbach, Jonathan 1933- .... **CLC 6, 23**
See See also CA 13-16R; CAAS 5; CANR 12, 66; DLBY 80; INT CANR-12; MTCW 1

Bausch, Richard (Carl) 1945- .... **CLC 51**
See See also CA 101; CAAS 14; CANR 43, 61; DLB 130

Baxter, Charles (Morley) 1947- ..... **CLC 45, 78; DAM POP**
See See also CA 57-60; CANR 40, 64; DLB 130; MTCW 2

Baxter, George Owen
See See Faust, Frederick (Schiller)

Baxter, James K(eir) 1926-1972 ...... **CLC 14**
See See also CA 77-80

Baxter, John
See See Hunt, E(verette) Howard, (Jr.)

Bayer, Sylvia
See See Glassco, John

Baynton, Barbara 1857-1929 .... **TCLC 57**

Beagle, Peter S(oyer) 1939- .... **CLC 7, 104**
See See also CA 9-12R; CANR 4, 51, 73; DA3; DLBY 80; INT CANR-4; MTCW 1; SATA 60

Bean, Normal
See See Burroughs, Edgar Rice

Beard, Charles A(ustin) 1874-1948 ... **TCLC 15**
See See also CA 115; DLB 17; SATA 18

Beardsley, Aubrey 1872-1898 .... **NCLC 6**

Beattie, Ann 1947- .... **CLC 8, 13, 18, 40, 63; DAM NOV, POP; SSC 11**
See See also BEST 90:2; CA 81-84; CANR 53, 73; DA3; DLBY 82; MTCW 1, 2

Beattie, James 1735-1803 .... **NCLC 25**
See See also DLB 109

Beauchamp, Kathleen Mansfield 1888-1923
See See Mansfield, Katherine
See See also CA 104; 134; DA; DAC; DAM MST; DA3; MTCW 2

Beaumarchais, Pierre-Augustin Caron de 1732-1799 .... **DC 4**
See See also DAM DRAM

Beaumont, Francis 1584(?)-1616 ...... **LC 33; DC 6**
See See also CDBLB Before 1660; DLB 58, 121

Beauvoir, Simone (Lucie Ernestine Marie Bertrand) de 1908-1986 ... **CLC 1, 2, 4, 8, 14, 31, 44, 50, 71, 124; DA; DAB; DAC; DAM MST, NOV; SSC 35; WLC**
See See also CA 9-12R; 118; CANR 28, 61; DA3; DLB 72; DLBY 86; MTCW 1, 2

Becker, Carl (Lotus) 1873-1945 .... **TCLC 63**
See See also CA 157; DLB 17

Becker, Jurek 1937-1997 .... **CLC 7, 19**
See See also CA 85-88; 157; CANR 60; DLB 75

Becker, Walter 1950- .... **CLC 26**

Beckett, Samuel (Barclay) 1906-1989 .. **CLC 1, 2, 3, 4, 6, 9, 10, 11, 14, 18, 29, 57, 59, 83; DA; DAB; DAC; DAM DRAM, MST, NOV; SSC 16; WLC**
See See also CA 5-8R; 130; CANR 33, 61; CDBLB 1945-1960; DA3; DLB 13, 15; DLBY 90; MTCW 1, 2

Beckford, William 1760-1844 .... **NCLC 16**
See See also DLB 39

Beckman, Gunnel 1910- .... **CLC 26**
See See also CA 33-36R; CANR 15; CLR 25; MAICYA; SAAS 9; SATA 6

Becque, Henri 1837-1899 .... **NCLC 3**
See See also DLB 192

Becquer, Gustavo Adolfo 1836-1870
See See also DAM MULT; HLCS 1

Beddoes, Thomas Lovell 1803-1849 .. **NCLC 3**
See See also DLB 96

Bede c. 673-735 .... **CMLC 20**
See See also DLB 146

Bedford, Donald F.
See See Fearing, Kenneth (Flexner)

Beecher, Catharine Esther 1800-1878 .... **NCLC 30**
See See also DLB 1

Beecher, John 1904-1980 .... **CLC 6**
See See also AITN 1; CA 5-8R; 105; CANR 8

Beer, Johann 1655-1700 .... **LC 5**
See See also DLB 168

Beer, Patricia 1924- .... **CLC 58**
See See also CA 61-64; CANR 13, 46; DLB 40

Beerbohm, Max
See See Beerbohm, (Henry) Max(imilian)

Beerbohm, (Henry) Max(imilian) 1872-1956 .... **TCLC 1, 24**
See See also CA 104; 154; CANR 79; DLB 34, 100

Beer-Hofmann, Richard 1866-1945 ... **TCLC 60**
See See also CA 160; DLB 81

Begiebing, Robert J(ohn) 1946- ...... **CLC 70**
See See also CA 122; CANR 40

Behan, Brendan 1923-1964 .... **CLC 1, 8, 11, 15, 79; DAM DRAM**
See See also CA 73-76; CANR 33; CDBLB 1945-1960; DLB 13; MTCW 1, 2

Behn, Aphra 1640(?)-1689 ...... **LC 1, 30, 42; DA; DAB; DAC; DAM DRAM, MST, NOV, POET; DC 4; PC 13; WLC**
See See also DA3; DLB 39, 80, 131

Behrman, S(amuel) N(athaniel) 1893-1973 . **CLC 40**
See See also CA 13-16; 45-48; CAP 1; DLB 7, 44

Belasco, David 1853-1931 .... **TCLC 3**
See See also CA 104; 168; DLB 7

Belcheva, Elisaveta 1893- .... **CLC 10**
See See also Bagryana, Elisaveta

Beldone, Phil "Cheech"
See See Ellison, Harlan (Jay)

Beleno
See See Azuela, Mariano

Belinski, Vissarion Grigoryevich 1811-1848 .... **NCLC 5**
See See also DLB 198

Belitt, Ben 1911- .... **CLC 22**
See See also CA 13-16R; CAAS 4; CANR 7, 77; DLB 5

Bell, Gertrude (Margaret Lowthian) 1868-1926 .... **TCLC 67**
See See also CA 167; DLB 174

Bell, J. Freeman
See See Zangwill, Israel

Bell, James Madison 1826-1902 .. **TCLC 43; BLC 1; DAM MULT**
See See also BW 1; CA 122; 124; DLB 50

Bell, Madison Smartt 1957- .... **CLC 41, 102**
See See also CA 111; CANR 28, 54, 73; MTCW 1

Bell, Marvin (Hartley) 1937- ..... **CLC 8, 31; DAM POET**
See See also CA 21-24R; CAAS 14; CANR 59; DLB 5; MTCW 1

Bell, W. L. D.
See See Mencken, H(enry) L(ouis)

Bellamy, Atwood C.
See See Mencken, H(enry) L(ouis)

Bellamy, Edward 1850-1898 .... **NCLC 4**
See See also DLB 12

Belli, Gioconda 1949-
See See also CA 152; HLCS 1

Bellin, Edward J.
See See Kuttner, Henry

Belloc, (Joseph) Hilaire (Pierre Sebastien Rene Swanton) 1870-1953 ..... **TCLC 7, 18; DAM POET; PC 24**
See See also CA 106; 152; DLB 19, 100, 141, 174; MTCW 1; YABC 1

Belloc, Joseph Peter Rene Hilaire
See See Belloc, (Joseph) Hilaire (Pierre Sebastien Rene Swanton)

Belloc, Joseph Pierre Hilaire
See See Belloc, (Joseph) Hilaire (Pierre Sebastien Rene Swanton)

Belloc, M. A.
See See Lowndes, Marie Adelaide (Belloc)

Bellow, Saul 1915- . **CLC 1, 2, 3, 6, 8, 10, 13, 15, 25, 33, 34, 63, 79; DA; DAB; DAC; DAM MST, NOV, POP; SSC 14; WLC**
See See also AITN 2; BEST 89:3; CA 5-8R; CABS 1; CANR 29, 53; CDALB 1941-1968; DA3; DLB 2, 28; DLBD 3; DLBY 82; MTCW 1, 2

Belser, Reimond Karel Maria de 1929-
See See Ruyslinck, Ward
See See also CA 152

Bely, Andrey .... **TCLC 7; PC 11**
See See also Bugayev, Boris Nikolayevich
See See also MTCW 1

Belyi, Andrei
See See Bugayev, Boris Nikolayevich

Benary, Margot
See See Benary-Isbert, Margot

Benary-Isbert, Margot 1889-1979 ... **CLC 12**
See See also CA 5-8R; 89-92; CANR 4, 72; CLR 12; MAICYA; SATA 2; SATA-Obit 21

Benavente (y Martinez), Jacinto 1866-1954 . **TCLC 3; DAM DRAM, MULT; HLCS 1**
See See also CA 106; 131; CANR 81; HW 1, 2; MTCW 1, 2

Benchley, Peter (Bradford) 1940- .... **CLC 4, 8; DAM NOV, POP**
See See also AAYA 14; AITN 2; CA 17-20R; CANR 12, 35, 66; MTCW 1, 2; SATA 3, 89

Benchley, Robert (Charles) 1889-1945 .... **TCLC 1, 55**
See See also CA 105; 153; DLB 11

Benda, Julien 1867-1956 .... **TCLC 60**
See See also CA 120; 154

Benedict, Ruth (Fulton) 1887-1948 ... **TCLC 60**
See See also CA 158

Benedict, Saint c. 480-c. 547 .... **CMLC 29**

Benedikt, Michael 1935- .... **CLC 4, 14**
See See also CA 13-16R; CANR 7; DLB 5

Benet, Juan 1927- .... **CLC 28**
See See also CA 143

Benet, Stephen Vincent 1898-1943 .... **TCLC 7; DAM POET; SSC 10**
See See also CA 104; 152; DA3; DLB 4, 48, 102; DLBY 97; MTCW 1; YABC 1

Benet, William Rose 1886-1950 .. **TCLC 28; DAM POET**
See See also CA 118; 152; DLB 45

Benford, Gregory (Albert) 1941- .... **CLC 52**

See See also CA 136

Bitov, Andrei (Georgievich) 1937- .. **CLC 57**
See See also CA 142

Biyidi, Alexandre 1932-
See See Beti, Mongo
See See also BW 1, 3; CA 114; 124; CANR
81; DA3; MTCW 1, 2

Bjarme, Brynjolf
See See Ibsen, Henrik (Johan)

Bjoernson, Bjoernstjerne (Martinius)
1832-1910 .... **TCLC 7, 37**
See See also CA 104

Black, Robert
See See Holdstock, Robert P.

Blackburn, Paul 1926-1971 .... **CLC 9, 43**
See See also CA 81-84; 33-36R; CANR 34;
DLB 16; DLBY 81

Black Elk 1863-1950 .... **TCLC 33; DAM
MULT**
See See also CA 144; MTCW 1; NNAL

Black Hobart
See See Sanders, (James) Ed(ward)

Blacklin, Malcolm
See See Chambers, Aidan

Blackmore, R(ichard) D(oddridge)
1825-1900 .... **TCLC 27**
See See also CA 120; DLB 18

Blackmur, R(ichard) P(almer) 1904-1965 ...
CLC 2, 24
See See also CA 11-12; 25-28R; CANR 71;
CAP 1; DLB 63

Black Tarantula
See See Acker, Kathy

Blackwood, Algernon (Henry) 1869-1951 ....
TCLC 5
See See also CA 105; 150; DLB 153, 156,
178

Blackwood, Caroline 1931-1996 .. **CLC 6, 9,
100**
See See also CA 85-88; 151; CANR 32, 61,
65; DLB 14, 207; MTCW 1

Blade, Alexander
See See Hamilton, Edmond; Silverberg,
Robert

Blaga, Lucian 1895-1961 .... **CLC 75**
See See also CA 157

Blair, Eric (Arthur) 1903-1950
See See Orwell, George
See See also CA 104; 132; DA; DAB;
DAC; DAM MST, NOV; DA3; MTCW 1,
2; SATA 29

Blair, Hugh 1718-1800 .... **NCLC 75**

Blais, Marie-Claire 1939- ... **CLC 2, 4, 6, 13,
22; DAC; DAM MST**
See See also CA 21-24R; CAAS 4; CANR
38, 75; DLB 53; MTCW 1, 2

Blaise, Clark 1940- .... **CLC 29**
See See also AITN 2; CA 53-56; CAAS 3;
CANR 5, 66; DLB 53

Blake, Fairley
See See De Voto, Bernard (Augustine)

Blake, Nicholas
See See Day Lewis, C(ecil)
See See also DLB 77

Blake, William 1757-1827 ...... **NCLC 13, 37,
57; DA; DAB; DAC; DAM MST,
POET; PC 12; WLC**
See See also CDBLB 1789-1832; CLR 52;
DA3; DLB 93, 163; MAICYA; SATA 30

Blasco Ibanez, Vicente 1867-1928 ..... **TCLC
12; DAM NOV**
See See also CA 110; 131; CANR 81; DA3;
HW 1, 2; MTCW 1

Blatty, William Peter 1928- ... **CLC 2; DAM
POP**
See See also CA 5-8R; CANR 9

Bleeck, Oliver
See See Thomas, Ross (Elmore)

Blessing, Lee 1949- .... **CLC 54**

Blish, James (Benjamin) 1921-1975 ..... **CLC
14**
See See also CA 1-4R; 57-60; CANR 3;
DLB 8; MTCW 1; SATA 66

Bliss, Reginald
See See Wells, H(erbert) G(eorge)

Blixen, Karen (Christentze Dinesen)
1885-1962
See See Dinesen, Isak
See See also CA 25-28; CANR 22, 50; CAP
2; DA3; MTCW 1, 2; SATA 44

Bloch, Robert (Albert) 1917-1994 ... **CLC 33**
See See also AAYA 29; CA 5-8R, 179; 146;
CAAE 179; CAAS 20; CANR 5, 78;
DA3; DLB 44; INT CANR-5; MTCW 1;
SATA 12; SATA-Obit 82

Blok, Alexander (Alexandrovich) 1880-1921
.... **TCLC 5; PC 21**
See See also CA 104

Blom, Jan
See See Breytenbach, Breyten

Bloom, Harold 1930- .... **CLC 24, 103**
See See also CA 13-16R; CANR 39, 75;
DLB 67; MTCW 1

Bloomfield, Aurelius
See See Bourne, Randolph S(illiman)

Blount, Roy (Alton), Jr. 1941- .... **CLC 38**
See See also CA 53-56; CANR 10, 28, 61;
INT CANR-28; MTCW 1, 2

Bloy, Leon 1846-1917 .... **TCLC 22**
See See also CA 121; DLB 123

Blume, Judy (Sussman) 1938- . **CLC 12, 30;
DAM NOV, POP**
See See also AAYA 3, 26; CA 29-32R;
CANR 13, 37, 66; CLR 2, 15; DA3; DLB
52; JRDA; MAICYA; MTCW 1, 2; SATA
2, 31, 79

Blunden, Edmund (Charles) 1896-1974 ....
CLC 2, 56
See See also CA 17-18; 45-48; CANR 54;
CAP 2; DLB 20, 100, 155; MTCW 1

Bly, Robert (Elwood) 1926- ..... **CLC 1, 2, 5,
10, 15, 38; DAM POET**
See See also CA 5-8R; CANR 41, 73; DA3;
DLB 5; MTCW 1, 2

Boas, Franz 1858-1942 .... **TCLC 56**
See See also CA 115; 181

Bobette
See See Simenon, Georges (Jacques
Christian)

Boccaccio, Giovanni 1313-1375 .. **CMLC 13;
SSC 10**

Bochco, Steven 1943- .... **CLC 35**
See See also AAYA 11; CA 124; 138

Bodel, Jean 1167(?)-1210 .... **CMLC 28**

Bodenheim, Maxwell 1892-1954 ... **TCLC 44**
See See also CA 110; DLB 9, 45

Bodker, Cecil 1927- .... **CLC 21**
See See also CA 73-76; CANR 13, 44; CLR
23; MAICYA; SATA 14

Boell, Heinrich (Theodor) 1917-1985 .. **CLC
2, 3, 6, 9, 11, 15, 27, 32, 72; DA; DAB;
DAC; DAM MST, NOV; SSC 23; WLC**
See See also CA 21-24R; 116; CANR 24;
DA3; DLB 69; DLBY 85; MTCW 1, 2

Boerne, Alfred
See See Doeblin, Alfred

Boethius 480(?)-524(?) .... **CMLC 15**
See See also DLB 115

Boff, Leonardo (Genezio Darci) 1938-
See See also CA 150; DAM MULT; HLC
1; HW 2

Bogan, Louise 1897-1970 ...... **CLC 4, 39, 46,
93; DAM POET; PC 12**
See See also CA 73-76; 25-28R; CANR 33,
82; DLB 45, 169; MTCW 1, 2

Bogarde, Dirk 1921-1999 .... **CLC 19**
See See also Van Den Bogarde, Derek Jules
Gaspard Ulric Niven

See See also CA 179; DLB 14

Bogosian, Eric 1953- .... **CLC 45**
See See also CA 138

Bograd, Larry 1953- .... **CLC 35**
See See also CA 93-96; CANR 57; SAAS
21; SATA 33, 89

Boiardo, Matteo Maria 1441-1494 ...... **LC 6**

Boileau-Despreaux, Nicolas 1636-1711 ... **LC
3**

Bojer, Johan 1872-1959 .... **TCLC 64**

Boland, Eavan (Aisling) 1944- . **CLC 40, 67,
113; DAM POET**
See See also CA 143; CANR 61; DLB 40;
MTCW 2

Boll, Heinrich
See See Boell, Heinrich (Theodor)

Bolt, Lee
See See Faust, Frederick (Schiller)

Bolt, Robert (Oxton) 1924-1995 .... **CLC 14;
DAM DRAM**
See See also CA 17-20R; 147; CANR 35,
67; DLB 13; MTCW 1

Bombal, Maria Luisa 1910-1980 .... **SSC 37;
HLCS 1**
See See also CA 127; CANR 72; HW 1

Bombet, Louis-Alexandre-Cesar
See See Stendhal

Bomkauf
See See Kaufman, Bob (Garnell)

Bonaventura .... **NCLC 35**
See See also DLB 90

Bond, Edward 1934- .... **CLC 4, 6, 13, 23;
DAM DRAM**
See See also CA 25-28R; CANR 38, 67;
DLB 13; MTCW 1

Bonham, Frank 1914-1989 .... **CLC 12**
See See also AAYA 1; CA 9-12R; CANR 4,
36; JRDA; MAICYA; SAAS 3; SATA 1,
49; SATA-Obit 62

Bonnefoy, Yves 1923- . **CLC 9, 15, 58; DAM
MST, POET**
See See also CA 85-88; CANR 33, 75;
MTCW 1, 2

Bontemps, Arna(ud Wendell) 1902-1973 .....
**CLC 1, 18; BLC 1; DAM MULT, NOV,
POET**
See See also BW 1; CA 1-4R; 41-44R;
CANR 4, 35; CLR 6; DA3; DLB 48, 51;
JRDA; MAICYA; MTCW 1, 2; SATA 2,
44; SATA-Obit 24

Booth, Martin 1944- .... **CLC 13**
See See also CA 93-96; CAAS 2

Booth, Philip 1925- .... **CLC 23**
See See also CA 5-8R; CANR 5; DLBY 82

Booth, Wayne C(layson) 1921- .... **CLC 24**
See See also CA 1-4R; CAAS 5; CANR 3,
43; DLB 67

Borchert, Wolfgang 1921-1947 .... **TCLC 5**
See See also CA 104; DLB 69, 124

Borel, Petrus 1809-1859 .... **NCLC 41**

Borges, Jorge Luis 1899-1986 .. **CLC 1, 2, 3,
4, 6, 8, 9, 10, 13, 19, 44, 48, 83; DA;
DAB; DAC; DAM MST, MULT; HLC
1; PC 22; SSC 4; WLC**
See See also AAYA 26; CA 21-24R; CANR
19, 33, 75; DA3; DLB 113; DLBY 86;
HW 1, 2; MTCW 1, 2

Borowski, Tadeusz 1922-1951 .... **TCLC 9**
See See also CA 106; 154

Borrow, George (Henry) 1803-1881 .. **NCLC
9**
See See also DLB 21, 55, 166

Bosch (Gavino), Juan 1909-
See See also CA 151; DAM MST, MULT;
DLB 145; HLCS 1; HW 1, 2

Bosman, Herman Charles 1905-1951 . **TCLC
49**
See See also Malan, Herman
See See also CA 160

Bosschere, Jean de 1878(?)-1953 .. **TCLC 19**
See See also CA 115

Boswell, James 1740-1795 .... **LC 4, 50; DA;
DAB; DAC; DAM MST; WLC**
See See also CDBLB 1660-1789; DLB 104,
142

Bottoms, David 1949- .... **CLC 53**
See See also CA 105; CANR 22; DLB 120;
DLBY 83

Boucicault, Dion 1820-1890 .... **NCLC 41**

Boucolon, Maryse 1937(?)-
See See Conde, Maryse
See See also BW 3; CA 110; CANR 30, 53,
76

Bourget, Paul (Charles Joseph) 1852-1935 .
TCLC 12
See See also CA 107; DLB 123

Bourjaily, Vance (Nye) 1922- ...... **CLC 8, 62**
See See also CA 1-4R; CAAS 1; CANR 2,
72; DLB 2, 143

Bourne, Randolph S(illiman) 1886-1918 .....
TCLC 16
See See also CA 117; 155; DLB 63

Bova, Ben(jamin William) 1932- .... **CLC 45**
See See also AAYA 16; CA 5-8R; CAAS
18; CANR 11, 56; CLR 3; DLBY 81; INT
CANR-11; MAICYA; MTCW 1; SATA 6,
68

Bowen, Elizabeth (Dorothea Cole) 1899-1973
.... **CLC 1, 3, 6, 11, 15, 22, 118; DAM
NOV; SSC 3, 28**
See See also CA 17-18; 41-44R; CANR 35;
CAP 2; CDBLB 1945-1960; DA3; DLB
15, 162; MTCW 1, 2

Bowering, George 1935- .... **CLC 15, 47**
See See also CA 21-24R; CAAS 16; CANR
10; DLB 53

Bowering, Marilyn R(uthe) 1949- ... **CLC 32**
See See also CA 101; CANR 49

Bowers, Edgar 1924- .... **CLC 9**
See See also CA 5-8R; CANR 24; DLB 5

Bowie, David .... **CLC 17**
See See also Jones, David Robert

Bowles, Jane (Sydney) 1917-1973 .... **CLC 3,
68**
See See also CA 19-20; 41-44R; CAP 2

Bowles, Paul (Frederick) 1910- ... **CLC 1, 2,
19, 53; SSC 3**
See See also CA 1-4R; CAAS 1; CANR 1,
19, 50, 75; DA3; DLB 5, 6; MTCW 1, 2

Box, Edgar
See See Vidal, Gore

Boyd, Nancy
See See Millay, Edna St. Vincent

Boyd, William 1952- .... **CLC 28, 53, 70**
See See also CA 114; 120; CANR 51, 71

Boyle, Kay 1902-1992 .... **CLC 1, 5, 19, 58,
121; SSC 5**
See See also CA 13-16R; 140; CAAS 1;
CANR 29, 61; DLB 4, 9, 48, 86; DLBY
93; MTCW 1, 2

Boyle, Mark
See See Kienzle, William X(avier)

Boyle, Patrick 1905-1982 .... **CLC 19**
See See also CA 127

Boyle, T. C. 1948-
See See Boyle, T(homas) Coraghessan

Boyle, T(homas) Coraghessan 1948- ... **CLC
36, 55, 90; DAM POP; SSC 16**
See See also BEST 90:4; CA 120; CANR
44, 76; DA3; DLBY 86; MTCW 2

Boz
See See Dickens, Charles (John Huffam)

Brackenridge, Hugh Henry 1748-1816 ....
NCLC 7
See See also DLB 11, 37

Bradbury, Edward P.
See See Moorcock, Michael (John)
See See also MTCW 2

Bradbury, Malcolm (Stanley) 1932- .... **CLC
32, 61; DAM NOV**
See See also CA 1-4R; CANR 1, 33; DA3;
DLB 14, 207; MTCW 1, 2

Bradbury, Ray (Douglas) 1920- ... **CLC 1, 3,
10, 15, 42, 98; DA; DAB; DAC; DAM
MST, NOV, POP; SSC 29; WLC**
See See also AAYA 15; AITN 1, 2; CA
1-4R; CANR 2, 30, 75; CDALB 1968-
1988; DA3; DLB 2, 8; MTCW 1, 2; SATA
11, 64

Bradford, Gamaliel 1863-1932 ..... **TCLC 36**
See See also CA 160; DLB 17

Bradley, David (Henry), Jr. 1950- . **CLC 23,
118; BLC 1; DAM MULT**
See See also BW 1, 3; CA 104; CANR 26,
81; DLB 33

Bradley, John Ed(mund, Jr.) 1958- . **CLC 55**
See See also CA 139

Bradley, Marion Zimmer 1930- ..... **CLC 30;
DAM POP**
See See also AAYA 9; CA 57-60; CAAS
10; CANR 7, 31, 51, 75; DA3; DLB 8;
MTCW 1, 2; SATA 90

Bradstreet, Anne 1612(?)-1672 ..... **LC 4, 30;
DA; DAC; DAM MST, POET; PC 10**
See See also CDALB 1640-1865; DA3;
DLB 24

Brady, Joan 1939- .... **CLC 86**
See See also CA 141

Bragg, Melvyn 1939- .... **CLC 10**
See See also BEST 89:3; CA 57-60; CANR
10, 48; DLB 14

Brahe, Tycho 1546-1601 .... **LC 45**

Braine, John (Gerard) 1922-1986 .... **CLC 1,
3, 41**
See See also CA 1-4R; 120; CANR 1, 33;
CDBLB 1945-1960; DLB 15; DLBY 86;
MTCW 1

Bramah, Ernest 1868-1942 .... **TCLC 72**
See See also CA 156; DLB 70

Brammer, William 1930(?)-1978 ..... **CLC 31**
See See also CA 77-80

Brancati, Vitaliano 1907-1954 ...... **TCLC 12**
See See also CA 109

Brancato, Robin F(idler) 1936- .... **CLC 35**
See See also AAYA 9; CA 69-72; CANR
11, 45; CLR 32; JRDA; SAAS 9; SATA
97

Brand, Max
See See Faust, Frederick (Schiller)

Brand, Millen 1906-1980 .... **CLC 7**
See See also CA 21-24R; 97-100; CANR
72

Branden, Barbara .... **CLC 44**
See See also CA 148

Brandes, Georg (Morris Cohen) 1842-1927
.... **TCLC 10**
See See also CA 105

Brandys, Kazimierz 1916- .... **CLC 62**

Branley, Franklyn M(ansfield) 1915- ... **CLC
21**
See See also CA 33-36R; CANR 14, 39;
CLR 13; MAICYA; SAAS 16; SATA 4,
68

Brathwaite, Edward (Kamau) 1930- ... **CLC
11; BLCS; DAM POET**
See See also BW 2, 3; CA 25-28R; CANR
11, 26, 47; DLB 125

Brautigan, Richard (Gary) 1935-1984 . **CLC
1, 3, 5, 9, 12, 34, 42; DAM NOV**
See See also CA 53-56; 113; CANR 34;
DA3; DLB 2, 5, 206; DLBY 80, 84;
MTCW 1; SATA 56

Brave Bird, Mary 1953-
See See Crow Dog, Mary (Ellen)
See See also NNAL

Braverman, Kate 1950- .... **CLC 67**
See See also CA 89-92

Brecht, (Eugen) Bertolt (Friedrich)
1898-1956 .... **TCLC 1, 6, 13, 35; DA;
DAB; DAC; DAM DRAM, MST; DC 3;
WLC**
See See also CA 104; 133; CANR 62; DA3;
DLB 56, 124; MTCW 1, 2

Brecht, Eugen Berthold Friedrich
See See Brecht, (Eugen) Bertolt (Friedrich)

Bremer, Fredrika 1801-1865 .... **NCLC 11**

Brennan, Christopher John 1870-1932 ....
TCLC 17
See See also CA 117

Brennan, Maeve 1917-1993 .... **CLC 5**
See See also CA 81-84; CANR 72

Brent, Linda
See See Jacobs, Harriet A(nn)

Brentano, Clemens (Maria) 1778-1842 ....
NCLC 1
See See also DLB 90

Brent of Bin Bin
See See Franklin, (Stella Maria Sarah)
Miles (Lampe)

Brenton, Howard 1942- .... **CLC 31**
See See also CA 69-72; CANR 33, 67; DLB
13; MTCW 1

Breslin, James 1930-1996
See See Breslin, Jimmy
See See also CA 73-76; CANR 31, 75;
DAM NOV; MTCW 1, 2

Breslin, Jimmy .... **CLC 4, 43**
See See also Breslin, James
See See also AITN 1; DLB 185; MTCW 2

Bresson, Robert 1901- .... **CLC 16**
See See also CA 110; CANR 49

Breton, Andre 1896-1966 . **CLC 2, 9, 15, 54;
PC 15**
See See also CA 19-20; 25-28R; CANR 40,
60; CAP 2; DLB 65; MTCW 1, 2

Breytenbach, Breyten 1939(?)- . **CLC 23, 37,
126; DAM POET**
See See also CA 113; 129; CANR 61

Bridgers, Sue Ellen 1942- .... **CLC 26**
See See also AAYA 8; CA 65-68; CANR
11, 36; CLR 18; DLB 52; JRDA; MAI-
CYA; SAAS 1; SATA 22, 90; SATA-Essay
109

Bridges, Robert (Seymour) 1844-1930 ....
TCLC 1; DAM POET; PC 28
See See also CA 104; 152; CDBLB 1890-
1914; DLB 19, 98

Bridie, James .... **TCLC 3**
See See also Mavor, Osborne Henry
See See also DLB 10

Brin, David 1950- .... **CLC 34**
See See also AAYA 21; CA 102; CANR 24,
70; INT CANR-24; SATA 65

Brink, Andre (Philippus) 1935- ...... **CLC 18,
36, 106**
See See also CA 104; CANR 39, 62; INT
103; MTCW 1, 2

Brinsmead, H(esba) F(ay) 1922- ..... **CLC 21**
See See also CA 21-24R; CANR 10; CLR
47; MAICYA; SAAS 5; SATA 18, 78

Brittain, Vera (Mary) 1893(?)-1970 . **CLC 23**
See See also CA 13-16; 25-28R; CANR 58;
CAP 1; DLB 191; MTCW 1, 2

Broch, Hermann 1886-1951 .... **TCLC 20**
See See also CA 117; DLB 85, 124

Brock, Rose
See See Hansen, Joseph

Brodkey, Harold (Roy) 1930-1996 .. **CLC 56**
See See also CA 111; 151; CANR 71; DLB
130

Brodskii, Iosif
See See Brodsky, Joseph

Brodsky, Iosif Alexandrovich 1940-1996
See See Brodsky, Joseph

See See also CA 106; CANR 24, 49, 75; HW 1; MTCW 1, 2

Bufalino, Gesualdo 1920(?)- .... **CLC 74**
See See also DLB 196

Bugayev, Boris Nikolayevich 1880-1934 ...... **TCLC 7; PC 11**
See See also Bely, Andrey
See See also CA 104; 165; MTCW 1

Bukowski, Charles 1920-1994 .. **CLC 2, 5, 9, 41, 82, 108; DAM NOV, POET; PC 18**
See See also CA 17-20R; 144; CANR 40, 62; DA3; DLB 5, 130, 169; MTCW 1, 2

Bulgakov, Mikhail (Afanas'evich) 1891-1940 . **TCLC 2, 16; DAM DRAM, NOV; SSC 18**
See See also CA 105; 152

Bulgya, Alexander Alexandrovich 1901-1956 .... **TCLC 53**
See See also Fadeyev, Alexander
See See also CA 117; 181

Bullins, Ed 1935- .... **CLC 1, 5, 7; BLC 1; DAM DRAM, MULT; DC 6**
See See also BW 2, 3; CA 49-52; CAAS 16; CANR 24, 46, 73; DLB 7, 38; MTCW 1, 2

Bulwer-Lytton, Edward (George Earle Lytton) 1803-1873 .... **NCLC 1, 45**
See See also DLB 21

Bunin, Ivan Alexeyevich 1870-1953 .. **TCLC 6; SSC 5**
See See also CA 104

Bunting, Basil 1900-1985 ... **CLC 10, 39, 47; DAM POET**
See See also CA 53-56; 115; CANR 7; DLB 20

Bunuel, Luis 1900-1983 . **CLC 16, 80; DAM MULT; HLC 1**
See See also CA 101; 110; CANR 32, 77; HW 1

Bunyan, John 1628-1688 .. **LC 4; DA; DAB; DAC; DAM MST; WLC**
See See also CDBLB 1660-1789; DLB 39

Burckhardt, Jacob (Christoph) 1818-1897 .. **NCLC 49**

Burford, Eleanor
See See Hibbert, Eleanor Alice Burford

Burgess, Anthony . **CLC 1, 2, 4, 5, 8, 10, 13, 15, 22, 40, 62, 81, 94; DAB**
See See also Wilson, John (Anthony) Burgess
See See also AAYA 25; AITN 1; CDBLB 1960 to Present; DLB 14, 194; DLBY 98; MTCW 1

Burke, Edmund 1729(?)-1797 .... **LC 7, 36; DA; DAB; DAC; DAM MST; WLC**
See See also DA3; DLB 104

Burke, Kenneth (Duva) 1897-1993 .. **CLC 2, 24**
See See also CA 5-8R; 143; CANR 39, 74; DLB 45, 63; MTCW 1, 2

Burke, Leda
See See Garnett, David

Burke, Ralph
See See Silverberg, Robert

Burke, Thomas 1886-1945 .... **TCLC 63**
See See also CA 113; 155; DLB 197

Burney, Fanny 1752-1840 . **NCLC 12, 54, 81**
See See also DLB 39

Burns, Robert 1759-1796 . **LC 3, 29, 40; DA; DAB; DAC; DAM MST, POET; PC 6; WLC**
See See also CDBLB 1789-1832; DA3; DLB 109

Burns, Tex
See See L'Amour, Louis (Dearborn)

Burnshaw, Stanley 1906- ...... **CLC 3, 13, 44**
See See also CA 9-12R; DLB 48; DLBY 97

Burr, Anne 1937- .... **CLC 6**
See See also CA 25-28R

Burroughs, Edgar Rice 1875-1950 . **TCLC 2, 32; DAM NOV**
See See also AAYA 11; CA 104; 132; DA3; DLB 8; MTCW 1, 2; SATA 41

Burroughs, William S(eward) 1914-1997 .... **CLC 1, 2, 5, 15, 22, 42, 75, 109; DA; DAB; DAC; DAM MST, NOV, POP; WLC**
See See also AITN 2; CA 9-12R; 160; CANR 20, 52; DA3; DLB 2, 8, 16, 152; DLBY 81, 97; MTCW 1, 2

Burton, SirRichard F(rancis) 1821-1890 ..... **NCLC 42**
See See also DLB 55, 166, 184

Busch, Frederick 1941- ... **CLC 7, 10, 18, 47**
See See also CA 33-36R; CAAS 1; CANR 45, 73; DLB 6

Bush, Ronald 1946- .... **CLC 34**
See See also CA 136

Bustos, F(rancisco)
See See Borges, Jorge Luis

Bustos Domecq, H(onorio)
See See Bioy Casares, Adolfo; Borges, Jorge Luis

Butler, Octavia E(stelle) 1947- .... **CLC 38, 121; BLCS; DAM MULT, POP**
See See also AAYA 18; BW 2, 3; CA 73-76; CANR 12, 24, 38, 73; DA3; DLB 33; MTCW 1, 2; SATA 84

Butler, Robert Olen (Jr.) 1945- ...... **CLC 81; DAM POP**
See See also CA 112; CANR 66; DLB 173; INT 112; MTCW 1

Butler, Samuel 1612-1680 .... **LC 16, 43**
See See also DLB 101, 126

Butler, Samuel 1835-1902 . **TCLC 1, 33; DA; DAB; DAC; DAM MST, NOV; WLC**
See See also CA 143; CDBLB 1890-1914; DA3; DLB 18, 57, 174

Butler, Walter C.
See See Faust, Frederick (Schiller)

Butor, Michel (Marie Francois) 1926- . **CLC 1, 3, 8, 11, 15**
See See also CA 9-12R; CANR 33, 66; DLB 83; MTCW 1, 2

Butts, Mary 1892(?)-1937 .... **TCLC 77**
See See also CA 148

Buzo, Alexander (John) 1944- .... **CLC 61**
See See also CA 97-100; CANR 17, 39, 69

Buzzati, Dino 1906-1972 .... **CLC 36**
See See also CA 160; 33-36R; DLB 177

Byars, Betsy (Cromer) 1928- .... **CLC 35**
See See also AAYA 19; CA 33-36R; CANR 18, 36, 57; CLR 1, 16; DLB 52; INT CANR-18; JRDA; MAICYA; MTCW 1; SAAS 1; SATA 4, 46, 80; SATA-Essay 108

Byatt, A(ntonia) S(usan Drabble) 1936- ...... **CLC 19, 65; DAM NOV, POP**
See See also CA 13-16R; CANR 13, 33, 50, 75; DA3; DLB 14, 194; MTCW 1, 2

Byrne, David 1952- .... **CLC 26**
See See also CA 127

Byrne, John Keyes 1926-
See See Leonard, Hugh
See See also CA 102; CANR 78; INT 102

Byron, George Gordon (Noel) 1788-1824 .... **NCLC 2, 12; DA; DAB; DAC; DAM MST, POET; PC 16; WLC**
See See also CDBLB 1789-1832; DA3; DLB 96, 110

Byron, Robert 1905-1941 .... **TCLC 67**
See See also CA 160; DLB 195

C. 3. 3.
See See Wilde, Oscar

Caballero, Fernan 1796-1877 .... **NCLC 10**

Cabell, Branch
See See Cabell, James Branch

Cabell, James Branch 1879-1958 ... **TCLC 6**

See See also CA 105; 152; DLB 9, 78; MTCW 1

Cable, George Washington 1844-1925 .... **TCLC 4; SSC 4**
See See also CA 104; 155; DLB 12, 74; DLBD 13

Cabral de Melo Neto, Joao 1920- . **CLC 76; DAM MULT**
See See also CA 151

Cabrera Infante, G(uillermo) 1929- . **CLC 5, 25, 45, 120; DAM MULT; HLC 1**
See See also CA 85-88; CANR 29, 65; DA3; DLB 113; HW 1, 2; MTCW 1, 2

Cade, Toni
See See Bambara, Toni Cade

Cadmus and Harmonia
See See Buchan, John

Caedmon fl. 658-680 .... **CMLC 7**
See See also DLB 146

Caeiro, Alberto
See See Pessoa, Fernando (Antonio Nogueira)

Cage, John (Milton, Jr.) 1912-1992 . **CLC 41**
See See also CA 13-16R; 169; CANR 9, 78; DLB 193; INT CANR-9

Cahan, Abraham 1860-1951 .... **TCLC 71**
See See also CA 108; 154; DLB 9, 25, 28

Cain, G.
See See Cabrera Infante, G(uillermo)

Cain, Guillermo
See See Cabrera Infante, G(uillermo)

Cain, James M(allahan) 1892-1977 . **CLC 3, 11, 28**
See See also AITN 1; CA 17-20R; 73-76; CANR 8, 34, 61; MTCW 1

Caine, Hall 1853-1931 .... **TCLC 99**

Caine, Mark
See See Raphael, Frederic (Michael)

Calasso, Roberto 1941- .... **CLC 81**
See See also CA 143

Calderon de la Barca, Pedro 1600-1681 . **LC 23; DC 3; HLCS 1**

Caldwell, Erskine (Preston) 1903-1987 . **CLC 1, 8, 14, 50, 60; DAM NOV; SSC 19**
See See also AITN 1; CA 1-4R; 121; CAAS 1; CANR 2, 33; DA3; DLB 9, 86; MTCW 1, 2

Caldwell, (Janet Miriam) Taylor (Holland) 1900-1985 . **CLC 2, 28, 39; DAM NOV, POP**
See See also CA 5-8R; 116; CANR 5; DA3; DLBD 17

Calhoun, John Caldwell 1782-1850 .. **NCLC 15**
See See also DLB 3

Calisher, Hortense 1911- .... **CLC 2, 4, 8, 38; DAM NOV; SSC 15**
See See also CA 1-4R; CANR 1, 22, 67; DA3; DLB 2; INT CANR-22; MTCW 1, 2

Callaghan, Morley Edward 1903-1990 . **CLC 3, 14, 41, 65; DAC; DAM MST**
See See also CA 9-12R; 132; CANR 33, 73; DLB 68; MTCW 1, 2

Callimachus c. 305B.C.-c. 240B.C. ... **CMLC 18**
See See also DLB 176

Calvin, John 1509-1564 .... **LC 37**

Calvino, Italo 1923-1985 .. **CLC 5, 8, 11, 22, 33, 39, 73; DAM NOV; SSC 3**
See See also CA 85-88; 116; CANR 23, 61; DLB 196; MTCW 1, 2

Cameron, Carey 1952- .... **CLC 59**
See See also CA 135

Cameron, Peter 1959- .... **CLC 44**
See See also CA 125; CANR 50

Camoens, Luis Vaz de 1524(?)-1580
See See also HLCS 1

Camoes, Luis de 1524(?)-1580
See See also HLCS 1

Campana, Dino 1885-1932 .... **TCLC 20**
See See also CA 117; DLB 114

Campanella, Tommaso 1568-1639 ..... **LC 32**

Campbell, John W(ood, Jr.) 1910-1971 ....
CLC 32
See See also CA 21-22; 29-32R; CANR 34;
CAP 2; DLB 8; MTCW 1

Campbell, Joseph 1904-1987 .... **CLC 69**
See See also AAYA 3; BEST 89:2; CA
1-4R; 124; CANR 3, 28, 61; DA3; MTCW
1, 2

Campbell, Maria 1940- .... **CLC 85; DAC**
See See also CA 102; CANR 54; NNAL

Campbell, (John) Ramsey 1946- ... **CLC 42;
SSC 19**
See See also CA 57-60; CANR 7; INT
CANR-7

Campbell, (Ignatius) Roy (Dunnachie)
1901-1957 .... **TCLC 5**
See See also CA 104; 155; DLB 20; MTCW
2

Campbell, Thomas 1777-1844 ...... **NCLC 19**
See See also DLB 93; 144

Campbell, Wilfred .... **TCLC 9**
See See Campbell, William

Campbell, William 1858(?)-1918
See See Campbell, Wilfred
See See also CA 106; DLB 92

Campion, Jane .... **CLC 95**
See See also CA 138

Campos, Alvaro de
See See Pessoa, Fernando (Antonio
Nogueira)

Camus, Albert 1913-1960 ..... **CLC 1, 2, 4, 9,
11, 14, 32, 63, 69, 124; DA; DAB; DAC;
DAM DRAM, MST, NOV; DC 2; SSC
9; WLC**
See See also CA 89-92; DA3; DLB 72;
MTCW 1, 2

Canby, Vincent 1924- .... **CLC 13**
See See also CA 81-84

Cancale
See See Desnos, Robert

Canetti, Elias 1905-1994 . **CLC 3, 14, 25, 75,
86**
See See also CA 21-24R; 146; CANR 23,
61, 79; DA3; DLB 85, 124; MTCW 1, 2

Canfield, Dorothea F.
See See Fisher, Dorothy (Frances) Canfield

Canfield, Dorothea Frances
See See Fisher, Dorothy (Frances) Canfield

Canfield, Dorothy
See See Fisher, Dorothy (Frances) Canfield

Canin, Ethan 1960- .... **CLC 55**
See See also CA 131; 135

Cannon, Curt
See See Hunter, Evan

Cao, Lan 1961- .... **CLC 109**
See See also CA 165

Cape, Judith
See See Page, P(atricia) K(athleen)

Capek, Karel 1890-1938 .. **TCLC 6, 37; DA;
DAB; DAC; DAM DRAM, MST, NOV;
DC 1; SSC 36; WLC**
See See also CA 104; 140; DA3; MTCW 1

Capote, Truman 1924-1984 ...... **CLC 1, 3, 8,
13, 19, 34, 38, 58; DA; DAB; DAC;
DAM MST, NOV, POP; SSC 2; WLC**
See See also CA 5-8R; 113; CANR 18, 62;
CDALB 1941-1968; DA3; DLB 2, 185;
DLBY 80, 84; MTCW 1, 2; SATA 91

Capra, Frank 1897-1991 .... **CLC 16**
See See also CA 61-64; 135

Caputo, Philip 1941- .... **CLC 32**
See See also CA 73-76; CANR 40

Caragiale, Ion Luca 1852-1912 .... **TCLC 76**
See See also CA 157

Card, Orson Scott 1951- .... **CLC 44, 47, 50;
DAM POP**
See See also AAYA 11; CA 102; CANR 27,
47, 73; DA3; INT CANR-27; MTCW 1,
2; SATA 83

Cardenal, Ernesto 1925- ...... **CLC 31; DAM
MULT, POET; HLC 1; PC 22**
See See also CA 49-52; CANR 2, 32, 66;
HW 1, 2; MTCW 1, 2

Cardozo, Benjamin N(athan) 1870-1938 .....
TCLC 65
See See also CA 117; 164

Carducci, Giosue (Alessandro Giuseppe)
1835-1907 .... **TCLC 32**
See See also CA 163

Carew, Thomas 1595(?)-1640 .... **LC 13**
See See also DLB 126

Carey, Ernestine Gilbreth 1908- ..... **CLC 17**
See See also CA 5-8R; CANR 71; SATA 2

Carey, Peter 1943- .... **CLC 40, 55, 96**
See See also CA 123; 127; CANR 53, 76;
INT 127; MTCW 1, 2; SATA 94

Carleton, William 1794-1869 .... **NCLC 3**
See See also DLB 159

Carlisle, Henry (Coffin) 1926- .... **CLC 33**
See See also CA 13-16R; CANR 15, 85

Carlsen, Chris
See See Holdstock, Robert P.

Carlson, Ron(ald F.) 1947- .... **CLC 54**
See See also CA 105; CANR 27

Carlyle, Thomas 1795-1881 . **NCLC 70; DA;
DAB; DAC; DAM MST**
See See also CDBLB 1789-1832; DLB 55;
144

Carman, (William) Bliss 1861-1929 .. **TCLC
7; DAC**
See See also CA 104; 152; DLB 92

Carnegie, Dale 1888-1955 .... **TCLC 53**

Carossa, Hans 1878-1956 .... **TCLC 48**
See See also CA 170; DLB 66

Carpenter, Don(ald Richard) 1931-1995 .....
CLC 41
See See also CA 45-48; 149; CANR 1, 71

Carpenter, Edward 1844-1929 ...... **TCLC 88**
See See also CA 163

Carpentier (y Valmont), Alejo 1904-1980 ....
**CLC 8, 11, 38, 110; DAM MULT; HLC
1; SSC 35**
See See also CA 65-68; 97-100; CANR 11,
70; DLB 113; HW 1, 2

Carr, Caleb 1955(?)- .... **CLC 86**
See See also CA 147; CANR 73; DA3

Carr, Emily 1871-1945 .... **TCLC 32**
See See also CA 159; DLB 68

Carr, John Dickson 1906-1977 .... **CLC 3**
See See also Fairbairn, Roger
See See also CA 49-52; 69-72; CANR 3,
33, 60; MTCW 1, 2

Carr, Philippa
See See Hibbert, Eleanor Alice Burford

Carr, Virginia Spencer 1929- .... **CLC 34**
See See also CA 61-64; DLB 111

Carrere, Emmanuel 1957- .... **CLC 89**

Carrier, Roch 1937- .... **CLC 13, 78; DAC;
DAM MST**
See See also CA 130; CANR 61; DLB 53;
SATA 105

Carroll, James P. 1943(?)- .... **CLC 38**
See See also CA 81-84; CANR 73; MTCW
1

Carroll, Jim 1951- .... **CLC 35**
See See also AAYA 17; CA 45-48; CANR
42

Carroll, Lewis ... **NCLC 2, 53; PC 18; WLC**
See See also Dodgson, Charles Lutwidge
See See also CDBLB 1832-1890; CLR 2,
18; DLB 18, 163, 178; DLBY 98; JRDA

Carroll, Paul Vincent 1900-1968 ..... **CLC 10**
See See also CA 9-12R; 25-28R; DLB 10

Carruth, Hayden 1921- .... **CLC 4, 7, 10, 18,
84; PC 10**
See See also CA 9-12R; CANR 4, 38, 59;
DLB 5, 165; INT CANR-4; MTCW 1, 2;
SATA 47

Carson, Rachel Louise 1907-1964 . **CLC 71;
DAM POP**
See See also CA 77-80; CANR 35; DA3;
MTCW 1, 2; SATA 23

Carter, Angela (Olive) 1940-1992 .... **CLC 5,
41, 76; SSC 13**
See See also CA 53-56; 136; CANR 12, 36,
61; DA3; DLB 14, 207; MTCW 1, 2;
SATA 66; SATA-Obit 70

Carter, Nick
See See Smith, Martin Cruz

Carver, Raymond 1938-1988 .... **CLC 22, 36,
53, 55, 126; DAM NOV; SSC 8**
See See also CA 33-36R; 126; CANR 17,
34, 61; DA3; DLB 130; DLBY 84, 88;
MTCW 1, 2

Cary, Elizabeth, Lady Falkland 1585-1639 .
LC 30

Cary, (Arthur) Joyce (Lunel) 1888-1957 .....
TCLC 1, 29
See See also CA 104; 164; CDBLB 1914-
1945; DLB 15, 100; MTCW 2

Casanova de Seingalt, Giovanni Jacopo
1725-1798 .... **LC 13**

Casares, Adolfo Bioy
See See Bioy Casares, Adolfo

Casely-Hayford, J(oseph) E(phraim)
1866-1930 ..... **TCLC 24; BLC 1; DAM
MULT**
See See also BW 2; CA 123; 152

Casey, John (Dudley) 1939- .... **CLC 59**
See See also BEST 90:2; CA 69-72; CANR
23

Casey, Michael 1947- .... **CLC 2**
See See also CA 65-68; DLB 5

Casey, Patrick
See See Thurman, Wallace (Henry)

Casey, Warren (Peter) 1935-1988 ... **CLC 12**
See See also CA 101; 127; INT 101

Casona, Alejandro .... **CLC 49**
See See also Alvarez, Alejandro Rodriguez

Cassavetes, John 1929-1989 .... **CLC 20**
See See also CA 85-88; 127; CANR 82

Cassian, Nina 1924- .... **PC 17**

Cassill, R(onald) V(erlin) 1919- .. **CLC 4, 23**
See See also CA 9-12R; CAAS 1; CANR 7,
45; DLB 6

Cassirer, Ernst 1874-1945 .... **TCLC 61**
See See also CA 157

Cassity, (Allen) Turner 1929- ...... **CLC 6, 42**
See See also CA 17-20R; CAAS 8; CANR
11; DLB 105

Castaneda, Carlos (Cesar Aranha)
1931(?)-1998 .... **CLC 12, 119**
See See also CA 25-28R; CANR 32, 66;
HW 1; MTCW 1

Castedo, Elena 1937- .... **CLC 65**
See See also CA 132

Castedo-Ellerman, Elena
See See Castedo, Elena

Castellanos, Rosario 1925-1974 ..... **CLC 66;
DAM MULT; HLC 1**
See See also CA 131; 53-56; CANR 58;
DLB 113; HW 1; MTCW 1

Castelvetro, Lodovico 1505-1571 .... **LC 12**

Castiglione, Baldassare 1478-1529 ..... **LC 12**

Castle, Robert
See See Hamilton, Edmond

Castro (Ruz), Fidel 1926(?)-
See See also CA 110; 129; CANR 81; DAM
MULT; HLC 1; HW 2

Castro, Guillen de 1569-1631 .... **LC 19**

Dexter, John
  See See Bradley, Marion Zimmer
Dexter, Martin
  See See Faust, Frederick (Schiller)
Dexter, Pete 1943- . **CLC 34, 55; DAM POP**
  See See also BEST 89:2; CA 127; 131; INT 131; MTCW 1
Diamano, Silmang
  See See Senghor, Leopold Sedar
Diamond, Neil 1941- .... **CLC 30**
  See See also CA 108
Diaz del Castillo, Bernal 1496-1584 . **LC 31; HLCS 1**
di Bassetto, Corno
  See See Shaw, George Bernard
Dick, Philip K(indred) 1928-1982 .. **CLC 10, 30, 72; DAM NOV, POP**
  See See also AAYA 24; CA 49-52; 106; CANR 2, 16; DA3; DLB 8; MTCW 1, 2
Dickens, Charles (John Huffam) 1812-1870 . **NCLC 3, 8, 18, 26, 37, 50; DA; DAB; DAC; DAM MST, NOV; SSC 17; WLC**
  See See also AAYA 23; CDBLB 1832-1890; DA3; DLB 21, 55, 70, 159, 166; JRDA; MAICYA; SATA 15
Dickey, James (Lafayette) 1923-1997 .. **CLC 1, 2, 4, 7, 10, 15, 47, 109; DAM NOV, POET, POP**
  See See also AITN 1, 2; CA 9-12R; 156; CABS 2; CANR 10, 48, 61; CDALB 1968-1988; DA3; DLB 5, 193; DLBD 7; DLBY 82, 93, 96, 97, 98; INT CANR-10; MTCW 1, 2
Dickey, William 1928-1994 .... **CLC 3, 28**
  See See also CA 9-12R; 145; CANR 24, 79; DLB 5
Dickinson, Charles 1951- .... **CLC 49**
  See See also CA 128
Dickinson, Emily (Elizabeth) 1830-1886 ...... **NCLC 21, 77; DA; DAB; DAC; DAM MST, POET; PC 1; WLC**
  See See also AAYA 22; CDALB 1865-1917; DA3; DLB 1; SATA 29
Dickinson, Peter (Malcolm) 1927- . **CLC 12, 35**
  See See also AAYA 9; CA 41-44R; CANR 31, 58; CLR 29; DLB 87, 161; JRDA; MAICYA; SATA 5, 62, 95
Dickson, Carr
  See See Carr, John Dickson
Dickson, Carter
  See See Carr, John Dickson
Diderot, Denis 1713-1784 .... **LC 26**
Didion, Joan 1934- .... **CLC 1, 3, 8, 14, 32; DAM NOV**
  See See also AITN 1; CA 5-8R; CANR 14, 52, 76; CDALB 1968-1988; DA3; DLB 2, 173, 185; DLBY 81, 86; MTCW 1, 2
Dietrich, Robert
  See See Hunt, E(verette) Howard, (Jr.)
Difusa, Pati
  See See Almodovar, Pedro
Dillard, Annie 1945- . **CLC 9, 60, 115; DAM NOV**
  See See also AAYA 6; CA 49-52; CANR 3, 43, 62; DA3; DLBY 80; MTCW 1, 2; SATA 10
Dillard, R(ichard) H(enry) W(ilde) 1937- ... **CLC 5**
  See See also CA 21-24R; CAAS 7; CANR 10; DLB 5
Dillon, Eilis 1920-1994 .... **CLC 17**
  See See also CA 9-12R; 182; 147; CAAE 182; CAAS 3; CANR 4, 38, 78; CLR 26; MAICYA; SATA 2, 74; SATA-Essay 105; SATA-Obit 83
Dimont, Penelope
  See See Mortimer, Penelope (Ruth)
Dinesen, Isak .... **CLC 10, 29, 95; SSC 7**

  See See also Blixen, Karen (Christentze Dinesen)
  See See also MTCW 1
Ding Ling .... **CLC 68**
  See See also Chiang, Pin-chin
Diphusa, Patty
  See See Almodovar, Pedro
Disch, Thomas M(ichael) 1940- .. **CLC 7, 36**
  See See also AAYA 17; CA 21-24R; CAAS 4; CANR 17, 36, 54; CLR 18; DA3; DLB 8; MAICYA; MTCW 1, 2; SAAS 15; SATA 92
Disch, Tom
  See See Disch, Thomas M(ichael)
d'Isly, Georges
  See See Simenon, Georges (Jacques Christian)
Disraeli, Benjamin 1804-1881 . **NCLC 2, 39, 79**
  See See also DLB 21, 55
Ditcum, Steve
  See See Crumb, R(obert)
Dixon, Paige
  See See Corcoran, Barbara
Dixon, Stephen 1936- .... **CLC 52; SSC 16**
  See See also CA 89-92; CANR 17, 40, 54; DLB 130
Doak, Annie
  See See Dillard, Annie
Dobell, Sydney Thompson 1824-1874 .... **NCLC 43**
  See See also DLB 32
Doblin, Alfred .... **TCLC 13**
  See See also Doeblin, Alfred
Dobrolyubov, Nikolai Alexandrovich 1836-1861 .... **NCLC 5**
Dobson, Austin 1840-1921 .... **TCLC 79**
  See See also DLB 35; 144
Dobyns, Stephen 1941- .... **CLC 37**
  See See also CA 45-48; CANR 2, 18
Doctorow, E(dgar) L(aurence) 1931- ... **CLC 6, 11, 15, 18, 37, 44, 65, 113; DAM NOV, POP**
  See See also AAYA 22; AITN 2; BEST 89:3; CA 45-48; CANR 2, 33, 51, 76; CDALB 1968-1988; DA3; DLB 2, 28, 173; DLBY 80; MTCW 1, 2
Dodgson, Charles Lutwidge 1832-1898
  See See Carroll, Lewis
  See See also CLR 2; DA; DAB; DAC; DAM MST, NOV, POET; DA3; MAICYA; SATA 100; YABC 2
Dodson, Owen (Vincent) 1914-1983 ..... **CLC 79; BLC 1; DAM MULT**
  See See also BW 1; CA 65-68; 110; CANR 24; DLB 76
Doeblin, Alfred 1878-1957 .... **TCLC 13**
  See See also Doblin, Alfred
  See See also CA 110; 141; DLB 66
Doerr, Harriet 1910- .... **CLC 34**
  See See also CA 117; 122; CANR 47; INT 122
Domecq, H(onorio Bustos)
  See See Bioy Casares, Adolfo
Domecq, H(onorio) Bustos
  See See Bioy Casares, Adolfo; Borges, Jorge Luis
Domini, Rey
  See See Lorde, Audre (Geraldine)
Dominique
  See See Proust, (Valentin-Louis-George-Eugene-) Marcel
Don, A
  See See Stephen, SirLeslie
Donaldson, Stephen R. 1947- .... **CLC 46; DAM POP**
  See See also CA 89-92; CANR 13, 55; INT CANR-13

Donleavy, J(ames) P(atrick) 1926- ... **CLC 1, 4, 6, 10, 45**
  See See also AITN 2; CA 9-12R; CANR 24, 49, 62, 80; DLB 6, 173; INT CANR-24; MTCW 1, 2
Donne, John 1572-1631 .... **LC 10, 24; DA; DAB; DAC; DAM MST, POET; PC 1; WLC**
  See See also CDBLB Before 1660; DLB 121, 151
Donnell, David 1939(?)- .... **CLC 34**
Donoghue, P. S.
  See See Hunt, E(verette) Howard, (Jr.)
Donoso (Yanez), Jose 1924-1996 .. **CLC 4, 8, 11, 32, 99; DAM MULT; HLC 1; SSC 34**
  See See also CA 81-84; 155; CANR 32, 73; DLB 113; HW 1, 2; MTCW 1, 2
Donovan, John 1928-1992 .... **CLC 35**
  See See also AAYA 20; CA 97-100; 137; CLR 3; MAICYA; SATA 72; SATA-Brief 29
Don Roberto
  See See Cunninghame Graham, R(obert) B(ontine)
Doolittle, Hilda 1886-1961 ...... **CLC 3, 8, 14, 31, 34, 73; DA; DAC; DAM MST, POET; PC 5; WLC**
  See See also H. D.
  See See also CA 97-100; CANR 35; DLB 4, 45; MTCW 1, 2
Dorfman, Ariel 1942- ..... **CLC 48, 77; DAM MULT; HLC 1**
  See See also CA 124; 130; CANR 67, 70; HW 1, 2; INT 130
Dorn, Edward (Merton) 1929- .. **CLC 10, 18**
  See See also CA 93-96; CANR 42, 79; DLB 5; INT 93-96
Dorris, Michael (Anthony) 1945-1997 . **CLC 109; DAM MULT, NOV**
  See See also AAYA 20; BEST 90:1; CA 102; 157; CANR 19, 46, 75; CLR 58; DA3; DLB 175; MTCW 2; NNAL; SATA 75; SATA-Obit 94
Dorris, Michael A.
  See See Dorris, Michael (Anthony)
Dorsan, Luc
  See See Simenon, Georges (Jacques Christian)
Dorsange, Jean
  See See Simenon, Georges (Jacques Christian)
Dos Passos, John (Roderigo) 1896-1970 ...... **CLC 1, 4, 8, 11, 15, 25, 34, 82; DA; DAB; DAC; DAM MST, NOV; WLC**
  See See also CA 1-4R; 29-32R; CANR 3; CDALB 1929-1941; DA3; DLB 4, 9; DLBD 1, 15; DLBY 96; MTCW 1, 2
Dossage, Jean
  See See Simenon, Georges (Jacques Christian)
Dostoevsky, Fedor Mikhailovich 1821-1881 .... **NCLC 2, 7, 21, 33, 43; DA; DAB; DAC; DAM MST, NOV; SSC 2, 33; WLC**
  See See also DA3
Doughty, Charles M(ontagu) 1843-1926 ...... **TCLC 27**
  See See also CA 115; 178; DLB 19, 57, 174
Douglas, Ellen .... **CLC 73**
  See See also Haxton, Josephine Ayres; Williamson, Ellen Douglas
Douglas, Gavin 1475(?)-1522 .... **LC 20**
  See See also DLB 132
Douglas, George
  See See Brown, George Douglas
Douglas, Keith (Castellain) 1920-1944 .... **TCLC 40**

See See also DLB 194; MTCW 1

Ellis, Bret Easton 1964- ... **CLC 39, 71, 117; DAM POP**
See See also AAYA 2; CA 118; 123; CANR 51, 74; DA3; INT 123; MTCW 1

Ellis, (Henry) Havelock 1859-1939 .... **TCLC 14**
See See also CA 109; 169; DLB 190

Ellis, Landon
See See Ellison, Harlan (Jay)

Ellis, Trey 1962- .... **CLC 55**
See See also CA 146

Ellison, Harlan (Jay) 1934- . **CLC 1, 13, 42; DAM POP; SSC 14**
See See also AAYA 29; CA 5-8R; CANR 5, 46; DLB 8; INT CANR-5; MTCW 1, 2

Ellison, Ralph (Waldo) 1914-1994 ... **CLC 1, 3, 11, 54, 86, 114; BLC 1; DA; DAB; DAC; DAM MST, MULT, NOV; SSC 26; WLC**
See See also AAYA 19; BW 1, 3; CA 9-12R; 145; CANR 24, 53; CDALB 1941-1968; DA3; DLB 2, 76; DLBY 94; MTCW 1, 2

Ellmann, Lucy (Elizabeth) 1956- .... **CLC 61**
See See also CA 128

Ellmann, Richard (David) 1918-1987 .. **CLC 50**
See See also BEST 89:2; CA 1-4R; 122; CANR 2, 28, 61; DLB 103; DLBY 87; MTCW 1, 2

Elman, Richard (Martin) 1934-1997 ... **CLC 19**
See See also CA 17-20R; 163; CAAS 3; CANR 47

Elron
See See Hubbard, L(afayette) Ron(ald)

Eluard, Paul .... **TCLC 7, 41**
See See also Grindel, Eugene

Elyot, Sir Thomas 1490(?)-1546 .... **LC 11**

Elytis, Odysseus 1911-1996 ...... **CLC 15, 49, 100; DAM POET; PC 21**
See See also CA 102; 151; MTCW 1, 2

Emecheta, (Florence Onye) Buchi 1944- ..... **CLC 14, 48; BLC 2; DAM MULT**
See See also BW 2, 3; CA 81-84; CANR 27, 81; DA3; DLB 117; MTCW 1, 2; SATA 66

Emerson, Mary Moody 1774-1863 .... **NCLC 66**

Emerson, Ralph Waldo 1803-1882 .... **NCLC 1, 38; DA; DAB; DAC; DAM MST, POET; PC 18; WLC**
See See also CDALB 1640-1865; DA3; DLB 1, 59, 73

Eminescu, Mihail 1850-1889 .... **NCLC 33**

Empson, William 1906-1984 .. **CLC 3, 8, 19, 33, 34**
See See also CA 17-20R; 112; CANR 31, 61; DLB 20; MTCW 1, 2

Enchi, Fumiko (Ueda) 1905-1986 ... **CLC 31**
See See also CA 129; 121; DLB 182

Ende, Michael (Andreas Helmuth)
1929-1995 .... **CLC 31**
See See also CA 118; 124; 149; CANR 36; CLR 14; DLB 75; MAICYA; SATA 61; SATA-Brief 42; SATA-Obit 86

Endo, Shusaku 1923-1996 .... **CLC 7, 14, 19, 54, 99; DAM NOV**
See See also CA 29-32R; 153; CANR 21, 54; DA3; DLB 182; MTCW 1, 2

Engel, Marian 1933-1985 .... **CLC 36**
See See also CA 25-28R; CANR 12; DLB 53; INT CANR-12

Engelhardt, Frederick
See See Hubbard, L(afayette) Ron(ald)

Enright, D(ennis) J(oseph) 1920- . **CLC 4, 8, 31**
See See also CA 1-4R; CANR 1, 42, 83; DLB 27; SATA 25

Enzensberger, Hans Magnus 1929- ...... **CLC 43; PC 28**
See See also CA 116; 119

Ephron, Nora 1941- .... **CLC 17, 31**
See See also AITN 2; CA 65-68; CANR 12, 39, 83

Epicurus 341B.C.-270B.C. .... **CMLC 21**
See See also DLB 176

Epsilon
See See Betjeman, John

Epstein, Daniel Mark 1948- .... **CLC 7**
See See also CA 49-52; CANR 2, 53

Epstein, Jacob 1956- .... **CLC 19**
See See also CA 114

Epstein, Jean 1897-1953 .... **TCLC 92**

Epstein, Joseph 1937- .... **CLC 39**
See See also CA 112; 119; CANR 50, 65

Epstein, Leslie 1938- .... **CLC 27**
See See also CA 73-76; CAAS 12; CANR 23, 69

Equiano, Olaudah 1745(?)-1797 .... **LC 16; BLC 2; DAM MULT**
See See also DLB 37, 50

ER .... **TCLC 33**
See See also CA 160; DLB 85

Erasmus, Desiderius 1469(?)-1536 ..... **LC 16**

Erdman, Paul E(mil) 1932- .... **CLC 25**
See See also AITN 1; CA 61-64; CANR 13, 43, 84

Erdrich, Louise 1954- .... **CLC 39, 54, 120; DAM MULT, NOV, POP**
See See also AAYA 10; BEST 89:1; CA 114; CANR 41, 62; CDALBS; DA3; DLB 152, 175, 206; MTCW 1; NNAL; SATA 94

Erenburg, Ilya (Grigoryevich)
See See Ehrenburg, Ilya (Grigoryevich)

Erickson, Stephen Michael 1950-
See See Erickson, Steve
See See also CA 129

Erickson, Steve 1950- .... **CLC 64**
See See also Erickson, Stephen Michael
See See also CANR 60, 68

Ericson, Walter
See See Fast, Howard (Melvin)

Eriksson, Buntel
See See Bergman, (Ernst) Ingmar

Ernaux, Annie 1940- .... **CLC 88**
See See also CA 147

Erskine, John 1879-1951 .... **TCLC 84**
See See also CA 112; 159; DLB 9, 102

Eschenbach, Wolfram von
See See Wolfram von Eschenbach

Eseki, Bruno
See See Mphahlele, Ezekiel

Esenin, Sergei (Alexandrovich) 1895-1925 .. **TCLC 4**
See See also CA 104

Eshleman, Clayton 1935- .... **CLC 7**
See See also CA 33-36R; CAAS 6; DLB 5

Espriella, Don Manuel Alvarez
See See Southey, Robert

Espriu, Salvador 1913-1985 .... **CLC 9**
See See also CA 154; 115; DLB 134

Espronceda, Jose de 1808-1842 .... **NCLC 39**

Esquivel, Laura 1951(?)-
See See also AAYA 29; CA 143; CANR 68; DA3; HLCS 1; MTCW 1

Esse, James
See See Stephens, James

Esterbrook, Tom
See See Hubbard, L(afayette) Ron(ald)

Estleman, Loren D. 1952- .... **CLC 48; DAM NOV, POP**
See See also AAYA 27; CA 85-88; CANR 27, 74; DA3; INT CANR-27; MTCW 1, 2

Euclid 306B.C.-283B.C. .... **CMLC 25**

Eugenides, Jeffrey 1960(?)- .... **CLC 81**

See See also CA 144

Euripides c. 485B.C.-406B.C. ..... **CMLC 23; DA; DAB; DAC; DAM DRAM, MST; DC 4; WLCS**
See See also DA3; DLB 176

Evan, Evin
See See Faust, Frederick (Schiller)

Evans, Caradoc 1878-1945 .... **TCLC 85**

Evans, Evan
See See Faust, Frederick (Schiller)

Evans, Marian
See See Eliot, George

Evans, Mary Ann
See See Eliot, George

Evarts, Esther
See See Benson, Sally

Everett, Percival L. 1956- .... **CLC 57**
See See also BW 2; CA 129

Everson, R(onald) G(ilmour) 1903- ..... **CLC 27**
See See also CA 17-20R; DLB 88

Everson, William (Oliver) 1912-1994 .. **CLC 1, 5, 14**
See See also CA 9-12R; 145; CANR 20; DLB 212; MTCW 1

Evtushenko, Evgenii Aleksandrovich
See See Yevtushenko, Yevgeny (Alexandrovich)

Ewart, Gavin (Buchanan) 1916-1995 .. **CLC 13, 46**
See See also CA 89-92; 150; CANR 17, 46; DLB 40; MTCW 1

Ewers, Hanns Heinz 1871-1943 .... **TCLC 12**
See See also CA 109; 149

Ewing, Frederick R.
See See Sturgeon, Theodore (Hamilton)

Exley, Frederick (Earl) 1929-1992 ... **CLC 6, 11**
See See also AITN 2; CA 81-84; 138; DLB 143; DLBY 81

Eynhardt, Guillermo
See See Quiroga, Horacio (Sylvestre)

Ezekiel, Nissim 1924- .... **CLC 61**
See See also CA 61-64

Ezekiel, Tish O'Dowd 1943- .... **CLC 34**
See See also CA 129

Fadeyev, A.
See See Bulgya, Alexander Alexandrovich

Fadeyev, Alexander .... **TCLC 53**
See See also Bulgya, Alexander Alexandrovich

Fagen, Donald 1948- .... **CLC 26**

Fainzilberg, Ilya Arnoldovich 1897-1937
See See Ilf, Ilya
See See also CA 120; 165

Fair, Ronald L. 1932- .... **CLC 18**
See See also BW 1; CA 69-72; CANR 25; DLB 33

Fairbairn, Roger
See See Carr, John Dickson

Fairbairns, Zoe (Ann) 1948- .... **CLC 32**
See See also CA 103; CANR 21, 85

Falco, Gian
See See Papini, Giovanni

Falconer, James
See See Kirkup, James

Falconer, Kenneth
See See Kornbluth, C(yril) M.

Falkland, Samuel
See See Heijermans, Herman

Fallaci, Oriana 1930- .... **CLC 11, 110**
See See also CA 77-80; CANR 15, 58; MTCW 1

Faludy, George 1913- .... **CLC 42**
See See also CA 21-24R

See See also CA 45-48; 29-32R; CANR 2, 35; DLB 72; MTCW 1

Giovanni, Nikki 1943- ...... **CLC 2, 4, 19, 64, 117; BLC 2; DA; DAB; DAC; DAM MST, MULT, POET; PC 19; WLCS**
See See also AAYA 22; AITN 1; BW 2, 3; CA 29-32R; CAAS 6; CANR 18, 41, 60; CDALBS; CLR 6; DA3; DLB 5, 41; INT CANR-18; MAICYA; MTCW 1, 2; SATA 24, 107

Giovene, Andrea 1904- .... **CLC 7**
See See also CA 85-88

Gippius, Zinaida (Nikolayevna) 1869-1945
See See Hippius, Zinaida
See See also CA 106

Giraudoux, (Hippolyte) Jean 1882-1944 ......
TCLC 2, 7; DAM DRAM
See See also CA 104; DLB 65

Gironella, Jose Maria 1917- .... **CLC 11**
See See also CA 101

Gissing, George (Robert) 1857-1903 . **TCLC 3, 24, 47; SSC 37**
See See also CA 105; 167; DLB 18, 135, 184

Giurlani, Aldo
See See Palazzeschi, Aldo

Gladkov, Fyodor (Vasilyevich) 1883-1958 ...
TCLC 27
See See also CA 170

Glanville, Brian (Lester) 1931- .... **CLC 6**
See See also CA 5-8R; CAAS 9; CANR 3, 70; DLB 15, 139; SATA 42

Glasgow, Ellen (Anderson Gholson)
1873-1945 .... **TCLC 2, 7; SSC 34**
See See also CA 104; 164; DLB 9, 12; MTCW 2

Glaspell, Susan 1882(?)-1948 . **TCLC 55; DC 10**
See See also CA 110; 154; DLB 7, 9, 78; YABC 2

Glassco, John 1909-1981 .... **CLC 9**
See See also CA 13-16R; 102; CANR 15; DLB 68

Glasscock, Amnesia
See See Steinbeck, John (Ernst)

Glasser, Ronald J. 1940(?)- .... **CLC 37**

Glassman, Joyce
See See Johnson, Joyce

Glendinning, Victoria 1937- .... **CLC 50**
See See also CA 120; 127; CANR 59; DLB 155

Glissant, Edouard 1928- . **CLC 10, 68; DAM MULT**
See See also CA 153

Gloag, Julian 1930- .... **CLC 40**
See See also AITN 1; CA 65-68; CANR 10, 70

Glowacki, Aleksander
See See Prus, Boleslaw

Gluck, Louise (Elisabeth) 1943- . **CLC 7, 22, 44, 81; DAM POET; PC 16**
See See also CA 33-36R; CANR 40, 69; DA3; DLB 5; MTCW 2

Glyn, Elinor 1864-1943 .... **TCLC 72**
See See also DLB 153

Gobineau, Joseph Arthur (Comte) de
1816-1882 .... **NCLC 17**
See See also DLB 123

Godard, Jean-Luc 1930- .... **CLC 20**
See See also CA 93-96

Godden, (Margaret) Rumer 1907-1998 ....
CLC 53
See See also AAYA 6; CA 5-8R; 172; CANR 4, 27, 36, 55, 80; CLR 20; DLB 161; MAICYA; SAAS 12; SATA 3, 36; SATA-Obit 109

Godoy Alcayaga, Lucila 1889-1957
See See Mistral, Gabriela

See See also BW 2; CA 104; 131; CANR 81; DAM MULT; HW 1, 2; MTCW 1, 2

Godwin, Gail (Kathleen) 1937- .... **CLC 5, 8, 22, 31, 69, 125; DAM POP**
See See also CA 29-32R; CANR 15, 43, 69; DA3; DLB 6; INT CANR-15; MTCW 1, 2

Godwin, William 1756-1836 .... **NCLC 14**
See See also CDBLB 1789-1832; DLB 39, 104, 142, 158, 163

Goebbels, Josef
See See Goebbels, (Paul) Joseph

Goebbels, (Paul) Joseph 1897-1945 ... **TCLC 68**
See See also CA 115; 148

Goebbels, Joseph Paul
See See Goebbels, (Paul) Joseph

Goethe, Johann Wolfgang von 1749-1832 ...
NCLC 4, 22, 34; DA; DAB; DAC; DAM DRAM, MST, POET; PC 5; WLC
See See also DA3; DLB 94

Gogarty, Oliver St. John 1878-1957 .. **TCLC 15**
See See also CA 109; 150; DLB 15, 19

Gogol, Nikolai (Vasilyevich) 1809-1852 ....
NCLC 5, 15, 31; DA; DAB; DAC; DAM DRAM, MST; DC 1; SSC 4, 29; WLC
See See also DLB 198

Goines, Donald 1937(?)-1974 . **CLC 80; BLC 2; DAM MULT, POP**
See See also AITN 1; BW 1, 3; CA 124; 114; CANR 82; DA3; DLB 33

Gold, Herbert 1924- .... **CLC 4, 7, 14, 42**
See See also CA 9-12R; CANR 17, 45; DLB 2; DLBY 81

Goldbarth, Albert 1948- .... **CLC 5, 38**
See See also CA 53-56; CANR 6, 40; DLB 120

Goldberg, Anatol 1910-1982 .... **CLC 34**
See See also CA 131; 117

Goldemberg, Isaac 1945- .... **CLC 52**
See See also CA 69-72; CAAS 12; CANR 11, 32; HW 1

Golding, William (Gerald) 1911-1993 . **CLC 1, 2, 3, 8, 10, 17, 27, 58, 81; DA; DAB; DAC; DAM MST, NOV; WLC**
See See also AAYA 5; CA 5-8R; 141; CANR 13, 33, 54; CDBLB 1945-1960; DA3; DLB 15, 100; MTCW 1, 2

Goldman, Emma 1869-1940 .... **TCLC 13**
See See also CA 110; 150

Goldman, Francisco 1954- .... **CLC 76**
See See also CA 162

Goldman, William (W.) 1931- ..... **CLC 1, 48**
See See also CA 9-12R; CANR 29, 69; DLB 44

Goldmann, Lucien 1913-1970 .... **CLC 24**
See See also CA 25-28; CAP 2

Goldoni, Carlo 1707-1793 .... **LC 4; DAM DRAM**

Goldsberry, Steven 1949- .... **CLC 34**
See See also CA 131

Goldsmith, Oliver 1728-1774 . **LC 2, 48; DA; DAB; DAC; DAM DRAM, MST, NOV, POET; DC 8; WLC**
See See also CDBLB 1660-1789; DLB 39, 89, 104, 109, 142; SATA 26

Goldsmith, Peter
See See Priestley, J(ohn) B(oynton)

Gombrowicz, Witold 1904-1969 ... **CLC 4, 7, 11, 49; DAM DRAM**
See See also CA 19-20; 25-28R; CAP 2

Gomez de la Serna, Ramon 1888-1963 . **CLC 9**
See See also CA 153; 116; CANR 79; HW 1, 2

Goncharov, Ivan Alexandrovich 1812-1891
.... **NCLC 1, 63**

Goncourt, Edmond (Louis Antoine Huot) de
1822-1896 .... **NCLC 7**
See See also DLB 123

Goncourt, Jules (Alfred Huot) de 1830-1870
.... **NCLC 7**
See See also DLB 123

Gontier, Fernande 19(?)- .... **CLC 50**

Gonzalez Martinez, Enrique 1871-1952 ......
TCLC 72
See See also CA 166; CANR 81; HW 1, 2

Goodman, Paul 1911-1972 .. **CLC 1, 2, 4, 7**
See See also CA 19-20; 37-40R; CANR 34; CAP 2; DLB 130; MTCW 1

Gordimer, Nadine 1923- .... **CLC 3, 5, 7, 10, 18, 33, 51, 70; DA; DAB; DAC; DAM MST, NOV; SSC 17; WLCS**
See See also CA 5-8R; CANR 3, 28, 56; DA3; INT CANR-28; MTCW 1, 2

Gordon, Adam Lindsay 1833-1870 ... **NCLC 21**

Gordon, Caroline 1895-1981 ...... **CLC 6, 13, 29, 83; SSC 15**
See See also CA 11-12; 103; CANR 36; CAP 1; DLB 4, 9, 102; DLBD 17; DLBY 81; MTCW 1, 2

Gordon, Charles William 1860-1937
See See Connor, Ralph
See See also CA 109

Gordon, Mary (Catherine) 1949- .. **CLC 13, 22**
See See also CA 102; CANR 44; DLB 6; DLBY 81; INT 102; MTCW 1

Gordon, N. J.
See See Bosman, Herman Charles

Gordon, Sol 1923- .... **CLC 26**
See See also CA 53-56; CANR 4; SATA 11

Gordone, Charles 1925-1995 .... **CLC 1, 4; DAM DRAM; DC 8**
See See also BW 1, 3; CA 93-96, 180; 150; CAAE 180; CANR 55; DLB 7; INT 93-96; MTCW 1

Gore, Catherine 1800-1861 .... **NCLC 65**
See See also DLB 116

Gorenko, Anna Andreevna
See See Akhmatova, Anna

Gorky, Maxim 1868-1936 ... **TCLC 8; DAB; SSC 28; WLC**
See See also Peshkov, Alexei Maximovich
See See also MTCW 2

Goryan, Sirak
See See Saroyan, William

Gosse, Edmund (William) 1849-1928 . **TCLC 28**
See See also CA 117; DLB 57, 144, 184

Gotlieb, Phyllis Fay (Bloom) 1926- . **CLC 18**
See See also CA 13-16R; CANR 7; DLB 88

Gottesman, S. D.
See See Kornbluth, C(yril) M.; Pohl, Frederik

Gottfried von Strassburg fl. c. 1210- . **CMLC 10**
See See also DLB 138

Gould, Lois .... **CLC 4, 10**
See See also CA 77-80; CANR 29; MTCW 1

Gourmont, Remy (-Marie-Charles) de
1858-1915 .... **TCLC 17**
See See also CA 109; 150; MTCW 2

Govier, Katherine 1948- .... **CLC 51**
See See also CA 101; CANR 18, 40

Goyen, (Charles) William 1915-1983 ... **CLC 5, 8, 14, 40**
See See also AITN 2; CA 5-8R; 110; CANR 6, 71; DLB 2; DLBY 83; INT CANR-6

Goytisolo, Juan 1931- . **CLC 5, 10, 23; DAM MULT; HLC 1**
See See also CA 85-88; CANR 32, 61; HW 1, 2; MTCW 1, 2

See See also AAYA 14; CA 138; CANR 47, 69; DA3; MTCW 2

Grossman, David 1954- .... **CLC 67**
See See also CA 138

Grossman, Vasily (Semenovich) 1905-1964 . **CLC 41**
See See also CA 124; 130; MTCW 1

Grove, Frederick Philip .... **TCLC 4**
See See also Greve, Felix Paul (Berthold Friedrich)
See See also DLB 92

Grubb
See See Crumb, R(obert)

Grumbach, Doris (Isaac) 1918- ...... **CLC 13, 22, 64**
See See also CA 5-8R; CAAS 2; CANR 9, 42, 70; INT CANR-9; MTCW 2

Grundtvig, Nicolai Frederik Severin 1783-1872 .... **NCLC 1**

Grunge
See See Crumb, R(obert)

Grunwald, Lisa 1959- .... **CLC 44**
See See also CA 120

Guare, John 1938- . **CLC 8, 14, 29, 67; DAM DRAM**
See See also CA 73-76; CANR 21, 69; DLB 7; MTCW 1, 2

Gudjonsson, Halldor Kiljan 1902-1998
See See Laxness, Halldor
See See also CA 103; 164

Guenter, Erich
See See Eich, Guenter

Guest, Barbara 1920- .... **CLC 34**
See See also CA 25-28R; CANR 11, 44, 84; DLB 5, 193

Guest, Edgar A(lbert) 1881-1959 . **TCLC 95**
See See also CA 112; 168

Guest, Judith (Ann) 1936- .... **CLC 8, 30; DAM NOV, POP**
See See also AAYA 7; CA 77-80; CANR 15, 75; DA3; INT CANR-15; MTCW 1, 2

Guevara, Che .... **CLC 87; HLC 1**
See See also Guevara (Serna), Ernesto

Guevara (Serna), Ernesto 1928-1967 ... **CLC 87; DAM MULT; HLC 1**
See See also Guevara, Che
See See also CA 127; 111; CANR 56; HW 1

Guicciardini, Francesco 1483-1540 ... **LC 49**

Guild, Nicholas M. 1944- .... **CLC 33**
See See also CA 93-96

Guillemin, Jacques
See See Sartre, Jean-Paul

Guillen, Jorge 1893-1984 ..... **CLC 11; DAM MULT, POET; HLCS 1**
See See also CA 89-92; 112; DLB 108; HW 1

Guillen, Nicolas (Cristobal) 1902-1989 . **CLC 48, 79; BLC 2; DAM MST, MULT, POET; HLC 1; PC 23**
See See also BW 2; CA 116; 125; 129; CANR 84; HW 1

Guillevic, (Eugene) 1907- .... **CLC 33**
See See also CA 93-96

Guillois
See See Desnos, Robert

Guillois, Valentin
See See Desnos, Robert

Guimaraes Rosa, Joao 1908-1967
See See also CA 175; HLCS 2

Guiney, Louise Imogen 1861-1920 .... **TCLC 41**
See See also CA 160; DLB 54

Guiraldes, Ricardo (Guillermo) 1886-1927 . **TCLC 39**
See See also CA 131; HW 1; MTCW 1

Gumilev, Nikolai (Stepanovich) 1886-1921 . **TCLC 60**
See See also CA 165

Gunesekera, Romesh 1954- .... **CLC 91**
See See also CA 159

Gunn, Bill .... **CLC 5**
See See also Gunn, William Harrison
See See also DLB 38

Gunn, Thom(son William) 1929- . **CLC 3, 6, 18, 32, 81; DAM POET; PC 26**
See See also CA 17-20R; CANR 9, 33; CDBLB 1960 to Present; DLB 27; INT CANR-33; MTCW 1

Gunn, William Harrison 1934(?)-1989
See See Gunn, Bill
See See also AITN 1; BW 1, 3; CA 13-16R; 128; CANR 12, 25, 76

Gunnars, Kristjana 1948- .... **CLC 69**
See See also CA 113; DLB 60

Gurdjieff, G(eorgei) I(vanovich) 1877(?)-1949 .... **TCLC 71**
See See also CA 157

Gurganus, Allan 1947- . **CLC 70; DAM POP**
See See also BEST 90:1; CA 135

Gurney, A(lbert) R(amsdell), Jr. 1930- . **CLC 32, 50, 54; DAM DRAM**
See See also CA 77-80; CANR 32, 64

Gurney, Ivor (Bertie) 1890-1937 .. **TCLC 33**
See See also CA 167

Gurney, Peter
See See Gurney, A(lbert) R(amsdell), Jr.

Guro, Elena 1877-1913 .... **TCLC 56**

Gustafson, James M(oody) 1925- . **CLC 100**
See See also CA 25-28R; CANR 37

Gustafson, Ralph (Barker) 1909- ... **CLC 36**
See See also CA 21-24R; CANR 8, 45, 84; DLB 88

Gut, Gom
See See Simenon, Georges (Jacques Christian)

Guterson, David 1956- .... **CLC 91**
See See also CA 132; CANR 73; MTCW 2

Guthrie, A(lfred) B(ertram), Jr. 1901-1991 . **CLC 23**
See See also CA 57-60; 134; CANR 24; DLB 212; SATA 62; SATA-Obit 67

Guthrie, Isobel
See See Grieve, C(hristopher) M(urray)

Guthrie, Woodrow Wilson 1912-1967
See See Guthrie, Woody
See See also CA 113; 93-96

Guthrie, Woody .... **CLC 35**
See See also Guthrie, Woodrow Wilson

Gutierrez Najera, Manuel 1859-1895
See See also HLCS 2

Guy, Rosa (Cuthbert) 1928- .... **CLC 26**
See See also AAYA 4; BW 2; CA 17-20R; CANR 14, 34, 83; CLR 13; DLB 33; JRDA; MAICYA; SATA 14, 62

Gwendolyn
See See Bennett, (Enoch) Arnold

H. D. .... **CLC 3, 8, 14, 31, 34, 73; PC 5**
See See also Doolittle, Hilda

H. de V.
See See Buchan, John

Haavikko, Paavo Juhani 1931- . **CLC 18, 34**
See See also CA 106

Habbema, Koos
See See Heijermans, Herman

Habermas, Juergen 1929- .... **CLC 104**
See See also CA 109; CANR 85

Habermas, Jurgen
See See Habermas, Juergen

Hacker, Marilyn 1942- ..... **CLC 5, 9, 23, 72, 91; DAM POET**
See See also CA 77-80; CANR 68; DLB 120

Haeckel, Ernst Heinrich (Philipp August) 1834-1919 .... **TCLC 83**
See See also CA 157

Hafiz c. 1326-1389 .... **CMLC 34**

Hafiz c. 1326-1389(?) .... **CMLC 34**

Haggard, H(enry) Rider 1856-1925 .. **TCLC 11**
See See also CA 108; 148; DLB 70, 156, 174, 178; MTCW 2; SATA 16

Hagiosy, L.
See See Larbaud, Valery (Nicolas)

Hagiwara Sakutaro 1886-1942 .... **TCLC 60; PC 18**

Haig, Fenil
See See Ford, Ford Madox

Haig-Brown, Roderick (Langmere) 1908-1976 .... **CLC 21**
See See also CA 5-8R; 69-72; CANR 4, 38, 83; CLR 31; DLB 88; MAICYA; SATA 12

Hailey, Arthur 1920- .... **CLC 5; DAM NOV, POP**
See See also AITN 2; BEST 90:3; CA 1-4R; CANR 2, 36, 75; DLB 88; DLBY 82; MTCW 1, 2

Hailey, Elizabeth Forsythe 1938- .... **CLC 40**
See See also CA 93-96; CAAS 1; CANR 15, 48; INT CANR-15

Haines, John (Meade) 1924- .... **CLC 58**
See See also CA 17-20R; CANR 13, 34; DLB 212

Hakluyt, Richard 1552-1616 .... **LC 31**

Haldeman, Joe (William) 1943- ...... **CLC 61**
See See also Graham, Robert
See See also CA 53-56; 179; CAAE 179; CAAS 25; CANR 6, 70, 72; DLB 8; INT CANR-6

Hale, Sarah Josepha (Buell) 1788-1879 .... **NCLC 75**
See See also DLB 1, 42, 73

Haley, Alex(ander Murray Palmer) 1921-1992 . **CLC 8, 12, 76; BLC 2; DA; DAB; DAC; DAM MST, MULT, POP**
See See also AAYA 26; BW 2, 3; CA 77-80; 136; CANR 61; CDALBS; DA3; DLB 38; MTCW 1, 2

Haliburton, Thomas Chandler 1796-1865 ... **NCLC 15**
See See also DLB 11, 99

Hall, Donald (Andrew, Jr.) 1928- .... **CLC 1, 13, 37, 59; DAM POET**
See See also CA 5-8R; CAAS 7; CANR 2, 44, 64; DLB 5; MTCW 1; SATA 23, 97

Hall, Frederic Sauser
See See Sauser-Hall, Frederic

Hall, James
See See Kuttner, Henry

Hall, James Norman 1887-1951 ... **TCLC 23**
See See also CA 123; 173; SATA 21

Hall, Radclyffe
See See Hall, (Marguerite) Radclyffe
See See also MTCW 2

Hall, (Marguerite) Radclyffe 1886-1943 ...... **TCLC 12**
See See also CA 110; 150; CANR 83; DLB 191

Hall, Rodney 1935- .... **CLC 51**
See See also CA 109; CANR 69

Halleck, Fitz-Greene 1790-1867 ... **NCLC 47**
See See also DLB 3

Halliday, Michael
See See Creasey, John

Halpern, Daniel 1945- .... **CLC 14**
See See also CA 33-36R

Hamburger, Michael (Peter Leopold) 1924- .... **CLC 5, 14**
See See also CA 5-8R; CAAS 4; CANR 2, 47; DLB 27

Hamill, Pete 1935- .... **CLC 10**
See See also CA 25-28R; CANR 18, 71

Hamilton, Alexander 1755(?)-1804 .... **NCLC 49**
See See also DLB 37

Hawkes, John (Clendennin Burne, Jr.)
1925-1998 . **CLC 1, 2, 3, 4, 7, 9, 14, 15,
27, 49**
See See also CA 1-4R; 167; CANR 2, 47,
64; DLB 2, 7; DLBY 80, 98; MTCW 1, 2

Hawking, S. W.
See See Hawking, Stephen W(illiam)

Hawking, Stephen W(illiam) 1942- ...... **CLC
63, 105**
See See also AAYA 13; BEST 89:1; CA
126; 129; CANR 48; DA3; MTCW 2

Hawkins, Anthony Hope
See See Hope, Anthony

Hawthorne, Julian 1846-1934 .... **TCLC 25**
See See also CA 165

Hawthorne, Nathaniel 1804-1864 ...... **NCLC
39; DA; DAB; DAC; DAM MST, NOV;
SSC 3, 29; WLC**
See See also AAYA 18; CDALB 1640-1865;
DA3; DLB 1, 74; YABC 2

Haxton, Josephine Ayres 1921-
See See Douglas, Ellen
See See also CA 115; CANR 41, 83

Hayaseca y Eizaguirre, Jorge
See See Echegaray (y Eizaguirre), Jose
(Maria Waldo)

Hayashi, Fumiko 1904-1951 .... **TCLC 27**
See See also CA 161; DLB 180

Haycraft, Anna 1932-
See See Ellis, Alice Thomas
See See also CA 122; CANR 85; MTCW 2

Hayden, Robert E(arl) 1913-1980 .... **CLC 5,
9, 14, 37; BLC 2; DA; DAC; DAM
MST, MULT, POET; PC 6**
See See also BW 1, 3; CA 69-72; 97-100;
CABS 2; CANR 24, 75, 82; CDALB
1941-1968; DLB 5, 76; MTCW 1, 2;
SATA 19; SATA-Obit 26

Hayford, J(oseph) E(phraim) Casely
See See Casely-Hayford, J(oseph)
E(phraim)

Hayman, Ronald 1932- .... **CLC 44**
See See also CA 25-28R; CANR 18, 50;
DLB 155

Haywood, Eliza (Fowler) 1693(?)-1756 .. **LC
1, 44**
See See also DLB 39

Hazlitt, William 1778-1830 ..... **NCLC 29, 82**
See See also DLB 110, 158

Hazzard, Shirley 1931- .... **CLC 18**
See See also CA 9-12R; CANR 4, 70;
DLBY 82; MTCW 1

Head, Bessie 1937-1986 ... **CLC 25, 67; BLC
2; DAM MULT**
See See also BW 2, 3; CA 29-32R; 119;
CANR 25, 82; DA3; DLB 117; MTCW 1,
2

Headon, (Nicky) Topper 1956(?)- ... **CLC 30**

Heaney, Seamus (Justin) 1939- .... **CLC 5, 7,
14, 25, 37, 74, 91; DAB; DAM POET;
PC 18; WLCS**
See See also CA 85-88; CANR 25, 48, 75;
CDBLB 1960 to Present; DA3; DLB 40;
DLBY 95; MTCW 1, 2

Hearn, (Patricio) Lafcadio (Tessima Carlos)
1850-1904 .... **TCLC 9**
See See also CA 105; 166; DLB 12, 78,
189

Hearne, Vicki 1946- .... **CLC 56**
See See also CA 139

Hearon, Shelby 1931- .... **CLC 63**
See See also AITN 2; CA 25-28R; CANR
18, 48

Heat-Moon, William Least .... **CLC 29**
See See also Trogdon, William (Lewis)
See See also AAYA 9

Hebbel, Friedrich 1813-1863 .... **NCLC 43;
DAM DRAM**
See See also DLB 129

Hebert, Anne 1916- ... **CLC 4, 13, 29; DAC;
DAM MST, POET**
See See also CA 85-88; CANR 69; DA3;
DLB 68; MTCW 1, 2

Hecht, Anthony (Evan) 1923- .... **CLC 8, 13,
19; DAM POET**
See See also CA 9-12R; CANR 6; DLB 5,
169

Hecht, Ben 1894-1964 .... **CLC 8**
See See also CA 85-88; DLB 7, 9, 25, 26,
28, 86

Hedayat, Sadeq 1903-1951 .... **TCLC 21**
See See also CA 120

Hegel, Georg Wilhelm Friedrich 1770-1831
.... **NCLC 46**
See See also DLB 90

Heidegger, Martin 1889-1976 .... **CLC 24**
See See also CA 81-84; 65-68; CANR 34;
MTCW 1, 2

Heidenstam, (Carl Gustaf) Verner von
1859-1940 .... **TCLC 5**
See See also CA 104

Heifner, Jack 1946- .... **CLC 11**
See See also CA 105; CANR 47

Heijermans, Herman 1864-1924 ... **TCLC 24**
See See also CA 123

Heilbrun, Carolyn G(old) 1926- ..... **CLC 25**
See See also CA 45-48; CANR 1, 28, 58

Heine, Heinrich 1797-1856 ...... **NCLC 4, 54;
PC 25**
See See also DLB 90

Heinemann, Larry (Curtiss) 1944- . **CLC 50**
See See also CA 110; CAAS 21; CANR 31,
81; DLBD 9; INT CANR-31

Heiney, Donald (William) 1921-1993
See See Harris, MacDonald
See See also CA 1-4R; 142; CANR 3, 58

Heinlein, Robert A(nson) 1907-1988 .... **CLC
1, 3, 8, 14, 26, 55; DAM POP**
See See also AAYA 17; CA 1-4R; 125;
CANR 1, 20, 53; DA3; DLB 8; JRDA;
MAICYA; MTCW 1, 2; SATA 9, 69;
SATA-Obit 56

Helforth, John
See See Doolittle, Hilda

Hellenhofferu, Vojtech Kapristian z
See See Hasek, Jaroslav (Matej Frantisek)

Heller, Joseph 1923- . **CLC 1, 3, 5, 8, 11, 36,
63; DA; DAB; DAC; DAM MST, NOV,
POP; WLC**
See See also AAYA 24; AITN 1; CA 5-8R;
CABS 1; CANR 8, 42, 66; DA3; DLB 2,
28; DLBY 80; INT CANR-8; MTCW 1, 2

Hellman, Lillian (Florence) 1906-1984 . **CLC
2, 4, 8, 14, 18, 34, 44, 52; DAM DRAM;
DC 1**
See See also AITN 1, 2; CA 13-16R; 112;
CANR 33; DA3; DLB 7; DLBY 84;
MTCW 1, 2

Helprin, Mark 1947- ...... **CLC 7, 10, 22, 32;
DAM NOV, POP**
See See also CA 81-84; CANR 47, 64;
CDALBS; DA3; DLBY 85; MTCW 1, 2

Helvetius, Claude-Adrien 1715-1771 . **LC 26**

Helyar, Jane Penelope Josephine 1933-
See See Poole, Josephine
See See also CA 21-24R; CANR 10, 26;
SATA 82

Hemans, Felicia 1793-1835 .... **NCLC 71**
See See also DLB 96

Hemingway, Ernest (Miller) 1899-1961 ....
**CLC 1, 3, 6, 8, 10, 13, 19, 30, 34, 39, 41,
44, 50, 61, 80; DA; DAB; DAC; DAM
MST, NOV; SSC 1, 25, 36; WLC**
See See also AAYA 19; CA 77-80; CANR
34; CDALB 1917-1929; DA3; DLB 4, 9,
102, 210; DLBD 1, 15, 16; DLBY 81, 87,
96, 98; MTCW 1, 2

Hempel, Amy 1951- .... **CLC 39**

See See also CA 118; 137; CANR 70; DA3;
MTCW 2

Henderson, F. C.
See See Mencken, H(enry) L(ouis)

Henderson, Sylvia
See See Ashton-Warner, Sylvia (Constance)

Henderson, Zenna (Chlarson) 1917-1983 ....
SSC 29
See See also CA 1-4R; 133; CANR 1, 84;
DLB 8; SATA 5

Henkin, Joshua .... **CLC 119**
See See also CA 161

Henley, Beth .... **CLC 23; DC 6**
See See also Henley, Elizabeth Becker
See See also CABS 3; DLBY 86

Henley, Elizabeth Becker 1952-
See See Henley, Beth
See See also CA 107; CANR 32, 73; DAM
DRAM, MST; DA3; MTCW 1, 2

Henley, William Ernest 1849-1903 . **TCLC 8**
See See also CA 105; DLB 19

Hennissart, Martha
See See Lathen, Emma
See See also CA 85-88; CANR 64

Henry, O. .... **TCLC 1, 19; SSC 5; WLC**
See See also Porter, William Sydney

Henry, Patrick 1736-1799 .... **LC 25**

Henryson, Robert 1430(?)-1506(?) ..... **LC 20**
See See also DLB 146

Henry VIII 1491-1547 .... **LC 10**
See See also DLB 132

Henschke, Alfred
See See Klabund

Hentoff, Nat(han Irving) 1925- .... **CLC 26**
See See also AAYA 4; CA 1-4R; CAAS 6;
CANR 5, 25, 77; CLR 1, 52; INT CANR-
25; JRDA; MAICYA; SATA 42, 69;
SATA-Brief 27

Heppenstall, (John) Rayner 1911-1981 . **CLC
10**
See See also CA 1-4R; 103; CANR 29

Heraclitus c. 540B.C.-c. 450B.C. . **CMLC 22**
See See also DLB 176

Herbert, Frank (Patrick) 1920-1986 .... **CLC
12, 23, 35, 44, 85; DAM POP**
See See also AAYA 21; CA 53-56; 118;
CANR 5, 43; CDALBS; DLB 8; INT
CANR-5; MTCW 1, 2; SATA 9, 37;
SATA-Obit 47

Herbert, George 1593-1633 .... **LC 24; DAB;
DAM POET; PC 4**
See See also CDBLB Before 1660; DLB
126

Herbert, Zbigniew 1924-1998 .... **CLC 9, 43;
DAM POET**
See See also CA 89-92; 169; CANR 36, 74;
MTCW 1

Herbst, Josephine (Frey) 1897-1969 .... **CLC
34**
See See also CA 5-8R; 25-28R; DLB 9

Heredia, Jose Maria 1803-1839
See See also HLCS 2

Hergesheimer, Joseph 1880-1954 .. **TCLC 11**
See See also CA 109; DLB 102, 9

Herlihy, James Leo 1927-1993 .... **CLC 6**
See See also CA 1-4R; 143; CANR 2

Hermogenes fl. c. 175- .... **CMLC 6**

Hernandez, Jose 1834-1886 .... **NCLC 17**

Herodotus c. 484B.C.-429B.C. ..... **CMLC 17**
See See also DLB 176

Herrick, Robert 1591-1674 .... **LC 13; DA;
DAB; DAC; DAM MST, POP; PC 9**
See See also DLB 126

Herring, Guilles
See See Somerville, Edith

Herriot, James 1916-1995 .... **CLC 12; DAM
POP**
See See also Wight, James Alfred

See See also AAYA 11; CA 21-24R, 181; CAAE 181; CANR 10, 25, 47; CLR 57; JRDA; MAICYA; SATA 8, 70; SATA-Essay 103

Holland, Marcus
See See Caldwell, (Janet Miriam) Taylor (Holland)

Hollander, John 1929- .... **CLC 2, 5, 8, 14**
See See also CA 1-4R; CANR 1, 52; DLB 5; SATA 13

Hollander, Paul
See See Silverberg, Robert

Holleran, Andrew 1943(?)- .... **CLC 38**
See See also CA 144

Hollinghurst, Alan 1954- .... **CLC 55, 91**
See See also CA 114; DLB 207

Hollis, Jim
See See Summers, Hollis (Spurgeon, Jr.)

Holly, Buddy 1936-1959 .... **TCLC 65**

Holmes, Gordon
See See Shiel, M(atthew) P(hipps)

Holmes, John
See See Souster, (Holmes) Raymond

Holmes, John Clellon 1926-1988 ..... **CLC 56**
See See also CA 9-12R; 125; CANR 4; DLB 16

Holmes, Oliver Wendell, Jr. 1841-1935 .... **TCLC 77**
See See also CA 114

Holmes, Oliver Wendell 1809-1894 ... **NCLC 14, 81**
See See also CDALB 1640-1865; DLB 1, 189; SATA 34

Holmes, Raymond
See See Souster, (Holmes) Raymond

Holt, Victoria
See See Hibbert, Eleanor Alice Burford

Holub, Miroslav 1923-1998 .... **CLC 4**
See See also CA 21-24R; 169; CANR 10

Homer c. 8th cent. B.C. . **CMLC 1, 16; DA; DAB; DAC; DAM MST, POET; PC 23; WLCS**
See See also DA3; DLB 176

Hongo, Garrett Kaoru 1951- .... **PC 23**
See See also CA 133; CAAS 22; DLB 120

Honig, Edwin 1919- .... **CLC 33**
See See also CA 5-8R; CAAS 8; CANR 4, 45; DLB 5

Hood, Hugh (John Blagdon) 1928- ...... **CLC 15, 28**
See See also CA 49-52; CAAS 17; CANR 1, 33; DLB 53

Hood, Thomas 1799-1845 .... **NCLC 16**
See See also DLB 96

Hooker, (Peter) Jeremy 1941- .... **CLC 43**
See See also CA 77-80; CANR 22; DLB 40

hooks, bell .... **CLC 94; BLCS**
See See also Watkins, Gloria
See See also MTCW 2

Hope, A(lec) D(erwent) 1907- ..... **CLC 3, 51**
See See also CA 21-24R; CANR 33, 74; MTCW 1, 2

Hope, Anthony 1863-1933 .... **TCLC 83**
See See also CA 157; DLB 153, 156

Hope, Brian
See See Creasey, John

Hope, Christopher (David Tully) 1944- .... **CLC 52**
See See also CA 106; CANR 47; SATA 62

Hopkins, Gerard Manley 1844-1889 . **NCLC 17; DA; DAB; DAC; DAM MST, POET; PC 15; WLC**
See See also CDBLB 1890-1914; DA3; DLB 35, 57

Hopkins, John (Richard) 1931-1998 . **CLC 4**
See See also CA 85-88; 169

Hopkins, Pauline Elizabeth 1859-1930 .... **TCLC 28; BLC 2; DAM MULT**

See See also BW 2, 3; CA 141; CANR 82; DLB 50

Hopkinson, Francis 1737-1791 .... **LC 25**
See See also DLB 31

Hopley-Woolrich, Cornell George 1903-1968
See See Woolrich, Cornell
See See also CA 13-14; CANR 58; CAP 1; MTCW 2

Horatio
See See Proust, (Valentin-Louis-George-Eugene-) Marcel

Horgan, Paul (George Vincent O'Shaughnessy) 1903-1995 ...... **CLC 9, 53; DAM NOV**
See See also CA 13-16R; 147; CANR 9, 35; DLB 212; DLBY 85; INT CANR-9; MTCW 1, 2; SATA 13; SATA-Obit 84

Horn, Peter
See See Kuttner, Henry

Hornem, Horace Esq.
See See Byron, George Gordon (Noel)

Horney, Karen (Clementine Theodore Danielsen) 1885-1952 .... **TCLC 71**
See See also CA 114; 165

Hornung, E(rnest) W(illiam) 1866-1921 ...... **TCLC 59**
See See also CA 108; 160; DLB 70

Horovitz, Israel (Arthur) 1939- ..... **CLC 56; DAM DRAM**
See See also CA 33-36R; CANR 46, 59; DLB 7

Horvath, Odon von
See See Horvath, Oedoen von
See See also DLB 85, 124

Horvath, Oedoen von 1901-1938 .. **TCLC 45**
See See also Horvath, Odon von
See See also CA 118

Horwitz, Julius 1920-1986 .... **CLC 14**
See See also CA 9-12R; 119; CANR 12

Hospital, Janette Turner 1942- .... **CLC 42**
See See also CA 108; CANR 48

Hostos, E. M. de
See See Hostos (y Bonilla), Eugenio Maria de

Hostos, Eugenio M. de
See See Hostos (y Bonilla), Eugenio Maria de

Hostos, Eugenio Maria
See See Hostos (y Bonilla), Eugenio Maria de

Hostos (y Bonilla), Eugenio Maria de 1839-1903 .... **TCLC 24**
See See also CA 123; 131; HW 1

Houdini
See See Lovecraft, H(oward) P(hillips)

Hougan, Carolyn 1943- .... **CLC 34**
See See also CA 139

Household, Geoffrey (Edward West) 1900-1988 .... **CLC 11**
See See also CA 77-80; 126; CANR 58; DLB 87; SATA 14; SATA-Obit 59

Housman, A(lfred) E(dward) 1859-1936 ..... **TCLC 1, 10; DA; DAB; DAC; DAM MST, POET; PC 2; WLCS**
See See also CA 104; 125; DA3; DLB 19; MTCW 1, 2

Housman, Laurence 1865-1959 ...... **TCLC 7**
See See also CA 106; 155; DLB 10; SATA 25

Howard, Elizabeth Jane 1923- .... **CLC 7, 29**
See See also CA 5-8R; CANR 8, 62

Howard, Maureen 1930- .... **CLC 5, 14, 46**
See See also CA 53-56; CANR 31, 75; DLBY 83; INT CANR-31; MTCW 1, 2

Howard, Richard 1929- .... **CLC 7, 10, 47**
See See also AITN 1; CA 85-88; CANR 25, 80; DLB 5; INT CANR-25

Howard, Robert E(rvin) 1906-1936 .. **TCLC 8**

See See also CA 105; 157

Howard, Warren F.
See See Pohl, Frederik

Howe, Fanny (Quincy) 1940- .... **CLC 47**
See See also CA 117; CAAS 27; CANR 70; SATA-Brief 52

Howe, Irving 1920-1993 .... **CLC 85**
See See also CA 9-12R; 141; CANR 21, 50; DLB 67; MTCW 1, 2

Howe, Julia Ward 1819-1910 .... **TCLC 21**
See See also CA 117; DLB 1, 189

Howe, Susan 1937- .... **CLC 72**
See See also CA 160; DLB 120

Howe, Tina 1937- .... **CLC 48**
See See also CA 109

Howell, James 1594(?)-1666 .... **LC 13**
See See also DLB 151

Howells, W. D.
See See Howells, William Dean

Howells, William D.
See See Howells, William Dean

Howells, William Dean 1837-1920 . **TCLC 7, 17, 41; SSC 36**
See See also CA 104; 134; CDALB 1865-1917; DLB 12, 64, 74, 79, 189; MTCW 2

Howes, Barbara 1914-1996 .... **CLC 15**
See See also CA 9-12R; 151; CAAS 3; CANR 53; SATA 5

Hrabal, Bohumil 1914-1997 ...... **CLC 13, 67**
See See also CA 106; 156; CAAS 12; CANR 57

Hroswitha of Gandersheim c. 935-c. 1002 .. **CMLC 29**
See See also DLB 148

Hsun, Lu
See See Lu Hsun

Hubbard, L(afayette) Ron(ald) 1911-1986 .. **CLC 43; DAM POP**
See See also CA 77-80; 118; CANR 52; DA3; MTCW 2

Huch, Ricarda (Octavia) 1864-1947 .. **TCLC 13**
See See also CA 111; DLB 66

Huddle, David 1942- .... **CLC 49**
See See also CA 57-60; CAAS 20; DLB 130

Hudson, Jeffrey
See See Crichton, (John) Michael

Hudson, W(illiam) H(enry) 1841-1922 .... **TCLC 29**
See See also CA 115; DLB 98, 153, 174; SATA 35

Hueffer, Ford Madox
See See Ford, Ford Madox

Hughart, Barry 1934- .... **CLC 39**
See See also CA 137

Hughes, Colin
See See Creasey, John

Hughes, David (John) 1930- .... **CLC 48**
See See also CA 116; 129; DLB 14

Hughes, Edward James
See See Hughes, Ted
See See also DAM MST, POET; DA3

Hughes, (James) Langston 1902-1967 . **CLC 1, 5, 10, 15, 35, 44, 108; BLC 2; DA; DAB; DAC; DAM DRAM, MST, MULT, POET; DC 3; PC 1; SSC 6; WLC**
See See also AAYA 12; BW 1, 3; CA 1-4R; 25-28R; CANR 1, 34, 82; CDALB 1929-1941; CLR 17; DA3; DLB 4, 7, 48, 51, 86; JRDA; MAICYA; MTCW 1, 2; SATA 4, 33

Hughes, Richard (Arthur Warren) 1900-1976 .... **CLC 1, 11; DAM NOV**
See See also CA 5-8R; 65-68; CANR 4; DLB 15, 161; MTCW 1; SATA 8; SATA-Obit 25

Hughes, Ted 1930-1998 . **CLC 2, 4, 9, 14, 37,**

Jabran, Kahlil
See See Gibran, Kahlil

Jabran, Khalil
See See Gibran, Kahlil

Jackson, Daniel
See See Wingrove, David (John)

Jackson, Jesse 1908-1983 .... **CLC 12**
See See also BW 1; CA 25-28R; 109;
CANR 27; CLR 28; MAICYA; SATA 2,
29; SATA-Obit 48

Jackson, Laura (Riding) 1901-1991
See See Riding, Laura
See See also CA 65-68; 135; CANR 28;
DLB 48

Jackson, Sam
See See Trumbo, Dalton

Jackson, Sara
See See Wingrove, David (John)

Jackson, Shirley 1919-1965 ...... **CLC 11, 60,
87; DA; DAC; DAM MST; SSC 9;
WLC**
See See also AAYA 9; CA 1-4R; 25-28R;
CANR 4, 52; CDALB 1941-1968; DA3;
DLB 6; MTCW 2; SATA 2

Jacob, (Cyprien-)Max 1876-1944 ... **TCLC 6**
See See also CA 104

Jacobs, Harriet A(nn) 1813(?)-1897 .. **NCLC 67**
See See also CA 97-100; INT 97-100

Jacobs, Jim 1942- .... **CLC 12**
See See also CA 97-100; INT 97-100

Jacobs, W(illiam) W(ymark) 1863-1943 ......
TCLC 22
See See also CA 121; 167; DLB 135

Jacobsen, Jens Peter 1847-1885 ... **NCLC 34**

Jacobsen, Josephine 1908- .... **CLC 48, 102**
See See also CA 33-36R; CAAS 18; CANR 23, 48

Jacobson, Dan 1929- .... **CLC 4, 14**
See See also CA 1-4R; CANR 2, 25, 66;
DLB 14, 207; MTCW 1

Jacqueline
See See Carpentier (y Valmont), Alejo

Jagger, Mick 1944- .... **CLC 17**

Jahiz, al- c. 780-c. 869 .... **CMLC 25**

Jakes, John (William) 1932- . **CLC 29; DAM NOV, POP**
See See also AAYA 32; BEST 89:4; CA 57-60; CANR 10, 43, 66; DA3; DLBY 83;
INT CANR-10; MTCW 1, 2; SATA 62

James, Andrew
See See Kirkup, James

James, C(yril) L(ionel) R(obert) 1901-1989
.... **CLC 33; BLCS**
See See also BW 2; CA 117; 125; 128;
CANR 62; DLB 125; MTCW 1

James, Daniel (Lewis) 1911-1988
See See Santiago, Danny
See See also CA 174; 125

James, Dynely
See See Mayne, William (James Carter)

James, Henry Sr. 1811-1882 .... **NCLC 53**

James, Henry 1843-1916 .... **TCLC 2, 11, 24,
40, 47, 64; DA; DAB; DAC; DAM MST,
NOV; SSC 8, 32; WLC**
See See also CA 104; 132; CDALB 1865-1917; DA3; DLB 12, 71, 74, 189; DLBD 13; MTCW 1, 2

James, M. R.
See See James, Montague (Rhodes)
See See also DLB 156

James, Montague (Rhodes) 1862-1936 ....
TCLC 6; SSC 16
See See also CA 104; DLB 201

James, P. D. 1920- .... **CLC 18, 46, 122**
See See White, Phyllis Dorothy James
See See also BEST 90:2; CDBLB 1960 to
Present; DLB 87; DLBD 17

James, Philip
See See Moorcock, Michael (John)

James, William 1842-1910 ...... **TCLC 15, 32**
See See also CA 109

James I 1394-1437 .... **LC 20**

Jameson, Anna 1794-1860 .... **NCLC 43**
See See also DLB 99, 166

Jami, Nur al-Din 'Abd al-Rahman
1414-1492 .... **LC 9**

Jammes, Francis 1868-1938 .... **TCLC 75**

Jandl, Ernst 1925- .... **CLC 34**

Janowitz, Tama 1957- . **CLC 43; DAM POP**
See See also CA 106; CANR 52

Japrisot, Sebastien 1931- .... **CLC 90**

Jarrell, Randall 1914-1965 .. **CLC 1, 2, 6, 9,
13, 49; DAM POET**
See See also CA 5-8R; 25-28R; CABS 2;
CANR 6, 34; CDALB 1941-1968; CLR 6; DLB 48, 52; MAICYA; MTCW 1, 2;
SATA 7

Jarry, Alfred 1873-1907 . **TCLC 2, 14; DAM DRAM; SSC 20**
See See also CA 104; 153; DA3; DLB 192

Jaynes, Roderick
See See Coen, Ethan

Jeake, Samuel, Jr.
See See Aiken, Conrad (Potter)

Jean Paul 1763-1825 .... **NCLC 7**

Jefferies, (John) Richard 1848-1887 . **NCLC 47**
See See also DLB 98, 141; SATA 16

Jeffers, (John) Robinson 1887-1962 . **CLC 2,
3, 11, 15, 54; DA; DAC; DAM MST,
POET; PC 17; WLC**
See See also CA 85-88; CANR 35; CDALB
1917-1929; DLB 45, 212; MTCW 1, 2

Jefferson, Janet
See See Mencken, H(enry) L(ouis)

Jefferson, Thomas 1743-1826 .... **NCLC 11**
See See also CDALB 1640-1865; DA3;
DLB 31

Jeffrey, Francis 1773-1850 .... **NCLC 33**
See See also DLB 107

Jelakowitch, Ivan
See See Heijermans, Herman

Jellicoe, (Patricia) Ann 1927- .... **CLC 27**
See See also CA 85-88; DLB 13

Jen, Gish .... **CLC 70**
See See also Jen, Lillian

Jen, Lillian 1956(?)-
See See Jen, Gish
See See also CA 135

Jenkins, (John) Robin 1912- .... **CLC 52**
See See also CA 1-4R; CANR 1; DLB 14

Jennings, Elizabeth (Joan) 1926- ..... **CLC 5, 14**
See See also CA 61-64; CAAS 5; CANR 8, 39, 66; DLB 27; MTCW 1; SATA 66

Jennings, Waylon 1937- .... **CLC 21**

Jensen, Johannes V. 1873-1950 ..... **TCLC 41**
See See also CA 170

Jensen, Laura (Linnea) 1948- .... **CLC 37**
See See also CA 103

Jerome, Jerome K(lapka) 1859-1927 . **TCLC 23**
See See also CA 119; 177; DLB 10, 34, 135

Jerrold, Douglas William 1803-1857 . **NCLC 2**
See See also DLB 158, 159

Jewett, (Theodora) Sarah Orne 1849-1909 .
TCLC 1, 22; SSC 6
See See also CA 108; 127; CANR 71; DLB 12, 74; SATA 15

Jewsbury, Geraldine (Endsor) 1812-1880 ...
NCLC 22
See See also DLB 21

Jhabvala, Ruth Prawer 1927- . **CLC 4, 8, 29,**

94; DAB; DAM NOV
See See also CA 1-4R; CANR 2, 29, 51, 74; DLB 139, 194; INT CANR-29;
MTCW 1, 2

Jibran, Kahlil
See See Gibran, Kahlil

Jibran, Khalil
See See Gibran, Kahlil

Jiles, Paulette 1943- .... **CLC 13, 58**
See See also CA 101; CANR 70

Jimenez (Mantecon), Juan Ramon
1881-1958 .... **TCLC 4; DAM MULT,
POET; HLC 1; PC 7**
See See also CA 104; 131; CANR 74; DLB 134; HW 1; MTCW 1, 2

Jimenez, Ramon
See See Jimenez (Mantecon), Juan Ramon

Jimenez Mantecon, Juan
See See Jimenez (Mantecon), Juan Ramon

Jin, Ha 1956- .... **CLC 109**
See See also CA 152

Joel, Billy .... **CLC 26**
See See also Joel, William Martin

Joel, William Martin 1949-
See See Joel, Billy
See See also CA 108

John, Saint 7th cent. - .... **CMLC 27**

John of the Cross, St. 1542-1591 .... **LC 18**

Johnson, B(ryan) S(tanley William)
1933-1973 .... **CLC 6, 9**
See See also CA 9-12R; 53-56; CANR 9;
DLB 14, 40

Johnson, Benj. F. of Boo
See See Riley, James Whitcomb

Johnson, Benjamin F. of Boo
See See Riley, James Whitcomb

Johnson, Charles (Richard) 1948- ... **CLC 7,
51, 65; BLC 2; DAM MULT**
See See also BW 2, 3; CA 116; CAAS 18;
CANR 42, 66, 82; DLB 33; MTCW 2

Johnson, Denis 1949- .... **CLC 52**
See See also CA 117; 121; CANR 71; DLB 120

Johnson, Diane 1934- .... **CLC 5, 13, 48**
See See also CA 41-44R; CANR 17, 40, 62; DLBY 80; INT CANR-17; MTCW 1

Johnson, Eyvind (Olof Verner) 1900-1976 ..
CLC 14
See See also CA 73-76; 69-72; CANR 34

Johnson, J. R.
See See James, C(yril) L(ionel) R(obert)

Johnson, James Weldon 1871-1938 ... **TCLC 3, 19; BLC 2; DAM MULT, POET; PC 24**
See See also BW 1, 3; CA 104; 125; CANR 82; CDALB 1917-1929; CLR 32; DA3;
DLB 51; MTCW 1, 2; SATA 31

Johnson, Joyce 1935- .... **CLC 58**
See See also CA 125; 129

Johnson, Judith (Emlyn) 1936- .. **CLC 7, 15**
See See Sherwin, Judith Johnson
See See also CA 25-28R; 153; CANR 34

Johnson, Lionel (Pigot) 1867-1902 .... **TCLC 19**
See See also CA 117; DLB 19

Johnson, Marguerite (Annie)
See See Angelou, Maya

Johnson, Mel
See See Malzberg, Barry N(athaniel)

Johnson, Pamela Hansford 1912-1981 . **CLC 1, 7, 27**
See See also CA 1-4R; 104; CANR 2, 28;
DLB 15; MTCW 1, 2

Johnson, Robert 1911(?)-1938 ...... **TCLC 69**
See See also BW 3; CA 174

Johnson, Samuel 1709-1784 . **LC 15, 52; DA;
DAB; DAC; DAM MST; WLC**
See See also CDBLB 1660-1789; DLB 39, 95, 104, 142

See See also CA 5-8R; CANR 6, 57; MTCW 1

Kavanagh, Dan
See See Barnes, Julian (Patrick)

Kavanagh, Julie 1952- .... **CLC 119**
See See also CA 163

Kavanagh, Patrick (Joseph) 1904-1967 ....
CLC 22
See See also CA 123; 25-28R; DLB 15, 20; MTCW 1

Kawabata, Yasunari 1899-1972 ... **CLC 2, 5, 9, 18, 107; DAM MULT; SSC 17**
See See also CA 93-96; 33-36R; DLB 180; MTCW 2

Kaye, M(ary) M(argaret) 1909- ...... **CLC 28**
See See also CA 89-92; CANR 24, 60; MTCW 1, 2; SATA 62

Kaye, Mollie
See See Kaye, M(ary) M(argaret)

Kaye-Smith, Sheila 1887-1956 ...... **TCLC 20**
See See also CA 118; DLB 36

Kaymor, Patrice Maguilene
See See Senghor, Leopold Sedar

Kazan, Elia 1909- .... **CLC 6, 16, 63**
See See also CA 21-24R; CANR 32, 78

Kazantzakis, Nikos 1883(?)-1957 .. **TCLC 2, 5, 33**
See See also CA 105; 132; DA3; MTCW 1, 2

Kazin, Alfred 1915-1998 .... **CLC 34, 38, 119**
See See also CA 1-4R; CAAS 7; CANR 1, 45, 79; DLB 67

Keane, Mary Nesta (Skrine) 1904-1996
See See Keane, Molly
See See also CA 108; 114; 151

Keane, Molly .... **CLC 31**
See See also Keane, Mary Nesta (Skrine)
See See also INT 114

Keates, Jonathan 1946(?)- .... **CLC 34**
See See also CA 163

Keaton, Buster 1895-1966 .... **CLC 20**

Keats, John 1795-1821 .... **NCLC 8, 73; DA; DAB; DAC; DAM MST, POET; PC 1; WLC**
See See also CDBLB 1789-1832; DA3; DLB 96, 110

Keene, Donald 1922- .... **CLC 34**
See See also CA 1-4R; CANR 5

Keillor, Garrison .... **CLC 40, 115**
See See also Keillor, Gary (Edward)
See See also AAYA 2; BEST 89:3; DLBY 87; SATA 58

Keillor, Gary (Edward) 1942-
See See Keillor, Garrison
See See also CA 111; 117; CANR 36, 59; DAM POP; DA3; MTCW 1, 2

Keith, Michael
See See Hubbard, L(afayette) Ron(ald)

Keller, Gottfried 1819-1890 .. **NCLC 2; SSC 26**
See See also DLB 129

Keller, Nora Okja .... **CLC 109**

Kellerman, Jonathan 1949- . **CLC 44; DAM POP**
See See also BEST 90:1; CA 106; CANR 29, 51; DA3; INT CANR-29

Kelley, William Melvin 1937- .... **CLC 22**
See See also BW 1; CA 77-80; CANR 27, 83; DLB 33

Kellogg, Marjorie 1922- .... **CLC 2**
See See also CA 81-84

Kellow, Kathleen
See See Hibbert, Eleanor Alice Burford

Kelly, M(ilton) T(errence) 1947- ..... **CLC 55**
See See also CA 97-100; CAAS 22; CANR 19, 43, 84

Kelman, James 1946- .... **CLC 58, 86**
See See also CA 148; CANR 85; DLB 194

Kemal, Yashar 1923- .... **CLC 14, 29**
See See also CA 89-92; CANR 44

Kemble, Fanny 1809-1893 .... **NCLC 18**
See See also DLB 32

Kemelman, Harry 1908-1996 .... **CLC 2**
See See also AITN 1; CA 9-12R; 155; CANR 6, 71; DLB 28

Kempe, Margery 1373(?)-1440(?) .... **LC 6**
See See also DLB 146

Kempis, Thomas a 1380-1471 .... **LC 11**

Kendall, Henry 1839-1882 .... **NCLC 12**

Keneally, Thomas (Michael) 1935- .. **CLC 5, 8, 10, 14, 19, 27, 43, 117; DAM NOV**
See See also CA 85-88; CANR 10, 50, 74; DA3; MTCW 1, 2

Kennedy, Adrienne (Lita) 1931- .... **CLC 66; BLC 2; DAM MULT; DC 5**
See See also BW 2, 3; CA 103; CAAS 20; CABS 3; CANR 26, 53, 82; DLB 38

Kennedy, John Pendleton 1795-1870 . **NCLC 2**
See See also DLB 3

Kennedy, Joseph Charles 1929-
See See Kennedy, X. J.
See See also CA 1-4R; CANR 4, 30, 40; SATA 14, 86

Kennedy, William 1928- . **CLC 6, 28, 34, 53; DAM NOV**
See See also AAYA 1; CA 85-88; CANR 14, 31, 76; DA3; DLB 143; DLBY 85; INT CANR-31; MTCW 1, 2; SATA 57

Kennedy, X. J. .... **CLC 8, 42**
See See Kennedy, Joseph Charles
See See also CAAS 9; CLR 27; DLB 5; SAAS 22

Kenny, Maurice (Francis) 1929- .... **CLC 87; DAM MULT**
See See also CA 144; CAAS 22; DLB 175; NNAL

Kent, Kelvin
See See Kuttner, Henry

Kenton, Maxwell
See See Southern, Terry

Kenyon, Robert O.
See See Kuttner, Henry

Kepler, Johannes 1571-1630 .... **LC 45**

Kerouac, Jack ..... **CLC 1, 2, 3, 5, 14, 29, 61**
See See also Kerouac, Jean-Louis Lebris de
See See also AAYA 25; CDALB 1941-1968; DLB 2, 16; DLBD 3; DLBY 95; MTCW 2

Kerouac, Jean-Louis Lebris de 1922-1969
See See Kerouac, Jack
See See also AITN 1; CA 5-8R; 25-28R; CANR 26, 54; DA; DAB; DAC; DAM MST, NOV, POET, POP; DA3; MTCW 1, 2; WLC

Kerr, Jean 1923- .... **CLC 22**
See See also CA 5-8R; CANR 7; INT CANR-7

Kerr, M. E. .... **CLC 12, 35**
See See also Meaker, Marijane (Agnes)
See See also AAYA 2, 23; CLR 29; SAAS 1

Kerr, Robert .... **CLC 55**

Kerrigan, (Thomas) Anthony 1918- . **CLC 4, 6**
See See also CA 49-52; CAAS 11; CANR 4

Kerry, Lois
See See Duncan, Lois

Kesey, Ken (Elton) 1935- ... **CLC 1, 3, 6, 11, 46, 64; DA; DAB; DAC; DAM MST, NOV, POP; WLC**
See See also AAYA 25; CA 1-4R; CANR 22, 38, 66; CDALB 1968-1988; DA3; DLB 2, 16, 206; MTCW 1, 2; SATA 66

Kesselring, Joseph (Otto) 1902-1967 ... **CLC 45; DAM DRAM, MST**

See See also CA 150

Kessler, Jascha (Frederick) 1929- ..... **CLC 4**
See See also CA 17-20R; CANR 8, 48

Kettelkamp, Larry (Dale) 1933- ..... **CLC 12**
See See also CA 29-32R; CANR 16; SAAS 3; SATA 2

Key, Ellen 1849-1926 .... **TCLC 65**

Keyber, Conny
See See Fielding, Henry

Keyes, Daniel 1927- ..... **CLC 80; DA; DAC; DAM MST, NOV**
See See also AAYA 23; CA 17-20R, 181; CAAE 181; CANR 10, 26, 54, 74; DA3; MTCW 2; SATA 37

Keynes, John Maynard 1883-1946 .... **TCLC 64**
See See also CA 114; 162, 163; DLBD 10; MTCW 2

Khanshendel, Chiron
See See Rose, Wendy

Khayyam, Omar 1048-1131 .... **CMLC 11; DAM POET; PC 8**
See See also DA3

Kherdian, David 1931- .... **CLC 6, 9**
See See also CA 21-24R; CAAS 2; CANR 39, 78; CLR 24; JRDA; MAICYA; SATA 16, 74

Khlebnikov, Velimir .... **TCLC 20**
See See also Khlebnikov, Viktor Vladimirovich

Khlebnikov, Viktor Vladimirovich 1885-1922
See See Khlebnikov, Velimir
See See also CA 117

Khodasevich, Vladislav (Felitsianovich) 1886-1939 .... **TCLC 15**
See See also CA 115

Kielland, Alexander Lange 1849-1906 .... **TCLC 5**
See See also CA 104

Kiely, Benedict 1919- .... **CLC 23, 43**
See See also CA 1-4R; CANR 2, 84; DLB 15

Kienzle, William X(avier) 1928- .... **CLC 25; DAM POP**
See See also CA 93-96; CAAS 1; CANR 9, 31, 59; DA3; INT CANR-31; MTCW 1, 2

Kierkegaard, Soren 1813-1855 .... **NCLC 34, 78**

Kieslowski, Krzysztof 1941-1996 .. **CLC 120**
See See also CA 147; 151

Killens, John Oliver 1916-1987 .... **CLC 10**
See See also BW 2; CA 77-80; 123; CAAS 2; CANR 26; DLB 33

Killigrew, Anne 1660-1685 .... **LC 4**
See See also DLB 131

Kim
See See Simenon, Georges (Jacques Christian)

Kincaid, Jamaica 1949- .. **CLC 43, 68; BLC 2; DAM MULT, NOV**
See See also AAYA 13; BW 2, 3; CA 125; CANR 47, 59; CDALBS; DA3; DLB 157; MTCW 2

King, Francis (Henry) 1923- ...... **CLC 8, 53; DAM NOV**
See See also CA 1-4R; CANR 1, 33, 86; DLB 15, 139; MTCW 1

King, Kennedy
See See Brown, George Douglas

King, Martin Luther, Jr. 1929-1968 .... **CLC 83; BLC 2; DA; DAB; DAC; DAM MST, MULT; WLCS**
See See also BW 2, 3; CA 25-28; CANR 27, 44; CAP 2; DA3; MTCW 1, 2; SATA 14

King, Stephen (Edwin) 1947- ... **CLC 12, 26, 37, 61, 113; DAM NOV, POP; SSC 17**

Kristeva, Julia 1941- .... **CLC 77**
　See See also CA 154
Kristofferson, Kris 1936- .... **CLC 26**
　See See also CA 104
Krizanc, John 1956- .... **CLC 57**
Krleza, Miroslav 1893-1981 ...... **CLC 8, 114**
　See See also CA 97-100; 105; CANR 50;
　DLB 147
Kroetsch, Robert 1927- .... **CLC 5, 23, 57;**
　DAC; DAM POET
　See See also CA 17-20R; CANR 8, 38;
　DLB 53; MTCW 1
Kroetz, Franz
　See See Kroetz, Franz Xaver
Kroetz, Franz Xaver 1946- .... **CLC 41**
　See See also CA 130
Kroker, Arthur (W.) 1945- .... **CLC 77**
　See See also CA 161
Kropotkin, Peter (Aleksieevich) 1842-1921 .
　TCLC 36
　See See also CA 119
Krotkov, Yuri 1917- .... **CLC 19**
　See See also CA 102
Krumb
　See See Crumb, R(obert)
Krumgold, Joseph (Quincy) 1908-1980 ....
　CLC 12
　See See also CA 9-12R; 101; CANR 7;
　MAICYA; SATA 1, 48; SATA-Obit 23
Krumwitz
　See See Crumb, R(obert)
Krutch, Joseph Wood 1893-1970 .... **CLC 24**
　See See also CA 1-4R; 25-28R; CANR 4;
　DLB 63, 206
Krutzch, Gus
　See See Eliot, T(homas) S(tearns)
Krylov, Ivan Andreevich 1768(?)-1844 ....
　NCLC 1
　See See also DLB 150
Kubin, Alfred (Leopold Isidor) 1877-1959 ..
　TCLC 23
　See See also CA 112; 149; DLB 81
Kubrick, Stanley 1928-1999 .... **CLC 16**
　See See also AAYA 30; CA 81-84; 177;
　CANR 33; DLB 26
Kumin, Maxine (Winokur) 1925- .... **CLC 5,**
　13, 28; DAM POET; PC 15
　See See also AITN 2; CA 1-4R; CAAS 8;
　CANR 1, 21, 69; DA3; DLB 5; MTCW
　1, 2; SATA 12
Kundera, Milan 1929- . **CLC 4, 9, 19, 32, 68,**
　115; DAM NOV; SSC 24
　See See also AAYA 2; CA 85-88; CANR
　19, 52, 74; DA3; MTCW 1, 2
Kunene, Mazisi (Raymond) 1930- .. **CLC 85**
　See See also BW 1, 3; CA 125; CANR 81;
　DLB 117
Kunitz, Stanley (Jasspon) 1905- . **CLC 6, 11,**
　14; PC 19
　See See also CA 41-44R; CANR 26, 57;
　DA3; DLB 48; INT CANR-26; MTCW 1,
　2
Kunze, Reiner 1933- .... **CLC 10**
　See See also CA 93-96; DLB 75
Kuprin, Aleksander Ivanovich 1870-1938 ...
　TCLC 5
　See See also CA 104; 182
Kureishi, Hanif 1954(?)- .... **CLC 64**
　See See also CA 139; DLB 194
Kurosawa, Akira 1910-1998 ... **CLC 16, 119;**
　DAM MULT
　See See also AAYA 11; CA 101; 170;
　CANR 46
Kushner, Tony 1957(?)- .... **CLC 81; DAM**
　DRAM; DC 10
　See See also CA 144; CANR 74; DA3;
　MTCW 2
Kuttner, Henry 1915-1958 .... **TCLC 10**
　See See also Vance, Jack

See See also CA 107; 157; DLB 8
Kuzma, Greg 1944- .... **CLC 7**
　See See also CA 33-36R; CANR 70
Kuzmin, Mikhail 1872(?)-1936 ..... **TCLC 40**
　See See also CA 170
Kyd, Thomas 1558-1594 .... **LC 22; DAM**
　DRAM; DC 3
　See See also DLB 62
Kyprianos, Iossif
　See See Samarakis, Antonis
La Bruyere, Jean de 1645-1696 .... **LC 17**
Lacan, Jacques (Marie Emile) 1901-1981 ...
　CLC 75
　See See also CA 121; 104
Laclos, Pierre Ambroise Francois Choderlos
　de 1741-1803 .... **NCLC 4**
La Colere, Francois
　See See Aragon, Louis
Lacolere, Francois
　See See Aragon, Louis
La Deshabilleuse
　See See Simenon, Georges (Jacques
　Christian)
Lady Gregory
　See See Gregory, Isabella Augusta (Persse)
Lady of Quality, A
　See See Bagnold, Enid
La Fayette, Marie (Madelaine Pioche de la
　Vergne Comtes 1634-1693 .... **LC 2**
Lafayette, Rene
　See See Hubbard, L(afayette) Ron(ald)
La Fontaine, Jean de 1621-1695 .... **LC 50**
　See See also MAICYA; SATA 18
Laforgue, Jules 1860-1887 . **NCLC 5, 53; PC**
　14; SSC 20
Lagerkvist, Paer (Fabian) 1891-1974 .. **CLC**
　7, 10, 13, 54; DAM DRAM, NOV
　See See also Lagerkvist, Par
　See See also CA 85-88; 49-52; DA3;
　MTCW 1, 2
Lagerkvist, Par .... **SSC 12**
　See See also Lagerkvist, Paer (Fabian)
　See See also MTCW 2
Lagerloef, Selma (Ottiliana Lovisa)
　1858-1940 .... **TCLC 4, 36**
　See See also Lagerlof, Selma (Ottiliana
　Lovisa)
　See See also CA 108; MTCW 2; SATA 15
Lagerlof, Selma (Ottiliana Lovisa)
　See See Lagerloef, Selma (Ottiliana Lovisa)
　See See also CLR 7; SATA 15
La Guma, (Justin) Alex(ander) 1925-1985 ..
　CLC 19; BLCS; DAM NOV
　See See also BW 1, 3; CA 49-52; 118;
　CANR 25, 81; DLB 117; MTCW 1, 2
Laidlaw, A. K.
　See See Grieve, C(hristopher) M(urray)
Lainez, Manuel Mujica
　See See Mujica Lainez, Manuel
　See See also HW 1
Laing, R(onald) D(avid) 1927-1989 . **CLC 95**
　See See also CA 107; 129; CANR 34;
　MTCW 1
Lamartine, Alphonse (Marie Louis Prat) de
　1790-1869 . **NCLC 11; DAM POET; PC**
　16
Lamb, Charles 1775-1834 ... **NCLC 10; DA;**
　DAB; DAC; DAM MST; WLC
　See See also CDBLB 1789-1832; DLB 93,
　107, 163; SATA 17
Lamb, Lady Caroline 1785-1828 . **NCLC 38**
　See See also DLB 116
Lamming, George (William) 1927- .. **CLC 2,**
　4, 66; BLC 2; DAM MULT
　See See also BW 2, 3; CA 85-88; CANR
　26, 76; DLB 125; MTCW 1, 2
L'Amour, Louis (Dearborn) 1908-1988 ....
　CLC 25, 55; DAM NOV, POP

See See also AAYA 16; AITN 2; BEST
　89:2; CA 1-4R; 125; CANR 3, 25, 40;
　DA3; DLB 206; DLBY 80; MTCW 1, 2
Lampedusa, Giuseppe (Tomasi) di 1896-1957
　.. **TCLC 13**
　See See also Tomasi di Lampedusa,
　Giuseppe
　See See also CA 164; DLB 177; MTCW 2
Lampman, Archibald 1861-1899 .. **NCLC 25**
　See See also DLB 92
Lancaster, Bruce 1896-1963 .... **CLC 36**
　See See also CA 9-10; CANR 70; CAP 1;
　SATA 9
Lanchester, John .... **CLC 99**
Landau, Mark Alexandrovich
　See See Aldanov, Mark (Alexandrovich)
Landau-Aldanov, Mark Alexandrovich
　See See Aldanov, Mark (Alexandrovich)
Landis, Jerry
　See See Simon, Paul (Frederick)
Landis, John 1950- .... **CLC 26**
　See See also CA 112; 122
Landolfi, Tommaso 1908-1979 .. **CLC 11, 49**
　See See also CA 127; 117; DLB 177
Landon, Letitia Elizabeth 1802-1838 . **NCLC**
　15
　See See also DLB 96
Landor, Walter Savage 1775-1864 .... **NCLC**
　14
　See See also DLB 93, 107
Landwirth, Heinz 1927-
　See See Lind, Jakov
　See See also CA 9-12R; CANR 7
Lane, Patrick 1939- .. **CLC 25; DAM POET**
　See See also CA 97-100; CANR 54; DLB
　53; INT 97-100
Lang, Andrew 1844-1912 .... **TCLC 16**
　See See also CA 114; 137; CANR 85; DLB
　98, 141, 184; MAICYA; SATA 16
Lang, Fritz 1890-1976 .... **CLC 20, 103**
　See See also CA 77-80; 69-72; CANR 30
Lange, John
　See See Crichton, (John) Michael
Langer, Elinor 1939- .... **CLC 34**
　See See also CA 121
Langland, William 1330(?)-1400(?) .. **LC 19;**
　DA; DAB; DAC; DAM MST, POET
　See See also DLB 146
Langstaff, Launcelot
　See See Irving, Washington
Lanier, Sidney 1842-1881 .... **NCLC 6; DAM**
　POET
　See See also DLB 64; DLBD 13; MAICYA;
　SATA 18
Lanyer, Aemilia 1569-1645 .... **LC 10, 30**
　See See also DLB 121
Lao-Tzu
　See See Lao Tzu
Lao Tzu fl. 6th cent. B.C.- .... **CMLC 7**
Lapine, James (Elliot) 1949- .... **CLC 39**
　See See also CA 123; 130; CANR 54; INT
　130
Larbaud, Valery (Nicolas) 1881-1957 . **TCLC**
　9
　See See also CA 106; 152
Lardner, Ring
　See See Lardner, Ring(gold) W(ilmer)
Lardner, Ring W., Jr.
　See See Lardner, Ring(gold) W(ilmer)
Lardner, Ring(gold) W(ilmer) 1885-1933 ....
　TCLC 2, 14; SSC 32
　See See also CA 104; 131; CDALB 1917-
　1929; DLB 11, 25, 86; DLBD 16; MTCW
　1, 2
Laredo, Betty
　See See Codrescu, Andrei

Larkin, Maia
See See Wojciechowska, Maia (Teresa)
Larkin, Philip (Arthur) 1922-1985 .. CLC 3, 5, 8, 9, 13, 18, 33, 39, 64; DAB; DAM MST, POET; PC 21
See See also CA 5-8R; 117; CANR 24, 62; CDBLB 1960 to Present; DA3; DLB 27; MTCW 1, 2
Larra (y Sanchez de Castro), Mariano Jose de 1809-1837 .... NCLC 17
Larsen, Eric 1941- .... CLC 55
See See also CA 132
Larsen, Nella 1891-1964 ... CLC 37; BLC 2; DAM MULT
See See also BW 1; CA 125; CANR 83; DLB 51
Larson, Charles R(aymond) 1938- . CLC 31
See See also CA 53-56; CANR 4
Larson, Jonathan 1961-1996 .... CLC 99
See See also AAYA 28; CA 156
Las Casas, Bartolome de 1474-1566 . LC 31
Lasch, Christopher 1932-1994 ...... CLC 102
See See also CA 73-76; 144; CANR 25; MTCW 1, 2
Lasker-Schueler, Else 1869-1945 .. TCLC 57
See See also DLB 66, 124
Laski, Harold 1893-1950 .... TCLC 79
Latham, Jean Lee 1902-1995 .... CLC 12
See See also AITN 1; CA 5-8R; CANR 7, 84; CLR 50; MAICYA; SATA 2, 68
Latham, Mavis
See See Clark, Mavis Thorpe
Lathen, Emma .... CLC 2
See See also Hennissart, Martha; Latsis, Mary J(ane)
Lathrop, Francis
See See Leiber, Fritz (Reuter, Jr.)
Latsis, Mary J(ane) 1927(?)-1997
See See Lathen, Emma
See See also CA 85-88; 162
Lattimore, Richmond (Alexander) 1906-1984
.... CLC 3
See See also CA 1-4R; 112; CANR 1
Laughlin, James 1914-1997 .... CLC 49
See See also CA 21-24R; 162; CAAS 22; CANR 9, 47; DLB 48; DLBY 96, 97
Laurence, (Jean) Margaret (Wemyss) 1926-1987 . CLC 3, 6, 13, 50, 62; DAC; DAM MST; SSC 7
See See also CA 5-8R; 121; CANR 33; DLB 53; MTCW 1, 2; SATA-Obit 50
Laurent, Antoine 1952- .... CLC 50
Lauscher, Hermann
See See Hesse, Hermann
Lautreamont, Comte de 1846-1870 ... NCLC 12; SSC 14
Laverty, Donald
See See Blish, James (Benjamin)
Lavin, Mary 1912-1996 . CLC 4, 18, 99; SSC 4
See See also CA 9-12R; 151; CANR 33; DLB 15; MTCW 1
Lavond, Paul Dennis
See See Kornbluth, C(yril) M.; Pohl, Frederik
Lawler, Raymond Evenor 1922- ..... CLC 58
See See also CA 103
Lawrence, D(avid) H(erbert Richards) 1885-1930 ... TCLC 2, 9, 16, 33, 48, 61, 93; DA; DAB; DAC; DAM MST, NOV, POET; SSC 4, 19; WLC
See See also CA 104; 121; CDBLB 1914-1945; DA3; DLB 10, 19, 36, 98, 162, 195; MTCW 1, 2
Lawrence, T(homas) E(dward) 1888-1935 .. TCLC 18
See See also Dale, Colin
See See also CA 115; 167; DLB 195

Lawrence of Arabia
See See Lawrence, T(homas) E(dward)
Lawson, Henry (Archibald Hertzberg) 1867-1922 .... TCLC 27; SSC 18
See See also CA 120; 181
Lawton, Dennis
See See Faust, Frederick (Schiller)
Laxness, Halldor .... CLC 25
See See also Gudjonsson, Halldor Kiljan
Layamon fl. c. 1200- .... CMLC 10
See See also DLB 146
Laye, Camara 1928-1980 .. CLC 4, 38; BLC 2; DAM MULT
See See also BW 1; CA 85-88; 97-100; CANR 25; MTCW 1, 2
Layton, Irving (Peter) 1912- ...... CLC 2, 15; DAC; DAM MST, POET
See See also CA 1-4R; CANR 2, 33, 43, 66; DLB 88; MTCW 1, 2
Lazarus, Emma 1849-1887 .... NCLC 8
Lazarus, Felix
See See Cable, George Washington
Lazarus, Henry
See See Slavitt, David R(ytman)
Lea, Joan
See See Neufeld, John (Arthur)
Leacock, Stephen (Butler) 1869-1944 . TCLC 2; DAC; DAM MST
See See also CA 104; 141; CANR 80; DLB 92; MTCW 2
Lear, Edward 1812-1888 .... NCLC 3
See See also CLR 1; DLB 32, 163, 166; MAICYA; SATA 18, 100
Lear, Norman (Milton) 1922- .... CLC 12
See See also CA 73-76
Leautaud, Paul 1872-1956 .... TCLC 83
See See also DLB 65
Leavis, F(rank) R(aymond) 1895-1978 . CLC 24
See See also CA 21-24R; 77-80; CANR 44; MTCW 1, 2
Leavitt, David 1961- ... CLC 34; DAM POP
See See also CA 116; 122; CANR 50, 62; DA3; DLB 130; INT 122; MTCW 2
Leblanc, Maurice (Marie Emile) 1864-1941
.... TCLC 49
See See also CA 110
Lebowitz, Fran(ces Ann) 1951(?)- .. CLC 11, 36
See See also CA 81-84; CANR 14, 60, 70; INT CANR-14; MTCW 1
Lebrecht, Peter
See See Tieck, (Johann) Ludwig
le Carre, John .... CLC 3, 5, 9, 15, 28
See See also Cornwell, David (John Moore)
See See also BEST 89:4; CDBLB 1960 to Present; DLB 87; MTCW 2
Le Clezio, J(ean) M(arie) G(ustave) 1940- .. CLC 31
See See also CA 116; 128; DLB 83
Leconte de Lisle, Charles-Marie-Rene 1818-1894 .... NCLC 29
Le Coq, Monsieur
See See Simenon, Georges (Jacques Christian)
Leduc, Violette 1907-1972 .... CLC 22
See See also CA 13-14; 33-36R; CANR 69; CAP 1
Ledwidge, Francis 1887(?)-1917 ... TCLC 23
See See also CA 123; DLB 20
Lee, Andrea 1953- .. CLC 36; BLC 2; DAM MULT
See See also BW 1, 3; CA 125; CANR 82
Lee, Andrew
See See Auchincloss, Louis (Stanton)
Lee, Chang-rae 1965- .... CLC 91
See See also CA 148
Lee, Don L. .... CLC 2

See See also Madhubuti, Haki R.
Lee, George W(ashington) 1894-1976 . CLC 52; BLC 2; DAM MULT
See See also BW 1; CA 125; CANR 83; DLB 51
Lee, (Nelle) Harper 1926- . CLC 12, 60; DA; DAB; DAC; DAM MST, NOV; WLC
See See also AAYA 13; CA 13-16R; CANR 51; CDALB 1941-1968; DA3; DLB 6; MTCW 1, 2; SATA 11
Lee, Helen Elaine 1959(?)- .... CLC 86
See See also CA 148
Lee, Julian
See See Latham, Jean Lee
Lee, Larry
See See Lee, Lawrence
Lee, Laurie 1914-1997 .... CLC 90; DAB; DAM POP
See See also CA 77-80; 158; CANR 33, 73; DLB 27; MTCW 1
Lee, Lawrence 1941-1990 .... CLC 34
See See also CA 131; CANR 43
Lee, Li-Young 1957- .... PC 24
See See also CA 153; DLB 165
Lee, Manfred B(ennington) 1905-1971 . CLC 11
See See also Queen, Ellery
See See also CA 1-4R; 29-32R; CANR 2; DLB 137
Lee, Shelton Jackson 1957(?)- ..... CLC 105; BLCS; DAM MULT
See See also Lee, Spike
See See also BW 2, 3; CA 125; CANR 42
Lee, Spike
See See Lee, Shelton Jackson
See See also AAYA 4, 29
Lee, Stan 1922- .... CLC 17
See See also AAYA 5; CA 108; 111; INT 111
Lee, Tanith 1947- .... CLC 46
See See also AAYA 15; CA 37-40R; CANR 53; SATA 8, 88
Lee, Vernon .... TCLC 5; SSC 33
See See also Paget, Violet
See See also DLB 57, 153, 156, 174, 178
Lee, William
See See Burroughs, William S(eward)
Lee, Willy
See See Burroughs, William S(eward)
Lee-Hamilton, Eugene (Jacob) 1845-1907 ... TCLC 22
See See also CA 117
Leet, Judith 1935- .... CLC 11
Le Fanu, Joseph Sheridan 1814-1873 .... NCLC 9, 58; DAM POP; SSC 14
See See also DA3; DLB 21, 70, 159, 178
Leffland, Ella 1931- .... CLC 19
See See also CA 29-32R; CANR 35, 78, 82; DLBY 84; INT CANR-35; SATA 65
Leger, Alexis
See See Leger, (Marie-Rene Auguste) Alexis Saint-Leger
Leger, (Marie-Rene Auguste) Alexis Saint-Leger 1887-1975 . CLC 4, 11, 46; DAM POET; PC 23
See See also CA 13-16R; 61-64; CANR 43; MTCW 1
Leger, Saintleger
See See Leger, (Marie-Rene Auguste) Alexis Saint-Leger
Le Guin, Ursula K(roeber) 1929- .... CLC 8, 13, 22, 45, 71; DAB; DAC; DAM MST, POP; SSC 12
See See also AAYA 9, 27; AITN 1; CA 21-24R; CANR 9, 32, 52, 74; CDALB 1968-1988; CLR 3, 28; DA3; DLB 8, 52; INT CANR-32; JRDA; MAICYA; MTCW 1, 2; SATA 4, 52, 99

Lucas, George 1944- .... **CLC 16**
See See also AAYA 1, 23; CA 77-80; CANR 30; SATA 56

Lucas, Hans
See See Godard, Jean-Luc

Lucas, Victoria
See See Plath, Sylvia

Lucian c. 120-c. 180 .... **CMLC 32**
See See also DLB 176

Ludlam, Charles 1943-1987 ...... **CLC 46, 50**
See See also CA 85-88; 122; CANR 72, 86

Ludlum, Robert 1927- ... **CLC 22, 43; DAM NOV, POP**
See See also AAYA 10; BEST 89:1, 90:3; CA 33-36R; CANR 25, 41, 68; DA3; DLBY 82; MTCW 1, 2

Ludwig, Ken .... **CLC 60**

Ludwig, Otto 1813-1865 .... **NCLC 4**
See See also DLB 129

Lugones, Leopoldo 1874-1938 ..... **TCLC 15; HLCS 2**
See See also CA 116; 131; HW 1

Lu Hsun 1881-1936 .... **TCLC 3; SSC 20**
See See also Shu-Jen, Chou

Lukacs, George .... **CLC 24**
See See also Lukacs, Gyorgy (Szegeny von)

Lukacs, Gyorgy (Szegeny von) 1885-1971
See See Lukacs, George
See See also CA 101; 29-32R; CANR 62; MTCW 2

Luke, Peter (Ambrose Cyprian) 1919-1995
.... **CLC 38**
See See also CA 81-84; 147; CANR 72; DLB 13

Lunar, Dennis
See See Mungo, Raymond

Lurie, Alison 1926- .... **CLC 4, 5, 18, 39**
See See also CA 1-4R; CANR 2, 17, 50; DLB 2; MTCW 1; SATA 46

Lustig, Arnost 1926- .... **CLC 56**
See See also AAYA 3; CA 69-72; CANR 47; SATA 56

Luther, Martin 1483-1546 .... **LC 9, 37**
See See also DLB 179

Luxemburg, Rosa 1870(?)-1919 .... **TCLC 63**
See See also CA 118

Luzi, Mario 1914- .... **CLC 13**
See See also CA 61-64; CANR 9, 70; DLB 128

Lyly, John 1554(?)-1606 .... **LC 41; DAM DRAM; DC 7**
See See also DLB 62, 167

L'Ymagier
See See Gourmont, Remy (-Marie-Charles) de

Lynch, B. Suarez
See See Bioy Casares, Adolfo

Lynch, B. Suarez
See See Bioy Casares, Adolfo; Borges, Jorge Luis

Lynch, David (K.) 1946- .... **CLC 66**
See See also CA 124; 129

Lynch, James
See See Andreyev, Leonid (Nikolaevich)

Lynch Davis, B.
See See Bioy Casares, Adolfo; Borges, Jorge Luis

Lyndsay, Sir David 1490-1555 .... **LC 20**

Lynn, Kenneth S(chuyler) 1923- ..... **CLC 50**
See See also CA 1-4R; CANR 3, 27, 65

Lynx
See See West, Rebecca

Lyons, Marcus
See See Blish, James (Benjamin)

Lyre, Pinchbeck
See See Sassoon, Siegfried (Lorraine)

Lytle, Andrew (Nelson) 1902-1995 .. **CLC 22**

See See also CA 9-12R; 150; CANR 70; DLB 6; DLBY 95

Lyttelton, George 1709-1773 .... **LC 10**

Maas, Peter 1929- .... **CLC 29**
See See also CA 93-96; INT 93-96; MTCW 2

Macaulay, Rose 1881-1958 .... **TCLC 7, 44**
See See also CA 104; DLB 36

Macaulay, Thomas Babington 1800-1859 ....
NCLC 42
See See also CDBLB 1832-1890; DLB 32, 55

MacBeth, George (Mann) 1932-1992 ... **CLC 2, 5, 9**
See See also CA 25-28R; 136; CANR 61, 66; DLB 40; MTCW 1; SATA 4; SATA-Obit 70

MacCaig, Norman (Alexander) 1910- . **CLC 36; DAB; DAM POET**
See See also CA 9-12R; CANR 3, 34; DLB 27

MacCarthy, Sir(Charles Otto) Desmond 1877-1952 .... **TCLC 36**
See See also CA 167

MacDiarmid, Hugh .... **CLC 2, 4, 11, 19, 63; PC 9**
See See also Grieve, C(hristopher) M(urray)
See See also CDBLB 1945-1960; DLB 20

MacDonald, Anson
See See Heinlein, Robert A(nson)

Macdonald, Cynthia 1928- .... **CLC 13, 19**
See See also CA 49-52; CANR 4, 44; DLB 105

MacDonald, George 1824-1905 ...... **TCLC 9**
See See also CA 106; 137; CANR 80; DLB 18, 163, 178; MAICYA; SATA 33, 100

Macdonald, John
See See Millar, Kenneth

MacDonald, John D(ann) 1916-1986 ... **CLC 3, 27, 44; DAM NOV, POP**
See See also CA 1-4R; 121; CANR 1, 19, 60; DLB 8; DLBY 86; MTCW 1, 2

Macdonald, John Ross
See See Millar, Kenneth

Macdonald, Ross ..... **CLC 1, 2, 3, 14, 34, 41**
See See also Millar, Kenneth
See See also DLBD 6

MacDougal, John
See See Blish, James (Benjamin)

MacEwen, Gwendolyn (Margaret) 1941-1987 .... **CLC 13, 55**
See See also CA 9-12R; 124; CANR 7, 22; DLB 53; SATA 50; SATA-Obit 55

Macha, Karel Hynek 1810-1846 .. **NCLC 46**

Machado (y Ruiz), Antonio 1875-1939 ....
TCLC 3
See See also CA 104; 174; DLB 108; HW 2

Machado de Assis, Joaquim Maria 1839-1908 .... **TCLC 10; BLC 2; HLCS 2; SSC 24**
See See also CA 107; 153

Machen, Arthur .... **TCLC 4; SSC 20**
See See also Jones, Arthur Llewellyn
See See also CA 179; DLB 36, 156, 178

Machiavelli, Niccolo 1469-1527 ... **LC 8, 36; DA; DAB; DAC; DAM MST; WLCS**

MacInnes, Colin 1914-1976 .... **CLC 4, 23**
See See also CA 69-72; 65-68; CANR 21; DLB 14; MTCW 1, 2

MacInnes, Helen (Clark) 1907-1985 .... **CLC 27, 39; DAM POP**
See See also CA 1-4R; 117; CANR 1, 28, 58; DLB 87; MTCW 1, 2; SATA 22; SATA-Obit 44

Mackenzie, Compton (Edward Montague) 1883-1972 .... **CLC 18**
See See also CA 21-22; 37-40R; CAP 2; DLB 34, 100

Mackenzie, Henry 1745-1831 .... **NCLC 41**
See See also DLB 39

Mackintosh, Elizabeth 1896(?)-1952
See See Tey, Josephine
See See also CA 110

MacLaren, James
See See Grieve, C(hristopher) M(urray)

Mac Laverty, Bernard 1942- .... **CLC 31**
See See also CA 116; 118; CANR 43; INT 118

MacLean, Alistair (Stuart) 1922(?)-1987 .....
CLC 3, 13, 50, 63; DAM POP
See See also CA 57-60; 121; CANR 28, 61; MTCW 1; SATA 23; SATA-Obit 50

Maclean, Norman (Fitzroy) 1902-1990 . **CLC 78; DAM POP; SSC 13**
See See also CA 102; 132; CANR 49; DLB 206

MacLeish, Archibald 1892-1982 .. **CLC 3, 8, 14, 68; DAM POET**
See See also CA 9-12R; 106; CANR 33, 63; CDALBS; DLB 4, 7, 45; DLBY 82; MTCW 1, 2

MacLennan, (John) Hugh 1907-1990 .. **CLC 2, 14, 92; DAC; DAM MST**
See See also CA 5-8R; 142; CANR 33; DLB 68; MTCW 1, 2

MacLeod, Alistair 1936- ...... **CLC 56; DAC; DAM MST**
See See also CA 123; DLB 60; MTCW 2

Macleod, Fiona
See See Sharp, William

MacNeice, (Frederick) Louis 1907-1963 ......
CLC 1, 4, 10, 53; DAB; DAM POET
See See also CA 85-88; CANR 61; DLB 10, 20; MTCW 1, 2

MacNeill, Dand
See See Fraser, George MacDonald

Macpherson, James 1736-1796 .... **LC 29**
See See also Ossian
See See also DLB 109

Macpherson, (Jean) Jay 1931- .... **CLC 14**
See See also CA 5-8R; DLB 53

MacShane, Frank 1927- .... **CLC 39**
See See also CA 9-12R; CANR 3, 33; DLB 111

Macumber, Mari
See See Sandoz, Mari(e Susette)

Madach, Imre 1823-1864 .... **NCLC 19**

Madden, (Jerry) David 1933- ..... **CLC 5, 15**
See See also CA 1-4R; CAAS 3; CANR 4, 45; DLB 6; MTCW 1

Maddern, Al(an)
See See Ellison, Harlan (Jay)

Madhubuti, Haki R. 1942- ... **CLC 6, 73; BLC 2; DAM MULT, POET; PC 5**
See See also Lee, Don L.
See See also BW 2, 3; CA 73-76; CANR 24, 51, 73; DLB 5, 41; DLBD 8; MTCW 2

Maepenn, Hugh
See See Kuttner, Henry

Maepenn, K. H.
See See Kuttner, Henry

Maeterlinck, Maurice 1862-1949 .. **TCLC 3; DAM DRAM**
See See also CA 104; 136; CANR 80; DLB 192; SATA 66

Maginn, William 1794-1842 .... **NCLC 8**
See See also DLB 110, 159

Mahapatra, Jayanta 1928- .. **CLC 33; DAM MULT**
See See also CA 73-76; CAAS 9; CANR 15, 33, 66

Mahfouz, Naguib (Abdel Aziz Al-Sabilgi) 1911(?)-
See See Mahfuz, Najib
See See also BEST 89:2; CA 128; CANR 55; DAM NOV; DA3; MTCW 1, 2

Mahfuz, Najib .... **CLC 52, 55**
See See also Mahfouz, Naguib (Abdel Aziz Al-Sabilgi)
See See also DLBY 88

Mahon, Derek 1941- .... **CLC 27**
See See also CA 113; 128; DLB 40

Mailer, Norman 1923- . **CLC 1, 2, 3, 4, 5, 8, 11, 14, 28, 39, 74, 111; DA; DAB; DAC; DAM MST, NOV, POP**
See See also AAYA 31; AITN 2; CA 9-12R; CABS 1; CANR 28, 74, 77; CDALB 1968-1988; DA3; DLB 2, 16, 28, 185; DLBD 3; DLBY 80, 83; MTCW 1, 2

Maillet, Antonine 1929- . **CLC 54, 118; DAC**
See See also CA 115; 120; CANR 46, 74, 77; DLB 60; INT 120; MTCW 2

Mais, Roger 1905-1955 .... **TCLC 8**
See See also BW 1, 3; CA 105; 124; CANR 82; DLB 125; MTCW 1

Maistre, Joseph de 1753-1821 ...... **NCLC 37**

Maitland, Frederic 1850-1906 ...... **TCLC 65**

Maitland, Sara (Louise) 1950- .... **CLC 49**
See See also CA 69-72; CANR 13, 59

Major, Clarence 1936- . **CLC 3, 19, 48; BLC 2; DAM MULT**
See See also BW 2, 3; CA 21-24R; CAAS 6; CANR 13, 25, 53, 82; DLB 33

Major, Kevin (Gerald) 1949- . **CLC 26; DAC**
See See also AAYA 16; CA 97-100; CANR 21, 38; CLR 11; DLB 60; INT CANR-21; JRDA; MAICYA; SATA 32, 82

Maki, James
See See Ozu, Yasujiro

Malabaila, Damiano
See See Levi, Primo

Malamud, Bernard 1914-1986 . **CLC 1, 2, 3, 5, 8, 9, 11, 18, 27, 44, 78, 85; DA; DAB; DAC; DAM MST, NOV, POP; SSC 15; WLC**
See See also AAYA 16; CA 5-8R; 118; CABS 1; CANR 28, 62; CDALB 1941-1968; DA3; DLB 2, 28, 152; DLBY 80, 86; MTCW 1, 2

Malan, Herman
See See Bosman, Herman Charles; Bosman, Herman Charles

Malaparte, Curzio 1898-1957 .... **TCLC 52**

Malcolm, Dan
See See Silverberg, Robert

Malcolm X .... **CLC 82, 117; BLC 2; WLCS**
See See also Little, Malcolm

Malherbe, Francois de 1555-1628 .... **LC 5**

Mallarme, Stephane 1842-1898 ..... **NCLC 4, 41; DAM POET; PC 4**

Mallet-Joris, Francoise 1930- .... **CLC 11**
See See also CA 65-68; CANR 17; DLB 83

Malley, Ern
See See McAuley, James Phillip

Mallowan, Agatha Christie
See See Christie, Agatha (Mary Clarissa)

Maloff, Saul 1922- .... **CLC 5**
See See also CA 33-36R

Malone, Louis
See See MacNeice, (Frederick) Louis

Malone, Michael (Christopher) 1942- . **CLC 43**
See See also CA 77-80; CANR 14, 32, 57

Malory, (Sir) Thomas 1410(?)-1471(?) ... **LC 11; DA; DAB; DAC; DAM MST; WLCS**
See See also CDBLB Before 1660; DLB 146; SATA 59; SATA-Brief 33

Malouf, (George Joseph) David 1934- . **CLC 28, 86**
See See also CA 124; CANR 50, 76; MTCW 2

Malraux, (Georges-)Andre 1901-1976 . **CLC 1, 4, 9, 13, 15, 57; DAM NOV**
See See also CA 21-22; 69-72; CANR 34, 58; CAP 2; DA3; DLB 72; MTCW 1, 2

Malzberg, Barry N(athaniel) 1939- .. **CLC 7**
See See also CA 61-64; CAAS 4; CANR 16; DLB 8

Mamet, David (Alan) 1947- . **CLC 9, 15, 34, 46, 91; DAM DRAM; DC 4**
See See also AAYA 3; CA 81-84; CABS 3; CANR 15, 41, 67, 72; DA3; DLB 7; MTCW 1, 2

Mamoulian, Rouben (Zachary) 1897-1987 .. **CLC 16**
See See also CA 25-28R; 124; CANR 85

Mandelstam, Osip (Emilievich) 1891(?)-1938(?) .... **TCLC 2, 6; PC 14**
See See also CA 104; 150; MTCW 2

Mander, (Mary) Jane 1877-1949 .. **TCLC 31**
See See also CA 162

Mandeville, John fl. 1350- .... **CMLC 19**
See See also DLB 146

Mandiargues, Andre Pieyre de .... **CLC 41**
See See also Pieyre de Mandiargues, Andre
See See also DLB 83

Mandrake, Ethel Belle
See See Thurman, Wallace (Henry)

Mangan, James Clarence 1803-1849 . **NCLC 27**

Maniere, J.-E.
See See Giraudoux, (Hippolyte) Jean

Mankiewicz, Herman (Jacob) 1897-1953 .... **TCLC 85**
See See also CA 120; 169; DLB 26

Manley, (Mary) Delariviere 1672(?)-1724 ... **LC 1, 42**
See See also DLB 39, 80

Mann, Abel
See See Creasey, John

Mann, Emily 1952- .... **DC 7**
See See also CA 130; CANR 55

Mann, (Luiz) Heinrich 1871-1950 .. **TCLC 9**
See See also CA 106; 164; 181; DLB 66; 118

Mann, (Paul) Thomas 1875-1955 .. **TCLC 2, 8, 14, 21, 35, 44, 60; DA; DAB; DAC; DAM MST, NOV; SSC 5; WLC**
See See also CA 104; 128; DA3; DLB 66; MTCW 1, 2

Mannheim, Karl 1893-1947 .... **TCLC 65**

Manning, David
See See Faust, Frederick (Schiller)

Manning, Frederic 1887(?)-1935 .. **TCLC 25**
See See also CA 124

Manning, Olivia 1915-1980 .... **CLC 5, 19**
See See also CA 5-8R; 101; CANR 29; MTCW 1

Mano, D. Keith 1942- .... **CLC 2, 10**
See See also CA 25-28R; CAAS 6; CANR 26, 57; DLB 6

Mansfield, Katherine . **TCLC 2, 8, 39; DAB; SSC 9, 23; WLC**
See See also Beauchamp, Kathleen Mansfield
See See also DLB 162

Manso, Peter 1940- .... **CLC 39**
See See also CA 29-32R; CANR 44

Mantecon, Juan Jimenez
See See Jimenez (Mantecon), Juan Ramon

Manton, Peter
See See Creasey, John

Man Without a Spleen, A
See See Chekhov, Anton (Pavlovich)

Manzoni, Alessandro 1785-1873 ... **NCLC 29**

Map, Walter 1140-1209 .... **CMLC 32**

Mapu, Abraham (ben Jekutiel) 1808-1867 .. **NCLC 18**

Mara, Sally
See See Queneau, Raymond

Marat, Jean Paul 1743-1793 .... **LC 10**

Marcel, Gabriel Honore 1889-1973 . **CLC 15**
See See also CA 102; 45-48; MTCW 1, 2

March, William 1893-1954 .... **TCLC 96**

Marchbanks, Samuel
See See Davies, (William) Robertson

Marchi, Giacomo
See See Bassani, Giorgio

Margulies, Donald .... **CLC 76**

Marie de France c. 12th cent. - .... **CMLC 8; PC 22**
See See also DLB 208

Marie de l'Incarnation 1599-1672 ..... **LC 10**

Marier, Captain Victor
See See Griffith, D(avid Lewelyn) W(ark)

Mariner, Scott
See See Pohl, Frederik

Marinetti, Filippo Tommaso 1876-1944 .... **TCLC 10**
See See also CA 107; DLB 114

Marivaux, Pierre Carlet de Chamblain de 1688-1763 .... **LC 4; DC 7**

Markandaya, Kamala .... **CLC 8, 38**
See See also Taylor, Kamala (Purnaiya)

Markfield, Wallace 1926- .... **CLC 8**
See See also CA 69-72; CAAS 3; DLB 2, 28

Markham, Edwin 1852-1940 .... **TCLC 47**
See See also CA 160; DLB 54, 186

Markham, Robert
See See Amis, Kingsley (William)

Marks, J
See See Highwater, Jamake (Mamake)

Marks-Highwater, J
See See Highwater, Jamake (Mamake)

Markson, David M(errill) 1927- ..... **CLC 67**
See See also CA 49-52; CANR 1

Marley, Bob .... **CLC 17**
See See also Marley, Robert Nesta

Marley, Robert Nesta 1945-1981
See See Marley, Bob
See See also CA 107; 103

Marlowe, Christopher 1564-1593 ..... **LC 22, 47; DA; DAB; DAC; DAM DRAM, MST; DC 1; WLC**
See See also CDBLB Before 1660; DA3; DLB 62

Marlowe, Stephen 1928-
See See Queen, Ellery
See See also CA 13-16R; CANR 6, 55

Marmontel, Jean-Francois 1723-1799 . **LC 2**

Marquand, John P(hillips) 1893-1960 . **CLC 2, 10**
See See also CA 85-88; CANR 73; DLB 9, 102; MTCW 2

Marques, Rene 1919-1979 ... **CLC 96; DAM MULT; HLC 2**
See See also CA 97-100; 85-88; CANR 78; DLB 113; HW 1, 2

Marquez, Gabriel (Jose) Garcia
See See Garcia Marquez, Gabriel (Jose)

Marquis, Don(ald Robert Perry) 1878-1937 .... **TCLC 7**
See See also CA 104; 166; DLB 11, 25

Marric, J. J.
See See Creasey, John

Marryat, Frederick 1792-1848 .... **NCLC 3**
See See also DLB 21, 163

Marsden, James
See See Creasey, John

Marsh, Edward 1872-1953 .... **TCLC 99**

Marsh, (Edith) Ngaio 1899-1982 ...... **CLC 7, 53; DAM POP**
See See also CA 9-12R; CANR 6, 58; DLB 77; MTCW 1, 2

Marshall, Garry 1934- .... **CLC 17**
See See also AAYA 3; CA 111; SATA 60

Marshall, Paule 1929- . **CLC 27, 72; BLC 3; DAM MULT; SSC 3**
See See also BW 2, 3; CA 77-80; CANR 25, 73; DA3; DLB 157; MTCW 1, 2

Marshallik
See See Zangwill, Israel
Marsten, Richard
See See Hunter, Evan
Marston, John 1576-1634 .... **LC 33; DAM DRAM**
See See also DLB 58, 172
Martha, Henry
See See Harris, Mark
Marti (y Perez), Jose (Julian) 1853-1895 ....
NCLC 63; DAM MULT; HLC 2
See See also HW 2
Martial c. 40-c. 104 .... **CMLC 35; PC 10**
See See also DLB 211
Martin, Ken
See See Hubbard, L(afayette) Ron(ald)
Martin, Richard
See See Creasey, John
Martin, Steve 1945- .... **CLC 30**
See See also CA 97-100; CANR 30; MTCW 1
Martin, Valerie 1948- .... **CLC 89**
See See also BEST 90:2; CA 85-88; CANR 49
Martin, Violet Florence 1862-1915 .... **TCLC 51**
Martin, Webber
See See Silverberg, Robert
Martindale, Patrick Victor
See See White, Patrick (Victor Martindale)
Martin du Gard, Roger 1881-1958 ... **TCLC 24**
See See also CA 118; DLB 65
Martineau, Harriet 1802-1876 ..... **NCLC 26**
See See also DLB 21, 55, 159, 163, 166, 190; YABC 2
Martines, Julia
See See O'Faolain, Julia
Martinez, Enrique Gonzalez
See See Gonzalez Martinez, Enrique
Martinez, Jacinto Benavente y
See See Benavente (y Martinez), Jacinto
Martinez Ruiz, Jose 1873-1967
See See Azorin; Ruiz, Jose Martinez
See See also CA 93-96; HW 1
Martinez Sierra, Gregorio 1881-1947 .... **TCLC 6**
See See also CA 115
Martinez Sierra, Maria (de la O'LeJarraga) 1874-1974 .... **TCLC 6**
See See also CA 115
Martinsen, Martin
See See Follett, Ken(neth Martin)
Martinson, Harry (Edmund) 1904-1978 ...... **CLC 14**
See See also CA 77-80; CANR 34
Marut, Ret
See See Traven, B.
Marut, Robert
See See Traven, B.
Marvell, Andrew 1621-1678 . **LC 4, 43; DA; DAB; DAC; DAM MST, POET; PC 10; WLC**
See See also CDBLB 1660-1789; DLB 131
Marx, Karl (Heinrich) 1818-1883 . **NCLC 17**
See See also DLB 129
Masaoka Shiki .... **TCLC 18**
See See also Masaoka Tsunenori
Masaoka Tsunenori 1867-1902
See See Masaoka Shiki
See See also CA 117
Masefield, John (Edward) 1878-1967 .. **CLC 11, 47; DAM POET**
See See also CA 19-20; 25-28R; CANR 33; CAP 2; CDBLB 1890-1914; DLB 10, 19, 153, 160; MTCW 1, 2; SATA 19
Maso, Carole 19(?)- .... **CLC 44**
See See also CA 170

Mason, Bobbie Ann 1940- . **CLC 28, 43, 82; SSC 4**
See See also AAYA 5; CA 53-56; CANR 11, 31, 58, 83; CDALBS; DA3; DLB 173; DLBY 87; INT CANR-31; MTCW 1, 2
Mason, Ernst
See See Pohl, Frederik
Mason, Lee W.
See See Malzberg, Barry N(athaniel)
Mason, Nick 1945- .... **CLC 35**
Mason, Tally
See See Derleth, August (William)
Mass, William
See See Gibson, William
Master Lao
See See Lao Tzu
Masters, Edgar Lee 1868-1950 ...... **TCLC 2, 25; DA; DAC; DAM MST, POET; PC 1; WLCS**
See See also CA 104; 133; CDALB 1865-1917; DLB 54; MTCW 1, 2
Masters, Hilary 1928- .... **CLC 48**
See See also CA 25-28R; CANR 13, 47
Mastrosimone, William 19(?)- .... **CLC 36**
Mathe, Albert
See See Camus, Albert
Mather, Cotton 1663-1728 .... **LC 38**
See See also CDALB 1640-1865; DLB 24, 30, 140
Mather, Increase 1639-1723 .... **LC 38**
See See also DLB 24
Matheson, Richard Burton 1926- ... **CLC 37**
See See also AAYA 31; CA 97-100; DLB 8, 44; INT 97-100
Mathews, Harry 1930- .... **CLC 6, 52**
See See also CA 21-24R; CAAS 6; CANR 18, 40
Mathews, John Joseph 1894-1979 . **CLC 84; DAM MULT**
See See also CA 19-20; 142; CANR 45; CAP 2; DLB 175; NNAL
Mathias, Roland (Glyn) 1915- .... **CLC 45**
See See also CA 97-100; CANR 19, 41; DLB 27
Matsuo Basho 1644-1694 .... **PC 3**
See See also DAM POET
Mattheson, Rodney
See See Creasey, John
Matthews, (James) Brander 1852-1929 .... **TCLC 95**
See See also DLB 71, 78; DLBD 13
Matthews, Greg 1949- .... **CLC 45**
See See also CA 135
Matthews, William (Procter, III) 1942-1997 .... **CLC 40**
See See also CA 29-32R; 162; CAAS 18; CANR 12, 57; DLB 5
Matthias, John (Edward) 1941- .... **CLC 9**
See See also CA 33-36R; CANR 56
Matthiessen, Peter 1927- .. **CLC 5, 7, 11, 32, 64; DAM NOV**
See See also AAYA 6; BEST 90:4; CA 9-12R; CANR 21, 50, 73; DA3; DLB 6, 173; MTCW 1, 2; SATA 27
Maturin, Charles Robert 1780(?)-1824 .... **NCLC 6**
See See also DLB 178
Matute (Ausejo), Ana Maria 1925- . **CLC 11**
See See also CA 89-92; MTCW 1
Maugham, W. S.
See See Maugham, W(illiam) Somerset
Maugham, W(illiam) Somerset 1874-1965 .. **CLC 1, 11, 15, 67, 93; DA; DAB; DAC; DAM DRAM, MST, NOV; SSC 8; WLC**
See See also CA 5-8R; 25-28R; CANR 40; CDBLB 1914-1945; DA3; DLB 10, 36, 77, 100, 162, 195; MTCW 1, 2; SATA 54
Maugham, William Somerset
See See Maugham, W(illiam) Somerset

Maupassant, (Henri Rene Albert) Guy de 1850-1893 . **NCLC 1, 42, 83; DA; DAB; DAC; DAM MST; SSC 1; WLC**
See See also DA3; DLB 123
Maupin, Armistead 1944- .... **CLC 95; DAM POP**
See See also CA 125; 130; CANR 58; DA3; INT 130; MTCW 2
Maurhut, Richard
See See Traven, B.
Mauriac, Claude 1914-1996 .... **CLC 9**
See See also CA 89-92; 152; DLB 83
Mauriac, Francois (Charles) 1885-1970 ...... **CLC 4, 9, 56; SSC 24**
See See also CA 25-28; CAP 2; DLB 65; MTCW 1, 2
Mavor, Osborne Henry 1888-1951
See See Bridie, James
See See also CA 104
Maxwell, William (Keepers, Jr.) 1908- . **CLC 19**
See See also CA 93-96; CANR 54; DLBY 80; INT 93-96
May, Elaine 1932- .... **CLC 16**
See See also CA 124; 142; DLB 44
Mayakovski, Vladimir (Vladimirovich) 1893-1930 .... **TCLC 4, 18**
See See also CA 104; 158; MTCW 2
Mayhew, Henry 1812-1887 .... **NCLC 31**
See See also DLB 18, 55, 190
Mayle, Peter 1939(?)- .... **CLC 89**
See See also CA 139; CANR 64
Maynard, Joyce 1953- .... **CLC 23**
See See also CA 111; 129; CANR 64
Mayne, William (James Carter) 1928- . **CLC 12**
See See also AAYA 20; CA 9-12R; CANR 37, 80; CLR 25; JRDA; MAICYA; SAAS 11; SATA 6, 68
Mayo, Jim
See See L'Amour, Louis (Dearborn)
Maysles, Albert 1926- .... **CLC 16**
See See also CA 29-32R
Maysles, David 1932- .... **CLC 16**
Mazer, Norma Fox 1931- .... **CLC 26**
See See also AAYA 5; CA 69-72; CANR 12, 32, 66; CLR 23; JRDA; MAICYA; SAAS 1; SATA 24, 67, 105
Mazzini, Guiseppe 1805-1872 .... **NCLC 34**
McAlmon, Robert (Menzies) 1895-1956 ...... **TCLC 97**
See See also CA 107; 168; DLB 4, 45; DLBD 15
McAuley, James Phillip 1917-1976 . **CLC 45**
See See also CA 97-100
McBain, Ed
See See Hunter, Evan
McBrien, William Augustine 1930- . **CLC 44**
See See also CA 107
McCaffrey, Anne (Inez) 1926- .... **CLC 17; DAM NOV, POP**
See See also AAYA 6; AITN 2; BEST 89:2; CA 25-28R; CANR 15, 35, 55; CLR 49; DA3; DLB 8; JRDA; MAICYA; MTCW 1, 2; SAAS 11; SATA 8, 70
McCall, Nathan 1955(?)- .... **CLC 86**
See See also BW 3; CA 146
McCann, Arthur
See See Campbell, John W(ood, Jr.)
McCann, Edson
See See Pohl, Frederik
McCarthy, Charles, Jr. 1933-
See See McCarthy, Cormac
See See also CANR 42, 69; DAM POP; DA3; MTCW 2
McCarthy, Cormac 1933- .... **CLC 4, 57, 59, 101**
See See also McCarthy, Charles, Jr.
See See also DLB 6, 143; MTCW 2

McCarthy, Mary (Therese) 1912-1989 . CLC **1, 3, 5, 14, 24, 39, 59; SSC 24**
See See also CA 5-8R; 129; CANR 16, 50, 64; DA3; DLB 2; DLBY 81; INT CANR-16; MTCW 1, 2

McCartney, (James) Paul 1942- ..... CLC **12, 35**
See See also CA 146

McCauley, Stephen (D.) 1955- .... CLC **50**
See See also CA 141

McClure, Michael (Thomas) 1932- .. CLC **6, 10**
See See also CA 21-24R; CANR 17, 46, 77; DLB 16

McCorkle, Jill (Collins) 1958- .... CLC **51**
See See also CA 121; DLBY 87

McCourt, Frank 1930- .... CLC **109**
See See also CA 157

McCourt, James 1941- .... CLC **5**
See See also CA 57-60

McCourt, Malachy 1932- .... CLC **119**

McCoy, Horace (Stanley) 1897-1955 . TCLC **28**
See See also CA 108; 155; DLB 9

McCrae, John 1872-1918 .... TCLC **12**
See See also CA 109; DLB 92

McCreigh, James
See See Pohl, Frederik

McCullers, (Lula) Carson (Smith) 1917-1967
.. CLC **1, 4, 10, 12, 48, 100; DA; DAB; DAC; DAM MST, NOV; SSC 9, 24; WLC**
See See also AAYA 21; CA 5-8R; 25-28R; CABS 1, 3; CANR 18; CDALB 1941-1968; DA3; DLB 2, 7, 173; MTCW 1, 2; SATA 27

McCulloch, John Tyler
See See Burroughs, Edgar Rice

McCullough, Colleen 1938(?)- .... CLC **27, 107; DAM NOV, POP**
See See also CA 81-84; CANR 17, 46, 67; DA3; MTCW 1, 2

McDermott, Alice 1953- .... CLC **90**
See See also CA 109; CANR 40

McElroy, Joseph 1930- .... CLC **5, 47**
See See also CA 17-20R

McEwan, Ian (Russell) 1948- .. CLC **13, 66; DAM NOV**
See See also BEST 90:4; CA 61-64; CANR 14, 41, 69; DLB 14, 194; MTCW 1, 2

McFadden, David 1940- .... CLC **48**
See See also CA 104; DLB 60; INT 104

McFarland, Dennis 1950- .... CLC **65**
See See also CA 165

McGahern, John 1934- .. CLC **5, 9, 48; SSC 17**
See See also CA 17-20R; CANR 29, 68; DLB 14; MTCW 1

McGinley, Patrick (Anthony) 1937- ..... CLC **41**
See See also CA 120; 127; CANR 56; INT 127

McGinley, Phyllis 1905-1978 .... CLC **14**
See See also CA 9-12R; 77-80; CANR 19; DLB 11, 48; SATA 2, 44; SATA-Obit 24

McGinniss, Joe 1942- .... CLC **32**
See See also AITN 2; BEST 89:2; CA 25-28R; CANR 26, 70; DLB 185; INT CANR-26

McGivern, Maureen Daly
See See Daly, Maureen

McGrath, Patrick 1950- .... CLC **55**
See See also CA 136; CANR 65

McGrath, Thomas (Matthew) 1916-1990 ....
CLC **28, 59; DAM POET**
See See also CA 9-12R; 132; CANR 6, 33; MTCW 1; SATA 41; SATA-Obit 66

McGuane, Thomas (Francis III) 1939- . CLC **3, 7, 18, 45, 127**

See See also AITN 2; CA 49-52; CANR 5, 24, 49; DLB 2, 212; DLBY 80; INT CANR-24; MTCW 1

McGuckian, Medbh 1950- ... CLC **48; DAM POET; PC 27**
See See also CA 143; DLB 40

McHale, Tom 1942(?)-1982 .... CLC **3, 5**
See See also AITN 1; CA 77-80; 106

McIlvanney, William 1936- .... CLC **42**
See See also CA 25-28R; CANR 61; DLB 14, 207

McIlwraith, Maureen Mollie Hunter
See See Hunter, Mollie
See See also SATA 2

McInerney, Jay 1955- .. CLC **34, 112; DAM POP**
See See also AAYA 18; CA 116; 123; CANR 45, 68; DA3; INT 123; MTCW 2

McIntyre, Vonda N(eel) 1948- .... CLC **18**
See See also CA 81-84; CANR 17, 34, 69; MTCW 1

McKay, Claude . TCLC **7, 41; BLC 3; DAB; PC 2**
See See also McKay, Festus Claudius
See See also DLB 4, 45, 51, 117

McKay, Festus Claudius 1889-1948
See See McKay, Claude
See See also BW 1, 3; CA 104; 124; CANR 73; DA; DAC; DAM MST, MULT, NOV, POET; MTCW 1, 2; WLC

McKuen, Rod 1933- .... CLC **1, 3**
See See also AITN 1; CA 41-44R; CANR 40

McLoughlin, R. B.
See See Mencken, H(enry) L(ouis)

McLuhan, (Herbert) Marshall 1911-1980 ...
CLC **37, 83**
See See also CA 9-12R; 102; CANR 12, 34, 61; DLB 88; INT CANR-12; MTCW 1, 2

McMillan, Terry (L.) 1951- ...... CLC **50, 61, 112; BLCS; DAM MULT, NOV, POP**
See See also AAYA 21; BW 2, 3; CA 140; CANR 60; DA3; MTCW 2

McMurtry, Larry (Jeff) 1936- . CLC **2, 3, 7, 11, 27, 44, 127; DAM NOV, POP**
See See also AAYA 15; AITN 2; BEST 89:2; CA 5-8R; CANR 19, 43, 64; CDALB 1968-1988; DA3; DLB 2, 143; DLBY 80, 87; MTCW 1, 2

McNally, T. M. 1961- .... CLC **82**

McNally, Terrence 1939- .. CLC **4, 7, 41, 91; DAM DRAM**
See See also CA 45-48; CANR 2, 56; DA3; DLB 7; MTCW 2

McNamer, Deirdre 1950- .... CLC **70**

McNeal, Tom .... CLC **119**

McNeile, Herman Cyril 1888-1937
See See Sapper
See See also DLB 77

McNickle, (William) D'Arcy 1904-1977 ......
CLC **89; DAM MULT**
See See also CA 9-12R; 85-88; CANR 5, 45; DLB 175, 212; NNAL; SATA-Obit 22

McPhee, John (Angus) 1931- .... CLC **36**
See See also BEST 90:1; CA 65-68; CANR 20, 46, 64, 69; DLB 185; MTCW 1, 2

McPherson, James Alan 1943- . CLC **19, 77; BLCS**
See See also BW 1, 3; CA 25-28R; CAAS 17; CANR 24, 74; DLB 38; MTCW 1, 2

McPherson, William (Alexander) 1933- ......
CLC **34**
See See also CA 69-72; CANR 28; INT CANR-28

Mead, George Herbert 1873-1958 ..... TCLC **89**

Mead, Margaret 1901-1978 .... CLC **37**

See See also AITN 1; CA 1-4R; 81-84; CANR 4; DA3; MTCW 1, 2; SATA-Obit 20

Meaker, Marijane (Agnes) 1927-
See See Kerr, M. E.
See See also CA 107; CANR 37, 63; INT 107; JRDA; MAICYA; MTCW 1; SATA 20, 61, 99; SATA-Essay 111

Medoff, Mark (Howard) 1940- .. CLC **6, 23; DAM DRAM**
See See also AITN 1; CA 53-56; CANR 5; DLB 7; INT CANR-5

Medvedev, P. N.
See See Bakhtin, Mikhail Mikhailovich

Meged, Aharon
See See Megged, Aharon

Meged, Aron
See See Megged, Aharon

Megged, Aharon 1920- .... CLC **9**
See See also CA 49-52; CAAS 13; CANR 1

Mehta, Ved (Parkash) 1934- .... CLC **37**
See See also CA 1-4R; CANR 2, 23, 69; MTCW 1

Melanter
See See Blackmore, R(ichard) D(oddridge)

Melies, Georges 1861-1938 .... TCLC **81**

Melikow, Loris
See See Hofmannsthal, Hugo von

Melmoth, Sebastian
See See Wilde, Oscar

Meltzer, Milton 1915- .... CLC **26**
See See also AAYA 8; CA 13-16R; CANR 38; CLR 13; DLB 61; JRDA; MAICYA; SAAS 1; SATA 1, 50, 80

Melville, Herman 1819-1891 ... NCLC **3, 12, 29, 45, 49; DA; DAB; DAC; DAM MST, NOV; SSC 1, 17; WLC**
See See also AAYA 25; CDALB 1640-1865; DA3; DLB 3, 74; SATA 59

Menander c. 342B.C.-c. 292B.C. .. CMLC **9; DAM DRAM; DC 3**
See See also DLB 176

Menchu, Rigoberta 1959-
See See also HLCS 2

Menchu, Rigoberta 1959-
See See also CA 175; HLCS 2

Mencken, H(enry) L(ouis) 1880-1956 . TCLC **13**
See See also CA 105; 125; CDALB 1917-1929; DLB 11, 29, 63, 137; MTCW 1, 2

Mendelsohn, Jane 1965(?)- .... CLC **99**
See See also CA 154

Mercer, David 1928-1980 .... CLC **5; DAM DRAM**
See See also CA 9-12R; 102; CANR 23; DLB 13; MTCW 1

Merchant, Paul
See See Ellison, Harlan (Jay)

Meredith, George 1828-1909 . TCLC **17, 43; DAM POET**
See See also CA 117; 153; CANR 80; CDBLB 1832-1890; DLB 18, 35, 57, 159

Meredith, William (Morris) 1919- ... CLC **4, 13, 22, 55; DAM POET; PC 28**
See See also CA 9-12R; CAAS 14; CANR 6, 40; DLB 5

Merezhkovsky, Dmitry Sergeyevich 1865-1941 .... TCLC **29**
See See also CA 169

Merimee, Prosper 1803-1870 .. NCLC **6, 65; SSC 7**
See See also DLB 119, 192

Merkin, Daphne 1954- .... CLC **44**
See See also CA 123

Merlin, Arthur
See See Blish, James (Benjamin)

Merrill, James (Ingram) 1926-1995 . CLC **2,**

3, 6, 8, 13, 18, 34, 91; DAM POET; PC
28
    See See also CA 13-16R; 147; CANR 10,
    49, 63; DA3; DLB 5, 165; DLBY 85; INT
    CANR-10; MTCW 1, 2

Merriman, Alex
    See See Silverberg, Robert

Merriman, Brian 1747-1805 .... NCLC 70

Merritt, E. B.
    See See Waddington, Miriam

Merton, Thomas 1915-1968 ... CLC 1, 3, 11,
    34, 83; PC 10
    See See also CA 5-8R; 25-28R; CANR 22,
    53; DA3; DLB 48; DLBY 81; MTCW 1,
    2

Merwin, W(illiam) S(tanley) 1927- .. CLC 1,
    2, 3, 5, 8, 13, 18, 45, 88; DAM POET
    See See also CA 13-16R; CANR 15, 51;
    DA3; DLB 5, 169; INT CANR-15;
    MTCW 1, 2

Metcalf, John 1938- .... CLC 37
    See See also CA 113; DLB 60

Metcalf, Suzanne
    See See Baum, L(yman) Frank

Mew, Charlotte (Mary) 1870-1928 . TCLC 8
    See See also CA 105; DLB 19, 135

Mewshaw, Michael 1943- .... CLC 9
    See See also CA 53-56; CANR 7, 47;
    DLBY 80

Meyer, Conrad Ferdinand 1825-1905 ....
    NCLC 81
    See See also DLB 129

Meyer, June
    See See Jordan, June

Meyer, Lynn
    See See Slavitt, David R(ytman)

Meyer-Meyrink, Gustav 1868-1932
    See See Meyrink, Gustav
    See See also CA 117

Meyers, Jeffrey 1939- .... CLC 39
    See See also CA 73-76, 181; CAAE 181;
    CANR 54; DLB 111

**Meynell, Alice (Christina Gertrude
    Thompson)** 1847-1922 .... TCLC 6
    See See also CA 104; 177; DLB 19, 98

Meyrink, Gustav .... TCLC 21
    See See Meyer-Meyrink, Gustav
    See See also DLB 81

Michaels, Leonard 1933- ... CLC 6, 25; SSC
    16
    See See also CA 61-64; CANR 21, 62; DLB
    130; MTCW 1

Michaux, Henri 1899-1984 .... CLC 8, 19
    See See also CA 85-88; 114

Micheaux, Oscar (Devereaux) 1884-1951 ....
    TCLC 76
    See See also BW 3; CA 174; DLB 50

Michelangelo 1475-1564 .... LC 12

Michelet, Jules 1798-1874 .... NCLC 31

Michels, Robert 1876-1936 .... TCLC 88

Michener, James A(lbert) 1907(?)-1997 ....
    CLC 1, 5, 11, 29, 60, 109; DAM NOV,
    POP
    See See also AAYA 27; AITN 1; BEST
    90:1; CA 5-8R; 161; CANR 21, 45, 68;
    DA3; DLB 6; MTCW 1, 2

Mickiewicz, Adam 1798-1855 .... NCLC 3

Middleton, Christopher 1926- .... CLC 13
    See See also CA 13-16R; CANR 29, 54;
    DLB 40

Middleton, Richard (Barham) 1882-1911 ....
    TCLC 56
    See See also DLB 156

Middleton, Stanley 1919- .... CLC 7, 38
    See See also CA 25-28R; CAAS 23; CANR
    21, 46, 81; DLB 14

Middleton, Thomas 1580-1627 .... LC 33;
    DAM DRAM, MST; DC 5
    See See also DLB 58

Migueis, Jose Rodrigues 1901- .... CLC 10

Mikszath, Kalman 1847-1910 .... TCLC 31
    See See also CA 170

Miles, Jack .... CLC 100

Miles, Josephine (Louise) 1911-1985 ... CLC
    1, 2, 14, 34, 39; DAM POET
    See See also CA 1-4R; 116; CANR 2, 55;
    DLB 48

Militant
    See See Sandburg, Carl (August)

Mill, John Stuart 1806-1873 ... NCLC 11, 58
    See See also CDBLB 1832-1890; DLB 55,
    190

Millar, Kenneth 1915-1983 .. CLC 14; DAM
    POP
    See See also Macdonald, Ross
    See See also CA 9-12R; 110; CANR 16,
    63; DA3; DLB 2; DLBD 6; DLBY 83;
    MTCW 1, 2

Millay, E. Vincent
    See See Millay, Edna St. Vincent

Millay, Edna St. Vincent 1892-1950 .. TCLC
    4, 49; DA; DAB; DAC; DAM MST,
    POET; PC 6; WLCS
    See See also CA 104; 130; CDALB 1917-
    1929; DA3; DLB 45; MTCW 1, 2

Miller, Arthur 1915- ..... CLC 1, 2, 6, 10, 15,
    26, 47, 78; DA; DAB; DAC; DAM
    DRAM, MST; DC 1; WLC
    See See also AAYA 15; AITN 1; CA 1-4R;
    CABS 3; CANR 2, 30, 54, 76; CDALB
    1941-1968; DA3; DLB 7; MTCW 1, 2

Miller, Henry (Valentine) 1891-1980 ... CLC
    1, 2, 4, 9, 14, 43, 84; DA; DAB; DAC;
    DAM MST, NOV; WLC
    See See also CA 9-12R; 97-100; CANR 33,
    64; CDALB 1929-1941; DA3; DLB 4, 9;
    DLBY 80; MTCW 1, 2

Miller, Jason 1939(?)- .... CLC 2
    See See also AITN 1; CA 73-76; DLB 7

Miller, Sue 1943- .... CLC 44; DAM POP
    See See also BEST 90:3; CA 139; CANR
    59; DA3; DLB 143

Miller, Walter M(ichael, Jr.) 1923- .. CLC 4,
    30
    See See also CA 85-88; DLB 8

Millett, Kate 1934- .... CLC 67
    See See also AITN 1; CA 73-76; CANR 32,
    53, 76; DA3; MTCW 1, 2

Millhauser, Steven (Lewis) 1943- ... CLC 21,
    54, 109
    See See also CA 110; 111; CANR 63; DA3;
    DLB 2; INT 111; MTCW 2

Millin, Sarah Gertrude 1889-1968 . CLC 49
    See See also CA 102; 93-96

Milne, A(lan) A(lexander) 1882-1956 . TCLC
    6, 88; DAB; DAC; DAM MST
    See See also CA 104; 133; CLR 1, 26; DA3;
    DLB 10, 77, 100, 160; MAICYA; MTCW
    1, 2; SATA 100; YABC 1

Milner, Ron(ald) 1938- ..... CLC 56; BLC 3;
    DAM MULT
    See See also AITN 1; BW 1; CA 73-76;
    CANR 24, 81; DLB 38; MTCW 1

Milnes, Richard Monckton 1809-1885 ....
    NCLC 61
    See See also DLB 32, 184

Milosz, Czeslaw 1911- .... CLC 5, 11, 22, 31,
    56, 82; DAM MST, POET; PC 8; WLCS
    See See also CA 81-84; CANR 23, 51;
    DA3; MTCW 1, 2

Milton, John 1608-1674 .... LC 9, 43; DA;
    DAB; DAC; DAM MST, POET; PC 19;
    WLC
    See See also CDBLB 1660-1789; DA3;
    DLB 131, 151

Min, Anchee 1957- .... CLC 86
    See See also CA 146

Minehaha, Cornelius
    See See Wedekind, (Benjamin) Frank(lin)

Miner, Valerie 1947- .... CLC 40
    See See also CA 97-100; CANR 59

Minimo, Duca
    See See D'Annunzio, Gabriele

Minot, Susan 1956- .... CLC 44
    See See also CA 134

Minus, Ed 1938- .... CLC 39

Miranda, Javier
    See See Bioy Casares, Adolfo

Miranda, Javier
    See See Bioy Casares, Adolfo

Mirbeau, Octave 1848-1917 .... TCLC 55
    See See also DLB 123, 192

Miro (Ferrer), Gabriel (Francisco Victor)
    1879-1930 .... TCLC 5
    See See also CA 104

Mishima, Yukio 1925-1970 .. CLC 2, 4, 6, 9,
    27; DC 1; SSC 4
    See See also Hiraoka, Kimitake
    See See also DLB 182; MTCW 2

Mistral, Frederic 1830-1914 .... TCLC 51
    See See also CA 122

Mistral, Gabriela .... TCLC 2; HLC 2
    See See also Godoy Alcayaga, Lucila
    See See also MTCW 2

Mistry, Rohinton 1952- .... CLC 71; DAC
    See See also CA 141; CANR 86

Mitchell, Clyde
    See See Ellison, Harlan (Jay); Silverberg,
    Robert

Mitchell, James Leslie 1901-1935
    See See Gibbon, Lewis Grassic
    See See also CA 104; DLB 15

Mitchell, Joni 1943- .... CLC 12
    See See also CA 112

Mitchell, Joseph (Quincy) 1908-1996 .. CLC
    98
    See See also CA 77-80; 152; CANR 69;
    DLB 185; DLBY 96

Mitchell, Margaret (Munnerlyn) 1900-1949
    .... TCLC 11; DAM NOV, POP
    See See also AAYA 23; CA 109; 125;
    CANR 55; CDALBS; DA3; DLB 9;
    MTCW 1, 2

Mitchell, Peggy
    See See Mitchell, Margaret (Munnerlyn)

Mitchell, S(ilas) Weir 1829-1914 .. TCLC 36
    See See also CA 165; DLB 202

Mitchell, W(illiam) O(rmond) 1914-1998 ....
    CLC 25; DAC; DAM MST
    See See also CA 77-80; 165; CANR 15, 43;
    DLB 88

Mitchell, William 1879-1936 .... TCLC 81

Mitford, Mary Russell 1787-1855 .. NCLC 4
    See See also DLB 110, 116

Mitford, Nancy 1904-1973 .... CLC 44
    See See also CA 9-12R; DLB 191

Miyamoto, (Chujo) Yuriko 1899-1951 ....
    TCLC 37
    See See also CA 170, 174; DLB 180

Miyazawa, Kenji 1896-1933 .... TCLC 76
    See See also CA 157

Mizoguchi, Kenji 1898-1956 .... TCLC 72
    See See also CA 167

Mo, Timothy (Peter) 1950(?)- .... CLC 46
    See See also CA 117; DLB 194; MTCW 1

Modarressi, Taghi (M.) 1931- .... CLC 44
    See See also CA 121; 134; INT 134

Modiano, Patrick (Jean) 1945- .... CLC 18
    See See also CA 85-88; CANR 17, 40; DLB
    83

Moerck, Paal
    See See Roelvaag, O(le) E(dvart)

Mofolo, Thomas (Mokopu) 1875(?)-1948 ....
    TCLC 22; BLC 3; DAM MULT

Mossgiel, Rab
See See Burns, Robert
Motion, Andrew (Peter) 1952- .... **CLC 47**
See See also CA 146; DLB 40
Motley, Willard (Francis) 1909-1965 ... **CLC 18**
See See also BW 1; CA 117; 106; DLB 76, 143
Motoori, Norinaga 1730-1801 .... **NCLC 45**
Mott, Michael (Charles Alston) 1930- .**CLC 15, 34**
See See also CA 5-8R; CAAS 7; CANR 7, 29
Mountain Wolf Woman 1884-1960 . **CLC 92**
See See also CA 144; NNAL
Moure, Erin 1955- .... **CLC 88**
See See also CA 113; DLB 60
Mowat, Farley (McGill) 1921- .... **CLC 26; DAC; DAM MST**
See See also AAYA 1; CA 1-4R; CANR 4, 24, 42, 68; CLR 20; DLB 68; INT CANR-24; JRDA; MAICYA; MTCW 1, 2; SATA 3, 55
Mowatt, Anna Cora 1819-1870 .... **NCLC 74**
Moyers, Bill 1934- .... **CLC 74**
See See also AITN 2; CA 61-64; CANR 31, 52
Mphahlele, Es'kia
See See Mphahlele, Ezekiel
See See also DLB 125
Mphahlele, Ezekiel 1919- . **CLC 25; BLC 3; DAM MULT**
See See also Mphahlele, Es'kia
See See also BW 2, 3; CA 81-84; CANR 26, 76; DA3; MTCW 2
Mqhayi, S(amuel) E(dward) K(rune Loliwe) 1875-1945 ..... **TCLC 25; BLC 3; DAM MULT**
See See also CA 153
Mrozek, Slawomir 1930- .... **CLC 3, 13**
See See also CA 13-16R; CAAS 10; CANR 29; MTCW 1
Mrs. Belloc-Lowndes
See See Lowndes, Marie Adelaide (Belloc)
Mtwa, Percy (?)- .... **CLC 47**
Mueller, Lisel 1924- .... **CLC 13, 51**
See See also CA 93-96; DLB 105
Muir, Edwin 1887-1959 .... **TCLC 2, 87**
See See also CA 104; DLB 20, 100, 191
Muir, John 1838-1914 .... **TCLC 28**
See See also CA 165; DLB 186
Mujica Lainez, Manuel 1910-1984 . **CLC 31**
See See also Lainez, Manuel Mujica
See See also CA 81-84; 112; CANR 32; HW 1
Mukherjee, Bharati 1940- ...... **CLC 53, 115; DAM NOV**
See See also BEST 89:2; CA 107; CANR 45, 72; DLB 60; MTCW 1, 2
Muldoon, Paul 1951- ...... **CLC 32, 72; DAM POET**
See See also CA 113; 129; CANR 52; DLB 40; INT 129
Mulisch, Harry 1927- .... **CLC 42**
See See also CA 9-12R; CANR 6, 26, 56
Mull, Martin 1943- .... **CLC 17**
See See also CA 105
Muller, Wilhelm .... **NCLC 73**
Mulock, Dinah Maria
See See Craik, Dinah Maria (Mulock)
Munford, Robert 1737(?)-1783 .... **LC 5**
See See also DLB 31
Mungo, Raymond 1946- .... **CLC 72**
See See also CA 49-52; CANR 2
Munro, Alice 1931- .. **CLC 6, 10, 19, 50, 95; DAC; DAM MST, NOV; SSC 3; WLCS**
See See also AITN 2; CA 33-36R; CANR 33, 53, 75; DA3; DLB 53; MTCW 1, 2; SATA 29

Munro, H(ector) H(ugh) 1870-1916
See See Saki
See See also CA 104; 130; CDBLB 1890-1914; DA; DAB; DAC; DAM MST, NOV; DA3; DLB 34, 162; MTCW 1, 2; WLC
Murdoch, (Jean) Iris 1919-1999 .. **CLC 1, 2, 3, 4, 6, 8, 11, 15, 22, 31, 51; DAB; DAC; DAM MST, NOV**
See See also CA 13-16R; 179; CANR 8, 43, 68; CDBLB 1960 to Present; DA3; DLB 14, 194; INT CANR-8; MTCW 1, 2
Murfree, Mary Noailles 1850-1922 .. **SSC 22**
See See also CA 122; 176; DLB 12, 74
Murnau, Friedrich Wilhelm
See See Plumpe, Friedrich Wilhelm
Murphy, Richard 1927- .... **CLC 41**
See See also CA 29-32R; DLB 40
Murphy, Sylvia 1937- .... **CLC 34**
See See also CA 121
Murphy, Thomas (Bernard) 1935- . **CLC 51**
See See also CA 101
Murray, Albert L. 1916- .... **CLC 73**
See See also BW 2; CA 49-52; CANR 26, 52, 78; DLB 38
Murray, Judith Sargent 1751-1820 ... **NCLC 63**
See See also DLB 37, 200
Murray, Les(lie) A(llan) 1938- .... **CLC 40; DAM POET**
See See also CA 21-24R; CANR 11, 27, 56
Murry, J. Middleton
See See Murry, John Middleton
Murry, John Middleton 1889-1957 ... **TCLC 16**
See See also CA 118; DLB 149
Musgrave, Susan 1951- .... **CLC 13, 54**
See See also CA 69-72; CANR 45, 84
Musil, Robert (Edler von) 1880-1942 . **TCLC 12, 68; SSC 18**
See See also CA 109; CANR 55, 84; DLB 81, 124; MTCW 2
Muske, Carol 1945- .... **CLC 90**
See See also Muske-Dukes, Carol (Anne)
Muske-Dukes, Carol (Anne) 1945-
See See Muske, Carol
See See also CA 65-68; CANR 32, 70
Musset, (Louis Charles) Alfred de 1810-1857 .... **NCLC 7**
See See also DLB 192
Mussolini, Benito (Amilcare Andrea) 1883-1945 .... **TCLC 96**
See See also CA 116
My Brother's Brother
See See Chekhov, Anton (Pavlovich)
Myers, L(eopold) H(amilton) 1881-1944 ..... **TCLC 59**
See See also CA 157; DLB 15
Myers, Walter Dean 1937- .... **CLC 35; BLC 3; DAM MULT, NOV**
See See also AAYA 4, 23; BW 2; CA 33-36R; CANR 20, 42, 67; CLR 4, 16, 35; DLB 33; INT CANR-20; JRDA; MAICYA; MTCW 2; SAAS 2; SATA 41, 71, 109; SATA-Brief 27
Myers, Walter M.
See See Myers, Walter Dean
Myles, Symon
See See Follett, Ken(neth Martin)
Nabokov, Vladimir (Vladimirovich) 1899-1977 ..... **CLC 1, 2, 3, 6, 8, 11, 15, 23, 44, 46, 64; DA; DAB; DAC; DAM MST, NOV; SSC 11; WLC**
See See also CA 5-8R; 69-72; CANR 20; CDALB 1941-1968; DA3; DLB 2; DLBD 3; DLBY 80, 91; MTCW 1, 2
Naevius c. 265B.C.-201B.C. .... **CMLC 37**
See See also DLB 211
Nagai Kafu 1879-1959 .... **TCLC 51**
See See also Nagai Sokichi

See See also DLB 180
Nagai Sokichi 1879-1959
See See Nagai Kafu
See See also CA 117
Nagy, Laszlo 1925-1978 .... **CLC 7**
See See also CA 129; 112
Naidu, Sarojini 1879-1943 .... **TCLC 80**
Naipaul, Shiva(dhar Srinivasa) 1945-1985 .. **CLC 32, 39; DAM NOV**
See See also CA 110; 112; 116; CANR 33; DA3; DLB 157; DLBY 85; MTCW 1, 2
Naipaul, V(idiadhar) S(urajprasad) 1932- .. **CLC 4, 7, 9, 13, 18, 37, 105; DAB; DAC; DAM MST, NOV**
See See also CA 1-4R; CANR 1, 33, 51; CDBLB 1960 to Present; DA3; DLB 125, 204, 206; DLBY 85; MTCW 1, 2
Nakos, Lilika 1899(?)- .... **CLC 29**
Narayan, R(asipuram) K(rishnaswami) 1906- . **CLC 7, 28, 47, 121; DAM NOV; SSC 25**
See See also CA 81-84; CANR 33, 61; DA3; MTCW 1, 2; SATA 62
Nash, (Fredric) Ogden 1902-1971 . **CLC 23; DAM POET; PC 21**
See See also CA 13-14; 29-32R; CANR 34, 61; CAP 1; DLB 11; MAICYA; MTCW 1, 2; SATA 2, 46
Nashe, Thomas 1567-1601 .... **LC 41**
Nashe, Thomas 1567-1601(?) .... **LC 41**
See See also DLB 167
Nathan, Daniel
See See Dannay, Frederic
Nathan, George Jean 1882-1958 .. **TCLC 18**
See See also Hatteras, Owen
See See also CA 114; 169; DLB 137
Natsume, Kinnosuke 1867-1916
See See Natsume, Soseki
See See also CA 104
Natsume, Soseki 1867-1916 ...... **TCLC 2, 10**
See See also Natsume, Kinnosuke
See See also DLB 180
Natti, (Mary) Lee 1919-
See See Kingman, Lee
See See also CA 5-8R; CANR 2
Naylor, Gloria 1950- ... **CLC 28, 52; BLC 3; DA; DAC; DAM MST, MULT, NOV, POP; WLCS**
See See also AAYA 6; BW 2, 3; CA 107; CANR 27, 51, 74; DA3; DLB 173; MTCW 1, 2
Neihardt, John Gneisenau 1881-1973 .. **CLC 32**
See See also CA 13-14; CANR 65; CAP 1; DLB 9, 54
Nekrasov, Nikolai Alekseevich 1821-1878 ... **NCLC 11**
Nelligan, Emile 1879-1941 .... **TCLC 14**
See See also CA 114; DLB 92
Nelson, Willie 1933- .... **CLC 17**
See See also CA 107
Nemerov, Howard (Stanley) 1920-1991 .... **CLC 2, 6, 9, 36; DAM POET; PC 24**
See See also CA 1-4R; 134; CABS 2; CANR 1, 27, 53; DLB 5, 6; DLBY 83; INT CANR-27; MTCW 1, 2
Neruda, Pablo 1904-1973 . **CLC 1, 2, 5, 7, 9, 28, 62; DA; DAB; DAC; DAM MST, MULT, POET; HLC 2; PC 4; WLC**
See See also CA 19-20; 45-48; CAP 2; DA3; HW 1; MTCW 1, 2
Nerval, Gerard de 1808-1855 . **NCLC 1, 67; PC 13; SSC 18**
Nervo, (Jose) Amado (Ruiz de) 1870-1919 .. **TCLC 11; HLCS 2**
See See also CA 109; 131; HW 1
Nessi, Pio Baroja y
See See Baroja (y Nessi), Pio
Nestroy, Johann 1801-1862 .... **NCLC 42**

O'Connor, (Mary) Flannery 1925-1964 ....
**CLC 1, 2, 3, 6, 10, 13, 15, 21, 66, 104;
DA; DAB; DAC; DAM MST, NOV;
SSC 1, 23; WLC**
See See also AAYA 7; CA 1-4R; CANR 3,
41; CDALB 1941-1968; DA3; DLB 2,
152; DLBD 12; DLBY 80; MTCW 1, 2

O'Connor, Frank .... **CLC 23; SSC 5**
See See also O'Donovan, Michael John
See See also DLB 162

O'Dell, Scott 1898-1989 .... **CLC 30**
See See also AAYA 3; CA 61-64; 129;
CANR 12, 30; CLR 1, 16; DLB 52;
JRDA; MAICYA; SATA 12, 60

Odets, Clifford 1906-1963 .... **CLC 2, 28, 98;
DAM DRAM; DC 6**
See See also CA 85-88; CANR 62; DLB 7,
26; MTCW 1, 2

O'Doherty, Brian 1934- .... **CLC 76**
See See also CA 105

O'Donnell, K. M.
See See Malzberg, Barry N(athaniel)

O'Donnell, Lawrence
See See Kuttner, Henry

O'Donovan, Michael John 1903-1966 . **CLC
14**
See See also O'Connor, Frank
See See also CA 93-96; CANR 84

Oe, Kenzaburo 1935- .... **CLC 10, 36, 86;
DAM NOV; SSC 20**
See See also CA 97-100; CANR 36, 50, 74;
DA3; DLB 182; DLBY 94; MTCW 1, 2

O'Faolain, Julia 1932- ... **CLC 6, 19, 47, 108**
See See also CA 81-84; CAAS 2; CANR
12, 61; DLB 14; MTCW 1

O'Faolain, Sean 1900-1991 .... **CLC 1, 7, 14,
32, 70; SSC 13**
See See also CA 61-64; 134; CANR 12, 66;
DLB 15, 162; MTCW 1, 2

O'Flaherty, Liam 1896-1984 ...... **CLC 5, 34;
SSC 6**
See See also CA 101; 113; CANR 35; DLB
36, 162; DLBY 84; MTCW 1, 2

Ogilvy, Gavin
See See Barrie, J(ames) M(atthew)

O'Grady, Standish (James) 1846-1928 ....
TCLC 5
See See also CA 104; 157

O'Grady, Timothy 1951- .... **CLC 59**
See See also CA 138

O'Hara, Frank 1926-1966 ...... **CLC 2, 5, 13,
78; DAM POET**
See See also CA 9-12R; 25-28R; CANR
33; DA3; DLB 5, 16, 193; MTCW 1, 2

O'Hara, John (Henry) 1905-1970 .... **CLC 1,
2, 3, 6, 11, 42; DAM NOV; SSC 15**
See See also CA 5-8R; 25-28R; CANR 31,
60; CDALB 1929-1941; DLB 9, 86;
DLBD 2; MTCW 1, 2

O Hehir, Diana 1922- .... **CLC 41**
See See also CA 93-96

Ohiyesa
See See Eastman, Charles A(lexander)

Okigbo, Christopher (Ifenayichukwu)
1932-1967 . **CLC 25, 84; BLC 3; DAM
MULT, POET; PC 7**
See See also BW 1, 3; CA 77-80; CANR
74; DLB 125; MTCW 1, 2

Okri, Ben 1959- .... **CLC 87**
See See also BW 2, 3; CA 130; 138; CANR
65; DLB 157; INT 138; MTCW 2

Olds, Sharon 1942- .. **CLC 32, 39, 85; DAM
POET; PC 22**
See See also CA 101; CANR 18, 41, 66;
DLB 120; MTCW 2

Oldstyle, Jonathan
See See Irving, Washington

Olesha, Yuri (Karlovich) 1899-1960 . **CLC 8**
See See also CA 85-88

Oliphant, Laurence 1829(?)-1888 . **NCLC 47**
See See also DLB 18, 166

Oliphant, Margaret (Oliphant Wilson)
1828-1897 ...... **NCLC 11, 61; SSC 25**
See See also DLB 18, 159, 190

Oliver, Mary 1935- .... **CLC 19, 34, 98**
See See also CA 21-24R; CANR 9, 43, 84;
DLB 5, 193

Olivier, Laurence (Kerr) 1907-1989 ..... **CLC
20**
See See also CA 111; 150; 129

Olsen, Tillie 1912- .... **CLC 4, 13, 114; DA;
DAB; DAC; DAM MST; SSC 11**
See See also CA 1-4R; CANR 1, 43, 74;
CDALBS; DA3; DLB 28, 206; DLBY 80;
MTCW 1, 2

Olson, Charles (John) 1910-1970 . **CLC 1, 2,
5, 6, 9, 11, 29; DAM POET; PC 19**
See See also CA 13-16; 25-28R; CABS 2;
CANR 35, 61; CAP 1; DLB 5, 16, 193;
MTCW 1, 2

Olson, Toby 1937- .... **CLC 28**
See See also CA 65-68; CANR 9, 31, 84

Olyesha, Yuri
See See Olesha, Yuri (Karlovich)

Ondaatje, (Philip) Michael 1943- .. **CLC 14,
29, 51, 76; DAB; DAC; DAM MST; PC
28**
See See also CA 77-80; CANR 42, 74;
DA3; DLB 60; MTCW 2

Oneal, Elizabeth 1934-
See See Oneal, Zibby
See See also CA 106; CANR 28, 84; MAI-
CYA; SATA 30, 82

Oneal, Zibby .... **CLC 30**
See See also Oneal, Elizabeth
See See also AAYA 5; CLR 13; JRDA

O'Neill, Eugene (Gladstone) 1888-1953 ....
**TCLC 1, 6, 27, 49; DA; DAB; DAC;
DAM DRAM, MST; WLC**
See See also AITN 1; CA 110; 132; CDALB
1929-1941; DA3; DLB 7; MTCW 1, 2

Onetti, Juan Carlos 1909-1994 ... **CLC 7, 10;
DAM MULT, NOV; HLCS 2; SSC 23**
See See also CA 85-88; 145; CANR 32, 63;
DLB 113; HW 1, 2; MTCW 1, 2

O Nuallain, Brian 1911-1966
See See O'Brien, Flann
See See also CA 21-22; 25-28R; CAP 2

Ophuls, Max 1902-1957 .... **TCLC 79**
See See also CA 113

Opie, Amelia 1769-1853 .... **NCLC 65**
See See also DLB 116, 159

Oppen, George 1908-1984 ..... **CLC 7, 13, 34**
See See also CA 13-16R; 113; CANR 8,
82; DLB 5, 165

Oppenheim, E(dward) Phillips 1866-1946 ...
TCLC 45
See See also CA 111; DLB 70

Opuls, Max
See See Ophuls, Max

Origen c. 185-c. 254 .... **CMLC 19**

Orlovitz, Gil 1918-1973 .... **CLC 22**
See See also CA 77-80; 45-48; DLB 2, 5

Orris
See See Ingelow, Jean

Ortega y Gasset, Jose 1883-1955 .. **TCLC 9;
DAM MULT; HLC 2**
See See also CA 106; 130; HW 1, 2;
MTCW 1, 2

Ortese, Anna Maria 1914- .... **CLC 89**
See See also DLB 177

Ortiz, Simon J(oseph) 1941- . **CLC 45; DAM
MULT, POET; PC 17**
See See also CA 134; CANR 69; DLB 120,
175; NNAL

Orton, Joe .... **CLC 4, 13, 43; DC 3**
See See also Orton, John Kingsley

See See also CDBLB 1960 to Present; DLB
13; MTCW 2

Orton, John Kingsley 1933-1967
See See Orton, Joe
See See also CA 85-88; CANR 35, 66;
DAM DRAM; MTCW 1, 2

Orwell, George .... **TCLC 2, 6, 15, 31, 51;
DAB; WLC**
See See also Blair, Eric (Arthur)
See See also CDBLB 1945-1960; DLB 15,
98, 195

Osborne, David
See See Silverberg, Robert

Osborne, George
See See Silverberg, Robert

Osborne, John (James) 1929-1994 ... **CLC 1,
2, 5, 11, 45; DA; DAB; DAC; DAM
DRAM, MST; WLC**
See See also CA 13-16R; 147; CANR 21,
56; CDBLB 1945-1960; DLB 13; MTCW
1, 2

Osborne, Lawrence 1958- .... **CLC 50**

Osbourne, Lloyd 1868-1947 .... **TCLC 93**

Oshima, Nagisa 1932- .... **CLC 20**
See See also CA 116; 121; CANR 78

Oskison, John Milton 1874-1947 . **TCLC 35;
DAM MULT**
See See also CA 144; CANR 84; DLB 175;
NNAL

Ossian c. 3rd cent. - .... **CMLC 28**
See See also Macpherson, James

Ostrovsky, Alexander 1823-1886 . **NCLC 30,
57**

Otero, Blas de 1916-1979 .... **CLC 11**
See See also CA 89-92; DLB 134

Otto, Rudolf 1869-1937 .... **TCLC 85**

Otto, Whitney 1955- .... **CLC 70**
See See also CA 140

Ouida .... **TCLC 43**
See See also De La Ramee, (Marie) Louise
See See also DLB 18, 156

Ousmane, Sembene 1923- .. **CLC 66; BLC 3**
See See also BW 1, 3; CA 117; 125; CANR
81; MTCW 1

Ovid 43B.C.-17 . **CMLC 7; DAM POET; PC
2**
See See also DA3; DLB 211

Owen, Hugh
See See Faust, Frederick (Schiller)

Owen, Wilfred (Edward Salter) 1893-1918 .
**TCLC 5, 27; DA; DAB; DAC; DAM
MST, POET; PC 19; WLC**
See See also CA 104; 141; CDBLB 1914-
1945; DLB 20; MTCW 2

Owens, Rochelle 1936- .... **CLC 8**
See See also CA 17-20R; CAAS 2; CANR
39

Oz, Amos 1939- .... **CLC 5, 8, 11, 27, 33, 54;
DAM NOV**
See See also CA 53-56; CANR 27, 47, 65;
MTCW 1, 2

Ozick, Cynthia 1928- .... **CLC 3, 7, 28, 62;
DAM NOV, POP; SSC 15**
See See also BEST 90:1; CA 17-20R;
CANR 23, 58; DA3; DLB 28, 152; DLBY
82; INT CANR-23; MTCW 1, 2

Ozu, Yasujiro 1903-1963 .... **CLC 16**
See See also CA 112

Pacheco, C.
See See Pessoa, Fernando (Antonio
Nogueira)

Pacheco, Jose Emilio 1939-
See See also CA 111; 131; CANR 65; DAM
MULT; HLC 2; HW 1, 2

Pa Chin .... **CLC 18**
See See also Li Fei-kan

Pack, Robert 1929- .... **CLC 13**
See See also CA 1-4R; CANR 3, 44, 82;
DLB 5

Peck, Robert Newton 1928- ... **CLC 17; DA; DAC; DAM MST**
See See also AAYA 3; CA 81-84, 182; CAAE 182; CANR 31, 63; CLR 45; JRDA; MAICYA; SAAS 1; SATA 21, 62, 111; SATA-Essay 108

Peckinpah, (David) Sam(uel) 1925-1984 ...... **CLC 20**
See See also CA 109; 114; CANR 82

Pedersen, Knut 1859-1952
See See Hamsun, Knut
See See also CA 104; 119; CANR 63; MTCW 1, 2

Peeslake, Gaffer
See See Durrell, Lawrence (George)

Peguy, Charles Pierre 1873-1914 . **TCLC 10**
See See also CA 107

Peirce, Charles Sanders 1839-1914 ... **TCLC 81**
See See also CA 153; 69-72; HLCS 2; HW 1

Pellicer, Carlos 1900(?)-1977
See See also CA 153; 69-72; HLCS 2; HW 1

Pena, Ramon del Valle y
See See Valle-Inclan, Ramon (Maria) del

Pendennis, Arthur Esquir
See See Thackeray, William Makepeace

Penn, William 1644-1718 .... **LC 25**
See See also DLB 24

PEPECE
See See Prado (Calvo), Pedro

Pepys, Samuel 1633-1703 . **LC 11; DA; DAB; DAC; DAM MST; WLC**
See See also CDBLB 1660-1789; DA3; DLB 101

Percy, Walker 1916-1990 ..... **CLC 2, 3, 6, 8, 14, 18, 47, 65; DAM NOV, POP**
See See also CA 1-4R; 131; CANR 1, 23, 64; DA3; DLB 2; DLBY 80, 90; MTCW 1, 2

Percy, William Alexander 1885-1942 . **TCLC 84**
See See also CA 163; MTCW 2

Perec, Georges 1936-1982 .... **CLC 56, 116**
See See also CA 141; DLB 83

Pereda (y Sanchez de Porrua), Jose Maria de 1833-1906 .... **TCLC 16**
See See also CA 117

Pereda y Porrua, Jose Maria de
See See Pereda (y Sanchez de Porrua), Jose Maria de

Peregoy, George Weems
See See Mencken, H(enry) L(ouis)

Perelman, S(idney) J(oseph) 1904-1979 .... **CLC 3, 5, 9, 15, 23, 44, 49; DAM DRAM; SSC 32**
See See also AITN 1, 2; CA 73-76; 89-92; CANR 18; DLB 11, 44; MTCW 1, 2

Peret, Benjamin 1899-1959 .... **TCLC 20**
See See also CA 117

Peretz, Isaac Loeb 1851(?)-1915 . **TCLC 16; SSC 26**
See See also CA 109

Peretz, Yitzhok Leibush
See See Peretz, Isaac Loeb

Perez Galdos, Benito 1843-1920 . **TCLC 27; HLCS 2**
See See also CA 125; 153; HW 1

Peri Rossi, Cristina 1941-
See See also CA 131; CANR 59, 81; DLB 145; HLCS 2; HW 1, 2

Perrault, Charles 1628-1703 .... **LC 3, 52**
See See also MAICYA; SATA 25

Perry, Anne 1938- .... **CLC 126**
See See also CA 101; CANR 22, 50, 84

Perry, Brighton
See See Sherwood, Robert E(mmet)

Perse, St.-John
See See Leger, (Marie-Rene Auguste) Alexis Saint-Leger

Perutz, Leo(pold) 1882-1957 .... **TCLC 60**
See See also CA 147; DLB 81

Peseenz, Tulio F.
See See Lopez y Fuentes, Gregorio

Pesetsky, Bette 1932- .... **CLC 28**
See See also CA 133; DLB 130

Peshkov, Alexei Maximovich 1868-1936
See See Gorky, Maxim
See See also CA 105; 141; CANR 83; DA; DAC; DAM DRAM, MST, NOV; MTCW 2

Pessoa, Fernando (Antonio Nogueira) 1888-1935 ..... **TCLC 27; DAM MULT; HLC 2; PC 20**
See See also CA 125

Peterkin, Julia Mood 1880-1961 ..... **CLC 31**
See See also CA 102; DLB 9

Peters, Joan K(aren) 1945- .... **CLC 39**
See See also CA 158

Peters, Robert L(ouis) 1924- .... **CLC 7**
See See also CA 13-16R; CAAS 8; DLB 105

Petofi, Sandor 1823-1849 .... **NCLC 21**

Petrakis, Harry Mark 1923- .... **CLC 3**
See See also CA 9-12R; CANR 4, 30, 85

Petrarch 1304-1374 .... **CMLC 20; DAM POET; PC 8**
See See also DA3

Petronius c. 20-66 .... **CMLC 34**
See See also DLB 211

Petrov, Evgeny .... **TCLC 21**
See See also Kataev, Evgeny Petrovich

Petry, Ann (Lane) 1908-1997 .. **CLC 1, 7, 18**
See See also BW 1, 3; CA 5-8R; 157; CAAS 6; CANR 4, 46; CLR 12; DLB 76; JRDA; MAICYA; MTCW 1; SATA 5; SATA-Obit 94

Petursson, Halligrimur 1614-1674 .... **LC 8**

Peychinovich
See See Vazov, Ivan (Minchov)

Phaedrus c. 18B.C.-c. 50 .... **CMLC 25**
See See also DLB 211

Philips, Katherine 1632-1664 .... **LC 30**
See See also DLB 131

Philipson, Morris H. 1926- .... **CLC 53**
See See also CA 1-4R; CANR 4

Phillips, Caryl 1958- . **CLC 96; BLCS; DAM MULT**
See See also BW 2; CA 141; CANR 63; DA3; DLB 157; MTCW 2

Phillips, David Graham 1867-1911 ... **TCLC 44**
See See also CA 108; 176; DLB 9, 12

Phillips, Jack
See See Sandburg, Carl (August)

Phillips, Jayne Anne 1952- .... **CLC 15, 33; SSC 16**
See See also CA 101; CANR 24, 50; DLBY 80; INT CANR-24; MTCW 1, 2

Phillips, Richard
See See Dick, Philip K(indred)

Phillips, Robert (Schaeffer) 1938- ... **CLC 28**
See See also CA 17-20R; CAAS 13; CANR 8; DLB 105

Phillips, Ward
See See Lovecraft, H(oward) P(hillips)

Piccolo, Lucio 1901-1969 .... **CLC 13**
See See also CA 97-100; DLB 114

Pickthall, Marjorie L(owry) C(hristie) 1883-1922 .... **TCLC 21**
See See also CA 107; DLB 92

Pico della Mirandola, Giovanni 1463-1494 . **LC 15**

Piercy, Marge 1936- ... **CLC 3, 6, 14, 18, 27, 62**
See See also CA 21-24R; CAAS 1; CANR 13, 43, 66; DLB 120; MTCW 1, 2

Piers, Robert
See See Anthony, Piers

Pieyre de Mandiargues, Andre 1909-1991
See See Mandiargues, Andre Pieyre de
See See also CA 103; 136; CANR 22, 82

Pilnyak, Boris .... **TCLC 23**
See See also Vogau, Boris Andreyevich

Pincherle, Alberto 1907-1990 ... **CLC 11, 18; DAM NOV**
See See also Moravia, Alberto
See See also CA 25-28R; 132; CANR 33, 63; MTCW 1

Pinckney, Darryl 1953- .... **CLC 76**
See See also BW 2, 3; CA 143; CANR 79

Pindar 518B.C.-446B.C. .. **CMLC 12; PC 19**
See See also DLB 176

Pineda, Cecile 1942- .... **CLC 39**
See See also CA 118

Pinero, Arthur Wing 1855-1934 .. **TCLC 32; DAM DRAM**
See See also CA 110; 153; DLB 10

Pinero, Miguel (Antonio Gomez) 1946-1988 .... **CLC 4, 55**
See See also CA 61-64; 125; CANR 29; HW 1

Pinget, Robert 1919-1997 ...... **CLC 7, 13, 37**
See See also CA 85-88; 160; DLB 83

Pink Floyd
See See Barrett, (Roger) Syd; Gilmour, David; Mason, Nick; Waters, Roger; Wright, Rick

Pinkney, Edward 1802-1828 .... **NCLC 31**

Pinkwater, Daniel Manus 1941- ...... **CLC 35**
See See Pinkwater, Manus
See See also AAYA 1; CA 29-32R; CANR 12, 38; CLR 4; JRDA; MAICYA; SAAS 3; SATA 46, 76

Pinkwater, Manus
See See Pinkwater, Daniel Manus
See See also SATA 8

Pinsky, Robert 1940- ...... **CLC 9, 19, 38, 94, 121; DAM POET; PC 27**
See See also CA 29-32R; CAAS 4; CANR 58; DA3; DLBY 82, 98; MTCW 2

Pinta, Harold
See See Pinter, Harold

Pinter, Harold 1930- . **CLC 1, 3, 6, 9, 11, 15, 27, 58, 73; DA; DAB; DAC; DAM DRAM, MST; WLC**
See See also CA 5-8R; CANR 33, 65; CDBLB 1960 to Present; DA3; DLB 13; MTCW 1, 2

Piozzi, Hester Lynch (Thrale) 1741-1821 .... **NCLC 57**
See See also DLB 104, 142

Pirandello, Luigi 1867-1936 .... **TCLC 4, 29; DA; DAB; DAC; DAM DRAM, MST; DC 5; SSC 22; WLC**
See See also CA 104; 153; DA3; MTCW 2

Pirsig, Robert M(aynard) 1928- .. **CLC 4, 6, 73; DAM POP**
See See also CA 53-56; CANR 42, 74; DA3; MTCW 1, 2; SATA 39

Pisarev, Dmitry Ivanovich 1840-1868 .... **NCLC 25**

Pix, Mary (Griffith) 1666-1709 .... **LC 8**
See See also DLB 80

Pixerecourt, (Rene Charles) Guilbert de 1773-1844 .... **NCLC 39**
See See also DLB 192

Plaatje, Sol(omon) T(shekisho) 1876-1932 .. **TCLC 73; BLCS**
See See also BW 2, 3; CA 141; CANR 79

Plaidy, Jean
See See Hibbert, Eleanor Alice Burford

Planche, James Robinson 1796-1880 . **NCLC 42**

Plant, Robert 1948- .... **CLC 12**

See See also CA 61-64; 157; CANR 31, 63; DA3; DLB 15, 139; MTCW 1, 2

Private 19022
See See Manning, Frederic

Probst, Mark 1925- .... **CLC 59**
See See also CA 130

Prokosch, Frederic 1908-1989 ..... **CLC 4, 48**
See See also CA 73-76; 128; CANR 82; DLB 48; MTCW 2

Propertius, Sextus c. 50B.C.-c. 16B.C. ....
CMLC 32
See See also DLB 211

Prophet, The
See See Dreiser, Theodore (Herman Albert)

Prose, Francine 1947- .... **CLC 45**
See See also CA 109; 112; CANR 46; SATA 101

Proudhon
See See Cunha, Euclides (Rodrigues Pimenta) da

Proulx, Annie
See See Proulx, E(dna) Annie

Proulx, E(dna) Annie 1935- . **CLC 81; DAM POP**
See See also CA 145; CANR 65; DA3; MTCW 2

Proust, (Valentin-Louis-George-Eugene-) Marcel 1871-1922 ...... **TCLC 7, 13, 33; DA; DAB; DAC; DAM MST, NOV; WLC**
See See also CA 104; 120; DA3; DLB 65; MTCW 1, 2

Prowler, Harley
See See Masters, Edgar Lee

Prus, Boleslaw 1845-1912 .... **TCLC 48**

Pryor, Richard (Franklin Lenox Thomas) 1940- .... **CLC 26**
See See also CA 122; 152

Przybyszewski, Stanislaw 1868-1927 . **TCLC 36**
See See also CA 160; DLB 66

Pteleon
See See Grieve, C(hristopher) M(urray)
See See also DAM POET

Puckett, Lute
See See Masters, Edgar Lee

Puig, Manuel 1932-1990 ... **CLC 3, 5, 10, 28, 65; DAM MULT; HLC 2**
See See also CA 45-48; CANR 2, 32, 63; DA3; DLB 113; HW 1, 2; MTCW 1, 2

Pulitzer, Joseph 1847-1911 .... **TCLC 76**
See See also CA 114; DLB 23

Purdy, A(lfred) W(ellington) 1918- .. **CLC 3, 6, 14, 50; DAC; DAM MST, POET**
See See also CA 81-84; CAAS 17; CANR 42, 66; DLB 88

Purdy, James (Amos) 1923- ... **CLC 2, 4, 10, 28, 52**
See See also CA 33-36R; CAAS 1; CANR 19, 51; DLB 2; INT CANR-19; MTCW 1

Pure, Simon
See See Swinnerton, Frank Arthur

Pushkin, Alexander (Sergeyevich) 1799-1837 ...... **NCLC 3, 27, 83; DA; DAB; DAC; DAM DRAM, MST, POET; PC 10; SSC 27; WLC**
See See also DA3; DLB 205; SATA 61

P'u Sung-ling 1640-1715 ...... **LC 49; SSC 31**

Putnam, Arthur Lee
See See Alger, Horatio Jr., Jr.

Puzo, Mario 1920-1999 ...... **CLC 1, 2, 6, 36, 107; DAM NOV, POP**
See See also CA 65-68; CANR 4, 42, 65; DA3; DLB 6; MTCW 1, 2

Pygge, Edward
See See Barnes, Julian (Patrick)

Pyle, Ernest Taylor 1900-1945
See See Pyle, Ernie
See See also CA 115; 160

Pyle, Ernie 1900-1945 .... **TCLC 75**
See See also Pyle, Ernest Taylor
See See also DLB 29; MTCW 2

Pyle, Howard 1853-1911 .... **TCLC 81**
See See also CA 109; 137; CLR 22; DLB 42, 188; DLBD 13; MAICYA; SATA 16, 100

Pym, Barbara (Mary Crampton) 1913-1980
.... **CLC 13, 19, 37, 111**
See See also CA 13-14; 97-100; CANR 13, 34; CAP 1; DLB 14, 207; DLBY 87; MTCW 1, 2

Pynchon, Thomas (Ruggles, Jr.) 1937- . **CLC 2, 3, 6, 9, 11, 18, 33, 62, 72; DA; DAB; DAC; DAM MST, NOV, POP; SSC 14; WLC**
See See also BEST 90:2; CA 17-20R; CANR 22, 46, 73; DA3; DLB 2, 173; MTCW 1, 2

Pythagoras c. 570B.C.-c. 500B.C. ..... **CMLC 22**
See See also DLB 176

Q
See See Quiller-Couch, SirArthur (Thomas)

Qian Zhongshu
See See Ch'ien Chung-shu

Qroll
See See Dagerman, Stig (Halvard)

Quarrington, Paul (Lewis) 1953- .... **CLC 65**
See See also CA 129; CANR 62

Quasimodo, Salvatore 1901-1968 .... **CLC 10**
See See also CA 13-16; 25-28R; CAP 1; DLB 114; MTCW 1

Quay, Stephen 1947- .... **CLC 95**

Quay, Timothy 1947- .... **CLC 95**

Queen, Ellery .... **CLC 3, 11**
See See also Dannay, Frederic; Davidson, Avram (James); Lee, Manfred B(ennington); Marlowe, Stephen; Sturgeon, Theodore (Hamilton); Vance, John Holbrook

Queen, Ellery, Jr.
See See Dannay, Frederic; Lee, Manfred B(ennington)

Queneau, Raymond 1903-1976 .... **CLC 2, 5, 10, 42**
See See also CA 77-80; 69-72; CANR 32; DLB 72; MTCW 1, 2

Quevedo, Francisco de 1580-1645 ..... **LC 23**

Quiller-Couch, SirArthur (Thomas) 1863-1944 .... **TCLC 53**
See See also CA 118; 166; DLB 135, 153, 190

Quin, Ann (Marie) 1936-1973 .... **CLC 6**
See See also CA 9-12R; 45-48; DLB 14

Quinn, Martin
See See Smith, Martin Cruz

Quinn, Peter 1947- .... **CLC 91**

Quinn, Simon
See See Smith, Martin Cruz

Quintana, Leroy V. 1944-
See See also CA 131; CANR 65; DAM MULT; DLB 82; HLC 2; HW 1, 2

Quiroga, Horacio (Sylvestre) 1878-1937 ...... **TCLC 20; DAM MULT; HLC 2**
See See also CA 117; 131; HW 1; MTCW 1

Quoirez, Francoise 1935- .... **CLC 9**
See See also Sagan, Francoise
See See also CA 49-52; CANR 6, 39, 73; MTCW 1, 2

Raabe, Wilhelm (Karl) 1831-1910 ..... **TCLC 45**
See See also CA 167; DLB 129

Rabe, David (William) 1940- . **CLC 4, 8, 33; DAM DRAM**
See See also CA 85-88; CABS 3; CANR 59; DLB 7

Rabelais, Francois 1483-1553 ..... **LC 5; DA;**

DAB; DAC; DAM MST; WLC

Rabinovitch, Sholem 1859-1916
See See Aleichem, Sholom
See See also CA 104

Rabinyan, Dorit 1972- .... **CLC 119**
See See also CA 170

Rachilde 1860-1953 .... **TCLC 67**
See See also DLB 123, 192

Racine, Jean 1639-1699 . **LC 28; DAB; DAM MST**
See See also DA3

Radcliffe, Ann (Ward) 1764-1823 . **NCLC 6, 55**
See See also DLB 39, 178

Radiguet, Raymond 1903-1923 ..... **TCLC 29**
See See also CA 162; DLB 65

Radnoti, Miklos 1909-1944 .... **TCLC 16**
See See also CA 118

Rado, James 1939- .... **CLC 17**
See See also CA 105

Radvanyi, Netty 1900-1983
See See Seghers, Anna
See See also CA 85-88; 110; CANR 82

Rae, Ben
See See Griffiths, Trevor

Raeburn, John (Hay) 1941- .... **CLC 34**
See See also CA 57-60

Ragni, Gerome 1942-1991 .... **CLC 17**
See See also CA 105; 134

Rahv, Philip 1908-1973 .... **CLC 24**
See See also Greenberg, Ivan
See See also DLB 137

Raimund, Ferdinand Jakob 1790-1836 ....
NCLC 69
See See also DLB 90

Raine, Craig 1944- .... **CLC 32, 103**
See See also CA 108; CANR 29, 51; DLB 40

Raine, Kathleen (Jessie) 1908- .... **CLC 7, 45**
See See also CA 85-88; CANR 46; DLB 20; MTCW 1

Rainis, Janis 1865-1929 .... **TCLC 29**
See See also CA 170

Rakosi, Carl 1903- .... **CLC 47**
See See also Rawley, Callman
See See also CAAS 5; DLB 193

Raleigh, Richard
See See Lovecraft, H(oward) P(hillips)

Raleigh, Sir Walter 1554(?)-1618 . **LC 31, 39**
See See also CDBLB Before 1660; DLB 172

Rallentando, H. P.
See See Sayers, Dorothy L(eigh)

Ramal, Walter
See See de la Mare, Walter (John)

Ramana Maharshi 1879-1950 .... **TCLC 84**

Ramoacn y Cajal, Santiago 1852-1934 ....
TCLC 93

Ramon, Juan
See See Jimenez (Mantecon), Juan Ramon

Ramos, Graciliano 1892-1953 .... **TCLC 32**
See See also CA 167; HW 2

Rampersad, Arnold 1941- .... **CLC 44**
See See also BW 2, 3; CA 127; 133; CANR 81; DLB 111; INT 133

Rampling, Anne
See See Rice, Anne

Ramsay, Allan 1684(?)-1758 .... **LC 29**
See See also DLB 95

Ramuz, Charles-Ferdinand 1878-1947 ....
TCLC 33
See See also CA 165

Rand, Ayn 1905-1982 ..... **CLC 3, 30, 44, 79; DA; DAC; DAM MST, NOV, POP; WLC**
See See also AAYA 10; CA 13-16R; 105; CANR 27, 73; CDALBS; DA3; MTCW 1, 2

Randall, Dudley (Felker) 1914- .... CLC 1; BLC 3; DAM MULT
See See also BW 1, 3; CA 25-28R; CANR 23, 82; DLB 41

Randall, Robert
See See Silverberg, Robert

Ranger, Ken
See See Creasey, John

Ransom, John Crowe 1888-1974 . CLC 2, 4, 5, 11, 24; DAM POET
See See also CA 5-8R; 49-52; CANR 6, 34; CDALBS; DA3; DLB 45, 63; MTCW 1, 2

Rao, Raja 1909- .... CLC 25, 56; DAM NOV
See See also CA 73-76; CANR 51; MTCW 1, 2

Raphael, Frederic (Michael) 1931- .. CLC 2, 14
See See also CA 1-4R; CANR 1, 86; DLB 14

Ratcliffe, James P.
See See Mencken, H(enry) L(ouis)

Rathbone, Julian 1935- .... CLC 41
See See also CA 101; CANR 34, 73

Rattigan, Terence (Mervyn) 1911-1977 . CLC 7; DAM DRAM
See See also CA 85-88; 73-76; CDBLB 1945-1960; DLB 13; MTCW 1, 2

Ratushinskaya, Irina 1954- .... CLC 54
See See also CA 129; CANR 68

Raven, Simon (Arthur Noel) 1927- . CLC 14
See See also CA 81-84; CANR 86

Ravenna, Michael
See See Welty, Eudora

Rawley, Callman 1903-
See See Rakosi, Carl
See See also CA 21-24R; CANR 12, 32

Rawlings, Marjorie Kinnan 1896-1953 .... TCLC 4
See See also AAYA 20; CA 104; 137; CANR 74; DLB 9, 22, 102; DLBD 17; JRDA; MAICYA; MTCW 2; SATA 100; YABC 1

Ray, Satyajit 1921-1992 . CLC 16, 76; DAM MULT
See See also CA 114; 137

Read, Herbert Edward 1893-1968 .... CLC 4
See See also CA 85-88; 25-28R; DLB 20, 149

Read, Piers Paul 1941- .... CLC 4, 10, 25
See See also CA 21-24R; CANR 38, 86; DLB 14; SATA 21

Reade, Charles 1814-1884 .... NCLC 2, 74
See See also DLB 21

Reade, Hamish
See See Gray, Simon (James Holliday)

Reading, Peter 1946- .... CLC 47
See See also CA 103; CANR 46; DLB 40

Reaney, James 1926- . CLC 13; DAC; DAM MST
See See also CA 41-44R; CAAS 15; CANR 42; DLB 68; SATA 43

Rebreanu, Liviu 1885-1944 .... TCLC 28
See See also CA 165

Rechy, John (Francisco) 1934- ..... CLC 1, 7, 14, 18, 107; DAM MULT; HLC 2
See See also CA 5-8R; CAAS 4; CANR 6, 32, 64; DLB 122; DLBY 82; HW 1, 2; INT CANR-6

Redcam, Tom 1870-1933 .... TCLC 25

Reddin, Keith .... CLC 67

Redgrove, Peter (William) 1932- . CLC 6, 41
See See also CA 1-4R; CANR 3, 39, 77; DLB 40

Redmon, Anne .... CLC 22
See See also Nightingale, Anne Redmon
See See also DLBY 86

Reed, Eliot
See See Ambler, Eric

Reed, Ishmael 1938- . CLC 2, 3, 5, 6, 13, 32, 60; BLC 3; DAM MULT
See See also BW 2, 3; CA 21-24R; CANR 25, 48, 74; DA3; DLB 2, 5, 33, 169; DLBD 8; MTCW 1, 2

Reed, John (Silas) 1887-1920 .... TCLC 9
See See also CA 106

Reed, Lou .... CLC 21
See See also Firbank, Louis

Reeve, Clara 1729-1807 .... NCLC 19
See See also DLB 39

Reich, Wilhelm 1897-1957 .... TCLC 57

Reid, Christopher (John) 1949- ...... CLC 33
See See also CA 140; DLB 40

Reid, Desmond
See See Moorcock, Michael (John)

Reid Banks, Lynne 1929-
See See Banks, Lynne Reid
See See also CA 1-4R; CANR 6, 22, 38; CLR 24; JRDA; MAICYA; SATA 22, 75, 111

Reilly, William K.
See See Creasey, John

Reiner, Max
See See Caldwell, (Janet Miriam) Taylor (Holland)

Reis, Ricardo
See See Pessoa, Fernando (Antonio Nogueira)

Remarque, Erich Maria 1898-1970 ..... CLC 21; DA; DAB; DAC; DAM MST, NOV
See See also AAYA 27; CA 77-80; 29-32R; DA3; DLB 56; MTCW 1, 2

Remington, Frederic 1861-1909 ... TCLC 89
See See also CA 108; 169; DLB 12, 186, 188; SATA 41

Remizov, A.
See See Remizov, Aleksei (Mikhailovich)

Remizov, A. M.
See See Remizov, Aleksei (Mikhailovich)

Remizov, Aleksei (Mikhailovich) 1877-1957 .... TCLC 27
See See also CA 125; 133

Renan, Joseph Ernest 1823-1892 . NCLC 26

Renard, Jules 1864-1910 .... TCLC 17
See See also CA 117

Renault, Mary .... CLC 3, 11, 17
See See also Challans, Mary
See See also DLBY 83; MTCW 2

Rendell, Ruth (Barbara) 1930- ...... CLC 28, 48; DAM POP
See See also Vine, Barbara
See See also CA 109; CANR 32, 52, 74; DLB 87; INT CANR-32; MTCW 1, 2

Renoir, Jean 1894-1979 .... CLC 20
See See also CA 129; 85-88

Resnais, Alain 1922- .... CLC 16

Reverdy, Pierre 1889-1960 .... CLC 53
See See also CA 97-100; 89-92

Rexroth, Kenneth 1905-1982 ... CLC 1, 2, 6, 11, 22, 49, 112; DAM POET; PC 20
See See also CA 5-8R; 107; CANR 14, 34, 63; CDALB 1941-1968; DLB 16, 48, 165, 212; DLBY 82; INT CANR-14; MTCW 1, 2

Reyes, Alfonso 1889-1959 . TCLC 33; HLCS 2
See See also CA 131; HW 1

Reyes y Basoalto, Ricardo Eliecer Neftali
See See Neruda, Pablo

Reymont, Wladyslaw (Stanislaw) 1868(?)-1925 .... TCLC 5
See See also CA 104

Reynolds, Jonathan 1942- .... CLC 6, 38
See See also CA 65-68; CANR 28

Reynolds, Joshua 1723-1792 .... LC 15

See See also DLB 104

Reynolds, Michael Shane 1937- ...... CLC 44
See See also CA 65-68; CANR 9

Reznikoff, Charles 1894-1976 .... CLC 9
See See also CA 33-36; 61-64; CAP 2; DLB 28, 45

Rezzori (d'Arezzo), Gregor von 1914-1998 . CLC 25
See See also CA 122; 136; 167

Rhine, Richard
See See Silverstein, Alvin

Rhodes, Eugene Manlove 1869-1934 . TCLC 53

Rhodius, Apollonius c. 3rd cent. B.C.- .... CMLC 28
See See also DLB 176

R'hoone
See See Balzac, Honore de

Rhys, Jean 1890(?)-1979 .... CLC 2, 4, 6, 14, 19, 51, 124; DAM NOV; SSC 21
See See also CA 25-28R; 85-88; CANR 35, 62; CDBLB 1945-1960; DA3; DLB 36, 117, 162; MTCW 1, 2

Ribeiro, Darcy 1922-1997 .... CLC 34
See See also CA 33-36R; 156

Ribeiro, Joao Ubaldo (Osorio Pimentel) 1941- .... CLC 10, 67
See See also CA 81-84

Ribman, Ronald (Burt) 1932- .... CLC 7
See See also CA 21-24R; CANR 46, 80

Ricci, Nino 1959- .... CLC 70
See See also CA 137

Rice, Anne 1941- .... CLC 41; DAM POP
See See also AAYA 9; BEST 89:2; CA 65-68; CANR 12, 36, 53, 74; DA3; MTCW 2

Rice, Elmer (Leopold) 1892-1967 .... CLC 7, 49; DAM DRAM
See See also CA 21-22; 25-28R; CAP 2; DLB 4, 7; MTCW 1, 2

Rice, Tim(othy Miles Bindon) 1944- .... CLC 21
See See also CA 103; CANR 46

Rich, Adrienne (Cecile) 1929- .. CLC 3, 6, 7, 11, 18, 36, 73, 76, 125; DAM POET; PC 5
See See also CA 9-12R; CANR 20, 53, 74; CDALBS; DA3; DLB 5, 67; MTCW 1, 2

Rich, Barbara
See See Graves, Robert (von Ranke)

Rich, Robert
See See Trumbo, Dalton

Richard, Keith .... CLC 17
See See also Richards, Keith

Richards, David Adams 1950- .... CLC 59; DAC
See See also CA 93-96; CANR 60; DLB 53

Richards, I(vor) A(rmstrong) 1893-1979 ..... CLC 14, 24
See See also CA 41-44R; 89-92; CANR 34, 74; DLB 27; MTCW 2

Richards, Keith 1943-
See See Richard, Keith
See See also CA 107; CANR 77

Richardson, Anne
See See Roiphe, Anne (Richardson)

Richardson, Dorothy Miller 1873-1957 .... TCLC 3
See See also CA 104; DLB 36

Richardson, Ethel Florence (Lindesay) 1870-1946
See See Richardson, Henry Handel
See See also CA 105

Richardson, Henry Handel .... TCLC 4
See See also Richardson, Ethel Florence (Lindesay)
See See also DLB 197

Richardson, John 1796-1852 .... NCLC 55; DAC

See See also CA 25-28R; CANR 23, 53

Roosevelt, Franklin Delano 1882-1945 .... **TCLC 93**
See See also CA 116; 173

Roosevelt, Theodore 1858-1919 .... **TCLC 69**
See See also CA 115; 170; DLB 47, 186

Roper, William 1498-1578 .... **LC 10**

Roquelaure, A. N.
See See Rice, Anne

Rosa, Joao Guimaraes 1908-1967 . **CLC 23; HLCS 1**
See See also CA 89-92; DLB 113

Rose, Wendy 1948- . **CLC 85; DAM MULT; PC 13**
See See also CA 53-56; CANR 5, 51; DLB 175; NNAL; SATA 12

Rosen, R. D.
See See Rosen, Richard (Dean)

Rosen, Richard (Dean) 1949- .... **CLC 39**
See See also CA 77-80; CANR 62; INT CANR-30

Rosenberg, Isaac 1890-1918 .... **TCLC 12**
See See also CA 107; DLB 20

Rosenblatt, Joe .... **CLC 15**
See See also Rosenblatt, Joseph

Rosenblatt, Joseph 1933-
See See Rosenblatt, Joe
See See also CA 89-92; INT 89-92

Rosenfeld, Samuel
See See Tzara, Tristan

Rosenstock, Sami
See See Tzara, Tristan

Rosenstock, Samuel
See See Tzara, Tristan

Rosenthal, M(acha) L(ouis) 1917-1996 . **CLC 28**
See See also CA 1-4R; 152; CAAS 6; CANR 4, 51; DLB 5; SATA 59

Ross, Barnaby
See See Dannay, Frederic

Ross, Bernard L.
See See Follett, Ken(neth Martin)

Ross, J. H.
See See Lawrence, T(homas) E(dward)

Ross, John Hume
See See Lawrence, T(homas) E(dward)

Ross, Martin
See See Martin, Violet Florence
See See also DLB 135

Ross, (James) Sinclair 1908-1996 .. **CLC 13; DAC; DAM MST; SSC 24**
See See also CA 73-76; CANR 81; DLB 88

Rossetti, Christina (Georgina) 1830-1894 ... **NCLC 2, 50, 66; DA; DAB; DAC; DAM MST, POET; PC 7; WLC**
See See also DA3; DLB 35, 163; MAICYA; SATA 20

Rossetti, Dante Gabriel 1828-1882 .... **NCLC 4, 77; DA; DAB; DAC; DAM MST, POET; WLC**
See See also CDBLB 1832-1890; DLB 35

Rossner, Judith (Perelman) 1935- .... **CLC 6, 9, 29**
See See also AITN 2; BEST 90:3; CA 17-20R; CANR 18, 51, 73; DLB 6; INT CANR-18; MTCW 1, 2

Rostand, Edmond (Eugene Alexis) 1868-1918 ...... **TCLC 6, 37; DA; DAB; DAC; DAM DRAM, MST; DC 10**
See See also CA 104; 126; DA3; DLB 192; MTCW 1

Roth, Henry 1906-1995 ... **CLC 2, 6, 11, 104**
See See also CA 11-12; 149; CANR 38, 63; CAP 1; DA3; DLB 28; MTCW 1, 2

Roth, Philip (Milton) 1933- . **CLC 1, 2, 3, 4, 6, 9, 15, 22, 31, 47, 66, 86, 119; DA; DAB; DAC; DAM MST, NOV, POP; SSC 26; WLC**

See See also BEST 90:3; CA 1-4R; CANR 1, 22, 36, 55; CDALB 1968-1988; DA3; DLB 2, 28, 173; DLBY 82; MTCW 1, 2

Rothenberg, Jerome 1931- .... **CLC 6, 57**
See See also CA 45-48; CANR 1; DLB 5, 193

Roumain, Jacques (Jean Baptiste) 1907-1944 .... **TCLC 19; BLC 3; DAM MULT**
See See also BW 1; CA 117; 125

Rourke, Constance (Mayfield) 1885-1941 ... **TCLC 12**
See See also CA 107; YABC 1

Rousseau, Jean-Baptiste 1671-1741 ..... **LC 9**

Rousseau, Jean-Jacques 1712-1778 .. **LC 14, 36; DA; DAB; DAC; DAM MST; WLC**
See See also DA3

Roussel, Raymond 1877-1933 .... **TCLC 20**
See See also CA 117

Rovit, Earl (Herbert) 1927- .... **CLC 7**
See See also CA 5-8R; CANR 12

Rowe, Elizabeth Singer 1674-1737 .... **LC 44**
See See also DLB 39, 95

Rowe, Nicholas 1674-1718 .... **LC 8**
See See also DLB 84

Rowley, Ames Dorrance
See See Lovecraft, H(oward) P(hillips)

Rowson, Susanna Haswell 1762(?)-1824 ...... **NCLC 5, 69**
See See also DLB 37, 200

Roy, Arundhati 1960(?)- .... **CLC 109**
See See also CA 163; DLBY 97

Roy, Gabrielle 1909-1983 .... **CLC 10, 14; DAB; DAC; DAM MST**
See See also CA 53-56; 110; CANR 5, 61; DLB 68; MTCW 1; SATA 104

Royko, Mike 1932-1997 .... **CLC 109**
See See also CA 89-92; 157; CANR 26

Rozewicz, Tadeusz 1921- . **CLC 9, 23; DAM POET**
See See also CA 108; CANR 36, 66; DA3; MTCW 1, 2

Ruark, Gibbons 1941- .... **CLC 3**
See See also CA 33-36R; CAAS 23; CANR 14, 31, 57; DLB 120

Rubens, Bernice (Ruth) 1923- .. **CLC 19, 31**
See See also CA 25-28R; CANR 33, 65; DLB 14, 207; MTCW 1

Rubin, Harold
See See Robbins, Harold

Rudkin, (James) David 1936- .... **CLC 14**
See See also CA 89-92; DLB 13

Rudnik, Raphael 1933- .... **CLC 7**
See See also CA 29-32R

Ruffian, M.
See See Hasek, Jaroslav (Matej Frantisek)

Ruiz, Jose Martinez .... **CLC 11**
See See also Martinez Ruiz, Jose

Rukeyser, Muriel 1913-1980 . **CLC 6, 10, 15, 27; DAM POET; PC 12**
See See also CA 5-8R; 93-96; CANR 26, 60; DA3; DLB 48; MTCW 1, 2; SATA-Obit 22

Rule, Jane (Vance) 1931- .... **CLC 27**
See See also CA 25-28R; CAAS 18; CANR 12; DLB 60

Rulfo, Juan 1918-1986 ..... **CLC 8, 80; DAM MULT; HLC 2; SSC 25**
See See also CA 85-88; 118; CANR 26; DLB 113; HW 1, 2; MTCW 1, 2

Rumi, Jalal al-Din 1297-1373 ...... **CMLC 20**

Runeberg, Johan 1804-1877 .... **NCLC 41**

Runyon, (Alfred) Damon 1884(?)-1946 .... **TCLC 10**
See See also CA 107; 165; DLB 11, 86, 171; MTCW 2

Rush, Norman 1933- .... **CLC 44**
See See also CA 121; 126; INT 126

Rushdie, (Ahmed) Salman 1947- ... **CLC 23,**

31, 55, 100; DAB; DAC; DAM MST, NOV, POP; WLCS
See See also BEST 89:3; CA 108; 111; CANR 33, 56; DA3; DLB 194; INT 111; MTCW 1, 2

Rushforth, Peter (Scott) 1945- .... **CLC 19**
See See also CA 101

Ruskin, John 1819-1900 .... **TCLC 63**
See See also CA 114; 129; CDBLB 1832-1890; DLB 55, 163, 190; SATA 24

Russ, Joanna 1937- .... **CLC 15**
See See also CANR 11, 31, 65; DLB 8; MTCW 1

Russell, George William 1867-1935
See See Baker, Jean H.
See See also CA 104; 153; CDBLB 1890-1914; DAM POET

Russell, (Henry) Ken(neth Alfred) 1927- ..... **CLC 16**
See See also CA 105

Russell, William Martin 1947- .... **CLC 60**
See See also CA 164

Rutherford, Mark .... **TCLC 25**
See See also White, William Hale
See See also DLB 18

Ruyslinck, Ward 1929- .... **CLC 14**
See See also Belser, Reimond Karel Maria de

Ryan, Cornelius (John) 1920-1974 ... **CLC 7**
See See also CA 69-72; 53-56; CANR 38

Ryan, Michael 1946- .... **CLC 65**
See See also CA 49-52; DLBY 82

Ryan, Tim
See See Dent, Lester

Rybakov, Anatoli (Naumovich) 1911-1998 .. **CLC 23, 53**
See See also CA 126; 135; 172; SATA 79; SATA-Obit 108

Ryder, Jonathan
See See Ludlum, Robert

Ryga, George 1932-1987 ...... **CLC 14; DAC; DAM MST**
See See also CA 101; 124; CANR 43; DLB 60

S. H.
See See Hartmann, Sadakichi

S. S.
See See Sassoon, Siegfried (Lorraine)

Saba, Umberto 1883-1957 .... **TCLC 33**
See See also CA 144; CANR 79; DLB 114

Sabatini, Rafael 1875-1950 .... **TCLC 47**
See See also CA 162

Sabato, Ernesto (R.) 1911- .... **CLC 10, 23; DAM MULT; HLC 2**
See See also CA 97-100; CANR 32, 65; DLB 145; HW 1, 2; MTCW 1, 2

Sa-Carniero, Mario de 1890-1916 ..... **TCLC 83**

Sacastru, Martin
See See Bioy Casares, Adolfo

Sacastru, Martin
See See Bioy Casares, Adolfo

Sacher-Masoch, Leopold von 1836(?)-1895 . **NCLC 31**

Sachs, Marilyn (Stickle) 1927- .... **CLC 35**
See See also AAYA 2; CA 17-20R; CANR 13, 47; CLR 2; JRDA; MAICYA; SAAS 2; SATA 3, 68; SATA-Essay 110

Sachs, Nelly 1891-1970 .... **CLC 14, 98**
See See also CA 17-18; 25-28R; CAP 2; MTCW 2

Sackler, Howard (Oliver) 1929-1982 ... **CLC 14**
See See also CA 61-64; 108; CANR 30; DLB 7

Sacks, Oliver (Wolf) 1933- .... **CLC 67**
See See also CA 53-56; CANR 28, 50, 76; DA3; INT CANR-28; MTCW 1, 2

Sadakichi
See See Hartmann, Sadakichi
Sade, Donatien Alphonse Francois, Comte de 1740-1814 .... **NCLC 47**
Sadoff, Ira 1945- .... **CLC 9**
See See also CA 53-56; CANR 5, 21; DLB 120
Saetone
See See Camus, Albert
Safire, William 1929- .... **CLC 10**
See See also CA 17-20R; CANR 31, 54
Sagan, Carl (Edward) 1934-1996 .. **CLC 30, 112**
See See also AAYA 2; CA 25-28R; 155; CANR 11, 36, 74; DA3; MTCW 1, 2; SATA 58; SATA-Obit 94
Sagan, Francoise .... **CLC 3, 6, 9, 17, 36**
See See also Quoirez, Francoise
See See also DLB 83; MTCW 2
Sahgal, Nayantara (Pandit) 1927- .. **CLC 41**
See See also CA 9-12R; CANR 11
Saint, H(arry) F. 1941- .... **CLC 50**
See See also CA 127
St. Aubin de Teran, Lisa 1953-
See See Teran, Lisa St. Aubin de
See See also CA 118; 126; INT 126
Saint Birgitta of Sweden c. 1303-1373 .... **CMLC 24**
Sainte-Beuve, Charles Augustin 1804-1869 . **NCLC 5**
Saint-Exupery, Antoine (Jean Baptiste Marie Roger) de 1900-1944 .. **TCLC 2, 56; DAM NOV; WLC**
See See also CA 108; 132; CLR 10; DA3; DLB 72; MAICYA; MTCW 1, 2; SATA 20
St. John, David
See See Hunt, E(verette) Howard, (Jr.)
Saint-John Perse
See See Leger, (Marie-Rene Auguste) Alexis Saint-Leger
Saintsbury, George (Edward Bateman) 1845-1933 .... **TCLC 31**
See See also CA 160; DLB 57, 149
Sait Faik .... **TCLC 23**
See See also Abasiyanik, Sait Faik
Saki .... **TCLC 3; SSC 12**
See See also Munro, H(ector) H(ugh)
See See also MTCW 2
Sala, George Augustus .... **NCLC 46**
Salama, Hannu 1936- .... **CLC 18**
Salamanca, J(ack) R(ichard) 1922- . **CLC 4, 15**
See See also CA 25-28R
Salas, Floyd Francis 1931-
See See also CA 119; CAAS 27; CANR 44, 75; DAM MULT; DLB 82; HLC 2; HW 1, 2; MTCW 2
Sale, J. Kirkpatrick
See See Sale, Kirkpatrick
Sale, Kirkpatrick 1937- .... **CLC 68**
See See also CA 13-16R; CANR 10
Salinas, Luis Omar 1937- .... **CLC 90; DAM MULT; HLC 2**
See See also CA 131; CANR 81; DLB 82; HW 1, 2
Salinas (y Serrano), Pedro 1891(?)-1951 ..... **TCLC 17**
See See also CA 117; DLB 134
Salinger, J(erome) D(avid) 1919- . **CLC 1, 3, 8, 12, 55, 56; DA; DAB; DAC; DAM MST, NOV, POP; SSC 2, 28; WLC**
See See also AAYA 2; CA 5-8R; CANR 39; CDALB 1941-1968; CLR 18; DA3; DLB 2, 102, 173; MAICYA; MTCW 1, 2; SATA 67
Salisbury, John
See See Caute, (John) David
Salter, James 1925- .... **CLC 7, 52, 59**

See See also CA 73-76; DLB 130
Saltus, Edgar (Everton) 1855-1921 . **TCLC 8**
See See also CA 105; DLB 202
Saltykov, Mikhail Evgrafovich 1826-1889 ... **NCLC 16**
Samarakis, Antonis 1919- .... **CLC 5**
See See also CA 25-28R; CAAS 16; CANR 36
Sanchez, Florencio 1875-1910 .... **TCLC 37**
See See also CA 153; HW 1
Sanchez, Luis Rafael 1936- .... **CLC 23**
See See also CA 128; DLB 145; HW 1
Sanchez, Sonia 1934- ... **CLC 5, 116; BLC 3; DAM MULT; PC 9**
See See also BW 2, 3; CA 33-36R; CANR 24, 49, 74; CLR 18; DA3; DLB 41; DLBD 8; MAICYA; MTCW 1, 2; SATA 22
Sand, George 1804-1876 ... **NCLC 2, 42, 57; DA; DAB; DAC; DAM MST, NOV; WLC**
See See also DA3; DLB 119, 192
Sandburg, Carl (August) 1878-1967 .... **CLC 1, 4, 10, 15, 35; DA; DAB; DAC; DAM MST, POET; PC 2; WLC**
See See also AAYA 24; CA 5-8R; 25-28R; CANR 35; CDALB 1865-1917; DA3; DLB 17, 54; MAICYA; MTCW 1, 2; SATA 8
Sandburg, Charles
See See Sandburg, Carl (August)
Sandburg, Charles A.
See See Sandburg, Carl (August)
Sanders, (James) Ed(ward) 1939- . **CLC 53; DAM POET**
See See also CA 13-16R; CAAS 21; CANR 13, 44, 78; DLB 16
Sanders, Lawrence 1920-1998 .... **CLC 41; DAM POP**
See See also BEST 89:4; CA 81-84; 165; CANR 33, 62; DA3; MTCW 1
Sanders, Noah
See See Blount, Roy (Alton), Jr.
Sanders, Winston P.
See See Anderson, Poul (William)
Sandoz, Mari(e Susette) 1896-1966 . **CLC 28**
See See also CA 1-4R; 25-28R; CANR 17, 64; DLB 9, 212; MTCW 1, 2; SATA 5
Saner, Reg(inald Anthony) 1931- ...... **CLC 9**
See See also CA 65-68
Sankara 788-820 .... **CMLC 32**
Sannazaro, Jacopo 1456(?)-1530 .... **LC 8**
Sansom, William 1912-1976 .... **CLC 2, 6; DAM NOV; SSC 21**
See See also CA 5-8R; 65-68; CANR 42; DLB 139; MTCW 1
Santayana, George 1863-1952 .... **TCLC 40**
See See also CA 115; DLB 54, 71; DLBD 13
Santiago, Danny .... **CLC 33**
See See also James, Daniel (Lewis)
See See also DLB 122
Santmyer, Helen Hoover 1895-1986 ..... **CLC 33**
See See also CA 1-4R; 118; CANR 15, 33; DLBY 84; MTCW 1
Santoka, Taneda 1882-1940 .... **TCLC 72**
Santos, Bienvenido N(uqui) 1911-1996 . **CLC 22; DAM MULT**
See See also CA 101; 151; CANR 19, 46
Sapper .... **TCLC 44**
See See also McNeile, Herman Cyril
Sapphire
See See Sapphire, Brenda
Sapphire, Brenda 1950- .... **CLC 99**
Sappho fl. 6th cent. B.C.- .... **CMLC 3; DAM POET; PC 5**
See See also DA3; DLB 176

Saramago, Jose 1922- .... **CLC 119; HLCS 1**
See See also CA 153
Sarduy, Severo 1937-1993 .... **CLC 6, 97; HLCS 1**
See See also CA 89-92; 142; CANR 58, 81; DLB 113; HW 1, 2
Sargeson, Frank 1903-1982 .... **CLC 31**
See See also CA 25-28R; 106; CANR 38, 79
Sarmiento, Domingo Faustino 1811-1888
See See also HLCS 2
Sarmiento, Felix Ruben Garcia
See See Dario, Ruben
Saro-Wiwa, Ken(ule Beeson) 1941-1995 ...... **CLC 114**
See See also BW 2; CA 142; 150; CANR 60; DLB 157
Saroyan, William 1908-1981 .. **CLC 1, 8, 10, 29, 34, 56; DA; DAB; DAC; DAM DRAM, MST, NOV; SSC 21; WLC**
See See also CA 5-8R; 103; CANR 30; CDALBS; DA3; DLB 7, 9, 86; DLBY 81; MTCW 1, 2; SATA 23; SATA-Obit 24
Sarraute, Nathalie 1900- . **CLC 1, 2, 4, 8, 10, 31, 80**
See See also CA 9-12R; CANR 23, 66; DLB 83; MTCW 1, 2
Sarton, (Eleanor) May 1912-1995 .... **CLC 4, 14, 49, 91; DAM POET**
See See also CA 1-4R; 149; CANR 1, 34, 55; DLB 48; DLBY 81; INT CANR-34; MTCW 1, 2; SATA 36; SATA-Obit 86
Sartre, Jean-Paul 1905-1980 .... **CLC 1, 4, 7, 9, 13, 18, 24, 44, 50, 52; DA; DAB; DAC; DAM DRAM, MST, NOV; DC 3; SSC 32; WLC**
See See also CA 9-12R; 97-100; CANR 21; DA3; DLB 72; MTCW 1, 2
Sassoon, Siegfried (Lorraine) 1886-1967 ...... **CLC 36; DAB; DAM MST, NOV, POET; PC 12**
See See also CA 104; 25-28R; CANR 36; DLB 20, 191; DLBD 18; MTCW 1, 2
Satterfield, Charles
See See Pohl, Frederik
Saul, John (W. III) 1942- ..... **CLC 46; DAM NOV, POP**
See See also AAYA 10; BEST 90:4; CA 81-84; CANR 16, 40, 81; SATA 98
Saunders, Caleb
See See Heinlein, Robert A(nson)
Saura (Atares), Carlos 1932- .... **CLC 20**
See See also CA 114; 131; CANR 79; HW 1
Sauser-Hall, Frederic 1887-1961 ..... **CLC 18**
See See also Cendrars, Blaise
See See also CA 102; 93-96; CANR 36, 62; MTCW 1
Saussure, Ferdinand de 1857-1913 ... **TCLC 49**
Savage, Catharine
See See Brosman, Catharine Savage
Savage, Thomas 1915- .... **CLC 40**
See See also CA 126; 132; CAAS 15; INT 132
Savan, Glenn 19(?)- .... **CLC 50**
Sayers, Dorothy L(eigh) 1893-1957 ... **TCLC 2, 15; DAM POP**
See See also CA 104; 119; CANR 60; CDBLB 1914-1945; DLB 10, 36, 77, 100; MTCW 1, 2
Sayers, Valerie 1952- .... **CLC 50, 122**
See See also CA 134; CANR 61
Sayles, John (Thomas) 1950- . **CLC 7, 10, 14**
See See also CA 57-60; CANR 41, 84; DLB 44
Scammell, Michael 1935- .... **CLC 34**
See See also CA 156
Scannell, Vernon 1922- .... **CLC 49**

Smith, David (Jeddie) 1942-
See See Smith, Dave
See See also CA 49-52; CANR 1, 59; DAM POET

Smith, Florence Margaret 1902-1971
See See Smith, Stevie
See See also CA 17-18; 29-32R; CANR 35; CAP 2; DAM POET; MTCW 1, 2

Smith, Iain Crichton 1928-1998 ...... CLC 64
See See also CA 21-24R; 171; DLB 40, 139

Smith, John 1580(?)-1631 .... LC 9
See See also DLB 24, 30

Smith, Johnston
See See Crane, Stephen (Townley)

Smith, Joseph, Jr. 1805-1844 .... NCLC 53

Smith, Lee 1944- .... CLC 25, 73
See See also CA 114; 119; CANR 46; DLB 143; DLBY 83; INT 119

Smith, Martin
See See Smith, Martin Cruz

Smith, Martin Cruz 1942- ... CLC 25; DAM MULT, POP
See See also BEST 89:4; CA 85-88; CANR 6, 23, 43, 65; INT CANR-23; MTCW 2; NNAL

Smith, Mary-Ann Tirone 1944- ...... CLC 39
See See also CA 118; 136

Smith, Patti 1946- .... CLC 12
See See also CA 93-96; CANR 63

Smith, Pauline (Urmson) 1882-1959 . TCLC 25

Smith, Rosamond
See See Oates, Joyce Carol

Smith, Sheila Kaye
See See Kaye-Smith, Sheila

Smith, Stevie .... CLC 3, 8, 25, 44; PC 12
See See also Smith, Florence Margaret
See See also DLB 20; MTCW 2

Smith, Wilbur (Addison) 1933- .... CLC 33
See See also CA 13-16R; CANR 7, 46, 66; MTCW 1, 2

Smith, William Jay 1918- .... CLC 6
See See also CA 5-8R; CANR 44; DLB 5; MAICYA; SAAS 22; SATA 2, 68

Smith, Woodrow Wilson
See See Kuttner, Henry

Smolenskin, Peretz 1842-1885 ...... NCLC 30

Smollett, Tobias (George) 1721-1771 .. LC 2, 46
See See also CDBLB 1660-1789; DLB 39, 104

Snodgrass, W(illiam) D(e Witt) 1926- . CLC 2, 6, 10, 18, 68; DAM POET
See See also CA 1-4R; CANR 6, 36, 65, 85; DLB 5; MTCW 1, 2

Snow, C(harles) P(ercy) 1905-1980 .. CLC 1, 4, 6, 9, 13, 19; DAM NOV
See See also CA 5-8R; 101; CANR 28; CD-BLB 1945-1960; DLB 15, 77; DLBD 17; MTCW 1, 2

Snow, Frances Compton
See See Adams, Henry (Brooks)

Snyder, Gary (Sherman) 1930- .... CLC 1, 2, 5, 9, 32, 120; DAM POET; PC 21
See See also CA 17-20R; CANR 30, 60; DA3; DLB 5, 16, 165, 212; MTCW 2

Snyder, Zilpha Keatley 1927- .... CLC 17
See See also AAYA 15; CA 9-12R; CANR 38; CLR 31; JRDA; MAICYA; SAAS 2; SATA 1, 28, 75, 110

Soares, Bernardo
See See Pessoa, Fernando (Antonio Nogueira)

Sobh, A.
See See Shamlu, Ahmad

Sobol, Joshua .... CLC 60

Socrates 469B.C.-399B.C. .... CMLC 27

Soderberg, Hjalmar 1869-1941 .... TCLC 39

Sodergran, Edith (Irene)
See See Soedergran, Edith (Irene)

Soedergran, Edith (Irene) 1892-1923 . TCLC 31

Softly, Edgar
See See Lovecraft, H(oward) P(hillips)

Softly, Edward
See See Lovecraft, H(oward) P(hillips)

Sokolov, Raymond 1941- .... CLC 7
See See also CA 85-88

Solo, Jay
See See Ellison, Harlan (Jay)

Sologub, Fyodor .... TCLC 9
See See also Teternikov, Fyodor Kuzmich

Solomons, Ikey Esquir
See See Thackeray, William Makepeace

Solomos, Dionysios 1798-1857 ...... NCLC 15

Solwoska, Mara
See See French, Marilyn

Solzhenitsyn, Aleksandr I(sayevich) 1918- .. CLC 1, 2, 4, 7, 9, 10, 18, 26, 34, 78; DA; DAB; DAC; DAM MST, NOV; SSC 32; WLC
See See also AITN 1; CA 69-72; CANR 40, 65; DA3; MTCW 1, 2

Somers, Jane
See See Lessing, Doris (May)

Somerville, Edith 1858-1949 .... TCLC 51
See See also DLB 135

Somerville & Ross
See See Martin, Violet Florence; Somerville, Edith

Sommer, Scott 1951- .... CLC 25
See See also CA 106

Sondheim, Stephen (Joshua) 1930- ...... CLC 30, 39; DAM DRAM
See See also AAYA 11; CA 103; CANR 47, 68

Song, Cathy 1955- .... PC 21
See See also CA 154; DLB 169

Sontag, Susan 1933- ... CLC 1, 2, 10, 13, 31, 105; DAM POP
See See also CA 17-20R; CANR 25, 51, 74; DA3; DLB 2, 67; MTCW 1, 2

Sophocles 496(?)B.C.-406(?)B.C. .. CMLC 2; DA; DAB; DAC; DAM DRAM, MST; DC 1; WLCS
See See also DA3; DLB 176

Sordello 1189-1269 .... CMLC 15

Sorel, Georges 1847-1922 .... TCLC 91
See See also CA 118

Sorel, Julia
See See Drexler, Rosalyn

Sorrentino, Gilbert 1929- . CLC 3, 7, 14, 22, 40
See See also CA 77-80; CANR 14, 33; DLB 5, 173; DLBY 80; INT CANR-14

Soto, Gary 1952- . CLC 32, 80; DAM MULT; HLC 2; PC 28
See See also AAYA 10; CA 119; 125; CANR 50, 74; CLR 38; DLB 82; HW 1, 2; INT 125; JRDA; MTCW 2; SATA 80

Soupault, Philippe 1897-1990 .... CLC 68
See See also CA 116; 147; 131

Souster, (Holmes) Raymond 1921- .. CLC 5, 14; DAC; DAM POET
See See also CA 13-16R; CAAS 14; CANR 13, 29, 53; DA3; DLB 88; SATA 63

Southern, Terry 1924(?)-1995 .... CLC 7
See See also CA 1-4R; 150; CANR 1, 55; DLB 2

Southey, Robert 1774-1843 .... NCLC 8
See See also DLB 93, 107, 142; SATA 54

Southworth, Emma Dorothy Eliza Nevitte 1819-1899 .... NCLC 26

Souza, Ernest
See See Scott, Evelyn

Soyinka, Wole 1934- .. CLC 3, 5, 14, 36, 44; BLC 3; DA; DAB; DAC; DAM DRAM, MST, MULT; DC 2; WLC
See See also BW 2, 3; CA 13-16R; CANR 27, 39, 82; DA3; DLB 125; MTCW 1, 2

Spackman, W(illiam) M(ode) 1905-1990 ..... CLC 46
See See also CA 81-84; 132

Spacks, Barry (Bernard) 1931- .... CLC 14
See See also CA 154; CANR 33; DLB 105

Spanidou, Irini 1946- .... CLC 44

Spark, Muriel (Sarah) 1918- ... CLC 2, 3, 5, 8, 13, 18, 40, 94; DAB; DAC; DAM MST, NOV; SSC 10
See See also CA 5-8R; CANR 12, 36, 76; CDBLB 1945-1960; DA3; DLB 15, 139; INT CANR-12; MTCW 1, 2

Spaulding, Douglas
See See Bradbury, Ray (Douglas)

Spaulding, Leonard
See See Bradbury, Ray (Douglas)

Spence, J. A. D.
See See Eliot, T(homas) S(tearns)

Spencer, Elizabeth 1921- .... CLC 22
See See also CA 13-16R; CANR 32, 65; DLB 6; MTCW 1; SATA 14

Spencer, Leonard G.
See See Silverberg, Robert

Spencer, Scott 1945- .... CLC 30
See See also CA 113; CANR 51; DLBY 86

Spender, Stephen (Harold) 1909-1995 . CLC 1, 2, 5, 10, 41, 91; DAM POET
See See also CA 9-12R; 149; CANR 31, 54; CDBLB 1945-1960; DA3; DLB 20; MTCW 1, 2

Spengler, Oswald (Arnold Gottfried) 1880-1936 .... TCLC 25
See See also CA 118

Spenser, Edmund 1552(?)-1599 .... LC 5, 39; DA; DAB; DAC; DAM MST, POET; PC 8; WLC
See See also CDBLB Before 1660; DA3; DLB 167

Spicer, Jack 1925-1965 .... CLC 8, 18, 72; DAM POET
See See also CA 85-88; DLB 5, 16, 193

Spiegelman, Art 1948- .... CLC 76
See See also AAYA 10; CA 125; CANR 41, 55, 74; MTCW 2; SATA 109

Spielberg, Peter 1929- .... CLC 6
See See also CA 5-8R; CANR 4, 48; DLBY 81

Spielberg, Steven 1947- .... CLC 20
See See also AAYA 8, 24; CA 77-80; CANR 32; SATA 32

Spillane, Frank Morrison 1918-
See See Spillane, Mickey
See See also CA 25-28R; CANR 28, 63; DA3; MTCW 1, 2; SATA 66

Spillane, Mickey .... CLC 3, 13
See See also Spillane, Frank Morrison
See See also MTCW 2

Spinoza, Benedictus de 1632-1677 .... LC 9

Spinrad, Norman (Richard) 1940- . CLC 46
See See also CA 37-40R; CAAS 19; CANR 20; DLB 8; INT CANR-20

Spitteler, Carl (Friedrich Georg) 1845-1924 .... TCLC 12
See See also CA 109; DLB 129

Spivack, Kathleen (Romola Drucker) 1938- .... CLC 6
See See also CA 49-52

Spoto, Donald 1941- .... CLC 39
See See also CA 65-68; CANR 11, 57

Springsteen, Bruce (F.) 1949- .... CLC 17
See See also CA 111

Spurling, Hilary 1940- .... CLC 34
See See also CA 104; CANR 25, 52

See See also CA 104; 131; HW 1

Stoughton, William 1631-1701 .... **LC 38**
See See also DLB 24

Stout, Rex (Todhunter) 1886-1975 .... **CLC 3**
See See also AITN 2; CA 61-64; CANR 71

Stow, (Julian) Randolph 1935- . **CLC 23, 48**
See See also CA 13-16R; CANR 33;
MTCW 1

Stowe, Harriet (Elizabeth) Beecher
1811-1896 ...... **NCLC 3, 50; DA; DAB;
DAC; DAM MST, NOV; WLC**
See See also CDALB 1865-1917; DA3;
DLB 1, 12, 42, 74, 189; JRDA; MAICYA;
YABC 1

Strabo c. 64B.C.-c. 25 .... **CMLC 37**
See See also DLB 176

Strachey, (Giles) Lytton 1880-1932 ... **TCLC
12**
See See also CA 110; 178; DLB 149; DLBD
10; MTCW 2

Strand, Mark 1934- .... **CLC 6, 18, 41, 71;
DAM POET**
See See also CA 21-24R; CANR 40, 65;
DLB 5; SATA 41

Straub, Peter (Francis) 1943- . **CLC 28, 107;
DAM POP**
See See also BEST 89:1; CA 85-88; CANR
28, 65; DLBY 84; MTCW 1, 2

Strauss, Botho 1944- .... **CLC 22**
See See also CA 157; DLB 124

Streatfeild, (Mary) Noel 1895(?)-1986 . **CLC
21**
See See also CA 81-84; 120; CANR 31;
CLR 17; DLB 160; MAICYA; SATA 20;
SATA-Obit 48

Stribling, T(homas) S(igismund) 1881-1965
.... **CLC 23**
See See also CA 107; DLB 9

Strindberg, (Johan) August 1849-1912 ....
**TCLC 1, 8, 21, 47; DA; DAB; DAC;
DAM DRAM, MST; WLC**
See See also CA 104; 135; DA3; MTCW 2

Stringer, Arthur 1874-1950 .... **TCLC 37**
See See also CA 161; DLB 92

Stringer, David
See See Roberts, Keith (John Kingston)

Stroheim, Erich von 1885-1957 .... **TCLC 71**

Strugatskii, Arkadii (Natanovich) 1925-1991
.... **CLC 27**
See See also CA 106; 135

Strugatskii, Boris (Natanovich) 1933- . **CLC
27**
See See also CA 106

Strummer, Joe 1953(?)- .... **CLC 30**

Strunk, William, Jr. 1869-1946 .... **TCLC 92**
See See also CA 118; 164

Stryk, Lucien 1924- .... **PC 27**
See See also CA 13-16R; CANR 10, 28, 55

Stuart, Don A.
See See Campbell, John W(ood, Jr.)

Stuart, Ian
See See MacLean, Alistair (Stuart)

Stuart, Jesse (Hilton) 1906-1984 .. **CLC 1, 8,
11, 14, 34; SSC 31**
See See also CA 5-8R; 112; CANR 31;
DLB 9, 48, 102; DLBY 84; SATA 2;
SATA-Obit 36

Sturgeon, Theodore (Hamilton) 1918-1985 .
CLC 22, 39
See See also Queen, Ellery
See See also CA 81-84; 116; CANR 32;
DLB 8; DLBY 85; MTCW 1, 2

Sturges, Preston 1898-1959 .... **TCLC 48**
See See also CA 114; 149; DLB 26

Styron, William 1925- .. **CLC 1, 3, 5, 11, 15,
60; DAM NOV, POP; SSC 25**

See See also BEST 90:4; CA 5-8R; CANR
6, 33, 74; CDALB 1968-1988; DA3; DLB
2, 143; DLBY 80; INT CANR-6; MTCW
1, 2

Su, Chien 1884-1918
See See Su Man-shu
See See also CA 123

Suarez Lynch, B.
See See Bioy Casares, Adolfo; Borges,
Jorge Luis

Suassuna, Ariano Vilar 1927-
See See also CA 178; HLCS 1; HW 2

Suckow, Ruth 1892-1960 .... **SSC 18**
See See also CA 113; DLB 9, 102

Sudermann, Hermann 1857-1928 . **TCLC 15**
See See also CA 107; DLB 118

Sue, Eugene 1804-1857 .... **NCLC 1**
See See also DLB 119

Sueskind, Patrick 1949- .... **CLC 44**
See See also Suskind, Patrick

Sukenick, Ronald 1932- ...... **CLC 3, 4, 6, 48**
See See also CA 25-28R; CAAS 8; CANR
32; DLB 173; DLBY 81

Suknaski, Andrew 1942- .... **CLC 19**
See See also CA 101; DLB 53

Sullivan, Vernon
See See Vian, Boris

Sully Prudhomme 1839-1907 .... **TCLC 31**

Su Man-shu .... **TCLC 24**
See See also Su, Chien

Summerforest, Ivy B.
See See Kirkup, James

Summers, Andrew James 1942- ...... **CLC 26**

Summers, Andy
See See Summers, Andrew James

Summers, Hollis (Spurgeon, Jr.) 1916- . **CLC
10**
See See also CA 5-8R; CANR 3; DLB 6

**Summers, (Alphonsus Joseph-Mary
Augustus) Montague** 1880-1948 ....
TCLC 16
See See also CA 118; 163

Sumner, Gordon Matthew .... **CLC 26**
See See also Sting

Surtees, Robert Smith 1803-1864 . **NCLC 14**
See See also DLB 21

Susann, Jacqueline 1921-1974 .... **CLC 3**
See See also AITN 1; CA 65-68; 53-56;
MTCW 1, 2

Su Shih 1036-1101 .... **CMLC 15**

Suskind, Patrick
See See Sueskind, Patrick
See See also CA 145

Sutcliff, Rosemary 1920-1992 .... **CLC 26;
DAB; DAC; DAM MST, POP**
See See also AAYA 10; CA 5-8R; 139;
CANR 37; CLR 1, 37; JRDA; MAICYA;
SATA 6, 44, 78; SATA-Obit 73

Sutro, Alfred 1863-1933 .... **TCLC 6**
See See also CA 105; DLB 10

Sutton, Henry
See See Slavitt, David R(ytman)

Svevo, Italo 1861-1928 .... **TCLC 2, 35; SSC
25**
See See also Schmitz, Aron Hector

Swados, Elizabeth (A.) 1951- .... **CLC 12**
See See also CA 97-100; CANR 49; INT
97-100

Swados, Harvey 1920-1972 .... **CLC 5**
See See also CA 5-8R; 37-40R; CANR 6;
DLB 2

Swan, Gladys 1934- .... **CLC 69**
See See also CA 101; CANR 17, 39

Swarthout, Glendon (Fred) 1918-1992 . **CLC
35**
See See also CA 1-4R; 139; CANR 1, 47;
SATA 26

Sweet, Sarah C.
See See Jewett, (Theodora) Sarah Orne

Swenson, May 1919-1989 ..... **CLC 4, 14, 61,
106; DA; DAB; DAC; DAM MST,
POET; PC 14**
See See also CA 5-8R; 130; CANR 36, 61;
DLB 5; MTCW 1, 2; SATA 15

Swift, Augustus
See See Lovecraft, H(oward) P(hillips)

Swift, Graham (Colin) 1949- .... **CLC 41, 88**
See See also CA 117; 122; CANR 46, 71;
DLB 194; MTCW 2

Swift, Jonathan 1667-1745 ... **LC 1, 42; DA;
DAB; DAC; DAM MST, NOV, POET;
PC 9; WLC**
See See also CDBLB 1660-1789; CLR 53;
DA3; DLB 39, 95, 101; SATA 19

Swinburne, Algernon Charles 1837-1909 ....
**TCLC 8, 36; DA; DAB; DAC; DAM
MST, POET; PC 24; WLC**
See See also CA 105; 140; CDBLB 1832-
1890; DA3; DLB 35, 57

Swinfen, Ann .... **CLC 34**

Swinnerton, Frank Arthur 1884-1982 . **CLC
31**
See See also CA 108; DLB 34

Swithen, John
See See King, Stephen (Edwin)

Sylvia
See See Ashton-Warner, Sylvia (Constance)

Symmes, Robert Edward
See See Duncan, Robert (Edward)

Symonds, John Addington 1840-1893 ....
NCLC 34
See See also DLB 57, 144

Symons, Arthur 1865-1945 .... **TCLC 11**
See See also CA 107; DLB 19, 57, 149

Symons, Julian (Gustave) 1912-1994 ... **CLC
2, 14, 32**
See See also CA 49-52; 147; CAAS 3;
CANR 3, 33, 59; DLB 87, 155; DLBY
92; MTCW 1

Synge, (Edmund) J(ohn) M(illington)
1871-1909 . **TCLC 6, 37; DAM DRAM;
DC 2**
See See also CA 104; 141; CDBLB 1890-
1914; DLB 10, 19

Syruc, J.
See See Milosz, Czeslaw

Szirtes, George 1948- .... **CLC 46**
See See also CA 109; CANR 27, 61

Szymborska, Wislawa 1923- .... **CLC 99**
See See also CA 154; DA3; DLBY 96;
MTCW 2

T. O., Nik
See See Annensky, Innokenty (Fyodorovich)

Tabori, George 1914- .... **CLC 19**
See See also CA 49-52; CANR 4, 69

Tagore, Rabindranath 1861-1941 .. **TCLC 3,
53; DAM DRAM, POET; PC 8**
See See also CA 104; 120; DA3; MTCW 1,
2

Taine, Hippolyte Adolphe 1828-1893 . **NCLC
15**

Talese, Gay 1932- .... **CLC 37**
See See also AITN 1; CA 1-4R; CANR 9,
58; DLB 185; INT CANR-9; MTCW 1, 2

Tallent, Elizabeth (Ann) 1954- ...... **CLC 45**
See See also CA 117; CANR 72; DLB 130

Tally, Ted 1952- .... **CLC 42**
See See also CA 120; 124; INT 124

Talvik, Heiti 1904-1947 .... **TCLC 87**

Tamayo y Baus, Manuel 1829-1898 .. **NCLC
1**

Tammsaare, A(nton) H(ansen) 1878-1940 ...
TCLC 27
See See also CA 164

Thomson, James 1700-1748 .. **LC 16, 29, 40; DAM POET**
See See also DLB 95

Thomson, James 1834-1882 .... **NCLC 18; DAM POET**
See See also DLB 35

Thoreau, Henry David 1817-1862 . **NCLC 7, 21, 61; DA; DAB; DAC; DAM MST; WLC**
See See also CDALB 1640-1865; DA3; DLB 1

Thornton, Hall
See See Silverberg, Robert

Thucydides c. 455B.C.-399B.C. ... **CMLC 17**
See See also DLB 176

Thurber, James (Grover) 1894-1961 ... **CLC 5, 11, 25, 125; DA; DAB; DAC; DAM DRAM, MST, NOV; SSC 1**
See See also CA 73-76; CANR 17, 39; CDALB 1929-1941; DA3; DLB 4, 11, 22, 102; MAICYA; MTCW 1, 2; SATA 13

Thurman, Wallace (Henry) 1902-1934 .... **TCLC 6; BLC 3; DAM MULT**
See See also BW 1, 3; CA 104; 124; CANR 81; DLB 51

Tibullus, Albius c. 54B.C.-c. 19B.C. . **CMLC 36**
See See also DLB 211

Ticheburn, Cheviot
See See Ainsworth, William Harrison

Tieck, (Johann) Ludwig 1773-1853 ... **NCLC 5, 46; SSC 31**
See See also DLB 90

Tiger, Derry
See See Ellison, Harlan (Jay)

Tilghman, Christopher 1948(?)- ...... **CLC 65**
See See also CA 159

Tillinghast, Richard (Williford) 1940- . **CLC 29**
See See also CA 29-32R; CAAS 23; CANR 26, 51

Timrod, Henry 1828-1867 .... **NCLC 25**
See See also DLB 3

Tindall, Gillian (Elizabeth) 1938- ..... **CLC 7**
See See also CA 21-24R; CANR 11, 65

Tiptree, James, Jr. .... **CLC 48, 50**
See See also Sheldon, Alice Hastings Bradley
See See also DLB 8

Titmarsh, Michael Angelo
See See Thackeray, William Makepeace

Tocqueville, Alexis (Charles Henri Maurice Clerel, Comte) de 1805-1859 . **NCLC 7, 63**

Tolkien, J(ohn) R(onald) R(euel) 1892-1973 .... **CLC 1, 2, 3, 8, 12, 38; DA; DAB; DAC; DAM MST, NOV, POP; WLC**
See See also AAYA 10; AITN 1; CA 17-18; 45-48; CANR 36; CAP 2; CDBLB 1914-1945; CLR 56; DA3; DLB 15, 160; JRDA; MAICYA; MTCW 1, 2; SATA 2, 32, 100; SATA-Obit 24

Toller, Ernst 1893-1939 .... **TCLC 10**
See See also CA 107; DLB 124

Tolson, M. B.
See See Tolson, Melvin B(eaunorus)

Tolson, Melvin B(eaunorus) 1898(?)-1966 ... **CLC 36, 105; BLC 3; DAM MULT, POET**
See See also BW 1, 3; CA 124; 89-92; CANR 80; DLB 48, 76

Tolstoi, Aleksei Nikolaevich
See See Tolstoy, Alexey Nikolaevich

Tolstoy, Alexey Nikolaevich 1882-1945 .... **TCLC 18**
See See also CA 107; 158

Tolstoy, Count Leo
See See Tolstoy, Leo (Nikolaevich)

Tolstoy, Leo (Nikolaevich) 1828-1910 . **TCLC 4, 11, 17, 28, 44, 79; DA; DAB; DAC; DAM MST, NOV; SSC 9, 30; WLC**
See See also CA 104; 123; DA3; SATA 26

Tomasi di Lampedusa, Giuseppe 1896-1957
See See Lampedusa, Giuseppe (Tomasi) di
See See also CA 111

Tomlin, Lily .... **CLC 17**
See See also Tomlin, Mary Jean

Tomlin, Mary Jean 1939(?)-
See See Tomlin, Lily
See See also CA 117

Tomlinson, (Alfred) Charles 1927- .. **CLC 2, 4, 6, 13, 45; DAM POET; PC 17**
See See also CA 5-8R; CANR 33; DLB 40

Tomlinson, H(enry) M(ajor) 1873-1958 .... **TCLC 71**
See See also CA 118; 161; DLB 36, 100, 195

Tonson, Jacob
See See Bennett, (Enoch) Arnold

Toole, John Kennedy 1937-1969 .... **CLC 19, 64**
See See also CA 104; DLBY 81; MTCW 2

Toomer, Jean 1894-1967 .. **CLC 1, 4, 13, 22; BLC 3; DAM MULT; PC 7; SSC 1; WLCS**
See See also BW 1; CA 85-88; CDALB 1917-1929; DA3; DLB 45, 51; MTCW 1, 2

Torley, Luke
See See Blish, James (Benjamin)

Tornimparte, Alessandra
See See Ginzburg, Natalia

Torre, Raoul della
See See Mencken, H(enry) L(ouis)

Torrence, Ridgely 1874-1950 .... **TCLC 97**
See See also DLB 54

Torrey, E(dwin) Fuller 1937- .... **CLC 34**
See See also CA 119; CANR 71

Torsvan, Ben Traven
See See Traven, B.

Torsvan, Benno Traven
See See Traven, B.

Torsvan, Berick Traven
See See Traven, B.

Torsvan, Berwick Traven
See See Traven, B.

Torsvan, Bruno Traven
See See Traven, B.

Torsvan, Traven
See See Traven, B.

Tournier, Michel (Edouard) 1924- ... **CLC 6, 23, 36, 95**
See See also CA 49-52; CANR 3, 36, 74; DLB 83; MTCW 1, 2; SATA 23

Tournimparte, Alessandra
See See Ginzburg, Natalia

Towers, Ivar
See See Kornbluth, C(yril) M.

Towne, Robert (Burton) 1936(?)- .... **CLC 87**
See See also CA 108; DLB 44

Townsend, Sue .... **CLC 61**
See See also Townsend, Susan Elaine
See See also AAYA 28; SATA 55, 93; SATA-Brief 48

Townsend, Susan Elaine 1946-
See See Townsend, Sue
See See also CA 119; 127; CANR 65; DAB; DAC; DAM MST

Townshend, Peter (Dennis Blandford) 1945- .... **CLC 17, 42**
See See also CA 107

Tozzi, Federigo 1883-1920 .... **TCLC 31**
See See also CA 160

Traill, Catharine Parr 1802-1899 . **NCLC 31**
See See also DLB 99

Trakl, Georg 1887-1914 ..... **TCLC 5; PC 20**
See See also CA 104; 165; MTCW 2

Transtroemer, Tomas (Goesta) 1931- ... **CLC 52, 65; DAM POET**
See See also CA 117; 129; CAAS 17

Transtromer, Tomas Gosta
See See Transtroemer, Tomas (Goesta)

Traven, B. (?)-1969 .... **CLC 8, 11**
See See also CA 19-20; 25-28R; CAP 2; DLB 9, 56; MTCW 1

Treitel, Jonathan 1959- .... **CLC 70**

Tremain, Rose 1943- .... **CLC 42**
See See also CA 97-100; CANR 44; DLB 14

Tremblay, Michel 1942- .... **CLC 29, 102; DAC; DAM MST**
See See also CA 116; 128; DLB 60; MTCW 1, 2

Trevanian .... **CLC 29**
See See also Whitaker, Rod(ney)

Trevor, Glen
See See Hilton, James

Trevor, William 1928- . **CLC 7, 9, 14, 25, 71, 116; SSC 21**
See See also Cox, William Trevor
See See also DLB 14, 139; MTCW 2

Trifonov, Yuri (Valentinovich) 1925-1981 .... **CLC 45**
See See also CA 126; 103; MTCW 1

Trilling, Lionel 1905-1975 ..... **CLC 9, 11, 24**
See See also CA 9-12R; 61-64; CANR 10; DLB 28, 63; INT CANR-10; MTCW 1, 2

Trimball, W. H.
See See Mencken, H(enry) L(ouis)

Tristan
See See Gomez de la Serna, Ramon

Tristram
.. See See Housman, A(lfred) E(dward)

Trogdon, William (Lewis) 1939-
See See Heat-Moon, William Least
See See also CA 115; 119; CANR 47; INT 119

Trollope, Anthony 1815-1882 .. **NCLC 6, 33; DA; DAB; DAC; DAM MST, NOV; SSC 28; WLC**
See See also CDBLB 1832-1890; DA3; DLB 21, 57, 159; SATA 22

Trollope, Frances 1779-1863 .... **NCLC 30**
See See also DLB 21, 166

Trotsky, Leon 1879-1940 .... **TCLC 22**
See See also CA 118; 167

Trotter (Cockburn), Catharine 1679-1749 .. **LC 8**
See See also DLB 84

Trotter, Wilfred 1872-1939 .... **TCLC 99**

Trout, Kilgore
See See Farmer, Philip Jose

Trow, George W. S. 1943- .... **CLC 52**
See See also CA 126

Troyat, Henri 1911- .... **CLC 23**
See See also CA 45-48; CANR 2, 33, 67; MTCW 1

Trudeau, G(arretson) B(eekman) 1948-
See See Trudeau, Garry B.
See See also CA 81-84; CANR 31; SATA 35

Trudeau, Garry B. .... **CLC 12**
See See also Trudeau, G(arretson) B(eekman)
See See also AAYA 10; AITN 2

Truffaut, Francois 1932-1984 .. **CLC 20, 101**
See See also CA 81-84; 113; CANR 34

Trumbo, Dalton 1905-1976 .... **CLC 19**
See See also CA 21-24R; 69-72; CANR 10; DLB 26

Trumbull, John 1750-1831 .... **NCLC 30**
See See also DLB 31

van Ostaijen, Paul 1896-1928 .... **TCLC 33**
See See also CA 163

Van Peebles, Melvin 1932- .... **CLC 2, 20; DAM MULT**
See See also BW 2, 3; CA 85-88; CANR 27, 67, 82

Vansittart, Peter 1920- .... **CLC 42**
See See also CA 1-4R; CANR 3, 49

Van Vechten, Carl 1880-1964 .... **CLC 33**
See See also CA 89-92; DLB 4, 9, 51

Van Vogt, A(lfred) E(lton) 1912- .... **CLC 1**
See See also CA 21-24R; CANR 28; DLB 8; SATA 14

Varda, Agnes 1928- .... **CLC 16**
See See also CA 116; 122

Vargas Llosa, (Jorge) Mario (Pedro) 1936-
..... **CLC 3, 6, 9, 10, 15, 31, 42, 85; DA; DAB; DAC; DAM MST, MULT, NOV; HLC 2**
See See also CA 73-76; CANR 18, 32, 42, 67; DA3; DLB 145; HW 1, 2; MTCW 1, 2

Vasiliu, Gheorghe 1881-1957
See See Bacovia, George
See See also CA 123

Vassa, Gustavus
See See Equiano, Olaudah

Vassilikos, Vassilis 1933- .... **CLC 4, 8**
See See also CA 81-84; CANR 75

Vaughan, Henry 1621-1695 .... **LC 27**
See See also DLB 131

Vaughn, Stephanie .... **CLC 62**

Vazov, Ivan (Minchov) 1850-1921 ..... **TCLC 25**
See See also CA 121; 167; DLB 147

Veblen, Thorstein B(unde) 1857-1929 ....
TCLC 31
See See also CA 115; 165

Vega, Lope de 1562-1635 ... **LC 23; HLCS 2**

Venison, Alfred
See See Pound, Ezra (Weston Loomis)

Verdi, Marie de
See See Mencken, H(enry) L(ouis)

Verdu, Matilde
See See Cela, Camilo Jose

Verga, Giovanni (Carmelo) 1840-1922 ....
TCLC 3; SSC 21
See See also CA 104; 123

Vergil 70B.C.-19B.C. ... **CMLC 9; DA; DAB; DAC; DAM MST, POET; PC 12; WLCS**
See See also Virgil
See See also DA3

Verhaeren, Emile (Adolphe Gustave) 1855-1916 .... **TCLC 12**
See See also CA 109

Verlaine, Paul (Marie) 1844-1896 . **NCLC 2, 51; DAM POET; PC 2**

Verne, Jules (Gabriel) 1828-1905 .. **TCLC 6, 52**
See See also AAYA 16; CA 110; 131; DA3; DLB 123; JRDA; MAICYA; SATA 21

Very, Jones 1813-1880 .... **NCLC 9**
See See also DLB 1

Vesaas, Tarjei 1897-1970 .... **CLC 48**
See See also CA 29-32R

Vialis, Gaston
See See Simenon, Georges (Jacques Christian)

Vian, Boris 1920-1959 .... **TCLC 9**
See See also CA 106; 164; DLB 72; MTCW 2

Viaud, (Louis Marie) Julien 1850-1923
See See Loti, Pierre
See See also CA 107

Vicar, Henry
See See Felsen, Henry Gregor

Vicker, Angus
See See Felsen, Henry Gregor

Vidal, Gore 1925- ..... **CLC 2, 4, 6, 8, 10, 22, 33, 72; DAM NOV, POP**
See See also AITN 1; BEST 90:2; CA 5-8R; CANR 13, 45, 65; CDALBS; DA3; DLB 6, 152; INT CANR-13; MTCW 1, 2

Viereck, Peter (Robert Edwin) 1916- .. **CLC 4; PC 27**
See See also CA 1-4R; CANR 1, 47; DLB 5

Vigny, Alfred (Victor) de 1797-1863 . **NCLC 7; DAM POET; PC 26**
See See also DLB 119, 192

Vilakazi, Benedict Wallet 1906-1947 . **TCLC 37**
See See also CA 168

Villa, Jose Garcia 1904-1997 .... **PC 22**
See See also CA 25-28R; CANR 12

Villarreal, Jose Antonio 1924-
See See also CA 133; DAM MULT; DLB 82; HLC 2; HW 1

Villaurrutia, Xavier 1903-1950 ..... **TCLC 80**
See See also HW 1

Villiers de l'Isle Adam, Jean Marie Mathias Philippe Auguste, Comte de 1838-1889
.... **NCLC 3; SSC 14**
See See also DLB 123

Villon, Francois 1431-1463(?) .... **PC 13**
See See also DLB 208

Vinci, Leonardo da 1452-1519 .... **LC 12**

Vine, Barbara .... **CLC 50**
See See Rendell, Ruth (Barbara)
See See also BEST 90:4

Vinge, Joan (Carol) D(ennison) 1948- . **CLC 30; SSC 24**
See See also AAYA 32; CA 93-96; CANR 72; SATA 36

Violis, G.
See See Simenon, Georges (Jacques Christian)

Viramontes, Helena Maria 1954-
See See also CA 159; DLB 122; HLCS 2; HW 2

Virgil 70B.C.-19B.C.
See See Vergil
See See also DLB 211

Visconti, Luchino 1906-1976 .... **CLC 16**
See See also CA 81-84; 65-68; CANR 39

Vittorini, Elio 1908-1966 .... **CLC 6, 9, 14**
See See also CA 133; 25-28R

Vivekananda, Swami 1863-1902 ... **TCLC 88**

Vizenor, Gerald Robert 1934- ...... **CLC 103; DAM MULT**
See See also CA 13-16R; CAAS 22; CANR 5, 21, 44, 67; DLB 175; MTCW 2; NNAL

Vizinczey, Stephen 1933- .... **CLC 40**
See See also CA 128; INT 128

Vliet, R(ussell) G(ordon) 1929-1984 .... **CLC 22**
See See also CA 37-40R; 112; CANR 18

Vogau, Boris Andreyevich 1894-1937(?)
See See Pilnyak, Boris
See See also CA 123

Vogel, Paula A(nne) 1951- .... **CLC 76**
See See also CA 108

Voigt, Cynthia 1942- .... **CLC 30**
See See also AAYA 3, 30; CA 106; CANR 18, 37, 40; CLR 13, 48; INT CANR-18; JRDA; MAICYA; SATA 48, 79; SATA-Brief 33

Voigt, Ellen Bryant 1943- .... **CLC 54**
See See also CA 69-72; CANR 11, 29, 55; DLB 120

Voinovich, Vladimir (Nikolaevich) 1932- ..... **CLC 10, 49**
See See also CA 81-84; CAAS 12; CANR 33, 67; MTCW 1

Vollmann, William T. 1959- . **CLC 89; DAM NOV, POP**
See See also CA 134; CANR 67; DA3; MTCW 2

Voloshinov, V. N.
See See Bakhtin, Mikhail Mikhailovich

Voltaire 1694-1778 .... **LC 14; DA; DAB; DAC; DAM DRAM, MST; SSC 12; WLC**
See See also DA3

von Aschendrof, BaronIgnatz
See See Ford, Ford Madox

von Daeniken, Erich 1935- .... **CLC 30**
See See also AITN 1; CA 37-40R; CANR 17, 44

von Daniken, Erich
See See von Daeniken, Erich

von Heidenstam, (Carl Gustaf) Verner
See See Heidenstam, (Carl Gustaf) Verner von

von Heyse, Paul (Johann Ludwig)
See See Heyse, Paul (Johann Ludwig von)

von Hofmannsthal, Hugo
See See Hofmannsthal, Hugo von

von Horvath, Odon
See See Horvath, Oedoen von

von Horvath, Oedoen
See See Horvath, Oedoen von

von Liliencron, (Friedrich Adolf Axel) Detlev
See See Liliencron, (Friedrich Adolf Axel) Detlev von

Vonnegut, Kurt, Jr. 1922- . **CLC 1, 2, 3, 4, 5, 8, 12, 22, 40, 60, 111; DA; DAB; DAC; DAM MST, NOV, POP; SSC 8; WLC**
See See also AAYA 6; AITN 1; BEST 90:4; CA 1-4R; CANR 1, 25, 49, 75; CDALB 1968-1988; DA3; DLB 2, 8, 152; DLBD 3; DLBY 80; MTCW 1, 2

Von Rachen, Kurt
See See Hubbard, L(afayette) Ron(ald)

von Rezzori (d'Arezzo), Gregor
See See Rezzori (d'Arezzo), Gregor von

von Sternberg, Josef
See See Sternberg, Josef von

Vorster, Gordon 1924- .... **CLC 34**
See See also CA 133

Vosce, Trudie
See See Ozick, Cynthia

Voznesensky, Andrei (Andreievich) 1933- ... **CLC 1, 15, 57; DAM POET**
See See also CA 89-92; CANR 37; MTCW 1

Waddington, Miriam 1917- .... **CLC 28**
See See also CA 21-24R; CANR 12, 30; DLB 68

Wagman, Fredrica 1937- .... **CLC 7**
See See also CA 97-100; INT 97-100

Wagner, Linda W.
See See Wagner-Martin, Linda (C.)

Wagner, Linda Welshimer
See See Wagner-Martin, Linda (C.)

Wagner, Richard 1813-1883 .... **NCLC 9**
See See also DLB 129

Wagner-Martin, Linda (C.) 1936- .. **CLC 50**
See See also CA 159

Wagoner, David (Russell) 1926- . **CLC 3, 5, 15**
See See also CA 1-4R; CAAS 3; CANR 2, 71; DLB 5; SATA 14

Wah, Fred(erick James) 1939- .... **CLC 44**
See See also CA 107; 141; DLB 60

Wahloo, Per 1926-1975 .... **CLC 7**
See See also CA 61-64; CANR 73

Wahloo, Peter
See See Wahloo, Per

Wain, John (Barrington) 1925-1994 .... **CLC 2, 11, 15, 46**

See See also CA 5-8R; 145; CAAS 4; CANR 23, 54; CDBLB 1960 to Present; DLB 15, 27, 139, 155; MTCW 1, 2

Wajda, Andrzej 1926- .... **CLC 16**
See See also CA 102

Wakefield, Dan 1932- .... **CLC 7**
See See also CA 21-24R; CAAS 7

Wakoski, Diane 1937- .... **CLC 2, 4, 7, 9, 11, 40; DAM POET; PC 15**
See See also CA 13-16R; CAAS 1; CANR 9, 60; DLB 5; INT CANR-9; MTCW 2

Wakoski-Sherbell, Diane
See See Wakoski, Diane

Walcott, Derek (Alton) 1930- ... **CLC 2, 4, 9, 14, 25, 42, 67, 76; BLC 3; DAB; DAC; DAM MST, MULT, POET; DC 7**
See See also BW 2; CA 89-92; CANR 26, 47, 75, 80; DA3; DLB 117; DLBY 81; MTCW 1, 2

Waldman, Anne (Lesley) 1945- .... **CLC 7**
See See also CA 37-40R; CAAS 17; CANR 34, 69; DLB 16

Waldo, E. Hunter
See See Sturgeon, Theodore (Hamilton)

Waldo, Edward Hamilton
See See Sturgeon, Theodore (Hamilton)

Walker, Alice (Malsenior) 1944- .. **CLC 5, 6, 9, 19, 27, 46, 58, 103; BLC 3; DA; DAB; DAC; DAM MST, MULT, NOV, POET, POP; SSC 5; WLCS**
See See also AAYA 3; BEST 89:4; BW 2, 3; CA 37-40R; CANR 9, 27, 49, 66, 82; CDALB 1968-1988; DA3; DLB 6, 33, 143; INT CANR-27; MTCW 1, 2; SATA 31

Walker, David Harry 1911-1992 ..... **CLC 14**
See See also CA 1-4R; 137; CANR 1; SATA 8; SATA-Obit 71

Walker, Edward Joseph 1934-
See See Walker, Ted
See See also CA 21-24R; CANR 12, 28, 53

Walker, George F. 1947- . **CLC 44, 61; DAB; DAC; DAM MST**
See See also CA 103; CANR 21, 43, 59; DLB 60

Walker, Joseph A. 1935- ...... **CLC 19; DAM DRAM, MST**
See See also BW 1, 3; CA 89-92; CANR 26; DLB 38

Walker, Margaret (Abigail) 1915-1998 . **CLC 1, 6; BLC; DAM MULT; PC 20**
See See also BW 2, 3; CA 73-76; 172; CANR 26, 54, 76; DLB 76, 152; MTCW 1, 2

Walker, Ted .... **CLC 13**
See See also Walker, Edward Joseph
See See also DLB 40

Wallace, David Foster 1962- ... **CLC 50, 114**
See See also CA 132; CANR 59; DA3; MTCW 2

Wallace, Dexter
See See Masters, Edgar Lee

Wallace, (Richard Horatio) Edgar 1875-1932
.... **TCLC 57**
See See also CA 115; DLB 70

Wallace, Irving 1916-1990 .... **CLC 7, 13; DAM NOV, POP**
See See also AITN 1; CA 1-4R; 132; CAAS 1; CANR 1, 27; INT CANR-27; MTCW 1, 2

Wallant, Edward Lewis 1926-1962 .. **CLC 5, 10**
See See also CA 1-4R; CANR 22; DLB 2, 28, 143; MTCW 1, 2

Wallas, Graham 1858-1932 .... **TCLC 91**

Walley, Byron
See See Card, Orson Scott

Walpole, Horace 1717-1797 .... **LC 49**
See See also DLB 39, 104

Walpole, Hugh (Seymour) 1884-1941 . **TCLC 5**
See See also CA 104; 165; DLB 34; MTCW 2

Walser, Martin 1927- .... **CLC 27**
See See also CA 57-60; CANR 8, 46; DLB 75, 124

Walser, Robert 1878-1956 ... **TCLC 18; SSC 20**
See See also CA 118; 165; DLB 66

Walsh, Jill Paton .... **CLC 35**
See See also Paton Walsh, Gillian
See See also AAYA 11; CLR 2; DLB 161; SAAS 3

Walter, Villiam Christian
See See Andersen, Hans Christian

Wambaugh, Joseph (Aloysius, Jr.) 1937- .... **CLC 3, 18; DAM NOV, POP**
See See also AITN 1; BEST 89:3; CA 33-36R; CANR 42, 65; DA3; DLB 6; DLBY 83; MTCW 1, 2

Wang Wei 699(?)-761(?) .... **PC 18**

Ward, Arthur Henry Sarsfield 1883-1959
See See Rohmer, Sax
See See also CA 108; 173

Ward, Douglas Turner 1930- .... **CLC 19**
See See also BW 1; CA 81-84; CANR 27; DLB 7, 38

Ward, E. D.
See See Lucas, E(dward) V(errall)

Ward, Mary Augusta
See See Ward, Mrs. Humphry

Ward, Mrs. Humphry 1851-1920 . **TCLC 55**
See See also DLB 18

Ward, Peter
See See Faust, Frederick (Schiller)

Warhol, Andy 1928(?)-1987 .... **CLC 20**
See See also AAYA 12; BEST 89:4; CA 89-92; 121; CANR 34

Warner, Francis (Robert le Plastrier) 1937-
.... **CLC 14**
See See also CA 53-56; CANR 11

Warner, Marina 1946- .... **CLC 59**
See See also CA 65-68; CANR 21, 55; DLB 194

Warner, Rex (Ernest) 1905-1986 .... **CLC 45**
See See also CA 89-92; 119; DLB 15

Warner, Susan (Bogert) 1819-1885 ... **NCLC 31**
See See also DLB 3, 42

Warner, Sylvia (Constance) Ashton
See See Ashton-Warner, Sylvia (Constance)

Warner, Sylvia Townsend 1893-1978 ... **CLC 7, 19; SSC 23**
See See also CA 61-64; 77-80; CANR 16, 60; DLB 34, 139; MTCW 1, 2

Warren, Mercy Otis 1728-1814 .... **NCLC 13**
See See also DLB 31, 200

Warren, Robert Penn 1905-1989 . **CLC 1, 4, 6, 8, 10, 13, 18, 39, 53, 59; DA; DAB; DAC; DAM MST, NOV, POET; SSC 4; WLC**
See See also AITN 1; CA 13-16R; 129; CANR 10, 47; CDALB 1968-1988; DA3; DLB 2, 48, 152; DLBY 80, 89; INT CANR-10; MTCW 1, 2; SATA 46; SATA-Obit 63

Warshofsky, Isaac
See See Singer, Isaac Bashevis

Warton, Thomas 1728-1790 ... **LC 15; DAM POET**
See See also DLB 104, 109

Waruk, Kona
See See Harris, (Theodore) Wilson

Warung, Price 1855-1911 .... **TCLC 45**

Warwick, Jarvis
See See Garner, Hugh

Washington, Alex
See See Harris, Mark

Washington, Booker T(aliaferro) 1856-1915
.... **TCLC 10; BLC 3; DAM MULT**
See See also BW 1; CA 114; 125; DA3; SATA 28

Washington, George 1732-1799 .... **LC 25**
See See also DLB 31

Wassermann, (Karl) Jakob 1873-1934 ....
.... **TCLC 6**
See See also CA 104; 163; DLB 66

Wasserstein, Wendy 1950- . **CLC 32, 59, 90; DAM DRAM; DC 4**
See See also CA 121; 129; CABS 3; CANR 53, 75; DA3; INT 129; MTCW 2; SATA 94

Waterhouse, Keith (Spencer) 1929- ..... **CLC 47**
See See also CA 5-8R; CANR 38, 67; DLB 13, 15; MTCW 1, 2

Waters, Frank (Joseph) 1902-1995 . **CLC 88**
See See also CA 5-8R; 149; CAAS 13; CANR 3, 18, 63; DLB 212; DLBY 86

Waters, Roger 1944- .... **CLC 35**

Watkins, Frances Ellen
See See Harper, Frances Ellen Watkins

Watkins, Gerrold
See See Malzberg, Barry N(athaniel)

Watkins, Gloria 1955(?)-
See See hooks, bell
See See also BW 2; CA 143; MTCW 2

Watkins, Paul 1964- .... **CLC 55**
See See also CA 132; CANR 62

Watkins, Vernon Phillips 1906-1967 .... **CLC 43**
See See also CA 9-10; 25-28R; CAP 1; DLB 20

Watson, Irving S.
See See Mencken, H(enry) L(ouis)

Watson, John H.
See See Farmer, Philip Jose

Watson, Richard F.
See See Silverberg, Robert

Waugh, Auberon (Alexander) 1939- . **CLC 7**
See See also CA 45-48; CANR 6, 22; DLB 14, 194

Waugh, Evelyn (Arthur St. John) 1903-1966
... **CLC 1, 3, 8, 13, 19, 27, 44, 107; DA; DAB; DAC; DAM MST, NOV, POP; WLC**
See See also CA 85-88; 25-28R; CANR 22; CDBLB 1914-1945; DA3; DLB 15, 162, 195; MTCW 1, 2

Waugh, Harriet 1944- .... **CLC 6**
See See also CA 85-88; CANR 22

Ways, C. R.
See See Blount, Roy (Alton), Jr.

Waystaff, Simon
See See Swift, Jonathan

Webb, Beatrice (Martha Potter) 1858-1943
.... **TCLC 22**
See See also CA 117; 162; DLB 190

Webb, Charles (Richard) 1939- .... **CLC 7**
See See also CA 25-28R

Webb, James H(enry), Jr. 1946- ..... **CLC 22**
See See also CA 81-84

Webb, Mary Gladys (Meredith) 1881-1927
.... **TCLC 24**
See See also CA 182; 123; DLB 34

Webb, Mrs. Sidney
See See Webb, Beatrice (Martha Potter)

Webb, Phyllis 1927- .... **CLC 18**
See See also CA 104; CANR 23; DLB 53

Webb, Sidney (James) 1859-1947 . **TCLC 22**
See See also CA 117; 163; DLB 190

Webber, Andrew Lloyd .... **CLC 21**
See See also Lloyd Webber, Andrew

Weber, Lenora Mattingly 1895-1971 ... **CLC 12**
See See also CA 19-20; 29-32R; CAP 1; SATA 2; SATA-Obit 26

Author Index

Weber, Max 1864-1920 .... **TCLC 69**
See See also CA 109

Webster, John 1579(?)-1634(?) . **LC 33; DA; DAB; DAC; DAM DRAM, MST; DC 2; WLC**
See See also CDBLB Before 1660; DLB 58

Webster, Noah 1758-1843 .... **NCLC 30**
See See also DLB 1, 37, 42, 43, 73

Wedekind, (Benjamin) Frank(lin) 1864-1918
.... **TCLC 7; DAM DRAM**
See See also CA 104; 153; DLB 118

Weidman, Jerome 1913-1998 .... **CLC 7**
See See also AITN 2; CA 1-4R; 171; CANR 1; DLB 28

Weil, Simone (Adolphine) 1909-1943 . **TCLC 23**
See See also CA 117; 159; MTCW 2

Weininger, Otto 1880-1903 .... **TCLC 84**

Weinstein, Nathan
See See West, Nathanael

Weinstein, Nathan von Wallenstein
See See West, Nathanael

Weir, Peter (Lindsay) 1944- .... **CLC 20**
See See also CA 113; 123

Weiss, Peter (Ulrich) 1916-1982 . **CLC 3, 15, 51; DAM DRAM**
See See also CA 45-48; 106; CANR 3; DLB 69, 124

Weiss, Theodore (Russell) 1916- .. **CLC 3, 8, 14**
See See also CA 9-12R; CAAS 2; CANR 46; DLB 5

Welch, (Maurice) Denton 1915-1948 . **TCLC 22**
See See also CA 121; 148

Welch, James 1940- ... **CLC 6, 14, 52; DAM MULT, POP**
See See also CA 85-88; CANR 42, 66; DLB 175; NNAL

Weldon, Fay 1931- . **CLC 6, 9, 11, 19, 36, 59, 122; DAM POP**
See See also CA 21-24R; CANR 16, 46, 63; CDBLB 1960 to Present; DLB 14, 194; INT CANR-16; MTCW 1, 2

Wellek, Rene 1903-1995 .... **CLC 28**
See See also CA 5-8R; 150; CAAS 7; CANR 8; DLB 63; INT CANR-8

Weller, Michael 1942- .... **CLC 10, 53**
See See also CA 85-88

Weller, Paul 1958- .... **CLC 26**

Wellershoff, Dieter 1925- .... **CLC 46**
See See also CA 89-92; CANR 16, 37

Welles, (George) Orson 1915-1985 . **CLC 20, 80**
See See also CA 93-96; 117

Wellman, John McDowell 1945-
See See Wellman, Mac
See See also CA 166

Wellman, Mac 1945- .... **CLC 65**
See See also Wellman, John McDowell; Wellman, John McDowell

Wellman, Manly Wade 1903-1986 .. **CLC 49**
See See also CA 1-4R; 118; CANR 6, 16, 44; SATA 6; SATA-Obit 47

Wells, Carolyn 1869(?)-1942 .... **TCLC 35**
See See also CA 113; DLB 11

Wells, H(erbert) G(eorge) 1866-1946 . **TCLC 6, 12, 19; DA; DAB; DAC; DAM MST, NOV; SSC 6; WLC**
See See also AAYA 18; CA 110; 121; CD-BLB 1914-1945; DA3; DLB 34, 70, 156, 178; MTCW 1, 2; SATA 20

Wells, Rosemary 1943- .... **CLC 12**
See See also AAYA 13; CA 85-88; CANR 48; CLR 16; MAICYA; SAAS 1; SATA 18, 69

Welty, Eudora 1909- .... **CLC 1, 2, 5, 14, 22, 33, 105; DA; DAB; DAC; DAM MST, NOV; SSC 1, 27; WLC**

See See also CA 9-12R; CABS 1; CANR 32, 65; CDALB 1941-1968; DA3; DLB 2, 102, 143; DLBD 12; DLBY 87; MTCW 1, 2

Wen I-to 1899-1946 .... **TCLC 28**

Wentworth, Robert
See See Hamilton, Edmond

Werfel, Franz (Viktor) 1890-1945 .. **TCLC 8**
See See also CA 104; 161; DLB 81, 124

Wergeland, Henrik Arnold 1808-1845 ....
NCLC 5

Wersba, Barbara 1932- .... **CLC 30**
See See also AAYA 2, 30; CA 29-32R, 182; CAAE 182; CANR 16, 38; CLR 3; DLB 52; JRDA; MAICYA; SAAS 2; SATA 1, 58; SATA-Essay 103

Wertmueller, Lina 1928- .... **CLC 16**
See See also CA 97-100; CANR 39, 78

Wescott, Glenway 1901-1987 . **CLC 13; SSC 35**
See See also CA 13-16R; 121; CANR 23, 70; DLB 4, 9, 102

Wesker, Arnold 1932- .. **CLC 3, 5, 42; DAB; DAM DRAM**
See See also CA 1-4R; CAAS 7; CANR 1, 33; CDBLB 1960 to Present; DLB 13; MTCW 1

Wesley, Richard (Errol) 1945- .... **CLC 7**
See See also BW 1; CA 57-60; CANR 27; DLB 38

Wessel, Johan Herman 1742-1785 .... **LC 7**

West, Anthony (Panther) 1914-1987 .... **CLC 50**
See See also CA 45-48; 124; CANR 3, 19; DLB 15

West, C. P.
See See Wodehouse, P(elham) G(renville)

West, (Mary) Jessamyn 1902-1984 .. **CLC 7, 17**
See See also CA 9-12R; 112; CANR 27; DLB 6; DLBY 84; MTCW 1, 2; SATA-Obit 37

West, Morris L(anglo) 1916- .... **CLC 6, 33**
See See also CA 5-8R; CANR 24, 49, 64; MTCW 1, 2

West, Nathanael 1903-1940 ..... **TCLC 1, 14, 44; SSC 16**
See See also CA 104; 125; CDALB 1929-1941; DA3; DLB 4, 9, 28; MTCW 1, 2

West, Owen
See See Koontz, Dean R(ay)

West, Paul 1930- .... **CLC 7, 14, 96**
See See also CA 13-16R; CAAS 7; CANR 22, 53, 76; DLB 14; INT CANR-22; MTCW 2

West, Rebecca 1892-1983 .. **CLC 7, 9, 31, 50**
See See also CA 5-8R; 109; CANR 19; DLB 36; DLBY 83; MTCW 1, 2

Westall, Robert (Atkinson) 1929-1993 . **CLC 17**
See See also AAYA 12; CA 69-72; 141; CANR 18, 68; CLR 13; JRDA; MAICYA; SAAS 2; SATA 23, 69; SATA-Obit 75

Westermarck, Edward 1862-1939 ..... **TCLC 87**

Westlake, Donald E(dwin) 1933- ..... **CLC 7, 33; DAM POP**
See See also CA 17-20R; CAAS 13; CANR 16, 44, 65; INT CANR-16; MTCW 2

Westmacott, Mary
See See Christie, Agatha (Mary Clarissa)

Weston, Allen
See See Norton, Andre

Wetcheek, J. L.
See See Feuchtwanger, Lion

Wetering, Janwillem van de
See See van de Wetering, Janwillem

Wetherald, Agnes Ethelwyn 1857-1940 ....
TCLC 81

See See also DLB 99

Wetherell, Elizabeth
See See Warner, Susan (Bogert)

Whale, James 1889-1957 .... **TCLC 63**

Whalen, Philip 1923- .... **CLC 6, 29**
See See also CA 9-12R; CANR 5, 39; DLB 16

Wharton, Edith (Newbold Jones) 1862-1937
... **TCLC 3, 9, 27, 53; DA; DAB; DAC; DAM MST, NOV; SSC 6; WLC**
See See also AAYA 25; CA 104; 132; CDALB 1865-1917; DA3; DLB 4, 9, 12, 78, 189; DLBD 13; MTCW 1, 2

Wharton, James
See See Mencken, H(enry) L(ouis)

Wharton, William (a pseudonym) . **CLC 18, 37**
See See also CA 93-96; DLBY 80; INT 93-96

Wheatley (Peters), Phillis 1754(?)-1784 .. **LC 3, 50; BLC 3; DA; DAC; DAM MST, MULT, POET; PC 3; WLC**
See See also CDALB 1640-1865; DA3; DLB 31, 50

Wheelock, John Hall 1886-1978 ..... **CLC 14**
See See also CA 13-16R; 77-80; CANR 14; DLB 45

White, E(lwyn) B(rooks) 1899-1985 ..... **CLC 10, 34, 39; DAM POP**
See See also AITN 2; CA 13-16R; 116; CANR 16, 37; CDALBS; CLR 1, 21; DA3; DLB 11, 22; MAICYA; MTCW 1, 2; SATA 2, 29, 100; SATA-Obit 44

White, Edmund (Valentine III) 1940- . **CLC 27, 110; DAM POP**
See See also AAYA 7; CA 45-48; CANR 3, 19, 36, 62; DA3; MTCW 1, 2

White, Patrick (Victor Martindale) 1912-1990 . **CLC 3, 4, 5, 7, 9, 18, 65, 69**
See See also CA 81-84; 132; CANR 43; MTCW 1

White, Phyllis Dorothy James 1920-
See See James, P. D.
See See also CA 21-24R; CANR 17, 43, 65; DAM POP; DA3; MTCW 1, 2

White, T(erence) H(anbury) 1906-1964 .... **CLC 30**
See See also AAYA 22; CA 73-76; CANR 37; DLB 160; JRDA; MAICYA; SATA 12

White, Terence de Vere 1912-1994 . **CLC 49**
See See also CA 49-52; 145; CANR 3

White, Walter
See See White, Walter F(rancis)
See See also BLC; DAM MULT

White, Walter F(rancis) 1893-1955 ... **TCLC 15**
See See also White, Walter
See See also BW 1; CA 115; 124; DLB 51

White, William Hale 1831-1913
See See Rutherford, Mark
See See also CA 121

Whitehead, Alfred North 1861-1947 . **TCLC 97**
See See also CA 117; 165; DLB 100

Whitehead, E(dward) A(nthony) 1933- ....
CLC 5
See See also CA 65-68; CANR 58

Whitemore, Hugh (John) 1936- ...... **CLC 37**
See See also CA 132; CANR 77; INT 132

Whitman, Sarah Helen (Power) 1803-1878 .
NCLC 19
See See also DLB 1

Whitman, Walt(er) 1819-1892 . **NCLC 4, 31, 81; DA; DAB; DAC; DAM MST, POET; PC 3; WLC**
See See also CDALB 1640-1865; DA3; DLB 3, 64; SATA 20

Whitney, Phyllis A(yame) 1903- .... **CLC 42; DAM POP**

Wintergreen, Jane
See See Duncan, Sara Jeannette

Winters, Janet Lewis .... **CLC 41**
See See also Lewis, Janet
See See also DLBY 87

Winters, (Arthur) Yvor 1900-1968 .. **CLC 4, 8, 32**
See See also CA 11-12; 25-28R; CAP 1; DLB 48; MTCW 1

Winterson, Jeanette 1959- ... **CLC 64; DAM POP**
See See also CA 136; CANR 58; DA3; DLB 207; MTCW 2

Winthrop, John 1588-1649 .... **LC 31**
See See also DLB 24, 30

Wirth, Louis 1897-1952 .... **TCLC 92**

Wiseman, Frederick 1930- .... **CLC 20**
See See also CA 159

Wister, Owen 1860-1938 .... **TCLC 21**
See See also CA 108; 162; DLB 9, 78, 186; SATA 62

Witkacy
See See Witkiewicz, Stanislaw Ignacy

Witkiewicz, Stanislaw Ignacy 1885-1939 ..... **TCLC 8**
See See also CA 105; 162

Wittgenstein, Ludwig (Josef Johann) 1889-1951 .... **TCLC 59**
See See also CA 113; 164; MTCW 2

Wittig, Monique 1935(?)- .... **CLC 22**
See See also CA 116; 135; DLB 83

Wittlin, Jozef 1896-1976 .... **CLC 25**
See See also CA 49-52; 65-68; CANR 3

Wodehouse, P(elham) G(renville) 1881-1975 . **CLC 1, 2, 5, 10, 22; DAB; DAC; DAM NOV; SSC 2**
See See also AITN 2; CA 45-48; 57-60; CANR 3, 33; CDBLB 1914-1945; DA3; DLB 34, 162; MTCW 1, 2; SATA 22

Woiwode, L.
See See Woiwode, Larry (Alfred)

Woiwode, Larry (Alfred) 1941- .. **CLC 6, 10**
See See also CA 73-76; CANR 16; DLB 6; INT CANR-16

Wojciechowska, Maia (Teresa) 1927- .. **CLC 26**
See See also AAYA 8; CA 9-12R; CANR 4, 41; CLR 1; JRDA; MAICYA; SAAS 1; SATA 1, 28, 83; SATA-Essay 104

Wolf, Christa 1929- .... **CLC 14, 29, 58**
See See also CA 85-88; CANR 45; DLB 75; MTCW 1

Wolfe, Gene (Rodman) 1931- .... **CLC 25; DAM POP**
See See also CA 57-60; CAAS 9; CANR 6, 32, 60; DLB 8; MTCW 2

Wolfe, George C. 1954- .... **CLC 49; BLCS**
See See also CA 149

Wolfe, Thomas (Clayton) 1900-1938 . **TCLC 4, 13, 29, 61; DA; DAB; DAC; DAM MST, NOV; SSC 33; WLC**
See See also CA 104; 132; CDALB 1929-1941; DA3; DLB 9, 102; DLBD 2, 16; DLBY 85, 97; MTCW 1, 2

Wolfe, Thomas Kennerly, Jr. 1930-
See See Wolfe, Tom
See See also CA 13-16R; CANR 9, 33, 70; DAM POP; DA3; DLB 185; INT CANR-9; MTCW 1, 2

Wolfe, Tom .... **CLC 1, 2, 9, 15, 35, 51**
See See also Wolfe, Thomas Kennerly, Jr.
See See also AAYA 8; AITN 2; BEST 89:1; DLB 152

Wolff, Geoffrey (Ansell) 1937- .... **CLC 41**
See See also CA 29-32R; CANR 29, 43, 78

Wolff, Sonia
See See Levitin, Sonia (Wolff)

Wolff, Tobias (Jonathan Ansell) 1945- . **CLC 39, 64**

See See also AAYA 16; BEST 90:2; CA 114; 117; CAAS 22; CANR 54, 76; DA3; DLB 130; INT 117; MTCW 2

Wolfram von Eschenbach c. 1170-c. 1220 ... **CMLC 5**
See See also DLB 138

Wolitzer, Hilma 1930- .... **CLC 17**
See See also CA 65-68; CANR 18, 40; INT CANR-18; SATA 31

Wollstonecraft, Mary 1759-1797 ... **LC 5, 50**
See See also CDBLB 1789-1832; DLB 39, 104, 158

Wonder, Stevie .... **CLC 12**
See See also Morris, Steveland Judkins

Wong, Jade Snow 1922- .... **CLC 17**
See See also CA 109

Woodberry, George Edward 1855-1930 ...... **TCLC 73**
See See also CA 165; DLB 71, 103

Woodcott, Keith
See See Brunner, John (Kilian Houston)

Woodruff, Robert W.
See See Mencken, H(enry) L(ouis)

Woolf, (Adeline) Virginia 1882-1941 . **TCLC 1, 5, 20, 43, 56; DA; DAB; DAC; DAM MST, NOV; SSC 7; WLC**
See See also Woolf, Virginia Adeline
See See also CA 104; 130; CANR 64; CD-BLB 1914-1945; DA3; DLB 36, 100, 162; DLBD 10; MTCW 1

Woolf, Virginia Adeline
See See Woolf, (Adeline) Virginia
See See also MTCW 2

Woollcott, Alexander (Humphreys) 1887-1943 .... **TCLC 5**
See See also CA 105; 161; DLB 29

Woolrich, Cornell 1903-1968 .... **CLC 77**
See See also Hopley-Woolrich, Cornell George

Woolson, Constance Fenimore 1840-1894 ... **NCLC 82**
See See also DLB 12, 74, 189

Wordsworth, Dorothy 1771-1855 . **NCLC 25**
See See also DLB 107

Wordsworth, William 1770-1850 . **NCLC 12, 38; DA; DAB; DAC; DAM MST, POET; PC 4; WLC**
See See also CDBLB 1789-1832; DA3; DLB 93, 107

Wouk, Herman 1915- .. **CLC 1, 9, 38; DAM NOV, POP**
See See also CA 5-8R; CANR 6, 33, 67; CDALBS; DA3; DLBY 82; INT CANR-6; MTCW 1, 2

Wright, Charles (Penzel, Jr.) 1935- . **CLC 6, 13, 28, 119**
See See also CA 29-32R; CAAS 7; CANR 23, 36, 62; DLB 165; DLBY 82; MTCW 1, 2

Wright, Charles Stevenson 1932- .. **CLC 49; BLC 3; DAM MULT, POET**
See See also BW 1; CA 9-12R; CANR 26; DLB 33

Wright, Frances 1795-1852 .... **NCLC 74**
See See also DLB 73

Wright, Frank Lloyd 1867-1959 .. **TCLC 95**
See See also CA 174

Wright, Jack R.
See See Harris, Mark

Wright, James (Arlington) 1927-1980 . **CLC 3, 5, 10, 28; DAM POET**
See See also AITN 2; CA 49-52; 97-100; CANR 4, 34, 64; CDALBS; DLB 5, 169; MTCW 1, 2

Wright, Judith (Arandell) 1915- .... **CLC 11, 53; PC 14**
See See also CA 13-16R; CANR 31, 76; MTCW 1, 2; SATA 14

Wright, L(aurali) R. 1939- .... **CLC 44**

See See also CA 138

Wright, Richard (Nathaniel) 1908-1960 ...... **CLC 1, 3, 4, 9, 14, 21, 48, 74; BLC 3; DA; DAB; DAC; DAM MST, MULT, NOV; SSC 2; WLC**
See See also AAYA 5; BW 1; CA 108; CANR 64; CDALB 1929-1941; DA3; DLB 76, 102; DLBD 2; MTCW 1, 2

Wright, Richard B(ruce) 1937- .... **CLC 6**
See See also CA 85-88; DLB 53

Wright, Rick 1945- .... **CLC 35**

Wright, Rowland
See See Wells, Carolyn

Wright, Stephen 1946- .... **CLC 33**

Wright, Willard Huntington 1888-1939
See See Van Dine, S. S.
See See also CA 115; DLBD 16

Wright, William 1930- .... **CLC 44**
See See also CA 53-56; CANR 7, 23

Wroth, LadyMary 1587-1653(?) .... **LC 30**
See See also DLB 121

Wu Ch'eng-en 1500(?)-1582(?) .... **LC 7**

Wu Ching-tzu 1701-1754 .... **LC 2**

Wurlitzer, Rudolph 1938(?)- ... **CLC 2, 4, 15**
See See also CA 85-88; DLB 173

Wyatt, Thomas c. 1503-1542 .... **PC 27**
See See also DLB 132

Wycherley, William 1641-1715 ..... **LC 8, 21; DAM DRAM**
See See also CDBLB 1660-1789; DLB 80

Wylie, Elinor (Morton Hoyt) 1885-1928 ...... **TCLC 8; PC 23**
See See also CA 105; 162; DLB 9, 45

Wylie, Philip (Gordon) 1902-1971 .. **CLC 43**
See See also CA 21-22; 33-36R; CAP 2; DLB 9

Wyndham, John .... **CLC 19**
See See also Harris, John (Wyndham Parkes Lucas) Beynon

Wyss, Johann David Von 1743-1818 . **NCLC 10**
See See also JRDA; MAICYA; SATA 29; SATA-Brief 27

Xenophon c. 430B.C.-c. 354B.C. .. **CMLC 17**
See See also DLB 176

Yakumo Koizumi
See See Hearn, (Patricio) Lafcadio (Tessima Carlos)

Yamamoto, Hisaye 1921- ...... **SSC 34; DAM MULT**

Yanez, Jose Donoso
See See Donoso (Yanez), Jose

Yanovsky, Basile S.
See See Yanovsky, V(assily) S(emenovich)

Yanovsky, V(assily) S(emenovich) 1906-1989 .... **CLC 2, 18**
See See also CA 97-100; 129

Yates, Richard 1926-1992 .... **CLC 7, 8, 23**
See See also CA 5-8R; 139; CANR 10, 43; DLB 2; DLBY 81, 92; INT CANR-10

Yeats, W. B.
See See Yeats, William Butler

Yeats, William Butler 1865-1939 ... **TCLC 1, 11, 18, 31, 93; DA; DAB; DAC; DAM DRAM, MST, POET; PC 20; WLC**
See See also CA 104; 127; CANR 45; CD-BLB 1890-1914; DA3; DLB 10, 19, 98, 156; MTCW 1, 2

Yehoshua, A(braham) B. 1936- . **CLC 13, 31**
See See also CA 33-36R; CANR 43

Yellow Bird
See See Ridge, John Rollin

Yep, Laurence Michael 1948- .... **CLC 35**
See See also AAYA 5, 31; CA 49-52; CANR 1, 46; CLR 3, 17, 54; DLB 52; JRDA; MAICYA; SATA 7, 69

Yerby, Frank G(arvin) 1916-1991 .... **CLC 1, 7, 22; BLC 3; DAM MULT**

See See also BW 1, 3; CA 9-12R; 136; CANR 16, 52; DLB 76; INT CANR-16; MTCW 1

Yesenin, Sergei Alexandrovich
See See Esenin, Sergei (Alexandrovich)

Yevtushenko, Yevgeny (Alexandrovich) 1933- . **CLC 1, 3, 13, 26, 51, 126; DAM POET**
See See also CA 81-84; CANR 33, 54; MTCW 1

Yezierska, Anzia 1885(?)-1970 .... **CLC 46**
See See also CA 126; 89-92; DLB 28; MTCW 1

Yglesias, Helen 1915- .... **CLC 7, 22**
See See also CA 37-40R; CAAS 20; CANR 15, 65; INT CANR-15; MTCW 1

Yokomitsu Riichi 1898-1947 .... **TCLC 47**
See See also CA 170

Yonge, Charlotte (Mary) 1823-1901 .. **TCLC 48**
See See also CA 109; 163; DLB 18, 163; SATA 17

York, Jeremy
See See Creasey, John

York, Simon
See See Heinlein, Robert A(nson)

Yorke, Henry Vincent 1905-1974 .... **CLC 13**
See See also Green, Henry
See See also CA 85-88; 49-52

Yosano Akiko 1878-1942 .. **TCLC 59; PC 11**
See See also CA 161

Yoshimoto, Banana .... **CLC 84**
See See also Yoshimoto, Mahoko

Yoshimoto, Mahoko 1964-
See See Yoshimoto, Banana
See See also CA 144

Young, Al(bert James) 1939- . **CLC 19; BLC 3; DAM MULT**
See See also BW 2, 3; CA 29-32R; CANR 26, 65; DLB 33

Young, Andrew (John) 1885-1971 ..... **CLC 5**
See See also CA 5-8R; CANR 7, 29

Young, Collier
See See Bloch, Robert (Albert)

Young, Edward 1683-1765 .... **LC 3, 40**
See See also DLB 95

Young, Marguerite (Vivian) 1909-1995 .... **CLC 82**
See See also CA 13-16; 150; CAP 1

Young, Neil 1945- .... **CLC 17**
See See also CA 110

Young Bear, Ray A. 1950- ... **CLC 94; DAM MULT**
See See also CA 146; DLB 175; NNAL

Yourcenar, Marguerite 1903-1987 . **CLC 19, 38, 50, 87; DAM NOV**
See See also CA 69-72; CANR 23, 60; DLB 72; DLBY 88; MTCW 1, 2

Yuan, Chu 340(?)B.C.-278(?)B.C. ..... **CMLC 36**

Yurick, Sol 1925- .... **CLC 6**
See See also CA 13-16R; CANR 25

Zabolotsky, Nikolai Alekseevich 1903-1958 . **TCLC 52**
See See also CA 116; 164

Zagajewski, Adam .... **PC 27**

Zamiatin, Yevgenii
See See Zamyatin, Evgeny Ivanovich

Zamora, Bernice (B. Ortiz) 1938- . **CLC 89; DAM MULT; HLC 2**
See See also CA 151; CANR 80; DLB 82; HW 1, 2

Zamyatin, Evgeny Ivanovich 1884-1937 ...... **TCLC 8, 37**
See See also CA 105; 166

Zangwill, Israel 1864-1926 .... **TCLC 16**
See See also CA 109; 167; DLB 10, 135, 197

Zappa, Francis Vincent, Jr. 1940-1993
See See Zappa, Frank
See See also CA 108; 143; CANR 57

Zappa, Frank .... **CLC 17**
See See also Zappa, Francis Vincent, Jr.

Zaturenska, Marya 1902-1982 .... **CLC 6, 11**
See See also CA 13-16R; 105; CANR 22

Zeami 1363-1443 .... **DC 7**

Zelazny, Roger (Joseph) 1937-1995 . **CLC 21**
See See also AAYA 7; CA 21-24R; 148; CANR 26, 60; DLB 8; MTCW 1, 2; SATA 57; SATA-Brief 39

Zhdanov, Andrei Alexandrovich 1896-1948 .... **TCLC 18**
See See also CA 117; 167

Zhukovsky, Vasily (Andreevich) 1783-1852 .... **NCLC 35**
See See also DLB 205

Ziegenhagen, Eric .... **CLC 55**

Zimmer, Jill Schary
See See Robinson, Jill

Zimmerman, Robert
See See Dylan, Bob

Zindel, Paul 1936- ... **CLC 6, 26; DA; DAB; DAC; DAM DRAM, MST, NOV; DC 5**
See See also AAYA 2; CA 73-76; CANR 31, 65; CDALBS; CLR 3, 45; DA3; DLB 7, 52; JRDA; MAICYA; MTCW 1, 2; SATA 16, 58, 102

Zinov'Ev, A. A.
See See Zinoviev, Alexander (Aleksandrovich)

Zinoviev, Alexander (Aleksandrovich) 1922- .... **CLC 19**
See See also CA 116; 133; CAAS 10

Zoilus
See See Lovecraft, H(oward) P(hillips)

Zola, Emile (Edouard Charles Antoine) 1840-1902 .... **TCLC 1, 6, 21, 41; DA; DAB; DAC; DAM MST, NOV; WLC**
See See also CA 104; 138; DA3; DLB 123

Zoline, Pamela 1941- .... **CLC 62**
See See also CA 161

Zorrilla y Moral, Jose 1817-1893 .. **NCLC 6**

Zoshchenko, Mikhail (Mikhailovich) 1895-1958 .... **TCLC 15; SSC 15**

See See also CA 115; 160

Zuckmayer, Carl 1896-1977 .... **CLC 18**
See See also CA 69-72; DLB 56, 124

Zuk, Georges
See See Skelton, Robin

Zukofsky, Louis 1904-1978 .. **CLC 1, 2, 4, 7, 11, 18; DAM POET; PC 11**
See See also CA 9-12R; 77-80; CANR 39; DLB 5, 165; MTCW 1

Zweig, Paul 1935-1984 .... **CLC 34, 42**
See See also CA 85-88; 113

Zweig, Stefan 1881-1942 .... **TCLC 17**
See See also CA 112; 170; DLB 81, 118

Zwingli, Huldreich 1484-1531 .... **LC 37**
See See also DLB 179

Literary Criticism Series
Cumulative Topic Index

This index lists all topic entries in Gale's *Classical and Medieval Literature Criticism, Contemporary Literary Criticism, Literature Criticism from 1400 to 1800, Nineteenth-Century Literature Criticism,* and *Twentieth-Century Literary Criticism.*

Topic Index

Topic Index

CMLC Cumulative Nationality Index

CMLC Cumulative Title Index

461

Title Index

Title Index

Title Index

ISBN 0-7876-4379-3

90000